Prophets Unarmed

Historical Materialism Book Series

The Historical Materialism Book Series is a major publishing initiative of the radical left. The capitalist crisis of the twenty-first century has been met by a resurgence of interest in critical Marxist theory. At the same time, the publishing institutions committed to Marxism have contracted markedly since the high point of the 1970s. The Historical Materialism Book Series is dedicated to addressing this situation by making available important works of Marxist theory. The aim of the series is to publish important theoretical contributions as the basis for vigorous intellectual debate and exchange on the left.

The peer-reviewed series publishes original monographs, translated texts, and reprints of classics across the bounds of academic disciplinary agendas and across the divisions of the left. The series is particularly concerned to encourage the internationalization of Marxist debate and aims to translate significant studies from beyond the English-speaking world.

For a full list of titles in the Historical Materialism Book Series available in paperback from Haymarket Books, visit:
www.haymarketbooks.org/category/hm-series

Prophets Unarmed

Chinese Trotskyists in Revolution, War, Jail, and the Return from Limbo

Edited by
Gregor Benton

Haymarket Books
Chicago, IL

First published in 2015 by Brill Academic Publishers, The Netherlands
© 2015 Koninklijke Brill NV, Leiden, The Netherlands

Published in paperback in 2017 by
Haymarket Books
P.O. Box 180165
Chicago, IL 60618
773-583-7884
www.haymarketbooks.org

ISBN: 978-1-60846-554-5

Trade distribution:
In the US, Consortium Book Sales, www.cbsd.com
In Canada, Publishers Group Canada, www.pgcbooks.ca
In the UK, Turnaround Publisher Services, www.turnaround-uk.com
In all other countries, Publishers Group Worldwide, www.pgw.com

Cover design by Jamie Kerry of Belle Étoile Studios and Ragina Johnson.

This book was published with the generous support of Lannan Foundation and the Wallace Action Fund.

Printed in Canada by union labor.

10 9 8 7 6 5 4 3 2 1

Library of Congress Cataloging-in-Publication data is available.

Contents

Acknowledgements   xvii

Editor's Introduction   1
       Gregor Benton

PART 1
Purgatory: The Chinese Trotskyists' Ordeal and Struggle
       Wu Jimin

Preface   43
       Chen Sihe

Moscow's Sun Yat-sen University   47

The Year 1931   60

Chen Duxiu   73

Peng Shuzhi   77

The Chinese Trotskyists' Unification Congress   85

Traitors and Informers   90

Chen Duxiu's Last Years   94

Chen Qichang   102

Zheng Chaolin   110

Huang Jiantong   118

Du Weizhi   126

Wang Guolong, Zhou Rensheng, and Zhou Lüqiang   137

Epilogue   148

Postscript   152

PART 2
Autobiographical Accounts of Chinese Trotskyists' Early Years

Unfinished Autobiography   159
  Chen Duxiu

A Consciousness Awakes   172
  Zheng Chaolin

My First Contact With New Ideas   213
  Wang Fanxi

PART 3
Chinese Trotskyists in the Revolution of 1925–7

Before and After May Thirtieth   225
  Zheng Chaolin

Two Years at University   272
  Wang Fanxi

PART 4
Chinese Trotskyists in Moscow

Twelve People   295
  Zheng Chaolin

KUTV   303
  Zheng Chaolin

Chinese Students in Moscow   327
  Wang Fanxi

My Second Year in Moscow   333
   Wang Fanxi

Chinese Students at the International Lenin School in Moscow, 1926–38:
   Light from the Russian Archives   366
      Alexander V. Pantsov and Daria A. Spichak

Stalin and the Chinese Communist Dissidents   389
   Alexander V. Pantsov

PART 5
The Unification of the Chinese Trotskyists

Appeal to All Comrades of the Chinese Communist Party
   (10 December 1929)   399
      Chen Duxiu

An Ebbing or a Flowing Tide?   417
   Zheng Chaolin

The Left Opposition   451
   Zheng Chaolin

Unification of the Four Groups   478
   Wang Fanxi

PART 6
Chinese Trotskyism in the 1930s and the 1940s

The Founding of *Struggle* and the Darkest Days of My Life   507
   Wang Fanxi

Chen Duxiu, the Chinese Trotskyists, and the War of Resistance   532
   Wang Fanxi

The Pacific War and a New Split in the Organisation   557
   Wang Fanxi

From War to Revolution   568
    Wang Fanxi

The Communist League of China (January 1940)   576
    Frank Glass

PART 7
Chen Duxiu

Chen Duxiu, Founder of Chinese Communism   585
    Wang Fanxi

Chen Duxiu and the Trotskyists   594
    Zheng Chaolin

Chen Duxiu Had No Wish to Rejoin the CCP on Leaving Jail   685
    Zheng Chaolin

Preface to the Collected Poems of Chen Duxiu (June 2, 1993)   691
    General Xiao Ke

PART 8
Chen Duxiu's Last Articles and Letters (1937–42)

Editor's Introduction to Chen Duxiu's Last Articles and Letters   697
    Gregor Benton

Letter to Chen Qichang and Others (21 November 1937)   709

Letter to Leon Trotsky (3 November 1938)   713

Letter to Xiliu and Others (1 March 1940)   719

Letter to Xiliu and Others (24 April 1940)   723

Letter to Xiliu (3 November 1938)   725

Letter to Liangen (31 July 1940)   728

Letter to Xiliu (September 1940)   731

My Basic Views (28 November 1940)   738

Letter to Y (19 January 1941)   743

Letter to H and S (19 January 1941)   744

A Sketch of the Post-War World (10 February 1942)   746

Once Again on the World Situation (19 April 1942)   756

The Future of the Oppressed Nations (13 May 1942)   762

My Feelings on the Death of Mr Cai Jiemin   768
    Chen Duxiu

On Chen Duxiu's Last Views   773
    Shuang Shan [Wang Fanxi]

PART 9
Peng Shuzhi and Wang Fanxi on Leon Trotsky

Introduction to *Leon Trotsky on China* (1974)   777
    Peng Shuzhi

Introduction: Leon Trotsky and Chinese Communism (1980)   819
    Wang Fanxi

PART 10
Peng Shuzhi and Wang Fanxi: A Confrontation

Trotskyism in China (1947)   851
    Peng Shuzhi

Problems of Chinese Trotskyism (1947)   863
    Wang Fanxi

PART 11
Some Articles and Speeches by Trotsky about the Chinese Trotskyists and Some Correspondence between Him and Them

The Speech of Comrade Chen Duxiu on the Tasks of the Chinese Communist Party (17 May 1927)   885

A Remarkable Document on the Policy and the Régime of the Communist International (4 October 1928)   892

Peasant War in China and the Proletariat (22 September 1932)   903

A Strategy of Action and Not of Speculation: Letter to Beijing Friends. What are, at Present, the Chief Elements of the Political Situation in China? (3 October 1932)   912

Excerpts from Letters from China Written or Copied to Trotsky (1934)   920

Chen Duxiu and the General Council (10 August 1935)   925

Introduction to Harold R. Isaacs, *The Tragedy of the Chinese Revolution* (1938)   928

Letter to Frank Glass (11 March 1939)   941

China and the Russian Revolution (July 1940)   943

PART 12
Chinese Trotskyist Reflections on Mao Zedong's Revolution

The Causes of the Victory of the Chinese Communist Party over Chiang Kai-shek, and the CCP's Perspectives. Report on the Chinese Situation to the Third World Congress of the Fourth International, August–September 1951 (1952)   949
    Peng Shuzhi

Thinking in Solitude (1957)   967
    Wang Fanxi

PART 13
Chinese Trotskyism and Guerrilla Warfare

The Real Lesson of China on Guerrilla Warfare: Reply to a 'Letter from a Chinese Trotskyist' (1971)   985
  Chen Bilan

On the Causes of the CCP's Victory and the Failure of the Chinese Trotskyists in the Third Chinese Revolution: A Reply to Peng Shuzhi (1973)   1001
  Wang Fanxi

PART 14
Chinese Trotskyism and Literature

Chinese Trotskyism and the World of Letters   1027
  Gregor Benton

Wild Lily (1942)   1048
  Wang Shiwei

Politicians, Artists (1942)   1055
  Wang Shiwei

PART 15
Prefaces and Introductions to Chinese Trotskyist Memoirs and Biographies

Editor's Introduction to Zheng Chaolin's *Memoirs*   1061
  Gregor Benton

Peng Shuzhi and the Chinese Revolution: Notes Towards a Political Biography   1075
  Joseph T. Miller

Zheng Chaolin's 1945 Preface to the Unpublished Manuscript of His *Memoirs* (1945)   1103

Zheng Chaolin's 1987 Postscript to the English Edition of His *Memoirs*
    (1987)   1105

A Self-Description at the Age of Ninety (1 May 1990)   1108
    Zheng Chaolin

Postscript to the 1980 Oxford Edition of *Memoirs of a Chinese Revolutionary*
    (1980)   1116
    Wang Fanxi

Preface to the 1987 French Edition of *Memoirs of a Chinese Revolutionary*
    (1987)   1118
    Wang Fanxi

Preface to the 1991 Morningside Edition of *Memoirs of a Chinese Revolutionary* (1990)   1120
    Wang Fanxi

PART 16
The Chinese Trotskyists' Imprisonment and Release From Prison

Statement by Chinese Trotskyists Overseas on the CCP's Release of Zheng Chaolin and Other Trotskyist Political Prisoners
    (24 July 1979)   1127

A Brief Account of My Third Spell in Prison   1132
    Zheng Chaolin

PART 17
Wang Fanxi Reviews Tang Baolin's *History of Chinese Trotskyism*

Interviews With Wang Fanxi on Tang Baolin's *Zhongguo Tuopai shi* ('History of Chinese Trotskyism')   1149

PART 18
Obituaries

Oration at the Funeral of Mr [Chen] Duxiu (1879–1942) 1165
   Gao Yuhan

Wu Jingru (1907–79)   1170
   Wang Fanxi

Frank Glass (Li Furen) (1901–88)   1173
   Wang Fanxi

Lou Guohua (1906–95)   1176
   Wang Fanxi

Zheng Chaolin (1901–98)   1178
   Wang Fanxi

Peng Shuzhi (1895–1983) and Chen Bilan (1902–87)   1182
   Cheng Yingxiang and Claude Cadart

Wang Fanxi (1907–2002)   1191
   Gregor Benton

Bibliographical Note   1195
Biographical List   1200
References   1215
Index   1233

Acknowledgements

Sebastian Budgen, David Broder, and Danny Hayward at HM and Gera van Bedaf and Debbie de Wit at Brill steered this book through to publication. Mike Taber produced the index. Louisa Wei made the photo collage of the main Trotskyist leaders for the frontispiece. At Nanyang Technological University, Professor Hong Liu and Professor K. K. Luke provided generous support. So did Professor Emile Kok-Kheng Yeoh of the University of Malaya's Institute of China Studies. Mr Wang Xufeng, the son of Wang Shiwei, and Dr Feng Xue, Wang Fanxi's grandson, gave their permission for the publication of excerpts from their deceased relatives' published work. John Sexton read and commented on the introduction. To all these people I am deeply grateful.

Editor's Introduction

Gregor Benton

My connection with Chinese Trotskyism began in 1975, when Wang Fanxi left Macao and came to live in Leeds, in our spare room, to escape Communist agents plotting to spirit him across the border into the Mainland. For more than a quarter of a century, until his death in 2002, I was his close friend and collaborator and translated many of his writings, some excerpted in this volume. Through him, I also got to know Zheng Chaolin in Shanghai, after Zheng's release from a labour camp in 1979. In the mid-1990s, I worked with Zheng and Wang to produce an uncensored and authoritatively annotated version of Zheng's memoir (also excerpted here) of early Chinese communism and Chinese Trotskyism, and his description of the Trotskyists' destruction in 1952.

Given my long association with Wang and Zheng, I was delighted to see Wu Jimin's new study on Chinese Trotskyism, the movement they helped found and lead. It is the first independent work in Chinese to raise the matter of the Chinese Trotskyists' rehabilitation, and so a milestone in their history. Here, it forms the centrepiece of a new sourcebook on their movement, alongside texts and documents drawn from publications on and by the Chinese Trotskyists.

My aim in writing, translating, and editing the materials collected in this volume was to rescue from oblivion the history of Chinese Trotskyism in the period between its birth in 1927 and its elimination in 1952. The materials are mainly analysis and reminiscence rather than primary documentation, for most of the Trotskyists' archive has been lost or destroyed over the years, or it disappeared behind bars together with its owners in 1952 and remained there even after their release.[1] I have not included writings on the consolidated Mao-régime written by Wang Fanxi and Peng Shuzhi, the only two leaders of the movement still free after 1952 (in exile) to voice an opinion on it, for the focus of the volume is on Chinese Trotskyism as an active political force rather than as detached commentary. For example, I have excluded their writings on the Great Leap Forward and the Cultural Revolution, since, by that time, neither could do more than watch and comment on events in China from a distance

---

1 An exception is Wang Fanxi's surviving papers (mostly from after 1949), together with letters to Wang from Zheng Chaolin and Lou Guohua, held in the Brotherton Library at the University of Leeds in England, and papers of Peng Shuzhi (see Bibliographical Note).

and in isolation.² However, I have included representative statements by each reflecting in the 1950s from the standpoint of their own earlier political missions on the causes and character of the revolution Mao brought about.

The Chinese Trotskyists have been among China's most persecuted political minorities under the Chinese Communist Party (CCP), which classed them as counter-revolutionaries, and under Chiang Kai-shek's Guomindang (or Nationalist Party), which classed them as dangerous revolutionaries, essentially indistinguishable from the CCP. In the early 1930s, scores and perhaps hundreds of Chinese Trotskyists were sent to prisons and labour camps in China, by Chiang, and in the Soviet Union, by Stalin, where an unknown number died. Others were persecuted or killed in the CCP's rural bases in the 1930s and 1940s, along with hundreds or even thousands of orthodox Communists (we have no way of knowing how many) falsely accused of being Trotskyists. Colonial police also helped hunt them down. The arrest of Chen Duxiu and Peng Shuzhi in 1932 was masterminded by French and British Intelligence in collaboration with the Guomindang authorities.³ In exile after 1949, the persecution continued. In Vietnam in 1950, Ho Chi Minh's security police murdered the Trotskyist Liu Jialiang. The colonial authorities in Hong Kong harassed Wang Fanxi and deported him to Macao, where he was threatened and victimised by the Maoists. In France, Stalinist agents plotted to assassinate Peng Shuzhi.⁴

The final persecution happened in China under Mao in December 1952, three years after the victory of the Revolution, when one thousand Trotskyists and their sympathisers and relatives were netted up in a nation-wide raid and sent to jails and labour camps. Not until June 1979, after twenty-seven years in Mao's jails, did Zheng Chaolin, aged seventy-nine, and a dozen other elderly survivors step into relative freedom in Shanghai.⁵ The Chinese Trotskyists were one of the few groups not rehabilitated after 1978. Wu Jimin confirms they were treated as badly as or worse than Guomindang 'war-criminals' after 1949.

2 For those interested in Peng Shuzhi's later writings, see P'eng Shu-tse 1980a; for Wang Fanxi's, see *inter alia* Shuang Shan 1973; for Zheng Chaolin's, see Zheng Chaolin 1998.
3 Wakeman 1995, p. 22.
4 For Liu Jialiang: Chen Bilan 2010, pp. 512–14, and Ngo Van 2010, pp. 149 and 175–6. For Peng Shuzhi: Chen Bilan 2010, p. 520, and Chen Bilan n.d. [1961]. In the case of Wang Fanxi, I am repeating what he told me in personal conversations.
5 *Amnesty International Newsletter*, Volume 9, No. 9 (1979), and Benton 1977 and 1979.

which more or less followed the Leninist position, was based on resolutions of the Moscow Toilers' Congress.[16]

The defeat of the Chinese Communists in 1927 led to a protracted dispute between Trotsky and Stalin. Trotsky believed the CCP should recognise a defeat had happened, draw its lessons, and rethink the way forward, but Stalin argued that the revolution was in a trough between waves and victory was still possible. In China, Chen Duxiu arrived, independently of Trotsky, at a position not incompatible with his. He believed there was no immediate prospect of a new 'high tide' of revolution and proposed concentrating on economic issues, as a way of reconstituting the smashed labour movement. Two of his four sons had been killed by Chiang Kai-shek during the bloodbath, and their deaths threw him into deep despair. For the time being, he stayed aloof from active opposition to the official line, busying himself instead with a study of Chinese philology. He also pondered basic questions in the Chinese revolution, including the extent of his own responsibility for the defeat, for he was after all the executor – although a reluctant one – of the strategy that had led to it.

While Chen Duxiu himself remained temporarily passive, a group of his supporters tried to rally an opposition within the CCP. In the mid-1920s, a so-called Moscow group, comprising people like Peng Shuzhi, Luo Yinong, and Zheng Chaolin sent back from Moscow to China in the mid-1920s to staff the CCP, had congregated around Chen Duxiu. The group remained tightly knit until 1926, when it began to disintegrate. The surviving core of loyalists became known as the Chen Duxiu-ites. They included Peng Shuzhi, Wang Ruofei, Yin Kuan, Zheng Chaolin, Chen Qiaonian, Chen Bilan, He Zishen, Cai Zhende, Ma Yufu, and Liu Bozhuang.[17]

The Chen Duxiu-ites agreed the revolution was in a trough. They lacked clarity and a strong basis in theory for their thinking, but they had organisational support in the Jiangsu Provincial Committee, which was controlled by their leader Wang Ruofei. In 1927, Wang Ruofei wrote the well-known Resolution of the Jiangsu Provincial Committee, which Trotsky saw as matching his own ideas on the situation in China. The Chen Duxiu-ites criticised the CCP leaders who replaced Chen Duxiu at the Emergency Conference on 7 August 1927, for denying that a defeat had happened and sticking to a policy that was costing lives and for blaming Chen Duxiu for mistakes the Comintern had forced

---

16   Wilbur and How (eds) 1989, pp. 30–2, 35, and 46.
17   Ren Jianshu and Tang Baolin 1989, Volume 2, p. 17.

Until the 1980s, the fate of the Chinese Trotskyists was practically unknown in China. Even today, few people are familiar with them except in political caricature, as supposed national and political traitors. So Wu Jimin's new study is particularly welcome, and I hope signals the start of a long overdue recognition – posthumous in nearly all cases – of the Chinese Trotskyists' place in modern Chinese history. Even so, the CCP's party history establishment has so far refused to allow Wu's work to be published in China because anti-Trotskyism is still automatic in official circles, at a time when other political and cultural taboos have been breached or flattened. Instead, it had to come out in Singapore.

Although Chinese Trotskyism as such continues to be problematic, the 'emancipation' of Chinese historiography after Mao's death in 1976 led to a partial rehabilitation of Chen Duxiu, founder of the CCP in 1921 and China's best-known Trotskyist, and this helped mitigate the Chinese Trotskyists' treatment by officials and scholars. Their long-standing description as a 'counter-revolutionary bandit-gang' and 'Japanese agents' was removed from the annotation to Mao Zedong's *Selected Works* in 1991, and they were instead described as merely 'wrong'.[6] Writings by Wang Fanxi, Zheng Chaolin, and other Trotskyist leaders and by Chen Duxiu from his Trotskyist period appeared in China, and foreign writings by Trotskyists or about Trotskyism appeared in Chinese translation. However, the reassessment of Chinese Trotskyism never stretched to their formal rehabilitation.

The Chinese Revolution played a key role in the emergence of the Trotskyist Opposition in the Soviet Union after 1923. On Comintern instructions and against the better judgement of its own leaders, in particular Chen Duxiu, in 1924 the CCP joined an alliance (known as the First United Front, to distinguish it from the Second United Front formed in 1937 at the start of the Japanese War) with the Guomindang, an authoritarian party populist in rhetoric but tied in practice to defending the economic interests of Chinese business-groups, financial circles, and rural élites. The terms of this united front were, in practice, disadvantageous to the Communist Party. They required its strict subordination to the Nationalist leaders and the submersion of important sections of its membership into the Guomindang.

The Soviet leaders' aim in promoting the united front was to gain Chinese allies against the West, so for reasons of self-interest they turned a blind eye

---

6 Zheng Chaolin 1991.

to the friction that grew up between the Chinese parties in 1926 and insisted on maintaining the arrangement despite the dangers. In April 1927, Chiang Kai-shek unilaterally ended the united front and slaughtered large numbers of Communists in Shanghai and elsewhere.

In the period leading up to these events, Trotsky called for the CCP's withdrawal from the Guomindang.[7] It is well known that Trotsky challenged the way the united front was put into practice in China, and he himself later claimed in a letter to Max Shachtman to have opposed 'from the very beginning, that is, from 1923', the CCP's entry into the Guomindang.[8] However, documents in the Soviet and Comintern archives suggest that the earliest indisputable challenge by Trotsky (and Zinoviev) to the official line was probably on 1 April 1926, by which time Trotsky perceived that the gulf between the bourgeoisie and the proletariat in China was rapidly widening. Trotsky's own explanation for his failure to call earlier and publicly for the CCP's withdrawal was that he was under factional constraints due to his alliance with the Zinovievists (although factional constraints cannot explain his silence before the founding of the anti-Stalin pact).[9] Yet, despite his failure to speak out openly, there was a clear difference of opinion between him and Stalin and Bukharin on how to characterise the Guomindang. Trotsky criticised the Soviet majority's description of the Guomindang as a bloc of four classes (workers, peasants, urban petty-bourgeois, and national bourgeois), a definition used to justify the CCP's presence in it. He said it was a bourgeois party, susceptible to 'the danger of a national-democratic degeneration'.[10] Many Communists both in China and the Soviet Union blamed Stalin for the defeat in 1927 and were impressed by Trotsky's prescient criticism of the strategy of entering the Guomindang.

After Chiang Kai-shek's Shanghai coup, Stalin instructed the CCP to switch its allegiance to the Guomindang's seemingly friendlier faction under Wang Jingwei in Wuhan, several hundred miles to the west, now identified by the Soviet majority leaders as the 'revolutionary Guomindang', its 'revolutionary

---

7   Trotsky 1957 [1928].
8   Quoted in Shachtman 1969 [1931], p. 19.
9   Pantsov and Benton 1994. In the China section of the Programme of the United Opposition, drafted by Trotsky and signed by Zinoviev, Trotsky, Radek, and others on 2 July 1927, Trotsky noted that 'one of our number [Trotsky himself] had already in 1925 demanded an organisational break with all Guomindang leaders and the replacement of cooperation within the Guomindang by cooperation outside the party'. The text of the China section can be found in Chinese translation in Tuoluociji 1947 [1927], pp. 36–53; the passage cited is on p. 47. This document is not in the Russian original, so it is not included in the supposedly definitive collection of Trotsky's writings on China (Trotzki 1990).
10 Trotsky 1973 [1924], p. 8; Wang Fanxi 1990, pp. 14–15.

centre purged of right-wing elements'. For several months, Wang Jingwei preserved the alliance with the Communists. Thousands of Communist survivors fled Shanghai and other parts of China under Chiang Kai-shek's terror régime to Wuhan, where they continued cooperating with Stalin's 'tried and true' ally. In May 1927, Trotsky and his supporters in the Opposition warned against this policy, which they described as replacing one hangman with another. Instead, they demanded the CCP's 'complete independence' from Wang Jingwei's 'left' Guomindang. However, Stalin and Bukharin denounced this call as 'an attack upon the Chinese revolution'.[11] In July 1927, Wang Jingwei also turned against the Communists, killing thousands more in fulfilment of Trotsky's warning, and eventually reunited with Chiang Kai-shek in Nanjing under a government controlled by Chiang.

Leaders of the CCP had opposed joining the Guomindang several years before Trotsky raised the issue publicly, and the Comintern agent Sneevliet managed to persuade them to give up their independence only by bullying them or playing on their sense of discipline.[12] In 1922, meetings of Communists in Guangdong, Shanghai, Beijing, Changsha, and Wuhan expressed hostility to the policy. Throughout the period of the united front, Chinese Communist leaders kept up their opposition, and repeated it at regular intervals.[13] In this sense, they were Trotskyists *avant la lettre*. However, their opposition to entry at such an early point was mainly a result of their first-hand encounter with the Guomindang, which they knew from this experience to be 'dead' even in the early 1920s, rather than of any theoretical understanding or strategic vision. According to Wang Fanxi, 'their opinion of the Guomindang and of the relationship that the newly founded CCP could and should have with it was based on empirical observation'.[14] Even so, the Chinese Communists' view was actually more in line with Lenin's strategy, of cooperating with nationalist democrats while at the same time organising independently of them for class struggle, first adopted at the Second Comintern Congress in 1920 and readopted at the Congress of the Toilers of the Far East held in Moscow in early 1922.[15] According to Chen Duxiu, the Manifesto of the CCP's Second Congress,

---

11   Trotsky 1973 [1927], Part 3, Chapter 9.
12   Saich (ed.) 1991.
13   For instances of CCP opposition to joining the Guomindang: Wilbur and How (eds) 1989, pp. 52, 84–5, 105, 123, 184, and 291; and Wang Fanxi 1990, pp. 15–16.
14   Wang Fanxi, personal communication. See also Wang Fanxi 1990, p. 11.
15   In practice, Communists were pushed to subordinate themselves to nationalist movements even at Comintern congresses Lenin attended; an example is the Turkish Communists' subordination to Kemal Atatürk.

on him. They also criticised what they saw as the Party's moral degeneration, its denial of democracy, and its descent into warring cliques. The Chen Duxiu-ites' views therefore corresponded with Trotsky's on three main points, although the correspondence was coincidental. They thought the CCP should have remained independent of the Guomindang, that its immersion in the Guomindang had caused its defeat, and that its organisational norms were in decay. What they lacked was political confidence and a justification in Marxist theory for their beliefs.

This political confidence and justification in theory arrived eventually from Moscow, where a strong Trotskyist group formed among hundreds of young Chinese Communists sent to study at schools and universities set up by the Comintern. A Left Opposition first sprang up among Chinese students at Moscow's Sun Yat-sen University while it was under the direction of the Trotskyist Karl Radek, who invited Trotsky and Bukharin to give lectures.[18] The Opposition was strengthened by Chiang Kai-shek's anti-Communist coup in Shanghai on 12 April 1927.

In 1927, Radek was replaced at Sun Yat-sen University by Pavel Mif, a Stalin supporter who substituted Stalinists for Trotskyist teachers and expelled Trotskyist students from the CCP and deported them to Siberia or China. However, it was not long before new arrivals from China learned of the controversy between Stalin and Trotsky. Because of their experience of events in China, they were far more attracted by Trotsky's views than other foreign students in Moscow. Hundreds of them became Trotskyists, whereas few of the non-Chinese did.

The conversion was not easy, for the Opposition had been denounced in Russia as disloyal and even 'counter-revolutionary'. In the end, the students were convinced not just by the debate on Stalin's policy for China but also as a result of their indignation at the high-handed ways of the Moscow leaders and the University authorities, including Chinese 'Red compradors' like Wang Ming, who used his links to the Soviet Stalinists to build a power-base in the CCP. Nearly all the second batch of Chinese Trotskyists formed in Moscow had personally experienced the Revolution of 1927, whereas none of the five main leaders of Moscow's Chinese Stalinist faction (known as the Twenty-Eight Bolsheviks) had. By the summer of 1928, most Chinese students in Moscow reportedly sympathised with the Trotskyists, and, in the early autumn, a dozen

---

18   Kuhfus 1985, p. 258.

of them secretly elected a committee to support the Opposition and arrange for the translation of Oppositionist writings into Chinese.

The Stalinist authorities at Sun Yat-sen University organised beatings and took administrative measures to try to stop the Trotskyists. For example, they prevented suspected Trotskyists from transferring into membership of the Communist Party of the Soviet Union (CPSU) (seen as political promotion). Some were even stripped of their 'second-class' membership of the CCP. The Trotskyists responded with a boycott of the transfer process; nine out of ten students were said to have supported the boycott. The Wang Ming group also stopped sending known Trotskyists back to China and instead kept them in Moscow, where they could be controlled.[19]

In late 1929, scores of Chinese Trotskyists in Moscow were seized by the Soviet political police. They had taken elaborate precautions against discovery, building their organisation vertically rather than laterally and skilfully covering their underground activities. However, they were no match for the veteran GPU commissars 'toughened in numerous struggles' (including intelligence-operations in China) who had been detailed to crack their group. Some were imprisoned for a while, expelled from the Party after recanting, and deported (these numbered fewer than ten). Others were sent to labour camps in Siberia or the Arctic Circle, whence two escaped back to China after 1949 to tell their story. Some were shot. According to Wang Fanxi, those who made it to China at the time were fewer than twenty.

In early 1929, Chinese Trotskyists deported from the Soviet Union in early 1928 formed Oppositionist nuclei in Shanghai, Hong Kong, and Beijing and started publishing a journal, *Women de hua* ('Our Word'). They claimed five hundred members (actually an exaggeration) and began recruiting people who had never been to Moscow. They also corresponded with the second generation of Chinese Trotskyists still in Moscow.

However, they had no contact with Chen Duxiu's supporters, whom they distrusted and despised as 'old opportunists' and blamed for the 1927 defeat. Their attitude to Chen Duxiu can be gauged from their demands on him after he and his supporters set up their own Trotskyist organisation: that he publicly declare Stalin's leadership opportunist, criticise his own past opportunist errors, and disband his group.[20] The distrust between them and the Chen

---

19 Wang Fan-hsi 1991, p. 97.
20 Shuang Shan (ed.) 1981, pp. 15–16, fn. 2, where a relevant passage is translated from the *Bulletin of the Opposition*, February–March 1930.

Duxiu-ites was mutual. For example, the Chen Duxiu-ite Zheng Chaolin criticised the Our Word group for arguing that the Chinese revolution was 'still in spate or already on its way up after a period of ebb', while Peng Shuzhi reportedly said the Our Word group 'was led by people without experience and ability'.

So there were big obstacles in the way of a union of the Chen Duxiu-ites and the Russia-returned Trotskyists. Not until March or April 1929 did Oppositionist documents reach Chen Duxiu, after the veteran Communist Yin Kuan (leader of the CCP's Shandong Committee and later a Trotskyist convert) received them from the Russia-returned Shandong Communist Wang Pingyi and passed them on to Peng Shuzhi and Wang Zekai, who passed them on to Chen Duxiu. After several weeks of deliberation, in May and June 1929, Chen Duxiu and most of the Chen Duxiu-ites came round to Trotsky's point of view, which provided support for Chen Duxiu's contention that the revolution in China was in a deep trough. In November 1929, Chen Duxiu and his supporters were expelled from the CCP and set up a formal Oppositionist organisation, with branches, district committees, and a journal, *Wuchanzhe* ('Proletarian').

Secret Chinese Trotskyists trickled back into China from the Soviet Union. The Trotskyist Liu Renjing arrived after visiting the exiled Trotsky in Turkey, bringing with him documents by Trotsky. Others from the second batch of Chinese Trotskyist students, including Wang Fanxi, returned from Moscow to work clandestinely in the official Party until their discovery and expulsion. Some joined Chen Duxiu's Proletarian group, others joined Our Word. By the summer of 1930, the number of rival organisations had risen to four.

These groups were divided by personal ambition and factional prejudice rather than ideology, but all three groups with Russia-returned members agreed that the Chen Duxiu-ites were 'opportunists' who bore responsibility for the 1927 defeat. They also opposed Chen's call for a 'democratic dictatorship' as opposed to a 'dictatorship of the proletariat', which was Trotsky's slogan, and saw it as an insuperable obstacle to unity.

To resolve the difference, Trotsky wrote to tell Liu Renjing that Chen Duxiu's position was 'absolutely correct' and 'simply a popularisation and amplification of the "dictatorship of the proletariat" formula'.[21] In later years, however, the way in which Chen's views on the Soviet Union and the future shape of revolutionary state power in China evolved suggests that the original difference was not just of style but indicated a fundamental disagreement between him and Trotsky on the relationship between socialism and democracy, a

---

21 Shuang Shan (ed.) 1981, p. 23; Wang Fan-hsi 1991, p. 139. Durand 1990, pp. 13–14, quotes from Trotsky's correspondence regarding Chen Duxiu.

divergence that emerged most clearly in Chen's last letters and articles (included in this volume).

On 8 January 1931, Trotsky wrote from Turkey urging the Trotskyists in China to unite,[22] and, within weeks, a unification campaign got under way. The youthful enthusiasm of the Russia-returned Trotskyists reminded Chen Duxiu of young people at the time of China's May Fourth Movement of 1919,[23] and he favourably contrasted them with the 'old men' of his own 'Proletarian group'. Peng Shuzhi reportedly took the view that the younger Trotskyists were too 'young and politically inexperienced to lead us old cadres who have participated in the revolution, [and] that they can only be led by us'.[24] Differences of interest and opinion hindered the negotiations, until Chen finally managed to get the four groups to form a Preparatory Committee for a Unification Congress.

The seventeen delegates at the Congress, held between 1 and 3 May 1931, claimed to represent 483 members in China.[25] They formed a Central Committee and a Standing Committee of Chen Duxiu, Chen Yimou, Zheng Chaolin, Wang Fanxi, and Song Fengchun,[26] merged the branches of the four organisations, and set up a journal, *Huohua* ('Spark'). However, on the night

---

22 Shuang Shan (ed.) 1981, pp. 33–40; Wang Fan-hsi 1991, p. 139.
23 Ren Jianshu and Tang Baolin 1989, Volume 2, p. 71; and Part V. Both Chen Bilan (quoted in Kuhfus 1985, p. 263) and Pu Qingquan (quoted in Part VII) say Chen Duxiu scorned these young Trotskyists: Chen Bilan because they had gained their Trotskyist convictions in the relative security of Moscow; Pu Qingquan because they were 'monkey-pups still smelling of their mothers' milk'. Zheng Chaolin and Wang Fanxi say the young Trotskyists' real detractor was Peng Shuzhi, Chen Bilan's husband.
24 Ren Jianshu and Tang Baolin 1989, Volume 2, pp. 70 and 93.
25 'Report No. 1' by the Secretariat of the Left Opposition of the CCP to the International Secretariat of the Left Opposition and Trotsky, May 9, 1931. Copies of this document, in Russian and English, are in Wang Fanxi's personal archive; a Chinese version was published in Beijing in 1993 by Wang Fanxi (translator) and Tang Baolin (editor) under the title 'Xin faxian de Zhongguo Tuopai chengli shi zhi Tuoluociji de liangfeng xin' ('Two newly discovered letters sent to Trotsky by the Chinese Trotskyists at the time of the establishment [of their organisation]', in *Guowai Zhonggong dangshi yanjiu dongtai* ('Overseas trends in research on the history of the CCP'), no. 6, pp. 22–3. According to Ren Jianshu and Tang Baolin 1989, Volume 2, p. 107, the new organisation had some five hundred members.
26 According to Wang Fanxi, the Committee comprised Chen Duxiu, Luo Han, Song Fengchun, Chen Yimou, Zheng Chaolin, and Zhao Ji.

of 21 May, all the members of the Central Committee except Chen Duxiu were arrested and later jailed for between six and fifteen years. In the autumn of 1932, Chen Duxiu and Peng Shuzhi were also seized.

A handful of Trotskyists escaped the dragnet, as Wu Jimin explains. However, attempts in 1933 to restore Trotskyist organisation in Shanghai failed because of internal wrangling.[27] Liu Renjing and Peng Shuzhi attacked Chen Duxiu on questions such as the meaning of the call for a constituent assembly, economic revival, and common action with bourgeois liberals. In the polemic, Chen Duxiu (who smuggled out messages to his comrades from his prison-cell) displayed greater realism and flexibility than his opponents, although he remained within the broad framework of Trotskyist analysis. Liu Renjing said economic revival was essential for a revival of the revolutionary movement. Chen criticised this as economic determinism and said that, wherever a proletarian movement exists and can find allies, revolution is conceivable. This was especially true 'in an economically backward country like China, where through the democratic movement – the road to a constituent assembly – the proletariat can achieve power earlier than in advanced countries'. On joint action, Liu wanted to maintain the gap between the classes, while Chen said that revolutionaries should act together with bourgeois liberals where possible.[28] As a result, Liu Renjing announced that 'Comrade Chen Tu-hsiu's [Chen Duxiu's] role as revolutionary leader is finished' and called for a complete break with Chen Duxiu-ism.[29]

A new Trotskyist body was set up in Shanghai in 1934 with the help of the English-born South African Trotskyist Cecil Frank Glass (Chinese name Li Furen) and his American friend Harold Isaacs, Liu Renjing's close political associates in the Opposition.[30] Under Liu Renjing's influence, the new organisation expelled Chen Duxiu for refusing to criticise himself for 'opportunism'.[31] It also expelled his supporters Chen Qichang and Yin Kuan, for proposing joint action with anti-Japanese politicians and military leaders in 1933 at the time of

---

27 Ren Jianshu and Tang Baolin 1989, Volume 2, pp. 185–6.
28 Ren Jianshu and Tang Baolin 1989, Volume 2, pp. 186–90.
29 Niel Sih (Liu Renjing) 1934.
30 On the relationship between Glass and Liu Renjing, see Hirson 2003. For short biographies of Glass, see *Revolutionary History*, Volume 1, No. 2 (1988), pp. 1–4, and Hirson 1988.
31 The charge of 'opportunism' was based on the policies Chen pursued in 1932, before his arrest in October of that year (Ren Jianshu and Tang Baolin 1989, Volume 2, p. 130).

the anti-Japanese Fujian Incident.[32] But the expulsions meant little in practice, for in March 1935 the new organisation was raided and destroyed.[33]

Another Provisional Central Committee was set up in the summer of 1935 by Wang Fanxi (after his release from jail) with the help of Chen Qichang, Yin Kuan, and Frank Glass, who in the meantime had been reconciled to one another. This group published a monthly journal, *Douzheng* ('Struggle'), and a theoretical journal, *Huohua* ('Spark'), from early 1936 to late 1942. But in May 1941, the group again split. A faction around Wang Fanxi argued that once a wider Pacific War started, the Guomindang would become a 'junior partner of American imperialism', so its war would no longer be progressive and revolutionaries would then have to 'lay more stress on the victory of the revolution than of the war'. Another faction around Peng Shuzhi said the Guomindang's war would remain progressive unless British or US troops started fighting Japan on Chinese soil.[34] The group around Wang Fanxi started publishing their own paper, *Guoji zhuyizhe* ('Internationalist'), when the majority refused to let them argue their position in a column in *Struggle*.[35]

In late 1948, the Peng Shuzhi group set up the Revolutionary Communist Party; in April 1949, the Wang Fanxi group set up the Internationalist Workers' Party. Together, the two parties had a membership of around two hundred. Thereafter, the Chinese Trotskyist movement in Hong Kong and the diaspora stayed split along lines that had their origin in the disputes of 1941. The leadership of Peng Shuzhi's group left China to escape repression in late 1948, just before Mao's armies swept into Shanghai. Zheng Chaolin's group remained in the country, to try to organise a workers' movement independent of the Communists.[36]

---

32   Ren Jianshu and Tang Baolin 1989, Volume 2, pp. 192–4.
33   Wang Fan-hsi 1991, pp. 172–3; Part VI. According to Ren Jianshu and Tang Baolin 1989, Volume 2, p. 197, Isaacs and Glass were among those arrested, though as foreigners they were soon released; but according to Alex Buchman, another foreign Trotskyist present in Shanghai at the time, Isaacs and Glass were not arrested. Buchman's recollection is borne out (in a letter to Buchman dated 20 October 1992) by Viola Robinson, Harold Isaacs's widow.
34   For Peng's view on the war see his report 'Trotskyism in China'. For Wang's view, see 'Chinese Trotskyism in the War'. Both are in this volume.
35   Peng Shuzhi 1982–3 [1942], Volume 2, pp. 172–80.
36   Wang Fanxi was chosen to staff the coordinating centre of his organisation in Hong Kong. 'As I was no deserter', he wrote, 'I must admit that I was moved by the spirit of St Peter [displayed by the future Trotskyist martyr Zheng Chaolin] and retreated to my "safe place" only with extreme reluctance. Ironically, the place to which I had gone proved in the space of a mere four months to be anything but "safe". The authorities there, hypersensitive as a result of the dramatic changes that were taking place in China, did not allow me

At first, Zheng Chaolin's old friends in the new régime urged him to join them. However, he refused their overtures, and on the night of 22 December 1952, he and up to one thousand other Trotskyists and their relatives and sympathisers disappeared into prison, in a raid coordinated at national level and carried out more or less simultaneously in different cities. The arrested relatives were soon released,[37] and some of the other prisoners were freed after a brief 're-education'. 'Some of our young people', wrote Zheng Chaolin, 'were sent on courses for surveillance and training, where they were ordered to "disclose" each other's (and other people's) [crimes]. The courses lasted six months.... Of those [sent on such courses], only a few were finally sentenced on account of their bad "attitude", while most were freed after completing the course'.[38] Trotskyists were seized in places as far apart as Guangxi, Guangdong, Fujian, Anhui, Zhejiang, Yunnan, Beijing, Shanghai, and the Northeast. Some were removed from where they were arrested to other places to serve their sentences. For example, those arrested in Guangdong were taken to Wuhan, those in north China to Beijing, and those in Wenzhou and Anhui to Shanghai; but those in Yunnan were detained locally.[39] At least a dozen veterans (including Zheng Chaolin) were detained until June 1979. Seven were supporters of the group led by Wang Fanxi and Zheng Chaolin, five were Peng-ites.[40]

The Trotskyist impact on the CCP in 1928 and 1929 was considerable. Those who became Trotskyists included Chen Duxiu, founder of the CCP; a score of senior veteran Communists; and around half the Chinese students in Moscow. Chen's defection worried Stalin, who enquired about his intentions and resources.[41] Even many Communists who did not become Trotskyists wanted to see the rift healed, and believed it had been wrong to expel Chen Duxiu.[42] For example, the three CCP martyrs Peng Pai, Yang Yin, and Yan Changyi, betrayed and arrested in 1929, sent out a last testament from their death-cells imploring the Central Committee to solve its dispute with the Chen Duxiu-ites by peaceful

---

to stay, while the comrades who had stayed behind [like St Peter] in "Rome" continued in operation until the night of 22 December 1952' (Wang Fan-hsi 1991, p. 252).

37   Wang Fanxi, personal communication.
38   Zheng Chaolin, letter, 30 December 1993.
39   Wang Fanxi, personal communication.
40   Wang Fanxi received this information from Zheng Chaolin. Zheng was unable to give the ratio between Peng's followers and followers of the Zheng-Wang group among those arrested (Wang Fanxi, letter, February 9, 1994).
41   Chang Kuo-t'ao 1971–2, Volume 2, p. 115.
42   Ren Jianshu and Tang Baolin 1989, Volume 2, p. 65.

means.⁴³ Because of Chen's special standing and the sympathy he enjoyed in all circles, the CCP treated him cautiously, at least until after the return to China of the arch-Stalinist Wang Ming in late 1937.⁴⁴

At the time of their Unification Congress in 1931, the Trotskyists' prospects looked relatively bright, especially given the disarray of the official Party, to which they continued to vow allegiance. The official Party had changed its leader four times in four years and was racked by factionalism. In 1929 many of its branches had not yet discussed the policies decided at the Sixth Congress in Moscow; other branches were inactive.⁴⁵ The ultra-left Li Lisan line endangered the Party's security and standing and demoralised its urban members, particularly after the capture of its Jiangsu group under He Mengxiong, which some blamed on Wang Ming. Leaders of the CCP warned members that the Trotskyists could take advantage of the fact that 'the theoretical level among our ranks is still low and disputes left over from historical problems have not yet quite settled, [so] it is quite possible for them to join up with party members who are backward and pessimistic, who have left their posts and are resentful towards the Party's leading organs in order to aid the formation of small groups and factions in the Party which would constitute an opposition to the Chinese Party'.⁴⁶ Even Communists like Zhang Guotao who did not sympathise with the Trotskyists agreed with them that the revolution had been defeated and the tactics proposed by Wang Ming were no way out.⁴⁷

The Trotskyists, in contrast, were freshly united under the Party's founding father and had an explanation for the defeats and claimed to have a way forward. So Chen Duxiu's challenge to the Party threw it into confusion, and, according to a party resolution, 'caused a mighty uproar among middle and senior cadres'.⁴⁸ However, his organisation did not live up to its early promise.

The Chinese Trotskyists failed in 1929 and 1930 partly because of the disciplinary measures Zhou Enlai took against them and also because they had no money or resources to maintain their activities. (Their poverty explains why nearly all were writers and intellectuals – people who could support themselves and their organisation independently.) But the main reason they failed was Guomindang repression. 'Following [Chen Duxiu's] arrest', wrote Xu Enzeng, Chiang Kai-shek's security chief at the time, 'all Trotskyite activities

---

43 Benton (ed.) 1997, p. 242.
44 Ren Jianshu and Tang Baolin 1989, Volume 2, pp. 65–6.
45 Zhou Enlai 1981 [1929], pp. 57–60.
46 Zhonggong liujie erzhong quanhui de 'zuzhi jueyian' 1985, p. 24.
47 Chang Kuo-t'ao 1971–2, Volume 2, p. 64.
48 Ren Jianshu and Tang Baolin 1989, Volume 2, p. 56.

in China came to a halt. I still doubt whether Chen's arrest was really profitable to our work. Maybe I should receive a medal from [Mao Zedong], since I silenced one of his most formidable enemies'.[49] By the time Chen Duxiu and the Trotskyists were freed in 1937, China was at the point of war with Japan and the CCP was no longer vulnerable to the Trotskyists' infection, especially since they were unable to develop a strategy for the war.

In later years, the Trotskyists were denounced by leaders of the CCP as counter-revolutionaries and traitors. This campaign, started by Wang Ming's Returned Students in 1930, generated a deep fear and hatred of Trotskyists among party members and turned them into pariahs. In 1938, when Wang Ming returned to China for a second time, the word 'Trotskyist' became synonymous in CCP usage with 'Japanese spy', just as Trotsky himself was called a Hitlerite agent in the Soviet Union.[50] Although the charge was ludicrous, some mud stuck, so that even today many veteran Communists question whether the Chinese Trotskyists should be rehabilitated.

However, the CCP's China-based leaders were not all as opposed to the Trotskyists as Wang Ming and his followers. Privately, Mao criticised the Moscow show-trials and Stalin's campaign to 'suppress counter-revolutionaries'. He must have known that he himself was the main indirect target of Wang Ming's second anti-Trotskyist campaign in 1938, because his own policies were more radical than Wang's and seemed closer to the Trotskyists'; and because the Central Committee under him had rashly conceived of allowing Chen Duxiu back into the Party, and had even included the 'Chinese Trotskyist League' among the addressees of an appeal 'to all parties' for unity against Japan it issued in April 1936.[51] Wang's aim was to finish off all the left-wing opponents of his 'accommodationist' view of the anti-Japanese united front, starting with the Trotskyists and ending if possible with Mao, but instead

---

49   U. T. Hsu n.d., p. 77.
50   See, for example, Sun Qiming 1980 and Tang Baolin 1980. For the original charge against Chen Duxiu, see Kang Sheng 1938. There was a special reason why Deng Xiaoping and others were prepared to be fair to Chen Duxiu on this question after Mao's death in 1976. The man who started the main anti-Trotskyist campaign in 1938 in China was Kang Sheng, just back from Moscow where he had been trained by Wang Ming and the NKVD. Kang Sheng later switched his allegiance from Wang Ming to Mao and was the Maoists' chief inquisitor in the Cultural Revolution, when he victimised Deng and others. When Kang died in 1975, he was among those most hated by the Deng group, which expelled him posthumously from the Party. When the time came to expose Kang's frame-ups, consistency required that his first great frame-up (of Chen Duxiu in 1938) also be exposed.
51   Wang Fan-hsi 1991, p. 223; Ren Jianshu and Tang Baolin 1989, Volume 2, p. 266. For the appeal, see Zhongguo gongchan dang zhongyang weiyuan hui 1991 [1936], pp. 17–19.

Mao finished him off, and no doubt took satisfaction in labelling him a 'Chen Duxiu-style right opportunist'. Yet Mao stepped into line when pressed to do so by Wang Ming, and he tolerated Wang Ming's campaign to defame Chen Duxiu as a Japanese agent.[52]

In recent years, some Chinese scholars have insisted that, following his release from jail in 1937, Chen Duxiu expressed a desire to return to the Communist Party but was unable to meet Mao's conditions, in particular that he publicly repent his errors. However, in an article republished in this volume, Zheng Chaolin convincingly rebuts the idea that Chen wanted to renew his membership in 1937 and says that Chen dismissed the CCP as 'reactionary', although he was not opposed to cooperating with it against Japan.

Trotskyism is usually seen by mainstream commentators as a form of political extremism, intolerant, authoritarian, and the absolute opposite of a democracy movement. In China, however, its association with democracy was always exceptionally strong. This association can be projected back to the early political career of Chen Duxiu. It continued to resonate throughout the history of the Chinese Trotskyist movement.

Chen Duxiu, the best-known Chinese Trotskyist, began his political career as a revolutionary patriot and democrat, a stand he maintained throughout his life. He said in 1918 that '[t]here are now two roads in the world, one is the road of light which leads to democracy, science, and atheism; and the other, the road of darkness leading to despotism, superstition, and divine authority'.[53] During his leadership of the CCP, he insisted that the General Secretary should be elected by and responsible to the different committee heads. According to his North American biographer Lee Feigon, 'The qualifications for membership in Chen's new party would certainly have made Lenin blanch'.[54] Even Mao Zedong recognised that under Chen, the Party was 'rather lively' and free from dogmatism.[55] In September 1940, not long before his death, Chen more or less repeated the formula he had proposed in 1918: 'Science, modern democracy, and socialism are three main inventions, precious beyond measure, of the genius of modern humankind'.[56]

---

52   Chang Kuo-t'ao 1971–2, Volume 2, p. 567.
53   Quoted in Yu-Ju Chih 1965, p. 68.
54   Feigon 1983b, p. 153.
55   Mao Zedong 1969 [1958], p. 160.
56   See the letter to Xiliu in Benton (ed.) 1998.

The 'Bolshevisation' of the CCP, which started around 1924, brought authoritarian habits into the Party that were magnified by Moscow's requirement that the party work as a disciplined, secretive faction within the Guomindang. Chen Duxiu's exit from the leadership in 1927 speeded its drift towards bureaucratic centralism, both because he was among its most committed democrats and because the Party's rejection of him coincided with its formal resolution to ban factions and hence democratic discussion and debate. Moreover, Chen was a man of independent stature who did not need to look to Moscow for backing – something that could be said of none of the lesser leaders who succeeded him over the next few years, before power in the Party eventually fell to Mao Zedong in the late 1930s. A second and more engulfing wave of 'Bolshevisation' hit the CCP in 1930, when Wang Ming took over the leadership and handed an even more complete mastery over it to the Comintern.

The Chinese Trotskyists believed in 1927 that the Chinese revolution had been defeated and profoundly disagreed with the official expectation of a 'new high tide' and the call for urban insurrections backed by peasant armies. They said the immediate task should be to rebuild the trade unions and re-establish the Party in the towns by campaigning for an all-powerful national (or constituent) assembly elected by universal secret ballot to bring together China's disparate economic and political struggles. This meant relegating the call for socialism, proletarian dictatorship, and soviets to general propaganda. That was their strategy until 1937.

The CCP's failure to recognise the defeat it had suffered and to issue a call for democracy capable of unifying the struggles in town and countryside and undermining the Guomindang in the cities left it increasingly isolated. That was partly why, in late 1934, it was defeated in its rural bases in south China and forced to go on the Long March (often portrayed as a victorious advance, but, in reality, at first a disorderly retreat). It faced military obliteration in the countryside and had already suffered political obliteration in the cities, where its underground organisation had become extinct. Only the Japanese invasion of 1937 and its own decision to revive its united front with the Guomindang and wage a 'democratic' struggle in the towns saved it from complete destruction.

The Chinese Trotskyists' campaign after 1929 for a constituent assembly got nowhere, given that most of them were in jail. Their campaign seemed to be no more than a tactical adjustment to the 1927 defeat. However, what attracted many of the Chen Duxiu-ites to the Opposition after 1927 was not just Trotsky's analysis of the failure of the Chinese revolution but above all his advocacy of the democratic slogan for China. On the whole in China, Trotskyism stood historically for the democratic movement, unlike the CCP, which opposed democracy and accused the Trotskyists of 'liquidationism' precisely because of their democratic policy.

Trotskyists in China also energetically discussed the role of democracy in the revolutionary party. This issue was suppressed in the CCP, which was run after 1927 as an élite dictatorship modelled on the Soviet Communist Party. Its leaders ignored Chen Duxiu when he warned them in 1929, at the time of his expulsion, that 'democracy is a necessary instrument for any class that seeks to win the majority to its side' and that suppressing dissident views would lead to a régime of bureaucratic centralism.[57] Until Mao's rise to power in the late 1930s, it was plagued by factionalism, both self-inflicted and imported. All its leaders after 1927 used methods learned from Moscow, plus some they invented independently, to resolve conflict and crush minority opinions. Each new candidate for leader contested Moscow's favours by tailoring his policies to suit the Kremlin; so party politics became increasingly irresponsible and unaccountable.

The Trotskyists' unification in 1931 was a process of 'purification and selection' during which some sectarians incapable of accepting the idea of a broad regroupment left the movement of their own accord. Delegates to the Unification Congress were allotted to the four contributing groups in proportion to their size. According to Wang Fanxi, the Conference 'put an end to the rivalry..., and the atmosphere afterwards was one of harmony, solidarity, and hope'.[58]

But very soon, the Chinese Trotskyists were behind bars. After their release, they were unable to maintain their pluralism. As soon as major differences of opinion arose, in 1941, they split into rival camps that remained in existence ever after. The minority in 1941 agreed to accept the decision of the more youthful majority (soon itself to become a minority) under Peng Shuzhi but requested specific minority rights. The majority refused, so a split took place and became permanent when other differences later arose.[59]

Peng Shuzhi's view of the party had been formed in Moscow, where he had led the Chinese students in 1923–4. Perhaps as a result of his training, he seems to have had less sympathy than other Chinese Trotskyists for the idea of inner-party pluralism. In jail in 1933, he criticised his fellow prisoner Chen Duxiu for refusing to promote himself as a 'natural leader' and failing to 'stand firm', a position Chen rejected (in his reply to Peng) as 'a world apart' from Lenin's

---

57 Chen Duxiu 1987 [1929], p. 449.
58 Wang Fan-hsi 1991, p. 139.
59 For an account of the dispute by a member of Peng Shuzhi's group, see Chen Bilan 2010, pp. 469–75.

idea of leadership.⁶⁰ In 1941, Peng's rallying call was again the need to 'establish authority' in the Trotskyist organisation and fight against 'petty-bourgeois concepts' of organisation. At the Shanghai congress of Trotskyists, where followers of Peng adopted the name Revolutionary Communist Party of China in August 1948, his supporter Liu Jialiang argued in a resolution that

> as a result of the long-term struggle against Stalinist bureaucracy and conditions of isolation, an extreme liberal tendency has grown up among intellectual propagandists in the Trotskyist movement... that has progressed from opposing bureaucratic centralism to opposing Leninist democratic centralism.... Freedom and democracy are counterposed to the centralist mechanism.⁶¹

The resolution went on to claim that 'the tendency represented during the war against Japan by Chen Duxiu' now blamed Bolshevism for Stalinism, a reference to views Chen Duxiu developed towards the end of his life (see Part X of this volume). It argued that 'the party organ should be under the absolute control of the party leadership' rather than become an 'indiscriminating liberal publication', and that 'petty-bourgeois liberal' Trotskyists should be deprived of party membership and reduced to the status of 'sympathisers'. According to Wang Fanxi, Peng Shuzhi's 'Leninist line' on party organisation formed the main issue in the split.⁶²

Thirty years later, in Hong Kong in 1978, an attempt was made to build a new Chinese Trotskyist movement by unifying all those outside China who claimed to be Trotskyists, regardless of where they had stood in the movement's old debates. Peng Shuzhi's supporters in Hong Kong republished the 1948 resolution. Wang Fanxi (in Leeds) and Lou Guohua (in Hong Kong) countered by arguing that Lenin's model of organisation had been developed to meet the specific needs of early twentieth-century Russia, that the Leninist formula of democratic centralism did not mean that the proportion of democracy to centralism should not vary with circumstances, that inner-party democracy should never be suppressed entirely even under conditions of extreme state

---

60   Peng Shuzhi 1982–3 [1933]; and Chen Duxiu 1982–3 [1933].
61   The resolution was published in Shanghai in a 17-page mimeographed pamphlet titled *Zhongguo geming gongchandang jianli zhi zuzhi yuanze yu fangfa: Jianli dang dahui* (*yiji-usiba nian bayue ershiri zhi jiuyue bari*) *yizhi tongguo* ('Organisational principles and methods for setting up the Revolutionary Communist Party of China: Unanimous resolution of the Party's Founding Congress [20 August–8 September 1948]').
62   Wang Fanxi, personal communication; see also Wang Fan-hsi 1991, pp. 236–7.

repression, that the party press should present a spread of opinions (including those of minorities), and that 'the leadership of a revolutionary party must be formed and established from the bottom up, naturally and gradually, in the course of the revolutionary struggle'.[63] Not surprisingly, the unification campaign stalled.

So the Trotskyists spent much of the Japanese War and all of the ensuing civil war divided and have remained divided ever since, both in China and in exile. Had they achieved critical mass in the 1930s, would their early momentum have become self-sustaining and led to unity and growth? Perhaps, but it is hard to avoid concluding that fractiousness was to some extent ingrained on them, and that the split was foreshadowed in earlier divisions.

The induction of Peng Shuzhi into revolutionary politics was quite different from that of the other Chinese Trotskyist leaders. At the age of twenty-five, in 1921, he went straight to Moscow, where he joined the CCP without first serving a revolutionary apprenticeship in China.[64] In Moscow, he became an official leader of the community of Chinese students. He stayed in the Soviet capital for three years. In 1924, he returned to Shanghai, but first the Comintern schooled him in a new line for the CCP stressing 'proletarian hegemony' and trained him in the version of democratic centralism that it introduced first in Russia and then exported to its worldwide sections – Bolshevisation, in the jargon of the day, which Peng Shuzhi helped take back to China. In Shanghai, he entered the top leadership of the CCP, where he served for a while as a protégé of Voitinsky, the Soviet emissary in China at the time. According to his constant critic Zheng Chaolin, he 'tightly latched onto Chen Duxiu in order to make himself more important', so, when the Central Committee fell into the hands of Qu Qiubai, Zhang Guotao, and Tan Pingshan in 1927, he and the rest of Chen's retinue were elbowed out of office.[65]

Most of Chen Duxiu's other supporters in the CCP who became Trotskyists had a difficult relationship with Peng Shuzhi. In Moscow, his alleged élitism and high-handedness alienated many of his fellow-students, particularly those like Zheng Chaolin who had earlier spent time working and studying in France, where they had been free to devote themselves to argument and debate.

---

63 Shuang Shan 1978, Wang Fan-hsi 1991, pp. 236–7, and Lian Gen and Gu He 1978.
64 See Cadart and Cheng 1983 for Peng's own account of his years in Russia; and Benton 1985 for a critical review of this book.
65 Part V.

Zheng's habit of questioning accepted beliefs and values inclined him to an affinity with Chen Duxiu, Chinese Communism's most critical, free-thinking, and iconoclastic leader, and preconditioned him to be out of sympathy with Peng Shuzhi, who put greater emphasis on the need for discipline. What distinguished most members of the Chen Duxiu group is that they had been both in Paris and in Moscow, so they experienced the Soviet Union in a different way from those Chinese students who had not known the 'bourgeois individualism' of bohemian France.

Relations between Peng Shuzhi and Chen Duxiu also became increasingly strained. After the arrest of the Trotskyists' first Central Committee in May 1931, Chen and Peng were practically the only Trotskyist leaders still at large, but they found it hard to remain on friendly terms, perhaps in part because Chen had denounced Peng as a 'rotten water-melon' during the unity negotiations in 1931.[66] After their arrest in 1932, they were at first put together in one cell, but their relationship collapsed and they were allowed separate rooms.

The Left Opposition in China started as a somewhat unwilling coalition jelled into shape mainly by the intervention of Trotsky, whose prestige among the Oppositionists was sufficient to convince them of the need to unite under Chen Duxiu. But because Chen Duxiu's followers in the Trotskyist camp were in many ways quite different in character, outlook, and experience from Peng Shuzhi's, old antagonisms reawakened after the formation of the Chinese Opposition. When the split widened and became fixed in 1941, it is not surprising that most of the old French-educated members of the Moscow group found themselves in the opposite camp to Peng Shuzhi, along with most of the 1929 Russia-returned Trotskyists (such as Wang Fanxi), whom Peng is said to have alienated by his overbearing manner. Having earned his credentials in Moscow as a Bolsheviser, Peng Shuzhi was more orthodox in his opinions and had a less liberal view of party organisation than the democratically minded Chen Duxiu and than younger Trotskyists like Zheng Chaolin and Wang Fanxi. So it is also not surprising that the 1941 split happened on the question of party democracy, with Peng Shuzhi insisting on authority and his opponents insisting on debate.

Whereas I knew Wang Fanxi personally and visited Zheng Chaolin more than once in Shanghai and was responsible for bringing out translations of some of Wang and Zheng's post–1952 work, I never met Peng Shuzhi, who spent much of his exile in the United States, and I had nothing to do with the publication of his writings. It is a striking fact that, after 1949, Peng Shuzhi

---

66   Ren Jianshu and Tang Baolin 1989, Volume 2, pp. 110–12.

published very little in languages other than Chinese about his Trotskyist activities in China. His memoirs (which appeared in 1983 in French) end in January 1925 and do not deal with the Opposition period. The promise in 1983 of further volumes to cover the years 1925–49 has not yet been realised, and perhaps never will be (although there are apparently copious notes in existence, both by him and of interviews with him). As for the Chinese-language memoirs by Chen Bilan, his wife and comrade, which do cover the two Trotskyist decades, they did not appear until 1992 (second edition 2010) and have not so far been translated.[67] So this sourcebook inevitably focuses more on the tradition of Chinese Trotskyism pioneered by Chen Duxiu and associated with Wang Fanxi and Zheng Chaolin, and less so on the Peng group. However, where possible, I have included material by and about Peng: his 1947 essay on the history of Chinese Trotskyism (and Wang Fanxi's riposte); lengthy excerpts from his 1951 evaluation of Mao's revolution (which can also be compared with Wang's roughly contemporaneous reflections); the account of the 'lives and times' of Peng Shuzhi and Chen Bilan by their daughter Cheng Yingxiang and her husband Claude Cadart; and an article by Joe Miller that is sympathetic to Peng. I have also included an article on guerrilla war by Chen Bilan in which she criticises a letter by Wang Fanxi on the same subject.

It is also a fact that Peng Shuzhi and Chen Bilan were too old and physically too far removed from the scene of action to play an important role in the campaign to restore Trotskyism to visibility and respectability in China after Mao's death, and they died before it first started to bear fruit in the late 1980s. Because of their absence from this effort, Chinese commentators and historians know far less about them than about the group associated with Zheng Chaolin, whose link with Chen Duxiu and refusal to leave China in 1949 earned him a reputation for integrity. Moreover, Zheng was available in Shanghai for historians to interview after 1979 and lived long enough (until 1998) to contribute to the discussion in China about the nature of Chinese Trotskyism and to campaign for the Trotskyists' rehabilitation. For all these reasons, there were fewer materials available concerning the Peng group when I collected the sources presented in this volume. However, for the sake of completeness and as a guide for those interested in studying its contribution to Chinese Trotskyism, I have included an extensive inventory of materials on it in the Bibliographical Note.

---

67   Chen Bilan 1992 and 2010. Mike Taber, who did the index for this book, has pointed out that an English-language translation in manuscript form does in fact exist. Formerly in possession of Pathfinder Press, it's currently in the Hoover Institution holdings (http://oac.cdlib.org/findaid/ark:/13030/kt638ncokw/entire_text/). Mike Taber can't say whether it's complete.

Chen Duxiu's preoccupation with the relationship between socialism and democracy eventually led him in the late 1930s to rethink his opinion of some aspects of the politics of Lenin and Trotsky. In the wake of the Moscow show-trials and Stalin's alliance with Hitler, he drew a link between Lenin's denial of democracy and Stalin's crimes and gave up distinguishing between bourgeois and proletarian democracy. He expressed these views in an exchange of letters with Wang Fanxi and others between 1936 and 1938, and again in late 1939 and early 1940, by which time he had been freed from prison and was living in a small town in Sichuan. His last articles and letters were later edited by He Zishen and published in a posthumous collection.

Wang Fanxi and other Trotskyists said that, after his move to Sichuan, Chen Duxiu had reverted to his youthful belief in 'pure democracy', which they criticised as abstract and transcendental. Even so, they respected his formulations and tried to preserve those elements in them they found to be of value. In 1957, Wang summarised his side of the exchange, in seven theses. Some of the correspondence, and Wang's theses, are contained in this volume.

In the ten years between the defeat of 1927 and the outbreak of all-out war between China and Japan on 7 July 1937, the CCP struggled to survive, but the war changed its fortunes and set it on the road to power. The Chinese Trotskyists viewed the CCP's decision in 1937 to resume the united front with the Guomindang (now morphed into an alliance against Japan) as a surrender to Stalin and thus a repeat of the errors of the mid–1920s. This was because, on paper, the united front allowed for the reorganisation of the Red Army under Chiang, the winding up of the Chinese soviets, an end to class struggle, and the merging of CCP and Guomindang territories. Watching from the towns, the Trotskyists failed to understand the CCP's strategy in the war, and accused it of 'converting the peasant armies ... into pawns in the hands of the Moscow military strategists' and delivering them into the hands of Chiang Kai-shek, an act of 'vilest betrayal'.[68] What they could not know was that Mao Zedong, although reluctant to be seen disagreeing openly with Stalin, had no intention of sacrificing his bases and forces and resolutely retained his party's independence of Chiang Kai-shek. Moreover, during the war, he won ground by actively championing the resistance to Japan and criticising Guomindang passivity and corruption.

---

68   *Spark* (Cape Town), Volume 2, no. 7 (16) (July 1936).

The Trotskyists, in contrast, spent the war in Shanghai organising workers, although the workers' movement had been shut down by the Japanese occupation. They failed to develop armed forces and therefore took little part in the military resistance.

Some Chinese Trotskyists, including Chen Duxiu, were aware that the war had rendered old formulae out of date and tried to strike out in new directions. Chen Duxiu's anti-Japanese engagement was unrelenting, throughout and beyond the period of his Trotskyist commitment. When a protest-movement swept China after Japan's seizure of Shenyang on 18 September 1931, as a first step towards seizing the whole of northeastern China, he wrote some forty articles for *Huohua* and the Trotskyists' internal bulletin, and on 5 December 1931, he founded *Rechao* ('Hot Tide'), in which he published 102 'contemporary comments' denouncing Japanese aggression, UK and US complicity in it, and the Guomindang's 'treasonous' failure to stand up against it. At the same time, he welcomed the military resistance to Japan spearheaded by the Guomindang's maverick Nineteenth Route Army, then stationed in Shanghai, in defiance of the Guomindang government's orders. He condemned peaceful petitioning of the Guomindang government and said that national salvation could be achieved only through the struggle of 'the lower stratum of the toiling masses.... It is definitely wrong to depend on the rulers'. He again called for a constituent assembly to 'rival the Nationalists' traitor-government', act as a general command for the whole of China, organise armed forces, organise the state, exterminate the organisations of Japan's running dogs, refuse to negotiate with the Japanese, and give land to the peasants. He called on patriotic junior officers of the Nationalist armed forces to disobey orders and prevent compromise.

Up to then, the constituent assembly slogan, adopted on Trotsky's recommendation, had failed to find an echo in society, but Chen Duxiu breathed new life into Trotsky's orthodox conception by adapting it to China's changing politics. It seemed to him that the revolution was once again in flow and the time had come to sweep the Guomindang from power, even by organising soviets among anti-Japanese troops susceptible to revolutionary influence and among striking workers and peasants.

At the time, the CCP was set on a sectarian course that prevented it from taking full advantage of the turmoil caused by Japanese aggression. Conscious of its failings, Chen Duxiu issued a call for joint action with bourgeois, petty-bourgeois, and other parties and close cooperation and unity with the CCP in the struggle against Japan. Earlier, he had denounced the CCP's peasant war as a betrayal of the workers' movement and predicted that its Red Army of 'lumpenproletarians' would collapse or become a 'White Army' of the rural petty bourgeoisie. Now, he proposed that, once urban soviets or anti-Japanese volunteer forces had been established, 'in parts of provinces where there were already peasant soviets, they should converge with the Red Army to occupy the cities'. However, the CCP rejected his overtures and compared the Trotskyists to Guomindang reformists and the Third Party, 'the most dangerous enemy, which we should attack... with might and main'.

Chen Duxiu's willingness and ability to rethink his ideas and to respond creatively to new developments led him into fights with his more orthodox comrades. He was no ideologist or theoretician and never able to develop a sustained and systematic Marxist analysis, but he was a political observer of great perspicacity and one of China's least dogmatic and least sectarian Communists. Sadly, few of the minority of Trotskyists still at large in late 1931 and early 1932 supported him. Some, including Liu Renjing, condemned his search for joint action against Chiang Kai-shek with 'patriotic soldiers' and petty-bourgeois parties as 'tailism' and 'thorough-going opportunism' and implied that his call for joint action with the CCP and his changed attitude towards Mao's Red Army was a 'capitulation'. Understandably, Chen set greater store by campaigning for his policies among the 'nationalist-democratic movement of the students' and the railway and industrial workers than by compromising with the 'liquidationist waitists' and 'ultra-leftists' who dominated what was left of his own organisation and appeared to disrespect him.[69]

Chen Duxiu's dispute with Liu Renjing was short lived, for in October 1932 Chen was arrested and disappeared for the next five years into jail, but the Japan question continued to divide the movement. In 1934, followers of Liu Renjing expelled Chen Duxiu for refusing to criticise himself for 'opportunism'. They also expelled Chen Qichang and Yin Kuan (both Chen Duxiu supporters) for trying to join the pro-Communist Song Qingling's Congress Against Imperialist War and Fascism and for contacting dissident and nationalist-minded Guomindang military leaders in November 1933 during the Fujian Incident, when a Fujian People's Revolutionary Government was declared in opposition to Chiang Kai-shek, at a time when the CCP's policy towards the Fujian rebels was sectarian and dismissive.[70]

---

69   Ren Jianshu and Tang Baolin 1989, Volume 2, pp. 78 and 114–30. Chen Duxiu first revised his view on the Chinese Red Army in January 1931, when he recommended an 'absolutely friendly attitude towards the peasant guerrillas' and said that 'to stand on the sidelines and view them with hostility is not the attitude of a Communist' (Ren Jianshu and Tang Baolin 1989, Volume 2, p. 104).

70   See Ren Jianshu and Tang Baolin 1989, Volume 2, pp. 192–4. The woman Trotskyist Li Cailian went to Fuzhou during the rebellion. The Opposition's positive attitude towards the rebellion helped swing Harold Isaacs towards it (Wang Fanxi, personal communication).

In July 1936, when moves towards a Second United Front first got under way, Chen Duxiu had denounced the CCP's rapprochement with the Guomindang, but, a few months later, he himself expressed support for the government as long as it remained committed to resistance. However, he continued to criticise Chiang Kai-shek's other policies and to demand democracy, opposition rights (including for the CCP), a multi-party system, an end to dictatorship, a lessening of the burden on the people, and a resolution of the land problems of the poor peasants.[71]

During the war, Chen Duxiu dreamed of building a united front of all democratic parties independent of the Guomindang and the CCP, for he believed there could be no revolution while the Guomindang continued to resist Japan and the cities were under Japanese occupation. This idea had its pedigree in the Trotskyists' old fight for a constituent assembly. Later, Wang Fanxi and others admitted that Chen Duxiu's policy was 'tactically... right and we were wrong', but at the time they rejected it. In any case, the CCP's united front foredoomed any attempt by the Trotskyists to create a revolutionary-democratic alliance, in that it offered the smaller parties an apparently similar but far more viable alternative. So, when Trotskyists in Shanghai announced on 20 January 1939 that they would cooperate with the Guomindang and the CCP in a popular movement in support of the war as long as it guaranteed all parties freedom of action, they received no response.[72]

At the same time as proposing an alliance with the minor democratic parties, Chen Duxiu tried to infiltrate some of his Trotskyist followers into existing anti-Japanese armed forces as advisers, in an attempt to influence them politically. But this scheme also failed, when Chen's target in the army was relieved of his command, probably by government agents who had been alerted to the scheme.[73] His military plan was all the more remarkable given his doctrinal

---

71   Ren Jianshu and Tang Baolin 1989, Volume 2, pp. 207–27. According to Tang Baolin, Chen Duxiu concluded after leaving prison that 'Chiang Kai-shek's rule seemed to be rather stable; it is not as frail as we analysed it to be'. However, his source is an article written by Pu Qingquan that contains numerous errors and was apparently designed to confirm CCP prejudices about Chen Duxiu.

72   Ren Jianshu and Tang Baolin 1989, Volume 2, p. 279. Tang Baolin argues that the Trotskyists changed their attitude towards cooperation after Chen Duxiu denounced their position in a letter to Trotsky, but actually, there was no contradiction on this question between the earlier and later positions of the Shanghai Trotskyists, who (with the exception of Zheng Chaolin) all along supported the war but would not cooperate with either of the bigger parties.

73   Ren Jianshu and Tang Baolin 1989, Volume 2, p. 235.

repugnance for 'military' revolution, either by Chiang Kai-shek at the time of the Northern Expedition or by the Chinese Red Army.

Only in Shandong[74] and in Zhongshan county in Guangdong[75] did small groups of Trotskyists cut off from Shanghai by the war organise guerrilla-detachments, but those in Shandong were destroyed by the CCP and those in Zhongshan by the Japanese. Despite these defeats, Wang Fanxi later concluded that the Trotskyist leaders should have set up more armed detachments:

> Naturally we can't say for certain that we would have built up a force strong enough to compete with the CCP, but at least we would not have ended up as we did: during the war, our organisation practically collapsed, some cadres even starved to death, and we made no contribution in action to the anti-Japanese effort, while in the postwar period, despite the favourable prerevolutionary situation, our revived organisation (or rather, two organisations) was too weak to profit from it, and we adopted an entirely passive attitude towards the civil war between the CCP and the KMT, in which we played the role of bystanders.[76]

Other Trotskyists like Peng Shuzhi continued to believe they had been right to oppose guerrilla war waged from the villages, that their 'orthodox' strategy had been right, and that the CCP's victory had had nothing to do with guerrilla war but was a result of 'exceptional historical circumstances'.[77]

The Chinese Trotskyists' links to Trotsky's Fourth International were tenuous. Contact was slow, unreliable, and dependent mainly on foreign seafarers. When the Chinese Trotskyists were not in prison, they were usually cut off from the outside world, by war or poor communications. So they played

---

74 An intelligence report (No. 270,10491) in the archive of the Guomindang's Intelligence Bureau in Taibei mentions an incident on the border between Shandong and Jiangsu in 1939 in which about one hundred and fifty Trotskyists were killed. However, Qian Jun 1985, pp. 102–3, denies that the ringleaders of a 'Trotskyist' conspiracy (perhaps but not necessarily the same incident) at around this time were Trotskyists.

75 Wang Fan-hsi 1991, p. 214. For a contemporary account of Trotskyist guerrillas in Zhongshan, see Frank Glass's report on the Communist League of China, written towards the end of 1939 and sent to Trotsky, in whose archive in the Houghton Library of Harvard University it can now be found; the report is reproduced under the title 'The Communist League of China' in *Revolutionary History* Vol. 2, No. 4 (1990), pp. 26–8.

76 This volume, p. 1018.

77 For criticism of these views, see Wang Fanxi 1973, in this volume, pp. 1003–26.

little part in the debates of the world Trotskyist movement, and few non-Chinese Trotskyists knew much about them. After 1949, of course, those in China became incommunicado.

Just before the final Communist victory, Peng Shuzhi and his Political Bureau transferred to Hong Kong,[78] and Wang Fanxi was sent to Hong Kong to coordinate from a 'safe place' the activities of his own organisation, which stayed behind in China.[79] Peng Shuzhi landed up in Paris via Vietnam and then went to the US; Wang Fanxi was deported to Macao and later left for Leeds. Wang Fanxi wrote several books and many articles and pamphlets, but only his *Memoirs* were published in translation (in 1980); Peng Shuzhi had greater access to English-language outlets run by his comrades in New York. Partly because the Chinese Trotskyists were so isolated, the thinking of some of them developed along independent lines, reworking old ideas and developing new ones when necessary.

One example of a radical modification of an existing strategy is the idea of 'victoryism' developed by Wang Fanxi and Zheng Chaolin in the war against Japan, as a play on the 'defeatism' advocated by Lenin in the First World War. 'Defeatism' was not appropriate in a semi-colony like China, whose resistance to Japan was progressive, but to support it was not the same as uncritically supporting the leadership of Chiang Kai-shek. To win the war, a revolutionary government was needed, so revolution could not wait on victory. Revolutionaries should support the Chinese side but maintain their independence and the right to criticise the conduct of the war. The problem was, said Wang Fanxi, 'how to transform the "arms of criticism" into the "criticism of arms"', so that it becomes revolution.[80] Peng Shuzhi, in contrast, emphasised the progressive nature of the war against Japan and opposed trying to win it through revolution.

Some Chinese Trotskyists also developed original analyses of the nature of the CCP's revolution and the reasons for its victory. For years, they had argued that Stalinist parties like the CCP had degenerated into 'petty-bourgeois' parties and could no longer carry out revolutions,[81] so the Maoist victory threw them into confusion. If the Mao régime was 'bourgeois', how had it been able to overthrow the Guomindang?

---

78   Ch'en Pi-lan 1980, p. 41.
79   Wang Fan-hsi 1991, pp. 251–2.
80   This volume, p. 1026.
81   This volume, pp. 1003–26.

Peng Shuzhi clung to the traditional characterisation of the CCP as a 'petty-bourgeois, peasant' party, arguing that it had won less through its 'subjective' efforts than because of 'exceptional' historical circumstances, including the disintegration of the Chiang Kai-shek régime, Washington's decision to abandon the Guomindang, the Japanese invasion (which had worked to the advantage of the CCP), and Russian aid.[82] When the new state moved in an anticapitalist direction, he said it had changed in nature because of the large numbers of workers that joined it and was 'in transition towards becoming a workers' party'.[83] His arguments about the CCP – its 'peasant class-nature' in the 1930s and 1940s, its victory in 1949, and its evolution after 1949 – can be criticised as mechanistic, in that they looked to its 'objective' determinants for explanations rather than to the men and women who led it.

Wang Fanxi, on the other hand, took greater pains to reconcile anti-Stalinism with the reality of what had happened in the Chinese Revolution. Did the CCP's victory mean it had abandoned Stalinism and become revolutionary, as Michel Pablo, leader of the Fourth International in Paris, argued? Was it simply a switch of power among bourgeois, as Peng Shuzhi originally concluded? Or was the new régime one led by bureaucratic collectivists, as the US Trotskyist Max Shachtman believed – a qualitative change, although not the sort Wang had fought for? At first, Wang followed Shachtman – the CCP was bureaucratic collectivist, and so was the Soviet Union, which Wang (following Trotsky) had previously characterised as a 'degenerated workers' state'. This option seemed to solve the intellectual riddle, but Wang quickly dropped it, for it could not provide a prescription for revolutionary action.[84]

In the end, Wang revised his view of the CCP. Yes, it was Stalinist, that is, profoundly bureaucratic and nationalist, but it was not a petty-bourgeois party that had given up class struggle, as Trotskyists had previously argued. This was because it had withdrawn to the countryside not as part of a strategic reorientation but to escape government repression. In the villages, it continued to carry out class struggle. The Second United Front had been a tactical manoeuvre,

---

82 This volume, pp. 998–9.

83 This volume, p. 968.

84 Yi De 1950. Zheng Chaolin explained his view of the CCP victory in Zheng Chaolin 1950, where he argued that the new régime was thoroughly reactionary and state-capitalist. Zheng had all along believed that the Chinese Revolution died in the countryside after the defeat of 1927. Whereas Wang saw the events of 1949 as a step forward, Zheng saw them as a 'natural disaster'. Of the Chinese Trotskyist thinkers, Zheng was beyond doubt the most stubbornly consistent.

not a strategic turn. The CCP had remained an organisation of revolutionaries that recruited members and soldiers on a class basis. So it remained a working-class party, for a political party is defined not just by its social composition but by 'the people who lead it'. Yet, although Wang thought Maoism had proved to be more resourceful than Trotsky's view of Stalinism implied, he still thought the Trotskyists had been right to form a separate and independent party in China, for even where Stalinist parties do overthrow capitalism, the methods they use lead to a 'socialism' deformed by bureaucracy and despotism.[85]

The Chinese Left Opposition was among the largest of the Trotskyist organisations outside Russia, and the best prepared and the most mature and able. Trotsky himself saw it as the cream of the crop.[86] So why was it ultimately so ineffective?

If analytical and prognostic skill determined the fate of political parties, the Chinese Trotskyists might have made a greater mark, for their criticisms of the official party's errors, false promises, and excesses were often incisive. They rightly predicted the defeat of the Chinese soviets after 1927 (yet failed to see that even so, a peasant army in China could still make a revolution). Although they themselves achieved nothing in the Japanese War, their comments on the terms of the Second United Front as it was publicly presented by CCP spokespersons in 1937 and 1938 unwittingly replicated those of Mao Zedong, who behind closed doors took a similar view of the 'accommodationist' proposals made by Wang Ming on behalf of the Kremlin and vigorously resisted their implementation. After 1949, the Trotskyists' argument that any true revolution must be radically anticapitalist and their criticism of Mao's idea that capitalism and class collaboration would last for 'several decades' was soon confirmed, when Mao took rapid steps to curb the capitalists, in defiance of his own earlier promises and predictions. So too was their prediction that socialism without democracy would meet with endless crises.

But, although many of their arguments and forecasts about the CCP and the future of Mao's government were borne out, their own strategy and tactics in the revolution, especially during the period of the anti-Japanese resistance, were short-sighted and doctrinaire by comparison with his. They failed to see the workers had been neutralised as a cumulative effect of the 1927 defeat, the ensuing Guomindang repression, and – most decisively of all – the Japanese occupation of China's industrial centres; and that, for the revolution

---

85 Wang Fan-hsi 1991, pp. 265–6.
86 Letter to the Chinese Opposition (January 8, 1931), in Evans and Block (eds) 1976, p. 500.

to succeed, it was essential to start organising the peasants even before the movement in the towns revived. So they pinned their hopes exclusively on the urban proletariat, a tiny class (reckoned by Mao Zedong in a famous essay to comprise less than half of one per cent of the population),[87] and continued to do so even after the start of the Japanese War in 1937, when the proletariat was further disabled by the invasion, and during the ensuing civil war.

At the root of this failure lay an excess of orthodoxy. The mission of the CCP in its infancy, shouldered in 1931 by Chen Duxiu's Trotskyists, was to undo the pattern of the Chinese past, which seemed to the early Communists to be set in an endless cycle of dynastic decay, peasant revolt, and renewal under a new despotic line. Chen's comrades in 1921 thought they had found in the modern urban classes – the bourgeoisie, the proletariat, and the critical intelligentsia – a way to break this vicious circle. The Chinese Trotskyists' unremitting commitment to this belief explains why they insisted – save for a brief interval in 1938, under the exceptional circumstances of the Japanese invasion – on sticking to the cities, and why they never once considered forsaking them in the long term for the villages.

They were Marxists in the classic mould. Although they understood the need for agitation in the villages, first they wanted to sink roots in the cities, for their members were too few to dissipate across the vast Chinese countryside. Even after the Japanese invasion in 1937, Chen Duxiu stuck firmly to his belief that there could be no revolution outside urban culture. Unlike his younger comrades, he was deeply pessimistic about the chances of revolution breaking out in the War, for China's industrial base along the coast had been destroyed and unrest in the countryside could not (he believed) make a proletarian revolution. 'In numbers, in material strength, and in spirit', he wrote to Trotsky on 3 November 1939, '[the workers] have gone back to where they were thirty to forty years ago'.[88]

The popular view is that Mao quickly saw through the bankruptcy of an urban strategy after 1927 and turned to the villages, whereas Chen Duxiu, who 'did not understand the peasants', was incapable of Mao's leap in imagination. But, in reality, Mao arrived only gradually and empirically at his strategy of encircling the cities with the villages, after he had been forced by circumstance to move into the countryside, and for several years he continued to talk in terms of the city leading the village. Nor is it true that Chen Duxiu failed to

---

87 Mao Zedong 1970–2 [1926], Volume 1, pp. 161–74. A later version of this article, heavily edited to make the younger Mao conform to the Mao-Stalin political canon, appeared in Mao Zedong's *Selected Works* after 1949.

88 Shuang Shan (ed.) 1981, p. 77.

understand the role of the peasantry in Chinese history. On the contrary, from his own point of view, he understood it all too well. The Chinese Trotskyists, far from ignoring the villages as a result of intellectual stiffness, actively resisted a turn to the countryside and insisted on striving for a new way to redeem Chinese society and the Chinese nation, rather than follow what they saw as the old and fruitless one. They failed, partly because the class of industrial workers on which they tried to fasten was too small, too little spread (in just three or four big cities), and too demoralised by defeat and terror to pay much attention to them. When the repression came, unlike the official party, they had no rural sanctuaries to retreat to.

Because of their excessive orthodoxy, the Chinese Trotskyists were, as Wang Fanxi conceded, relegated to the role of bystanders in China's national and social movements in the late 1930s and the 1940s. Even those few who tried to create armed forces and foment revolution in the villages failed. This was partly because they lacked the necessary human skills and material resources. Most were *literati* with no experience of bearing arms. Mao and Zhu De formed their Red Army around the remnants of renegade Guomindang divisions, workers' armed pickets, and local bandit forces, and obtained financial and other support from the Russians.[89] The Trotskyists had neither weapons nor people capable of bearing them. They remained unarmed at a time when arms decided all, and so they failed, for 'all armed prophets have been victorious, and all unarmed prophets have been destroyed'.[90]

However, the main reason for their failure to make a political impression was the massive opposition they faced on all sides. The Guomindang's summary justice and 'scientifically organised' state terror defeated the Trotskyists in the cities, while the CCP killed those it encountered in the villages and finished them off nationwide by slandering them as agents of Japan. Revolutionaries in many countries have faced state terror, but the Chinese Trotskyists were equally hated both by the government and by a highly organised and influential opposition that had its own mechanisms of repression. It is probably impossible to find the same pattern anywhere else in the world save Vietnam (where, after 1945, the Trotskyists, despite their relative strength, were likewise crushed).[91]

---

89   That the Russians aided the CCP after 1945 is well known; for the help they gave it during the war against Japan, see Garver 1988, p. 158.
90   Machiavelli, *The Prince*.
91   On the Vietnamese Trotskyists, see Ngo Van 1995 and 2010.

All parties of the democratic centre that tried to follow a third way in China suffered obliteration. Only those that leaned to one side, that of the Guomindang or the CCP, could hope to survive. The Trotskyists refused to compromise, and took the consequences.

So the Chinese Trotskyists never achieved their aim of building a workers' movement, and were tested more in jail than in struggle. At most, they remained a propaganda group. They never realised their programme, which remained abstract and failed (unlike Mao's) to acquire genuinely Chinese features. It was therefore easy for the Maoists to denigrate them as foreign tools and put them down the memory hole after 1949.

What of the Chinese Trotskyists today? The old Trotskyist polemic about the nature of the Chinese Revolution is now only of historical interest, but the other issue that most exercised them, the relationship between socialism and democracy, is more relevant than it ever was. So is the role of the workers, who they always believed to be central to the revolution, for today the industrial proletariat in China is numerically stronger and better educated than ever. But, disappointingly for those who value the Chinese Trotskyists' integrity, courage, and vision, there is no sign of a revival of the Trotskyist tradition in China, and not even much sign of their posthumous recognition, as prophets in their own land. The most that can be said is that a faint ghost of Trotskyism continues to haunt some political, cultural, and intellectual circles.

In the late 1970s and the 1980s, some well-known dissidents and oppositionists like Wang Xizhe, Chen Fu, and Shi Huasheng were attracted by the Trotskyists' views on socialist democracy. However, they were usually careful not to say so openly, because the topic remained sensitive and even dangerous.[92] Critical and creative writers in the official world wrote sympathetic stories about Trotskyists loosely based on the autobiographies of Zheng Chaolin[93] and Wang Fanxi.[94]

Probably the first veteran party leader to call for a reassessment of the role Chen Duxiu and the Chinese Trotskyists played in the revolution was General Xiao Ke in a speech made in 1981 to mark the sixtieth anniversary of the founding of the CCP. Xiao Ke asked seven questions:

---

92 Lau Sanching 1992, p. 20; Benton 1985, p. 19; Miller 1979, pp. 13–15.
93 Zhou Meisen 1997.
94 Wang Ruowang 1989.

What were the differences between China's Trotsky-Chen liquidationist faction and foreign Trotskyists? How was their programme? What was their attitude to Chiang Kai-shek's Guomindang régime? What was their attitude to the Communist Party? What was their attitude to imperialism and in particular to Japanese imperialism? How did they acquit themselves in the jails of the Guomindang? What was [Chen's] political attitude between his release from prison [in 1937] and his death?[95]

But, as the treatment by the CCP's official historians of Wu Jimin's manuscript shows, Xiao Ke's questions remain unanswered, at least in public.[96]

Zheng Chaolin's release from prison in 1979 and the publication in China of his and Wang Fanxi's memoirs had an impact in some university history-schools. Quite a few scholars and historians visited Zheng to ask him about events in France (of which after Deng Xiaoping's death he was the sole surviving witness) and in the Soviet Union in the mid–1920s and in China.[97]

But the most important factor in the reconsideration of Trotskyism in China was the rediscovery of Chen Duxiu. 'In the late 1920s Chen was kicked out of the party as a "Trotskyist deviationist and opportunist" for advocating many of the same ideas proposed by the students in 1989', wrote the US historian Lee Feigon. 'In the 1980s some of those interested in reform looked to Chen Duxiu's ideas to demonstrate a tradition within the Party for openness and democracy'.[98] Many books on Chen Duxiu and collections of his last articles and letters have appeared in China over the past thirty years. Several highlight his discussion of the relationship between socialism and democracy.[99] According to the

---

95 Xiao Ke 1994, pp. 32–3.
96 In 2013, an article in a mainstream news journal noted what it called the 'rehabilitation' of the Trostkyists in the former Soviet Union and sketched a history of the treatment of Trotsky by Maoist historiographers since 1949. According to this article, Zheng Yifan, the main translator of Trotsky's writings into Chinese (originally published in just fifty copies, for top cadres), ended up concluding, in his preface to a *Tuoluociji duben* ('Trotsky reader'), published in 2008, that Trotsky 'was undoubtedly a revolutionary' (Xu Tian 2013).
97 For an extremely sympathetic account of Zheng Chaolin's political calvary, published in one of China's most popular contemporary magazines, see Jin Shupeng 1993. As Wu Jimin points out, among those who consulted Zheng Chaolin about his days in France was Mao Mao, who quoted his comments in her filial biography of Deng Xiaoping (Mao Mao 1993).
98 Feigon 1990, p. ix.
99 Wang Guangyuan (ed.) 1987; Tang Baolin and Lin Maosheng 1988; and Ren Jianshu and Tang Baolin 1989. An early and perhaps the best available chronology of Chen's life is Zhi Yuru 1974. In Taiwan, there is Zheng Xuejia 1989. See also Guo Chengtang 1992, a translation of Thomas Kuo 1975, based on Kuo's 1969 PhD.

orthodox historian Tang Baolin, Chen's positions on 'the five great issues of progress, democracy, science, patriotism, and socialism ... were all essentially in accordance with the truth'.[100] The partial rehabilitation of Chen Duxiu has inevitably contributed to a greater tolerance for Chinese Trotskyism, which is an essential part of his biography.

The rediscovery in China since the death of Mao of the martyred dissident Wang Shiwei also helped boost the Trotskyists' reputation. Wang Shiwei was a close friend of Wang Fanxi – the two studied together in the same class in Beijing University's Department of Letters in the mid-1920s. Although Wang Shiwei never formally joined the Trotskyists, he worked with them before slipping away in the late 1930s to join the Mao-led anti-Japanese resistance, and he shared their approach to literature and their opposition to bureaucracy and élitism. He was arrested in 1942 in Yan'an, the CCP's wartime capital, for criticising privilege and 'bureaucratic tendencies' in the Party and for making the Trotskyist argument that the role of literature in a revolutionary society should be to monitor abuses by the leadership and creative writing should be free to explore the complexities of the soul. He was put before a Moscow-style show-trial in Yan'an and denounced among other things for opposing Stalin's purges. At his trial, he defended the Trotskyists Wang Fanxi and Chen Qichang as 'Communists of humanity'. He was put to the sword in 1947. In China, in 1957, during the Hundred Flowers campaign, and again in the 1980s, under Deng Xiaoping, radical activists and thinkers elevated him into a symbol of the struggle for cultural and political freedom and saw him as one of the earliest victims of its suppression under the Communists. So it is right that he is represented in this volume, by the two Trotskyist-inspired essays written in Yan'an that led to his arrest and execution and that were hailed fifty years after his murder as antecedents of contemporary dissent.[101]

Today, no one in China seriously believes Chen Duxiu worked for the Japanese in the 1930s, just as no one in Russia seriously believes Trotsky was a Hitlerite agent. However, in 2005, the historian Zuo Shuangwen, writing in the party history journal, cited evidence suggesting that, at the end of his life, Chen Duxiu knowingly took money from the Guomindang.[102] Zuo says five files in the archives of the Institute of Modern History in the Academia Sinica in

---

100 Tang Baolin (ed.) 1993, p. 17.
101 See Part XIV.
102 Zuo Shuangwen 2005. See <http://dangshi.people.com.cn/GB/144956/10847969.html>, accessed 17 August 2010.

Taipei, marked 'secret', show that the Guomindang, acting 'in the name of Zhu Jiahua', gave Chen sums of 1,000, 5,000, and 8,000 yuan in 1940, 1941, and 1942 (a relatively paltry amount, it must be said), which Chen 'reluctantly accepted'. This evidence supposedly overturned the scholarly consensus of the previous twenty years, which had absolved Chen of all such charges. Thus a final assault was launched on Chen's reputation: if not a 'national traitor', was he not perhaps a class traitor?

In fact, Zhu Jiahua, a professor of geology, had been Chen Duxiu's colleague at Peking University before the founding of the CCP and in 1940 was appointed acting president of the Academia Sinica. Although a prominent member of the Guomindang, his academic tie to Chen would explain why Chen (living in poverty and ill health in Jiangjin, a county town near Chongqing) was prepared to accept his help. Would Chen have accepted it if he had known or suspected the money's actual source? Almost certainly not, for it had always been his principle never to take money of any political colour, whether from Zhou Enlai (representing the CCP) or from people like Hu Zongnan, Dai Li, and Zhang Guotao (representing the Guomindang). One can therefore agree with the findings of another senior Chinese scholar, the historian Zeng Yanxiu (writing in *Yanhuang chunqiu*, one of China's most important radical-reformist journals), that Chen's acceptance of Zhu's gift did not impugn his personal integrity, 'which was as the sun and the moon'.[103]

At the end of their lives, both Wang Fanxi and Zheng Chaolin, the only Chinese Trotskyist leaders to survive into the second decade of the post-Mao reforms, campaigned simultaneously, 'from both within [in Shanghai] and without [in Leeds]', for the complete rehabilitation of their movement. By this, they meant the restoration of its members to a state of acquittal on all criminal charges against them, rather than a mere amnesty of the sort Mao and Deng instituted, which did not necessarily entail exoneration. In the 1990s, officials wrote to Wang urging him to return to China to live out his final years there. Wang made no secret of his wish to rejoin his wife and children in Shanghai after fifty years of exile, but in his reply he made the Trotskyists' rehabilitation a condition for doing so, to chime with letters Zheng Chaolin wrote to party congresses after 1979 also demanding rehabilitation. Neither Wang nor Zheng received an answer.

Today, after a sad crescendo of deaths at around the turn of the century, as far as I know only one Trotskyist veteran remains alive in China. He is Zhou

---

103   Ibid.

Lüqiang, born in Wenzhou in 1927. Zhou joined the Trotskyist movement as a student in Shanghai in 1947 and narrowly escaped execution during Chiang Kai-shek's evacuation of the city in 1949. He was arrested and jailed by the Communists in 1952. In his book, Wu Jimin calls Zhou Lüqiang and his wife Qian Huichu 'birds of passage', on account of their annual north-south migrations to meet one another after Zhou's release from prison in 1959, when he was transferred to a labour camp in Inner Mongolia. For the next two decades, each winter he made the days-long journey down from the icy Hulunbeir grasslands to Shanghai; while, each summer, she toiled up the long, hot, lonely road from Shanghai to Hulunbeir, until her death in 1981. In 1987 Zhou Lüqiang finally returned south to live with his son in Shanghai, where I met him several years ago, still staunchly committed to the Trotskyist cause. Zhou would probably be the sole direct beneficiary of any rehabilitation (not that such a consideration would occur to him). However, even posthumous rehabilitation in China (as in the old Soviet Union) can benefit victims' surviving relatives, who, if they are lucky, might get a pension, better accommodation, and a better job.[104]

In his book, Wu Jimin mentions the Soviet rehabilitations of 1988, arguing that the same treatment should be extended to the Chinese Trotskyists, 'who drew their inspiration from the Soviet Trotskyists'. So does Chen Sihe, in his Preface. But, in reality, Gorbachev never formally rehabilitated Trotsky, the only old Bolshevik not restored to the Party. Logically, the rehabilitation of Trotsky's alleged co-conspirators cannot but also apply to him, their 'ringleader' and the key defendant in Stalin's show-trials, and there can be no doubt of his civil rehabilitation in the glasnost-era. However, it is hard to avoid the impression that Gorbachev's opposition to militant Bolshevism so prejudiced him against Trotsky's left-wing, 'unpatriotic' views that his failure to sanction political rehabilitation of the fiery old revolutionary was more than a mere formality, and that he would rather rehabilitate people like Bukharin, whose memory could be mobilised under perestroika in support of market-socialism and 'democracy'.[105] For the Soviet reformers of the 1980s, Trotsky was the worst of the Bolsheviks, and he was one of the few leaders of the Soviet Left Opposition never to recant.

In any case, there is no obvious reason why the Chinese leaders should accept Trotsky's rehabilitation in Moscow, any more than Mao accepted Khrushchev's denunciation of Stalin in his secret speech to the Twentieth Congress of the Soviet Communist Party in 1956. Studies on the history of the CCP have noted the divisions and conflicts in Mao's relations with Stalin, but one must not

---

104 For Soviet practice, which Chinese practice roughly follows, see Van Goudoever 1983.
105 Thatcher 2002, p. 19, has a discussion.

lose sight of the basic affinity between the two men. Since Mao's death, the leadership has tried to legitimise its rule by increasing political participation and seeking ways other than naked repression. Like Mao in his day, who risked allowing occasional expressions of dissent, today's leaders are prepared to tolerate 'the conspicuous exercise of rights' as long as it avoids open sedition and sticks to sheltering behind officially approved reformist criticism.[106] However, this relaxation is designed to ensure the leadership retains its monopoly on power at the centre, any threat to which is met with a crackdown like that in 1989 on the protestors in Beijing.

The Chinese Trotskyists were never compatible with such an arrangement. They were not a 'within-system opposition' loyal to the régime in some respects and critical of it in others, for they had the 'will to power' that distinguishes an opposition from a movement of dissent.[107] They never sought to shelter behind sympathetic forces in the official world or to borrow or adapt official arguments. Instead, they advanced their own full and coherent political programme.

Why is anti-Trotskyism such an enduring part of the CCP's political constitution and so hard for it to disown, even though most of the Chinese Trotskyists are dead? Probably, because it is a badge of commitment to political monolithism. One can even surmise that the shift towards capitalism since Mao's death, China's massive and ever increasing polarisation into winners and losers, and the looming prospect of an independent workers' movement, have intensified hostility to Trotskyism among those in the leadership familiar with its tenets, which include labour internationalism as well as political democracy. If so, the Chinese Trotskyists' rehabilitation, in the sense of their complete exoneration from all criminal charges and a disowning of the political slanders against them, is unlikely to take place, short of a major political change.

This book uses the Hanyu Pinyin system to romanise Chinese, except in citations (where Wang Fanxi, for example, is given where appropriate as Wang Fan-hsi, its Wade-Giles spelling, and Peng Shuzhi as P'eng Shu-tse, a hybrid spelling) and in the case of some historical figures (like Sun Yat-sen and Chiang Kai-shek) and places (Hong Kong) better known in other transcriptions. I have unified the spelling across the texts, for the convenience of readers who might

---

106   These are the characteristics of dissent under Stalinism as defined by the Hungarian political philosopher G. M. Tarás (1993).
107   This is the argument of another Hungarian oppositionist, the political scientist Rudolf. L. Tökés (1974).

otherwise be confused by the different transcriptions used by different writers to romanise Chinese characters. Readers can find out the older spellings of people's names by consulting the appendix containing the short biographies, where the Wade-Giles transcription is given in parentheses. The short biographies also give the names in Chinese characters.

Most of the texts (documents and excerpts) are integral. A few have been slightly shortened, by the removal of material I thought repetitive (including of material contained elsewhere in the volume), merely illustrative, or less centrally relevant. Editorial excisions are shown by ellipses.

Much of the work incorporated in this volume would have been impossible without the advice and guidance of Wang Fanxi. Wang Fanxi was probably the only living person besides Zheng Chaolin capable of explicating the precise meaning of Chen Duxiu's last writings, which are written in a style that is frequently elliptical or arcane. He was also one of the few people capable of deciphering the handwriting of Zheng Chaolin, who was practically blind towards the end of his life and could no longer write clearly. Wang Fanxi monitored my translation of his own and of Chen Duxiu's and Zheng Chaolin's writings and clarified difficult or obscure passages and references. Where necessary, he passed on requests for information to Zheng Chaolin (in Shanghai) and others. This book is dedicated to his memory.

PART 1

Purgatory: The Chinese Trotskyists' Ordeal and Struggle

Wu Jimin

∴

Preface

Chen Sihe

In his postscript, the author reproduces verbatim the opinion of Zheng Yifan on the significance of this study, so there is no need to say anything further on that point. I am no expert in this field. All I can do, as Wu Jimin's friend, is express my feelings on reading this text. Wu Jimin had the chance as a result of working at Shanghai's Historical Studies Institute to hear veteran survivors tell the story of the Trotskyists' years of hardship, especially after the 'great Trotskyist purge' of 22 December 1952. They had continued to uphold their beliefs, a secret about which only a tiny number of people knew. The purpose in righting wrongs committed more than half a century ago is not to elicit cheap sighs of disapproval or even to achieve belated justice for those who suffered. Most of the Trotskyists are now dead: only a handful remain alive. Rehabilitation has therefore lost much of its meaning. So what can we learn from this book?

The Chinese Trotskyists were staunch believers in their cause, prepared to shed their last drop of blood for China's socialist revolution. Their conflict with the Third International, which led to clashes between them and the Chinese Communist Party, was a contradiction within the world communist movement. Today, it is common knowledge in Party history circles that errors in the Third International's line on China led to tragic losses. The crimes Stalin committed after the establishment of Soviet power were criticised by the Soviet Communist Party as early as the 1950s. However, our party history workers have not reflected to the extent they should have done on the splits these errors caused in the Chinese Party and the emergence of the Trotskyists. Even more distressing (as this book shows), these splits and conflicts in the revolutionary movement led to attacks on the Trotskyists that far surpassed in their intensity those on real enemies of the revolution.

Over the last few years, various studies on Trotskyism have appeared in China, but to no great fanfare. One example is a book on Lenin's testament, which shows in detail how Stalin falsified it to attack Trotsky. Then there is Isaac Deutscher's *Trotsky Trilogy*, which exposes Stalin's framing of his enemies and reign of terror. Sadly, the Chinese Communist Party copied these methods. The classic example is Wang Ming's speech at the Politburo in December 1937: 'In opposing Trotskyism we cannot be charitable. Even if Chen Duxiu is not a Japanese agent, we must say he is'. The framing of Chen Duxiu, leader of the May Fourth Movement, founder of the Communist Party, its General Secretary for several years, led to the perpetration of a general injustice against all Trotskyists.

But that is not the end of the story of the framing. Today, all studies on Chen Duxiu blame the framing on Wang Ming and Kang Sheng, carrying out Stalin's leftist line. They argue that when Chen Duxiu left jail in 1937, he and the Chinese Communist state in Yan'an could have established cooperative relations – as this study explains, in its analysis of the article 'Where is Mr Chen Duxiu Going?' (*Liberation Weekly*, 20 November 1937). This article suggested in a mild and roundabout way that as long as Chen Duxiu acknowledged his errors, he could 'regenerate his old militant spirit and rejoin the ranks of the revolution'. But, just after that, Wang Ming and Kang Sheng returned from the Soviet Union to Yan'an and Wang Ming shouted: 'Stalin is resolutely opposing Trotskyism but we want to liaise with them, that's terrible! If Stalin knew, the consequences would be hard to imagine'. Wang Ming's remarks were probably directed at the article in *Liberation*, so Kang Sheng published a long article in *Liberation* on 28 January and 8 February 1938, viciously framing Chen Duxiu as a Japanese spy and thus initiating the gross injustice. However, what Wang Ming said about Stalin was true. Even if Chen Duxiu and the Chinese Communist Party had established some sort of cooperation in the Resistance War, Stalin would have torpedoed it, and it might have brought disaster to an even greater number of Chinese Communist leaders.

The article about Chen Duxiu in *Liberation* and the three conditions the Chinese Communist leaders set Chen Duxiu followed the same line. Although they knew Chen Duxiu would not accept the conditions, the article signalled their misgivings about this 'commander-in-chief' of the May Fourth New Culture Movement. However, things were extremely complicated. In his biography of Chen Duxiu, *Prometheus Bound: A Life of Chen Duxiu*, so far not openly published on the Chinese Mainland, Wang Guanquan reveals that on 5 October 1936, in issue no. 59 of the Chinese Communist Party's journal *National Salvation*, based in Paris, a lengthy and tedious article denounced the Trotskyists for 'willingly acting as spies for the Japanese bandits'. The main evidence was Feng Xuefeng's 'Letter Replying to the Trotskyites', which he wrote on behalf of Lu Xun in August 1936 after returning to Shanghai from Mao's base in Wayaobao, levelling various charges against the Trotskyists. So Lu Xun was also drafted into the campaign to surround and exterminate the Trotskyists. Wang Guanquan writes:

> In August 1936, that is, before the Xi'an Incident had broken out, the idea of cooperation between the Guomindang and the Chinese Communist

Party to resist Japan was merely at the stage of public opinion or something about which Zhang Xueliang and Yang Hucheng were conferring secretly together; even less could one foresee the Marco Polo Bridge Incident [which triggered war with Japan], and there was still a year and a half to go before Kang Sheng slandered Chen Duxiu as a Japanese spy. Chen Duxiu still had another full year to spend in a Guomindang jail for his Communism. At this point Feng Xuefeng went from [Mao's base in] northern Shaanxi to Shanghai on his mission to frame Chen Duxiu as a national traitor, and to shut Chen up by using Lu Xun's name.

It is easy to understand Wang Guanquan's indignation. Whether Feng Xuefeng's framing of the Trotsky-Chen group as national traitors was an arbitrary act or part of a special mission still needs to be ascertained on the basis of evidence. However, Wang Guanquan has shown that Chen Duxiu's opponents were already conspiring to put him beyond redemption, as a national traitor, in 1936, while he was still serving his sentence in a Guomindang jail, and this added fuel to the flames of Wang Ming and Kang Sheng's despicable campaign.

During the period of the Great Revolution, the Comintern repeatedly suppressed Chen Duxiu's correct proposals for a policy of acting independently and on one's own initiative and instead followed a right-opportunist line, leading to the 1927 split and the crushing defeat of the defenceless Communist Party. Chen Duxiu's own sons died as a result. In 1926, at the time of the Zhongshan Gunboat Incident and Chiang Kai-shek's 'Party readjustment', Chen Duxiu repeatedly asked the Soviet advisors and the Soviet Government for permission to retain 5,000 guns so the Communists could arm themselves in self-defence, but the Comintern and big-brother party said no. After the crushing defeat, Chen Duxiu was scapegoated and cast aside. In that situation, Chen Duxiu and his comrades chose Trotsky's analysis of the China question over Stalin's, and subsequently made their own further explorations.

History cannot repeat itself. That Stalinism has been exposed and criticised does not necessarily mean Trotskyism was correct and would inevitably have led to the success of the Communist movement. Yet it is important that we understand and ponder the tragic fate of Trotsky, commander of the October Revolution, and his loyal followers, and of the Chinese Trotskyists who suffered for their ideals and beliefs. Do they deserve our sympathy, or even a conscientious rethink?

So after reading Wu Jimin's book, I feel that if these materials can induce the Chinese Communist Party to follow the example of the former Communist Party of the Soviet Union in the 1980s, when they redressed the gross injustice perpetrated against Trotsky, and resolve the Chinese Trotskyist question, some honour would be redeemed. The book mentions the case of Zheng Chaolin, a veteran cadre of the Chinese Communist Party and a staunch Trotskyist, who in his eighties and nineties, observing organisational principles, several times wrote to National Congresses of the Chinese Communist Party demanding rehabilitation of the Chinese Trotskyist organisation. He said:

> I make this request not only because of the wrongs we have suffered but also in the interests of the Chinese Communist Party and the People's Republic of China.... [I]f there is a miscarriage of justice in the country and its victims are not rehabilitated, that shames those who hold the reins of government.

No Chinese of conscience could ignore the sincerity of this statement. An independent, vital Marxist party would face up squarely to its own history and rectify prejudices and errors, treat generously those who have opposed it, and unite with all possible forces. Then and only then could such a party serve as a mainstay of Marxist ideology in the complex conditions of today's world. In so doing, it would – to quote the Trotskyist Lou Guohua, in his Preface to Wang Fanxi's *Memoirs* – 'let the broad working masses know that the collapse of Stalinism is in no way equivalent to the bankruptcy of socialism and communism'.

Moscow's Sun Yat-sen University

On 12 March 1925, Sun Yat-sen, pioneer of the Chinese Revolution, died in Beijing, leaving China and the Chinese people in turmoil. Just before dying, he signed a number of documents. The best-known were his testament, drafted by Wang Jingwei, and a letter to the Central Executive of the Soviet Socialist Republic, drafted by Eugene Chen. The letter read:

> Dear Comrades,
>
> I have firm confidence in the reliable support you have given my country to this day. In bidding you farewell, dear comrades, allow me to express the hope that the day will soon come when the Soviet Union will be able to greet a friend and ally in the shape of a powerful and free China, and that the two united countries will march hand in hand in the great struggle for the emancipation of the oppressed peoples of the world. I leave behind a Party that, as has always been my wish, will be bound with you in the historic work of the final liberation from the imperialist order of China and other exploited nations. By the will of fate, I must leave my work unfinished and hand it over to those who, remaining true to the Party's principles and teachings, will show themselves to be my true followers.
>
> Sun Yat-sen

This was Soviet Russia and the Chinese revolutionaries' honeymoon period. However, the love-affair went through difficult times. In July 1912, after the 1911 Revolution, Lenin read Sun Yat-sen's 'On the Social Meaning of the Chinese Revolution' and wrote 'Democracy and Narodnism in China', in which he expressed infinite respect for Sun and China in the wake of the Revolution:

> In China, the Asiatic provisional President of the Republic is a revolutionary democrat, endowed with the nobility and heroism of a class that is rising, not declining, a class that does not dread the future, but believes in it and fights for it selflessly, a class that does not cling to maintenance and restoration of the past to safeguard its privileges, but hates the past and knows how to cast off its dead and stifling decay.
>
> Does that mean, then, that the materialist West has hopelessly decayed and that light shines only from the mystic, religious East? No, quite the

opposite. It means that the East has definitely taken the Western path, that new *hundreds of millions* of people will from now on share in the struggle for the ideals the West has already worked out for itself. What has decayed is the Western bourgeoisie, which is confronted by its grave-digger, the proletariat. But in Asia there is *still* a bourgeoisie capable of championing sincere, militant, consistent democracy, a worthy comrade of France's great men of the Enlightenment and great leaders of the close of the eighteenth century. The chief representative, or the chief social bulwark, of this Asian bourgeoisie that is still capable of supporting a historically progressive cause, is the peasant.

Sadly, Sun Yat-sen had not experienced such support from faithful friends during his years of suffering and frustration. Having embraced the West's civilisation and revolutionary ideals, Sun naturally turned towards the West. In 1917, however, the October Revolution was victorious in Russia. Surrounded by imperialist powers, Soviet Russia under Lenin again turned its attention to its neighbours, particularly China, the largest country in Asia. In 1920, at the Second Congress of the Comintern, Lenin put forward his ideas on the 'national and colonial question'. He proposed an alliance between Soviet Russia and China's revolutionaries and again wooed Sun. At this very moment, Sun Yat-sen, bogged down in the quagmire of the Chinese revolution and repeatedly disappointed in his dealings with the Western powers, turned his attention for the first time to Soviet Russia. China and the Soviet revolutionaries immediately warmed to each other. With Li Dazhao, co-founder of the Chinese Communist Party, acting as go-between, on 27 January 1923, Joffe, representing the Central Committee of the Russian Communist Party and the Soviet Government, met Sun Yat-sen in his residence, where they issued a joint declaration. (Later, Joffe became an Oppositionist: he was expelled from the Party by Stalin and committed suicide.) General Borodin then went to Guangzhou, to act as Sun's advisor. In 1924, the Guomindang underwent reorganisation, after which it adopted Sun's Three Great Policies of 'alliance with Soviet Russia, alliance with the Communists, and support for the workers and peasants'. The two parties cooperated and a vigorous revolutionary movement ensued.

When the Guomindang and the Communists split and the civil war started, Chiang Kai-shek slandered the Chinese Communists as the 'rouble party'. Actually, the Guomindang was also a 'rouble party', indeed much more so than the Chinese Communists. The Comintern and the Soviet Government thought that both Chinese parties opposed imperialism and warlordism and supported both with huge resources. We know from recently opened archives of the Comintern and the Soviet Union that the Chinese Communist Party benefitted enormously from Soviet support, from the year of its founding right up to 1949.

After the Chinese Communist Party's First Congress, Chen Duxiu reported to the Comintern that the Party's central organs 'had spent 17,655 yuan and received 16,655 yuan from the Comintern, together with one thousand dollars it raised itself'. In October 1923, at the Chinese Communist Party's Third Congress, Chen Duxiu said that in the first eight months of 1923 alone, the Central Committee had received 'expenses of about 15,000 yuan from the Comintern'. By this time, Moscow usually provided labour movement funds separately. For example, Maring, the Comintern delegate in China, noted in May 1923 that 'today £2,000.78 were transferred to Beijing', of which two thirds were used to organise the labour movement. One thousand US dollars were also donated, 'to help comrades persecuted by the Chinese government', and another thousand 'to help the Chinese Communist Party'.

In 1924, the Chinese Communist Party received around 36,000 yuan from the Comintern to cover its day-to-day running costs. This figure rose steadily, to an average of 10,000 yuan a month in 1927. After 1927, the Chinese Communists received hundreds of thousands of yuan for 'special expenditure'. The Comintern allocated 30,000 yuan for organising the three armed workers' uprisings in Shanghai in 1927, said to have been donated by Leningrad (that is, St Petersburg) party members, who contributed additional monthly dues. Ten thousand yuan were contributed to help pay for the Autumn Harvest Uprising and more than 100,000 yuan for the Guangzhou Uprising.

Over the same period, the Comintern and the Soviet Government gave ten times more financial support to the Guomindang than to the Chinese Communist Party. The first allocation for the establishment of the Huangpu [Whampoa] Military Academy alone was worth more than one million yuan, not to mention 5,000 tons of ammunition.

Early in 1924, Chiang Kai-shek went on Sun Yat-sen's instructions on an inspection-tour of the Soviet Union. Sun Yat-sen wrote repeatedly in letters to him: 'The future revolution my party makes must learn from Russia, or it will not succeed'. This comment was sincerely meant.

On 12 March 1925, Sun Yat-sen died. The Russian Communist Party and the Soviet Government expressed their grief. The Central Committee of the Russian Communist Party and its General Secretary Stalin decided to set up Sun Yat-sen University in Moscow, to recruit Chinese students and train them as cadres for the Chinese revolution. They set up a special selection committee with the Guomindang veterans Tan Yankai, Gu Yingfen, and Wang Jingwei as members, and with General Borodin as advisor. On 7 October 1925, at a plenary meeting of the Guomindang in Guangzhou, Borodin formally announced this decision on behalf of the Soviet Government and proposed enrolling a first batch of 340 students. They included 180 recruited from Guangzhou, ten from each of the military academies at Huangpu and in Yunnan and Hunan, fifty each from the Beijing-Tianjin area and Shanghai, and thirty accepted on Borodin's personal recommendation. After the news spread, students across the country, the overwhelming majority of them members of the Chinese Communist Party, the Communist Youth League, or the Guomindang, welcomed the news. The students Borodin recommended were all relatives of members of the Guomindang élite. They included Chiang Kai-shek's son Chiang Ching-kuo, Shao Lizi's son Shao Zhigang, Liao Zhongkai's son Liao Chengzhi, Li Zongren's wife Wei Shuying and his brother-in-law Wei Yuncheng, Zhang Fakui's brother Zhang Faming, Deng Yanda's brother Deng Mingqiu, Chen Shuren's son Chen Fu, Ye Chulun's son Ye Nan, and General Gu Zhenglun's two younger brothers Gu Zhenggang and Gu Zhengding. In the autumn of 1926, Shao Lizi visited Russia and also studied at Sun Yat-sen University, so father and son were fellow-students for a while. Shao Lizi, a widower, married Fu Xuewen, a member of the Communist Youth League and also a student at Sun Yat-sen University, and took her back to China. There were far more men than women at the University – the number of women students was fewer than sixty. When the male students saw an old man take Fu Xuewen away, many were depressed. Shao Lizi remained a leftist. In April 1949 he held talks with the Chinese Communists, broke with the Guomindang, and stayed in Beijing, a development not unconnected with his wife.

When Chiang Kai-shek heard about the founding of the University, he sent his fifteen-year-old son Chiang Ching-kuo to be a student, Sun Yat-sen University's youngest. On the other hand, students of the Huangpu Military Academy were strictly forbidden to study at Sun Yat-sen University. This was because its graduates were to form the backbone of Chiang Kai-shek's army. Even so, a few slipped away to Moscow. One of the best-known was Deng Wenyi, Chiang's trusted subordinate and a Huangpu man. Kang Ze and Zheng Jiemin, important backbone-cadres of the Chiang clique, also went.

Later, the Chinese Communist Party's Central Committee sent some of its members studying in Europe to Moscow's Sun Yat-sen University, to strengthen it. They included Deng Xiaoping, Zuo Quan, and Fu Zhong. In Moscow, Deng Xiaoping met the beautiful woman Communist Zhang Xiyuan and her younger sister Zhang Xirui. At the time, Deng was 23 and Zhang Xiyuan was 19. Later, in Shanghai, they married.

The preparations for Sun Yat-sen University were completed in October 1925. It was situated in the centre of Moscow. It occupied a three-storey building once owned by an aristocrat. The rooms were high and spacious. There was a big hall in the middle, decorated with huge crystal chandeliers and luxurious fittings. It had once been a ballroom; Pushkin and his wife are said to have held their wedding party there.

The lives of the Soviet people were still extremely hard, but they were nevertheless very generous towards the Chinese students, who enjoyed excellent living conditions. In *My Father Deng Xiaoping*, Mao Mao wrote:

> At that time the Soviet Union was still recovering from the trauma of civil war and imperialist armed intervention, but the young Soviet state fully guaranteed those foreign students their livelihood and learning. The Soviet Union set up an association to raise funds for Sun Yat-sen University. Its annual budget was about 10 million roubles. To provide the students with the foreign exchange necessary (for example) for repatriation, it had to use scarce foreign currency reserves. The Soviet Government did everything possible to guarantee the students' livelihood. Foreign students enjoyed better living conditions than Russian teachers and students. A Chinese student recalled: 'We were never short of eggs, poultry, fish, or meat, which were not readily available in 1926. Despite economic difficulties, we got three meals a day, adequate in quantity and quality. I don't think even a rich man would have eaten a better breakfast'. The school gave the students suits, overcoats, leather-shoes, raincoats, winter-clothing, and all daily necessities, as well setting up clinics where they could see a doctor. It organised ballet, opera and other performances for the students, holiday visits to sanatoria, and summer-camps, as well as visits to famous places and tours of Moscow and Leningrad. My father said in 1926 he joined the school trip to Leningrad.

In his memoir *My Life in the Soviet Union*, Chiang Ching-kuo wrote:

> Soviet people themselves lived a hard life, but they were exceptionally generous towards Chinese students. At first, we received five meals a day, which later changed to three. For breakfast we usually had bread, butter, or milk, sometimes with rice gruel and millet gruel. If you didn't like butter they gave you a fried egg. At mid-day everyone got soup, vegetables, and a cup of tea. The soup contained beef, potatoes, and

tomatoes. For dinner we had a big bowl of soup. The staple food was white or black bread, you could have it any time. I was a foreigner, but I didn't have to spend a cent. I ate so well in their country, while their own students lived hard lives.

In November 1925, Sun Yat-sen University held a grand opening ceremony in the hall of the famous Moscow Trade Union building. The building had been redecorated and the hall was hung with portraits of Lenin and Sun Yat-sen. On opposite walls were the flags of Russia and China. Radek, the school's first principal, presided over the opening. A Jew, born in Poland in 1885, he had joined the Social-Revolutionary Party in 1904. He had taken part in the October Revolution and the German Revolution of 1918. He had sneaked into Germany as a delegate of the Central Committee of the Russian Communist Party. He reorganised the German Communist Party and was one of its three giants. After the murder of Luxemburg and Liebknecht, he returned to the Soviet Union, where he specialised in research on China. A scholar, a professor, and a leading expert on China in the Comintern, he was Trotsky's comrade-in-arms and follower. Because he refused to give up his Trotskyism, in late 1927 he was removed as school principal and expelled from the Party. His successor at Sun Yat-sen University was Mif. In 1942, Radek was killed in prison – needless to say, this was not made public until much later. Numerous guests attended the opening. They included Trotsky and Zinoviev.

Trotsky was a main leader of the October Revolution. He was one of the most important revolutionaries and theoreticians in the Central Committee of the Russian Communist Party, and Lenin's close ally. His actual name was Bronstein. He was born in Russia on 7 November 1879. His father was a wealthy Jewish merchant from Russia's southern steppes. At the age of seventeen, he joined a socialist group and became a Marxist. Two years later, he was arrested and exiled to Siberia. Four years later, he escaped to London on a false passport in the name of Trotsky. In his later political career, this is the name under which he became famous.

In October 1902, he founded the revolutionary newspaper *Iskra* in London together with Lenin, whom he had not known previously. When the 1905 Revolution broke out, he returned to St Petersburg from abroad and was the main spokesman for the St Petersburg workers' soviet. Subsequently, he was arrested and exiled several times; each time he fled abroad. When the February Revolution broke out in 1917, he hurried back to Russia from the United States. The Kerensky Government arrested him, but in September he was released. With Jacob Sverdlov and others, he planned and led the October Revolution and welcomed Lenin back to St Petersburg from the Gulf of Finland. On the night of the victory of the October Revolution, while Lenin and Trotsky were awaiting the convening of the All-Russian Soviet Congress, they were exceptionally close to one another. In his *My Life*, Trotsky recalled:

> Late thát evening, as we were waiting for the opening of the congress of the Soviets, Lenin and I were resting in a room adjoining the meeting hall, a room entirely empty except for chairs. Someone had spread a blanket on the floor for us; someone else, I think it was Lenin's sister, had brought us pillows. We were lying side by side; body and soul were relaxing like overtaut strings. It was a well-earned rest. We could not sleep, so we talked in low voices. Only now did Lenin become reconciled to the postponement of the uprising. His fears had been dispelled. There was a deep sincerity in his voice. He was interested in knowing all about the mixed pickets of the Red Guards, sailors, and soldiers that had been stationed everywhere. 'What a wonderful sight: a worker with a rifle, side by side with a soldier, standing before a street fire!' he repeated with deep feeling. At last the soldier and the worker had been brought together!

On the first anniversary of the victory of the October Revolution, Stalin wrote:

> All practical work in connection with the organisation of the uprising was done under the immediate direction of Comrade Trotsky, the president of the Petrograd Soviet. It can be stated with certainty that the Party is indebted primarily and principally to Comrade Trotsky for the rapid going over of the garrison to the side of the Soviet and the efficient manner in which the work of the Military Revolutionary Committee was organised.

After the victory of the October Revolution, Trotsky was appointed People's Commissar for Foreign Affairs. In 1918, he chaired the Military Revolutionary Commission and was known as 'father of the Red Army'. He was second only to Lenin. Every day he and Lenin 'met in the corridors of the Kremlin at least a dozen times... to discuss issues and exchange views'. When the Comintern was established in 1919, he was one of its leaders and drafted its founding declaration. He was a propagandist, the most enthusiastic agitator for the revolutionary cause; and an organiser, the greatest organiser of revolutionary war and the revolutionary armed forces. But he was no conspirator. So, in January 1924, after the death of Lenin, Trotsky lost out to Stalin in the power struggle.

Trotsky was a speaker and writer of great eloquence and inspirational power. At Sun Yat-sen University's opening ceremony, he described the excellent situation of the Chinese Revolution and the world revolution to the students, and urged them to attack relentlessly. From that day onwards, Trotsky sowed 'Trotskyist' seeds and ideals in the hearts of the Chinese students.

The Chinese students' study-régime was intense. Of the many courses taught, the most popular was Radek's 'History of the Chinese Revolutionary Movement'. Radek was short and looked rather odd. He had a broad forehead and a narrow jaw. He was eloquent, humorous, and expressive, and often made his audiences laugh. Every time he taught his course on the 'History of the Chinese Revolutionary Movement', Chinese students from Moscow's University of the East also attended. There was never an empty seat. Radek's great fund of knowledge infected nearly everyone. That Sun Yat-sen University later became a hotbed of Trotskyism had much to do with Radek's teaching.

In 1927, the Chinese Revolution went through a period of great turmoil. The revolutionary upheaval in China affected the world, including the Soviet Union. It also affected Sun Yat-sen University, already in a state of agitation.

On 21 March 1927, the Shanghai working class staged its third armed uprising under the leadership of the Communist Party, and at one fell stroke seized power in the city. When the news broke, people were inspired. When it reached Moscow, the city boiled with excitement. Sheng Zhongliang (also known as Sheng Yue), later Secretary of the Shanghai Bureau of the Chinese Communist Party, writing in his book *Sun Yat-sen University in Moscow and the Chinese Revolution*, recalled the events as follows:

> The news of the great victory of the Chinese Revolutionary Army spread like lightning to every corner of the world. At Sun Yat-sen University the news was like 'a thunderbolt from a clear sky'. We heartily congratulated ourselves, shook hands with one another, and embraced one another with joy and excitement. Our enthusiasm was such that sparkling tears ran down many happy faces.
>
> The secretary of the CPSU organisation at the university walked towards a huge map of China and bowed in deep reverence. He then took down the little black flag, which was a symbol of warlord occupation, from the part of the map where Shanghai was located. He tore the flag to shreds and threw it to the floor. We all rushed to stamp on it with our feet. Within seconds there was hardly anything left of the flag. In a mood of wild celebration we thronged into the auditorium and held a jubilant meeting. The big hall reverberated with uproarious talk and loud laughter. The speakers' repeated attempts to talk were drowned out by deafening applause. One of my classmates leapt to the podium, shrieked 'Comrades', and then, literally, was so stricken with emotion that he could

not go on. He just stood there, his mouth frozen in an ecstatic grin. He looked rather like the beaming worker in the front-page cartoon in *Pravda* the next day, who proclaimed, 'Shanghai is ours'. Somehow, some order eventually descended on the meeting, and we voted to send two effusive congratulatory telegrams. One telegram was sent to the commander of the Northward Expeditionary Force, Generalissimo Chiang Kai-shek, and the other to the workers of Shanghai. After the meeting was adjourned we pushed through the gate of the university and quickly formed lines for a demonstration, which eventually included thousands of Moscow residents. Two stout northerners carrying huge banners led the march to the Comintern building. The students of Sun Yat-sen University marched in front of everyone else in the demonstration. *International Press Correspondence*, in what strikes me as a reasonably accurate account of what happened, described the demonstration in the following manner: 'The news of the seizure of Shanghai by the insurrectionary workers spread this morning in Moscow and was received with the greatest enthusiasm by the population. After the close of work, meetings took place in the factories where speakers explained the significance of the new victory of the Nationalist troops. At four pm a mass meeting of many thousands of workers took place in the square before the Comintern building. The students of Sun Yat-sen University marched at the head of the demonstration. Comrades Murphy, Kolarov, Duncan, and a representative of the Communist Party of China spoke to the masses. The demonstrations lasted until late in the evening, workers streamed to them from the factories on the farthest outskirts of the town'.

In the square in front of the Comintern building, people gathered by the thousands. Banners were flying high in the sky. After Murphy's speech the president of the university, Radek, spoke to the massed demonstrators, among whom were five hundred young Chinese patriots: 'Shanghai is now in the hands of the Chinese, but when the revolutionary army marched into Shanghai they could still see the barbed wire set up by the British soldiers! The revolution in China is still in its embryonic stage; the counter-revolutionary forces have not been driven out. The troops of Zhang Zuolin still threaten Wuhan. But the Chinese Revolutionary Movement is growing stronger every day, and no doubt it will be able to conquer all the obstacles and difficulties that lie in its future. The workers of Moscow received the news of the taking of Shanghai only this morning [21 March] at 10 am; already they are streaming to you in celebrating this great victory. Moreover, they adopted resolutions extending greetings and brotherly love to the Shanghai revolutionary proletariat. Let the imperialists be aware that in case of necessity, the proletariat of Soviet Russia will not hesitate to support the Chinese Revolutionary Movement'.

His speech greatly moved us, and our spirits rose still higher.

The marchers continued on towards the headquarters of the CC of the CPSU. As we passed through the Ileinka zone, someone in the Soviet Department of Finance building waved to us and shouted at the top of his voice, 'Long live the youth of China!' We became more and more exuberant. Finally we made a turn and halted in the old square in front of the building of the CC. CC member Andreev appeared on the balcony of the building to welcome us and to deliver a speech of encouragement and praise. Here, the demonstration dispersed, and each group made its own way back home. On our way we were stopped by the crowds. They cheered us and some even seized some of my fellow students, threw them in the air and caught them as they fell. Many Russian girls innocently threw us kisses and flirted with us coquettishly.

But just twenty days later, Chiang Kai-shek and his armed forces colluded with the imperialists and the big bourgeois to launch a counter-revolutionary coup and drowned Shanghai in a pool of blood. The news spread to the Soviet Union. The students of Sun Yat-sen University expressed their unfathomable indignation. Sheng Zhongliang recalled:

> The events at Shanghai came as a sickening shock to Moscow and the students of Sun Yat-sen University. Neither the Comintern nor the university had any forewarning of the coup. On the evening of 12 April we held another meeting. Instead of the celebration of some twenty days before cold anger reigned in the assembly-hall. No trace of a smile was visible on any of our youthful faces. With great fury we adopted a resolution to send a telegram to the Nationalist government at Wuhan, demanding severe punishment for the traitors of the revolution. The cable read: 'Present developments of the Chinese revolution have provoked counter-attacks from the Imperialists and their loyal lackeys. Chiang Kai-shek and his colleagues, the pseudo-revolutionaries, have violated the principles and discipline of the Party; they have betrayed our revolution, massacred the Shanghai revolutionary workers, and have thus become the lackeys of the imperialists. Now they constitute an obstacle on our revolutionary path. But we feel confident that the Central Executive Committee of the Guomindang and the Nationalist government will, with the support of our worker-masses and revolutionary army, bravely and steadfastly

pursue the struggle against the counter-revolutionary Chiang Kai-shek and his colleagues. We are sure that we shall attain the final victory. From all the members of the Guomindang and the Chinese Communist Party at Sun Yat-sen University'.

Many students, including sons of Guomindang leaders, delivered speeches excoriating the 12 April coup. Among them was Chiang Ching-kuo, at the time a member of the Chinese Socialist Youth League. His speech was greeted with thunderous applause.

A few days later, Chiang Ching-kuo published a famous 'public statement' in the press. It was translated into many languages and reprinted in newspapers around the world. It read as follows:

> Chiang Kai-shek's betrayal is not surprising. At the same time as he was talking about revolution, he was gradually beginning to betray the revolution. He was anxious for a compromise with Zhang Zuolin and Sun Chuanfang. Chiang Kai-shek has already ended his revolutionary career. As a revolutionary, he is dead. He has already gone over to the counter-revolution and is an enemy of the Chinese working masses. Chiang Kai-shek was my father and revolutionary friend. He has already gone over to the counter-revolutionary camp. Now he is my enemy.

On 15 July 1927, Wang Jingwei in Wuhan launched a counter-revolutionary coup. At roughly the same time, Feng Yuxiang, of whom the Russian Communist Party had had high hopes, also openly 'purged the Communists'. The revolutionary movement had ended in failure. Feng Yuxiang's son Feng Hongguo, also studying at Sun Yat-sen University in Moscow, like Chiang Ching-kuo, made a public statement saying:

> Father: Now it is quite clear that you have deserted the revolutionary front and become a counter-revolutionary leader. You have become the workers and peasants' enemy and a traitor to Sun Yat-sen-ism. In the past, when I was studying at the old school, I knew very little about revolutionary principles. Now, after coming to Sun Yat-sen University to study revolutionary theory and practice, I have grasped the line that the Chinese Revolution must follow. At the same time you were running after the counter-revolutionaries, I had already become a revolutionary. As a revolutionary, I have nothing other in mind than the interests of the revolution and do not think in the slightest about my relationship with you,

my father. Now I am going to sever all relations with you, my counter-revolutionary father. From now on, I consider you as one of Chiang Kai-shek and Zhang Zuolin's gang of counter-revolutionaries.

Now, you and I belong to opposed camps. You are in the counter-revolutionary camp. In future, I must struggle against my father, who has become an enemy of the workers and peasants. These are my final words to my counter-revolutionary father!

Feng Hongguo
15 August 1927, Moscow

The defeat of the revolutionary movement caused a huge shock in the Chinese Communist Party and led directly to the loss of dozens of outstanding leaders. Party membership fell from 60,000 to 10,000 and there was a major reorganisation of the Party's Central Committee. Chen Duxiu, one of the Party's founders and its General Secretary ever since its founding, stepped down and was later expelled.

At the same time, inside the Comintern, the Central Committee of the Russian Communist Party launched a major debate about the defeat, led on opposing sides by Stalin and Trotsky. Stalin, who had a firm grip on power, expelled Trotsky from the Party, exiled him to Alma Ata, and later deported him. Finally, in 1940, he sent someone to Mexico to murder him.

The Chinese students at Sun Yat-sen University were drawn into this great vortex. According to Sheng Zhongliang, more than half supported Trotsky's viewpoint. Four or five hundred of them, including Chiang Ching-kuo, backed him. Because of this, on the afternoon of 13 May 1927, Stalin personally went to Sun Yat-sen University to deliver a report and answer questions raised by the Chinese students, in an attempt to win them over. The result was simply that their anger subsided a little for the time being. On 18 May, at the Eighth Plenary of the Comintern, Trotsky again went on the offensive with a long speech 'On the Chinese Revolution' in which he directly attacked Stalin, after which Trotskyist activity at Sun Yat-sen University flared up again.

On 7 November 1927, the tenth anniversary of the October Revolution, the Soviet people held a big parade in Moscow's Red Square. When the Sun Yat-sen University students marched past the review stand, they suddenly displayed banners saying 'Support Trotsky' and 'Oppose Stalin', and dozens chanted slogans. This was a slap in the face for Stalin and an enormous shock to him. On 14 November, the Central Committee decided to expel Trotsky from the Party. Then they removed Radek from his post at Sun Yat-sen University and put him in prison. They appointed Mif dean of the university and launched a thorough investigation into the activities of the Trotskyists there. After Mif took office, he deported back to China group after group of Chinese students who were Trotskyists and secretly supported Trotsky's ideas. They included Lu Yuan, Liang Ganqiao, Wang Wenyuan (that is, Wang Fanxi), Fan Jinbiao, Ou Fang, Zhang Fang, Li Ping, Song Fengchun, Chen Yimou, Li Meiwu, Xu Zheng'an, and Fu Renlin. In 1930, Stalin ordered the disbanding of Sun Yat-sen University. The Chinese students returned from Russia, taking Trotsky's ideas with them to sow in Chinese soil. Stalin never dreamed that Sun Yat-sen University, which he had established to aid the Chinese revolution, would not only nurture Wang Ming (Chen Shaoyu), Bo Gu (Qin Bangxian), Zhang Wentian, Wang Jiaxiang, Xia Xi, Shen Zemin, and other left-opportunist followers of Mif, who were versed only in Marxist dogma, had not the slightest practical experience, and later almost ruined the Chinese revolution, but would also sow the seeds of Chinese Trotskyism and nurture its cadres. Sun Yat-sen University became the cradle of the Chinese Trotskyist movement.

The Year 1931

1931 was a very important year in modern Chinese history – not just for the Guomindang and the Communist Party, but also, and especially, for the Chinese Trotskyists.

Early on the morning of 1 January 1931, from his heavily guarded field headquarters in Nanjing, Chiang Kai-shek published his New Year message in all major national newspapers. It was titled 'Two Issues of Vital Importance in the Twentieth Year of the Republic – Respect Learning and Promote Farming'. The message was a Confucian-style admonition to the people of the whole country and was summed up in two slogans, respect education and pay attention to farming. It said nothing at all about the bloody 'large-scale campaign of extirpation' then being carried out against the Chinese Communist Party. Chiang Kai-shek smugly believed that in this way he could unite the people of the whole country and realise his wish to make China rich and strong.

At the time, Chiang Kai-shek was in a good position to issue such a proclamation. On 12 April 1927, he had seized power in a military coup. Under the banner of the Three People's Principles, he had proclaimed himself successor to Sun Yat-sen. Relying on military men of the Huangpu clique whom he had personally trained, for more than one year he carried out numerous military campaigns coupled with political manoeuvres, until finally, on 18 September 1928, northeast China's Zhang Xueliang switched flags and went over to the central government and the Guomindang and the whole of China was formally reunited.

The decade from 1927 to 1936 was the Guomindang's best period and both Chinese and foreigners have called it a 'golden age'. In the past, textbooks described it as 'the civil-war decade', as if the only thing Chiang Kai-shek did was hunt down the Communists. That he suppressed the Communists is a fact, but, at the time, they occupied no more than a few remote and backward mountain regions, far from China's political and economic centre, and formed no threat to the Guomindang's rule. Chiang Kai-shek's early advisor Yang Yongtai, from Jiangxi, likened them to a disease of the skin, not of the heart, and therefore not fatal, although when they began to itch they discomforted the whole body and could become intolerable. The analogy was apt.

From 1927 to 1936, China's industry grew at an average annual rate of more than 8 per cent. In 1936, industrial output was 83 per cent higher than in 1927 and agricultural output was 107 per cent higher. By the end of 1936, the country's rail-network had grown from 8,000 kilometres in 1927 to 13,000; highways had extended even more quickly, from just over 1,000 kilometres to

115,700. Education had also made substantial progress. Whereas there were only 74 universities and colleges in 1928, there were 108 in 1936. The Guomindang showed in those few years that it was serious about reconstruction.

However, the Japanese imperialists were not happy to see China develop. On 18 September 1931, three years after Zhang Xueliang's switch of allegiance, Japan's Kwantung [Guandong] Army launched its long-planned '18 September Incident' in Shenyang and began its campaign to annex China. Chiang Kai-shek mismanaged the incident and created an even greater crisis that eventually changed the course of Chinese history.

On 7 January 1931, on a cold, wet morning in Shanghai, a group of men and women slipped quietly into a newly built lane house in a workers' district near Huxi to hold a very important meeting in the history of the Chinese Communist Party, the Fourth Plenary Session of the Sixth Congress. Mao Zedong was in his red base in the Jinggang Mountains, but the 37 who attended included Zhou Enlai, Qu Qiubai, Xiang Zhongfa, Ren Bishi, Li Weihan, He Chang, Gu Shunzhang, Guan Xiangying, Chen Yun, Wang Ming, Bo Gu, Shen Zemin, Xia Xi, and Wang Jiaxiang, some of the Communist Party's most important leaders, and the Comintern's Pavel Mif, representing the Russian Communist Party. The causes and consequences of the meeting were complex. Mao Zedong bitterly resented it, but it was legally constituted. Its sole purpose was to allow Mif's students at Moscow's Sun Yat-sen University – Wang Ming, Bo Gu, Luo Fu (Zhang Wentian), Xia Xi, Wang Jiaxiang, and others – to assume power in the Chinese Communist Party.

The meeting lasted all day, until ten at night. Mif achieved his objective. Qu Qiubai was removed from the Politburo, along with Li Weihan and He Chang.

Qu Qiubai was born in Changzhou in 1899. He and two others born in Changzhou, Zhang Tailei and Yun Daiying, were known to the Chinese Communist Party's early leaders as the 'three heroes of Changzhou'. After the defeat of the Great Revolution of 1927, Qu Qiubai convened the 7 August Conference in Wuhan, after which the Chinese Communist Party fired its first bullet at the Guomindang and began an independent struggle for revolutionary power. From the 7 August Conference to the Sixth Congress in 1928, Qu Qiubai was the actual leader of the Chinese Communist Party, General Secretary in all but name. In late July 1930, he and Zhou Enlai were urgently called back from Moscow to Shanghai to convene the Third Plenary Session of the Sixth Congress, to correct Li Lisan's left-opportunist errors (on the orders of the Comintern). From 24 to 28 September, the conference met in a small Western-style house on today's Taixing Road. According to Nie Rongzhen's reminiscences, Zhou Enlai constantly pushed Qu Qiubai to the fore while he himself hid behind the scenes. Perhaps he was being modest, but it is a fact that

Qu Qiubai was pushed up against the wall. The meeting concluded by adopting a resolution Qu Qiubai had drawn up on behalf of the Central Committee. Li Lisan was sent to the Soviet Union, where he remained for fifteen years. Just three and a half months later, Mif, representing the Comintern, convened the Fourth Plenum, at which Qu Qiubai himself was ousted. As for Zhou Enlai, he chose to 'consider the overall situation and make concessions for the sake of the Party' and made a self-criticism. In the words of the Wang Ming gang, Zhou Enlai ought to 'have his arse kicked'. He did not have to go, but he did need to rectify his errors...

When Qu Qiubai heard Zhou Enlai's self-vindication, he could not help saying Zhou was the most despicable of all, a fence-sitter, a follower of trends. Even so, Zhou has always been regarded by outsiders as 'broad-minded'.

At a subsequent meeting of the Central Committee, Wang Ming was elected to the Politburo. In the Politburo, Wang Ming assumed the crucial post of Secretary of the Party's Jiangsu Provincial Committee. There, he sowed the seeds of the Chinese Communist Party's historic defeat.

On 21 April 1931, Gu Shunzhang, an alternate member of the Politburo and responsible in the underground Central Committee for security work, turned traitor in Wuhan and gave away the Party's secrets, causing its collapse in Shanghai. Zhou Enlai, responsible for security, did not forget about Qu Qiubai when organising the retreat of the Central Committee's main leaders.

Mao Dun recalls that, at the time, he was writing his novel *Midnight*. That day, he and his wife Kong Dezhi were visiting Qu Qiubai in his lodgings, and had specially brought some of the later sections of *Midnight* to ask Qu Qiubai to comment. Qu Qiubai was delighted to see his old acquaintances. He told his wife Yang Zhihua to prepare some dishes, but just as they were sitting down to eat, an urgent message arrived: 'Your mother is ill, hurry back to her'. Qu Qiubai knew it was a warning from the Party. They fled to Mao Dun's home, where Qu Qiubai and his wife stayed for about ten days. Afterwards, they were looked after by Feng Xuefeng, who arranged for them to stay with Xie Danru.

Xie Danru, whose family came from Fujian, was born in Shanghai in 1904. His father ran an old-style bank, his family was well-off. At the age of fifteen, he joined the bank to study business, but his true love was writing. A founder of two bookshops, he made friends with Ying Xiuren, Lou Shiyi, and other poets, and especially with Gao Yuhan.

Gao Yuhan and his wife Wang Lingjun were Chen Duxiu's close friends. Gao Yuhan was an early member of the Communist Party and had come under Chen's influence. He also embraced Trotskyist ideas – for a while, he and his wife were Trotskyists. Xie Danru was a progressive, and a potential revolutionary. After the martyring of the five members of the Leftwing Writers'

Association, he personally financed the publication of a special issue of *Vanguard* commemorating them. Only a specialised researcher could distinguish between a Communist and a Trotskyist. Who could blame Xie Danru for joining the Trotskyists under Gao Hanyu's influence?

Xie Danru's residence was extensive. It had a big courtyard and housed a large collection of books. It was in a secluded location. Qu Qiubai lived there for nearly two years, a relatively stable and happy period in his life. He was unrestrained and undisturbed. He did a lot of writing while in Xie Danru's home, much of it subsequently published in his *Collected Essays*.

Xie Danru needed extraordinary courage to shelter Qu Qiubai, after Chiang Kai-shek had offered a reward of 20,000 silver dollars for his capture, twice as much as for Zhou Enlai. By Guomindang law, it was a serious crime to conceal a Communist leader. Xie Danru was brave enough to take the risk. He showed courage in other ways, too, as we shall see.

Gu Shunzhang's turning traitor put the Party's underground Central Committee in Shanghai in grave danger. On 22 June, its General Secretary Xiang Zhongfa was arrested in Shanghai; he too turned traitor. The next day, Chiang Kai-shek ordered his execution in Longhua Prison. In August, Wang Ming decided to leave Shanghai for Moscow and to serve on the Comintern as delegate of the Central Committee of the Chinese Communist Party. Shortly before leaving, he met with Zhou Enlai and Li Zhusheng (also a returned student from Moscow's Sun Yat-sen University, and, at the time, a member of the Politburo) in a small restaurant, where a decision was made that had a direct impact on the Party's future: the appointment of the 24-year-old Bo Gu (Qin Bangxian) as head of its Central Committee. Bo Gu told a meeting of the Politburo in Yan'an on 31 November 1943 that Wang Ming, Zhou Enlai, Lu Futan, and Bo Gu decided not to appoint a General Secretary but to make him, Bo Gu, Secretary, and, in effect, General Secretary. Two years later, Bo Gu, who was good at quoting authoritative texts and high-flown language but devoid of practical experience, entered the Central Soviet area and, as a matter of course, became leader of the Central Committee. After that, he laid waste the central base that Mao Zedong had opened up and allowed to thrive.

Zhou Enlai did not stay long in Shanghai. One evening, towards the end of November 1931, he was alone with just one bodyguard on a boat sailing from Shantou to the Jinggang Mountains region. As he stood looking out into the Huangpu River, he must have wondered when he would ever return to Shanghai.

On 7 January 1934, Qu Qiubai, suffering from a serious lung-disease, left Shanghai on the orders of the Central Committee to go to the Central Soviet, as head of the Chinese Soviet Government's education commission. At the time, many people, among them his best friend Lu Xun, were confused by the decision to order Qu Qiubai to leave Shanghai. Lu Xun told Qu's wife Yang Zhihua: 'It's not right for someone in Qu's state of health to go to the Soviet area. It would be better to send him to the Soviet Union'. On 4 January, when Qu Qiubai took his leave of Lu Xun, Lu Xun let Qu Qiubai sleep in his bed while he and Xu Guangping spent the night on bedding laid out on the floor, to demonstrate his deep feelings for Qu.

In October 1934, the Red Army set out on the Long March, leaving Qu Qiubai behind. Qu Qiubai personally told Mao he wanted to join the march, but Mao could do nothing – after all, he himself was almost left behind. According to Zhang Wentian, all the preparations for the march were made by Otto Braun (Li De), Bo Gu, and Zhou Enlai, who decided which of the senior cadres left and which stayed. After Mao reached Yan'an, he said several times that Wang Ming and Bo Gu had behaved in a sectarian manner and left Qu Qiubai behind in the Soviet to be killed by the enemy.

He Shuheng, a veteran of the First Congress, was also left behind and sacrificed. He Shuheng, Dong Biwu, Lin Boqu, Xu Teli, and Xie Juezai were known to youngsters in the Soviet area as the 'five veterans'. Dong, Lin, Xu, and Xie joined the Long March and reached northern Shaanxi under the protection of the young revolutionary fighters: only He Shuheng stayed and died at the hands of the Guomindang butchers.

After the start of the Long March, Qu Qiubai went to see Chen Yi, who had remained in Ruijin due to a leg injury. Chen Yi was shocked to him. He asked Qu Qiubai why he had stayed, and pointed out that Qu was not fit enough to wage guerrilla war. He got his groom to fetch his big white horse and told Qu Qiubai to ride off and catch up with the main force. Qu Qiubai rode off, but later he rode back and said to Chen Yi: 'They don't want me, what's the point of catching up with them!' Having said that, he left, heartbroken.

On 23 April 1935, he was arrested at Tingshui in Fujian and taken to Changting. Before he died, he wrote a famous memoir, *Superfluous Words*, published in the semi-legal publication *Social News* and in *Yi Jing*. It caused a sensation.

In July 1943, when Zhou Enlai returned to Yan'an, he participated in the campaign to criticise the Wang Ming Line and the Rectification Campaign, part of the preparations for the Seventh Congress. From 15 to 19 November, Zhou Enlai made a speech to a meeting of top cadres in which he systematically reviewed the background to the leftist line and made a thorough-going self-criticism. Unfortunately, even though more than sixty years have passed, the materials have still not been made fully public. To clarify the Qu Qiubai question, the Central Committee made a careful study of *Superfluous Words*.

Mao Zedong, Liu Shaoqi, Zhou Enlai, Ren Bishi, and Kang Sheng read it, and confirmed that Qu Qiubai remained a great Communist fighter throughout his life. In fact, as early as 1938, Ding Ling had read a copy of *Superfluous Words* in the library of the Central Propaganda Department in Yan'an and discussed it with Zhang Wentian. Zhang Wentian ordered Li Kenong to get the original manuscript from the Guomindang, but unfortunately Li failed.

In the summer of 1966, Mao Zedong launched the Cultural Revolution, bringing great suffering to the Chinese people. However, in the early period of the Cultural Revolution, Mao revealed his actual aim to only a handful of people, among them Zhou Enlai. Zhou Enlai spent days and nights agonising over what to do, and eventually decided to 'consider the overall situation and make concessions for the sake of the Party' and stand by Mao. Not long afterwards, at a speech to Red Guards, he praised them for their contribution to the Great Proletarian Cultural Revolution. Shortly before his speech, the Red Guards found a copy of Qu's *Superfluous Words*. Zhou said: 'Like Chen Boda, Kang Sheng, and others of my generation, this is the first time I have seen this work. It shows that Qu Qiubai was a big traitor'. This was, of course, a lie.

When Mao first decided to launch the Cultural Revolution, the Central Committee held a very important conference, in May 1966. On 21 May, after Lin Biao published his famous 'coup' speech on 18 May, Zhou Enlai spoke for a second time, saying the most important thing was to 'maintain integrity to the end'. He said: 'Otherwise we write everything off at a single stroke'. And: 'One cannot be finally judged even after death, even after cremation'. Later, he proposed 'moving Qu Qiubai from the Babaoshan Cemetery and destroying [the Taiping leader] Li Xiucheng's palace in Suzhou', because neither had stood firm at the end and both had betrayed the revolution. Qu Qiubai had written *Superfluous Words*, Li Xiucheng had written his Self-Description for the Qing court after his arrest. Both had betrayed the cause, 'both were shameless'.

As a direct result of Zhou Enlai's words, Qu's tomb was smashed and his remains were burned. Even his mother's tomb was not spared. Red Guards throughout the country started seizing 'traitors'. All those imprisoned under the Guomindang were labelled 'traitors' and trampled on. Sadly, the sword of Damocles also hung over the head of Zhou Enlai, when the Red Guards found a 'declaration' dated 18 February 1932, which Zhang Chong and other Guomindang agents had forged and published in *Shenbao*. (In it, Zhou Enlai and 242 others purportedly renounced the Communist Party.) The Red Guards handed it to Jiang Qing and Mao Zedong. On 17 May 1967, Jiang Qing personally wrote to Lin Biao, Zhou Enlai, and Kang Sheng to tell them. Although it was plainly a forgery, for the next eight or more years, until his death on 8 January 1976, the word 'traitor' dogged this faithful Communist fighter.

On 1 July 1975, when Zhou Enlai was in hospital and met the Thai Prime Minister, someone suggested a photo be taken of the two men. Afterwards, Zhou said: 'This is the last time I will be photographed with you, I hope in future you don't scratch an X on my face'. On 20 September, before his final operation, Zhou Enlai exclaimed in a loud voice: 'I am loyal to the Party and to the people, I am not a traitor, I am not a capitulationist!' Such was his tragedy.

It is said that, just before his death, Zhou Enlai told his bodyguard: 'I am not a traitor, and nor was Qu Qiubai. The Red Guards didn't find his *Superfluous Words*, I read this work a long time ago, I let him down'.

'The words of a man about to die ring true' – this brings me back to the Trotskyist Xie Danru. In June 1935, after he had received the news of Qu's death, he handed over the manuscripts of all Qu's translations to Lu Xun, keeping the rest in a suitcase. When the war reached Shanghai in August 1937, the part of the city Xie Danru lived in was devastated, and Xie fled with nothing but the suitcase. After Pearl Harbor, wandering from place to place in desperation, he remembered Lu Xun's injunction that 'paper and ink vanquish metal and stone', and realised he could not let the martyrs' legacy sink into oblivion. So he published Qu's precious manuscript *On Luantan Opera and Other Things* and his *Introduction to Social Science* under the name 'Xia Publishing House'. He also published Fang Zhimin's testament, 'Beloved China!' This is an example of Xie's nobility of heart. Sometimes even the sentiments of great revolutionaries fail to match those of ordinary people such as some of the Trotskyists.

Let us return to 1931, the Chinese Trotskyists' most important year. At noon on 1 May in a workers' district in Hudong in Shanghai, seventeen delegates from across China representing 483 Trotskyists nationwide, together with four non-voting delegates, held their Unification Congress.

The emergence of Chinese Trotskyism was due to a number of complex factors, principal among them the defeat of the Chinese revolution. On 12 April 1927, Chiang Kai-shek launched a counter-revolutionary military coup in Shanghai, followed on 15 April by another in Nanjing. On the same day, in Guangzhou, the Guangdong warlord Li Jishen purged the Communists. On 21 May, the Guomindang reactionary Xu Kexiang launched the bloody 'Horse Day Incident' in Changsha. On 15 July, the self-proclaimed 'leftist' Wang Jingwei launched a counter-revolutionary coup in Wuhan. So, by then, almost all the Nationalists had raised their butchers' knives against the Communists, and the Chinese revolutionary movement had finally petered out. In that period, dozens of the Communist Party's outstanding leaders – including Li Dazhao, Wang Shouhua, Zhao Shiyan, Luo Yinong, Hou Shaoqiu, Peng Pai, Yang Yin, Cai Hesen, Xiang Jingyu, and Chen Duxiu's sons Chen Yannian and Chen Qiaonian – were killed by the Guomindang authorities, and membership of the Chinese Communist Party abruptly slid from sixty thousand at the height of the revolution to just over ten thousand.

Most Chinese Communists were keen to know why the revolution had failed. Chen Duxiu, the Party's founder and General Secretary for its first five Congresses, bore the brunt of the criticism. His secretary Huang Jieran described the events in his memoirs:

> On the night of July 9 or 10, 1927, I hid with Mr Chen Duxiu in the attic above a restaurant. The next day, we moved to the paper-store of the East Asia Bookshop Publishing Company and stayed there until we left Wuhan.... During that time, Chen Duxiu sat quietly all day, wracking his brains. I was downstairs and could hear him pacing back and forth upstairs. The worst thing was we were so isolated, we knew nothing about what was going on in the outside world. For example, we only found out about the Nanchang Uprising, a major event, at the 7 August Conference.... I was very depressed. I had lots of questions I couldn't answer and that I would have liked to discuss with Chen Duxiu. One day, I took advantage of the maid's absence to go upstairs and ask him three questions: Why did the revolution come to such an end? What lessons should we learn? What should we do next? After Chen Duxiu had heard me out, he stared at me for a long time and finally gave me a wry smile, but he didn't say a word.

In September 1927, Chen Duxiu and Huang Jieran moved secretly from Wuhan to Shanghai and went to live in a three-storey house off Jiangxi North Road. Chen was like an angry lion locked in a cage. Every day he paced up and down his tiny room, thinking constantly.

In July 1922, at its Second Congress, the Chinese Communist Party had resolved to join the Third International, as its 'Chinese branch'. According to the Third International's Twenty-One Regulations, adopted in July 1920, the constitution of the party in each country must be approved by the International; all the International's resolutions must be carried out by the various national parties; and any party that refused to carry out its duties should be expelled. In other words, the party's fundamental rights in each country were vested in the Comintern, and a legal basis was established for the Russian Communist Party and Stalin to interfere at will in the affairs of its national sections.

Acting on the Comintern's instructions, the Politburo of the Chinese Communist Party met in Hankou on 7 August 1927, to criticise Chen Duxiu and remove him as General Secretary. Even though Chen was in Wuhan, no one notified him of the meeting. After his removal, no one told him why. He was perplexed and unhappy, in addition to which he fell seriously ill in the intense Wuhan heat. After that, again in accordance with Comintern instructions, the Central Committee tried several times to get him to go to the Soviet Union to study. Each time he refused. He told Huang Jieran: 'What does Moscow want me to study? Problems of the Chinese Revolution? Who understands Chinese history better, a Chinese or a foreigner? If we have to ask foreigners about China's problems, should foreigners ask Chinese about foreign questions?' In June 1928, the Chinese Communist Party held its Sixth Congress in Moscow. On Comintern instructions, it told Chen Duxiu to attend. (It also told Zhang Guotao and Peng Shuzhi, who had served on the Standing Committee of the Politburo.) However, Chen Duxiu continued to refuse to go, despite Qu Qiubai's and Zhou Enlai's efforts to mobilise him. Qu Qiubai even got Chen Duxiu's good friend Wang Ruofei to try, again to no effect. According to Zheng Chaolin, who took part in the 7 August Conference and was a lifelong follower of Chen Duxiu, Chen thought that because the Chinese revolution had failed, the Comintern wanted to save face by sacrificing him and Tan Pingshan. That judgement would seem to be justified.

According to materials released only recently, the Politburo of the Soviet Communist Party discussed the Chinese revolution at 122 meetings and passed 738 resolutions on it between 1923 and 1927. That figure does not include resolutions and decisions of the Comintern Executive. Whether on big matters such as the Chinese Communists joining the Guomindang in their own name or small ones such as when the Chinese Communist Party should send students to the Soviet Union and how many it should send, and even regarding when to talk with Chiang Kai-shek, who should talk with him, and what to talk about, in all such matters detailed instructions were issued that had under all circumstances to be obeyed. It should be clear from this what 'hegemonic party' meant. Even a great intellectual like Chen Duxiu, a great scholar, known for his fiery temper, had no choice other than to submit in the face of the Comintern and the Russians. Now that the revolution had been defeated, the first thing they did was kick Chen Duxiu out, as a scapegoat.

The causes of the defeat of the Chinese revolution were hotly debated within the Soviet Party, mainly by Stalin and Trotsky. Stalin published major works on the Chinese Revolution, including numerous directives issued in the Comintern's name. Trotsky also made many speeches (collected in two pamphlets) on the Chinese revolution, 'On the Chinese Question After the Comintern's Sixth Congress' and 'Summary and Prospects of the Chinese Revolution', later circulated by his Chinese followers under the title *Problems of the Chinese Revolution*. His proposals regarding the Chinese revolution were as follows. (1) He insisted that the Chinese Communist Party should not join the Guomindang during the period of the Great Revolution, a position that happened to chime with Chen Duxiu's view. Chen Duxiu got into fierce arguments with delegates of the Comintern about whether or not Communists should join the Guomindang. (2) He said the revolutionary nature of the Guomindang should not be overestimated, and there should be no yielding to the Guomindang's and especially not to Chiang Kai-shek's overbearing manner. That was also consistent with Chen Duxiu's view. For example, after the Zhongshan Gunboat Incident, Chen proposed a counterattack but was reprimanded by the Comintern representative, Borodin, who told him that, at that particular moment, the Communist Party should act as the Guomindang's coolies. (3) After the defeat of the Great Revolution, the revolutionary situation ebbed and was 'in a period of transition between two revolutions'. The Chinese Communist Party should not overestimate its own strength or underestimate Chiang Kai-shek's. It should 'first go on the defensive and then attack', a position Chen Duxiu also adopted. (4) Finally, Trotsky did not believe that feudalism dominated the Chinese economy and superstructure, so he argued capitalist relations were in the ascendancy in China and in a position of direct dominance. Based on that analysis, he believed that in the then stage of the Chinese revolution one should be active within the bourgeois state's 'national assembly', gather strength, and win over the people, whereas 'armed uprisings' and 'setting up soviets' were for the future. Chen Duxiu agreed with this too. So they opposed Mao Zedong's policy of establishing rural base-areas and seizing political power through armed struggle. That is why people later ridiculed Chen Duxiu and the Trotskyists as the 'Trotsky-Chen liquidationists'. Needless to say, on this point Mao Zedong, in practice, proved them wrong.

In 1956, at the Twentieth Congress of the Soviet Communist Party, the Soviet leader Nikita Khrushchev delivered his famous 'secret report' on Stalin. This was the first time Stalin's abuse of power and brutal repression of oppositionists in the Party, including Trotsky, was systematically made public, and it set off a wave of anti-Stalinism. Zhu De and Deng Xiaoping, who had been invited to participate in the meeting, received copies of the 'secret report' and took them back to China. Mao Zedong read the Chinese translation the same night and felt an upsurge of emotion. After discussing it with Liu Shaoqi, Zhou Enlai, and others, a decision was taken to continue to publicly defend Stalin's image. Mao uttered a well-known phrase: 'The pictures in Tian'anmen Square of the five dead – Marx, Engels, Lenin, Stalin and Sun Yat-sen – and the one living – the one called Mao Zedong – will continue to hang. Not one will be withdrawn'. However, he held repeated talks with Yudin, the Soviet philosopher and Ambassador to China, and later with Soviet Communist Party leaders, about Stalin's mistakes concerning the Chinese Revolution. They can be summed up as follows: in the Great Revolution, he overestimated the revolutionary character of the Guomindang, he invariably yielded to the Guomindang, and, after the defeat of the Revolution, he blamed everything on Chen Duxiu. That judgement was almost exactly the same as Chen Duxiu's, who said in 1928 that 'he and Tan Pingshan had been sacrificed'. None of this was made public until after the collapse of the Soviet Union.

Arguments about theory can end up as political showdowns. By the end of 1927, Stalin, whose misleadership of the Chinese revolution had ended in its defeat and who had also suffered defeat in the theoretical debate, used his power to expel Trotsky from the Party at its Fifteenth Congress and exiled him the following year to Alma Ata, while launching a nationwide purge of the Trotskyists. I have already mentioned how Shi Tang, Liang Ganqiao, Ou Fang and other students were expelled from the Party and sent home in late 1927. After their return, they set up China's first Trotskyist organisation, the Chinese Bolshevik-Leninist Opposition, in Shanghai and published a mimeographed journal, *Our Word*. Chen Duxiu first came into contact with Trotsky's theory and viewpoint through this publication.

Zheng Chaolin tells the story:

> Probably in mid or late May 1929, Yin Kuan brought some unusual mimeographed documents for us to see, documents of the Trotskyist Opposition in the Soviet Union. They were poorly translated and poorly mimeographed, but still they were intelligible. Yin Kuan had obviously been affected by them. He excitedly introduced them to us....
>
> After discussing and exchanging ideas for just a week or two, we basically became Trotskyists. But Chen Duxiu held out for longer than the rest of us.... After reading each of Trotsky's documents, Chen would raise a disagreement...; but the next time he came he had abandoned his previous disagreement and would raise a new one on the shoulders of the old argument. In the course of his gradual conversion to their point of view, he never once yielded to them in their presence, but next time he came face to face with them he raised new differences on the basis of what they had previously told him. And so it went on.

Trotsky's ideas resolved Chen's dilemmas and showed him the way forward. He felt the questions he had agonised over for more than a year had finally been answered. It seemed to him he could see 'clouds and rainbows in the great drought'. He fully embraced what Trotsky proposed. On 5 August 1929, he wrote a 'Letter to the Central Committee of the Chinese Communist Party on the Chinese Revolution' that symbolised his turn to Trotskyism. In it, he systematically put forward his own ideas about the Chinese revolution and the defeat of the Great Revolution, aiming his spearhead at the Comintern. The letter ended as follows:

> Because I cannot bear to see the Party (created by the warm blood of innumerable comrades) destroyed and ruined by the enduring and essentially false line, I have no choice but to write this letter to you.... I hope you will publish it in its entirety in the party press, so it can be discussed by the whole Party.

By that time, Trotsky had been expelled by the Soviet Government, first to Turkey, then to Norway, and finally to Mexico, where Stalin's assassin killed him.

Once he had accepted Trotsky's proposals, Chen Duxiu's political evolution was unstoppable. Apart from the 5 August letter, he put his name to other documents. In September, together with Peng Shuzhi (who had been on the Politburo and the Standing Committee and had headed the Propaganda Department) and others, he organised the Left Opposition of the Chinese Communist Party, also known as the Chinese Bolshevik-Leninist Faction, with Chen as General Secretary. On 10 and 26 October, he wrote two more letters to the Central Committee stating his views even more clearly. According to Wang Fanxi's *Memoirs of a Chinese Revolutionary*, when Zhou Enlai, head of the Organisation Department of the underground Central Committee in Shanghai, read the letters, he ridiculed them: 'Let the opportunists go to the Trotskyists for a way out!' More and more people in the Chinese Communist Party were embracing Trotsky's theories and ideas. As well as Peng Shuzhi, Yin Kuan (who had been on the Politburo), Zheng Chaolin (who had edited the Central Committee journal *Bolshevik*), Wang Zekai, Ma Yufu, and many other senior leaders of the Chinese Communist Party joined the Trotskyists.

The Central Committee launched a fierce counterattack against Chen Duxiu and the Trotskyists. On 5 October, it passed a resolution 'Opposing the Opportunists and Trotskyist Oppositionists in the Party' and made three decisions: (1) Oppositionist cells must immediately disband; (2) party members who subscribed to liquidationist ideology 'should be expelled from the Party without further ado'; (3) 'Comrade Duxiu must immediately comply with the Central Committee's resolution, accept its warning, work under its line, and cease all anti-party propaganda and activities'. On 6 October, the Central Committee wrote Chen Duxiu a letter: 'The Central Committee has decided to ask you to do editing work in the Central Committee under the political line of the Party, and to write an article "Against the Opposition" within a week'. I have been unable to find out which member of the Central Committee wrote this letter, but it is more than a little ridiculous, especially since it was addressed to the standard-bearer of the New Culture Movement and the Chinese Communist Party's General Secretary at five consecutive congresses. Chen immediately wrote back: 'I would never have thought you would end up making such fools of yourselves'.

At this point, the Central Committee of the Chinese Communist Party copied the Soviet Communist Party and began a ruthless attack on the Opposition. On 21 October, its Jiangsu Provincial Committee passed a resolution expelling Peng Shuzhi, Wang Zekai, Ma Yufu, and Cai Zhende and 'requesting the Central Committee to expel Chen Duxiu'.

However, the Central Committee bided its time, waiting for the Comintern's final decision on Chen Duxiu. On 26 October, the Comintern wrote to the Central Committee of the Chinese Communist Party: 'The Party should carry out a merciless struggle against the Chen Duxiu liquidationist proposals'. On 15 November, the Chinese Party's Politburo passed a resolution expelling Chen Duxiu and agreeing with the decision of the Jiangsu Provincial Committee to expel Peng Shuzhi and the three others.

From then on, Chen Duxiu and the party he had founded went separate ways. Also from then on – in Shanghai, where nearly all China's major parties and political factions originated – Chen Duxiu threw himself wholeheartedly into unifying the Chinese Trotskyists.

Chen Duxiu

In the early spring of 1930, on Shanghai's Dent Road off Seward Road (today's Changzhi East Road and Dantu Road), in the front part of an old-style lane house, stood a man in his fifties, a recluse who went out only occasionally to stroll around the courtyard. He had few friends, and usually few visitors. He lived a frugal life, eating simply, and each day he read books and newspapers, or bent over his desk writing. His neighbour was a 20-year-old divorcee called Pan Lanzhen, a worker, who lived in a small room in the basement. She noticed the old man had no one to look after him, so she got into the habit of helping him with his cleaning, and sometimes she cooked for him. Feelings developed, and the two became a couple. Such a relationship was unusual at the time, but people got used to it. However, the old man never told her his real name. He simply said he was a businessman from Nanjing called Li. So Pan Lanzhen called her husband 'Old Man Li'.

In fact, 'Old Man Li' was Chen Duxiu. After his expulsion from the Party, the Central Committee stopped supporting him, the Party's trump-card in dealing with opposition, since it paid the living expenses of professional revolutionaries. Professional revolutionaries who carried out revolutionary activities and, at the same time, had to support their families were vulnerable to capture by the Guomindang. Fortunately, Chen Duxiu was a prolific writer who could live off the royalties of his writings published in 1922 by the East Asia Book Company and other royalties from new writings. At the time, however, he was writing little, for he was putting his main effort into studying Trotsky's theories and organising the Trotskyist movement throughout China.

In December 1928, the Our Word group, China's first Trotskyist organisation, was established in Shanghai. When Chen Duxiu turned to Trotskyism, Communist leaders like Peng Shuzhi, Zheng Chaolin, and Yin Kuan were more or less in step with him ideologically. Although they had their differences, generally speaking they followed his lead. They were the Chen Duxiu faction, and some of them (like Zheng Chaolin) followed him for the rest of their lives. When I first met Zheng Chaolin, he was already more than ninety years old, but if anyone evinced the slightest disrespect towards Chen Duxiu, he would purse his lips and seem unhappy. In August 1929, the Chen Duxiu-ites asked to join Our Word, but Our Word 'not only did not welcome the Chen Duxiu-ites' turn towards Trotskyism but even resented it'. According to the Trotskyist Wang Fanxi, writing in his *Memoirs*, they saw Chen Duxiu 'as an inveterate opportunist trying to find his way out of a blind alley'. Peng Shuzhi was furious. According to his wife Chen Bilan, in her *Recollections of a Chinese Revolutionary*:

> These young people thought they were the true Trotskyists. Because they hadn't taken part in the revolutionary movement between 1925 and 1927, they felt they bore no responsibility for its defeat, so only they were worthy of the name Trotskyist.... When Duxiu and Shuzhi proposed a meeting to seek ways of cooperating, they arrogantly put themselves forward as the orthodox Trotskyists and didn't want to negotiate cooperation with anyone.

But Chen Duxiu, despite his reputation for hot-headedness, didn't seem to mind. He repeatedly and magnanimously discussed with members of the Our Word group. He even agreed to 'review his past mistakes' and joined Our Word under his own name.

Another important figure in the Trotskyist movement, Liu Renjing, turned up in Shanghai. He had been a delegate at the Party's First Congress, when only nineteen years old and still a student at Beijing University. At the time, the Communist group in Beijing had been so full of talent that it was never Liu Renjing's turn. After Liberation, Liu Renjing recalled:

> No one then thought the meeting would be so significant. I remember the voting went like this: first Zhang Guotao was chosen unanimously as delegate. Then Deng Zhongxia and Luo Zhanglong were proposed, but each modestly declined, on the grounds that they were busy working, so eventually it was decided I would be the second delegate.

In that way, his name was inscribed in perpetuity in the annals of the Chinese Communist Party. After the defeat of the 1927 Revolution, Liu Renjing became a Trotskyist while studying at the Lenin Academy in the Soviet Union. In April 1929, he finished his studies and made a diversion by way of Europe with the secret support and connivance of the Comintern delegates Zhang Guotao and Wang Ruofei, including a special trip to Turkey, where he visited Trotsky on Prinkipo Island. Because of this, the Comintern criticised and punished Zhang Guotao and Wang Ruofei. Liu Renjing had good English and Russian, and Trotsky was immediately smitten by his new 'Chinese comrade'. The two men held long conversations. The more they talked, the closer they became. After nearly a month of 'accelerated training', Liu Renjing became Trotsky's loyal follower. As the only Chinese Trotskyist who had met Trotsky and learned his Trotskyism from the man himself, he became Trotsky's link and spokesperson in China.

In August 1929 Liu Renjing went back to Shanghai, and, not long afterwards, he met Chen Duxiu in Zheng Chaolin's home. If, in the past, Chen Duxiu had experienced his Trotskyism second-hand from the Our Word group, now Liu

Renjing brought back the original doctrine as well as a number of Trotsky's 'latest directives', an eye-opener for the Chinese Trotskyists. It is important not to underestimate Liu Renjing's role in helping the Chinese Opposition to understand and accept Trotskyism, which they only really did after his return to China. Chen Duxiu resolved to arm his followers with Trotsky's theories. He got Liu Renjing to retranslate Trotsky's 'Summary and Prospects of the Chinese Revolution' and Zheng Chaolin to retranslate Trotsky's 'On the Chinese Question After the Comintern's Sixth Congress', the publication of which he funded from his own pocket, as *Problems of the Chinese Revolution*. He also decided to publish his own journal, *Proletarian*, which he also paid for. On 15 December 1929, Chen Duxiu finalised the text of 'Our Political Views', which was signed by 87 people, with his name at the top (it was initially drafted by Liu Renjing). More than fifty signed with their real names. Apart from Chen Duxiu, they included Peng Shuzhi, who had worked in the Central Committee, Peng's wife Chen Bilan, Zheng Chaolin and his wife Liu Jingzhen, Yin Kuan, Li Ji, He Zishen, Gao Yuhan, Wang Duqing, Chen Qingchen, and Ma Yufu. They signed as the Left Opposition of the Chinese Communist Party, and because their publication was called *Proletariat*, they were known as the Proletarian Society. According to Zheng Chaolin, speaking in September 1988 in Shanghai: 'The list of 81 was drawn up by me and the old gentleman [Chen Duxiu] in the old gentleman's home. Actually only two thirds of the signatures were real, the others were fake, to give the impression there were lots of us'.

The strange thing is that Liu Renjing did not sign the document he drafted. Boasting that he was Trotsky's 'imperial envoy', he tried to bring Our Word and the Proletarian Society together, but to no effect. Angry at this rebuff, he formed a new organisation with a few young Trotskyists, called the October Group after their journal, *October*. Another group composed of people who walked out of the three existing factions set up a fourth faction, the Militant Group, named after their publication, *Militant*.

In his *Memoirs*, Wang Fanxi reflected thus on the Chinese Trotskyist scene at the time:

> People's motives for becoming Trotskyists in the first place varied enormously. Some joined because they found it difficult to realise their ambitions within the Party, and thought that the best thing would be to branch out in a new direction; others were intimidated by the intensity of the White Terror, and used the Opposition as a stage in their retreat from the Revolution; and still others took advantage of the left-wing reputation of the Trotskyist movement to retreat into a world of 'revolutionary' mouthings, with no practical consequences. But although many sorry types were coming over to our side, the overwhelming majority of

Opposition supporters in China at that time were sincere revolutionaries driven by the best of motives, who firmly supported Trotsky's proposals for the Chinese Revolution and considered them far better suited to the conditions of China than those of Stalin. It was for this reason that they gave up their established positions in the Party and devoted themselves wholeheartedly to the Oppositionist cause.

Chen Duxiu was just such a person. He too gave up his established position in the Party and devoted himself wholeheartedly to the Oppositionist cause. However, at times, he was deeply depressed. When he tried to unite with Our Word, denounced by Peng Shuzhi as 'a bunch of simple-minded children', he was repeatedly rebuffed. Liu Renjing was also dissatisfied. Chen Duxiu's only real pleasure was watching the pure-hearted Pan Lanzhen, his lover, on whom he was practising his mild deception. Only when she naïvely called him Old Man Li would a smile light up his face, the only comic line in the drama being acted out at the time on the Shanghai stage.

Peng Shuzhi

On 20 October 1932, the Shanghai press published a photo of two important Communist prisoners who had been taken into custody in the middle of the night and were being escorted to Nanjing. The two were Chen Duxiu and Peng Shuzhi. Chen Duxiu was 53 and Peng was 37, but they looked more or less the same age in the photo. Later, many historians got the two men mixed up, and 'put Zhang's hat on Li's head'.

Were it not for the Chinese Communist Party's professional researchers, even fewer people would know the name Peng Shuzhi. However, he was an important figure in the Party's early history. He was a staunch supporter of Chen Duxiu and attended the Fourth National Conference, when he was elected the Party's no. 2.

Peng Shuzhi, from Baoqing in Hunan, was born in 1895. He joined the Chinese Socialist Youth League in 1920, and was later assigned to study at the University for the Toilers of the East in Moscow. Along with Liu Shaoqi and Ke Qingshi, he joined the Chinese Communist Party in Moscow and led its branch there. Afterwards, Peng Shuzhi, Qu Qiubai, and Luo Yinong were known as the Chinese Communist Party's 'three Soviet-educated leaders'.

When I interviewed Zheng Chaolin in the late 1990s, he described Peng Shuzhi as follows: 'He was a typical old Confucian gentleman. He was short and swarthy, but with fine, delicate features. He liked to wear a leather-coat and hat. He was very learned, and had attended a small private school where he studied the Confucian *Four Books* and *Five Classics*. He had also read lots of Marxist books, and could quote them readily. He had written quite a lot too, and his *Imperialism and the Boxer Movement* and *Who is the Leader of the National Revolution* were important works at the time of the Great Revolution. He was an eloquent speaker, although it was not easy to understand his Baoqing accent. Even so, he loved to hold forth, and could never resist the chance to address a meeting. He was very popular with the Soviet authorities, and even the Comintern's Zinoviev called him "Confucius". His Russian name was Petrov. The Chinese students in Moscow held him in high regard. He was one of their leaders'.

In September 1924, the Comintern assigned Peng Shuzhi to return to China. In Shanghai, he joined the Party's Municipal Committee and helped edit the Party's *Guide* and *New Youth* magazines. He accepted Chen Duxiu's leadership and became his staunch supporter.

From 11 to 22 January 1925, the Chinese Communist Party held its Fourth Congress in the area between the British Concession and the Chinese-governed district, in a lane house. Twenty delegates attended, representing the Communist Party's 994 members. In addition to Mao Zedong, they included nearly all the Party's early leaders: Chen Duxiu, Qu Qiubai, Cai Hesen, Li Dazhao, Zhou Enlai, Xiang Ying, Li Lisan, Luo Zhanglong, Li Weihan, Zhu Jintang, Wang Hebo, Deng Zhongxia, Ren Bishi, Peng Shuzhi, Zhang Tailei, Wang Shouhua, Xiang Zhongfa, Yin Kuan, Chen Qiaonian, and Shen Xuanlu. The young and inexperienced Peng Shuzhi headed the Congress Secretariat. The Congress discussed the labour movement and cooperation with the Guomindang, and elected Chen Duxiu, Li Dazhao, Cai Hesen, Zhang Guotao, Xiang Ying, Peng Shuzhi, Qu Qiubai, Tan Pingshan, and Li Weihan to the Central Committee, with Chen Duxiu, Zhang Guotao, Peng Shuzhi, Cai Hesen, and Qu Qiubai as its five-member Central Bureau. Chen Duxiu was General Secretary. He concurrently headed the Organisation Bureau, with Zhou Enlai as his deputy; Peng Shuzhi headed the Propaganda Department, with Cai Hesen and Qu Qiubai as his deputies. Peng Shuzhi prided himself to the end of his life on having served as second in command in the Chinese Communist Party.

Peng Shuzhi became Cai Hesen's immediate superior, and the two of them spent a lot of time together with Cai's wife Xiang Jingyu. Then the unexpected happened: Peng and Xiang had an 'extramarital affair'.

Xiang Jingyu was the Chinese Communist Party's main early woman-activist. From Guanzhen in Xupu in Hunan, she was a member of the Tujia minority, and Cai Hesen's fellow-student. After the May Fourth Movement, she went together with Cai Hesen and his younger sister Cai Chang to France to study. Xiang Jingyu was petite, outgoing, and extremely active. Before boarding the ship, she declared ardently to her fellow-passengers: 'We are going to the European home of Marxism to fetch the revolutionary scripture, we are not yet married, nor will we marry until the revolution has succeeded'. But after more than a month at sea, just before disembarking, she again loudly announced: 'I have formed a revolutionary partnership with Cai Hesen!'

Cai Hesen was Mao Zedong's early best friend and an important early leader of the Chinese Communists. He joined the Party in 1921, and was elected to the Standing Committee of the Politburo (then called the Central Executive Committee) at the Second Congress and made head of the Propaganda Bureau and editor of *Guide Weekly*. His wife Xiang Jingyu was put in charge of the Women's Bureau. Many in the Party admired and wished to emulate Cai and Xiang's marriage. However, Cai Hesen developed severe asthma, and because of the poor environment and unavailability of treatment, he was short of breath. Also, Cai paid little attention to his health. Whenever he was busy, he skipped meals. He did not care about his appearance either, and his bedroom was piled high with books and newspapers. He lived an irregular life, and often slept fully clothed. He rarely took a bath, and wouldn't wash his feet for a whole week at a time. Zhang Guotao wrote in his memoirs that Cai Hesen 'cannot be regarded as a husband likely to make his wife happy'.

Peng Shuzhi was quite different. He had just returned from Moscow, and was riding the crest of success. Nicknamed Confucius, he behaved like a gentleman. He spoke and wrote well, and this attracted Xiang Jingyu, so the two fell hopelessly in love. Xiang Jingyu wrote to tell the Central Committee: 'I have fallen in love with Peng Shuzhi. He is so witty and interesting that I cannot resist my feelings for him.... But I cannot bear to hurt Cai Hesen.... So I beseech the Central Committee to send me to Moscow to study'. This caused a stir in the Party. According to Zheng Chaolin, working in the Central Committee at the time, Chen Duxiu was dumbfounded. He was himself a romantic by nature, but he took this love-triangle involving members of the Politburo very seriously. He specifically sought the views of Qu Qiubai, and sent Xiang Jingyu to Moscow. After the defeat of the Great Revolution, Xiang Jingyu was arrested in Wuhan, in 1928, and died a hero on 1 May. In 1931, the Party sent Cai Hesen to Guangzhou to lead the Guangdong Provincial Committee. The traitor Gu Shunzhang found out about this. On 10 June, Cai was entrapped and arrested in Hong Kong, escorted back to Guangzhou, and bayoneted to death in prison on orders of the warlord Chen Jitang.

The affair did not seem to have much effect on Peng Shuzhi. In December, he started living with Chen Bilan, editor of *Chinese Women*.

Chen Bilan was one of the Chinese Communist Party's talented early women-activists. A native of Huangpo in Hubei, she was from a wealthy family. She went to Shanghai to escape an arranged marriage, and joined the revolution. In 1923, she became a Communist. At the time the Party's top leaders, including Chen Duxiu, Qu Qiubai, and Deng Zhongxia, were fond of the pretty 21-year-old. After arriving in Shanghai, she lived for a long time with Cai Hesen and Xiang Jingyu. In the spring of 1924, the Central Committee decided to send Li Dazhao and Zhang Tailei to Moscow to attend the Comintern's Fifth Congress, and to send Chen Bilan with them to study at the University for the Toilers of the East. Needless to say, she was delighted. However, because the Party had limited funds, people had to pay for their own travel to Moscow, a total of 200 yuan. The comrades in the Central Committee had a whip-round for Chen Bilan. Besides Qu Qiubai, Deng Zhongxia, Shi Cuntong, and others, even Mao Zedong contributed twenty silver dollars. Chen Bilan was greatly moved. She benefitted much from her year in Moscow, principally by getting to know many of the Party's early activists such as Chen Duxiu's son, Chen Qiaonian, Luo Yinong, Wang Yifei, Liu Bojian, and Wang Ruofei. She was able to hear with her own ears speeches by Stalin, Trotsky, Bukharin, and Zinoviev, main leaders of the Soviet Communist Party and the Comintern, which left a deep impression on her. In the summer of 1925, she returned from Moscow to work for the Party. In Shanghai, after a short break, she was sent to Kaifeng to work in the Henan Provincial Committee. A few months later, she was transferred back to Shanghai to edit *Chinese Women* under Peng Shuzhi, who headed the Party's Propaganda Department. Peng Shuzhi was attracted by her beauty and talent, and this attraction was mutual. A few months later, they started living together. Chen Bilan was good at keeping him on a short leash, and there was never again any talk of his womanising, right up until after Liberation in 1949, when the two fled to Western Europe by way of Vietnam.

The year 1926 was eventful in the Chinese Revolution. As a main leader of the Chinese Communist Party, Peng Shuzhi was at the centre of a turbulent and difficult situation.

On 20 March 1926, the famous Zhongshan Gunboat Incident took place in Guangzhou. Chiang Kai-shek deployed his troops to Huangpu, where he arrested Li Zhilong, the acting Communist captain of the gunboat, and declared martial law in Guangzhou. The same night, a large number of Chiang Kai-shek loyalists belonging to the First Army entered Guangzhou, disbanded the armed workers' pickets, seized the Chinese Communists in the First Army and the Huangpu Military Academy, surrounded the Soviet Consulate and the headquarters of the Guangzhou-Hong Kong strike-committee and the home of the Soviet advisor Bubnov, and put Bubnov under house-arrest. The Central Committee of the Chinese Communist Party in Shanghai unanimously agreed that Chiang Kai-shek's action amounted to a 'counter-revolutionary coup d'état', and prepared to fight back. In mid-April, Chen Duxiu received a detailed report from the Guangdong Party Secretary, his older son Chen Yannian. The Chinese Communist leaders in Guangzhou, like Tan Pingshan, head of the Organisation Department in the National Government, Mao Zedong, deputy-head of the Propaganda Department, Lin Boqu, head of the Peasant Department, and Yun Diying, an important figure in the Huangpu Military Academy, demanded tough measures against Chiang Kai-shek, to limit the expansion of his powers. Chen Duxiu called a meeting of the Central Committee and decided to adopt the following four counter-measures:

(1) unite with the Guomindang left wing and resist and isolate Chiang Kai-shek;
(2) strengthen Li Zongren's Second Army, Tang Shengzhi's Sixth Army and other leftist forces with material and human resources, so that if necessary they can strike against Chiang Kai-shek;

(3) expand as much as possible [the leftist] Ye Ting's forces and the pickets under the command of the Guangzhou-Hong Kong strike-committee, so they become a fundamental force of the revolution;

(4) set up a special committee of the Central Committee of the Chinese Communist Party in Guangzhou formed by Peng Shuzhi, Zhang Guotao, Tan Pingshan, Chen Yannian, Zhou Enlai, and Zhang Tailei, with Peng Shuzhi as secretary.

Chen Duxiu also proposed leaving the Guomindang and switching from inner-party co-operation to an extra-party alliance. This was actually Chen's consistent position. At the time of the Second Congress, the Comintern-representative wielded the stick of the Comintern at Chen Duxiu, forcing him to agree to party members joining the Guomindang in a personal capacity, which then became the basis for cooperation between the Guomindang and the Chinese Communist Party.

In late April, Peng Shuzhi and Chen Bilan went by boat from Shanghai to Guangzhou carrying directives of the Central Committee. The journey took four days. On 29 April, the Guangdong Government's Soviet political advisor Borodin arrived back in Guangzhou with decisions of the Soviet Politburo.

Borodin was a legend of the Great Revolution. He was the Soviet Government's and the Comintern's 'incarnation', who always overrode the Central Committee of the Chinese Communist Party and its Secretary Chen Duxiu. Born in Russia in 1884, he was big, tall, and imposing. In 1903, he joined Lenin in leading the Bolsheviks. He moved to America, but in 1918 he returned to Russia. After the establishment of the Comintern, he took up a post in its central organ. In September 1923, General Borodin went to China as representative of the Russian Government and the Central Committee of the Soviet Communist Party, and was appointed Special Advisor to the Guomindang by Sun Yat-sen, with important powers. For example, in the absence of Sun Yat-sen, Borodin would preside over meetings of the Guomindang's Central Executive. Resolutions adopted by the Guomindang needed Borodin's agreement. Even more importantly, Borodin controlled Soviet aid to the National Revolutionary Army, amounting to tens of millions of dollars a year and tens of thousands of tons of arms and materials.

The Central Committee of the CPSU was divided on what course the Chinese Revolution should follow. Trotsky and Zinoviev wanted the Chinese Communist Party to withdraw from the Guomindang, but Stalin and Bukharin insisted it stay in the Guomindang, and they prevailed. When Borodin arrived in Guangzhou, he held back the Chinese Communist Party and supported the

Guomindang, giving full support to Chiang Kai-shek, so that the right wing under Chiang Kai-shek kept the upper hand. On 15 May 1926, the Guomindang Central Committee held its Second Plenum, which adopted Chiang Kai-shek, Zhang Jingjiang, and Sun Ke's proposal to 'reorganise the Party'. It was decided that Communists who joined the Guomindang should not be allowed to lead ministries; Communists not be allowed to occupy more than one third of executive posts in the Guomindang's Central Committee, Provincial Committees, or special municipal bodies; a list of Communists who joined the Guomindang be handed over to the Chairman of the Guomindang's Central Committee; and directives from the Comintern and the Central Committee of the Communist Party to Communists who joined the Guomindang be discussed in advance at a joint meeting of the two parties. Under Borodin's pressure, Communist delegates at the Third Plenum agreed to this – all except Mao Zedong, who did not raise his hand. In this way, Chiang Kai-shek took a step closer to his dictatorial goal.

At the meeting, Chen Duxiu's proposal, passed on to Peng Shuzhi, to withdraw collectively from the Guomindang was suppressed by Borodin. Borodin even proposed that 'Communist Party members should act as coolies for the Guomindang'. So Borodin sacrificed the interests of the Chinese Communist Party and the working class to those of the Soviet Government and the Soviet Communist leadership, thus foreshadowing the defeat of the Great Revolution. Peng Shuzhi's trip to Guangzhou achieved nothing, and, in early June, he and Chen Bilan returned to Shanghai, angry and resentful.

On 1 July 1926 the National Revolutionary Army in Guangzhou took a mass pledge to carry out the Northern Expedition, and the Great Revolution reached its climax. Chen Duxiu and Peng Shuzhi still wanted to withdraw from the Guomindang, but the situation developed so quickly they were unable to adapt to or control it. In July 1926, the Chinese Communist Party held its Third Enlarged Executive Conference in Shanghai, at which Chen and Peng jointly proposed 'leaving the Guomindang'. The proposal was rejected. When Chen and Peng sent the proposal to the Comintern, it was even more severely criticised, by Bukharin.

In August 1926, the Chinese Communist Party's Central Executive convened an important meeting in Shanghai to discuss the Northern Expedition. Chen Duxiu wanted to oppose it, and Peng Shuzhi supported him; but Zhang Guotao and Qu Qiubai opposed Chen's views and supported the Northern Expedition. The vote was two for, two against. Chen Duxiu was furious and shouted abuse, an example of what has often been called his 'patriarchal' style. Zhang Guotao dared not respond to the name-calling, but he refused to change his mind, so, at this critical juncture, the Chinese Communist Party lacked an actual resolution. Chen Duxiu's son Chen Yannian came up with a resolution 'supporting the Northern Expedition' in the name of the Party's Guangdong Provincial Committee.

On 31 July 1926, with the Comintern's support and the backing of the great majority of members of the Chinese Communist Party, the Central Committee of the Chinese Communist Party, following the then trend, issued a circular publicly approving the Northern Expedition. This was undoubtedly a heavy blow at Chen Duxiu and Peng Shuzhi. It also showed that General Borodin and other representatives of the Comintern and Soviet Russia in China were already preparing to ditch Chen Duxiu and had started looking for a new leader.

In late December 1926, the Soviet Government sent three representatives to China to guide the Chinese revolution. In Wuhan, they got together with Borodin, and agreed that the Chinese Communist Party's main task should be to support the Northern Expedition. They liaised with Qu Qiubai and got him to write an article opposing Chen Duxiu's line. A report the three Soviet representatives submitted to the Central Committee of the CPSU in March 1927 said: 'Since Chen Duxiu's prestige in the Chinese Communist Party is too great, at present it's not really possible to change the leader, all one can do is attack Chen Duxiu by innuendo, by opposing Peng Shuzhi'.

Qu Qiubai was ordered to pretend he was 'not feeling well, and needed to rest', so he could request leave from the Central Committee and slip off to Lushan to start his pamphlet *Against Peng Shuzhi-ism*. Chen Duxiu and Peng Shuzhi were in Shanghai, where together with Luo Yinong, Zhao Shiyan, and Wang Shouhua of the Party's Shanghai District Committee and Zhou Enlai, in charge of military affairs on the Central Committee, they were making feverish preparations for the Shanghai workers' third armed uprising.

In early April 1927, Chen Duxiu and Zhou Enlai held talks in Shanghai with Wang Jingwei and published the famous 'Wang-Chen Manifesto'. After that, they went to Wuhan, to prepare for the Party's Fifth Congress. The Congress met in Hankou from 27 April to 9 May. In advance of the Congress, Qu Qiubai's pamphlet *Some Controversial Questions in the Chinese Revolution* was widely distributed among delegates and party activists, and Peng Shuzhi was made the scapegoat for the Chen Duxiu line. At the Congress, Qu Qiubai and nearly twenty others were on the platform, while Peng Shuzhi, elected to the Central Executive Committee (that is, the Politburo's Standing Committee) at the Fourth Congress, sat in the hall. There was no longer any room for Peng Shuzhi at the top of the Chinese Communist Party....

After the Fifth Congress, Peng Shuzhi and his wife Chen Bilan went to Tianjin, where Peng was deputy secretary of the Party's newly established Northern Bureau, with Wang Hebo as secretary. Less than six months later,

Peng returned to Shanghai. From then on, he began to embrace Trotskyism, and became Chen Duxiu's most effective helper in his efforts to establish a unified Trotskyist organisation.

All the Comintern's representatives in China during the Great Revolution met a tragic end. After returning home, General Borodin worked for a long time editing *Moscow News* with the American reporter Anna Louise Strong, and was shot by Stalin in 1950; Joffe became a Trotskyist and committed suicide in 1927; General Karakhan, who issued two China declarations, was also implicated in Trotskyism, and was executed in the 1937 purge; Marshal Galen was secretly executed in 1938. Pavel Mif was also executed in 1938. The Dutchman Maring, who took part in the Chinese Communist Party's First Congress, became a Trotskyist and was executed by the Nazis in the Netherlands in 1942, where he had gone to fight fascism. So many loyal Communist revolutionaries (Mif excluded) were killed by Stalin as Trotskyists.

The Chinese Trotskyists' Unification Congress

In the second half of 1930, China's four small Trotskyist organisations, which were engaged in violent disputes with one another, received a letter from Trotsky in Turkey that showed Trotsky's high hopes for their movement.

On 22 August, Trotsky wrote to Liu Renjing:

> Today I finally received the 'Letter to All Comrades' written on 10 December 1929, by Comrade Chen Duxiu. I think this letter is a very good document. On all important questions it takes a perfectly clear and correct position. Comrade Duxiu has adopted an absolutely correct position, particularly on the question of the democratic dictatorship.... When an outstanding revolutionary like Chen Duxiu formally breaks with the Party, so that he is expelled from it, and ends up announcing that he completely agrees with the International Opposition – why do we ignore him? Can you find many Communists as experienced as Chen Duxiu? He made many mistakes in the past, but he has already understood his errors. It is a very precious thing when revolutionaries and leaders understand their own mistakes. Many young people in the Opposition can and must learn from Comrade Chen!

The same day, the Our Word group also received a letter from Trotsky. It said: 'I absolutely cannot agree with your position', that is, that 'the other two factions must first admit their mistakes to you before you allow them to join your organisation'. This attitude of 'first humiliate them and then unite with them is impermissible and unacceptable'. Trotsky referred specially to Chen Duxiu, saying he 'has plenty of political experience, which the overwhelming majority of Oppositionists in China lack'. Trotsky's letter sounded the alarm for Shi Tang, Liang Ganqiao, Ou Fang, and others who had returned to China from Moscow's Sun Yat-sen University.

On 1 September, Trotsky wrote a letter to the October Group in which he said:

> Comrade Chen's views on fundamental issues are entirely consistent with our own general positions. Given that, I cannot understand why certain of our Chinese comrades call Comrade Chen Duxiu a 'rightist'.... I therefore feel that the four groups should, on the basis of a common principled stand, publicly and sincerely unite.

But that the problem of the Chinese Trotskyist organisations and their unification could be resolved only from afar by Trotsky suggests they lacked certain basic talents. It also shows Trotsky's absolute authority over them. Whatever the case, their unification was greatly accelerated as a result. In October 1930, the four groups each sent two representatives to form a negotiating committee to discuss unification. On 8 January 1931, Trotsky sent another letter asking them to put aside their prejudices and endless arguments and to act decisively and unite. He again beseeched them: 'Dear friends, merge your organisations and journals this very day!' After receiving Trotsky's letter, Chen Duxiu was deeply convinced and determined to use radical means to resolve 'past and present disputes'. He and Yin Kuan, an honest and sincere person, personally acted as the Proletarian Society's delegates in negotiations and sought out the other delegates for discussions. As a result of the deployment of Chen Duxiu's prestige and talents, coupled with his extreme modesty, a unified Chinese Trotskyist organisation finally came into being, on 1 May 1931.

This first meeting was quite different in character from that of the Chinese Communist Party a decade earlier. The Chinese Trotskyists lacked external support (Trotsky was in exile, and his support was merely moral), and the Unification Congress was difficult to organise – even the expenses. According to Zheng Chaolin,

> [t]he negotiating committee made the Proletarian Society responsible for arranging the venue. The Proletarian Society gave the responsibility to He Zizhen [who succeeded Mao Zedong as Secretary of the Party's Hunan Provincial Committee]. Li Zhongsan brought a gown lined with lynx-fur that I pawned for 200 yuan to help pay for the meeting. He Zishen sent Comrade Wang Zhihuai's whole family to live as tenants in the house we rented. Wang Zhihuai himself was a Proletarian Society delegate. The other delegates gathered in groups of three or four and were then conducted to the house. Once you entered it, you were not allowed out again until after the congress had finished, three or four days later. The only exception was Chen Duxiu, who was allowed to go home after every session.

Those attending the Unification Congress were Chen Duxiu, Zheng Chaolin, Wang Zhihuai, Jiang Zhendong, Jiang Changshi, and Peng Shuzhi (who arrived late), representing the Proletarian Society; Liang Ganqiao, Chen Yimou, Song Jingxiu, Luo Han, and two workers from Hong Kong (one, according to Wang Fanxi, was called Zhang Jiu, the name of the other is not known), representing Our Word; Wang Fanxi, Song Fengchun, and Pu Dezhi, representing the October Society; and Zhao Ji and Lai Yantang, representing Militant.

After a heated debate, the conference adopted Chen Duxiu's political report and the name he had proposed for the organisation, the Left Opposition of the Chinese Communist Party. It elected a Central Committee of nine people by secret ballot: Chen Duxiu, Peng Shuzhi, Zheng Chaolin, Wang Fanxi, Song Fengchun, Pu Dezhi, Chen Yimou, Ou Fang, and Luo Han.

Peng Shuzhi was not originally a delegate, but to balance the representation, his name was added as a representative of the Proletarian Society. He was unaware of this at first, and as a rather serious political thinker and a one-time member of the Standing Committee of the Politburo of the Chinese Communist Party and Chen Duxiu's no. 2, he was unhappy at his exclusion. He wrote a letter for He Zishen to pass on to Chen Duxiu in which he talked disparagingly of the conference as a 'division of the spoils'. Always a master of surprise, Chen Duxiu read out the letter to the conference and asked Peng if he stood by it. Amid laughter, Peng went bright red. His wife Chen Bilan claimed in her memoirs that Wang Fanxi had engaged in a conspiracy to vilify Peng.

After the election, Luo Han and Pu Dezhi feared that Liu Renjing and Liang Ganqiao's failure to get elected might lead in future to unnecessary arguments and quarrels, so they offered to step down in their favour. Chen Duxiu said: 'Your sincerity is commendable, but the Central Committee has been elected, so to tamper with it would indeed turn it into a "division of the spoils"'. This again provoked laughter, and Luo Han and Pu Dezhi withdrew their proposal. However, Liang Ganqiao saw himself as a founder of the Chinese Trotskyist movement, and reacted to the perceived rebuff by seeking refuge in the Guomindang. He later changed his name to Ye Qing and became a Guomindang agent.

On 5 May, the Central Committee held its first meeting and elected Chen Duxiu, Chen Yimou, Zheng Chaolin, Wang Fanxi, and Song Fengchun to its Standing Committee, with Chen Duxiu as General Secretary, Chen Yimou as head of the Organisation Department, Zheng Chaolin as head of the Propaganda Department, Wang Fanxi as editor of the party journal, and Song Fengchun as head of the Secretariat. On behalf of the conference, Wang Fanxi wrote two letters to Trotsky, which read as follows:

> Executive Committee of the Left Opposition of the Chinese Communist Party to Trotsky
>
> Dear Comrade Trotsky,
>
> We understand from the bourgeois press that your precious library has been burned, and this news has been confirmed by the International Secretariat [of the Left Opposition]. We deplore this loss. To rebuild your library, we have set up a special committee to raise money.

The four Chinese oppositionist groups are now united. We hope that this good news will in some way compensate for your great loss.

The Unification Congress was held on 1 May, an historic anniversary. Seventeen delegates represented the various opposition groups, plus another four delegates. Our common platform (drafted in advance) and other resolutions were adopted by the congress. These documents will be translated in the near future. From now on, the Chinese Opposition is a single organisation.... Regarding the general situation in China and the special circumstances of our movement, we will provide you and the International Secretariat with a detailed report.

A communist salute,

The Executive Committee of the Left Opposition of the Chinese Communist Party

5 May 1931, Shanghai

Unification Congress of the Left Opposition of the Chinese Communist Party (First Report) to the International Secretariat and Trotsky

Dear Comrades of the Secretariat,
Dear Comrade Trotsky:

The Unification Congress of the Chinese Opposition took place on May Day, that historic anniversary, in Shanghai. Seventeen delegates and four non-voting delegates attended, representing 483 members (formerly belonging to the four different groups). Congress adopted a common platform and passed several other resolutions previously drafted by the unification committee. Congress elected a National Executive Committee (with nine full members and four alternates). The National Executive Committee elected five of them to form the Secretariat. Our organisation has already adopted the name Left Opposition of the Chinese Communist Party. Its organ is *Spark*. Our platform and the resolutions will be translated into European languages in the near future.

The unification of the Chinese Opposition attracted the attention of the reactionaries, and also of the workers. We believe that, under the leadership of the International Left Opposition, it will be able to complete its great historic task. We hope in future the Secretariat [of the

International] will be able to establish regular and close ties with its Chinese section.

We learned from the bourgeois press about the burning of Comrade Trotsky's library, now confirmed by your announcement. We have set up a special committee to raise funds for the reconstruction of Comrade Trotsky's library.

We salute the Opposition

The Secretariat of the Left Opposition of the Chinese Communist Party
Secretary of the Secretariat Chen Duxiu
Director of the Organisation Department Chen Yimou
Director of the Propaganda Department Zheng Chaolin
Editor of the party newspaper Wang Fanxi
Head of the Secretariat Song Fengchun

Shanghai, 9 May 1931

(The originals of both letters and the congress documents are held by Harvard University.)

For Chinese revolutionaries, whether members of the official Communist Party or of the Left Opposition, May 1931 in Shanghai was one of the darkest months. Because of Gu Shunzhang's betrayal, the underground leadership of the Central Committee of the Chinese Communist Party in Shanghai was thrown into panic and confusion. The butcher's knife of the Guomindang hung permanently above every Communist's head. However, the newly unified Chinese Trotskyists were full of excitement. The two letters show how optimistic and naïve they were after their unification. Not long after the Unification Congress, the first issue of *Spark* appeared. Chen Yimou actively worked to unite the grass-roots of the four groups in Shanghai. Even Chen Duxiu evinced excitement and passion for the first time since the defeat of the Great Revolution in 1927. However, this was only a brief glimmering before the long night of darkness. A fresh blow quickly struck down the newly unified Trotskyists.

Traitors and Informers

Late at night on 21 May 1931 (Zheng Chaolin's *Memoirs* says the 21st, Pu Dezhi and Wang Fanxi say the 22nd, Peng Shuzhi and Chen Bilan say the 23rd: the archives confirm the 21st), just twenty days after their unification, the Trotskyists received their first big blow when five of the nine members of the Central Committee were arrested, including all the entire Standing Committee apart from Chen Duxiu. The four members of the Standing Committee arrested were Zheng Chaolin, Wang Fanxi, Chen Yimou, and Song Fengchun. The others arrested were Pu Dezhi (a Central Committee member), He Zishen and his wife Zhang Yisen, Zheng Chaolin's wife Liu Jingzhen, Lou Guohua, Jiang Changshi, and Wang Zhihuai and his wife and daughter, thirteen in all. Suddenly, the Chinese Trotskyists had been hit by a disaster.

In fact, the destruction could have been avoided.

After 5 May, the Trotskyists' Standing Committee met once again in Wang Zhihuai's home, to prepare for a meeting the following day to discuss a draft of the first issue of *Spark*. They decided to hold a bigger conference on 22 May in the original venue to discuss propaganda. Naturally, Chen Duxiu wanted to be present.

On 21 May, Zheng Chaolin held a meeting in his own home to discuss propaganda work. Zhao Ji, Wu Jiyan, and Yan Lingfeng (who had not yet joined the Trotskyist movement) attended. After the meeting, Zhao Ji left and Yan Lingfeng and Wu Jiyan stayed behind to play mahjong. Half way through the game, the Trotskyist Peng Guiqiu rushed in. He took Zheng Chaolin to one side and said: 'Yu Mutao has turned traitor. The police will come tonight at ten to make arrests'. He then hurried off. Zheng Chaolin told Yan Lingfeng and Wu Jiyan the news and pointed out that he himself had just moved, and Yu Mutao did not know his new address. Yan Lingfeng went home, and Wu Jiyan stayed with Zheng Chaolin to await further news.

Zheng Chaolin thought that, before anything else, Chen Duxiu should be told, so he would not turn up at Wang Zhihuai's home the following day. Only Zheng Chaolin knew Chen Duxiu's address, so he rushed off and told him. After leaving Chen Duxiu's house, he went to see Peng Guiqiu, to ask him where he got the information. At Peng Guiqiu's place he bumped into Xie Depan. He questioned him, and discovered that Peng Shuzhi had been the first to receive the news about the planned raid. That Yu Mutao was the traitor was merely Peng Shuzhi's inference.

Zheng Chaolin became worried. Who was the traitor? No one knew. Perhaps the traitor knew Zheng Chaolin's address. He immediately took his leave of

Xie Depan and Peng Guiqiu and hurried home. On the way, he informed Liu Renjing and his wife, who lived nearby. There were no taxis, and even if there had been, he could not have afforded one. Because of all the rushing about, it was past ten o'clock before he reached home. Wu Jiyan and his wife were still waiting, but they hurried away when they heard about the change. Zheng Chaolin discussed the situation with his wife Liu Jingzhen, and, although it was late, they decided it would be best to look for a hotel. While they were packing, a team of Chinese and foreign police burst in and took them away to the police-station at Tilanqiao.

Peng Shuzhi's wife Chen Bilan was working as a teacher in a middle school of which the Trotskyist Lu Chen was principal. That night she was with her two-year-old daughter having dinner at Lu's home when the Trotskyist Ma Renzhi came running in and told her someone had turned traitor and the police were going to her home to arrest Peng Shuzhi. Who the informer was remained unclear. Ma Renzhi also told Chen Bilan that he had received the information from his friend Pan Guzhi. Pan had a close friend who was working as a senior staff-officer in the Guomindang's Longhua command-headquarters. This man had told Pan that someone dressed as a worker had turned up that afternoon and defected. He had handed in a list of names, including Peng Shuzhi's. He had said he did not know Chen Duxiu's address, but added that Chen often went to the home of a man called Zheng – Zheng Chaolin – and that if they waited there, they would be able to catch Chen. On hearing the news, Ma Renzhi had hurried over to Lu Chen's home to discuss with Lu how to inform Peng Shuzhi, and there he had found Chen Bilan.

Chen Bilan rushed home, where she found Peng Shuzhi talking with Xie Depan. Peng Shuzhi had decided that Xie Depan should tell Zheng Chaolin, and he himself would sleep at Lu Chen's house. However, it turned out not to be practical for him and Chen Bilan to sleep in Lu Chen's guest-room, from where they could hear Lu's wife in the nearby bedroom complaining all night, so they got up early the next day and moved to a hotel, to escape the ordeal.

If Zhou Enlai, who was also in Shanghai at the time, had been in charge, the Guomindang would probably have captured no one. Unfortunately, things were in the hands of a collection of inexperienced Trotskyist scholars who were good at talking but little else.

In fact, the informer was not Yu Mutao but Ma Yufu.

Ma Yufu was a native of Hubei. He was an early member of the Chinese Communist Party and had sailed to France with Deng Xiaoping to take part in the work-study programme. Later, together with Deng Xiaoping, Zuo Quan, Fu Zhong, and others, he had gone from France to Moscow, where he studied at the University for the Toilers of the East. After returning to China, he was allocated to the Shanghai underground-party where he led the labour movement. He knew little about theory, but he was a good activist, prominent in grass-roots workers' organisations. He was a follower of Chen Duxiu, and, after joining the Trotskyists, he remained a diligent industrial organiser. He was responsible for developing worker-branches for the Trotskyists in Shanghai. He was proud of his achievements, and when he failed to be chosen as a delegate for the Unification Congress or any of the Trotskyist leading organs, he went to the Guomindang authorities and turned informer.

The Guomindang authorities did not know the difference between Trotskyists and Communists and punished both groups equally in their prisons. Using regulations designed to deal with the Chinese Communist Party, they sentenced Zheng Chaolin to fifteen years, He Zishen to ten years, and Wang Fanxi and others to five years. Nor did the Communist Party let Ma Yufu go just because he had betrayed the Trotskyists. After a long period of planning, they used a hit-man to finish him off.

Chen Duxiu, who had slipped through the net, continued to fight for his Trotskyist ideals in China. In July 1931, he and Peng Shuzhi, together with Yin Kuan, Cai Zhendong, and others, re-established the Trotskyist organisation. However, just one month later, Yin Kuan, Cai Zhendong, and six others were arrested by the Guomindang authorities, another heavy blow. Chen Duxiu painstakingly reassembled the scattered pieces of the wreckage and re-formed a Central Executive consisting of Song Fengchun (who had been bailed from prison due to illness), Pu Dezhi, Peng Shuzhi, Luo Shifan, and himself and continued to be active. He himself funded the activities of the Trotskyists, while leading a very difficult life. According to his wife Pan Lanzhen, household-expenses were covered by the pittance she earned by laundering and sewing. Later, Kang Sheng and his ilk spread the slander that Chen Duxiu was a traitor and received a monthly allowance of three hundred yuan from the Japanese secret service. On 18 September 1931, the Japanese imperialists launched the Shenyang Incident and occupied the whole of Northeast China. At this time of national crisis, Chen Duxiu, having already been expelled from the Party, took the initiative in early January 1932 to publish in the name of the Chinese Trotskyist centre a 'Letter to All Comrades' in which he expressed the hope that all Chinese Communists would unite against Japanese imperialism. Shortly afterwards, he wrote to the Politburo of the Central Committee of the Chinese Communist Party proposing cooperation. However, the Central Committee of the Chinese Communist Party was at the time dominated by Wang Ming's left opportunists, who regarded the Trotskyists as 'the most dangerous enemy of the Chinese revolution' and flatly rejected Chen's call. On 15 October 1932, at the time of Xie Depan's betrayal, the central leaders of the Trotskyist organisation were arrested in Shanghai. Xie Depan personally led the agents to Chen Duxiu's address, which he alone knew. Chen Duxiu was arrested and Xie Depan received a big reward, amounting to fifty ounces of gold. Xie Depan changed his name, to Xie Ligong, meaning 'he who renders meritorious service'. Although the Chinese Trotskyists subsequently continued to engage in sporadic activity, as a political force they (and the drama they had just begun to stage) came to a more or less permanent end in early 1931, after just one year.

Chen Duxiu's Last Years

Chen Duxiu's arrest was a major event. The press carried lengthy reports on it, in which the Trotskyist leader was described as a 'Communist prisoner' and as founder of the Chinese Communist Party and its General Secretary at its first five congresses, for whose arrest the Guomindang had offered a reward of 30,000 silver dollars. On 19 October 1932, he was taken at night to Nanjing. On the 20th, *Shenbao* carried a report saying that Chen Duxiu and 'another important Communist Party leader' (Peng Shuzhi) had been sent by night-train to the capital, and the North Station (from where the train left) had been put under martial law, 'in case anything unexpected happened'.

On 25 October, He Yingqin, the Guomindang military leader, invited Chen Duxiu on Chiang Kai-shek's orders to a reception-room in his Department for an hour-long meeting described by Chen as 'half chat, half interrogation'. Although Chen Duxiu talked with ease and confidence and gave a detailed account of the Chinese Communist Party's policies and the Trotskyists' policies, He Yingqin was unable to make head or tail of it. Finally, it dawned on him that Chen Duxiu would have nothing to do with Chiang Kai-shek's campaign to eradicate the Chinese Red Army. After the meeting, a dramatic scene ensued: He Yingqin's officers beseeched Chen Duxiu to write some characters for them. He said: 'Thank you for your kind affection, which is deeply gratifying. Surrounded on all sides by you, my younger brothers, I am overwhelmed'. Chen Duxiu, a good calligrapher, wrote: 'Only when the ink is exhausted will I escape your encirclement'. (See Chen Duxiu's letter to Gao Yuhan's wife.) Something similar had happened at the time of Qu Qiubai's arrest. Qu Qiubai was a famous seal-maker, and officers under Chiang Kai-shek's Commander Song Xilian asked him to make seals for them. By the time of his death, he had carved at least one hundred. For a master is a master, whether Guomindang or Communist.

Later, Chiang Kai-shek had Xie Depan sent to Jiujiang to work at the front 'exterminating the Communists' and investigate the relationship between Chen Duxiu and the Red Army in Jiangxi. Only when he was sure there was not the slightest contact between Chen Duxiu and the Chinese Red Army did he relax.

On 26 April 1933, the Jiangsu Supreme Court sentenced Chen Duxiu to thirteen years in prison and fifteen years' deprivation of civil rights. Chen Duxiu appealed, but his appeal was rejected on 22 June; after a further appeal, and interventions by various individuals, the sentence was commuted to eight years, and Chen was taken to Jiangsu's No. 1 Model Prison. According to his 'accomplice' Pu Dezhi, Chen Duxiu received preferential treatment. He had his own cell and was allowed to leave the prison-dormitory. At the same time, Pan Lanzhen was allowed to visit him. Normally, Pu Dezhi and Luo Shifan took turns at looking after him. Pu Dezhi was Chen Duxiu's junior cousin, and cared for Chen 'in every way possible'. In prison, Chen Duxiu's life was bearable, apart from the loss of liberty. In his letter to Gao Yuhan's wife he said: 'Every day I can walk for a few minutes and do a bit of exercise. I'm no different in health, looks, and spirit from when I first arrived here'. Chen Duxiu put a desk and bookshelf in his cell, which was around a dozen square metres, and got people (even Hu Shi) to buy him a great number of books so he could begin a study of Chinese language and phonology. He turned his cell into a study, and, from the summer of 1933 to the summer of 1937, when he was released, he wrote six works on classical Chinese phonology and linguistics.

In his memoirs, published in his old age, Xu Enzeng, head of the Central Investigations Bureau, talked about the esteem in which members of the Guomindang ruling élite held Chen Duxiu, and their disappointment in him:

> He is so well read in Chinese literature, he had the traditional manners of a literatus, he had a strong national self-confidence, he made a seminal contribution to the New Culture Movement in his 1919, and even today he continues to enjoy the admiration of young people. He was different from most Communists. At the same time, he gave me the impression that one could prevail upon him to give up his past political views. But after our conversation, my confidence in him was shaken. I found his attitude was very stubborn. He wasn't prepared to give up his belief in Marxism. Although he had been expelled from the Communist Party, he still proclaimed himself a true Marxist. I failed to persuade him, so numerous old friends who had been colleagues of his at Beijing University from before and after 1919 [such as Jiang Menglin, who became Dean of Beijing University in 1930] were invited to talk with him, but he continued his stubbornness. Afterwards we stopped putting pressure on him, and merely let him live a quiet life in Nanjing and pursue his research.

In prison, Chen Duxiu did not give up his Trotskyist ideas, but the Trotskyists themselves failed to appreciate him. After 15 October 1932, when Chen Duxiu and all the Chinese Trotskyist leaders were rounded up by the Guomindang, two men stood out, but for different reasons. One was Chen Qichang, an earnest and down-to-earth person who quietly laboured for his beliefs, of whom more later. The other, floating along the surface and determined to enjoy the limelight as a Trotskyist leader, was Liu Renjing.

I mentioned earlier that Liu Renjing had been a delegate at the First Congress and that he went in person to Turkey to receive Trotsky's teachings at first hand and claimed to be the only genuine Chinese Trotskyist. Liu Renjing was very keen to be a leader, and good at empty verbiage. When the four Chinese Trotskyist factions united, they all rejected Liu Renjing. He was thus excluded from the Trotskyist leadership, which he took to heart. At the time of the Shanghai War, which started on 28 January 1932, Chen Duxiu proposed 'allying and cooperating with the bourgeoisie', a slogan Liu Renjing seized on and described as 'petty-bourgeois romanticism'. At a meeting of the Trotskyists' Shanghai branch on 23 January 1935, he expelled Chen Qichang, who supported Chen Duxiu's position, and also wrote to tell Chen Duxiu that 'unless he completely changed his stance, our organisation would be unable to continue links with him'. The meeting changed the name of the Chinese Trotskyist organisation from 'Left Opposition of the Chinese Communist Party' to 'Chinese Communist League' and made Liu Renjing leader. In March 1935, Liu Renjing was arrested in Beijing, sentenced to two and a half years in prison, and sent to Suzhou to be detained so he could carry out introspection. The 'Chinese Communist League' vanished from sight. He was rumoured to have 'surrendered', but the evidence is unclear.

With Chen Duxiu and Liu Renjing arrested, one after the other, all China's Trotskyist leaders were behind bars and there was no central organisation or activity to speak of, except for a few stalwarts engaged in sporadic and scattered activities in Guangxi, Wenzhou, and other places. They fought to realise their ideals, and were later tempered in jail by a never-ending purgatory.

On 7 July 1937, at the time of the Lugou Bridge Incident, when China joined war with Japan, various political forces tried to convince Chen Duxiu of their arguments. On 23 August, Chen Duxiu was released from prison. He declined the invitation of the Guomindang intelligence-chief Ding Mocun to move into the guest-house of the Guomindang Central Committee and, instead, went to stay with his student Chen Zhongfan. An American publisher sent someone to invite him to the United States to write his autobiography, but he declined. Some Trotskyists asked him to return to Shanghai to reorganise the Trotskyist group, but he said there was no way forward for 'Trotskyist sectarian methods', and said no. On 3 November 1938, in a letter to Trotsky, he wrote: 'A closed-door ultra-left sect (with a few rare exceptions) obviously cannot hope to develop; and if it could, it would be an obstacle to the Chinese revolutionary movement'. This shows his thorough disappointment with and decisive split from the 'closed-door' Liu Renjing school of Chinese Trotskyism. This is an important letter. It shows the founder of Chinese Trotskyism was disillusioned with the organisation he had so painstakingly built up. Afterwards, all

Chen Duxiu's activities were carried out in a personal capacity, although the Trotskyism represented by Zheng Chaolin always held high the great banner of Chen Duxiu. Such was the tragedy of Chen Duxiu and of Chinese Trotskyism. When Hu Shi and Zhou Fohai, representing important personages, invited him to join the national-defence advisory council and hinted he would get a high position in it, he replied:

> Chiang Kai-shek killed many of my comrades. He also killed my two sons. He and I are absolutely irreconcilable. Now that the great enemy stands before us, and the Guomindang and the Communist Party have formed a second United Front, since it is necessary to work with him in the anti-Japanese cause, I do not oppose it, that is enough.... Under no circumstances will I become an official.

Such was Chen Duxiu's integrity.

Chen Duxiu was the founder of the Chinese Communist Party and its General Secretary for its first five congresses, so the Chinese Communist Party could hardly be indifferent to him. The two sides began extending olive branches to each other. In August 1937, shortly after Chen Duxiu's release from prison, the heads of the Chinese Communist Party Office in Nanjing, Bo Gu and Ye Jianying, met with him. Chen Duxiu said: From now on, 'I will speak for the majority, I will not be bound by any party'. This was good news for the Communists, who had struggled against him as the Trotskyist leader. On 20 November, Yan'an's *Liberation Weekly* (no. 24) published an unprecedented article titled 'Where Is Mr Chen Duxiu Going?' The article expressed the hope that he would 'restore his old militant spirit and return to the ranks of the revolution'.

At that point, another figure, Luo Han, made a reappearance. Luo Han was a Hunanese who knew Mao Zedong. An early member of the Chinese Communist Party, he was also familiar with Zhou Enlai, Ye Jianying, and others. He was a follower of Chen Duxiu and in 1931 attended the 1 May Unification Congresses as a member of the Proletarian Society. He was elected onto the Central Executive, but the next year he left the movement and became a teacher in Suzhou. His intervention was designed to restore relations between Chen Duxiu and the Central Committee of the Chinese Communist Party, particularly Mao Zedong. He met Chen Duxiu in Nanjing, and Chen showed him 'seven opinions' about the Resistance-War he had written in prison for the Central Committee of the Communist Party. Luo Han was overjoyed, and took them to Ye Jianying in the Communist Party Office. Ye Jianying was an honest and sincere person. According to Wang Fanxi's *Memoirs*, Ye Jianying ran around trying to rescue Wang from prison in 1937. This shows senior Communists at the time viewed the Trotskyists not as criminals but as friends. When Ye Jianying saw Chen Duxiu's 'seven opinions', he thought it worth a try. On 30 August 1937, Luo Han received travel-expenses and a letter of introduction from the Communist Party Office and headed for Yan'an, in a state of high excitement. On the way, he met his old friend Lin Boqu in Xi'an. Because of flooding, the road between Yan'an and Xi'an was cut, so the contact had to be by radio. On 10 September, Lin Boqu received a message from Luo Fu and Mao Zedong in which Mao set Chen Duxiu three conditions: '(1) Publicly renounce and resolutely oppose all Trotskyist theories and activities, publicly announce an organisational break with the Trotskyists, and admit your own past mistake in joining the Trotskyists. (2) Publicly express support for the policy of the anti-Japanese national United Front. (3) Demonstrate through action the sincerity of that support'. I do not know who drafted these three points, but they are consistent with Mao Zedong's character, especially his habit of demanding 'public recognition' of one's errors.

When Luo Han saw the three points, it was as if he had been hit by a hammer. He was familiar with Chen Duxiu's hot temper. There was no chance of Chen publicly announcing in the press that he admitted making mistakes. All Luo Han could do was return crestfallen to Nanjing. When Luo Han showed Bo Gu the message, Bo Gu told him repeatedly: 'It would be better to tell him verbally, no need for the time being to show Duxiu the original telegram'.

In October, Luo Han bumped into Chen Duxiu in Hankou. Skipping polite preliminaries, Luo Han told Chen what had happened on the journey from Nanjing to Xi'an. Chen Duxiu was unhappy with the tone of Luo Fu and Mao Zedong's message, but he was aware of the primacy of the anti-Japanese issue, so he wrote a letter to the Central Committee of the Chinese Communist Party saying he agreed with its line of resistance. However, he said a statement admitting past mistakes was out of the question. He had spent several years in a Guomindang prison, and having been expelled first from the Communist Party and then from the Trotskyist group, his temper had changed radically. Gone was the patriarchal style: all that was left was a modicum of self-esteem. He was not prepared to admit mistakes, so his cooperation with the Chinese Communist Party was temporarily shelved. Luo Han went back to his teaching. Later, he fled with his students up the Yangtze River to Wuhan and then to Chongqing, evading the Japanese advance, and disappeared from sight. Relatives and friends sought high and low for him until Liberation, but to no avail. Most think he died in the Japanese bombing of Chongqing.

Just a few months later, the climate suddenly changed. In late November 1937, Wang Ming and Kang Sheng returned to Yan'an from Moscow. In December, Wang Ming told the Politburo of the Chinese Communist Party that Stalin was vigorously opposing the Trotskyists while they are allying with them, how terrible! 'We can cooperate with anyone against the Japanese, but not with the Trotskyists'.

In hoisting the banner of anti-Trotskyism, Wang Ming, Kang Sheng, and their ilk were not just attacking Chen Duxiu and the handful of Trotskyists. Wearing Stalin's anti-Trotsky tiger-skin, they attacked and killed as Trotskyists all the revolutionary comrades who had opposed Wang Ming in the past. In October 1937, together with Kang Sheng and Chen Yun, Wang Ming went from Moscow to Yan'an by way of Dihua (now Urumqi, in Xinjiang), where they rested for a week. In Dihua, they met Yu Xiusong and Dong Yixiang, doing secret work for the Party in Sheng Shicai's Xinjiang Office. Yu Xiusong was one of the earliest members of the Chinese Communist Party and founder of the Chinese Communist-Youth League. However, he had opposed Wang Ming while at Sun Yat-sen University in Moscow, so Wang Ming did not hesitate to vilify Yu and Dong as Trotskyists. They got Sheng Shicai to arrest them secretly and had them deported to the Soviet Union. After being tortured by the KGB, Yu was killed and buried in a mass-grave, so that even his bones could not be found. When his wife An Zhijie talked with me about it in her old age, she broke down in tears.

Apart from Yu Xiusong, the Wang Ming gang seized many Trotskyists, including Zuo Quan, one of the Eighth Route Army's senior generals, branded a Trotskyist. Zuo Quan was sacrificed in the Taihang Mountains, under the suspicion of being a Trotskyist, and has never been rehabilitated. Wang Ming also considered denouncing Mao Zedong as a Trotskyist, as I shall show. So it is not surprising that he and Kang Sheng were so ferociously opposed to Chen Duxiu after their return to China.

In January 1938, Kang Sheng published a long article titled 'Eradicate the Trotskyite Criminals, Who Are Enemies of the Nation and Spies of the Japanese' in *Liberation Weekly*, nos. 29–30. In it, he claimed that 'Japan gives Chen Duxiu's "Trotskyite Central Committee" a subsidy of 300 yuan a month', and that Chen Duxiu was a Japanese spy and a traitor to the Chinese nation. Chen Duxiu ignored this slander, but a group of his friends came to the rescue and wrote an open letter in his defence. Wang Ming published a commentary in *New China Daily* that forced Chen Duxiu to defend himself against the charge. Things got lively and there was a big argument. Shi Ximin, head of the news-desk at *New China Daily*, later recalled:

> *New China Daily* suddenly announced that Chen Duxiu was a traitor, arousing suspicion and concern among knowledgeable people. Even Professor Zhang Ximan, a famous scholar and social activist who was close to our Party, expressed dissatisfaction with this peremptory

approach.... Comrade Zhou Enlai was in a very difficult situation. He had to work hard to reduce the damage to the Party.

Zhou Enlai frequently got people to visit Chen Duxiu and urge him 'not to be active, not to publish articles'. That was consistent with Zhou Enlai's character. So Chen Duxiu lay low and did not defend himself. However, Zhou Enlai was too wily to come out in public support of Chen Duxiu, so the error was compounded and the baseless assertion that the Chinese Trotskyists 'were cooperating with the Japanese secret service, receiving a Japanese subsidy, and engaging in a variety of activities beneficial to the Japanese aggressors', that is, they were traitors, was a hat they wore for the next few decades, until the Third Plenum in 1978, when it was finally removed.

In the summer of 1938, Chen Duxiu left Wuhan and travelled upriver to Jiangjin, a small county-town one hundred miles from Chongqing, where he went to stay in a stone-walled courtyard in Yang Qinqyu's home in nearby Heshanping, to live out his final years in poverty and ill health. He could, of course, have been rich. Top officials of the Guomindang, including even Chiang Kai-shek, frequently sent him money, but he invariably returned it. Ye Qing (that is, Ren Zhuoxuan), a former Trotskyist who went over to the Guomindang after his arrest and became a secret-service leader, also sent him money, which he also sent back. He basically lived by writing articles. He was self-reliant, although he occasionally accepted help from old friends like Bao Huizeng, who had attended the First Congress of the Chinese Communist Party, and members of the local gentry. His life was extremely hard. One night, thieves broke into his home and ransacked several boxes, but could not find a single dollar, just a dozen or so old clothes and a roll of manuscripts, the loss of which upset him for a while. Chen Duxiu put his main effort into primary research on language and phonology, including his famous *Etymological Studies*, written in the courtyard. He also wrote a number of political articles and letters, including 'A Sketch of the Postwar World-Situation' and 'Once Again on the World-Situation'. In his articles, he proposed a united front, demonstrating his political wisdom. In Jiangjin, he associated chiefly with gentry and peasants. He was lonely and unhappy, and would have liked his friends in the Chinese Communist Party to visit him. According to one of its earliest members, Xu Meikun (Chen had introduced him to the Party and worked together with him in Shanghai), writing in his memoirs:

> In Chongqing, at one point I received a letter from Chen Duxiu, who was living in Jiangjin in Sichuan. He wanted me and Shi Fuliang to go and see him. Shi Fuliang and his wife went first, and they urged me to go too.

> I went to the office to see Comrade Zhou Enlai and discuss it with him. Comrade Zhou thought it best not to go. Out of respect for his views, I didn't go.

Obviously, Zhou Enlai erred on the side of caution.

Mao Zedong was under no such constraints. He evaluated Chen Duxiu, still alive at the time, very highly. On 30 March 1942, in a speech to the Central-Committee Study Group in Yan'an, he said:

> At the time of the May Fourth Movement, the Chinese proletariat began to become conscious. The May Fourth Movement was in 1919, and in 1921 the Chinese Communist Party arose.... Chen Duxiu was Commander-in-Chief of May Fourth. Now is not the time to propagate the history of Chen Duxiu. In future, when we write the history of China, we must talk about his contribution.

In April 1945, three years after Chen Duxiu's death, Mao Zedong said:

> He was Commander-in-Chief at the time of the May Fourth Movement, he actually led the entire campaign.... We are the students of that generation. The May Fourth Movement prepared the cadre for the Chinese Communist Party. At the time, *New Youth* magazine was edited by Chen Duxiu. That magazine and the May Fourth Movement woke people up, and later some joined the Communist Party. These people were greatly influenced by Chen Duxiu and his entourage. You could say he gathered them together. Only then could the Party be established. He created the Party, that was his achievement. In some respects, Chen Duxiu was like Russia's Plekhanov, he did the work of the Enlightenment.

But Chen Duxiu did not hear what Mao said, even before his death. On 27 May 1942, he died. His funeral was paid for by two of his admirers among the Jiangjin gentry.

Chen Qichang

On 1 May 1931, at the time of the Trotskyists' Unification Congress, Chen Qichang was one of just a handful of people who knew about the meeting but did not attend in person. He was one of Chen Duxiu's loyal followers, and also a man of action. In 1930, he left the Chinese Communist Party to follow Chen Duxiu into the Trotskyist Proletarian Society. After that, he spent his whole life working at the grassroots. Zheng Chaolin drafted him in to help prepare the Trotskyists' Congress. On the night of 30 April, Chen Qichang checked the venue for the next day's meeting one last time and then left.

Chen Qichang came from a poor family, but was admitted to Beijing University in 1922 to study law. At university, he joined the Communist Party and threw himself single-mindedly into working for it. As an early revolutionary activist, he worked for a long time in the student-movement and the labour movement, and was secretary of the Communist Party branch at Beijing University and a member of the party committee in Beijing's Dongcheng district. After the defeat of the Great Revolution, he fled with his wife and newborn child to Shanghai, where, in addition to carrying out revolutionary activities, he agonised over the causes of the defeat. In the meantime, he came across one of Trotsky's pamphlets, accepted the Trotskyist perspective, and (in 1929) joined Chen Duxiu and Peng Shuzhi as a backbone member of the Proletarian Society.

On 1 May 1931, the day of the Unification Congress, Chen Qichang was greatly excited. He worked hard for the organisation. He excelled at activity in the grassroots, educating and developing party members and expanding Trotskyist organisation. However, on 21 May, the Trotskyist leadership was smashed, and four out of five members of its Central Executive were arrested, including Chen Qichang's friend Zheng Chaolin. In October 1932, the reconstituted central leadership was again betrayed, and even Chen Duxiu was caught. At this critical juncture, Chen Qichang came forward, and together with Zhao Ji reformed the Trotskyist leadership and regrouped the remnant forces, but, by that time, they numbered fewer than one hundred.

Chen Qichang's eldest son Chen Daotong told me his father was a man of few words. He knew only how to work for the Party, and had no small talk. At the time, there were anyway few people he could talk with. His wife was uneducated, and his son was in his teens.

Chen Qichang's greatest enemy was loneliness. Although fighting for his ideals, he was lonely and depressed. He saw darkness on all sides. His leaders and commanders were in prison and out of reach; comrades and friends had scattered or gone into hiding. He longed for his friends, for the understanding and sympathy of friendship, and, at that point, he thought of Lu Xun.

On 3 June 1936, despite the opposition of Zhao Ji, he wrote a letter to Lu Xun, using the name Chen Zhongshan. As a result of that letter, he was criticised by many of those still in prison, including Zheng Chaolin. I asked Zheng Chaolin about Chen Qichang. After praising Chen Qichang's loyalty and dedication, Zheng Chaolin repeatedly criticised his naïveté and stupidity. Chen Qichang cannot have known when he wrote his letter that it would become famous, together with its author, despite his usual reticence.

The letter read:

Dear Mr Lu Xun,

After the failure of the 1927 Revolution, instead of withdrawing in order to prepare for a come-back, the Chinese Communists took to military adventurism. Abandoning work in the cities, they ordered Party members to rise everywhere although the tide of revolution had ebbed, hoping to make Reds out of the peasants, to conquer the country. Within seven or eight years, hundreds of thousands of brave and useful young people were sacrificed on account of this policy, so that now in the high tide of the nationalist movement there are no revolutionary leaders for the city-masses, and the next stage of the revolution has been postponed indefinitely.

Now the Reds' movement to conquer the country has failed. But the Chinese Communists who blindly take orders from the Moscow bureaucrats have adopted a 'New Policy'. They have made *a volte-face*, abandoned their class-stand, issued new declarations and sent representatives to negotiate with the bureaucrats, politicians and warlords, including those who slaughtered the masses, in order to form a 'united front' with them. They have put away their own banner and confused the people's mind, making the masses believe that all those bureaucrats, politicians and executioners are national revolutionaries who will resist Japan too. The result can only be to deliver the revolutionary masses into the hands of those executioners for further slaughter. These shameless acts of betrayal on the part of the Stalinists make all Chinese revolutionaries blush with shame.

Now the bourgeois liberals and upper strata of the petty bourgeoisie of Shanghai welcome this 'New Policy' of the Stalinists. And well they might. The traditional prestige of Moscow, the blood shed by the Chinese Reds and their present strength – what could play better into their hands? But the greater the welcome given to this 'New Policy', the greater the damage that will be done to the Chinese Revolution.

Since 1930, under the most difficult conditions, our organisation has made unremitting efforts to fight for our ideals. Since the defeat of the Revolution we have opposed the recklessness of the Stalinists and advocated a 'revolutionary-democratic struggle'. We believe that since the Revolution has failed, we must start all over again, from the beginning. We have never ceased to gather together revolutionary cadres to study revolutionary theory, accepting the lessons of defeat to educate revolutionary workers so that during this difficult period of counter-revolution we may lay a firm foundation for the next stage of the revolution. The events of the past few years have proved the correctness of our political line and method of work. We were against the opportunist and reckless policies and bureaucratic party system of the Stalinists. Now we resolutely attack its treacherous 'New Policy'. But precisely because of this we are under fire from all sorts of careerists and party bureaucrats. Is this our good fortune or is it a misfortune?

For the last decade and more, sir, I have admired your scholarship, writing and moral integrity, for while many thinking men have fallen into the quagmire of individualism you alone have fought on without respite to express your own views. We should count it a great honour to hear your criticism of our political views. I am sending you a few of our recent publications, which I beg you to accept and read. If you are good enough to write a reply, please leave it with Mr X – I shall go to his house within three days to fetch it.

With best wishes,

Chen xx, 3 June

Chen Qichang could never have imagined that, a few weeks later, Lu Xun would publish Chen's letter and Lu Xun's reply. The reply, published on 1 July 1936, in *Literary Anthology*, no. 4, and in *Realist Writing*, no. 1, read as follows:

Dear Mr Chen,

I have received your letter and the copies of *Struggle* and *Spark* you sent me.

I take it that the main drift of your letter is contained in these two points: You consider Stalin and his colleagues bureaucrats, and the proposal of Mao Zedong and others – 'Let all parties unite to resist Japan' – as a betrayal of the cause of revolution.

I certainly find this 'confusing'. For do not all the successes of Stalin's Union of Soviet Socialist Republics show the pitifulness of Trotsky's exile, wanderings and failure that 'forced' him in his old age to take money from the enemy? His conditions as an exile now must be rather different from conditions in Siberia before the Revolution, for, at that time, I doubt if anyone so much as offered the prisoners a piece of bread. He may not feel so good, though, because now the Soviet Union has triumphed. Facts are stronger than rhetoric; and no one expected such pitiless irony. Your 'theory' is certainly much loftier than that of Mao Zedong; yours is high in the sky, while his is down-to-earth. But admirable as is such loftiness, it will unfortunately be just the thing welcomed by the Japanese aggressors. Hence I fear that it will drop down from the sky, and when it does it may land on the filthiest place on earth. Since the Japanese welcome your lofty theories, I cannot help feeling concern for you when I see your well-printed publications. If someone deliberately spreads a malicious rumour to discredit you, accusing you of accepting money for these publications from the Japanese, how are you to clear yourselves? I say this not to retaliate because some of you formerly joined certain others to accuse me of accepting Russian roubles. No, I would not stoop so low, and I do not believe that you could stoop so low as to take money from the Japanese to attack the proposal of Mao Zedong and others to unite against Japan. No, this you could not do. But I want to warn you that your lofty theory will not be welcomed by the Chinese people, and that your behaviour runs counter to present-day Chinese people's standards of morality. This is all I have to say about your views.

In conclusion, this sudden receipt of a letter and periodicals from you has made me feel rather uncomfortable. There must be some reason for it. It must be because some of my 'comrades-in-arms' have been accusing me of certain faults. But whatever my faults, I am convinced that my views are quite different from yours. I count it an honour to have as my comrades those who are now doing solid work, treading firmly on the ground, fighting and shedding their blood in the defence of the Chinese people. Excuse me for making this an open reply, but since more than three days have passed you will probably not be going to that address for my answer.

Yours faithfully,
Lu Xun, 9 June

(This letter was dictated by Lu Xun and taken down by O. V.)

According to Zhao Ji, Chen Qichang was shocked and pained by Lu Xun's reply. He put his head in his hands and said again and again: 'How can this be?' Needless to say, Chen Qichang's letter contained various errors, reflecting the Trotskyists' wrong understanding of the Chinese Revolution. However, he was at heart sincere.

Lu Xun's reply to Chen Qichang contains his sole public reference to Mao Zedong. He called Mao Zedong his 'comrade-in-arms', to which Mao responded by saying on more than one occasion that his heart and Lu Xun's were linked. Lu Xun's letter, titled 'Reply to a Trotskyite', was included in middle-school literature textbooks after the founding of New China, especially during the Cultural Revolution. Millions of Chinese (including me) were familiar with Chen Qichang's name as a result.

But research shows that this letter was not written by Lu Xun, nor was it 'dictated by Lu Xun and taken down by O. V.'. In fact it was written entirely by O. V., that is, Feng Xuefeng.

In his memoirs, Hu Feng wrote about the letter as follows:

> *Realistic Literature* published Lu Xun's 'Letter to the Trotskyites' and 'On Our Current Literary Movement'. The two articles both made it appear that they had been dictated by him [Lu Xun] and transcribed by O. V. Actually, both were drafted by Feng Xuefeng. O. V. was an attempt at rendering my name, so that no one would guess that it was actually he [Feng Xuefeng]. He was a party leader, so I felt it was my duty to do all I could to shield him.
>
> After the question of the slogans had arisen, the literature of national-defence faction went onto the all-out offensive. Feng Xuefeng flew into something of a panic, and wanted to take steps to stem the offensive. At the time, Lu Xun was seriously ill and could neither sit up nor speak, it was not even possible to discuss with him. Just then the foolish Trotskyists, believing the rumours, thought they might be able to profit from the situation, and wrote a letter hoping to 'draw' Lu Xun over to their side. Lu Xun was angry when he read the letter, and Feng Xuefeng drafted this reply after he himself had read it. The 'literature of national defence' faction were spreading rumours to the effect that 'literature of the masses for national-revolutionary war' was a Trotskyist slogan. Feng Xuefeng's reply was intended as a rebuttal of this slander. He arranged for us to go together with his draft [letter] to see Lu Xun and read it out to him. Lu Xun listened with his eyes closed and said nothing, but simply nodded to indicate agreement.

After Feng Xuefeng had gone back, he felt that he ought to provide some theoretical basis for the slogan [of 'literature for the masses'], so he drafted 'On Our Current Literary Movement', and again arranged to go with me to read it to Lu Xun. Lu Xun was clearly weaker than the previous evening and was even less capable of speaking, all he did was nod to indicate agreement, but he also showed some slight signs of impatience. After we had left, Xuefeng suddenly said to me: I hadn't expected Lu Xun to be so difficult, he's not as good as Gorky; Gorky's political comments are all written by the secretary assigned to him by the Party, all Gorky does is sign them.

Hu Feng's recollections show the letter was written by Feng Xuefeng, on Feng's initiative, and later released above Lu Xun's name. Lu Xun did not express any opinion: he just nodded in agreement, but he also 'showed some slight signs of impatience'.

But he did nod, which means the letter must count as Lu Xun's.

In fact, Chen Qichang was right to suppose that Lu Xun had spent his entire life in struggle and solitude, and in his old age, when he became seriously ill, he was attacked not just by his enemies but even by friends. Not surprisingly, he became depressed. He had no idea who Chen Qichang was. By signalling his agreement to the letter, he greatly wronged Chen Qichang. Chen Qichang admired him, and had heard him speak at Beijing University. He loved Lu Xun's writings and his strength of character. He imagined that he knew Lu Xun well, which is why he wrote the letter, so when he saw Lu Xun's (actually Feng Xuefeng's) sarcastic and cynical reply, his pain and disappointment were beyond comprehension by ordinary people. Although a Trotskyist, Chen Qichang was first and foremost a Chinese patriot, who never took a penny from the Japanese. In his *Memoirs*, Wang Fanxi rebutted Lu Xun's comments about the Trotskyists' 'well-printed publications'. He pointed out that to print *Struggle*, the Trotskyists rented premises costing thirteen yuan a month. Ink and paper cost more than ten yuan a month. They lived off selling articles. The South African Trotskyist Frank Glass (whose Chinese name was Li Furen) met the shortfall, from his income as editor of an English-language newspaper in Shanghai, where he earned about 400 yuan a month. Later, as an editor of *Weekly Review*, he earned 300 yuan a month. Frank Glass became a Trotskyist in the late 1920s and came to Shanghai in the 1930s. As for Chen Qichang, he was tortured to death by the Japanese.

In 1937, war broke out and Shanghai became the front line. After China's defeat in the Battle of Shanghai, the Japanese put Chen Qichang on a blacklist.

His family was too poor to redeem him and the Trotskyists were in no position to help, so Chen Qichang had to increase his vigilance. According to his son Chen Daotong, in the four years between the outbreak of war and his arrest, they moved home five times, into ever smaller and more remote premises with ever less furniture. Finally, they arrived at a lane off Xikang Road, a garret of less than twelve square metres. Chen Qichang and his wife and five children lived separately, because of their economic difficulties. Under the bed were two wooden boxes crammed with copies of *Struggle* and *Spark*.

In early 1940, Chen Qichang's elder brother Chen Qilun arrived in Shanghai. He was working in a bank as a cover for collecting economic intelligence, which he secretly radioed to Chongqing. At the end of 1941, Chen Qilun returned to Chongqing, and before leaving entrusted this work to Chen Qichang. At first Chen Qichang refused, but later he reluctantly agreed to take over the job for three months. When the three months were up, Chen Qilun was unable to return, so the job was extended. At this point, the man in charge of the secret transmission station was arrested and betrayed Chen Qichang.

On 30 June 1942, Chen Qichang was arrested. The Japanese military police, accompanied by a gang of traitors, searched Chen Qichang's home and found the copies of *Struggle* and *Spark*. Collecting economic intelligence for Chongqing was not a major crime and you could buy your release for a relatively small sum, but the discovery of magazines advocating communist revolution made it serious. (The Japanese were unable to distinguish between the Chinese Communist Party and the 'Chinese Communist Party – Leninist Left Opposition', so Chen Qichang was executed as a member of the Communist Party, a tragic irony.) Chen Qichang was tortured, but revealed nothing. One day in September, the Japanese military police put him in a sack, bayoneted him to death, and threw his body in the sea at Wusongkou.

Chen Qichang was a Trotskyist fighter, and his death robbed the Trotskyists of a true down-to-earth activist. In his *Memoirs*, Wang Fanxi described his death as 'another tragic loss' after that of Chen Duxiu. Zheng Chaolin and Huang Jiantong (a later Trotskyist leader, whom I interviewed many times in the 1980s) wept bitter tears when they spoke of him in their old age. Why did he die? The Guomindang had nothing good to say about him because he was a 'Communist', and the Communist Party regarded him as a mortal enemy because of his Trotskyism. Especially after Lu Xun's letter, he was considered a 'traitor who took money from the Japanese', a hat he wore for decades, even after his death. Even his son became implicated. In 1946, Chen Daotong was introduced to Trotskyism by his father's friend Zheng Chaolin. Later, he worked in a Trotskyist bookshop, while continuing his studies. On the eve of Liberation he withdrew, and in the autumn of 1950 he was admitted to Beijing University's law school. Two years later he transferred to People's University to do graduate studies. In pledging allegiance to the Party, he voluntarily revealed that he had previously been a Trotskyist. As a small organisation, the Trotskyists kept no archive, so if he had stayed quiet no one would ever have known of his Trotskyist activities. At the time, the Party treated him leniently, as naïve, ignorant, and misguided, and told him that as long as he talked about it, it would be alright. Chen Daotong really was 'naïve and ignorant'. In December 1952, he was arrested during the 'big purge' of the Trotskyists and given four years. After that he returned to Shanghai, where he worked for a team of builders, first producing metal-strips and later as a designer, thus wasting his life. When I interviewed him, he had retired and was helping people renovate their houses, but his main job was working on materials about his father, although he was never able to find a publisher. I end this chapter by telling you, dear readers, that although Chen Qichang was a Trotskyist, he sacrificed his life for the freedom and liberation of the Chinese people.

Zheng Chaolin

When I visited Zheng Chaolin in the summer of 1996, more than sixty years after the Trotskyists' Unification Congress on 1 May 1931, his enthusiasm was undimmed. In his thick Minnan accent, he shouted: 'That was the day the Chinese Trotskyists united, what exciting times! Trotskyism could have had such a bright future, but unfortunately...'.

'Who caused the arrests on 21 May?'

'Ma Yufu. He betrayed the revolution, but we expected too much of him. He was not a staunch revolutionary, and when his wishes were not met, he defected. Peng Shuzhi was to blame. When he received information, the person he sent to tell me had nothing to do with us. Peng did this because he wanted to escape. Also, he gave us wrong intelligence, so everyone was left guessing. As a result, we lost time...'.

Peng Shuzhi was the first to hear of Ma Yufu's defection, but he did not come forward himself and instead got Xie Depan, who just happened to be in his home, to inform people. Peng himself went into hiding, with his wife Chen Bilan. Xie Depan got Peng Guiqiu to tell Zheng Chaolin. Zheng Chaolin went round telling everyone. Short-sighted and impractical as he was, he rushed about in the night telling Chen Duxiu, Liu Renjing, and Wang Shuhuai. Not long after he got home, he was arrested. He did not have time to inform the central leadership, four out of five of whom were arrested.

To the outside world, Zheng Chaolin is known as the 'father' of Chinese Trotskyism, and for two reasons. First, because of his seniority. He joined the Chinese Communist Party in 1922 in France, together with Zhou Enlai. He took part in the Chinese Communist Party's Fifth National Congress, and not long after that he was Hubei delegate to the Party's 7 August Conference. When I interviewed him, he was the sole surviving participant of the 7 August Conference. While working for the Central Committee of the Communist Party in Shanghai, he attended the wedding celebrations of Comrade Deng Xiaoping and his first wife, Zhang Xiyuan. He recalled that when other people got married everyone clubbed together, but not in Deng Xiaoping's case, for people thought his family would send money for the banquet. In her book *My Father Deng Xiaoping*, Deng's daughter Mao Mao mentions Zheng Chaolin several times. The TV documentary *Deng Xiaoping* interviewed him on several occasions. As a result, a man sealed off from the world for so many years entered the limelight and, because of his rich experience, attracted public interest.

The second reason he was revered as the 'father' of Chinese Trotskyism was because of his great age (he died in 1998, aged 98). Throughout most of his adult life he fought for his Trotskyist ideals, never once betraying his faith.

Zheng Chaolin was born in Fujian at the start of the previous century, into a declining landlord-family in Zhangping. Zhangping was rich in resources and its people were by no means poor, but they tended to go overseas to make a living. If a family had no one living overseas, it was considered a source of shame. In recent years, human trafficking has flourished in the region. Naturally Zheng Chaolin was not trafficked overseas, but he did go abroad – honestly and openly, on a scholarship provided by Chen Jiongming, to study in France. Once there, he and Deng Xiaoping and others worked in a factory outside Paris – Deng Xiaoping earned more than 200 francs a month, but the short-sighted Zheng Chaolin could only earn just over 100 francs. Deductions were made for food. In 1922, he, Zhou Enlai, Zhao Shiyan, Wang Ruofei, Chen Yannian, and others set up the Communist Youth Party; later, he and others were sent to Moscow to study at the University for the Toilers of the East. In 1924, when China's Great Revolution started, the Party needed cadres, so Zheng Chaolin was summoned home.

In fact, Zheng Chaolin was a scholar, and his scholarly temperament remained with him all his life. He loved translating and writing. Chen Duxiu wanted to promote him, but he never achieved a post higher than head of the Publications Bureau of the Central Committee of the Communist Party, and he worked longest as editor of *Bolshevik* magazine. During the Great Revolution, he translated Bukharin's famous *ABC of Communism*.

Zheng Chaolin and Chen Duxiu became Trotskyists at almost the same time. In May 1931, at the Trotskyists' Unification Congress, Zheng Chaolin was elected to the Central Executive, where he was responsible for party publications. In just twenty days, he edited three issues, but only one was printed before his arrest. He spent longer in prison under the Guomindang than Chen Duxiu. After 21 May 1931, he was sentenced to fifteen years, but in fact he was released after six years and three months, in August 1937, after the outbreak of war with Japan.

When Zheng Chaolin left prison, the Shanghai-Nanjing region was in flames and his Trotskyist comrades were scattered. He had no choice but to flee with his wife, also a firm believer in Trotskyism, to an isolated part of southern Anhui, where they ended up staying for three years and where their son was born.

But Zheng Chaolin craved political engagement, so in the winter of 1940 he and his wife and son went to Zhejiang and took a boat from Ningbo to

Shanghai, under Japan's brutal fascist rule. Even the Communist Party had withdrawn its underground activists to its rural bases in northern Jiangsu, and for the Trotskyists things were even more difficult. In 1942, at the time of Chen Duxiu's death, there cannot have been more than one thousand Trotskyists in the whole of China, and the Trotskyist organisation consisted of a handful of branches and little more than one hundred members. Sadly, despite their small numbers, they were internally divided into factions. The great tragedy of Chinese Trotskyism is that it was never really united and always racked by endless disputes. At the time, it was split into a group around Peng Shuzhi, Yin Kuan, and Jiang Zhendong, the 'practical' faction, with several factory-branches and the line that 'the Resistance War is correct, but we should resist independently'; and another around Zheng Chaolin and Wang Fanxi, the 'theorists', who believed that 'the Resistance War is part of the Second World war, we should prepare in the war to carry out proletarian-socialist revolution'. This 'theory' was, needless to say, a pipedream. Zheng Chaolin's greatest contribution to Trotskyist theory and one might even say to Chinese thought and culture was his translation and publication, under conditions of extreme difficulty, of Trotsky's *History of the Russian Revolution*.

On 17 April 1949, when the People's Liberation Army was preparing to liberate Shanghai, the Trotskyists held their first National Congress. Formally speaking, this was their Second Congress, following the one held on 1 May 1931. Earlier, in November 1948, Peng Shuzhi's group had also held a 'delegates' congress' that renamed the Trotskyist organisation 'Revolutionary Communist Party of China', but after the meeting all the delegates fled abroad and the 'Revolutionary Communist Party of China' vanished. Peng Shuzhi and Chen Bilan took their family into exile in Vietnam, where they remained for nearly a year and a half, before moving on to France, where they settled in Paris. Peng established a link with the Trotskyist Fourth International and joined its leadership, as a member of its Executive, its Standing Committee, and its Secretariat. At the time, he was its most senior member. Peng lived off his writing. His wife Chen Bilan's *Recollections of a Chinese Revolutionary* contains much valuable information about the early history of the Chinese Communist Party. In 1973, Peng Shuzhi moved to the United States, where he died on 28 November 1983.

Many people were unhappy when Peng Shuzhi left China and stayed abroad. Some, like Jiang Zhendong, joined the Zheng Chaolin group and participated in its Congress. Zheng Chaolin organised the Congress single-handedly. He chose Zhonglu Middle School as the venue – the school's principal was Jiang Zhendong, a member of Peng Shuzhi's faction. The Chinese Revolution was on the point of victory and New China was about to be born – a New China the Chinese Trotskyists were also looking forward to, and for which many

Trotskyists had sacrificed their lives. Mao Zedong, the leader of that revolution, was suspected by Stalin of being a Trotskyist (as Khrushchev revealed in his memoirs), but China's true Trotskyists had no reason to share the general happiness, for the victory of the Chinese Revolution showed that Mao's line of 'establishing workers and peasants' armed forces and encircling the cities from the countryside' was right and the Trotskyists' line of 'carrying out workers' uprisings in the cities and establishing proletarian dictatorship' was wrong. According to Zheng Chaolin's *Memoirs*, the meeting lasted for one day, and the mood was depressed. Zheng Chaolin, Wang Fanxi, He Zishen, Huang Jiantong, and Yu Shuowei were elected as the five-person executive. The meeting ended by singing the *Internationale*. Wang Fanxi went to Hong Kong and finally settled in Macao, where he wrote his *Memoirs*, an objective account of the development and dénouement of Chinese Trotskyism. According to Huang Jiantong, Wang Fanxi went abroad at Zheng Chaolin's insistence. He felt that Wang Fanxi would be able to write and at least leave a valuable record of the Trotskyist movement. Wang Fanxi did not let his old friends down. Born in 1907 into a small merchant's family in western Zhejiang, he started studying at Beijing University in 1925 and joined the Communist Party. In July 1927, the Party sent him to Moscow to study at Sun Yat-sen University. In early 1929, he became a Trotskyist, and in July he was sent back to Shanghai to work for the Chinese Revolution. The Party's underground Central Committee allocated him to the Organisation Department. His powers were extensive: his colleagues were Yun Daiying, Chen Tanqiu, and Zhou Enlai, who headed the Department. In 1930, Wang was expelled as a Trotskyist. Zhou Enlai was said to have been upset, for he valued talent and regretted losing it. Yun Daiying and the others invited Wang Fanxi for a meal in a restaurant, so they could part on good terms. Wang Fanxi was a Trotskyist theorist. His 1957 *Memoirs* were scratched onto wax-stencils by comrades, yielding a mere twenty copies. But before long they reached the Mainland, where 10,000 copies were printed for circulation within the Communist Party. Later, it was translated into English, French, German, and Japanese and became the most authoritative work on Chinese Trotskyism. Wang Fanxi died on 30 December 2002, in Leeds, England, aged 95.

Another important memoir on the growth and development of Chinese Trotskyism is Chen Bilan's *Recollections of a Chinese Revolutionary*, written in exile in France in 1954 but not published until 1992. By then, both Peng Shuzhi and Chen Bilan had died. The book contains exaggerations, especially regarding Peng Shuzhi, as well as numerous inaccuracies.

After the Liberation of Shanghai, the Trotskyist leadership there co-opted Jiang Zhendong onto the executive. On 22 December 1952, in a nationwide raid whose details have not yet been made public, all the Trotskyists left on the Mainland and their sympathisers, about one thousand people in all, were arrested and imprisoned. Zheng Chaolin described it in his memoirs:

> At just after ten o'clock at night on 22 December 1952, I was seized on my way home and taken directly to be locked up in No. 1 Detention Centre. No one asked me any questions. I was simply placed in an empty cell on the second floor. A card bearing my name had already been attached to the cell-door. The cell was some sixteen square metres and could have housed a dozen or so people, but I was its sole occupant. I asked myself whether only I had been arrested, or whether the entire group had been rounded up. Surely my wife had not been arrested too?

Yin Kuan recalled:

> On the evening of 22 December, I invited some friends for a game of mah-jong in my home. There was a knock at the door and I heard the voice of Zheng, director of the police-station. Even though I wondered why he was coming so late at night, I opened the door anyway, and lots of military police rushed in, armed with guns. They took out photos, checked us one by one, and questioned us, but took only me away.

Zheng Chaolin, Yin Kuan, and Huang Jiantong were not actually sentenced as 'criminals'. The reason for the decision not to prosecute them was that 'their crime was too great, there was no penalty commensurate with it'. Yin Kuan was a senior veteran of the Chinese Communist Party, which he had joined in 1923. Later, he served as Secretary of its Shandong Provincial Committee and of the Shanghai District Committee. After the defeat of the Revolution, he was made Secretary of the Anhui Provincial Committee. He was therefore one of few early Chinese Communists who had occupied the main leadership post in three important provincial and municipal party bodies, and Mao Zedong held him in high regard. Under Chen Duxiu's leadership, he took part in the third Shanghai workers' armed uprising. He accepted Trotskyist ideas in 1929 and later joined the Trotskyists. He worked effectively under Chen Duxiu. Before Liberation, he was arrested several times by the Guomindang. After Liberation, he returned to his hometown, Tongcheng in Anhui, where the arrest took place. He was later taken to Tilanqiao Prison in Shanghai. He was never sentenced, but he received quite good treatment. In 1965, he was released on bail due to illness. He died at home in 1967. In 1972, Mao Zedong proposed releasing all the Trotskyists, but the directive was not implemented because of the turbulence and chaos of the Cultural Revolution. In 1975, the Central

Committee of the Chinese Communist Party proposed the release of all Guomindang and Trotskyist prisoners, and Zheng Chaolin was sent to work in the Shanghai Reform-through-Labour Factory in Qingpu, where he was joined by his wife, sent to take care of him. His civil rights were not restored until after the Third Plenum of the Eleventh Congress in 1978. Later, he was elected a member of the Shanghai Chinese People's Political Consultative Conference.

On 15 August 1987, when the Chinese Communist Party held its Thirteenth National Congress, Zheng Chaolin, who had joined the Party in 1922, wrote a letter to the Congress asking it to rehabilitate the Chinese Trotskyists. This was Zheng Chaolin's most important work in his old age. The main contents of his letter were as follows:

> In late December 1952, there was a purge of the Trotskyists in China. In the course of a few days, organised and unorganised Trotskyists across the whole country were arrested and later sentenced, one after the other (as well as some who were never sentenced), to reform through labour. In 1972, exactly twenty years later, apart from those prisoners who had died or been released after completing their sentences, our detention was commuted into strict control. Not until 1979 were our civil rights restored, in accordance with a decision of the Third Plenary Session of your Eleventh Congress. But when our civil rights were restored in 1979, there was no declaration that we Trotskyists were innocent. Instead it was said that we had repented in custody and had therefore been dealt with leniently. In other words, even after the restoration of our civil rights we were still 'counter-revolutionaries', that is, we had committed counter-revolutionary crimes and had not been rehabilitated....
>
> Why are the Chinese Trotskyists a counter-revolutionary organisation?
>
> I have asked the Public Security Bureau, the prison authorities, the interrogators of the control authority, the supervisors, and the guidance-officials, but as a rule they will not give a formal answer to this question. It seems as if Trotskyists are counter-revolutionaries, and there is no need for any further explanation. However, occasionally, in the course of conversation, they touch on reasons why the Trotskyists are counter-revolutionary. These reasons can be summarised in the following three points: (1) The Chinese Trotskyist leader Chen Duxiu asked the Japanese secret service on the Trotskyists' behalf for a monthly subsidy of 300 yuan as payment for traitorous activities; (b) Trotskyists participated in Guomindang spy-organisations and carried out reactionary activities;

(c) Trotsky, the founder of the Trotskyist movement, was a German Fifth Columnist.

Later in his letter, after refuting these charges, Zheng Chaolin continued:

> I ask the Thirteenth Congress of the Chinese Communist Party to declare the Chinese Trotskyist organisation innocent.
> I make this request not only because of the wrongs we have suffered but also in the interests of the Chinese Communist Party and the People's Republic of China. We who were wronged are now living a reasonable life from a material point of view, and we are all old (I am 87) and will soon be dead. If we have been subjected to visible and invisible forms of discrimination and have not had our full civil rights restored, so be it. But if there is a miscarriage of justice in the country and its victims are not rehabilitated, that shames those who hold the reins of government.

He addressed the same demand for the rehabilitation of the Chinese Trotskyists to the Fourteenth and Fifteenth Congresses, the Party's supreme authority. At the time of the Fifteenth Congress, the world was in the throes of great changes and events, including the declaration by the Soviet Supreme Court in 1988 that the 1938 case against the 'anti-Soviet right-wing Trotskyist group' was mistaken and the 'Trotsky-Zinoviev anti-Soviet bloc' was a fabrication. Those implicated were rehabilitated. But if those people were rehabilitated, why not the Chinese Trotskyists, who drew their inspiration from the Soviet Trotskyists? In ancient Egypt there was a saying: People fear time, and time fears the pyramid. Only in China are people not afraid of time. What are eight or nine years in the five thousand years of Chinese history? When Mao Zedong was quarrelling with the Central Committee of the CPSU in the 1960s, did he not say with pride that the struggle would continue for ten thousand years? So Zheng Chaolin's letters fell on barren soil and were never mentioned. All the Trotskyists grew old, and the oldest of all was Zheng Chaolin. At dawn on 1 August 1998, Zheng Chaolin's hard life finally ended, putting a last full stop to the life of Chinese Trotskyism.

7 August 1998, happened to be 71st anniversary of Zheng Chaolin's attendance at the emergency conference in 1927, and that was the day the Shanghai People's Political Consultative Conference held a memorial service for him. The ceremony was grand and well attended. Because Zheng Chaolin had featured in the TV-documentary about Deng Xiaoping, China Central Television and Shanghai Television both sent crews to film the service. But because

he was a Trotskyist and his case was therefore sensitive, the documentaries were never screened. Some remnants of the old Trotskyist movement living in Shanghai and in Jiangsu and Zhejiang came to say farewell. Looking at his painted face, people could be forgiven for thinking that he might suddenly sit up and say loudly: '1 May 1931, they could have had such a bright future, but unfortunately...'.

Huang Jiantong

Guangxi is a region of unending mountains, numerous ethnic groups, fighters, sturdy people, and hard living. It has never produced politicians or thinkers, but it has produced many military strategists. Guangxi soldiers are known for their physical endurance and fighting strength, a product of the extreme poverty of the region, where joining the army is the sole option for many. Then, when a new ruler comes to power and reduces the size of the army, soldiers become bandits, and Guangxi became notorious for its 'bandit-problem'. To be a scholar in Guangxi is not a promising career. However, between 1931 and 1932, when the Chinese Trotskyist leadership received two heavy blows at the hands of the Guomindang and all were imprisoned, so that its original bases in Shanghai, Hong Kong, Beijing, and Tianjin were destroyed, only in Guangxi and Wenzhou was the movement able to revive. In his *Memoirs*, Wang Fanxi recalled that in those areas several Trotskyist branches were established and became active, and provided cadres for the future development of Trotskyism. In Guangxi, the most important Trotskyist was Shi Tang.

I mentioned Shi Tang earlier, in connection with Sun Yat-sen University in Moscow, where he was active as a Trotskyist. On 7 November 1927, on the tenth anniversary of the October Revolution, he was among the Chinese students in Red Square shouting 'Down with Stalin!' and 'Up with Trotsky!' At the end of 1927, he and Liang Ganqiao were repatriated by Stalin, and he was immediately expelled by the Party's underground Central Committee. He then published China's first Trotskyist journal, *Our Word*, and founded China's first Trotskyist group, of the same name. He did not attend the Unification Congress in May 1931 and naturally did not gain a post on the Central Executive, but he was not a Peng Shuzhi, so that did not worry him. He was a cultured person who taught and wrote for a living, winning praise both as teacher and writer. After 1932, when the white terror in Shanghai became intense, the entire Trotskyist organisation took flight. Shi Tang escaped to Guangxi, where he resumed teaching.

In old China, Guangxi was Li Zongren and Bai Chongxi's territory. Li and Bai relied on the hardened soldiers of Guangxi. They entered into an apparent alliance with Chiang Kai-shek, but in fact they were his rivals, and occasionally they warred with him. In the early 1930s, they raised their standard against Chiang and attracted many leftists to Guangxi. At the time, Li and Bai had a favourite called Huang Gongdu, who had also studied at Sun Yat-sen University in Moscow. Although he had not joined the Trotskyist organisation, ideologically he was a staunch Trotskyist. Li Zongren's wife and her younger brother had also been at Sun Yat-sen University and come under Trotskyist influence, so Trotskyists from other places in China without means of subsistence went to Guangxi, Shi Tang among them. In Guangxi, Shi Tang trained numerous aspiring young Trotskyists, including Lin Huanhua, Mao Hongjian, and Mai Junqi. Later, Lin and Mao were sent to Shanghai, where they were made responsible for printing and publishing Trotskyist literature, with outstanding results. Even Lu Xun read their publications, sighed at their fine binding and the neat, careful way in which they had been printed, and wrongly thought they must have had Japanese financial support.

Shi Tang's best-known student was Huang Jiantong. Huang Jiantong, a member of the Zhuang ethnic minority, was born in Wuming in Guangxi in 1918. His father was a teacher in an old-style private school; it was he who initiated his son into learning. In 1935, at the age of seventeen, he went to Nanning to study at the Provincial Teachers' Training College, where he got to know Shi Tang and, under his influence, became a Trotskyist.

In the autumn of 1982, I met Huang Jiantong while working in the Shanghai Historical Studies Institute. Thin as a rake, with barely an ounce of fat on him, he looked as if the wind could blow him over. He was employed at the Institute, and was also responsible for his team-members' political study. He was very talkative, and at meetings he would always chatter away in his Guangxi-accented Chinese, not always easy to understand. There was a lot of unnoticed talent at the Historical Studies Institute, including many former Guomindang politicians and members of the Guomindang secret service, prominent figures from all walks of life in the old society. Many liked to talk about history and boast of their exploits. Huang Jiantong was the only one who never mentioned his own past. Some of the old politicians and spies who knew about it occasionally raised it, but then he would abruptly stop talking, as if closely guarding a secret. Not until a long time later did I learn that Huang Jiantong was a member of the only group not in any way rehabilitated in 1978, when the Chinese Communist Party began a comprehensive review of its history and fully corrected its past mistakes at the Third Plenum of the Eleventh Congress – he was a Trotskyist.

In 1937, Huang Jiantong went home to Wuming and became a teacher in a national elementary school, where he set up a Trotskyist branch. However, he was soon arrested on charges of organising on behalf of the Chinese Communist Party and encouraging rebellion. As I mentioned before, many Trotskyists were charged and sentenced and even executed by the Guomindang as Communists, yet since the founding of New China, all the Trotskyists left in the country were, without exception, jailed by the Communists. A tragic irony.

The War of Resistance had already started. The Guomindang and the Chinese Communist Party once again shook hands, and the 'Communist' Huang Jiantong was released from prison. At the time he was twenty. His family had long ago bought him a child-bride, and tried to persuade him to first get married and then decide what to do. Huang Jiantong told them he could not return home until the invader had been vanquished, so he exchanged the pen for the sword and swore not to return to marry until after victory. His child-bride waited desperately for him to return and eventually died of grief. Huang Jiantong never married and his funeral was arranged by his colleagues at the Historical Studies Institute.

In the spring of 1941, Huang Jiantong was invited by Chiang Ching-kuo to go to southern Jiangxi and work with Cao Juren, Gao Suming, Guo Dali, Wang Lixi, and others on *Justice*, to write the editorials.

Chiang Ching-kuo was, in essence, also a Trotskyist. I explained earlier that in 1925, when he was only fifteen, he had gone to Moscow to study at Sun Yat-sen University, as its youngest student. Before he went, his father had given him a personal letter for Trotsky. In August 1923, Sun Yat-sen sent Chiang Kai-shek to the Soviet Union on an inspection tour. The only major leader he met was Trotsky, on 27 November in Moscow. Afterwards Chiang Kai-shek said: 'I think Trotsky is very straightforward in both words and deeds'. He also said: Trotsky is 'fervent and lively of speech. "A revolutionary must be steadfast and persevering": These were his parting words'. Chiang Ching-kuo frequently heard Trotsky speak at Sun Yat-sen University and was deeply impressed. At Sun Yat-sen University, he most liked the Trotskyist Radek's course 'On the Chinese Revolution'. Although there is no evidence as yet that he participated in the Trotskyist organisation, it was not until 7 December 1936 that he joined the Soviet Communist Party (five days after the Xi'an Incident). Wang Ming, Chinese representative on the Comintern, was convinced that Chiang Ching-kuo was a Trotskyist and got the Soviet secret police to send him to a concentration-camp in Siberia, where Soviet Trotskyists ended up. He barely survived in the Altai mines, but was finally released after Stalin's intervention.

In June 1939, Chiang Kai-shek arranged for his son to lead work in southern Jiangxi. The region was sparsely populated. Its eleven counties, a land-area of 23,000 square kilometres, had a population of just 1.6 million. When Chiang Ching-kuo took office, he ambitiously proclaimed he would 'implement a new politics and construct a new southern Jiangxi'. In the spirit of 'suffering hardship, daring to take risks, and engaging in creative activities', he would reconstruct southern Jiangxi in line with Sun Yat-sen's Three People's Principles, so 'everyone has a job, everyone is fed, everyone is clothed, everyone is housed, and everyone has the chance to study'. He proclaimed this policy throughout southern Jiangxi and summoned talent from across the nation, especially those who had studied together with him in Moscow. Huang Jiantong responded to this appeal.

These were probably the best years of Huang Jiantong's life. In addition to writing editorials, he also did reporting, and he spent time in all southern Jiangxi's eleven counties. He had a ready pen. His then editor, Cao Juren, highly praised his writing. In 1942, a delegation led by Chiang Ching-kuo included Huang Jiantong. Huang Jiantong told me he wrote nearly 2,000 articles during his five years in southern Jiangxi, an average of one a day.

Women love gifted scholars. Huang Jiantong was not a handsome man, but that was an age full of idealism in which passion reigned and literary talent was respected and admired. Many people loved and admired a brilliant journalist like Huang, and his most fervent admirer in southern Jiangxi was Wu Yuefang, daughter of a wealthy Shanghai merchant. According to Zhou Rensheng, who had been in Tilanqiao Prison with Huang Jiantong, Wu Yuefang was very beautiful. She was taller than Huang Jiantong. She worked in the Southern Jiangxi Youth Service-Corps and went almost every day to Huang Jiantong's home to cook and clean for him. They seemed a perfect match, an ideal pair. Many advised Huang Jiantong to marry her, but he thought of his lonely child-bride in Wuming and dared not transgress the bounds of rectitude. He was like a monk, dedicated to his ideals, never once contaminated by sex.

Chiang Ching-kuo was a tolerant person. He did not mind whether you were Guomindang, a Communist, a member of the Nationalist Youth Corps, or a Trotskyist, as long as you were prepared to resist Japan and build a 'new southern Jiangxi'. But above Chiang Ching-kuo loomed his father Chiang Kai-shek, who would not allow his son to overstep certain limits. While Chiang Ching-kuo was working in southern Jiangxi, Chiang Kai-shek recalled him three times to Chongqing for a lecture, and each time he came back depressed and even burst into tears in front of his men. In early 1945, Chiang Kai-shek transferred him to Chongqing to lead the Youth Corps' Central Cadre School. So he decided to let matters rest in southern Jiangxi, in whose towering mountains he left behind a group of intellectuals that included the fervent Huang Jiantong.

After victory over Japan, all political parties hoped to make advances in China, which had been devastated by the War, and the tiny Trotskyist organisation was no exception. On Peng Shuzhi's instructions, Huang Jiantong went in the spring of 1946 to Changchun in northeastern China, to edit the newly founded *Youth* journal. When that closed down, he got a job teaching in a middle school in Changchun, where he propagated Trotskyist ideas and built the Trotskyist organisation. But the northeast was a main focus of the civil war between the Guomindang and the Chinese Communist Party and a brutal cockpit, as well as a cold, harsh place for Huang Jiantong, who had lived so long in the south. Also, as a scholar, he found it hard to cope with the complex political environment. After two years trying to do so, at the end of 1948, when the war had reached a critical juncture, he returned to Shanghai, where with his comrade Jiang Zhendong's help he got another teaching job and waited to see how things would turn out.

The Chinese Trotskyists' tragedy was that they were a leaderless throng, quarrelling constantly and never truly united. In May 1931, under Trotsky's personal supervision and in the presence of Chen Duxiu, they held their first national congress and elected Chen Duxiu as leader. However, after Chen Duxiu's death what was already a weak body disintegrated into factions, and was unable to reunite.

After the victory over Japan, faced with a revolutionary situation, the Chinese Trotskyists again split into two factions. The majority under Peng Shuzhi published *Seek the Truth*, edited by Peng Shuzhi, and *Youth and Women*, edited by Peng's wife Chen Bilan. The minority under Zheng Chaolin published *New Banner*. In August 1948, the majority held its first national congress in Shanghai and adopted a new constitution and a new name, the Revolutionary Communist Party of China. The meeting elected a political bureau comprising Peng Shuzhi, Chen Bilan, Liu Jialiang, Yin Kuan, and someone called Jiao. The congress decided, in light of the military situation, that the five leaders and other activists would relocate to the south, while all those Trotskyists not publicly exposed as such were to join the Chinese Communist Party, to prepare for the victory of the Chinese Revolution. By the end of 1948, everyone apart from Yin Kuan was in Guangzhou. Soon they left the Mainland entirely, some to Hong Kong, some to Macao, while Peng Shuzhi and his wife went to Vietnam, from where they eventually reached France.

On 17 April 1949, while the People's Liberation Army was crossing the Yangtze, the minority also held a national congress in Shanghai. It was organised by He Zishen and held in Jiang Zhendong's elementary school. It met for one day. Ten delegates attended, representing 64 members in Shanghai. It adopted the name Internationalist Workers' Party of China, and elected Zheng Chaolin, Wang Fanxi, He Zishen, Yu Shuoyi, and Huang Jiantong to its central committee. (Wang Fanxi's *Memoirs* list Lin Huanhua in place of Huang Jiantong, but this is wrong.) Following the precedent set by Peng Shuzhi and the others, some proposed that the central committee should go abroad, but Zheng Chaolin strongly disagreed. However, Zheng did propose that Wang Fanxi should go, which he did (first to Macao and later to England). Jiang Zhendong was chosen to replace Wang Fanxi on the central committee.

After Liberation, Huang Jiantong remained in Shanghai. His emotions were complex. He was inspired by the thought that the people, and in particular the working class, were now in charge, but he grieved for his shattered Trotskyist ideals, for which he had struggled tirelessly all his adult life. He also cherished the illusion that the victory of the Chinese Communist Party was not yet complete and the Chinese Revolution would go down Trotsky's road of 'permanent revolution', that by way of struggle in a political assembly a proletarian state would be established and 'universal harmony' achieved. . . .

He stayed in Shanghai and continued to teach, but he was not politically active, nor could he have been. In October 1949, several Trotskyists, including Qian Chuan, Zhao Yangxing, and Zhou Lüqiang, mimeographed a publication titled *Study* in Qian Chuan's home. The People's Police found out and they were taken to the police-station. Qian Chuan spent thirteen days in detention, but the rest were released the next day. The police told them all their activities and views were known, in other words 'everything was under control'. 'We don't intend to arrest you, but this time you exposed yourselves, by publishing this journal . . .'.

This was a clear warning of which nearly all the Trotskyists were made aware. Afterwards, they waited three years, their emotions switching between excitement, anguish, hope, disillusion, indecision, and hesitation, until finally everything came to a head on 22 December 1952.

That night, Huang Jiantong was already in bed in his room in the school-dormitory, preparing to sleep. He heard a knock at the door. He opened it and a team of police entered. Without a word they took him to the detention-centre on Sinan Road and put him in a single cell. A piece of paper with his name on it had been affixed to the cell-door. All his books and correspondence were removed from the dormitory. He Zishen recalled:

> That autumn, Yu Shuoyi was sent by his work-unit to Anhui to investigate health-work, and not long after that he was arrested. On 10 December Zheng Chaolin hurried to my house and told me he knew from reliable sources that the Communist Party might be about to act against us. I thought to myself, our organisation is small, we're not engaged in sabotage, and many people in the Chinese Communist Party are still our old friends, even Chairman Mao and I worked together in Hunan during the most difficult period of the Great Revolution, so I didn't take what Zheng Chaolin said to heart, which didn't make Zheng happy. . . . I never imagined they would come and get us. . . . (See He Zishen's prison-confessions.)

Huang Jiantong later told me that 'after Yu Shuoyi's arrest, I knew it was just a matter of time before the same happened to me. But I was amazed that they used so many military police to arrest such a frail scholar'.

After Huang Jiantong was locked up, nothing happened either that night or the following day. He heard people singing the *Internationale* (a sad irony, in a Communist prison). He wanted to join in, but he had a bad cough and was unable to raise his voice. So he settled down to wait, anxious about what might happen. No one came on the third day either. Unable to contain himself, Huang Jiantong asked the guard who delivered his food. The guard answered with a joke: 'First we're going to let you celebrate New Year, then we'll deal with it...'.

This was China's 'big Trotskyist purge', staged the day after Stalin's birthday (21 December). It was synchronised across the country. All the Trotskyists who had stayed in China, together with their sympathisers, totalling more than one thousand people, were netted in one fell swoop. Details of this incident remain secret to this day.

After more than two years, all the Trotskyists had finally been dealt with. Because of Chairman Mao's injunction that 'no one should be killed', the Trotskyists were sentenced to three, five, ten, fifteen, and twenty years in prison and even – in the case of eight – life-imprisonment. A few of the Trotskyists' relatives and Trotskyist suspects were released. Huang Jiantong, Zheng Chaolin, Yin Kuan, and Yu Shuoyi were left in limbo, on the grounds that their crimes 'were so heinous no punishment was commensurate with them'. They were kept in prison, but their status was as 'prisoners whose cases have not been decided', that is, they had been neither charged nor sentenced, a strange phenomenon.

In May 1964, in line with a decision of the Ministry of Public Security, all the remaining Trotskyists (twenty in all) were sent to a prison in Shanghai. (The exception was Du Weizhi, an outstanding linguist, who was sent to prison in Beijing, to work as a translator.) The twenty included one woman. Of the rest, four had been sentenced to twelve years, three to fifteen years, and eight to life, while the cases of four 'had not been decided'. In prison they studied, laboured, and reformed their thinking, and were allowed out once a year for visits. But whatever their sentence, because of the Cultural Revolution they were all held until September 1972, when they were released, in accordance with Chairman Mao's directive that 'all the Trotskyist elements in prison should be released'. At the time, it was said that 'when Chairman Mao speaks, one sentence tops ten thousand', but when the dozen or so Trotskyists in custody received their release certificates on 28 September 1972, they continued to be kept under supervision, some in a reform-through-labour glass-factory and some on a reform-through-labour farm (at Qingdong). Huang Jiantong was sent to Qingdong. The work was not hard and the pay was sixty yuan a month, no small sum (the equivalent of what a university-graduate might receive). They were allowed to bring family-members to live with them. Zheng Chaolin, who worked at the glass-factory, was allowed to live with his wife. But they had no freedom of action. Once a month they were allowed to go to town to buy household-items, but only if accompanied by security officers. Then, on 5 June 1979, the twelve surviving Trotskyists still living under supervision were gathered together in a small hall in Qingdong for a ceremony at which their civil rights were formally restored. They received identity cards. After a short stay at the Oriental Hotel, they went to Nanjing and Suzhou on a tour. Huang Jiantong was invited to work at the Shanghai Historical Studies Institute.

In the early summer of 1985, I visited Huang Jiantong in the Historical Studies Institute. I asked him: 'Do you regret the life you have led?' He smiled and said: 'I do not regret it. In prison, I wrote many confessions repenting my errors, but they were written under brutal political pressure and cannot be taken as true'. I asked: 'So do you still believe in Trotskyism? Do you stick to Trotsky's way and ideas?' He looked at me and did not answer. He turned towards the window, and the verdant array of trees and bushes beyond it. A ray of sunlight lit up his face with a strange aura, like that of a martyred saint.

In 1987, Huang Jiantong died in Shanghai. He had no family to grieve his passing. His funeral was arranged by the staff of the Shanghai Historical Studies Institute.

Du Weizhi

In Beijing in October 1986, ten years after the smashing of the Gang of Four and shortly after National Day, Vice-Chairman Wulanfu and General Wu Xiuquan received two guests from the United States, Gao Suming and his wife Luo Lanying. This was an unusual meeting, for the four had been students together at Moscow's Sun Yat-sen University sixty years earlier. It was also unusual in that Gao Suming had a Trotskyist background. By 1986, most miscarriages of justice had been righted; people who for decades had been declared non-people had been rehabilitated. Only the Trotskyists continued to be ignored. Whether Wulanfu and Wu Xiuquan discussed these matters with Gao Suming and his wife is not known.

When old friends meet, they like to talk. During the conversation, Gao Suming raised the case of Du Weizhi and handed Wulanfu a letter from Du Weizhi, which can be summarised as follows:

Respected Chairman Wulanfu:

I don't know if you still remember your fellow-student Tu Qingqi at Sun Yat-sen University sixty years ago, who everyone called 'beancurd'?

A few days ago, two old classmates, Gao Suming and Luo Lanying, came to Shanghai, and seeing how difficult my life was, they encouraged me to write to you and ask you to help relieve my plight, hence this letter.

I have three problems.

The first is political. Thirty-four years ago, in 1952, I was arrested and sentenced to life imprisonment for having joined Chen Duxiu's Trotskyists. Twenty years later, in October 1972, the Chairman said we should be released. I have been free for fourteen years, but according to the files of the public-security organs I am still one of the 'four elements' (landlords, rich peasants, counter-revolutionaries, and bad elements), and the Shanghai Public-Security Bureau often come to my house to question me, which puts great mental pressure on me. If you ask me what my subjective wish is, it is to return to the Party. That is, of course, a dream. But at least I should be able to become an ordinary citizen, and I should not be made to wear a 'four elements' hat. So I ask to be incorporated into the 'united-front' system and to be allowed to participate in one of the democratic parties.... In short, I must get rid of this 'four elements' hat.

My second problem is economic. After I was released in 1972, the Government gave me eighty yuan a month to live on. At the time, I was living in Beijing and the money was enough. In 1976, after I moved to Shanghai, it was no longer enough. In 1983, I had no choice but to write a letter to Xiaoping, asking for more living expenses, and I got a rise of forty yuan, making 120 yuan a month. But over the last two years, prices have risen a lot, and 120 is also no longer enough. My wife has hardly any income. She has lots of illnesses and takes medicine regularly, which makes things even harder.... So my second request is for an increase in my living expenses, so I get a bit more money each month to mitigate my economic difficulties.

My third problem is accommodation. The house I live in is only 27 square metres. I share it with my son and granddaughter, so it's very crowded. There's nowhere to do any writing, and if guests come, there's nowhere to sit. So I am requesting slightly bigger accommodation, so I can have a small study and somewhere to sit if guests come.

I am in good health, and I can work for at least another ten years. I would really like to do something for the motherland. But as things now stand, there's nothing I can do. The past fourteen years have been wasted, I don't want to waste the next ten. That is why I have been so bold as to write this letter, in the hope of receiving your assistance and removing these difficulties.

Gao Suming and Luo Lanying naturally said many good things about Du Weizhi, and Wulanfu and Wu Xiuquan took what they said seriously. After seeing off their guests, they discussed what to do, and then drafted a letter to Rui Xingwen, the Secretary of the Shanghai Municipal Committee of the Chinese Communist Party, and Jiang Zemin, the city's Mayor. The letter said:

Comrade Xingwen, Comrade Zemin:

After National Day, we met with the Chinese American Gao Suming, who handed over a letter Mr Du Weizhi wrote to Comrade Wulanfu. We enclose it.

We discussed it, and we thought that relevant policies of the Party should continue to be implemented in regard to Du, so we propose:

First, Du's case should be transferred to the Department for United-Front Work of the Shanghai Municipal Committee for them to deal with. Arrange for Du to do work commensurate with his ability in a translation-unit or a history unit in the city, and take care of him politically.

Second, consider increasing his subsidy by eighty yuan, or give his wife eighty yuan a month, so that together they would have an income of about 200 yuan a month.

Third, make appropriate adjustments to Du's accommodation, and if possible give him three rooms.

These observations are for your reference.

Greetings,

Wulanfu
Wu Xiuquan

Moscow's Sun Yat-sen University was established by the Soviet Party and Government in commemoration of Sun Yat-sen, to train cadres for the Chinese Revolution. The Guangzhou Revolutionary Government organised a selection committee consisting of Tan Yankai, Gu Yingfen, and Wang Jingwei, with Borodin as advisor. Of the first 340 students, 280 were from Guangzhou, Shanghai, and Beijing. Others were children of Guomindang officials. Students from among the common people or selected from the localities were rare. Wulanfu, Wu Xiuquan, Du Weizhi, and Gao Suming were all children of the common people, so their feelings for one another were especially deep.

Du Weizhi was originally known as Tu Qingqi. Du Weizhi was his pen name, which he used after 1930 – after a while, few knew his old name. Du Weizhi was a native of Yonghe in Henan Province. His father was a small merchant. In 1919, Du Weizhi passed the examination for a school in Kaifeng that prepared students for study in Europe and the United States. However, because of the First World war and the worsening economic situation in Europe, the study abroad did not happen, so he enrolled at Southeastern University in Nanjing and Zhongzhou University in Kaifeng, and in early 1925 he joined the Communist Youth League. The League sent him to work under the cover of a teacher in his hometown, where he set up the League's first ever branch.

In the early autumn of 1925, the Soviet Government in Moscow began enrolling for Sun Yat-sen University and the news reached China. A recruitment-station was established in Tianjin. Du Weizhi was very excited, and went to Tianjin to register, carrying a letter of introduction from the Henan Provincial Committee of the Communist Youth League. To his surprise, he was accepted. On 28 October 1925, Du Weizhi set out by boat from Shanghai for Moscow, together with Wang Ming, Zhang Wentian, Wang Jiaxiang, Yu Xiusong, Wulanfu, Wu Xiuquan, and others, almost all famous names in the history of the Chinese Revolution. The journey took a month, and they finally reached Moscow on 28 November. Because he was good at languages, Du Weizhi was assigned to a small Russian-language class with around ten other people. His classmates included Wang Ming, Yu Xiusong, Liu Shaowen, and Li Peizhi. Apart from studying, members of the class were expected to act as a bridge between teachers and the Chinese students. Not long after arriving, Du Weizhi transferred into the Communist Party.

Du Weizhi was a talented linguist. In China he had learned English and Russian, and in Moscow he learned German and French. He attained a high proficiency in all four languages. Later he learned how to read Polish, Czech, Spanish, Italian, Romanian, and other languages, thus laying a solid foundation for his later career as a translator.

People's material existence in the Soviet Union at the time was extremely hard. Food was scarce. Soviet students at a college near Sun Yat-sen University ate only twice a day, mainly black bread. But the students at Sun Yat-sen University were treated more generously, and often ate beef. Du Weizhi did not like Western food, and used to reminisce about the various kinds of beancurd in Yongcheng – salted beancurd, green onion beancurd, and so on, so the other students nicknamed him Beancurd. Probably not many knew who Tu Qingqi was, but everyone knew who Little Beancurd was.

While Du Weizhi was in Moscow studying, the Chinese Revolution went through its most tempestuous period, including the capture and then loss of Shanghai. The success of the Shanghai workers' third armed uprising led to a carnival atmosphere in Moscow, followed by tremendous shock and a wave of protests after Chiang Kai-shek's 12 April coup. There was a big debate in the Comintern and the CPSU about the causes of the defeat of the Chinese Revolution, with Stalin on one side and Trotsky on the other. The students at Sun Yat-sen University formed into two factions, one for Stalin, the other for Trotsky. To Stalin's surprise, the Trotsky faction preponderated over the Stalin faction among the Chinese students. Du Weizhi supported Trotsky, but his main thoughts were on his studies. Others saw him as a diligent student, ideologically pure and a good party member. In September 1927, Sun Yat-sen University produced its first batch of graduates in Moscow, and the great majority of those with Trotskyist ideas were sent back to China, taking their Trotskyism with them. However, Du Weizhi stayed on as an interpreter, as did Wang Ming, Zhang Wentian, Wang Jiaxiang, and Shen Zemin. At the same time, Wulanfu (then known as Yun Ze) went to work as an interpreter at the Communist University for the Toilers of the East and Wu Xiuquan went to Moscow's Infantry-Academy.

In the summer of 1928, the Chinese Communist Party held its crucial Sixth Congress at an old aristocrat's estate on the outskirts of Moscow. Eighty-four delegates attended together with 34 alternate delegates, representing more than 40,000 party members engaged in a difficult struggle back in China. Du Weizhi interpreted.

On 12 June 1928, when Stalin met Qu Qiubai, Zhou Enlai, Li Lisan, Deng Zhongxia, and Su Zhaozheng in the Kremlin, Du Weizhi was the interpreter. Stalin and the Chinese Communist leaders focussed on two main issues. One was the nature of the Chinese Revolution. Stalin believed that although the Chinese Revolution had been defeated and the Guomindang had betrayed it, it remained bourgeois-democratic in character. Du Weizhi translated carefully. He noticed the Chinese Communist leaders listened to Stalin like primary-school students to their teacher. From time to time they made notes, but no one said anything. However, when Stalin got round to the second question, whether the Chinese Revolution was at high tide or low tide, things changed.

Stalin said the Chinese Revolution, which had just experienced the 12 April massacre and the defeats of the Nanchang Uprising and the Guangzhou Uprising, was at a low ebb. Suddenly, Li Lisan interrupted him. He said: 'Comrade Stalin, the Chinese Revolution is still at high tide, in Shanghai, Guangzhou, Wuhan, Changsha, ... and many other places, the workers and peasants' struggle is surging forward, in wave after wave'.

'Surging forward, in wave after wave?' Stalin probably thought he must have misheard. He looked at his own interpreter, who looked for help to Du Weizhi. Du Weizhi immediately repeated: 'Surging forward, in wave after wave'.

Stalin sneered sarcastically: 'That's not waves, that's foam! When the revolution is at low tide, there can sometimes be a bit of spray...'.

Li Lisan muttered something, but Zhou Enlai stopped him.

This exchange left an unforgettable impression on Du Weizhi and shaped his future life.

The Sixth Congress in Moscow lasted from 18 June to 18 July. After it was over, Du Weizhi was sent back to China. At first, he was put to work for a while in the central organ of the Communist Youth League in Shanghai, where he familiarised himself with the situation in China. He was then sent to Zhengzhou to head the Propaganda-Department of the Communist Youth League's Henan Provincial Committee. In the summer of 1929, he returned once more to Shanghai, where he became Secretary of the Organisation Department of the Central Committee of the Communist Youth League.

In early 1930, as a result of the development of the revolution, leftist ideology began to appear in the Chinese Communist Party, mainly around Li Lisan, an important leader at the time. In May, Li Lisan published a long article in the Communist Party organ *Bolshevik* titled 'Problems in the Face of a New Revolutionary Upsurge'. In it, he argued that 'the high tide of the Chinese

Revolution has already arrived'. On 8 June, Li Lisan made similar points in a report to a Politburo meeting. On 11 June, the Politburo adopted Li Lisan's resolution titled 'Resolution on the Current Political Tasks: The New Revolutionary High Tide and Victory Initially in One or More Provinces'. Fortuitously, the Fifth Red Army under Peng Dehuai had just captured Changsha, and although the occupation lasted only three days, it was a source of great encouragement to Li Lisan. He was preparing to organise a series of major actions, including seizing Nanchang, attacking Jiujiang, joining forces at Wuchang, and encouraging insurrections by Nanjing's rank-and-file troops.

Du Weizhi, who had personally witnessed the dispute in Moscow between Stalin and Li Lisan, expressed his views at a party meeting and told the 'wave' and 'foam' story, when Stalin had criticised Li Lisan. Someone told the Central Committee what Du Weizhi had said, and Li Lisan was furious. He suspended Du Weizhi from the Party and then expelled him. Du Weizhi's wife Liang Shiwei, who was from a working-class background and had joined the Party in 1925, was also suspended because she was unwilling to sever ties with Du Weizhi. She was forced to leave the Party in early 1931.

The early 1930s were a period of unbridled and intense ideological struggle in the Party. Those who opposed Li Lisan's leftism included Wang Ming, Bo Gu, Wang Jiaxiang, and He Zishu from Sun Yat-sen University in Moscow; and long-term members of the central trade unions and the Party and the League, like He Mengxiong, Li Qiushi, Luo Zhanglong, and Xu Xigen. Similarly, the Trotskyists were very active, and the alliance of the four Trotskyist organisations was campaigning for its ideas. In theory, Du Weizhi and Wang Ming and the others were in the same boat: they had studied at the same university and had close relationships with one another. However, Du Weizhi was an intellectual, aloof from politics in the worldly sense. He looked down on Li Lisan and also on Wang Ming, and instead became interested in Trotskyism. In May 1931, shortly after the Trotskyists held their Unification Congress, he became a Trotskyist. Unlike the Chinese Communist Party, the Chinese Trotskyists received no external material support, so with the help of friends Du Weizhi went to Anqing (then the capital of Anhui Province) to be a professor in the Department of Philosophy at Anhui University, and at the same time to devote himself to translation-work.

In April 1931, Gu Shunzhang, an alternate member of the Politburo and the most important person responsible for security-work in the Chinese Communist Party, turned traitor in Wuhan and gave away the Party's secrets. Gu Shunzhang's arrest ended up implicating Du Weizhi.

On the afternoon of 2 July 1932, Du Weizhi received a phone-call from Peng Shuzhi, who told him to go to Zhaofeng Park (now Zhongshan Park) in west

Shanghai for a meeting to discuss propaganda-work. As I explained earlier, not long their Unification Congress on 1 May 1931, the Chinese Trotskyists suffered two heavy blows. One was in late May, when four of their five main leaders were arrested. In July, Chen Duxiu united with Peng Shuzhi to draw in Yin Kuan and Cai Zhendong and reorganise the Central Executive, but just one month later, a second blow struck, when Yin Kuan, Cai Zhendong, and six others were arrested. Chen Duxiu was not discouraged and insisted they 'keep fighting', and again he united with Peng Shuzhi and with Song Fengchun, Pu Dezhi, and Luo Shifan in a five-member Standing Committee, with Peng Shuzhi in charge of propaganda. Zhaofeng Park was a fairly secluded place. Both Peng Shuzhi and Chen Duxiu were short of money and lived in cramped accommodation, so they had little choice other than to hold their meetings in a park.

Four people attended the meeting: Peng Shuzhi, Li Ji, Wu Jiyan, and Du Weizhi. They pretended to be sightseers. They talked for about an hour, and then the meeting ended. Peng Shuzhi and Li Ji stayed behind in the park to talk about the philosophy of Laozi. Wu Jiyan and Du Weizhi went off together to the park-gate. At the gate, someone patted Wu Jiyan's shoulder: 'It's been a long time since we met, shall we have a cup of tea?' Wu Jiyan and Du Weizhi were astonished, it was Gu Shunzhang! Gu Shunzhang was familiar with the way in which Communist activities were staged, and after turning traitor he regularly took Guomindang secret agents to places Communists might frequent. Whoever he approached was surrounded and arrested, and so were Wu Jiyan and Du Weizhi. But Peng Shuzhi and Li Ji, busy discussing Laozi, got away.

Wu Jiyan and Du Weizhi were taken to a police-station. After a protracted interrogation, it became clear that the two were no longer Communists but Trotskyists. Trotskyists were also liable to be sentenced, but fortunately Du Weizhi's appointment at Anhui University protected him, and after repeated interventions by others he was freed on bail, in late 1932. After that Du Weizhi left the Chinese Trotskyist organisation and gave himself up to his studies, to teaching, and to translating. So he lost in the beginning but gained in the long run. He was not really a political activist but a scholar. In later years, he buried himself in translation. His main translations were Engels's *Dialectics of Nature*, Lenin's *The Development of Capitalism in Russia*, Plekhanov's *Militant Materialism*, Romanov's *Russia in Manchuria*, and dozens of other works, all Marxist classics that were extremely difficult to translate and only someone like him proficient in a dozen languages could manage. These translations were Du Weizhi's contribution to Chinese culture and the spread of Marxism to China. Even today, his versions remain authoritative.

In October 1949, New China was born. On the eve of Liberation, some important figures in Chinese Trotskyism like Peng Shuzhi and Wang Fanxi went overseas. As a linguist, Du Weizhi had many friends in foreign countries and was well equipped to make a living overseas, but he did not go. He rejoiced at the victory of the Chinese Revolution, and seemed to have long forgotten that he himself had once been a Trotskyist for a little more than a year. He had been persecuted under the Li Lisan line and had joined the Chinese Communist Party very early on. He had translated a number of Marxist works, and endured his share of suffering under the Guomindang. Because of this, in the early years after Liberation he sought out the party organisational department and asked for his membership to be restored.

On 20 December 1950, *People's Daily* published a statement by the Trotskyist leaders Liu Renjing and Li Ji, together with an extremely harsh Editorial Note quoting Stalin's well-known denunciation of Trotskyism:

> Present-day Trotskyism is not what it was, let us say, seven or eight years ago; Trotskyism and the Trotskyists have, during this time, undergone a serious evolution that has radically altered the face of Trotskyism; in view of this, in the struggle against Trotskyism, the methods of struggle likewise must be radically altered. Our party comrades have failed to notice that Trotskyism has ceased to be a political tendency within the working class, that from that political tendency within the working class that it was seven or eight years ago, Trotskyism has transformed into a frenzied and unprincipled band of wreckers, diversionists, spies, and killers, acting upon the instructions of the intelligence-service organs of foreign states.

So the situation suddenly worsened. As I mentioned earlier, Liu Renjing had attended the Chinese Communist Party's First Congress and was the only Chinese Trotskyist to have gone to Turkey to visit Trotsky. In 1937, he stopped being a Trotskyist, and worked thereafter for the Guomindang. After Liberation, he wrote to the Central Committee acknowledging his errors. Liu Shaoqi met him and made a severe criticism of him. On 20 December 1950, after the publication of Liu Renjing and Li Ji's statement, he was unable to stay on at Beijing Normal University and was transferred to the People's Publishing House, as an editor and translator. In December 1952, at the time of the purge of the Trotskyists, Liu Renjing, who had already publicly capitulated, was severely criticised and developed a mental illness. After the outbreak of the Cultural Revolution, he was arrested and kept in detention from 1966 to 1978. He was initially held in Qincheng Prison, but when that became overcrowded, Mao Zedong said some old Trotskyists like Liu Renjing no longer needed to be detained. So Liu Renjing was moved from Qincheng Prison to another prison.

Unlike other prisoners, he was allowed to read books and newspapers and go to Beijing once a month, in a special car with his own guard. Liu Renjing obtained his freedom in 1978, and returned home to live with his family. On 1 July 1981, on the sixtieth anniversary of the founding of the Chinese Communist Party, a Chinese News reporter interviewed him as the only surviving delegate at the First Congress and published a report titled 'A Visit to Liu Renjing'. He wrote:

> Not until after New China was founded in 1949 did he wake from his dream, abandon his reactionary stance, and go over to the side of the people. From 1951 until now, he has been engaged in translation-work for the People's Publishing House [this was, of course, untrue – WJM]. He has translated more than a dozen important documents and works.

In 1986, aged 84, Liu Renjing was appointed as an advisor to the State Council. The following year, on 5 August, he was killed by a car at the entrance to Beijing Normal University. Li Ji was also a veteran member of the Chinese Communist Party, which he joined in the early 1920s. He joined the Trotskyists in 1931, withdrew in 1934, and spent his entire life as a translator, also after Liberation.

On 22 December 1952, during the purge of the Trotskyists the day after Stalin's 73rd birthday, Du Weizhi was locked up in the Detention Centre near Shanghai Station. In 1955, he was sentenced to life imprisonment. This was completely unexpected, and put Du Weizhi among those Trotskyists sentenced most heavily, apart from Zheng Chaolin, Huang Jiantong, Yin Kuan, and Yu Shuoyi. He had been a Trotskyist for just one year and had never occupied a position in the Trotskyist organisation. Why the heavy sentence? Perhaps because he was well known. Apart from a small handful of people like Chen Duxiu, he was the best-known Trotskyist, due to his prolific output. And to think that his translations were mostly of Marxist classics – what a tragedy!

'Raised up by Xiao He, cast down by Xiao He'. Because of his outstanding language-skills, Du Weizhi did not suffer greatly in prison. According to his Trotskyist fellow-prisoners Wang Guolong and Zhou Rensheng, at Tilanqiao Prison he was put in charge of a prisoners' translation unit, which mainly translated scientific and technical materials, including equipment specifications for imported machinery. In 1963, at the time of the dispute between the Chinese Communist Party and the CPSU regarding the international movement, senior translators who understood Marxist theory were in great demand to help spread China's views to the world. Chen Boda and Kang Sheng independently thought of Du Weizhi's rare talent locked up in Tilanqiao Prison in

Shanghai, so they urgently sent for him to be brought to Beijing and locked him up in the famous Qincheng Prison, where he continued his old line of work, heading the translation team. During the Cultural Revolution, when Qincheng Prison became overcrowded, Du Weizhi was temporarily sent to Fushun in Liaoning and held in a prison for war-criminals. Apart from a little more than one year spent in Fushun, he was kept for eight years in Qincheng Prison. In October 1972, in accordance with Chairman Mao's proposal to release all the Trotskyists, Du Weizhi left Qincheng Prison, and four years later his civil rights were restored.

In Qincheng prison, an extraordinary incident took place. On 13 September 1971, Lin Biao fled China and died when his plane crashed near Öndörkhaan in Mongolia, and an investigation into Chen Boda, who supported the Lin Biao clique, gathered pace. Someone said Chen Boda had joined the Trotskyists at Sun Yat-sen University in Moscow – that person was a former student at Sun Yat-sen University, Wang Zhiling, together with his former wife Hu Peiwen. They both provided written evidence that Chen Boda (then known as Chen Shangyou) had taken part in the Trotskyist organisation and contributed two or three roubles to its operating expenses. Both sets of materials were published in the report on the investigation into Chen Boda's counter-revolutionary crimes circulated by the Central Committee's special investigation team. Naturally the secretary of the team, Kang Sheng's secretary Li Xin, contacted Du Weizhi, and asked him to write an exposé of Chen Boda and 'redeem himself by good service'. Du Weizhi was surprised, and thought: why has Chen Boda, a great Marxist theoretician and militant anti-revisionist, suddenly become a counter-revolutionary and a Trotskyist? After thinking it through, he provided a truthful account: 'lots of people at Sun Yat-sen University in Moscow were sympathetic to Trotsky or agreed with Trotsky, and including myself. Maybe Chen Shangyou did a bit too, but certainly no one ever joined a Trotskyist organisation. This is because there was no Trotskyist organisation in the Chinese Communist Party at the time. China's first Trotskyist organisation was founded in Shanghai in 1929, when the Our Word group was set up. By that time, both I and Chen Shangyou had already returned home...'. Later, Chen Boda read these two sets of materials and said: 'Wang Zhiling and Hu Peiwen's exposés don't match the facts, who would have thought that Du Weizhi, who was treated so unjustly, would tell the truth!'

Years later, in October 1986, the Communist Party's Shanghai Municipal Committee received Wulanfu and Wu Xiuyuan's personal letter, which they took to heart. After an investigation, they took speedy measures. In January 1987, Mayor Jiang Zemin personally presented a letter appointing Du Weizhi to the Shanghai Historical Studies Institute. In early 1990, Du Weizhi joined the Shanghai Translators' Association. In June 1992, this extraordinary polymath died after a life of terrible hardship, although compared with the Trotskyists Wang Guolong, Zhou Rensheng, and Zhou Lüqiang, who were still struggling in poverty, he at least finally enjoyed a happy old age.

Wang Guolong, Zhou Rensheng, and Zhou Lüqiang

Wenzhou is a city in Zhejiang near the border with Fujian, surrounded by mountains and the sea. The Siming Mountains isolate the region from other parts of the country. Communications are not easy. For a long time there was only one poorly-built road to the provincial capital, and the journey could take days. In the past, Wenzhou maintained many of its ties to the outside world by water, but even sailing to Shanghai could take four days. Since the reforms and opening up, Wenzhou has become a prosperous city and now has an airport and is connected by inter-provincial highways. You can fly to Shanghai in forty minutes, although the train still takes more than ten hours.

But, despite being cut off for so long, its people are open-minded. In their pursuit of truth and wealth they have crossed oceans and arrived at Ningbo, Shanghai, London, and Paris. At the time of the Great Revolution in the 1920s, some went to study in France and at Moscow's Sun Yat-sen University, where they were influenced by Trotskyism. In his *Memoirs*, Wang Fanxi noted that when the Trotskyist leadership was smashed in Shanghai in the early 1930s, in Guangxi and Wenzhou the Trotskyists remained buoyant and nurtured and delivered cadres for the organisation. In Guangxi, this was due mainly to Shi Tang, who went to Guangxi from Shanghai, taught at Guangxi Teachers' College, and sowed the seeds of Trotskyist thinking. In Wenzhou, the spread and development of Trotskyist ideas was due mainly to Zeng Meng.

Zeng Meng was a native of Wenzhou, an early member of the Chinese Communist Party, and one of the first Chinese students at Moscow's Sun Yat-sen University. According to his student and comrade Wang Guolong, Zeng Meng did not live up to his name, which means 'fierce': he had a pale face and was quiet and gentle. In the early 1930s, when Wang Guolong first met Zeng Meng in Wenzhou, he gained the impression that Zeng Meng was a 'scholar who had met with misfortune'.

Zeng Meng had long credentials in the Party. When he returned to China from Moscow, he first served as Chen Duxiu's secretary and later as Zhou Enlai's. His personal relations with Zhou Enlai and Zhou's wife Deng Yingchao were excellent. In November 1929, when Chen Duxiu was expelled from the Party, Zeng Meng was unhappy. He had been influenced by Trotskyist ideas in Moscow, so he left the Communist Party and joined the Trotskyists. On 15 October 1932, when Chen Duxiu was arrested, Zeng Meng was also arrested. However, Zeng Meng was soon released by Zhang Chong, the head of the Guomindang's secret police. Zhang Chong told him to tell the press he was politically 'demoralised'. After he had done so, he returned with his wife Qiu Jun to Wenzhou.

What he had said was not true and a subterfuge, but even Wang Fanxi was taken in, and wrote in a Trotskyist publication that Zeng Meng had 'gone home as a retired scholar'. In fact he became a teacher, and spread Trotskyist ideas among the students and other teachers. He won more than thirty people to the organisation, and at the same time built peripheral organisations including a National Salvation Alliance and a Book Club. There were more Trotskyists in Wenzhou than Communists and more Trotskyist sympathisers than Communist sympathisers. The Wenzhou women's knitting workers' strike, noted in the annals of the Wenzhou labour movement, was led by Trotskyists.

In 1937 and 1938, the Trotskyists in the Wenzhou area organised two 'general councils' at Zeng Meng's home attended by members of the Trotskyist branches. Five people were at the first: Zeng Meng, He Zishen, He Shufen, Zhu Qian, and Li Guodong. Two more, Qian Chuan and Wang Guolong, attended the second. In March 2003, when I went to Wenzhou to interview Wang Guolong, he recollected the events with great enthusiasm, although by then he was in his nineties. He told me the meetings had lasted a whole day, and because material circumstances were difficult, Zeng Meng's wife Qiu Jun had only been able to provide two meals of rice gruel and sweet potatoes. Even so, everyone was as if on fire. China was in crisis, territory had been lost, and the Guomindang, the Japanese, and Chinese collaborators were riding roughshod over people. All the participants believed that only Marxism and Trotskyism could save China, and they were busy realising their ideals in practice.

Unfortunately, in the autumn of 1939, an accidental error caused havoc in the Trotskyist organisation in Wenzhou, although it could have been avoided. That day a young female follower of Zeng Meng called Li Wenting had asked Zeng Meng's help after fleeing her forced marriage, and Zeng Meng had allowed her to stay in his home. Li's husband was a Guomindang Party boss, and when he came knocking at Zeng Meng's door, he saw some Trotskyist publications and denounced Zeng Meng to the Guomindang authorities. Zeng Meng was taken away to Jinhua and then escorted back to Wenzhou, where he was detained until after the victory over Japan.

After this, Zeng Meng was, indeed, a little 'demoralised', and it seems he was never again active. Fortunately, a new leader emerged from among the Wenzhou Trotskyists. This was Zhou Rensheng, who in the winter of 1945 set up the Marxist Advance Association. In March 2003, I interviewed Zhou Rensheng in Wenzhou. When I mentioned Zeng Meng, it was clear he still respected him deeply: Zeng Meng had sown the seeds.

In May 1949, when Wenzhou was liberated, Zeng Meng was immediately arrested, not because he was a Trotskyist but because of his awkward relationship with Zhang Chong, the Guomindang's secret-service chief. His wife Qiu Jun wrote to Zhou Enlai, and Deng Yingchao soon wrote back on behalf of Zhou Enlai, after which Zeng Meng was released. In the autumn of 1950, he was arrested a second time. This time his wife wrote to Deng Xiaoping, who had studied with Zeng Meng in Moscow and worked with him in the underground Central Committee in Shanghai after returning to China. Deng wrote personally, and recommended he work as an advisor for the State Council. So Zeng Meng was again released and went to Beijing. However, he did not get a position working for the State Council. He then returned to Wenzhou. On 22 December 1952, at the time of nationwide Trotskyist purge, he was again arrested. This time no one interceded, and in 1958 he died in prison.

Compared with Zeng Meng, Wang Guolong was a tall, strapping figure. When I interviewed him in March 2003 in Wenzhou, friends were meeting to celebrate his ninetieth birthday. Straight-backed but walking with a stick, he was on his way to Zhou Rensheng's home. His voice was loud and clear. If you wanted to be heard, you had to shout.

In 1931, a key year for the Chinese Trotskyists, the seventeen-year-old Wang Guolong left Wenzhou for Shanghai to serve as an apprentice. He was poor and by no means reconciled with his destiny. He contacted the Guomindang, the Communist Party, and the Trotskyists, and finally he concluded that only the Trotskyists could change his life and save China. Seventy or eighty years later, when talking about his choice, he thought that of all the people and parties, the Trotskyists were the poorest, the most dedicated, and the hardest working. This was true both of grassroots party members and of the cadres, without exception. He recalled that when he had gone to visit Peng Shuzhi, he was amazed that such an important cadre lived in a garret, utterly destitute, not knowing where his next meal would come from... and poor people are most likely to want to change their destiny. Wang Guolong was not wrong. In China, both the Guomindang and the Chinese Communist Party, generally speaking, were heavily subsidised by the Soviet Union. Only the Chinese Trotskyists received no external support. All the Trotskyist revolutionaries, whether Zheng Chaolin, Peng Shuzhi, or even Chen Duxiu, lived off their writing, part of the income from which they used to support the revolution. They were truly loyal to their beliefs. In choosing Trotskyism, Wang Guolong chose a life of hardship.

Wang Guolong became very active in the Trotskyists' grassroots organisations. In the 'golden age' of Chinese Trotskyism in Shanghai, there were more than twenty branches with more than one thousand members and sympathisers. However, from May 1931 to October 1932, the Trotskyist leadership was ravaged in Shanghai, so Wang Guolong and Zeng Meng had to return to Wenzhou. There Wang was arrested a few months later for 'harming the Republic' and given two-and-a-half years in prison. He was a robust and dauntless character and in prison he did his best to stand up for others. As a result, his sentence was steadily increased, so he ended up spending more than four years in prison, before his release on the outbreak of the Resistance-War.

After his release, Wang Guolong received a directive from Zeng Meng telling him to join the labour movement and help build a Trotskyist organisation among the workers. He was again arrested and spent six months in prison, so he missed the Trotskyists' first general council in Wenzhou. However, shortly after his release he attended the second general council and was elected to its leadership. Then, in the autumn of 1939, he was again arrested in the course of the third destruction of Wenzhou's Trotskyist organisation.

This time, Wang Guolong suffered greatly in prison. Needless to say, he was beaten and tortured. Because of the poor conditions, in May 1940 he contracted severe malaria and his temperature reached 42 degrees. According to the doctor, if it stayed that high, he would never recover. So a friend sought out the prison-director and pointed out that if a prisoner died, it would be bad for the director's career. The director saw his point, and agreed to 'medical parole'. Wang Guolong was taken from prison to a hospital run by the Catholic Church, and his life was saved.

By late 1940, Wang Guolong had finally recovered. Wenzhou was bleak and desolate. Wang Guolong left once again for Shanghai and ran into Peng Shuzhi. Peng persuaded him to return to Wenzhou to develop the Trotskyist organisation. Peng Shuzhi had a big plan: having parted ways with Chen Duxiu, he was now the senior person. He had played a main part in the Chinese Communist Party's Central Committee and its Propaganda Department, but he had never fulfilled his ambition in the Trotskyist movement. Now most of the older Trotskyists had either died or gone away, Peng was determined to gather together the remnants and to train and develop a youth-movement and establish his absolute authority over it. The idea looked fine, but Peng Shuzhi was a scholar and talker rather than a doer. China was like a heap of firewood: in many areas, such as Wenzhou, neither the Guomindang nor the Communist Party were aware of what was going on. But the Trotskyists also failed to ignite a general conflagration.

Wang Guolong returned to Wenzhou full of enthusiasm, but when he learned from Zhou Rensheng, nearly ten years younger than he, that Peng Shuzhi had said 'Don't trust old people, now we must rely on young people to conquer the world', he was deeply disappointed and became depressed. After that he worked as a tutor for a family, and also taught at a Normal School. Finally, he got a job editing a local newspaper.

Shortly after Liberation, he went to Shanghai, where he stayed with his sister and earned a living as a writer. Several of his Trotskyist friends, including Qian Chuan, Zhao Yangxing, and Zhou Lüqiang, published a mimeographed journal titled *Study*. Wang Guolong also wrote some articles for it arguing that according to Marxism, socialism cannot be built in a single country. Was what the Chinese Communist Party was doing socialist? He argued we would have to wait and see. He said in the past the Trotskyists had always said political power could not come from the barrel of a gun, but now the Chinese Communists had won power with guns.... New things were emerging one after another, and the Trotskyist classics could not provide an answer, so we would have to engage in study....

This thinking was widespread in the Trotskyist movement at the time. According to Wang Fanxi, writing in his *Memoirs*, the establishment of New China threw the Chinese Trotskyist movement 'into a period of intellectual ferment'. This was, of course, right. To be cynical, they were keeping abreast of the times. However, what they were doing was considered a counter-revolutionary act, and Wang Guolong, Zhou Lüqiang, Qian Chuan, and Zhao Yangxing were arrested. Qian Chuan was held for thirteen days, because he had engraved the wax-paper and done the mimeographing, the others for just one day. After their release, the public security cadres went to talk with them. The man who visited Wang Guolong said: 'You Trotskyists are against the Guomindang, so you are friends of our Communist Party. You are poor, you should concentrate on survival. Don't write any more of this kind of article. Find a proper job'. Zhou Lüqiang also said that the police told him the Trotskyists were the Communist Party's friends, although they should stop their activities. This suggests that in the early days after Liberation, the prevailing view of the Trotskyists was relatively relaxed. On 22 December 1952, however, everything changed. Wang Guolong was arrested in Shanghai, sentenced to life in 1955, and not released until 1972. His civil rights were not restored until after 1975.

During my long interview with Wang Guolong, he particularly mentioned his wife Liu Manzhuang. Liu Manzhuang, unlike the wives of many other Trotskyists, was not an educated woman. They married in 1937. Liu Manzhuang remained unswervingly loyal during Wang Guolong's 33 years in prison. She raised their three children by working as a maid. Her younger brother Liu Zhishan, an office-worker, chose not to marry so he could help her with the children. In December 1825 in Russia, some democratic-minded aristocrats rose up to resist the tyranny of the Tsar and became known as the Decembrists.

When their uprising failed, they were exiled to Siberia. Not one of their wives betrayed them, and many abandoned their lives of luxury and accompanied their husbands to Siberia. The Chinese Trotskyists' wives were even stauncher than the Decembrists', a Russian symbol for the devotion of a wife to her husband: as far as I know, not one betrayed her husband in his hour of need. Liu Manzhuang was such a woman. Ten years ago she died. Wang Guolong, now 95, lives in an old people's home in Wenzhou.

Zhou Rensheng (Zhou Renxin) is the last of the Wenzhou Trotskyists, and one of their most important leaders. He enjoyed a high standing, but he and his wife live in very modest circumstances. In March 2003, I interviewed him in Wenzhou, in his home. I never imagined that right in the centre of Wenzhou there could be such a dilapidated small courtyard. In the middle of the courtyard is a well, overgrown with weeds and moss. The wall along the side of a room of fifteen square metres looks as if about to tumble. Along it is a two-doored cupboard, also crooked and twisted, and nailed and wired to wooden posts in the wall so that it is impossible to say which supports which. Apart from a black-curtained bed, there is nothing else. Zhou Rensheng has lived here since the early 1930s.

Zhou Rensheng was born into a poor family that lived by making oil-cloth umbrellas of the sort you no longer see in the big cities. His father Zhou Lizhai had only a slight education. By dint of a lifetime of hard work, his father finally set up his own umbrella workshop and sent Zhou Rensheng to school. He desperately wanted him to become a student and 'pass the examination, bring glory to the family-line'. He achieved his first aim – Zhou Rensheng took an excellent degree – but not his second. Because Zhou Rensheng believed in a certain doctrine and insisted on pursuing his ideals, far from bringing glory to the family name, he visited a great scourge on it.

In 1939, Zhou Rensheng passed the entrance-examination to Xiamen University, to study in the English Department. He studied hard, and his talents were widely recognised in the department. One day, a fellow-student showed him an English translation of Trotsky's *Son, Friend, Fighter*, which moved him deeply. The writing was beautiful, and Trotsky affectionately recalled his elder son's development from a lively child to a friend and comrade-in-arms and finally to a victim of Stalin's brutal killing machine. Zhou Rensheng read it again and again, and was filled with complex emotions. This book influenced his life more than any other. Seventy years later, he sat in his courtyard under a withered vine reciting in English passages from it he had learned by heart.

In the summer of 1940, when Zhou Rensheng returned to Wenzhou for the summer-holidays, Lin Songqi introduced him to Wang Guolong and he joined the Trotskyists. He still believes his choice was right. He subsequently devoted his life to Trotskyism. 'Our goal and the Chinese Communist Party's was the same – to liberate the people from Guomindang slavery and eventually realise communism. Only the methods we adopted and the road we took differed from those of the Communist Party'.

While at university, Zhou Rensheng met a beautiful young woman called Zhao Qingyin. They married just before graduating. Zhou Rensheng persuaded Zhao Qingyin of Trotskyism, and she too joined the organisation.

After graduating, Zhou Rensheng taught at Wenzhou Middle School, where he himself had studied, and also at Zhejiang University and Jingjiang Middle School in Jiangsu, where he propagated Trotskyism.

The Marxist Advance Association Zhou Rensheng set up in 1945 was one of the most important of the later Trotskyist organisations. It organised workers' and students' strikes against hunger and civil war in Wenzhou. Many of the workers and students who participated in these activities thought they were led by the Communist Party.

In 1949, Zhou Rensheng went to Haidun in Fujian to be principal of Haidun Middle School (now Longhai Middle School, in Longhai). In July 1949, he joined the Chinese Communist Party and was appointed head of the propaganda department in Haidun, but at the same time he was a Trotskyist leader in Haidun. Haidun had not yet been liberated. Joining the Communist Party was said to have been Peng Shuzhi's idea. In late 1948, after Peng Shuzhi had convened a conference of the majority group in Shanghai, he and his wife Chen Bilan fled overseas with their children. At the same time, he called on Trotskyists to join the Communist Party. 'At the time of the Great Revolution, lots of people were members of two parties, we Trotskyists can do that too. We can go into the Communist Party to study and engage in activities, and to develop our organisation'.

On 22 December 1952, Zhou Rensheng and his wife Zhao Qingyin were arrested in the nationwide purge of the Trotskyists. The arrests caused uproar throughout Haidun Middle School. Neither teachers nor students believed their principal Zhou Rensheng, head of the county propaganda department, was a 'heinous criminal' and a Trotskyist. In November 1954, he was sentenced to life-imprisonment as a 'backbone element of the Trotskyite bandits' and Zhao Qingyin got five years. Zhou Rensheng was initially held in Zhangzhou in Fujian and was later transferred to Linping in Zhejiang. In 1963, he was sent with other Trotskyists to Tilanqiao Prison in Shanghai. He was released in 1972, and his civil rights were restored in 1975. Because of his excellent English, in Tilanqiao Prison he was assigned to the translation team. He said the most interesting work he did during his later period in prison was to translate Isaac

Deutscher's authoritative *Trotsky Trilogy* (Zhou Rensheng was one of three translators, the others being Wang Guolong and Shi Yongqin).

In the winter of 1956, while Zhou Rensheng was being moved from Zhangzhou to Linping, he passed through Wenzhou and stayed for several days. Through the kindness of his guards, he was able to meet his father Zhou Lizhai. Zhou Lizhai was not yet sixty, but he seemed much older to Zhou Rensheng, who felt deeply guilty. He knew he had been his parents' hope, and instead he had brought them misery. Not long after, Zhao Qingyin won a year's remission for good conduct and was released early. When Zhou Rensheng saw her thin face, he reminded her of the ancient story of 'The Woman of Zhao who Entrusts the Orphan', a tale of loyalty and moral rectitude. Finally, he said: 'It's easy to die, what is difficult is to live. My heart has already died. I kept the easy things for myself and left the suffering for you'.

Zhao Qingyin understood Zhou Rensheng's meaning. She returned home and quietly assumed the task of raising their young son and caring for Zhou Rensheng's parents. Naturally she could no longer teach, so she got a daytime job in a neighbourhood printing factory and in the evenings she worked as a maid. Some of leaders repeatedly urged her to divorce Zhou Rensheng, and promised that if she did, they would arrange for her to get another teaching job. But she turned them down. She chose loyalty: loyalty to her husband and to her own beliefs; and she chose extreme poverty. She worked hard all day, at whatever jobs came up. She even worked at the hospital, emptying the night-soil pails of people with infectious diseases. She made every cent count twice. Although she was utterly destitute and every piece of clothing had been endlessly patched, she kept the house fastidiously clean and tidy and always made sure her child and mother-in-law maintained basic human dignity. As a result of the privations, she became bent and her hair turned white. The skin on her hands cracked and became rough as a rasp. Only when she narrowed her eyes and smiled did you catch a glimpse of the beautiful young woman student in the English Department at Xiamen University. However, those narrow and bony shoulders bore the burden of supporting the whole family, until Zhou Rensheng's final return. In the spring of 1976, Zhou Rensheng went home to Wenzhou. When he saw his elderly mother, old, ailing, and white-haired, and his equally white-haired wife, who had always cared for her, he knelt down and wept.

On 27 January 2004, Zhou Rensheng died peacefully in his home, while his wife continued to live in that dilapidated building.

How Zhou Lüqiang came to join the Trotskyists is hard to understand. He was born in Wenzhou, but he did not know Zeng Meng, Wang Guolong, or Zhou Rensheng, nor had he been influenced by them. In 1947, he graduated from high school and left Wenzhou for Shanghai, where he studied at Shanghai Teachers' College. At the college, the Guomindang Youth League and the underground Communist Party were both very active, whereas the Trotskyists had only a tiny impact. Yet of these three organisations, Zhou Lüqiang opted for the Trotskyists.

The original emergence of Chinese Trotskyism was closely connected with the defeat of the Chinese Revolution. Many older Trotskyists split from the Chinese Communist Party because they were dissatisfied with the Comintern and Stalin's cover-up and refusal to take responsibility: that was why they turned to Trotskyism. By 1947, however, people were no longer concerned about the reasons for the defeat of the Great Revolution. The Communist-led People's Liberation Army had swept through half of China. The victory of the Chinese Revolution was dawning before the Chinese people. Youth in pursuit of revolution were turning their sights to the Chinese Communist Party. Who, ostrich-like, would tie his or her star to the Chinese Trotskyists, who never believed in armed revolution and in encircling the cities with the villages?

When Zhou Lüqiang went to Shanghai, he studied at the Normal College. The Communist underground was very active, and he made contact with the Communist Party. However, he got to know a teacher who was a Trotskyist. He was conquered by the teacher's charisma: the teacher was poor, honest, knowledgeable, self-abnegating, self-sacrificing, and always true to his beliefs. He was the sort of person one very rarely meets in this world, but of whom there are quite a few among the Trotskyists. Later, I got to know Zheng Chaolin and Zhou Rensheng, people of that sort. At the time, Peng Shuzhi used to give lecture-courses at a school at the intersection of North Sichuan Road and Wujin Road, doing one lecture every Sunday morning. The teacher took Zhou to listen. The first lecture was about dialectical materialism; the second, about the history of the development of society; the third, about the history of the Chinese Revolution. Even before he had completed the course, Zhou joined the Trotskyists' Socialist Youth League, together with his classmate Qian Huichu, later his wife.

In joining the Trotskyists, Zhou Lüqiang believed he was participating in the revolution and pursuing the same objectives as the Chinese Communist Party. Little did he realise that the choice he made would condemn him to a life of suffering.

Normal College students at the time were poor, and they were also very active ideologically. The underground Communist Party launched a massive campaign against 'hunger and civil war' in which many students participated. The Trotskyist branch in the Normal College had only three members, all of whom joined in the revolutionary activities organised by the Communist Party.

On the eve of the Liberation of Shanghai, on 25 April 1949, Chiang Kai-shek ordered Guomindang agents in Shanghai to launch one last crazed effort in which they arrested, in one fell swoop, hundreds of students, including fifteen Normal College students and two Trotskyists, Zhou Lüqiang and Qian Huichu. Those arrested were taken to the Guomindang Police Academy on Jianguo Road. Chiang Kai-shek wanted them shot, but the underground Communist Party skilfully publicised the incident in the press with the help of Yan Duhe, a well-known figure, so there was a public outcry. Many professors joined the protests, and many heads of families gathered at the police-station to demand their children's return. The People's Liberation Army had just crossed the Yangtze. The rumble of artillery could be heard in Shanghai suburbs. The Guomindang authorities lost their nerve, and the arrested patriotic students were all released with the exception of the Jiaotong University students Mu Hanxiang and Shi Xiaowen, who were shot, and were thus among the last martyrs before the Liberation of Shanghai.

After Liberation, the Trotskyists left several people behind in Shanghai to run *Study*, a small mimeographed publication. Zhou Lüqiang, who narrowly escaped a martyr's death at the hands of the Guomindang, also participated. *Study* came out twice before it was banned, and in October 1949, Zhou Lüqiang, Wang Guolong, and Qian Chun were arrested and locked up for a day. While giving an account of himself in the detention centre, Zhou Lüqiang mentioned he had participated in the student movement and been arrested by the Guomindang on 25 April 1949. The public security officer was sympathetic. He said: 'you Trotskyists are the Communist Party's friends'. When he heard the word 'friend', Zhou Lüqiang was overcome by feelings of warmth. The policeman said: 'In future make sure you reform, don't be active again'. He took the advice to heart, and when he left the detention centre he went to Xiamen to teach, until his arrest on 22 December 1952, during the big Trotskyist purge. Two years later, he received seven years, a relatively light sentence. His wife Hui Qianchu received an even lighter sentence, and was released after just a few months. She later taught at Shanghai Girls' Middle School No. 2.

However, Zhou Lüqiang's life in prison was far less fortunate than that of his fellow Wenzhounese Zeng Meng, Wang Guolong, and Zhou Rensheng. In April 1955, he was sent to Jining in Inner Mongolia to build the Jining railway. At the end of April, it was still snowing, which was hard for a young southerner like Zhou, but he soldiered on. After that, he was sent to Baotou to build the Baotou-Lanzhou Railway, and in late 1957 he was sent to a remote labour camp in the Jalaid Banner near Hulunbeier in Inner Mongolia, where it was winter seven months of the year, a vast wasteland. Every night he heard wolves howl. Not until 1987 did he return to Shanghai.

For the first five years after his arrest, he lost all contact with his family in Shanghai. He did not know whether they were dead or alive. He was the only Trotskyist in the labour camp. He had no companions, no friends, no faith, and no support. He survived by animal instinct: he was still young, and he simply refused to die. Every day he laboured interminably, supported only by his instinct, until in early 1958 he finally made contact with his wife.

From then on, he and his wife Qian Huichu became birds of passage. Every summer, she travelled all the way from Shanghai to Hulunbeir to visit him. Zhou Lüqiang was released from prison in 1959, having served his sentence. Every winter, he went all the way from Inner Mongolia to Shanghai, to visit his wife and children. This happened year after year until 1981, when his wife passed away.

In 1987, he retired and went back to Shanghai, where he went to live in his son's home. The youngest of the Trotskyists, he is restless by nature, so he resumed contact with his remaining comrades. I got know him in Zheng Chaolin's home. He was Zheng Chaolin's staunch admirer, and his Wenzhou dialect was not too far removed from Zheng Chaolin's Fujian dialect, so he could understand Zheng Chaolin when he spoke his native tongue. Once a week, he visited Zheng Chaolin's home to do little jobs around the house. Most recently, however, one of his main tasks has been to make funeral arrangements for his friends. Some were his teachers, some strangers to him. However, as soon as he received the news, he would rush from the ends of the earth to do what was required. For he understood: all those dying had the same beliefs as he, and had suffered the same hardship. He was even the first among his friends in China to know of Wang Fanxi's death in England. At the time of the big Trotskyist purge in 1952, he was one of more than one thousand people seized, and today fewer than ten remain. Who will speak at his funeral? When I asked him this, he fell deep into thought.

Epilogue

On 12 March 2003, I took the night train to Wenzhou to interview a number of elderly Trotskyists, preceded by Zhou Lüqiang, their youngest member.

I should have gone much earlier – my visit was long overdue. I had contacted them long before, by phone, but I kept on having to postpone the visit, for personal reasons. Zhou Lüqiang called me early in March to say Wang Guolong was ninety and hard of hearing. Zhou Rensheng's memory was excellent, but he had contracted prostate cancer, and could die anytime. (He died in Wenzhou on 27 January 2004: Zhou Lüqiang saw him off.) Two years earlier, I had intended going to Guangdong to interview the veteran Trotskyist Liu Pingmei, but he died before I could make the trip. I also wanted to go to Guangxi to interview the elderly Trotskyist Jiang Junyang, but just after I got in touch, he too passed away. Wang Guolong and Zhou Rensheng were probably the sole surviving members in mainland China of the early generation of Chinese Trotskyists. I immediately decided to drop all other tasks and go with Zhou Lüqiang to Wenzhou.

As the train chugged across the Hangjiahu Plain, Zhou Lüqiang and I fell to talking about past events and people. Suddenly he said the following, which struck me to the heart:

> I joined the Socialist Youth League [the Trotskyist majority's youth organisation] to make revolution, to get rid of the Guomindang. Actually, I didn't really understand what Trotskyism was, or what the Communist Party was. I loved my country so much that I almost gave my life so that New China could be born. Under no circumstances am I a counter-revolutionary!

My heart trembling, I watched his old and wrinkled face and could find no words.

The Chinese Trotskyist movement arose for a complex set of reasons that I have tried to explain. Most early Trotskyists were major figures in the Chinese Communist Party who (for various reasons) split from it. However, they never wavered in their opposition to the Guomindang's brutal rule. Later, some passionate youngsters joined the Trotskyists, also for the revolution. Apart from a handful of traitors like Ma Yufu and Xie Depan, the rest consistently fought alongside the Chinese Communists, in the Soviet concentration camps in Siberia and in the Guomindang's Longhua Prison, Baigongguan Prison, and

Zhazidong Prison in Shanghai. Their blood mingled with that of Chinese Communists. In his old age, Zheng Chaolin wrote: 'There is also Trotskyist martyrs' blood on the Five-Starred Red Flag'. (He had just read a report in *People's Daily* about Baigongguan and Zhazidong mentioning the martyr Zhang Luping, a Trotskyist, and was moved to write these words.) This is an indisputable fact. So is it right to continue to treat them as 'the most vicious enemy', 'traitors and spies', and 'murderous thugs' (as Wang Ming and his gang did) rather than as comrades or at least as friends?

By this time, it was deep in the night and the train gathered speed. It was pitch-black outside the window. Zhou Lüqiang, used to the life of a migratory bird, had long since fallen asleep and was snoring. I could not sleep, and once again fell deep into thought.

The big Trotskyist purge of 22 December 1952, was a product of Mao Zedong's policy in the early days after Liberation of 'leaning to one side', that is, full reliance on the Soviet Union. Mao had proclaimed this policy on 1 July 1949, the twenty-eighth anniversary of the Chinese Communist Party. Before that, US Ambassador John Leighton Stuart had written a letter that he asked a Chinese 'democratic personage' to pass on to Zhou Enlai in which he explained that the US Government wanted to offer a low-interest loan of US$1–2 bn in the hoping of establishing friendly relations with New China (see *My Father Ji Chaozhu*). The 'democratic personage' went to Beijing, but when he saw Chairman Mao's article, he quietly returned south. In June 1950, the Korean War began; on 15 October, the Chinese People's Volunteers arrived in Korea. In 1951, the Central Committee of the Chinese Communist Party decided to launch a vigorous thought reform campaign among the nation's intellectuals. Hu Shi's son published a letter to his father in *People's Daily* making a clean break. In the United States, Hu read the letter and wept. Fei Xiaotong, Feng Youlan, Zhu Guangqian, Liang Sicheng, and Yu Guoen all published articles claiming they would reform their thoughts and make a clean break with the culture of US imperialism. However, all this was wishful thinking on the part of Mao Zedong. Stalin was deeply suspicious of him, and wondered whether China would take the 'Yugoslav road' and Mao would be a 'second Tito'. Some in Stalin's inner circle, such as Nikita Khrushchev, even suspected Mao might be a Trotskyist. This was mainly due to Wang Ming's influence. According to Mao Zedong's interpreter Shi Zhe: 'To seize power and gain the leadership of the Chinese Communist Party, Wang Ming constantly bad-mouthed Mao Zedong to Stalin'. In late 1939, in Yan'an, Wang Ming wrote a poem titled 'The Theory of New Democracy: On the Fundamental Errors in Mao Zedong's Article'. Part of it went like this:

> The theory of New Democracy comes from Trotsky and Chen Duxiu.
> After the success of the bourgeois revolution,
> It's fine for the capitalists, but not for the socialists.
> We take pains to advocate change,
> But persuasion is met with anger.
> Leninism is revised, the future is obscure.

This piece of doggerel, not even remotely comparable as poetry with Mao Zedong's majestic verse, attacks Mao Zedong as China's Trotsky. And, as Shi Zhe pointed out, 'Stalin's view of Mao Zedong came mainly from Wang Ming'. To remove Stalin's doubts, the Chinese Trotskyists were sent as sacrifice.

In the early days of national reconstruction, the Trotskyists who stayed behind on the Mainland were not active. At the very beginning, some printed a small publication, but then even that stopped. They abided by the law. The students studied (like Chen Daotong, son of the well-known Trotskyist Chen Qichang, whom Zheng Chaolin introduced to Trotskyism, and who became a research student at People's University), the teachers taught (like Zhou Lüqiang and Zhou Rensheng), and the scholars wrote scholarly works (like Zheng Chaolin and Du Weizhi). The Government more or less tolerated them, and most engaged in 'painful reflection' (in Wang Fanxi's words) about the road they had taken and the ideology they had upheld. In 1952, during the Korean War, to get even more Soviet support and as a gift for Stalin on the day after his birthday, the Trotskyists and their sympathisers all over China were arrested and their leaders were given heavy sentences (though none was killed).

The purge was nothing like the anti-rightist campaign and even less like the Cultural Revolution in terms of the number of people involved, and it did not even achieve the scale of the campaign against Hu Feng's 'counter-revolutionary clique'. They were a tiny handful and could have been ignored, for nearly all were feeble scholars, politically inactive and in no way engaged in sabotaging China's socialist revolution and reconstruction. Arresting and jailing them had only symbolic value. Even so, the Government seized them, and a life of extreme hardship ensued. Fewer than ten survive, in the twilight of their lives.

The arrests were conducted in secret. There was no mention of them in the press. The trial too was conducted in secret. The entire case was wrapped in layer upon layer of secrecy. The campaign was unlike any other. Most campaigns were carried out to great fanfare, but not that against the Chinese Trotskyists. Even when Zhou Lüqiang was sent to a labour camp in Inner Mongolia after sentencing, the leadership repeatedly stressed that it could only be announced that he had been sentenced as a counter-revolutionary.

EPILOGUE

To this day, hardly anybody knows there are still Trotskyists in China, people who endured terrible suffering for more than half a century, who have still not been rehabilitated, and who continue to be ignored and have been left to fend for themselves until they die.

In the 1960s, China and the Soviet Union quarrelled publicly about issues concerning the international Communist movement. In his old age, Deng Xiaoping said: 'Actually, we did not know how to understand and develop Marxism under changed circumstances'. He also said: 'Both sides engaged in much empty talk'. We called Khrushchev a revisionist. He replied with epithets, including that the Chinese Communist Party was Trotskyist. In a letter to Communist Parties and Workers' Parties throughout the world and to the people of the Soviet Union, Khrushchev said again and again that he intended to launch a 'struggle against the chauvinist, Trotskyist, and factionalist viewpoints of the Chinese leadership'. Mao Zedong was accused of having Trotskyist beliefs. But the tragic thing is that China's few dozen actual Trotskyists were rotting in Mao Zedong's and the Chinese Communist Party's prisons.

Nowadays, we acknowledge the diversity of the world and the right of the world's people to make their own choices. In the last century, the Trotskyists lay low for a long time, but at the end of the century they began to make a come-back. Now the biggest country in Latin America, Brazil, is ruled by the Workers' Party, which has Trotskyist tendencies; the Brazilian President Lula da Silva, a former industrial worker, has Trotskyist tendencies.

Twenty years ago, in Shanghai's Historical Institute, I got to know the mysterious Huang Jiantong and began to find out about Chinese Trotskyism. In the 1990s, while I was working with the cultural historian Professor Yu Qiuyu on the TV series *Shanghai's Ark*, Professor Yu asked about my future plans. I told him I had two topics in mind: a book on Shanghai's old houses; and a book on Chinese Trotskyism, its origins and development, and the Trotskyists' suffering. Professor Yu applauded the idea of a book on the Trotskyists. He said: 'even if you don't write the book on Shanghai's old houses, someone else will; but if you don't write about the Chinese Trotskyists, perhaps no one will. And they're the sort of people someone should write about'.

Professor Yu's words set me thinking.

For more than ten years, I concentrated almost all my spare time on this book. I read everything published in China and abroad about the Chinese Trotskyists, interviewed survivors and their families, and wrote this book. I want it to be known that in the last hundred years of modern Chinese history there were people of inestimable integrity who chose a belief and stood by it all their lives, with no regrets. They fought, sacrificed their lives, and left their mark on history. We should not forget them.

Postscript

It is ten years since I decided to write a book on the Chinese Trotskyists. I experienced various difficulties in researching it – in regard, for example, to the interviews – but here I want to talk about just one thing, my difficulties and frustrations in getting it published.

I hoped I would be able to publish it in China. I therefore held back some source materials, playing down the inhuman treatment and extreme torture to which Trotskyists were subjected in prison and labour camps. The people this book is about were born and bred in China, and even though they suffered terrible humiliation and ill-treatment, they loved their country. If the Chinese Trotskyists' problem is to be resolved, it will require wisdom, farsightedness, and tolerance on the part of the Chinese Communist Party.

When I finished a first draft, I handed it to a friend who works for a big Shanghai publishing house. This friend read the entire manuscript and said it was good, moving, and worth publishing. But it turned out to be harder than one might think. You also work in the media, I was told. You should know....

I understood what my friend meant, and took the manuscript back.

Several months later, Yan Xiaoling, a senior editor at Beijing's Masses Press, called to ask me if I had any manuscripts, and I mentioned this book. She was interested and said her press published that sort of thing. She told me to send her the manuscript. I carefully revised it, quietly removing some sensitive bits, and sent it to her. A long wait ensued.

Several months later, Yan Xiaoling phoned and said she was in Shanghai. She told me excitedly there should be no problem in publishing the manuscript. I was delighted, and invited her for a coffee in Xintiandi. As we sat in a super-modern café, I fell to thinking of Chen Duxiu, Mao Zedong, Zhou Enlai, Qu Qiubai, Liu Renjing, and the others. Nearby was the building where the First Congress was held. Could any of them ever have imagined that China would undergo such massive changes? Yan Xiaoling told me one of their senior editors was an old comrade familiar with the period in my manuscript, he was interested in it and had written a passionate memo in its favour. He had then passed it on to the General Administration of Press and Publication, which also approved it. For safety's sake, they had passed it and the reviews to the Central Committee's Party History Research Centre. This was more than a month ago. As a general rule, if manuscripts cannot be published, the Party History Research Centre sends them back within a couple of days.... Afterwards, she asked me to give her all the photographic material so she could take it to Beijing to prepare it for publication.

POSTSCRIPT

That was the only time my manuscript got anywhere near being published without restrictions within China. Although it never came to anything, I am still grateful to Yan Xiaoling and her senior colleague, who behaved honourably. I never believed my manuscript was particularly well written, but it was after all the first time that these events had been brought to light, the first time that the existence in the motherland of this group of people willing to fight and sacrifice themselves for their communist ideals, a few of whom still survived, would be made known to ordinary people

A fortnight later, my hopes were dashed. Yan Xiaoling phoned to say the view of the Party History Research Centre thought my manuscript should not be published in China, and she had no choice but to convey this 'view' to me. She passed on to me the opinions of some experts on party history. They are not long, so I reproduce them in full:

Readers' comments on *Bringing to Light a Long Ignored History*.

This book is an account of the history of Chinese Trotskyism and of some Chinese Trotskyists. The author has taken a lot of trouble to track down and interview the dwindling number of Trotskyists and, on the basis of their oral testimony, writings, and other historical documents, to clarify their emergence, rise and fall, and eventual demise. The description of the Trotskyists' later and recent situation is uniquely valuable and places this book in a class virtually of its own. The book is well structured and the chapters are well arranged. It contains rich historical material and is written in clear, plain language. It is a valuable source on Chinese Trotskyist history. However, the book should not be openly published, because the Central Committee has not yet reached a formal decision on the rehabilitation of the Trotskyists. As the book itself points out, the full circumstances of the 'great Trotskyist purge' of 22 December 1952, 'have still not been released to the public'. Essentially, the book affirms the Chinese Trotskyists and reverses the sentence against them. Precisely because the Central Committee has not reached a formal conclusion regarding the Trotskyists, the book's standpoint and tendency cannot be sustained. This standpoint and tendency are contrary to vol. 1 of the *History of the Chinese Communist Party*, so until the Central Committee reaches a conclusion, the book is not suitable for open publication.

Later, Yan Xiaoling returned the photos, but for some reason I never received them. What grieves me most is that the photos of Huang Jiantong and Du

Weizhi, which my friends had obtained for me despite great difficulties, have also disappeared.

What I could never understand was why the leadership of the Party History Research Centre and the experts were unable to take an open-minded view consonant with the times. The world has changed greatly, and so has the evaluation of the Trotskyists. Was it not their responsibility to revise party history in line with new developments? I always believed the Hu Jintao-Wen Jiabao Government was close to the people and pragmatic. But if party history experts cannot propose the righting of a gross injustice perpetrated nearly sixty years ago or at least display a modicum of leniency and allow people in the unofficial world to express views different from those in official 'party history', how will senior levels of Government ever get to know that sixty years ago in China such a thing happened and even today some people continue to live in humiliation and misery?

Another long wait followed.

During this period, Professor Yu Qiuyu met the head of a Taiwan publishing group, but this person told him the atmosphere in Taiwan was not then right for such a book, that the only issue people were interested in was the conflict between the 'blue' parties (that tend towards China) and the 'green' (that tend towards a Taiwanese national identity). All he could do regarding the book was apologise.

Last year was the year of my birth sign. Everything was going fine for me, except for the book I had so taken to heart. My son comforted me: could I not bring it out through the Internet? He said he would give me money so I could contact a company and have a couple of hundred copies privately printed. He even offered it as a birthday present, to set my mind at rest and for the sake of my Trotskyist friends. True to his word, he found a company on the Internet and made detailed enquiries about how much it would cost to design and print an edition of the book.

'When you are at the end of your tether, a glimmer of hope suddenly appears'. When I had all but given up, my elder brother Wu Weimin returned to Shanghai from the United States on a family visit. He came by way of Singapore to take part in celebrations for Dr Yang Zhenning. My brother is a well-known high-energy physicist, a man of great enthusiasm who also likes to write, including about subjects other than physics. I knew that in Singapore he had a good friend called Pan Guoju, a leading figure in the World Scientific Publishing Company in Singapore, which had a subsidiary (Global Publishing) that specialises in cultural studies. I gave my brother the manuscript, thinking I might as well try – and he agreed to help. He went to Shenzhen to stay with our younger sister and stayed up half the night reading it. Deeply moved, he called me early the next morning and said he would discuss it in Singapore with Mr Pan and urge him to publish it. A few days later, he called me from Singapore and said Pan Guoju had been very straightforward about it and had already agreed to publish. He had delegated his editor He Hua to read it carefully. He had passed on the manuscript to well-known scholars in China, including Zheng Yifan, a researcher at the Central Translating and Editing Office, for him to scrutinise.

Zheng Yifan and I have never met, but I could see that he took his job as a reviewer seriously and made a fair and objective assessment. The assessment is not long, so I reproduce it here in full:

> Reader's comments on the manuscript *Purgatory*
>
> For a long time, the Soviet Union did not mention the role played by the Trotskyists in the Russian Revolution and building the Soviet Union, and finally Stalin characterised them as 'imperialist spies' and wiped them out. The Chinese Trotskyists suffered the same tragic fate. They were persecuted by the Guomindang and repressed by the Communist Party. Kang Sheng fabricated the charge that they accepted funds from Japanese imperialism and acted as Japan's agents, so Trotskyists were all along equated with counter-revolution. In reality, they too fought for the revolution and for communism. They emerged as a political force due to Stalin's errors in regard to the leadership of the Chinese Revolution, when Trotsky's ideas were correct and Stalin's were wrong. As a result, large numbers of Chinese students became Trotskyists. However, in the subsequent revolution Mao Zedong's policy of encircling the cities from the countryside proved to be more correct than Trotsky's and better suited to Chinese realities. Yet this concerned different approaches to revolution and had nothing to do with the question of counter-revolution.
>
> This book uses archival sources and its author has consulted many Trotskyist materials. Particularly valuable are the author's interviews with some Trotskyist survivors, by means of which he retrieved and secured valuable information about the Chinese Trotskyists. Apart from Wu Jimin's work, very few people have done anything on this subject (apparently Ye Yonglie also came across the Chinese Trotskyists). So from an historical point of view, this book is well worth publishing. The notes on the Trotskyists in Mao's *Selected Works* have already been revised, and no one now repeats the nonsense about them being Japanese spies. So far, however, there has been no formal rehabilitation of the Chinese Trotskyists, and none would seem to be imminent, which is why this

book cannot be published on the Mainland. It is a worthwhile book, and I very much hope you can publish it, as part of modern Chinese history.

Zheng Yifan (researcher, Central Translating and Editing Office)
1 December 2007

Zheng Yifan's assessment must have played a big part in persuading Pan Guoju to publish *Purgatory*. I thank him for standing up for me, and I am also grateful to Pan Guoju for his generous and gallant heart. Laozi said: 'The highest good is like water'. Without Pan Guoju's benevolent heart, this book would never have been published.

I would also like to thank my colleague Professor Chen Sihe, Chairman of Fudan University's Chinese Department and a well-known specialist in contemporary Chinese literature. He read the manuscript with an expert eye and wrote an enthusiastic preface. 'Great love cannot be expressed in words'. I will never forget his kindness.

I would also like to thank my family and friends for their support while I was carrying out the interviews, writing the book, and waiting and waiting for an outcome.

Finally, I wish to thank Zheng Chaolin, Huang Jiantong, Du Weizhi, Wang Guolong, Zhou Rensheng, Zhou Lüqiang, Zhao Qingyun, and other Trotskyist friends, some of whom have passed away (may their souls rest in peace in the soil of the motherland), and some of whom are still alive, for letting me interview them, for exposing the traumas, for clarifying to me this period of history, and for telling me about their suffering and hardship. Through a life of suffering, they kindled life's radiance. By means of their own destiny, they revealed to others a simple truth: life is beautiful; as long as life goes on, there is hope.

PART 2

Autobiographical Accounts of Chinese Trotskyists' Early Years

∴

Unfinished Autobiography

Chen Duxiu

Adapted from the translation by Richard C. Kagan, The China Quarterly, *no. 50 (April 1972), pp. 295–314.*

Hume began his autobiography by saying:

> It is difficult for a man to speak long of himself without vanity; therefore, I shall be short. It may be though an instance of vanity that I pretend at all to write my life: but this narrative shall contain little more than the history of my writings; as, indeed, almost all my life has been spent in literary pursuits and occupations. The first success of most of my writings was not such as to be an object of vanity.[1]

For the last few years, many of my friends have done their best to get me to write my autobiography. I delayed this project not to avoid vanity, for vanity did not prompt me to begin it. Hume devoted most of his life to the letters, and most of my life has been devoted to politics. My political defeats and failures are hardly a reason for being vain. While writing my autobiography, I intend to adhere to Hume's guidance and be 'short' when discussing my personal affairs. I want to concentrate on describing for the benefit of modern youth the social and political changes I have witnessed during my life.

People who write autobiographies usually begin by describing their childhood, but I have almost forgotten mine. Benjamin Franklin begins his autobiography by saying [to his son]: 'I have ever had a pleasure in obtaining any little anecdotes of my ancestors. You may remember the inquiries I made among the remains of my relations when you were with me in England, and the journey I undertook for that purpose'.[2]

I am not able to do this, nor would I wish to do this. I will simply sketch various events that made a deep impression on me when I was young.

The first thing is that I was a fatherless child.

In 1921, I was at a supper-party in Guangdong. Chen Jiongming said: 'People say you have organised an "association for attacking fathers." Is that true?'

---

1 Hume 1854, p. xiii.
2 Franklin 1953, p. 3.

I replied in a serious vein: 'My sons have the qualification to organise such an association, I do not even have the proper qualifications to join, since as a child I had no father'. Some of the people sitting around me laughed energetically, others stared silently at me as if they did not understand what I had said, or perhaps could not make out my dialect or thought my answer begged the question.

Several months after I was born my father died. When I was young, we lived in Huaining county in Anhui province, in the town of Huaining. I had a stern grandfather on my father's side, an able and affectionate mother, and an indulgent elder brother.

My relatives called my grandfather 'Old White Beard'. If the children cried, as soon as someone said 'Old White Beard' is coming, everyone would shut up and not dare to make another whimper. 'Old White Beard' had two perversities: he hated dirt and noise. If there was the slightest dirt in any part of the house, my mother and big sister would be in serious trouble. He did not permit the sound of footsteps in the house. When my second elder sister was young she did not understand the consequences of making noise, so each time she walked noisily she was beaten fiercely. She never understood why. Even my maternal grandmother would have to sneak by him on tiptoe like a thief, for fear of his cursing.

This grandfather who was bent on cleanliness and quietness was an opium-smoker. For him to smoke opium at home was not fulfilling. He frequently went downtown to a filthy, noisy opium-den. Only then could he satisfy his desires. So what happened to his passion for cleanliness and quietness? One answer is that men have a gregarious nature; even when smoking opium, they gather together for enjoyment. Then there is the mutual enjoyment in lighting up. For the smoker, everything outside his artistic world is forgotten. Perhaps others will think I am joking. I fear only my friend Liu Shuya[3] will be able to understand this philosophy.

From the time I was five until I was seven or eight, 'Old White Beard' was my teacher. Although I was just a little intelligent, I suffered even for that. When my elder brother read, my grandfather paid little attention to him; he picked me out, and on account of his own pride, forced me to read the *Four Books* and the *Five Classics* in just one year. I finished the *Four Books* and the *Classic of Poetry*, and looked ahead with trepidation to the *Zuo Zhuan*. Fortunately, my grandfather did not understand the importance of the three books on propriety,

---

3 Liu Wendian (*zi* Shuya), 1893–1958. His native town was Hefei in Anhui. He studied in Japan, and was a pupil of Zhang Bingling (Zhang Taiyan). Beginning in 1929, he taught in the Chinese literature department at Tsinghua University.

or the struggle to read them under his guidance would have driven me to death. If I failed to memorise the whole lesson he became terribly angry and slapped me. What made him most angry was not my deficient memory but my failure to cry out, however hard he hit me. He would draw back his lips, revealing his gritted teeth, his face contorted with rage, so that everyone was terrified. He would swear at me with a mixture of anger and sadness, 'You little bastard, when you grow up you will become an evil robber and a cold blooded killer. That will be a real tragedy for our family'.

I don't know how many tears my mother shed on account of my beatings and my grandfather's predictions. But my mother was not as pessimistic about me as he. She always used kind words to encourage me: 'My little child, you must study conscientiously, and when you have completed your studies, you can become a *juren*[4] and obtain merit for your father. Your father studied all his life, but he never passed the *juren* examination, that was a great burden for him right through until his death'. When I saw my mother crying, I too cried. My mother would wipe my tears and rebuke me, saying: 'You are mischievous. You don't cry when your grandfather beats you, but now you cry for no reason'. My mother's tears carried more authority than my grandfather's stick: even now I am not afraid of people beating and killing, but I cannot bear them crying, especially women.

My mother's tears drove me to study diligently. We know that many children do not cry when beaten, but even if they don't become persons of note, they do not necessarily turn into robbers. My grandfather's prediction was evidently wrong; I have not become a robber, and I detest killing more than anything. However, in this age we still cannot avoid war. Even though killing in revolutionary wars is bloody and barbaric, such wars have a progressive function. Other types of killing, like political assassination and legal murder as rationalised by capital punishment, merely draw out people's cruel and barbaric natures and have no beneficial effect. There is no need to discuss other kinds of killing.

I don't know much about my father's character. As for my mother's character, she was capable, generous, and a champion of justice, ever ready to take up cudgels against injustice. Our relatives and clan called her 'the heroine'. Actually she was a complaisant person for she lacked firmness when confronting evil. Two incidents drawn from my memory bear out this weakness.

A relative of my grandfather's generation was head of our clan. In the local dialect of Huaining, he was a *fangzun* (a venerable). Among the gentry in the town of Lushui he had a good reputation and was considered a pillar of

---

4 An academic degree-holder under the imperial system.

society. My mother greatly respected him; the feelings of the younger generation go without saying. One year, probably around the 12th year of the Guangxu reign [1886], a big flood broke the Guangji dyke and the entire Lushui area near Huaining was inundated. The clan-head told my mother about the bitter experiences of her neighbours. Following this tale, he asked for a loan to help the suffering members of his family. My mother was respectful but never responded to his question. After he had gone, I said to her: 'Our family is poor, but we are still better off than the families ruined by the floods. Why won't you give him anything?' My mother wrinkled her brow and said nothing. I understood her temperament. If she did not want to talk, there was no point in insisting. My doubts bothered me. My mother often pawned clothing to get money for people in distress. She always told us not to look down on the poor and didn't let us curse beggars. So why was she so unwilling to give money to the clan-head for the victims of the flood, when she was usually so respectful towards him?

Not until a few years later did I come to understand our clan-head's behaviour. Whenever a dispute had to be handled within the clan or the neighbourhood, everyone would ask him to determine what was right and what was wrong. In making his decisions he did not distinguish between relatives and outsiders. His sole standard of judgement was the number of chickens or the amount of rice, opium, or money he received from the litigants. Because of this, sometimes his own relatives were declared guilty. The villagers in the area praised him as an upright and unselfish member of the gentry!

Whenever the dykes needed repairing or money was required for flood-victims, he was always more enthusiastic than anyone in soliciting contributions. In the depths of the winter or the oppressive heat of summer, he would scurry around performing meritorious service for the people. But the sections of the dykes under his management were in worse repair than those under any other clan-head. Maybe he thought that if he seriously attended to the problem, he would lose revenue and the chance for further charity collections if the dykes held, and thus suffer financial loss. His conscience could not permit such unfairness to himself. Only after I realised these things did I understand why my mother had furrowed her brow and remained silent: she was well aware of the behaviour of this clan-head, yet she treated him with great respect – is this not a weakness?

The clan-head had an underling whose job was to carry out assignments of clan-elders, arrest the clan's unfilial sons and grandsons, and send them to the ancestral hall for punishment. He was also a messenger from Hades – he brought news of death from the king of hell. He often came to our house to say he had seen our ancestors in hell and they had asked him to ask us to pay him to buy spirit-money to burn for them. My mother respectfully entertained him and gave him the money he requested. It is obvious what happened with it. After he left, my mother would always say that she did not believe his wild talk.

One day he came to our home and began conducting a séance with the spirit-world. His mouth opened, and he yawned, went stiff, and fell over onto the bed. He uttered nonsense that no one could understand. They were probably the dialect of the dead in Fengdu [where spirits go when they leave the body, before entering hell]. I was overcome with rage and went out and called together a dozen children from our compound and the neighbourhood. I told them to rush in through both doors shouting that a fire had broken out. He stopped his noises and hurried back to earth, issuing small yawns. With his eyes shut he asked, 'Is there really a fire?' My mother, standing near the bed smiling, said yes. He instantly replied, 'that's just the way it was. I already heard about it in the underworld'. I stood aside, bent double and with my shoulders hunched, suppressing a laugh with my hand. My mother grabbed a broom of chicken-feathers and drove us away. Also trying not to laugh, she said 'you are such little devils'. But she still treated this man reverently, with wine and meat, and helped him buy spirit-money. This is another example of my mother's toleration of evil.

Some people praise me for being a righteous man who cannot tolerate evil, others criticise me for being hot-tempered. Maybe I am hot-tempered, but it is not entirely true that I am a righteous man who can tolerate no evil. In this respect, I am like my mother: I lack resolution, and sometimes I too tolerate evil. Because of this, I have ruined many important political affairs, and have been used badly. Although I understand this, I am unable to reform. The main reason is I am unsure about politics and lack resolve. My mother's character must have influenced me.

Fortunately, I was not at all influenced by my mother's respect for the examination system. But we should not excessively blame the older generation for their foolish beliefs – especially women who have received no education, either old-style or modern.

The traditional examination system not only made people vain but controlled almost every aspect of their lives. Only if one became a degree-holder by examination could one become a big official. (At the time, people who paid contributions to become officials were not highly thought of, and could achieve only petty rank; the big officials had to take the orthodox road through the examination system to obtain a degree and thus a high post. As for foreign PhDs, they were as yet unknown in China.) Once you became a big official, you could make a lot of money; once you were rich, you could invest in land; once you were a landlord (at that time wealth did not yet derive from banking and trade) you could build a big house (western-style houses had not yet been introduced), swindle the oppressed, and glorify your ancestors and family.

When a child was born, only Chinese in the foreign parts of Shanghai would think to flatter the parents by predicting that it might become a comprador. Outside Shanghai, neighbours would say the infant will become a district-graduate, and maybe a provincial or even a metropolitan graduate; and maybe even a 'scholar of the realm'. Mothers-in-law would judge their daughters-in-law entirely on the basis of whether their sons achieved a respectable rank and position. If they did achieve high rank, the parents-in-law would respect the daughter-in-law and the son; otherwise, the daughter-in-law and the son would be treated with contempt and even the servants would look down on them. We need not even consider the possibility of poor peasants' children winning higher degrees; they would not even dream of passing the lowest examination. If a family employed the power of nine oxen and two tigers to support their peasant son for several years at school or with a tutor, he would be revered as a genius, no matter how little he knew – even if he could only write eighty out of one hundred characters. If he went to the city in the company of his teacher and took the district examination, and if he managed to write several hundred characters of complete nonsense, then even if he failed so miserably that his name was not even on the list at the end of the first section of the examination, everyone would treat him with respect when he returned home; even the vicious and evil landlords would treat such a peasant's family better. In our region, there was the saying:

> Even though you go to the examination-hall and only fart,
> By gaining glory for your ancestors, you will have done your part.

If the son of a peasant passed the district examination, he went straight to heaven; he also laid the foundation for a future life of merciless squeezing of others, as a landlord and member of the gentry. He would never again have to worry about food. So no matter whether in the city or the country, people who failed the examinations again and again would blame it on the geomancer who had told them where to bury their ancestors. They would disinter the bodies and rebury them in more propitious locations; this was how the disciples of Confucius practised filial piety, by enhancing their name in order to bring glory to their ancestors. In such an atmosphere, people – especially women – saw preparing for the examinations as a sacred occupation.

Although my mother received no education, she knew all the orthodox educational tags – loyalty, filial piety, chastity, and decency. I thank her for never teaching us these sayings. She only wanted us to take the examinations and become successful at least at the provincial level to bring honour to our father. When my brother passed the district examination, my mother was very happy. I, however, was both happy and fearful. Happy because my mother was happy; fearful because I would soon have to study the lifeless eight-legged essay[5] myself and prepare for the torture of examination.

After my grandfather died, I had several tutors, but I was satisfied with none of them. When I reached the age of twelve or thirteen *sui*, my elder brother taught me. He knew I disliked the eight-legged essay. Apart from studying the classics, I learned the selections of prose in the *Zhaoming wenxuan*, an anthology from the sixth century. When I began reading them, I developed a slight headache, but after a while I acquired a taste for them and grew even more disdainful of the eight-legged essay. This caused my indulgent brother much embarrassment, for while he was under strict orders from our mother to teach me the eight-legged essay and prepare me for the examinations, he knew how much I loathed it.

By the 22nd year of Guangxu [1896] I was already seventeen *sui*, and it was only one or two months to the district examination. My brother could hold back no further: 'The examinations are about to start, don't you think you should study the eight-legged essay?' I remained silent. He knew my temperament – my silence expressed acknowledgement, not opposition. Cheerfully, he gave me Lu De's examination essays, which were useful in preparing for the *xiucai* degree. I listened inattentively, for I was still thinking about the *Zhaoming wenxuan*. After a while, my brother noticed I could not stomach Lu De, so for the next lesson he used the eight-legged essay styles of Jin Huang and Yuan Mei. I found their writing styles vaguely interesting, but even so they repulsed me. My brother could think of no other method to use on his intractable pupil, so he gave up and let things take their course. Although honourable and honest, he must have thought up a story to tell my mother, for I could see from her cheerful face that she thought I was hard at work mastering the eight-legged essay.

With my proficiency in the eight-legged essay such as it was, I was bound to come bottom in the first and second preliminary examinations for the *xiucai* degree. At the third and final *xiucai* examination, I discovered the question had been chosen by the Director of Education. It was a selection of incomplete phrases from Mencius: 'We will have enough fish and turtle to eat.... Wood ...'. A crazy question deserved a crazy answer. I wrote out a list of obscure terms for birds, animals, and bamboo drawn from the *Wenxuan*, padded out with absurd

---

5   An essay rigidly divided into eight sections, mastery of which was necessary to pass the imperial examinations. A byword in modern China for pedantry and empty rhetoric.

characters from the Kangxi Dictionary. I paid no attention to coherence; whether a cow's head could be matched with a horse's mouth, or whether or not there was a connection between the start and the conclusion.

Just as I was tidying up my examination materials and preparing to hand in my paper, the Provincial Director of Education, a big fellow from Shandong called Mr Li, personally came over to take my examination booklet. (I and several others were sitting at the front of the hall, either because we were young and had achieved first place in the county and prefectural exams, or because we had already done well in the preparatory examination in the classics. Since we were sitting in front of his desk, it made sense for him to collect our papers personally. I hadn't signed up for the children's examination and hadn't shone in the county and prefectural exams, but when I entered the examination-hall I had seen a note on my exam booklet telling me to sit at the front of the room, so I knew I had passed in classics. Needless to say, the compiler of the *Wenxuan* should take the credit.) Mr Li tore the seal from my paper, read a few lines, and said: 'Stand still, don't rush off'. This scared me. I had no idea what kind of calamity I had rushed into. Skimming the essay, he looked me up and down and asked me how old I was and why I hadn't entered the children's examination. I told him my age. He nodded and said: 'You're still young. Go home, be diligent'.

I went home and showed my brother a draft of my essay. After reading it, he frowned and stayed silent for a full hour. I had only done the exam for mother's sake. I hadn't taken it seriously. When I saw how disappointed my brother was, I started to have regrets. No one would ever have thought that my muddled essay would deceive the Provincial Director of Education, but he gave me first place in the examination. This made me despise the system even more. When the news came, my mother was so happy she nearly cried.

'People's power of observation is shallow'. This criticism was even admitted by the natives of Huaining. When a catastrophe occurred, relatives and neighbours would exaggerate it more than one hundred-fold. When someone became a little prosperous, they would make his wealth seem more than ten times greater than it was. Our Chen clan was insignificant in Huaining. The gentry always looked down on us. In the history of our clan, my father was the first degree-holder, a *xiucai*. His younger brother also obtained a degree, as *juren*. Now that we two brothers were *xiucai*, not only did the gentry pay special attention to us but they came up with a lot of nonsense about how the *fengshui* of our ancestors' graves had been propitious, how the pagoda in the suburbs of Huaining stood erect like a writing brush in front of the burial-plot of the Chen clan, and how my mother had supernatural dreams on the eve of my birth.

It never occurred to them that later I would frighten them all by becoming a member of Kang Youwei's party, a revolutionary, and a Communist, instead of climbing up the examination ladder to become a provincial graduate, a metropolitan graduate, and a scholar of the realm, as they had pictured. Most interesting were the several rich families who suddenly noticed this penniless, fatherless child. Racing to be first, fearful of being last, they sent matchmakers to discuss betrothal. This was the social cause for my mother's great happiness. Since my mother was happy, I too was happy. What I feared was the ordeal of the Jiangnan provincial exams, due to catch up with me the following year.

Although we had lost the war with Japan [1895], people were still as if in a dream, and considered the Jiangnan provincial examination a very important affair. The torture I had imagined was far less than I actually experienced in the examination stalls. However, I knew it was unavoidable and decided to make the best of it by working hard to obtain the second degree and satisfy my mother's wish; afterwards, I could do some serious and worthwhile work. So in the year leading up to the exam I rigorously prepared for it, although I was often sick. Fortunately, I had some interest in two areas – the classics and applied knowledge. I even forced myself to study the eight-legged essay. As for writing styles, I enjoyed imitating the calligraphy texts on memorial tablets. My brother advised me to practise the official and formal form of writing, but I had already decided to opt out of the struggle to become an official after the exam, so I found it hard to focus on studying and considered the bureaucratic forms a pointless exercise. The relationship between my brother and me was extremely good. Although we had different viewpoints on everything and I rejected all his advice, I maintained a friendly attitude towards him so as to preserve our close relations.

It was probably around the seventh month of the 23rd reign year of Guangxu [July–August, 1897] that I had to leave my mother for the first time and travel to Nanjing for the provincial examinations. I was accompanied by my elder brother, his teacher, the teacher's brothers, and my elder brother's fellow-candidates. We planned to travel by steamship, which was faster than by junk. At the time, people travelling to Nanjing for the examinations liked to go by junk, not to preserve the traditional way, but to make a killing: on the mast they would raise a yellow flag with large characters saying 'by imperial decree we are travelling to the Jiangnan provincial examinations'. The guards at the custom-points knew the students were smuggling goods, but didn't dare check. The students were even more proud and fearless than the Japanese smugglers of today. We, on the contrary, did not want to make fortunes in that way and can be considered upright!

I was leaving home for the first time, but the rest of our group of gentlemen had been in Nanjing for previous provincial examinations. On reaching the city, the view of the big walled gates, for example the Phoenix Gate, was truly a great awakening for a country-boy like me. I was proud of Anqing, a provincial city of nine *li* and 13 steps in circumference. When I viewed these gates, Anqing changed in my imagination into a small frontier town. As I approached the city on the back of a donkey, I imagined that the street-markets and buildings of Nanjing would be unbelievably beautiful, and because I had heard that Shanghai was even more prosperous than Nanjing, I imagined that the gates of Shanghai would be even higher and wider. But, when I saw the city, I was disappointed. Although the streets in the northern section were far more level and wider than Anqing's, the buildings were just as small and cracked. Nanjing's only special feature was its size. The buildings were ramshackle, and the western-style buildings that would later be built with the blood of the people did not yet exist.

Both outside and inside the city only one form of transport operated – the donkey, which could be heard running along the roads – the 'ling-ling' of the bells round its neck harmonising with the 'clip-clop' of its four hooves. To the person riding, these sounds were like poetry. At the time, rickshaws and horse-carts were not used. Nor were automobiles, today called 'tigers in the city' by the Cantonese and cursed as 'coffins' by the residents of Nanjing. In the southern sections of Nanjing, the main streets were as narrow as Anqing's. The expansion of the small streets into large thoroughfares had not yet begun.

Because of the large indemnity paid after the Sino-Japanese war, prices were rising daily. The population of Nanjing at the time had increased temporarily by more than 10,000. Rice sold at 50 or 80 cash a pint; pork sold at 100 cash a pound. Everywhere people were complaining about this. Now, when I recall the situation, you could still say the people of Nanjing were free and happy. When they looked at one another, at least they did not suspect each other of being pick-pockets or secret policemen. Does this condition result from the evils of materialism and revolution? Absolutely not. It has other causes.

Our group of upright gentlemen spent the first night in Nanjing on the floor, on the upper storey of the home of a friend's family. On the second day we rose early. Three remained in the house to look after the baggage while the others went to look for a place to stay. Of the three baggage-watchers, one was my elder brother's teacher. He was the highest authority in our group of upright gentlemen, so naturally it was inconvenient for him to go out on this expedition – he would lose his dignity. The second was my elder brother, who was not good at expressing himself. I was too young to take responsibility for finding a house, so I was the third watcher. In the afternoon, the others found a place to stay, and we immediately moved. As soon as we entered our new room, the upright gentlemen who had gone to look for lodgings opened their eyes wide, looked at each other, and exclaimed, 'This room is expensive and bad, we've been deceived!' I was confused. Hadn't they personally seen this house? Why did they suddenly feel they had been deceived? Overhearing a conversation among fellow candidates three or four days later, I discovered what had happened. When these upright gentlemen had first arrived at the house, they had noticed an attractive girl sat sewing on the windowsill of the landlord's room, but when they moved in, this 'little angel' had disappeared with the wind. It seems engaging a beautiful girl to attract boarders was a ploy used by Nanjing landlords. Some of the girls used as decoys were the landlord's relatives, others were local prostitutes. We were not the only ones taken in.

Although many of the candidates were stung, so were some landlords. If they really did have a young woman in their house, or if they were careless and left salted fish and dried meat hanging in the kitchen or under the eaves, the girl and the provisions were wont to vanish without trace. The candidates were protected by their exalted status as 'intelligentsia', so the landlords did not dare charge them with crimes like seduction or theft. While they were out shopping, if the candidates had the chance they would shoplift, concealing objects in their sleeves. If the shopkeeper saw this and protested, the culprits would say, 'We have received the Imperial order to enter the provincial examinations: insulting us as thieves is insulting the Emperor'. But heaven is high and the Emperor is far away, so these taunts didn't frighten the merchants.

What the merchants feared were our numbers. Any affront could stir the candidates into a mêlée. Passing students, even strangers, would jump into the fray. The merchants knew the real reason the other candidates joined in was not to help in the battle but to steal as much as they could in the confusion. So the merchant's loss would be even greater. Even if the magistrate was informed of the theft, he could do nothing. The influx of students and their escorts temporarily increased the population by ten thousand or more, and the average person spent fifty yuan, so the city's income rose by 500,000 yuan and temporary stores spread everywhere, especially around Zhuangyuan. As long as the merchants made money, they did not consider theft so terrible, even if it meant they had to take some abuse.

But these erudite and rowdy gentlemen lost all their toughness when whoring in Nanjing's Diaoyu Alley. There they proclaimed they were poor students and begged the madam for a discount. Perhaps they thought they had to be like this or lose the quality of refinement so basic to the scholar-class.

Our room was shabby and expensive. But the story of my being cheated along with the others was nothing compared to the problem of relieving my bowels – even now I groan when I think about it. We didn't have a common toilet in the room and the gentlemen had never used a women's night stool; they simply went outside the front door to relieve themselves. I remember on the outskirts of town the gates of all the houses were covered with droppings – ours was not the only one.

Our elder teacher was a typical orthodox Confucian scholar. Whenever he spoke, it was to talk about Confucius and Mencius, or Chen Yi and Zhu Xi.[6] Not only had he read the utterances of Song dynasty Neo-Confucianism, but he also knew about the 'proprieties concerning the sexes' and Mencius's saying that 'men and women should not get too close'. Even so, he went out in daylight to an empty place by the side of the road and relieved himself. Whenever a girl passed by, he pretended he had not seen her. Pranksters in our rooming house would shout out the eight-legged essay about Confucian principles: rites and propriety, purity and shame, upright mind and refined body. If they saw a young girl approaching, he would run out and let down his trousers to get ready to empty his bowels; it seemed he couldn't wait to show off his precious cargo.

As for me, I always put it off until evening. Only then did I dare go out to defecate. Because of this I would sometimes step right into a pile of it. This was unpleasant enough, but I had to endure the taunts of the others who ridiculed me for being hypocritical and asked why I didn't go out to relieve myself during the day instead of returning at night with my feet covered in mess and stinking up the room. Was I a hypocrite? I was experienced in worldly things and at times masturbated fiercely, and probably would not have refused the chance to make love to a woman. But to display my precious load to a strange girl on the street was, to me, disgusting.

On the seventh day of the eighth month we prepared to enter the examination hall. On my back I carried an examination basket, books, writing materials, food, provisions, a cooking stove, and an oil-cloth. This exhausted me. If my elder brother hadn't helped by fetching my examination scroll, I would have been crushed to death in the crowd. Two-and-a-half of my three souls fled in fright as I entered the examination pen. Each alley of more than one hundred feet was sectioned off into one hundred or so small stalls, each the size of a policeman's guard-house. The ceilings were so low that a tall person had to stoop. This is the so-called 'low room' spoken of with such pride by the big men who have made it through the examination system. Three sides of this narrow stall consisted of an uneven brick-wall that had never been whitewashed. The inside was full of cobwebs and dust, and difficult to sweep clean. I entered, sat

---

6   Neo-Confucian philosophers.

down, and created a desk by placing a piece of board in front of me. I had to sleep in this sitting position.

Each aisle had one or two vacant stalls that served as toilets, known as 'excrement rooms'. After the candidate had taken the first examination, his name would be posted up on the list of those who had passed, unless he had been stupid enough to confess on the examination sheet about his immoral acts or had smudged it with ink. If assigned to an 'excrement room' for the second examination, he would have to put up with a terrible stink for three days, and everyone would say he deserved this punishment for some disgraceful act committed in a previous existence.

The weather in Nanjing was still terribly hot. Everyone had brought with them an oil-cloth that they hung up to block out the sun. The stalls were strung along a high wall. In between was a narrow path barely wide enough to pass through, and above a strip of sky you could no longer see when the oil-cloths went up. The air stagnated. Everyone hung a cooking stove on the wall. The heat of the cooking and of the sun turned the long passageway into a fire alley. I didn't know anything about cooking, so after the three examinations, lasting nine days, I had eaten nothing but half-cooked, overcooked, or lumpy noodles.

One incident made a deep impression on me. At the first examination was a fat candidate from Xuzhou who was stark naked except for a pair of broken shoes and a big pig-tail coiled over his head. In his hand he held an examination paper. Walking up and down the fire alley, with his large head and his small member wagging to and fro, he read out his favourite essay, in a strange drawl. Reaching his favourite place, he would slap his thigh, lift his thumb, and say, 'Great! This time I will make it!' Staring at him, I began to think about the whole strange phenomenon of the examination system, and how my country and its people would suffer when these animals won positions of power. I started questioning the selection of men of talent by examination. It was like a circus performed once every few years. Was it not as defective as every other system in the nation? I concluded that the writings of men like Liang Qichao in the *Shiwu* newspaper made sense. Resolving my problems in this way caused me to turn from being a disciple of the examination system into an advocate of the party of Kang Youwei and Liang Qichao.[7] This meditation of a couple of hours determined my activities for more than ten years. So although I had unwillingly taken the examination, I received unforeseen benefits from it.

---

7   Reformist advocates of constitutional monarchy.

A Consciousness Awakes

Zheng Chaolin

Source: An Oppositionist for Life: Memoirs of the Chinese Revolutionary Zheng Chaolin.

In the eighth year of the Chinese Republic, more easily remembered as 1919, Chinese became collectively aware and my own small consciousness awoke.

If I had written these memoirs ten or more years ago, in the early 1930s, I would have had no need to remind readers that the May Fourth Movement broke out in 1919. But few of today's youth, for whom this book is written, know when the May Fourth Movement happened, let alone what it meant.

In 1919, I was nineteen years old. In April, the sixth class of Fujian's Ninth Provincial Middle School (in Longyan) finished its studies and was granted special leave so that we students could go home and await the final examinations in June. I returned to Zhangping and relaxed. Sometime in May, an old gentleman came to our home to chat with my father. He said that there was trouble in Beijing among the students, that they were beating people, burning houses, and boycotting lectures. After he had finished speaking, he shook his head and sighed. This old gentleman was one of just a handful of people in our town who frequently read a newspaper. My father did not read one, nor did I. Even at school, I rarely went to the reading room. It held one or two Fuzhou newspapers, but as far as I know, there were none from Beijing or Shanghai, and even the Fuzhou ones were usually out-of-date. In those days, few students ever went to the reading room to look at newspapers.

There were three primary schools in Zhangping, one run by the county-government, one by a clan, and one by evangelists. There were several middle school graduates in town, together with five or six people – like me – waiting to graduate. There was a student association, but it had not met for a long time. We barely responded to the hurricane from Beijing. Other places were erupting with lecture-strikes, demonstrations, and anti-Japanese consumer boycotts. Our schoolmates left behind in Longyan wrote to tell us that they had led a demonstration of all the local primary schools and had set up a checkpoint for Japanese goods outside town on the road to Zhangzhou. They had also invaded the Chamber of Commerce, where they had banged on the table, brandished teacups, and sworn at the chairman. But we students in Zhangping had barely lifted a finger. True, pupils of the New People's Primary School run by evangelists outside the West Gate marched into town on one occasion, and the pastor apparently gave each a bag of sweets and made them promise never to buy Japanese products again. But that was the church-school.

When I went to take the examinations in June, the movement in Longyan had already died down. Our schoolmates told those of us who had gone home some anecdotes about what had happened, that student-pickets were still active outside town, that the student association was still meeting, but that it was not holding demonstrations, boycotting classes, or causing trouble. Even so, the climate had changed dramatically in those two months. Students who normally never stirred were now active, students who never spoke were now voluble, the reading room was crowded, current events were common knowledge, and most important of all, the students themselves now controlled their own association. Pinned to the association notice-board were letters from people who had gone off to study in the big cities.

That was May Fourth as I experienced it. At the time, I knew nothing about May Fourth other than the anti-Japanese boycott, the attacks on traitors, the refusal to sign the treaty,[1] and things of that sort. It is unlikely that anyone else in Zhangping was any better informed. And Longyan? Had people in Longyan read *Xin qingnian* ('New Youth') and been carried along by the new tide? I cannot say. But even if some had, they were a rarity.

After graduating from middle school, I became unaccountably depressed. I wanted to fly, I wanted to quit the narrow cage of Zhangping, even of Fujian. While still at school, I had resolved along with several others to go to Beijing and enrol at normal school – not because I felt some 'sacred calling' to become a scholar but because I had heard that normal schools demanded no tuition fees or board expenses and even provided a small subsidy, so that one ended up paying scarcely more than I had paid at middle school. But my father could not help me, and neither he nor I could get our hands on any other source of funds. A Longyan student who had gone ahead sent me a postcard from Shanghai describing his visit to the New World Recreation Centre. Once again I became agitated. Just at that moment, something entirely unexpected happened.

---

1 In 1914, Japan seized German-controlled territory in Shandong. In 1917, Britain, France, and Italy secretly agreed to support Japan's claim to this territory, and in 1918, the Government in Beijing secretly acquiesced in this; in 1919, the Paris Peace Conference agreed to transfer German rights in China to Japan. On 4 May 1919, three thousand students demonstrated in Beijing against this 'national betrayal', and beat a pro-Japanese official. There followed a nationwide movement of strikes, lecture-strikes, and anti-Japanese boycotts. On 28 June, the Beijing Government gave in to the protest-movement and refused to sign the Peace Treaty with Germany. So the May Fourth Movement in its narrowest sense had been brought to a successful end. In its broadest sense, May Fourth was a movement of cultural renewal and revolution.

The county education inspector in Zhangping, a man called Chen Hua, was a friend of my grandfather. My father and I were both put out because I could not go to Beijing. Luckily, Mr Chen intervened to dispel our worries. Mr Chen was anyway against me going to Beijing, because he thought that the climate in the colleges there was too turbulent. One day, he told me that Commander Chen had issued a proclamation ordering the local magistrate, a man called Xiong, to send two students to study in France, where half their expenses would be met from public funds.

Commander Chen was, of course, Chen Jiongming, Commander-in-Chief of the 'Guangdong Army Relieving Fujian'. Sometime later, Chiang Kai-shek's Nanjing Government promulgated a decree amnestying political offenders, but the 'Communist bandits' and Jiongming were on the list of those pardoned. Chen Jiongming's crime was to have incited his subordinate Ye Ju to surround Generalissimo Sun Yat-sen's headquarters in Guangzhou and force him aboard a battleship.[2] But all these things happened several years after the events I am describing. In 1919, Chen Jiongming, far from being a traitor to the Guomindang, commanded its sole armed force. (In reality the Guomindang did not then exist outside a few factions around Sun Yat-sen.) When Guangdong was occupied by the Guangxi Army, the Guangdong Army (which had a revolutionary history) was unable to hold out in its native province and was forced to add the words 'Relieving Fujian' to its battle-standard and snatch a corner of Fujian from the Beiyang warlords.[3] It occupied the old Tingzhou-Zhangzhou-Longyan district and set up its general command at Zhangzhou.

Chen Jiongming was a new-style army man[4] who preached socialism and even anarchism. As soon as he got to Zhangzhou, he built carriageways in the city, opened a park, and started running athletics meetings and publishing a daily newspaper. Rickshaw-pullers were banned from the highway; a stone obelisk was placed in the park inscribed with the words 'Freedom', 'Equality', 'Fraternity', and 'Mutual Aid'. Here, the anarchist influence of Wu Zhihui and Li Shizeng is discernible. To chime in with Wu and Li's work-study programme,[5]

---

2 In June 1922, troops under Chen Jiongming, who had previously supported Sun Yat-sen, surrounded Sun's residence. Sun then escaped to a gunboat anchored off Guangzhou and remained there for more than two months, after which he left for Hong Kong.

3 Beiyang is the Qing dynasty name for the northern coastal provinces of Liaoning, Hebei, and Shandong. The Beiyang warlords were a military clique split into the Zhili and Anhui factions.

4 In the last years of the Qing (1644–1911), China began to modernise its armies. New-style officers became a mainstay of the radical movement that toppled the Qing in 1911.

5 In June 1915, Li Shizeng, Cai Yuanpei, Wu Zhihui and others founded the Society for Frugal Study by Means of Labour (in French, the *Société rationnelle des étudiants-travailleurs en*

Chen Jiongming ordered each county magistrate in the region under his jurisdiction to send two or three people to France to study. That instruction was the origin of Fujian's programme of officially subsidised study abroad.

Wu and Li conceived the work-study programme at the end of the First World War. During the War, France was short of labour, so one hundred thousand or so Chinese workers were recruited to go there. Financial assistance to Chinese studying in France dried up, so students, too, started looking for jobs in French factories. The French workers, through their sacrifices, had achieved far better working conditions than in China; the Chinese students were happy to take advantage of this. So the idea arose that Chinese students going to France would work half their time in factories and use what they earned to subsidise their studies in the other half. Li Shizeng stayed in France to organise this programme. He helped people enter the country, find work, and find a school. In a Shanghai newspaper, Wu Zhihui, already back in China, published *Cuoan kezuo tanhua* ('Random Talks on Different Subjects'), part of which consisted of propaganda for the idea of work-study. *Random Talks* also appeared separately as a pamphlet; it sold well. According to estimates, because of the fall in the value of the French franc, you could study in France on an income of just six hundred Chinese silver dollars, even without working.

So, on the basis of these estimates Chen Jiongming asked each student's family to raise $300 and got the county magistrate to contribute the rest.

On the eighteenth day of the seventh lunar month, I and another student boarded a boat outside Zhangping's Middle Water-Gate. My father, my third uncle, and my second younger brother had come to send me off; it was the last time I ever saw them. Students from several different counties in Fujian met up at Zhangzhou, where they were welcomed by Chen Jiongming at his headquarters in the former Daotai Yamen. There was a group photograph and a banquet with speeches, including one by Zhu Zhixin, but I have no memory of either event.

Altogether more than thirty of us sailed to Hong Kong to await the boat for France. After a few days, Chen Jiongming's representative in Guangzhou, Huang Qiang, invited us up to Guangzhou, where we stayed at the Zengbu Technology College, of which he was principal. He got a local woman to teach us French. We studied it for three weeks. While we were in Guangzhou, Fujianese members of the National Parliament (among them Lin Sen) held a valedictory meeting in our honour.

France). The aim of the society was to help poor students study in France by working part-time in factories.

Finally, on 4 November, we boarded a *messager maritime*, the Paul Lecat. This ship had started out from Shanghai and already had one to two hundred students aboard. By the time fifty or sixty more of us from Fujian and Guangdong had joined them, the fourth-class deck was full to bursting.

The thirty-three days aboard that ship sealed my fate. I experienced my personal May Fourth aboard that packet-liner.

Before climbing aboard, I had no idea that May Fourth meant anything other than patriotism. True, you could already buy new books and journals in Hong Kong and Guangzhou, but neither I nor my companions had bought any, and even if we had, it is unlikely that we would have read them. In Hong Kong, I had bought pirated Shidetang editions of *Laozi*, *Zhuangzi*, and *Liezi*, as well as Commercial Press editions of *Jingshi baijia zachao* ('An Anthology of Classics, Histories, and Other Writings') and a small-character edition of *Laocan youji* ('Travels of Laocan'). In addition, I had taken with me from home a Guoxue Fulun edition of Gong Dingan's *Collected Works* and a badly printed edition of *Bai xiang cipu* ('*Ci* Patterns'). These I took with me to France. Apart from *Laozi*, *Zhuangzi*, and *Liezi*, to which I shall return in a moment, I lost the rest in 1927, when Tang Shengzhi's troops occupied the Communist Party's Hubei Committee headquarters in Hankou.

At sea, I had my first real contact with students from 'across the river'.[6] I met a new sort of student, not just different from the sort I had known at home but also different from how I had imagined students from 'across the river', after reading *Liu dong waishi* ('Informal History of Chinese Students in Japan').[7] They were farsighted and intellectually lively. I learned many new things from listening to them: about many ancient and modern books I had never previously heard anyone mention, and that a new life awaited us in France, quite different from the one to which we had been accustomed. They showed me many newly published journals; I read a great many of their magazines. Some had large circulations. I was astonished at this, and at how little known were the Saturday Press group publications I usually read.

One day on the ship, I borrowed a magazine called *New Youth*. Leafing through it, I came across an article by someone called Chen Duxiu. I forget the title, but I remember the subject, Confucianism.

My Chinese language teacher at middle school, Mr Huang Baoshu, once set me an essay on making Confucianism the state religion. Naturally, I supported this idea of Kang Youwei's. Mr Huang covered my essay with circles and underlinings indicating approval, but when he met me later on the playing field, he said: 'Confucius was an educationalist, his theories should not be turned into

---

6 A Fujianese term meaning 'from other provinces'.
7 By Xiang Kairan.

a state religion'. That was the first time I realised that, among my old teachers, there was at least one who opposed making a cult of Confucius. Now, reading this article by Chen Duxiu, I thought to myself, 'It's that same discussion again'. Only when I read further did I realise that the article was completely against Confucius. Even in ancient times, learned people had opposed Confucius. For example, Zhuangzi had opposed him. But what annoyed me was the last sentence of the article. It said: If the way of Confucius is not blocked, the way of democracy will not flow; if the way of Confucius is not stopped, the way of democracy will not be open. 'If this is not blocked, that will not flow; if this is not stopped, that will not be open' was first said by Han Yu against Buddhism and Daoism in *Yuan dao* ('The Original Way').[8] Now, Chen Duxiu was using Han's text to attack Confucius! My first day aboard ship I started writing a diary. In it, I loudly cursed Chen Duxiu.

But on the outside, I showed no sign of all this inner dismay. None of my fellow Fujianese on board was interested in subjects of this sort. Some had never even heard of *The Original Way*. As for the students from 'across the river', the more I heard them talk, the quieter I fell. Actually, I was not a good talker, and in any case my 'Mandarin' was not yet fluent enough to handle complicated issues. But *New Youth* and other periodicals of that sort fascinated me, and the more I reacted against them, the more I wanted to borrow and read them, so gradually I lost interest in the classics I had previously valued. On 7 December, when we stepped ashore at Marseilles, I may have looked the same person that had stepped aboard in Hong Kong, but inwardly I had changed. Secretly, my consciousness had flowered; from now on, I was my own master. I was in charge of my own fate, I would never again be a mere link in the chain forged for me by my father, my teacher, and former generations of my lineage.

Perhaps I should mention some of the special factors that lay behind my coming to awareness. Needless to say, it was mainly a result of the epoch we were living in; the proof is that of the thirty-odd Fujianese who went to France, after six months or a year all but a handful had learned to write in the vernacular,[9] could talk intelligently about the new wave of thought, and in some cases had even joined the Communist Party. But to illustrate the

---

8 The article that Zheng here quotes, called 'Xianfa yu Kongjiao' ('The Constitution and Confucianism'), appeared in *Xin qingnian* ('New Youth'), Volume 2, no. 2, on 1 January 1916.

9 Before May Fourth, most writing was in classical Chinese, a dead language 'no longer spoken by the people'. The new literature movement that started in 1916 argued that writing should approximate to the spoken language. One of May Fourth's greatest victories was its 'literary revolution': the creation of 'a literature in the national language and a national language suitable for literature'. This switch to the vernacular also spread to the Chinese students in France.

seriousness and radical depth of the change from being a link in someone else's chain to becoming a new-style human being, I can do no better than take my own individual case as an example.

I was born the eldest son in an old-style landlord family, then in decline. For many generations, we had been scholars, addicted to the fragrance of the printed book. At school, I was by no means stupid. Naturally, my grandfather and my father vested their hopes in my young person. These hopes were typical of traditional landlord families in old China: to win merit by proceeding along the proper path, to go 'across the river' and be an official in a place or two, and then to return home to buy land and build a house. When the imperial examinations were abolished, these hopes were, of course, dashed. My grandfather said: 'You were born a few years too late, otherwise....' But the education I received was still the old-style education from the days before abolition. We were not only taught the text of the Four Books[10] but we studied Zhu Xi's annotation[11] of them, together with other commentaries. Of the Five Classics, we read the *Book of Songs*, the *Book of History*, the *Book of Changes*, and the *Spring and Autumn Annals*, but not the *Book of Rites*. We also studied Lin Yunming's *Guwen xiyi* ('Analysis of Ancient Literature'). Fortunately, we did not learn how to write eight-legged essays[12] or commentaries; instead, we just wrote a few discursive essays. In our county, there was already an official primary school (called county primary school following the founding of the Republic in 1911). My grandfather was an elder of the school and my father was treasurer and manager of its property, but curiously, they allowed neither me nor my brothers to attend. Even after three generations had graduated from the primary school, we and others in the same position were still enrolled in a local *sishu* or private academy. This was because it was considered that, in the primary school, we would not be in a position to acquire the 'necessary' knowledge. But in 1914, the primary school was reorganised and our *sishu* teacher Liu Cenzhong was appointed to teach Chinese there. In any case, by then our fathers and grandfathers had realised that the only way left of 'winning merit by proceeding along the proper path' lay in the primary school, so we followed our teacher. I went straight into the upper-third form and gradu-

---

10   The *Great Learning*, the *Analects*, the *Doctrine of the Mean*, and *Mencius*, that is, the basic texts of Confucian orthodoxy from the Song dynasty onwards.

11   Zhu Xi (1130–1200) wrote a new philosophical commentary on the Four Books to replace the old Han dynasty explanation. Zhu's school, called Neo-Confucianism in the West, became orthodox (and sterile) in the fourteenth and fifteenth centuries.

12   See fn. 5, p. 165.

ated after just six months. In 1915, I left home for the first time to go to middle school in Longyan, sixty kilometres from my native town. The Chinese teachers there were even more progressive, for they taught Yao Nai's *Guwen cilei zuan* ('Selections from Ancient Literature') and Wang Xianqian's *Xu guwen cilei zuan* ('Further Selections'). True, we still had to write descriptions, narratives, and essays in the old way, but we also dealt with issues of contemporary interest.

Even more important than formal education in either the old school or the new was the upbringing I received at home and in society. Consciously and unconsciously, directly and indirectly, people inculcate you with the worldview and morality requisite to their own small sphere, and so turn you into a fresh link in their chain.

Did I live up to their expectations? Generally speaking, I did. Both my grandfather and my father were satisfied with my progress. I was quiet and obedient, I was making headway, and I was always prepared to give in to their manipulation. I never refused to play any of the roles they forced on me. I thought it was quite natural to play these roles, as natural as dressing or eating. I could see no point in resisting, and, moreover, I was incapable of doing so. The only thing that dissatisfied them was my great reticence and inability to perform in the company of guests. My mother was unhappy to see me always with a book in my hand. I am convinced that what made me the person I am today had much to do with 'always having a book in my hand'.

Before my tenth birthday, I was no different from other children. I liked being naughty, I liked eating between meals, and I was particular about what clothes I wore. I was not especially keen on watching operas and listening to stories. But at eleven, I changed. One day that summer I was lying ill in bed in third uncle's house. I could not play with my cousins, and I was bored. Under the pillow I found a copy of the novel *Xue Rengui zhengdong* ('Xue Rengui Marches East'). Third uncle had been reading it. He had got as far as the fourth chapter and had rolled it up and put it under the pillow. I looked at it and was surprised to find that I could understand it, even though it contained many characters for vernacular words like 'this' or 'what' that I had never come across in the classics. I had heard the story many times and had often seen it on the stage, so I was able to guess characters I did not know. I could not put the volume down. I carried on reading late into the night, and by the end of the next day, I had finished all four volumes. So I started pestering third uncle for more novels, and later, I started buying them myself. They were old-fashioned books of the sort that go on for dozens and even hundreds of chapters. After that, I no longer had any interest in children's play, so I became steadily more alienated from my cousins and younger brothers.

Today there is nothing unusual in children reading novels, and even in my day, children in other parts of China read them. But in Zhangping, it was anything but usual. Everyone in that small place who had studied knew each other. For an eleven-year old child to read novels – lots of novels – and never to be without a book in his hand, for him to pay not the slightest attention to the hubbub outside or even to an opera performance but to hide indoors with his novel was quite unknown in my home-town. Very soon, my house had become a centre for books (meaning novels). Adults who read novels also borrowed my books.

Novels opened a new world to me: an unreal world, an imaginary world. I was so entranced by it that I forgot the real world. This created, and strengthened, my weakness: taciturnity, an inability to socialise, a general isolation from others. Novels stopped me having friends. My childhood playmates had already deserted me, and my schoolmates did not understand me, for they had read no novels, or not many. Most had only read the books set them by their teachers. But in another way, novels made me dissatisfied with reality, with the life and thinking of our circle, with the future others had marked out for me, and they even caused me to doubt the sacred tradition of the classics. I kept this dissatisfaction and these doubts completely to myself. However, my preference for Laozi and Zhuangzi[13] and my wish to leave for distant parts after graduating, including my wish to go to France, were probably manifestations of my inner feeling. (That was the first time I decided my own fate, previously I had let my father decide everything on my behalf, but now, he did not actually oppose my suggestion, though he was not enthusiastic about it.)

I should add that I did not just read novels. Though I started with novels, I later progressed to literary sketches, essays, the pre-Qin philosophers, and the dynastic histories. In sum, the sort of books that neither my teachers nor my schoolfriends read. On the contrary, I had an immediate prejudice against any book they recommended to me, and read it (if at all) only as a duty. So I acquired nearly all my knowledge from self-study; I looked on school as a place to sleep, eat, and take my leisure; I seriously believed that the education I got there was useless. Thinking back, that was a one-sided view. Since the books I read were different from those that others read – in sentiment, taste, and intellectual direction – it's not surprising that though I never sought conflict and had no enemies, I was incapable of dissolving into the community and had not a single friend. On the surface, I was slow and impassive, and I took things as

---

13   The Daoist teachings of Laozi and Zhuangzi are generally considered to be more creative and libertarian than the teachings of Confucius. They promote independence, spontaneity, freedom, and happiness as opposed to morality and rites.

they came, but I lived another life inside. Had I been born in another age, my imagination would gradually have been ground away by the millstones of the real world, I would sooner or later have compromised with the rest, I would have learned the social graces, I would have become good at receiving guests, I would have melted into my environment, I would gradually have stopped being a bookworm, and through slow tempering, I would have learned to become competent in everyday life, so that I could follow in my grandfather's and my father's footsteps and become a minor *shenshi*[14] in a minor county capital.

Luckily, May Fourth saved me. By May Fourth I do not mean the thrashing handed out to Zhang Zongxiang,[15] the lecture-strike, the boycott of Japanese goods, or the patriotic movement. Instead, I mean the May Fourth that sought the help of Messrs Science and Democracy to overthrow the Confucian family-shop.[16] I heaved aside the Confucianism that weighed like a nightmare on my shoulders, I even abandoned Laozi and Zhuangzi, those appendages of the Confucian Way. From then on, I lived only one life: what I did and what I thought were one and the same thing. I got there by serious meditation and inner struggle: not by following the times, following the crowd.

The struggle lasted more than just a day or two. Several months elapsed between my cursing Chen Duxiu in my diary and my complete acceptance of his views. During that time, not until I had finished reading Hu Shi's *Zhongguo zhexue shi dagang* ('Outline History of Chinese Philosophy') were my doubts finally dispelled. Even though after arriving in France I felt that the French were stronger than we in many things, that Confucius was no match for Messrs Science and Democracy, I still believed in a 'national essence', an oriental culture, a spiritual civilisation, a sacred thing that the West did not have.[17] That thing was contained in works of the Zhou and Qin philosophers. For in middle school, I had read a book that argued that Buddhism was not as good as our Laozi, Zhuangzi, Yangzi, and Mozi; as for philosophy, that is, Western rational philosophy, Socrates, Plato, and Aristotle were dilettantes compared to our own thinkers. But Hu Shi taught me that the ancient Chinese masters were also

---

14   The *shenshi* or gentry-class in Imperial China was the class of officials and of degree-holders in and out of office.

15   Zhang Zongxiang was the pro-Japanese official beaten to the ground by students during the May Fourth Movement in 1919.

16   In other words, Zheng means the May Fourth Movement in its broad rather than its narrow sense. (See fn. 1, p. 173.)

17   Partly as a reaction to the First World war, which disillusioned many Chinese who had previously looked to the West as a model for their own country, some thinkers after 1919 began to stress the superiority of the Chinese tradition and 'national essence' over the mechanical, mercantile civilisation of the West.

philosophers, that they could be examined and researched by scientific methods, that Western philosophers had not only dealt with many of the problems thrown up by the Chinese masters but had gone even further than them. So the 'national essence' lost its mystery.

We stayed in Paris for a week. On 15 December, the thirty or so students from Fujian were sent away from the Sino-French Education Association[18] to the Collège de Garçons in Saint-Germain-en-Laye. Saint-Germain is three-quarters of an hour from Paris by train, and an hour by tram. There is a palace there where kings used to live. Louis XIV was born there. Now, it has been turned into a museum. The palace and the town are on a hill that looks onto the Seine and the plain beyond the opposite bank. To get under the river and up the hill, the train from Paris had to shed a few coaches and add a locomotive at the rear. At the top of the hill is the terminus. The station is near the palace, and the palace park is above the tunnel. The park is rather small, but along the raised bank of the river runs a long road, straight as an arrow, through a large forest where kings used to hunt. The whole of Saint-Germain is surrounded by forest. The highway from the railway station through the town and out past our school also enters the forest at a certain point. Every spring at weekends and on holidays, Parisians come here to walk among the trees and flowers. Three months before we arrived, the Allies signed a peace-treaty with Austria in that palace.

Our dormitory was inside the school grounds. We were given a special room to live in, a refectory to eat in, and a classroom for our lessons. We studied only French. Our French teacher had been in the army and claimed to have killed many Germans. He was a perfect chauvinist. The French students were all younger than we and lived a completely separate life. There were three Serbs, two Albanians, and a Persian at the school, but they studied together with the French.

For a while, we Fujianese were held together by the fact that Chen Jiongming had sent someone with us from Zhangzhou to see us aboard the liner in Hong Kong. This man remitted our first year's allowance directly to the Sino-French Education Association. We had asked him to remit our own money to France, so he paid that in for us, too. Everything was arranged for us by the Association; we had no choice in the matter. The Association sent all of us (bar one woman student) to the same school. The Saint-Germain middle school was a provisional arrangement. We were the first Chinese to go there. At first, all of us were

---

18   In 1915, Li Shizeng, Wu Zhihui, Cai Yuanpei, and Wang Jingwei organised the Societé Franco-Chinoise d'éducation in Paris. In 1920, Li, Cai, and Wu founded the Sino-French University near Beijing and the Institut Franco-Chinois de Lyon in France.

Fujianese, save for one person from 'across the river'. But a month later, thirty or forty non-Fujianese arrived, from a mixture of provinces.

The Fujianese students actively discriminated against students from 'across the river'. If they were together in a group, they would often begin to ridicule outsiders. As a result, the other students turned against us and called us 'barbarians'. This meant not only that we were crude and rough but that we were culturally benighted and backward. When a Hunanese student voiced an opinion of this sort, the Fujianese would gang up against him and there would almost be a riot. That is not to say that we Fujianese were united. We were divided into Tingzhou and Zhangzhou factions, and the Zhangzhou faction was further subdivided into an eastern and a southern party. The factional struggle had begun as early as Guangzhou and Hong Kong. There were numerous altercations on board ship during elections for the Student Association. People got up to even worse tricks in Saint-Germain. This division by provenance might appear inexplicable, but it had an objective basis. For a start, we were divided by language. Students from counties in the old Tingzhou prefecture spoke Hakka – only one or two spoke the dialect of the Zhangzhou-Quanzhou region.[19] None of the students from the old Zhangzhou prefecture spoke Hakka. The two groups were forced to communicate in Mandarin. Secondly, and even more importantly, we had received different sorts of education. The Tingzhou students had attended primary schools typical of the hinterland, not so very different from the school I had gone to. Schools of that sort stressed Chinese language and literature. The teachers were old men who had got their learning from stitched books. The Zhangzhou students, in contrast, had enjoyed a seaport-education, a church-style education as in the treaty ports. They had learned their Chinese from young men in Western suits and leather shoes. They had probably never read *Selections from Ancient Literature*. The Tingzhou students considered the Zhangzhou students superficial, the Zhangzhou considered the Tingzhou students backward. For example, most of the Tingzhou students had read the *Original Way*. When they saw that I had copies of Laozi and Zhuangzi in my suitcase, they knew that these thinkers were against Confucius, because Han Yu had told them so.[20] This fact meant nothing to the Zhangzhou students. When they saw my copy of Bai Xiang's *Ci Patterns*, they even insisted

---

19   The linguistic map of southern and western Fujian is extremely complicated. A large number of mutually unintelligible dialects, including Hakka, flourish in its separate valleys.

20   Han Yu (768–824), an orthodox Confucianist, was a notorious scourge of non-Confucian thought in China.

that it was written by Bai Letian.[21] But neither the students from Zhangzhou nor those from Tingzhou had ever heard of Gong Dingan.[22] The Zhangzhou students called me Academician Zheng because I had brought stitched books with me. Unlike the Tingzhou group, they despised stitched books. I was a bystander to their struggles. I was from neither Tingzhou nor Zhangzhou but from the region directly under the jurisdiction of the provincial government – Longyan, midway between the two rival prefectures. My educational background was the same as that of the Tingzhou students, but I spoke no Hakka (though I could speak Zhangzhou dialect). A fellow student of mine from Zhangping could speak both Hakka and Zhangzhou dialect. He switched between the factions and caused all sorts of trouble. I remember once that when both groups were shaping up for battle in the classroom, I hid in the corner and just watched. The headmaster wrote to the Association about us. The Guomindang veteran Zhang Boquan, in Paris at the time, came in person to Saint-Germain to sort us out.

The students from 'across the river' took their lessons in a separate classroom. They had brought large numbers of new publications with them, mainly journals but also some stitched volumes. Though they thought we were barbarians, they by no means excluded us. They were like medieval missionaries spreading the word. We Fujianese gradually caught up on May Fourth. It was probably about this time (the spring of 1920) that May Fourth penetrated Fujian, for schoolmates back home wrote us letters about the new tide.

Though writing in the vernacular and talking about new culture became the rage, the struggle between the prefectures continued. By the start of the summer holidays, the Association had run out of money, so we had to begin fending for ourselves. The Fujian link finally snapped; we had to seek our own way out. What happened to the other Fujianese is largely a mystery to me. One joined the Communist Party in my footsteps, but after suffering some blows, he returned to the path his father had marked out for him, and devoted himself to working for the greater glory of his family.

After the summer holidays, I and two other Fujianese were the only Chinese students still left in Saint-Germain, so we joined the French students instead of attending separate classes. We had studied physics, chemistry, and maths in China, and we benefited little from studying French history and geography. Nor were we particularly interested in reading the French classics. When the winter

---

21 Actually, it was compiled not by Bai Letian, the great Tang dynasty poet, but by Shu Menglan, of the Qing dynasty.
22 Gong Dingan, alias Gong Zizhen (1792–1841), was a Qing dynasty thinker, writer, and poet.

holidays arrived, we left Saint-Germain and went to Melun, two hours by train to the southeast of Paris. A middle school in Melun also took Chinese students, but we did not enrol in it. Instead, we rented accommodation for ourselves where we could cook and study. Melun is capital of a department, less beautiful than Saint-Germain.

I had not left Saint-Germain in the summer because I was short of money. I left Saint-Germain in the winter because my money was up.

Before the War, the Mexican silver dollars we used in China were worth 2.5 francs each. In 1919, the year of the Versailles peace treaty, while we were still in Hong Kong, one dollar was worth eight or nine francs. By now, the franc had lost greatly in value and stood at fifteen to the dollar. While we were in Paris an official of the Association told us, 'The cost of living has gone up. In Paris you need 300 francs a month to live'. He added: 'But 300 francs is only thirty Chinese dollars, you could never live on that in Shanghai'. Yet in Saint-Germain, we had paid on average 150 francs a month for bed, board, fees, and laundry. The Association had paid this amount on our behalf as a lump sum. Other expenses we had to meet from our own pockets, that is, from the money that the Association kept for us, which we withdrew at regular intervals. By the end of 1920, having too little money to pay for the following term, I had no choice but to leave school. I and my two friends estimated that we would be able to live more frugally if we cooked for ourselves. Since Melun is rather far from the capital, the cost of living there was lower. We each had our own room. I lived in the attic, whence I could see through a dormer-window onto a canal. I paid 35 francs a month in rent; my friend on the second floor paid forty. Rent was our biggest outlay; we economised on the rest. In all, we got by on 100 francs a months. That sum paid for haircuts, baths, laundry, and postage to China. The only things it did not include were clothes, books, travel, and medicine. We skimped on food. In our case, the saying 'not a taste of meat for three months' was true. We rarely ate breakfast; our other two meals consisted of bread and mashed potato, with an occasional plate of stir-fried cabbage as a special treat, done in pig-fat rather than olive oil. I still remember that the bread cost 1.3 francs a pound. After three months of this, we could stand it no longer and started adding meat to our diet once every few days. Our other expenses also increased. Our monthly budget soared by thirty per cent.

Melun straddles the Seine. Once when walking along its banks, we met a sickly looking Chinese who told us he was called Zeng Qi and was a member of the Young China Association. He had gone to Melun for a cure. His living conditions were far superior to ours. He became our friend. We used to visit each other and go for outings together. He lent us issues of *Shaonian Zhongguo*

('Young China') and gave us copies of his *qijue*[23] to criticise; I gave him some of mine in return. At the time, he was writing a column for a newspaper in China in which he said that students on the work-study programme in France could get by on one hundred francs a month, that is, six or seven Chinese dollars. When the other students heard about this article, they cursed him as a blockhead. They were not to know that we were the cause of his claim.

Li Shizeng and Wu Zhihui were no longer publishing *Xin shiji bao* ('Nouveau siècle'), but the Chinese printshop in Tours was still in existence and every week published a magazine similar in format to a Shanghai tabloid. I cannot remember what it was called, but I remember that the editor was Zhou Taixuan. He was also a member of the Young China Association and a friend of Zeng Qi. Zeng Qi often wrote articles for Zhou's magazine. I think it was Zeng Qi who wrote an article analysing Chinese students in France into three 'classes': officially sponsored students; semi-officially sponsored students and self-financing students; and work-study students. He said that the first group was bourgeois, the last group was proletarian, and the two middle groups were petty-bourgeois. That meant that he and I were 'petty-bourgeois'.

There were statistics that showed the different sorts of students in percentages. I have forgotten the exact figures, but I remember that work-study students were in the majority, and far outnumbered the other groups. There were some three thousand of them from every one of China's eighteen provinces save Gansu. The biggest groups were from Sichuan and Hunan. Most of them had been leaders of or activists in the May Fourth Movement. They were like me: they wanted to fly from their provinces and even fly abroad, but also like me they lacked wings. The cry 'hard work and frugal study' was certainly no voice in the wilderness. Most of them gathered at Shanghai to await the boat, but some waited in Beijing or Baoding. Two or three batches had preceded me to France; even more came after me. In the autumn of 1920, the flow ebbed or stopped.

The reason was that the ideal had been shattered. True, schools all over France threw open their gates to us – after all, we were worth good money; but the factories remained closed to us. It was nearly two years since the War. The French economy was in recession and workers were being laid off. Why should they make room for us yellow-skins? After the work-study students had used up the money they had brought with them from China, they became real 'proletarians' and were forced to seek help from the Association. A tiny minority found factory jobs; the rest had to make do with a subsidy of two

---

23   A poem of four regular lines, each consisting of seven characters arranged in a strict tonal pattern and rhyme scheme.

to three francs a day for bread and hot water. Some lived in the Education Association building. The Education Association was actually a unit of the Overseas-Chinese Association. Apparently, a rich widow who sympathised with China had donated the building. On my second day in Paris, this lady made a speech at our reception. The Overseas-Chinese Association was at 39 Rue de la Pointe in Lagarenne-Colombes, 20 minutes from Paris by train, not far from the famous Beancurd Company.[24] The reason I remember this location so clearly is because it was my mailing address for more than three years. The Association was in a three-storey building in its own grounds. By that time, the cellar was full of work-study students. Others lived in a marquee in the garden. A rope was strung between two trees where students hung out their shirts, socks, trousers, and sheets to dry. The constant hubbub in the garden disturbed the neighbours, who petitioned the police to intervene. Once, an official of the Association said to us: 'The neighbours say we Chinese are not clean. Not clean? Chinese not clean? When the toilet seat gets wet, no one wants to sit on it any longer, so they squat on it instead, and break it. Then other people use the toilet standing up. It gets dirty so people start pissing in from the door. The entrance gets wet so people start pissing in the corridor'. This was an exaggeration. I often used to go to the Association, and though the toilet was not exactly clean, it was not as dirty as this man made out, and there was no sign of shit or piss in the corridor.

The work-study students had been activists in the student movement in China; they were 'student rabble, worse than soldiers'. Barred from work, they were unable to continue with their studies, so they became resentful. Li Shizeng had already gone back to Beijing University to become a professor. His friend Liu Hou became the students' stand-in target. Liu Hou had to put up with all sorts of problems. When Cai Yuanpei and Wu Zhihui came to France, they held a meeting to try to sort things out.

These luminaries came to China in connection with their campaign to force France to pay back the Boxer Indemnity Fund.[25] They intended to use the fund to finance a new batch of Chinese students. The work-study students naturally protested. They said that the aim of sending them there in the first place

---

24   In 1919, Li Shizeng set up a soybean factory (the Usine Caseo Sojaine) at Colombes; its more than thirty workers used their wages to pursue their studies in France.

25   In 1901, China paid 450 million silver taels to the Western Allies at the time of their invasion of Hebei to crush the Boxers. With interest, the actual sum rose to 982 million. After protracted negotiations, Li Shizeng finally secured the return of the French portion of this fund, to be used for cultural and educational purposes, in 1925.

had been to force France to pay back the fund. Now that the aim had been achieved, they were being ditched.

There were two struggles I should mention.

One was the '28 Movement' that happened on 28 February 1921, when work-study students from all over France crowded into Paris to petition the Chinese Minister Chen Lu and to raise demands. The result was that they were scattered by a police charge.

The other was the 'Lyons University movement'. This Chinese University overseas had already been established by the autumn of 1921. It was housed in the Fort Sainte Irène on a small hill across the river from Lyons. Wu Zhihui had brought some students to France who were probably already living at the University. The work-study students had been abandoned. One day, the Lyons police were shocked to see a train pull in at the station from which stepped group after group of Chinese students bound for the fortress (still under renovation in preparation for its new role). The students marched up to the fortress, entered it, and refused to leave. The police surrounded the fortress and held the Chinese prisoner in it. A few days later, the French Government ordered their repatriation to China.

I took part in neither of these movements, for I was 'petty bourgeois' (to use the terminology of Zeng Qi or his friends), not 'proletarian'.

After the Lyons movement and the deportation of some of the troublemakers, the morale of the work-study students dropped even further, but the economic depression lifted and we yellow-skins gradually became welcome again in the factories. The mass movement had passed its peak.

As for me, I had descended from the 'petty bourgeoisie' into the 'proletariat'; simultaneously – was there a connection? – I stopped thinking as a mere democrat and starting thinking as a socialist, and I even started acting as a socialist.

The Communist Youth Party

Is a long period of capitalist democracy necessary to get from Chinese society with its 'feudal remnants' to socialism? This is still a controversial question. As for me, I personally got from feudal ideology to socialist ideology without a 'long and stable' intervening stage of bourgeois ideology. The same is true of the collective awakening of Chinese consciousness – at least of its main current – in the May Fourth era. Like me, it skipped the 'long and stable' period of bourgeois democratic ideology.

I said earlier that while at Saint-Germain, the students from 'across the river' had the attitude of medieval missionaries towards us Fujianese 'barbarians'.

Naturally, this statement was not true of all of them, but a few names of those of whom it was true still spring to mind. One was Xiong Xiong from Jiangxi. He had served in the army under Li Liejun, and was a model officer of the early Republic. He wrote beautiful calligraphy, and was a poet in the classical style and an avid admirer of everything new and revolutionary, but he lacked an analytical brain. Another was the Sichuanese Qin Zhigu. Qin liked to spin a yarn. He was a sincere person who spoke good English and was fond of discussing issues in the New Culture Movement. Another was Wang Songlu from Guizhou. His old-style learning was rather shallow, but he enjoyed visiting people who inclined towards the new thinking. There were others, too, but I have forgotten their names. I do not mean to give the impression that apart from these people no one else from 'across the river' wanted dealings with us Fujianese. Even though my fellow-Fujianese used to make fun of students from 'across the river' behind their backs or even (in dialect) to their faces, the two sides were not averse to passing the time of day together. But their conversation rarely lifted above the weather, the Paris sights, or women. The people I mentioned had no interest in talking about such subjects. Xiong Xiong was always welcome among the Fujianese. Many Fujianese made friends with him, chiefly on the grounds that he was a military officer. Qin Zhigu and Wang Songlu, in contrast, were mainly unsuccessful in their overtures to the Fujianese. Whenever they started talking about culture or ideology, the Fujianese would constantly butt in to ask them what subject they were planning to study. 'I'm going to go to university', the Fujianese would add, 'I'm going to study chemistry or engineering'. Apart from my given name, I had another name (as was often the custom in those days). This name was Zelian. Most of my fellow-Fujianese knew the name, but none could guess why I had chosen it. Wang Songlu and I used to smile at one another about this. Later, Wang told me that one of his teachers called Huang was coming to Paris. This man had called himself Qisheng, with the same meaning.[26] Huang Qisheng was Wang Ruofei's maternal uncle; later, I shall return to him.

One day, Wang Songlu took me into the corridor outside a classroom and introduced me to a tall thin man with a flat face and high cheekbones. He had an unhealthy flush, the colour of a parboiled crab. Wang told me, 'This is Mr

---

26 During the Warring States period (403–221 BC), a man called Lu Zhonglian in the State of Qi (now Shandong) achieved fame by his distinguished and selfless efforts to resolve disputes among warring states. He was admired throughout history as a peace-maker and a unique hero. Three names mentioned in this passage are related to his name. *Zelian* means to take Lu Zhong*lian* as an example; Song*lu* means to praise Lu; and *Qisheng* means man of the State of Qi.

Yin Kuan, from Tongcheng [in Anhui]'. I found it hard not to laugh, for Kuan means broad, and Yin Kuan was anything but broad. Chang (meaning tall) would have been a better name for him. Yin Kuan immediately sounded off on a long but well-organised speech about some subject or other. Later, the three of us often used to meet together to hold discussions. Gradually, we arrived at the idea of setting up a research group. We decided that we three would form the nucleus and that each of us would try to recruit new members. One day, we met in the woods outside Saint-Germain and sat down among the trees to discuss the name and constitution of our group. I suggested calling it the Self-Enlightenment Society; the others immediately agreed.

Why 'Self-Enlightenment'? The name requires an explanation. Though we were studying in France, the literature we read consisted mainly of periodicals posted to us from China and books published by Beijing University. In China, new thought was in its heyday. Students everywhere were challenging established authority and their unions were even taking over the day-to-day administration of the schools. That was democracy, modelled on Europe and America. Moreover, Li Shizeng's people had settled on France as the future model for China's development. But what about the France that we saw around us? Solemnly pacing Catholic priests in black robes came to the school each day to preach to the students; the students viewed the principal and the housemaster as mice view cats; they had not the slightest notion of how to run a movement, and never talked about resistance, revolution, socialism, atheism, anarchism, and the rest; the books and magazines they read never broached such subjects. Could it be that France had not yet had its May Fourth? That French students had no *New Youth*, no Chen Duxiu, no Hu Shi? Luckily, a recently arrived issue of *New Youth* carried a translation by Zhang Songnian of a 'Manifesto of Independence of Spirit' signed by Romain Rolland, Henri Barbusse, Bertrand Russell, and a host of others I had never heard of. Zhang Songnian had added a note explaining who these people were. He said that Barbusse had recently set up an organisation in Paris called the Society of Light that published a magazine called *Clarté*.

I lost no time in going to Paris, where I somehow managed to track down the Librairie Clarté. I bought a year's subscription to the magazine, and took the most recent issue home with me. It was in newspaper format, rather like *Shenbao*, and came out weekly. I took out my dictionary and began to wade my way through my purchase. It was exactly what we wanted; I conveyed the contents to like-minded friends. But the next issue did not arrive, nor the next. I wrote to the bookshop, which wrote back inviting me to Paris. I went. They told me that they been posting my subscription and that the headmaster was probably confiscating it, and advised me to use another address. It so happened that a friend of mine from Fujian who could not settle down to dormitory life had decided to rent a room outside the school. His landlord was an engineer. I went to discuss my problem with them. The landlord readily agreed to let me use his address for my subscription. He let fly a torrent of abuse at the school authorities. It turned out that he was a member of the Socialist Party. Later, the people at the Librairie Clarté wrote to me a second time inviting me to Paris to attend a course of lectures by distinguished speakers. I knew I would understand little of what I heard, but I went anyway a few times. I bought four postcards at the bookshop, of Lenin, Trotsky, Lunacharsky, and Kollontai. Needless to say, I got the idea for the name Self-Enlightenment from the Society of Light. I was the first of the sixty or seventy Chinese students in Saint-Germain to subscribe to a French magazine and the first to make contact with French socialists. My fellow-Fujianese considered my behaviour highly eccentric and thought there must be something wrong with me.

The Self-Enlightenment Society was a secret cabal that never developed beyond the three of us. I am not sure why we kept it secret. It was not illegal, either in France or in China. Perhaps we were afraid that people would sneer at us or pass comments. When we formed our society, the summer holidays were almost upon us. Before we could meet a second time, Wang Songlu had gone to Paris and Yin Kuan had gone to Melun. I was the only one of us left in Saint-Germain. We continued to stay in touch by letter.

In the course of our correspondence, Yin Kuan and I entered into a dispute. I forget who opened fire first. Yin Kuan contended that emotions govern reason, I argued the opposite. Yin's position led him to approve of religious fervour. He said people needed religion. I, on the contrary, argued that religion was a disaster for humanity. So the debate came to centre on religion. Yin told me in one of his letters that he was planning to write some essays on the difference between religious rites and religious spirit. Wang Songlu mediated between us. I kept copies of my own letters, and naturally I saved Yin's. Later, when I got to know Zeng Qi in Melun, I discovered that he, too, was against religion. He told me that *Young China* was planning to bring out two special issues on religion, one to be edited in China, the other in France, by him. I showed him the correspondence. He wanted to publish it, but when I told Yin Kuan, Yin was against the idea. 'It's too immature', he told me. I burned it, either when I left France or when I left Russia.

The work-study students were split by violent factional disputes, but the factions were based on politics, unlike the 'struggle between the prefectures' that tore us Fujianese apart. Early on during my stay in France, I heard that there was an 'eccentric' among the work-study students called Cai Hesen. He had taken his mother (who had bound feet) and his younger sister to Paris to share in his 'hard work and frugal study'. He never washed his face, had his hair cut, changed his clothes, or paid attention to women. He was once seen together with a group of people in a coffee bar. When it was time to pay the bill, he sat there without moving, and let his sister pay instead. Xiang Jingyu, a woman student in Paris, loved him. They were already living together. Xiang Jingyu was learned, pretty, competent, and an excellent speaker. Many of the best work-study students, mainly Hunanese, were under her spell and at her command. They organised an association called the Work-Study World Society. Cai Hesen and most of his acolytes studied at Montargis Middle School.

I heard all this from others. Montargis was even smaller than Melun. It was capital of an arrondissement, not of a departement. Like Melun, it was on the Paris-Lyons-Marseilles line, an hour or so further along the track from Melun. Montargis was especially popular with Chinese students because it was run by M. Chapeau, a socialist, who was a friend of Li Shizeng and a patron of Chinese people. Later, when I went to Montargis, I met him once. A work-study student called Ouyang had died in hospital and M. Chapeau made a grave-side speech. He was connected in some way with the rubber factory in Montargis and with the middle school, though I do not know exactly how. The work-study students used to malign him behind his back, but I don't know why.

The representatives, manifesto, and proposals of the Montargis students during the '28 Movement' were quite unlike those of the rest of us. Wang Zekai was a man of rhetoric with a loud, clear voice that combined a sense of agitation and of indignation. The Montargis manifesto said that work-study students have a right to exist and a right to study, and that the Chinese Government should support us. This amounted to a frontal attack on the work-study ideal and the principle of self-reliance. For it was becoming ever plainer that it was not possible to rely on one's own labour, to scrimp and save, and eventually to go to school and return to China after finishing. When the Montargis proposals became known, not only the minister and the consul shook their heads, but so did the people from the Sino-French Association. Even some of the work-study students shook their heads. The Association bulletin rebutted the proposal, as, too, did many of the duplicated news-sheets put out by students in the different towns and cities. These people stuck by their anarchist ideal of hard work and frugal study. They saw labour as sacred and thought that it was shameful to live and study on the backs of others. They saw the Montargis proposal as parasitism.

This anti-Montargis group had no particular centre. Its leaders were the Sichuanese Zhao Shiyan, the Hunanese Li Longzhi (who later changed his name to Li Lisan), Xiong Zhinan and Wang Ruofei from Guizhou, Wu Ming, and also perhaps Luo Han. The two sides clashed furiously in print and speeches. The antis often changed their point of view, but the Montargis people stuck to their guns throughout. Each side tried to defame the other, for example, accusing it of being in someone else's pay.

Yin Kuan was connected to the Montargis group. Either he had a meeting with the leaders of the group during the '28 Movement' or he went to Montargis at a later date and met Cai Hesen; Wang Songlu was from the same place as Xiong Zhinan, a leader of the other faction. I had nothing to do with this particular conflict, for my 'right to exist' and my 'right to study' were guaranteed by my official scholarship and money from home. But in May or June 1921, three or four months after the '28 Movement', Xiong Zhinan came to Melun to see Wang Songlu and at the same time to see me and Yin Kuan. He told us that he wanted to organise a society to exchange books and magazines and was inviting Chinese students everywhere to join it. He wanted people to make a list of what they had and then to arrange by post to swap and borrow. This was the first time I had come across such an organisation, but still I agreed to join. Naturally, Wang Songlu joined. Yin Kuan hesitated at first, but he, too, agreed to go to Paris that same day. The meeting was held in Xiong Zhinan's room. He was a painter. He painted porcelain in a factory in Saint-Cloud, in the southwestern suburbs of Paris, where there is a beautiful palace with a hill and woods. Xiong Zhinan lived in a *pension* at the foot of the hill. It was there that I first met Zhao Shiyan, Wang Ruofei, Wu Ming, and many others. Yin Kuan kept quiet for most of the meeting, but just before the end of it, he stood up and declared that he had come just to listen, not to join. Everyone reacted with surprise, but only for a while. Afterwards, I learned that the meeting had something to do with the campaign against the Montargis group, with whose members Yin was on friendly terms. But to this day, it beats me why Yin came 'just to listen'.

When I received the stencilled membership list, I saw many familiar names, for example, Li Longzhi and Xiong Xiong. My three books in the catalogue – Laozi, Zhuangzi, and Liezi – provoked sneers from Xiong Zhinan. Actually, others had listed the same titles, but my pirate editions of the Shidetang imprint were the best.

Several months after this meeting – I cannot remember whether it was before or after the Lyons campaign – I received a very pessimistic letter from Xiong Zhinan asking to borrow my three books. I posted them, and he replied thanking me. The tone of his letter was still extremely pessimistic. A short while later, I heard that he had been taken to hospital. Apparently, he had fallen in love with a French girl and agreed to meet her on such-and-such a day in front of a railway station somewhere in Belgium to get married in the nude, but she had failed to turn up. He had then come back to France and got drunk in a café at the border and refused to pay, saying: 'Why should I pay you?' It was then that he went mad.

Actually, this anecdote was something of a fairy-tale. Later, I asked Zhao Shiyan about it. He said he didn't know, but that the last time he met Zhinan, he had thought him a bit strange in the head.

During the Lyons campaign the two factions worked together; what brought that cooperation about, I'm not sure. Cai Hesen and his wife Xiang Jingyu, Luo Xuezan, Li Longzhi, Wu Ming, and Luo Han were all deported as a result of the campaign.

After the Lyons campaign, the remnants of the two factions, having already begun to cooperate, merged into one organisation. So a new unitary chapter began in the life of the Chinese in France. Even I climbed down from my book-worm's attic to join in.

Cai Hesen's secret was Marxism. On the French course at Baoding (or Beijing) others concentrated on learning how to speak; he, however, paid sole attention to learning how to read. After just a few days of learning French, he started reading theoretical publications, with the aid of a dictionary. I do not know exactly what books he read. In those days, all sorts of socialist ideas were current in China, particularly anarchist ideas. Apparently, Cai Hesen became a Marxist even before leaving China.[27] In short, he was the first Marxist among the work-study students and among overseas Chinese of any description. You could say that he was founder of the Communist movement that later emerged among Chinese in France. At Montargis Middle School, other students were busy planning how to use the money they would save while working to finance their further education, and worrying about how to use the time they set aside from learning French to study other subjects that would be useful for getting into university or technical college, or even for becoming engineers. Cai Hesen,

---

27 According to a friend of mine who is familiar with the early development of Cai's thinking, Cai was essentially a Modi-ist (a follower of the school of thought founded by Modi, a philosopher and a contemporary of Confucius who emphasised the concept of *boai* or 'universal love') when he was in China and remained such during the early days of his stay in France, though he had already studied Marxism at that time. He finally and definitively became a Marxist only in 1920, when the French Socialist Party decided to join the Comintern and renamed itself at its Tours Congress the Communist Party of France. [Note added by Zheng Chaolin in the early 1980s.]

meanwhile, spent his time diving into dictionaries and reading the newly published French translation of Lenin's *State and Revolution* and similar texts. He and others close to him pointed out: hard work and frugal study is an illusion, a fraud; they decided early on what attitude to take towards the struggle of the work-study students. Though their proposals did not get majority support, and on the contrary provoked fierce opposition, they were very influential among Chinese circles overseas. Under the pressure of events, opponents of Cai like Zhao Shiyan, Li Longzhi, and Wang Ruofei gradually came round to Cai's way of thinking and accepted his proposals – or at least his main proposal, which was Marxism.

After the Lyons campaign, the factional struggle stopped. The main leaders of the anti-Montargis group became Marxists. The Chinese Communist Party had already been founded,[28] and Zhang Songnian (who later called himself Zhang Shenfu) was its Europe correspondent. He and Liu Qingyang lived together in Germany as man and wife. Zhang and Liu were not work-study students, but self-financing. However, they had come to Europe on the same boat as work-study students, and had later transferred to Germany. Zhang and Liu had got to know each other only on the boat; there was much salacious gossip about them. Later, they married. After the May Thirtieth Movement in 1925, they were attacked for this in the Beijing press, and Zhang had to write a letter to the *Chenbao* (or some other similar newspaper) in self-defence.

Zhang Songnian introduced Zhao Shiyan to the Chinese Communist Party and Zhao became its France correspondent. Under Zhang's direction, Zhao started organising for the Communist Youth in France. In June 1922, he set up its founding congress. I was among the eighteen delegates.

Here I must pause to explain how it was that I came down from my attic.

Chen Jiongming had already ceded to the Beiyang warlord Li Houji the part of Fujian that he had occupied, and had led his Guangdong Army back to Guangdong, where he chased Lu Rongting's Guangxi Army back to Guangxi.[29] Though the northerners took back southern Fujian, they continued paying subsidies to those of us studying in France. My father collected $300 a year from the county yamen, right through to the time I left Moscow and returned to

---

28   The Chinese Communist Party's First Congress met in Shanghai, on 23 July 1921, though 1 July has been settled on as the official date of its founding.

29   In August 1920, Chen Jiongming, having decided to support Sun Yat-sen's plan to establish a national government at Guangzhou, advanced into Guangdong at Sun's behest and defeated Lu.

Shanghai. He posted one instalment to me and even added some money of his own, though it was less than the $300 he was supposed to send. Later, however, he kept the lot. Some people in Zhangping blame him for that, but I forgive him. I was unlikely to starve to death without the money, and even if he had sent it, I still could not have got into university or technical college, for the cost of living in France had shot up in the meantime. But $300 meant a lot to a big family back in China, and it set my mind at rest to know that it was available to them. In late 1921, I was still expecting to get my money the following year. One other student from Fujian was in the same position as I; another had put his money in the Sino-French Industrial Bank and got into difficulties when the bank went into liquidation. At that time, Lyons University had already started accepting students. Lyons University was not against accepting Chinese students in France in principle, nor was it against accepting work-study students; the only qualification one needed was the ability to pay fees. Some fee-paying students had already passed the examinations and joined, among them one or two who were short of funds and who had promised to pay their fees as soon as their remittances arrived. Two of the students at Lyons University who had come direct from China were from the same place as Wang Songlu; it was through them that we learned about this. Wang Songlu and we three Fujianese hoped to solve our problem in the same way, by promising to pay as soon as our money arrived. I was chosen to go to Lyon to scout things out. Armed with an introductory letter from Wang Songlu, I sought out his two contacts and learned that the students without funds were a special case, but that if we moved to Lyons we could perhaps find some way of achieving our aim. I took this information back to Melun. The general opinion was that though rents in Lyons were higher than in Melun, other living expenses were more or less the same, so we decided to move there. In early January 1922, we rented accommodation near the university. We got to know some students recently arrived from China. To us, they seemed like a new breed of student: affable, courteous, content, and fond of talking about how science and industry would save China. I felt that there was a high barrier between us and them. There was no such barrier between us and the students at Lyons who had come on work-study schemes. Outside the university, there were some work-study students who had come to take care of unfinished business in the wake of the defeat of the movement. In a coffee-bar at the entrance to the university I met Liu Bojian, a pock-marked fellow from Sichuan. Being the work-study students' representative, he despised those of them who had enrolled at the university. Once, I and a few others met Wu Zhihui, dean of the university, in the university courtyard, and demanded that he let us enrol even though we could not yet pay our fees, but he refused. Wang Songlu said he knew the dean or registrar, Chu Minyi, and invited us to go along with him to meet Chu. We met Chu in the office. Wang said nothing about enrolling. All he said was: 'We have no food to eat, we want you to do something about it!' Chu replied that he could do nothing. Wang banged on the table and called him a rascal. Chu, too, banged on the table. Liu Hou, former secretary of the Sino-French Education Committee, tried to calm things down. Chu went into a side-room. Wang stormed out, still cursing. We three Fujianese had not uttered a word, for Wang had failed to tell us that he had come with the intention of having a row. He was merely reflecting the anger of the great mass of work-study students.

After the defeat of the Lyons campaign, the work-study students hated university officials like Wu Zhihui, Chu Minyi, and Zeng Zhongming, but they also hated the minister Chen Lu, who they said was the source of the idea to deport them. There were also conflicts between the university and the minister's office. The minister represented the Beijing Government, the university had historical connections to the southern Guomindang Government. Which side was the more contemptible? In my view, Wu Zhihui. The idea of work-study was his creation, two to three thousand passionate youngsters had believed in him. They had scraped together the money to get to France and now they had neither work nor any means of livelihood. Having got back the Boxer Indemnity Fund, Wu was not prepared to enrol them. The decision of the French parliament to hand back the money had been taken under the pressure of public opinion, which had been greatly influenced in its turn by the presence in France of two to three thousand work-study students. But no one ever intended to assassinate Wu Zhihui, whereas someone did assassinate Chen Lu.

The Sichuanese Li Heling (who later changed his name to Helin, written with simpler characters, thus saving himself no fewer than twenty seven penstrokes each time he wrote it) was young, handsome, clever, articulate, a first-class writer, and an anarchist. He wanted to kill Chen Lu, and spent several months preparing his attempt. He got someone to introduce him to Madam Zheng Yuxiu, whose secretary he became. Then he waited for his chance. Madam Zheng was a *politicante* who later became Chief Justice of Shanghai District Court. Many people knew her. Her Paris salon was constantly full of politicians in or out of office on visits to France. One day, Chen Lu had dinner in her home. On his way back by car, a shot rang out behind him. It missed him and hit someone else, newly arrived in France on a mission for the Beijing Government, but the wound was superficial. Later, Li Helin said that when he saw at the banquet how lovingly Chen Lu behaved towards his daughter, it affected him, so his shot went wide. Li Helin was sent to prison for nine months and then deported to Belgium. His article on the incident was published in the Commercial Press' *Xuesheng zazhi* ('Students' Journal'), edited by Yang

Xianjiang. It's probably available somewhere in one of the big libraries. Later, I shall have more to say about Li Helin. As for Chen Lu, even though he did not die that time, a few years ago he was shot dead at a banquet in Shanghai, while serving as minister of foreign affairs in the pro-Japanese puppet government.[30]

Li Helin brings to mind the Russian nihilists and the articles by Lenin and Trotsky opposing individual terror. Li's attempt to assassinate Chen Lu was a clear expression of disillusion after the defeat of a mass movement; but there can be no doubt that even had Li's bullet found its mark, it would have made no difference.

The defeat of the Lyons campaign sped the unification of the Marxists. The arguments were no longer about work-study but about isms.[31]

Anarchism. Here I do not mean the anarchism that had got its hands on the Boxer funds, but the anarchism that grew up among the work-study students. After the defeat of the Lyons campaign, students in each region received a mimeographed publication called *Gongyu* ('After Work') brought out by Li Zhuo, Chen Yannian, and others. This was the first-ever publication by work-study students. Earlier, there had been only stencilled manifestos, open letters, and the like voicing individual or group opinions. *After Work* was warmly welcomed. As far as I remember, it did not clearly espouse anarchism, nor did it oppose Marxism. A few months later, after Chen Yannian and his brother had come over to Marxism, Li Zhuo continued to bring out *After Work* and called Chen Yannian a traitor.

Nationalism. A long time after the unification of the Marxists, the nationalists also set up an organisation that had almost certainly been long fomenting. It was the child of self-financing students like Zeng Qi.

As a serious political organisation, the Guomindang only really got going in China after the 1924 reform.[32] The Communists supported it in its initial stages, and later, it became an important political force. But at that time, in 1922, there was no trace of the Guomindang among Chinese in France.

In late February or early March 1922, we three Fujian students who had moved to Lyons were living on just bread and water. I wrote to Qin Zhigu at the

---

30 Chen was killed in February 1939 by the Iron and Blood Army, which had undertaken to assassinate various prominent Chinese who collaborated with the Japanese occupiers.

31 In July and August 1919, Hu Shi broke with the radicals of May Fourth when he wrote an article attacking the 'slaves of Marx and Kropotkin' who tried to provide 'fundamental solutions' for all society's problems by resort to totalistic 'isms'.

32 In 1924, the Russian Borodin drafted a new constitution for the Guomindang based on that of the Communist Party of the Soviet Union, after which the Guomindang became a mass organisation with a centralist structure and a systematic ideology.

Montargis rubber factory. He wrote back saying that the factory was recruiting hands, so I packed my bags and went to Montargis. The factory, about a mile away from the town, employed one thousand-odd workers, most of them women and children, and including thirty Chinese, all of them work-study students. I worked in the tires section, where I was the sole Chinese; there were a few more Chinese in the raincoats section; the rest were concentrated in galoshes and overshoes. After three or four months, the tires section contracted and I was transferred to galoshes and overshoes, where I stayed until I left. In the tires section I was on a ten-hour day and paid at the rate of one franc an hour, including on Saturday mornings. In the footwear section, a piece-work system applied, but only after you had worked yourself in. I produced ten pairs of boots a day. The others produced twenty-five or even thirty-five. They were three times as productive as I, but they earned only fifty or sixty per cent more. Needless to say, the factory was happy about this. After one or two months, the foreman tried to get me to switch to piece-work, but I refused. Later, he told me one or two more times to switch, but I ignored him, and he left it at that. So I stayed on time-rate, and in that sense I was an anomaly. Every other Saturday was pay-day. Wage packets were invariably right, to the last centime.

I lived in a spacious wooden shed made available by the factory, with room in it for forty-odd beds, ten of which were empty when I arrived. All my roommates were Chinese. The shed was in a wood, five minutes' walk from the factory. Some Chinese preferred their comfort and rented accommodation (at about thirty francs a month) in the town. It took them thirty or forty minutes to get to work. We shed-people ate collectively. We chose two cooks and paid them by the hour, like in the factory. They had to account publicly for their expenditure. We each paid about three francs a day. We had bread and coffee for breakfast and meat at midday and in the evening. The food was much better than when I had been cooking for myself. The shed was free. After paying the cooks, I could still send 150 francs a month to two friends of mine from Fujian who were in Lyons. But I only sent money for a month or two. One of my friends got a remittance from his relatives in China and enrolled at a middle school in Orleans. The other came to Montargis to work in the rubber factory.

Most of the other Chinese in the rubber-factory were from Anhui. Some had heard about me through Yin Kuan. Li Weinong from Chaoxian invited me to the middle school to meet the Montargis faction: Li Weihan, Xue Shilun, Wang Zekai, his lineage mate Wang Zewei, and another person called Zhang, none of whom was any longer attending classes. I do not know why they were still living in the school. Very soon, they rented rooms in town, and after that, they came to work in the rubber factory. Soon Yin Kuan and Wang Ruofei came too. For some reason, the people in the shed stayed aloof from them and never even mentioned them. But they got on well with Li Weinong. They used to tease him mercilessly about his socialism and enjoyed making him lose his temper.

One day, a Sunday, Xue Shilun came out from town and invited Li Weinong, Han Qi, and me to go to a forest south of the railway line. He told us he was preparing to set up a Communist youth organisation and asked if we would join. Li Weinong said he would, and so did I after a moment's reflection. Han Qi took longer to make up his mind, but he, too, eventually agreed to join. Li Weinong's agreement was a formality: the real targets were Han Qi and I.

In 1931, in White Cloud Temple,[33] the head of the Investigation Team of the Garrison Headquarters in Shanghai asked me:

'When did you join the Communist Party'.
'1922'.
'Who introduced you?'
'Li Weinong'.
'Where's Li Weinong now?'
'He led a strike in Qingdao. Zhang Zongchang had him shot'.

We held our founding conference in Paris, in June. Montargis sent a large delegation, including Yin Kuan, Wang Ruofei, Li Weinong, Li Weihan, Xue Shilun, and me. We told other people that we were going to the annual meeting of the Work-Study World Society, even though in reality the society had long since been defunct. Zhao Shiyan fetched us from Lyons railway station and we went together to his home in the treizième quartier at 17 Rue Godfroy. Yuan Qingyun, too, lived there. The next day, we held a meeting in the Bois de Boulogne in Paris' western suburbs. As we were entering the woods, we met a pale-looking young man introduced to us as Ren Zhuoxuan. He led us to a swarthy-looking fellow who he said was Chen Yannian. As we walked on, Ren pointed to a man in a yellow overcoat in the group in front and said he was Zhou Enlai, representative of the German branch. It was the first time that I had heard the name. We reached a glade where somehow or another a couple of dozen steel-framed chairs were waiting. We arranged them in a circle and sat down.

There were eighteen of us. Can I remember all the names?

First, there was Zhao Shiyan, of course, and his fellow-townsman Yuan Qingyun, who shared digs with him. Wang Linghan, a cripple, from Xichong in Sichuan. The Cantonese Xiong Rui. Ren Zhuoxuan from Sichuan. Li Weihan and Xue Shilun from Hunan. Zhou Enlai, whose family was from Zhejiang but who had been brought up in Tianjin. Chen Yannian, the son of Chen Duxiu. Pock-marked Liu Bojian, representing the Belgian branch. Wang Ruofei from

---

33   Baiyunguan, then used by the Shanghai secret police as an interrogation centre.

Guizhou. The Sichuanese Xiao Pusheng. Yin Kuan and Li Weinong from Anhui. And me. That accounts for fifteen of us. I no longer remember who the other three were. Perhaps they were Xiong Weigeng, Li Fuchun, and Lin Wei.

Zhao Shiyan presided over the morning session and Ren Zhuoxuan over the afternoon session. I forget what we did for lunch. Of the eighteen, only Zhou Enlai spoke northern Chinese. Sometimes, we had to ask him to repeat himself or even to write things down before we could understand what he was saying. For example, he had to repeat the word *yunniang* ('fomentation') many times before we understood it. Another word we had difficulty with was *xuanshi* ('oath'). When we finally did understand what he meant, almost all of us were against it. After all, we were atheists. Who would we swear our oath to? The most violently against was Ren Zhuoxuan, supported by me. But Zhou Enlai explained that it was necessary and important. He gave as an example Sun Yat-sen's resignation in favour of Yuan Shikai, when Sun made Yuan swear loyalty to the Republic. Later, when Yuan proclaimed himself emperor, people were able to accuse him of going back on his oath, so he could not proceed with his plan. Zhou Enlai refused to drop his proposal. When the chairman called for a vote on it, the majority was against.

But the most heated argument was about the name of the organisation. Everyone wanted to call it Communist Youth Party. Zhou Enlai was against this proposal, on the grounds that we could not use the word party since one country could not have two parties. Moreover, our organisation would be doing youth-work under the leadership of the Party, so it should be called the Communist Youth League. Again, we voted; again, Zhou lost. Later, Li Weihan went back to China and discussed our joining the Socialist Youth League with its secretary, Shi Cuntong. Only then did we stop calling ourselves the Communist Youth Party and change our name instead to the European Branch of the Chinese Socialist Youth League.

The next day, the conference reconvened to discuss a constitution and elect officials, but I went back to Montargis the same night, and my place at the conference was taken by someone else. I cannot remember why I left early. Perhaps it was because it was difficult to get time off from the rubber factory. As far as I remember, the first session was on a Sunday. Since I had Saturday afternoons and Sundays free, I had no need to ask for leave to go to Paris, but there would have been problems had I stayed until Monday.

Five people were elected to the leading body, the name of which I have forgotten. Zhao Shiyan became 'General Secretary'; under him were Zhang Bojian, Chen Yannian, Li Weihan, and one other, perhaps Zhou Enlai.

Zhang Bojian, a Yunnanese, had not taken part in the founding conference. He was chosen as General Secretary on the grounds that he was leader of a large secret association that would join the new organisation en masse. He was made head of the organisation bureau. Until he got back to Paris, Li Weihan stood in for him. After the conference and the election, Zhang returned to Paris (I have no idea where he had been in the meantime). The new leaders wanted him to hand over his membership, but he kept stalling. Finally, he was unmasked as a paper tiger: there was no association, and he represented no one but himself, so he was punished by being relieved of his job, which Li Weihan took over. But being infinitely resourceful, he was very soon in Moscow, where he blazed the trail for the rest of us. Whether in Moscow, Shanghai, or Guangzhou, he never became important. In 1926, he died of TB in a Guangzhou hospital.

The founding of the 'Communist Youth Party' was a big event among Chinese in Europe. The Party grew in leaps and bounds. In the period up to 1925, when almost the entire membership went back to China after the jailing of Ren Zhuoxuan, probably three to four hundred people joined the Party or the League. But at the time of its founding, it was very small. The original eighteen delegates were not chosen on a proportional basis: anyone who wanted to take part was welcome. It is doubtful whether we had another eighteen supporters in the whole of Europe. As far as I know, the German branch had four or five members, the Belgian branch was even smaller, and of the Montargis branch, only Wang Zekai, his lineage mate Wang Zewei, and Han Qi had not attended; there were others in the Creusot branch represented by Xiao Pusheng, but otherwise, probably only a few isolated individuals had not been able to attend because they lived too far away from Paris or for some other reason. Chen Yannian's younger brother, Chen Qiaonian, had also not attended. The bulk of us were members or friends of the old Montargis faction together with Zhao Shiyan and his fellow-provincials and friends, Chen Yannian and a few anarchists he had brought along, and those from Germany who had nothing whatsoever to do with the work-study movement.

After setting up the organisation, we started up activity in various fields. Our general headquarters was in Zhao Shiyan's boarding house. We had a mimeograph on which we produced *Shaonian* ('Youth') and internal bulletins.

Everyone received his or her own copy of the bulletin, which was kept absolutely secret. In one issue, we all received false names that we were told to use both in the organisation and outside it, including on articles for *Youth*. This was the idea of the Montargis branch, where Han Qi had proposed it.

Han Qi was from Jiangsu (probably Haimen), but he used to tell people that he was from Anhui. Later, when the Anhui provincial government started giving its students subsidies, he got one, too, since his father Han Qibo, a well-known revolutionary, had been killed at Anqing in the early years of the Republic and counted as an Anhui martyr. When I first went to Montargis, Qin Zhigu told me confidentially that Han 'has a rather complicated brain'. Among us, he was probably the only one to realise that people who engage in revolution are likely to end up losing their lives. That statement means not that the rest of us were unaware that revolution demands sacrifice, but that our understanding of this fact was still abstract, whereas Han Qi's father had given his life for the revolution. That's probably why he very soon clashed with the organisation, left it, changed his name, graduated, returned to China, and became not only an engineer but (according to what I have heard) a county magistrate under the Guomindang.

Even so, his proposal was very useful. All of us in the organisation changed our names. I'm sure that many young people today have heard of Wu Hao[34] and Luo Mai,[35] false names that accompanied their owners back to China. But the rest of us kicked off our pseudonyms, like dirt on shoes, before leaving France. While preparing this chapter, I had to think for a long time before I remembered that my own pseudonym was Si Lian. I formed it by changing one syllable of my assumed name, Zelian; it had no deeper significance. Many others also chose names at random. One man chose the name S.3 by picking up two leads in the printshop where he worked. Chen Yannian wanted a name that was quick to write, so he chose Lin Mu, which means forest and comprises only twelve strokes. But some people took a long time over their choice. Li Weinong spent several days trying to think up a name, but to no avail; eventually, he decided to call himself Chu Fu ('hoe-axe') after studying the emblem on the masthead of our paper *Youth*, even though in reality the emblem showed not a hoe but a sickle and not an axe but a hammer. Wang Zekai called himself Luo Ti ('naked'); he had often represented political movements in the past and been wrongly accused of various crimes, so he wanted to show that he was above reproach. Zhang Songnian called himself R, apparently an abbreviation of the English word 'realist'. Zhou Enlai called himself Wu Hao (which sounds like 'number five' in Chinese) – people said that he chose this name because he had been the fifth person to join a secret student association in Tianjin. Later, a comrade from Fuzhou, Fang Erhao ('number two Fang'), also chose his name for the same sort of reason; he had been the second person to join a secret organisation, and apparently he still felt the event was worth commemorating. Zhang Bojian was called Hong Hong ('red swan'). In those days, names with 'red' in them were very popular, like, for example, Jiang Guangchi (Jiang 'gloriously red'). In Germany, Zhang had this name transcribed into English when he went to get a Russian passport. Later, in Moscow, we used to call him Hong Hong, but the students from Russia and other countries called him

---

34 Zhou Enlai.
35 Li Weihan.

Hunge-Hunge. Some people's pseudonyms were clearly related to their real names, for example, Xiong Xiong called himself Qi Guang (both names meaning 'big flame'). Xiao Zizhang called himself Ai Mier and Chen Qiaonian called himself Luo Re, since most people knew that Ai's and Chen's French names were Emile and Roger (of which their pseudonyms were Chinese transcriptions). When Xiong Rui called himself Yin Chang, Yin Kuan said: 'When people see it, they're bound to think it's me'. Li Weihan called himself Luo Man, which according to some people stood for the first two syllables of the word 'romanticism'. Wang Ruofei was called Lei Yin ('thunderous noise'), but I do not know why.

Youth was produced in large format as a sextodecimo. It had an eye-catching cover, which showed a crossed hammer and sickle and carried the slogan 'Proletarians of the world, unite!' Under the title it said in smaller letters, 'Organ of the Communist Youth Party'. I went to Place d'Italie to watch while the first issue was being written and printed. Chen Yannian was cutting the stencils; Wang Ruofei, Zhao Shiyan, and Zhou Enlai were sitting round the table having a discussion. Someone – I cannot remember who – said we should add the word 'newspaper' to the subheading, or rather, 'Newspaper of the Organ'. Zhou Enlai disagreed. He said that in German 'organ' was enough, there was no need to say 'newspaper'. Zhou had brought the theoretical articles with him from Germany; the articles written by the people in France were about current affairs. Zhang Songnian made a list of 'books to read', with titles in English, German, and French. Chen Yannian, head of the propaganda department, wrote no articles himself but was responsible for cutting the stencils. His cutting was clearer than lead-type, and more beautiful. It was the first time I had ever seen a mimeographed publication that could compare with a typeset one. Apart from items like reports on party affairs, which Zhao Shiyan cut directly onto stencils, everything else was the work of Chen Yannian.

Originally, the work-study students had not had a publication of their own. Sometimes, the newspaper put out in Tours published some of their contributions, but their literary battles were waged on wax. When someone or some group wanted to publicise a point of view, they had to go to the stationer to buy two or three stencils, a bottle of chemicals, and a few sheets of special paper. First, the article was written on the special paper with the chemicals, then it was printed on the stencil, and then the stencil was used to print on ordinary letter-paper. Each stencil could print forty to fifty sheets. Then the sheets were put in envelopes and posted to schools or factories where there were Chinese working, or to individuals. Such publications were, of course, irregular, rather like the circular telegrams that warlords used to send out. After the defeat of the Lyons campaign, *After Work* had started up, and now, we had *Youth*, which was a comparatively attractive publication. It helped greatly in developing our political work.

The two main fields of activity apart from internal education were among work-study students and the *Huagong*, or Chinese workers recruited during the War.[36] For some reason that I have now forgotten, the work-study movement suddenly flared up again after remaining dormant for one year. Montargis published a flurry of stencils, and Chinese in other places responded by sending delegates to Paris to organise a Work-Study Association. They elected some officials to staff the association office, among them Han Qi and Ren Zhuoxuan (there were others, too, but Han and Ren ran everything). They were new to this sort of work. Li Weihan, Wang Zekai, Zhao Shiyan, and Wang Ruofei did not dare show their faces, having been responsible for the movement during its previous defeat. But behind the scenes, they controlled Han and Ren. Han Qi had ideas of his own and was not willing to be someone else's cat's-paw, so he soon clashed with Wang Ruofei and either resigned or was expelled. This was a blow to our forces in the Work-Study Association.

After the 'hundred thousand' Chinese workers had 'taken part' in the War, the majority of them were sent back to China when their contracts expired, but a few thousand or even a few tens of thousands of free labourers stayed behind in France after they had served their time. The YMCA sent people to work among them. The newly established Communist organisation could hardly afford to ignore this target. Zhao Shiyan, our general secretary, worked hardest at it, and made friends with large numbers of Chinese workers. In one issue of *Youth*, Zhou Enlai wrote an article about our trade union work among them.

Chen Qiaonian worked in a glass factory near Place d'Italie. Quite a few other Chinese worked there, too, including some comrades, one of whom had his middle finger cut off by a machine. Zhao Shiyan and Chen Yannian were kept by the organisation. Those of us in work used to pay dues to the Party, a few francs a month, I cannot remember exactly, but not just a nominal amount. Every time I went to Paris I visited them, but I never once saw them eat. Mr Huang Qisheng went to see his nephew Wang Ruofei; when he returned to China, he praised them as 'Puritans'. 'Chen Duxiu's two sons live such a hard

---

36   By 1918, between 140,000 and 175,000 Chinese workers had been recruited to help the war-effort in France and elsewhere. This large-scale labour migration had a big impact on the development of the Chinese radical movement, for it gave Chinese students in France the chance to live with and to lead these workers, who as a result took back with them to China Communist, anarchist, and nationalist ideas. On the *Huagong*, see Griffin 1973 and Summerskill 1982.

life! They eat nothing but bread and sauce!' This was not Chinese soy-sauce but a solid mixture that was added to water and gradually dissolved into a salty brew used for flavouring. The two Chens and Zhao Shiyan really were Puritans. The treizième quartier was a poor people's area.

Mr Huang Qisheng and Mr Xu Teli were 'veteran work-study students', probably in their fifties. Xu Teli often wrote articles for that lead-type newspaper (whose name I have forgotten) and used to make propaganda for his work-study students and to spur on young people. He deeply hated Cai Hesen's Montargis movement. We used to consider Xu an enemy. I believe he was involved in the Lyons defeat. In 1927, in Changsha, he was a leader of the Guomindang left wing.[37] At around the time of the defeat of the revolution (I cannot remember whether it was before or after), he joined the Communist Party. Later, he took part in the Long March (or went to Moscow).[38] Today he is a Communist Party veteran.

During the May Fourth Movement, Huang Qisheng led a group of students from Guizhou around China. They visited Kang Youwei, Zhang Taiyan, and other famous people. When the work-study movement started, Huang brought his students to France. Probably all the students from Guizhou were brought by him. Later, someone in China wrote an article saying that while he was in France, he had set his students an essay 'On Qin Shihuang'.[39] That claim is untrue. All his students had exceeded him. Even his nephew Wang Ruofei showed no respect for his teachings. He was not like Xu Teli, who could never stop flaunting his status as a work-study student. At the time of the Lyons campaign, he and Shi Ying from Hubei mediated between representatives of the work-study students and Wu Zhihui, but Wu showed him no respect. Before I myself went to Montargis to work, he had already started working there. He had a small goatee and wore a top hat and a swallow-tail suit; not exactly appropriate for life in a factory. We urged him to live with us in the hut and eat with us, and told him he did not need to work in the factory. He accepted our proposal. In his free time, he used to clean up for us and tidy our things away. In the evenings, he talked to us about Gong Yang's commentary on the *Spring and Autumn Annals* and about modern history. When we met to discuss household affairs, he would also proffer his opinions, with great intensity and in a loud, clear voice. He was against Marxism, but when he read in Chen

---

37 See the chapter on Wuhan in Zheng's book.
38 In fact, he first went to Moscow, and later went on the Long March after going back to China.
39 At the time, to have students write articles on such a subject was considered old-fashioned and an echo of the old system of imperial examinations.

Duxiu's pamphlet on Marx how Marx's landlord had once confiscated his children's toys, he was immediately on Marx's side. After returning to China, he became Dean of China College in Shanghai, or of some similar institution.

The Montargis branch used to hold regular meetings. Mostly, we met in the woods or in the open countryside; we rarely met indoors. To this day, I clearly recall two meetings of the branch. One was when we met to say goodbye to Li Weihan, who was going back to China. He wrote a farewell letter to the comrades in Europe and asked for our views on a draft of it. The letter was very long. I forget what it said, but I recall Li walking up and down as he spoke (in those days, we used to meet standing). He gave us his views on certain comrades. Some, he said, were able but unwilling to learn, and others were willing to learn but not able; the latter held out more hope than the former.

The other time was when we discussed the question of the Communist Party joining the Guomindang.[40] That discussion took place after the debate had already started back in China. I expressed a few doubts, whereas Yin Kuan defended this policy. I remember he used two arguments to support his case. One was that if we joined the Guomindang, we could gradually increase our forces, like a snowball rolling down a hill. Perhaps those were not his exact words, but I still recall the simile. Another was based on the example of the French Communist Party. Yin said that though it was public, part of it was so secret that even party members were unaware of its existence. These arguments were designed to rebut various opinions the substance of which I no longer recall.

We started up a research society. Li Weinong and I got some others to join, including Qin Zhigu, but the membership stayed small. We held our meetings in the shed. All the leaders who were unpopular with the shed people used to attend. Everyone was asked to raise an issue to discuss. I was asked first. I proposed that there were three possible attitudes: help the capitalists against the proletariat, help the proletariat against the capitalists, or transcend the struggle of the two classes. I intended clarifying my own view, that is, that we should support the proletariat against the capitalists, but the others did not wait for that; they said even before I had finished speaking that there were only two possible standpoints, and no third view that transcended the others. I argued that the transcendent view did exist and that it had its supporters, for example, Romain Rolland. They immediately thought that I backed this point of view, and stood up one after the other to insist that such an attitude did not exist. What they should have said is that the attitude was not correct, or that it was

---

40   This policy was imposed on the Chinese Communist Party in 1922 by Henk Sneevliet (alias Maring), a representative in China of the Moscow-based Communist International.

wrong, or that it was reactionary. They left in a huff without giving me a chance to defend myself. A few days later, they criticised me at the branch meeting and said that even non-comrades had opposed this point of view. Why, then, had I supported it? I replied that I, too, opposed it and had simply raised it for the sake of discussion, but they had not bothered to hear me out and instead, had started arguing against me. They were still not satisfied. From then on, I became known as Romain Rolland. Admittedly, I was reading *Jean Christophe* at the time, but my aim in raising the question had been to oppose Romain Rollandism.

The revolution in European thought, from the rejection of Catholic theology to the emergence of Marxism, lasted three to four centuries, during which time it passed through an entire historical stage, that of bourgeois democracy. In China, we ought not to and moreover cannot go through such a long and complicated stage to get from Confucianism to Marxism. Chen Duxiu's development during the May Fourth Movement is clear proof of that fact. I myself, after having just accepted the argument against feudalism set out in *New Youth*, had only the anticapitalist *New Youth* to read. The editions of *New Youth* I got to read in France were no longer written by Hu Shi, Qian Xuantong, Liu Fu, Lu Xun, Shen Yinmo, and Zhou Zuoren, but by Li Da, Zhou Fuhai, Li Hanjun, Shi Cuntong, and, of course, Chen Duxiu.[41] But what caused my thinking to develop even further was not this Marxism of the Second International imported from Japan but Marxism of the Third International as propagated by the magazine *Clarté*. At first, *Clarté* was a weekly news-sheet, but later, it became a fully fledged fortnightly on sale at every kiosk in Paris (though I myself had a personal subscription). Barbusse was even more progressive than Romain Rolland, but he rarely wrote for *Clarté*, even though he was billed on the cover as its editor. Frequent contributors included Vaillant-Couturier (who had been to China to chair a conference against imperialism), Raymond Lefebvre (who attended the Third Congress of the Third International and drowned in the Black Sea on the way back), and Victor Serge (who later joined the Left Opposition and spent many years in Stalin's jails). They were all Communists (at the time Barbusse had not yet joined the Party), and they were all even more progressive than Barbusse. But in the view of Marxists in France, *Clarté* was a 'con-

---

41 By 1920, the left wing of the New Youth group, especially those around Chen Duxiu in Shanghai, thought their liberal partners around Hu Shi too conservative, whereas the liberals thought Chen too political. By May 1922, the alliance between the two groups had finally collapsed altogether.

fused' publication. Through *Clarté*, I got to read many Marxist writings. I also read *L'Humanité* (organ of the French Socialist Party, later of the Communist Party) and *Communist Bulletin* (edited by supporters of the Comintern in the French Socialist Party, under Valliant-Couturier). I bought a complete set of cheap pamphlets including the *Communist Manifesto*, *Socialism Utopian and Scientific*, and some current propaganda. On Yin Kuan's advice, I conscientiously read through the *Communist Manifesto*; Yin Kuan himself had read it at the urging of Cai Hesen or someone else in the Montargis faction.

I read *Jean Christophe* to improve my French and to widen my knowledge of French literature, but how could I have accepted Romain Rollandism when at the same time I was under the influence of Marxism? In my view, Montesquieu, Voltaire, Rousseau, and Diderot were no better than Kang Youwei and Liang Qichao.

When I first arrived in France, Liang Qichao was in Paris collecting materials for a book called *Ou you xinjing lu* ('Reflections on a Tour of Europe'). 'Western and Oriental culture' was a fashionable theme in those days. In France (and in other countries too), many Chinese students on government scholarships wrote their dissertations on this subject. Back in China, many journals (with the exception of *New Youth*) were constantly discussing the issue. Liang Shuming published his *Dong xi wenhua jiqi zhexue* ('Eastern and Western Culture and Philosophy'), which became as popular as Hu Shi's earlier *Outline History of Chinese Philosophy*. But I could work up no interest in this subject. Reading Hu's *Outline History* resolved the issue for me. There was nothing mysterious or inexplicable about Eastern civilisation. I was astonished that scholars like Liang Qichao and Liang Shuming could not see this. When I think today about this attitude, I know that it was a reaction against May Fourth, one that aimed at blocking the thought newly liberated from Confucian orthodoxy and preventing it from developing quickly in the direction of Marxism. This reaction was the product not of 'feudal vestiges' but of the newly arisen bourgeoisie, which – being incapable of producing its own stable ideology, of containing liberated thought within its own ideological domain for any period of time – had no choice other than to seek the help of feudal notions in order to hold back the quickening movement of ideas. Sun Yat-sen, leader of the Guomindang, had the same idea. Later, Dai Tianqiu[42] tried to include Sun Yat-sen in the pantheon of Yao, Shun, Yu, Tang, Wen, Wu, Zhou Gong,[43] and Confucius. That

---

42 Dai Jitao, a sponsor of the infant Chinese Communist Party, who immediately retreated to the Guomindang.

43 Yao and Shun were the last two of the eight 'culture heroes' of Chinese pseudohistory. Yu founded the Xia dynasty (2205–1766 BC); Tang founded the Shang dynasty (1600–1028

attempt is clear proof that Sun Yat-sen shared the same opinion as the two Liangs. This fact implies certain things about the Guomindang, but to spell them out here would lead us too far afield.

The reason China has no stable bourgeois ideology is because it has no capitalist future. Chinese capitalism developed so late that it can no longer catch up with the advanced countries, in the way that Russia and Japan caught up. The Russian proletariat has already seized state power and the proletariats of the other advanced countries have put proletarian dictatorship on the order of the day, but China is still only at the beginning of its 'modernisation'! The rapid development of the Chinese proletariat and the aid it is receiving from its brothers and sisters throughout the world will not permit the Chinese bourgeoisie to complete the path taken by the bourgeoisies of the advanced countries. From another point of view, the violence of social development has produced a violent development of thought in China. Recently, while re-reading a speech by Trotsky that I translated twenty years ago, I came across a passage that is very relevant to this question:

> ... [H]uman consciousness [is] in general frightfully conservative. When economic development proceeds slowly and systematically it tends to find it hard to break through human skulls. Subjectivists and idealists in general say that human consciousness, critical thought and so on and so forth draw history forward like a tug towing a barge behind it. This is untrue. You and I are Marxists and we know that the motive power of history consists of the productive forces which have up until now taken shape behind man's back and with which it tends to be very difficult to smash through man's conservative skull in order to produce the spark of a new political idea there and especially, let me repeat, if the development takes place slowly, organically and imperceptibly. But when the productive forces of a metropolis, of a classic land of capitalism, like Britain, encroach upon a more backward country, as with Germany in the first half of the 19th century, and with ourselves on the watershed of the 19th and the 20th centuries, and at the present time with Asia; when economic factors intrude in a revolutionary way cracking the old régime, when development takes places not gradually, not 'organically' by means of terrible shocks, and abrupt shifts in the old social layers, then critical thought finds its revolutionary expression incomparably more easily and

---

BC); Wu, the son of Wen, founded the Zhou dynasty in either 1122 or 1027 BC; and Zhou Gong was the consolidator of the Zhou.

rapidly, providing there are of course the necessary theoretical prerequisites for this.⁴⁴

That the May Fourth Movement, as evidenced in the development of my own thinking, did not pass from feudalism to socialism through a stable bourgeois-democratic stage was therefore only natural and logical. The forces that initially drove us to reject Confucianism were after all the same forces that drove us to reject democratism.⁴⁵ We must not forget that May Fourth happened after Russia's October Revolution.

I went through intense inner struggle to step from Confucianism to democratism, but I passed almost organically from democratism to socialism.

In November 1922, I read in *L'Humanité* that the Third International was holding its Fourth Congress in Moscow. A few days later, I went to Paris, where I saw a letter that Chen Duxiu had written to Zhao Shiyan from Moscow. The letter said that Chen was representing the Communist Party and Liu Renjing was representing the Communist Youth League at the Congress. He had seen how the Soviet state was already consolidated in Russia. He urged Zhao Shiyan to go back to China. Zhang Bojian had already gone to Moscow by this time, so Chen Duxiu certainly knew about the organisation in France, about Zhao Shiyan, and about Zhao's fondness for working among the Chinese labourers in France. The letter also said that there were very few comrades active back in China, and – comparing workers in China with Chinese workers in France – it added that the labour movement in China needed Zhao Shiyan more. Shortly after reading this letter, I heard from people in the Party that Chen Duxiu had already negotiated some places at Moscow's University of the East and that he wanted the comrades in Western Europe to send people to fill them. The rumour was confirmed when people came to ask me if I wanted to go. Of course, I said yes. In late February or early March 1923, I collected my last wage-packet at the rubber factory and moved to Paris.

Before the first batch of comrades set out, the Communist Youth Party held another conference in Paris. This time, it was not in the woods or in the countryside but in a police-station at Billancourt in the western suburbs of Paris, where there was a hall there that could be hired for meetings. Next door was the police-station. Yuan Qingyun hired the hall saying he was from the Chinese

---

44   Trotsky 1973 [1924], pp. 4–5.
45   By 'democratism', Zheng Chaolin means bourgeois democracy.

Students' Association. The French police do not understand Chinese, but of course we could not sing the Internationale.

Even more people attended this conference, for in the previous six months we had recruited many new comrades. But my recollections of it are not as clear as they are of the first conference. All I remember is that two Chinese labourers took part: Yuan Zizhen and Wang Ziqing. I remember that some new comrades got up to speak, among them Liu Bozhuang; I also remember that the conference expelled Zhang Songnian.

I cannot recall exactly why Zhang was expelled. I already knew before the conference that he had clashed with the leadership. He had planned to control the organisation by manipulating Zhou Enlai and Zhao Shiyan from behind the scenes, but Zhou and Zhao were unwilling to act as his puppets. Finally, Zhang tried to use his status as correspondent in Western Europe of the Chinese Communist Party, but it did not help him. The conference decided to expel him. During the vote, Zhao Shiyan stepped down from the chair, unwilling to take responsibility for such a move. Almost everyone voted for the expulsion. Only Zhou Enlai and one or two northerners opposed it. Zhang's most fervent opponents were Chen Yannian and Yin Kuan, but later, Zhang Songnian blamed Zhou Enlai, saying that he had secretly stirred things up against him, and broke off relations with Zhou.

In 1923, Zhang Songnian and his wife passed through Moscow on their way back to China. Despite the incident in Paris, the 'Moscow branch'[46] still received him as a comrade. Zhao Shiyan and Chen Yannian both joined in the meeting to welcome him. After he got back to China, he went to Shanghai, where he attended the Fourth Congress of the Chinese Communist Party, but without voting rights. He was the last person to speak out against entering the Guomindang. After returning to Beijing, he failed to realise his ambition. Gradually, he fell into the orbit of Zhang Shizhao and became a minor official in the Education Ministry of the Beiyang Government. He received a warning from the Party's Northern District Committee but he ignored it and was finally expelled. Today, he is a member of the Guomindang's Consultative Assembly.

---

46   See Part IV, p. 327.

My First Contact With New Ideas

Wang Fanxi

Source: Memoirs of a Chinese Revolutionary (1957).

The town in which I was born was a strange mixture of backwardness and enlightenment. Xiashi lies on the railway line between Shanghai and Hangzhou, and it was one of the main rice-markets in Western Zhejiang. Silk produced by the peasants from quite a wide area around it was bought by local merchants to be resold in Shanghai. Commercial capital had therefore long been dominant in the area, and all the most powerful figures in the community were merchants. For centuries, local scholars had been looked down on unless they also owned a pawnshop, bank, or large amounts of land. The stench of money prevailed over the fragrance of the book, and there was no cultural life to speak of. In a town of 30,000 inhabitants there were only two higher primary schools. Mine was regarded as the highest educational institution in the town since its headmaster was both rich and learned – he had passed the second grade in the Imperial examinations and most of the teaching staff were respected members of the local gentry. But the headmaster's methods were very old-fashioned. In the school-hall there was a tablet in honour of Confucius inscribed with the words 'Divine Sage of the Greatest Perfection', and we children had to bow down in front of it when we arrived in the morning and before we went home in the afternoon. Although the curriculum included natural science, music, and English for the older pupils, pride of place still belonged to Chinese literature, and in particular to the *Analects* of Confucius and Mencius. I only studied the *Analects*, which were taught by an old *xiucai* (a holder of the lowest degree in the Imperial examinations), who was versed in the Confucian classics and in traditional Chinese medicine. He was a very conscientious and fastidious teacher, and made us learn Zhu Xi's textual commentary by heart.

In 1919, when the May Fourth Movement[1] broke out, I was twelve years old. News from the Shanghai market could cause a commotion within a matter of hours in the local tea-shops, but 'trouble-making' by Beijing students attracted little attention. Shut up as we were inside the four walls of the school, it is not

---

1 On 4 May 1919, Beijing students went on strike, demonstrating against the decision reached on China at the Versailles Peace Conference and against the Chinese Government's acceptance of Japanese demands. May Fourth represented a turning point in Chinese history, and signalled the awakening of many Chinese intellectuals to the need for change.

surprising that the ideological ferment of the outside world took some time to seep through to us. But there was no way of holding up the inevitable, and a year or two later the new ideas took the school by storm.

It so happened that at the time the county's Education Inspector was eager to seize control of our primary school. With the support of a member of the local gentry, he managed to oust the old headmaster from his post. But he was unable to gain the sympathy of the rest of the townspeople, and when he came to take over as headmaster the teachers resigned *en masse*, and local scholars declined his offers of appointments. As he was therefore forced to seek his teaching staff elsewhere, he recruited a batch of recent graduates of the Hangzhou First Normal School to teach us.

Hangzhou First Normal School, a training college for secondary-school teachers, was the Beijing University of Zhejiang province. With Changsha First Normal School, where Mao Zedong studied, it was one of the two most powerful provincial outposts of the new ideological movement which centred on Beijing University. The Principal of Hangzhou First Normal School, Jing Hengyi, was rather similar in character to the President of Beijing University, Cai Yuanpei. He harboured no prejudices, and was prepared to tolerate all outstanding individuals, whatever their views. His own thinking was enlightened and democratic. One of his best-known students, Shi Cuntong, became famous for an anti-Confucian article he wrote, 'Against Filial Piety'. This was published in the school magazine and gained the First Normal School quite a reputation among radical intellectuals of the period. But the military, civil, and police authorities in Zhejiang Province, who had long considered the Hangzhou First Normal School a thorn in their flesh, seized this chance to start up a campaign of harassment. To protect his teachers and students, Jing Hengyi threatened to resign, and eventually did so. The students, who wanted him to stay on, boycotted lectures and demonstrated. After they had assembled on the school playing fields, they were surrounded by soldiers and police. This confrontation, which became famous throughout China, went on for several days.

One of the graduates from the Hangzhou First Normal School that our new headmaster appointed was a leader of that struggle, and he became my teacher in the graduation-class. The others were also followers of the new movement. On the first day of term we noticed that the tablet to Confucius had been removed, and that the Confucian classics had been taken off the curriculum. The four or five new teachers were only about ten years older than we were. Standing there in their long linen-gowns, they did not seem at all forbidding. The solemn atmosphere of the school under the old headmaster was clearly a thing of the past, and those of us who were now under the 'new dynasty' could not help feeling rather upset by what we saw. Students whose families could afford private tuition stayed away from school out of loyalty to the old headmaster. Most of us who remained were poor, and at first we received these representatives of the May Fourth Movement with a mixture of disappointment and apprehension. This feeling did not last for long, however, and after a couple of months we began to hero-worship them.

We no longer feared our teachers, as we had in the old days. On the contrary, they were like friends to us. We found it easy to grasp the things they taught us, unlike the classical texts we had studied previously. We greedily devoured Chen Duxiu's and Hu Shi's articles on the literary revolution, Zhou Zuoren's essays, and the poems in modern Chinese by Liu Bannong and others. (I should add that the teachers never once told us about Lu Xun's writings, and we did not even hear his name mentioned; I myself only heard of Lu Xun and began to read him after 1925.) We were especially fond of hearing them talk about their lives as students and the struggle in Hangzhou. It was not long before we began to experiment with new activities inside our own school: we set up a school-council, ran our first library, subscribed to newspapers and magazines from Shanghai and Hangzhou, wrote out our own school newspaper by hand and pasted it up on the school wall. We even opened a school-shop (dubbed the 'business-management training department' by our English teacher) where we sold exercise books, pencils, and sweets.

I left primary school at the age of fourteen, and like many others of my generation clashed with my father about my future career. He was something of a scholar, and had gained the degree of *xiucai* during the last Imperial examinations ever held. He had many friends among the educated local gentry, but because he was not from a wealthy background they never really accepted him as an equal, even when he was drinking and swapping poems with them, and he resented this. Hence the two sides to his character: he looked down upon his friends as merchants pretending to be scholars, but he was also determined to compete with them in amassing a fortune. When he got drunk he often used to remark cynically to us children: 'There's not much percentage in being a scholar, they'll only respect you if you've got money'. When I had finished my primary-school studies (generally considered as the equivalent of a *xiucai* degree under the old Qing dynasty), he insisted that I should study business and refused to let me go on to middle school. Another reason for his decision was the state of our family finances: my father simply did not have enough money to pay for me to study at Hangzhou, the provincial capital. He therefore arranged for me to receive training in an import-and-export business in Shanghai.

In my outlook and my aspirations I was very unlike my father. I think I must have been born an idealist. As a child, I loved novels of heroism, and adored a great-uncle who had been in the army and told me about his father's adventures fighting for the Taipings.[2] Now a year or so of education in the spirit of the May Fourth Movement had turned me into a high-flying idealist 'infected with the sickness of the epoch'. Given my mental state, it was inevitable that I would refuse to accept the future my father had mapped out for me. When he told me that he had found me an apprenticeship in Shanghai where I could study English and learn about the import-export trade I found the courage to blurt out: 'I don't want to go into business, I want to go to Hangzhou to study!' Relations between us became tense and remained so for months. Finally we arrived at a compromise: he would let me go on to middle school as long as I agreed to study commerce. I therefore entered Hangzhou Commercial Middle School.

This school was on the same site as Hangzhou First Normal School. Both used the buildings which under the Qing dynasty had housed the Imperial examination rooms, and were separated by a wall. Physically, I was on the eastern side of the wall, but my heart was on the western side. The curriculum of the commercial school did not arouse the slightest spark of interest in me. I especially detested book-keeping, abacus work, and the course on how to recognise counterfeit coins. The atmosphere in the school was utterly philistine. There were no student activities, and even less intellectual life than there had been in my primary school under the old régime. After over a year breathing the fresh air of the May Fourth Movement, I felt suffocated in my new surroundings. I still had no definite idea about what I wanted to study, and I was not in the least concerned about what profession I should follow. What I really cared about was scholarship and knowledge in general, especially the 'new' variety. Therefore I read every modern book I could get my hands on, not caring whether it was literature, philosophy, or science. Since I could not afford to buy books, I would go and browse in the bookshops every Sunday, or borrow from the West Lake Library. Few of these books were easy to understand, and some of them were very difficult, often as a result of bad translation; but, whether I could digest them or not, I swallowed them all. In my two years at the commercial school I did not even learn how to use the book-keeper's ruler for drawing lines in the account books. But I already knew the names of a string of famous thinkers, from John Dewey and Bertrand Russell to Henri Bergson and Rabindranath Tagore, as well as classical thinkers like Socrates and Plato. I had even read some of their works in Chinese translation. My interests were moving further and further away from commerce, and to stay on in that school would have been pure torture for me.

---

2 The great peasant rebellion (1850–64) against Manchu rule, led by Hong Xiuquan.

Fortunately, that was not to happen. During the second term of my second year, we students went on strike against the Principal, and I was elected as one of our representatives. We achieved our demands, but, at the end of term, our representatives were all expelled. I was originally among those expelled but, because the Chinese literature teacher, who was a friend of my father, spoke up for me, I was in the end quietly advised to leave. To my surprise, my father was not at all angry, and he willingly allowed me to transfer to a privately run, ordinary middle school. After that I had nothing more to do with commerce.

A year later, my father died, and the next year, 1925, just before I graduated from middle school, the May Thirtieth Movement erupted. On 30 May 1925, Shanghai students staged a mass demonstration in support of workers on strike at a Japanese cotton-mill. While marching into the city centre, they were fired on by British police. Several died and still more were wounded. As a result, a furious anti-imperialist movement swept first Shanghai and then the rest of China. This was the prologue to the Second Chinese Revolution.

I was then eighteen years old. In the two years leading up to May Thirtieth, I had continued to read indiscriminately whatever came to hand, but like many other young people of my generation I came under the influence of the newly-formed Creation Society[3] and gradually developed a particular interest in literature. I was very fond of Yu Dafu's work and whether I was aware of it or not I was profoundly influenced by his romantic and decadent style. Because of my father's death and my family's worsening financial plight, I was all the more ready to identify with the unhappy hero of Yu Dafu's novel *Degradation*. Among my fellow students there were some who liked to write, and there were even one or two adherents of the new school. Six months before the events of May Thirtieth, three other students and I produced a paper called *Red News*. I cannot say for certain why we used the word 'red' – our thinking was still far from 'red', and so were the contents of the paper. I recall that one of the articles was a translation from the English I made of the introduction to a history of philosophy published in the Home University Library series. Those of us who collaborated on the paper had no fixed ideological positions, and our politics could best be described as nationalist. But the name of the paper created considerable alarm and, as it was banned by the school principal, the first issue was also the last.

---

3 The Creation Society was a literary group, organised in the summer of 1921 by Guo Moruo, Yu Dafu, and other students returned from Japan and France. At first it espoused 'art for art's sake' and romanticism, but later it moved to the left and finally advocated 'proletarian literature'.

Red ideas were in fact already circulating in Hangzhou at that time. The address of the Communist Party organ *Guide Weekly* was given openly as Hangzhou Law School. An Cunchen (later renamed An Tiren), one member of the teaching staff (later murdered by Chiang Kai-shek in Shanghai), was a well-known member of the Communist Party, and several people from my home-town were carrying out Communist activities under the guise of doing Guomindang work. The Socialist League of Youth was already in existence, and had a small group at Hangzhou First Normal School, run by my childhood friend Xu Zhixing. I was in constant touch with this group, but I never joined it, since I used to look down upon people who engaged in political activity. I believed strongly in 'study for study's sake', and I felt that the pursuit of politics and the search for knowledge were mutually exclusive. I had chosen the latter, and intended to devote myself heart and soul to research. One or two of the students in my middle school had become politically active and joined the Guomindang: they thought themselves a cut above everyone else, but they were very poor students, which only strengthened my prejudices.

These views of mine reflected the differentiation taking place within the main current of the new ideological movement, although it was not until some years after May Fourth that I personally came into contact with the ideas it represented. By the time that I caught up with and came to accept these ideas, the new ideology had itself changed and developed further. The *New Youth*[4] group had split, and its two leading figures, Chen Duxiu and Hu Shi, had parted company and gone their separate ways. The former advanced towards Marxism, while the latter remained stuck at the bourgeois-democratic stage. The former made the leap from thought into action, and from the literary to the political revolution; the latter wanted to conserve the 'purity' of ideology, and was opposed to scholars sullying themselves with politics. Chen Duxiu, Li Dazhao, and others had set up the Chinese Communist Party (CCP) in 1921, and made an alliance with the revolutionary nationalist Sun Yat-sen and his Guomindang in the south; Hu Shi and others had joined Liang Qichao's 'Study Clique', which based its political hopes on the warlord government in the north.

I was completely unaware of this process of differentiation and regrouping in the Chinese intellectual world. Even though Hangzhou was a provincial capital where new publications from Beijing could quite easily be obtained, it was still very backward. Insofar as the teachers and students of Hangzhou were of the new school, most of them did not advance beyond accepting the general spirit of May Fourth. In Hangzhou the dividing line between the new and the old was, and remained, between those who were for Science and Democracy,

---

4   *New Youth* was the name of a magazine published by Chen Duxiu.

MY FIRST CONTACT WITH NEW IDEAS

and those who were against them, between those who attacked Confucius and those who revered him. It was therefore only natural that the young people ideologically awakened by the May Fourth Movement in Hangzhou tended to drift into Hu Shi's camp (that is, Liang Qichao's camp), rather than Chen Duxiu's. Their attitude towards the handful of 'Guomindang elements' was hostility and contempt. This was because the latter were not 'faithful to the cause of learning' and instead spent their time 'messing about' with politics.

Before the spring of 1925, I was also one such unwitting follower of the Hu Shi school. However, the experience of the May Thirtieth Movement brought a radical and decisive change in me. When the tragic events of May Thirtieth took place in Shanghai, we were busy taking our end of school examinations. At first, we did not pay much attention to what was happening, but when we heard that the protests were gathering momentum, and that students, merchants, and workers were staging strikes and creating unprecedented turmoil, we felt we had to do something, if only not to be outdone by the Shanghai students. The atmosphere in my school became heated and the students excited. Contacts began to grow between one school and another, and everyone thirsted for action. Some three or four days after the Shanghai killings, a delegation from the Shanghai Students' Union arrived in Hangzhou and told me in detail what had happened. Hangzhou students responded immediately by electing two delegates from each school to form the Hangzhou Students' Union (representing middle school and college students). Since I used to take part in public-speaking competitions, and had once won the all-Hangzhou schools public-speaking prize, my fellow students considered that I had the necessary qualifications for being a delegate and duly elected me. The other delegate was one of the Guomindang 'elements'. At first I was not too keen on being a delegate, because of the prejudice I mentioned earlier: I was afraid of appearing vain. And to my surprise, at the inaugural meeting of the Hangzhou Students' Union I was put in charge of the propaganda department. This both alarmed and embarrassed me: how on earth would I be able to revise for the school-leaving examinations, let alone prepare for university entrance? But these feelings were short-lived. As soon as I started work, the struggle between the students and the local authorities in Hangzhou intensified daily, and I threw myself wholeheartedly into my new role, putting the question of examinations and university to one side for the moment.

My work for the Hangzhou Students' Union lasted only two months, from the beginning of June until I left Hangzhou at the end of August to sit the entrance examinations for Beijing University. But my experiences in those two months profoundly influenced my life and my thinking. In short, I left the Hu Shi camp for that of Chen Duxiu. During those two months my whole time was taken up with work, and yet the experience taught me more than ten years' reading. The struggles which take place during periods of great historical importance are like huge furnaces which instantly reduce to ashes all unhealthy or inappropriate thoughts or feelings and enhance one's better qualities. A student movement in a provincial capital, especially at that time, was not particularly significant, either in itself or in terms of its wider repercussions. But, because this movement occurred within the context of other epoch-making struggles and was seen to be part of a nation-wide anti-imperialist and anti-warlord upsurge, it took on a very different meaning. For someone like me, who had only just taken the first step into the realm of ideas, it was of decisive significance. I very soon realised that the theory of 'study for study's sake' was a false one; true learning should be integrated into and should serve action. I also realised that people who are politically oppressed cannot possibly engage in pure scholarship, as what they learn must have as its focal point the struggle to remove that oppression. I reached this awareness partly through my own experience in the course of the struggle and partly through my contacts with those people whom I had formerly looked down on as 'show-offs'. I found that most of them were not only more able than I but also more learned. The 'true' learning which had for several years now been my declared aim in life – a hotchpotch of Dewey, Russell, Bergson, and others – was now revealed as an ill-informed mess of confused ideas. It was during this period that I first came into contact with Marxism. Two friends from my home-town who were working in the Guomindang lent me some elementary social science pamphlets which struck me as examples of practical and useful learning, worlds apart from what I had been studying before.

My short period of student activity in Hangzhou taught me something which has stood me in good stead all my life: that it is impossible to draw any distinguishing line between struggles waged against internal enemies and those waged against external ones. Victory over the first is an indispensable pre-condition for victory over the second. I remember that at the first meeting of the Hangzhou Students' Union one important question under discussion was whether or not to express solidarity with the Shanghai students by boycotting lectures. The delegates were split two ways on this question. Some argued that, since the struggle was against an external adversary (British imperialism), we should not use the boycott weapon, which was more suited to dealing with internal matters such as government corruption or reactionary measures by the school administration. In their opinion, to go on a lecture-strike to oppose the British in the international settlements in Shanghai was the equivalent of shooting an arrow without a target. 'The British won't care if you boycott classes', they said. 'You will simply be spiting yourselves. If we really want to

MY FIRST CONTACT WITH NEW IDEAS

oppose imperialism, we must drop the idea of a lecture strike and study harder in order to arm ourselves'. Arguments of this sort were very attractive at first. But those delegates who in one way or another had connections with outside political organisations were firmly in favour of the boycott. Their argument was quite simple: if we did not go on strike, then all talk of resisting imperialism was hot air. I was among those in favour of going on strike, but in my heart of hearts I was more convinced by the other argument; I only favoured a boycott because I wanted to see some action.

The strike-resolution was passed by a narrow majority, and the entire student body was organised into hundreds of small units, each of which agitated in theatres, tea-shops, parks, and on the streets. The mobilisation was very thorough. It even affected the students of the ultra-conservative girls' middle schools in Hangzhou. At first we even tried to get the shopkeepers to close down their shops, but without much success. Finally, the Hangzhou students' movement held its biggest demonstration ever, numbering seven to eight thousand people, including primary school pupils in their early teens and a number of townspeople.

The Military Governor of Zhejiang province was a very shrewd and cunning northern warlord called Sun Chuanfang. Since the whole country was in a mood of extreme militancy, he did not dare to repress us openly and even came to us to express his 'sympathy'. During the demonstration he sent soldiers with loaded rifles slung over their shoulders to 'protect' us. He also summoned a delegation of students, and told them that he was as patriotic as the next man, but that we should leave foreign affairs to the responsible authorities and devote our energies to our studies. At first it was very difficult, especially for those of us who were teenagers, to see through his treachery; but we gradually became aware of what he was up to behind the scenes. The delegates of a physical training college, whose principal was in collusion with the provincial authorities, began to sabotage the Students' Union by behaving disruptively. Then a teacher at my school who was an ardent supporter of the students' movement was sacked, and I myself received a warning in a roundabout way. I was told that if I did not forgo my political activities I would be refused a graduation certificate.

By the time I handed over my responsibilities in the Hangzhou Students' Union propaganda department to my successor and left for Beijing, I had already purged myself of the last vestiges of Hu Shi's and Liang Qichao's values, and had gone over completely to the left-wing positions of Chen Duxiu, even though I had still not yet joined the Communist Party.

PART 3

Chinese Trotskyists in the Revolution of 1925–7

Before and After May Thirtieth

Zheng Chaolin

Source: *An Oppositionist for Life: Memoirs of the Chinese Revolutionary Zheng Chaolin* (1945).

I arrived in Shanghai just at the time of the war between Qi Xieyuan and Lu Yongxiang.[1] There were notices pasted up along the roads declaring martial law in the name of the Shanghai Municipal Council. Lu Yongxiang was in a weak position and the war was gradually getting closer to Shanghai. But, within the International Settlement, things were calm. The house on Moulmein Road was double-fronted with a wing-room abutting onto the road and a bridging room over the alley, so that you could cross the alley from the upper wing-room. Peng Shuzhi lived in this bridging room. The wing-room was empty save for a large table, several untidy rows of chairs, and an empty bed next to the bridging room, on which I spread my bedding. The rear wing-room was Qu Qiubai's bedroom. His wife had died not long before. He was a widower. Cai Hesen and his wife Xiang Jingyu lived in the upstairs middle guest-room. Li Longzhi[2] and his wife lived in the downstairs guest-room. Zhang Tailei's mother, wife, and child occupied the whole of the downstairs wing-room. Two maidservants lived in the small room off the landing.[3] One looked after Qu Qiubai; the other, Auntie

---

1 Qi Xieyuan, a warlord of the Zhili faction, was Military Governor of Jiangsu. Lu Yongxiang, Military Governor of Zhejiang, controlled the Shanghai area. In September 1924, Qi attacked Lu and defeated him (though the victory was short-lived).
2 Li Lisan.
3 Zheng Chaolin is describing a lane house, typical of Shanghai, Hankou, Tianjin, and other foreign settlements in China in the early twentieth century. These houses were generally owned by foreign estate companies (Shanghai's best-known landlords being Hadoon and Sassoon, both British Jews). But, save for a few White Russians, they were occupied almost exclusively by Chinese of the middle and lower classes. (Most foreigners lived in apartments, European style terraced houses, or detached cottages in the suburbs.) There is no space between these lane houses; each gives onto a common lane. Most lane houses have a small front courtyard and a passage (which may or may not be roofed and contains a water-tap and a brick-basin) leading to the back door. They have no toilets. All lane houses have two storeys, with a big room on each. The downstairs room can be used as a parlour or dining room; the upstairs one, as a bedroom. The small room off the landing is known as the pavilion room; being cheapest, in the old days it was usually let to a single person (often a student or jobless intellectual; hence the term 'pavilion room writer'). Generally, all these rooms (including the

Long, had been brought by Mao Zedong from Hunan, and now cooked for us. We took our meals in Li Longzhi's room. While we were eating, we could see Li Yichun's bulging belly sticking out from the bed on which she was sleeping. We received guests not in the guest-room but in the upstairs wing-room. The big table alongside my bed was for receiving guests and also for holding meetings of the Central Committee's Presidium. Besides this, it doubled as my work-desk. There was no electrical light in this room, so at night we lit oil-lamps.

Li Longzhi shook hands with Chen Yannian, and also with me. We had already met in France. Li was from Liling in Hunan. He was tall and strong with rather white skin. He had a loud, clear voice, flashing eyes, and heavy red lips. I have already talked about his time in France. After being deported back to China, he worked in the Anyuan collieries in Jiangxi fomenting strikes and organising unions and cooperatives; later, he went to Hankou,[4] and during or after the Beijing-Hankou rail-strike, he was almost arrested; now, he was responsible together with Xiang Delong[5] for the workers' movement in Shanghai. He took Cai Zhihua, who had arrived together with us, to live in a workers' club in Xiaoshadu.[6]

In the afternoon, Qu Qiubai returned from teaching at Shanghai University. I had never seen a comrade as neat as Qu. He was wearing a hat, a Western suit, and leather shoes. No one introduced us. All he saw was a newly arrived 'child' proof-reading *Guide Weekly* at the table for receiving visitors in the guest-room. As for me, I realised that he was Qu Qiubai, the brilliant student of the Beijing Russian-language school, the publisher together with Zheng Zhenduo and Geng Jizhi during the May Fourth Movement of *Shuguang* ('Dawn') magazine, who had later become a journalist for *Chenbao* and been sent to Russia as a reporter. In Russia, he had been won to Marxism, joined the Communist Party, interpreted for Chinese students at KUTV, and written *Chi chao ji* ('Red Tide') and *Chidu xinshi* ('An Inside History of the Red Capital'). After returning to China, he edited *New Youth*. He was our theoretician, and now, he was Director of the Sociology Department at Shanghai University. It was a long time before I learned that during that period he was very unhappy. He had just been urgently

---

attic where there was one) were partitioned (sometimes more than once), with more than one family inhabiting each floor. The lane house described at the beginning of this excerpt is a duplex variant on this pattern, with an extension reaching across the alley from part of the upper floor.

4   Wuhan is on the middle reaches of the Yangtze. Hankou is part of the tri-city of Wuhan, which comprises Hankou, Hanyang, and Wuchang.
5   Xiang Ying.
6   A workers' district in west Shanghai.

summoned back to Shanghai from Guangdong, where under the direction of Borodin, he was engaged as a representative of the Communist Party's Central Committee in various activities of which the Central Committee disapproved.

Cai Hesen was suffering from his old ailment, asthma. He was lying on his bed, served by an old-fashioned girl-student wearing a white blouse and a black skirt, who entered and left by the side-door of the wing-room. This girl-student ignored the fact that there was bedding on the empty bed in the wing-room. I already knew that she was Xiang Jingyu. The next day or the day after, a guest came and Auntie Long sent up his name-card. It was Lin Zuhan. Xiang Jingyu asked the guest to wait at the table where I was working. After a while, a tall thin man emerged from the upstairs guest-room. He was breathing asthmatically, but began conversing animatedly with the new arrival. He spoke rather more than the guest. Finally, the guest fell silent and took his leave. Just at that moment, Zhang Bojian arrived, probably to fetch the galley-proofs, and asked Cai Hesen – for it was he – who the guest had been. Cai Hesen had still not apparently had enough of talking, so the torrent continued for a while. He said among other things, 'He's a centrist'. Having proof-read *Guide Weekly*, I already knew that Cai divided the Guomindang into three factions: the anti-Communists were the right wing, those who approved of the proposals contained in *Guide Weekly* were the left wing, and the rest were centrists. Actually, Lin Zuhan had already joined the Communist Party (as I learned later), but Cai Hesen still did not recognise him as a true comrade.

I was rather surprised that this was Cai Hesen. In my mind's eye, Cai had been a new Wang Anshi, who talked about Marxism with tousled hair and a dirty face.[7] When I saw him that day, his face was clean, his hair was not particularly long, and he was dressed like a country *xiucai*,[8] quite the opposite of Qu Qiubai, who looked like one of the talented scribblers in the foreign settlement.

Cai Hesen was general editor of *Guide Weekly*. From an organisational point of view, he was my and Zhang Bojian's 'direct superior'. I was in charge of proof-reading and collecting material; Zhang was in charge of printing and distribution, and before my arrival, he had also proof-read. He rented a room elsewhere for himself. Although from Yunnan, he had several Sichuanese characteristics. He became my close friend. We spoke to one another without the slightest reservation about people and issues. He had arrived in Shanghai more than two months earlier than I. He told me everything he had learned during

---

7   Wang Anshi was a Northern Song dynasty reformer who according to conservatives never washed his face.
8   The holder of a low-level imperial degree under the dynasties.

that period, for example, that the house on Moulmein Road was a well-known centre of Bolshevism and that the reactionaries kept a close eye on it.

Whenever the Presidium met, Chen Duxiu came, Wang Hebo came, Lin Yunan came, Cai Hesen emerged through the side-door of the guest-room, Peng Shuzhi emerged from the bridging room, and together they took over my working table. I automatically retreated to the room of Qu Qiubai, who was mostly away from home. Chen, Wang, and Cai formed the Presidium; Lin Yunan represented the Youth League. And in what capacity did Peng Shuzhi attend? He had been sent by the Comintern, and attended these meetings as a future member of the Central Committee.

Yuan Qingyun was also a painter. He had painted a portrait of Chen Duxiu from a photograph, framed it, and hung it in our KUTV dormitory. I could now see that his portrait was a good likeness, though the real Chen looked even older than the painted one. Chen was only forty-odd, but his hair had already begun to thin. He was of medium build and rather swarthy; his eyes slanted; he spoke with an Anqing accent. When he laughed, he revealed a set of neat white teeth. He did not like wearing Western clothes. When I first met him, he was wearing a traditional long gown, a mandarin jacket, and a hat. Later, when winter came, he wrapped a scarf round his neck. In the summer, he wore a long gown woven from grass linen. This was the man whom all China's revolutionary youth considered as their leader, and whom Confucian gentlemen everywhere heartily despised. Even then, there were already many myths and legends about him. Now, I could see him with my own eyes, hear him with my own ears. The first time I had come across the name of this man, while reading an article by him, I had cursed him in my diary; later, I had gradually come to feel that what he said was not unreasonable, and later still, that it was eminently reasonable. Now, I was carrying out revolutionary work under his direction.

In the autumn of 1924, everyone felt that China was on the brink of a revolution or a great movement; at the very least I felt that, and so did people I was close to. On the one hand, the government, inherited from Yuan Shikai, of the Beiyang warlords was already in decline and splitting; clearly, it would not last long. On the other hand, a new force was emerging that China had never before known: a modern proletariat. China had long known economic strikes; and by May Fourth at the latest we had begun to witness mass political strikes, the Shanghai strikes in support of the demands of the students' movement. In 1922, there was the great Hong Kong seamen's strike that finally forced British imperialism to submit. In 1923, there was the great Beijing-Hankou rail-strike,[9] which ended in a massacre but did not lead to the demoralisation of the working class – on the contrary, it infused the workers with new ardour. Even more important, China already had a proletarian political party. The Chinese Communist Party led not only the economic struggles of the proletariat but the struggles of the people of the entire country, and it took part in and developed the national and the democratic struggle. In the face of the workers' struggle and Communist activity, the whole of the petty bourgeoisie and part of the big bourgeoisie gradually lost their fear of the Beiyang warlords and dared to rise up against them and to seek a way out for themselves. The awakening of the middle classes found its expression in the reorganisation of the Guomindang. Before reorganisation, in effect, the Guomindang did not exist. At around the time of the 1911 Revolution, this revolutionary organisation rapidly crumbled as a result of the defeat of the revolution[10] and of betrayals by its members. There was Sun Yat-sen and a number of people close to him and there was a vague democratic programme and a faint memory of the revolution, but there was no Guomindang. It was the experience, funds, and firepower of the Soviet proletariat and the efforts of the Chinese Communist Party that fashioned a new political party, modelled on the organisation of the Russian Bolsheviks, under the old and vacant signboard of the Guomindang. In January 1924, this party held its *first* all-China congress – it was only then that a Guomindang organisation came into being; the Central Committee was set up in Guangzhou, and branches were set up at provincial, municipal, county, and district levels all over China. The Communists were in a small minority on the Guomindang's Central Executive Committee and Control Committee, but all major decisions were in the hands of Borodin, who was adviser to the Guomindang Government. The local branches were almost exclusively under Communist control. The main exceptions were Guangzhou and Shanghai, where some so-called 'rightist elements' could match the Communists. Apart from the Guomindang organisation, a military academy funded and armed by the Soviet Union was set up at Huangpu in Guangzhou. Its main instructors were from the Soviet Union, but its head was Chiang Kai-shek. The Communist Zhou Enlai, newly returned from Europe, was also assigned to work there.

---

9   On 7 February 1923, Zhili warlords bloodily suppressed a Communist-led strike of railmen. In Wuhan itself, the labour movement never really recovered from this blow until the arrival of the Guomindang's Northern Expedition in the city in September 1926.
10 In 1913, Yuan Shikai, first President of the Chinese Republic, suppressed the Guomindang and started a reign of terror.

After the defeat on 7 February 1924 of the great Beijing-Hankou rail-strike,[11] the Chinese Communist Party decided to take the path of 'national revolution'. The Chinese Communist movement was originally a product of the May Fourth Movement. After a short while, this patriotic movement, which opposed feudal Confucian ritual, which reformed the Chinese language, and which proposed science and democracy, turned into a socialist or communist movement. Chen Duxiu and Li Dazhao, professors at Beijing University, went from democratism to communism and extreme leftists among the leaders of the students at Beijing University – people like Zhang Guotao, Deng Zhongxie,[12] Fan Hongjie, Gao Shangde, and Luo Zhanglong – went from the patriotic movement to the labour movement. There were no factories in Beijing, so they decided to leave the city and organise the railway workers. Changxingdian Railway Station became the hub from which they spread outwards across railway lines throughout the north. The labour movement in the north was virgin territory. Things went less smoothly for the Communists in the south, where they met competition from remnants of the Chinese Socialist Party[13] formed in the early years of the Republic, and from Guomindang members who had become active in the labour movement before the reorganisation of their party. These people had set up labour unions or workers' associations, but they had no followers. In Guangdong, there were some workers' organisations similar to the old-style guilds under the leadership of the Mechanics' Union. These bodies constituted a mass organisation, but resisted encroachment by the Communist Party.

At the time of its founding, the Chinese Communist Party naturally took as its banner proletarian-socialist revolution. The Guomindang did not exist; the Communist leaders and rank and file looked down with contempt on its remnants, including Sun Yat-sen. They considered them to be yesterday's people, whereas they thought that they themselves were taking giant steps towards the future. Had anyone said at that time that China first needed to go through a bourgeois-democratic revolution before carrying out proletarian-socialist revolution, so the Guomindang should be revived and the Communists should join that 'revolutionary organisation' and lead it, they would have been laughed at. In short, at the time of the Party's First Congress, no one proposed anything

---

11   The warlord Wu Peifu executed two leaders of the strike on that day.
12   Deng Zhongxia.
13   The Chinese Socialist Party was founded in 1911 by Jiang Kanghu, who had encountered anarchist and socialist ideas in Japan and Europe. In 1913, Jiang claimed that his party had 400,000 members, but he was almost certainly exaggerating. His party went into decline after 1913, when he retired to the United States. His attempt to revive it in the early 1920s came to grief after his relationship with Puyi, the deposed emperor, was exposed.

of the sort. Later, when such proposals finally surfaced, they came not from the Chinese Communists but from the Dutch Communist Maring,[14] who had been commissioned by the Comintern to direct the young Chinese Communist Party and by the Soviet Ministry of Foreign Affairs to liaise with China's democratic leaders. Maring proposed that the Chinese Communist Party should take part in the 'national-revolutionary' movement and join Sun Yat-sen's Guomindang, the revival of which Maring had urged and plotted. After its Second Congress, the Chinese Communist Party had already issued a circular telling party and league branches to discuss joining the Guomindang. At the Third Congress,[15] Maring demanded that the Party formally resolve to adopt such a line. He met with opposition, not only from Li Hanjun but from Zhang Guotao and even Chen Duxiu. Finally, Maring took out his order from the Comintern. More than ten years later, a historian[16] went to Holland to interview Maring about this. Maring denied that he had used the authority of the Comintern to force the Chinese Communist Party to accept this line. But, at that time, Russian diplomatic interests required a government in China like Kemal's in Turkey, so Russian diplomats needed the Comintern and its Chinese section[17] to do their utmost to make such a government come about; this is an undeniable fact. No one raised the question of whether another position might not have served the Chinese and the world revolution better, for everyone without exception believed that the interests of Soviet diplomacy and of world revolution were identical. But in reality, it was exactly in that period that the interests of the Soviet Union and of world revolution began to part.

When I first got back to China, the Chinese Communist Party had already completed this evolution, or rather this regression. After the 7 February defeat, the labour movement went through a temporary depression. Zhang Guotao began to show some passivity and was soon arrested and sent to jail; Li Hanjun, who was the fiercest opponent of joining the Guomindang, quit the Communist Party. The Comintern line was passed, party opinion was unanimous, and the Party's entire work pressed on in this new direction. The Communist Party had originally set up *Guide Weekly* to the express end of serving the 'national revolution'; now, *Guide Weekly* became the Party's official organ. I personally had

---

14 Hendricus Sneevliet.
15 Here I am wrong. It was at the West Lake (Hangzhou) Conference, held shortly after the Second Congress, that Maring insisted on this point. By the time of the Third Congress, Chen Duxiu had already been persuaded, and no longer opposed joining the Guomindang. [Note added by Zheng Chaolin in 1989.]
16 Harold Isaacs.
17 That is, the Chinese Communist Party.

already gone through this 'evolution' in France, so when I returned home, I took the national revolution and joining the Guomindang for granted, even though deep inside I still had reservations about it. For I had come to Communism as a result of my study of the world's general development, not of China's special development.

In Shanghai, what first attracted my attention was the struggle within the Guomindang between the Communists (or leftists) and the rightists. This struggle took place at the Guomindang headquarters at 44 Route Vallon. Before I reached Shanghai, some rightists beat up Shao Lizi there. At first, they had thought that he was a Guomindang veteran. Only now did they discover that he had joined the Communist Party. Of *Republic Daily*'s two chief editors, Ye Chucang was a rightist and Shao Lizi a leftist. They were old friends, but under the control of their respective factions, they began to fight; of the rest of the editors, Zhang Tailei and Shen Zemin were leftists and Chen Dezheng was a rightist. The Principal of Shanghai University, Yu Youren, was a figurehead who sympathised with the leftists; the Dean, Deng Zhongxia (that is, Deng Zhongxie), the Director of the Sociology Department, Qu Qiubai, and Professors Shi Cuntong, Zhang Tailei, Yun Daiying, Peng Shuzhi, and Jiang Guangchi were leftists; the Director of the Department of Chinese Literature, Chen Wangdao, sympathised with the leftists, but the Director of the Department of English Literature, He Shizhen, was a rightist. In the struggle between these various bodies, the Left invariably had the upper hand, for the Right was made up of old public figures who were disunited, lacked a central leadership, and above all, lacked followers. They were furious, but could resort only to thuggery. Before I went to Shanghai, they had already beaten up Shao Lizi; a fortnight or so after I arrived, they beat to death the Shanghai University student Huang Ren. That happened on Double Tenth,[18] at a commemoration held at Tianhougong in Shanghai. The chairman of the meeting was Yu Yuzhi; Tong Lizhang was secretary or some such – both were rightists. A Shanghai University student raised a point of view from the floor and Tong shouted, 'Beat him!' Whereupon, a group of tattooed thugs set about a dozen or so students, wounding them. The same day, the Sichuanese Huang Ren died of his wounds. The Party Presidium happened to be meeting round my table. Chen Duxiu still had not arrived. Someone came rushing in, furious, to report the incident. That man was Shi Cuntong.

The Left went onto the counteroffensive. Ye Chucang was kicked off *Republic Daily* and He Shizhen was kicked out of Shanghai University. He Shizhen took the English Department students with him and set up a Chizhi University,

---

18   10 October, the anniversary of the 1911 Revolution, China's National Day.

but on condition that Qu Qiubai left too.[19] Qu Qiubai did leave, and was soon followed by Deng Zhongxia. Deng was replaced as Dean by Han Juemin, a Communist; Zhou Yueran, a centrist, was the new Director of the Department of English Literature; and Shi Cuntong was the new Director of the Department of Sociology. Shanghai University students said that Shi Cuntong had secretly had a hand in Qu Qiubai's resignation because he wanted the directorship for himself. Though, by that time, I was in the Shanghai University branch of the Communist Party, I knew nothing of any such thing. The Left ended up winning the struggle at the Guomindang headquarters on Vallon Road, but I do not know the ins and outs of the victory.

A struggle also took place in the labour movement, but that struggle was not carried out in the name of the Guomindang. The Communist Party was active under its own banner in the labour movement. There had already been a Federation of Workers' Associations in Shanghai, but it was an empty shell. We had thought of taking it over, but it proved impossible, so we concentrated our activity on factories. Li Longzhi and Xiang Delong were in charge of this work: one from Hunan, one from Hubei: one in charge of west Shanghai, the other of east Shanghai. Though the strike at the Nanyang Tobacco Company failed, it increased our following. After that, our activity gradually spread and almost surpassed our capacity. The other labour movement activists[20] were no longer able to compete with us.

After the death of Huang Ren and the intensification of the struggle, for security purposes *Guide Weekly*'s editorial department moved from Moulmein Road to South Minhouli off Hadoon Road. Zhang Bojian had found the place. The rent was high: $40 a month for two flats on the first floor. The sub-lessors were two generations of widows who lived beneath Cai Hesen and his wife. Peng Shuzhi and I lived in another flat, also on the first floor, with some other tenants downstairs. Auntie Long cooked for us; Mao Zedong had returned to Hunan and left her behind to work for Xiang Jingyu. Zhang Bojian, too, moved to South Minhouli, but lived in a pavilion room over the kitchen in a house two alleys further up. South Minhouli was very famous in those days. If you called a rickshaw you only had to say Minhouli; you did not need to say which road it was on, all the rickshaw men knew where it was. The newly published *Xing shi* ('Awakening Lion') weekly and its editor Zeng Qi also had their offices there; luckily, I never met him. Zhang Bojian said that the population of South

---

19   The implication is that otherwise He Shizhen would have refused to go quietly.
20   Those of the Guomindang.

Minhouli was extremely diverse. A strikingly large number of bureaucratic politicians lived there, for further west, there were no lane houses, and to the east, there were none until Seymour Road. For miles around, there was nothing but Western-style mansions and empty spaces. Shanghai University was on Seymour Road, so large numbers of students lived in South Minhouli. We often used to hear them singing the *Internationale*.

After a while, when the Central Committee met, I no longer left the room, but after the move it started meeting somewhere else. At first, it met in a flat over a coal-and-firewood store on Weihaiwei Road, and then it moved to Guangdong Road in Zhabei. That was where the Secretariat was. The Secretary (who doubled as Treasurer) was first Xue Shilun and then Ren Zuomin. The Party's entire expenses in those days amounted to a little over $900 a month. I do not know if that sum included expenses incurred in Beijing and Guangzhou, but it certainly included everywhere else. Chen Duxiu, Cai Hesen, and Peng Shuzhi got $40 a month; Zhang Bojian, Xiang Jingyu, and I got $30. We did our own cooking – each of us used to chip in six or seven dollars a month. Though we were not overworked, we were certainly not idle. Apart from *Guide Weekly*, I also proofread *New Youth* and occasional pamphlets, for example, the proclamation and resolutions of the Fourth Congress. As for collecting material, I used to buy and save magazines like *Yinhang zhoukan* ('Bankers' Weekly') and *Qianye gongbao* ('Official Bulletin of the Old-Style Bankers' Guild') dealing with economic issues, and annual customs' reports. I bought them secondhand as well as new. Often, I bought runs covering five or six years. No one ever used to read or use these things. Apart from this activity, I also used to cut out articles from newspapers and paste them in scrap-books.

I also used to write articles for *Guide Weekly*. At first, I forged readers' letters under the pen-name Ma Daofu; later, I wrote articles on questions of minor importance using my real name, and during the events of May Thirtieth, I started writing reports. Sometimes, I wrote articles on international questions, and I also translated articles from foreign languages. After arriving in Shanghai, I answered all but two of the readers' letters. Chen Duxiu was responsible for the column 'Inch of Iron', but I also wrote it on a few occasions. *Guide Weekly* did not publish theoretical articles, and I was not up to writing articles on political subjects. I translated quite a few articles for *New Youth*; those that I wrote myself had something of the flavour of KUTV or Shanghai University lectures. But I put considerable effort into the articles I wrote for *Zhongguo qingnian* ('Chinese Youth'), under the name Zelian.

The moving spirit behind *Guide Weekly* was Cai Hesen, who wrote the lead-articles for every issue. Chen Duxiu's articles were short and perfunctory, as if he were going through the motions rather than applying himself seriously. But

Chen's 'Inch of Iron' column, which he monopolised, was a brilliant literary exercise in just forty or so characters.

Peng Shuzhi achieved his aim of wresting *New Youth* from Qu Qiubai. After we moved premises, an issue appeared around the theme of 'national revolution' (issue number four of the quarterly). Its lead article was an essay Peng had brought back from Moscow titled 'Who Is the Leader of the National Revolution?' This essay later became the target of an attack by Qu Qiubai in his pamphlet *Against Peng Shuzhi-ism*, to which I shall return later. For the time being, I shall merely mention Zhang Songnian's reaction to the issue. He wrote a letter to Chen Duxiu protesting at its vulgar style, and mentioned as an example the statement on page one. This announced that *New Youth* was going to stop publishing as a quarterly and to start up again as a monthly. It was written in a semi-literary style[21] and full of clichés like '*shouren aidai*' ('having enjoyed readers' esteem and appreciation'). Zhang Songnian had been a pillar of the old *New Youth* and thought that style was very important. He wanted *New Youth* to be a model of vernacular Chinese and thought that it should avoid literary terms in its statements, but if it was to publish writing in the literary style, then it should be good literary style. It is superfluous to add that the statement to which Zhang took exception was from the pen of the new editor, Peng. The first issue of the new monthly was the 'Lenin issue'. It consisted mostly of texts that we had brought back from Moscow. After that, Peng Shuzhi fell ill, and the next three issues were haphazardly thrown together by Qu Qiubai and me.

Apart from internal publications, I wrote articles for the *Awakening* supplement of *Republic Daily* and entered into a polemic with a journalist on the Shanghai French-language newspaper about Sun Yat-sen's passage through Shanghai. I wrote several letters in French, all of which were published.

On 21 January 1925, the first anniversary of the death of Lenin, the Chinese Communist Party held its Fourth Congress.[22]

The venue was a three-storey lane house along the railway line behind Guangdong Street in Zhabei where delegates from outside Shanghai ate and slept. The dormitory was on the second floor and the meeting was held on the

---

21   The literary revolution of the late 1910s and early 1920s was aimed at replacing *wenyan* or 'literary Chinese', based on the old classical language, with a new style based on the vernacular. Zhang Songnian's complaint was apparently that Peng Shuzhi's style was regressing in the direction of a vulgar variant of literary Chinese.

22   Here my memory betrayed me. The Fourth Congress opened on 11 January and closed on 22 January. [Note added by Zheng Chaolin in 1980.]

first floor, which was arranged like a classroom; downstairs was the guest-room. Hanging at the mouth of the stairway was a string tied to a bell that could be pulled if anything untoward happened; then the delegates upstairs would have time to put away their conference papers and take out their English textbooks or some other innocent 'classroom' reading. The meeting went on for three or four days; nothing happened to disturb it.

The first floor 'classroom' was almost full, but I cannot remember exactly how many people came. All I remember is that the following people took part in the meeting: Chen Duxiu, Cai Hesen, and Qu Qiubai for the Central Committee; Li Weihan and Zhu Jintang representing Hunan; Chen Tanqiu representing Hubei; Yang Yin representing Guangdong; Gao Shangde representing the north; Peng Shuzhi representing Moscow; He Jinliang representing Vladivostok; Zhou Enlai representing France; Yin Kuan representing Shandong; and Zhang Tailei representing Socialist Youth. I do not remember who the Shanghai representative was. Li Qihan also took part in the meeting, but I do not recall what he represented. Zhang Guotao wrote a respectful letter to the Congress, but did not attend. Zhang Songnian and his wife, Shen Xuanlu and his wife, and Huang Ping attended once or twice in a non-voting capacity. Zhang Bojian and I attended as minute-takers. Zhang only took minutes at one or two sessions; I did the rest. The minutes were never sorted out and edited. Peng Shuzhi, representing the Moscow branch, concurrently headed the Congress Secretariat.

The Comintern representative Voitinsky attended once and Qu Qiubai interpreted his speech. Voitinsky drafted the political resolution and other important documents; Qu Qiubai translated them into Chinese. On theoretical and political questions, the Congress simply accepted Comintern instructions. None of the members of the Central Committee expressed views that differed from these instructions, nor did any of the delegates. The Congress ran so smoothly that it was more like a ceremonial assembly than a political discussion, so even though I minuted 80 or 90 per cent of the Congress proceedings, they left no deep impression on me. But I clearly remember some minor details. For example, when Zhang Songnian got up to speak as a visitor, he spoke among other things about joining the Guomindang. This issue had been at the heart of the debates at the Third Congress, but now, no one save Zhang even mentioned it. We considered that the argument had been settled; it no longer interested us. Moreover, Zhang Songnian, the person who had raised the issue, had no formal right to speak at the meeting. Even so, Qu Qiubai got up to reply to him. Qu was the best person to do so, for he was the staunchest supporter of the policy. We were familiar with his arguments even in advance of his reply, but he added an example by way of proof. To this day, I remember it: 'For instance, if we want to get a seal cut, and it has words like Communist Party on it, in Shanghai, you could not take it to the seal-carver, though you could in Guangzhou. That proves that the policy is beneficial to us'.

I also recall the Comintern representative proposing a resolution attacking Trotsky. The other resolutions had all been drafted beforehand, mimeographed, and handed out to delegates; this was the only unscheduled resolution. The chairman (I forget who) read it out and asked if anyone wanted to oppose it. Although everyone at the meeting knew that there were differences of opinion in the CPSU, few had any idea what they were. I was a regular reader of *Correspondance internationale*,[23] which brimmed with articles against Trotskyism. Because the issues at stake in the CPSU had already become public and had spread to the Comintern, Communist parties in the various countries were formally passing 'anti-Trotskyist' resolutions to send to Moscow, and, of course, the Chinese Communist Party had to be among them, even though (as I have said) few of us knew what the controversy was about. After the draft had been read out, it was a long time before anyone spoke. Finally, Peng Shuzhi got up and made a speech on the lines of Trotsky is wrong on this or that point and must be opposed. The result was that the resolution was passed unanimously. I do not know how the delegates felt about this at the time. Later, when the North China Regional Committee of the Chinese Communist Party sent someone to talk with Zhang Songnian before expelling him, Zhang expressed his dissatisfaction with the Party on several points. Among other things, he said: 'Trotsky was a leader of the October Revolution, and now, we've turned against him!' Perhaps he was referring to the translations of articles by Zinoviev, Stalin, and others that later appeared in *New Youth* or to this resolution, but at the Congress he had failed to speak up for Trotsky. (It is possible that he failed to turn up on the day the resolution was adopted.)

The third thing I recall is a clash between Zhang Tailei and some delegates from minor places. Zhang Tailei was a good-looking fellow, and some delegates inevitably lacked the urban graces. Zhang frequently made fun of these people and invented nicknames for them that were very much to the point. For example, he called Li Weihan 'real powerholder'. Li Weihan attracted much attention at the Congress. Though there were no theoretical or political disputes at it, there were some disputes about minor practical matters. Every time a dispute arose, Li Weihan would at first keep silent and only later come out with a few clear-cut sentences meant to decide the issue. Was this because he had good judgment and was a fluent speaker, or because he commanded a

---

23   This is probably a reference to the French edition of *International Press Correspondence*, a news publication put out by the Comintern.

following? Zhang Tailei thought that the reason Li Weihan's speeches were so important was purely because he had a following. But Li Weihan loathed his nickname.

The last thing I remember is that Yang Yin was beaten up and injured by fellow Cantonese in Shanghai. This probably had something to do with clashes between the two trade union factions in Guangzhou. Yang arrived at the Congress only on the last day, his head wrapped in bandages.

On the last day, the Congress elected nine people onto the Central Committee, together with four alternate members. The nine were Chen Duxiu, Li Dazhao, Qu Qiubai, Cai Hesen, Zhang Guotao, Peng Shuzhi, Tan Pingshan, Li Weihan, and someone else (I forget who).[24] Of the four alternates, I recall only Wang Hebo and Zhu Jintang. The five people – Chen, Cai, Qu, Zhang, and Peng – permanently stationed in Shanghai formed the Presidium. In the almost two and a half years that elapsed between the Fourth and Fifth Congresses, the Central Committee met only two or three times in plenary session. If the revolution that took place in those years had been led by the Chinese Communist Party, it would have been led in effect by this five-member Presidium.

Chen Duxiu was a militant of the 1911 Revolution, commander-in-chief of the May Fourth Movement, founder of the Chinese Communist Party, and General Secretary several times in succession. He was the living embodiment of China's permanent revolution, he symbolised the rapid transition from China's bourgeois revolution to its proletarian revolution. There is no denying that he had a revolutionary history, a following, and experience of revolutionary activity.

Zhang Guotao had been a student leader at Beijing University during the May Fourth Movement. He had been in the vanguard of the move from the universities to industry. He was in charge of the Secretariat of Chinese Trade unions and had led many strikes. He had been arrested by Cao Kun and Wu Peifu[25] because of his revolutionary activity, though he had later been released. He was a leader thrown up by the mass movement.

Cai Hesen was the first of the work-study students in France to become a Marxist. He had been a leader of the work-study movement and a harbinger of the Communist movement among Chinese students in France, whence the French Government deported him back to China because of his involvement in the Lyons University movement. He, too, had been produced as leader by a mass movement, though its scope and nature were different from the one that produced Zhang Guotao.

---

24 The ninth was Xiang Ying.
25 Cao Kun and Wu Peifu headed the Zhili clique of warlords.

Qu Qiubai had participated in the May Fourth cultural movement. He was a Beijing journalist, clever, learned, and popular among students. That he had now become a Communist leader was due to his history and his ability, but also to his close relations with the Comintern and the Russian comrades.

Peng Shuzhi was a newcomer. Before he got to China he was unknown in the Communist Party, not to mention outside it. He had never taken part in any mass movement. What forces did he represent in the leadership? He had been appointed by the Comintern. He represented the Comintern line as it then was. He took part in Central Committee meetings even before he had been elected onto it by Congress, and acted as head of its Propaganda Department.

In Shanghai, I met these five men almost daily. (Zhang Guotao did not come to Shanghai until a long time after the Congress.) The Presidium met roughly once a week to discuss big and small questions, from organising a National Government to comrades' love-entanglements. Chen Duxiu's opinion was decisive. The meetings were rarely attended by disputes, though thinking back on those days, it is now clear to me that the unanimity was only on the surface and that below it lurked differences of opinion.

Under the General Secretary was a Secretariat that at first comprised just one person, Ren Zuomin, who served as both bookkeeper and secretary; later, Wang Ruofei was specially transferred to this office and a separate secretariat was established, independent of the accounts section. Wang Ruofei had two or three office-staff to attend to secret correspondence, maintain the party archive, and work the mimeograph machine. Chen Duxiu was not only General Secretary but *de facto* head of the organisation department, for in practice, no formal organisation department had been established. In late 1926 or early 1927, Zhou Enlai was assigned to take charge of organisational affairs, though he was not on the Central Committee. But Zhou was occupied with more urgent matters. The Propaganda Department had been set up before the Fourth Congress and was headed by Peng Shuzhi. Nominally, I was its secretary, but my work consisted solely of looking after *Guide Weekly*, *New Youth*, and the publication of party pamphlets. Not until later, in Wuhan, did I learn from the wife of Pavel Mif what propaganda work was about; during my time in Shanghai, neither I nor the head of the Propaganda Department had much idea. In any case, shortly after taking up his post, Peng Shuzhi fell seriously ill and spent eight months in hospital before returning to work. Zhang Guotao was in charge of the Workers' and Peasants' Department, which in reality did little more than receive comrades working in trade unions in various parts of China. The Women's Department was for a time in the handbag of Yang Zhihua, Qu Qiubai's wife; and for a time in that of Peng Shuzhi's wife Chen Bilan.

The Youth League led an independent life. After the Party's Fourth Congress, the League also held a Congress and changed its name from Socialist to Communist. Zhang Tailei was its Secretary. But Zhang was soon replaced by others, including Ren Bishi, He Chang, Liu Changqun, and Lu Dingyi. Liu Renjing edited *Chinese Youth*, the League's magazine. I was not familiar with the League's internal life, but its officials became my good friends. I often visited them in their homes to talk about films, novels, and women; we were like school-friends.

After the Fourth Congress, party activity developed rapidly. In the spring of 1924, when I formally joined the Party, it claimed more than three hundred members in China and abroad, one in ten of them in the Moscow branch. According to Congress statistics, it now had more than nine hundred members. By the time of the Fifth Congress, it had claimed more than 100,000.[26] Before and after the Fourth Congress, the most important jobs in the Party were almost all in the hands of comrades who had returned to China from Moscow, and in particular of those who had returned from France via Moscow. Peng Shuzhi was already a member of the Central Committee waiting to be elected onto it. Zhao Shiyan was in charge of northern China, Chen Yannian of Guangdong, Yin Kuan of Shandong, and Wang Ruofei of Henan. Not long afterwards, Luo Jiao took over Shanghai; and Li Weihan in Hunan had been in France. There were Moscow branch people in Hubei, too, though they played no important role there. There were even more of them in the smaller places, like Wang Zekai in Anyuan, Gao Feng in Baoding, and Li Weinong in Qingdao. After this batch of comrades had returned from abroad, the comrades in China stepped aside one after the other to make way for them. The name 'Moscow branch group' or 'Moscow group' was current in the Party; they were like a faction that dominated all other factions.

Actually, before we returned to China the Party had few cadres. The main source of cadres had been Zhang Guotao's connections, that is, the comrades who had spread out from Beijing to agitate among the railway workers. Under Zhang Guotao were Luo Zhanglong, Li Zhenying, Zhang Kundi, Wu Yuming, and others. Because they had worked together in the past, these people were virtually a faction, and sometimes they actually did clash with the Moscow returners. Those working in the labour movement in southern China could not boast the same achievements as those in the north, so they did not form a faction. Li Longzhi, Liu Shaoqi, and Lu Chen had been active together in the trade unions and the workers' clubs in Anyuan, so they had some mutual ties. Apart from these groups, there were local cells in Guangdong, Beijing, Hunan, Hubei,

---

26   The actual membership at the time of the Fifth Congress was 57,900.

Shandong, and other places. They were pleased to receive the comrades from Moscow.

The machine was ready, waiting for raw materials to process. By coincidence, the materials had been prepared and were on their way.

I arrived back in China at exactly the time of the Jiangsu-Zhejiang war. Lu Yongxiang, who was in alliance with Sun Yat-sen, had been forced onto the defensive. He had abandoned Hangzhou and retreated to Shanghai to dig in. Not long after that, he had even had to give up Shanghai. The Fengtian Army[27] in the north was also on the defensive. We were worried that the Zhili warlords, boosted by their string of victories, might nip the revolution in the bud. But just a few days after the end of the Shanghai war, the Zhili warlords unexpectedly fell from power. President Cao Kun was taken prisoner, and Wu Peifu fled. They had been overthrown by their own generals: Feng Yuxiang, Hu Jingyi, and Sun Yue.[28] It all happened so suddenly and unexpectedly that Cai Hesen was thrown off balance. He wrote an article for *Guide Weekly* that attacked US imperialism for plotting to take over China, for he believed that the US had been behind Feng Yuxiang's betrayal of Cao and Wu. Shao Lizi came to party headquarters to protest. He said that Feng's coup, far from being instigated by America, was good for the revolution, and we should refrain from criticising it. Cai Hesen said angrily, 'Is Comrade Shao implying that it's possible that Chinese warlords could act without imperialists pulling the strings?' Whether Feng Yuxiang was acting independently or being stage-managed from abroad I still do not know even today, twenty years after the event. But it's a fact that not long afterwards, *Guide Weekly* abandoned Cai Hesen's position. Reports from Beijing and Guangdong and information provided by the Soviet Consulate or Voitinsky in Shanghai were incompatible with Cai's view. Shortly after that, Sun Yat-sen left Guangdong and went to Beijing via Shanghai and Japan. He issued slogans calling for the convention of a National Assembly and the abolition of the unequal treaties.[29] In the spring of 1925, he died in Beijing. The Society to Promote a National Assembly and the movement to commemorate the death of Sun Yat-sen were launched and led by the Communist Party. These two national movements spread the Party's influence, developed its

---

27   Under Zhang Zuolin.
28   Feng Yuxiang, the 'Christian General', occupied Beijing on 23 October 1924, and forced Cao Kun to dismiss Wu Peifu from his posts and to resign as President.
29   The 'unequal treaties' were imposed on China by foreign powers; these treaties gave foreigners special status and privileges in China.

organisation, and increased its membership. But it was a national movement, promoted under the banner of the Guomindang.

In the labour movement, the Communist Party showed its true face. Two years after the February Seventh defeat, the labour movement revived. This time it was a movement not of transport workers but of factory workers in the big cities, starting with the Shanghai cotton mills. This was the fruit of the hard efforts of Li Longzhi and Xiang Delong; the two workers' clubs in east and west Shanghai played an important role in the events. The clubs drew in the factory-workers; strikes took place, and workers influenced by the clubs immediately began to play a role in them; in the background, we controlled these workers. The capitalists reckoned on the basis of past experience that the strikes would cave in after two or three days, but they were wrong: the strikes went on and on, though the workers had no unions and no reserves. Finally, the capitalists had no choice but to give in, to negotiate with the workers' representatives, to accede to their conditions, and to sign agreements. The workers' representatives did not omit to include union recognition among their conditions. The capitalists, foreign and Chinese, were surprised by all this. Where did the workers get the funds to tide them through the strike? Where did they learn these new methods of struggle? Moreover, workers in different factories had adopted more or less similar tactics. The workers were exhilarated by their victory. They were not only happy that their demands had been met but delighted that they had the power and the means to make the factories submit. The more progressive workers joined the Communist Party. Alongside the Society to Promote a National Assembly, in Shanghai and other cities there arose a labour movement that aided the development of the Communist Party in even greater measure. The biggest strike was in a Japanese-owned cotton mill in Xiaoshadu.

I myself did not directly participate in these two mass movements, but I often attended the Congresses of the two organisations as an anonymous observer. On one occasion, I, Jiang Guangchi, and Shen Zemin organised a propaganda team. We got some paper-flags and leaflets from the headquarters of the Society to Promote a National Assembly and addressed passers-by on the road near the West Gate. A group of naughty children crowded round us asking for leaflets to wrap their sweets and peanuts in. I and Wang Ruofei, newly back in China, attended the meeting at Tanziwan in memory of Gu Zhenghong,[30] but we nearly caused a serious incident. We were both wearing Western suits. As soon as we arrived at the meeting, people began noticing us. A group of workers came over to keep an eye on us. Large numbers of people were scattered across the open ground, in the middle of which was a makeshift

---

30   A worker whose killing by the Japanese marked the start of the May Thirtieth Movement.

platform, on which stood Li Longzhi. Li was dressed in a blue shirt and trousers, like the workers round the platform listening to the speeches. Just as Liu Hua was speaking, two of the group supervising us asked us to follow them to an empty spot beyond the edge of the crowd.

They asked whether we were Japanese.

I said, 'We're Shanghai University students'.

A pock-marked youth said, 'Then you must know the name of the man who's speaking now'.

I said, 'He's a student too. His name is Liu Hua'.

To dispel their doubts I added, 'Look, that's Li Cheng,[31] he is also our friend'.

The two men seemed to have calmed down. Not long after that, Li Longzhi stepped down from the platform and asked us over to a room near where the meeting was taking place. This room was the union office. He asked us to go back to headquarters and report on a few things for him.

Supreme commander of the strikes was Chen Duxiu. Every time an important decision was needed, for example, on whether to strike or not, what demands to raise, how to conduct negotiations, and whether or not to sign an agreement, the labour movement cadres took it in consultation with Chen. The usual venue for these meetings, which mostly took place at night, was a comrade's house south of Baoshan Road. One evening, Xiang Jingyu once told me, the meeting did not finish until very late. Chen Duxiu walked along the alley saying, 'I missed the triple prize, what a shame, all I needed were the last seven stripes, I was sure they had come, but they just would not come....' He talked non-stop about this imaginary game of mahjong until the keeper of the iron gate at the end of the alley let them out; only then did he stop.

After the end of each big strike or movement, whether won or lost, the Shanghai District Committee[32] met in plenary session to assess the outcome. The meetings were convened in a primary school in the Chinese territory in the Hengbin Bridge area. They were plenary sessions in the true sense of the term, that is, all party members had to attend them, but in effect attendance was limited by the size of the classroom. On several occasions, I took the minutes at these meetings. Chen Duxiu made the political report, the District Secretary Zhuang Wengong made the work-report, and Zhuang or someone else made

---

31   Alias Li Lisan, alias Li Longzhi.
32   Before the Fifth Congress [of April–May 1927], the District Committee was bigger than the Provincial Committee. The Shanghai District Committee controlled the organisation in Jiangsu, Zhejiang, and Anhui. Later, district committees became constituent parts of the municipal committees, for example, the east Shanghai district or the district covering the French Concession and south Shanghai. [Note added by Zheng Chaolin in 1980.]

additional reports on the movement or the strike. Sometimes, punishments or expulsions were announced. On one occasion, Qu Qiubai made a theoretical report in which he talked about the history of world communism, starting with Plato's *Republic*. After the end of each report, people raised questions or points of view. I remember once Shao Lizi angrily standing up to denounce our discrimination against Guomindang members in the labour movement. I cannot remember how his point was dealt with. Even though we had not formally decided not to let Guomindang members take part in the labour movement, in reality the labour movement in Shanghai was completely in Communist hands. I do not know whether this was because the Guomindang members did not want to join or because we did not let them join.

The District Secretary Han Baihua, a man from Zhejiang, a student of the First Provincial Normal School, had gone to Moscow to study but had soon returned; when *Guide Weekly* first appeared, he had been responsible for it. After the 7 February defeat, he was arrested in Shanghai, and spent several months in prison before being bailed out. By this time, he had changed his name to Zhuang Wengong. He was like a primary school teacher, loyal and hardworking but with little real ability. After the expansion of the Party as a result of the May Thirtieth movement, he was unable to cope and was replaced.

Great movements and revolutions often catch people unawares. This generalisation also holds for the Chinese Revolution of 1925 to 1927. That does not mean that the revolution itself came unexpectedly. Quite the contrary, we had known for a long time that a great movement was about to burst forth in China. I had said to Zhang Bojian: 'Eight years after the Revolution of 1911 there was the May Fourth Movement. Quite a while has elapsed between May Fourth and now. Some sort of movement *must* be in the offing'. Needless to say, my argument was based on a calculation not just of spans of time but of various underlying factors in the situation. Yet no one imagined that the revolution would break out on 30 May 1925, and in such a form.

I know nothing of the preparations that were made for May Thirtieth. After breakfast that morning, Cai Hesen said to me: 'Chaolin, if you've got nothing planned, you can go into town and watch, today the students are going to the International Settlement to make propaganda'. I immediately dressed and went out. Though Cai Hesen had not said as much, I already understood that our Central Committee had prepared this event. The All-China Students' Federation was under our control, as was the Shanghai Students' Federation. There were Communist Youth branches in a large number of schools. We controlled nearly all the Guomindang branches in the schools. We had already mobilised the students several times to go out onto the streets and make propaganda, for example, at the time of the campaign for a National Assembly, at the time of the death of Sun Yat-sen, and during the movement to aid the striking workers. But those mobilisations had been in Chinese-controlled territory. We had staged several mass rallies and demonstrations, but always outside the West Gate, at the Public Sports Ground. We had never held a rally, a congress, or a demonstration inside the area of the International Settlement. Shanghai University students had, on one occasion, marched with banners to the area north of Suzhou Creek to take part in a commemorative meeting and the police had intervened and arrested four of them while they were passing by the Gordon Road Police Station. 'When will we be able to hold a mass meeting at the race course?'[33] I asked Zhang Bojian.

Making public speeches in the International Settlement was certainly a novelty. When I reached the Nanjing Road, nothing was afoot; I turned onto Fuzhou Road, and still saw nothing; not until I reached the intersection between Qipan Street and Jiaotong Road did I see a student dressed in Western clothes standing on a stool making a speech. An Indian policeman was arresting him and demanding that he go with him to the police-station. I learned from passers-by that the same thing had already happened many times that day, also on the Nanjing Road. I returned to the Nanjing Road and met Yu Xiusong at the Sunrise Pavilion. He said that there would be a demonstration at three o'clock that afternoon at the New Yamen.[34] The two of us walked over to the Magistrate's Court on the North Zhejiang Road. We waited there for a long time, but nothing happened, so we crossed back slowly to the Nanjing Road. But when we reached the Sincere Department Store, we saw a great crowd of people, all very agitated and all speaking of only one thing: that there had just been some firing at the entrance to Laozha Police Station and that a large number of students had been shot dead. We hurried to the place mentioned – not today's entrance but the old entrance on the Nanjing Road, which is now a clock-and-watch shop. There were no longer any crowds. There was blood on the pavement; the bodies had been carted off. I and Yu Xiusong parted company. I walked along thinking to myself, more material for anti-imperialist propaganda. I went to the Northern Railway Station. While passing by the small station for Wusong-bound trains, I came across a group of students telling each other about the massacre. Some of them had witnessed it with their own eyes. I discovered that after large number of students had been arrested for making speeches on the streets and taken off to Laozha Police Station, other students had crowded into

---

33 Modern-day People's Park.
34 The New Magistracy.

the entrance demanding the release of those seized. Passers-by had stopped, too, to watch the hubbub or join in the shouting. The crowd quickly swelled. A foreign police officer with three stripes on his sleeve gave the order to open fire. That's how the massacre began.

I later discovered that the great majority of casualties had been citizens who had stopped to watch the uproar and that only a handful of students had been killed. Among the dead students was the Communist He Bingyi of Shanghai University.

I went home and wrote an account of the massacre, based on my own observations and on the next day's press reports, for publication in the following issue of *Guide Weekly*. Later, Hua Gang copied my account in its entirety in his history of the Great Revolution.[35]

The massacre happened at just the right time to detonate an accumulation of explosives. It was not simply that massacre could trigger revolution. History is littered with massacres of an even greater scope and brutality that triggered no revolution. The revolution made use of the occasion of the Shanghai massacre of 30 May 1925.

One reason it could do so was because the Shanghai bourgeoisie nursed grievances against the International Settlement authorities. The bourgeoisie had gone into opposition and begun to raise all sorts of demands. The Chinese bourgeois, originally under the wing of foreign capital, had by this time already accumulated considerable wealth. They demanded independence, or the right to exploit on a rather greater scale than previously. They could not but notice the spread of the national movement with Communist support, and the victories of the strikers in the foreign factories in Shanghai. This encouraged them to raise their heads. A few days before the massacre, the Chinese press opposed the increase in the police-levy and the new publishing regulations imposed by the directors' board of the Municipal Council of the International Settlement and demanded the right of Chinese to join the directors' board. At that time, they had a new organisation called the Federation of Merchants of All Streets, set up in opposition to and to the left of the official General Chamber of Commerce. This organisation had links to Guomindang veterans and was beyond the Communist Party's control. When the massacre took place, the members of this organisation were extremely angry; they also reflected the feelings of the shop-assistants. They agreed to go on a business strike. The General Chamber of Commerce refused to support this proposal, but the same day, the same night, students' and workers' representatives went to its headquarters and begged on their knees, with tears in their eyes, for action. Before

---

35   That of 1925–7.

long, the deputy-leader of the Chamber, Fang Jiaobo, agreed to order a shutdown. The next day, business throughout Shanghai ground to a halt. The newspapers stopped publishing their 'arse-end',[36] and though shops selling daily necessities did not shut down completely, they remained outwardly closed and boarded. Foreign troops patrolled the silent streets, as if before a great enemy.

Another even more important reason the revolution could break out was because the proletariat had just finished preparing its combat organisation. It was as if the Communist Party had known that a revolution would break out between May and June. It had already completed its preparations. Even more surprising than the massacre and the shop-strike, the following day a Shanghai General Labour Union emerged to issue orders to the Shanghai workers. Every sector of workers submitted to it, carried out its commands, and reported to it. It became like a soviet in the Russian Revolution. The Shanghai workers' general command appeared as if from a conjurer's hat, and enjoyed absolute authority. How did this come to be?

On 1 May 1925, the Second All-China Labour Congress had convened in Guangzhou. Even though not all the delegates and the others present were Communists, all were susceptible to Communist control. By this time, the other faction of labour movement activists, who were Guomindang veterans, had been excluded; it had become clear during the workers' struggles that they lacked effective strength. When the workers at the Japanese cotton mills went on strike, these Guomindang veterans drove round in motor cars distributing leaflets in workers' areas warning workers not to fall into the Communists' trap. The workers understood without our having to explain that these people were nothing but 'running dogs'. From the Labour Congress emerged the All-China General Labour Union; the Congress decided that the Shanghai delegation should organise a Shanghai General Labour Union after returning home. At the end of May, the delegation had already returned from Guangzhou and was in the process of preparing such an organisation. There were already no few legal and illegal mass unions produced by the spring strike-wave, in many different places, all under Communist influence. The Shanghai General Labour Union was to become a federation and general command for these factory-committees (for they were organised by factory rather than by industry or profession; actually, they were factory committees, not industrial unions). The original plan was to inaugurate this general command at the beginning of June, for some formal procedures had still not been completed. But as soon as the massacre happened, the procedures were dispensed with and the General

---

36   A supplement rather like a gossip column, often consisting of reports on society scandals, literary wrangles, and the like, but sometimes serious.

Labour Union was instantly proclaimed. Its order to go on strike was instantly obeyed. Its leader Li Lisan instantly became the leader of workers throughout Shanghai. Li Lisan was a false name, created just a few hours before it was made public; if the Xiaoshadu workers had seen this Li Lisan, they would have recognised him as Li Cheng, another false name; if the Anyuan miners had seen him, they would have recognised him as Li Longzhi, which was his real name. Naturally, the workers' strike was not as orderly as the shopkeepers', which was suddenly total, from one day to the next; the workers' strike was ragged and irregular, and spread over a considerable period of time. The merchants had decades of organisation behind them and their street federations were also of comparatively long standing, whereas the workers' General Labour Union was just a few hours old.

Similar in nature to the General Labour Union was the National Press Agency and *Rexue ribao* ('Hot Blood Daily').[37] Just a short time before, a sum of money had been allocated for running the 'national movement', and the Central Committee had decided to launch a Press Agency and a small-format newspaper. This agency and newspaper had been under preparation even before the massacre, but now, their appearance was speeded up. Yet there is no way of speeding up the appearance of a print-shop, so the newspaper could not be published until just over three weeks later.

The press agency and the newspaper were run from the same office by the same people. I dropped propaganda work and joined the paper. The editorial office was alongside Xiangshan Road in Zhabei, close to the Party's district headquarters but a long way from my lodgings in Hadoon Road. The editor-in-chief was Qu Qiubai; apart from me, the editorial board comprised two comrades assigned by the District Committee: Shen Zemin[38] and He Weixin. Zhang Bojian looked after distribution. Why was the newspaper called *Hot Blood Daily*? Because there was already a *Gongli ribao* ('Justice Daily'), published by the Commercial Press with an allocation of $10,000 from the Commercial Press senior management and edited by Shen Yanbing[39] and others. Though Shen was a comrade, in his position, he had no choice but to speak grey.[40] Qu Qiubai said, 'What justice is there in this world? Hot blood will decide things!' *Hot Blood*'s circulation was higher than *Justice Daily*'s. The printers (not of the Party) were almost unable to keep up with the demand,

---

37   *Hot Blood Daily* was the name of the strike-journal edited by Qu Qiubai during the events of May Thirtieth. Twenty four issues came out in June and July.
38   The younger brother of the writer Mao Dun.
39   Mao Dun.
40   Not to speak red, but to disguise his Communist convictions.

but twenty days later, they were tracked down by the police and the owner was jailed for two days. The print-shop was closed and the case was settled with a fine. We recompensed the owner for his losses. Our own printers managed with difficulty to put out one more issue, after which *Hot Blood* stopped appearing. Qu Qiubai personally wrote nearly all the editorials. I and Shen Zemin wrote general articles and edited reports from the District Committee and the General Labour Union. He Weixin specialised in editing news-stories. Sometimes, he wrote anti-imperialist songs to the tune of popular melodies like *Eighteen Gropes* and *Mengjiang nü*.[41]

The strike-movement spread out in waves, from the foreign-owned factories to the foreigners' servants and amahs; workers at the electric light company and the waterworks awaited the order to come out, but the General Labour Union let them work on so as not to inconvenience the general public. Even some policemen contacted the Union to say that they were prepared to agitate for a police-strike. The General Labour Union split into a large number of sections to deal with the rush of business; even so, it was almost overwhelmed. Li Lisan spent his whole time rushing between Chen Duxiu and Yu Qiaqing. The Chinese factories had not been called out, so Yu 'sympathised' with the labour movement and contributed towards the strike-fund. He also contributed some opinions; when Li Lisan went to Beijing on business, he even wrote him a letter of introduction to Li Sihao, Minister of Finance in the Beijing Government. It was very much in the interests of the Chinese capitalists that the strikes in the British cotton mills and tobacco factories should continue. No one was any longer smoking Daying[42] cigarettes, so the British-American Tobacco Company had no choice but to change the brand-name to Hongxibao[43] and to launch an advertising campaign to announce that the brand was registered in New York (though the packet still said London).

The people actually responsible for the General Labour Union were Liu Shaoqi and some other labour movement activists under the direct command of Zhang Guotao. He Jinliang returned from Vladivostok and was assigned to the General Labour Union; he changed his name to He Songlin. He had become very experienced in Russia; even Zhang Guotao was impressed by his ability. So he became inseparable from the Shanghai General Labour Union. A large group of Shanghai University students worked for the union. On one occasion, some thugs smashed up the union headquarters and injured some of these students; on another occasion, Li Lisan was kidnapped by thugs, dragged off

---

41 Popular songs of the period, one of them sexually explicit.
42 'Great Britain' brand.
43 'Red Tin Wrapped'.

to see Chang Yuqing,[44] owner of the Daguanyuan Bath-house, and forced to call him 'laotouzi' ('chief'). During that period, the Chinese police had not yet intervened. After September, when the Beijing Government ordered the closing down of the General Labour Union and the arrest of Li Lisan, the situation changed. The union went underground; two mass demonstrations to unseal its headquarters failed.

Though the merchants and workers were unable to get results and the strikes came to a ragged end, this movement in Shanghai had an enormous impact on the rest of China. In Guangzhou, there was the 23 June Shakee Road Bridge massacre, and the ensuing Hong Kong strike; in Hankou, too, there was a massacre and there were strikes. There was a sensational response in the interior of the country to these goings-on: everyone was eager to read the newly published books and newspapers and young people streamed out into the coastal provinces, most of them in the direction of Huangpu.[45]

After *Hot Blood* had ceased publishing, I withdrew from the National Press-Agency, too, but there was no chance of a return to the days of ease and leisure before May Thirtieth. In early June, Cai Hesen went to Beijing's Western Hills to recuperate from illness. Peng Shuzhi was in hospital. Only Chen Duxiu and Qu Qiubai were writing articles for *Guide Weekly*. They handed in their copy and then paid no further attention to the matter, so editorial responsibility inevitably devolved on me. To fill each issue, I translated articles from foreign languages or wrote about extraneous matters. When Chen and Qu were particularly busy, they wrote no articles at all, and I became responsible for the entire enterprise. Luckily, apart from this, I had no other agitprop-work to distract me. But I was often busy with local work in Shanghai. I joined the reorganised District Committee. The Secretary was still Zhuang Wengong, Xie Wenjin was in charge of the organisation department, I was in charge of propaganda, Li Lisan was in charge of the labour movement, and Xiang Jingyu was in charge of women's work. Two worker-comrades, Gu Shunzhang and Zhang Zuochen, joined the committee. Li Lisan was simply a figurehead, he rarely attended meetings. My job was rather straightforward: to write propaganda-outlines, to represent the District Committee at sub-district meetings, to lead the Commercial Press branch, and to do various other odd jobs. For example, when the order went out for Li Lisan's arrest, I escorted him to safety, booked a cabin for him on a steamship, and assigned a worker-comrade to accompany

---

44   A leader of the Green Gang in the International Settlement.
45   To enrol in the Huangpu Military Academy.

him secretly to Hankou. But I did not let Li share a cabin with his wife Yichun. When the worker-comrade got back, he told me that Li Lisan had joined Yichun immediately the ship cast off, for Yichun's cabin-mate had turned out to be male, which made Li Lisan nervous. The reorganised District Committee was still not equal to its tasks, for both Zhuang Wengong and Xie Wenjin were mediocrities; so a second reorganisation took place in November. Yin Kuan was transferred from Shandong, Zhuang Wengong was transferred to Zhejiang, and I stayed put. Soon after that, Yin Kuan come under attack from Shandong comrades for having fallen in love in Shandong. He resigned his posts on the grounds – feigned or otherwise – of illness, and was replaced by Wang Yifei. I, too, then stepped down from the District Committee, because Qu Qiubai wanted me to. He thought that propaganda work was being neglected. Only in the spring of 1926, when Luo Jiao came down to Shanghai from the north, was Shanghai local work properly led and did it resume its stride. Not long after that, Luo Jiao intercepted Zhao Shiyan on his way through Shanghai and kept him behind to take charge of organisational work. Yin Kuan took over local propaganda-work from me. At this point, the golden age of Shanghai work started. Luo Jiao used another name after his return to China: he called himself Luo Yinong.[46]

After that, I worked exclusively for the party journal and agitprop (save for teaching a few hours a week at Shanghai University). Before May Thirtieth, I had been a substitute lecturer. Peng Shuzhi taught 'sociology', but less than a month after the start of the spring term of 1925, he fell ill and recommended me as his replacement. By sociology we meant the materialist conception of history, that is, the historical materialism propagated by Bukharin. I taught three classes, amounting to nine hours a week in all. After the summer vacation, Shanghai University moved to Qingyun Road in Zhabei. After his recovery, Peng taught the third year, and I continued to teach the first and second years, no longer as a substitute. By that time, Shanghai University was almost a Communist Party school. The Principal Yu Youren[47] did not reside in Shanghai; the Deputy Principal Shao Zhonghui (Shao Lizi) was a Communist; the Dean, Han Juemin, was a Communist; Shi Cuntong, the Director of the Sociology Department, was a Communist; the lecturers in the Sociology Department – Li Ji, Gao Yuhan, Jiang Guangchi, Yin Kuan, Wang Yifei, Xiao Pusheng, Peng Shuzhi, and I – were Communists; Chen Wangdao, Director of the Department of Chinese Literature, had been a Communist and was now working together with the Communist Party, but the students believed that he was secretly

---

46   Written sometimes with one set of characters, sometimes with another.
47   A veteran Guomindang supporter.

plotting to destroy Communist Party influence; Zhou Yueran, Director of the Department of English Literature, was non-partisan – the students in his Department tended towards anti-Communism and had left the University together with its ex-Director, He Shizhen. Of the students, the overwhelming majority in the Sociology-Department were Communists, and so were a good many in the other two Departments; most of the rest were sympathisers. Shanghai University was not registered with the Beijing Government's Ministry of Education. The élite universities looked down on it as a 'pheasant university'.[48] It's true that the curriculum was not as it should have been, the dormitories on the Qingyun Road were dilapidated, and more students came from provinces – especially Sichuan and Hunan – other than Jiangsu and Zhejiang.[49] In a word, Shanghai University was a miniaturised replica of the work-study movement in France. The role played by Shanghai University students in the lower ranks of the revolutionary cadre was akin to that played by cadets of the Huangpu Military Academy in the lower ranks of the military cadre of the armies that carried out the Northern Expedition. What's more, a few former Shanghai University students (for example Ouyang Jixiu) taught politics at Huangpu. The difference was that the Huangpu students gained their military expertise in the classroom, whereas the Shanghai University students got their political knowledge not in the classroom, or at least not from formal classes, but from extracurricular activities and research. Apart from Li Ji, the other Communist lecturers approached their teaching in a perfunctory and light-minded way. Li Ji translated *Students' Capital* as teaching material but the rest of us openly declared that we would not write special lectures and did little by way of preparation. If the students got anything from us, it was less from our formal appearances in the classroom than from the speeches we delivered at commemorative events, for we prepared such speeches rather more conscientiously. After a while, Peng Shuzhi even delegated third-year teaching to me. When Li Hanjun arrived, I let him take over all these classes, but he left again after a couple of months, so I resumed my sociology-teaching and stuck with it right up until Shanghai University was finally shut down.

Peng Shuzhi was not discharged from hospital until just before National Day[50] in 1925. He had been there since early February. Not a single drop of the great wave of May Thirtieth sprayed his person. When he came out, the Propaganda

---

48   In Shanghai dialect, a 'pheasant' was a lower-class prostitute. The implication is that Shanghai University was not institutional and was second class.

49   That is, they came from the interior rather than from the relatively prosperous and open provinces of central eastern China.

50   10 October.

Department had just moved to a house on Fusheng Road. Fusheng Road is a small road that runs between Range Road and Zhabei. It was close to the Secretariat of the Central Committee, the Workers' and Peasants' Department, the District Committee, and the Shanghai General Union; it was much more convenient to live there than at Hadoon Road. The building was a three-storey lane house. We met, ate, received visitors, and on occasions played mahjong on the ground floor; Peng Shuzhi occupied the whole of the first floor; the second floor was reserved for Cai Hesen and his wife Xiang Jingyu, but while Cai was still in Beijing, Xiang lived there by herself; I lived in the pavilion room. Xiang Jingyu brought in a Shanghai University woman student called Yang Fulan to do secretarial work – mainly clipping and pasting newspaper reports – for two or three hours a day. Not long afterwards Yang left and Shen Yanbing or Yang Xianjiang brought in an old lady to do this work. Both Yang and the old lady were comrades. Zhang Guotao ate there and Chen Duxiu often used to come, either for meetings of the Presidium or for an idle chat. Very soon, Cai Hesen returned. Qu Qiubai was living at Rue du Marché in the French Concession. He did not often visit us.

After the end of the great movement, our life slipped back into a routine. Apart from when I had to get up early to give lectures, I spent my mornings in bed until ten or eleven o'clock. Before lunch, I used to read the newspapers; in the afternoons, I used to go to the print-shop, go for a stroll, or look up old friends for a chat. I always used to work at night, until two or three o'clock in the morning. I smoked, drank alcohol, went to the cinema, went to the amusements centre, or played mahjong. Sometimes, I went for walks, including some very long ones, in the countryside around Shanghai. I very rarely spent my free time on my own. I had drinking companions, opera-going companions, and fellow walking enthusiasts to accompany me on my excursions. All my friends were single men or men like Jiang Guangchi, Yin Kuan, Wang Ruofei, Yan Changyi, and Shi Qiong whose wives or sweethearts were resident outside Shanghai. At the Secretariat, I read reports from different places and learned about developments in the Party all over China; I heard from Luo Yinong, Zhao Shiyan, and Yin Kuan about the situation of the Party in Shanghai; chatting together with Qu Qiubai in his home in the French Concession was quite different – he was immensely knowledgeable and witty and used to regale us with anecdotes about himself and others. He also kept us abreast of the literary journals, for apart from politics, we read nothing.

When Jiang Guangchi's novel came out, almost none of us bothered to read it. We were all deeply prejudiced against Jiang Guangchi himself, against his poems and novels, and against new literature in general. Even when we had the time to read his books, we lacked the inclination. Chen Duxiu flicked through

Shaonian piaopozhe ('Young Wanderers') and said: 'Even in hot weather I get goose-pimples when I read this sort of stuff'. Jiang gave me a copy and I managed to struggle through it, but the next time I met him, I failed to give him the praise he was clearly seeking. He often said, 'Foreign writers frequently get fan-mail from their women readers, but Chinese women never write to authors'. I realised he was complaining about his own feeling of neglect. Qu Qiubai was more sympathetic to him than the rest of us, and was able to converse with him about the literary world. One day, after Jiang had left, Qu said, 'That man really has no talent!' Jiang wrote a novel about our life in Shanghai in those years. Qu Qiubai played the main role in it, and there was even a faint shadow of me among its pages. Jiang asked Qu Qiubai what he should call the book. 'Short-Trouser Party', said Qu. That was a mistranslation of the French *sans-culottes*. But in spite of his failings, Jiang pioneered the unblazed paths of revolutionary literature; the Creation Society's shift in line[51] did not happen until a year later.

Living as I did, I could still make time free each month to work on a translation of *The ABC of Communism*.[52] The reason I started work on this translation was because there was spare capacity in our print shop. The movement had quietened down a bit, there was less call for leaflets, and the setters and printers were often idle. When the comrades in charge of managing the print shop asked me if I had anything to publish, I said I had nothing ready-made but that I could provisionally do some translating and they could print the text as I delivered it, in batches. I settled on the ABC, which expounds the political programme of the Russian Bolshevik Party. The introduction explains what a party programme is, the second section is the ABC, and after that comes the party programme itself. The section on the party programme is about the same length as the ABC. The Russian, French, English, and German versions were all like that. I ventured to dispense with the introduction and the party programme and kept only the second, explanatory section. It was translated, set, proofread, and printed bit by bit, and it was a long time before the entire text was finally published. I had never imagined that this book would have such a tremendous impact! In 1927, a Shanghai newspaper published a list of the last few years' best-sellers. Top of the list was inevitably Sun Yat-sen's *Sanmin zhuyi* ('Three People's Principles'), but most copies of this book had been printed at official expense and distributed free. Next was the ABC; our central distribution department had no rules governing complimentary copies, but the book was cheap (at 20 cents) and I do not know whether reprints in other cities were

---

51   That is, its conversion to 'proletarian literature'.
52   By N. I. Bukharin and E. A. Preobrazhensky.

distributed free or not. Third was Zhang Jingsheng's *Xing shi* ('Stories of Sex Lives').[53]

Few people have noticed the significance of the ABC in the revolution of 1925 to 1927 – namely, that it was the only book that told people what communism really was about. The awakening masses of the towns and villages had a great thirst for knowledge. They wanted to know where the revolution was taking them, but they could find no satisfactory answer in Guomindang propaganda, even when compiled by Communists. They could not even find one in the Communists' own publications like *Guide Weekly*, like Beijing's *Zhengzhi shenghuo* ('Political Life'), or like Guangzhou's *Renmin zhoukan* ('People's Weekly'), for these publications simply said that 'We are going to overthrow imperialism, we are going to overthrow the warlords'. Was that all the Communists were after? Was that what the word 'communism' meant? When the ABC was finally published, people at long last discovered that the Communist Party was out to abolish the system of private property, that it wanted 'communal ownership', and that the revolution was the necessary product of objective developments, that it was inevitable. Thereafter, workers and peasants plunged into the daily struggle, which was against only the imperialists and the warlords, with this final goal in mind. Later, the Hunan peasants went even further than the party leaders in promoting land revolution, and at the 7 August Conference and thereafter, the Party took its 'semi-Trotskyist' leap. These developments, too, were not unconnected with the appearance in Chinese of the ABC, which sowed seeds of revolution across the whole of China.

After the ABC, I translated other books like Bukharin's *Lenin as a Marxist* and his *The Peasant Problem* and, finally, Stalin's *Problems of Leninism*. I set down two principles for myself: I would leave my name off my translations; and I would never take a fee. There were reasons for this decision.[54]

---

53   Zhang Jingsheng was a Professor of Philosophy at Beijing University. After returning to China from France, he became one of the first people to campaign against traditional ideas about sex in China. He edited many sex-stories, the first collection of which became a best-seller. He championed the exaltation of sex and wanted to create a utopian society founded on sex.

54   Here I am referring to malpractices already evident at the time among Communist Party members, namely, fame-seeking and the demand for extra pay for overtime. I particularly disapproved of Shi Cuntong. He was in bad health and wanted to return to his home-town to recuperate, but he had no money. He asked Peng Shuzhi for a loan from the Central Committee on condition that he would repay the money after selling one of his translation manuscripts. Peng acceded to this request without consulting me. [Note added by Zheng Chaolin in 1989.]

Before a year was up we moved from Fusheng Road to a foreign-style lane house near Hengbin Bridge. Each house had a small front garden. The rooms were Western-style, with bath-tubs and flush-toilets. The house we rented had direct access to a large bridging room attached to the house next door. Most of the other tenants in the terrace were Japanese people or Western prostitutes. Peng Shuzhi had proposed this move so that the Propaganda Department could be expanded and its staff accommodated in one office. The bridging room was used for writing and equipped with four or five desks. The back part was screened off and turned into a library, with shelves to hold the economic journals I had purchased earlier and Russian books that people had brought back from Moscow. Qu Qiubai introduced Yang Muzhi, an administrative worker at Shanghai University from the same native place as Qu, to help run things; the District Committee assigned the Shanghai University student Huang Wenrong to take charge of administration at a slightly higher level, and Shen Yanbing to run the Bureau of Information. Everyone save Shen lived in this house. Shen attended the office for several hours each day. I had no choice but to change my life-style. But by then we were already in the 'insurrectionary' period.

The idea of a Shanghai 'insurrection' came up at the time of Sun Chuanfang's 'autumn exercises'. In the autumn of 1925, Sun, the Military Governor of Zhejiang province, massed his troops on the pretext of holding 'autumn exercises' and launched a surprise attack on the Fengtian Army in Jiangsu. A couple of days later, he took Shanghai almost without a fight, drove the Fengtian Army from Jiangsu, and declared himself Commander-in-Chief of the Allied Army of Five Provinces. Zhang Guotao said: 'Next time there is a war in Shanghai, we should make preparations to disarm the defeated troops, equip ourselves at their expense, and then hold talks with the victor-warlord'. It had not yet occurred to him that 'next time' would be the war between the Northern Expedition and the Beiyang warlords.

Preparations for the insurrection were made by the Military Committee. This was a secret body: secret not only to the outside world but also to party comrades. At that time, there were three sorts of organisation in the Chinese Communist Party: the Youth League, the Party, and the Military Committee, the Committee being most rigidly disciplined and the League least. But the Committee was not established until a long time after my return to China. When I was in Moscow, the Russian Military Academy was not yet open to Chinese students, and became so only during or after my departure. This development was doubtless connected with the founding of the Military

Academy at Huangpu. Among those studying military science in Moscow were newly arrived Chinese students like Yan Changyi; Chinese students like Nie Rongzhen who had gone to Moscow from Western Europe; and ex-KUTV students like Xiao Jingguang. Wang Yifei was transferred from KUTV to the Military Academy to be an interpreter, so he also learned some military science. A strict selection procedure governed admission to the Academy. You had to be fit and strong, but even more important, you had to be from a poor family background with no rich relatives or ties to high officials. I do not know how many people studied military science, nor do I remember precisely when a Military Committee was set up under the Central Committee. I have an idea that it was at the end of 1925 or the beginning of 1926. At first, it was under Wang Yifei and Yan Changyi. The comrades on the Military Committee did not belong to ordinary branches. In principle, neither its members nor its work were known to ordinary party members, so I did not know about the Committee's activities or the military preparations for the Shanghai insurrection, though some people close to me did give me an inkling of what was going on. Yan Changyi often took me to the Military Committee's headquarters and asked me to attend his training course – a lecture on 'secret correspondence' was in Russian, and since Wang Yifei and the other comrades who knew Russian could not get round to dealing with it, he gave it to me and asked me to teach it. So I also learned something about secret correspondence, though unfortunately I have now forgotten the names of many of the chemicals. During the 'insurrectionary period' in Shanghai, the Military Committee was specially enlarged and Zhou Enlai became an important figure in it. Hangzhou's insurrection in response to the Northern Expedition was the Committee's work. After Gu Shunzhang returned from Hangzhou, he also joined the committee leadership, to help prepare the Shanghai insurrection. But the political preparations for the insurrection were made by the District Committee.

When Luo Yinong became Secretary of the District Committee, its style changed radically. Luo had guts. He acted boldly and resolutely. He put the Party's internal organisation into the capable and reliable hands of Zhao Shiyan; He Jinliang easily coped with day-to-day union business, while Zhao Shiyan decided the important questions. The scope of our work grew daily, and our administration became increasingly accomplished; the Communist Party in Shanghai became a powerful force. Luo Yinong did not immerse himself in Shanghai work, unlike several of his predecessors. He participated in 'diplomatic' work, which in the past had been the Central Committee's remit. For example, he liaised with important members of the Shanghai Guomindang, kept up contact with left-wing capitalists, and tried to make friendly contacts with gangsters so as to win their neutrality or support. During Chen Duxiu's 'disappearance',[55] he practically took over this side of party work. For that purpose, he got himself an even more luxurious residence than ours and lived there with his wife, his mother-in-law, and his brother-in-law. He used to wear a long gown and a mandarin jacket. He had bushy eyebrows and a big mouth. He looked awe-inspiring when he did not smile, very much like a middle-class family patriarch. Zhao Shiyan lived together with him, but much more simply and frugally than he. He Songlin, Wang Ruofei, Yin Kuan, and I were frequent guests in this house. We used to order food from nearby restaurants, drink alcohol, and play mahjong with Luo's mother-in-law.

By this time, the Northern Expedition had already made considerable progress. It had occupied Hunan and Jiangxi, and not long after that, it took Hankou. The Party in Shanghai had already put the insurrection at the top of its agenda. The Guangdong Government[56] sent Niu Yongjian to Shanghai to take secret command; Du Yuesheng acted as his protector. In the course of our cooperation with Niu, we, too, developed relations with Du. In October or November 1926, we proposed staging an immediate insurrection and occupying Shanghai, but Niu would have none of it. We made preparations to act secretly. We had comrades on a battleship anchored off Gaochangmiao, and on land, we had already made some preparations. We hoped that if just a few people dared to act, we might sway the northern armies[57] and cause them to collapse, disintegrate, or surrender, for at the same time, Niu Yongjian was lobbying the Shanghai garrison. But when the navy loosed off a few salvoes, there was no response on land. A few comrades of the Military Committee were locked in stalemate for a while with a police contingent in the Nantao district of Shanghai,[58] but they were defeated and Xi Zuoyao was seized and subsequently shot at Longhua.[59] Just a few days earlier, I had played mahjong with Xi in the Military Committee headquarters. This was what was later known as

---

55   In early 1926, Chen Duxiu fell ill with typhoid fever and went to hospital. He stayed there for more than a month. Before going, he told Ren Zuomin, but he did not say that he was entering hospital. While in hospital, he wrote no letters. We all thought he had been assassinated. Everyone was extremely worried. We made enquiries everywhere, but there was no news of his whereabouts. When Chen Yannian left Guangdong for Beijing, he passed through Shanghai and helped in the search. Finally, after he had already boarded the steamship for Tianjin, a messenger rushed to the quayside to tell him that his father had 'emerged'. [Note added by Zheng Chaolin in 1980.]

56   That is, the Guomindang.
57   These armies were occupying Shanghai.
58   The Chinese territory, south of the French Concession.
59   Longhua was the site of the garrison headquarters.

the first insurrection. When the navy opened fire, Luo Yinong was visiting Niu Yongjian in his home. When Niu heard the firing, he blanched. He knew that it was our doing, and blamed us for not letting him know about it in advance.

The second insurrection, in February 1927, was better prepared. Hangzhou had already fallen to the Northern Expeditionaries. We called a general strike; at the same time, our armed squads attacked police stations. That night, I was at command headquarters, helping out at the new party school in Guanhua Alley off Route Lafayette. I watched as group after group was dispatched to its position. No one dared sleep. Everyone was waiting for good news to arrive, but none came. I went to the second floor to listen. I seemed to hear firing, but I could not be sure. The next morning, the various groups came back. Some said that the people they had been waiting for had not arrived, others that the police stations had been prepared for them, that no one had dared move, and that some people had fired a few shots and then backed off. Wang Hebo's younger brother turned up in a furious temper. He said that he had already prepared weapons aboard the battleship, but no boat had arrived from Pudong to fetch them.

In March 1927, the third insurrection finally succeeded. We captured all the police stations, surrounded the garrison occupying the Oriental Library and the Northern Railway Station, captured large numbers of weapons, and set up an armed picket of two to three thousand men.

The insurrection began at midday. During the afternoon and night, the fighting intensified. We drove to Zhabei to see what was going on; dusk set in. During the night, I constantly crossed back and forth between the Propaganda Department and Hengfeng Alley in Scott Road. At that time, Chen Duxiu was living in the Propaganda Department building, and the District Committee had one of its offices in Hengfeng Alley so as to be able to pass on news from the front. We could hear firing from Zhabei throughout the night, sometimes heavy, sometimes light. On occasions, it was so heavy that it sounded like strings of fire-crackers going off. People were sent out from Hengfeng Alley to take news of the battle to the Propaganda Department; sometimes Chen Duxiu sent back directives. I, too, passed on several notes. At around three o'clock in the morning, Chen sent a note to the people in Zhabei proposing that they withdraw to Dachang in order to avoid sacrifices. But the people at the front failed to act on the proposal. After we had stabilised our position, the northern troops were gradually overcome. The following afternoon, I returned to Zhabei to take a second look. The northerners inside the Oriental Library had still not surrendered. The iron-gate in front of the building was firmly shut. There were a dozen or so soldiers on one of the upper storeys who fired whenever anyone passed by this gate. The besiegers lurked behind street corners or in the printing factory of the Commercial Press on the other side of the road. People warned me not to cross in front of the Library, so I took the long way round to the back of the Commercial Press building. Inside was a command post of the insurrection, where I saw Zhao Shiyan and Zhou Enlai. Soon afterwards, Gu Shunzhang arrived to report on his negotiations with the troops occupying the Library. After the sealing of the General Labour Union in 1925, a warrant had been issued for Gu's arrest because of his union activities or for some other reason, so he had fled Shanghai; when the Northern Expedition reached Hangzhou, he had greeted it by organising an insurrection in the city; now, he was one of the main organisers of the Shanghai insurrection. He wrote a note and took it personally to the iron gate in front of the Library advising the soldiers to surrender and informing them that the garrison at the Northern Railway Station had already laid down its arms. (Actually, the troops at the station were still holding out.) He brought back the troops' reply, which was that they would not surrender. While our people were discussing what to do, I and some other comrades went on an observation tour of the Zhabei streets, which were quiet save for occasional groups of three or four people armed with rifles and revolvers. We turned into a small road to the west of the Oriental Library, where there was an insurrection post manned by several dozen armed workers; Zhao Shiyan, too, was there. A Commercial Press worker protested furiously that someone had taken his pistol and said that we should send people out to take revenge. It turned out that there were other units active on the Zhabei streets who did not consider themselves under the jurisdiction of the General Labour Union. They had come not to take part in the insurrection but to take away the northerners' weapons for purposes of their own. There were far fewer of them than there were of us, and they had no liaison network, but Zhao Shiyan restrained the angry workers and refused to let them cause a provocation. Just at that moment, there was a hubbub in front of the Oriental Library and shots rang out. We rushed over to see what was happening. Either the Library had fallen to an attack or its occupiers had surrendered, for a large crowd of workers surrounded a knot of northern soldiers and accompanied them away from the Library. By that time, the whole of Zhabei except for the Northern Railway Station was in the hands of insurrectionaries. I wanted to go to the station to see what was happening, but was ordered not to. After that, we went back to North Sichuan Road. While we were crossing the railway line, we suddenly heard volleys of rifle fire from the direction of the Northern Railway Station. The firing got nearer and nearer; we all fled into an alley, locked the iron gate, and peered out to see what was happening. Very soon, crowds of northern troops came running down the track, some armed with rifles, others not. Some had patches of fresh blood on their grey cotton-padded greatcoats. Obviously, it was not they who had opened fire. Not long after they had run by, people outside the alley began to spread the word that the northern troops were squatting on the track and no longer moving. We went out to see for ourselves. Sure enough, just three or four hundred paces from where we had been sheltering, these northern troops were sitting down with their rifles on the ground, to show that they had surrendered. Crowds of citizens jostled round them and took their weapons; they did not resist. By the time the General Labour Union sent someone to accept their surrender, many of the rifles had been taken away by people who had nothing to do with the insurrection. We crossed the railway line back into Zhabei and went down Baoshan Road to the Northern Railway Station, which General Xue Yue had already occupied. A handful of Hunanese troops recounted the fighting to us. In front of the station were some trenches that the northerners had started but not finished. Two headless corpses hung from the railing along the International Settlement. They were naked from the waist up, but from their leggings and trousers you could see that they were policemen, not troops. There were eight or nine corpses – northerners who had been shot trying to escape into the International Settlement – hanging from the barbed wire that spread across North Henan Road. Behind the barbed wire, foreign soldiers manned machine-guns. We went back to the headquarters on Xiangshan Road, planning to return from there to North Sichuan Road. As dusk approached, I suddenly heard rifle-fire from the east. Everyone was puzzled. Soon, reports arrived to say that the firing was coming from a trainload of northerners who had arrived from Wusong, and that they had already left the train and were attacking in our direction. An urgent order went out to take up defensive positions, and we outsiders ran off to hide. It was not until later that I learned that these were troops who had fled to Wusong by train that morning but had found that the track was up and managed some way or other to get back to Shanghai. When their train reached the area behind the Commercial Press building, they found that the track there had also been dug up, so they had no choice but to retreat to the Railway Station at Tiantongan Road and dig in. There were quite a few of them, and they were well armed. If they attacked Zhabei, the insurrectionaries would be in no position to resist. Luckily, the troops' morale was gone. They had no idea of the real situation in Shanghai; night had already fallen, so they adopted a defensive strategy. Later, the northern soldiers at the Tiantongan Railway Station gave their weapons to the Japanese and withdrew into the International Settlement. The Central Committee of the Communist Youth had its headquarters near the Tiantongan Railway Station. Xiao Zizhang and his Russian wife, who lived there, spent the whole night in terror.

The next day, the situation in Zhabei had completely changed. The streets were bustling with people: not shoppers but armed workers, unarmed workers, students, and women marching up and down on demonstrations. I followed them from Baoshan Road past the Northern Railway Station towards Xinzha Bridge. The armed men were dressed in short gowns; some wore the green uniforms of postmen. After the demonstrations were over, I went to the new headquarters of the Shanghai General Labour Union, housed in the building of the Huzhou Fellow Townsmen's Association, and also to the general command post of the workers' picket in the Oriental Library. The entrances to both these places were guarded by machine-guns. The people at the General Labour Union asked me to stay behind to help them; I spent the night there. We passed the whole night in fear and alarm. People brought reports saying that a group of ruffians were on their way to attack the building and disarm us. Actually, we had no weapons and no men, in spite of the fact that the gate to our building was guarded by machine-guns. We asked the people at the Oriental Library for reinforcements; for some reason or another no pickets came, but a dozen or so troops of the Sappers' Battalion of the First Division eventually arrived. I and Long Dadao jointly welcomed the squad or platoon commander who had led these troops over to our side.

Victory in Shanghai was now assured, and Suzhou and Nanjing also fell. After Chiang Kai-shek arrived in Shanghai, Bai Chongxi took over as garrison-commander. It became rapidly clear that they intended to treat us as enemies. One night, Zhou Enlai arrived at our house near Hengbin Bridge, where ever since the start of the insurrection, Chen Duxiu had stayed together with us. He slept in my bed, so I slept in the office room on a bamboo bed. We had still not retired to sleep when Zhou arrived. Chen Duxiu, I, and other officials of the Propaganda Department were all busy in the office.

Zhou Enlai said,

> Three drops of water[60] has arrived. The Russian comrades told me. I was the first person to meet him. No one else knows he is here yet. He is on our side. He asked me whether comrades back in China resented the fact that he had gone abroad before the start of the Northern Expedition and only returned after its successful conclusion. I explained to him that the comrades back in China all hoped that he would quickly start to lead them. He voiced some dissatisfaction with the Russian comrades. He said that the comrades responsible for getting him back to China had treated him like a prisoner, both on the train in Siberia and on the steamship from Vladivostok to Shanghai.

---

60 Wang Jingwei. The character Wang is written with the water radical, which consists of three dots representing three drops of water.

Zhou Enlai proposed sending Wang directly to Hankou and not letting him meet Chiang Kai-shek and the other Guomindang leaders in Shanghai. Chen Duxiu agreed. After that, Zhou Enlai came every day without fail, sometimes more than once. I was not present during discussions, but I do know that his proposal was not implemented. One day, he went out together with Chen Duxiu. When Chen came back, he said that he had been to see Wang Jingwei and that Wang had told him that he had already met Chiang Kai-shek, that Wu Zhihui and others had also been present at the meeting, that Wu had loudly cursed the Communist Party, and that Chiang had kept quiet. Chen Duxiu said: Wu and Chiang are of one mind, this one plays the red-faced part, that one plays the white.[61] That night, Chen Duxiu spent a long time at his desk penning his 'Wang-Chen Joint Manifesto'. The next day, when Zhou Enlai brought it back, I noticed that Wang had endorsed it, leaving a big white space on the front. The implication was that Chen Duxiu should sign the front. But Chen signed his name beneath Wang's. When the newspapers published the manifesto, Chen Duxiu said to me: 'It's a long time since the big newspapers[62] published anything by me!'

The aim of the manifesto was to scotch rumours, ensure that cooperation between the two parties continued to the end, and explain that the General Labour Union pickets had no intention of attacking the garrison headquarters at Longhua. Actually, these rumours had been deliberately put about by Chiang Kai-shek to prepare the way for an attack on the pickets.

After the transfer of the First Division from Zhabei, the Second Division arrived to replace it. The Divisional Commander Liu Zhi was an anti-Communist. One day, I was helping out Mao Zemin[63] in our newly opened bookshop. A soldier bought a book and then, instead of leaving, indicated that he wanted to talk with us.

Standing by the side of the counter, he said in a low voice, 'Be careful, the pickets should keep their guns and ammunition by their side when they go to sleep'.

'Why?' I asked.

He was unwilling to elaborate. Actually, we had known for a long time from other sources that Chiang Kai-shek was planning to attack us. A Huangpu student called Jiang Youliang was a Communist. At an officers' meeting at

---

61 In Beijing opera, the character in the red mask is the good man, the character in the white mask, the bad man. Here, however, the reference simply means that Wu and Chiang played the same role – that of the Communist Party's deadly enemy – in different guises.
62 Chen means the 'respectable' press.
63 Mao Zedong's younger brother.

command headquarters when Pan Yizhi, Director of the Political Department, had expressed anti-Communist opinions, Jiang Youliang had stood up to rebut him. The order had immediately gone out for Jiang's arrest, but his fellow-students secretly allowed him to escape. He had sought out Zhou Enlai and told him of Chiang Kai-shek's conspiracy. Needless to say, we got reports from other channels too. Zhou Enlai wrote a 'Letter to Messrs Chen Duxiu and Chiang Kai-shek'. The letter was very long and agitated. It was not published anywhere. I was worried and told Yin Kuan so. He consoled me, saying: 'Even if Chiang's attack on us succeeds, it will be only a temporary military victory; politically, he will have lost and we will have won'. The organ of the District Committee that Yin edited had already secretly begun to attack Chiang Kai-shek. This newspaper was published using the types and printing press of the Commercial Press.

On the morning of 12 April, I awoke in the house near Hengbin Bridge to the sound of firing from the direction of Zhabei. I asked the others what was happening. They told me that the firing had started at midnight. Soon after that, Zhao Shiyan's wife Xia Zhixu came from the District Committee with an order for me to go and work there. According to her, the firing was by thugs belonging to the Green Gang; they were using pistol-carbines and there were not many of them. We prepared to rush out and disarm them. I asked her about the attitude of the garrison army. She said they were sticking to a neutral course. By the time I arrived in Zhabei, the situation had changed dramatically. The 26th Army, under General Zhou Fengqi, had joined in the thugs' attack on the Oriental Library, the Huzhou Fellow Townspeople's Association building, and other picket centres. When I went to Baoshan Road to look for Zhou Enlai, he was just coming out from the hospital opposite the Commercial Press building. He told me we should give out leaflets along the streets and paste up slogans opposing the new warlords, and that there was no longer any need to worry about maintaining our collaboration with Chiang Kai-shek. I immediately got to work. I did not witness the demonstration and massacre on Baoshan Road.

Early one morning two or three days after the massacre, three people came to the house near Hengbin Bridge to waken me. One was Chen Yannian, one was Li Lisan, one was Nie Rongzhen. They had just arrived from Hankou. En route, they had heard about the 12 April counter-revolution and reckoned that the Propaganda Department where I lived would be comparatively safe, which was why they were there. They wanted me to take them to see Luo Yinong and Zhao Shiyan. I asked them to wait inside the house while I went off by myself to where Luo lived. Zhao, too, was there. I told them about the arrival of Chen, Li, and Nie, and that the three were at my house waiting to see them. Luo looked at Zhao, Zhao looked at Luo; both realised what the visit was about. Luo told me to bring the three to his home, so I went back to fetch them. Only then did I discover that the Central Committee in Hankou had sacked Luo Yinong and sent Chen Yannian to replace him. When the three set out from Hankou, news of the massacre of 12 April had not yet reached them. Apart from this development, Chen Yannian brought an order from the Central Committee that concerned me. It said that all Central Committee officials still in Shanghai – Zheng Chaolin of the Propaganda Department, Luo Yan of the Peasant Department, and Yang Zhihua of the Women's Department – should proceed forthwith to Hankou. I left Luo Yinong's house and went with Li Lisan to the Three Friends' Industrial Society to buy a new quilt; even more important, I visited an optician to buy a pair of sunglasses.

On around 22 April, I and Comrade Lu Dingyi of the Central Committee of Communist Youth reluctantly set out for Wuhan. Chen Duxiu had already left for Hankou after issuing the Wang-Chen joint manifesto. In Hankou, we heard reports of the August First Incident. Qu Qiubai had already returned from Wuhan, but he was the only one to do so, for all the rest had joined the Ye-He army. One or two days before 7 August, Luo Yinong told me that the Central Committee was about to hold an important meeting at which I was to represent Hubei. That was the famous 7 August Conference.

The Conference was held in a Western-style hostel in Hankou's former Russian Concession. We had to climb a staircase alongside a Western-style shop. In the front room a foreigner sat reading; he paid no attention to us. This man, an American citizen and the owner of the building, later wrote a pamphlet on the Chinese Revolution. I forget what he was called. We went through into the back room, which was full of Chinese. Still more arrived later. When everyone was present, a huge and unusually fair-skinned Russian entered the room. Just as Qu Qiubai was about to introduce him, the Russian himself told us that his name was Nikola, which was later shortened to N. in some documents. Actually, he was Lominadze, shot by Stalin ten years later for 'semi-Trotskyism'.[64]

Apart from me and Peng Gongda, representing the Hunan Provincial Committee, all the others at the meeting were members of the Central Committee elected by the Fifth Congress. Chen Duxiu was the only member still in Hankou who did not attend. There were eighteen of us in all, including me and Peng. I do not remember who they all were. The meeting was very brief and not

---

64   Actually, Lominadze was not shot but committed suicide before the secret police could arrest him. His draft of the 7 August Conference document was titled 'Letter to Comrades'. [Note added by Zheng Chaolin in the early 1980s.]

many people spoke, so it left no deep impression on me. Qu Qiubai interpreted, so naturally, he was there; Luo Yinong was there, and so were Mao Zedong and Li Zhenying. I cannot remember who the rest were.[65]

The sole aim of this meeting was to pass a lengthy resolution that Lominadze had already drafted and Qu had translated into Chinese; it was written very clearly and placed on the table. Lominadze addressed the meeting; Qu read out the resolution and invited contributions. Mao Zedong spoke, though I forget what he said. Luo Yinong also spoke, and I still recall his words. He said: 'The Guomindang won't be able to stay in power', which statement he then translated into Russian. Lominadze reproached him, saying: 'It's quite possible that the Guomindang will stabilise its rule'.

Lominadze had been sent to China to take over from Roy. He brought with him the new Comintern line and told us to accept it and to present it as our own resolution. Actually, many comrades knew nothing about the new Comintern line before Lominadze spoke about it and Qu read it out. When it came to the vote, I, too, raised my hand in favour, my sole reason being that the Comintern representative had proposed it; I did not do so because I had given the matter deep thought or because I believed in my heart of hearts that it was right. In my opinion, a true revolutionary party should call things by their right names; if top leaders order lesser leaders to accept something, then they should do so in the form of an order or a directive. The 7 August Resolution (or 'Letter to All Comrades') was later printed in many copies, so historians will probably be able to find one. I cannot remember the exact contents of the new line,[66] but I do know that there was no proposal to quit the Guomindang. The directive to quit the Guomindang was not received until September. I still remember how I and Qu Qiubai went to the Russian Consulate in Hankou in mid September. I sat in the waiting room, and he went through the door. After he had come out again, he told me, 'The International has wired to say that we should withdraw from the Guomindang'. Both the right-wing and the left-wing Guomindang had already expelled us, but the August 7 Resolution was still saying that under no circumstances would we abandon the Guomindang flag.

Chen Duxiu was in Hankou during the 7 August Conference, but he did not attend, even though he was a member of the Central Committee. This meeting

---

65   They were Cai Hesen, Xiang Zhongfa, Li Weihan, Su Zhaozheng, Zhang Tailei, Ren Bishi, and Deng Zhongxia.
66   The Conference issued four documents. One denounced the old leadership, in particular Tan Pingshan and Chen Duxiu, for opportunism. The others called for insurrections to overthrow both the Nanjing and the Wuhan régimes under the banner of the 'revolutionary-left Guomindang'.

was called precisely to oppose 'his' line, but from beginning to end, he was never once named,[67] either in speeches or in writing. No one explained why he, a member of the Central Committee, had not been invited, and no one asked, either. I already knew privately that the International had suspended him because of his 'mistakes'. Not long after the meeting, he returned to Shanghai together with Huang Wenrong, his personal secretary.

Sometime before the conference, Zhou Enlai invited me, Luo Yinong, and Liu Bojian to a Sichuanese restaurant (the Jiaxiu Lou?) at the corner of Tianlong Alley. He began in a guarded and roundabout way to discuss the inner-party struggle. He criticised past mistakes and concluded by saying that we should not deal too harshly with the 'two old men', by which he meant Chen Duxiu and Tan Pingshan. The latter, once earmarked by Moscow to replace Chen Duxiu as leader, was now also under attack from the International. Liu Bojian had not been in Hankou for long. He was unaware of the situation in the Party and naïve to boot, so he flew into a rage when he heard Zhou say this. As for me, I just sat there, wearing a meaningful smile.

After the 7 August Conference, Qu Qiubai, in fact if not in name, occupied the position in the Party previously held by Chen Duxiu. Tan Pingshan and Zhang Guotao were both with the Communist armed forces; I don't know where Cai Hesen was.[68] Apart from Qu, the only member of the Central Committee in Hankou was Li Weihan. Later, Luo Yinong joined the Standing Committee, but neither his status nor Li's were as high as Qu's. He wanted to sort out things after the chaos, so I stopped doing local work and returned to the Central Committee.

Luo Yinong told me that Qu Qiubai wanted me back on the Central Committee to revive *Guide Weekly*. Luo said he did not want to let me go, but Qu had insisted; he had no choice but to accept, so he proposed swapping me for Chen Qiaonian. This account is not necessarily reliable. I think what actually happened is that Luo, seeing that Liu Bojian lacked the competence to run the Organisation Department, had asked the Central Committee for Chen Qiaonian, whereupon Qu proposed swapping Chen for me. The swap went ahead, and Liu Bojian was transferred to some other office. Li Weihan had many people under him and could easily replace Chen Qiaonian. Hua Lin took over from me as head of the Provincial Committee's Propaganda Department.

---

67 According to Wilbur 1983, p. 150, Chen was named, along with Tan Pingshan.
68 After the 7 August Conference, Cai Hesen went first to Beijing and then to Tianjin, where together with Wang Hebo and others, he restored the Party's Northern Bureau.

By then, *Guide Weekly* had been dormant for quite some time. After Chen Duxiu's downfall, Zhang Guotao took over everything, including *Guide Weekly*. Manuscripts edited by other people were sent to him for checking. He stuffed them in his portfolio and it would be a week or two before he found time to look at them. So gradually, *Guide Weekly* stopped appearing, and the editorial office was disbanded. In the meantime, there had been several attempts to find someone to edit it and get it going again. One suggestion was that Shen Yanbing should be editor, but Shen was married and had children to fend for, and Zhang Guotao could not afford to pay that sort of wage. I heard from others that they had had me in mind for a long time, for I was a bachelor. After Qu Qiubai had taken real power in the Central Committee from Zhang Guotao, the plan was realised. But as soon as I got to work, it became apparent to me that as things stood, there was no hope whatsoever of reviving *Guide Weekly*. The tide of reaction was gradually flowing. Our publishing enterprise was already paralysed. I controlled three organisations: the Chang Jiang Bookshop, the print-shop, and a paper-supplier. The bookshop had already closed down, and its stock had been either removed or stolen; it was in complete chaos, and I could not but ignore it. The print-shop and the paper-business were also in a mess. Former comrades were blackmailing us by threatening to report us to the army and get us closed down as 'Communist organs' if we did not agree to their demands. So I wound up the paper-business and crated the printing machinery, in preparation for sending it back to Shanghai. At the same time, I dismissed the staff and workers, for the Central Committee, too, as I had heard, was to be transferred back to Shanghai. 'There is no way we can revive *Guide Weekly*', I told Qu Qiubai.

Qu and his wife invited me to stay with them in a newly built Western-style hostel in the former British Concession. They had four big rooms – a guest-room, a dining room, and two bed-rooms – on the first floor. Each bed-room had an adjoining bathroom and trunk-room. The kitchen had gas; in wintertime, there was steam-heating. There was a similar suite of rooms on the second floor lived in by a landlord family from Hunan; in the middle of a pebbled terrace roof were two more rooms for sleeping in during the summer months, with tiled floors and glass windows on three sides. One room belonged to the first floor, the other to the second floor.

I and Pan Jiachen lived together in the guest-room. Little Pan was working for the Russians as an interpreter; he also acted as a courier between Qu Qiubai and the Russians. After we had been there for a few days, Pan brought in a girl called Zhuang Dongxiao who had just got back from Moscow. Many other women had returned together with Zhuang across the Mongolian desert into Gansu and south via Shaanxi and Henan. Feng Yuxiang had already gone over to the other side by that time, but he did not harm these women and even protected them as they crossed the region under his control. By the time they reached Hankou, it, too, was in the grip of reaction.

Qu and his wife slept in one bedroom and the fifteen year-old younger sister of Yang Zhihua[69] slept in the other. There was also a young man of around twenty who Yang Zhihua said was her relative; he was called Sheng and came from a rich family, but had run away to become a revolutionary. Sleeping in the same room, Sheng and the girl quickly became lovers and decided to marry without asking the consent of their parents. Yang Zhihua began to arrange for an old-style wedding to increase their protective cover. One day, the boy, who worked for the Central Committee as a secret courier, arrived home in a panic. 'Everything's ruined!' he said. He said that he had been carrying $5,000 back from the Russians rolled up in a newspaper when he was robbed on the street. He did not dare report the robbery to Qu Qiubai but hurriedly packed his things and fled without a backward glance. When Qu and his wife got home and heard the news, they were rather distrustful. The girl was in tears, fearful that the boy would kill himself. Yang Zhihua's older brother, a petty functionary in the Ministry of Agriculture or of Labour, went out to search for him and found him on board a boat bound for Shanghai. When he came over next day to report the fact, Yang Zhihua told him off for not dragging the boy ashore. The girl protested the innocence of her fiancé, but later, back in Shanghai, she met him and discovered that he had opened an account at the post office. Only then was she prepared to believe that he was guilty. The boy had already forgotten his betrothal.

Luo Yinong said to me, 'Qu Qiubai loves employing his relatives!' The next day, the Russians made good the missing sum.

'That money will spoil the boy's whole life', said Qu Qiubai. 'A similar thing happened in one of Dostoevsky's novels. The criminal continued to feel the prick of conscience until his dying day...'.

After the print-shop and the paper-business had been wound up, I was once again at a loose end. I frequently ate well at Qu Qiubai's place or at Luo Yinong's. Every day, I went out sight-seeing with Pan Jiachen, along the streets or along the banks of the Yangtze.

After the summer heat had passed its peak and the autumn breezes were starting to blow, the evening crowds along the river gradually thinned. When the winds came up, Wuhàn assumed a desolate air. The desolation was born not just of the changing seasons. After a lively spell as capital, Wuhan had once again reverted to its original status – a provincial city of the interior. One

---

69   Qu Qiubai's wife.

afternoon, in the cool air, I slowly made my way from Qu Qiubai's place to Luo Yinong's in Lanling Gardens, for that day, the Central Committee was meeting there and Luo had invited me for a meal. Entering the Garden, I saw two men sitting on a bench on the lawn in front of the entrance to Luo's home. At first, I paid little attention to them, but suddenly one of them called out my name. It turned out to be Li Heling. The man talking with him was Ouyang Qin of the Military Committee. Li Heling was weeping bitterly and confessing that he had made mistakes. He said that he had been overcome by a sudden fit of emotion, that he had behaved petulantly like a spoiled young master and posted an advertisement to say that he had broken with the Party; but that he had done nothing else of a reactionary nature.

'A few days ago, someone fired a shot at me at my home', he continued. 'But I do not hold it against the Party, I deserve to be punished. Luckily, the shot only grazed me, I'm all right again now. I want the Party to restore my membership. I'll go anywhere and do anything'. He told me that he had bumped into Ouyang Qin on the street and invited him into the Garden for a chat.

'If you write a letter, I can pass your views on', I told him.

He agreed, and made a date to meet Ouyang two or three days later, at dusk, on one of the wharves along the Yangtze, to give him his report. Just as we were speaking, Li Weihan came walking over from the other side of the Garden. When he saw that it was me standing there, he entered Luo's house without further ado. When I, too, went in, they asked me what had kept me so long. I told them; they flew into a panic, convinced that Li Heling was acting insincerely. Li Heling had noticed Li Weihan come into the house, so he would surely guess that it was an important headquarters of the Party. (I myself had deliberately strolled round the Garden after Li Heling had left, and only then gone into Luo's house.) So we abandoned an excellent meal and slipped off at intervals through the back door. The other side of the street happened to be the back door of the building where we had held the 7 August Conference. By then, the Americans had left Hankou and the premises housed the Central Committee's Workers' Department or Workers' and Peasants' Department under Li Zhenying.

Ouyang Qin met Li Heling as planned. The report was unsigned, but I recognised Li Heling's handwriting. The Central Committee decided to send him to Hailufeng,[70] where he could more easily be kept under supervision. A few days after arriving in Shanghai, I was told at the Central Committee office that Li and his wife were also in the city, and that they were staying at such-and-such

---

70   Hailufeng, in Guangdong, was the site of the first Chinese Soviet Government, founded in 1927 by Peng Pai and suppressed in February 1928.

a hotel. Not long after that, they went to Guangdong. A long time later, I cannot remember when, I heard that Li had been shot by Peng Pai. Was it for a new crime or for the old one? Or was it simply because he was unreliable and had shown that he was capable of going against the revolution? I fear that I have no answer to these questions.

On or around 20 September, I and Qu Qiubai boarded the ship for Shanghai. Yang Zhihua stayed on for a few days in Hankou, to fix the baggage and get the furniture sent on. The two of us sailed first class. Qu Qiubai had all his meals brought directly to the cabin, which he never left throughout the voyage. As for me, I strolled round the ship, but apart from a comrade in steerage who had previously managed the Party's paper-business in Hankou, I saw no one else I knew. Everyone else was just a normal passenger. Compared with the outward voyage, this Yangtze steamship, too, had reverted to its old ways.

Two Years at University

Wang Fanxi

Source: *Memoirs of a Chinese Revolutionary* (1957).

Graduating from middle school was for me a very different experience from primary school graduation, since by then there was no one attempting to map out my future. My father had been dead for more than a year, and, in that respect, I was completely free to do as I chose, but family finances were much worse than before and this placed new constraints on me.

My brother, who was only six years older than I, had assumed the heavy burden of supporting the family. A young man in his early twenties, he was expected to deal with the many financial problems which arose after my father's death. In a little town like ours, where money was so important, it was humiliating for him to have to face our father's creditors, and he became very aware of the cruelty of human and social relations. He constantly grumbled about this to me and declared that it was his intention to restore the family fortunes. As a part of his plan, he approved of my wish to sit the university entrance examination, and promised to do everything he could to help me.

Five members of the graduation class, myself included, were going to sit the examinations in Beijing. Just before I left, my brother and my mother managed to scrape together fifty silver dollars for me. Since a third-class ticket to Beijing cost nearly twenty dollars, I had no idea how I would manage on only thirty dollars after I arrived in Beijing. The other four students started out from Hangzhou, and we met up together on the way. My brother came along to the station to see me off, and travelled with me for a short stretch before returning home. On the train neither of us spoke a word, except when he urged the other four to look after me. He got off at Jiaxing and waited for a while at the train-window, not knowing what to say. As the train moved off, he stood there in the sunset watching me. I leaned out of the window. On his face I could read the expectations he had of me, and this put me in a solemn frame of mind; it was as if we were comrades-in-arms, and I was off to the front to fight to restore the fortunes of the family. However, I completely failed to fulfil those expectations. As time went by, our ideas grew further and further apart, and after many disappointments his brotherly affection towards me cooled considerably.

My long-cherished dream materialised: I passed the entrance examination to Beijing University. I was very happy and excited, rather like a Christian must feel on entering a great cathedral. Beijing University was a very different place from what it had been at the time of the May Fourth Movement. Cai Yuanpei had already resigned as president, and Chen Duxiu had long since left Beijing to devote himself to Communist Party work. Hu Shi was said to be at odds with those professors who were members of the Guomindang, and had asked for extended leave, but there were still many other professors working at the university whom I looked up to. And then there was the library, stacked high with books I had never seen or even heard of before, and the porter's lodge, where many different sorts of publications were on sale. I was deeply impressed by the magnificence of China's highest educational institution, and as I drank in the air of learning and culture I felt that I was close to the vital pulse of the nation, the epoch, and the world. I think that this combination of reverence and exhilaration was felt by many of the young people who came to Beijing from all over China in search of knowledge.

The political situation in Beijing at that time was rather unstable, and was moving quickly to the left. As a result of the warlord Feng Yuxiang's change of allegiance, the confused war between the Fengtian and the Zhili warlords had come to an end; Puyi, the last emperor of the Qing dynasty, had been swept out of the Forbidden City in Beijing; the political reverberations of the campaign launched by the Left after Sun Yat-sen's death could still be felt, and political life was in a state of lively ferment.[1] The May Thirtieth incident in Shanghai, the world-famous Guangzhou-Hong Kong general strike of 1925–6 and the Shaji shootings in Guangzhou on 23 June stimulated and reinforced political developments among the intellectuals in Beijing.[2] The Duan Qirui régime in Beijing was nothing more than an empty shell propped up by a number of

---

1 On 15 September 1924, Zhang Zuolin (1875–1928), head of the Fengtian warlord-clique, declared war on the Zhili warlords headed by Cao Kun (1862–1938), then President of the Beijing Government. This, the second Fengtian-Zhili war, was brought to an end within a month by the defection to the Zhili forces of one of the three top commanders, Feng Yuxiang (1880–1948). Having established secret contact with the Guomindang, Feng called for the cessation of the war and moved his forces back to Beijing, driving Puyi (1906–67), the former emperor of the Qing dynasty, out of the Forbidden City and inviting the Guomindang leader, Dr Sun Yat-sen, to Beijing. Duan Qirui (1865–1936), leader of the Anhui clique of northern warlords, came to Beijing to be 'Provisional Executive Chief of State'. Dr Sun came to Beijing with the aim of convoking a national congress, but fell ill and died on 12 March 1925.

2 In response to the May Thirtieth Incident in Shanghai, 250,000 Hong Kong workers staged a general strike, beginning on 19 June 1925. They left *en masse* for Guangzhou. At the same time workers in Shamian, a settlement for foreigners in Guangzhou, also joined the strike. On 23 June, when the strikers together with peasants, students, and soldiers, were marching along Shaji (opposite Shamian), British and French marines behind barricades in Shamian machine-gunned the demonstrators, killing 52 of them, and badly wounding more than 170.

mutually hostile military forces. Powerless to act by itself, it could not intervene in the process of differentiation and regrouping taking place in the ideological and political spheres.

The various cliques and factions of the northern warlords who at that time controlled the Government in Beijing lacked any conception of ideology. The politicians in their pay regularly published articles attacking the 'red menace', but they were so absurdly argued that people simply laughed at them. However, the warlord government did benefit indirectly from the activities of Liang Qichao's 'Study Clique' and Hu Shi's faction. Liang Qichao's advocacy of reform, rather than revolution, and Shih's call for a 'government of good men' won some support among students, and the negative tactics (such as the slogan of 'study for study's sake') with which they opposed revolutionary activity had even more influence. On the other hand, the Left in Beijing was much stronger, but had not yet clarified its ideas to the same extent as the Right.

At that time Beijing was the publication centre of the whole of China. Nearly every party, group, or tendency had its own paper or magazine. According to statistics published in the *China Year Book*, 1925 (compiled by the English *Peking-Tientsin Times*), there were over 220 dailies and periodicals published in the city. But the two ideological persuasions I have just mentioned were mainly represented by the newspapers *Chenbao* ('Morning Post') and *Jingbao* ('Peking News'), and in particular by the supplements they published. Two popular weeklies, Hu Shi and Chen Xiying's *Xiandai pinglun* ('Contemporary Review') and Lu Xun and Zhou Zuoren's *Yusi* ('Thread of Talk'), also more or less represented the two rival tendencies.

These supplements and periodicals were mainly literary in character, and rarely dealt with serious ideological or political questions. The disputes that broke out between them, such as the denunciations of Lu Xun in Chen Xiying's gossip column and Lu Xun's spirited counter-attacks, were often rather trivial and mostly revolved around personalities, but young people followed them as avidly as if they were affairs of state, and they were as influential as any weighty political controversy. It was in fact through these literary 'cold wars' that people learned to distinguish between new and old, progressive and reactionary, revolutionary and conservative. Together with a number of other literary publications like *Mangyuan* ('Deserted Plain') and *Mengjin* ('Forward'), these periodicals succeeded in creating a renaissance of sorts in literature and art.

The Hong Kong-Guangzhou general strike lasted for over two years and played an important role in the Second Chinese Revolution.

All these publications made a big impression on those of us who had just arrived in the capital. We eagerly awaited each new issue, and as soon as we got hold of a copy we would read it straight through from cover to cover, more assiduously than any university textbook. I think this was the highpoint of my love for literature. From being just an ardent reader of these publications I soon became a contributor to them, at first writing for *Xiandai pinglun*, and then for *Yusi*.

The Han Gardens and the Horse Spirit Temple area where the university was located could be compared in some ways to the Montmartre district of Paris. Apart from university students, all sorts of young intellectuals lived there. Most of them were very poor, interested in letters and disdainful of all conventions. The people one came across in the street were usually carrying weighty books under their arms or holding the latest issue of some periodical. They seldom bothered to comb their hair, and dressed untidily in long blue gowns and worn-out shoes or sandals. Only a few of them wore Western-style clothes. The hotels and cheap restaurants were full of every kind of aspiring scholar, artist, and rebel, chatting away in a mixture of dialects. For a long time I had been attracted by the romanticism of the Creation Society, and I had a weak spot for this sort of bohemian existence. The world I now found myself in was in many ways an embodiment of my long-cherished dreams, and I was naturally very happy. I was eager to approach these young intellectuals, and soon made friends with some of them. Among those living in this 'Montmartre' of Beijing were Feng Xuefeng and Pan Xun, two of the leading figures in the West Lake Poetry Society set up at Hangzhou First Normal School. I got to know both of these men, especially Pan Xun (later Mo Hua), with whom I was on the best of terms.

Apart from the West Lake Poetry Society there were many other literary groups in this part of Beijing. Some published journals, and others simply held discussions. I was interested in all these groups to some extent, but I never joined any of them. In my class, I was closest to Wang Shiwei, and on good terms with Zhang Guangren (later known as Hu Feng). By a strange coincidence, both these men later became victims of CCP literary policy.[3]

But my craze for literature and art did not last long, and my exhilaration at being a contributor to famous publications soon passed. Because of my financial plight, I was forced to write for those newspaper supplements which, unlike *Yusi* and *Contemporary Review*, paid fees for the articles they published.

---

3 Wang Shiwei became famous for his article 'Wild Lily', published in Yan'an in 1942, for which he was bitterly criticised and later killed. Zhang was arrested by the CCP authorities in the early fifties as the leader of a literary dissident group.

I soon discovered that it was a real chore having to sell articles in this way, and the humiliation of hawking them around quickly dispelled all the feelings of vanity I had developed on becoming a writer.

An even more important reason why I did not continue as a writer was the fact that, shortly after enrolling at the university, I joined the then underground Communist Party. I became more and more involved in working for the revolution, and found I no longer had any time for dabbling in literature. My transformation from a bohemian scribbler into a disciplined revolutionary brought about parallel changes in other spheres of my life, including my leisure-time interests and activities. After the winter vacation of 1926, I wrote hardly anything of a literary nature and did not even read any literature, despite the fact that I remained enrolled in the Department of Letters until I left Beijing.

The tragic events of 18 March 1926,[4] which resulted in the deaths of forty-seven young men and women and the wounding of one hundred or so more, had a decisive influence on Beijing and on me as well. It would not be an exaggeration to say that March Eighteenth marked the end of an era as far as the intellectual youth of Beijing was concerned. From the May Fourth Movement right down to the eve of March Eighteenth, the Beijing student movement never appeared to move beyond the limits of a revolution in ideology and literature. Even though the May Fourth Movement was in one important sense a political struggle, the political activities of the Beijing students lagged far behind Shanghai and Guangzhou over the following five or six years. Their social analysis lacked any real depth, and they confined their activities to rallies in Tian'anmen Square and petitions to the government. Even though the political atmosphere in the capital livened up after Sun Yat-sen's visit to Beijing and his death there in 1925, political life remained superficial. There was a festive spirit in the air, and after the temporary reconciliation of the warring factions, it was as if a national reunion was taking place. Feng Yuxiang's clique (which held military power), the Anfu clique (which held political power) and the leaders of the Guomindang, the Study Clique and the Communist Party seemed to be getting on so well together that it was hard to imagine that there could be any irreconcilable differences between them. Relations between the various individuals involved were complex and ideological divisions blurred. A few of the top-level leaders and most of the rank and file believed that it was possible for the problems of the revolution to be solved through personal

---

4   Beijing students staged a huge demonstration to protest against imperialist violation of Chinese sovereignty. They were beaten and fired on by troops of the 'Provisional Executive' Duan Qirui, thus ending the more or less liberal interlude that had existed since the spring of 1925.

contact and literary polemic, and that the revolution itself could achieve its aim through demonstrations and petitions. This was the honeymoon period of the revolution, its romantic and literary phase. Periods of this sort are generally brought to a close by bullets and bloodshed, and the tragic events of March Eighteenth supplied these two missing ingredients. That day – called by Lu Xun the 'darkest day in the history of the Republic' – the grief and indignation shown by Beijing youth defied description in its intensity, and in the university dormitories the general feeling was that book-learning was absolutely useless. In the course of those days, Lu Xun wrote many excellent articles in which he gave voice to our feelings:

> 'All we have at present are a few poems and essays, a few more topics for conversation'.
> 'What use is that which is written with the pen?'
> 'I want no more petitions of this sort'.
> 'The legacy which those who have died have bequeathed to the future is...to have taught those who continue the struggle to adopt other means'.
> 'A debt of blood must be repaid in the same currency'.

Three months later, the revolutionary struggle which had started in the South, launched by the Guomindang with CCP and Soviet support from Guangzhou, began to spread like a prairie fire. Across the whole of south China the sky was ablaze. We watched from the darkness of the North, and were all the more deeply impressed by what we saw. We now had an additional reason to turn our backs on the sterile literary squabbles of the capital. We thirsted for action, and we desperately searched around for any revolutionary ideology or theory which could be linked to practice. It was then that many students wanted to join the Communist Party.

Contrary to what most people believed, there was only a handful of 'rebels' at Beijing University in the period 1925 to 1926. When I first joined the Party, as a rank-and-file member, I had no means of knowing what the actual situation was, and it was not until I was brought into the leadership of the university-branch that I discovered that of nearly two thousand students only twenty or thirty were party members. I was told that there were more originally, but after the May Thirtieth Movement in Shanghai developments in the South called for more cadres, so that many comrades were either sent south or went there of their own accord. But at that time there was no need to worry about a shortage of members, since the tide was moving in our favour and many young people were very anxious to join. The Party did not open its doors widely, and had a very cautious recruitment policy in order to prevent an influx of careerists. There were many memorable figures in the Party's ranks at that time. As far as I know, none of the ones I knew in the early days in Beijing were fortunate enough to survive and to find their way into the top echelons of the Party; many of them died a martyr's death. Among those whose memories are still dear to me are: Peng Shuchun, a brilliant student in the mathematics department, who was shot with Professor Gao Renshan in 1928; Du Hongyuan, another student of mathematics, murdered by Chiang Kai-shek; Zhang Jingchen, executed at Kunming in 1931; and Chen Qichang, murdered in the headquarters of the Japanese gendarmes in Shanghai in 1943.

At first, branch activities were centred on the university, and our main aim was to extend our influence within the Students' Union. During that period, our only rivals were the Guomindang rightists who belonged to the Western Hills Conference faction,[5] but since they had no mass support, they were no real match for us. The Students' Union and the various bodies under it all came under our control. During the period in which I was politically active in the university, there were no great political storms to arouse the students, so we never had the chance to use the Students' Union as a weapon to carry on the struggle. Our main field of work in the university was education and training. We ran useful evening classes in which we taught members of the maintenance, cleaning, and service staff of the university, and poor people from the neighbourhood, to read and write. At the same time we organised and kept close contact with a great number of drinking-water vendors who worked in the vicinity of the university. During this period, our most important task was to educate ourselves as revolutionaries and to win over the best of our fellow-students to the Party. In the long term, this work was of crucial significance, since, for a whole number of reasons, Beijing University had long since become one of the two most important sources of top-level cadres for the Communist Party. (Shanghai College, nominally under Guomindang control but effectively run by the Communists, was the other.) The North China Bureau of the CCP, under Li Dazhao, attached great importance to this work, and meetings for theoretical study were held frequently, but they were not very satisfactory. The member of the Beijing committee responsible for branch education was Chen Weiren, who had returned from France after being sent there by the Society for

---

5   The Western Hills Conference faction was a right-wing Guomindang group that met in the Western Hills outside Beijing in May 1925 and for the first time voiced opposition within the Guomindang to the policy of co-operation with the CCP.

Frugal Study.[6] We respected him as an individual: he knew how to suffer hardship, and was without the slightest trace of romanticism; his character was the precise opposite of us Han Garden Bohemians. He was our first glimpse of a professional revolutionary, and it was from him that we first heard such expressions as 'iron discipline' and 'absolute obedience'. We had never come across anyone like him before, and he made a deep initial impression on us. But before long it became obvious to us that his general learning and in particular his grasp of revolutionary theory was weak, and we were all very disappointed. He often used to give us lectures on questions of theory and on current political topics, but he was clearly only acting as a transmitter of other people's ideas. Worse still, he was only capable of reproducing about half of what he had heard elsewhere. Not only was he incapable of conveying these ideas to us, but he did not even understand them all himself. As a result, when we asked him about points which we did not grasp, he would answer evasively, or accuse us of asking too many questions. Liu Bozhuang, another member of the Beijing committee, was a lot better than Chen Weiren, but he rarely came to speak to us. As for Li Dazhao, he had long since gone underground as a security precaution, and I never once met him all the time I was in Beijing.

We had taken the first step towards becoming activists, but we did not have even a rudimentary grasp of theory. This was a source of great worry to us members of the Party who were intellectuals. At that time, it was impossible to buy new books on social science in Beijing. As far as I remember, all we had read by the end of 1926 was *A History of the Development of Society* edited by Cai Hesen. There had been some Marxist writings in foreign languages in Beijing University library, but because of the advance of the Northern Expedition and the Beijing warlord Government's phobia about the 'red menace' those books had been removed from the shelves and were no longer available to borrow.

Depressed by my lack of theoretical training, bored by the monotony of the student movement in Beijing compared with the heated struggles going on in the south of the country, and on the verge of starvation as a result of my financial plight, I began to think of leaving Beijing.

During my seventeen months or so in the capital, I was often very short of money. My elder brother kept his promise and did his best to supply me with adequate funds, but his own financial situation was bad, and he was not in a position to send me money every month; moreover, the money he did send was not always sufficient to meet my needs. I managed to supplement my income

---

6 On the Society for Frugal Study by Means of Labour, see fn. 5, p. 174.

to a certain extent by writing, but the pay was pitifully low – the publishing houses themselves were extremely hard pressed. Even if a writer did manage to get two or three dollars for an article, the publisher would often pay part of the fee in postage stamps or in small change. On many occasions, I did not even have the four dollars for a month's meals in the university refectory. Life dragged on in this way until the late autumn of 1926. I even had to pawn my winter-gown, and did not have the money to redeem it. Since it was impossible for me to carry on in this way, I decided to give up my studies and ask the Party for permission to go to Guangzhou.

I arrived in Guangzhou by ship. At that time the Northern Expedition had already got as far as the Yangtze Valley. Wuhan had just fallen, and Chiang Kai-shek's main forces were massing around Nanchang. The Guomindang Central Committee and the National Government had not yet moved north from Guangzhou, which was nominally still the capital of the revolution. But it was already clear that Guangzhou was in the process of losing its former status, and its main role was now that of rearguard of the revolution and its logistical centre. Politically, real power in the city had already fallen into the hands of General Li Jishen, who was then very close to Chiang Kai-shek and a member of the right wing of the Guomindang. The forces of the Left, however, were still very strong; the Guangzhou-Hong Kong general strike was still on and the strike committee could still insist on equal standing with the Nationalist Government in Guangzhou.

The Guangzhou I now saw was very different from the revolutionary Mecca I used to dream of when I was in north China, but it still aroused my enthusiasm and emotions. As soon as I got settled in I went on a tour of the bookstores. I was like a mole emerging into the sunlight: everywhere I looked there were all kinds of revolutionary newspapers, and the sight of them made me feel quite dizzy. I came across the communist *New Youth* for the first time, and I was pleasantly surprised to see *Guide Weekly*[7] displayed on the counter like any other magazine. Wherever one looked there were piles of books with words like 'Communism' and 'Marx' printed in bold characters on the covers. Ten days before, we only dared to mention such words in whispers behind closed doors. Almost without discriminating I bought up a great pile of literature, and came near to spending my last cent.

I was deeply impressed by *New Youth*, the current issue of which was entirely devoted to world revolution. Up to then, I had never realised that there were so many or such profound theories about the revolution. All I had were a few

---

7 The political organ of the CCP, founded in September 1922 and appearing until July 1927.

general ideas, or rather simple convictions. I felt that it was impossible for people to go on living in the same old way, that darkness should not be allowed to hold sway any longer, and that imperialist oppression should no longer be tolerated; we should therefore make a revolution and as thoroughgoing a one as possible. The main reason we had joined the Communist Party was not because we had a deep understanding of things, but because it was the most consistent and the most revolutionary political organisation we had ever come across. Some party leaders in the North had even told us there was no need for understanding, and that all that was necessary were these simple convictions, since revolution was first and foremost a question of action. Too much study, they told us, could turn people into 'academics', good only for spouting hot air. Even then we found this sort of attitude unconvincing, and we were dissatisfied with the 'pure activism' of Chen Weiren and others like him. We suspected that this was nothing more than a theoretical justification for their own lack of learning. We afterwards discovered that this was not just the isolated prejudice of one or two cadres in north China, but an important political tendency in the Party during the years 1925–7. For me, reading these issues of *New Youth* was like entering a completely new world, and I came into contact with many questions I had never thought about before. For the first time, such problems as the character of the revolution, the nature of Chinese society, the leadership of the revolution, and the relationships between the classes within the revolution and between the Chinese and the world revolution, began to invade my brain and engage my intellect. These problems have been the main themes of my ideological life ever since.

Many of my old teachers and friends from Hangzhou were then in Guangzhou. Some had already joined the Guomindang and were high or middle-level cadres in it or in the Government. They lived fairly well, and during the first few days after my arrival I was warmly received by my friends, so I had no problems in that respect. Through them I was able to get a clear picture of the internal functioning of the revolutionary institutions. I discovered that there was a world of difference between the cadres working for the Revolutionary Government in Guangzhou and those of us working underground in north China. In my rather puritanical eyes, the revolutionaries I met in Guangzhou did not entirely deserve that name. They were not sufficiently serious or vigilant, and they were not fired by great feelings of anger and sorrow. They appeared to spend their time enjoying themselves, and they lived a rather carefree life. For me the books and periodicals I bought in Guangzhou were priceless treasures, but it seemed to me that there were very few people there who studied them seriously. Whenever young men got together they were much more interested in discussing women than in discussing politics.

In Guangzhou, Sun Yat-sen's famous slogan 'The revolution has not yet been achieved; comrades must still bend every effort' had been given a new twist: 'Love has not yet been achieved, comrades must still bend every effort'. No one ever discussed questions of revolutionary theory, and the main after-work activities of revolutionary cadres were eating out in restaurants or the pursuit of pleasure. Even though everyone admired the austerity of the Communist leader Yun Daiying, few followed his example. I found the situation more and more painful, since it presented such a stark contrast to the unrewarding labours of my comrades in the north. What distressed me most was the attitude towards revolutionary work I found in Guangzhou. It was considered as a means of entering the bureaucracy, and those who wished to participate in the revolution were looked upon as job-seekers.

One of the reasons I had gone south in the first place had been my financial situation, but the main reason had been that I wanted to participate more directly, more whole-heartedly, and more effectively in the revolution. Now, when I arrived in Guangzhou, everyone thought I had come looking for a job. My friends told me that they would try to find me a 'superior position' in the administration. The more kindness and sympathy they showed me, the more embarrassed they made me feel. As a matter of fact, there were more people than jobs in Guangzhou at that time, for although the revolutionary centre had moved north, all sorts of people – sincere revolutionaries and careerists, young and middle-aged alike – were still flooding in from all parts of China. It was not that there was no work in Guangzhou, but that most people were after a 'better type of job', and these had generally been snatched up by early arrivals and those with good connections.

During my first fortnight in Guangzhou I was absorbed in the books and periodicals I had bought, and, since I had no immediate worries about food and lodgings, I paid no attention to the problem of getting a position. A little later, I was offered a choice of three different jobs: one as editor of a paper published by a certain military organisation; another as Guomindang representative in an army unit; and, finally, the chance to return north and work underground. At that time many of the Communists who were working externally (that is, in Guomindang military or civilian organs) had been allotted their jobs through friends or contacts, and then had gone to the Party for confirmation. Of the three jobs I mentioned above, the first two were suggested to me by friends who were also members of the Party. I was keen to take the editing job, but since one of my friends also wanted it, and was more experienced than I was, I decided not to apply. The second job was with Commander Yan Zhong's newly established Independent Division. One of my old teachers in Hangzhou was now Yan Zhong's secretary, and one of my old friends, Fan Jinbiao, was Guomindang representative in one of the regiments in the division. These two men wanted me to take over as Guomindang representative in another of the division's three regiments. I had received no military training, but neither had many of the other comrades in similar jobs. They urged me not to worry, and to take it anyway. For my part, I was quite attracted to the idea of trying something new, but after I had discussed the matter with leading members of the Communist Party, I changed my mind. They were not opposed to my joining the army, but they told me that if I really wanted to do something of value for the revolution, then I should go back to Beijing and work underground behind enemy lines. I decided without hesitation to take this course.

My trip to Guangzhou was by no means a wasted journey, despite what some of my friends said. I had seen the revolution with my own eyes, I had broadened my vision, I had increased my awareness, and I had dispelled some illusions: for all these reasons I was more confident than ever. Before I had gone south, the revolution was not exactly an abstract concept in my mind, but I was very hazy about its concrete form and its internal structure. I was completely ignorant about the internal contradictions that existed between the various wings of the revolutionary movement, and I was even so naive as to think that no such contradictions existed. At this time the most important task of the Northern Bureau of the CCP, as I and my comrades in Beijing had discovered from reports sent down from higher levels, had been to win over General Feng Yuxiang and oppose the Western Hills Faction. We had therefore been under the impression that, apart from a handful of old men around Zou Lu and Zhang Ji, the whole of the Guomindang was on the side of the revolution. Before I went south, I never heard a single word of criticism voiced against Chiang Kai-shek at branch meetings, but as soon as I arrived in Guangzhou I discovered that reality was very different from what we had imagined. The forces of the Right were very strong, and real military power lay in their hands. Chiang Kai-shek's positions, far from being revolutionary, were similar to those of the Western Hills Faction. Chiang Kai-shek's combat organisation in the Guomindang at Guangzhou was the influential Society for the Study of Sun Yat-sen's Thought, with the right-wing ideologue Dai Jitao as its moving spirit. The so-called left wing of the Guomindang was made up of Communists working 'externally', who were on bad terms with Chiang Kai-shek: in fact there was no independent left wing. Those individuals who did hold left-wing positions were a tiny minority, and would never constitute a force to be reckoned with. When I first arrived in Guangzhou, I often heard my friends expressing fears and anxieties about Chiang Kai-shek's increasingly obvious disloyalty, but I never came across anyone who had the slightest idea of how to forestall him or strike a blow against him. In party speeches and publications, even these fears and anxieties were not expressed. It was as if everyone was counting on the setting up and consolidation of a revolutionary government in Wuhan, and when Chiang was 'forced to agree' to the removal of the National Government to that city everyone heaved a sigh of relief, thinking that the right wing had been brought to heel.

The strike committee of the Guangzhou-Hong Kong general strike, whose headquarters were in Guangzhou, and its constituent bodies (the workers' tribunals and militia, the huge strikers' canteens, and so on), particularly impressed me. I had never seen anything of the sort before. By then, the resources at the disposal of the strike committee had been depleted by the recruitment of workers to the Northern Expeditionary forces, but even so it was still a very impressive organisation. On my second day in Guangzhou I looked across the creek to the British concession on the island of Shamian, where I saw all the doors and windows of the Western-style houses sealed and shuttered. There was not a sign of life, and in the open spaces between the houses the grass was growing knee-high. The effects of the strike were to be seen everywhere. I had no opportunity to take an active part in that movement. All I saw were some of its external manifestations: I paid a visit to the communal canteen, which was capable of seating several hundred workers at a time, and I took part in lively mass meetings of the strikers. I remember vividly to this day the activities of the local strike committee branches in Guangzhou. In each branch there was a long table covered with red cloth, and on the walls were the pictures of revolutionary leaders framed in red. Sometimes there were groups of workers sitting around these tables discussing political issues of the day; at other times they would arbitrate on the disputes that arose between local workers and employers, and even put troublemakers (mainly hooligans) on trial. I was amazed to see how knowledgeable and capable the Guangzhou workers were, but it was only after I got hold of some of the internal discussion documents on that period, published in Moscow in 1928, that I realised the true significance of what had happened: the strike committee was in fact rivalling the authority of the National Government in a situation of dual power, and had even taken the law into its own hands. This was the first time I understood what the theory of the hegemony of the working class meant in practice.

My stay in Guangzhou also taught me that the Chinese and the Russian revolutions were intimately linked. This gave me much to think about. Questions such as that of Soviet aid to the revolution – a longstanding source of contention between the reactionary and the revolutionary parties – had played on my mind for a long time. Even before I joined the Party, I had strongly resented the uproar that the papers of the Study Clique and the Young China Party[8] raised when they called the Communists and even the Guomindang 'rouble-traitors'. I was angered not only because of my vague admiration for the October Revolution, but also because those people I knew who openly professed to being Communists, friends from my home-town, were in my opinion entirely incorruptible. They would never have sold their souls for a few roubles. For that reason, I fervently hoped that all the talk about roubles would be proved untrue, so that there would no longer be any grounds for criticism on that score. By the time I arrived in Guangzhou, my ideas had obviously matured a little, but I still could not help feeling uneasy at some of the things I saw: as my ship sailed into the Pearl River, a Soviet freighter passed the other way; when we anchored, I saw more freighters flying red flags anchored in mid-stream; after disembarking I frequently came across Westerners wearing Guomindang military uniforms; and later, when I walked over to the Dongshan area where all the foreigners and high officials used to live, I saw Russian advisers speeding by in motorcars, with pistol-toting Chinese bodyguards on the running boards. It seemed to me that this was harmful to national honour and to the long-established Chinese concepts of frugality and integrity.

Fortunately, it did not take long for me to shake off these remnants of nationalist thinking. After a few weeks, I realised, through study and discussion, that the Chinese Revolution was part of the world revolution, and that it could only triumph in the context of the world revolution. From that moment on, I no longer had any doubts about Soviet aid. Whether or not this aid was used in the right way is, of course, another question, and one which at the time never occurred to me. It was only in 1928, after I had arrived in the Soviet Union, that I read about this question in internal CPSU (Communist Party of the Soviet Union) documents.

While I was in Guangzhou I naturally learned more about the Russian Revolution and the Soviet Union, but, because of the brevity of my stay and the lack of literature on the subject and of people qualified to talk about it with authority, what I learned was extremely limited and mostly inaccurate anyway. We got the impression that Borodin, the Russian political adviser in Guangzhou, was more important than Lenin, and that General Galen (as Blücher was known when in China as chief Russian military adviser) eclipsed

---

8 Young China Party. Also known as the 'Nationalist of the Awakening Lions'. Organised in Paris in 1923 by Zeng Ji (1892–1951) and others. Advocating nationalism, it fought not only against the CCP but also against the Guomindang by aligning itself with various groups of Beiyang warlords.

Trotsky as a military strategist. No one as much as mentioned the internal disputes that were going on within the Soviet Party.

In the winter of 1926, after my pilgrimage to the Mecca of the revolution, I returned to Beijing University a more hardened and convinced revolutionary. I wrapped myself up in my lined gown against the bitter winter cold. The political climate in the ancient capital of China was equally bleak. The Fengtian warlords who controlled Beijing were living on fear, caught unawares by the speed with which the revolutionary forces were advancing in the south. At first they panicked completely, but their confidence gradually returned when they realised that the revolutionary forces were not a unified bloc, and that the faction which controlled the army was in reality anti-Communist. After the conclusion of the Jiangxi campaign in November 1926, Chiang Kai-shek prepared to march on Nanjing and Shanghai, while at the same time establishing secret links with Beijing; as a result, the Fengtian clique launched a wave of frantic anti-Communist activity, with the covert support of the Japanese imperialists.

Japanese imperialism had become the main enemy of the Chinese Revolution after the advance guard of the Northern Expeditionary armies crossed the Yangtze from the British sphere of influence to the Japanese sphere of influence. In Beijing, Japanese special agents actively co-operated with the local warlord Zhang Zuolin's police spies, and devoted all their efforts to dealing with the 'red menace'. Since Beijing University was well known as a Communist Party base, these agents made it their main target. Plain-clothes men lurked in every corner, especially in the restaurants and hostels of the Han Garden area, and it became more and more difficult for us to engage in any political activity. After my two months away I noticed that many changes had taken place in methods of party work in the capital. In the past, we had usually held our meetings in rooms in the university, but this was no longer possible. Some of the leading comrades of the university branch, who had previously lived like other students, now no longer dared to attend classes or to sleep in the student dormitories. Formerly we had been able to leave our mimeograph printing machine in the workers' night-school which we had set up, and our work was semi-legal. Now we were forced to move it to a special place. Comrades were kidnapped while they were walking along the street by men who followed them in cars. We became more and more tense, and our communications more and more secretive. This was my first taste of both the fear and the excitement of real underground work.

After I had worked for a period in the leadership of the university branch the Party transferred me to the district committee, probably because of my experience in Guangzhou. The work was nerve-racking and exhausting, with meetings and contact work from early in the morning until late at night. As a result, my studies came to a halt and I began my new life as a professional but unpaid revolutionary. We had to find our own means of livelihood. As far as I knew, only the members of the Beijing city committee received payment from the Party. It was no longer possible for me to earn my living by writing articles, not only because I was too busy, but also because the publishing world was subject to more and more repression. One-time booming literary activities were now in sharp decline. For the first few months of 1927, my food was paid for by an old fellow-student of mine from Hangzhou, who was studying on an unofficial basis at the university.

Despite the fact that life was hard and I was overburdened with work, I still felt very happy. Finally purged of the decadent and romantic ideas of the Creation Society, I was seized by a new sort of optimism and filled with confidence. The history of China was leaping forward, and the old was being replaced by the new at a dramatic pace. It seemed to us that we could already look to the day when a rejuvenated China would become free and liberated from imperialist oppression, and even to the day when China would become communist. Though we were still living under the muddle-headed and barbaric rule of the warlords and suffering daily persecution at the hands of spies and gendarmes, we knew quite clearly that the days of the régime were numbered, so we did not allow ourselves to be intimidated by such repressive measures, even learning to laugh at them. We joyfully got on with our underground work, and good-humouredly put up with the hardships of life. The revolution was in its ascendancy, and the honeymoon was not yet over. We revolutionaries who were working behind enemy lines were full of illusions: in our view the prospects were excellent.

Despite increasing repression, many young people were eagerly joining the Party. When I had joined it in the winter of 1925, the university branch only had twenty or thirty members, but by the early spring of 1926 membership had shot up to more than two hundred. Most of the 'aspiring scholars' of the university quarter left their ivory towers to engage in the real struggle, and even after the arrest and assassination of our leader Li Dazhao this influx of new blood into the Party continued.

But there were two things which worried me: the relations between the Communist Party and the Guomindang, and the general contempt for theory in the Party. Among the revolutionaries actively working underground in Beijing at that time there was not a single real member of the Guomindang, which apart from a handful of rightwing officials did not exist there as a separate organisation. None of the young students had any confidence in the Guomindang or even respected Sun Yat-sen, even though there was a flood of propaganda after he died and he was described in the most reverent terms. We found much of what we read in his lectures on the 'Three People's Principles' – nationalism, democracy, and people's livelihood – too laughable for words. Nevertheless we were forced to join the Guomindang. When we were engaged in certain types of activity, we had to say that we were Guomindang members and we were even forced to set up phoney Guomindang meetings. I remember that shortly after I joined the Communist Party I was ordered to attend a meeting of this sort. The first item on the agenda was to bow down in front of a portrait of Sun Yat-sen and listen in respectful silence while his political testament was read out. After that, we listened to a number of reports on the situation in the south. I later learned that of the fifteen or twenty people at that meeting, only one was a real Guomindang member, and all the rest were Communists. I could not for the life of me understand the necessity for such a charade, and I found it even more ridiculous when the real Guomindang members we had invited failed to turn up, so that everyone at such a meeting was really a member of the Party. The fact that we still bowed down in front of Sun's portrait and read out his will made some of us burst out laughing. When I mentioned my reservations to leading comrades, they explained that this was necessary on account of the united front. 'But there is no Guomindang to unite with', I protested. 'The whole thing is a farce'. 'The situation is different in the south, where the Guomindang is a real force', they would reply. 'We have to carry out the national line'.

In Beijing, or at least in the branches under the district committee for eastern Beijing, there were only two books of a theoretical character in circulation at that time. One was the first part of Bukharin's *ABC of Communism*, and the other was Burkhardt's *The Student's 'Capital'*. The first of these was very popular with party members because it was written in a style that was easy to understand, and we mimeographed several copies of it. But Burkhardt's book was heavy going, and, since we had no time to make a proper study of it, we read it without understanding it. So from an ideological point of view we were not qualified to be called Communists. We were fighting for communism, but none of us really understood what communism was. We were all very aware of this deficiency, and hoped for more books to read and people to teach us; above all we wanted the Party to set up a short training course. But, because of the increasingly difficult situation and the negligence of higher-level party members, none of this was done.

There we were, working away in an almost light-heartedly optimistic frame of mind, under a régime of intensifying terror, inspired by an ideology we barely understood. Our goal was clear and simple: opposition to imperialism and warlordism. Our task was simply to expand the organisation. It was only in April 1927, when Li Dazhao was arrested and killed, that our style of work, and more particularly our state of mind, changed. Our easy-going mood gave way to a profound sense of tragedy and anger.

As a middle-level cadre, I did not know whether the Party had taken any precautionary measures in advance of this incident, but it seemed to me that the organisation was aware that the authorities had something planned. Several weeks before it happened, we were all told to be especially careful in our movements. Two days before the arrest, Tan Zuyao, who, a few days later, was to be hanged together with Li Dazhao, told me he was going to hide in a safe place, the Legation Quarter, and urged me not to sleep in my lodgings. But we had no way of knowing the enemy was to strike precisely in that place we usually considered safest. According to the 1901 treaty forced on China after the Boxer Rebellion, the Legation Quarter was not subject to Chinese sovereignty, but, with Japanese help, the warlord Zhang Zuolin got permission from all the signatories to the Treaty to send troops and police into the area on 6 April 1927. They openly violated the diplomatic immunity of the Soviet Embassy and arrested the Communists who were in the Chinese Eastern Bank adjacent to the embassy building.

Many accounts have already been written of this incident. Future historians, basing their conclusions on archive materials and eyewitness reports, will undoubtedly write more detailed accounts of the martyrdom of Li Dazhao and his nineteen comrades. This is not the place for me to write down my fragmentary recollections. But there is one point, widely talked about in Beijing party organisations at the time, which I think should be raised. After the arrests, there was a storm of protest, both at home and abroad, and considerable pressure from public opinion. Zhang Zuolin was therefore in a quandary: what was he to do with the Communists he had arrested? It was said that elements within his clique, in particular his leading adviser Zhao Xinbo, were speaking up for Li Dazhao and the others, and urging that they should not be executed. Zhang Shizhao, one of Duan Qirui's ex-ministers, also recommended strongly that the prisoners' lives be spared. As a result, Zhang Zuolin was said to be in favour of sending them to Shenyang to sit out long prison sentences. But the 'Supreme Commander of the Revolutionary Armies', Chiang Kai-shek, urged Zhang Zuolin through secret channels to have them killed, thus helping Zhang Zuolin to reach his final decision. This information came from very reliable sources close to the Fengtian clique. The execution of Li Dazhao and the others in Beijing on 28 April came within days of Chiang Kai-shek's massacre of the Shanghai workers on 12 April, and the two incidents were clearly linked.

It was the start of a bloodbath. It had an enormous effect on the revolutionary camp, in particular on young revolutionaries like me, proving that revolution was not a game in which youthful romantics could indulge their imagination or get rid of surplus energy. Those of us with a more utilitarian outlook began to weigh up the advantages and disadvantages of continuing the fight. The merciless face of the class struggle revealed itself to everyone, acutely posing the question of whether or not to follow the revolution. We were all forced to make a decision, influenced by factors such as the background we came from, the depth of our understanding, and our strength of character. In other words, with the deepening and differentiation of the revolution, a differentiation also began to take place in the revolutionary ranks.

But, in Beijing, the arrest of Li Dazhao and the others did not immediately result in the collapse of the local party organisation. Our work carried on as usual, and, in the short term at least, the bloody repression did not cause any wavering in our ranks. On the contrary, we became much more serious, and not a single comrade was driven out of the organisation by fear. The warlord system was in its death agony, and was totally incapable of evoking panic. What shook Communists in the north more, and created uneasiness and confusion in our ranks, was the news of the savage purges that were taking place in the south as the leaders of the Guomindang turned on all popular organisations. We were not prepared for this either ideologically or emotionally, and found it hard to believe that the leader of the revolutionary army could massacre the workers. The younger comrades were particularly embittered by the anti-Communist articles of the former radical Wu Zhihui which were published in the Beijing press, since we had always looked up to him as a progressive and admired his personality and lively literary style. We ran around commiserating with each other about the shocking news, and found it impossible to explain the sudden transformation in our former idol. Naturally enough, none of the people I was in contact with was in sympathy with Chiang Kai-shek or Wu Zhihui: there was a widespread sense of regret and even betrayal, and a feeling that their actions could only benefit the enemy. We wanted an explanation for what had happened and instructions on what our attitude towards Chiang should be in the future. But the only explanation I could get from the Beijing committee was that Chiang had capitulated to imperialism and the rightists and betrayed the revolution. I conveyed these remarks to the comrades in the branches. Shortly, however, we received the following consolation from the same source: 'Chiang's defection is not important; the Guomindang still has a left wing, there is still Wang Jingwei. They are our trusted allies. The centre of the revolution is now Wuhan'. This seemed to clear up our confusion. We resumed our work, and turned our eyes towards Wuhan. There was an immense amount of work to be done there, and not enough people to do it, so the Party asked the

Beijing committee to send some comrades south. It was decided to send those, myself included, most likely to be marked out for surveillance by the Beijing police. There were ten of us in all, including Peng Lianqing, the famous student leader of the Beijing Women's Normal University, and Zhang Jingchen, chairman of the Beijing University Students' Union. Early one morning in July 1927, we quietly slipped out of Beijing. Thus ended my life as a university student.

PART 4
Chinese Trotskyists in Moscow

Twelve People

Zheng Chaolin

Source: An Oppositionist for Life: Memoirs of the Chinese Revolutionary Zheng Chaolin (1945).

On 18 March 1923, we set out from Gare du Nord in Paris, armed with passports issued by the Chinese Consulate. We had said that we were going back to China via Siberia. Actually, we were going to Moscow to enrol in the University of the East. Zhou Enlai travelled with us, bound for Germany. We were to be a group of twelve: Xiong Xiong and Wang Gui were already in Berlin, and Yuan Qingyun had gone ahead to Berlin to get our Russian visas. So only nine of us set out from Paris, but Zhou Enlai made ten.

Zhao Shiyan was our leader. He had just stopped being secretary of the 'Communist Youth Party' and was in charge of our small group. He did most of the negotiating for us, especially when English was required, for only he spoke it. Zhao was a Sichuanese, the son of a big family. His family home was in Tianjin or Qingdao. He had learned to speak northern Chinese, but he still had a Sichuan accent. I got to know many 'Sichuan rats' in France. You could tell a Sichuan rat not only by his accent and vocabulary but by his character. What do I mean by that? I think anyone who has made friends with a Sichuanese will know what I mean, but it is very hard to put into words. I knew Zhao Shiyan was from Sichuan as soon as he opened his mouth, but, after a while, I discovered that his character was quite unlike that of other Sichuanese I had known. He was a born leader: he could reconcile differences of opinion without violating big principles, he could place a person in the right job, he was vigilant, he knew how to deal with every contingency, he was a good speaker, and he was the most obvious choice to preside over meetings and deal with the outside world. I once mentioned to him that in character he was different from other Sichuanese. He replied that he was from such-and-such a county in Sichuan, that it was on the Sichuan border, and that this county was closer in the attitudes and behaviour of its people to other provinces; in addition, he had grown up outside Sichuan.

At that time, he was 23 or 24 years old. On the train, he tapped the homburg he was wearing and said he had searched nearly every hat shop in Paris before finding it. He could not wear a normal-sized hat. But though his head was big, his face and body were not. His face was positively small, tapering to a pointed chin. He looked a bit like the cartoonist Ye Qianyu's Mr Wang. I never saw him wearing glasses; his eyes, his nose, and his cheeks were plain. You could not call him handsome, but when he gave speeches he was not unattractive. He was not in bad health, but nor was he strong. I know nothing about his life before he went to France; I have an idea he studied at a middle school in Beijing and played a prominent role in the May Fourth Movement. He was friends with Deng Zhongxia and Xu Deheng, student leaders at Beijing University.

Chen Yannian and Chen Qiaonian did not look like brothers. In 1927, Wu Zhihui, ranting against Chen Duxiu and his two sons, said: 'In my view, his son Chen Yannian, another called Chen Something-or-another Nian, and the father had the ugliest faces on earth. Even if they wore long silk gowns, people would still call them thieves'.[1] Wu Zhihui was talking nonsense. Chen Duxiu was not ugly. Anyone who never saw him can consult the photo on the cover of *Shi An zizhuan* ('Autobiography of Chen Duxiu'), published by the Oriental Book Company. A woman comrade once said that his eyes were especially likeable. Chen Qiaonian was a handsome young man, not only the best-looking of the twelve of us, but, in my view, the best-looking Chinese student in the whole of Moscow. Even Li Heling (who was constantly admiring himself in the mirror) could not compare with Chen Qiaonian. Chen was strong-looking and his skin was white. His cheeks were as rosy as a pair of apples. His elder brother Chen Yannian was the complete opposite. He was in poor health; he had a fat belly, spindly legs, and a swarthy complexion, with thick eyebrows and slanting eyes; and he was short-sighted. Sometimes, when you thought that he was looking at you, it turned out he was looking at the person next to you. He was lethargic in his movements, as if unable to brace himself. After he reached Moscow, Yuan Qingyun nicknamed him 'Corruption'. But he certainly was not as ugly as Wu Zhihui made out. He was by no means the ugliest of the twelve of us. Apart from looks, these two brothers also differed in other regards. Yannian loved to talk and to tell stories about the 1911 Revolution or his family. Whenever a group of people got together, you could always hear him talking away in his low voice. Qiaonian, in contrast, was forever tongue-tied. He did not speak at meetings or even at private gatherings. Only when Wang Ruofei started his horseplay did Qiaonian speak or smile. Later, he gradually overcame his shyness and started speaking in public. He spoke rather well, though less so than his older brother. The two brothers got on extremely well. They had left home together, and distanced themselves not only from the bureaucratic tradition of their family but from their father. Chen Duxiu had already become famous as a rebel against the family. For several years people everywhere had been saying that he denounced 'filial piety' as 'the worst

---

[1] See *Wu Zhihui baihua wenchao* ('An Anthology of Writings by Wu Zhihui in the Vernacular').

of ten thousand vices'[2] and that he had organised an 'anti-fathers league'. In 1921, Chen Jiongming asked Chen Duxiu about this. Chen replied: 'My sons are qualified to set up such a league, but I'm not even qualified to be a member'.[3] (See Chen Duxiu's *Autobiography*.) Though, in fact, his sons had never organised such a league, their attitude to Chen Duxiu before they left for France was no less antagonistic than their father's attitude to his grandfather. The clash between them was about politics. The father was a democrat, the sons were anarchists. Later, Chen Duxiu was among the first to become a Communist; the sons, too, in France, retreated from anarchism to Communism, and as a result both sides completely overcame their mutual alienation. Qiaonian went along in everything with Yannian. Yannian's conversion had a big impact on the Chinese anarchists, even in Southeast Asia and the Americas.

The two brothers were Puritans. They ate poorly, dressed poorly, and never showed the slightest interest in women. Yannian died a virgin. The first time I ever heard Yannian express dissatisfaction with his younger brother was when Qiaonian started living with Shi Jingyi in Beijing. Qiaonian was everyone's 'younger brother'. Yannian called him *frère*, as we did, too. After we got to Moscow, we called him *Yabloko* ('apple' in Russian), on account of his rosy cheeks. (There may have been another reason, but I forget.) That year, Yannian was 25 and Qiaonian was 22.

Wang Ruofei's age was hardest to estimate. At first glance he seemed to be the same age as the rest of us, that is, in his mid-twenties, but if you looked carefully at his wrinkles and his stained teeth and if you took into account his experience and behaviour, he was clearly much older. He was around 30, certainly no younger than 28. He had learned a lot about political dirty tricks from his uncle Huang Qisheng and the other Guizhou politicians, but he was an able person, and no less loyal to Communism than youngsters fresh from school. He was short, with a squat neck, plump fingers, a slightly twisted nose, and white skin. He spoke Guizhou-style Mandarin. He was fond of drinking, like me, and liked to joke. He was boisterous and fun-loving, and the most interesting of the twelve.

The second most interesting was Yuan Qingyun. He, too, was boisterous and playful, but unfortunately, he was afflicted like me with a stammer. He was a typical 'Sichuan rat', with all the strengths and weaknesses that epithet implies. He was Zhao Shiyan's friend, and had become a Communist together with Zhao Shiyan. As far as I know, this conversion was not due just to the fact that they came from the same province, but resulted from genuine political

---

2 This is a parody on the old adage 'Adultery is the worst of ten thousand vices'.
3 Chen Duxiu's father died when Chen was only a few months old.

and intellectual conviction. Yuan was a tall man, lively and extremely popular. He especially liked to make friends with foreigners. Despite his stammer, he was not afraid of speaking. In Moscow, he learned Russian sooner than I. It was he who found the meeting place for the second conference of the Communist Youth Party, alongside the police-station. He was the most often criticised in the Party's Moscow branch.

Yuan Qingyun's fellow-provincial Wang Linghan was an even more typical Sichuan rat. He was a cripple. He joined every organisation that Zhao Shiyan joined, so he ended up in the Communist Youth Party. He loved to hold the floor at meetings, but he tended to ramble. At a meeting of the Montargis branch, Yin Kuan said that at the founding conference some people had not yet grasped in what ways this new organisation was different from the old ones. The example he gave was Wang Linghan.

Zhao Shiyan, Yuan Qingyun, Wang Ruofei, and the Chen brothers lived in Paris, so they were already waiting there at the time of our departure. I had met them several times during my visits to the capital and knew them well. Wang Linghan did not live in Paris, but I had met him once at the founding conference.

The three people I am about to describe were new to me, for they had lived in the provinces. However, I had met them at the second conference before setting out for Moscow.

She Liya was a Hunanese, tall, broad-framed, enthusiastic, and strong. In that regard he was a typical Hunanese, but there was no trace about him of the Hunanese character as represented by Cai Hesen, Li Weihan, and Wang Zekai. He rarely spoke at meetings, for he lacked systematic views of his own; he bowed to the leadership of others, and loyally carried out the missions entrusted to him.

Gao Feng was also from Hunan and was also enthusiastic and strong, but unlike She Liya, he loved to discuss theoretical questions, from the origins of the universe to philosophies of life. None of the rest of us was interested in such questions, which rather disappointed him. I knew his name even before I knew him, for he had published an article or a letter in the internal bulletin proposing that we set a date for declaring war on the ruling classes, and when that day came we should start the insurrection.

Inseparable from Gao Feng was Chen Jiuding from Henan, the only northerner among us twelve. Gao and Chen had worked in the same factory, and because they both liked discussing world views and outlooks on life, they gradually became firm friends. Even their names were inseparable. We often said Gao Feng and Chen Jiuding in one breath, as if they were one name, not two. Gao Feng was a sturdy peasant type, whereas Chen Jiuding was thin, short, and pigeon-chested.

These eight (including Yuan Qingyun, who was in Berlin waiting for us), together with me and Zhou Enlai, left Paris by train for Germany. Our tickets were valid for three days, which meant that we could leave the train en route as long as we got to Berlin in time. We had a branch at the University of Labour in Charleroi in Belgium. The comrades there had written to us asking us to visit them, so we went. Liu Bojian, Xiong Weigeng, and others organised a meeting to welcome us. They showed us the university and the town and we went out into the countryside for a photo. I forget whether we stayed in Charleroi overnight, but early the next morning we arrived in Cologne and changed the same afternoon into another train, so I know for certain that we did not stay the night in Cologne. Cologne is not far from the Belgian border, but when we got off the train, it was as if we were in another world. First, the language was different. In France and in Belgium everyone spoke French, so there was no problem, but once we reached Germany, we were at a loss, for none of us spoke German. Though Zhou Enlai was resident in Berlin, he spoke German worse than we spoke French and could only handle the simplest things, like ordering food and paying bills. One restaurant bill in Cologne came to fifty or sixty thousand Marks. We were astonished. This was only the first stage of inflation in Germany – in October it got much, much worse. But when we reached Moscow, one small loaf cost seven million roubles! We also visited the famous Cologne Cathedral.

In Berlin, we stayed separately in several small groups. I stayed in Xiong Xiong's place, at Kantstrasse in Charlottenburg. Charlottenburg was also known as New Berlin. From there to old Berlin you had to pass through a forest, but there was an underground and also an overhead railway. In France, I had never lived in such a splendid house. None of the work-study students, semi-official students, and self-financing students had ever, as far as I know, lived in such beautiful accommodation. The landlady was an army officer's widow. Her daughter, who was engaged to be married, used to play the piano every day in the drawing room. To supplement their income, they rented out their best rooms to foreigners. I forget what they charged, but converted into francs it would have rented only a room fit for a work-study student. Xiong Xiong cooked for himself. He lived very modestly, quite out of keeping with his grand surroundings. He had originally lived in France, and had supplied Li Heling with the pistol Li used when he tried to assassinate Chen Lu. After the attempt, he fled to Germany, but in his depositions to the police Li Heling avoided implicating him. The incident had a romantic, anarchistic flavour. By the time I arrived in Berlin, Xiong Xiong had already joined the Communist Party. He recounted the events to me with an air of self-satisfaction. He had no idea that Marxism opposed individual terror. To tell the truth, he never learned what Marxism was about until the day he died. He was childishly naïve: sincere, innocent, pure, ardent, and immature. He pursued everything that was new and revolutionary and made friends with everyone who was fervent, brave, and rebellious, but he lacked judgement and was unable to distinguish between Marx and Kropotkin. He always wore hunter's clothes and long boots. A whip hung in his room. Every day, he would copy stone-rubbings of the works of famous calligraphers, in big and small characters, for example, Yue Fei's *Manjianghong ci*.[4] He rose early, and if it was snowing, he would go far out into the countryside before dawn to walk across the snow. He was terrible at languages, and even spoke Chinese with a strong Jiangxi accent. Later, in Moscow, if you ever asked him a question during classes or discussions, he would stand up wide-eyed and wide-mouthed and finally say: 'I've forgotten'.

Yuan Qingyun and Wang Ruofei stayed in Wang Gui's lodgings. Wang Gui, a Hunanese, spoke fluent German and was our sole interpreter. Without him, we would have been as mute. Zhao Shiyan said he understood some German because it often sounded like English. He wanted to study German, but no one else was interested. We were simply passing through Germany. Our only reason for stopping in Berlin was to get a Russian visa. There was no Soviet representative in Paris, for at that time, France had not yet recognised the USSR. Berlin was the obvious alternative. Wang Gui knew some Comintern officials through connections bequeathed by Zhang Bojian and Xiao Zizhang, who had already left Germany. The visa took many days to get, so we had plenty of time on our hands. Wang Gui and Zhou Enlai took us to the museums, the zoo, and various famous and historic sites. One day, we went to Potsdam where there is a palace built in the manner of Versailles, but far less impressive.

Zhou Enlai also took us to a Chinese restaurant. The restaurant was not a shop on a street like most restaurants but in a private house. The waitresses were all Germans. The menu was in Chinese and German and each dish had a number by which you ordered it. We met several Chinese students there, and got the chance to read some newspapers posted out from China. Indignantly, we read the reports of Wu Peifu's massacre of striking railway workers on the Beijing-Hankou line.

Zhou Enlai took us to the Chinese restaurant for a meeting. Since Zhou's arrival back in Berlin, Zhang Songnian and his wife had snubbed him, and they would not meet us, either. Zhou Enlai called a meeting of the German branch

---

4 Yue Fei (1103–41), one of China's most famous generals, was distinguished not only for his brilliant victories over the Jin invaders but also for his poems and calligraphy. *Manjianghong* is a beautifully composed *ci*, bursting with heroism and patriotism, that was said to have been written in Yue Fei's own hand and later engraved on a stone tablet.

of the Youth League to explain his attitude to the decision at the second conference to expel Zhang Songnian. The German branch was quite small. Perhaps it had some members outside Berlin, but in Berlin there was only one other person (whose name I forget) besides Zhang and his wife, Zhou Enlai, Wang Gui, and Xiong Xiong. This person arrived late at the meeting and said nothing. Zhou Enlai defended himself vigorously. Xiong Xiong and Wang Gui naturally agreed with him. The other comrade raised some simple questions and then fell silent again. Clearly, he did not agree with Zhou. After we had left Berlin, this comrade withdrew from the Communist Youth Party.

There are two ways to Moscow from Berlin: the land-route, via the Polish corridor, Lithuania, and Latvia; and the sea-route, from Stettin to Petrograd, whence by train on to Moscow. We chose the land-route. After ten days in Berlin, we resumed our journey east. We stopped in neither Poland nor Lithuania, and did not get off the train until we reached Riga in Latvia. We arrived in the morning, and had to wait until the afternoon or evening for the train to Russia. It was already spring in Paris and Berlin and the trees were green, but in Riga it was still winter. We stood on an iron-bridge over a river and watched large lumps of ice drift slowly by. French and German were useless here, and we spoke no Russian, but we got by on Zhao Shiyan's English. When Zhao spoke to the waiters in English while we were eating in a coffee-bar, two dancing girls who understood some English came over and asked him to dance. He blushed, and after that, we often teased him about the incident. If it had been Wang Ruofei, he would not have blushed, but he could not dance, either.

When we reached the Russian border, we climbed down from the train and our luggage was inspected, for the first time ever. We had crossed many frontiers in the past, but only our passports had been inspected. As soon as the inspectors learned that we were bound for the University of the East, they stopped checking. This was the first time we had seen Red Army men. They were dressed in coarse-cloth overcoats and peaked caps adorned with a red star. The other passengers got back on the train, but we could not do so, for we lacked sufficient money for the ticket. At the station we were attentively received and promised free or concessionary tickets for the further journey, but told that we would have to wait for authority to be given, which would take at least a day. We sent a telegram to the Chinese students at the University of the East and spent the night in an empty railway carriage.

The Chinese students met us at the station in Moscow. Among them was Xiao Zizhang who had gone there from France and whom we knew. All the others had come to Russia straight from China. There were many of them. I remember only Ren Bishi, who had a high-pitched voice, and Wang Yifei, who had a low-pitched voice. When we left the station Wang Yifei walked with me arms linked and with his hand twined round my waist. We had never seen anyone walk like that in France and Germany or in China, but in Russia it was common to do so.

Our life of travel was at an end, and a new life was beginning. We had not only gone for the first time from a capitalist country to a proletarian country but we had passed from factory life to a life of study, from a life of unsystematic self-study to one of set classes and curricula. We knew that we were not about to get an MA or a PhD, for we were to live the life of revolutionaries. Ahead lay struggle, insurrection, revolution, jail, bloodshed, sacrifice.

Twelve people! But where have they ended up, those twelve?

Yuan Qingyun joined the Northern Expedition in 1926,[5] and died of cholera in Chenzhou in Hunan.

Gao Feng was arrested at Baoding in the same year and shot by the Beiyang warlords.

Xiong Xiong escaped from the Huangpu Military Academy[6] after 15 April 1927, but was seized and shot by Li Jishen.

Chen Yannian was arrested and shot by Yang Hu in Shanghai, in late April or early May of the same year.

Zhao Shiyan was seized and shot by Yang Hu not long after the death of Chen Yannian.

She Liya also died at the hands of Yang Hu at around the same time.

Chen Qiaonian was arrested in Shanghai in 1928 and shot by Xiong Shihui.

Wang Linghan disappeared while working in Wuxi in 1928. He was said to have been assassinated by local strongmen, but later, it turned out that he had given up and fled to Sichuan.

I know nothing of Chen Jiuding.

I met Wang Gui once during the Wuhan period, when he was some sort of army officer, but I have heard nothing of him since.

Wang Ruofei was still in Yan'an in 1937, but today I do not know whether he is alive or dead.[7]

---

5 The Northern Expedition was launched by Chiang Kai-shek in 1926 from Guangzhou, to overthrow the warlords and unify China.
6 The Huangpu (also transcribed as Whampoa) Military Academy was organised for the Guomindang in 1924 by the Russians, who also subsidised its subsequent running. Its mission was 'the training for the army of junior officers, well educated in the political sense'. The Huangpu clique, denoting former faculty and students of the Academy, later became a main political support of Chiang Kai-shek, who was the Academy's founding principal.
7 He died in an air crash in 1946.

Finally, there is me, writing about the twelve.

In the Central Military Prison, I was under the impression that Wang Linghan, Chen Jiuding, and Wang Gui were all dead, and there were rumours that Stalin had exiled Wang Ruofei to Siberia on suspicion of being a member of the Left Opposition. Needless to say, I felt even more emotional then than I do today. I thought of us as a small company of privates with Zhao Shiyan as our captain; we had marched shoulder to shoulder into the line of fire and all had fallen save one or two who had been captured. But now, one prisoner has regained his freedom, and though some others are without trace, there is as yet no record of their death. Only seven definitely died, but even that represents more than one in two.

KUTV

KUTV, the Communist University for the Toilers of the East, also known as Stalin University, was founded in April 1921. Its main purpose was to educate toilers from backward nationalities in the Caucasian and Siberian regions of the old Russian Empire, just like the Communist University for the Toilers of the West, set up for toilers from Latvia and Lithuania in the western part of the Empire. Students from parts of the East outside the old Russian Empire, for example, Chinese, Japanese, Koreans, Mongols, Indians, Persians, and Turks, were a minority in it. Many of these foreign students had come to Russia in the first instance to take part in the Baku Conference of the Peoples of the East or the Petrograd Conference of the Peoples of the Far East; some had even been delegates to Congresses of the Third International.

The Chinese students, like us work-study students from France, had been swept to Shanghai or Beijing by the tide of May Fourth, but had arrived there a little later than we and had therefore missed the work-study wave. So they were better versed than we in the new socialist thought in China. After Chen Duxiu came out of jail, he gave up being Dean of Letters at Beijing University[8] and left for Shanghai; these students, or at least the most progressive among them, had no longer searched out people like Li Shizeng or Wu Zhihui but had looked to Chen Duxiu. Chen Duxiu was running a sort of work-study scheme in Shanghai. Many of its students had come to form the basic ranks of the

---

8 According to recently uncovered literature, Chen had already been removed as Dean of Letters by Cai Yuanpei, President of the University, nearly a month before the May 4 demonstrations. Cai was acting under pressure from the reactionaries. [Note added by Zheng Chaolin in 1989.]

Socialist Youth League. The Socialist Youth League was, of course, under the leadership of the newly formed Chinese Communist Party, but at first, it was not called the Communist Youth League, and for two reasons. One was that the aim was to be a public organisation; another was that some of its members were anarchists who were only prepared to cooperate under the socialist, not the Communist, banner. The students who went directly from China to Russia were members of this Socialist Youth League, and had come out in several batches. At that time, you still had to cross territory controlled by the White Army to get to Moscow; the road was sown with difficulties and dangers. One batch of students detained by armed units along the way could not speak Russian and had no way of knowing whether their interceptors were Reds or Whites. The troops searched them thoroughly and found in the heel of the shoe of one of them a pass issued by representatives of the Third International. It turned out that the troops were Reds, so the prisoners instantly became honoured guests. Many students were delayed for long periods along the way. One batch was kept in Chita or Irkutsk for several months before it was able to travel on to Moscow. Some students never reached Moscow at all, but were kept in the Far East of the Soviet Union to perform various tasks.

When we arrived in Moscow in the spring of 1923, there were thirty-odd Chinese students at KUTV. Some were from Hunan, mostly students of the School of the Common People run by Mao Zedong in Changsha, others were Zhejiangese from Hangzhou's First Normal School. There were people from other provinces, too, and four Chinese labourers from Siberia, including two Red Beards.[9]

These people were those who had been left over after much sifting. How many Chinese students were at KUTV when the University opened? I do not know, but there were certainly many, at least twice as many as when we arrived. They were probably engaged in unremitting internal struggles from the very moment that they left China. One obvious division was between Communists and anarchists, though there were other grounds, too, for division. Differences in outlook were inextricably intertwined with personal animosities; public differences were mixed with private plots and schemes. From chaos was born order, from equality were born leaders and led, the givers and the receivers of commands. When we arrived in Moscow, the struggle had already been resolved. The losers had been elbowed out and had left the

---

9   The Red Beards of Manchuria were said to be remnants of the White Lotus rebellion; they now lived by robbery. In Chinese opera, a red beard signifies that a character is fierce and lawless, whence the name.

movement after returning home. Some of the winners had also gone home, but most had stayed. We only heard the winners' version of events, but it was clear from their tone of voice that the struggle had been extremely intense. I never got to know the losers, but from what I saw of the winners, together with inferences from the logic of such struggles and my personal experience of them, I can permit myself a judgment on the contest among the Chinese students at KUTV before my arrival in Moscow. This contest, looked at from an overall point of view, was neither entirely worthless and purely personal nor an ideological struggle between Communism and anarchism. Instead, it was a struggle between two types of student. One type was sensitive, lively, intelligent, many-sided, and lofty-minded, and loved freedom and opposed authority. But such people lacked stability, they were excessively flexible and given to empty talk. The other type was stubborn, self-assured, and courageous but at the same time dull, narrow-minded, superficially informed, and a worshipper of authority who easily buckled under it. In Russia as it then was, the former group was destined to lose out. It would be an exaggeration to describe what happened as class struggle. Both groups were from broadly similar class backgrounds, though there was a herdsman and a menial among the victors. The losers were somewhat more cultured than the winners.

By the time that we arrived, the main struggle was already over, but it had left clear scars on the minds of those thirty-odd people. In the first place, they were divided into leaders and masses. The leaders gave the orders, the masses followed. The leaders behaved not like the masses' fellow-students but like their teachers. However much they feigned gentleness, there was always something unapproachable about them. In France, we had also had leaders and had all along looked up to Zhao Shiyan, but our leaders had gained their status naturally in the course of their political activity (among work-study students and Chinese labourers). We genuinely recognised them as our leaders, but we also saw them as our own sort: more capable, perhaps, but nevertheless, our own sort. We saw Zhao Shiyan as our squad commander, and moreover as our elected squad commander; we did not see him as our imposed squad-commander, and we saw him even less as our brigade commander, our divisional commander, our army commander, or our commander-in-chief. The Moscow students' view of leaders was completely alien to us. We had expelled Zhang Songnian precisely because he had wanted us to treat him as that sort of leader. But what really surprised us was not so much the Moscow leaders as the masses, with their attitude of absolute submission. They not only submitted publicly but did not even dare express their dissatisfaction in private. But deeds and words apart, I could tell from various subtle signs that they were not happy about subjecting themselves in this way. On the contrary, deep inside they were full of rancour and contempt. All this emotion was the aftermath of the great internal struggles of the previous months and years.

These struggles had thrown up three leaders: Bu Shiqi, Luo Jiao,[10] and Peng Shuzhi, all of them from Hunan. Bu Shiqi had left for China shortly before I arrived. I never met him. When he got back to Beijing, he became entangled in a love affair with He Mengxiong's wife Miao Boying, which created a scandal in the Party. Later, he went to Guangzhou and left the Party to work as some sort of official for the Guomindang government.

The big chief was Luo Jiao. He was from a poor peasant family in Xiangtan, but he invariably hid his background. I remember the first time I met him he was wearing a thick hat and had more clothes on than the rest of us. He was tall and thin, with a pale complexion and a large mouth. When he talked, you could see that the inside of his lips were red and he had large teeth. When he saw you, he would first give a loud laugh and then become serious and get down to what he had to say. He loved to tell people that he was in bad health, that he was always getting ill, that he often had to go to sanatoria for treatment. And it's a fact that we rarely saw him. He was Secretary of the 'Branch of the Chinese Communist Party in Moscow' and a member of the presidium of the KUTV branch of the Russian Communist Party. He represented the Chinese students to the outside world. Foreigners called him Bukharov, but we Chinese continued to call him Luo Jiao.

Second fiddle was Peng Shuzhi. Luo Jiao was tall and pale, Peng was short and dark. He wore leather clothes and a flat leather-cap. He was hard to understand, for he spoke with a heavy Baoqing accent. He insisted on speaking whenever we met, and at great length. He was a bookworm. As a child he had worshipped Wei Moshen,[11] an illustrious son of Baoqing, and his personal ambition had been to become (like Wei) a commentator on the Confucian classics. After May Fourth, he put aside his stitched volumes and began reading magazine translations and exegeses of the essays of Dewey and Russell; later, he became a Marxist (though I do not know under what circumstances).[12] He was the most cultured of the Moscow victors. During the great struggle, he had not immediately joined the victors. At first, he was pushed aside by them; it was some time before he stood shoulder to shoulder with them. Luo Jiao called him Confucius, a nickname that was supposed to represent both his 'culture'

---

10   Alias Luo Yinong.
11   A famous late nineteenth century scholar, among the first Chinese to awaken to the need to learn from the West.
12   See Cadart and Cheng 1983 for Peng's own account of his political conversion.

and the contempt with which the victors viewed people of learning. We did not dare call him Confucius to his face; instead, we addressed him as Comrade Shuzhi. Foreigners called him Petrov.

Luo Jiao inhabited the lofty heights, and saw little of us. Peng Shuzhi was the opposite. Although he lived in separate accommodation, he often called in for individual chats with those of us who had come to Russia from France. He used to visit each of us in turn, many times. He gave the impression of being an old-style middle school supervisor (today called an 'overseer of students' behaviour').

Apart from Luo and Peng, the rest of us were 'rank-and-file masses'. True, there were some special people, but the great majority were absolutely submissive. Wang Yifei and Ren Bishi were in charge of the Youth League, but in everything, no matter how big or small, they had to seek permission; they had no freedom of action whatsoever. Wang Yifei, from Zhejiang, had studied at Hangzhou's First Normal School. He was short in stature and mediocre in personality. He spoke and wrote Russian rather well. He had no Russian name, and was listed in the register as Wang Yifei. Ren Bishi, a Hunanese, was in everything like a small child. He was given the Russian name Belinsky (after the famous Russian critic), but people invariably got it wrong and called him Prinsky instead. Few of the other students from Hunan and Zhejiang were in any way remarkable.

Among the special people I mentioned earlier was Li Zhongwu. Li was the pampered son of an influential family, the nephew or some relative of Liang Qichao. He had studied together with Qu Qiubai at the Russian Language School in Beijing and come to Russia with Qu Qiubai as a journalist. Qu had gone back to China, but Li had stayed on to study at KUTV. He spoke excellent Russian, and adapted brilliantly to his surroundings. Later, back in China, he acted as interpreter for General Galen. Not long after that, he resigned and went to Haining to get married, and we saw nothing more of him. In 1926, we tried hard to track him down, but without success.

Another was Peng Zexiang, from Yuezhou. He had come to Russia from Beijing. He always wore a closed-neck jacket. His style was in every way that of an opportunist Chinese politician. We all found it odd to have such a person in our midst. I learned only later that when he first arrived in Russia, he was a member of the *Jinri* ('Today') faction, and wrote articles for it, though he had already 'renounced' *Today*'s politics. His nickname was 'Fascist'; we even used to call him it to his face. He was able and knowledgeable. On one occasion, he started talking with me about Hu Shi's *Outline History of Chinese Philosophy*. He said he wanted to write a history of Chinese philosophy based on an economic analysis. He could have become the leader of an opposition (that is, to Luo Jiao and Peng Shuzhi), but he lacked mass support. Apart from this, the leaders viewed him as exceptional. Soon, after the reorganisation of the Youth League, he was made 'training organiser'. After his appointment, he started summoning us for individual lectures. He acted more like a judge at a court martial than like a supervisor.

Of the four Chinese labourers, two adapted and two did not. Those who did not had been Red Beards. Eventually, they rose in open revolt and were sent to Vladivostok to work.

The real oppositionists were Jiang Guangchi and Bao Pu. They were the remnants of another sort of student. You could see at a glance that they were by nature incompatible with the rest. We lived at 15 Tverskaya Street, but these two lived by themselves in the convent near Pushkin Square. They were intelligent and lively, unlike both the Hunanese and the Zhejiangese. Jiang Guangchi was from Lu'an in Anhui, Bao Pu was from Wuxi in Jiangsu. Jiang was the only poet among us, Bao the only Esperantist. They both spoke good Russian and could communicate directly with the Russians, they did not need Luo Jiao to represent them. They deliberately stayed away from meetings. When we met them, we perhaps exchanged a joke or two, but we never talked about anything serious. A few months later, Bao Pu returned to China. He wrote a letter from Vladivostok attacking Luo and company and even attacking Communism. But the 'Moscow branch' had already decided to expel him even before he wrote the letter, for secretly inciting the two Red Beards to oppose the leadership. At a meeting the following year, just before he returned to China, Jiang Guangchi also came out as an oppositionist. He said that we would have to wait until we got back to China to see who were the real party loyalists.

When Jiang got back to China, he was definitely not a good party member. At first, he continued to work in the Party; later, however, he became a litterateur – albeit a 'revolutionary' litterateur. Luo Jiao and Peng Shuzhi became important cadres of the revolution, and we students from France also provided a large number of revolutionary cadres. But almost all the students (save Luo and Peng) originally in Moscow, especially the absolute submitters, disappeared from sight, with the exception of Ren Bishi and Wang Yifei.

The twelve of us first arrived in Moscow during the spring holidays. The KUTV students were preparing to go on a trip to Petrograd. We hurried through the registration procedure so that we could join them.

In connection with registration, I should say something about our names. Either because our Chinese names were hard to remember or for some other reason, the registrar Vaks gave each of us a Russian name. According to Li Zhongwu, who interpreted for us, our new names were based on those of the twelve members of the Petrograd Soviet Executive arrested in 1905. Zhao Shiyan was Radin, Chen Yannian was Sukhanov, Chen Qiaonian was Krassin, Wang Ruofei was Nemchev, Yuan Qingyun was Yanovsky,[13] Xiong Xiong was Silverstrov, Chen Jiuding was Shiskin, and I was Marlotov. I forget what the other four were called.

On the train and in Petrograd, we gradually got to know the students who gone to Moscow straight from China. We stayed on the second floor of the Smolny Institute. We discovered only later that this had been Trotsky's command post in the October Revolution. Petrograd was neater and cleaner than Moscow. We visited the Winter Palace, the Peter-Paul Fortress (which was empty), some factories, and a museum containing some futurist paintings. We saw a play (Molière's *Le bourgeois gentilhomme*) and went outside the city to visit Tsarskoeselo. We walked along the Nevsky Prospect almost every day. We knew little at the time about the events of the Revolution, so the places we visited left no great impression on us.

When we got back to Moscow, the spring holiday was already over and we began our studies. The curriculum covered economics, historical materialism, the history of class struggle, the history of the labour movement, the history of the Russian Communist Party, natural science, and Russian language. As far as I remember, that was all. Most of us had learned the Russian alphabet in France, and I myself had got half way through a Russian grammar. Even so, our teachers began teaching us from scratch. In the first lesson, we were taught the meaning of the abbreviation KUTV. Abbreviations became very popular after the Russian Revolution. They were formed by taking the first letter of every word, writing them all as capitals, and separating them by full stops (though these were optional), so you could tell at a glance whether something was an abbreviation or not. For example, the Communist Party of the Soviet Union was known as the CPSU and the Central Executive Council of the Union of Soviet Socialist Republics was known as the CEC-USSR. (This is how the Guomindang, or Kuomintang as it was then spelt in Western languages, came to be called the KMT.) Another fashion was to join the first syllables of two or more words to form an acronym. Sometimes, if you did not know that you were dealing with one of these acronyms you could waste much time searching for it in a dictionary. Examples are Konsomol (the Communist Youth League) and Comintern (the Communist International). On our curriculum at KUTV, political economy was called *politekonom* and historical materialism was called *istomat*. Traditionalists shook their heads and said that this practice was destroying

---

13 Trotsky sometimes used this name.

the integrity of the Russian language. The name of our university was also an abbreviation: *K*omunisticheski *U*niversitet *T*rudiashikhsia *V*ostoka, that is, KUTV or University for the Toilers of the East. At our first Russian lesson, the teacher spoke only Russian, but still he managed to get the meaning of KUTV across to us. Later, however, we benefited little from our Russian classes. Some of us thought that the pace was too slow, others that it was too fast. I myself got nothing from these classes. We learned to speak and understand by practising on other foreign students, and we learned to read by studying grammars and learning new words off by heart. Those like Chen Jiuding and Xiong Xiong who were incapable of self-study got nowhere, however attentively they listened to the teachers.

Apart from at Russian classes, we always had interpreters. The interpreters were Li Zhongwu, Wang Yifei, Ren Bishi, and Bao Pu. Very occasionally, Luo Jiao helped out; even more occasionally, Jiang Guangchi did so. This was because Luo Jiao was busy with other things and Jiang was frequently in hospital. Peng Shuzhi and the others never interpreted for us; on the contrary, they needed interpreters themselves when they attended classes. The teachers would say something, and then the interpreter would repeat it in Chinese. This meant that one hour of teaching actually became half an hour. What's more, you could not always understand the translation, and it was not necessarily faithful. Our economics teacher was a girl and our *istomat* (historical materialism) teacher was an old lady. They treated us like schoolchildren and gave us only a smattering of general knowledge. There was a Jew called Something-stein who taught us the history of the international labour movement. He taught in French, and I was chosen to interpret. This man brought new materials and viewpoints into his lectures, and I had to concentrate hard to interpret them, so he left an even deeper impression on me. Unfortunately, he worked for the Profintern[14] and often arrived late – after a few months he stopped coming altogether. (I once saw a photo of him with Lenin and some guests from Western Europe.) Right through until the time we left for China, we never mixed in class with students from other nationalities. One reason was that few of us could independently understand Russian-language lectures, another was that there were enough Chinese to form a class on our own; apart from the twelve of us, another twenty or thirty later arrived from France, and a dozen or so more came straight from China.

Needless to say, the university fed, clothed, and housed us. We could get tobacco too. Every month we got 1.5 new roubles in pocket money, which later went up to 3 roubles. Haircuts, baths, and laundry were also free. It was hard to

---

14   The Profintern was the Moscow-based Red Trade Union International.

find anywhere to spend the pocket money. I myself spent it all on books. Some people bought chocolate with it; at most it stretched to two or three packets a months. Li Zhongwu and Peng Zexiang often ate in Chinese restaurants with money they had taken with them from China. The rest of us did not dare do so, for the restaurants were too expensive. I did not even know where the Chinese restaurants were.

A few days after we arrived, Chen Yannian told me that he had never lived so well in his life, meaning the food. By 'life' he meant since he and his brother had left home. In Shanghai, they had still worn unlined clothes even in the depth of winter, and I believe they cooked for themselves throughout their stay in France. Naturally, they ate poorly. As for the rest of us, we did not share their enthusiasm. True, the food was a little better than what work-study students ate in France, but when we first arrived, our bread was black rather than white and full of stalks. We had often heard people sing the praises of black bread, but now that we got to know it, we found it barely palatable. At first, we were constipated for three or four days, in some cases, for nearly a week. It was a month or two before our bowels settled. The veterans told us that we had nothing to complain about, that when they had first arrived there were even more stalks in the bread, the food was even worse, and there was never enough of it. After our first summer in Russia, we gradually started getting white bread, and the year after that, we stopped getting black bread altogether. You could also see from the improved clothes that things were getting better in the Soviet Union. The first year, we wore thick Red Army hempen overcoats and Red Army peaked caps of all different shapes and sizes; the second year, we wore more or less uniform homespun black trousers and overcoats, though still of rough material. At first, people used old roubles on the streets, in denominations of hundreds of thousands and of millions, but later, the new rouble came in and chervonets were used.[15]

Kitchen duty was a particular drudgery. Apart from Luo Jiao, everyone had to do it, even Peng Shuzhi. We used to take turn once every three weeks or so. You had to turn up in the kitchen before dawn to cut firewood, peel potatoes, fetch bread from the store-room, slice the bread, put on white smocks three times a day at mealtimes, lay the tables, dish out the soup and food, and keep a smile on your face while people shouted at you from all directions. After serving seven or eight sittings, you yourself were finally allowed to eat. You could sleep for an hour or two after lunch. You were only released at eleven o'clock at night.

---

15 'Chervonets' means 'roubles in gold', though it was actually a sort of bank-note issued in November 1922. One chervonets was equal to ten new roubles.

For entertainment, there were free film shows and sometimes free tickets for plays or operettas. In springtime, we went on outings to Sparrow Hill in the western suburbs, whence Napoleon is said to have watched Moscow burn.

What did the Russian people think of us foreign students? Once Bao Pu met some ordinary citizens while he was attending hospital outside the college. According to him, ordinary people resented us. They said the Soviet Government was giving foreign students Russian people's bread and money, and the Russians were starving as a result.

The Chinese students at KUTV formed a separate unit. True, the Japanese, Korean, Indian, Turkish, and Persian students also tended to stick together in their own national groups, but only in the same way as Cantonese or Yunnanese stick together in (say) Beijing or Shanghai. The Chinese students, however, had their own separate political organisation, known as the 'Moscow branch of the Chinese Communist Party'. According to the statutes of the Third International, Communists living in a country other than their own must join that country's party. So members of the Chinese Communist Party or the Socialist Youth League in Moscow who could furnish proof and references should have joined the Russian organisation rather than set up branches of their own. How did the 'Moscow branch' come into being? Was its status legal? Was it recognised by the Russian Communist Party? I cannot answer these questions, and at the time, no one asked them – no one dared ask them. We were all members of China's Socialist Youth League, but we took no part in the KUTV branch of the Russian Youth League. In foreign comrades' eyes, we were mere sympathisers. Zhao Shiyan and Xiong Xiong were members of the Chinese Communist Party, but they, too, had no relations with the KUTV-branch of the Russian Communist Party.

In foreigners' eyes, we were sympathisers, but in Chinese eyes, we were comrades. We were divided into several cells, each with four or five members. Old and new comrades, familiar and unfamiliar comrades, were cleverly mixed. Each cell met once or twice a week, and there were plenary sessions and other sorts of meetings. Each meeting lasted two, three, or four hours. The atmosphere at them was tense, excited, and ardent. What were our activities? There were none. What theoretical research did we do? We did none. Most of the time was given over to 'individual criticism'. The criticism was never about specific issues but about abstract psychological attitudes: you're too individualistic, you're too arrogant, you're too petty-bourgeois, you have anarchist tendencies, and so on. The ones who were criticised would think up similar criticisms to hurl back against their critics. The result was that everyone ended up blushing and seeds of hatred were sown in people's hearts. In short, everyone learned to expose motives (*zhu xin*), like Confucius in the *Spring and Autumn Annals*; and to rectify the mind (*zheng xin*), like the Song Confucianists; but the object was to upbraid others, never oneself.

The commanding and submitting among the Chinese students and this sort of personal criticism was what I found most novel after arriving in Russia. True, Russian life was new, but I had been able to imagine it in advance. Only the commanding, the submitting, and the criticising had been beyond the power of my imagination. Whether or not the other students from France or the students direct from China thought the same way, I do not know. I suspect that, like me, they thought that this was an experience of the Russian Revolution that we ought to emulate and take back to China with us. We all learned to adapt to the environment, to recognise established authority, and to delve deep into the innermost recesses of the mind in order to criticise others' weak spots. Zhao Shiyan, Wang Ruofei, and later, Yin Kuan, Wang Zekai, and others who in France had been like tigers no longer dared to challenge authority now that they had arrived in Russia. They had opposed Zhang Songnian, but they did not dare oppose Luo Jiao or Peng Shuzhi. But there was at least one difference between us newcomers and the old crowd: we may have submitted, but we never did so blindly.

Zhang Bojian, now called Hunge-Hunge, was the first person to resist. He was often ill and in hospital, so he rarely attended classes with us. He came out against Luo Jiao and wrote letters cursing him and demanding that he answer. We knew about this, but we had not read the letters and did not know what was in them. Luo Jiao refused to reply to Zhang Bojian. He said that literary wrangles were a bad habit of Chinese intellectuals that he did not intend to emulate. Xiao Zizhang also came out in opposition and was severely criticised. Zhao Shiyan and Chen Yannian had their own positions, but they knew how to push them through under the guise of compliance. I was the one who found it hardest to adapt. I was criticised more than anyone else at cell meetings. I accepted most of the criticisms, but there were two that I would never accept.

The first criticism was that I read too much, studied too much Russian, was not active enough, and did not speak often enough with other people. According to a slogan popular in the 'Moscow branch', we had come here not to become 'academics' but for 'training'. Training meant meetings and criticism; 'academic study' meant learning Russian and reading books on theory. Peng Shuzhi made no secret of this fact. He said: 'You won't be here long. Russian is not an easy language. Fortunately, there are already people among the Chinese students who know Russian well, who know theory well, and who are experienced. It's enough to learn from them'. I am convinced that, had the school authorities allowed, Peng would have proposed cancelling the six hours of Russian we did each week. We already spent more time and energy on meetings than on classes. What we learned in the classroom was crude and superficial, and here were people who wanted even fewer classes and even more meetings. They considered that it was enough to read *Zhengzhi changshi* ('The Rudiments of Politics'), jointly translated by Qu Qiubai and Wang Yifei. Several copies of this manuscript had been made and distributed to us. Though I thought that this proposal was unreasonable, I did not openly oppose it. I simply carried on with my Russian and my other studies and paid no attention to the cajoling and criticising. People gave me the nickname 'Professor', in English.

The second criticism concerned my friendship with Bao Pu. When we first got to Moscow, we knew nothing of personal relations among the Chinese students. Everyone came to welcome us. We had no idea who were the leaders and the led, who were the people in power and the people out of power. Chen Jiuding came from the crowd and pointed out someone called Bao Pu, who he said spoke Esperanto. I went up to him and said, '*Ĉu vi parolas Esperanton?*' (Do you speak Esperanto?) He said he did, so we became good friends. He was the only Esperantist among the Chinese students in Moscow, and I the only one among the Chinese students from France. Later, I found that he was more knowledgeable than other people and that he was neither unapproachable, like the leaders of the Moscow branch, nor bossy. He lived in the Convent, in the same room as Jiang Guangchi and a worker comrade. Jiang was in hospital having his eyes seen to; not until a long time afterwards did I meet him. It later turned out that the worker had been sent to keep an eye on the two of them. I often went there to chat for a few hours; Bao used to take me round Moscow to see the sights. He also took me to meet some Moscow Esperantists: Polakov, Nekrassov, and a Hungarian refugee who could also speak Esperanto. We often went to evening parties of Esperantists or non-Esperantists. At that time, an organisation had split away from the international Esperanto organisation. It was called SAT[16] ('International Association of Non-Nationals'). This organisation had its office in France. There were Communists in it and it was sympathetic to the Soviet Union. The editor of the SAT journal had recently come back from the Soviet Union and published articles in the journal about

---

16 In Esperanto, Sennacieca Asocio Tutmonda. SAT's inaugural meeting in 1921 emphasised the use of Esperanto in the class struggle, urged all class-conscious proletarians to join SAT, and condemned the mainstream Universal Esperanto Association for its political neutrality.

his travels in that country. I learned a lot from those articles. I corresponded with the editor (unfortunately, I forget his name) and he set me up as pen-pal with an Esperantist worker in Paris. When I mentioned this editor to the Esperantists in Moscow, they said they had had a visit from him just a short time before. They took me to see their editorial board and their print shop. Polakov wrote articles and Nekrassov wrote poems. They set their own type and did their own printing and distribution. None of them was a Communist, but a high Communist official who was an Esperantist acted as their patron. I once heard this man give a speech in Esperanto. He had a bureaucratic manner and was not approachable like the rest of them. Bao Pu also knew an Outer Mongolian who had relations with the Outer Mongolian Government. I used to speak Esperanto with this Mongol; Bao Pu spoke Russian with him, for the Mongol's Esperanto was poor. The Mongol often looked me up at school and later asked me for news of the Beijing Government. Gradually, I became estranged from him.

It was not long before I learned about Bao Pu's position in the Moscow branch, but it made not the slightest difference to our friendship. People warned me, and at criticism meetings they obliquely criticised me. Finally, Peng Shuzhi sought me out for a private chat. He told me straight out that Bao Pu was on a dangerous political course, and he wanted me to break with him. I refused. I said Bao was a party member and I was only a league member. I ought to accept his leadership. If Bao was wrong, why did not the Party put him right? Several months later, after Bao Pu had returned to China, the Moscow branch announced his expulsion. He went back to Shanghai and wrote articles opposing Communism and the Soviet Union for the *Xuedeng* ('Lamp of Knowledge') supplement of *Shishi xinbao* ('New Current Affairs Daily'). Qu Qiubai rebutted him in the *Juewu* ('Awakening') supplement of *Minguo ribao* ('Republic Daily') and the two men became embroiled in a long literary wrangle. In Moscow, they had been good friends. In 1925, Bao Pu had gone to Russia for a second time as a staff member in the Chinese Consulate in Vladivostok. After that, I heard nothing more of him. On 29 August 1937, while I was being released from Nanjing's Central Military Prison, someone handed me a letter as I passed the reception desk. It was from a person called Qin Diqing of the Guomindang's Central Propaganda Bureau. It said that this man Qin had been busy trying to arrange for my release. I had never heard of anyone by that name, but luckily, there was a note on the back of the letter explaining that it was Bao Pu. I tore it up at the prison gate.

My friendship with Bao Pu delayed my promotion from League to Party. When we first arrived in Moscow, as far as I remember, only Zhao Shiyan and

Xiong Xiong were in the Party. Before the start of the summer holidays the Chen brothers, Wang Ruofei, and Yuan Qingyun were all promoted.[17] During the vacation, down in the countryside, Luo Jiao visited me one day wreathed in smiles and invited me and She Liya to go for an outing with him in the forest. I did not go. I was a bit surprised by the invitation. Later, She Liya told me that Luo Jiao had spoken to him on behalf of the party organisation. After that, She, too, joined. I myself only formally joined the following year, after Lenin's death. The rest joined either at the same time as I or later.

During the summer vacation of 1923, the entire school went down to the countryside to escape the heat. It took one or two hours by train to reach our destination, and another couple of hours' walk from the railway station. Finally, we arrived at the KUTV estate, in a small village. I forget what the village was called, but I remember a landlord's mansion at the side of a forest. In it was a big hall with four or six rooms along the two sides. Four or five hundred paces from the mansion was a two-storey house with seven or eight rooms on each floor. The Chinese students lived on the first floor of this building. Apart from this, there were some typically Russian wooden cabins called *isba*. Each day, we did several hours' 'physical labour' on the school farm – digging, weeding, ploughing, and the like. We spent most of the time planting sweet radishes. The food was more or less the same as in the city, but we started getting white bread.

During the summer vacation, the Chinese class acquired a new member called Lin Keyi, who had come straight from China. He had studied in Japan and had then taught at some private university in Beijing. Now, he had come to Russia to study Marxism. He was not in the Communist Party but was a member of the *Today* group. In China, apart from the Communist Party there was a Marxist organisation that published a journal called *Jinri* ('Today'). Its leader was the member of parliament Hu Egong. Its rank and file consisted of some people who had studied in Japan and some Beijing bureaucrats. *Today* adopted a leftwing position and was against the Communist Party entering the Guomindang. *Xiangdao* ('Guide Weekly'), replying to this attack, pointed out that Hu Egong was a parliamentary hack in the pay of the Beiyang government; whereupon, Hu defended himself by quoting from Lenin's newly published *Left-Wing Communism: An Infantile Disorder* on parliamentary movements.

---

17 Here I am wrong. In fact, these people were accepted into the Party immediately after arriving in Moscow, for they had already joined the Communist Party of either France or Germany. [Note added by Zheng Chaolin in 1989.]

The Third International's secret envoy in China tried to patch things up and even invited *Today* to send a representative to Moscow to take part in the Comintern Congress. I know little about what transpired behind the scenes. Perhaps Peng Zexiang, who came to Moscow with Chen Duxiu to attend the Fourth Congress, was the *Today* representative. By the time that we arrived, Peng had already joined the Communist Party. Later, nearly all Hu Egong's people joined the Party, but they played no role in the revolution.

Lin Keyi was the second *Today* representative to arrive in Moscow. The school authorities sent him down to the countryside to stay with us. We did not know before we arrived in the village that he would come to join us. Peng Shuzhi hurriedly called a plenary meeting to discuss how to handle this non-comrade. He said: 'Lin Keyi is a university professor. He has published articles in newspapers and magazines in China, whereas we're nobodies. Maybe he will look down on us. We must apply our collective strength to conquer him'. He then assigned tasks, for example, who was to talk with him and what sort of thing to talk about. I was one of the handful of people assigned to do this, for like me, Lin was a Fujianese. My mission was to discuss historical materialism with him, find out what he knew about it, and probe him about the *Today* group. A comrade was moved from my room to empty a bed for Lin. Lin turned out to be a white-faced bookworm, a typical Fuzhou man. As a fellow Fujianese, I looked after him. My other room-mates only talked with him about things like the weather, but I sometimes steered the conversation round to theoretical issues. After a few conversations, I discovered that he knew nothing about historical materialism. Other people were responsible for assessing his knowledge of economics and other subjects. When the subject got round to *Today*, he flatly denied having anything to do with that organisation.

A few weeks later, Peng Shuzhi announced that he was going to introduce Lin Keyi into the Youth League (even though he was already more than twenty-three years old). I was in the same cell as him. At the first meeting, he confessed that he had not only joined the *Today* group but was on its Central Committee. After the summer vacation, he attended classes together with me. He made me think of Liu Zongyuan's short masterpiece *Qianzhi lü* ('The Ass of Guizhou').[18]

During the summer vacation of 1924, he returned to China together with me. He did not want to go back, and when he got the order to return, he raised a great many counter-arguments, all to no avail. Eventually, he packed his bags and set out with the rest of us. When we reached Chita, he asked Chen Yannian,

---

18   *The Ass of Guizhou* is a famous fable written by Liu Zongyuan, one of the 'Eight Great Essayists of the Tang and Song'. *Ass of Guizhou* has since been used to denote someone who appears or pretends to be great or able yet actually is not.

leader of the group, if he could go with Li Zhongwu and return to China on the Chinese Eastern Railway via Manzhouli. We realised what he intended to do and proposed that he go back with the rest of us via Vladivostok, but Chen granted his request. The result was that Li Zhongwu returned to China and Lin stayed in Chita. Later, he went to Vladivostok and got mixed up with Bao Pu. After he got back to China, he wrote articles in the Beijing press attacking the Soviet Union. In 1926, he represented China in Japan at the Asian Nations' Conference. In 1927, he became a professor at Sun Yat-sen University in Wuhan and wrote to *Guide Weekly* explaining this 'misunderstanding'. In the autumn of the same year, when Tang Shengzhi massacred the Communists,[19] for some strange reason Lin, too, was taken off and shot. People said that just before he died, a Sun Yat-sen University student who was shot at the same time as Lin ridiculed him. Lin's sole reason for going to the Soviet Union was to acquire the status of a person who has studied abroad.

Writing about Lin Keyi leads me on quite naturally to Chen Qixiu. Chen, too, was a Beijing University professor and a returned student from Japan, and now he came to the Soviet Union to do research. He brought with him a letter of introduction from Li Dazhao and visited us in our dormitory at KUTV. He bowed formally in four directions and inquired, 'Which of you gentlemen is Mr Luo Jiao, which is Mr Peng Shuzhi?' We received him. He had not come to study at KUTV, and he rented accommodation outside the university. He did independent research, but he spent much of his spare time at KUTV. Naturally enough, some of us visited him frequently at his home. I had not been assigned to the campaign to win him over, for there were quite a few Sichuanese among us. Soon afterwards, he, too, joined the Communist Party. Either before or after joining (I cannot remember which), the Moscow branch asked him to give some lectures, which he did on five or six occasions. His topic was the Chinese economy. Each time Peng Shuzhi got up onto the platform after Chen had finished speaking and explained in a friendly manner where he disagreed. We got nothing from Chen's lectures, but Peng Shuzhi seized the chance to show us that he was on a par with the famous professors of Beijing University. After Chen returned to China, his relations with the Party were sometimes intimate, sometimes distant. Many people know about this, so there is no need for me to discuss it further.

Towards the end of the summer vacation, students who had gone up to the capital from the countryside brought back with them the news that Sun Yat-sen had sent a delegation to Moscow. The leader of the delegation was a man called Jiang. The other delegates were Shen Xuanlu, Zhang Tailei, and a man called

---

19   In July 1927, General Tang's commanders suppressed Communist organisations in Wuhan.

Huang. Xiong Xiong said: 'It will be great if this man called Jiang turns out to be Jiang Zungui, because he owes me $300. I can get it back from him and take you all out for a Chinese meal'. A few days after we had restarted classes we held a meeting in our dormitory to receive the four delegates. Guests and hosts sat each side of a long table, and people for whom there was no room sat on beds. Shen Xuanlu sported a beard. He looked magnificent. We had often read his articles in *New Youth*, but by this time, he had already withdrawn from the Communist Party. Zhang Tailei was a giant of a man, and extremely handsome. He was a leader of the Chinese Socialist Youth League.[20] Huang Dengren was a secretarial type, quite undistinguished. The leader of the delegation was also unimposing and undistinguished. He was thirty-odd years old, white-skinned and dapper, of medium build, and spoke non-standard Mandarin. To Xiong Xiong's disappointment (and to ours, for we had begun to look forward to our Chinese meal), he was not Jiang Zungui. Instead, he was called Chiang[21] Kai-shek, a name that few people had heard of at that time. Xiong Xiong had served as a military officer in the Guomindang, but even he had not heard of him. After the meeting, we discussed among ourselves why Sun Yat-sen had sent such a nonentity to lead the delegation. Some people suspected that the real leader of the delegation was Shen Xuanlu and that this Chiang Kai-shek was just a figurehead.

On National Day (the Double Tenth),[22] the delegation invited all the Chinese students at KUTV to a dinner. The delegation was housed in an aristocrat's mansion, which, though small, was exquisitely beautiful. We ate sumptuously in the great hall. After the meal, there were entertainments. Shen Xuanlu did a sword dance. The sword slipped from his hand and he picked it up and continued dancing; we did not dare laugh. Peng Shuzhi then danced a Caucasian dance and other people sang songs.[23] Chiang Kai-shek asked us into a small room at the side of the hall and lectured us on the history of the Guomindang, which he then asked us to join. He spoke on his feet, one hand resting on the back of a chair. He gave the impression of being honest but weak. We privately asked each other why Sun Yat-sen had sent such a useless person.

The Moscow branch appointed certain people to stay close to the delegates and try to win them over. Naturally, Luo Jiao and Peng Shuzhi were among these people. As a 'tactic', some people – I forget who – were chosen to 'enter'

---

20 The Socialist Youth League, founded on July 22, 1920, was renamed the Communist Youth League in 1925.
21 Jiang in Pinyin transcription.
22 10 October, commemorating the Revolution of 1911.
23 See Cadart and Cheng 1983, pp. 338–9, for another account of this party.

the Guomindang and to deal with the delegates as 'Guomindang comrades'. The result was that Shen Xuanlu rejoined the Party. After the Double Tenth, the only member of the delegation I saw was Zhang Tailei. I heard that the negotiations had not gone smoothly, and that the man called Chiang had complained. After a few weeks, they went back to China, but Zhang Tailei stayed on in the Hotel Lux as Moscow representative of the Chinese Socialist Youth League. We often visited him in his hotel. In the spring of 1925, Luo Jiao returned to China and met Chiang Kai-shek in the Huangpu Military Academy in Guangdong. When Luo Jiao came to Shanghai, he told me, 'As soon as he saw me he said, "Are you better?" He remembered from Moscow that I had been ill'.

Zhang Tailei brought with him news of the Third Congress of the Chinese Communist Party. Peng Shuzhi summoned a plenary assembly to report on it. He said that at the meeting, Li Hanjun had opposed the policy of joining the Guomindang, and that even though Li had contributed much to the Party (for example when the journal *Gongchan dang* ['The Communist Party'] had no money, Li paid the printing costs with fees he had got for his own articles), we should still oppose him. This was the first time I realised that there were internal struggles in the Party. But none of us in Moscow supported the opposition, for joining the Guomindang was a policy that we had already discussed and approved, and Li Hanjun had no authority as far as we were concerned.

After the summer, another batch of Chinese students reached Moscow from Western Europe. There were far more of them than there had been of us: twenty or thirty in all. Almost all the people I knew had come: Yin Kuan, Li Weinong, Wang Zekai, Xue Shilun, and Yu Lüzhong. Among those who arrived was Yuan Zizhen, one of the two worker delegates at the Second Congress. Another worker comrade among the new arrivals was Tang Ruxian. From Belgium, where they had joined the organisation, came Liu Bojian and Li Heling, the famous terrorist. The rest, who were all new to me, included Ma Yufu.[24] Like us, they were 'trained' by the Moscow branch, but Yin Kuan, Wang Zekai, and Xue Shilun all the same learned Russian and read theory. They paid no attention to the criticisms of the leaders and the rank and file. It was a shame they arrived late, for their Russian was not yet advanced by the time they returned to China, so they had to do all their theoretical study in French.

The people from France and Belgium had stayed in the homes of German Communists while crossing Germany on their way to Russia. The mark was devaluing uncontrollably and the German proletariat was trying to make a

---

24   Later to become a traitor to the Trotskyists.

revolution. Even down in the countryside, we had heard from city visitors that a revolution was going to break out in Germany. Some had heard Radek talking in Red Square about the situation in Germany, but neither *Pravda* nor *Izvestia* had published his speech. The newly arrived Chinese students said that in the German comrades' houses, they had seen people preparing first-aid materials, including bandages and medicines. We urgently read the news from Germany in the press, including news about the founding and dissolution of the Dresden workers' government and the fighting on the barricades in Hamburg. Peng Shuzhi even bought a book on the German language and studied a few chapters. After October, all our illusions about Germany were dispelled. Afterwards, we gradually learned about the internal struggle in the Russian Communist Party. The Communist Party branch at our 'Stalin University' was one of the few intensely anti-'Trotskyist' branches in Moscow. At one branch meeting,[25] Kamenev spoke for the faction in power and Radek for the opposition. Each set out his own position and there was a fierce exchange of views. As a member of Socialist Youth, I was not qualified to attend the meeting, but later, I heard Chinese students discussing the respective arguments. I have forgotten most of it, but I remember someone quoted Radek as saying, 'Kamenev, who's heard of you outside Russia? But Trotsky is a household name throughout the world!'

It was true – in France I had heard next to nothing about Kamenev. Admittedly, during Lenin's second illness, *L'Humanité* had listed the duties of the three men standing in for Lenin, and Kamenev was among the troika. But apart from that, he had left no impression on me. I did not know anything about Stalin. As for Trotsky, he was as famous as Lenin and had even made a slightly greater impression on me than had Lenin, because I had read more of his writings and been more stirred by them. I had read his *From the October Revolution to the Brest Peace Talks* (called *Avènement du bolchevisme* in French translation and *A Faithful Record of the Russian Revolution* in Chinese translation) and I had also bought *1905*, just then published in French, but I had not read it. I sensed an internationalist spirit in Trotsky's theses and pamphlets that went deeper than that of other writers. Perhaps Lenin surpassed Trotsky in his works, but I had not read them.

---

25   Here my memory deceived me. According to Cadart and Cheng 1983, pp. 345–6, there were two meetings at that time of cadres and activists in Moscow and they were not held in KUTV. Luo Jiao and Peng attended these meetings as representatives of the Chinese section of the KUTV party organisation. I heard of their proceedings later, during an informal chat with Peng. [Note added by Zheng Chaolin in 1989.]

At that time, white cloth-banners bearing Trotsky's portrait were still hanging across the streets, and although there were fewer of them than of Lenin, they were still quite plentiful. One hung in the square alongside KUTV. I never saw a portrait of Stalin, Kamenev, or Zinoviev on the street. At that time, I was reading the *History of the French Revolution*[26] and saw how Brissot, Danton, Robespierre, and Hébert slaughtered one another. I was astonished that such a thing could happen just three or four years after the start of the Revolution. The Russian Revolution had already been going on for six years, but I was convinced that it would never repeat the drama of the French Revolution, that the dispute would soon be peacefully resolved, and that as soon as Lenin recovered from his illness, all the problems would automatically disappear. How naïve I was!

Lenin never recovered. I had read even before setting out from France that Lenin was in his death agony. I said to people, we're going to Russia to attend Lenin's funeral. During the summer vacation, down in the countryside, some people had already heard rumours that Lenin would not recover; Bukharin was said to have announced in a speech that Lenin's brain had already been damaged, and that even if he did not die, he would be an idiot. On the morning of 22 January 1924, while we were breakfasting, rumours spread throughout the school that Lenin had died the day before. They were soon confirmed. The comrade in charge of the laundry, a lady in her fifties, cried and told us that she had once worked with Lenin. In the afternoon, we went out onto the streets, where a big white cloth announcing Lenin's death was hanging. The school-authorities assigned students to take charge of the telephone. Only people with official permits were allowed to use it. I also took my turn at the phone. Soon, Lenin's body was brought into Moscow from the countryside and laid in state in the great hall of the National Trade Unions' building. People from all the different factories, schools, and offices went to pay their respects to the body. We formed a long queue and waited for several hours before it was our turn to enter. We hurriedly filed through and out the other side. I saw Lenin's body laid out on a central bier surrounded by fresh flowers with only his face showing, just like on the ubiquitous portraits and on the postcard I had bought at the *Clarté* bookshop in Paris, save that the eyes were closed and the skin was bloodless. On 27 January, we went to the funeral. It was bitterly cold, the temperature was more than 20 degrees below Celsius. The procession shuffled slowly forward, sometimes coming to a halt; it took almost half a day to reach Red Square. One man who looked like a peasant carelessly knocked at his frozen ear and it dropped to the ground.

---

26   Mathiez 1922–7.

The day that Lenin was buried, Red Square was hung with huge slogans saying that now Lenin was dead, we should unite and carry out his will. But with Lenin dead, the Russian Communist Party rushed even faster towards a split. Even if the people had been able to support the opposition, the political police (the GPU) were still in the hands of those in power. At some point, Yuan Qingyun got orders to act for the GPU among the Chinese students. The authorities still did not feel at ease. They sent Zhang Kaiyun, from Xinjiang, to KUTV to study and keep an eye on all the Chinese.

I had seen the dead Lenin with my own eyes, but I also heard the living Trotsky speak. In April 1924, KUTV held a meeting to commemorate the third anniversary of its founding, and the party branch invited Trotsky to make a speech. He was a large, tall man with a ringing voice who dominated the platform like a fierce lion. By that time, I could almost follow a long speech in Russian. A few days later, the school journal printed the speech, which I translated into Chinese and took back to China with me. Later, it was published in issue no. 4 of *New Youth* quarterly.

Bukharin also came to KUTV to give a speech. After the assassination of Vorovsky in Switzerland, I heard Lunacharsky speak in a demonstration in Red Square. On the second anniversary of the Soviet Constitution, I heard Zinoviev speak somewhere in the suburbs. During demonstrations on 1 May and 7 November, I saw Stalin and other important leaders on the rostrum in Red Square. The veteran Japanese socialist Katayama Sen came to KUTV to talk to the Chinese students. He spoke in English and Zhao Shiyan translated.

A few days after Lenin's death, *Pravda* published a telegram from Sun Yat-sen saying that the First Congress of the reorganised Guomindang had adjourned for three days in mourning.

From then on, we paid even more attention to events in China. As for Chinese publications, we had all along regularly received internal bulletins and external dailies and magazines. One day, Peng Shuzhi told us angrily that *New Youth*, the Party's theoretical journal, had started publishing nothing but boring and vacuous articles on philosophy and literature. Actually, *New Youth*, which had stopped publishing for quite some time, had become a quarterly under the editorship of Qu Qiubai. It had already published its first and second issues. Starting with issue number two, it had begun to publish novels and literary criticism. At the same time, the internal publication *Dangbao* ('Party Report') had published an article titled 'Should there be a Chinese Communist Party?' This, too, made Peng angry. He said that the Party's very existence was now being put up for discussion. So the Moscow branch decided to contribute articles to the party press. I proposed that *New Youth* should bring out a special Lenin number, to commemorate the recent death of the leader of the world-revolution. People supported my proposal. Articles were assigned to various individuals and I was put in charge of sorting things out and pushing people to contribute. But no one started writing. As the deadline neared, I began to harass them, and they called me 'debt collector'. Even before the Lenin issue, I had to contribute a few things. I had translated an article by Plekhanov on dialectics, and Yin Kuan had translated another article on the same subject; Zhao Shiyan, too, had written an article. We posted these contributions back to China. At that time, Qu Qiubai was in Guangzhou, and Chen Duxiu had published the submissions from Moscow indiscriminately in the third issue of *New Youth* quarterly. Earlier, I had forged a bulletin from France for *Guide Weekly* on the basis of reports in *L'Humanité*, which I read regularly.

After the reorganisation of the Guomindang, our activities in China expanded and the Party needed personnel to take charge of them. Before the summer vacation of 1924, a batch of Chinese students at KUTV got the order to return to China. Among them were Jiang Guangchi, Xiao Zizhang, Yin Kuan, Xiong Xiong, and Zhang Bojian. For the holidays, we went to another village where there was a KUTV estate that was closer to the railway station. There were some wooden cabins in a small forest where we received military training.

Zhang Guotao had been arrested in Beijing; Li Dazhao fled to Moscow, and not long after that, Wang Hebo and a worker comrade called Yao also turned up. They had come to represent the Chinese Communist Party at the Fifth Congress of the Third International.

Before the end of the summer break, I received orders to return to China. Those who returned at the same time as I included Peng Shuzhi, Chen Yannian, Wang Zekai, Xue Shilun, Li Zhongwu, Lin Keyi, Yu Lüzhong, Cai Zhihua, Fu Daqing, and Zhou Yaoqiu. This list was decided by the Chinese delegation. My name was proposed by Peng Shuzhi. He was planning to take over the editorship of *New Youth*, and through my work on the Lenin issue I had demonstrated that I was not entirely useless.

All the delegates save Li Dazhao returned to China. Peng Shuzhi, alone among us students, travelled back with them. They went by the Chinese Eastern Railway and entered China through Manzhouli. The route they took was comparatively dangerous, but it was much quicker than the other routes; the rest of us first went to Vladivostok and then took the boat to Shanghai, which route was not in the least dangerous.

We set out from Moscow sometime in late July and took the train direct to Chita. At Chita, we changed onto a train bound for Vladivostok. We were some twenty days underway – this is the longest railway line in the world.

Chen Yannian was our group leader; I looked after the funds. I took charge of buying bread, sausage, and other sorts of cold food at stations along the line. Someone else took care of fetching water. The train did not stop for long at small stations, but at big stations it often stopped for two or three hours. At Irkutsk, it stopped for a whole day. We got off the train for a tour of this coldest city in the world and enjoyed a meal in a restaurant alongside Lake Baikal.

In Vladivostok, there was no boat going to Shanghai, so there was nothing for it but to wait patiently. We stayed there for more than a month, in the Sailors' Club on Lenin Street down by the sea. Life was by no means lonely during our month in Vladivostok. The Sailors' Club library had a large collection of French novels, and there was a Chinese workers' May First Club on Pekinskaya Ulitsa run by Liang Botai and He Jinliang. Liang and He had originally been on their way to KUTV three years earlier to study, but had stayed in the Soviet Far East to work among the Chinese community there. They were both from Zhejiang. Wu Fang, a Hunanese, had also come with them to Russia. He was working as an inspector of Chinese labourers in the Soviet Far East and did not often go to Vladivostok; there was also Ren Zuomin, another Hunanese, who worked in Khabarovsk. Then there was a man called Wang Jun, who worked in the May First Club in Vladivostok. He was a northerner who had worked on the railways and been a delegate at a conference of the Third International. He had fled to Russia after the defeat of the Beijing-Hankou rail-strike to seek refuge and to work for the movement. The club leaders wanted to keep us in Vladivostok, for they were short of officials. They had asked the Party in China to send them people, but to no effect. Just before we left, the Party in China did send someone, a man from Hubei called Zhang Jueyu, who had fled to Shanghai after the collapse of the rail-strike.

There were many overseas Chinese in Vladivostok, all of them northerners. They congregated in a part of the city where there were two Beijing opera theatres, several restaurants, several bath-houses, and innumerable shops. When you entered this district, it was as if you were in China. The streets in other districts preserved a Russian character. Wang Jun, Liang Botai, and He Jinliang invited us out for a meal at one of the restaurants, for a bath at one of the bathhouses, and for an evening at the opera. We received a warm reception everywhere, and we never once had to pay. When we ate, all we needed to say was 'Put it on my bill' and that was that. I asked them, 'Do you pay once every four months?' They replied, 'We never pay'. At first, I naïvely imagined that since the club worked for the interests of the Chinese workers and small merchants, these people naturally cherished its officials and were unwilling to take money from them. Later, I found out that this was not so. The Chinese feared and hated these people. The Chinese were actually opposed to the Soviet system;

many were Red Beards. One of the four workers who had studied at KUTV, a man called Lü Xianji, had gone to Vladivostok to work a year earlier and had been murdered just a few days after our arrival. The GPU already knew who had committed the murder, but were unable to catch this person. He Jinliang asked Chen Yannian and others to go to drink tea in a Chinese restaurant frequented by the assassin and gather information, since we were new arrivals and not known there. I do not know what the outcome was.

In September, Zhao Shiyan and Ren Bishi also arrived from Moscow. They stayed several days in Vladivostok, before going on by train to northeastern China via Yimianpo. The rest of us stayed on to await the boat, which finally arrived with twenty or thirty Chinese students on board, all bound for KUTV. Among them was Li Qiushi, a handsome young man, one of the five writers shot at Longhua in 1931.[27]

In mid September, a British coal freighter left Vladivostok for Shanghai without passengers. We sought out the Chinese crew to see if there was any way that we could travel on this vessel. They agreed to let only three or four of us stow away, so we split into two groups for the journey back to China. Wang Zekai, Xue Shilun, and some others went ahead, while I, Chen Yannian, and the rest left several days later, aboard a Russian ship. They slipped away like thieves, whereas we left legally and openly, sleeping on sofas in the ship's clubroom. On 29 September, we reached Shanghai.

Xue Shilun came to the Taian Hotel to seek us out. He had already been assigned to a job, as secretary to the central presidium; Wang Zekai had already gone to work in Anyuan.[28] In his capacity as secretary, Xue Shilun informed us of our new duties. Chen Yannian was to go to Guangzhou to be district party secretary, I was to stay in Shanghai, to work in the Central Committee's Propaganda Department. The next day, we moved together with our luggage to a lane house on Moulmein Road.

---

27   In early 1931, Li and thirty-five other people were arrested in Shanghai by the British police and handed over to the Guomindang. Most were shot on 7 February in Longhua Prison. Those shot included Li and four other writers.

28   The Anyuan coal mines in Jiangxi were one of the Party's main proletarian strongholds in the 1920s.

Chinese Students in Moscow

Wang Fanxi

Source: *Memoirs of a Chinese Revolutionary* (1957).

The Moscow branch of the CCP, which had flourished in the early 1920s, consisted exclusively of Chinese Communists resident in the Soviet Union. It had similar status to the former European branch of the CCP led by Zhou Enlai in Paris. Organisations of this sort were not strictly in keeping with the organisational principles of the Comintern, by which every Communist Party had equal rights as a section of the International, and every Communist, regardless of nationality, had the right and duty to participate in the life of the party organisation in the country where he or she lived. The European and Moscow branches of the CCP originally came into existence because of the special nature of their membership. Most of the Chinese Communists in Europe and Moscow at that time were students, who had gone or been sent there to receive theoretical and organisational training related to the problems of China. The Moscow branch was nominally under the direct leadership of the Comintern, but in practice it was a part of the CPSU. Its status was therefore rather unclear and confused. Normally, this was not a problem, but as the struggle among the Chinese students in Moscow became more heated it soon became one, as I shall explain later. The Moscow branch had been founded four or five years before we arrived, and was at first led by Liu Shaoqi, Peng Shuzhi and others. Afterwards Yu Xiusong became prominent in it, and, by our time, it was under the control of Wu Fujing. The power and influence of men like Wu was due to the fact that they had lived in Moscow for a comparatively long period of time, knew Russian well, and were known and trusted by the Soviet comrades. The way in which they ran the branch was chiefly aimed at maintaining their established position in Moscow and using it as a springboard for securing control of the CCP itself. They argued that it would be a waste of time for those Chinese students who arrived in Moscow after them to learn Russian, and they were against the study of theory on the grounds that it would turn us into useless academics.

The older members of the Moscow branch were about a dozen former students who had stayed on as party officials, translators, and interpreters. They were the middlemen between the Chinese students and the Russian comrades, and their role in the Party was similar to that of the compradors in the treaty ports at home. They had translated a number of elementary textbooks of communism and histories of the Communist Party of the Soviet Union and of the international workers' movement into Chinese. Whenever a new intake of Chinese students arrived in Moscow they would dole out these mimeographed textbooks, teach them a few rudiments supposed to be a 'must' for every party member, and then pack them back off to China to 'take part in the real struggle'. Anyone who dared to challenge this system by learning Russian or studying more theory than was thought necessary was looked upon as an unreliable intruder. Such people would be severely criticised and even sent back to China ahead of schedule as a punishment.

There had already been one struggle against the branch before we arrived in Moscow, waged by a group of older comrades around Luo Han, among them Li Xiagong, Wu Jixian, Zhu Danji, and others. These men had been politically active both inside and outside the Communist Party for many years. In experience and learning they were head and shoulders above the leadership of the branch. It was out of the question that men of their calibre would accept the petty restrictions that the latter tried to impose on them. They demanded changes in the curriculum and insisted on more time for private study. After a brief clash, they won some slight concessions from the party committee: they were allowed more time for learning Russian; the number of cell meetings was reduced, which also implied a reduction in the number of harrowing criticism sessions; and the atmosphere became less hostile to the study of theoretical questions. Party power, however, remained firmly in the hands of the middlemen.

It was this group that we finally confronted and fought. They were heavily outnumbered, and their influence was much less than that of the Moscow branch in its heyday. It was only later I realised why we had needed a bitter struggle to overthrow them. The entire administration of the Communist University for the Toilers of the East (KUTV) stood behind them, including the president, Boris Shumiatsky, an old Bolshevik and a staunch Stalinist, as well as the top officials of the party committee and the educational board of the university, who were all faithful Stalinists too. They were, almost without exception, loathsome bureaucrats. The head of the military training school affiliated to KUTV was a man called Maslov. He was the sort of officer who would have been more at home at a palace-ball than in a revolution. He knew nothing about China and her revolution, and assumed an air of extreme arrogance. He imposed exacting discipline on his students, but was very perfunctory where his own teaching duties were concerned. The course in military training was only scheduled to last six months, which is probably why it was so elementary. Since the lectures were given in Russian and interpreted into Chinese, they appeared even more trivial than they actually were.

Many of the students at the school had studied military affairs before coming to Moscow, and even more had first-hand experience of war from their time in the army. Not surprisingly, they were very dissatisfied with the way the course was run: they had not come to Russia to be taught trivia. But when they demanded an improvement, they were immediately rebuffed by the Chinese interpreters, who were time-servers, like the interpreters who used to work for the municipal council and the foreign firms in Shanghai, and who can still be found in Hong Kong. Above all they hated trouble, and they looked upon anyone who asked them to transmit a complaint as a trouble-maker. After trying and failing to deal with the military students' complaints themselves, they passed their demands to the Russian authorities, putting their own particular gloss on them. The Russian officials reacted in exactly the same way as their Chinese underlings, and flatly refused to consider the demands.

There was an eruption of anger as the students of the military school, backed by the KUTV students as a whole, declared war on the 'survivors' of the Moscow branch. Since nearly all the interpreters were 'survivors' it was only natural that the anger that was felt for Maslov should spill over onto the university's party committee. A delegation went to see Shumiatsky, who denounced their demands out of hand, thus adding fuel to the fire. The same day the students called an emergency general meeting and elected a new delegation. Yaroslavsky received them in person, and had a short talk with them, but nothing positive came of it. The next day, therefore, all the students from the military school marched in procession to the Comintern headquarters. Wildcat demonstrations of this sort had at one time been the vogue in China, but they had been strictly prohibited in the Soviet Union ever since Stalin's assumption of power. The sight of the Chinese students marching in procession through the main streets of Moscow caused quite a sensation, and was considered a very serious incident. Rumours were flying about that the students who had organised the demonstration would be severely punished, but nothing came of this threat. I later learned that this was because another faction in the Stalinist camp had attempted to turn the incident to its own advantage.

As soon as the two main CCP delegates to the Ninth Plenum of the Comintern's Executive Committee, Xiang Zhongfa and Li Zhenying, arrived in Moscow, they became involved in the struggle of the Chinese students. Xiang Zhongfa, a boatman from the Yangtze River, was head of the labour federation in the Wuhan area and had stood out as a workers' leader during the Revolution. He was an able and straightforward sort of person, but his weakness was that he was rather simple-minded. It was because he was a worker that he had been chosen as chief CCP delegate to the Comintern plenary session, as the predominance of intellectuals among the Party's leaders was then commonly regarded as the main cause of the defeat of the Revolution. Xiang had no personal relations with any members of the Moscow branch, whereas he did know a number of the KUTV students and had worked together with them in China. He therefore sided openly and unreservedly with the student rank and file as soon as he knew the situation. But this would not have sufficed to tip the balance our way. Our quick victory over the branch bureaucrats was due to the powerful forces behind Xiang.

The two main figures behind Xiang were Pavel Mif, the new head of Sun Yat-sen University who was later also to become head of the Eastern Department of the Comintern, and Wang Ming, a student leader at the same university and Mif's chief lieutenant. Mif's initial rise to fame was a result of his proficiency in Stalin-style 'Leninism'. It was this that first brought him to Stalin's attention. He was then made a lecturer at Sun Yat-sen University, where he taught a course in 'Problems of Leninism' (the title of a book by Stalin). Wang Ming was his favourite pupil. Before going to Moscow, Wang Ming had been a middle-school student in Wuhan. When Wang Ming arrived in Moscow he was not even a member of the Communist Youth League. A shrewd, ambitious man with a strong will, he was above all a master of flattery. Even in Radek's time as president of the university, Wang Ming had already sensed Mif's bright future, and deliberately played up to him by paying special attention to the 'Problems of Leninism' course. In the spring of 1927, the Comintern sent Mif on a mission to China, and he took Wang Ming with him as his interpreter. In Wuhan, Mif urged the Central Committee of the CCP to take on Wang as head of the Agit-Prop Department, but Chen Duxiu (then General Secretary of the Party) refused this and assigned him to a trainee post in the department instead. Wang Ming declined the job, and returned to Moscow with Mif. During the struggle against the Oppositionists at Sun Yat-sen University Mif and Wang Ming worked closely together and thereby cemented the alliance on which their clique was based. It was as a result of his role in this struggle that Mif gained promotion from lecturer to president of the university and leading Comintern official. Wang Ming's rise to power paralleled that of his teacher. He and his friends already-controlled the party committee at Sun Yat-sen University. Thus a new Moscow branch of the CCP came into being, to rival and eventually eclipse the 'survivors' of the KUTV branch.

News of our struggle against the KUTV 'survivors' rekindled the ambitions of the Mif/Wang Ming clique. Their aim was to gain complete control over all the Chinese students in Moscow as a spring-board for taking over the leadership of the CCP as a whole. A crucial first step was to detach the six or seven hundred Chinese students at KUTV from men like Shumiatsky, Maslov, and the 'survivors'. This is why, from the very first, they showed so much interest in our struggle. The arrival of Xiang Zhongfa and Li Zhenying in Moscow gave them the chance they were waiting for. They put forward a three-point proposal for bringing an end to the unrest at KUTV: 1) the 'survivors' should be sent back to China, where they could correct their mistakes by participating in the real struggle; 2) all the Chinese students at KUTV should be transferred to Sun Yat-sen University; 3) the military school (which had in fact just finished its scheduled six-month course) should be closed down and its students sent back to China, apart from a minority who should be transferred to Sun Yat-sen University, and an even smaller minority who should be sent to higher military academies for further training. These measures were pushed through quite easily, and we thought that we had emerged from the struggle as victors. But, before long, it became clear to us that the real victors were the Mif/Wang Ming clique. From then on, the education and training of Chinese Communists in Moscow was entirely in their hands.

After this initial victory, they proceeded to the second stage in their carefully prepared plan. When the other delegates returned to China after the meeting of the Comintern executive, they arranged for Xiang Zhongfa to stay behind in Moscow for further training, so that they could use him as a tool in the inner-party struggle. Six months later, at the Sixth Congress of the CCP in Moscow in June 1928, they succeeded in ousting Qu Qiubai from the leadership and made Xiang general secretary of the Party. In this way, they successfully laid the foundation for their subsequent influence in the Chinese Communist Party.

I was not neutral in the struggle I have just described, but neither was I particularly active. I did not like the 'survivors', mainly because of the way they behaved. They ingratiated themselves with their superiors and were arrogant towards ordinary students. As they themselves had never engaged in any serious study, they stopped others from doing so. The only thing they required of us was that we learn by heart the documents they handed round. I myself heartily despised them. But I could see no point in concentrating our efforts on struggling against the 'survivors' if this meant neglecting the much more central issues raised by the Russian Opposition.

I gradually became acquainted with the secret documents of the Trotskyists, and understood more clearly the problems at the heart of the Russian and Chinese Revolutions. On one occasion, I was selected to go on a delegation to see Yaroslavsky, chairman of the Central Control Commission of the CPSU. During the interview, one of my fellow delegates sought to win the Russians' support by explaining at great length that we had nothing to do with the Trotskyists, and boasting how active we had been in the anti-Trotskyist struggle at KUTV. I was nauseated by this display. After that, I became less active in the struggle against the 'survivors', and decided to devote my time instead to improving my Russian, studying the basic theories of Marxism, and reading Opposition documents that I obtained from one of my old friends, Fan Jinbiao, with whom I had worked together several years before in Hangzhou. We had met again a year later in Guangzhou, where he joined the Northern Expeditionary Army as a political commissar in a regiment of the Independent Division commanded by the left-wing Guomindang General Yan Zhong. After General Yan Zhong was stripped of his command by Chiang Kai-shek, Fan was also forced to quit the army, and shortly afterwards he returned to Taizhou county south of Hangzhou, where he spread revolutionary propaganda among the peasants and began to organise them. He arrived in Moscow a month after me, and was assigned to study at Sun Yat-sen University. There he established contact with those underground Oppositionists who had been lucky enough to survive the purge, and he therefore became a Trotskyist before I did.

The first opposition document that I read was Zinoviev's *Theses on the Chinese Revolution*. A little later I read Trotsky's *The Chinese Revolution and the Theses of Comrade Stalin*, and after that the *Platform of the United Opposition of the CPSU*. They had an enormous impact on me, because of their unassailable logic and also their superb style. They were a real contrast to the lifeless and insipid documents of the Central Committee. The arguments and warnings of the Opposition, especially those concerned with the Chinese Revolution, were so obviously true and had been so often confirmed in practice, that I could not help nodding vigorously in agreement as I eagerly pored over them. I was also deeply moved by Zinoviev's writings. When I read these documents it was as if the scales fell from my eyes. I now realised that on all fundamental questions the CCP leaders had been acting on orders from the Stalin faction; that the ill-conceived policies which had led to the defeat of the Chinese Revolution were far from being Chen Duxiu's mistakes; and that these mistakes had been warned against in advance, and could have been avoided. It was clear to me that on nearly all questions whether tactical or strategic concerning the Chinese Revolution, the Russian Opposition, and Trotsky in particular, had very different positions from those of the Stalinist Central Committee, and had given timely warnings about the consequences of the line Stalin was pursuing. It was only because of the stubborn refusal of the Stalin-Bukharin clique to acknowledge that the criticisms of the Opposition were correct that the leadership in China made so many disastrous mistakes, leading finally to the collapse of the Chinese Revolution.

I already knew something about the situation in Britain and the Soviet Union, and when I turned to the Oppositionist documents dealing with subjects such as the Anglo-Soviet Trade Union Committee and economic construction in the Soviet Union I again found myself in complete agreement with the criticisms raised.

From then on I became a 'Bolshevik-Leninist' (as the Oppositionists were called at that time). My ideological commitment soon became a practical one. This was towards the end of my second term at KUTV. By now, the struggle against the 'survivors' of the branch was over, and most of the Chinese students, myself among them, were about to be transferred to Sun Yat-sen University.

My Second Year in Moscow

In the summer of 1928 most of the students in Moscow were sent to the barracks for a month of military training. I and a few others were exempted on health grounds, and sent to a rest-house instead. We travelled there by train, and the journey took just over an hour. The rest-house was on a hill overlooking a river, and it commanded a splendid view. During my stay there, I came into contact for the first time with ordinary Russian working people, and got the chance to find out about the life of Russian peasants. I also made my first contact with the various factions which had formed among the students at Sun Yat-sen University, and which were later to influence the factional struggles within the CCP.

Among my companions at the rest-house were students from both KUTV and Sun Yat-sen University. Later, after their period of military training was over, we were joined by the other Chinese students from Moscow for the remainder of the summer holidays. It was a carefree life, with five meals a day and time for a nap after lunch. We spent our time swimming, rowing, playing volley-ball, going for outings in the woods, listening to music (there were improvised concerts most evenings of the week), and making friends with members of the opposite sex. To the casual observer, everything was happy and tranquil. But, beneath the surface, it was a hot-house of political activities.

Both in China and in the Soviet Union, the Communist movements were going through a difficult period and had reached important turning points. The Ninth Plenum of the Comintern Executive had met in the February of that year; in June and July, the CCP had held its Sixth Congress in Moscow; and, while we were staying in the rest-house, the Sixth Congress of the Comintern was in session. The two main items these three important meetings dealt with were the Chinese Revolution, and the Opposition within the CPSU. It was around these two questions that an important process of differentiation was taking place in the Chinese Party and in the International as a whole. At first, factional and even personal interests seemed to play a greater role than political considerations in shaping the alignment of forces among the Chinese students in Moscow.

I showed earlier how the Mif/Wang Ming group used events at KUTV to get the 'survivors' of the Moscow branch sent back to China, and thus to win complete control over the training of Chinese students in the Soviet Union. I also explained how this clique intended to make use of Xiang Zhongfa, chief delegate of the CCP to the Comintern Executive, in their bid for the leadership of the Party. This was quite a task, of course, and, in preparation for it, Wang Ming and his friends staged a dress-rehearsal at Sun Yat-sen University by starting up a campaign against what became known as the 'Jiangsu-Zhejiang Provincial Association'.

Many of the older generation of party members came from, or had connections with, one or other of the five central and southern provinces of Jiangsu, Zhejiang, Anhui, Hunan, and Guangdong. This was entirely natural, given that the Chinese Communist movement originated in these areas. It is an elementary principle of party life that Communists should never take into account regional loyalties or affiliations in their dealings with one another. But it was nonetheless inevitable that people who had been born in the same place or who had worked together in the same area would develop close personal ties. This is probably as true now as it was then, not only in China but also in Communist parties elsewhere in the world. To admit that this is so is not to deny that such a state of affairs is a symptom of extreme backwardness. But the only sure way of eliminating abuses of this sort is to educate party members thoroughly, and to make them politically more aware by plunging them into the fierce political struggles of the working class. Campaigns launched specifically against this sort of 'localism' are counterproductive, strengthening such relationships rather than weakening them. And this was precisely what happened when Wang Ming and his associates started up their campaign against the so-called 'Jiangsu-Zhejiang Provincial Association' in the summer of 1927.

When Sun Yat-sen University was set up in the winter of 1925, many of its students were teachers or students from the Shanghai College, an institution set up by the Party in Shanghai to meet the ever-growing demand for trained and educated cadres. They were for the most part natives of Jiangsu and Zhejiang provinces. There were also a number of worker Communists from factories in the Shanghai-Wuxi area of Jiangsu province. These facts explain how students from these two provinces made up the largest single regional grouping at the university. Among those from Shanghai were a number of fairly prominent intellectuals such as Dong Yixiang, Gu Guyi, and Yu Xiusong, and it was only natural that these men should play an important role in the party committee at the university during the first period. The name 'Jiangsu-Zhejiang Provincial Association', with its connotations of the regional clubhouses established by officials, merchants, and expatriates in general, was coined by a rival group of students, who aimed to seize power from Dong, Yu, and the others. Wang Ming and his group then used the name in their own attacks. But, in reality, there was no such 'Association', nor could there be. First, not all those accused of belonging came from Jiangsu or Zhejiang, although quite a few of Wang Ming's supporters did, among them Wang Ming's right-hand man Qin Bangxian, who was born in Wuxi, Jiangsu. Second, many interpreters like Zhang Wentian, Shen Zemin, Shen Zhiyuan, Wu Liping, and Zhu Tingzhang, accused of being members of the 'Association' because of where they were born, were in fact on very bad terms with Dong Yixiang, Gu Guyi, and other alleged leaders of the group.

By the time we were transferred to Sun Yat-sen University the attacks were over. The 'Anhui group' with Wang Ming, Wang Jiaxiang, and others as its leaders stood at the head of the party organisation there. But the ill-fated name of 'Provincial Association' was still hovering around like a spectre in search of a new victim. When I first heard people using the term, I had no idea what they were talking about. I found it impossible to understand why they spent so much effort on exorcising a devil which had never really existed. Later, I realised that the whole affair was part of a plot by the Wang Ming group to smear Qu Qiubai, Chen Duxiu's successor as the Party's general secretary, who was soon to be replaced by Xiang Zhongfa at the Sixth Congress of the CCP in Moscow. Wang Ming and his supporters used every opportunity to insinuate that Qu Qiubai, who came from Changzhou in Jiangsu province, was the real power behind this 'Association'.

The Sun Yat-sen University students I had met at the rest-house were among the main victims of the campaign against the 'Association'. My reason for getting in touch with them had nothing to do with the fact that I came from Zhejiang. It was rather because they were by that time out of power. In the eyes of the Wang Ming group, those of us who had studied at KUTV were alien and suspect elements anyway, and, since the 'Association' members had been driven out of power, they had nothing to lose by contacting us. Some of them were old friends of mine, and some were acquaintances. I was on very good terms with Dong Yixiang, who was a bitter enemy of Wang Ming's, and was eventually murdered by him in Xinjiang in 1937. Dong, a learned man with mild and patient manners, had lectured at the Party's Shanghai College before coming to Moscow, and was an old friend of Qu Qiubai. It was from him and his friends that I learned about the complicated relationships between the various student groups at Sun Yat-sen University.

I had disliked Wang Ming and his associates from the outset. I needed no encouragement from any fictitious 'Association' in my contempt for these mindless and arrogant young bureaucrats, who had never done a thing for the Chinese Revolution and who had only gained control of the party organisation at the university by toadying to their Comintern superiors. I based this judgement on something more than mere regional loyalty: I already had a political standpoint of my own. My first concern was therefore to enquire into the political differences that separated the 'Association' and Wang Ming's 'Anhui group'. To my disappointment, I discovered that the 'Association's' attitude towards the Opposition was at least as uncompromising as that of the 'Anhui group', if not more so. At first, I thought that this was to avoid laying themselves open to attack, but I soon found that I was mistaken. In private conversations, Dong Yixiang admitted to me that the Stalin-Bukharin leadership of the Comintern deserved some of the blame for the defeat of the Chinese Revolution, but he argued that, in the main, they had been right. He said that on most of the main questions, such as the entry of the CCP into the Guomindang and the attempt to create a new revolutionary centre in Wuhan after Chiang Kai-shek's betrayal, Stalin and Bukharin had been acting in accordance with Leninist principles. On the question of the nature of Chinese society, the 'Association' had some disagreements with the official view, and were inclined to accept the conclusion that capitalist relations predominated in China's economic life, but, at the same time, they were strictly opposed to calling for the dictatorship of the proletariat in China. They argued that the revolution in China would lead at most to the democratic dictatorship of the workers and peasants. In their assessment of the political situation in China at that time, they supported the resolutions passed at the Ninth Plenum of the International's Executive Committee even more unflinchingly than Wang Ming and his group.

I should explain at this point the controversies then raging on various questions relating to the Chinese Revolution. They were: the causes of the defeat of the Revolution and the lessons to be drawn from it; the political situation in China and the tactics that should be adopted by the CCP; and the character of the future revolution.

The Ninth Plenum of the Comintern's Executive Committee was held following the defeat of the Guangzhou insurrection. The Committee refused to acknowledge that the Chinese Revolution had been defeated. Instead, it put forward the well-known formula that the Revolution was passing through a short trough between two waves, and that a new rising wave was imminent. It therefore continued to uphold the policy of armed insurrection decided upon at the CCP's Emergency Party Conference of 7 August 1927.

The Sixth Congress of the CCP admitted the defeat of the Revolution, but failed to point out its real causes. The Congress heaped all the blame for the mistakes made during the Revolution on the shoulders of the 'opportunist' Chen Duxiu. Apart from this, the only other reason given for the defeat was that the imperialists had been too strong. They might just as well have said that the revolution in China was impossible as long as imperialist influence lasted. The Opposition's analysis, which located the real causes of the defeat in the wrong assessment of the role and character of the colonial bourgeoisie, the mistaken policy of CCP entry into the Guomindang, the failure to substitute a coalition with the peasantry and the urban poor for the coalition with 'petty bourgeois' politicians, and the failure to understand the role of soviets and the need to organise them, was deliberately distorted and denounced in the congress resolution, or else ignored. The Sixth Congress repeated the formulae laid down at the Ninth Plenum, although the word 'waves' was changed to 'tides'. Although the Congress formally condemned putschism, it still adopted a resolution endorsing a continuation of the policy of armed insurrection in China. While it argued the need for a democratic programme, it repudiated Trotsky's call for a national assembly. It therefore lacked a central political slogan with which to sum up and embrace all the other democratic demands. It predicted 'in accordance with Bolshevik tradition' that the coming revolution in China would be bourgeois-democratic in character, and that the revolutionary state would therefore be a 'democratic dictatorship of the workers and peasants', but it postponed the socialist revolution in China to the remote future.

The Russian Opposition had already expressed views on the events of 1925–7 in China. Its analysis of probable future developments there was to be found in the correspondence between Trotsky and his comrades in exile (particularly Preobrazhensky). All these views were repeated in a more precise and definitive way in Trotsky's *Critique of the Draft Programme of the Comintern*. Essentially, the Opposition's line was as follows: after the autumn of 1927 there could be no further doubt that the Chinese Revolution had been defeated; that the main cause of the defeat was the opportunist policy adopted by the Stalin-Bukharin faction; and that the Chinese Communists should now recognise the reality of the defeat and investigate its causes, in order to decide upon a correct course for the future. If they insisted on closing their eyes to what had happened and on dressing up the defeat as a 'development of the Revolution to a higher stage' they would lurch inevitably from opportunism into 'putschism', and thus prepare the way for an even worse defeat, squandering the forces of the revolution. Trotsky developed this line in his article 'The Problems of the

Chinese Revolution after the Sixth Congress', in which he called for the setting-up of a national assembly in China.

Trotsky's own assessment of the situation in China was summed up in the following passage:

> We are entering in China into a period of reflux, and consequently into a period in which the party deepens its theoretical roots, educates itself critically, creates and strengthens firm organizational links in all spheres of the working class movement, organizes rural nuclei, leads and unites partial, at first defensive and later offensive, battles of the workers and the peasant poor.

As for the contents and character of the coming revolution, he wrote:

> It is not excluded that the first stage of the coming third revolution may reproduce in a very abridged and modified form the stages which have already passed.... But this first stage will be sufficient only to give the Communist Party a chance to put forward and announce its 'April thesis', that is, its programme and tactics of the seizure of power.[1]

The position which the leaders of the 'Association' took up in this debate could be called 'centro-rightist'. In their view, the main responsibility for the defeat of the revolution belonged to Chen Duxiu, although Stalin and Bukharin shared some of the blame. As for the political situation in China, they too accused the Opposition of 'liquidationism' (as the Bolsheviks had done when the Mensheviks advocated exclusively legal activity after the failure of the 1905 Revolution in Russia), although they reluctantly admitted that the Chinese Revolution had indeed been defeated. As for the future of the revolution, they were more orthodoxly Leninist, in the peculiar sense that the word had by then acquired. They declared that there could be no question of establishing a dictatorship of the proletariat without first passing through a democratic dictatorship of the workers and peasants.

Since, by then, I had already accepted the analysis of the Opposition on these questions, I found myself in disagreement with the leaders of the 'Association' on these points. Through them, however, I did manage to get in touch with a group of Shanghai workers at the rest-house who had been under their influence. Among them was a former cotton-mill worker from Wuxi in Jiangsu prov-

---

1 Trotsky 1976 [1927].

ince called An Fu. He was the best-read and politically the most advanced of the group, and was already an Oppositionist or semi-Oppositionist. Since they were close to Dong Yixiang and his friends, An Fu and the other workers were regarded by the Wang Ming factions as the rank and file of the 'Association'. During the factional struggle at Sun Yat-sen University, An Fu and the others had taken the side of the 'Association' and were therefore plunged into a deep depression after its defeat. The more simple-minded among them even went so far as to believe that since the Party was now dominated by such a mean and worthless man as Wang Ming, there was no longer any hope for the revolution in China. But after a period of frustration and disappointment, the more far-sighted among them realised that the factional struggle at the university had to be seen in terms of the titanic struggle which was going on within both the CPSU and the Communist International as a whole, between the two camps of Stalinism and Trotskyism. Their struggle ended up in the same way as ours at KUTV, but with one difference: whereas we had turned to the Russian Opposition after prevailing over our opponents, they had done so after suffering defeat on their campus.

In the winter of 1927 more than ten well-known Oppositionists, among them Ou Fang, had been expelled from the Party and sent back to China. Two of those expelled, however, Chen Qi and Wen Yue, were not allowed to leave the Soviet Union. Isolated from the rest of the students, they were kept behind on the campus, awaiting further punishment. No one dared to approach them, and they made no attempt to speak to their fellow-students. They just sat in the library all day reading, contemptuously ignored by the 'loyal elements' (that is, the Stalinists of the Wang Ming group). They were regarded with curiosity by the uncommitted majority as museum specimens of the species 'Trotskyist'. While I was at KUTV and before I had any relations with the underground Trotskyist organisation, this is precisely how the two men had struck me during my occasional visits to Sun Yat-sen University. They seemed set apart from the others, so that I gained the impression that apart from them there were no other Trotskyists among the Chinese students, or that if there were, they had been eliminated. In fact, there were still quite a few secret Oppositionists among the teachers and the students at that time, and it was precisely these secret Oppositionists who won An Fu and others over to Trotskyism during the period leading up to the summer vacation of 1928. My old friend Fan Jinbiao also came under the influence of this group.

During the latter half of our stay in the rest-house, we went through a period of extremely strenuous political thinking and activity. After we had been there just over a month, we were joined by An Fu and his friends, who had by then completed their spell of military training. They brought with them to the rest-house tiny notebooks in which they had copied out the main Oppositionist documents, covering page after page with thousands of tiny Chinese characters. These notebooks were surreptitiously passed from hand to hand, and very soon they had influenced considerable numbers of Chinese students, especially those from KUTV, of whom there were over a hundred at the rest-house. A much greater number had been sent either back to China or on to higher military academies in Moscow and Leningrad at the end of the first school year. Most of the ex-KUTV students in the rest-house were incapable of putting up the slightest resistance to the ideological onslaught of the Opposition.

Within the ranks of the CPSU itself, a completely different mood prevailed. It was six months since the 'liquidation' of the Russian Opposition, when all Oppositionists had been driven out of the Party and some had been exiled or imprisoned under Article 58 of the criminal code. To make things worse, Zinoviev and Kamenev, two prominent leaders of the United Opposition, had capitulated and renounced their views. A wave of capitulations followed. Every day *Pravda* was full of humiliating statements by former members of the Opposition, which was to all appearances in a state of demoralisation and disintegration. But here were we Chinese Communists, stealthily and enthusiastically devouring these condemned and forbidden documents and turning *en masse* to the Opposition! On the surface, this seemed like a paradox. It certainly made a startling contrast with our frame of mind just after we had arrived in Moscow a year before. We were not really Stalinists then, but, because of our ill-informed prejudices about the two factions in the CPSU, we had supported Stalin in his struggle against Trotsky. During the discussions leading up to the Fifteenth Congress of the Russian Party some of us had doubted the correctness of the Comintern's policy in China, but few of us had thought the subject through to the end, or examined the arguments of the Opposition that emerged in fragmentary or distorted forms from the official party documents. Most of us had believed that to do so would be disloyal to the Party and therefore to the revolution. It had been drummed into us from the very beginning that any form of opposition or factional activity was harmful to the Party and the revolution, if not downright counter-revolutionary. Without thinking, therefore, we had regarded the Opposition as something poisonous and threatening, to be avoided at all costs. During the factional struggle at KUTV, both sides had refrained from smearing each other as 'Oppositionists', and both had been careful not to lay themselves open to such a charge, going out of their way to support the attacks on Trotsky. It was not that our support for Stalin had been insincere. In voting unanimously in favour of Stalin, we had been acting out of misconceived loyalty to the movement rather than from calculated obsequiousness to the leadership.

By the late summer of 1928, our attitude towards the defeated and 'liquidated' Opposition had changed. For those Chinese Communists at the rest-house, emotional embrace preceded ideological acceptance. The Opposition no longer seemed poisonous or untouchable to us. There was an almost holy aura about it, wronged and persecuted as it clearly was, and it quickly gained our sympathy and admiration. Our view of loyalty and disloyalty to the Party was now quite the opposite of what it had been. At first I thought that this change was simply due to disillusion as a result of the factional struggles at the two universities, but there was more to it than that. The main reason most of the Chinese students in Moscow began to go over to the Opposition after the spring of 1928 was, as I soon realised, because the events of the last six months in China and the Soviet Union had confirmed the analysis of the Opposition with surprising speed. In China the Autumn Harvest uprising and the Guangzhou insurrection in late 1927 demonstrated at terrible cost the failure of Stalin's policies. In the Soviet Union, the fallacies of the Stalinists were just as mercilessly exposed. We had been repeatedly told that the Opposition was stirring up trouble amongst the Russian peasantry. We were also told that (thanks to the purging of the Opposition) the peasants had been mollified. In reality, the opposite was true. The bread we ate was more and more often coarse and black. Emergency measures were introduced to ration food, and fruit had virtually disappeared from the market. After Trotsky's downfall, the kulaks went onto the offensive, forcing Stalin to launch a disorderly counter-attack of his own. It became obvious that the Opposition's warnings had been well-grounded. I learned later that during 1928, despite the wave of recantations by well-known Oppositionists, even larger numbers of rank-and-file members, especially young workers, joined or supported the underground-organisations of the Opposition.

As autumn advanced the new term began, and all the Chinese students returned from the rest-house to Sun Yat-sen University. By this time one could say without exaggeration that nine-tenths of the former KUTV students had been won over to Trotskyism. An organisation to unite them was urgently needed. One Sunday in late September or early October, a dozen or so of us travelled out of Moscow by tram in groups of two or three to have a picnic. We found somewhere quiet, and there we ate, laughed, and sang. As soon as there were no Russian holiday-makers within earshot, we got down to more serious business. We discussed and finally settled the problem of how to organise so many Trotskyists. Three of us – Fan Jinbiao, An Fu, and myself – were chosen from this conference of activists to form a leadership committee.

All this happened long ago, and I cannot remember all those who were present at this meeting. Luo Han had already returned to China. One comrade whose presence I particularly recall was Ji Dacai, a memorable man of outstanding character. During the Revolution, Ji Dacai was chairman of the Federation of Labour in Zhejiang province. He was a tough-looking individual, and his courage and loyalty to the movement had won him enormous respect from the Hangzhou workers. While he was in Moscow, he showed himself to be a good student, and made rapid progress in studying Marxist and Leninist theory. Another comrade at the meeting who made a big impression on me was a worker called Bian Fulin. He was a reticent man who seldom spoke his mind, but, when he did so, he spoke well and to the point. They were both later arrested and probably died in Stalin's prisons.

After the establishment of our three-man committee, the influence of the Opposition among the Chinese students in Moscow grew. The existence of our organisation was almost an open secret among ex-KUTV students. Oppositionist documents were openly discussed, even in the presence of students who had not yet become members of the organisation. It was at this time that we got hold of a mimeographed copy of Trotsky's *Critique of the Draft Programme of the Comintern* that had been widely but secretly circulated among Russian Communists. Since most Chinese students were unable to read Russian, I was assigned to translate the document into Chinese. I began to do this in the KUTV library, where there were no longer any Chinese students and where none of the other foreign students read Chinese. I hid the document in a big volume of *Capital* and translated it while pretending to take notes from Marx. At first, I ran no risk of being discovered. It was unlikely that any of the students of the other nationalities would suspect me, since most of them knew who I was. I explained to the librarian at KUTV, a very kind old lady, that I had decided to come back to my old college to do my reading because I enjoyed the quietness of her room. She welcomed me warmly. In this way, I managed to get most of the translation done. But then Professor Chen Hansheng, who had once taught modern history at Beijing University, also started to frequent the library, so I was forced to stop going there for fear of detection.

The link man between us and the Russian Trotskyists was a young man called Poliakov, who had lectured at Sun Yat-sen University when Radek was principal. During the struggle against the Opposition, he had been expelled from the Party and dismissed from his job. Now he was a shop-floor worker in a Moscow factory. When he heard that I could find nowhere safe to work on my translation, he invited me to use his home, a small room in an old-fashioned apartment block not far from the KUTV library. He had been married for about a year to a young woman who was still a student at Moscow University. The first day I arrived there, Mrs Poliakov was preparing a bottle for their baby, a little girl a few months old. She welcomed me warmly, and told me that my visit was very opportune, since she needed a baby-sitter that day. The baby was a beautiful child, lying asleep in her cot. 'If she cries when she wakes up', my young hostess said to me, 'give her this bottle. She's a very good little girl, I don't expect she'll give you any trouble'. She gave me a cup of tea and a sandwich and left the flat with her husband, locking the door as she went. I then got down to work, pausing every now and then to feed the baby or change its nappy. I stayed there until the young woman returned home towards evening. This routine continued for nearly a fortnight until one morning, just as I was leaving college on my way to Poliakov's flat, I heard a voice calling out my name. I turned round to see a woman standing with her head and shoulders wrapped in a shawl, so that I did not recognise her at first. It was only when I walked up to her that I realised it was Mrs Poliakov. She did not respond when I made to shake her hand, but beckoned me to follow her along the street. She was not her usual self: no joyous smile, no mischievous expression. Her eyes showed that she had been crying bitterly, and her face was pale with grief. We stopped at a corner of the street, where she told me that Poliakov had been arrested after leading a strike at his factory, and that she could no longer go back to university. She had no idea what to do next. Her only immediate plan was to return with the baby and her mother to her home-town on the Volga. After that we both fell silent. I could think of nothing to say that would comfort her. Finally she handed me a book which I had left at her home: a volume of Lenin's *Collected Works* with my name on it in Chinese. 'You're lucky', she told me, 'the GPU men didn't see it. Otherwise you might have been involved as well'. I was grateful beyond words for her consideration. She dared not stay too long, so she shook hands with me, pulled her shawl back over her head again, and walked off, after we had wished each other good luck. This was the first time I had witnessed the persecution of a family of revolutionaries by the Stalinist secret police, and, to this day, I can clearly recall every detail of the scene. Since then, I have heard nothing more of the fate of those women of three generations. I hope that they really did have the good luck that I wished them.

Poliakov was not the only one to be arrested. Along with him the entire underground committee of the Moscow Opposition, of which he was a member, had been rounded up by the GPU. Subsequently, even more people were implicated and taken off to prison. The fact that nothing happened to us Chinese Trotskyists shows that not a single one of those arrested betrayed our activities to the GPU.

Once again, I was without a place to work, and at a time when the demand for Chinese translations of Oppositionist literature was very great. The exiled leaders of the Opposition were at that time scattered all over the Asian part of the Soviet Union, from Central Asia and Siberia to the Caspian Sea. It was almost as if the clock had been turned back to the old Tsarist days. Here were these veteran revolutionaries, engaged in intense theoretical activity or political analysis of the world situation from a small town along the north-western border of China, a shabby hotel in Siberia or a ramshackle log-cabin in the ice-sealed tundra. Stalin did not yet dare to prevent them from putting their views in writing and circulating them among themselves. First among the questions they discussed was the Chinese Revolution. The second was the Soviet economy, and the beginnings of a Stalinist 'left turn' in economic policy. In these two discussions, there were sharp divergences among the leaders of the Opposition, with Trotsky and Rakovsky on one side and Radek and Preobrazhensky, who were later to capitulate to Stalin, on the other. The letters and articles which this debate produced were typed out in pamphlet form by underground Oppositionist groups and widely circulated among the masses. We also got hold of some of these publications, and naturally wanted to translate them into our own language. Again, the problem was to find a safe place to work in. Since we were foreigners, our only links in Russia were with the Party, so that it was impossible for us to find a room outside the university.

Much to our surprise, we did find a place, and a very good one at that, before long. But, before telling that story, I want to mention some other developments which took place during that period.

After the Sixth Congress of the CCP had taken place in Moscow in 1928, a few of the delegates stayed on for the Sixth Congress of the Comintern. Among them were Qu Qiubai, Zhou Enlai, Zhang Guotao, Wang Ruofei, Guan Xiangying, and Luo Zhanglong. Qu Qiubai had been stripped of the General Secretaryship of the Party at the Sixth Congress, and replaced, just as the Stalin/Mif/Wang Ming group had wanted, by the worker Communist Xiang Zhongfa. At the Sixth Congress of the Comintern, however, Qu continued to act as chief spokesman for the CCP delegation, because of his proficiency in Russian and his relatively good grasp of Marxism. Officially, Wang Ming's role at the Congress was that of interpreter, but, in actual fact, he and Mif began to play an important part in the Chinese delegation. They continued to edge Qu Qiubai further away from the levers of power in the Party, and this angered and upset some of the other delegates. Having brought Xiang Zhongfa into their orbit, Mif and Wang Ming set out to work on Zhou Enlai. Since he was a brilliant organiser and administrator, they wanted to win him over to accept their political and ideological leadership. Zhou was the member of the delegation most active among the Chinese students, and he received a particularly warm welcome from the party committee of the university, in other words the Wang Ming/Mif group. Qu Qiubai and Zhang Guotao were also invited to address us. But the manner in which the three meetings were arranged was very different. Qu Qiubai's reception was much cooler than Zhou Enlai's, and colder still was the reception given to Zhang Guotao.

Although Trotsky had submitted his *Critique of the Draft Programme of the Comintern* to its Sixth Congress, the presidium had decided that it should not be published or circulated. It was probably only after considerable pressure from some delegates that they decided to allow a few leading members of each delegation to see it, on condition that the document was returned after reading. But despite these restrictions, Trotsky's *Critique* had an important influence on the delegates. Nearly all those who read it were deeply impressed. Some of the delegations, for example the Americans and the Canadians, agreed with it immediately, smuggled a copy out of Russia and decided to struggle for its aims thenceforth.

As the member of the Chinese delegation who knew Russian, Qu Qiubai could read the document from beginning to end. The other delegates could only acquaint themselves with Trotsky's analysis at second-hand through a few quotations, mostly wrenched out of context, which Wang Ming and his friends had translated into Chinese.

I did not know Qu Qiubai personally, nor did I have a chance to talk with him at that time. According to a friend of mine who was close to him, Qu's first reaction to Trotsky's *Critique* was not entirely negative, and he said that some of the points it raised were worth considering. But when he spoke at the Congress itself, he sounded like a die-hard anti-Trotskyist, whole-heartedly supporting the official line of the Stalin-Bukharin leadership. Was Qu being true to himself in making such a speech? My answer is both yes and no. Although Qu is recorded in the history of the CCP as its leader in the period of armed putsches, he was both physically and spiritually a weak man. As was shown by his behaviour in later years, when he came under attack from his opponents in the Party, he succumbed to pressure relatively easily. It seems to me that this was why he sided with Stalin and Bukharin at the Congress, even though he might earlier have sympathised with some of Trotsky's positions. At the same time, however, the fact that he came out and denounced the Russian Opposition was not at all out of keeping with his beliefs, since, on the question of the bourgeois-democratic revolution, Qu Qiubai was a Leninist of the pre-1917 vintage. Trotsky's ideas seemed to him to contradict what Lenin had written. In this respect, one could call him a Chinese Communist of the Russian 'Old Bolshevik' type. It is true that he had made a fairly systematic study of

Lenin's works, but, like most Russian 'Old Bolsheviks', he failed to notice the change that had taken place in Lenin's thinking during and after the revolution of 1917. In my view this is the first reason why Qu openly came out in support of a policy which had actually betrayed the Chinese Revolution. The second reason for his attitude was probably the fact that he had been influenced by the campaign Stalin and Zinoviev had been carrying on ever since 1923: a campaign which falsified Trotsky's ideas and misrepresented them as the absolute antithesis of Leninism.

But, despite all this, Qu Qiubai's Stalinism was not entirely to Stalin's liking. Qu was a thinker, and he took up Stalin's policies in his own way and expressed them in his own words. He therefore became a target for personal attacks, and Mif and Wang Ming branded him a 'semi-Trotskyist'. In later years, Qu was very badly treated by the Party, and all those who had had links with him were cruelly persecuted. His younger brother Qu Jingbai was driven mad while still in Moscow, and died there.

Zhou Enlai was a man who had never shown any interest in revolutionary theory, but distinguished himself instead by his practical ability, his great energy, his shrewdness, his good looks (at this time he sported a long beard), and his eloquence. There is no denying that Zhou was a revolutionary of sorts, but, in the course of the ideological and political struggles that continuously rocked the inner life of the Party, he was never once to be found on the losing side, upholding some remote and lofty ideal. That would have been completely out of keeping with his character. He was strong and wanted to be so, and in disputes he therefore invariably sided with the strongest party. He was born to be a kingmaker, rather than a king. Every aspiring leader in the Party always wanted to win over Zhou and make use of his talents as an administrator. In the long history of intra-party struggles in the Chinese Revolution, the fact that Zhou emerged so often on the winning side earned him the nickname of *budaoweng* ('the old man who never falls down' – the name of a traditional Chinese toy). By comparison with Zhou Enlai, Wang Ming was a mere dwarf. There was only one area where Wang Ming clearly excelled: in the tenacity with which he strove after the top place in the Party. He would stop at nothing to achieve his aim, and considered any tactics legitimate, however damaging to the revolution and however shameful.

The 1928 attempt to raise Zhou Enlai's status at the expense of Qu Qiubai was largely the work of Wang Ming. Considering his low status in the Party, it might seem that Wang still had a very long way to go before reaching his goal. But, given his close links with the ruling group in the CPSU, he had every reason to make such preparations. In Wang Ming's timetable, the substitution of Xiang Zhongfa for Qu Qiubai was simply one step on the path towards the final seizure of power in the Party. Paying court to Zhou Enlai was simply the modern equivalent of the second-century would-be emperor Liu Bei paying court to the brilliant administrator Zhuge Liang. Zhou Enlai was naturally pleased by the attentions being paid to him. He could not but have a poor opinion of Wang Ming, but he was full of admiration for Stalin, Mif, and others, whose faction had won control of the CPSU and the Comintern. Under such circumstances, it was out of the question that Zhou would consider seriously the theoretical and political arguments of the Russian Opposition.

Zhang Guotao, who lacked Qu Qiubai's learning and Zhou Enlai's talents, inspired not the slightest fear in Wang Ming and his friends, who made no attempt to court him, but ignored and even despised him. Zhang was therefore the most lonely man in the Chinese delegation. I remember I once had a conversation with him in the room of an interpreter called Shi Yisheng. Since Shi and I were the only others present, Zhang, who was usually a very reticent man, dropped his guard a little and began to talk more freely. He complained of the frustration he felt in Moscow. He told us: 'Lenin once said that people who cannot read stand outside politics. In Moscow, people who cannot read Russian stand outside politics'. The implication of his remark was obvious. I realised at once that he was dissatisfied with the red compradors like Wang Ming. Shi responded to Zhang's remark with an embarrassed smile, and I too smiled and said nothing. Zhang seemed to sense that he had gone too far, so he suddenly changed the subject and began instead to talk about the one-eyed general Liu Bocheng, who was at that time attending a military academy in Moscow, and the delicious Sichuanese food that Liu could cook. Knowing that Zhang Guotao was out of favour and dissatisfied with the faction in power, one Chinese comrade had tried to win him over to the Opposition. But it turned out that Zhang was at least as unwilling as Zhou Enlai to side with 'the truth in defeat'.

Some of the Chinese delegates, however, were sincerely interested in finding out about the view of the Russian Opposition. Among them were Wang Ruofei, Guan Xiangying, and Luo Zhanglong. They came to the views of the Opposition without prejudice, and where they did not accept them were at least prepared to give them consideration. We gave all of them documents, which they read carefully and responded to rather favourably.

I have already described our difficulties in finding somewhere for me to do my translations after Poliakov's arrest. For about a fortnight after that I had found it impossible to do any work whatsoever. We searched high and low for a new place, and asked everyone we knew in Moscow. Then we were unexpectedly offered Wang Ruofei's room in the smart Europa Hotel. After he had read the Oppositionist writings on the Chinese Revolution, Wang Ruofei had been deeply impressed. His own experiences in China confirmed the truth of the

Oppositionist arguments. On other issues in the dispute – economic construction in the Soviet Union, problems of the British and German revolutions and so forth – Wang was more doubtful: because of his lack of theoretical training and his ignorance of world politics he found it impossible to say which side of the argument was right. On the current situation in China he did not accept completely the resolutions of the CCP Sixth Congress; but he did not agree with the criticisms Trotsky raised of the 'democratic dictatorship' slogan for China either. He had not formed any opinion of his own on the perspectives of the Chinese Revolution. Such was Wang Ruofei's position at that time, and it is therefore not surprising that he took a sympathetic attitude towards us. As soon as he heard of my problem, he made his room available to me during the day, while he was away at the office of the Comintern's Eastern Department. I would arrive at his room at about nine o'clock every morning, and he would leave shortly afterwards. I used to take a few slices of bread with me, so that I could work uninterruptedly until he returned in the afternoon. I worked in Wang Ruofei's room for several days, just long enough to complete my translation of that part of the *Critique* which dealt with the Chinese Revolution. Wang Ruofei was running something of a risk in helping us in this way, since his wife, Li Peize, a student at Sun Yat-sen University, was well known to be a staunch supporter of the Wang Ming group. Naturally, Wang Ruofei was well aware of his wife's political leanings, and was careful never to reveal his sympathies to her.

Wang Ruofei died for the CCP in 1946, killed in an air-crash while flying back from Chongqing to Yan'an (others killed in the crash included General Ye Ting and Bo Gu). I have decided to reveal this secret episode in Wang Ruofei's life for two main reasons: first, he is dead anyway, and no harm can come to him for his 'error'; and second, the fact that he committed such an 'error' shows to my mind that he was not a time-server, but a revolutionary of character and integrity.

Wang Ruofei and the other two delegates who had expressed sympathy for the Opposition (Guan Xiangying and Luo Zhanglong) returned to China one after the other. Once they plunged back into party work, they lost all interest in the 'unpractical' disputes on theoretical principles which had disturbed their thinking for a while. They reverted once again to the 'blind activities [*weigan zhuyi*]' at which they so excelled. They linked up with what was left of the party apparatus after the defeats that had been suffered and threw themselves back into the struggle. Through hard work and effort, they finally worked their way to the top of the party hierarchy, and after that they never again re-established contact with the Chinese Trotskyist movement. Luo Zhanglong's political evolution was rather different from that of Wang and Guan; he became the leader of a new faction in the Party, the so-called 'conciliationist' faction, as Wang Ming called those who opposed Li Lisan without whole-heartedly supporting himself. This grouping had no differences of principle with the ruling Stalinist faction, but, in the recalcitrance they displayed towards the Wang Ming clique, one could just catch a glimmer of the influences which their leader, Luo Zhanglong, had been exposed to in Moscow. Wang Ming and his friends attacked the 'conciliationists' in the most unscrupulous and treacherous way. Finally, Chiang Kai-shek intervened to assure Wang Ming of victory in the struggle by arresting and executing all of the 'conciliationists' with the sole exception of Luo Zhanglong. Even after his narrow escape, Luo refused to draw any lessons from his experience. He made no attempt to find a way to Trotskyism. Instead, utterly demoralised and disillusioned he opted for 'conciliation' with the Guomindang.

In the winter of 1928, the Opposition rapidly expanded its organisation among the Chinese students in Moscow. We had comrades everywhere: in the Lenin Institute, in the various military academies, and, in particular, at Sun Yat-sen University, where out of a total of four hundred students about one hundred and fifty were Trotskyists, either as members or as close sympathisers of the organisation. By then copies of Trotsky's famous article 'Problems of the Chinese Revolution after the Sixth Congress' had already arrived in Moscow, provoking a heated debate, particularly among us Chinese students. Trotsky's arguments did not win unanimous or immediate support. We were particularly reluctant to accept his central slogan, the call for a constituent, or national, assembly (to which I shall return shortly). We were mere novices in revolutionary theory at that time, and we knew even less about revolutionary strategy and tactics and the need to apply them flexibly and in accordance with changing circumstances. What little theory we had been taught at university was abstract and schematic, and our grounding in the history of Bolshevism was extremely shallow. Moreover, the fact that we had just left behind a defeated revolution meant that we were embittered and enraged, and as such unconditional 'leftists', whether or not we were aware of being so. We were ready to accept any slogan or position which appeared to be leftist, 'pure socialist', or tending towards direct action. By the same token, we found it very difficult to accept any tactic which could in any way be interpreted as 'rightist', moderate, or 'bourgeois' in character. Up to then, we had considered Trotsky's positions consistently 'left', but, on reading his article, and in particular the section on the constituent assembly slogan, it seemed to us young fanatics as if he had suddenly leapt to the right of Stalin.

At the Sixth Congress of the CCP, the call for establishing soviets in China was rejected as a slogan for direct action, but retained as a propaganda slogan to be acted upon when the next 'revolutionary wave' drew near. Thus, the Sixth Congress left the CCP without a central political slogan, although nominally the call for soviets continued to play that role. This disastrous decision had come about because Stalin and Bukharin had failed to understand the new situation that had emerged in China after the defeat of the revolution. The result was that the CCP pursued counter-productive putschist policies for a number of years afterwards.

It was not until years later, particularly after the Xi'an Incident of December 1936, that I realised just how profound and far-sighted Trotsky's thinking on this question had been. If Trotsky's views on the Chinese Revolution were, without exception, the embodiment of his political genius, then his decision to put forward the slogan of the constituent assembly in the autumn of 1928 was his boldest and most flexible policy stroke ever, if, at the same time, the most difficult for his followers to grasp. I sometimes thought that, if the CCP had accepted this policy at that time, that is to say if they had adopted the slogan of a constituent assembly and fought for it as Trotsky proposed, instead of waiting for seven years until 1935 before coupling the slogan with offers of a shameful capitulation to the Chiang Kai-shek régime, then the lives of many tens of thousands of revolutionaries would have been spared, Chiang Kai-shek's reactionary rule would have ended much sooner than it did, the Japanese militarists would perhaps not have acted so recklessly, and the situation in China and Asia as a whole in the next two or three decades would have been quite different.

At the time, however, not only Stalinists but even those of us who accepted Trotsky's positions on every other fundamental question thought that he had made a grave mistake in putting forward such an 'opportunist' slogan. Among the Trotskyists in Moscow, there was none who did not recognise that the counter-revolution had triumphed in China, and that its reign would last for some time.

However, none of us had gone on to ask what tactics we should adopt in our revolutionary work. We realised that, in such a situation, it was wrong to call for direct armed insurrection under the banner of soviets. Stalin and Qu Qiubai knew it too, which was why they decided to withdraw it for the time being as a slogan for immediate action. But what slogan should we use? What slogan covered all the features of the new situation in which the counter-revolution had triumphed, in which all the democratic tasks remained unresolved, and yet in which the revolutionary forces, despite their severe defeat, had somehow managed to survive? We Trotskyists were just as incapable as Stalin and

Qu Qiubai of providing an answer to this question. It was Trotsky who came up with the correct formula: a revolutionary-democratic programme, with the call for a constituent assembly as its central slogan. This was, of course, precisely what was needed to meet the circumstances, but Stalin, Qu Qiubai, and others rejected it as a 'liquidationist' or 'Social-Democratic' deviation. Cowed by these attacks and influenced by our own immature prejudices, we dared not accept the slogan. We Chinese Trotskyists were so puzzled by it that we continued to argue and quarrel heatedly over it even after our return to China.

The first to accept this slogan was the veteran Communist Liu Renjing. However, his interpretation of it astonished us all: he pointed to the stability of the Chinese bourgeoisie, and argued that China could only develop politically through parliamentarianism. A new revolution would break out only after such a development, and its problems would be solved only 'at a higher historical stage'.

In the eyes of most Chinese Trotskyists, Liu was advocating the abandonment of the revolution. A few of our sympathisers were frightened away by Liu's ultra-rightist interpretation of Trotsky's policy. After long discussions, the majority of us accepted Trotsky's slogan, but we understood it to mean that our chief aim in a democratic struggle for a constituent assembly would be to re-establish contact with the masses during a period of counter-revolution, to rally the revolutionary forces against the military dictatorship, and to prepare the way for a new revolutionary upsurge. This interpretation, despite its imperfections, was leftist in orientation and was, in our opinion, much closer to the spirit of the slogan than that of Liu.

In this way, the ideological confusion caused by the constituent assembly slogan was finally dispelled, and the organisation of the Opposition among the Chinese students in Moscow continued to grow. New names were added daily to our list of sympathisers. Despite its ambition of seizing the leadership of the whole of the Chinese Party, Wang Ming's university party committee neither led an ideological life of its own, nor allowed the students to lead theirs. It merely frittered away its time in trivialities. To take just one example: a girl student called Zhu was cruelly rebuked and tormented for several nights in succession before a general meeting of all the students of the university just because she had fallen in love with two men at the same time. The overwhelming majority of the students found this sort of 'party work' nauseating. Not surprisingly, the more serious minded among them turned towards the Opposition. We managed to keep our organisation secret, and the existence of our three-man committee was known only to a very few people. Nevertheless, nearly everyone was aware of the functioning of the Opposition, and Oppositionist documents were easily obtainable. Of the ex-KUTV students, only a handful stayed outside the orbit of the Opposition: most of them either joined us, or sympathised with our aims. As far as I remember, only two were worthless enough to turn towards the Wang Ming clique. One of these was nicknamed 'Old Widow' [*lao guafu*], a pun on his adopted Russian name of Logov. 'Old Widow' was a native of Shaanxi province, and a former political commissar with General Feng Yuxiang's army. He was now playing the part of double agent between us and the Wang Ming clique. It was he who a year or so later betrayed the whole of our Moscow organisation to the GPU.

By the end of 1928, the Stalinist party committee at the university became more and more aware of a growing silent opposition to its rule on the campus. They took many measures to stave off the threat from the Oppositionist forces. First, they organised 'shock troops' to beat up suspected Oppositionists and intimidate 'undesirable elements'. This policy was carried out under the pretext of 'selecting and cultivating worker comrades', by grouping together strong but dull-witted worker comrades as 'party activists'. Some of these comrades were natives of Shandong province who had been sent to work in France during the First World War and who had stayed on there after the Armistice, where they had been recruited by the CCP branch in Paris. Their main contribution to party work in France was to defend the organisation against attacks from thugs hired by the Chinese Nationalists. As comrades, they were sincere enough, but they unfortunately completely lacked understanding. They believed in communism and the Party, and were willing to support anything that was done in the name of the Party and anyone who sat in the party committee offices. In their eyes, especially after they had been 'educated' by Wang Ming and his friends, anyone who had differences with the committee was as much an enemy as the Nationalists had been, to be dealt with in the same way. Apart from these men, Wang Ming's 'shock troops' also included a small number of workers from Shanghai, the two best-known of which were Li Jianru and Wang Yuncheng. The 'shock troops' also served as Wang Ming's bodyguards. Wherever he went, his crack unit went with him. However, this display of force only made the Wang Ming clique even more abhorrent to the rank-and-file student body and helped the growth of the Opposition.

The second main measure used against those suspected of belonging to the Opposition was the so-called 'transference of party membership'. The aim of this manoeuvre was to purge Oppositionists from the Party without resorting to formal expulsion. In accordance with the principle of internationalism, members of one section of the world Communist movement automatically became members of another section when they passed from one country to another. In this way, CCP members studying in the Soviet Union for any length of time had till now been automatically considered to be members of the

CPSU, and, so far, no one had thought of questioning the procedure. All of a sudden, Wang Ming and his friends discovered that this was wrong, since, in their view, membership of the CCP could not be put on a par with membership of the CPSU. They argued that a Chinese Communist in Moscow had fewer rights than a Russian Communist, and if he wanted to live, study, and work in Russia as a Communist, he should have to apply to the CPSU for membership and be subjected to a careful examination. This process was called 'transference of party membership'. General meetings of the whole student body were convened, at which those students who had applied for transfer were called to the platform and asked to give a report on their own background and personal history. They were then subjected to criticism from the 'masses' (that is, the party committee), and were made to answer questions. If the 'masses' were satisfied with an applicant's report and with his answers to the questions and criticisms raised, his application for transfer was granted and he was thereafter regarded as a 'first-class party member'. But, if doubts were raised, his application was most unlikely to be accepted. In such cases, some of the unsuccessful applicants were allowed to retain their 'second-class' membership (that is, of the CCP), but others were stripped even of that. Needless to say, this was precisely why the 'transfer meetings' were held. However, the fact that Wang Ming and his friends were prepared to admit openly that the CPSU enjoyed a higher status than our own party clearly exposed their servility. It also showed how evil-intentioned they were, driving people into hell under the pretext of sending them on to heaven. They held several general meetings of this sort, and each one provoked more and more people to anger. Finally, we decided to boycott such sessions and to refrain from applying for transfer. Nine out of ten students supported this boycott, and the party committee was forced to abandon the transfer ceremony.

The frustration of this plot did not mean of course that Wang Ming and his friends gave up persecuting and oppressing their opponents on the campus. On the contrary, they continued to do so with redoubled efforts after the spring of 1929, but the methods that they adopted were no longer the same.

I mentioned earlier that by this time the influence of the Opposition in the Soviet Union was growing rapidly. As a result of the deepening crisis in the country, Stalin was forced to adopt some of the ideas of the Left Opposition, and to break with his right-wing Bukharinite allies. Trotsky's warnings against the danger from the Right, denounced as 'slanders against the Party' just a year ago, were suddenly 'confirmed'. These were now taken up by Stalin himself, who urged all party members to be ready to fight against a threat the existence of which he had denied right up to that very moment. Trotsky's prestige was therefore restored with surprising speed. The Russian people were more ready than ever to listen to what the Opposition had to say, and Trotsky's secretly circulated articles were in great demand. A similar shift of mood and sympathy also took place among the Chinese students in Moscow. Those who, a year ago, had half-heartedly supported Stalin began to turn towards Trotsky.

Clandestine Trotskyist organisations in Moscow were repeatedly raided, but new ones immediately sprang up to replace them. Trotsky himself was exiled to Alma Ata, a remote city in Soviet Central Asia near China's western border. He lived there under close surveillance, and his correspondence with friends was both censored and otherwise interfered with. But, despite this, his articles were invariably in wide circulation within a month of being written. Trotsky had supporters and sympathisers everywhere, and even some of the secret-police agents detailed to keep watch on him used to give him covert help on occasions. Since the struggle for power between the various factions had not yet finally been settled, some professional bureaucrats were continuing to hedge their bets in case of a sudden reversal of fortunes in the final round.

Every year, the Chinese students in Moscow had to spend a certain part of their time in productive work. Some of them were sent to work in the Moscow factories, while a smaller number, usually those who had lost their membership of the Party, were sent out to factories or gold-mines in the provinces. When they got back to Moscow, they brought with them information about the local situation and the mood of the workers. We learned from these sources that Russian workers were becoming more and more sympathetic to the Trotskyists, and were so dissatisfied with the Government that the smallest incident would often provoke a strike.

Naturally, Stalin was very worried by these developments. And yet he dared not put Trotsky in jail, let alone kill him. At first, he tried to silence his opponent by ordering him, in the name of the Central Committee, to put a stop to his political activities; but Trotsky refused to do so. Stalin therefore decided to deport him from the Soviet Union, a decision carried out in January 1929. The preparations for Trotsky's deportation were made in strict secrecy. We already knew that Stalin and the Central Committee would place harsher and harsher constraints on Trotsky's activities, and we fully expected that the persecution of the Opposition would increase. However, none of us imagined that they would go so far as to deport him. Naturally, the news was a great shock to the Oppositionists, but publicly people did not seem to be very much concerned by it. The report of the deportation was tucked away in an obscure corner of *Pravda* and we did not notice any particularly emotional reactions to it among any sections of the community. But, a fortnight or so later, something very different happened. We were on our way to the university one morning when we noticed clusters of people standing around newsstands reading, talking, and even arguing. Realising that something important must have happened, I bought a paper and found a piece by Yaroslavsky on the front page with the banner headline 'MR TROTSKY'S FIRST STEP ABROAD'. Alongside the article was a photographic reproduction of the front page of the London *Daily Express*, featuring an article by Trotsky. Without even revealing anything of the content of the article, Yaroslavsky claimed that no sooner was Trotsky out of the country than he was fighting against the Soviet Union and was in collusion with the imperialists.

Yaroslavsky's attack was a real blow below the belt. After ten years of outright hostility between the Soviet Union and the imperialist countries, there was a widespread misconception, especially among young people, that under no circumstances should a revolutionary make use of the bourgeois press. This misconception had been further strengthened by the fact that, in the Soviet Union, the press was controlled by the Communist Party. People were either unaware or had forgotten that revolutionaries under bourgeois régimes were sometimes compelled to make use of the bourgeois press, publish books through bourgeois publishing houses, and issue statements through the 'massmedia'. Taking advantage of this ignorance, Yaroslavsky and Stalin used the fact that Trotsky had granted an interview to a *Daily Express* correspondent and had contributed an article to the paper, to launch a smear campaign against him. The trick worked. The report caused a sensation, arousing suspicion not only among ordinary Russians but also among us Chinese Trotskyists. We regretted that Trotsky had committed a blunder, which, in our view, could only play into the hands of his enemies.

Trotsky had not yet been deprived of his citizenship and was living in the Soviet consulate in Constantinople. He was well informed about what was going on in Russia. As soon as he heard what had happened, he wrote an article titled 'An Open Letter to the Soviet Workers' in which he exposed the hypocrisy of Yaroslavsky and Stalin, accusing them of persecuting him in collusion with a reactionary foreign government, and protested against Stalin's criminal decision to deport one of the founders of the Soviet Union from his own country. He then went on to give examples from Lenin's life to show that it was common practice and entirely permissible for revolutionaries to grant interviews to bourgeois correspondents and write articles for the bourgeois press. His open letter was widely circulated among the masses, and was warmly received as it was brilliantly written and full of passion. I translated it into Chinese, and although it lost much of its original fire and beauty in the process, it still greatly charmed and moved our Chinese comrades, some of whom began to cry as they read it. It is a pity that neither the original nor the translation was ever sent to China. I remember it as one of the most moving things that Trotsky ever wrote, matched only by the article 'Son, Friend, and Fighter', which he wrote after the mysterious death of his son, Leon Sedov, in a Paris hospital in 1938.

However, Trotsky's deportation and Stalin's campaign against him could not prevent the further growth of the Opposition in the Soviet Union. By this time, the split between Stalin and Bukharin was an open secret. Bukharin wrote an article criticising Stalin's policy towards the peasants, and we were told that he had made secret contacts with Kamenev, his former opponent and now a capitulator to Stalin. Before long, we saw Stalin striking heavy blows at the rightist opposition. The quarrels between the Stalinists and the Bukharinites did much to open the eyes of the masses to the reality of the 'Leninist solidarity of the Central Committee of the Party'. Up to that time, there had been a feeling among the masses (in part created and encouraged by the bureaucracy) to the effect that, although Trotsky was an outstanding leader and a great hero, he was by nature an uncooperative trouble-maker. Some people therefore saw it as a regrettable necessity to get rid of him in order to maintain the 'Leninist' solidarity of the Central Committee and permit it to function as an efficient collective. Demagogic talk about the need for a collective leadership was one of Stalin's main weapons against Trotsky, and it was in the name of precisely such a 'collective leadership' by 'ordinary folk' that he denounced the Trotskyists for engaging in hero-worship and the cult of personality.

After the spring of 1929, however, naïve misconceptions and deliberate smears of this sort were refuted by events. The reason why a 'great hero' had been driven out of the country by 'ordinary folk' was by now clear: a thoroughly ordinary individual was himself anxious to lay claim to 'genius'. Although not everyone saw this immediately, they could hardly miss the fact that, only a month or so after the deportation of the 'trouble-maker' Trotsky, there was still no solidarity in the Central Committee: the differences between the various leaders were, if anything, more unprincipled than they had ever been. Lenin's 'faithful disciples' were behaving in a way unworthy of the name, fighting against each other at one moment and recanting and capitulating the next. The result was that the common people began to think more and more sympathetically of Trotsky. The deeper one went among the masses, the more often one would hear remarks such as: 'He alone was a real man'. This was particularly the case among those who had personally experienced the Revolution, and among ex-Red Army men who had fought under him. Although the few contacts I had in Moscow were for the most part party members, I also heard several remarks of this sort.

It was at about this time that we began to exchange correspondence with those Chinese Trotskyists who had been expelled and sent back to China a year before. From their letters, we learned that they had succeeded in organising Oppositionist nuclei in Shanghai, Hong Kong, and Beijing. In Shanghai, they had established a connection with a book company called New Universe, through which they were preparing to publish a few Oppositionist pamphlets. We were told that our Hong Kong friends were working in the docks, while those who had gone to Beijing were active among students, and had published a national magazine called *Our Word*. I sent the Chinese translations of the Oppositionist documents to Shi Tang, who was at that time responsible for the Shanghai organisation, through the New Universe Book Company.

A number of students were due to be sent back to China in May or June of that year. Some of them had been chosen by the party committee, while others were going of their own accord. The majority were either secret members of, or sympathisers with, the Opposition. We were faced with two questions: how we should work once we got back to China; and how we should go about setting up an all-China Trotskyist organisation. These questions were the two items on the agenda of a conference we convened at the campus of the Artillery School in Moscow. Besides the three leading members of the Oppositionist organisation at Sun Yat-sen University, representatives of Oppositionist groups at the various military schools also attended, together with Liu Renjing. We arrived at the following conclusions:

1. When we returned to China we should stay in the CCP and thereby prove ourselves to be good Communists. We reasoned that it was only by establishing our reputation as brave fighters, and by winning the respect and confidence of our fellow party members through our part in the actual revolutionary struggle, that we could earn the right to put forward our views and win support for them. But in order to remain within the Party we would have to hide the fact that we were Trotskyists, since the Party rules forbade the existence of factions. We therefore decided that, in our actions, we would abide by party discipline and obey the decisions of the majority, while, in ideological or political discussions, we would criticise the wrong tactical and strategic decisions adopted by the Sixth Congress of the CCP in such a way as would not immediately reveal us as Oppositionists.

2. Since we still considered ourselves to be a faction of the CCP, and saw our task as rectifying the mistakes in the Party caused by the dominant influence of Stalinism, we did not intend to form a new political party. If we were expelled (which was sooner or later inevitable, whether or not we abided by democratic-centralist principles), we would not make any attempt to set up a new Oppositionist organisation, but would continue

our revolutionary activities within the framework of the organisation already established by the Trotskyists who had returned to China before us.

With the sole exception of Liu Renjing, who declared that he had no intention of wasting time and energy on working in the CCP and would devote himself entirely to Oppositionist work once he got back to China, all those present at the meeting accepted these decisions and agreed to abide by them. Liu, who had only contempt for the 'callow youths' who were working for the Opposition in China, declared that it was impossible for him to say in advance whether he could work with them once he returned to China, or precisely what form his work for the Opposition would take. He could not be bound by any decision in this respect. We were very dissatisfied both with his attitude towards the CCP, which was in contradiction with that of the rest of the Opposition, and also with his arrogant attitude towards the Oppositionists who had returned to China before us. After a long discussion and considerable criticism, Liu finally agreed to submit to the majority, though his actions when he got back to China belied his apparent submission. He returned from the Soviet Union via Europe, and stopped off en route to pay a visit to Trotsky in Prinkipo. He spent some days with the Old Man, who took advantage of the occasion to write the 'Draft Programme of the Chinese Bolshevik-Leninists', which Liu Renjing afterwards brought back to China with him.

Most of us Chinese students in Moscow were very keen to get back to China as quickly as possible, so that we could put the political line of the Opposition into practice. We reasoned that, as we were first and foremost Chinese revolutionaries, our proper battlefield was China. If we stayed on in Moscow, we would undoubtedly increase our academic understanding of Marxism, but there would be less and less work for us to do there. Our activities were confined to the Chinese student body, whose numbers had dropped by the summer of 1929 from almost a thousand to only four or five hundred. Of that number, nearly a third had already been won over to our side. We believed returning to China was the only way we could prove the correctness of the platform of the Opposition and win new forces to it. True, it would be safer and more comfortable to remain in Moscow, since China was at that time in the grip of the white terror and revolutionaries were losing their lives every day and every hour. But only the sort of cowards who belonged to the Wang Ming clique would tremble at the idea of returning home, or would attempt to intimidate those they disliked by threatening to send them back. We despised them for their attitude, and the overwhelming majority of underground Oppositionists among the Chinese student body wanted to return to China as soon as the second academic year was over.

As our desire to return became more and more apparent, the members of the clique in charge of the party committee changed their attitude accordingly. If their aim had simply been to seize power at the university, as it had been eighteen months earlier, then they could easily have disposed of the problem by shunting all undesirable and 'unreliable' elements back home. But, now, their ambitions had swollen, and they looked upon the whole of the Chinese Party as their 'sphere of influence'. The methods they used to deal with their opponents, Trotskyists and non-Trotskyists alike, changed correspondingly. They would no longer just send us back, without regard for what we might get up to in the Party in China. They preferred to keep us in Moscow, where they could keep an eye on us and if necessary have us liquidated with the help of Stalin's secret police. It was therefore no easy matter for us to be sent home, especially for those of us considered by the party committee to be 'suspect' but politically able, and unlikely to quit the Party or go over to the reactionary camp once we got back to China. Those of us who were in this category would scarcely be allowed to return unless we managed in some way to win the confidence of the Wang Ming group.

Here I would like to relate two incidents which concern myself. My health had never been good and, while I was in Moscow, I used to go to see the university doctor once or twice a month. I was rarely seriously sick: most of my ailments were of a minor sort, such as colds and high temperatures brought on by fatigue, so I had never applied to go to a rest-home or a sanatorium. However, one day in the spring of 1929, I was unexpectedly informed by the head of the university hospital that I had been granted permission to go to a health resort on the Black Sea. It was like a gift from heaven! My destination was a place near the beautiful town of Feodosiya on the Crimean Peninsula, where I stayed for a month. It was a very picturesque little place, and must of the people taking cures there were high-ranking officials from factories and Party or government offices in Moscow and Leningrad. The only other Chinese there apart from me was an active supporter of the Wang Ming group. Obviously, to be sent to a resort such as this was a very different matter from being sent to a rest-home in a Moscow suburb, and was in fact a privilege reserved for the higher ranks. So why was I sent there, and even before the summer holidays had begun? Lying there on the sandy beach soaking up the warm Crimean sun, I could not help asking myself this question. It was obvious that the party committee must have spoken up on my behalf, or I would never have been so lucky. But my relations with the party committee were cool, not to say hostile. I had no personal contact with Wang Ming. We did not even acknowledge one another when we met on the street. I heartily despised him, and, for his part, he clearly had no reason to like me. He could not yet know for certain that I was a member of the Opposition, but he must have realised that I was not an active supporter of the party committee. The number two man in the hierarchy of the Wang Ming faction was He Zishu; he and I were in the same class together at Sun Yat-sen University and we were on fairly good terms with one another. Nevertheless, one could hardly call our relationship close, since he was a top member of the party committee while I was a 'non-activist'. Shortly before I was notified of my selection for a health cure, however, I noticed that he began to warm towards me, constantly asking after my health and chiding me for not looking after myself properly. It was therefore not very difficult for me to guess who I had to thank for my stroke of good luck. Then I realised that this unasked-for favour was actually part of a plan to win me over to the side of the Wang Ming group, and thus to strike a blow at the dissident camp among the Chinese students in Moscow, which they feared might provide the nucleus for a Chinese Trotskyist Opposition.

The second incident was even more unexpected than the first. One evening towards the end of July, not long after I had returned from the Crimea, I was called to the office of the party committee and told that I had been assigned to participate in a big anti-war and anti-imperialist demonstration in Leningrad on 1 August, as the CCP representative in a delegation that included several members of the Comintern and that was to be led by Ernst Thälmann, leader of the Communist Party of Germany. There were also a number of other well-known German leaders of the delegation, including Remmele, who was killed by Stalin a few years later. I was very surprised to find myself in such distinguished company; but even more so by the fact that the party committee had chosen me to represent them. After all, an assignment of this sort was far too good for someone who was not even a member of the Wang Ming clique. Members of such delegations would be entertained and cheered wherever they went, they would watch the demonstration from a special rostrum, and be expected to make short speeches at meetings and to pay visits to factories and other institutions. So how was it that I, a rank-and-file student who had no special links with the party committee, suddenly found myself singled out for such an honour? Was it because I knew a little Russian? But there were other followers of Wang Ming whose Russian was better than mine. In terms of seniority and work-record, my qualifications were rather meagre. So what, then, was the real cause of my sudden promotion? Without doubt, it was just one more step by the Wang Ming faction in their long-term strategy for fighting the Opposition. Nevertheless, it gave me a chance to see at close range something of the privileges which the Soviet bureaucrats enjoyed, at a time when the system of privileges in general had not yet fully developed. In addition to this, I also got the chance to visit the scene of the October Revolution.

Thälmann and others had just attended the Tenth Plenary Session of the Comintern Executive. This meeting was a landmark in the history of the Comintern, and represented an abrupt lurch to the left. It was at this plenum that the Communist International officially announced that the world revolution had entered its 'third period', during which world capitalism would collapse on all fronts and the revolution would go into a general offensive. Stalin also performed an important organisational manoeuvre at this session, officially removing Bukharin from the position as head of the Comintern to which he had been elected at its Sixth Congress. Perhaps it was as a reward for the services he rendered in this operation that Thälmann was chosen to officiate at the Leningrad demonstration on his way back to Germany. Two Italian students from the Communist University for the Toilers of the West (KUTZ) and I were added to the German delegation to give it a more international look.

On the night of 30 July, we travelled to Leningrad by train. I shared a compartment with an Italian comrade called Niccolo, who taught me how to sing *Avanti popolo!* (a song I can still sing even now). It was daybreak when we arrived in Leningrad. Outside the railway station were some cars waiting to take us to the Smolny Institute, where the headquarters of the October Revolution had been. I felt as if on a pilgrimage. Only a few months before, I had read John Reed's *Ten Days that Shook the World*, and I was therefore familiar with the role the building had played during the Revolution. I had a fresh impression in my mind of the corridors milling with workers and soldiers, and the rooms where Lenin, Trotsky, and the other Bolshevik leaders had worked. Now I had the chance to see with my own eyes what I had so far only read in books. It was a fascinating experience, but, at the same time, it set me thinking: the two giants who had planned and directed the Revolution from this place were now gone; one dead and the other deported.

Niccolo and I, together with another German comrade, were put up for the night in the 'Peasants' Home' in Smolny. It was a quiet place, ideal for resting in, which before the revolution had been a dormitory for senior nuns. Thälmann and the other VIPs stayed in a luxury hotel.

On the day that we arrived in Leningrad, a meeting of party activists was held in the Uritsky Palace to celebrate the approaching 1 August Anti-War Day. We were seated on the platform as part of the presidium. Kirov, who became famous a few years later after his assassination, officiated at the meeting, and Thälmann delivered the main address. There was no doubt about Thälmann's talents as a speaker. Unlike most Communist leaders in recent years, he did not read from a long prepared text, but spoke fluently and impromptu, with a lively style. He had a resounding voice, and gave an impression of real strength to his audience. What was more, he spoke briefly and to the point, which must have been a pleasant surprise for his listeners, for whom set speeches were generally a torture.

That afternoon or the next (the exact date escapes me), there was a demonstration of tens of thousands of workers through Leningrad. We were again invited to mount the rostrum, where we stood alongside all the dignitaries. We reviewed the procession, and received the cheers of the demonstrators. This was the last time I was to play such a role. Those of us on the rostrum were expected to acknowledge the cheering crowds by waving back at them and keeping fixed smiles on our faces for what seemed an interminable period. Of all the Stalinist ceremonial formalities, this was perhaps the commonest, and to review such a demonstration was regarded as a matter of the highest honour, by reviewers and reviewed alike. I saw things rather differently, however: in my opinion, the role was a painful one to play, and the performance as a whole quite meaningless. This is not to say, of course, that the demonstration itself was meaningless. But it does seem to me that once something becomes a mere formality, a pre-arranged ceremony in which every last detail is prescribed by some bureaucrat, it inevitably loses all its revolutionary significance. Worse still, this whole ridiculous performance could only serve a reactionary and counter-revolutionary purpose. It was precisely in rituals of this sort that the ugliness of the 'personality cult' and the ambitions of some leaders revealed themselves most clearly. As I write these lines in the autumn of 1956, the leaders of the CCP are busy expressing their opposition to Stalin's 'personality cult'. But the most fanatical and dramatic expression of that cult, the march past the reviewing stand, has been plagiarised to the letter in China on an even more massive and intimidating scale. One is forced to conclude that the CCP has yet to take the first step on the road to opposing the 'personality cult'.

The day after we reviewed the demonstration, we were taken to visit Tsarskoe Selo ('Tsar's Village') and a number of factories, including the Putilov steelworks, which had played such an important part in the October Revolution. The afternoon was free of official engagements, and we were allowed to go wherever we liked. I went to see a friend I had got to know during my stay in the Crimea, a leading trade unionist at the Red October Confectionery factory. He spent the afternoon showing me round Leningrad. First of all he took me to the Viborg district, which had provided the main forces for the revolution in 1917. Then, we went for a walk along the Neva River and the Nevsky Prospect. He took me to the world-famous Hermitage Museum. In the evening, he invited me to his home to have dinner with his family and some other men and women

I had met in the Crimea. His wife did the cooking, and it was the first and only time during my stay in the Soviet Union that I ate with a Russian family. Their kindness and hospitality, typical of all Russians, overwhelmed me. But it was clear from the way they behaved and talked that they were supporters of the 'Thermidor'.[2] I compared them with the few Russians I knew in Moscow, and found the differences striking. My Russian friends in Moscow were mostly Oppositionists. They too were young, but most of them had been in the Party for a long time. Nearly all had taken part in the Revolution or the Civil War, had suffered much, and had been tempered by their experiences. Naturally, they held firmly to revolutionary principles, knew more about politics, had a broader outlook, and paid less attention to the material pleasures of life. They had made friends with us Chinese Communists chiefly, even exclusively, because of our common position towards the Revolution. It was quite different, of course, with my Leningrad friends, who were very contented with their lot and hardly ever bothered to think about political questions. In fact, all of them, men and women alike, were much more interested in the latest fashions in clothes than they were in politics. They were good workers and activists in their various fields, but the main reason they worked so hard was because they wanted to improve their living standards. Nearly all of them were members of the Party or the Komsomol, but they knew little of the world and even less of China. Indeed, one pretty young girl, a Komsomol member and a clerk at the confectionery factory, asked me whether there was electric light in China and whether Chinese could live together with monkeys. My Leningrad friends were more typical of the new generation of Soviet youth than the Russians I knew in Moscow. Seeing them, it became clearer to me why Stalin had beaten Trotsky in the party struggle. Obviously Trotsky's theory of permanent revolution was neither to the liking nor in the interests of these young men and women.

We stayed in Leningrad for another four or five days, and spent much of our time travelling round the barracks on the outskirts of the city, making speeches to the soldiers. We visited several places a day, and once we even went as far as the Finnish border. Wherever we went, we were invariably welcomed by thousands of soldiers, whom we usually addressed very briefly from a makeshift platform in the barrack yard. What we said was rather commonplace, but needless to say in the spirit of Stalin's new left turn: we spoke of the imminence of war and the need for the solidarity of workers all over the world. The soldiers responded enthusiastically, and, after we had delivered our speeches, it was

---

2 Stalin's right turn in the mid-1920s was often compared with the right turn in France after the fall of Robespierre and the left-wing Jacobins in the month of Thermidor of Year II by the revolutionary calendar (July 1794).

usually impossible to break through the encirclement of the young Red Army men, who attacked us from all sides, captured us, tossed us repeatedly into the air amid great cheers, and finally carried each of us shoulder high across the parade ground. I remember that, on one occasion, Thälmann, who was a large and rather stout man, was spared this treatment, but only after a considerable amount of begging and pleading on his part. These displays of enthusiasm by the Red Army men were quite genuine, and there was no question of their being stage-managed by the officers. After all, the October Revolution was still only eleven years old, and despite the fact that Stalin's theory of 'socialism in one country' was beginning to have an effect in Russia, the internationalist ideas propagated during the revolutionary years before Lenin's death had captured the imagination of the ordinary Soviet people. They therefore still regarded us foreign Communists as comrades closely connected with their own life-and-death struggles. It was not until after 1935 that the bureaucracy began to regard every foreigner as a spy and every foreign Communist as a 'running dog' to be patted or kicked, favoured or put down at will.

I only attended one official dinner in Leningrad, and it was not particularly luxurious, quite unlike the unbelievably sumptuous feasts that the Stalinist bureaucrats in the Kremlin started to give in the late 1930s. But, even at that early date, it was obvious that the top bureaucrats lived far better than the ordinary Soviet people. Take my case, for example. As an ordinary student, I usually got ten roubles a month, but, while I was on the Leningrad delegation, I got that amount each day, supposedly to spend on food – which I was mostly given free anyway. By the time I got back to Moscow, I was therefore quite a rich man, with enough money in my pocket to treat my friends to Chinese meals.

On my return to Moscow, He Zishu was even more friendly towards me than before; he congratulated me on the success of my mission to Leningrad, and told me that he hoped that, from now on, I would be more active and take on more assignments from the party committee at the university. It was by then obvious that they were putting pressure on me to join the Wang Ming faction. I was quite familiar with their carrot-and-stick tactics: first a polite invitation, and then, should it prove necessary, crude harassment. They had extended their invitation: the next step was up to me. I raised the matter at a meeting of the clandestine committee of the Opposition, and it was unanimously agreed that it was no longer possible for me to stay on in Moscow. Certainly the party committee would no longer be prepared to tolerate my apparent inactivity. It was therefore decided that I should go back to China as soon as possible. Once the party committee had abandoned the carrot and taken up the stick, that would be the end of my hopes of returning home. But on what grounds should I apply to return? It was obvious that Wang Ming and his friends suspected that I might have something to do with the Opposition in the university, and it might well be that they would not allow me to leave.

Once again, the summer vacation came round, and this time the students were to be sent to the Crimea for their holidays. Since I had only just got back from there, I asked to be allowed to stay on in Moscow, and my request was granted. Apart from me, there were another dozen or so other students who had been allowed to stay behind in the capital, on the grounds that they were about to return to China. Some were Oppositionists, others Wang Ming supporters. Among them was a girl comrade called Ye whom I had married several months before, so I grasped the opportunity and asked to be sent back to China with her. It was a reasonable-sounding request, and, since all the Chinese members of the party committee had left for the Crimea, I was able to apply directly to a Russian comrade for permission to return. He consulted the Eastern Department of the Comintern, and it was granted. For the second time in my life, I set off on the Trans-Siberian Railway, thus bringing to an end my two-year stay in the Soviet capital.

Just before the holidays began, we had carried out a reorganisation of the Chinese Opposition in Moscow. In view of my decision to leave Russia, another conference of activists was convened at which a new member, Zhao Yanqing, was chosen to replace me on the leading committee of the organisation. Zhao, former principal of the First Normal School of Hubei province, was much older than most of us and a kind and popular man. Those of us who knew him were therefore dismayed as well as surprised to learn, six months or so later, that he was responsible for the smashing of the entire Moscow organisation, numbering some two to three hundred Chinese Trotskyists. This is a subject to which I shall return.

Chinese Students at the International Lenin School in Moscow, 1926–38: Light from the Russian Archives

Alexander V. Pantsov and Daria A. Spichak

Edited from an article first published in Twentieth Century China, *no. 2 (2008), pp. 29–50.*

Soviet support of the Chinese Communist movement in the 1920s and the 1930s was truly all-encompassing. Not only did the Comintern directly finance the Chinese Communist Party (CCP) but it also greatly helped the Party train its cadres in the USSR. This kind of help required a huge amount of money. By 1930, the Bolsheviks had spent five million roubles training Chinese revolutionaries at just one of the international schools.[1] Meanwhile, in the Soviet Union there was a vast network of such institutions. The largest international school in the Soviet Union was Sun Yat-sen University of the Toilers of China (UTK in Russian abbreviation), which operated from 1925 to 1930 (in 1928 it was renamed the Communist University of the Toilers of China [KUTK]). Various other schools also operated. These were the Communist University of the Toilers of the East (KUTV), the KUTV Military-Political Courses, the Nikolai G. Tolmachev Military Political Academy, the Mikhail V. Frunze Military Academy, the Military Engineers' School, the Moscow Artillery School, the Moscow Infantry School, the Leningrad Signalmen's School, the Kiev Military School, the Aeronautical Military-Theoretical School, the Borisoglebsk Pilot-School, the Kliment E. Voroshilov Third Orenburg Pilot and Air-Sentry School, the *Vystrel* (Shot) courses organised for Red Army commanders in Moscow Lefortovo district, and the Su Zhaozheng School in Vladivostok (the latter started in 1925 and was later renamed the Vladivostok Soviet Party Higher School and, in 1929, the Chinese Lenin Higher School).

Among these institutions, the International Lenin School (MLSh) occupied a distinctive place. It functioned longer than other schools, from 1926 to 1938, and was specially designated for the CCP and other foreign Communist parties' top cadres. In 1936–8, there was another important training centre for Chinese students in Moscow, the Scientific Research Institute of National and Colonial Issues (NIINKP). In the late 1930s and early 1940s, Chinese students in the Soviet Union received training at the secret Chinese Party School, also known

---

1 Titarenko et al. (eds) 1999, Volume 3, p. 457.

as the CCP Central Committee (CC) Party School, formally affiliated with the Central Committee of the USSR International Proletarian Revolutionaries' Aid Organisation (MOPR), located in Kuchino near Moscow, and secretly coded the 'NIINKP Seventh, Eighth, and Fifteenth Sections'.[2]

The post-1991 opening of the Soviet Communist Party and Comintern archives, including the archives of the Comintern international schools, has laid a new foundation for scholarly research into Chinese Communist history and the history of the training of Chinese revolutionary cadres in the USSR. Memoirs of former students and instructors at these schools are also of great significance. Among them are recollections by Chiang Ching-kuo (1910–88), Afanasii G. Krymov (Guo Zhaotang 1905–89), Liu Renjing (1902–87), Ma Yuansheng (1906–77), Sheng Yue (1907–2007), Shi Zhe (1905–98), Tang Youzhang (1906–2000), Wang Fanxi (1907–2002), Wang Jueyuan, Yang Xingfu, Zhang Guotao (1897–1979), and others.[3] In addition, the memoir of Lena Din-Savva (1937–), a daughter of two Chinese students of the Communist University of the Toilers of the East (KUTV), is also of enormous importance.[4]

A number of scholars have taken the first steps in researching these precious materials. They include Vladimir P. Galitskii, Alexander G. Larin, N.N. Timofeeva, Gerontii V. Yefimov, and Yu Minling as well as a group of historians at the Russian Academy of Sciences Institute of Far Eastern Studies Centre of Modern Chinese history. Vladimir N. Nikiforov and Victor N. Usov have also examined some issues connected with the CCP cadres' training.[5] These specialists, however, focused exclusively on the 1920s. Furthermore, they only examined the history of UTK/KUTK and KUTV.

The history of the International Lenin School, NIINKP, and the Chinese Party School has remained outside researchers' purview. Nonetheless, an examination of the MLSh documents helps us better understand the evolution of the Comintern system of supervision over the CCP. The history of NIINKP and the Chinese Party School also add important details to this analysis. This article seeks to shed light on a dramatic story of the MLSh Chinese sector that was at first an essential part of the 'élite' party school, but finally fell under total control of the Soviet Stalinists, who imposed a reign of terror on it.

---

2   Russian State Archives of Social and Political History (hereafter RGASPI), 531/1/1/8.
3   Chiang Ching-kuo 1963; Chang Kuo-t'ao 1971; Krymov 1989; 'Liu Renjing tan Tuoluociji pai zai Zhongguo' 1982; Ma Yuansheng 1987; Sheng Yueh 1971; Shi Zhe and Shi Qiulang 2001; Tang Youzhang 1988; Wang Fanxi 1980; Wang Jueyuan 1969; Yang Xingfu 1985.
4   Din-Savva 2000.
5   Galitskii 2003; Yefimov 1977; Larin 2003; Timofeeva 1976 and 1979; Yu Min-ling 1995; Nikiforov 1962; Usov 1987.

MLSh as the Comintern 'élite' Party School

The International Lenin School (MLSh) for top party officials was established in the mid-1920s, a turbulent time in the world revolutionary movement, by a resolution of the Comintern Fifth Congress.[6] In February 1925, the Comintern named the future school the International Party Higher Courses (VMPK),[7] but, in April 1925 it renamed it the International Party Courses (IPK), and, in April 1926, the International Lenin Courses (MLK).[8] The name 'International Lenin School' appeared in 1928,[9] but, in 1930, it was modified one more time, and the school became the International Communist University (MKU).[10]

The school was formally affiliated with the V. I. Lenin Institute, but it actually operated under the Executive Committee of the Comintern (ECCI) Presidium and its Agitation and Propaganda Department. The Soviet government financed the school according to its annual budget set up by the Politburo. The budget reached an impressive sum of 718,520 roubles.[11]

The Politburo appointed the school's rectors. From 1926 to 1930, the rector was Nikolai Ivanovich Bukharin (1888–1938), a party member from 1906 and a Politburo member from 1924–9. From 1918 to 1929, Bukharin edited the official party newspaper *Pravda*, and from 1919 to 1929, he served on the ECCI Presidium. In 1929, however, Stalin (1878–1953) expelled him from the Politburo and the ECCI for his opposition to the brutal Bolshevik collectivisation. Shortly thereafter, Bukharin lost his post at MLSh.[12] He was succeeded by Klavdia Ivanovna Kirsanova (1887–1947), a party member from 1904 and the wife of a famous party official, historian, and journalist Minei I. Gubelman (alias Yaroslavskii, 1878–1943). In late 1931, as a result of the intra-party and intra-school struggle, she was temporarily replaced by Wilhelm Pieck (1876–1960), a co-founder of the German Communist Party, who from 1931 on was a member of the ECCI Presidium and Secretariat. Pieck, however, remained in the office just a few months. In 1932, he yielded his post back to Kirsanova. In 1937, however, Kirsanova was arrested by the Stalin secret police on false charges of being a member of the Trotskyist opposition. A new and final rector of the school was then appointed: Vŭlko Chervenkov (1900–80, alias Vladimirov),

---

6   Babichenko 1989, p. 119.
7   RGASPI, 531/1/1/3.
8   RGASPI, p. 7.
9   Babichenko 1989, p. 120.
10   RGASPI, 531/1/21/2 verso.
11   Galitskii 2003, p. 18.
12   Cohen 1973.

a co-leader of the Bulgarian Communist Party and – most importantly – a close relative of the ECCI General Secretary Georgi Dimitrov (1882–1949) – Chervenkov was married to Dimitrov's sister, Elena (1902–74).[13]

The School was located at 25 Vorovskogo Street in downtown Moscow. It opened on 1 October 1926, and except for the early 1930s (when the students took three years to complete their studies) had a two-year curriculum.[14] There were also short nine-month courses and, in 1930, special Communist groups were open for twelve-month training.[15] In 1932, the School set up a two-year PhD programme.[16]

At first, in 1926, MLSh was divided into four language sectors: Russian, German, English, and French.[17] In 1928, all students were split into national groups named sector 'A' (German), 'G' (Hungarian), 'D' (American), 'I' (French), and so on. In all, there were nineteen sectors. The Chinese students belonged to the sector 'Ts' that was split into two short-term groups 'A' and 'B' and one long-term group. Later a post-graduate study group was added. In 1931, two more short-term groups were created, 'V' and 'G'.[18] There also was a group 'D' consisting of those Chinese graduates who wished to continue their education while working at Soviet factories.[19]

The MLSh curriculum focused on the Bolshevisation of the student body. Due to a Politburo decision, several top Soviet CC officials took part in developing the curriculum. From 1926 to 1930, Bukharin played the leading role by personally developing the school curriculum and many extra programmes. Karl B. Radek (1885–1939), rector of UTK in from 1925 to 1927, helped him greatly, although Radek took an active part in the intra-party Left Opposition. From 1926 to 1927 the course work included the following main subjects: history of the Bolshevik Party, economy of capitalism, history of the labour movement, and Leninism. In addition, the students also had to study political economy, imperialism and the world economy, economy of the transformational (that is, transitional from capitalism to socialism) period, world history, history of the Communist International, strategy and tactics of the world proletariat, history of socialist construction in the USSR, dialectical and historical materialism, and party building. This last course covered material on the organisational

---

13 Banac (ed.) 2003, pp. 456–7.
14 RGASPI, 531/1/3/25.
15 RGASPI, 531/1/18/2 and 531/1/230/8.
16 RGASPI, 531/1/233/4.
17 RGASPI, 531/1/71/30.
18 RGASPI, 531/1/11/30.
19 RGASPI, 531/1/220/48.

principles and structure of the Bolshevik Party and the Comintern.[20] From 1928 onwards, the curriculum included fifteen courses.[21] Learning Russian was not compulsory, but the students who mastered Russian could take a more active part in the party, labour union, and cultural life of the MLSh.[22] That was why most students wished to study the language of their hosts.

After the dismissal of Bukharin from office in 1930, the Stalinists revised the programme and the curriculum in the light of the new party line. From 1930 to 1935, Stalin's close associate and the secretary of the Moscow City Party Committee Lazar M. Kaganovich (1893–1991) supervised the development of the new MLSh programmes.[23] He began a propaganda campaign which emphasised Stalin's personal role in the October Revolution, the Civil War, and socialist construction in the USSR. 'One must sometimes correct history', Stalin said, letting the cat out of the bag one day.[24] Kaganovich, Kirsanova, Pieck and other bureaucrats at MLSh zealously strove to fulfil the leader's directive.

Class meetings included seminars and lectures. The students composed many papers and could visit their professors during their office hours.[25] The teachers were selected by the Bolshevik Party CC Agitation and Propaganda Department and the ECCI from the Institute of Red Professors. Some occupied important administrative positions. For example, head of the 'Ts' sector M. Raiskaia taught the Soviet economy and one of her aides, L. Ziman, taught political economy. The other aide, A. Chebukin, and the first associate chair of the Education Department, V. Altufov, both taught the history of the Bolshevik Party, and the second associate chair of the Education Department, Alerutov, taught Leninism.[26] In the 1920s and 1930s, the school administration invited leading members of the Bolshevik Party and the Comintern to participate as visiting lecturers. In this way, the students were able to listen to Grigorii E. Zinoviev (1883–1936), Josef I. Stalin, and Béla Kun (1886–1938).[27]

The School worked in a conspiratorial manner. The students had to submit all personal papers to the Education Department which kept them in the students' personal files. In place of their names, they received student identity-cards which bore their pseudonyms. On 5 April 1926, the MLK administration

---

20   RGASPI, 531/1/15/41.
21   McLoughlin 1997, p. 65.
22   RGASPI, 531/1/1/31.
23   Torchinov and Leontyuk 2000, pp. 237–9.
24   Cited in Banac 2003, p. 101.
25   McLoughlin 1997, p. 65.
26   RGASPI, 531/1/61/27.
27   RGASPI, 531/1/1/19.

decided that all students would bear pseudonyms 'which will not coincide with their real or passport surnames'.[28]

In 1927, the International Lenin Courses began to issue a journal *Leninskaia Shkola* (The Lenin School) in four languages: English, French, German, and Russian.[29] Its editorial board consisted of a party committee member who served as its chair, the pro-rector of the school, a member of the labour union committee, and representatives from each language sector. It was between twenty and thirty pages in length and it came out twice a month. The number of printed copies fluctuated between fifty and one hundred. The journal was disseminated among MLSh students, professors, and ECCI officials. The readers were supposed to give back their copies as soon as they finished reading them.[30]

In sum, MLSh did indeed become an 'elite' school that could give its students authentic Bolshevik ideological training. Its graduates were well-prepared and could compete for leading positions in their indigenous parties.

Sector 'Ts': Students and Faculty

At the beginning, in the first year (1926–7), only those Chinese who knew English could enrol at MLSh. The special Chinese sector at the time did not exist and all Chinese had to join a group where the British, American, Canadian, and Irish students took classes. In 1927, some Chinese who knew Russian better than English were transferred to the newly organised Russian sector. They studied there together with the Poles, Latvians, Lithuanians, Romanians, and Bulgarians, all of whom could speak satisfactory Russian.[31] Only in 1928, when the students split into national sectors, were all the Chinese united into their own sector under the designation 'Ts'. By 1931, ninety-five Chinese had studied at MLSh. According to our estimation, they constituted ten per cent of the entire student body. Of these students, twenty-eight persons had been transferred to MLSh from KUTK in 1929. Eight more had come from KUTK in 1930.[32] In 1931, six more Chinese enrolled at the School. In 1932, forty-three students joined the undergraduate and graduate programmes,[33] and in 1933 forty more

---

28   RGASPI, 531/1/2./2; 531/1/3/1 verso.
29   RGASPI, 531/1/257/1.
30   RGASPI, 531/1/257/2–4.
31   Ma Yuansheng 1987, p. 83.
32   RGASPI, 531/1/32, 20; 29/1.
33   RGASPI, 531/1/4, 12.

enrolled in the short-term groups.[34] In 1934, fifteen Chinese graduated from MKU, and in 1935 seventeen new students joined the short-term groups of the sector 'Ts'. Fifteen students enrolled at the long-term group.[35] At the same time, four Chinese received PhD candidate identity cards.[36] In 1936, there were twenty-nine Chinese at the sector 'Ts',[37] in 1937, twenty,[38] and in 1938, six.[39] Most came from workers' and peasants' families and all were members of the CCP or the Chinese Communist Youth League (CCYL). As a whole, in the period 1926 to 1938, according to various archival materials, over two hundred Chinese students graduated from the sector 'Ts'.

Among those who studied or worked at MLSh were many leading Chinese Communists: Dong Biwu (1886–1975, aliases Slukhov and Sleptsov, a delegate to the CCP's First Congress in 1921), Gao Zili (1900–50, alias Zhou Hesen, a member of the Central Executive Committee of the Chinese Soviet Republic and People's Commissar of Agriculture in the Chinese Soviet government; and a member of the CCP delegation to the ECCI from 1934 to 1938), Huang Ping (1901–81, alias Vorovskii, a member of the CCP CC from 1930 to 1931 and a member of the CCP delegation to the ECCI), Li Lisan (1899–67, aliases Alexander Lapin and Li Ming, a leader of the Chinese labour movement who was the second man in the CCP leadership from 1928 to 1930), Chen Yu (1901–74, alias Polevoi, a member of the CCP CC Politburo in 1931 and of the CCP delegation to the ECCI in 1933), Zhou Dawen (1903–38, alias Vladimir Vasilievich Chugunov, a chairman of the All-China student union in 1924), and Yu Xiusong (1899–1938, alias Ruben Narimanov, co-founder of the Chinese Socialist Youth League). The CCP Politburo members Zhang Guotao (alias Popov) and Li Weihan (1896–1984, alias Luo Mai and Izyumov) also studied there. In addition the following famous CCP activists studied or taught at MLSh: Wang Guanlan (1906–82), Wang Ruofei (1896–1946), Dong Yixiang (1896–1938), Kong Yuan (1906–90), Li Peize (1905–?), Liu Renjing, Liu Changsheng (1904–67), Ma Huizhi (1901–94), Song Yiping (1916–), Wu Kejian (1900–86), Chen Gang (1906–67), Chen Yun (1905–95), Yang Xiufeng (1897–1983), Yang Zhihua (1900–73), and Yan Hongyan (1902–67).

The sector 'Ts' was headed by a woman named Dr Minna Yakovlevna Raiskaia (1902–61), a party member from 1918 and a specialist in the Chinese

---

34   RGASPI, 531/1/47/28.
35   RGASPI, 531/1/50/3.
36   RGASPI, 531/1/84/6.
37   RGASPI, 531/1/106/9.
38   RGASPI, 531/1/131/15.
39   RGASPI, 531/1/143/6.

economy. In 1922, Raiskaia finished short-term courses at the Sverdlovsk Communist University, in 1925 she graduated from the Economics Department of Leningrad State University, and in 1933 she graduated from the Economics Department of the Institute of Red Professors. Until 1926, she had worked in the Leningrad Oblast Party School as head of a student group. Her aides were Afanasii Vasilievich Chebukin (1904–?) and Lev Yakovlevich Ziman (1900–56). Chebukin graduated from a party school in 1926 and from the Leningrad Institute of Oriental Studies and the Oriental Department of the Institute of Red Professors in 1934. He had worked at MLSh until its closing in 1938. Then, from May 1939 onwards, he served as a senior referent on China at the ECCI Cadres Department and head of the Chinese Party School at Kuchino.[40] In 1940, ECCI General Secretary Georgi Dimitrov transferred him to work in the Bolshevik Party CC.[41] As for Ziman, he was an economist, a geographer, and a cartographer. Before joining the MLSh faculty, he had worked at Yakov M. Sverdlov Communist University, at the Big Soviet Encyclopaedia, and had been a deputy head of the Diplomatic School and the editor-in-chief of the Main Administration of Geodesy and Cartography.[42] In the fall of 1931, a Chinese named Bu Shiji (1902–64, alias Evgenii Andreevich Proletariev) was appointed associate head of the sector. He was a KUTV and UTK graduate and a member of the CCP delegation to the ECCI. On 15 March 1933, however, the ECCI decided to dismiss him and he was sent back to China where the Guomindang's secret police arrested him and forced him to collaborate with them. In 1949, he fled to Taiwan where in 1961 he established the Institute of International Relations.[43]

On 21 December 1933, the Political Commission of the ECCI Political Secretariat appointed Kang Sheng (1898–1975) a curator of the MLSh sector 'Ts'.[44] At the time, Kang was a CCP CC Politburo member and – under pseudonyms Piatnitskii and Boss – a deputy head of the CCP delegation to the ECCI.[45] On 29 January 1937, taking into account that Kang Sheng was about to return to China, the ECCI Secretariat replaced him with Chen Tanqiu (1896–1943, alias Xu Jie), a former organiser of the Hubei Communist movement, a co-founder of the CCP, and a member of the CCP delegation to the ECCI.[46] Chen, however,

---

40 RGASPI, 495/18/1278/101.
41 RGASPI, 495/65a/2815/1.
42 Kipnis 1998, p. 251.
43 RGASPI, 495/4/225/275; Pantsov and Levine n.d., pp. 57–63.
44 RGASPI, 495/4/273/8.
45 RGASPI, 514/1/836/ 40.
46 Titarenko et al. (eds) Volume 4, p. 1096.

served in this capacity only until 16 January 1938, when he was transferred to the Chinese section of the Chinese Workers' Publishing House.[47]

There were several translators at the sector, some of them Russians, some Chinese. In the period 1933 to 1936, the leading interpreters were Lu Yongquan (1903–?, aliases Dmitrii Aleksandrovich Lobov and Wu Xingcai), Fu Qinghua (1906–71, alias Yakov Mikhailovich Dashevskii), V. N. Aduev, E. F. Pozin, and I. T. Khinchuk, who also taught political economy.[48]

In the 1920s, the school administration praised sector 'Ts' many times as a 'great success' in 'socialist competition'. The administration believed this group was unified 'around the party line and the Comintern'. It was especially proud of the fact that the Chinese students 'demonstrated great irreconcilability in the struggle against all kinds of opportunistic sentiments'.[49] At the same time, the administration criticised the sector for the 'insufficient development of party activity', emphasising that 'some instructors' did not actively participate in the sector's every-day political life.[50]

MLSh and the Stalinist Purges

The administration's positive evaluation of the sector 'Ts' was due mainly to the fact that it strictly believed there were no Chinese Trotskyists at MLSh. From the second half of the 1920s onwards, the school underwent a series of severe purges[51] that failed to uncover Trotskyists.

Nonetheless, Chinese Trotskyists did exist at MLSh. The leading figure among them was Liu Renjing (alias Lenskii) who later became one of the most famous Chinese adherents of Leon Trotsky and, in 1929, even visited him on Prinkipo Island in Turkey. It was Liu who involved some other MLSh-students in factional activity by disseminating Trotskyist views on the Chinese Revolution. Many of these students would be arrested and interrogated in late 1929 and early 1930 by the party Purge Commission. Among those who went through all circles of the abyss were Ma Yuansheng, Zhu Daijie, and others.[52]

Ma Yuansheng was the first to become interested in Liu's propaganda. He later recalled that Liu was very cautious and attracted his attention by talking

---

47   RGASPI, 495/225/2852.
48   RGASPI, 531/1/61/19.
49   RGASPI, 531/2/28/20.
50   RGASPI, 531/2/28/20.
51   RGASPI, 531/1/258/5.
52   For details, see Pantsov 2000, Chapter 6.

first about general political issues. Only after a few talks did he begin to 'drop phrases' in defence of Trotsky's opinion. When Ma agreed with him, Liu gave him some Trotskyist literature. Liu Renjing urged his friend to participate in the organisational activity by translating and disseminating the 'factional' (that is, Trotskyist) literature.[53] The minutes of Ma Yuansheng's interrogation preserved in the archives indicate that Liu 'used propaganda to involve' Kon (Zhu Daijie), Yang (Yang Zhongyi), and then Popov (Zhang Guotao), Nemtsev (Wang Ruofei), and Orlinskii (Dong Yixiang).[54]

In the meantime, on 7 November 1927 some Sun Yat-sen University students and instructors belonging to the Left Opposition took part in the Trotskyist-Zinovievist demonstration in Red Square. This protest attracted public attention. Shortly after the incident, most active Trotskyist adherents from UTK were deported to China.[55] However, in 1928, new groups of Oppositionists (that is, Trotskyists) enrolled at KUTV and KUTK. A big Trotskyist faction also functioned in the Moscow Infantry Military School. Its leader was Lu Yeshen (alias Nikonov).[56] Some Chinese Trotskyists also studied at the Engineers' and Artillery Schools. Oppositionists were still attending MLSh, too. After Liu Renjing's departure to China in April 1929, the leading Trotskyists were Ma Yuansheng and Zhu Daijie.

In the fall of 1929, however, the Stalinists decided to strike a blow at the dissidents, thereby initiating the first total purge of foreign Communists in the USSR. The purge took a few months and was especially harsh. By the spring of 1930 the underground Trotskyist organisations at MLSh and other schools had been crushed. The atmosphere at MLSh as well as in Moscow generally became very tense. Yu Xiusong recalled: 'For the prevailing years in this atmosphere.... I was literally afraid to meet any Chinese comrade. While studying at MLSh, I very rarely left school'.[57]

Ma Yuansheng's personal file in the Russian archives contains his letter of 10 February 1930. It is addressed to the Party Purge Commission after it 'unmasked' him. He writes about the reasons that caused him to join the Trotskyists, pointing to 'the process of his ideological transformation'.[58] This letter is very important for our understanding of the political situation in which many Chinese students found themselves. These students tried to understand

---

53 RGASPI, 495/225/954/21.
54 RGASPI, p. 77.
55 Pantsov 2000, pp. 183–8.
56 Pantsov 2000, p. 202.
57 RGASPI, 495/225/3001/7 verso.
58 RGASPI, 954/83.

the political platforms of the CCP, the Guomindang, the Bolshevik Party, and the Trotskyist-Zinovievist Opposition. For example:

> I arrived and enrolled at KUTV having been sent by the CCP CC in the spring of 1927. In a few months after my arrival, the Chiang Kai-shek (1887–1975) coup d'état took place. Then the Wuhan government revolted and the Chinese Revolution was defeated. These events made me study the Chinese question seriously. In particular, I began to investigate causes and lessons of the defeat. At the time, I maintained that the main task of comrades who stayed in Moscow must be to study [at school] as hard as possible. In the KUTV wall-newspaper I raised Lenin's slogan 'To learn, to learn, and to learn once again'.[59]

Ma and his co-thinkers were about to graduate when they asked the CCP delegation to the ECCI to send them back to China to work. Their request was denied. The Comintern officials told them that it was too early for them to return to their motherland and instead transferred them to MLSh, saying they had not studied hard enough. Ma continued:

> When I enrolled at MLSh, I was very much satisfied with the learning conditions and I was eager to study. [However,] during the first period I learned too little because of my poor knowledge of Russian. Besides, I [wanted to understand] the causes of the defeat of the Chinese Revolution. I knew that the Opposition had argued with the All-Union Communist Party (Bolsheviks) (AUCP[B]) CC for a long time. Although I had not known the essence of the Opposition, I had just voted for the CC while being at KUTV.

At the time, Ma Yuansheng was afraid to talk with the Oppositionists openly. He worried that the university administration would misinterpret his talks and accuse him of keeping ties with the Trotskyists. Ma wrote: 'I saw that the comrades who even unconsciously uttered one word were being accused. [That is why] I was afraid to speak up at all. So, I studied disputed questions secretly'.[60]

The letter shows that Ma Yuansheng could not understand why the Oppositionists were so severely repressed: 'There is only one thing I cannot understand. If a group of people whose opinion differs from the political views

---

59   RGASPI, 954/83.
60   RGASPI, 954/83.

of the government representatives, does not defend its beliefs by an armed uprising, and only conducts talks as relatives do among themselves, why would the government want to destroy it?'[61]

Ma Yuanshen's story was not unique. According to recollections of other Chinese students who attended the Soviet international schools, all arrived in the USSR to study seriously. However, they had to search for a proper place in the midst of the turmoil of the time. Ma claimed in his letter, 'I was eager to learn, but I found myself following absolutely the wrong way'.[62]

Ma Yuansheng wanted to discuss his doubts with Liu Renjing, but Liu refused. 'Then in the fall of 1928 after the closing of the Comintern's Sixth Congress and the CCP's Sixth Congress, I finally came to the Oppositionist views', wrote Ma.[63] Accidentally, Ma Yuansheng had discovered Trotsky's work *A Criticism of the Basic Points of the Programme of the Communist International* and was impressed by it. This work analysed the main reasons for the defeat of Communism in Germany, China, and France. Trotsky offered a new Comintern tactical line for the period following the debacle of the Chinese National Revolution. He believed that the CCP should develop a programme of serious democratic reforms including the call for a national assembly. He urged the Chinese Communists to pursue it.[64]

It was this Trotsky brochure that made Ma Yuansheng pose many questions. He wished to receive answers to them and that was why he again came to Liu Renjing. He shared his thoughts with him. He told Liu he disagreed with Trotsky's thesis to reject a slogan in favour of soviets after the CCP's rout in the Revolution. He did not want to replace it with a slogan in favour of a national assembly. At that time, Liu agreed to talk to him but he did not yet offer him new materials.[65] Only later did he give him another work written by Trotsky, *The Chinese Question After the Sixth Congress*. This work focused on the causes of the defeat of the Canton Uprising in December 1927. The uprising was organised by the CCP under Stalin's Comintern pressure.[66] Most likely, it was this work that Liu Renjing was translating at the time for secret dissemination among MLSh Chinese students. Thereafter Liu conducted a series of talks with Ma asking him what he would like to learn. In April 1929, Liu advised Ma to get in touch with Fan Wenhui (1904–56), who had enrolled at UTK in

---

61   Ma Yuansheng 1987, p. 94.
62   RGASPI, 495/225/954/86.
63   RGASPI, 495/225/954/86.
64   Trotsky 1993, pp. 64–233.
65   RGASPI, 495/225/954/84.
66   Trotsky 1993, pp. 234–80.

the mid-December 1927 under the pseudonym Aleksei Makarovich Fogel. He said that Fan could give him a lot of translated and original Oppositionist literature.[67]

Shortly thereafter some Chinese Oppositionists from KUTV were transferred to MLSh. They were Liu Yin (1906–40, aliases Gubarev and Kashin) and Cao Li.[68] Two Trotskyists, Zhang Hesheng and Li Guangti, then came from China.[69] Ma Yuansheng exchanged views with them, and they disagreed on many issues.[70] As a result, Ma failed to unify the Oppositionists at MLSh. The Chinese Trotskyists there just read forbidden books and participated in anti-Stalinist talks. Only in September 1929, with the help of Chinese Trotskyists from KUTK, did Ma Yuansheng and other MLSh Oppositionists manage to overcome their differences and then the Trotskyist faction at MLSh was formed under Ma's formal leadership.[71] It was tiny. Ma could enlist only ten or so people.

Despite all precautions, at the end of 1929, this organisation was crushed by Stalin's secret police. A former MLSh student, Australian Communist, Ted Tripp (1900–92), recalls:

> A few months before I finished the course, the school called all the students together in our large auditorium. We were addressed by the woman comrade who ran the Lenin School [Kirsanova]. She announced in a loud and accusing manner:
> 'We have just discovered that a faction has been formed of Zinoviev and Bukharin. We don't know how far it has gone, but it is permeating the ranks of the Party. We are determined that it is going to be wiped out. I have received instructions that all students at the School have to be examined to see if they have any germs of this faction in them. It is what we call a party *chistca*, a party cleansing, which has been ordered throughout the Soviet Union'.[72]

And here is what Zhang Guotao remembered:

> The purge at Lenin Academy [MLSh] was conducted by the Party Purification Committee appointed by the Comintern. Zinosanova

---

67 RGASPI, 495/225/954/77 verso.
68 There is no information about Cao Li in the archives.
69 RGASPI, p. 76.
70 RGASPI, p. 85.
71 RGASPI, p. 78.
72 Tripp n. d.

[Kirsanova], president of the academy, was the first to be purged at the investigation meeting. She recounted to the audience her entire political life, particularly all the errors that she had committed in the realm of politics. In the course of her hour-long confession, she even made mention of her private life during her younger days, which astonished foreign Communist party members. Next to be removed were other responsible persons of the academy and members of the party cell committee, followed by teachers and some students.... The campaign went on continuously, day and night, and all classes were practically suspended. The drive was concluded nearly two months later, after several persons had been removed.[73]

The Party Purge Commission interrogated students 'to test their solidity'. They asked twenty-five or thirty questions checking the financial status of the student's parents, the purpose of the student's arrival in the USSR, his or her reasons for joining the party, and his/her Communist activity. The Commission particularly wondered if the student had taken part in the struggle against the former CCP leader Chen Duxiu (1879–1942). They also asked the students about their behaviour during the anti-Trotskyist campaign in the Soviet Union and their 'deviations' from the party line.[74]

There is an interesting document in the archives, a list of MLSh Chinese students about whom the Commission could find compromising materials. The list reflects the new atmosphere of terror created at MLSh by the Soviet Stalinists. Dated 3 January 1930, it consists of ten surnames: Petukhov (Ma Yuansheng), a former student of KUTV who had 'connections with a Trotskyist, a former MLSh student Liu Renjing'; Kon (Zhu Daijie), 'a Trotskyist expelled from KUTV'; Kochergin (Wang Shiyuan), a son of a merchant, a CCP member, and a candidate member of the AUCP(B) who maintained 'written connections with Trotskyist students and who was undeveloped politically'; Vazhnov (Guo Miaogen 1907–?), a worker, a CCP member and a CCYL member from 1926, and a candidate member of the AUCP(B) from 1928 who was 'unreliable and had sympathy for the Trotskyists from 1927'; Nudelman (Jiang Yuanqing), a peasant, a CCP member from 1923, and a candidate member of the AUCP(B) from 1928 whose 'relatives were Guomindang members'; Chugunov (Zhou Dawen), an intellectual, a CCYL and Guomindang member from 1923 and a CCP member from 1924; Orlinskii (Dong Yixiang) who 'befriended' the 'right' Guomindang members Tolstoy (Gu Rongyi) and Polevoi (Deng Yisheng);

---

73   Chang Kuo-t'ao 1971, Volume 2, pp. 98–9.
74   RGASPI, 531/2/24/1–4; 25/42, 43.

Kliuev (Pan Kelu), a son of an aristocrat; Li Guoxuan (1898–?), a CCYL member from 1920 and a CCP member from 1923, who was 'an adherent of Chen Duxiu'; and Narimanov (Yu Xiusong).[75]

The document indicates that Wang Shiyuan, Zhou Dawen, Dong Yixiang, and Yu Xiusong were members of the so-called 'Solidarity Association' (other names were the 'Mutual Aid Fund' and the 'Jiangsu-Zhejiang Friendly Association'.) What was this organisation? From some Comintern officials' point of view, it was an illegal, anti-party group set up in 1927 and led by Sun Yat-sen University students Yu Xiusong, Zhou Dawen, Dong Yixiang and Chiang Ching-kuo (Chiang Kai-shek's oldest son). These ECCI officials believed that the aim of the group was to dismiss student leaders of UTK and MLSh who were active Stalinists in order to establish 'counter-revolutionary links' with the former CCP leaders Chen Duxiu and Tan Pingshan (1886–1956), both of them by this time deemed 'betrayers of the Revolution'. The 'Association' members were accused of maintaining links with the Opposition and 'Right' Guomindang members.[76]

There is no doubt that some sort of a student organisation called the 'Mutual Aid Fund' did exist among the Chinese students in Moscow. However, it was not at all 'counter-revolutionary'.[77] The students simply helped each other financially, kept friendly relations, and spent their leisure time together. Members of the group including Yu Xiusong, Zhou Dawen, and Dong Yixiang were all devoted Stalinists. The person who made 'a counter-revolution-story' out of this mutual-support society was a chairman of the UTK student commune Chen Shaoyu (1904–74, alias Ivan Andreevich Golubev; in 1931, he would become known under his pseudonym Wang Ming). Chen strove to establish his personal control over all Chinese students in Moscow and hated Yu Xiusong, Zhou Dawen, and Dong Yixiang for their zealous opposition to 'the Golubev dictatorship'. The UTK rector and the head of the University Stalinists Pavel Mif (1901–38, alias Mikhail Aleksandrovich Fortus) backed Chen Shaoyu, in spite of the fact that Yu, Zhou, and Dong were all old party members. As for Chen, he joined the Party only in 1926 in Moscow![78]

Chen managed to push his foes out of UTK by means of intrigues, having artificially united Yu, Zhou, and Dong with Chiang Ching-kuo. In 1927, Zhou Dawen, Dong Yixiang, and Yu Xiusong were transferred to the International Lenin School. 'Chugunov, Narimanov, and Orlinskii could not stay at KUTK any

---

75 RGASPI, 1/220/5.
76 Galitskii 2003, p. 43.
77 Galitskii 2003, p. 43.
78 See Wang Ming's three-volume personal file preserved in RGASPI (495/225/6).

longer', recalled Chen Shaoyu, who continued to attack his opponents.[79] In July 1928, Chen and Mif managed to win the new CCP General Secretary Xiang Zhongfa (1880–1931) over to their side, and he began to help them in their struggle. Yu, Zhou, and Dong were summoned to the Party Purge Commission and interrogated.

They stubbornly denied all charges, even the very existence of the 'Mutual Aid Fund'. Zhou Dawen wrote to the ECCI on 31 July 1928 as follows:

> For some recent months rumours about the existence of an alleged 'counter-revolutionary organisation' have become widespread. One said that this organisation was established by Chinese students who were party and Komsomol [Communist Youth League] members and lived on USSR territory. Some others said that even our renowned proletarian organisation GPU [State Political Directorate, Stalin's secret police] was warned about it. [Many people said that] the denunciation of this contemporary political conspiracy and the struggle against this conspiracy became one of the main everyday tasks of the Chinese University party committee. Taking it all into account, I consider it a very serious matter, but in fact I think it is not correct.... The very name 'Zhejiang Friendly Association' which many people like to use was taken very arbitrarily. Where did one get it? It is worth discovering.[80]

The Bolshevik Party Central Control Commission (CCC) adopted a resolution on the 'Mutual Aid Fund'. It read that the establishment of this fund was 'an attempt to render financial help to Chinese students at military and other Soviet schools'. The CCC had no reason to believe that 'the comrades pursued other goals'. It considered unjust and false all charges brought by some Communists against the students who were members of such a 'Fund'. The charges included an anti-party activity, supporting the Third Party (that is, Tan Pingshan's party), and attempting to seize power in the CCP. At the same time, the CCC decided to liquidate this and other kind of associations because

> any grouping among the Chinese Comrades, members and candidate members of the AUCP(B) and the Komsomol, may affect the struggle of the proletariat. The Chinese Comrades are preparing themselves for revolutionary activity in China where the CCP works under unusually difficult circumstances which demand extremely strict unity and discipline.... In

---

79 RGASPI, 495/225/932/38.
80 RGASPI, p. 85.

this situation, associations based on friendship rather than the party principle also hamper the CCP struggle.[81]

The CCC decision was read and discussed at general student meetings at KUTK and MLSh. Thus, the Comintern Executive put an end to Chen Shaoyu's further attempts to denounce old party members seemingly closed the 'Jiangsu-Zhejiang Association' case.[82] In 1929, Chen with his future wife Meng Qingshu (1911–83) returned to China. However, in 1930, during the new party purge at MLSh, conducted by the ECCI and the International Control Commission (ICC), the case resurfaced. The new Party Purge Commission now clearly wished to tie the 'Association' with the Ma Yuansheng Trotskyist group. Many members of the 'Mutual Fund' opposed such an approach, but in vain.[83] This time, they could not avoid punishment.

Real Trotskyists did not manage to save themselves either. After examination, for some reason, the Party Purge Commission 'approved' only three of them. These were 'the son of an aristocrat' Pan Kelu, who successfully graduated and was sent to work in a CCP cell,[84] Yu Xiusong, and Dong Yixiang (Yu and Dong both remained at MLSh).[85] As for Zhou Dawen, the Party Purge Commission adopted the following resolution: 'Due to new accusations brought against the Association, the Chugunov issue is to be transferred to the ICC'.[86] Only the Bolshevik Party and the ICC Appeal Commission finally decided to 'regard Comrade Chugunov approved'.[87] This decision was taken on 20 May 1930.

At the same time, four MLSh students, Wang Shiyuan, Guo Miaogen, Jiang Yuanqing, and Li Guoxuan, were charged as active Trotskyist fighters against the party leadership. The Commission reprimanded them severely and sent them to work in factories.[88] Zhu Daijie, deemed an active Trotskyist who 'was not sincere enough at the commission meeting', was expelled from the School.[89] The Commission also expelled Ma Yuansheng, who was soon arrested and on 26 June 1930 exiled to the city of Ivanovo.[90] In 1931, Ma appealed to the ECCI requesting he be allowed to re-enter the Communist Party. Strange as it may

---

81 Cited in Galitskii 2003, p. 43.
82 Pantsov and Levine n.d., pp. 275–7.
83 See RGASPI, 495/225/3001/7 verso.
84 RGASPI, 3024.
85 RGASPI, 3001/72; 932.
86 RGASPI, 932/7 verso.
87 RGASPI, 932/7 verso.
88 RGASPI, 3064, 3071, 3078.
89 RGASPI, 954/34.
90 RGASPI, 2.

seem, he was forgiven and readmitted to the Party in 1932. However, he was not allowed to return to China. Until September 1935, he worked as a mechanic at the Fourth Ivanovo industrial plant. Then he was re-arrested and imprisoned in a labour camp.

In February 1930, in addition to the above-mentioned MLSh students, thirty-one KUTK students were arrested for participation in the 'Jiangsu-Zhejiang Friendly Association' and the Trotskyist movement.[91] In April, the NKVD (People's Commissariat of Internal Affairs, a successor of GPU) sent five more KUTK students behind bars, and in July nineteen more students were imprisoned.[92]

Wang Ruofei and Zhang Guotao received serious reprimands as well. They were both accused of maintaining links with the Oppositionists. On 22 May 1930, the ICC and AUCP(B) Special Commission dealt with Wang's case and gave him a severe reprimand for his Trotskyist views and for rendering help to the Trotskyists.[93] As for Zhang Guotao, technically he did not have to go through the purge since he was not an official MLSh student. However, as a member of the CCP delegation to the ECCI and a candidate member of the ECCI Presidium, he was summoned by the ECCI secretary Joseph A. Piatnitskii (1882–1938) who informed him that the Commission had learned that Zhang maintained 'links' with Liu Renjing. This fact had become known from a real Chinese Trotskyist during his interrogation. This Trotskyist mentioned that Zhang had allegedly read secret Trotskyist documents given to him by Liu Renjing. Zhang recalled that he indeed read some papers, but insisted that Liu asked him to read them in order to correct the translation. According to Zhang, while reading, he did not get to the contents of the paper. 'One can see from this incident how the purge campaign could produce fantastic chain reactions', wrote Zhang in his memoirs.[94] Because of these 'reactions', Zhang finally had to prove his innocence before the Party Purge Commission.[95]

The CCP delegation to the ECCI played an instrumental role in the purge. The head of the delegation Qu Qiubai (1899–1935, alias Strakhov), a member of the CCP Politburo, was particularly rigorous. In 1928, at the Sixth Comintern Congress, Qu was elected a member of the ECCI Presidium and from 1928 to 1930 he taught at MLSh and KUTK. It was Qu who closely cooperated with Stalin's secret police and the International Control Commission

---

91   Galitskii 2003, p. 82.
92   Galitskii 2003, p. 83.
93   Pantsov 2000, p. 196.
94   Chang Kuo-t'ao 1971, Volume 2, p. 101.
95   Pantsov 2000, p. 196.

in denouncing Chinese Trotskyists.[96] Deng Zhongxia (1894–1933), the other member of the delegation, also demonstrated great anti-Trotskyist activity.[97] To be sure, they vigorously defended Zhou Dawen, Yu Xiusong, and Dong Yixiang, as they did not consider them Trotskyists. With Pavel Mif's support, Chen Shaoyu attacked Qu and Deng in 1929 before his return to China. In his secret letter to the ECCI denouncing 'errors' of the CCP delegation, he accused them of sympathising with the Trotskyists.[98] As a result, in 1930 both Qu and Deng were dismissed from their offices and sent back to China.

In 1931, following Kirsanova's temporary dismissal, Stalin's secret police arrested a number of MLSh teachers including pro-rector and chair of the Education Department Zinovii L'vovich Serebrianskii and chair of the Economics Department Lev Khanovich Segel.[99] In January 1937, the NKVD arrested Raiskaia's husband, Petr Nikolaevich Pozharskii, a former nobleman and a Tsarist Army officer. He was charged with being 'an enemy of the people and a participant in the anti-Soviet campaigns'. The MLSh party committee dealt with the 'Raiskaia affair' and charged her with keeping her husband's background a secret. The totally distraught woman wrote in her statement to the party committee:

> I believed that I have known [my husband] for twelve years. I trusted him as if he were an honest man.... Such a devilish disguise and such a terrible blindness of mine! The Party and the Revolution gave me so much, but I could not protect the Party from an enemy of the people.... How could I make a fool of myself after having received such a strong party education! I cannot imagine my life outside the Party.

Raiskaia asked 'the Party' to let her redeem herself. She wrote that, for the last five years, she and her husband had lived separately in different cities and she 'could not unmask him as an enemy in time'. She betrayed her husband, but 'the Party' did not forgive her. In November 1937, she was expelled from the Communist Party and dismissed from her office as the head of the 'Ts' sector. She was charged with lacking vigilance, keeping her husband's social origins a secret and even with violating the conspiracy rules. Some people recalled that

---

96　RGASPI, 495/225/1014; *Geming renwu* ('Figures of the Revolution'), no. 1, 1986, pp. 47–8.
97　RGASPI, 495/225/528.
98　Pantsov and Levine n.d., p. 126.
99　RGASPI, 495/225/44/8.

she had let her husband bid her farewell at a railway station when she and her students were leaving for summer practice.[100]

Nonetheless, Raiskaia managed to escape arrest. Many students and instructors at MLSh were not so lucky. The terror also extended to the KUTV and NIINKP. On 25 May 1936, the KUTV was divided into two independent institutions: the KUTV continued to train Soviet students and the Scientific Research Institute of National and Colonial Issues (NIINKP) grew up from the KUTV Foreign Department (at the time it was called the Cadres Department). All foreign students were transferred to the NIINKP. Pavel Mif was named its director. The 143 Chinese students at the newly organised school constituted about 80 per cent of the student body.[101]

The Russian State Archives of Social and Political History contain a fascinating list of nineteen NIINKP students arrested by the NKVD.[102] We know little about these people. One student began taking classes at the KUTV Foreign Department in 1934, another in 1935, and three more enrolled at the NIINKP in 1936. As for the other arrested persons, they arrived in the USSR in 1934, 1935, and 1936. All were CCP members. Some occupied important positions. These were a certain Jing Chang (alias Zhan Bei) who had served as a district-level party secretary in Harbin; Ma Youqing (alias Ma Ying) who had been a party cell secretary at the North Manchurian Special Committee and a district-level CCP secretary; Tian Qingguo (alias Tian Yongguang) who had worked as an instructor in the Military Department of the Harbin CCP City Committee; Zhang Yidian (alias Yang Toli) who had arrived in the USSR in 1935 as a delegate to the Seventh Comintern Congress and had been an officer and conducted party activity among the peasants; and Bai Qiangsheng (alias Cheng Yousheng), who had been a secretary of the CCYL Shanghai Committee. Apart from them, the NKVD arrested Jing Chang's wife Wen Suzen (alias Wang Nanpu), who had been a technical secretary with the Manchurian CCP Committee Special Department; Guang Pingyong (alias Li Fang), who had worked at the Harbin Party Committee and at the Manchuria railway station as the ECCI liaison-officer;[103] Duan Binghen (alias Zhang You), who had been a party agitator and a liaison-officer; Cheng Tifang (alias Yang Ming), who had worked on several CCP committees; and a former guerrilla Lu Liangsheng (alias Ba Bao). Justifications

---

100 RGASPI, 495/65a/7776; Kipnis 1998, p. 443.
101 Pantsov 2000, pp. 165 and 290; Timofeeva 1979, p. 41.
102 Among them there are ten Chinese (eight men and two women) and nine Koreans. (All names are in Russian; no characters are given.)
103 Ma Youqing (Ma Ying) and Guang Pingyong (Li Fang) were man and wife (Din-Savva 2000, pp. 133–73).

for arrests differed. For example, Ma Youqing was denounced to the ECCI as a Japanese spy by the CCP delegation, but Zhang Yidian 'aroused the suspicion' of the ECCI itself. The Comintern Executive rejected him as a delegate to the Seventh Comintern Congress.[104]

It is unknown how many such lists existed. However, there is no doubt this was not the only one. Books on victims of political repressions in the USSR published by the Memorial Society contain many names of Chinese students of the NIINKP who were arrested and shot in 1937 or 1938.[105] The Comintern's personal files of Chinese revolutionaries preserved in the archives also show that at least several dozen Chinese students and instructors lost their lives in the Soviet Union during the Stalin purges. On 11 December 1937, Mif himself was arrested and, on 28 July 1938, he was shot.[106]

A tide of Stalinist purges flooded MLSh and other Comintern schools, thus disorganising the educational process. In the spring of 1938, the AUCP(B) CC Politburo adopted a resolution to close the International Communist University (the Lenin School). At the time, such decisions could have been made only with Stalin's approval. Here, the resolution closing the International Lenin School stated:

> 1. To accept the NKVD suggestion with regard to the schedule of the departure from the USSR of the Lenin School students. To oblige Cmds. Manuilskii (1883–1959) [the ECCI secretary] and Frinovskii (1898–1940) [the first deputy of the head of NKVD] to finish the departure no later than 15 April this year. 2. To deliver the school buildings and property as follows: a) to deliver a building at 51 Hertsin St., three dachas in Tomilino and Kraskovo, a library, and the auto transport to the ECCI; b) to deliver buildings at 14 and 15 Gogol Boulevard and at 16 Volkhonka St. as well as a kindergarten in Tomilino and the Soloviev sanatorium in Gurzuf to the AUCP(B) CC Management Department.[107]

In September 1938, following the Politburo resolution, the Comintern Executive passed its own decision in this regard. At the same time it decided

---

104   RGASPI, 495/225/378/267.
105   *Knigi pamiati zhertv politicheskii repressii v SSSR. Bibliograficheskii ukazatel* ('Memorial Books on Victims of Political Repression in the USSR. Bibliographical Reference Book'), CD-rom, 1.
106   Pantsov 2000, p. 290.
107   RGASPI, 495/73/61/13.

to liquidate the NIINKP.[108] The Chinese students of the MLSh 'Ts' sector and the Chinese from the NIINKP who survived the 'Great Terror' were transferred to the newly organised secret USSR International Proletarian Revolutionaries' Aid Organisation (MOPR) CC Chinese party school in Kuchino. Later well-known Communists like Cai Chang (1900–90, alias Rosa Nikolaeva) and Lin Biao (1906 or 1907–71), alias Li Ting as well as Mao Zedong's (1893–1976) third wife He Zizhen (1909–84, alias Wen Yun) and Deng Xiaoping's (1904–97) ex-wife and Li Weihan's wife Jin Weiying (1904–41, aliases Li Sha and Lisa) studied here.[109]

Conclusion

A history of the Chinese international schools in the USSR highlights the significance of the Soviet factor in the ideological and political evolution of the Chinese Communist movement in the 1920s and 1930s. The Russian Communists tried to create the CCP cadres in their own image and likeness. To pursue this goal, they financed, directed, and supervised the Chinese Communists. For this reason, the Stalinisation of the Bolshevik Party that took place from 1924 to 1929 had a tremendous impact on the CCP. The Chinese students in Moscow were the first to feel it.

The MLSh Chinese sector 'Ts' underwent the same dramatic alteration. Those CCP students who rose in Trotskyist opposition perished; some were killed, some went through countless moral tortures. Others had to follow Bolshevik discipline. Thus, the sector along with the entire MLSh was transformed from an international communist institution into a university that trained Chinese Stalinists.

Nonetheless, unlike the returned students from KUTV and KUTK, returned students from MLSh did not create their own faction within the CCP. Neither did they join the Wang Ming group (the so-called Twenty-Eight Bolsheviks). Despite MLSh's 'élite' status, most of its graduates did not become party leaders. Only twenty people (fewer than ten per cent of all Chinese MLSh-students) became top CCP cadres and only those who had been famous beforehand continued to occupy leading positions after attending the International Lenin School. They included Dong Biwu, Gao Zili, Ma Huizhi, Liu Changsheng, Li Weihan, Kong Yuan, Song Yiping, Wang Guanlan, Wang Ruofei, and some others.

---

108   Adibekov, Shakhnazarova, and Shirinia 1997, pp. 208–9 and 247–8.
109   RGASPI, 495/225/53/1; 109; 420; 428/1–28; Shi Zhe and Shi Qiulang 2001, p. 45.

Most likely this was because the rectors of MLSh – Bukharin, Kirsanova, Pieck, and Chervenkov – were not as ambitious as KUTK's rector Pavel Mif, who zealously tried to push his alumni into the CCP leadership. As a result, most MLSh graduates and Chinese instructors did not oppose the rise of Mao Zedong, who, in the 1930s and 1940s, was no more than a Chinese Stalinist.[110] Only one Lenin School graduate tried to challenge Mao's leadership and establish his own dictatorship – Zhang Guotao. And he did not rely on the returned MLSh students – he used his army.

Overall, regardless of their future party ranking, most MLSh graduates made a contribution to the Communist victory in China. So, the MLSh itself played a substantial role in the Chinese Revolution, although its role was not as significant as that of the KUTK and the KUTV. Historically, it remained an exemplary Comintern party school that functioned longer than other Comintern institutions under the total control of the Soviet Stalinists, who imposed a particularly ruthless reign of terror on it.

---

110 For new documents on Mao, see Pantsov 2005 and 2007.

Stalin and the Chinese Communist Dissidents

Alexander Pantsov

First published in Reflections at the End of a Century, *edited by Morris Slavin and Louis Patsouras, Youngstown: Youngstown State University Press, 2002, pp. 28–40.*

The Trotskyist Left Opposition challenged the Stalinists on many issues. One of the most important was bureaucratisation of the Bolshevik party government apparatus. Trotsky and his co-thinkers did not accept Stalin's antidemocratic perceptions of the intra-party organisation. They contrasted his policy of tough centralisation with the romantic idea of a 'democratic' communist party in which, as they believed, 'the necessary balance between elements of democracy and centralism'[1] would be maintained. They also disagreed with Stalin's repudiation of world-wide revolution, arguing that without the victory of the proletariat in the main countries of Europe it was impossible to arrive at socialism in a backward Russia. The Trotskyists could find no ground with the Stalinists on various other issues of internal and foreign policy too, including the Chinese Communist Party's (CCP's) tactics in the Chinese Revolution. Trotsky, for example, supported the independence of the CCP in its 1924–7 united front with the Guomindang, underlining that the Communists' true aim was to prepare the workers' liberation.

The ideas of the Oppositionists affected all local sections of the Communist International. By the end of 1927, Trotskyist factions had emerged in most Communist parties. At that time, however, the Stalinists managed to suppress the Opposition in the Soviet Union itself. In November 1927, Trotsky was expelled from the Bolshevik Party. In 1928, other members of his group were deported to remote areas in the Soviet Union, and, early in 1929, Trotsky was deported. However, Oppositionist propaganda against Stalinism continued into the 1930s.

The Soviet secret police and intelligence service as well as the Comintern officials directed by Stalin himself did their best to stop anti-Stalin activity among dissident foreign Communists. Particular attention was paid to the Oppositionists in the CCP inasmuch as the CCP was the second biggest section – after the Bolshevik Party – of the Communist International.

---

1 Trotsky 1985 [1941], p. 140.

When did Stalin start persecuting the Chinese Communist dissidents and what was the outcome? The disclosing of the voluminous Stalin files shortly after the collapse of the USSR laid the foundation for a scholarly inquiry of this topic. These files are now preserved in the State Archives of Social and Political History (RGASPI in a Russian abbreviation.) This depository also received Stalin's documents from the top secret Archives of the President of the Russian Federation. Apart from the Stalin collections, invaluable material can also be found in the archives of the CCP's delegation to the Comintern Executive (ECCI), of the Soviet international schools of the 1920s and 1930s, and of the Internal Opposition in the Bolshevik Party. Personal dossiers of the members of the CCP, Soviet Communists, and employees of the Executive Committee of the Comintern are also interesting. Of interest also are the files of the head of the Comintern Executive Committee Georgi M. Dimitrov's Secretariat and the Comintern International Control Commission.

These collections contain minutes of interrogations and testimonies of arrested Chinese Trotskyists, coded telegrams from Soviet and Comintern agents in China, records of Stalin's meetings with Soviet and Chinese officials, information from the Soviet secret police and intelligence service, including Russian translations of foreign diplomatic letters intercepted by the police Foreign Department, as well as Chinese Communist and Comintern correspondence.

The evidence supports the view that the formation of the Chinese anti-Stalinist Communist Opposition was triggered by the activities of Soviet Stalinists who insisted in the autumn of 1926 on drawing Chinese students at Soviet international schools into their struggle against the Trotskyist minority in the Bolshevik Party. Until then, there were no supporters of the Opposition among the Chinese Communists either in China or in Russia, for the simple reason that they knew nothing about the debate. By October 1926, the Bolshevik Central Committee had decided to spread the struggle to the international schools. In the 1920s, Chinese revolutionaries studied at a number of these schools, including the Communist University of the Toilers of the East (established in April 1921), Sun Yat-sen University of the Toilers of China (opened in November 1925; in September 1928, it was renamed the Communist University of the Toilers of China), the International Lenin School (set up in 1925), and some others. Most were students at Sun Yat-sen University, where the rector was Karl Radek, a prominent Oppositionist. In 1919, Radek was a co-organiser of the Comintern and until 1923 worked as a secretary of this international organisation. Then he joined Trotsky in his struggle against Stalin and was dismissed from the office. He was rector of Sun Yat-sen University from 1925 until 1927 and considered by many in the Comintern as an expert in Chinese affairs. An outstanding orator and polemicist, he exerted a lot of influence on his Chinese students.[2]

In October 1926, however, an enlarged anti-Trotskyist meeting of the party committee was convened at Sun Yat-sen University. It was followed by a general meeting of all Communists. Radek was the main target of the Stalinists' attacks. This is how the former student of this school Meng Qingshu recalls the start of the anti-Trotskyist campaign at the University:

> At that time all that the students knew about Trotsky and the Trotskyists was what was contained in the history course on the Soviet Communist Party. We knew nothing of their activities in 1924–6. So after the party committee meeting, a general meeting of all Communists and young Communists at the University was called. Party secretary Ignatov addressed the gathering, delivering a lecture on Trotskyism. In this way the intense struggle against Trotskyism at the University began.[3]

The Stalinists employed the same methods as in their campaign in the broader party. The international schools were plunged into a constant round of meetings and worked up into a hysteria. The Stalinists expected the Chinese students to play the role of extras in the struggle against the Opposition. Reading Opposition material was forbidden and the students were constantly reminded of the need to observe discipline and to bind themselves to the leadership. A large proportion decided to toe the Comintern line, but others felt an increasing desire to examine for themselves the Opposition's documents and get to the root of the questions raised by Trotsky and Radek. It was within these circles that the Left Opposition in the CCP was born.

Until April 1927, the interest of the Chinese students in Trotskyist ideas remained academic. The situation was changed radically by the course of the Chinese National Revolution. On 12 April 1927, Chiang Kai-shek, who had previously collaborated with the Chinese Communists and been enthusiastically supported by Stalin and the Comintern, staged a bloody anti-communist coup d'état. Only after that did the critically minded section of the Chinese student body reject the Stalinist line on China. The first Chinese supporters of the Opposition were few in number; in August 1927, at Sun Yat-sen University, for example, including sympathisers and waverers, they numbered just over thirty persons or ten per cent of the student body.[4] They restricted themselves

---

2 For Chinese students' evaluation of Radek's teaching see RGASPI, 530/2/29, 32.
3 Meng Qingshu n.d., pp. 66–7.
4 Calculated from RGASPI, 530/l/42.

to ideological struggle and made no attempt to set up an organisation. They were not so concerned to make propaganda among their fellow-students as to influence the leadership of the CCP. The Opposition literature they translated was dispatched to the CCP Central Committee. Their most striking action was to participate in anti-Stalinist demonstration on 7 November 1927, in Red Square. Shortly after the demonstration, eight activists were expelled from Sun Yat-sen University and returned to China. At that time, none of the Chinese Oppositionists was arrested.

The expelled students did not abandon their anti-Stalinist activity. Upon arrival in China, they set up the Left Opposition. Chinese Trotskyists left behind in the Soviet Union formed their own centralised, conspiratorial organisation in the autumn of 1928. At first, it had about forty members. They directed their work towards laying the foundations for Oppositionist activity in China. The future struggle against Stalinism in the CCP would require great resources and the young Chinese Oppositionists did all in their power to lay the basis for it in advance. They studied, translated, and diffused anti-Stalinist literature, which they received from a group of Russian Trotskyists in Moscow. The clandestine links with the Russian Trotskyists were carried on via a former teacher at Sun Yat-sen University, Polyakov, who used to attend the meetings of the so-called General Committee (a ruling body) of the Chinese Trotskyist organisation as an associate member.[5] After Polyakov's arrest at the end of 1928, he was replaced by the widow of Trotsky's former confederate Adolf A. Joffe, Maria Mikhailovna.[6]

In 1929, the Chinese Oppositionists accelerated their work. While keeping up their preparation for the future struggle in China, they began developing their protest in the universities. In 1929 at the Communist University of the Toilers of China they formed a united front with those at odds with the university party committee. In addition to the General Committee, a new body, the 'Struggle Committee', was established. Its task was to coordinate the joint struggle of the Trotskyists and other disaffected elements against the Stalinists in the universities. The most significant result of the Struggle Committee's discussions with other student groups came at a general meeting of the university party branch in June 1929 when the Oppositionists and their allies made fierce and sustained criticisms of the party leadership of the Communist University of the Toilers of China.[7] Naturally, the Oppositionists did not advertise their

---

5 Vitin (An Fu), RGASPI, 514/l/1012/30.
6 RGASPI, 514/l/1012/30, 28; Wu K'un-jung 1974, p. 80.
7 For a stenographic record of this meeting, see RGASPI, 530/l/7071. See also recollections of this meeting of a former student of the Communist University of the Toilers of China Zhang

membership of the secret anti-Stalinist organisation. This stormy meeting lasted several days but ended in defeat for the Opposition. It proved impossible to overturn the Stalinist majority in the student body.

The Oppositionists were growing in number towards the beginning of 1930. Evidence points to a membership of about eighty.[8] In addition, there were scores of sympathisers.[9] The Trotskyists now accounted for more than twenty per cent of Chinese students in Moscow. The centre of the organisation was the Communist University of the Toilers of China, which had the greatest concentration of Oppositionists. The biggest of the groups outside the Communist University of the Toilers of China were the ten to fifteen Oppositionists at the Moscow Infantry School and others at the International Lenin School, the Artillery School, and the Military Engineering School.[10]

Such a large underground organisation created a potential menace for Stalinist domination. By February 1930, the secret police and the Comintern Executive had good intelligence about the individual membership of the Trotskyist organisation at the Communist University of the Toilers of China. The Stalinists were simply waiting for a suitable moment to deal the organisation a shattering blow. It came in early February 1930, when arrests took place at the Communist University of the Toilers of China. Twenty-five persons were detained. In the following three months, another eleven activists of the Chinese Left Opposition followed them into the cellars of the Lubyanka prison.[11] The Stalinists were now less mild than in 1927. In September 1930, twenty-four Chinese Trotskyists were sent to concentration camps or

---

Chunwen, published in *Zhonggong dangshi ziliao* (Materials on CCP History), Volume 37, Beijing, 1991, pp. 37–48.

[8] Testimony of Vitin [An Fu], 28; Testimony of a Student [Li Ping], RGASPI, 514/1/1012/17; Letter from V.I. Veger to the AUCP(B) CC addressed to L.M. Kagonovich, A.I. Stetsky; AUCP(B) Moscow Committee, K. Ya. Bauman, Kogan, 25 April 1930, RGASPI, 530/1/71.

[9] List of Trotskyists at the Communist University of the Toilers of China, RGASPI, 514/1/1010/38; List of Chinese Trotskyists in the USSR, RGASPI, 514/1/1010/44–56.

[10] Wang Fanxi 1980, p. 102; Ma Yuansheng 1987; Pantsov 1998. Testimony of Comrade Nekrasov [Qi Shugong], RGASPI, 514/1/1012/9–10; Record of Communication between the Student Donbasov [Zhao Yanqing] and a Member of the CCP Delegation, Comrade Deng Zhongxia, RGASPI, 514/1/1010/99; From the testimony of Vitin [An Fu], 26; Testimony of a student [Li Ping], 16.

[11] OGPU [Soviet Secret Police] on the List of Students Arrested at KUTK [the Communist University of the Toilers of China], RGASPI, 514/1/1010/36–37; 530/1/62; List of Those Arrested by the OGPU [Soviet Secret Police] on February 8 and 19, 1930, RGASPI, 514/1/1010/73–74; RGASPI, 495/225/1100.

into exile.¹² Fewer than ten survived. Thus, the Chinese Left Opposition on Soviet territory shared the fate of the Russian Trotskyists.

The Stalinists also launched a drive to repress the Left Opposition in China. In June 1929, the Second Plenum of the Sixth CCP Central Committee passed a special 'Resolution on the Organisational Question', saying that 'in the organisational field, we must carry out a severe purge of leading activists of the Opposition in the Party'.¹³

The former General Secretary of the CCP Central Committee and one of the first Chinese Bolsheviks, Chen Duxiu, along with four other prominent CCP activists, was expelled by the CCP Politburo for establishing a faction that opposed the CCP leadership. The resolution expelling them was confirmed by the Presidium of the Comintern Executive on 30 December 1929 and formally implemented on 11 June 1930. In December, other members of the Chen Duxiu's group were also purged.

Meanwhile, Chen Duxiu became acquainted with Trotsky's anti-Stalinist writings. Encouraged by the Trotskyist programme, he set up his own Opposition group and a pro-Trotskyist periodical, *Wuchanzhe (Proletarian)*. In May 1931, various Chinese Trotskyist groups merged in Shanghai,¹⁴ but it was smashed by the Guomindang's secret police.

The Soviet and Chinese Stalinists kept a close eye on the Chinese Left Opposition. The CCP delegation to the Comintern Executive regularly received Chinese Trotskyist literature, translated it, and sent copies of the translations to the top leadership of the Bolshevik Party and the Comintern, including Stalin, Molotov, Voroshilov, and later Dimitrov. The most serious attention was paid to Chen Duxiu.¹⁵ No practical actions, however, were taken. There is no archival evidence of a Stalinist involvement in the destruction of Chen's party.

Only occasionally did the Stalinists interfere. The best-known case is that of the American journalist Harold R. Isaacs, who came to Shanghai from the Philippines in early December 1930. Isaacs worked as a reporter, for the *Shanghai Evening Post and Mercury*, then as an editor for the *China Post*, and

---

12   OGPU on the List of Students Arrested at KUTK, 36–37; Supreme Court of the USSR, Ruling no. 4N–013598/57, RGSPI, 495/225/1100; ibid., 495/225/543; 495/225/1106, 1116, 1384, 2045.

13   'Zuzhi wenti juean' (Resolution on the Organisational Question), *Zhonggong zhongyang di erci quanti huiyi cailiao* (Materials of the Second CCP CC Plenum). Moscow: NII po Kitayu, 1930, p. 51.

14   Report no. 1 of the Secretariat of the CCP Left Opposition to the International Secretariat of the International Left Opposition and L. D. Trotsky, 9 May 1931, Trotsky Papers at Houghton Library, Harvard University, bMs Russ, 13.1, 1068, p. 1.

15   RGASPI, 514/1/997/1–93, 998/24–67, 999/1–44, 1005/1–10, 1017/40–531037/90–94.

finally as a translator for the French Havas News Agency. Shortly after his arrival, he met Agnes Smedley, an American Stalinist and a correspondent for the German *Frankfurter Zeitung*, who was not formally a member of any Communist party but maintained secret connections with the Comintern and the Communist Party of the USA. In the early 1930s, she was unofficial representative of the ECCI in China and served as a channel through which Comintern-agents passed money and directives to the Chinese communists. Under the alias Anna, she was also enmeshed in the Soviet spy-ring in Shanghai via the Soviet military intelligence agent Richard Sorge, then living under the alias of Johnson. In 1930, Agnes became one of Sorge's many lovers.[16] In the autumn of 1931, she introduced Isaacs to Soong Qingling, the widow of the late President Sun Yat-sen. Soong, who was openly leftist, maintained secret links with the Comintern representative in China, the American Communist Tim Rayn (alias Eugene Dennis) and some other Comintern and Soviet intelligence agents.[17] Through Soong Qingling, Stalinists came up with the idea that Isaacs might start a paper of his own, under their sponsorship. Isaacs's paper, called *China Forum*, started up on 13 January 1932.

However, a few months before that he met Frank Glass, who exerted a great influence on him. In 1933, Isaacs began to doubt Soviet Communism. He shared his hesitations with Soong Qingling, who informed Soviet agents. An unknown Soviet spy wrote to Moscow: 'The first signals about Isaacs's unreliability came from Soong Qingling who reproduced in detail her conversations with Isaacs to me and the ECCI representative. It became obvious from these conversations that he tried to influence her in a Trotskyist way'.[18] The Stalinists stopped financing *China Forum* and Isaacs had to cease publishing it. He never learned about Soong Qingling's betrayal and preserved friendly feelings for her until his death.[19]

Stalin once again began to worry about the Chinese Left Opposition after the release of Chen Duxiu and other Trotskyists from Guomindang jails in August 1937. Stalin himself tried to influence the Guomindang leadership against the Trotskyists. In November 1937, at a meeting with General Yang Jie and Zhang Chong, he said:

---

16   MacKinnon and MacKinnon 1988, pp. 146–9 and 182–7; Price 2005, pp. 171–208 and 303–20.
17   Secret report sent by Chinese Communists in 1936 to the Comintern Executive, RGASPI, 495/74/299/34.
18   RGASPI, 514/1/1037/53.
19   Isaacs 1985.

> We also have bad informers. One was our Ambassador Bogomolov.... Bogomolov greatly hampered our non-aggression treaty.... He turned out to be a Trotskyist. We arrested him. We arrest bad informers, even Ambassadors. Recently we have also received 'information' from Melamed, now acting as Ambassador. He told us that Bai Chongxi [a Chinese warlord] received a $50 m. bribe from Chiang Kai-shek.... What should we do with Melamed? Is your Yangtze River deep? Would it be better if we drowned him in this river?... Our Trotskyists killed a good man – Kirov. He was a big man. One should keep an eye on pro-Japanese types [that is, Trotskyists.] If you crush traitors, the people will say thank you.[20]

After the late 1930s, real Trotskyists were no longer a main concern for the Stalinists in China. However, the CCP's anti-Trotskyist campaign remained aggressive. The only difference was that the Trotskyist label was now mostly applied to 'honest Stalinists', who, for some reason or other, had lost their leaders' confidence. This 'anti-Trotskyist' campaign was led by Chen Shaoyu (Wang Ming). His personal file in the Comintern archives is full of false information about 'counter-revolutionary Oppositionists' and denunciations of people who were not actually Trotskyists.[21] His 'anti-Trotskyist' activity had nothing in common with Stalin's earlier fight against the Chinese Left Opposition.

---

20   RGSPI, 555/11/321/25–26.
21   RGASPI, 495/222/3.

PART 5

The Unification of the Chinese Trotskyists

Appeal to All Comrades of the Chinese Communist Party

Chen Duxiu

10 December 1929

> *Chen wrote this letter, published in English in the* Militant *(New York), 15 November and 1 December 1930, and 1 and 15 January and 1 February 1931 (and here slightly edited), after being ousted as General Secretary of the* CCP.

Since 1920 (the ninth year of the Republic) I have worked with the comrades, in founding the Party, in sincerely carrying out the opportunist policy of the [Third] International's leaders, Stalin, Zinoviev, Bukharin, and others, bringing the Chinese Revolution to a shameful and sad defeat. Though I have worked night and day, yet my demerits exceed my merits.

Of course, I should not imitate the hypocritical confessions of some of the ancient Chinese emperors: 'I, one person, am responsible for all the sins of the people', and take upon my own shoulders all the mistakes that caused the failure. Nevertheless, I feel ashamed to adopt the attitude of some responsible comrades at times – only criticising the past mistakes of opportunism and excluding oneself. Whenever my comrades have pointed out my past opportunist errors, I earnestly acknowledged them. I am absolutely unwilling to ignore the experiences of the Chinese Revolution obtained at the highest price paid by proletarians in the past. (From the 7 August Conference [1927] to the present time, I not only did not reject proper criticism against me, but I even kept silent about the exaggerated accusations against me.)

Not only am I willing to acknowledge my past errors, but now or in the future, if I should make any opportunist errors in thought or action, I likewise expect comrades to criticise me mercilessly with theoretical argument and facts. I humbly accept or shall accept all criticism, but not rumours and false accusations. I cannot have such self-confidence as Qu Qiubai and Li Lisan. I clearly recognise that it is never an easy thing for anybody or any party to avoid the errors of opportunism. Even such veteran Marxists as Kautsky and Plekhanov were guilty of unpardonable opportunism when they were old; those who followed Lenin for a long time like Stalin and Bukharin are now also acting like shameful opportunists. How can superficial Marxists like us be self-satisfied? Whenever a man is self-satisfied, he prevents himself from making progress.

Even the banner of the Opposition is not the incantation of the 'Heavenly Teacher' Zhang [the Taoist pope]. If those who have not fundamentally cleared out the ideology of the petty bourgeoisie, and have not plainly understood the system of past opportunism and decisively participated in struggles, merely stand under the banner of the Opposition to revile the opportunism of Stalin and Li Lisan, and then think that the opportunist devils will never approach, they are suffering under an illusion. The only way of avoiding the errors of opportunism is continually and humbly to learn from the teachings of Marx and Lenin in the struggles of the proletarian masses and in the mutual criticism of comrades.

I decisively recognise that the objective conditions were second in importance as the cause of the failure of the last Chinese revolution. The main cause was the error of opportunism, the error of our policy in dealing with the bourgeois Guomindang. All the responsible comrades of the Central Committee at that time, especially myself, should openly and courageously recognise that this policy was undoubtedly wrong. But it is not enough merely to recognise the error. We must sincerely and thoroughly acknowledge that the past error was the internal content of the policy of opportunism, examine the causes and results of that policy, and reveal them clearly. Then we can hope to stop repeating the errors of the past, and the repetition of former opportunism in the next revolution. When our party was first founded, though it was quite young, yet, under the guidance of the Leninist International, we did not commit any great mistakes. For instance, we decisively led the struggle of the workers and recognised the class nature of the Guomindang. In 1921, our party induced the delegates of the Guomindang and other social organisations to participate in the conference of the Toilers of the Far East, called by the Comintern. The conference resolved that in the colonial countries of the East the struggle for the democratic revolution must be carried out, and that, in this revolution, peasant soviets should be organised.

In 1922, at the Second Congress of the Chinese Party, the policy of the united front in the democratic revolution was adopted, and based upon this we expressed our attitude towards the political situation. At the same time, the representative of the Communist Youth International, Dalin, came to China and suggested to the Guomindang the policy of a united front of the revolutionary groups. The head of the Guomindang, Sun Yat-sen, stubbornly rejected this, agreeing only to allow the members of the Chinese Communist Party and the Youth League to join the Guomindang as individuals and obey it, denying any unity outside the Party.

Soon after the adjournment of our party congress the Communist International sent its delegate Maring to China. He invited all the members of the Central Committee of the Chinese Communist Party to hold a meeting at the West Lake in Hangzhou, in Zhejiang province, at which he suggested to the Chinese Party that it join the Guomindang organisation. He strongly contended that the Guomindang was not a party of the bourgeoisie but the joint party of various classes and that the proletarian party should join it in order to improve this party and advance the revolution.

At that time, the five members of the Central Committee of the Chinese Communist Party – Li Shouchang, Zhang Teli, Cai Hesen, Gao Junyu, and I – unanimously opposed the proposal. The chief reason was: to join the Guomindang was to confuse the class organisations and curb our independent policy. Finally, the delegate of the Third International asked if the Chinese Party would obey the decision of the International.

Thereupon, for the sake of respecting international discipline, the Central Committee could not but accept the proposal of the Communist International and agree to join the Guomindang. After this, the international delegate and the representatives of the Chinese Party spent nearly a year carrying out the reorganisation of the Guomindang. But, from the very outset, the Guomindang entirely neglected and resisted it. Many times, Sun Yat-sen said to the delegates of the International: 'Since the CCP has joined the Guomindang, it should obey the discipline of the Guomindang and should not openly criticise it. If the Communists do not obey the Guomindang I shall expel them from it; if Soviet Russia stands on the side of the CCP I shall immediately oppose Soviet Russia'. As a result, a dejected Maring returned to Moscow. Borodin, who took over Maring's post in China, brought with him a large sum of material aid for the Guomindang. It was then, in 1924, that the Guomindang began the policy of reorganisation and alliance with Soviet Russia.

At this time the Chinese Communists were not very much tainted with opportunism. We were able to lead the railroad workers' strike on 7 February 1923, and the May Thirtieth Movement of 1925, since we were not restrained by the Guomindang and at times severely criticised its compromising policy. But, as soon as the proletariat raised its head in the May Thirtieth Movement, the bourgeoisie was immediately aroused. In response, Dai Jitao's anti-Communist pamphlet appeared in July.

At the enlarged plenum of the Central Committee of the CCP held in Beijing in October of 1925, I submitted the following proposal to the Political Resolution Committee: Dai Jitao's pamphlet was not accidental but an indication that the bourgeoisie was attempting to strengthen its own power for the purpose of checking the proletariat and going over to the counter-revolution. We should be ready immediately to withdraw from the Guomindang. We should maintain our [public] political face, lead the masses, and not be held in check by the policy of the Guomindang.

At that time, both the delegate of the Comintern and the responsible comrades of the Central Committee unanimously opposed my suggestion, saying that it was to propose to the comrades and the masses to take the path of opposing the Guomindang. I, who had no decisiveness of character, could not insistently maintain my proposal. I respected international discipline and the opinion of the majority of the Central Committee.

Chiang Kai-shek's coup d'état on 20 March 1926 was made to carry out Dai Jitao's principles. Having arrested the Communists in large numbers and disarmed the Guangzhou-Hong Kong Strike Committee's guards for the visiting Soviet group (most of whom were members of the Central Committee of the Soviet Communist Party) and for the Soviet advisers, the Central Committee of the Guomindang decided that all Communist elements should be removed from the supreme party headquarters of the Guomindang, that criticism of Sun Yat-sen-ism by Communists should be prohibited, and that a list of the names of the members of the Communist Party and of the [Youth] League who had joined the Guomindang should be handed over to the latter. All these conditions were accepted.

At the same time, we resolved to prepare our independent military forces in order to be equal to the forces of Chiang Kai-shek. Comrade Peng Shuzhi was sent to Guangzhou as representative of the Central Committee of the Chinese Party to consult the international delegate about our plan. But the latter did not agree with us, and tried his best to continually strengthen Chiang Kai-shek. He insistently advocated that we use all our strength to support the military dictatorship of Chiang Kai-shek, to build up the Guangzhou government, and to carry on the Northern Expedition. We demanded that he take 5,000 rifles out of those given to Chiang Kai-shek and Li Jishen, so that we might arm the peasants of Guangdong province. He refused, saying:

'The armed peasants cannot fight against the forces of Chen Jiongming nor take part in the Northern Expedition, but they can incur the suspicion of the Guomindang and make the peasants oppose it'.

This was the most critical period. Concretely speaking, it was the period when the bourgeois Guomindang openly compelled the proletariat to follow its guidance and direction, when we formally called on the proletariat to surrender to the bourgeoisie, to follow it, and be willing to be subordinates of the bourgeoisie. (The international delegates said openly: 'The present period is a period in which the Communists should do coolie service for the Guomindang'.)

By this time, the Party was already not the party of the proletariat, having become completely the extreme left wing of the bourgeoisie, and beginning to fall into the deep pit of opportunism.

After the coup of 20 March, I stated in a report to the Comintern my personal opinion that cooperation with the Guomindang by means of joint work within it should be changed to cooperation from outside the Guomindang. Otherwise, we would be unable to carry out our own independent policy or win the confidence of the masses. After having read my report, the International published an article by Bukharin in *Pravda* severely criticising the Chinese Party on [the question of] withdrawing from the Guomindang, saying:

'There have been two mistakes: the advocacy of withdrawal from the yellow trade unions and from the Anglo-Russian Trade Union Unity Committee; now the third mistake has been produced: the Chinese Party advocates withdrawal from the Guomindang'. At the same time, the head of the Far Eastern Bureau, Voitinsky, was sent to China to correct our tendency to withdraw from the Guomindang. At that time, I again failed to maintain my proposal strongly, for the sake of honouring the discipline of the International and the opinion of the majority of members of the Central Committee.

Later on, the Northern Expedition army set out. We were very much persecuted by the Guomindang because in *Xiangdao* ('Guide') we criticised the curbing of the labour movement in the rear, and the compulsory collection of the military fund from the peasants for the use of the Northern Expedition. In the meantime, the workers in Shanghai were about to rise up to oust the Zhili-Shandong troops. If the uprisings were successful, the problem of the ruling power would be posed. At that time, in the minutes of the [discussion of the] political resolution of the enlarged plenum of the Central Committee I suggested:

The Chinese revolution has two roads: One is that it be led by the proletariat, then we can reach the goal of the revolution; the other is that it be led by the bourgeoisie, and in that case the latter must betray in the course of the revolution. And, though we may cooperate with the bourgeoisie at the present, we must nevertheless seize the leading power. However, all the members of the Far Eastern Bureau of the Comintern residing in Shanghai unanimously opposed my opinion, saying that such an opinion would influence our comrades to oppose the bourgeoisie too early. Further, they declared, if the Shanghai uprising succeeds, the ruling power should belong to the bourgeoisie and that it was unnecessary to have any participation by workers' delegates. At that time, I again could not maintain my opinion because of their criticism.

About the time the Northern Expedition army took Shanghai in 1927, [Qu] Qiubai paid great attention to the selection of the Shanghai municipal government and how to unite the petty bourgeoisie (the middle and small traders) in opposition to the big bourgeoisie. Peng Shuzhi and Luo Yinong were in agreement with my opinion, that the immediate problem was not the municipal elections. The central problem was that, if the proletariat was not strong enough to win a victory over Chiang Kai-shek's military forces, the petty bourgeoisie would not support us. Chiang Kai-shek, at the instigation of the imperialists, would be certain to carry out a massacre of the masses. Then not only would the municipal elections be reduced to empty talk, but we would face the beginning of a defeat throughout China. When Chiang Kai-shek openly betrayed the revolution, it could not be just an individual action but would be the signal for the bourgeoisie in the whole country to go over to the reactionary camp.

At that time, [Peng] Shuzhi went to Hankou to state our opinion before the international delegate and the majority of the members of the Central Committee of the Chinese Communist Party and to consult with them on how to attack Chiang Kai-shek's forces. But they did not care very much about the impending coup in Shanghai. They telegraphed me several times urging me to go to Wuhan. They thought that since the Nationalist government was then at Wuhan, all important problems should be solved there. At the same time, the International telegraphed instructing us to hide or bury all the workers' weapons to avoid a military conflict between the workers and Chiang Kai-shek, in order not to disturb the occupation of Shanghai by the armed forces. Having read this telegram, [Luo] Yinong became very angry, and threw it on the floor. At that time, I again obeyed the order of the International and could not maintain my own opinion. Based upon the policy of the International towards the Guomindang and the imperialists, I issued a shameful manifesto with Wang Jingwei.

At the beginning of April, I went to Wuhan. When I first met Wang Jingwei, I heard some reactionary things from him, far different from what he had said while in Shanghai. I told this to Borodin; he said that my observations were right and that as soon as Wang Jingwei reached Wuhan he was surrounded by Xu Qian, Gu Mengyu, Chen Gongbo, Tan Yankai, and others, and became gradually colder. After Chiang Kai-shek and Li Jishen began their massacre of the workers and peasants, the [Wuhan] Guomindang came to hate the power of the proletariat more every day, and the reactionary attitude of Wang Jingwei and of the Central Committee of the Guomindang rapidly hardened. At the meeting of our Political Bureau, I made a report on the status of the joint-meeting of our party and of the Guomindang:

> The danger involved in cooperation between our party and the Guomindang is more and more serious. What they tried to seize on seemed to be this or that small problem; what they really wanted was the whole of the central power. Now there are only two roads before us: either give up the authority of leadership or break with them.

Those attending the meeting answered my report with silence. After the coup [on 21 May at Changsha] in Hunan province, I twice suggested withdrawal from the Guomindang. Finally, I said: 'The Wuhan Guomindang has followed in the footsteps of Chiang Kai-shek! If we do not change our policy, we too will end up on the same road'.

At that time, only Ren Bishi said, 'That is so!' Zhou Enlai said, 'After we withdraw from the Guomindang the labour and peasant movement will be freer but the military movement will suffer too much'. All the rest still answered my suggestion with silence. At the same time, I discussed this with [Qu] Qiubai. He said: 'We should let the Guomindang expel us; we cannot withdraw by ourselves'. I consulted Borodin. He said: 'I quite agree with your idea but I know that Moscow will never permit it'.

At that time, I once more observed the discipline of the International and the opinion of the majority of the Central Committee and was unable to maintain my own opinion. From the beginning, I could not persistently maintain my opinion; but this time I could no longer bear it. I then tendered my resignation to the Central Committee. My chief reason for this was:

> The International wishes us to carry out our own policy, on the one hand, and does not allow us to withdraw from the Guomindang on the other. There is really no way out and I cannot continue with my work.

From the beginning to the end, the International recognised the Guomindang as the main body of the Chinese national-democratic revolution. In Stalin's mouth, the words 'leadership of the Guomindang' were shouted very loudly (see 'The Errors of the Opposition', in *Questions of the Chinese Revolution*). So it wished us throughout to surrender in the organisation of the Guomindang and to lead the masses under the name and the banner of the Guomindang. This was continued up to the time when the whole Guomindang of Feng Yuxiang, Wang Jingwei, Tang Shengzhi, He Jian, and so on, became openly reactionary and abolished the so-called three-point policy: unite with the Soviet Union, allow the CP to join the Guomindang, and help the labour and peasant movement. The International instructed us by telegram: 'Only withdraw from the Guomindang government, not from the Guomindang'.

So, after the 7 August Conference, from the Nanchang uprising to the capture of Shantou, the Communist Party still hid behind the blue-white banner of the left clique of the Guomindang. To the masses, it seemed that there was trouble within the Guomindang, but nothing more. The young Chinese Communist Party, produced by the young Chinese proletariat, had not had a proper period of training in Marxism and class struggles. Shortly after the founding of the Party, it was confronted by a great revolutionary struggle. The only hope of avoiding a very grave error was correct guidance by the proletarian policy of the International. But, under the guidance of such a consistently opportunist policy, how could the Chinese proletariat and the Communist Party clearly see their own future? And how could they have their own independent policy? They only surrendered to the bourgeoisie step by step and subordinated themselves to the bourgeoisie. So when the latter suddenly massacred us we did not know what to do about it. After the coup in Changsha, the policy given to us by the International was:

1. Confiscate the land of the landowners from the lower strata, but not in the name of the Nationalist government, and do not touch the land of military officers. (There was not a single one of the bourgeoisie, landlords, *dujun*, and gentry of Hunan and Hubei provinces who was not the kinsman, relative, or old friend of the officers of that time. All the landowners were directly or indirectly protected by the officers. To confiscate the land is only empty words if it is conditioned by 'do not touch the land of the military officers'.)
2. Restrain the peasants' 'over-zealous' actions with the power of the party headquarters. (We did execute this shameful policy of checking the peasants' over-zealous actions; afterwards, the International criticised the Chinese Party for having 'often become an obstacle to the masses' and considered it as one of the greatest opportunist errors.)
3. Destroy the present unreliable generals, arm twenty thousand Communists, and select fifty thousand worker-and-peasant elements from Hunan and Hubei provinces for organising a new army. (If we could get so many rifles, why should we not directly arm the workers and peasants and why should we still recruit new troops for the Guomindang? Why couldn't we establish soviets of workers, peasants, and soldiers? If there were neither armed workers and peasants nor soviets, how and with whom could we destroy the said unreliable generals? I suppose that we could have continued to pitifully beg the Central Committee of the Guomindang to discharge them. When the Comintern representative

Roy showed Wang Jingwei these instructions from the International it was, of course, for this purpose.)
4. Put new worker elements into the Central Committee of the Guomindang to take the place of old members. (If we had the power to deal freely with the old committee and reorganise the Guomindang, why could we not organise soviets? Why must we send our worker and peasant leaders to the bourgeois Guomindang, which has already been massacring the workers and peasants? And why should we decorate such a Guomindang with our leaders?)
5. Organise a revolutionary court with a well-known member of the Guomindang (one who is not a member of the CCP) as its chairman, in order to judge the reactionary officers. (How can an already reactionary leader of the Guomindang judge the reactionary officers in the revolutionary court?)

Those who attempted to implement such a policy within the Guomindang were still opportunists, of a left stripe. There was no change at all in the fundamental policy; it was like taking a bath in a urinal! At that time, if we wanted to carry out a genuinely left, that is, revolutionary policy, the fundamental line had to be changed. The Communist Party had to withdraw from the Guomindang and be really independent. It had to arm the workers and peasants, as many as possible, establish soviets of workers, peasants, and soldiers, and seize the leading power from the Guomindang. Otherwise, no matter what kind of left policy was adopted, there was no way to realise it.

At that time the Central Political Bureau wired the Communist International in answer to its instructions: we accept the instructions and will work according to their directions, but they cannot be realised immediately. All the members of the Central Committee recognised that the International's instructions were impractical. Even Fan Ke, a participant in the Central Committee meeting (said to be Stalin's special envoy), thought there was no possibility of carrying them out. He agreed with the telegraphic answer of the Central Committee, saying: 'This is the best reply we can give'.

After the 7 August Conference, the Central Committee tried to propagate the idea that the Chinese Revolution had failed because the opportunists did not accept the Communist International's instructions to immediately change tactics. (Of course, the instructions were the above mentioned ones; besides these, there were no instructions!) We did not know: how could the policy be changed from inside the Guomindang? And who were the so-called opportunists?

Once the Party had committed such a fundamental error, a continual series of other smaller or larger subordinate errors was naturally inevitable. I, whose perception was not clear, whose opinion was not decisive, became immersed in the atmosphere of opportunism and sincerely carried out the opportunist policy of the Third International. I unconsciously became the tool of the narrow faction of Stalin. I could not save the Party and the Revolution. For all this, both I and other comrades should be held responsible. The present Central Committee says: 'You attempt to place the failure of the Chinese Revolution on the shoulders of the Comintern in order that you might throw off your own responsibility!' This statement is ridiculous. One does not permanently lose his right to criticise the opportunism of the party leadership, or to return to Marxism and Leninism, because he has himself committed opportunist errors.

At the same time, nobody can take the liberty of avoiding his responsibility for executing an opportunist policy because the opportunism originated in high places. The source of the opportunist policy is the Comintern; but why did not the leaders of the Chinese Party protest against the Comintern, and instead loyally carry out its policies? Who can absolve us of this responsibility? We should very frankly and objectively recognise that all the past and present opportunist policies originated in the Communist International. The International should bear the responsibility. The young Chinese Party has not yet the ability of itself to invent any theories and settle any policy; but the leading organ of the Chinese Party ought to bear the responsibility for blindly implementing the opportunist policy of the Comintern without a little bit of judgement and protest.

If we mutually excuse each other and all of us think we have committed no mistakes, was it then the error of the masses? This is not only too ridiculous but also does not assume any responsibility towards the revolution! I strongly believe that if I, or other responsible comrades, could at that time have clearly recognised the falsity of the opportunist policy and made a strong argument against it, even to the point of mobilising the entire party for a passionate discussion and debate, as Comrade Trotsky has been doing, the result would inevitably have been a great help to the Revolution. It would not have made the Revolution such a shameful failure, though I might have been expelled from the Communist International and a split in the Party might have taken place. I, whose perception was not clear and whose opinion was not resolute, did not do so after all! If the Party were to base itself on such past mistakes of mine or on the fact that I strongly maintained the former erroneous line, as grounds for giving me some severe punishment, I would earnestly accept it without uttering a word.

But these are the reasons given by the present Central Committee for expelling me from the Party:

1. They said: 'Fundamentally, he is not sincere in recognising his own error of opportunist leadership in the period of the great revolution, and has not decided to recognise where his real past error lies, so it is inevitable that he will continue his past erroneous line'. In reality, I was expelled because I sincerely recognised where the error of the former opportunist leadership lay, and decided to oppose the present and future continuation of wrong lines.
2. They said: 'He is not satisfied with the decisions of the Communist International. He is obdurately unwilling to go to Moscow to be trained by the International'. I have been trained enough by the Communist International. Formerly, I made many mistakes because I accepted the opinions of the Third International. Now, I have been expelled because I am not satisfied with those opinions.
3. Last 5 August, I wrote a letter to the Central Committee in which there were the following sentences: 'Besides, what is the continuing fundamental contradiction of "economic class interests" between these two classes [the bourgeoisie and the landlords]?!' 'Before and after the Guangzhou uprising... I wrote several letters to the Central Committee pointing out that the ruling power of the Guomindang would not collapse as quickly as you estimated'. 'At present, though there are some mass struggles it is not enough to take them as the symptoms of the coming revolutionary wave'. 'The wholly legal movement, of course, is an abandonment of the attempt at revolution. But, under certain circumstances, when it is necessary to build up our strength, as Lenin said, except in eruptions of a white-hot intensity, we should also make use of all possible legal measures in this (transitional) period'.

    The Central Committee changed these sentences to read ambiguously:

    'There is no contradiction between the bourgeoisie and the feudal forces'. 'The present ruling class is not going to be overthrown and the revolutionary struggle is not beginning to revive but is declining more and more'. He advocates 'the adoption of legal forms'.

    Furthermore, they put quotation marks around each sentence so as to make them seem like my original statements. This is another reason for my expulsion.
4. I wrote another letter to the Central Committee on 10 October saying:

    The present period is not a period of the revolutionary wave, but a period of counter-revolution. We should elaborate democratic slogans as our general demands. For instance, besides the eight-hour-day demand and the confiscation of land, we should issue the slogans 'Nullify the unequal treaties', 'Against the military dictatorship of the Guomindang', 'Convoke the national assembly', and so on. It is necessary to bring the broad masses into activity under these democratic slogans; then we can shake the counter-revolutionary régime, go forwards to the revolutionary wave, and make our fundamental slogans – 'Down with the Guomindang government', 'Establish the soviet régime', and so on – the slogans of action in the mass movement.

On 26 October, Comrade Peng Shuzhi and I wrote a letter to the CC saying: 'This is not the transitional period to direct revolution, and we must have general political slogans adapted to this period; then we can win the masses. The workers' and peasants' soviets is merely a propaganda-slogan at present. If we take the struggle to organise soviets as a slogan of action, we will certainly get no response from the proletariat'. But the CC claimed that in place of the slogans 'Down with the Guomindang government' and 'Establish the soviet régime' we wish to substitute as the present general political slogan the demand 'Convoke the national assembly'. This is also one of the reasons for my expulsion.

5. I said in a letter that we should point out 'the policy of treason or spoliation of the country by the Guomindang in the handling of the Chinese Eastern Railroad', making the 'broad masses still imbued with nationalist spirit able to sympathise with us and oppose the manoeuvre of the imperialists to attack the Soviet Union by utilising the Guomindang and making the Chinese Eastern Railroad problem an excuse'. This was to help the slogan of defence of the USSR penetrate the masses. But the CC said I wanted to issue the slogan of opposing the spoliation of the country by the Guomindang in place of the slogan of supporting the USSR. This is another reason why I was expelled.

6. I wrote the CC several letters dealing with the serious political problems within the Party. The CC kept them from the Party for a long time. Further, the delegates of the Comintern and the CC told me plainly that the principle is that different political opinions cannot be expressed in the Party. Because there is no hope of correcting the mistakes of the Central Committee by means of a legal comradely discussion, I hold that I should not be bound by the routine discipline of the organisation, and still less should comrades be prevented from passing my letters to others to be read. This is also one of the reasons why I am expelled.

7. Since the 7 August Conference, the CC has not allowed me to participate in any meetings, nor has it given me any work to do. Then, on 6 October (only forty days before my expulsion), they suddenly wrote me a letter saying: 'The CC has decided to ask you to undertake the work of editing in the CC under the political line of the Party, and to write an article, "Against

the Opposition," within a week'. As I had criticised the Central Committee more than once for continuing the line of opportunism and putschism, they tried to create some excuse for my expulsion. Now I have recognised fundamentally that Comrade Trotsky's views are identical with Marxism and Leninism. How would I be able to write false words, contrary to my opinions?

8. We know that Comrade Trotsky has decisively opposed the opportunist policy of Stalin and Bukharin. We cannot listen to the rumours of the Stalin clique and believe that Comrade Trotsky, who led the October Revolution hand in hand with Lenin, really is a counter-revolutionist. (It may be 'proved' by rumours created about us by the Chinese Stalinist clique, Li Lisan, and so on) Because we spoke of Trotsky as a comrade, the Central Committee accused us of 'having already left the revolution, left the proletariat, and gone over to the counter-revolution', and expelled us from the Party.

Comrades! The Central Committee has now invented these false reasons in order to expel me from the Party and brand me as a 'counter-revolutionist' without any proof. I believe that most of the comrades are not clear about this case. Even the CC itself has said: 'There may be some who do not understand it!' But they expelled me and said I went over to the counter-revolution even though some comrades do not understand it. Nevertheless, I understand quite well why they falsely accuse us as 'counter-revolutionists'. This is a weapon created by up-to-date Chinese for attacking those who differ from them. For instance, the Guomindang accuses the communists of being 'counter-revolutionists' in order to cover its own sins. Chiang Kai-shek tries to deceive the masses with the signboard of revolution, portraying himself as the personification of revolution. Those who oppose him are 'counter-revolutionists' and 'reactionary elements'.

Many comrades know that the false reasons I have cited, given by the CC for expelling me, are only the formal and official excuse. In reality, they have become tired of hearing my opinions expressed in the Party and of my criticism of their continued opportunism and putschism and their execution of a bankrupt policy.

In any number of the bourgeois countries of the world, there are feudal survivals and methods of semi-feudal exploitation (blacks, and slaves of the South Sea archipelago, are like those of the pre-feudal slave system), and there exist remnants of feudal forces. China is even more like this. In the revolution, of course, we cannot neglect this; but the Comintern and the CC unanimously hold that in China the feudal remnants still occupy the dominant position in the economy and politics and are the ruling power. As a result, they consider these survivals as the object of the revolution and disregard the enemy, the suppressor of the revolution – the forces of the bourgeoisie. They pass off all reactionary actions of the bourgeoisie as those of the feudal forces.

They say that the Chinese bourgeoisie is still revolutionary, that it can never be reactionary, and that all those who are reactionary cannot be the bourgeoisie. Thus, they do not recognise that the Guomindang represents the interests of the bourgeoisie or that the Nationalist government is the régime representing the interests of the bourgeoisie. The conclusion must be that, besides the Guomindang, or the Nanjing section of it, there is or will be, now or in the future, a non-reactionary, revolutionary-bourgeois party. Therefore, in tactics and in practical actions, they now simply follow the Reorganisationists and do the military work of overthrowing Chiang Kai-shek. In the platform, they say that the character of the third revolution in the future must still be that of a bourgeois-democratic revolution, opposing anything that would antagonise the economic forces of the bourgeoisie and opposing issuing the slogan for the dictatorship of the proletariat. Such illusions in the bourgeoisie and such continual attraction to it are calculated not only to perpetuate the opportunism of the past but to deepen it. It must lead to a more shameful and miserable failure in the future revolution.

If we consider the slogan 'Establish the soviet régime' as a slogan of action, we can issue it only when the objective conditions have ripened into a revolutionary wave. It cannot be issued at any time at will. In the past, during the revolutionary wave, we did not adopt the slogans 'Organise soviets' and 'Establish the soviet régime'. Naturally, this was a grave error. In the future, when the revolution takes place, we shall immediately have to organise workers', peasants', and soldiers' soviets. Then we shall mobilise the masses to struggle for the slogan 'Establish the soviet régime'. Furthermore, it would be the soviet of the dictatorship of the proletariat, and not the soviet of the workers' and peasants' democratic dictatorship.

In the present period when the counter-revolutionary forces are entirely victorious and when there is no wave of mass revolutionary action, the objective conditions for 'armed uprising' and the establishment of soviets have not matured. At the present time, 'Organise soviets' is only a propaganda and educational slogan. If we use it as a slogan of action and mobilise the working class at once to struggle in practice to 'organise soviets', we will be completely unable to generate a response from the masses.

In the present situation, we should adopt the democratic slogan 'Struggle for the convocation of the national assembly'. The objective conditions for this movement have matured and at present only this slogan can take large masses through the legal political struggle and towards the revolutionary rise and the struggle for the 'armed uprising' and the 'establishment of the soviet régime'.

The present CC, continuing its putschism, does not do this. They consider that the rebirth of the revolution has matured, and reproach us for regarding the slogan of the 'Establishment of workers' and peasants' soviets' as only a propaganda slogan; thus, they logically consider it a slogan of action. In consequence, they are continually ordering party members into the streets for demonstrations in workers' quarters, and ordering employed comrades to strike. Every small daily struggle is artificially blown up into a big political battle, leading to more and more defections from the Party by the working masses and employed comrades.

More than that, at the Jiangsu representative conference recently, it was resolved 'to organise the great strike movement' and 'local uprisings'. Since last summer, there have been signs of small struggles among the Shanghai workers, but as they appear they have been defeated through the party's putschist policy. Henceforth, of course, they will all be crushed; if the resolutions of the Jiangsu representative conference are carried out, these workers' struggles will be destroyed. Our party is no longer the guide, helping the coming wave of workers' revolutionary struggles; it is becoming the executioner destroying the workers' struggles at their roots.

The present Central Committee, sincerely basing itself upon the bankrupt line of the Sixth Congress, and under the direct guidance of the Comintern, is executing the above bankrupt policy and capping the opportunism and putschism of the past by liquidating the Party and the revolution. No matter whether it was the Comintern or the Chinese Communist Party that committed the opportunist errors in the past and made the revolution fail, it was a crime. Now these errors have been pointed out plainly by the comrades of the Opposition, but they still do not acknowledge their past mistakes and consciously continue their past erroneous line. Moreover, for the sake of covering up the errors of a few individuals, they deliberately violate the organisational norms of Bolshevism, abuse the authority of the supreme party organs, and prevent self-criticism within the Party, expelling numerous comrades from the Party for expressing different political opinions and deliberately splitting the Party. This is the crime of crimes, the most stupid and the most shameful.

No Bolshevik should be afraid of open self-criticism before the masses. The only way for the Party to win the masses is to carry out self-criticism courageously, never losing the masses for fear of self-criticism. To cover up one's own mistakes, like the present Central Committee, is certainly to lose the masses.

The majority of comrades have felt these mistakes and the party crisis to varying degrees. As long we do not simply expect to make our living through the Party, as long as we have some feeling of responsibility for the Party and the revolution, any comrade should stand up and resolutely make a self-criticism of the Party in order to rescue it from this crisis. To silently watch, arms folded, while our party comes close to destruction would surely be criminal!

Comrades! We all know that whoever opens his mouth to express some criticism of the errors of the Party is himself expelled, while the mistake remains uncorrected. But we should draw a balance. Which is more important: to save the Party from danger or save ourselves from having our names dropped from the party list?

Since the 7 August Conference, which adopted the 'general line of armed uprising', and the uprisings that followed in several places, I have written many letters to the Central Committee, pointing out that the revolutionary sentiment of the masses was not then at a high point, that the Guomindang régime could not be quickly exploded, that uprisings that lacked objective conditions only weaken the power of the Party and isolate it further from the masses. I proposed that we change from the policy of uprisings to a policy of winning and uniting the masses in their daily struggles. The Central Committee thought that widespread uprisings were an absolutely valid new line for correcting opportunism, and that to take account of the objective conditions for the uprisings and to consider how to insure the success of the uprisings is opportunism. Of course, they never took my opinion into consideration and regarded my words as a joke. They propagated them everywhere, saying it was proof that I had not corrected my opportunist mistakes. At that time, I was bound by the discipline of the party organisation, and took a negative attitude, being unable to go over the head of the organisation to wage a determined struggle against the policy of the Central Committee which was destroying the Party.

I accept responsibility for this. After the Sixth Congress, I still had a false comprehension and still entertained the illusion that the new Central Committee had received so many lessons from events that they themselves would awaken to the fact that it was not necessary after all to follow blindly the erroneous line of the Comintern. I still continued my negative attitude and did not hold any different theories that would have involved a dispute within the Party, though I was fundamentally dissatisfied with the line of the Sixth Congress. After the war between Chiang Kai-shek and the Guangxi cliques and the anniversary of the 30 May Movement, I felt deeply that the Central Committee would obstinately continue its opportunism and putschism and manifestly could not change by itself: that, except through an open discussion and criticism by the party members, from the lowest to the highest ranks, the seriously false line of the leading organ could not be corrected. But all the party members are under the domination and restriction of party discipline, in a state of 'daring to be angry but not daring to speak'.

At that time, I could not bear to see the Party (created by the warm blood of innumerable comrades) destroyed and ruined by the enduring and essentially false line. Thus, I could not do otherwise than begin to express my opinion, from August onward, in order to fulfil my responsibility. Some comrades sought to dissuade me, saying that the people in the Central Committee regard the interests of a few leaders as more important than the interests of the Party and the revolution, that they have attempted everywhere to cover up their mistakes and could never accept the criticism of comrades, and that since I was criticising them so frankly, they would use it as an excuse to expel me from the party. But my regard for the Party compelled me to resolutely follow the path of not caring for my own interests.

The Communist International and the Central Committee have for a long time opposed any review of the record of failure of the Chinese Revolution. And now, because I have continued to criticise them, they have suddenly invented the following declaration: 'He [Chen Duxiu] is not sincere in recognising his own error of opportunist leadership in the period of the great revolution and has not decided to recognise where his real past error lies, so it is inevitable that he will continue his past erroneous line'.

These words are an accurate description of their authors. In reality, if I were to stultify my mind and care nothing about the interests of the proletariat, if I had not decided to recognise my real past errors and had been willing to do their dirty work and let them continue with their past false line, they would, as before, rely on the old opportunist's pen and mouth and use me to attack so-called Trotskyism in order to cover up their errors. How could they expel me from the Party?

Am I, who have struggled against evil social forces for the greater part of my life, willing to do such a base work – to confuse right and wrong? Li Lisan said: 'The Chinese opportunists are unwilling to absorb accurately the lessons of the failure of the past great revolution, but try to hide behind the banner of Trotskyism to cover up their own mistakes'. In reality, the documents of Comrade Trotsky censure me much more severely than do those of Stalin and Bukharin; and I could not but recognise that the lessons of the past revolution pointed out by him are one hundred percent correct, and I could never reject his words because he criticises me. I am willing to accept the severest criticism of my comrades, but unwilling to bury the lessons and experiences of the revolution. I would rather be expelled now by Li Lisan and a few others than see the party crisis without attempting to save the Party, and be blamed in future by the masses of party members.

I would much rather have peace of mind while suffering oppression by evil forces in my struggle for the interests of the proletariat. I am unwilling merely to go along with cruel and corrupt bureaucratic elements!

Comrades! I know that my expulsion from the party by the Central Committee is the act of a few men for the purpose of covering up their errors. They not only want to save themselves the 'trouble' of hearing my opinions expressed within the Party and hearing me advocate an open discussion on political problems, but also to demonstrate by my expulsion that all comrades must keep their mouths closed. I know the masses of party members never entertained the idea of expelling me. Though I have been expelled by a few leaders at the top, yet there has never been any hostility or bad feeling between the masses in the ranks and myself. I shall continue to serve the proletariat hand in hand with all those comrades both in the International and in China who are not following the opportunist policy of Stalin's clique.

Comrades! The present errors of the Party are not partial or accidental problems: as in the past, they are the manifestation of the whole opportunist policy conducted by Stalin in China. The responsible heads of the Central Committee of the Chinese Communist Party who are willing to be the phonograph of Stalin have never shown any political consciousness and are growing worse and worse: they can never be saved. At the Tenth Congress of the Russian Party [1921], Lenin said: 'Only when there exist within the Party fundamentally different political opinions and there is no other way to resolve them, then factional groupings are proper'. Based on this theory, he led the Bolshevik movement at that time.

Now, in our party, there is no other way permitted (legal or open discussion in the Party) to overcome the party crisis. Every party member has the obligation of saving the Party. We must return to the spirit and political line of Bolshevism, unite together solidly, and stand straightforward on the side of the International Opposition led by Comrade Trotsky, that is, under the banner of real Marxism and Leninism. We must decisively, persistently, and thoroughly fight against the opportunism of the Comintern and the Central Committee of the Chinese Party. We are opposed not only to the opportunism of Stalin and his like, but also to the compromising attitude of Zinoviev and others. We are not afraid of the so-called 'jumping out of the ranks of the Party' and do not hesitate to sacrifice everything in order to save the Party and the Chinese Revolution!

With proletarian greetings,

Chen Duxiu

An Ebbing or a Flowing Tide?

Zheng Chaolin

Source: *An Oppositionist for Life* (1945).

So I followed the Central Committee from Hankou back to Shanghai. Qu Qiubai told me to rent a small foreign-style house, for the Central Committee was preparing to move to Guangzhou when Guangdong fell to the Ye-He army,[1] in which case I would be left behind in Shanghai to run the Central Committee office, as a permanent contact point between Shanghai and other places. I rented the first house – a foreign-style terrace-house – in the last alley off Hengchang Road on the eastern side of Jessfield Park. I shared the place with Huang Wenrong. After we had been there for a few days, a woman comrade called Huang also came to live with us. Not long after that, she got married to Zhang Baoquan, who worked as liaison man for the Central Committee.

The plan to move the Central Committee to Guangdong came to nothing,[2] so our house became the editorial office of the party journal and also headquarters of the Propaganda Department. But, apart from the party journal, very little was actually done by way of propaganda.

I proposed bringing out another publication rather than reviving *Guide Weekly*, and Qu Qiubai agreed. The two of us drew up a list of possible names, and finally chose *Buersaiweike* ('Bolshevik'), which had been my suggestion. From the point of view of editing, *Bolshevik* was an advance on *Guide Weekly*. In the old days, articles had been thrown together quite haphazardly, but now they were properly coordinated, at least in form. Every issue carried an unsigned editorial, signed articles, letters from all over China, and the occasional obituary. It was in octavo like *Yusi* ('Threads of Talk'),[3] that is, a big newspaper cut from one sheet of newsprint into twenty-four pieces. We held editorial conferences once a week to check each other's articles and assign next week's articles. Qu Qiubai represented the editorial board on the Standing Committee of the Central Committee and reported to the editorial board on behalf of that body. He wrote all the editorials bar one. Apart from him and

---

1 The Ye (Ting)-He (Long) army staged the Nanchang Uprising on 1 August 1927, and then marched south to Guangdong.
2 The Ye-He army was defeated.
3 *Threads of Talk* was a weekly edited in the 1920s by Lu Xun and Zhou Zuoren.

me, the editorial board consisted of Cao Dianqi and Xue Juezai, who had both come over from Hunan, and Luo Qiyuan, who had come up from Guangdong.

In my capacity as editor-in-chief or Secretary of the Propaganda Department, I also ran a printing press and a publishing company. The printing press had been in Shanghai all along, the publishing company had been moved to Shanghai from Hankou, where it had been known as the Chang Jiang Bookshop. The printing equipment that I had sent from Hankou had still not been fetched from the customs. Not until a long time later did several comrades pool their capital and open a printing house for money-making purposes.

The situation was quite chaotic when the Central Committee first moved back to Shanghai: our theory was in chaos, our organisation was in chaos, and relations between people were in chaos. Qu Qiubai liaised with the Russians on behalf of the three-person Standing Committee, so he knew sooner than anyone about important new developments and was the first to see documents of the International. People gradually came to look on him as the political and theoretical centre of the Party, but he was not officially its General Secretary, and he was never able to establish for himself the same authority as Chen Duxiu had enjoyed. He was on the same level as the other two members of the Standing Committee. Luo Yinong gave the post of secretary of the Hubei Provincial Committee to Chen Qiaonian, and Wang Zekai took over the Organisation Department there. Luo himself came to Shanghai to join the Standing Committee. He not only represented real power in Hubei and Shanghai but was viewed as a representative of the 'Chen Duxiu group'. Gradually, he increased his authority. He set up a Chang Jiang Bureau and an Organisation-Bureau in the Central Committee, both of which he personally controlled. His position had come to resemble that of Stalin in the Soviet Union. Li Weihan, the third member of the Standing Committee, had brought a crowd of people with him from Hunan and assigned them to various bodies under the Central Committee. None had ever worked outside Hunan before.

If Qu Qiubai or Luo Yinong came up with a resolution, they had to rely on the apparatus of the Central Committee to carry it out, that is, they had to rely on Li Weihan's Hunanese. These people were well-disposed towards Qu but violently prejudiced against Luo, so Luo's Chang Jiang Bureau and his Organisation Bureau were of no avail to him.

The only way Luo could consolidate his position was by really becoming leader of the 'Chen Duxiu-ites'; that he was not prepared to do. After the Fifth Congress, he vacillated between the two factions. He had been moved from Jiangxi to become Secretary of the Provincial Committee in Hubei partly because he was needed there – people felt that Zhang Tailei's Guangdong style would get nowhere, so they replaced Zhang with Luo, who had earlier served as Secretary of the Shanghai Regional Committee. Another reason was that Luo had given Zhang Guotao and Qu Qiubai an undertaking never to stand against them on the side of Chen Duxiu. There was nothing that Luo would not tell me save this, about which he kept absolutely silent.

When I first got back to Shanghai, the two groups – for and against Chen Duxiu – were by no means clearly counterposed. The old conspiratorial organisation that had existed in Wuhan had by now already been disbanded. Qu Qiubai, Zhang Guotao, and Tan Pingshan – the three main figures in it – had gone their separate ways. Qu had at first stayed in Hankou, where he controlled the Central Committee; Zhang and Tan had both gone off to join the Ye-He army. Tan had been Chairman of the Revolutionary Committee of the Guomindang during the 1 August Nanchang Uprising, while Zhang had wielded the goose-feather fan behind the screen.[4] Had the Ye-He army succeeded in taking Guangzhou, Tan and Zhang would have set up a Central Committee there and excluded all those leaders who had not joined the army. But after Ye and He were routed in the Chaozhou-Shantou region, Tan and Zhang returned by a devious route to Shanghai, where they were blamed for the defeat. Tan was dismissed outright from the Party, whereas Zhang was kept under examination, I do not know for how long. They were made scapegoats for what had happened in Guangdong, just as Chen Duxiu had been made scapegoat for the Wuhan defeat. But there was more to it than that. The people on the Central Committee in Shanghai used the occasion to oust their rivals. Other people close to Tan were attacked too. To stop Tan's friends causing trouble in Guangdong, Zhang Tailei ordered Yang Bao'an and Luo Qiyuan to go to Shanghai, which is how Luo Qiyuan ended up in the Propaganda Department. Luo Qiyuan, who commanded a mass following in Guangdong, wrote well and had a good sense of humour. When he came to stay in the Propaganda Department, we told the neighbours that he was my cousin. Not long after that, my 'cousin's wife' turned up with four or five of my 'cousin's children'. He knew why the Central Committee had assigned him to the Propaganda Department. On one occasion, he told me that he was not a member of Tan Pingshan's group, and that he and Yang Bao'an had always despised Tan. The anti-Chen Duxiu mood started to evaporate. Actually, there had never been any document clearly opposing Chen, just some vague pronouncements against 'opportunism'. The resolution passed by the 7 August Conference had not mentioned Chen Duxiu by name. Perhaps the rank and file were baffled, but people close

---

4 A reference to Zhuge Liang, a statesman and strategist in the period of the Three Kingdoms (220–265), who masterminded things from behind the scenes and is represented in Chinese opera holding a fan made of goose-feathers.

to the Central Committee knew quite clearly that responsibility for the defeat at Wuhan could not be pinned on Chen Duxiu alone; and that the only reason Chen had withdrawn from the leadership was that the International had ordered it. After Qu Qiubai arrived in Shanghai, he also believed that theory, or at least he pretended to. After he had been back for two or three days, he visited Chen Duxiu and behaved respectfully towards him, just as in the old days in Shanghai. When Chen Duxiu sent back Huang Wenrong, his personal secretary, to the Central Committee, Qu accepted Huang, and assigned him to help me out. When *Bolshevik* appeared, he asked Chen to write for it, but Chen only contributed items along the lines of his old 'Inch of Iron' column under the name Sa Weng, together with space-fillers like a highly appreciated song that began 'The Three People's Principles are completely muddle-headed'. He lived on Fusheng Road near the building that had formerly housed the old Propaganda Department and rarely went out, save for once when he went to Luo Yinong's place for a meal and another occasion when he came to stay for three days at my house. I never heard anyone say anything disrespectful about him during the first six months after the Central Committee moved back to Shanghai, and I rarely saw any articles or proclamations attacking 'opportunism'. Every time something important happened he wrote to the Standing Committee giving his opinion, but it was never accepted.

All the same, he was frequently implicated in the inner-party struggle in this period. In reality, there was no such thing as a 'Chen Duxiu group'. In the first place, the Old Man himself was opposed to having one. In Wuhan, he had shown not the slightest intention of gathering a coterie of supporters to enable him to fight back against his detractors. He made no distinction between his opponents and his supporters – he looked on each and every one as a comrade. In Wuhan, he had carried out the new line, the Comintern line, the line represented by Qu Qiubai, but he did not consider that by doing so he was submitting to other people's judgment. On the contrary, he thought that it was right to do that, for the Northern Expedition had anyway been victorious and the revolution was anyway deepening as a result of it. True, it had produced the reactionary force of Chiang Kai-shek, but it had also borne us into power. He had a wealth of political experience and acute political antennae, but he was short of skill in basic and systematic theoretical analysis.

After the Wuhan debacle and the move to Shanghai, he developed new ways of looking at things and often expounded on them in his letters to the Standing Committee. Unfortunately, these letters have not been preserved, and even though I read them at the time, I can no longer recall their contents. All I remember is that the views expressed in them were disjointed and achieved no system or formula, though they were completely out of sympathy with those of the Standing Committee. At the time, he still had no intention of forming another small group. He was confident that Qu Qiubai and Luo Yinong were as objective, as sincere, and as public-spirited as he was, that they would gradually come round to his way of thinking and the old spirit would revive.

But, imperceptibly, a 'Chen Duxiu group' did exist, though it had no definite form. The Jiangsu Provincial Committee, that is, the old Shanghai Regional Committee, was almost solidly in support of Chen. Deng Zhongxia was its secretary, but main power over it was in the hands of Wang Ruofei, who had inherited Luo Yinong and Zhao Shiyan's old base. The rank-and-file cadres submitted to Wang just as they had originally submitted to Zhao Shiyan. Deng Zhongxia used to joke self-deprecatingly that he was 'only the Deputy Secretary' of the Committee. Actually, he was not even that. He tried hard to build himself a base to counter Wang, but he failed. On the Hubei Provincial Committee, Chen Qiaonian, Wang Zekai, and Ren Xu all supported Chen Duxiu, as did Peng Shuzhi in Beijing. On the Standing Committee, Luo Yinong was considered to belong to the Chen group. Had Chen really lived up to people's expectations, the Chinese Communist Party could without difficulty have restored the old pre-Wuhan style. This was what Wang Ruofei was working for, and after Chen Qiaonian arrived in Shanghai, Wang and Chen approached Luo Yinong for talks and tried to win him to their position. But Luo not only resisted but told Qu Qiubai about the approach, so the new Central Committee went on the alert and prepared for battle.

After the defeats suffered in various parts of the country, many leaders congregated in Shanghai; some were punished and some lost their jobs, after which most of them went to live in a big house with two first floors and two ground floors near the Chongqing Road, where they killed time playing mahjong. This group included no few confirmed opponents of Chen Duxiu, like Zhang Guotao and Li Lisan. They made it known that they supported the Central Committee line and that they wanted to help the Central Committee attack the 'Chen Duxiu group', starting with Luo Yinong. Zhou Enlai came to Shanghai and immediately went onto the Standing Committee. Everyone complained to him about Luo Yinong. The forces under Wang Ruofei and Chen Qiaonian were not prepared to back Luo, who became completely isolated. The Organisation Bureau was dissolved and the Chang Jiang Bureau was split between Luo and Li Weihan; in short, Luo was relegated to the role of an ordinary member of the Standing Committee, and gradually dropped deeper still.

Peng Shuzhi in Beijing also came under attack and brought his wife and daughter back to Shanghai; he, too, had time to kill. Luo Yinong and Peng were enemies. Wang Ruofei and Chen Qiaonian despised Peng, there was no way he could play any role in this struggle. All he could do was 'clasp the feet' of Chen

Duxiu.[5] If there was a 'Chen Duxiu group', then its leader was Wang Ruofei; as for the Old Man himself, he not only was not a member of it but he even opposed its activities.

I was not the slightest bit interested in this sort of organisational struggle. Wang Ruofei often dropped by for a drink and started complaining about this and that once he was in his cups; he told me a great deal. He knew that even though I was not minded to help him actively, I would never give away his plans. It seemed to me that there was little to choose between the political proposals of these various leaders, at least not insofar as they had revealed them, and that they were simply jockeying for positions in the Party. I got a headache just thinking about the situation. The Old Man came up with some uncommon ideas but they lacked system, so I paid no special attention to them. Thinking back on it, after the defeat of the Revolution he was the only person who ever did any thinking – none of the rest did. Certainly Qu Qiubai did not; he simply span Comintern directives into resolutions or essays of the Chinese Communist Party. Cai Hesen was lecturing on the history of Chinese opportunism at the party school in Beijing and later published his lectures in mimeograph-form. But his aim was not to do any original thinking about problems of the revolution but to attack Chen Duxiu and Peng Shuzhi. I leafed through Cai's pamphlet but put it to one side, unread. Qu Qiubai, on the other hand, read it carefully from start to finish.

'Cai's book is against me, too', he told me. 'Cai has always opposed me'.

I have no idea what part of Cai's book was directed against Qu. There were so many things in those days that required thought, but no one save Chen Duxiu was prepared to give them it.

Our thinking was in such a shambles that even I, the editor of the party journal, was unclear about what to write. I wrote an article for the inaugural issue of *Bolshevik* roughly titled 'What Should We Do Now the National Revolution Has Been Defeated?' The article's contents are clearly stated in the title. I argued that, since the Revolution had already been defeated, we would have to start again from scratch. After the article had appeared, a circular arrived from the Central Committee that seemed to say that the Revolution had not been defeated, that on the contrary, it had advanced to a new stage, and that we were now even closer to victory. I waited for a letter from the Central Committee or some other comrade opposing my article, but none came. The issue was never broached, and no one even drew attention to the fact that there was a contradiction between an article in the party journal and a circular of the Central Committee. Everyone was so caught up in the organisational struggle that they slighted thought and theory, so no one even noticed the contradiction!

---

5   A play on 'clasping the feet of Buddha', that is, trying to seek protection from Chen Duxiu.

But I had learned my lesson. 'From now on, I will be more careful when I write articles', I told myself. I was so careful that for the next few weeks, I wrote nothing. That is to say: I wrote only odds and ends, or general articles, or inconsequential articles on themes that would not get me into trouble. It was not that I suddenly believed through reading the circular that the Revolution had not been defeated after all. The opposite was true: I still thought that the Revolution had been defeated but that the International and the Central Committee (for the Central Committee had no views of its own – it got all its ideas on theory from Moscow, or from the Russians in Shanghai) must have some reason for saying that the victory of the Revolution was even closer; perhaps the reason was that in our position we could not proclaim the defeat of the Revolution. But, later, when I noticed that the Central Committee's plans were premised on the imminence of the victory of the Revolution, I started to have doubts. Did they really think that? How come I thought so differently from them? Not only the Central Committee was saying that the tide of revolution was rising – even opponents of the Central Committee, like Wang Ruofei and Chen Qiaonian of the Party's Jiangsu Provincial Committee, thought the same. One day, Wang brought some wine over to my place and we sat there drinking it and chatting about party matters. The conversation got round to Chen Duxiu's letters to the Central Committee. I told him that I thought that what he had written in the letters was simply a collection of odds and ends, that I understood some bits of it but not others. He said he by no means approved of what Chen had written in his letters.

'But sometimes Chen sees deeper than other people', he continued. 'For example, a few days ago, at his place, he told me that the Revolution was on the decline. I said no, it's rising. We got into an argument. He asked me: "Over the past few days most of the foreign troops in Shanghai have been sent home. Do you believe that the imperialists would withdraw most of their armies if the Chinese Revolution was still ascending?" I suddenly saw the light: the Revolution was on the decline'.

I simply replied that the observation was perceptive and did not mention my article in *Bolshevik*. But, after that, I took Chen's letters rather more seriously. Chen himself certainly had not committed this view to paper, nor did Wang Ruofei formally publicise his conviction. I do not know when it was that the struggle between the Jiangsu Provincial Committee and the Central Committee first began to take on political and theoretical dimensions. Perhaps it was after Wang Ruofei acquired that conviction.

For quite a few issues, I contributed nothing of any substance to the journal, yet I had no need to explain myself to anyone, for no one ever asked me why I had stopped writing. But, when news arrived of the Guangzhou insurrection, I had no choice but to put pen to paper. Qu Qiubai was busy holding meetings and had no time to write the editorials, so I had to write; in any case, I felt that my old attitude had been mistaken, for now, there could be no doubt that the revolution was in spate. I took up my pen to write the editorial. Previous editorials had analysed current Chinese or world affairs. I could not write an article of that sort, so I wrote about what was uppermost in my mind at the time. I cannot remember what I called the editorial, but I do remember that it used the insurrection to prove that China had only two possible futures: either the Great Dragon Empire that Zhang Zuolin was preparing to set up; or the 'dictatorship of the proletariat'. There could be no third way. I published it without having Qu Qiubai check it. At the next editorial conference, Qu – who presided – said nothing. At the conference after that, he delivered a report: 'On such-and-such a day at the Standing Committee Comrade Luo Man (that is, Li Weihan) raised the question of Comrade Chaolin's editorial in the last issue of *Bolshevik* opposing the line of the International. The International considers that the revolution in China is a bourgeois-democratic revolution that will lead in future to a workers' and peasants' democratic dictatorship, but Comrade Chaolin's article talks about proletarian dictatorship. The Standing Committee resolved that I should take the responsibility for making a correction. In this issue, I intend to write an editorial containing such a correction. But Comrade Chaolin's editorial was a very useful revelation to me. In the past, I could never find a suitable subject to write about in editorials. But from now on, we can use this column to discuss theoretical questions'. I raised a few doubts, and Qu replied that Lenin had issued the call for a workers' and peasants' democratic dictatorship in 1905. If, in those days, all that Russia could manage was a workers' and peasants' democratic dictatorship, surely the same applied all the more to a country like China? Qu said in his editorial that the editorial in such-and-such an issue of the journal had not been vetted by the editorial committee, and that though most of it was right, one section of it required correction, and so on. I planned to write an article for the following issue in the discussion column rebutting Qu, so I started searching for relevant passages from Lenin's *Selected Works* in Russian that we had in the bookcase. I found several articles on the workers' and peasants' democratic dictatorship and read them carefully. Then I lost heart and gave up, because Lenin argued that Russia could only implement a workers' and peasants' democratic dictatorship, just as Qu had said. After that, I became even more timorous about writing articles, and stayed so right through until the time I quit as editor of *Bolshevik*.[6]

---

6 My editorial, published in issue no. 11, was called 'Long Live Soviet State Power!' Qu's editorial, called 'Chinese Soviet State Power and Socialism', appeared in no. 14. I talked about the Great Dragon Empire and the Guomindang Government on the one hand, and proletarian

Seen from the point of view of past developments and the present Guangzhou insurrection, the Chinese revolutionary state could be only a dictatorship of the proletariat. But going by what Lenin wrote before the Russian Revolution, the Chinese revolutionary state could be only a workers' and peasants' democratic dictatorship. Could it be that Lenin was wrong? Or was the mistake mine?

This question continued to haunt me right through until 1929, when I read some of Trotsky's writings and resolved the problem.

But the polemic in *Bolshevik* – a polemic waged across two unsigned articles – attracted next to no attention. No one wrote a letter or an article in response to it, no one talked to me about it. Today, Qu Qiubai is dead, and though Li Weihan is still alive, it is likely that he has forgotten the whole business; but I still remember it quite clearly, for it obsessed me for many months to come.

This Chinese Revolution started on 30 May 1925, with the Shanghai massacre, and ended on 11 December 1927, with the defeat of the Guangzhou insurrection. The result was that the Guomindang replaced the Beiyang warlords as China's rulers and Nanjing took over from Beijing as its capital. Apart from that, almost nothing changed, though it is true that the Guomindang political system was more consonant with the interests of the Chinese bourgeoisie than was the political system of the Beiyang warlords.

What was the place of this Chinese Revolution in the general history of world revolution? On my way from Shanghai to Hankou, I had bumped into Pan Jiachen, just back from Russia. He explained to me as we paced the deck of the steamship how people in Moscow viewed the Chinese Revolution as it was then happening.

'The comrades in the International think that of the revolutions that have ever happened in the world, only the French Revolution of 1789, the Russian Revolution of 1917, and the present Chinese Revolution can be called "Great Revolutions"', he explained to me. This was the first time I realised that this revolution that I had personally experienced was deemed so important by other people. But I had my doubts about their estimation, though I did not tell Pan so. Four or five months earlier, I had given a lecture course on 'The History of World Revolution' at the party school run by the Shanghai Regional Committee; that lecture had given me the chance to make a general review of

---

dictatorship on the other, and I said that there could be no third way. [Note added by Zheng Chaolin in 1980.]

the subject, so the French and Russian Revolutions were still fresh in my mind. How could I compare our revolution with them? Moreover, for most comrades in those days – at least for those with Shanghai style – revolution meant the proletarian-socialist revolution that we ourselves would carry out after the conclusion of the Northern Expedition. However much effort the workers and peasants put into speeding the Expedition's victory, we still did not consider that it constituted the revolution as we understood it – at most it was a 'national revolution', that is, a transitional stage in the process leading from outright reaction to our own revolution, to the revolution without attributive. If to call this middle stage a 'revolution' was already to stretch the term, how on earth could one justify including it among the 'Great Revolutions'? After arriving in Wuhan and seeing so many causes for concern, I became all the more convinced that I was right. Later, after the defeat in Wuhan and then in Guangzhou, for me the question whether it was right or not to call the Chinese Revolution 'great' was finally disposed of. But others continued to talk of the 'Great Revolution', not only after the defeat at Guangzhou but even today, nearly twenty years later. The only Chinese author to write about the Revolution was Hua Gang. He called his book, which appeared in 1931, *Zhongguo da geming shi* ('History of the Great Chinese Revolution')! In my opinion, the view propagated by the International before was excusable up to the defeat of the Revolution, but to keep on calling it a 'Great Revolution' so many years later must have been due either to ignorance about the history of the Revolution or to a wrong view of what revolution is.

From a positive point of view, this Chinese Revolution was not a major event in the history of world revolution, but it was important in a negative sense, that is, from the point of view of the mistakes committed by its leaders, for the future Chinese revolution and for revolutions in countries in a similar position to that of China. The contest within the world communist movement between Stalinism and Trotskyism started around three issues, one of which was the Chinese Revolution. I shall have more to say in the chapter on the Left Opposition about the debate on the Chinese Revolution, but I shall start here with a general observation.

Errors committed by the leadership must bear a great deal of the responsibility for this defeat, for the Revolution broke out not as a spontaneous explosion provoked by objective factors but as a result of conscious preparation by revolutionaries. The relationship between subjective input by the revolutionary party and the objective facts of the Revolution was even more clearly visible in this revolution than in 1789 or 1917. The storming of the Bastille in Paris and the five-day strike, the demonstrations, and the insurrection in Petrograd were far more 'spontaneous' than the speeches in Shanghai's International Settlement on 30 May and the general strike triggered by the massacre. The speeches and strikes were consciously prepared and led by the Chinese Communist Party, whereas the insurrections in Paris and Petrograd were not prepared or led by a political party, even though they were the result of the efforts of revolutionaries. The 'planned' and 'conscious' nature of the Chinese Revolution was preserved even after the Revolution's outbreak and for a comparatively long period of time, right through until the Revolution's second stage, that is, the new wave set going by the Northern Expedition. That it was 'planned' and 'conscious' should by rights have guaranteed its victory, but actually, it brought about its downfall. Why so?

It is easy at this point to answer, 'Because the leadership made mistakes'. But different people have different views of 'what the mistakes were' and 'who the leaders were'.

The 'original sin' was the lack of a proper understanding of the relationship between bourgeois and proletarian revolution. The Third Congress of the Chinese Communist Party decided to join in the 'national revolution' and raised as its two main slogans 'Down with imperialism' and 'Down with the warlords'. This decision represented an epoch-making change. The Chinese Communist Party was a product of the October Revolution. Revolutionaries in China and abroad, discerning no future whatsoever in bourgeois thought or politics, became Communists after succumbing to the influence of the October Revolution and the soviet system. So they founded or joined the Communist Party. At first, they nurtured the ideal of proletarian-socialist revolution, but later, they stowed this ideal away and no longer talked about it, reverting, instead, to the struggle for China's independence and democracy. Save for a tiny minority, everyone agreed to the new line, though there was still no unanimity about when to fetch the old ideal from storage or about how to make the transition from 'national revolution' to proletarian revolution. Of the two main slogans, 'Down with the warlords' was subordinate to 'Down with imperialism'. People viewed the warlords as no more than tools through which the imperialists controlled China. What's more, every disaster, every potential cause of disquiet, was blamed on imperialism. The compradors were the tools of imperialism, the right-wing of the Guomindang were running dogs of imperialism, agricultural bankruptcy was the result of imperialist aggression, and so on. In a nutshell, people diverted the workers' and peasants' hatred for their Chinese oppressors onto the imperialists and the foreign oppressors. Perhaps it's true that, in the last resort, everything that is wrong with China is a result of imperialist aggression, but only to resist imperialism, and to fight back against Chinese oppressors only when they are tools of imperialism, can often lead to wrong conclusions. For example, since peasant misery is a result of agricultural bankruptcy and agricultural bankruptcy is a result of imperialist aggression, the natural target for the peasants will be imperialism and not their most intimate enemy, the landlords. If peasants join in the revolution, it will be to fight against imperialism, not to raise the land question. It was no accident that the Chinese Communist Party only raised the land question after the Hunan peasants had spontaneously expropriated the landlords' fields and divided them among the peasants; on the contrary, this delay was intimately related to the Party's exclusive stress on anti-imperialism at the expense of class struggle. When the Communists raised the land question in the peasants' wake, it was not according to them for the sake of land revolution in itself, but because expropriating the land would weaken the power of the landlord-class, which represented imperialism in the villages; so it would strengthen the fight against imperialism.

The national bourgeoisie was not generally considered to be a tool of imperialism. On the contrary, it was considered to be rather anti-imperialist, waking hopes that this bourgeoisie would join hands with the proletariat to complete the national revolution.

In and around 1925, the Chinese Communist Party prepared, launched, and led the Chinese Revolution according to this theory of 'national revolution'. In the event, the workers, the petty bourgeois, and part of the peasantry responded to the call. They vigorously fought back against the imperialists, who were shaken by the wave of strikes in Shanghai and Hong Kong. In this period, most people followed behind the Communist Party, and hardly any went ahead of it. So there was as yet no talk of 'excesses'.[7]

But there was no future for a revolution that concentrated only on imperialism. The strikes in Shanghai and Hong Kong got nowhere; the tide of revolution slowly ebbed; normality returned. By the early spring of 1926, the movement was like a bow-shot at the end of its flight.[8] When news of the Beijing massacre of 18 March reached Shanghai, Qu Qiubai sighed and said: 'Now that the tide has ebbed, not even a massacre can rouse the broad masses'. He was right. Only twenty or so people died in Shanghai's 30 May massacre, but still a great movement started; on 18 March 1926, in Beijing even more people died, but there were no more than a few vague protests in other parts of the country.

The Northern Expedition was a watershed in the Revolution. In a certain sense, we can say that the revolution that had broken out on 30 May was

---

7 In 1927, Chen Duxiu said that peasants in Hunan had committed 'excesses' during their land revolution.
8 According to a Chinese saying, at the end of its flight a bolt shot from a cross-bow cannot pierce even thin cloth.

already over; not until after the Northern Expedition did a new revolution burst forth. This new revolution was spontaneous. What I mean is: the masses raised even more radical demands than the Communist Party leaders, demands that these leaders had never even contemplated, and surged ahead of them. Strictly speaking, only this new revolution merits the name; the old one was simply a movement against imperialism.

The new revolution burst forth in the Hunan countryside. Hunan was a fountainhead of the Chinese Communist movement. At its epicentre in Changsha, from 4 May through to the birth of socialism, the growth of the revolution was no less tardy than that of its better-known counterpart represented in Beijing by *New Youth*. Hunanese predominate among the Chinese Communist Party's chief leaders. Geographically speaking, the Anyuan collieries are in Jiangxi, but most of the colliers are Hunanese, and Anyuan is linked by the Zhuzhou-Pingxiang Railway to Zhuzhou in Hunan. So, from the very beginning, Communists from Hunan were active there. Li Lisan is from Liling;[9] after he was deported from France, he was active in Anyuan fomenting strikes and organising workers' clubs and cooperatives. The Communist Party had one of its most important branches in Anyuan; and one of its members, the worker Zhu Jintang, was elected an alternate member of the Central Committee at the Fourth Congress. When Li Lisan left, Liu Shaoqi took over; after that, Wang Zekai (who came back from Russia together with me) was sent there by the Central Committee to be branch secretary; he, too, was from Liling. The Party launched a string of victorious struggles in the collieries, which became a very influential force in the movement; in the same year as May Thirtieth, that is, 1925, or in the spring of 1926, it was finally defeated. The owner, Sheng Xuanhuai's son, colluded with Jiangxi warlords to get the clubs disbanded, and their leader Comrade X was shot; a great many colliers returned to their villages. At Anyuan, they had received an education and training, so even though they had achieved nothing in the pits, these people – especially the activists among the colliers – became teachers and leaders back in the villages. That's why the peasant movement in Hunan was so much stronger than in other provinces. When the Northern Expedition reached Hunan, the students of the Peasant Training Institute that Mao Zedong had set up in Guangzhou followed on its heels. This, too, helped the peasant movement grow. The Hunan peasants were roused to greet and act in concert with the expeditionaries, to join in the fighting, and to disarm straggling northerners. But, to the surprise of the instigators, the instigated peasants refused to stop short at military actions of this sort and, instead, went on to raise their own demands. These demands

---

9 In Hunan.

rapidly escalated, and the peasants were soon demanding land and power; in parts of some counties, they even took land and power.

After the defeat of the revolution, historians delving into piles of old paper, from the Twenty-Four Histories[10] to the *Jiu tong*,[11] discovered that, on several occasions in ancient times, the peasants had staged land revolutions. We had known even before these revelations that there were peasant insurrections on several occasions in Chinese history, but we had always thought that they were carried out by 'roving bandits' like those at the end of the Ming dynasty – we had no idea that during them the peasants had demanded land. When we read in histories of the Russian revolutionary movement about the Russian peasants' thirst for land and about the prime place that the land question occupied in the organisation of the Narodniki,[12] we wondered why Chinese peasants had never demanded land and why Chinese revolutionaries never discussed the land question. Most Chinese revolutionaries knew nothing about the land question until the second half of 1926, when the Hunan peasants' fight for land shook the whole of China – not just the landlords, but the leaders of the Communist Party. The role played by the Communist Party in the peasant war for land was to pull it back. Even so, the movement still surged forward. Many of the Communist Party's minor officials and rank-and-file members approved of and led this spontaneous action, for they themselves lived cheek by jowl with the peasants. Peasant associations were organised in many parts of Hunan. They formed armed units; in some places, peasant associations took power. When the expeditionaries marched towards Jiangxi and Hubei, the land-struggle spread quickly in their wake. At the same time, the peasant movement under Peng Pai in the Dong Jiang region of Guangdong developed apace and also reached the stage of struggle for the land.

After the Northern Expedition reached Wuhan, that metropolis of central China, it triggered a series of mass movements. Artisans and shop-assistants started settling accounts with their masters. They demanded not only higher wages but back-payment of higher wages, in some cases going back several decades; in some cases, the eventual settlement was many times bigger than the original wage. This movement, too, was spontaneous, and even ran counter to what the Party's agitators had intended. There were similar movements in small towns all over Hubei.

---

10 Dynastic histories from remote antiquity through to the Ming dynasty.
11 Old encyclopaedia-style compilations divided into three sections dealing with manners, customs, costumes, and the like; biography; and geography.
12 The Russian Narodniki or Populists, derided by Marxists as 'utopian' and 'petty-bourgeois', had a predilection for the peasantry and terrorism.

Landlords and shop-owners who opposed these demands and people who had committed flagrant crimes were punished. Minor offenders were paraded round the streets wearing dunce's hats; major ones were shot. No few people were shot, notably, Ye Dehui,[13] a learned scholar of the old school; one other such scholar, Wang Guowei, drowned himself in a lake in Beijing[14] as a result of this incident. If scholars like Wang Guowei were so demoralised by the tragic fate of one of their ilk, how much more so must the landlords and the bourgeoisie have been? So the Chinese Revolution began to slip into 'civil war' mode. I do not mean the civil war between the armies of the Guomindang and of the Beiyang warlords, but that between the workers and peasants and the landlords and capitalists. Shanghai, that great anti-imperialist city, was rocked by a wave of 'economic' strikes, that is, strikes by workers out to better their lives regardless of whether the boss was an imperialist or a member of the national bourgeoisie. Shanghai workers had already started down this path in the interlude between May Thirtieth and the launching of the Northern Expedition, when the Communist Party was still in a position to control the strikes.

The special feature of this new revolution was class struggle, that is, the struggle between Chinese workers and peasants and Chinese capitalists and landlords, even to the point of civil war; compared with this, the revolution of the earlier period was no more than a national struggle, that is, a struggle between Chinese and imperialists. Anti-imperialism barely featured in the revolution that broke out later, save for the recovery of the concessions in Hankou, Jiujiang, and elsewhere.[15] It was this class struggle, not the national struggle, that decided Chiang Kai-shek, Wang Jingwei, Tang Shengzhi, and others to go over to the reaction and massacre people. If the revolution had not gone beyond its 'national' stage, if it had kept to slogans like 'Down with imperialism' and 'Down with the warlords' and only demanded national independence and national reform, then perhaps Chiang really would have waited until after taking Beijing before settling accounts with us. But the Chinese workers and peasants were not ready to do as the Comintern and the Communist Party wished; they were not ready to stay within the bounds of the 'national revolution'.

I know that some people say, 'By opposing capitalists and landlords the workers and peasants were opposing the Chinese representatives of imperialism, so they were opposing imperialism itself!' And that's true. But it is also

---

13   Ye Dehui was shot during the revolutionary turmoil not because he was a 'scholar of the old school' but because he had served as a high official under the Qing and was a big landowner and member of the so-called 'evil gentry'.
14   Kunming Lake in the Yiheyuan or Summer Palace.
15   Chinese demonstrators seized control of these concessions in January 1927.

true that 'During the revolution of the later period, when the concessions in Hankou and Jiujiang were recovered, the masses struggled against imperialism because it was helping their sworn enemies, the landlords and the capitalists. The masses were fighting against Chinese capitalists and landlords in the person of imperialism'. Without waging class struggle to the end, without seizing the land and taking over the factories, China will never be in a position to realise national independence and democratic reform, so it will not be able to make an effective stand against imperialism either. In other words, unless we step beyond the bounds of 'national revolution' to carry out proletarian-socialist revolution, we will not be able to complete the bourgeois-democratic revolution. The leadership of the Communist Party did not understand this fact during the events that I am describing, but the workers and peasants did, as they showed in action.

When I say the leadership, I mean not just the Chinese leaders but the Moscow leaders, the Third International and the CPSU, in a word, all those people who set a bourgeois-democratic term to the Chinese Revolution.

The second stage of the revolution that I have just described was triggered by the Northern Expedition. Some people may conclude that had there been no Northern Expedition to start with, this new revolution could not have happened. But they would be wrong. It's perhaps true that as long as the Communist Party leaders stuck to their wrong position, this new revolution needed the trigger of a Northern Expedition, or some other similar military action. But, if they had had a correct position, they could still have prepared, launched, and led this new revolution even without a Northern Expedition, for it could have burst forth just like May Thirtieth. In the event, the revolution that did take place bequeathed a pernicious legacy, for it left people with a wrong idea of revolution.

Before the Northern Expedition, most people – at least those party cadres with Shanghai style – thought (rightly) that revolution is in essence the product of mass insurrection. The Party allocates its main forces and its outstanding cadres to the basic levels of the mass movement and to its own internal organisation. It then sends its less capable members to work in the government or the army. The aim of this deployment is to prepare sufficient forces to carry out our own revolution. At the time, there was no other view of revolution than the one I have just described. But the question arose of whether or not a Northern Expedition should be undertaken. The Central Committee in Shanghai said no. Later, to everyone's surprise, the Expedition was successful and provoked an even more progressive mass movement of workers and peasants, whereupon most people (including the Shanghai-based Central Committee) changed their minds about the revolution. Occupy a territory, set up a government, organise an army, and then launch an expedition to seize state power at national level – this was now seen as the main way to make revolution; mass armed insurrection was relegated to the role of ancillary action, in support of the revolutionary army. Thereafter, the Party deployed its best cadres in the government and the army[16] and delegated its less capable ones to working in the mass movement. This concept of revolution even spread to the comrades of the Comintern. The Sixth Congress of the Chinese Communist Party, held in the countryside outside Moscow under Bukharin's tutelage, produced a theory that substantiated this view of revolution by appealing to China's special national circumstances. The theory went like this. The Chinese Revolution, unlike other revolutions, could 'win initial victory in one or more provinces'. In one sense, this idea was obviously a result of the influence of the Northern Expedition; in another sense, it was an imitation of Stalin's theory of 'socialism in one country'. The large-scale 'Red Army'[17] movement that started up after the Sixth Congress corresponded precisely to this concept of revolution. The Chinese Communist Party occupied one or more counties in Jiangxi and other provinces, set up soviet governments, organised red armies, and then set out on expeditions against Changsha, Nanchang, and even Nanjing. The workers' movement in big cities like Shanghai was relegated to an ancillary role, in support of the Red Army. Naturally, this 'revolution' later failed and the Red Army set out on the Long March to northern Shaanxi.[18] Now that the Guomindang and the Communists are once again cooperating, people no longer talk about revolution, but should they ever do so, then they do so in code, using words like occupy a 'border area', set up a 'border area government', organise an Eighth Route Army and a New Fourth Army, and when the time is ripe go on expeditions to the southwest, the southeast, or the northeast.[19] Even today, the mass movement in Guangdong is still seen as ancillary to the Eighth

---

16   In the first instance, before the final split in July 1927, this meant the government and army of the left-wing Guomindang.

17   Chinese Red Army.

18   The Long March beginning in southern China in October 1935 and ending in northwestern China a year later is portrayed by Chinese Communist historians as a victory march to open up a new front against the Japanese in northern China. Actually, it began as an evacuation of the old Central Soviet in southern China after the defeat of the Red Army by Chiang Kai-shek in the so-called Fifth Encirclement campaign. See Benton 1992, Chapter 1.

19   After the formation of the second united front between the Guomindang and the Communists in 1937, the Communists temporarily moderated their policies and changed the name of the territory they occupied from Soviet to 'border area' and the name of their Red Army to Eighth Route Army (later joined by the smaller New Fourth Army). Between

Route Army and the New Fourth Army. Unfortunately, there are antecedents in China for this view of revolution. Apart from the Northern Expedition there is the Revolution of 1911, which was also carried out by armies. The Chinese Revolution cannot hope for victory until Chinese revolutionaries relinquish this wrong idea of revolution.

But I am getting ahead of myself. In the period that I am now describing (late 1927 to early 1928), I could never have said what I have just said about the process and concept of revolution. I arrived at these ideas after reading Trotsky's speeches and writings about the Chinese Revolution some time later. These ideas were the fruit of my contemplation of problems of the revolution during my second spell in prison. Up to that time, even though I thought a great deal about it and had my doubts, I arrived at no firm conclusions.

By the spring of 1928, the state of the inner-party struggle had changed, to the disadvantage of the 'Chen Duxiu-ites'. The attacks came from the direction of the Shanghai Garrison Headquarters. The headquarters of the Jiangsu Provincial Committee were raided and many important party leaders were arrested, including Chen Qiaonian. Wang Ruofei escaped by a whisker. Rumours later circulated that if a ransom of $20,000 had been paid while those arrested were still in police custody, they would not have been extradited to the Chinese authorities,[20] but the Central Committee was not prepared to come up with $20,000. I myself believe that either it did not have the money or the Russians would not agree to pay it. But Wang Ruofei, who was incensed by the affair, accused the Central Committee of deliberately sacrificing these comrades to resolve the dispute in the Party. The result was that they were handed over. Chen Qiaonian, Xu Baihao, and Zheng Futa were shot at Longhua. The rest were sent to prison. Not long after the incident, Luo Yinong was also arrested and handed over to Longhua to be shot.

During this period, the Chinese Communist Party was preparing for its Sixth Congress, to be held in the Soviet Union. Starting in the spring, delegates set out one after the other from every part of China. The Russians wanted Chen Duxiu to go, but Chen refused. Qu Qiubai entreated Wang Ruofei to change Chen's mind.

'I originally thought he should go', Wang replied, 'but then I thought to myself that they're in the middle of a campaign against Trotsky in the Soviet

---

their arrival in the northwest and 1945, when Zheng finished this memoir, they expanded southward and eastward in the course of a series of expeditions and campaigns.

20   They were arrested in the International Settlement.

Union. If Chen goes, he is bound to stick to his own opinions and oppose those of the International, so people will attack him in order to attack Trotsky'.

'Not necessarily, not necessarily', said Qu.

What Wang meant was that, if the situation had not been complicated by the issue of the Soviet opposition, Chen's views might have won out. Ren Bishi, too, arranged to meet me in Jessfield Park for a chat, and tried to get me to persuade Chen to go to Moscow. I promised to pass on what he had said. Peng Shuzhi, too, refused an invitation to go to Moscow. The rest of the top leaders all went – of the Central Committee members, only Li Weihan was left behind. The people left in charge all over China had been newly promoted into the leadership, and were either inexperienced or incompetent; we all sensed a tremendous vacuum. I stayed behind in my old job. When the Standing Committee met, I was sometimes summoned to attend. The second person on the Standing Committee after Li was Luo Dengxian, a worker from Hong Kong, who had recently come up to Shanghai from Guangdong. There must have been a third, but I cannot remember who it was. We spent most of our time discussing trivialities. The only issue of political import that reached the agenda was the massacre at Jinan on 3 May; that was one of the meetings I attended.

Apart from attending the Standing Committee in my capacity as editor of the party journal, I received a new assignment, in my capacity as Secretary of the Propaganda Department. I was ordered to direct the activity of the Creation Society.[21]

The Creation Society had started out as a literary association. In the past, it had confined its activity to publishing literary books and journals, of which I had read hardly any; and if I read one by accident, I never liked it. I thought that even realism was obsolete, let alone romanticism. I especially disliked the poems of Guo Moruo, who adulterated the vernacular with classical verbosity. Besides, after returning to China, I was completely absorbed by revolution, and had no interest in literature. Before the Northern Expedition, Creation Society writers had no connection with the revolution, and were even against it. But the people in the Society for Literary Studies[22] were close to us; they included

---

21   The Creation Society was a literary group organised in 1921 by Guo Moruo, Yu Dafu, and other students returned from Japan and France. At first, it espoused 'art for art's sake' and romanticism, but later, it moved to the left and ended up advocating 'proletarian literature'.

22   The Society for Literary Studies, founded in Beijing in January 1921, promoted 'literature for life's sake' in opposition to the Creation Society's 'literature for art's sake'.

Shen Yanbing[23] and his brother Shen Zemin, who were our comrades. Needless to say, they were not close to us in a literary sense. On one occasion, Shen Yanbing and Jiang Guangchi were discussing literature in the office of the Propaganda Department on Fusheng Road. Shen Yanbing voiced some criticisms of the Creation Society; Jiang Guangchi defended it. 'What sort of a writer is he?' said Jiang after Shen had left. 'All he has done is introduce a few foreign writers to the Chinese public!' And it was true. In those days, Shen was no more than an 'introducer of foreign writers'. But he was a party veteran who had worked as Secretary of the Shanghai Regional Committee long before my own return to China. After I got back, he was Secretary of the Party's Commercial Press branch. He had also been active in the Guomindang in Shanghai; he was a very loyal and hardworking comrade. I used to attend the Commercial Press branch as Regional Committee representative, and on occasion, he attended to some business in the Propaganda Department. So we often met, though we never discussed literary questions. After the Wuhan debacle, he returned to Shanghai and became imperceptibly estranged from the Party. In November 1927, not long after I myself had returned to Shanghai, I bumped into Song Yunbin in a Shaoxing wine-bar on Fuzhou Road. (Song appeared as the character 'Yunlang' in one of Shen Yanbing's stories about Guling.) In the course of our conversation, Shen Yanbing's name came up, and Song gave me his address. A few days later, I went to visit Shen in his home on Jingxing (or Jingyun) Alley off Darroch Road. I took along a copy of the inaugural issue of *Bolshevik*. Shen lived in a two-storey house. His study was on the top floor. He told me that he had been back in Shanghai for more than fifty days, but that he had not once been outside his front-door for fear of being recognised. I asked him how he spent his time. He told me that he spent it writing stories.

'One of my stories is in the most recent issue of *Xiaoshuo yuebao* ('Novel Monthly')', he told me. 'Read it and see if you can guess which one it is'.

I was too busy to act on his suggestion; not until a long time afterwards did I discover that he had published his trilogy *Huanmie* ('Disillusion'), *Dongyao* ('Wavering'), and *Zhuiqiu* ('Pursuance') under the pseudonym Mao Dun, originally in serial form. Later, I read the trilogy when it came out in separate volumes. When I told Qu Qiubai about my visit to Shen Yanbing, Qu told me that someone writing under the pen-name Ding Ling had published a story in *Novel Monthly* that accurately depicted the popular mood at the time of the May Fourth Movement. He wondered who this Ding Ling was. In those days, I had so little interest in literature that I could not summon the energy to read this story. Only a long time later did I discover that this Ding Ling was the woman

---

23 Mao Dun.

Jiang Bingzhi, who at one time had run after Qu. On the day of my visit, Shen also told me something about his own political views. He complained about the positions that the Party had adopted after the 7 August Conference and opposed the policy of organising peasant insurrections everywhere. He said that, if one insurrection failed, the peasants would no longer be prepared to participate in insurrections even if the situation became revolutionary. That was the first time I had ever heard a comrade come out clearly against the new policies of the Central Committee. Later, he incorporated his view on insurrections into his essay *Cong Guling dao Dongjing* ('From Guling to Tokyo'). During the period of Li Lisan's ascendancy,[24] Party controlled literary publications attacked Shen and the Central Committee instructed the Japanese section of the Chinese Communist Party not to recognise him as a comrade. In 1929, I met Yang Xianjiang after he had just got back from Japan. When I asked him about Shen, he talked about him as if he were an enemy.

But all that happened later. Let's return to the subject of the Creation Society. When the Northern Expedition first set out, Guo Moruo somehow or other became Deputy Director of the main Political Department under Army Headquarters, so these romantic writers, who had never before shown any interest in politics, also began to discuss revolution. In late 1927 or early 1928, a new monthly publication began to appear alongside *Chuangzao* ('Creation'). I forget what it was called.[25] It was a Marxist discussion journal. The people who wrote for it were all nonentities. Members of the Creation Society like Cheng Fangwu contributed nothing more than the editorial notes. I found it hard to understand the articles in it; after I had struggled through a page or two, my head began to ache, for the articles were written in long, convoluted sentences with peculiar grammar and terminology. The other members of the Propaganda Department felt the same way as I did about the publication. We concluded that these people must just have got back to China after studying in Japan, and that though their Japanese may have been good, their Chinese was still extremely awkward. It never occurred to us that, in five years' time, this deliberately unreadable style would become fashionable in China among young people, and that it would stay so until checked by the 'popular language' movement.[26]

---

24 The 'ultra-left Li Lisan line', imposed on the Chinese Communist Party by Stalin, lasted from 1929 to 1930.

25 It was called *Wenhua pipan* ('Cultural Criticism'). [Note by the Chinese editors of Zheng's book.]

26 In 1928, a group of young supporters of the Creation Society returned from Japan and launched the magazine *Wenhua pipan* ('Cultural Criticism'). In it, they used a style of

But I could not help noticing some articles in this publication directed against Lu Xun and Jiang Guangchi that I felt were right.

Lu Xun adopted an aloof and cynical attitude towards this revolution. Later, people defended him by arguing that well in advance of anyone else, he had openly satirised the reactionary tendencies of the Guomindang Government in Guangzhou. Actually, he did not only satirise the reactionary tendency in the Guomindang Government – he satirised the entire revolution. After Jiang Guangchi's return to China, Jiang rejected the idea of working in the Party and set himself up in business under the shop-sign 'revolutionary man of letters', much to the disgust of most party members. He set up Sun Society and a like-named bookshop, and he began publishing a magazine called *Taiyang* ('Sun'). He was protected by the authority of the Party. Yang Chunren and Qian Xingchun, who worked under him, knew even less about Marxism and world-literature than he did. Undoubtedly, the Creation Society people were more knowledgeable than Yang and Qian in these two respects.

Two or three weeks before he left the country, Qu Qiubai told us at a meeting of the editorial board that the Creation-Society had asked the Central Committee to appoint someone to lead them. He added that Guo Moruo had links to the Party and that when he was in Shanghai, he had often gone to see Zhou Enlai; Guo had advised this group of returned students (from Japan) to work together with the Party, and had told them that there was no need to run a separate magazine. He also told us that we now had two comrades in the Creation Society, Li Minzhi and Ouyang Jixiu; Li had originally worked as Guo's secretary and Ouyang was a student at Shanghai University. These two men did bring out a separate small-format magazine. The meeting proposed me for the job, but I refused, and proposed Qu instead. I was unused to dealing with outsiders, especially writers. Qu declined, on the grounds that he was about to go abroad, so I had no choice but to accept. However, I procrastinated right through until the end of April or the beginning of May. Not until after the Jiangsu Provincial Committee had urged me several times to get on with the job did I finally fix a time to meet the writers.

The morning before my appointment with them, I received a brief note addressed to 'Comrade' Chaolin asking me to go to the sender's home at 12 Scott Road before going to meet the Creation Society people. The letter

---

writing strongly influenced by Japanese, in both terms and structure. As a result, their articles were practically unreadable and unintelligible. Not even book-trained intellectuals could understand them, let alone the workers for whom they had supposedly been written. About five years later, a campaign was started up by other left-wing writers (including Qu Qiubai) to promote a *dazhong yu*, a language for and of the masses.

was written casually, as if to a very old friend, and was signed Duqing, who I realised must be Wang Duqing. I had heard the name, though I had never met the person nor even dealt with him indirectly. In the event, I did not first go to Wang's house but, instead, went straight to Yongan Alley, either because I had already agreed a time with Li Minzhi, or for some other reason. There were a dozen or so people waiting for me. It was the first time I had met any of them, including Li Minzhi (that is, Li Yimang) and Ouyang Jixiu (that is, Hua Han). Among the members of the Creation Society present were Cheng Fangwu, Zheng Boqi, Zhang Ziping, Peng Kang, Li Chuli, Zhu Jingwo, Feng Naichao, and Li Tiesheng. Cheng Fangwu, who seemed to be acting as their spokesperson, said a few words of welcome and introduced me to the gathering. Then he said that they were intending to set up a research association or symposium to discuss various questions, and he hoped I would be its leader. At first, I politely refused, but naturally, I ended up by having to make a little speech. In it, I analysed Chinese social structure and the nature and future of the Chinese Revolution, as formulated in a number of Comintern circulars. My speech was on Comintern lines, so it was Stalinist. These people were not members of the Party, so I was constrained to stick to the official line. After I had finished, I asked for their opinions on what I had said. Li Chuli spoke up first. He said he had never heard anyone say such things before; all he had heard in the past was abstract theory, he had never heard anyone explain problems of the Chinese Revolution with such lucidity, he was deeply grateful. Clearly, he was just being polite. Others also spoke, but they had nothing relevant to say.

During my several years in the Party, I had never attended such a polite gathering. Once, in 1926, I was asked to speak at a Guomindang meeting in Zhabei. Liu Yazi introduced me and was also very polite, but after my speech was over, no one in the audience opened their mouths. I felt about the Creation Society meeting that it made no difference whether I had gone or not, for they had assigned tasks anyway in advance. Cheng Fangwu and Li Chuli's little speeches were set-pieces designed to please the Communist Party. They had welcomed me because through me, they were welcoming the Party. I continued to believe this until two years ago,[27] when I met a certain Mr Gao from Suzhou, who had spent some time with Li Chuli in Suzhou Reformatory. One day, the authorities in the Reformatory called all the prisoners together to hear speeches by prisoners eligible for release, to decide who should go and who not. Some grovelled shamelessly, but Li Chuli spoke out boldly and eloquently. He said that after returning from Japan, he had made an abstract study of social science, but that in Shanghai, he had met someone sent to talk to the Creation Society on behalf

---

27 In 1942.

of the Central Committee of the Chinese Communist Party (he said he could not remember the man's name) and this person had convinced him to become a Marxist. At this point, the man in charge of the rally told someone to help Li down from the platform, for he had become quite agitated. Mr Gao was full of admiration for Li Chuli; his story moved me. Assuming that Li meant me, his little speech that day in Yongan Alley was sincerely meant, and was not just spoken out of politeness. And that's quite possible, because outsiders never got to see Comintern circulars, nor did they necessarily become acquainted with the theoretical debate in the Party, even though it had been published in pamphlet form in Hankou. Later, I sent copies of the booklets by Qu Qiubai and Peng Shuzhi to the Creation Society. We had brought the plates with us from Hankou and reused them. Qu's was the second edition, but Peng's was in effect the first edition, for it had merely been typeset in Wuhan and not published. I was not in favour of publishing Peng's book, but Qu Qiubai read the plates and discovered a host of 'opportunist errors', so he was very keen to bring it out as a way of keeping up the offensive against Peng.

After the meeting in Yongan Alley, I went on alone to Scott Road. I went inside. A fat man got up from a bed, pulled on a pair of slippers, and said hello, all the while shooting me suspicious glances. When I told him my name, he warmly shook my hand, and we immediately became old friends. This Creation Society man was casually dressed in Chinese clothes, unlike the others I had already met, who wore neat Western-style suits. He talked volubly and unconstrainedly, whereas they had behaved with gentlemanly decorum and reserve. On later occasions, the same distinction held.

Wang Duqing had waited for me in his home, which was why he had not gone to Yongan Alley; he was a little disappointed when I told him that I had already been there. He said that there was much he wanted to talk to me about. First, we reminisced about France, Montargis, and common friends. We also talked about his wife, Wu Ruoying, the daughter of Wu Yu. But then, Cheng Fangwu and Zhang Ziping came in, doubtless to tell Wang what had happened at the meeting. I sat for a while and then took my leave.

From then on, I went to Yongan Alley once a fortnight. No one was ever absent, and Wang Duqing came too. Each time, we took up a new issue. Everyone said what they thought, there was some discussion; finally, I summed up. My judgment was definitive and incontrovertible. I realised that we were doing no more than perform a sort of ritual to show that the Creation Society accepted party leadership and that we were not really a debating society or research-group, so I gradually lost interest. We continued meeting until the end of July, when the Standing Committee sent me to Fujian to inspect our work there. During my absence, the group stopped meeting – proof that my suspicions were fully grounded.

Once when I went to see Wang Duqing, he asked me to go for a cup of coffee with him at the Xinya Restaurant, newly opened at the intersection of Sichuan Road North and Qiujiang Road. He told me the inside story of the Creation Society.

'You can divide the Creation Society into two groups', he started. 'One group consists of "established authors" like Guo Moruo, Cheng Fangwu, Zhang Ziping, Zheng Boqi, and me; then, there is a group of "unknowns" like Peng Kang, Li Chuli, and the rest. Apart from them, there are a few "young employees" like Cheng Fangwu's nephew Cheng Shaozong and like Qiu Yunduo and Gong Binglu. They, too, sometimes write. Some people in the Creation Society are ambitious and want the Creation Society to talk with the Communist Party on an equal footing. Zhang Ziping belongs to the Third Party. He is completely unreliable. Zheng Boqi is a petty politician. As for the "unknowns", most of them are newly graduated and quite pure. Only a few individuals are ambitious. We must take care to subdue Zheng'.

When I first started dealing with the Creation Society, it had already stopped attacking Lu Xun, and after that, we no longer discussed him. Nor did we discuss the Sun Society, though Jiang Guangchi and Qian Xingchun continued to complain to me about the Creation Society, and pointed out a number of mistakes in articles attacking the Sun Society in the magazine. For example, the first person in China to mention 'revolutionary literature' was Jiang Guangchi, but the Creation Society said it was Guo Moruo; also, an article in *Sun* had said that 'knowledge is born from experience', but the Creation Society publication called this 'an idealist error'. I cannot remember how I replied to these criticisms. But it required an even greater expenditure of energy to mediate the disputes within the Creation Society than to mediate those between it and the Sun Society. When Cheng Fangwu went abroad, Zhang Ziping imperceptibly drifted away from the Society, and Wang Duqing and Zheng Boqi – the two remaining 'established authors' – were constantly at loggerheads. What's more, the 'unknowns' made a common front against them. The issues were invariably personalised and trivial. For some reason or other, Li Minzhi and Ouyang Jixiu thought that I should intervene. In my name and at the Propaganda Department's expense, Li Minzhi invited them to a Sichuanese meal at his place. During the meal, we discussed their internal altercations and asked them to bring their differences out into the open and explain to one another what the problems were. But Wang Duqing did not want to.

'We're like a married couple', he said: 'before midnight we fight, after midnight we make love. There is no need to discuss anything'.

The rest of them aired their points of view, everyone smoothed out the misunderstandings, and we all parted amicably, though I do not know whether this reconciliation dinner was really effective. After each of the meetings

I attended, Wang Duqing would drag me off to his place, or to a coffee-parlour or sometimes to a bar or a dance-hall. It was obvious that I was closer to him than to the rest. Zheng Boqi was very unhappy about this, and the others said that I had been 'cordoned off'. Through me, Wang Duqing got back in touch with Wang Zekai, whom he had known in France. Wang Zekai introduced him to Peng Shuzhi and Li Ji, and at Peng's place, he met Chen Duxiu. So that was the beginning of his friendship with us, and of the association of this 'established author' of the Creation Society with Trotskyism. The tie survived attacks and blandishments, right through until his death.

Wang Duqing's famous long poem about the Guangzhou insurrection was written after I got to know him. He showed me the draft and asked me what he should call it. I suggested '11 Déc'.[28]

All along, I saw these writers as fellow-travellers and never planned to draw them into the Party. After the Sixth Congress, when Cai Hesen took over as head of the Propaganda Department, the Communist party caucus in the Creation Society asked him to attend their meeting. He adopted the same position as I had, and called them 'Democracy'. But, sometime after Li Lisan had taken over from Cai and I had quit the Propaganda Department, one after another these 'unknowns' were admitted to the Party. On the whole, it must be said that they did not fail their duty. I have already described Li Chuli's steadfastness in jail. While I was in the Central Military Prison in Nanjing, Zhu Jingwo happened to occupy the cell next to mine. We saw each other every day, and though we could agree on nothing, we were never divided by bad feelings. He joined the New Fourth Army after his release; it is said that he shot himself with his own revolver to avoid capture during the Southern Anhui Incident.[29] (According to another version, he committed suicide by pitching himself off a stretcher and rolling down a cliff.) Peng Kang was jailed for terrorism, and was at first held in a jail in the Shanghai Settlement. While I was in prison in Nanjing, I read an article by him on Laozi in the Suzhou Reformatory magazine, in which he claimed that Laozi's theories were consonant with Chen Lifu's 'vitalism'.[30] If the Chinese Communist Party does not take the things that comrades write

---

28   In French in the original. This is the day on which the Guangzhou insurrection started in 1927.

29   An incident that took place in January 1941, when superior Guomindang forces attacked and destroyed the Communist New Fourth Army headquarters in southern Anhui, after which the united front was over in all but name.

30   Chen Lifu led the Guomindang's Investigation Division for some ten years after 1928. His book *Weisheng lun* ('On Vitalism', translated into English as *Philosophy of Life*) was intended to restore a conservative interpretation of China's cultural tradition and provide a philosophical basis for the ideas of Sun Yat-sen.

in reformatory too seriously, then Peng Kang can be regarded as a good comrade following his release from jail.

After the defeat of the Guangzhou insurrection, confidence in the 'revolutionary high tide' seemed to ebb a little. In February 1928, Stalin, Bukharin, Xiang Zhongfa, and Li Zhenying put their names to a brief manifesto in Moscow that was already rather less optimistic in tone than earlier pronouncements. After the delegates to the Sixth Congress had left China for Moscow, Li Zhenying, who was not a delegate and was already back in China, specially looked me up in Shanghai for a talk and to give me a French-language *European Almanac*. He said that, according to Stalin, the Chinese Revolution was still not back at high tide, but that it had already passed its trough and was now once again rising. While Li was saying this, he formed a V with the thumb and index finger of his left hand and used the index finger of his right hand as a pointer.

'Comrade Stalin says that the revolution is no longer here', he said, tapping the bottom of the V. 'He says it's on its way up, somewhere around here', he continued, tapping a point half way up his index finger.

I do not recall Stalin or any other Comintern comrade ever saying that the Chinese Revolution was in the trough of a V. All I remember is seeing circulars that said that the Revolution was nearing a new high tide. Surely, it was not forbidden in these circulars to say that the Revolution had ebbed? And could it really be that, even if you had no choice but to admit that it had ebbed, you still had to add that it was 'now beginning to rise again'? I had had some illusions at the time of the Guangzhou insurrection, but afterwards, I no longer believed that nonsense about a 'high tide', and I used to hate hearing people use the term. Yet, I was unable to draw any systematic conclusions from all this theorising. After the delegates had returned to China, not only was the struggle on the outer front absolutely quiet, but even the Party's internal life seemed to have ebbed away to nothing. In July, Li Weihan sent me to Fujian to sort things out there, for a Provincial Committee member had defected to Zhang Zhen, a minor warlord in Zhangzhou, and as a result, the Party was in chaos.

I went by boat from Shanghai to Xiamen. Nine years earlier, I had set out from Xiamen for the continent of Europe; on my way back, I had then taken the Trans-Siberian Railway to Vladivostok, whence by boat to Shanghai. The only stretch I had not yet completed on my round-trip across Europe and Asia was between Shanghai and Xiamen; now, I was about to fill the gap. In those days, various counties in western Fujian were in insurrection.[31] The Xiamen

---

31   In 1929, the Red Army marched into western Fujian and founded a soviet base there in conjunction with local Communist forces.

press was constantly reporting on these insurrections, but the Provincial Committee had lost touch with the insurrectionary areas, so the Party in Xiamen and Zhangzhou (not to mention Fuzhou) was powerless to intervene. I called a conference of delegates from all over Fujian (but no one came from the insurrectionary areas), spurred on a few inactive comrades, had a new Provincial Committee elected, and went on an inspection tour of the villages outside Xiamen and Zhangzhou. I did not return to Shanghai until September. On my second day back, the newspapers reported that Communist Party offices in Xiamen had been raided. Several overseas Chinese students living in the Party's liaison centre had been arrested, and a party office outside Xiamen had been raided. But the main target had escaped: an official of the Central Committee on an inspection-tour of the region had already left Xiamen. No one on the Central Committee knew that I was back, so they were thrown into panic by the news.

At around this time, things began to liven up on the Central Committee. The Sixth Congress held in the Soviet Union had already elected a new Central Committee and the Standing Committee members had already come back to Shanghai.

I returned amid a great storm to my house on Yuyuan Road. I went upstairs, clasped Jing[32] in my arms, and wept for joy. This was the first time we had been apart since getting married, and it had been more than forty days since I had left Shanghai. Jing told me that Cai Hesen, the new head of the Propaganda Department, had already arrived. The new General Secretary was Xiang Zhongfa. Li Weihan had failed to be elected, even as an alternate member of the Central Committee, and was in the process of handing over to his successor. Qu Qiubai, Zhang Guotao, and Wang Ruofei had been kept in Moscow and not allowed to return. Li Lisan returned as an alternate member;[33] in the absence of one of the full members, he filled the vacancy. The new Central Committee had already decided at one of its first meetings to keep me on as editor of the party journal and Secretary of the Propaganda Department.

I was dismayed by what Jing told me, for I had no wish to continue working under Cai Hesen. His behaviour in Wuhan and his *Jihui zhuyi shi* ('History of Opportunism') had led me to despise him. Surely they could find someone else

---

32 Wu Jingru, Zheng's wife.
33 Here, my memory played a trick on me. Li was elected as an alternate member of the Politburo at the Sixth Congress. By the time he came to head the Propaganda Department, he had already been promoted to full membership of the Politburo after a certain other full member left. [Note added by Zheng Chaolin in 1989.]

to be secretary? After I had reported to Xiang Zhongfa on my inspection-tour of Fujian, I asked to be allowed to resign. But they would not let me.

Wang Zekai also got back to China and came to look me up. He told me all sorts of stories about what had happened at the Sixth Congress. The 'Chen Duxiu-ites' had united around Wang Ruofei and become the core opposition at the Congress. They had joined together with other opposition groups to attack the Central Committee. Qu Qiubai had been attacked so badly that he had not been allowed to leave Russia; Li Weihan had not been elected because of the criticism, and Li Lisan had just scraped in. Li Weihan had been completely smashed by He Zishen.

The Yunnan delegate Wang Maoting, Jing's fellow-provincial, came to see me. It was the first time that I had ever met him. He handed me a letter written in invisible ink and told me the formula. I bought the necessary chemicals and washed the paper with them; it turned out to be a long letter from Wang Ruofei to Chen Duxiu about developments at the Sixth Congress. It had originally been written as an open letter and given to the new Central Committee to be passed on to Chen, but because it contained some uncomplimentary comments about certain leaders or for some other reason, the Central Committee would quite probably have held on to it; so Wang Ruofei copied it in invisible ink and asked Wang Maoting to pass it on to me. Wang Maoting had not had any previous dealings with the 'Chen Duxiu-ites'; he had come out against the Central Committee as a result of his own experiences in the Party. In his theoretical thinking, he was even more progressive than the so-called 'Chen Duxiu-ites'. According to reports, at one of the Moscow meetings – either at the Sixth Congress of the Chinese Communist Party or at a meeting of the Chinese delegation to the Congress of the Third International – he had publicly demanded a discussion of Trotsky's views on the Chinese Revolution. Many delegates – members of both the Central Committee group and the opposition – mentioned this incident in private conversation as evidence of Trotskyist activity in the Soviet Union. 'Even a Chinese delegate has been influenced by it!' But because Wang Maoting had nothing to do with the 'Chen Duxiu-ites', he was not detained in Moscow like Wang Ruofei, Liu Bojian, and others, nor was he punished after getting back to China like Wang Zekai, Ren Xu, He Zishen, and others. He even returned to Yunnan and resumed his old job as Secretary of the Yunnan Provincial Committee. Perhaps the only reason he dared to speak out publicly in Moscow was precisely because he had nothing to do with the 'Chen Duxiu-ites', who were at that time suffering repression. Less than a year after returning to Yunnan, Wang Maoting was arrested by Long Yun and shot.

The new Central Committee refused to let me resign, but actually, I had nothing to do anyway, for after I got back to Shanghai from Fujian the party journal and the Propaganda Department came to a standstill. I had no idea how to break the deadlock. But, to everyone's surprise, shortly – probably less than a month – after I got back from Fujian, Cai Hesen was toppled. Not until after the Sixth Congress did the northern comrades[34] accuse Cai in a statement to the new Central Committee of various misdeeds committed before the Congress was held. I cannot remember what they were, for during the hubbub created by the inner-party struggle, I had no interest in the various accusations brought against comrades. The new Central Committee dealt with Cai in accordance with the charges and removed him from the Standing Committee; naturally, he could no longer lead the Propaganda Department.

The newly appointed head of the Propaganda Department was Li Lisan, who had played an important position in Cai Hesen's overthrow. The Sixth Congress had elected Li as an alternate member of the Central Committee; as far as I remember, he came last,[35] but many of those elected to full membership had already died, defected, become inactive, or been punished, so he was gradually promoted to full membership. By now, he was on the Standing Committee, and he was also head of the Propaganda Department. The first time he attended the Department for a meeting, he made a speech in which he said: 'Our Party lacks a theoretical and political centre'. In the rest of his speech, he more or less proposed himself as that centre. I laughed to myself. But it later turned out that I had laughed too soon. From then on, sure enough, Li Lisan became the Chinese Communist Party's 'theoretical and political centre'. Luo Qiyuan asked him about the inner-party struggle at the Sixth Congress. He made a short report, the gist of which was that some oppositionists had come together on an unprincipled basis and that factions formed on an unprincipled basis would not last. At the end of the meeting, I once again tried to resign, but he laughed away my request and started talking about some other subject. *Bolshevik* appeared for a few more issues at Li Lisan's insistence.

The inner-party struggle that had begun in Moscow spread to China and continued to develop. Chen Duxiu, as ever, stood outside it, though Wang Zekai had reported to him on the Sixth Congress and asked him to become active.

'I won't', said Chen Duxiu. 'If I do, it will be to create a new party'.

Wang Zekai reported this exchange to me, shaking his head the while. At that time, we still thought that we should fight for the leadership of the old party. The idea of setting up a new party was treason and heresy. Ever since withdrawing from the leadership in Wuhan, Chen Duxiu had done nothing to fight for the restoration of his old position or to collect supporters. He had

---

34 Cai Hesen had been leader of the Party's Northern Region.
35 Actually, Li Lisan came second to last, before Zhang Guotao.

even opposed Wang Ruofei and Chen Qiaonian's efforts to form a group. After his return to Shanghai, he devoted himself to a study of the alphabetisation of Chinese; he was the only member of the Communist Party to show any interest in this subject.[36] If someone visited him, he would almost immediately raise this question. If he met someone from Hubei, he would ask how this or that character was pronounced in Hubei dialect; if from Guangdong, how in Cantonese. He even asked me to take him to Shen Yanbing's place so that he could make a study of Jiangsu and Zhejiang pronunciation.[37] We had various theories about why he started this research. Yin Kuan thought that the best analogy was with Cao Can, whose story is told in the *Han shu*.[38] If anyone ever went to visit Cao with a suggestion, he had got them drunk to shut them up. In short, no one really believed that Chen Duxiu was serious about his phonological research. But I happen to know that, actually, he was quite accomplished in this field. More than a year later, he wrote up his research in a book in which he presented a new Chinese alphabet that he had invented. The alphabet had thirty-odd letters, most of them Roman, a few Greek, and one or two new inventions. The rules for spelling were rather complicated. The Chinese language was divided for the purposes of this study into four dialects: Beijing, Wu, Yue, and Min.[39] After he had finished this manuscript, Chen sent copies of it to some of his old friends at Beijing University; I seem to remember that they included the linguist Zhao Yuanren. If it was not destroyed during the Japanese invasion of 28 January 1932, this manuscript must still be extant. It should be clear from Chen's earlier work *Ziyi leili* ('A Philological Study of Chinese Characters') and from studies he wrote later, in prison, that his interest in linguistics was deeply rooted. His work on alphabetising Chinese was actually an extension of his promotion of the vernacular in the May Fourth era.

But though Chen's research was like Cao Can's wine, his decision to stand outside the factional struggle still requires an explanation. His enemies said that he was arrogant, that he looked down on them, that he would not stoop

---

36   A few years later, Qu Qiubai, too, became interested in the question of the Latinisation of Chinese.
37   Shen Yanbing was a native of Zhejiang.
38   Cao Can was a Prime Minister in the Han dynasty. The *Han shu* is a history in 120 chapters of the Former or Western Han dynasty (206 BC–23 AD).
39   Beijing speech is used as the basis for Modern Standard Spoken Chinese. The Wu languages (or 'dialects') of Chinese are spoken in eastern China; Suzhou (or ancient Wu) dialect is their best-known representative. The Yue languages, including Cantonese, are spoken in Guangdong and parts of Guangxi. The Min languages are spoken mainly in Fujian. Between them, these four language systems account for the majority of Chinese-speakers.

to enter the fray with them. Wang Ruofei told Chen about this prejudice in the long letter he wrote to him from Moscow. According to Peng Shuzhi, Chen had the 'political morality of an Oriental', which was out of place in the modern political arena. Let me try to offer a third view. In my opinion, Chen knew that Moscow was opposing him and not those Chinese leaders; he believed that Moscow was sincere about revolution, even though it was wrong about China, and that future developments would convince Moscow that he was right. On no account did he see Wang Ruofei and the others as 'his' base; for Chen, every party member was his base, including Qu Qiubai. He therefore devoted himself to studying script and confined himself to offering his opinion on quite specific questions; he was not prepared to organise an opposition.

So, the 'Chen Duxiu-ites' were bound to fail. But Li Lisan was also wrong when he said that the people Wang Ruofei gathered around him were united merely by personal ties and that Wang's coalition had no basis in principle. A careful examination of the facts shows that Wang's group was different from other factions of the period. It was bound not simply by personal ties but also by a sort of principle – a principle drawn from practical experience, or from pronouncements on various issues by Chen Duxiu (mainly his insistence that the revolution was in a trough rather than on the rise). True, the principle lacked clarity and no one overtly raised it as such, nor did anyone have the courage to think it through to the end. Even so, the group was grounded in principle, as evidenced not just by the fact that its members later joined the Trotskyists almost to a man and woman but also by the famous 'resolution of the Jiangsu Provincial Committee'. Wang Ruofei drafted this resolution before going to Russia for the Congress, but another group in the Jiangsu Committee headed by Xiang Ying refused to pass it. For some reason Sun Yat-sen University in Moscow translated it into Russian and made it available as material on the Chinese question. Trotsky was delighted, and specially wrote an article about it.[40] He thought that it was unwittingly in concert with the ideas of the Left Opposition. But Wang's group committed one fundamental error – it kept within the bounds of Comintern *légalité*,[41] and took as its target certain Chinese leaders rather than Stalin and Bukharin. It even borrowed Stalin and Bukharin's ideas to attack the Chinese leaders. Its attack was rather successful, and Qu Qiubai and Li Weihan fell as a result. But what came after Qu and Li was even worse: Li Lisan.

Wang Ruofei was not allowed to go back to China, and Xiang Ying – Li Lisan's competitor and rival – used the Jiangsu Provincial Committee's past opposition

---

40 This is a reference to the Appendix, titled 'A Remarkable Document on the Policy and the Régime of the Communist International', to Trotsky 1969 [1928].
41 This word is in French in the original.

to the Central Committee for his own purposes. In 1924, when I returned from Russia, the tiny Shanghai labour movement was under the leadership of Xiang and Li. One was in charge of east Shanghai, the other of west Shanghai; each tried to outdo the other, and Li Lisan won. Now that Li Lisan had become the Party's 'theoretical and political centre', Xiang Ying at first refused to submit. I do not know what job he had in the Party, probably it was in the All-China General Labour Union, but his base was in the Jiangsu Provincial Committee, of which he had been Secretary before the Congress, if my memory serves me rightly.[42] The new Secretary of the Provincial Committee was Li Fuchun. On the Committee, Li Fuchun was supported by He Mengxiong, but Cai Zhende and Ma Yufu continued to uphold the old Wang Ruofei tradition. Xiang Ying, Li Fuchun, and He Mengxiong united with Cai and Ma against the new Li Lisan Central Committee and declared their 'independence'. They had their own sources of finance, so they were not reliant on the Central Committee; they could communicate on their own account with other provinces, and they expected a response from several of them. They made much noise, but after a few days their revolt fizzled out. Zhou Enlai called a meeting in Shanghai of the other provinces and ensured their loyalty. Xiang Zhongfa, Li Lisan, and the others threatened Xiang Ying and accused him of manipulating people from behind the screens, whereupon, Xiang knuckled under. The one who had tied the bell to the tiger took it off,[43] and, as a result, the Jiangsu Provincial Committee was restored to its original condition, save for Cai Zhende and Ma Yufu, who resigned. While the storm was brewing, He Mengxiong constantly asked Cai Zhende, 'Why hasn't Zheng Chaolin come yet?' I do not know how Cai told He that I was with them. Li Fuchun came to my place to look me up, by which time, I had already resigned from agitprop work on the Central Committee and sold the lease on the house on Yuyuan Road and moved to Li Minzhi's place. Li Fuchun asked me to go and help out, and promised to make me head of the Jiangsu Committee's Propaganda Department. I was not surprised by his request, for it was an open secret that I felt wronged and was on a go-slow; but I was surprised by the offer of a quid pro quo. Perhaps it was a trick that Li had picked up while working as Political Director of the Guomindang's Second Army. All the same, I agreed to 'help'. Together with Peng Shuzhi, Liu Bozhuang, and Wang Zekai, I helped the Jiangsu Provincial Committee write some manifestos and resolutions in Cai Zhende's house, but

---

42 In late 1927 or early 1928, Xiang Ying replaced Deng Zhongxia as Secretary of the Jiangsu Committee.
43 The person who had begun the trouble ended it.

none was accepted, for they exceeded the political bounds set by Xiang Ying, Li Fuchun, and He Mengxiong.

All this happened in January or February 1929. That was a long time after I had quit the Propaganda Department. My first attempt to resign, after Li Lisan took power, was turned down; the second time, Li said there was no one to take over from me, so we should let the matter rest until someone suitable turned up; the third time, he still would not agree, but, a few days later, he sent Pan Wenyu, who had just got back from studying in Moscow, with a request that I assign work to him. It was obvious to me that Li had already found his 'suitable' person, so now I insisted on resigning and he agreed. They assigned me no new work but promised to send me and Jing to Moscow to study. First, we went to live at Li Minzhi's place; from there, we moved to Cai Zhende's place. Cai Zhende insisted that we come, while Li Minzhi and Pan Hannian insisted that we stay. Originally, we had lived in the room belonging to Pan Hannian and his wife, for they had gone back to Yixing for the time being. When they returned from Yixing, they would not let us move out and went, instead, to live in a big room under Li Minzhi's. I felt bad about this, but it was mainly for political rather than for personal reasons that we moved into the second storey of the house next door to where Chen Qiaonian was arrested, in Hengfeng Alley off Scott Road. On the first floor lived Cai Zhende and his wife. He Zishen's wife Zhang Yisen and her daughter – a newborn baby, who had not yet even been named – lived in the small room above the kitchen.

On 18 March, we were arrested there.

The Left Opposition

Zheng Chaolin

Source: *An Oppositionist for Life* (1945).

We were only forty days in jail, but coming out was like entering a new world. While driving along the Longhua Road, we saw that there was no longer any plum-blossom on the trees. The grass was high and the air was full of orioles; it was a typical late spring in Jiangnan.[1] I remember that, before we were arrested, there had been no air of spring in Shanghai, and the trees along the pavements had not yet put forth leaves. In Longhua Prison, no trees were to be seen, and the grass that grew in the prison courtyard was pitifully scant. At Qingming,[2] one of the guards had brought in a twig of plum-blossom, so in my heart I knew that it was now spring, but I had not imagined that it was so advanced. When we got to Shanghai, the noisy, bustling streets gave us a feeling we had never before experienced.

But something else, too, had changed: a change more abrupt than that between the seasons. Yin Kuan came to the New Hotel to visit us. He had originally planned to come to our house on 18 March, to play mahjong; I don't know whether it was because he had forgotten or because something else happened, but he had failed to show up, thus escaping the fate of Ma Yufu. We praised his good fortune. After some social talk, he took out a roll of mimeographed paper. It was an essay by Trotsky on the Chinese Revolution, later included in the first volume of *Zhongguo geming wenti* ('On the Problem of the Chinese Revolution'), that we published.[3] The essay was very poorly mimeographed, but even so, it made a much deeper impression on us than Qu Qiubai's well printed and well translated Comintern circulars put out by the Secretariat of the Central Committee. It was as if an electric-beam had been shone into our skulls. For a while, I was confused, unable to say whether the document was right or wrong. Later, when I met Peng Shuzhi and Wang Zekai, I discovered that they had already read some of these mimeographs; and that Chen Duxiu

---

1   Jiangnan is that part of eastern China directly south of the Yangtze.
2   Clear Brightness, the fifth solar term, roughly corresponding to our Easter time, around 5 April.
3   Here, I got the time and place wrong. Yin Kuan did not give us any Oppositionist documents when we first left jail. He only did so after we had moved home. [Note added by Zheng Chaolin in 1980.]

had also read them. They had got them from Yin Kuan, who had obtained them from the Shandong comrade Wang Pingyi, just back from Moscow. Yin Kuan had once taken me to see him, but we had not talked much.

After that, I read a whole series of such documents, together with one or two issues of *Womende hua* ('Our Word').[4] Since Yin Kuan had not sworn me to secrecy, I passed them on to Cai Zhende and Ma Yufu after reading them. Being newly out of jail, I had no idea that an opposition had already formed in the Chinese Communist Party, or what the Central Committee's attitude was towards it. I thought it was an open secret that comrades were passing round Trotsky's articles. On one occasion, Huang Wenrong came to visit me.

'Has there been any reply from the Central Committee to Trotsky's ideas?' I asked him.

'Who told you about Trotsky's ideas?'

I thought for a while and then said: 'Yin Kuan gave me an article of his to read'.

A few days later, Yin Kuan came to remonstrate with me, for after Huang had gone back and reported on our conversation, the Central Committee had interrogated Yin Kuan about the source of these articles. I apologised and said: 'I didn't know it was so serious'. Now, the Central Committee knew that we were already acquainted with Oppositionist documents.

We by no means accepted Trotsky's analysis overnight. Speaking personally, I only accepted it after repeated deliberation and repeated discussion. There were so many issues involved, and the issues were so complicated! The last to give in was Chen Duxiu. Every time he talked with Yin Kuan, he raised a different objection, and held to it even after listening to Yin's reply; but the next time they met and spoke, he no longer raised the same objection but raised a new one on the basis of what Yin (following Trotsky) had said the previous time. And so the discussion proceeded, layer by layer. By the time the rest of us were one hundred per cent convinced, Chen still had differences. Finally, he wrote an article saying that China could only carry out a workers' and peasants' dictatorship, not a proletarian dictatorship. The article was never published, but later, after he had come over completely to the Opposition, Liu Renjing attacked him on the basis of it. Apparently, Liu had not read it himself but had only heard about it from Yin Kuan.

---

4 *Our Word*, founded in 1928, was published by the first batch of Chinese Trotskyists to be deported back to China from the Soviet Union.

So what were Trotsky's views on the Chinese Revolution? A memoir is not the place for a detailed political analysis of such questions, but nor is it easy to describe them roughly, for they touch on such a broad range of issues. Later, we brought together in two volumes, titled *On the Problem of the Chinese Revolution*, the articles Trotsky wrote in those years; later still, we brought out a third volume. His views on China are set out in those three volumes. Besides that, three years ago I wrote a pamphlet titled *Buduan geming lun ABC* ('An ABC of the Theory of Permanent Revolution'), one chapter of which was devoted to the relevance of this theory to the Chinese Revolution and briefly reiterates Trotsky's views on this question.

But it's important to discuss these issues, at least briefly. Young people in the 1930s who were interested in politics and revolution were more or less acquainted with Trotsky's views on China; but young people today, in the 1940s, are not so fortunate, and some have never even heard his name. Since this memoir is written mainly with the young people of today in mind, I must devote at least a little space to explaining the differences between the Trotskyist and Stalinist views on the Chinese Revolution.

Three practical issues caused the Soviet Communist Party to split; they concerned the Soviet Union itself, the Anglo-Soviet Trade union Committee, and the Chinese Revolution. In 1923, when the Left Opposition first took shape, Soviet issues dominated the inner-party struggle; in 1927, when the new Opposition formed, the latter issues became central. Trotsky and Zinoviev, who together led this new Opposition, were by no means wholly in agreement about the Chinese Revolution. The Zinoviev group was unwilling to accept the theory of permanent revolution, so the views of the united opposition on questions of basic theory were often half-hearted and wrong. Only after the decisive split between Trotsky and Zinoviev was Trotsky able to present a thoroughgoing and systematic analysis of the Chinese Revolution. What I am about to say is based on what Trotsky said after going into exile.

In contrast to the schema that people had previously observed, Trotsky now said that the Chinese Revolution was proletarian-socialist. It did not need to complete the bourgeois-democratic stage before entering the proletarian-socialist one, contrary to what Stalin said. The bourgeois-democratic tasks of the Chinese Revolution, that is, the tasks of the so-called national revolution, could be fulfilled only under proletarian dictatorship; and, in order to set up and maintain a proletarian dictatorship, the revolution would have to go beyond bourgeois-democratic tasks and realise a number of tasks that belong properly to proletarian socialism.

Trotsky derived these conclusions from an analysis of Chinese class relations. China's semi-colonial status and imperialism's pressure on China made it impossible to unite 'all' China's classes, as the Stalinists were then claiming to want to do. Quite the contrary, the more the revolution developed, the more the capitalists would tend to ally with the imperialists against the toiling classes; and the harder would it be to achieve China's liberation. This statement held not only for the national question but also for the land-question. China had no independent landed aristocracy. The big and middle landlords in China were inextricably connected to the urban bourgeoisie. So land revolution in China was intrinsically anticapitalist in nature; the capitalists would not only disapprove of it but would actively try to stop it.

So the bourgeoisie cannot achieve national independence or resolve the land question. But that fact alone does not prove that the Chinese Revolution must be proletarian-socialist. Has there not been a view ever since Lenin that bourgeois-democratic revolutions are not necessarily led by the bourgeois themselves and are often achieved despite them? This was certainly how Lenin described the Russian Revolution before April 1917. His call was for a 'workers' and peasants' democratic dictatorship'. Since China and Russia are in many ways similar, can we not conclude, as Lenin did for Russia, that the Chinese Revolution is bourgeois-democratic in nature? And that it must aim for a 'workers' and peasants' democratic dictatorship'?

But first, the Russian Revolution did not result in a 'workers' and peasants' democratic dictatorship'. Lenin dropped this slogan immediately after returning to Russia in April 1917, and called for 'proletarian dictatorship'. The result was that the bourgeois-democratic tasks were achieved as a by-product of proletarian-socialist revolution. Second, before April 1917, the only reason Lenin had proposed and insisted on a 'workers' and peasants' democratic dictatorship' was because of the tradition in Russia of petty-bourgeois peasant movements. Russia had a landed aristocracy. Serfdom in Russia had only recently been abolished, and relations between landowners and the urban bourgeoisie were less intimate than in China. This is why Russia, unlike China, produced a Narodnik movement and a revolutionary party with a long history of struggle, namely, the Social Revolutionary Party, which claimed to represent the peasants and harboured the illusion that Russia could achieve socialism without first going through a stage of capitalism. Before the Revolution, Russian Marxists knew that Russia could not achieve socialism without first going through a capitalist stage, but they could not afford to overlook this petty-bourgeois revolutionary organisation and continued to come up with different formulae to express the nature of the relationship between the workers and the peasants; one of them being 'the proletariat leads the peasantry'. This was the source of Lenin's famous formula 'democratic dictatorship of the workers and peasants'. The Revolution of 1917 proved that despite all these formulae and slogans, the Russian peasants were still subordinate to the leadership of the proletariat and its political party, and that in the face of a real revolution, the petty-bourgeois Social Revolutionary Party, with its revolutionary traditions, would be revealed as impotent and disintegrate. So, when the Revolution finally broke out, Lenin said: 'He who *now* speaks of "revolutionary-democratic dictatorship of the proletariat and peasantry" only is behind the times, is therefore in practice on the side of the petty bourgeoisie and against the proletarian class struggle; such a one should be placed in the archive of "Bolshevik" pre-revolutionary antiques (it may be called the archive of "old Bolsheviks")'.[5]

If this is true of Russia, how much truer must it be of China! The Chinese agrarian economy has even fewer feudal relics than the Russian and no petty-bourgeois revolutionary party claiming to represent the interests of the peasantry; and events have proved that the Chinese peasants can submit to proletarian leadership. There is no future in China for a 'workers' and peasants' democratic dictatorship'. The only revolutionary state possible is one grounded in the 'dictatorship of the proletariat'. But, to set up and maintain a dictatorship of the proletariat, the revolution must exceed the limits of bourgeois democracy.

The Guangzhou Insurrection is living proof of this. The Guangzhou Soviet proclaimed as law among other things: factory committees should control production; big industry, communications, and the banks should come under state control; and the mansions of the big bourgeoisie should be confiscated to house the workers. Trotsky asked: if that's a bourgeois revolution, what will proletarian revolution in China look like?

Trotsky's views on the nature of the Chinese Revolution, though derived from an analysis of Chinese class relations and verified by the Guangzhou Insurrection, were fully in accord with his unique theory of 'permanent revolution'. There is no room here to elaborate on the development of this theory or its various implications. I shall simply say that it first took shape in Russia's 1905 Revolution, led by Trotsky, who on the basis of an analysis of Russian class-relations arrived at his conclusion that in a backward country like Russia the bourgeois-democratic revolution, having been excessively delayed, cannot – unlike in the advanced countries of Western Europe – be led and completed by the bourgeoisie. Though the immediate tasks of the Russian Revolution in its initial stages were bourgeois-democratic, they could be achieved only by a further unfolding of the Revolution in the direction of proletarian dictatorship and the realisation of certain socialist goals. Proletarian dictatorship was

---

5   Lenin 1960–72 [1917c].

a powerful guarantee that Russia's bourgeois revolution would cross over into proletarian revolution. Whether or not socialism, being the final goal of proletarian revolution, could be achieved in Russia, and to what extent it could be achieved, would depend partly on conditions within the country and partly on the Revolution's international environment. The Russian Revolution can be seen only as a constituent of world revolution. On the basis of this theory formed in 1905, Trotsky insisted that the revolution in Russia should carry out 'proletarian dictatorship' and would not need to go through the stage of 'workers' and peasants' democratic dictatorship'. The October Revolution of 1917 showed that he was right.

Trotsky was all along opposed to the Chinese Communist Party entering the Guomindang.[6] In 1923, when the Third International debated this question he alone resolutely opposed such a step; in 1925, he again formally proposed that the Chinese Communist Party should quit the Guomindang forthwith, but his proposal was not accepted. He saw clearly that the Guomindang represented China's bourgeoisie and that if the Chinese Revolution was to succeed, the proletariat should not only not support the bourgeoisie but should resolutely oppose it. Even before the massacre of 12 April 1927, Trotsky had pointed out that the Guomindang leaders would betray the revolution. He had demanded the immediate establishment of soviet organisations, and had said that the revolution should first be deepened and then spread. His views were rejected; not long after that, the Guomindang's 'left-wing' in Wuhan sure enough went over to the reaction. After the defeat of the Guangzhou Insurrection, Trotsky concluded that the revolution was already finished and raised the question of what tactics to pursue 'between two revolutions', in order to prepare for the third revolution.[7] But, instead, people now adopted his earlier proposals, and set about staging insurrections and organising soviets. They mistook the ebb for the flow; they met the ebb with tactics appropriate for the flow.

According to Lenin, 'An elementary truth of Marxism says that the tactics of the socialist proletariat cannot be the same in face of a revolutionary situation as when this situation does not exist'.[8]

Trotsky proposed the tactic of a 'national assembly'[9] for this period 'between two revolutions'. Seeing that the Chinese workers' and peasants' revolution

---

6 In fact, Trotsky probably did not oppose Communist entry into the Guomindang until April 1926. See Pantsov and Benton 1994.
7 China's first revolution had been in 1911, so the revolution between 1925 and 1927 counted as the second and the future revolution would be the third.
8 Quoted in Trotsky, *Problems of the Chinese Revolution*, p. 132.
9 Chinese Trotskyists preferred the term *guomin huiyi*, or 'national assembly', to the term *lixian huiyi*, or 'constituent assembly'. In China, the word *lixian* had been discredited as a result of

had been defeated, he thought that the ruling class would be able to achieve a measure of political stability, which would in its turn provide the basis for a revival of the economy. Industry and commerce, which had declined during the period of revolution and civil war, would gradually recover, the pool of unemployed would shrink, the workers' ranks would swell, and the proletariat's specific weight in Chinese social life would correspondingly increase and its self-confidence return. But barring unexpected developments, there could be no question, for the time being, of revolution, insurrection, and soviets. The Communist Party's immediate task was to lead the proletariat back onto the political stage. The best way to do so was by campaigning for a national assembly. Under conditions of political stability and economic revival, the ruling class itself also needed such an assembly, to help it clip the army's wings and lessen expenditure on unproductive ends; and it would also help in bargaining with the imperialists. The petty bourgeois, too, were now likely to spring back into action and raise even more democratic demands. To that end, they would probably try to ally with upper layers of the urban workers and the peasants. The Communist Party should not then stand by with folded arms, but should actively take part in such a movement, in order to combat the influence of the bourgeoisie and the petty bourgeoisie on it, and to lead the workers and peasants back into political life. The Communist Party should be in the forefront of the various classes and should call for a national assembly on their own account.

Trotsky spoke up about the nature of the Chinese Revolution before it was defeated; and proposed a national assembly after it was defeated, and, moreover, after the Sixth Congress of the Third International, that is, after the autumn of 1928. The import of his earlier analysis was strategic, whereas his later proposal was tactical. But both the strategic and the tactical proposals reached China simultaneously, and we embraced them simultaneously. In the meantime, this created no end of confusion, especially among the broader public, which knew little about the debates in the world communist movement.

---

successive attempts first by the dying Qing dynasty and then by Yuan Shikai and the warlords after the Revolution of 1911 to draft a constitution and convoke a constituent assembly. In the 1920s and the 1930s, the memory of these 'constitutional tricks' was still very fresh in China. The word *lixian* was not only unpopular but sounded positively reactionary. Trotsky accepted the arguments of his Chinese comrades on this question, and after 1930, he used the term national assembly instead of constituent assembly, which he had originally proposed.

On one occasion, Deng Yanda, leader of the Third Party,[10] arranged to meet Gao Yuhan for a discussion.

'You Trotskyists claim that the revolution in China is proletarian', he said, 'but you call for a national assembly; while the Stalinists say that it is bourgeois but call for soviets. Aren't the positions of both sides self-contradictory?'

What Deng meant was that if the Chinese Revolution was proletarian, then it should set up soviets; and if bourgeois, it should demand the convening of a national assembly. I can't remember how Gao answered him.

Even though by then we had all accepted Trotsky's analysis and proposals, not everyone understood and weighted them identically. In 1940, when I returned to Shanghai,[11] one of the first things that Peng Shuzhi said to me was: 'In the early days we understood the ideas of the Fourth International from a right-wing point of view'. Actually, that's wrong. Though it is true that Peng himself stopped being a Stalinist and became a Trotskyist 'from a right-wing point of view', the same is not true of other people. Peng Shuzhi not only accepted the 'national assembly' proposal but elevated it from the tactical to the strategic level. He saw it as the means by which the proletariat would take power in China's coming third revolution. But Trotsky was quite clear on this question. He systematically set out his views on the national assembly in 'The Chinese Question after the Sixth Congress',[12] under the sub-heading 'The Inter-Revolutionary Period and the Tasks that Present Themselves in the Course of It'. At the end of this essay, he returned to the theme with an explicit warning against potential misinterpretations of the slogan: 'The party must have in mind and must explain that in comparison with its principal aim, the conquest of power with arms in hand, the democratic slogans have only an auxiliary, a provisional, an episodic character. Their fundamental importance consists of the fact that they permit us to debouch on the revolutionary road'.[13] Peng Shuzhi agreed that the revolution was 'proletarian in nature', but he specifically attacked two points of view: that 'China's third revolution will be proletarian from the very start', and that 'in China bourgeois-democratic tasks will be achieved as a by-product of proletarian revolution'. He vigorously attacked

---

10 In November 1927, Deng Yanda called for the setting up of a 'provisional action committee' of the Guomindang to act as the true heirs of Sun Yat-sen against the usurpers in Nanjing. This later became known as the Third Party, whose goal was a socialist state, though it opposed the idea of class struggle and proletarian dictatorship.

11 After he was freed from prison in 1937, Zheng and his wife Jing went to Anhui, where Zheng recovered from his poor health.

12 Translated in Trotsky 1967 [1932], pp. 120–84.

13 Trotsky 1967 [1932], p. 167.

these ideas in the unification talks; in Nanjing Jail, he wrote articles attacking them; and in the 1941 debate, he attacked them for a third time. He failed to see that once these two ideas were dropped, there was nothing to distinguish Trotsky's analysis of this particular issue from Stalin's. The Stalinists never denied that, once China's third revolution reached its final stage, it would be proletarian-socialist in character; what distinguished them from Trotskyism on this point was their belief that only after solemnly completing the 'bourgeois-democratic tasks' could proletarian revolution be carried out. So it's true: Peng did interpret Trotsky's ideas 'from a right-wing point of view'.

Chen Duxiu agreed with Trotsky from a different angle. I mentioned earlier that the Chinese Communist Party followed a certain scheme in the revolution: its leaders considered that China must first pass through 'national revolution' before embarking on 'socialist revolution'. But there are two different ways of understanding this scheme. According to one, since China can carry out a national revolution, we should concentrate single-mindedly on doing so; for those who understand the scheme in this way, socialist revolution remains a vague idea that we need only think about after the achievement of national revolution. Others thought that, since China must first go through national revolution before it can carry out socialist revolution, then all right, let's carry out national revolution, but let us not forget that national revolution is not our revolution but a precondition for it, that we're only engaged in national revolution for the sake of the future socialist revolution.

Actually, these two interpretations are not opposites but Stalinist twins, for both split the Chinese Revolution into two stages: carry out first national revolution, then socialist revolution. But if we consider them more carefully, they differ in one regard: the latter can develop in the direction of the theory of permanent revolution if it jettisons the idea of two stages, whereas the former cannot. Chen Duxiu belonged to the latter tendency. For the sake of the future socialist revolution, he stressed the importance of the workers' and peasants' movement, even to the point where he opposed the Northern Expedition and secretly proposed to the Comintern that the Chinese Communist Party should withdraw from the Guomindang. But the Northern Expedition unexpectedly succeeded. Was not a revolution carried out by a trained standing army even more powerful than strikes and mass insurrections? So Chen Duxiu gradually switched from the latter to the former interpretation of national revolution. Only after the Wuhan debacle did he realise that revolution was impossible without the broad masses as its main force. Mercenaries, however steeled and trained, are in the long run unreliable. The ideas of the Left Opposition chimed in with this new realisation. Immediately he had accepted them, he wrote an essay opposing the 'Red Army' movement and opposing the wholesale abandonment of the urban labour movement by party organisations and members, who flocked to the villages to set up a 'Red Army'.

I know little about the Red Army's origins. Before the Fifth Congress, the only two leaders of the Chinese Communist Party who I knew merely by sight were Li Dazhao and Mao Zedong. Li Dazhao had always been based in Beijing. As for Mao, when I first got back to China, he was still in Shanghai, but he apparently held no office in the Party,[14] for I never saw him attend any of the Central Committee meetings. Not long after that, he returned to Hunan. He did not spend long there, and again, he apparently held no office in the Party. Later, I either read in a report from the Guangdong Regional Committee or heard from someone that in Guangzhou Mao had become Secretary of the Propaganda Department of the Central Committee of the Guomindang, and that his boss Wang Jingwei prized him highly; he also ran the Peasant-Movement Training Institute in Guangzhou. In April 1927, I saw him at the Wuchang Congress and gave him a letter from his younger brother Mao Zemin. By coincidence, it was also at around that time that I read his 'Report on the Hunan Peasant Movement'.[15] He was the first of the Party's main leaders to pay attention to the peasant movement.[16] He personally visited various counties in Hunan to investigate this movement at first hand. His booklet on the Hunan peasants was published without first going through the Central Committee's Propaganda Department, which in any case had not yet acquired the power of censorship. After the Fifth Congress, he was instructed to go to Hunan to take over from Li Weihan as Provincial Secretary, but he did not do so until after the Horse Night Incident, by which time, the Party in Hunan had gone underground. When Tang Shengzhi returned to Hunan, the Provincial Committee assigned party members to stick up posters 'welcoming Commander-in-Chief Tang, who has laboured so hard and achieved so much!' The people sticking up the posters were seized and roundly beaten by Tang's troops. It was only after He Zishen had protested to Mao about the slogan that he rescinded it. People were still hoping to rope in Tang against Xu Kexiang and He Jian![17]

---

14   Throughout this period, Mao held office not in the Communist Party but in the Guomindang.
15   For an expurgated version of this article, edited to make it seem more Marxist than it originally was, see Volume 1 of Beijing's English-language edition of Mao's *Selected Works*. For a translation of excerpts from the original article, see Schram (ed.) 1963.
16   Actually, the first important party leader to pay attention to organising peasants was not Mao but Peng Pai. Peng was a leader of the Guomindang's Peasant Department; the first director, before Mao, of the Peasant Movement Training Institute set up in 1924; and founder, in 1927, of the earliest Chinese soviet government, in Hailufeng.
17   Xu Kexiang and He Jian were military leaders who suppressed the Communists and their mass organisations in Hunan in mid 1927.

After the Fifth Congress, I do not know what role Mao played in the Party's internal scheming. Needless to say, he was dissatisfied with Chen Duxiu, but he did not merge with Qu Qiubai, Zhang Guotao, or Tan Pingshan. He was independent: his views and proposals were different from those of the Party's other leaders. He once said that 'power comes from the barrel of a gun'. He scorned the Communist leaders of the labour movement, and any movement unconnected to the gun. A founding member of the Party, he was unhappy and frustrated during the high tide of revolution and merely held a few unimportant posts. It was only when the Revolution ebbed that he really came into his own, only when the means of struggle changed that he leapt to pre-eminence in the Party. This might appear odd at first sight, but actually, it is wholly in accordance with his character and views.

After 15 July, when Zhang Tailei was about to hand over his job as Hubei Provincial Secretary, he reported to me on the intentions of various party leaders, including Mao Zedong. 'Runzhi[18] is planning to go to Sichuan to become a modern Shi Dakai',[19] he told me. Mao attended the 7 August Conference and spoke, but I cannot remember what he said. As far as I remember, he did not say anything about going to Sichuan. That was the last time I saw him. He Zishen was close to him. The two of them worked together for a while in Hunan after the Horse Night Incident. They got on well together and were united by their common dislike for the former provincial secretary.[20] In late 1927 or early 1928, they were both in Shanghai. When Mao Zedong was about to go back to Hunan, He Zishen – who was aware of Mao's plans – gave him a copy of *Shuihu zhuan* ('Water Margin') punctuated by Wang Yuanfang[21] for the Oriental Book Company, together with post-office maps of all the counties in Hunan. Mao treasured these gifts, especially the maps, which some comrades working for the post-office had given to the Party. They were not available for sale, and were hard to come by. They were much more detailed and reliable than other maps. They showed villages and small towns, and the distances between places.

---

18 Mao Zedong.
19 Shi Dakai was a leader of the Taiping Revolution (1851–64) who split with its main leader Hong Xiuquan and went to Sichuan.
20 Li Weihan.
21 *Water Margin* (translated into English by Pearl Buck as *All Men Are Brothers*) is about a group of bandit heroes who set up a mountain base from which they fought against injustice in society. Traditionally, this and other classical novels in China were published without punctuation, which was added (in the form of commas and full stops) by the reader. Wang Yuanfang, of the Oriental Book Company, helped introduce Western punctuation to China. His contribution to the movement for a modern literature was to punctuate the classics.

In Hunan, Mao unified the surviving armed forces of the peasant associations in the various counties and detached them from the villages, in order to keep them intact. This is one source of what later became the Red Army.

When Ye Ting and He Long staged their insurrection in Nanchang on 1 August, a dispute was said to have arisen among the staff officers about what direction the insurrectionary army should take. Liu Bocheng proposed going to Hunan to 'make land revolution', while the others wanted to go to Guangdong to seize Guangzhou, organise a government, swell their forces, and then launch a 'second Northern Expedition'. The latter view prevailed. Everyone knows the fate of the Ye-He Army,[22] so there is no need to go into it here. But a small part of it, under Zhu De,[23] escaped destruction and roamed between the borders of Guangdong, Jiangxi, and Hunan. For a while, they joined up with Fan Shisheng's Guomindang troops,[24] but after that, they somehow merged with the troops that Mao had salvaged from Hunan's peasant forces.[25] This is how the nucleus of the Red Army was formed. It slowly grew in strength, and after numerous setbacks, became what we now know as the Eighth Route Army and the New Fourth Army. But that's another story.

The Red Army was not a deliberate creation of the Central Committee or the Comintern. At first, the Central Committee had no interest in it, believing that it had no future. During the Li Lisan period, the Communist Party had not yet decided to abandon the big cities. But against all expectations, this tiny military nucleus managed to grow into an army, and Zhu and Mao assumed the mantle previously worn by Ye and He; at the same time, the Communist Party gradually found it impossible to keep up its work in the cities, so it switched

---

22   The Ye-He army marched south after the Nanchang Uprising on 1 August 1927, and captured Shantou on the Guangdong coast on 23 September, where it was defeated a week later.

23   Luo Yinong, who was Secretary of the Jiangxi Provincial Committee, knew Zhu De. Zhu had been a general in the Yunnan [warlord] Army. He had gone to Germany to study, where he apparently joined the Chinese Communist Party. After Luo Yinong was transferred to Hubei, on one occasion, he invited me to accompany him to a certain hotel to meet a comrade who was an army officer. When I got there, I discovered that it was Zhu De. We hastily exchanged a few words, and then I left. I seem to recall that he was thin, but apart from that I cannot remember anything about him. [Note by Zheng Chaolin.]

24   Fan Shisheng was a Guomindang commander and an old acquaintance of Zhu De from Yunnan. Zhu briefly 'allied' with Fan and got some supplies from him, but he soon broke the alliance when the Central Committee criticised it.

25   In early September 1927, Mao was sent to his native Hunan to lead peasant uprisings. The risings failed, but Mao took the survivors into the Jinggang Mountains and formed them into a guerrilla army.

its forces to the Red Army and pinned all its hopes on the Red Army. To the extent that it did continue to work in the cities, it was simply in order to prepare the workers to respond to the Red Army, just as they had responded to the Northern Expedition in earlier years. By the time we accepted Trotsky's views, the whole Party had come round to this way of thinking. Whenever we discussed political questions with other comrades, we always eventually came up against the same argument, to wit: whatever the mistakes of the Central Committee and the Comintern, the one undeniable truth was that the Red Army was going from strength to strength. Since the Party was going to seize power through the Red Army, what was the point of a national assembly? In this way, Mao Zedong-ism came to dominate the whole party. On one occasion, Xiang Zhongfa and Zhou Enlai went to talk to Chen Duxiu, just before the split. The conversation naturally got round to the Red Army.

'According to Marxism', said Chen, 'should the cities control the villages, or the villages the cities?'

'It's obvious', Xiang blurted out, 'the villages should control the cities!'

Zhou Enlai interrupted to correct him: 'Theoretically, the cities should control the villages. However...'.

We all thought that the idea of a Red Army was dangerous. We were afraid that as a result of it, the Party would abandon the real revolution and concentrate exclusively on military adventures, that it would abandon the proletariat and start representing the peasants or even bandits. At the time, we never imagined that the Party would degenerate to the point that it has now reached.

Chen Duxiu wrote a long essay opposing the Red Army campaign. It had a big impact. Needless to say, the Stalinist Central Committee was furious. The so-called 'Conciliationists', under the leadership of Xiang Ying and Luo Zhanglong, also thought that the Old Man was 'in his dotage'. When the Oppositionists apart from us[26] wrote to Trotsky criticising the 'opportunist' Chen Duxiu for his essay on the Red Army, Trotsky wrote back to say that we should not completely oppose the Red Army, for, in some ways, it was an important and positive movement. Under attack from several sides, we who had at first agreed with Chen's article now began to doubt it. Yin Kuan said that it was 'badly worded'. Later, Chiang Kai-shek had the article reprinted in large numbers and distributed in Jiangxi province.[27] Perhaps he smuggled some changes into it, I don't know. I don't have Chen's essay to hand, and I forget on what grounds he opposed the Red Army. But there can be no doubt that he

---

26   That is, apart from the Chen Duxiu group.

27   Jiangxi was the site of several Red Army bases, including of the Chinese Communists' Central Soviet and its capital Ruijin, in the late 1920s and early 1930s.

talked about the need to stress the urban workers, to base the revolution on the power of the broad masses, and to accord military might a secondary role in seizing power. These are the lessons that Chen drew from the Wuhan defeat, and the basis on which he embraced Trotskyism.

In my own case, Trotsky's ideas took me back to positions I had adopted ten years earlier, in France, when I had come out against joining the Guomindang. For me, Trotsky's ideas meant putting the Chinese Revolution on the same footing as revolutions in other countries rather than seeking differences between it and them or discovering 'special national characteristics' that restricted the application of Marxism to China. When I first retreated from 'socialist revolution' to 'national revolution', I had found it necessary to divide my Marxism into two parts: one part that could simultaneously be applied to China, and another part that could be applied only to the West. But now, everything I had learned in the past suddenly came to life and was of immediate practical relevance. Apart from this, the two main questions that had haunted me during my period as editor of *Bolshevik* – 'a rising or an ebbing tide?' and 'proletarian dictatorship or workers' and peasants' democratic dictatorship?' – had finally been answered.

In discussions with fellow-members of the Opposition or with other comrades, I paid special attention to the question of the nature of the revolution: bourgeois-democratic or proletarian-socialist. Cai Zhende and Ma Yufu did too. But Yin Kuan disagreed. He said: 'Trotsky never stressed that question, he only said incidentally that the Chinese Revolution is proletarian in nature. If you insist on arguing about it, you run the risk of turning a debate about politics into a debate about metaphysics'. The question Yin Kuan liked to emphasise was what should we promote, soviets or a national assembly? In those days, there was not much writing about the nature of the revolution, and Trotsky said different things at different times. It was not until after Liu Renjing got back to China that we became acquainted with the several long and systematic essays that Trotsky had written in Alma Ata. It was clear from those essays that the question of the nature of the revolution was not unimportant in Trotsky's thinking.

When Liu Renjing got back to China, he lived in a hostel in the French Concession, where Yin Kuan and I went to visit him. He spoke with us, and also with supporters of the Central Committee, from an openly Oppositionist standpoint. He told us that the day before Yun Daiying had been to see him, and that he had told Yun that in his view, the Party had become bureaucratised.

Yun had denied this and told Liu that he was free to express his criticisms and that he, Yun, could guarantee that the Central Committee would discuss them.

'And if the Central Committee isn't prepared to let my criticisms be known?' Liu had asked.

'Then I will fight alongside you'.

Liu Renjing also told us that he had been to Constantinople to see Trotsky on his way back to China. I agreed a time with Liu for him to meet Chen Duxiu at my place.

On our release from jail, Cai Zhende and I gave up the house on Hengfeng Alley and moved out our furniture and effects. We had nothing of any value. The only thing that had gone missing during our absence was a fur-coat that Jing had brought with her to Shanghai from her parents' home. At first, we rented the rear part of a wing-room on Wuchang Road, but two months later, Cai Zhende invited us to live together with him in his newly rented house in Yuqing Alley, off East Youheng Road. That was where Liu Renjing came to see us. It became the headquarters of our section of the Opposition. At first, we used to gather there informally; later, we held official meetings there. There can be no doubt that the Central Committee got to hear of it. It adopted a policy of trying to win us over. Pan Wenyu, Secretary of the Propaganda Department, came to visit me and very politely invited me to go back to work in his department; I refused to accept a fixed job, but agreed to do some translating for them. Every few days I used to deliver what I had done and fetch back new material. They gave me forty dollars a month to live off. He Mengxiong came, too, to see Cai Zhende, and introduced Cai to a job on a news-agency. The work was only for a few hours a day, but the pay was good. I translated these documents for the Party and used my spare time to carry on with my translation of *Religion, Philosophy, and Socialism*, of which I had already completed some two thirds before I was arrested. The Public Security Bureau had sent the manuscript to Longhua together with the documents seized in the raid, but I had got it back from the judge the day I was set free.

I asked many people to sell the manuscript for me, but to no avail. Eventually, Yang Xianjiang managed to sell it to the newly established Hubin Book Company. This company was managed by Ma Renzhi, who came from the same county as Peng Shuzhi. Not long after that, he, too, joined the Opposition. Yang Xianjiang was our branch secretary at the time. Wang Zekai and I, who were both in his branch, repeatedly argued about basic questions of the Chinese Revolution with people delegated to discuss with us by the Jiangsu Provincial Committee. Yang Xianjiang wavered between the two sides, so the branch never took a decision on these issues. Not long after that, Chen Duxiu,

Peng Shuzhi, and Wang Zekai were expelled by the Central Committee. I didn't see the circular, so I do not know on what grounds they were expelled. Five or six comrades protested to the Central Committee about these expulsions; my name was among the protesters, though I did not know so at the time, nor did I know who was responsible for putting it there. The first thing I knew of the protest was when I turned up at the Central Committee's Propaganda Department and Pan Wenyu asked me why I had put my name to it. But I was not going to deny it.

'I have the right to protest', I said.

'Of course, you have the right to protest at any irregularities surrounding the expulsion, but first you should say that you agree politically with the Central Committee'.

Now I knew that the protest was about procedures, not politics. 'I don't agree politically, either', I said. 'I've already raised it in my branch'.

There had not yet been any conclusion in our branch to the discussion of the political problems that Wang Zekai and I had raised. Though Wang had been expelled, I was still a member of the branch, and I still demanded an answer from the party leaders. Eventually, Wang Kequan, Secretary of the Provincial Committee, himself came to the branch together with Li Chuli, who made a transcript of my comments. After I had systematically explained my political opinions, I once again protested at procedural irregularities surrounding the expulsion of Chen, Peng, and Wang Zekai. Wang Kequan simply said that he would answer me officially at a meeting to be held the following week, but Yang Xianjiang finally chose sides: he stood with the Central Committee and thought that the expulsions were right. I was surprised at his change in attitude, but, not long afterwards, I discovered that before the meeting he had been put under pressure and even intimidated. The following week, when I and Jing turned up at his place for the meeting, Yang Xianjiang cordially welcomed us and explained that the others probably had some other business that temporarily prevented them from attending. We took our leave after fixing a time for the following week, but a few days later, I learned that I too had been expelled. I never received formal notification of my expulsion, nor did I see any notice of it in *Hongqi bao* ('Red Flag'),[28] but I heard from others that I had been charged with inciting the newspaper workers' branch and the Yunnan delegate (sent to Shanghai to make a report) to oppose the Central Committee.

And it was true. Under the influence of Ma Yufu and Cai Zhende, several branches – together with individuals such as Luo Shifan and Xue Nongshan –

---

28   In this period, *Red Flag* – the new party organ published after Zheng Chaolin quit the Department of Propaganda – regularly announced the names and offences (real or invented) of people expelled from the Party.

went over to the Opposition, among them the newspaper branch. The branch-secretary was Tu Yangzhi, a type-setter on *New Current Events*, who together with a number of other workers' leaders had followed Ma Yufu. Our people had elected me to represent the Opposition point of view at branch meetings. We met several times. The entire branch supported the Opposition. No one spoke up for the Central Committee. But someone told the Central Committee about our activities, so the branch was disbanded and Tu Yangzhi, too, was expelled. I forget the name of the Yunnan delegate. I spoke with him once at Liu Shaoyou's place. I do not know whether it was this person or Chen Jiru (the wife of Liu Shaoyou) who reported on my activities to the Central Committee or the Provincial Committee; whatever the case, I had been exposed. Those of us who had been expelled refused to recognise the validity of the decision, and still looked upon ourselves as members of the Chinese Communist Party; the new organisation we set up was not a second Party but an internal faction – 'the Chinese Communist Party's Left Opposition'. Chen Duxiu, father of the Chinese Communist Party, was with us. Trotsky, the second great leader of the October Revolution, was with us too. And if Lenin had still lived, so would he have been. His widow Krupskaya told people: 'If Lenin had not died, Stalin would have thrown him in jail!'

The struggle was worldwide. There was scarcely a section of the Third International that did not split. 'Left Oppositions' were formed in almost all them. These Oppositions elected leaderships, issued journals, and tried to promote international unity. The International Left Opposition, forerunner to the Fourth International, was also formed.

Had the struggle been not international but merely confined to China, things would have been completely different. We would not have so lightly abandoned the Comintern and the Party; and the Central Committee would not have dared to expel us without further ado. Our expulsion was ordered by the Comintern, it was not simply a decision of the Central Committee.

During the struggle, many honest revolutionaries were worried that the two sides would grow further and further apart. Even though they may not have agreed with us, they, too, opposed our expulsion. But, since the instruction to expel us had come from the International, there was nothing they could do about it. They did not even dare protest. I only know of three comrades who, under special circumstances, spoke out on this question. In the autumn of 1929, Peng Pai, Yang Yin, and Yan Changyi[29] were arrested. Peng and Yang I knew only by sight; Yan was a good friend of mine. These three fair-minded

---

29 Peng Pai and Yang Yin fled to Shanghai in 1928, after the suppression of the Hailufeng Soviet, which they had led. On 24 August 1929, they were arrested together with Yan Changyi; a week later, the three of them were executed.

comrades hated all plots and schemes in the Party. On one occasion, when I had gone to the Propaganda Department to fetch or hand over some materials, Pan Wenyu showed me a message that they had smuggled out from Longhua Prison. In it, they said that they knew that they themselves were already doomed, and they wanted to use what time remained to make propaganda for the revolution in jail; as for the Party itself, they hoped that the Central Committee would be able to resolve the present internal disputes by peaceful means. Such was the last testament of these three important leaders; but no one heeded their advice.

In those days, Zhou Enlai was the most influential figure in the Party. He was head of the Organisation Department and Director of the Military Commission, and organisationally responsible for our expulsion.

The Chinese Left Opposition had already been in existence in an organised way for quite some time; it was around even while we were still drowning in the Stalinist swamp. This organisation had its origins in Sun Yat-sen University in Moscow, where it already had a glorious history of struggle. I hope that at some future date, those qualified to tell the story will do so.[30] In late 1928 or early 1929, Left Oppositionist students returning from Moscow formally set up an organisation in China and started publishing a journal called *Our Word*. Gradually, people began to join who had never been abroad. This organisation was distributing the documents we had seen. Though we had accepted Trotsky's ideas, we were by no means satisfied with this Our Word society. Perhaps Yin Kuan, Peng Shuzhi, and the rest had other reasons to be dissatisfied with it, such as its being led by people without experience and ability or by people who were not prepared to subordinate themselves to one another, but I had only one reason, namely, *Our Word* claimed that the revolution in China was still in spate or already on its way up after a period of ebb. After reading Trotsky and then reading the articles in *Our Word*, it seemed to me that these self-styled 'Trotskyists' had completely failed to understand what Trotsky meant.

When Liu Renjing, on his way back to China via Western Europe, stopped off in Turkey to visit Trotsky, Trotsky asked him to be his China correspondent, so Liu went around claiming that he was 'Old Trotsky's representative' and was unwilling to submit to the existing Opposition's discipline. He brought together a number of Oppositionists outside the existing Oppositionist organisation and put out a journal called *Shiyue* ('October'). But Liu Renjing was unable to control the October society. Chen Duxiu or Yin Kuan told me that Liu Renjing was nothing more than an isolated figurehead and that the guiding spirit

---

30   See Part IV, pp. 327–65.

behind the October society was Wang Wenyuan,[31] a student who had returned from Moscow. This story reminded me of what Ma Renzhi had once said. The Hubin Book Company had published a Chinese edition of Plekhanov's *From Idealism to Materialism*. When I asked Ma who had translated it, he said a 'kid' just back from Moscow, and added that the kid was very bright and very able. Not long afterwards, Liu Renjing was kicked out of the October society, but he still claimed to be 'Old Trotsky's representative' and even issued his own journal, *Mingtian* ('Tomorrow').

Apart from these two Oppositionist organisations, there were a few undecided people like Liu Yin, Zhao Ji, and Wang Pingyi. They, too, decided to put out a journal. While discussing what to call it, they remembered that the magazine (regularly mailed to China) published by the American Left Opposition was called the *Militant*, so they decided to call their journal *Zhandou* ('Combat'), though actually *Zhanshi* would have been a better translation. The Combat-society had no distinctive and consistent political position that I need mention here.

Apart from these three organisations, there were still some people working in the official Party, including some in positions of responsibility. They had had no organisational ties to the Opposition in Moscow, but now that they were back in China they gradually began to declare themselves for the Opposition. They included Wu Jiyan and Tu Qingqi.

Though those of us who had been expelled from the official party as 'opportunists' agreed with Trotsky, in the eyes of the Oppositionists who had returned from Moscow we still did not count as part of the Left Opposition; they, too, denounced us as 'opportunists'. They may have welcomed our rank-and-file supporters, but they opposed us leaders, especially Chen Duxiu. When Liu Renjing wrote to Trotsky telling him about this attitude, Trotsky wrote back to correct it. He said that the line Chen Duxiu had followed in the past was not his own but the Comintern's, that Chen himself was a good revolutionary, and that you young people should learn from him. Trotsky proposed that representatives of the four societies should form a joint 'Negotiating Committee' to unify the societies. So the other three societies no longer had any choice but to consider us part of the Left Opposition, in the same way as they were.

By that time, we ourselves already had an official organisation that grouped together several branches and elected a Standing Committee. Chen Duxiu was naturally General Secretary, and the other members of the Standing Committee were Peng Shuzhi, Yin Kuan, Ma Yufu, and Luo Shifan; the Secretariat was headed first by Wu Jiyan and later by He Zishen. We issued a manifesto titled

---

31   Wang Fanxi.

'Our Political Views' that was signed by more than eighty people, including some worker comrades using false names. We, too, published a journal. While we were discussing what to call it, I proposed the name *Wuchan jieji geming* ('Proletarian Revolution') and everyone agreed, but for some reason it later got called *Wuchanzhe* ('Proletarian'). The first two issues were set in lead-type; after that, it was mimeographed.

The process of negotiations was extremely protracted, complicated, muddled, and a waste of time. The different organisations looked upon one another not as comrades but as enemies, and fought each other with diplomatic tricks. Meanwhile, struggles also broke out within the Proletarian society and the Our Word society, which were the two biggest organisations.[32] Wu Jiyan, one of the Proletarian society delegates, told me jokingly: 'These tricks will come in handy in any future parliament'. I was not the slightest bit interested in such disputes; secretly, I despised them. Nor was I interested in the controversies of that period about points of principle, for they were all tied up in one way or another with organisational squabbles and were artificially raised to serve organisational ends. I barely paid the slightest attention to the 'negotiations', but buried myself, instead, in translating saleable Marxist texts. I only finally decided to throw myself into the factional vortex after the Proletarian society split into two clearly differentiated wings.

The Proletarian society's first representatives on the Negotiating Committee were Ma Yufu and Wu Jiyan. They reported that the members of the three other societies had no intention of uniting, and I believed them. I did not know a single person in any of the other three societies. Since they had not previously recognised us as Oppositionists and were only negotiating because Trotsky had told them to, I thought it only natural that they would be against unification; as for us, I myself thought that unification was necessary, and the others thought the same. What's more, He Zishen told me that the tiny base we had salvaged from the old party was rapidly crumbling, and that if we did not unite soon, our organisation would become an empty shell. Chen Duxiu, too, was very worried. I knew that he was most anxious to achieve a united organisation. After Trotsky's letter, the October society and the Our Word society sent representatives to meet him. He bared his feelings to me.

---

32 At the time, each of the four organisations claimed the title 'Chinese Communist Left Opposition'. None called itself a *she* ('society'), which was a term used by outsiders. But to distinguish between them, even their members all tacitly accepted the term. [Note added by Zheng Chaolin in 1982.]

'These young people are like the young people I came into contact with at the time of May Fourth and May Thirtieth', he told me. 'They're full of youthful vigour and vitality'.

In one sense, this was an admission of his disappointment with the old cadres. Having been through one revolution, they had lost heart and lapsed into apathy. I, too, was dissatisfied with them, and also with myself; I looked for salvation to the new comrades, who I hoped would shake me from my lethargy. But, finally, I discovered that the main reason for the lack of progress towards unity lay in the bad faith not of the other three societies but of the representatives of our own Proletarian society. Ma Yufu and Wu Jiyan were tightly controlled by Peng Shuzhi, who was the chief obstacle to unity.

Chen Duxiu all along despised organisational plots. You have only to look at his attitude in the official party from the Wuhan period through to the time of the Sixth Congress to know that. But the same was not true of Peng Shuzhi. He craved to be leader. I have already described how he climbed into the leadership not because large numbers of people supported him but through organisational manoeuvres. He had created and maintained his leadership position among the twenty or thirty Chinese students in Moscow by those famous 'Moscow branch' training methods. After getting back to China, he was looked upon as a representative sent to China by the Comintern. In that capacity, he joined its Presidium and gained the confidence of Chen Duxiu. Later, he tightly latched onto Chen in order to make himself more important. 'The Old Man's views are identical with mine', he would say. In one period, between his coming out of hospital in 1925 and Qu Qiubai's attack on him in 1927, he was even crazy enough to believe that save for Chen Duxiu, he constituted the leadership of the Chinese Communist Party. Cai Hesen was then in Moscow and there were only four people on the Presidium.

'Qu Qiubai is a higher technician,[33] Zhang Guotao is a higher administrator', he used to say.

But to tell the truth, Cai, Qu, and Zhang (not to mention Chen Duxiu) were all far more able than Peng, who was the least distinguished of the five-member Presidium. After going to Wuhan, he was easily toppled. Even Wang Ruofei and Chen Qiaonian, who were trying to build a nucleus in the Party and to resist the anti-Chen Duxiu campaign within it, had no good feelings towards Peng. After his downfall, Peng clung even more tightly to Chen Duxiu. When Yin Kuan wanted to talk with Chen after getting hold of the Oppositionist documents, he had to go through Peng,[34] who remained in attendance every time

---

33   A translator and interpreter from and into Russian.
34   At the time, Peng was the only person who knew Chen's address.

the two men met, for Yin was unable to go directly to Chen's home. Peng's only hope of getting back into the leadership was by relying on Chen Duxiu.

When the question of unifying the four societies came up, what concerned us most was whether or not our political views were identical in principle. What animated Peng and the people under his influence, on the other hand, was the different question of how to unite. The Our Word society considered itself to be the orthodox opposition in China. Before the arrival of Trotsky's letter advocating negotiations, the Our Word society permitted the 'converted opportunists' to enter their organisation only individually, and reserved the right to take or leave them. Apart from this procedure, there could be no other form of 'unity'. Peng Shuzhi could not even bear to hear of this method of selection. After the arrival of Trotsky's letter, the Our Word society's status fell to the same level as the other three societies; the aim now was to unite in a new organisation – there could no longer be any talk of orthodoxy or unorthodoxy. But Peng Shuzhi opposed this approach as well. The real reason he slighted and mistrusted the other organisations was because he knew that most of the young people in them had no good feelings towards him and he was unlikely to become a leader of the new organisation. He dared not openly express his view that the Proletarian society was the orthodox opposition, so his only alternative was to spin out and sabotage the talks.

It was a long time before we realised this fact. Though Yin Kuan was not a delegate to the talks, he knew a large number of people in the other three societies, and often got together with them. So he found out that what our delegates were telling us was not true, and that Peng Shuzhi was staunchly opposed to unity. On one occasion, Yin managed (no easy matter) to meet Chen Duxiu independently of Peng, and arranged for Chen to go to his home for a discussion. He told Chen what he had found out. Chen was thoroughly awakened. At a meeting of the Standing Committee, he proposed recalling Ma Yufu and Wu Jiyan as delegates to the talks and replacing them with him and Yin Kuan as the Proletarian group delegates. After that, the talks went smoothly.

As soon as Chen Duxiu awoke, he immediately split from Peng Shuzhi and even ceased to be friends with him. Chen was a man of strong feelings. He easily trusted people and easily overestimated the value of those he trusted, but if he was ever disappointed, he quickly went over to the opposite extreme. Now, he hated Peng in the same way as he had once trusted him: to excess. He Zishen once said of Peng that he was a paper tiger, all teeth and claws but easy to punch holes in.

'He is not a paper tiger', replied Chen Duxiu, 'he's a rotten water melon. Paper tigers are full of air. Rotten melons are pretty on the outside but stink like hell if you burst them open'. After that, every time the Standing Committee of the Proletarian society met, there was inevitably a row, and a violent one at that. Chen Duxiu, Yin Kuan, and He Zishen were in favour of unity, Peng Shuzhi and Ma Yufu were against it; I cannot say for certain what Luo Shifan thought. Things carried on like this right through until unity was realised and the Proletarian group as a separate organisation came to a natural end.

The split between these two old friends was final. After I went to jail the second time, Peng Shuzhi rose once more to become a leader and once again cooperated with Chen Duxiu, but there was no longer any friendship between them. After they were arrested and sent to jail together, they quarrelled senselessly and interminably right through until their release. Chen Duxiu had no interest in discussing his and Peng's wrangles. When I met him after my release from jail, he never once mentioned Peng. Wang Wenyuan in Hankou once mentioned him to Chen. 'Don't use that man's name in my presence', said Chen. Peng Shuzhi, on the other hand, loved to talk about his prison clashes with Chen. In 1940, when I met him in Shanghai, he raised the subject many times. He even went so far as to calumniate Chen in the ugliest terms, and tried to pass off his petty wrangles as part of a battle between Peng's correct political position and Chen's wrong one. When news of Chen's death[35] reached Shanghai Peng wrote an essay to blacken him and a couplet in which he cursed him with the words 'He lost his integrity in his later years'.

Though most people on the Standing Committee of the Proletarian society favoured unification, in the branches they did not. The branches were made up partly of people that Cai Zhende and Ma Yufu had brought with them from the official party in Shanghai, and partly of cadres who in the past had worked for the Party in Shanghai or elsewhere in the country; the latter supported Chen Duxiu, but most had to do so through Peng Shuzhi. By this time, Cai Zhende had become apathetic, and Peng and Ma were opposed to unification. None of the old cadres trusted Yin Kuan. Yin was intelligent and quicker off the mark than Peng, both as a thinker and as an activist, but he was a cynic, actually a harmless one, and cynical not so much in dealing with other people as in selling himself as a person of great intelligence; but whatever the case, this cynicism caused people to dislike him. Peng could easily present the question of whether or not to unify as a dispute between him and Yin, and thus win support for his position.

In the several months that elapsed between the arrival of Trotsky's letter and the establishment of the Negotiating Committee, I stayed aloof from the various disputes. The Standing Committee of the Proletarian society sent me as a representative of the east Shanghai district organisation to discuss merging

---

35   Chen Duxiu died on 27 May 1942, in Jiangjin, Sichuan province.

with the east Shanghai district organisation of the Our Word society. I met Shi Tang in a primary school. That was the first I learned that he had worked as a type-setter in the printing factory that I had been responsible for running. He knew me, but I did not know him. In 1927, he had gone to study in Moscow, where he had joined the Opposition. After returning to China, he had taken on a responsible position in the Opposition. 'Why did I never hear your name during all these arguments over the last few months?' he asked me. I cannot remember how I answered him, but after that, my name did start to crop up in the discussions, for I became a firm supporter of unification. Supporters of unification gradually came to predominate in the branches of the Proletarian society. Among the delegates they elected to the Unification Congress were Chen Duxiu and I. Chen's election was a matter of course, as was Peng Shuzhi and Ma Yufu's non-election; it might seem strange that such a firm supporter of unification as Yin Kuan was not elected, but goes to show that, though people favoured unification, they still opposed Yin and thought that he was using the unification issue as part of his vendetta against Peng. As for me, no one suspected that I harboured any personal ambition.

In the course of the negotiations, the Our Word society also split. The Liang Ganqiao faction had its base in Guangdong and the Ou Fang faction in Shanghai, where many people joined the Opposition. At the time, Ou Fang was in Caohejing Prison. The person who represented the Ou Fang faction at the Unification Congress was Song Jingxiu, who had joined in Shanghai.[36]

The Unification Congress of the Left Opposition of the Chinese Communist Party was held in a newly rented lane house on Dalian Bay Road.

The Negotiating Committee gave the job of finding a venue to the Proletarian society, which gave it to He Zishen. We funded the Congress with the help of Li Zhongsan's lynx-fur gown, which I pawned for more than $200. He Zishen sent Wang Zhihuai's whole family to live as sublessors in the house we rented. Wang himself, a worker, was also a Proletarian society delegate. The other delegates gathered in groups of three or four and were then conducted to this house.

---

36   Wang Fanxi has written to me to say that there was no organisational split between the Guangdong faction (led by Liang Ganqiao) and the Shanghai faction (led by Ou Fang) in the Our Word group. The entire northern organisation of the Our Word group had split away nearly one year before the Unification Congress and become part of the founding nucleus of the October group, in whose name they participated in the unity negotiations and the Congress. This is the first I knew of this. [Note added by Zheng Chaolin in the early 1980s.]

Once you entered you were not allowed out again until after the Congress had finished, three or four days later. The only exception was Chen Duxiu, who was allowed to go home after every session.

I forget how many delegates attended, but I do know that they included Chen Duxiu, Jiang Changshi, Jiang Zhendong, Wang Zhihuai, and me for the Proletarian society;[37] Liang Ganqiao, Chen Yimou, Song Jingxiu, and four Hong Kong workers for the Our Word society; Wang Wenyuan, Pu Dezhi, Song Fengchun, and Luo Han for the October society; and Lai Yantang for the Combat society. I had never met any of the delegates of the other three societies before, nor had I met Jiang Zhendong representing our own group.

The resolutions had all been drafted by the Negotiating Committee and agreed by the main leaders of the four societies, most of whom were themselves delegates, so there was virtually no debate. All I remember is that while we were discussing the political resolution, I stood up to speak and got into an argument. It was about the relationship between political stability and the national assembly. It was now 1931. Two years had passed since 1929. In the months leading up to the Congress, the various societies had argued violently, verbally and in writing. Everybody had made progress in the course of these confrontations. *Our Word* was no longer claiming that the revolution was back in spate, and no one any longer denied that the Guomindang had already achieved political stability. But could it be maintained? Yes, and for quite a long time: that was what I believed. In my view, it was precisely because of this political stability that we must call for a national assembly. But others, including Liang Ganqiao and Song Fengchun, criticised my way of thinking, though I forget on what grounds.

The final session of the Congress was given over to elections. Some people were especially interested in this procedure, since more often than not, it is the reason they attend Congresses. I forget how many Central Committee members were chosen. Chen Duxiu and Wang Wenyuan got an equally high number of votes; every delegate voted for them. Of the other candidates, some got

---

37   After counting the membership of each group, the Negotiating Committee finally awarded the Proletarian and Our Word societies one extra delegate each. The Proletarian society then decided to send Peng Shuzhi, but he arrived either only on the second or third day of proceedings or not at all. [Note added by Zheng Chaolin in 1982.] As far as Wang Fanxi recalls, Peng did not attend this Congress. He also recalls that there were seventeen delegates in all: seven representing Our Word, six representing the Proletarian group, four representing the October group, and two representing the Combat group. Since one delegate was allowed for every twenty members, this means that there were approximately 340 Trotskyists in China in 1931.

more votes, some less. Peng Shuzhi and Liang Ganqiao came last among the successful candidates, with a tied number of votes, but in a run-off, Peng won. Liang's failure to get elected came as a surprise to many people. Later, Chen Yimou said it was due to a misunderstanding. The Hong Kong workers had not realised that Liang Ganqiao and Liang Daci were one and the same person, so they had not voted for him.

Even after the Negotiating Committee had decided in favour of unification, Peng Shuzhi still continued to oppose it. He said that 'on behalf of the rank and file' he opposed 'collusion by the high-ups'.

'Others may represent the rank-and-file, but it's hardly seemly for Peng to claim to do so', was Chen Duxiu's comment.

Even so, people feared that he would stir up trouble.

'It's easy to settle', I told them. 'Just guarantee him a seat on the Central Committee. Then he will be most unlikely to oppose anything'.

Yin Kuan and He Zishen told me not to talk such nonsense. They accused me of having a simplistic view of politics and of Peng Shuzhi.

'Perhaps it's true that I don't understand politics', I said, 'but I do understand Peng'.

After the start of the Congress on 1 May, when Chen Duxiu was back at home, He Zishen handed him a long letter by Peng that criticised unification as 'hypocritical' and 'meaningless', to name just two of the unpleasant epithets Peng used. The letter also said: 'I would rather die than recognise it'. But Peng had not expected that he would be elected. The first time the new Central Committee met, he came along. Chen Duxiu took out the letter, showed it round, and then asked Peng: 'Do you still think unification is "hypocritical", "meaningless", and all the rest of it?' I can see Peng to this day, sitting on the side of the bed, blushing violently and completely speechless. Finally, I intervened to help him out of his embarrassment and save him the trouble of a reply. Later, He Zishen told me angrily that to tolerate evil is to abet it, and that I was politically irresolute. He thought that people like Peng should be completely crushed, and that the letter had been the best chance of doing so. 'He has already suffered enough', I said. He Zishen now admitted that he had been wrong when he had said before the Congress that I had a simplistic view of Peng. But Yin Kuan never raised the matter again, so I do not know what he thought.

The first meeting of the Central Committee elected a Standing Committee made up of Chen Duxiu, Chen Yimou, Wang Wenyuan, Song Fengchun, and me. Chen Duxiu was General Secretary, Chen Yimou was in charge of organisation, I was in charge of propaganda, Wang took care of the party journal, and Song was head of the Secretariat.

Not long after that, just when we had begun our real work, our organisation was uncovered and the entire Standing Committee apart from Chen Duxiu was arrested, so I went to jail a second time. This time was less pleasant than the first, two years earlier. The first spell had lasted forty days: the second, six years and three months. I was freed only when the reactionary Guomindang government was preparing to abandon its capital at Nanjing under the bombardment of the Japanese imperialists.

Unification of the Four Groups

Wang Fanxi

Source: Memoirs of a Chinese Revolutionary (1957).

Although I had devoted myself full time to work for the Chinese Communist Party during the short period between my return to China and my expulsion from the Party, I had kept up regular contact with my fellow Oppositionists, and met the Our Word comrades about once a fortnight to exchange information. Like Shi Tang, Zhang Te, and the other comrades responsible at that time for the Our Word group in Shanghai, I recoiled from the idea that Chen Duxiu was moving towards Trotskyism. We saw him as an inveterate opportunist trying to find his way out of a blind alley. Hence our attitude and tactics towards the Chen group: we would do all we could to expose the base motives of its opportunist leadership, while trying to win over the rank and file under its control. Although this approach was totally misconceived, we clung stubbornly to it until Trotsky himself intervened in January 1931.

Some of the Oppositionists who had returned with me from Moscow, like Liu Renjing, Zhao Ji, and Liu Yin, had absolutely refused to participate in Communist Party work from the start. I have already mentioned that on his return Liu Renjing simply sent the Central Committee a statement declaring his allegiance to Trotskyism. Liu Yin and Zhao Ji had turned up at the educational course held shortly after our arrival in Shanghai, but later found pretexts for not taking up their assignments in Shanghai, where they had been apprenticed to the district and sub-district committees, and thus had made their exit from the Party. Together with Liu Renjing, they spent all their time discussing how to organise a new Trotskyist movement with Chen Duxiu and his friends. This implied, of course, that they did not recognise the Our Word group, despite the fact that it had already been active for a year or two, particularly in north and south China. Instead, they wanted to set up a new organisation, run not by 'childish amateurs' but by 'experienced politicians'. The supporters of the Our Word group viewed them with the same suspicion as we did Chen Duxiu. I felt the same way as the other comrades, not only because of my assessment of Chen Duxiu's group, but also because it seemed to me that Liu Renjing in particular had violated our Moscow agreement in starting up a new organisation, rather than joining Our Word, the existing Oppositionist group in China. In fact Liu Yin himself had never actually joined the Opposition in Moscow; his relationship with us there had been more social than political, so his posing as a veteran Trotskyist made him even more odious in my eyes.

Such was the state of the Opposition shortly before my expulsion from the Party. After I had been expelled and had recovered from my illness, the situation looked very different. Liu Renjing had broken with Chen Duxiu's group. Disputes had also broken out within the Our Word group, and the leaders of the north China, Shanghai, and south China groups eventually split on issues I did not properly understand at the time and have long since forgotten. The north China Trotskyists, under Song Fengchun and Dong Zicheng, linked up with Liu Renjing against both the Chen Duxiu group and the Shanghai-based part of the Our Word group under Ou Fang and Zhang Te. In order to justify the separate existence of his group, Liu Renjing drafted a political criticism of what he called the 'remnants of Chen Duxiu's opportunism'. Liu Yin and Zhao Ji also broke from Chen, although I am not quite sure on what grounds. They attracted a number of people to them and set up yet another group.

I learnt of all these splits and regroupings from comrades who came to visit me on my sick-bed, and the news depressed me immensely. Because of the prejudices I felt towards the Chen group, I wanted nothing to do with them, not even with those who were old friends or acquaintances. I considered myself a member of the Our Word group, but unfortunately lost contact with them when Shi Tang, my only acquaintance in the group, was imprisoned in the Shanghai International Settlement. The people I knew best were Liu Yin and Zhao Ji, but I had a very low opinion of Liu both from a political and a personal point of view. During my years as a revolutionary, I have seen many careerists drift in and out of the movement, but never such a self-seeking petty bourgeois as Liu Yin. At the time of the Northern Expedition, he had been a leader of the Wuhan student movement. He was a very good speaker and brilliant agitator, but more than anything else wanted to be a leader. He was very weak ideologically and lacked the spirit of self-sacrifice which marks a real revolutionary. It was therefore quite natural that he should go over to Chiang Kai-shek and become his hired intellectual stooge. While in Moscow he had called on the Opposition to 'unite' with him – more than two hundred people unite with one! – but what he really meant was that, if we invited him to become our leader, he would consider the offer. His suggestion made him the laughing stock of the Moscow Oppositionists, and infuriated Fan Jinbiao. I could not join an organisation led by someone like that, and thus the only group I could and would get into contact with was the one set up by Liu Renjing and Song Fengchun. Song had been one of the first to join the Opposition during his Moscow days. He had been expelled by the Party in the winter of 1927, and had been sent back to China together with Ou Fang and others. He had made his way to Beijing, with Ge Chonge and Xiao Changbin, where they met up with Luo Han, at that time a member of the Beijing District Committee of the CCP. They had immediately started to work among students, until Luo Han was arrested and Song Fengchun left for Shanghai, where he arrived sometime towards the end of 1929. Song had originally been the driving force in the Our Word group, but because of his unhappiness about the growing conflict between Ou Fang and Zhang Te, he went to work as a labourer in a cotton-mill. He was an excellent revolutionary, and an extremely modest man who could put up with every kind of hardship. Later, he was arrested with me and sent to Shanghai jail, but released about a year afterwards when influential friends of his family interceded on his behalf. A few days after his release, he was re-arrested together with Chen Duxiu. This was too much for him; he lost his faith in the revolution and left our ranks.

In the early summer of 1930, Song was the person I was closest to in the movement. He and other comrades from north China had joined with Liu Renjing to draft a collective political programme as a basis for uniting all the Oppositionists. When I came to read the programme, which was actually written by Liu Renjing, under the title 'An Open Letter to all Trotskyist Comrades', I found that Liu's line on the subject of the constituent assembly had not changed since his Moscow days, and that he still proposed limiting the aims of the struggle to the establishment of a parliamentary system in China. He quoted at length from Marx's *The Eighteenth Brumaire of Louis Bonaparte* to show that such a system would be qualitatively superior to Chiang Kai-shek's military dictatorship. I disagreed profoundly with his analysis, and, although he was usually intolerant of other people's views, he responded to my criticisms by proposing that I rewrite the part devoted to the question of the constituent assembly and submit it to the others for discussion. Urged on by Song Fengchun and others, my line was as follows: that as the counter-revolution had triumphed and the democratic tasks of the Revolution had not yet been completed, the only correct slogan was the call for a constituent assembly. This would make it possible to re-organise the scattered forces of the working class, bring together the separate struggles of the peasantry and the urban petty bourgeoisie, and clear the way for the CCP to re-enter the political arena – all with the ultimate aim of hastening the arrival of a new revolutionary storm. Whether or not it would prove possible in the course of such a struggle for a parliamentary system to come into being and establish itself was, of course, another question entirely, and one which could only be answered by events. The main reason for raising the slogan of a constituent assembly was to help the revolution mature in a period of counter-revolution, and to hasten the proletarian revolution.

The exact interpretation of this call for a constituent assembly was to remain a major controversy in Chinese Oppositionist ranks for many years. My own approach to the problem may not have been perfect, but, in my opinion, it was much closer to the spirit of Trotskyism than Liu Renjing's purely socialdemocratic interpretation. Song Fengchun and the others agreed with my draft, and Liu Renjing only put up token resistance before agreeing to substitute it for his own. My criticisms accepted, I added my name to the Open Letter together with those of the other comrades. As far as I can remember, there were nineteen signatories in all, including Li Cailian, a brilliant woman comrade. The north China Oppositionists also gave their support to the Open Letter as soon as they got hold of a copy, although they did not formally add their signatures to it. Liu Renjing and I then started up a journal which we called *October*, and we were soon dubbed 'Octobrists' by the other Trotskyist groups.

By the summer of 1930, four mutually hostile Oppositionist groups had emerged: the Octobrists; the Chen Duxiu group, which issued a journal called *The Proletarian* and went under the name of the Proletarian Society; the Our Word group, which continued to publish a periodical of that name; and finally Liu Yin and Zhao Ji, who with a handful of other comrades brought out one issue of a journal called the *Militant*, and therefore went under the name of the Militant group.

It seems to me in retrospect that the 'struggle' between these four groups was waged over trivial and petty issues with exaggerated intensity. As is not unusual in a political or ideological movement in its early stages of development, personal ambition and factional prejudice become entangled with genuine differences of opinion, and the best and the worst motives often become indissolubly mingled. When political activities are restricted to writing and discussion, it is difficult for any organisation to test the real strengths and weaknesses of its membership.

People's motives for becoming Trotskyists in the first place varied enormously. Some joined because they found it difficult to realise their ambitions within the Party, and thought the best thing would be to branch out in a new direction; others were intimidated by the intensity of the white terror, and used the Opposition as a stage in their retreat from the revolution; and still others took advantage of the left-wing reputation of the Trotskyist movement to retreat into a world of 'revolutionary' mouthings, with no practical consequences. But, although many sorry types were coming over to our side, the overwhelming majority of Opposition supporters in China at that time were sincere revolutionaries driven by the best of motives, who firmly supported Trotsky's proposals for the Chinese Revolution and considered them far better suited to the conditions of China than those of Stalin. It was for this reason that they gave up their established positions in the Party and devoted themselves wholeheartedly to the Oppositionist cause.

The problems I have just mentioned were more or less common to all four groups. During the period when fighting between factions was at its most intense, the pace was set by people driven by egotism and personal ambition, who gave little thought to the overall needs of the movement. Afterwards, under the pressure of the majority and more particularly as a result of the personal intervention of Trotsky himself, the unification campaign began, giving the signal for the genuine revolutionaries in our ranks to pull down the 'mountain strongholds' erected by the leaders of the four groups. The campaign soon succeeded in isolating the sectarians, so that they either left the movement to become inactive or defected to the reactionary camp.

The period in which the four factions each had their own separate existence lasted for just over a year, from early 1930 to 1 May 1931. This period can be subdivided into two: before January 1931, when the differences between the factions were exaggerated and inflated; and after 8 January, when a letter arrived from Trotsky urging us to unify our forces, and a period of 'negotiations' began. At first, the controversies centred on questions such as the slogan of a constituent assembly, the Chinese Red Army, the nature of the coming revolution, and the lessons of the defeat of the 1925–7 Revolution. There is no need to go into any detail about these old controversies, and I will restrict myself to pointing out that we deliberately exaggerated our differences in order to justify the existence of our various factions. Liu Renjing, for example, deliberately and wilfully exaggerated the differences that separated us. At first, he enthusiastically welcomed Chen Duxiu's conversion to Trotskyism, but when he failed to get what he was after, which was control of the propaganda department, he wrote an article in which he quoted the ancient Greek philosopher's remark 'I love my teacher, but I love the truth even more', implying he had had to break with Chen as a matter of principle. Afterwards, when he split from the Octobrists, he suddenly discovered that he could love both his teacher and the truth. People like Liu Renjing, however, were in a minority, so when the different factions came into more frequent contact with one another, these differences dwindled away.

During those years, controversy raged around the call for a constituent assembly more than any other issue, but, as Trotsky later pointed out, such discussions were for the most part purely hypothetical. For example, there was the question of whether a constituent assembly could ever actually be brought into being, and if so, whether it would ever be able to solve any of the problems facing the country. Then there was the question of the relationship between a constituent assembly and the soviets. Of course it was pointless, not to say ludicrous, to raise questions of this sort, which could only really be answered by events themselves. Anyway, there was broad agreement between all the Oppositionists except Liu Renjing on this question.

Questions such as the Chinese Red Army and the lessons to be drawn from the defeat of the 1925–7 Revolution were raised only to discredit Chen Duxiu. In *The Proletarian*, Chen wrote an article on the future prospects for the Red Army, arguing that, unless the peasant struggle was led by the urban proletariat, the Revolution would either degenerate or be destroyed. If Chen Duxiu was wrong on this point, then Marx, Engels, and Trotsky were wrong too. At the time, however, we did not realise the wider implications of this question, and all of us (myself included) attacked what we saw as Chen's slander of the Red Army. We seized on imperfections in the way in which he had worked his article and his one-sided slanting of the issue. In reality we were simply swelling the Stalinist anti-Chen chorus.

The question of the lessons to be learnt from the defeat of the 1925–7 Revolution was also raised to discredit Chen Duxiu, and was essentially a demand that Chen admit his share of the blame for the policy of the Stalinists. Many comrades felt that for Chen to admit to having been the executor of Stalin's policies was not only not enough, but was positively dishonest. In our view, Chen had been a conscious tool of Stalin. I am still convinced that our interpretation of his behaviour was not unreasonable. Chen Duxiu was no puppet, but a revolutionary with a mind and a will of his own. We have Chen's own word for it that although he carried out some of the Comintern directives and resolutions between 1923 and 1927 unwillingly, to others he gave his full assent and agreement. In my opinion it would have been a much more effective rebuttal of Stalinism and an important contribution to the historiography of modern China if Chen had distinguished between these two categories and compiled a detailed record of what happened, but, unfortunately, he never did so. However, it was completely wrong of us to demand that he should go down on his knees to confess his guilt to us as 'orthodox Trotskyists', since this only delayed the unification of our forces.

The dispute on the nature of the coming revolution was at first over whether to struggle for a 'dictatorship of the proletariat' or a 'dictatorship of the proletariat and the poor peasantry'. Later the crux of the argument was whether or not the third revolution would be socialist in character from the very outset. Chen Duxiu had argued in *Our Political Platform* that a successful third revolution would inevitably lead to the establishment of a dictatorship of the proletariat and the poor peasantry. Trotsky always talked of the 'dictatorship of the proletariat' or the 'dictatorship of the proletariat at the head of the poor peasantry'; but Chen Duxiu's formula appeared to give equal weight to both forces, and therefore to be making a concession to the outdated old Bolshevik slogan of the 'democratic dictatorship of the workers and the peasants'. (This problem is discussed fully in Trotsky's *The Permanent Revolution*.) This difference was first seized on by Liu Renjing, and was subsequently picked up by all the other Trotskyists outside the Chen camp. Liu accused Chen of attempting to smuggle the poison of the 'democratic dictatorship' into the ranks of the Opposition, and dismissed Chen's article as a 'pitiful and hypocritical document'. Although, unlike Liu Renjing, we had not originally intended to make this the sole basis for our attack on Chen's so-called left turn, we were influenced by Liu's criticisms. We felt that that Chen's formula was close to the 'democratic dictatorship', and in fundamental contradiction to the 'dictatorship of the proletariat' slogan. Trotsky, however, on reading Chen Duxiu's document, declared that it was simply a popularisation and amplification of the 'dictatorship of the proletariat' formula, and that, in his view, there was no contradiction between the two. Liu Renjing was left dumbfounded by Trotsky's intervention, but, for the rest of us, it was as if the scales had suddenly fallen from our eyes.

The last of the four differences that separated the various factions involved the nature of the coming (third) Chinese revolution. It was Trotsky himself who originally forecast that this revolution would be socialist in character from the very outset, and not one of us disagreed with his analysis. Where the disagreement arose, however, was over an interpretation of it advanced in an article I wrote after the unification campaign was already under way, to which I will return later.

In brief, the squabbles and disputes of this period did not, as Trotsky pointed out, involve any differences of principle, but were more often than not blown up for purely factional reasons. After he had studied the various documents we had sent him, Trotsky wrote a long letter to us on 8 January 1931 proposing that we should immediately unify our forces. His tone was very pressing and earnest: 'Dear friends, merge your organisations and your papers today! Don't delay too much in preparing for unification. Otherwise, you will unconsciously create artificial differences between yourselves'. His prestige among us was so high that even the most diehard sectarian could find no further excuse for delaying unification; and, shortly after receiving his letter, the four factions decided to set up a 'Committee to Negotiate Unifications', which would draw up documents and unify on a common platform.

As I said earlier, this unification campaign was very beneficial for our movement, strengthening and concentrating us numerically, and at the same time involving a process of purification and selection. The small minority of comrades who could not accept the loss of their 'mountain strongholds' left the unified Opposition of their own accord, unable to reconcile themselves to the idea of working in a broader and numerically stronger organisation. To clarify what went on during this period of regroupment, I would now like to say something about some of the individuals involved in the different organisations, beginning with the October group of which I myself was a member.

The natural leader of the Octobrists was Liu Renjing. He was older than the rest of us, and had better credentials. He had been one of the original twelve delegates at the First Congress of the CCP in 1921, and had also been General Secretary of the Chinese Communist Youth League. He had visited Trotsky at Prinkipo in Turkey, and even used to brag that Trotsky had chosen his pen-name, Niel Shih, for him. In Moscow, I had had my differences with Liu, but I had always respected him as a veteran of the movement. On returning to China, when we got together with other comrades to publish *October* and organise our group, I continued to hold him in fairly high regard, but, as soon as I and the other comrades began to work closely with him, we discovered he had many faults. As a theoretician, he was one-sided and unstable. Of Lenin's 'three component parts of Marxism', he was versed in only one – the history of the modern European revolutionary movement. He knew nothing of political economy and had only an elementary knowledge of philosophy. His instability in ideology enabled him to change his views according to his own ever-changing needs. However, what made us split from him after no more than a few months of co-operation was his way of working, which was entirely different from ours. He was obsessed with cultivating the famous, and he held himself aloof from the working class. He left our organisation after only two issues of *October* had appeared. After the split, we continued to publish under the new name of *The Road to October*. Liu Renjing brought out two issues of a one-man paper called *Tomorrow*. Later, he lapsed into inactivity after failing to win a place in the leadership when the four factions united. In 1934, he was hired by Harold Isaacs to translate material for his book *The Tragedy of the Chinese Revolution*. He was later arrested in Beijing, but let out of prison after a period of 'reflection'. In 1938 he joined General Hu Zongnan's Anti-Communist League. When the Communist Party took power in 1949 the first thing he did was to write a statement denouncing Trotskyism.

Fortunately, people like Liu Renjing were in a tiny minority in the movement, and of the eighty or more members of the October group in Shanghai and north China only one other, a man called Lu, went over to the counter-revolution. Among these eighty there were many truly heroic figures, such as Ge Chonge, Li Cailian, and Luo Han, all of them utterly dedicated.

The group which continued under the name of Our Word after 1930 was in effect confined to Shanghai and Hong Kong. Its leadership was made up of the first generation of Moscow Trotskyists, Sun Yat-sen University students sent back to China in 1927. They had already been working for a few years in the country, and in Hong Kong had established a particularly strong base after Ou Fang, Chen Yimou, and others went to work in the Taigu dockyards. In Shanghai, where Shi Tang and Lu Yiyuan were in overall charge of the activities of the Our Word group, there were fewer successes, but some contacts were established among workers and intellectuals.

Twenty-seven years later, at the time of writing, it is possible to look back on the events of those days dispassionately and to weigh up the merits of the various groups. It seems to me that the Our Word group was the healthiest of the four factions, more militant than the Chen Duxiu group and with a broader base than either the Octobrists or the Militant group. It had some outstanding leaders, among them Ou Fang, who was resilient, modest, optimistic by nature, and both a man of action and a thinker. He dressed just like a labourer and was a brilliant writer and speaker. Tragically, Ou Fang was arrested together with Ge Chonge of the October group before unification could be carried out, and both comrades died at the hands of the Guomindang in Shanghai jail. Then there was Chen Yimou, who, although not as good a thinker or writer as Ou Fang, had at least as much capacity to endure pain. Chen also died in jail. Song Jingxiu, another outstanding and determined revolutionary, was the leader of the workers' section of the Our Word group in Shanghai. He died in the same prison as Ou Fang and Chen Yimou. This is how the revolution always treats the people who take part in it, physically destroying the strong and the loyal, and spiritually destroying the weak and the bad. Other leaders of the Our Word group such as Shi Tang, Lu Yiyuan, Zhang Te, and Liang Ganqiao belonged to the latter category. Shi Tang and Lu Yiyuan were weak, and later dropped out of politics altogether, but Zhang Te and Liang Ganqiao actively went over to the counter-revolution, becoming 'specialists' in anti-communism for the Guomindang.

The Proletarian Society was made up of over eighty high- and middle-ranking cadres trained during the early period of the CCP, all of them experienced and able activists. They would have been a powerful asset to any ideological movement, especially with a man of Chen Duxiu's calibre at their head. Whatever his mistakes, Chen was still the symbol of China's progressive and revolutionary movement, both at home and abroad. The Proletarian Society might therefore have been expected to play an important role in the formation and development of the Chinese Trotskyist movement. But this never happened, the reason being that most of these old comrades were by now too apathetic.

During the long period of CCP Guomindang cooperation, many of them had adopted the style and attitudes of a bureaucrat or a member of the gentry, and having got used to working within a ready-made organisational apparatus found it hard to come to terms with the problems of building a new movement from scratch. As events were later to show, only a small minority of this organisation of officers and general staff were as capable of fighting in the ranks once unification had been achieved.

For a long period, the Militant group had only four members. Apart from Liu Yin and Zhao Ji, the other two members were called Wang and Xu. Wang and Xu went over to the Guomindang with Liu Yin shortly after unification, and only Zhao Ji continued to work alongside the other Oppositionists. While the unification campaign was gathering strength, a member of the Communist Party called Ming Yinchang, who was responsible for the workers' section of the CCP in north Shanghai, was recruited to the Militant group by Zhao Ji. Twenty or so other worker Communists joined with him, so the Militant group could boast a couple of dozen members by the time of the Unification Congress in 1931. But, of all the groups in existence at that time, the Militant group was without doubt the smallest.

The first concern of the more sectarian-minded comrades in the various groups was how to secure for themselves the best possible representation on the committee set up to negotiate unification. Should the various groups be represented on a proportional basis, which would work out to the advantage of the bigger organisations, or should the groups be represented equally, which would favour the smaller ones? After some preliminary discussions the decision was made to allot each organisation – regardless of size – two delegates. Originally Ou Fang and Shi Tang, who had just been released from the International Settlement prison in Shanghai, were chosen to represent the Our Word group; Wu Jixian and Ma Yufu, the Proletarian Society; Liu Yin and Zhao Ji, the Militant group; and Song Fengchun and myself, the Octobrists. Shortly afterwards the Our Word group's delegation was changed to Liang Ganqiao and Chen Yimou, after the arrest of Ou Fang and the desertion of Shi Tang, who secretly left Shanghai for his home town. The first few sessions of the unification negotiations committee were marred by quarrelling, and at meeting after meeting old issues were revived and old disputes re-enacted. These so-called negotiations (altercations would be a better word) dragged on for about two months, to the disappointment of many of the delegates and all the genuine Oppositionists in the four groups. The committee had originally set itself two tasks: to draw up a series of documents for voting on at a subsequent unification conference, and to organise such a conference. Both tasks were to prove difficult to achieve.

I was chosen to draw up the platform of the Chinese Left Opposition – not a particularly exacting task, since all it entailed was making a few editorial changes to the draft platform Trotsky had already sent us – on the 'Nature of the Coming Chinese Revolution'. Trotsky had written in his draft: 'Our strategic general line is directed towards the seizure of state power.... The dictatorship of the proletariat in China will without doubt make of the Chinese revolution a part of the world socialist revolution'. As it seemed to me that this formulation was not complete, I drew on a passage from Trotsky's *The Summary and Perspectives of the Chinese Revolution*: 'The third Chinese revolution ... will be forced from the very outset to effect the most decisive shake-up and abolition of bourgeois property in city and village'. On the basis of this I wrote, 'the coming Chinese revolution will be socialist in character from the very outset'.

To my surprise, this sentence raised a storm of protest, and Liu Renjing rose to denounce it as mechanical and ultra-leftist; he had himself long maintained that the Chinese revolution would inevitably go through a Kerensky stage. After this, *Our Word* and *The Proletarian* published articles both for and against my formulation. I have forgotten the details of the argument, but I do remember that the majority of the Our Word group supported me, whereas the majority of the Proletarian Society opposed me. My most uncompromising opponent was Peng Shuzhi, and my firmest supporter in the Proletarian Society was Zheng Chaolin, while Chen Duxiu wrote an article which fell between the two camps. Other theoretical problems of rather less importance were also argued over in the negotiating committee. Here, too, everyone refused to move from their positions, so it took a long time to draw up the documents to be voted on.

Organising the unification conference proved to be an even thornier problem. First, it was very difficult to work out just how many members there were in each group. On this point, Liang Ganqiao's attitude was particularly obstructive. Liang Ganqiao, a soldier who had been through the Huangpu Military Academy, showed not the slightest interest in theoretical questions, but, as soon as the discussion switched to questions which concerned the future control of any unified organisation that might be set up, he would immediately spring to life and devote his undivided attention to what was going on around him. For him, everything that anyone else might say was always part of a plot, so he had no scruples about carrying out cynical organisational manoeuvres. To ensure a dominant position in any future elections, he approached us Octobrists with proposals for an anti-Chen alliance; but, when we turned him down, he decided to adopt another tack, hugely exaggerating the strength of 'his' group and claiming without so much as a blush that its membership was equal to the rest of the three groups put together.

The general tone of the negotiations angered many of those present, and caused great anxiety to the more genuine comrades. Wu Jixian and Ma Yufu, the representatives of the Proletarian Society, were the first to lose their enthusiasm, and they decided to waste no more time attending the meetings. It seemed like the beginning of the end for the negotiations. At first, we thought that Wu and Ma were simply impatient at the lack of progress being made, but I afterwards learned that internal problems within the Proletarian Society probably also influenced their decision to resign. Trotsky's letter of 8 January 1931 had in fact changed the relationship of forces between the different Trotskyist groups. Before it, the Chen group had neither prestige nor status, and the other three factions (in particular the Our Word group) all prided themselves on their orthodoxy. Time and time again, Chen and his friends expressed their readiness to engage in joint activities and even to put their forces into the existing organisation, but their advances were turned down out of hand, and they were subjected to a ferocious political battering. But it was not long before Trotsky read Chen's document, praised it, and stretched out his hand to the former leader of the CCP in comradeship, at the same time strongly urging the other Chinese Trotskyists to unite with him immediately. After this, the situation was reversed. The other three groups accepted Trotsky's advice with extreme reluctance and not a little embarrassment. Chen's Proletarian Society entered the negotiations as victors, turning the tables on the rest of us, pretending they were the only orthodox Trotskyists, and trying to give the impression that they were above our 'childish nonsense'. Needless to say, none of them dared to express their feelings openly, but they wore superior smiles and turned up their noses at others. They had no confidence in the negotiations, and it was with little enthusiasm that they sent their representatives along. After weeks of unceasing bickering, the prospect of unification receded further and further. Their delegates would have liked nothing better than to withdraw from the negotiating committee, and they began to display their arrogance and superiority more and more openly. Worst of all was Peng Shuzhi, who argued that it was pointless to continue talking about unification, and that the groups should go back to working by themselves; any other Oppositionists who were sincere about working for the Revolution could join the Proletarian Society. These proposals found some support among the veteran cadres, especially Wu Jixian and Ma Yufu, but many others in the Proletarian Society, in particular Zheng Chaolin and Yin Kuan, opposed them. The negotiations temporarily broke down, and whether or not the unification movement would continue depended largely on the attitude of Chen Duxiu.

One day in March, Chen Qichang, an old friend of mine from Beijing University and a member of the Chen Duxiu group, paid me a visit and told me that Chen Duxiu would like to see me for a talk at the home of Yin Kuan. This was the first time I had ever met Chen Duxiu, and although I was no longer as hostile to him as I had been several months earlier, I was still critical of him.

As soon as I set eyes on him, however, I gained a most favourable impression. This middle-aged man in his early fifties, with his sincere and unassuming ways, swept all remaining traces of factional prejudice from me. We talked all afternoon, allowing our conversation to follow its own course, but dwelling chiefly on my own personal history, from the time I was at Beijing University down to when I worked under Zhou Enlai in the organisation department. He asked many questions and said little himself, but once a subject captured his interest he would join in with relish. I was particularly impressed by his straightforwardness – there was not the slightest trace of ceremony or pretentiousness about him. But, for all his frankness, I saw no signs of his notorious hot temper. On the contrary, it seemed to me that he was extremely considerate and modest in his attitude towards others. Finally we got around to talking about the question of unification. He asked me my opinion, and I gave it to him without hesitation. I explained how I had at first been opposed to cooperating with his group, but had afterwards changed my mind and was now looking forward to unification. He seemed pleased, and said that in his view it was absolutely imperative for the Chinese Trotskyist movement to unify its forces, as otherwise there would be no future for any of the groups. He added that this applied equally to the Proletarian Society, since it was mostly made up of 'old men', and the tasks confronting the Opposition in China could only be carried out by young people. After we had finished our conversation, we left separately. It was dusk by now, and as I walked home I was filled with rare emotions. I felt as though a big change had come over me. I had got to know a great figure in the history of revolutionary thought in modern China. The enormous respect I developed for Chen Duxiu remains with me to this day.

The following morning, Chen Qichang came back to see me, and told me what Chen Duxiu's impressions of the conversation had been. I was pleased to hear that Chen Duxiu had told him that I was 'the complete opposite of Liang Ganqiao', whom he had invited over for a similar talk the previous day. This was hardly surprising, as Liang was to defect to the Guomindang only a few weeks later and take over as head of Chiang's secret police: how could comparison of a revolutionary with a man like that even be considered? Chen Qichang also told me that the Proletarian Society had decided to replace its representatives on the negotiating committee with Chen Duxiu and Yin Kuan, hoping in this way to speed up progress towards unification.

There was a dramatic change once Chen Duxiu arrived at the negotiations. The squabbling stopped, and the determination to achieve unity infected all those present. Differences on theoretical questions were now resolved without the interminable disputes which used to accompany them, and exaggeration and hair-splitting were frowned upon. It was decided that the documents should be rewritten. Chen Duxiu was to write the political platform and the agrarian programme. I was chosen to draw up some theses on the question of the constituent assembly; if I remember rightly, Liang Ganqiao was assigned to write the organisational resolution, and Yin Kuan a resolution on the workers' movement. The resolutions were written and submitted in record time, and, after a frank and good-natured discussion, they were quickly voted on and passed. As for the controversial question of the nature of the third Chinese revolution, Chen Duxiu's draft reverted to Trotsky's original formulation, arguing that it would result from the very outset in a decisive shake-up of private property in both town and country. The platform was unanimously accepted.

After the political preparations for unification had been completed, the only problem outstanding was the election of delegates for the forthcoming unification conference. A sub-committee consisting of Yin Kuan, Zhao Ji, Liang Ganqiao, and myself was set up to deal with this. The simplest thing would have been to allocate delegates proportionately, according to the strength of the various groups, but the difficulty was that Liang Ganqiao had exaggerated the size of his group. As for the other three groups, there had originally been eighty signatories to the collective platform of the Proletarian Society, but during the last few months they had gained some adherents both in Hong Kong and north China, which had boosted their membership to over a hundred. The October group had originally collected nineteen signatures in Shanghai alone for its platform, and afterwards it won over a dozen or so new supporters in addition to the fifty or so members of the Our Word group in north China who came over to them, making about eighty in all. The Militant group had at most thirty members, all of them in Shanghai. The Our Word group had a similar membership there. In Hong Kong, their organisation was stronger, consisting of some seventy or eighty comrades. But Liang Ganqiao was insisting that their total membership was over three hundred. We asked him to supply a membership list, but he refused on the grounds that this would be dangerous. When Yin Kuan proposed sending someone to make an on-the-spot investigation he replied that this was impossible, since the comrades were scattered throughout the East River area and Zhongshan county in Guangdong province. After several days of haggling, we at last succeeded in making a deal with him, agreeing to grant the Our Word group representation on the basis of 120 to 140 members. One delegate was allowed for every twenty members, so the Our Word group got six or seven. The Proletarian Society had five delegates, the Octobrists four, and the Militant group two.

The problems of finance and venue were left to the Proletarian Society. I afterwards learnt that the money was provided by Li Zhongsan, a friend of the famous Guomindang general Yang Hucheng, who pawned his fur-coat to raise it, while He Zishen rented a house for the conference in the Dairen Bay Road area of east Shanghai. None of us knew in advance the exact location of the house.

The various factions soon elected their representatives to the conference. Chen Duxiu, Zheng Chaolin, Jiang Changshi, Wu Jixian, and the veteran railway worker Wang Zhihuai or He Zishen were chosen to represent the Proletarian Society. The Our Word group was represented by Liang Ganqiao, Chen Yimou, Lou Guohua, who was unable to attend for other reasons and whose place was taken by Song Jingxiu, Zhang Jiu, a worker from Hong Kong, and two or three other Hong Kong comrades. The Octobrists decided to send Luo Han, who had just got out of jail in Beijing, and represented the north China comrades, Song Fengchun, Pu Dezhi, and myself. The Militant group sent Zhao Ji and Lai Yantang.

The Unification Conference of the Chinese Left Opposition was called for 1 May 1931 and met for three days. The first two days were taken up with discussion and amendment of the various documents submitted by the negotiating committee, and, on the third and final day, a new leadership was elected. Chen Duxiu inaugurated the conference and delivered a short political report. During the subsequent debate, the only issue which caused any real controversy was whether or not the national unification of China could be achieved under Chiang Kai-shek. No one argued that none of the democratic tasks could be achieved except under the dictatorship of the proletariat, and Chen Duxiu's report did not exclude the possibility of at least the appearance of national unification under the existing régime, even though he agreed with our fundamental postulate. Most of the delegates, myself included, opposed this formulation, and so Chen allowed it to be struck out from his political report when it came to voting. All the other documents were approved unanimously.

The Unification Conference put an end to the rivalry between the four factions, and the atmosphere afterwards was one of harmony, solidarity, and hope. It was as if all of those present in that small room saw a bright future for the Chinese Bolshevik-Leninists (as Trotskyists throughout the world continued to call themselves at that time) and were convinced they would play a decisive role in the coming Chinese revolution. The only exception to this general mood of unity was Liang Ganqiao, who was so narrow-mindedly factionalist in his attitude that the very idea of a unified movement was distasteful to him. After the documents had been voted on, elections followed. All the delegates ignored previous factional demarcations and cast their votes regardless of old factional ties. The following comrades were elected to the formal leadership body of the new unified organisation: Chen Duxiu, Luo Han, Song Fengchun, Chen Yimou, Zheng Chaolin, Zhao Ji, and myself. Others were elected as alternate members. (Whether Peng Shuzhi was elected as a full or alternate member I can no longer say with certainty.) The most striking feature of these results was that the 'heroes' of the aimless factional skirmishing of the last year or so, men like Liang Ganqiao, Liu Renjing, Liu Yin, and Ma Yufu, who had bent all their efforts towards securing themselves positions of dominance in the movement, failed without exception to gain election to the new leadership body. The fact that manoeuvres got them nowhere confirms my earlier statement that unification was a process of natural selection, a remorseless and unerring process of purification. Less than a month after the conference, Liang Ganqiao made his way to Nanjing to seek out Chiang Kai-shek, who had been head of the Huangpu Military Academy when Liang was trained there, and issued a statement declaring that 'communism is not in harmony with the Chinese natural character'. Liu Renjing lapsed into complete apathy. Liu Yin bided his time, waiting for the highest bidder to buy him out of the movement. Ma Yufu immediately defected to the Wusong-Shanghai garrison headquarters of the Guomindang to join their special agents.

Now that unification had been achieved, the Left Opposition of the Chinese Communist Party made great progress in several fields. The new Central Committee made Chen Duxiu General Secretary; Zheng Chaolin was put in charge of propaganda; Chen Yimou was given responsibility for organisational work; Luo Han was made secretary of the Central Committee; and I was put in charge of our theoretical organ. At the first plenary session of the Central Committee, Luo Han drafted a telegram to Trotsky joyfully announcing that the Chinese comrades had taken a step of great significance, and that the banner of the Chinese Bolshevik-Leninists would soon be fluttering from one end of China to the other. The tone of this message reflected our boundless confidence. At that time, the Guomindang were toying with a provisional constitution, and a struggle for democracy was beginning at all levels of society, just as Trotsky had forecast. We therefore decided to launch a nationwide campaign for a genuine constituent assembly.

Our unification also came at a very opportune moment from the point of view of the internal struggle in the CCP. But, before I go into that question in more detail, I want to take another look at the doings of our old friend Wang Ming, who had returned to China only a few months after us. By early 1930, he was back in Shanghai, together with the other members of the so-called 'Twenty-Eight Bolsheviks' (or 'Returned Students') faction. Among these twenty eight were He Zishu, Qin Bangxian (alias Bo Gu), Chen Changhao, Chen Weiming, and Sun Jiming. I was very familiar with all these men, most of whom (with the sole exception of He Zishu) were very shallow-minded. When they first got back they were treated just as we had been several months before, and despite the fact that Wang Ming was in favour with Stalin and had excellent relations with Xiang Zhongfa, then General Secretary of the CCP, he was assigned to a very lowly position in the propaganda department under Li Lisan. However, a man of his ambition was not going to settle for such a humble situation.

At that time, Li Lisan was still leader of the Party, having imitated Stalin's 'Third Period' line with his theory of a 'new revolutionary high tide', and achieved an initial success for the revolution 'in one or several provinces'. In Shanghai, he tried to occupy the streets by mounting adventurist demonstrations along the Nanjing Road; and, nationally, he aimed at occupying Changsha and even Wuhan with the help of the Hunan and Hubei Red Armies. As defeat followed defeat, many comrades came to question the Li Lisan (or rather the Stalin) line. By September 1930, after the failure of the Red Army's second attack on Changsha, the failure of Li Lisan's policy was plain for all to see. At the Third Plenary Session of the Sixth Central Committee in the same month, a group of CCP leaders headed by Qu Qiubai put an end to the Li Lisan era. By this time, of course, we Trotskyists had been expelled from the Party, so I have no clear idea of what role Wang Ming and his group played in the overthrow of Li Lisan. But, judging from the factional changes in the leadership of the CCP over the previous year or two, Qu Qiubai, who had been removed as General Secretary at the Sixth Congress in Moscow in 1928, was hardly in a position to carry out such a coup without backing from elsewhere.

It seems to me that Wang Ming must have played a role behind the scenes through his protégé, General Secretary Xiang Zhongfa, and with the help of both the Comintern representative in Shanghai and of Moscow. Less than four months later, at the Fourth Plenary Session of the Sixth Central Committee held in January 1931, Wang Ming and his supporters emerged from the wings, overthrew Qu Qiubai, just as Li Lisan had been overthrown shortly before, and, with the active support of Xiang Zhongfa and the connivance of Zhou Enlai, snatched the leadership for themselves. Wang Ming, 'hero' of the battle against the Trotskyists at Sun Yat-sen University in 1927, victor over the 'Jiangsu-Zhejiang Provincial Association' and the 'survivors' of the Moscow Branch of the CCP, the man who amalgamated KUTV into Sun Yat-sen University and unified the leadership of the Chinese students in the Soviet Union into his own hands – this same Wang Ming had now won his biggest battle, the battle for the leadership of the whole party. From start to finish, it had only taken him four years, during which time this ambitious nonentity, this total outsider to the Chinese Revolution, had manoeuvred his way into the Politburo of the CCP. It was an amazing record. But, for anyone at all familiar with the reality of Stalinism, the paradox is only too easy to explain. Wang Ming's rapid rise to power had less to do with natural ability, which played only a very minor role in the whole enterprise, than with the fact that his ambitions fitted in very well with Stalin's needs.

After his victories over Trotsky and Bukharin, Stalin immediately set about Stalinising all the other Communist Parties in the Third International. The first to fall were the supporters of the Left Opposition, soon followed by all genuine Communists with minds of their own. It was during this campaign that Stalin raised the slogan in the Comintern of 'Bolshevisation', but what he meant by 'Bolsheviks' were only the docile and spineless supporters of his own factional interests. The best example of such a 'Bolshevik' was Wang Ming himself. Of the early leaders of the CCP, Chen Duxiu was definitely not a 'Bolshevik' of this sort, and Qu Qiubai was far too fond of expressing his own opinion. Zhou Enlai came a little closer to the mark, but he had no direct relations with the Stalinists, and, in any case, was far too able for Stalin to trust. Xiang Zhongfa was certainly qualified in one way to receive the appellation, but he had absolutely no talent at all and as far as theory went he was illiterate. Mao Zedong, of course, was less qualified than any of these last three for such a title.

Stalin, and his immediate entourage including Mif, had long intended to cultivate a loyal agent among the Chinese students in Moscow. Wang Ming's nomination as Stalin's Chinese puppet emperor had already been decided on by late 1927 and his performance at the Fourth Plenum of the Sixth Central Committee was stage-managed by Stalin through Mif, then the Comintern-agent in Shanghai. It was about this time that Wang Ming wrote his pamphlet *The Struggle for Bolshevisation of the CCP*. In his pamphlet, Wang Ming launched an attack on Li Lisan's 'ultra-left line' and raised the new charge of 'conciliationism' against Qu Qiubai. The result was that both men were kicked out of the leadership and made to confess their 'mistakes'. Zhou Enlai, also, was ordered to make a self-examination. Li Lisan was sent to Moscow to 'study'. Qu Qiubai's fate was different. It was almost as if he had been expelled from the Party completely: he lived in Shanghai at the house of a non-party friend called Xie Danru and engaged in left-wing literary activities.

Despite the fact that Wang Ming and his friends had never been elected to the Central Committee, they manipulated it at will. They were co-opted straight onto the Politburo and given posts of high responsibility. The most authoritative Maoist document available, ('Resolution on Certain Questions in the History of our Party') had the following to say on the coup carried out by Wang Ming and his friends in the guise of 'Bolshevisation':

> This new 'left' line [was carried out] under Comrade Chen Shaoyu's [Wang Ming's] leadership.... Organisationally, the exponents of this new 'left' line violated discipline, refused the work assigned them by the Party, committed the error of joining with a number of other comrades in factional activities against the central leadership, wrongly called upon the party membership to set up a provisional leading body and demanded

that 'fighting cadres' who 'actively support and pursue' their 'Left' line should be used to 'reform and strengthen the leading bodies at all levels'; they thereby created a serious crisis in the Party. Hence, generally speaking, the new 'Left' line was more determined, more 'theoretical', more domineering and more fully articulated in its 'leftism' than the Li Lisan line, even though it did not call for organising insurrection in the key cities and, for a time, did not call for concentrating the Red Army to attack those cities.

In January 1931, the Fourth Plenary Session of the Sixth Central Committee of the Party was convened under circumstances in which pressure was being applied from all directions by the 'left' dogmatist and sectarian elements headed by Comrade Chen Shaoyu and in which some comrades in the central leading body who had committed empiricist errors were compromising with these elements and supporting them. The convening of this session played no positive or constructive role; the outcome was the acceptance of the new 'left' line, its triumph in the central leading body and the beginning of the domination of a 'left' line in the Party for the third time during the period of the Agrarian Revolutionary War.... Under this programme, the Fourth Plenary Session and the subsequent central leadership promoted the 'left' dogmatist and sectarian comrades to responsible positions in the central leading body on the one hand; on the other, they excessively attacked those comrades headed by Qu Qiubai who were alleged to have committed the 'error of the line of conciliation', and immediately after the session the Central Committee wrongly attacked the great majority of the so-called 'rightist' comrades.[1]

Although most of what is said about Wang Ming in the piece I have just quoted is true, the really important things are left unsaid. Since it deliberately avoids naming the main instigator of these crimes, dressing up a mere pickpocket as a big-time criminal, it cannot therefore draw the correct lessons from the historical events it attempts to describe. Wang Ming's coup was not the mistaken action of an isolated individual, but part of a more general process of Stalinisation which was affecting all sections of the Comintern. When Lenin and Trotsky were in power, the Comintern was the supreme organ of power in the world communist movement. The CPSU was simply a subordinate section of the International, to which it looked for leadership, as did the whole Soviet Union, the state which it had created and which it controlled. All fraternal

---

1 This resolution was omitted from later editions of Mao's *Selected Works* because of its favourable references to Liu Shaoqi, Qu Qiubai, and others.

parties enjoyed equal status within the Comintern. As headquarters of the world revolution, the Comintern was made up of the most authoritative and talented revolutionaries, who had won the respect of the masses in their own countries. If Lenin played a leading role in the International, this was due to his superior talents and his unique experience, not to his position as leader of the Soviet state. From time to time, certain leaders were expelled from the International because they fell short of the standards required of them, but this was only after proper discussion and consultation and with the aim of advancing rather than harming the interests of the revolution. Gradually, however, the Soviet Union began to degenerate and the theory of 'socialism in one country' became an official tenet of the CPSU. The first thing that happened was that a change came about in the relationship between the CPSU and the Comintern, which, from being a headquarters of the world revolution, changed into an arm of Soviet diplomacy. At the same time, the trend towards degeneration which was becoming more and more apparent in the CPSU was paralleled in the Comintern and in the parties affiliated to it. But the Soviet bureaucrats could only really control the Comintern if the leaders of the various foreign sections submitted completely to their will. The old generation of Communists, who had inherited a revolutionary-socialist tradition going back for almost a century and who had been tempered in the struggles of the immediate postwar period, were hardly likely to change into yes-men overnight. The subjugation of the foreign parties required a long process of so-called 'Bolshevisation'. Stalin spared no effort to achieve this aim, working at it for months and even years, and not hesitating wherever necessary to sabotage any revolutions not under his immediate control. At the same time, he murdered countless thousands of foreign revolutionaries, either in the prison camps of Siberia or in the Lubianka Jail in Moscow (where, for example, the entire central committee of the Polish Communist Party were imprisoned), so that, by the early 1930s, Communist parties throughout the world were dominated exclusively by 'Bolsheviks' of the Wang Ming type.

I am not suggesting that Mao himself was unaware of who Wang Ming's patrons were, or of the true implications of the 'Bolshevisation' campaign. There were two main reasons why Mao put all the blame on Wang Ming: first, he was at the time of writing anxious not to impair Sino-Soviet friendship; and second, Mao Zedong was himself a Stalinist – ideologically, if not in terms of faction.

The Unification Conference of the Chinese Trotskyist movement took place three months after the CCP's Fourth Plenary Session. The CCP was still reeling from the after-effects of Wang Ming's coup. The tragic fate of the so-called 'conciliationist' or 'rightist' faction particularly saddened the middle and lower cadres of the Party. I will briefly explain what happened. Luo Zhanglong, He Mengxiong, Lin Yunan, Li Qiushi, and the group of Communists under them were all veteran cadres of the Party, most of them members of the Provincial Committee of Jiangsu province and some of them longstanding activists in the trade union movement. These men were outstanding professional revolutionaries and pillars of the workers' movement, down-to-earth, hard-working, and indissolubly linked to the proletariat. Even though none was an outstanding theoretician or could match Wang Ming in his manipulation of quotations from the 'classics', the fact that they lived like true revolutionaries and shared the day-to-day fate of the working class meant that they had a genuine feeling for the movement and were receptive to the smallest change in its mood. This was completely unlike the members of the Central Committee of the Party, who took as their starting point the telegrams and resolutions they received from Moscow. As early as 1928, when Stalin sent his 'prodigy' Lominadze to China to direct Qu Qiubai in a new putschist wave, the 'conciliationists' had voiced a number of correct and sharply worded criticisms. Their resolution of May of that year was quoted at length by Trotsky in his article 'The Chinese Question after the Sixth Congress', where he called it 'a remarkable document on the policy and the régime of the Communist International'. Independently, and on the basis of their own experience, the 'conciliationists' of the Jiangsu Provincial Committee had reached similar conclusions to those the Left Opposition had deduced from its broad theoretical analysis.

After the CCP Sixth Congress, some of these individuals became more interested in Trotskyist ideas, but their empiricism, or else their lack of courage, prevented them from breaking altogether with Stalinism. When the Stalinists came out with their 'Third Period' theory immediately after the Sixth Congress – a theory which in China was embodied in the 'Li Lisan Line' – they once again began to express deep dissatisfaction, and when the Li Lisan Line came under fire at the Third Plenum, the Jiangsu Committee supported Qu Qiubai. Afterwards, when Wang Ming began a more thoroughgoing purge of Li Lisan and his handful of supporters and moved to topple Qu Qiubai, they gave Wang their tacit support. But, as soon as Wang Ming and his friends took over the leadership, their even more absurdly 'leftist' line and domineering ways alienated their Jiangsu supporters. Wang Ming therefore counter-attacked, relying on Comintern support and his newly acquired position in the CCP leadership to launch a ferocious onslaught on the 'conciliationists', or 'rightists'. All the odds were on Wang Ming's side. But the 'rightists' showed considerable mettle, and refused to surrender. Even though they realised their cause was hopeless, they fought back heroically, and were even prepared at one point to organise a new Communist party as a vehicle for their ideas. But, before they could realise their plans, tragedy struck. While all the main leaders of the Jiangsu group were attending a meeting in the Eastern Hotel just behind the Sincere Department Store in Shanghai, they were surprised by agents from the Wusong-Shanghai Garrison Headquarters and arrested. Despite attempts to bribe and intimidate them, not one capitulated to the Guomindang, and they were all taken out and shot. Among the twenty-five martyrs were He Mengxiong, Lin Yunan, Li Qiushi, my old friend Zhao Pingfu, and Yun Yutang, who had come back from Moscow with me. The novelist Hu Yepin, husband of the writer Ding Ling, was also among the martyrs.

The death of these comrades caused grief and anger in the Party's ranks. There were rumours that Wang Ming was responsible for this incident, and had informed the police of their whereabouts as a way of getting rid of them. Such treachery was the normal practice of the Stalin/Wang Ming school, but there is no proof that it actually happened. It is undeniable, however, that their martyrdom was linked at least indirectly to the inner-party struggle, and that it had a demoralising and depressing effect on the party rank and file. Despite the crisis, Wang Ming and his friends did not let up for a moment in their campaign to seize control of the Chinese Party, ruthlessly persecuting, dismissing, and even expelling all those old cadres who proved 'uncooperative' or who fell foul of them in any way.

The Chinese Oppositionists presented a complete contrast to this picture of disarray. After May Day, 1931, we were united in one organisation, and led by the founder of the Chinese Communist movement, Chen Duxiu. The main reason why we did not make our influence felt more was that Chiang Kai-shek, with the help of the traitor Ma Yufu, unexpectedly came to Wang Ming's aid. Our newly elected leaders had been at their posts scarcely a month when almost all of them were arrested during a police raid on the night of 21 May, after Ma Yufu had tipped off the Guomindang. Apart from Chen Duxiu and Luo Han, the entire Standing Committee of the organisation was arrested, including Zheng Chaolin and his wife Wu Jingzhen [Wu Jingru], He Zishen and his wife Zhang Yisen, Song Fengchun, Chen Yimou, Lou Guohua, Jiang Shangshi, Pu Dezhi, Wang Zhihuai, and me. This crushing blow brought the activities of the newly unified Opposition to a temporary standstill. As for me, I was about to enter a new chapter in my life – a chapter mainly made up of long periods of imprisonment. But, before I go on to describe those experiences, I would like to say a few things about the literary activities of the Oppositionists, which is how many of us earned our living during that period.

In the history of revolutionary movements, revolutionary ideologies have generally tended to precede the actual implementation of revolution. China in the 1920s was an apparent exception to this rule. It is true that the May Thirtieth

Movement of 1925 was a natural development of the May Fourth Movement of 1919, and represented a transformation from bourgeois-democratic ideology to socialist consciousness – a transformation clearly embodied both in the person of Chen Duxiu, the most important ideologist of the period, and in the *New Youth* magazine he edited. In this sense, the Second Chinese Revolution, which started up at roughly the same time as the May Thirtieth movement, could be said to have been preceded by an ideological upsurge. But, in fact, the pace of events during the Chinese Revolution rapidly outstripped the range of previous revolutionary thinking.

After the end of the European War in 1918, and especially as a result of the October Revolution of 1917, socialist thinking found its way to China. It became the 'most fashionable decoration on the soul' of China's intellectuals. All sorts of Western ideologies were seized upon, some going back a hundred years or more, so long as they bore the label 'socialist'. It mattered little whether they were scientific, utopian, revolutionary, reformist, or even reactionary. So long as they fulfilled this minimum condition, they were translated into Chinese, published in all sorts of magazines, chatted about in bourgeois drawing-rooms, and even lectured on in the academies by young men anxious to make a name for themselves as progressives or simply to make money. As soon as they had been published and politely chatted about, they were immediately forgotten, and our 'socialist' heroes would go off to rejoin their warlord friends; or even, like Jiang Kanghu, the founder of the Chinese Social-Democratic Party, to visit the former Emperor in the Forbidden City.

Of course, not all intellectuals with socialist leanings were like this. The group around Chen Duxiu and Li Dazhao quickly opted for scientific socialism in its most modern form – Bolshevism. They set up the Chinese Communist Party, and began to establish contacts with China's newly emerging social force, the proletariat. But, because the Chinese Revolution developed so quickly, the first generation of socialist revolutionaries had no conception of how to lead the class struggle; in fact they could not even recognise the struggle when they came face to face with it. In Russia, the complete opposite had been the case. There, revolutionary intellectuals had investigated and thoroughly discussed all the fundamental problems of the Revolution some ten or twenty years before its actual outbreak. They already had both a strategic and a tactical programme, and a fighting organisation unifying all the most determined revolutionaries in its ranks, so that, when the Revolution actually arrived, it developed almost as if according to plan for Lenin, Trotsky and others, although not without the most bitter struggles. In China, things turned out differently. During the revolutionary years 1925 to 1927, most of the leaders of the CCP had only the sketchiest understanding of theory, culled from largely undigested foreign sources, and were incapable of adapting it to Chinese realities. The result was that Moscow did their thinking for them. As an internationalist, I consider that it is entirely permissible for national revolutions to receive direction from a world revolutionary headquarters. But, unfortunately, those doing the thinking were no longer Lenin and Trotsky, who had brought the revolution to fruition, but Stalin, who had betrayed it. Although Trotsky and his fellow-thinkers had a strategy which could have led the Chinese Revolution to victory, their views were suppressed by the Stalinists, who advanced what amounted to a Menshevik line for China. None of the leaders of the CCP was capable of distinguishing between these two positions and carried out this line more or less blindly, with the inevitable tragic results.

Wielding the big hammer of counter-revolution, Chiang Kai-shek broke and bloodied a great many revolutionary heads, but, at the same time, awakened many of those who were lucky enough to survive the bloodbath to the need for theory. During the darkest days of the defeat, many revolutionaries became profoundly aware that in the past they had acted blindly. Because of their lack of theoretical understanding, they had been forced to drift wherever the wind took them, like boats without rudders. It is a tragic fact that the Chinese socialists only went out in search of socialist theory after the defeat of the Revolution. But the socialist-cultural movement which started in Shanghai in 1929 was nevertheless of great historical significance, and the important role played in it by the Chinese Trotskyists is also worthy of note. It was not a movement consciously set in motion by any individual or group, but a reflex reaction by hundreds of revolutionaries to the defeat. Moreover, as a result of the defeat, many revolutionary intellectuals had been forced back to their studies, thus giving an added impetus to the cultural movement.

After 1929, small publishing houses sprang up everywhere in Shanghai, which had long been the main publishing centre of the country. All specialised in social-science publications. The men who provided the capital for these publishers came from many different walks of life: former bureaucrats and military men outnumbered ordinary merchants. These people had for one reason or another fallen out of favour with Chiang Kai-shek, and therefore come to form a sort of opposition to the Nanjing Government. During their enforced idleness many entrusted a small part of their accumulated wealth to friends or acquaintances to set up 'cultural enterprises'. Their real aim was to build a reputation for themselves on which they could capitalise during any future attempt at a political comeback. The friends and acquaintances to whom they entrusted their money were for the most part former subordinates – men who could deal only in bureaucratic niceties and were ignorant of the new cultural movement. These latter therefore sought out the help of people with some experience of the publishing world to do their editing and writing for them. Naturally, the majority of such people were intellectuals who had emerged from the revolutionary movement.

The largest of the new publishing houses was the Shenzhou Guoguang Company. The funds for it were put up by General Chen Mingshu, leader of the famous Nineteenth Route Army which, in 1932, waged a heroic resistance against the Japanese around Shanghai. Actual responsibility for the day-to-day running of the company was in the hands of Wang Lixi. I am not sure what Wang's background was, but he liked to think of himself as a classical poet. He knew nothing about publishing and the social sciences, but he was an honest enough man, and because he knew very little about politics he had few preconceptions. As long as you were a 'left-wing personality' or could trot out a few social-science terms he would immediately snatch you up to work for his firm. He liked to think of himself as a second Cai Yuanpei (the liberal Chancellor of Beijing University during and after the May Fourth Movement), and employed writers from right across the political spectrum, including the pro-Guomindang rightist Tao Xisheng, members of the Stalinist faction, and even Trotskyists. During the early part of 1930, his links with the Left Opposition were particularly close, and Liu Renjing, Li Ji, Wang Duqing, Peng Shuzhi, Du Weizhi, Peng Guiqiu, and Wu Jixian were among those who worked for him. Through Liu Renjing, I received a commission from Wang Lixi to edit and translate material for an illustrated history of the Russian Revolution. I was paid by the month at a rate of three dollars per thousand Chinese characters, which worked out on average at some sixty dollars a month, more than twice what my monthly party allowance had been. The history was based on Comintern produced material and John Reed's *Ten Days that Shook the World*. After it was completed, Wang Lixi sent the manuscript to the propaganda department of the Guomindang Central Committee in Nanjing for submission to the censors, where, unfortunately, it was confiscated. Up until my arrest in May 1931 this was my sole source of income.

All the other leading Oppositionists with any literary talent also earned their living by writing or translating social-science books. We were expected not only to keep ourselves and our families, but also to provide the necessary funds for the running of the organisation and for feeding and clothing those who worked full-time for it. No wonder, therefore, that the Opposition was renowned for its poverty. Nevertheless, our 'rice-bowl' literary activities during that period played no small part in popularising and deepening socialist thinking in China. Apart from the Shenzhou Guoguang company, the Hubin, 'New Universe', Qunqiu, and 'Oriental' publishing houses had links with the Oppositionists. (The Oriental Book Company had a special relationship with the Left Opposition, which I will return to later.) We also made use of other publishing houses, such as the 'New Life' company, run by Tao Xisheng and Fan Zhongyun. Our literary activities were not organised according to any plan, but separately decided on in discussions with the publishers themselves. However, we managed to bring out a varied collection of Marxist classics, including works by Marx, Engels, and Lenin. Trotsky's *My Life* was published simultaneously in no less than three different translations, all by Oppositionists. (This was before unification, of course.) We also translated many histories of the European revolutionary movement, including works by Kropotkin, Trotsky, and others. During the same period the Proletarian Society brought out an influential periodical called *Dongli* ('Motive Force'), which popularised Trotskyism and more general social science.

The CCP in Shanghai launched their own left-wing cultural movement, but they lagged a long way behind us in their publishing. Most of the officials of the CCP sponsored movement were men of letters, and their main focus was therefore 'proletarian literature'. They achieved nothing of note, just like similar 'proletarian literature' movements elsewhere in the world, and it was not until after 1933, when Qu Qiubai joined them, that their cultural movement began to show any real sign of life. By that time, however, all the main Trotskyist writers were in jail, and those claiming to represent Trotskyism in the famous debate on the nature of Chinese society in the pages of *Dushu zazhi* ('Study Magazine') were either pseudo-Trotskyists or former members of the movement.

PART 6

Chinese Trotskyism in the 1930s and the 1940s

∴

The Founding of *Struggle* and the Darkest Days of My Life

Wang Fanxi

Source: *Memoirs of a Chinese Revolutionary* (1957).

The Provisional Central Committee formed in late 1935 occupied an important position in the history of the Chinese Trotskyist movement. It was the most enduring and productive of all the bodies we established, reviving and expanding the organisation, both in Shanghai and nationally. We began publishing a series of writings by international Oppositionists, and even more important, we started bringing out a monthly political organ called *Douzheng* ('Struggle') and a theoretical organ called *Huohua* ('Spark'). Between spring 1936 and late 1942 these two periodicals were published almost without interruption.

The first task of the new leading body was to set up its own printshop. When Harold Isaacs left Shanghai for Beijing, he had handed over a small printing press to the organisation, but it had been sold to cover running expenses when Si Chaosheng and his three young comrades took over the leadership in 1934. We were not in a position to buy a new press, so some comrades who were printing workers rigged up a primitive wooden frame in which we inserted lead-type: the latter was in fact our sole outlay. With this contraption, we could turn out a reasonable-looking page of print in two colours. Our publications were so good, in fact, that Lu Xun accused us of receiving 'dirty money', implying we were financed by the Japanese. At first, our print-shop was looked after by two comrades who were printing workers, but when one defected he tried to steal the printing press from us. We therefore staged a raid. Li Furen, the foreign comrade, dressed up as an Inspector of the International Settlement police, and with two other Chinese comrades disguised as detectives burst into the defector's home and retrieved the press. For a long time after that, Comrades Lin Huanhua and Mao Hongjian were in charge of printing.

The second task of the new leading body was to put the organisation in order. In the Shanghai area we still had many contacts, and once the organisation was on its feet again it was a relatively easy matter to start up activities. We then began to turn our attention to Hong Kong, which had been one of the Opposition's earliest bases. Many workers there had been part of the organisation, but, over the years, most had lost contact with the centre, as a result of the repeated arrests of leading members in Shanghai and elsewhere. So, in May 1936, it was decided that I should go south to re-establish contact with them. I stayed a month in the colony, and worked with Comrade Luo, a former member of the Proletarian Society, and Comrade Chen Zhongxi, who later died at the head of a Trotskyist guerrilla unit during the War of Resistance against Japan. We reunited a dozen or so cadres, set up a local organisation and, following the example of Shanghai, built a primitive printing press with which we began to publish a paper called *Huoxing* ('Sparkle'). Earlier, after we had lost contact with Hong Kong, certain comrades there had ill-advisedly got mixed up with Zhang Bojun's Third Party. It was my first job therefore to draw the line clearly between ourselves and them and put an end to the attempts of some comrades to straddle the two parties. Reviving the tradition of the two Trotskyist martyrs, Ou Fang and Chen Yimou, the comrades immediately turned their efforts towards the industrial proletariat. Li Furen, who had gone with me to Hong Kong, made use of his special status as a foreigner to bring our south China friends large quantities of Oppositionist literature. It was the first time for many years that they had had a chance to read publications of this sort.

At the same time, our organisation was unexpectedly reinforced by an influx of young comrades in Guangxi, a province in which our leadership had never made any special efforts. Zhang Te, who, as I mentioned, abandoned Trotskyism after the unification of the four groups in 1931, had returned to Guangxi, where Huang Gongdu, a powerful associate of the leading local warlords, cultivated him. Although Huang had studied in Moscow, he had never had any links with the Opposition, and, as far as I know, did not even join the Communist Party, but, despite this, he made Zhang Te his confidant after his return to Guangxi. When the Guangxi warlords came out in open opposition to Chiang Kai-shek, putting on a left 'face' for the occasion, many Communists who had either left the Party or kept up their membership secretly were summoned to Guangxi to rally support for the local authorities. At the same time, a power struggle was going on inside the Guangxi clique between Huang Gongdu's group and another faction within the local bureaucracy. To strengthen his hand, Huang Gongdu managed to summon a number of ex-Trotskyists to Guangxi with the help of Zhang Te. None of those who accepted Zhang Te's invitation was still a member of the Opposition at that time. Most were assigned to work as teachers at Guangxi middle schools or universities, and among them was Shi Tang. Shi Tang had earlier left the movement but, as the saying has it, 'even when the lotus root breaks the fibres hold together'. In his contacts with students, he continued to propagate his old beliefs, and, as a result, won many over to

Trotskyism. By the time that we had set up the Provisional Central Committee, the Guangxi group had already established direct links with us in Shanghai, and before long they sent representatives to Shanghai for discussions. The two comrades mentioned above, Lin Huanhua and Mao Hongjian, were among the members of the delegation, and as I recall, the third member was a comrade called Mo Junqi.

There was no organisation of ours functioning in north China at this time. When the four factions had unified in 1931, the former Octobrist and Proletarian groups had been quite strong in north China, especially in Beijing. I had heard while in prison that, after the arrest of Chen Duxiu and others, big campaigns to free Chen had been launched in Beijing. In many universities, students supporting Chen and Stalinist students who opposed him had demonstrated in equal strength at a number of rallies. But, around 1934, after Si Chaosheng and others went south to Shanghai and Liu Renjing was arrested and thrown in jail, the activities of the organisation in Beijing had come to a halt. In Shandong, a group of comrades kept up political work and succeeded in building a base in many counties of the region. After the establishment of the Provisional Central Committee – I think it was in the summer of 1936 – they sent a delegation to Shanghai to re-establish links with the centre. Among the delegates was Comrade L., one of the few comrades who has survived and remained loyal to the cause to this day.

Trotskyist activities in Wenzhou, the ancient city in southeast Zhejiang province, were still only in their infancy during this period. The comrades there did not establish contact with us until sometime later. Events in the Wenzhou area had taken a similar course to those in Guangxi, and it was almost as if a group of young Trotskyists had sprung up spontaneously from nowhere. The seeds of Trotskyism had in fact been planted in Wenzhou by a man called Zeng Meng, who like Shi Tang in Guangxi, had earlier left the movement. Zeng Meng had become a Trotskyist while in Moscow and had been arrested together with Chen Duxiu and the others, but he had soon been released when his family used contacts he had made during his days at the Huangpu Military Academy. Before leaving jail, he was made to sign a document denouncing Trotskyism, and naturally took steps to avoid meeting us; he returned instead to Wenzhou, his home-town, where he lived like a recluse. Eventually, he joined up with a group of young people, and explained the ideas of Trotskyism to them. Although he did not mean to spread propaganda on our behalf, many Wenzhou Middle School students came over to our side as a result of their contact with him. Together with Zhongshan county in Guangdong province, Guangxi, and Shandong, Wenzhou was later to become one of the four main areas from which the Chinese Trotskyist movement recruited its second and third generations of cadres.

Although it is not uncommon in the history of revolutionary parties for people to leave the organisation, either voluntarily or under pressure, to protect themselves and their families, they often secretly or unconsciously despise themselves for abandoning the cause. As reactionary political governments grow more and more corrupt, incompetent, and unpopular, such people's schizophrenia deepens. No matter how rich or successful the renegades become in their new professions, many find it impossible to shake off their earlier convictions. They often continue to sympathise with the aims of the revolution, maintain old friendships and, under certain conditions, even appear to make partial amends for their past weakness by making new recruits to the movement, as did Shi Tang and Zeng Meng. When the revolution once again enters a period of upsurge and the revolutionary party grows in influence, people of this sort more often than not return to the ranks and resume the struggle. It is true, of course, that careerism and human weakness can also play a part in this, and that such 'conversions' can be an important factor in speeding up the degeneration of the revolution. But the phenomenon of the return of the 'revolutionary prodigals' has its roots in the depths of society and human nature, and if the party is to be built there is, generally, nothing for it but to accept such people at face value.

When the leaders of the newly unified Chinese Opposition were rounded up, those members of the four organisations who had not by then been brought into the new structure often drifted off and lost all contact. Many were worthless, but some of these comrades were schizophrenics of the sort I have just mentioned. We were often approached by young people who had found their way to Trotskyism by involved and circuitous routes, and when we asked who had first introduced them to Trotskyist ideas they would mention some name we only vaguely remembered from the distant past, or, in some cases, had never heard before.

By the time our organisation had reunited, Hitler had already been in power for over a year, and Germany was advancing towards militarism, thus hastening the outbreak of the Second World war. The Japanese imperialists had already invaded Manchuria and parts of the Yellow River valley, and central China was clearly their next target.

Stalin responded to the military threats from Germany and Japan by raising the 'popular front' slogan at the Seventh Congress of the Comintern in August 1935. Now he was willing to collaborate not only with the Social Democrats, whom only yesterday he had derided as 'social fascists', but with all kinds of democrats, including 'democratic' imperialists, in the name of anti-fascism.

Meanwhile, at home, he was stepping up his persecution of revolutionaries and had begun to carry out his policy of killing off the entire generation of old Bolsheviks.

The Guomindang government, still pursuing its policy of 'internal pacification before resistance to the invader', made repeated concessions to the Japanese imperialists in order to concentrate all its forces against the Communist armies in Jiangxi province. In late 1934, it scored a decisive military victory, forcing the Red Army to set out on its famous Long March to the north.

In January 1935, at a meeting of the CCP Central Committee's Politburo at Zunyi in Guizhou province, during the Long March, Mao Zedong took over from Wang Ming as the real leader of the Party. This represented a victory of 'indigenous' Communists over Stalin's representatives in China. On 1 August of the same year, in line with Moscow's new 'popular front' policy, the CCP issued a manifesto calling for an end to the Civil War and unity with the Guomindang against Japan, an abandonment of the class struggle, and the drawing up of a programme for resistance. In October, the Communist armies established a new base in north Shaanxi province.

It was in this political climate that *Struggle* was born. Since I have lost all my records, I have no way of checking exactly when the first issue came out, but it was some time in the spring of 1936. The first article – which I wrote – was an open letter to the CCP, attacking the Party's new 'popular front' line.

The publication of *Struggle* fulfilled a very urgent political need, and could not have come at a better time. Both at home and abroad, a period of rapid change had begun. With each turn of events, people were becoming more and more confused. Everyone was keen to understand the situation and eager to get involved in some practical political activity. In a limited way, *Struggle* was the answer some of them were looking for. As far as we Trotskyists were concerned, this period had a special significance, since it confirmed in every detail the analysis of the future path of the Chinese Revolution which Trotsky had made in 1929. For the previous four or five years, the Stalinists had been calling us the 'Trotsky-Chen liquidationist faction'. We had argued that there was no longer even a revolutionary situation after the autumn of 1927, let alone the actual conditions for a revolutionary uprising; that the most one could hope for was a struggle along democratic or national lines; and that the Chinese proletariat and its party should put forward a revolutionary-democratic programme calling for an all-powerful constituent assembly, so that they could then lead such democratic struggles and prepare the way for a new socialist revolution. The Stalinists were fundamentally opposed to this approach, and for five long years had carried out their so-called 'leftist' line on the mistaken premise that a 'new high tide of revolution was imminent', so that, in the towns, the CCP organisation was completely smashed, and, in the countryside, their armed forces were on the brink of annihilation,

Meanwhile, as a result of continuous Japanese aggression against China and the creeping capitulation to it of the Guomindang, an upsurge of anti-Japanese and anti-Guomindang feeling was taking place in the cities, particularly among the petty bourgeoisie. This nationalist awakening was exploited by bourgeois politicians active in the National Salvation Association, a patriotic body formed in 1935, and by other organisations. Such developments were a complete vindication of what we in the Chinese Trotskyist movement had been arguing for years, and pointed clearly to the need for a revolutionary-democratic programme along the lines we had been proposing. But, when Stalin announced his change of policy, members of the CCP were transformed overnight from out and out 'leftists' into out and out rightists. For years, they had constantly misrepresented and caricatured our democratic programme, but, suddenly, they took up positions identical with all the worst features of the caricatures they had made of us. For years, they had been accusing us of 'liquidationism', and now they themselves were pursuing an active liquidationist line, disguised as a struggle for democracy. Only yesterday they had condemned any call for a constituent assembly as treason to the revolution. Now, they not only demanded a constituent assembly (devoid, of course, of any revolutionary content), but were even prepared to drop the class struggle, reorganise the Red Army, and swear allegiance to Sun Yat-sen's Three People's Principles (nationalism, livelihood, and democracy), all in order to get the Guomindang to join in a popular front with them. The change was so dramatic and so sudden that not only people outside the Party but even party members themselves were left dazed. Mao Zedong himself was taken aback. In *Thirty Years of the Chinese Communist Party* the orthodox-Maoist historian Hu Qiaomu described these events as follows:

> At that time there was a pressing need to make a correct analysis of the situation in the country following on the Japanese invasion, to decide on party policy and to rectify the prevailing current of 'left' closed-door sectarianism in the Party. The Party's Central Committee had proved incapable of completing these tasks during the years 1931 to 1934, and Comrade Mao Zedong was also unable to complete them in the course of the Long March of 1935. It was only with the help of the Comintern's correct policy of the anti-fascist united front that this need could be met.[1]

---

1 *Thirty Years of the Chinese Communist Party*, first published in Beijing, June 1951, and reprinted by the People's Publishers, Guangzhou, July 1951.

From this extremely guarded passage it is possible to discern that it was not Mao who 'completed' the new liquidationist policy towards the Guomindang, but the Comintern (that is, Stalin), and that the new line in China simply followed the one adopted by Communist Parties throughout the world.

We were the only group capable of expressing a critical view of the party line – in the pages of our organ *Struggle*. The tragedy was that our equipment was primitive and our 'productive forces' undeveloped, so the best we could bring out was a four-page monthly with a run of 200 copies. But, because *Struggle* appeared regularly over a period of years, it steadily grew in influence.

I would now like to recount an episode connected with the new turn taken by the CCP: the correspondence between Chen Qichang and Lu Xun on the question of the anti-Japanese united front. At the time, there were two different attitudes to the CCP's new turn among left-wing writers and intellectuals in Shanghai. Although I never had the chance to read all the relevant material on this debate, in essence it revolved around the problem of whether literature should encourage struggle or collaboration between classes. The main proponent of class struggle was Lu Xun, who was rather more insistent on the original position of the League of Left-Wing Writers.[2] The main advocates of class collaboration were Xu Maoyong and Zhou Qiying (better known as Zhou Yang), who unconditionally supported the CCP's new line on literature. Seen in its broader context, this struggle was simply a manifestation of the transition in Stalinist thinking from the 'Third Period' phase to the Popular Front. Lu Xun was unhappy with the new slogan of 'a literature of national defence' proposed by Xu Maoyong and Zhou Yang, and proposed instead the slogan 'a literature of the masses for revolutionary war'. In our view, the old 'Third Period' philosophy and the new 'Popular Front' line were equally disastrous, but we admired Lu Xun as a great writer who had sympathised all along with the struggle of the oppressed and downtrodden, and who had never capitulated to nationalism in any of its forms. Although never a Marxist, he had advocated 'proletarian literature' for many years and fought fiercely against both the Guomindang hack-writers and the advocates of a 'Third Line',[3] so it was not surprising that he bitterly resented the sudden change of front. When we heard about the dispute, Chen Qichang became very excited and wrote Lu Xun a letter, enclosing some back issues of *Struggle* and some Chinese translations of pamphlets

---

2 The League of Left-Wing Writers was inaugurated in March 1930 in Shanghai, and consisted of most of the pro-Communist writers of that time, including Lu Xun.

3 These were a group of writers in the mid-1930s in Shanghai, mainly represented by the magazine *Xiandai* ('Contemporary Magazine'). They rejected both Guomindang nationalism and 'proletarian literature'. Their leader was the poet Dai Wangshu.

by Trotsky. These were sent to the Uchiyama Book Company in Shanghai, a shop Lu Xun frequented. Lu Xun's reply was first published in the magazine *Xianshi* ('Reality'). The gist of his letter was that he was amazed to see how well *Struggle* was produced, and suspected that it was financed by the Japanese.

I was in Hong Kong when Chen Qichang wrote his letter.

Since he had not discussed its contents with any of the other members before sending it, he came in for heavy criticism from the rest of us. Chen Duxiu in particular, who was still in Nanjing jail at the time, flew into a rage when he heard the news, and demanded to know how we came to have illusions about Lu Xun. In his opinion, the relationship between Lu Xun and the Communist Party was the same as that between Wu Zhihui and the Guomindang: both of them were flattered by the attentions paid to them, eager to show their gratitude, and totally incapable of pursuing the truth for its own sake, without regard for the consequences. Chen Qichang, who idolised Lu Xun, felt very bitter when he read his reply, not so much because of the slanderous assertions it made against him personally, as because of the discovery that even a man of 'unbending morality' could end up parroting the party line and stooping to the sort of tactics he had hitherto despised, by hinting that we took Japanese money. Chen Qichang wrote another letter to Lu Xun, but received no reply. Shortly after this Lu Xun died, and, six years later, Chen Qichang was murdered by the Japanese in Shanghai. At the time, I also thought that Chen Qichang had acted rather rashly in writing the letter, but, since the correspondence was included in Lu Xun's *Collected Works* and readers can decide for themselves who was right, perhaps it was not such a bad thing to have done after all.

In their struggle against Trotskyism, the Chinese Stalinists never once met us on the theoretical plane, but jailed or executed our supporters in the areas they controlled; and, in areas they did not control, spread rumours and slanders about us, in particular the accusation that we took money from the enemy. To put the record straight, I will outline our financial situation when we were publishing *Struggle*. Our expenses totalled just over fifty dollars a month: thirteen for the rent of our print-shop in a small detached house in the French Concession in Shanghai; thirty to support the two printer comrades; and about ten for items such as newsprint and ink. We had no other expenses, since all our cadres were expected not only to earn their own living but also to give ten per cent of what they earned in party dues. Those of us in the leadership who earned our living through literary activities of one sort or another were often very poorly paid, and our meagre dues came nowhere near meeting organisational costs. Our expenses were therefore almost always met by the foreign comrade, Li Furen. Where did Li Furen get his money from? Was his money dirty? When he first came to Shanghai, Li Furen had been a reporter on the

Shanghai Evening Post and then on the *Shanghai Times*. During his last three years in Shanghai, he was the assistant editor of the *China Weekly Review*, with a monthly salary of some three hundred dollars. It was as a communist and a member of our organisation that Li Furen helped to finance our activities in China.

In August 1936, Moscow staged the notorious trial of the so-called 'anti-Soviet Trotsky centre'. Sixteen members of the Bolshevik Old Guard, headed by Lenin's comrade-in-arms Zinoviev and the top party theoretician Kamenev, were accused of organising a 'conspiracy to overthrow the Soviet government in order to restore capitalism in Russia', in collusion with Trotsky, then living abroad in Norway. If the charges were absurd, even more absurd was the way in which these old revolutionaries stepped forward one after another to plead guilty. As a result, all were sentenced to be shot. Apart from the religious Inquisition of the Middle Ages, the world had never seen such a spectacle. What was happening in Moscow, and how could it be accounted for? People all over the world were shocked at the news of the trials, and questions such as these plagued friends and foes alike of the Soviet Union. It was only natural, therefore, that *Struggle* should devote itself more and more to coverage of this issue. With what little knowledge of the situation we had, we advanced various explanations of the tragedy then unfolding in Moscow, and translated and published all that Trotsky himself wrote on the subject.

At this point, I want to introduce Wang Mengzou, owner of the Oriental Book Company, into my story. Wang Mengzou was a most remarkable man. His book company was in existence for over fifty years, from the late 1890s to 1952, but he was much too far ahead of his time to make any money. If a new ideological current was being persecuted and the authors associated with it could not find a publisher, then he would publish them. But, by the time such ideas had become the vogue, he would already have moved on, so the books which yesterday nobody had wanted to buy but which today were best sellers made fortunes not for him but for other companies. In the meantime, Wang Mengzou would be busy publishing some new item of avant-garde literature. Time passed and there were many changes, but Wang Mengzou's way of life stayed much the same, with the result that he always found himself in the company of the persecuted, and generally speaking shared their fate.

Wang Mengzou was a lifelong friend of Chen Duxiu, and I got to know him through Chen. I had just been released from Suzhou Jail, and was completely destitute. Wang Mengzou was planning to bring out a series titled *Lives of Bourgeois Democratic Revolutionaries*, and hoped to get his old friend Chen Duxiu, who at the time was still in Nanjing Jail, to be its chief editor. Chen Duxiu asked me to stand in for him, and to edit the series jointly with

Dr Tao Xingzhi, one of Chiang Kai-shek's political opponents and later a leader of the anti-Japanese National Salvation Society. In fact, the project never got off the ground, but Wang Mengzou and I became friends for life, and, for a long period, I depended on him for my livelihood, working as an 'editor' for his book company at a monthly salary of twenty dollars. During all that time, I never once edited a single volume for him, since he was very short of the necessary capital for new projects. But, in the autumn of 1936, after the Moscow trials had shaken world opinion, old Wang suddenly got very excited and decided that, whatever the cost, he must reveal the truth about what was going on in Stalinist Russia. We discussed the matter, and decided as a first step to bring out two small books, *The Moscow Trials and World Public Opinion* and *The Truth about the Moscow Trials*. They were to consist partly of original material, which I was to write, and partly of translations from the European and American left-wing press. The first book did not take long to produce, and I had already got some way through the second when I was once again arrested by Guomindang special agents and taken off to jail. Fortunately, Chen Qichang took over from where I had left off, and the second volume appeared soon afterwards. Chen Qichang also translated for Wang Mengzou Trotsky's famous speech *I Stake My Life*, and parts of the Dewey Commission report on the Moscow trials, which had found that the whole affair was a massive frame-up and exonerated Trotsky and his son Sedov completely.

As far as I remember, only two issues of our theoretical organ *Spark* came out before I was arrested for the third time. The most important articles in them concerned the preparations for the Fourth International and Trotsky's criticisms of both the 'Popular Front' and the new Soviet Constitution. Apart from these, I should also mention Chen Duxiu's thesis on democracy, which signalled an important change in his thinking, in effect representing a retreat on his part after two decades of uninterrupted advance. After his imprisonment and his enforced separation from the struggle, Chen Duxiu's thinking began to show signs of retrogression. At first, he voiced doubts on the nature of the Soviet Union, which, in his view, was no longer either a workers' state, or even, as Trotsky analysed it, a degenerated workers' state. He argued that, once the working class had been driven out of the state machinery, it could by definition no longer be called a proletarian state, and therefore characterised the Soviet Union under Stalin as a bureaucratic state. This was an emotional and instinctive response to the Moscow trials, rather than a thoroughly thought-out piece of historical and sociological research. Later, he made a serious study of the historical evolution of democracy, in which he concluded that the history of mankind was essentially the history of the development of democracy, and that, from the time when slave society had destroyed the democracy of primitive communism down to the present, the replacement of one social form by another had invariably signified a qualitative development and extension of democracy – even though historical development did not follow a linear path. This led him to his second conclusion; namely that democracy, apart from being the most reliable indicator of whether a given society is progressive or reactionary, was completely devoid of all class character, and certainly not specific to the bourgeoisie. It was reactionary for socialists to reject democracy on the grounds that it pertained to a class other than the proletariat, since a workers' state would by definition be much more democratic than a capitalist state.

Not one of us agreed with these views of his. We thought that, by raising democracy above class as a historical factor, he had reduced it to an abstraction. As I followed Lenin's line on democracy, it was decided that I should write a reply to Chen's article, to be published alongside it in *Spark*. At the time, I was in the middle of reading Trotsky's *Terrorism and Communism*, which contains many excellent arguments refuting Kautsky's ideas on democracy, so I translated a number of passages from the book and sent them to Chen Duxiu for him to read. They had no effect on him, however, and he stuck to his guns. After the signing of the Hitler-Stalin pact in 1939, he even began to urge support for the democratic powers against the Soviet Union, thus completing his ideological break from Trotskyism. Some of his writings from this period were afterwards published in Shanghai by his pupil He Zishen.

Between 1936 and 1937, the Guomindang carried out a number of important improvements to its machinery of repression, entering what I earlier called the 'fourth period' – the period of 'scientific repression'. Shortly after the new Provisional Central Committee of our organisation came into being, Yin Kuan suddenly disappeared, and, many weeks later, we learned that he was being held in the secret prison of the Guomindang special service. At about the same time, Han Jun happened to be released from another prison, so he took Yin Kuan's place on the Central Committee. Han Jun told us that special agents were everywhere, and were extremely interested in our group. He warned us to improve our security, but even he did not really know just how the special agents operated and what methods of surveillance they were using, so we were unable to take effective precautions against spying and infiltration. In March or April 1937, a worker who had been arrested together with Yin Kuan and later freed bumped into Chen Qichang and had a quiet conversation with him, explaining how he had been arrested, forced to recant his ideas, and subsequently released from prison. He warned Chen that we could not continue working in the old way, as we were already under close scrutiny from the special agents, who could finish us off whenever they chose. He told Chen that he wanted to wash his hands of the movement, and said he was only telling him all this for the sake of past friendship.

Chen immediately became very excited and rushed over to my place to tell me the news. We realised that the situation was serious, but suspected that the man who had given the warning might have become a special agent himself, and might therefore have been deliberately exaggerating the danger. We agreed that we had to be more vigilant, but that there could be no question of abandoning our old way of working. Shortly afterwards, Chen Qichang was on his way to visit Han Jun one afternoon when he spotted two men in workmen's overalls behaving suspiciously outside the front door of Han's house. He abruptly turned round and started walking back the way he had come, with the two agents closely shadowing him. After several hours, he managed to shake them off, and hurried back to Han Jun's place to warn him of the danger. Han Jun had no time to pack any of his belongings: if he had hesitated for a moment, he would almost certainly have been re-arrested. All the other comrades who might have been in danger of arrest were ordered to leave their homes immediately. Thus, we successfully weathered yet another storm.

The situation was indeed extremely serious. The CCP underground organisation in Shanghai had been defunct for many years, partly as a result of Guomindang repression and partly following the Party's decision to withdraw to their bases in the countryside. Now, the Guomindang clearly intended to uproot our organisation as well, fearing that we might benefit from the anti-imperialist mass movement growing up as a result of Japanese aggression in north China. We were very aware of the imminent danger, but there was little we could do. Calling a halt to our activities was obviously out of the question. Should we then follow the example of the CCP and leave the cities? But we had no bases to retreat to, and, in any case, our orientation towards the working class would not allow us to leave Shanghai. There was no alternative but to carry on and take the consequences. In May 1937, the inevitable happened and I was arrested by Guomindang special agents, exactly a year after I had married for the second time, and a few weeks after the birth of my daughter.

In a way, I profited from the disaster of my arrest, for I got to know a great deal about the new 'scientific' police techniques the Guomindang had learned from Stalin and Hitler. Today, Hitler and Stalin are dead, but their 'science' lives on in ever more parts of the world, and many of my close friends are even now suffering as a result. That is why I intend to devote rather more space to my experience of such methods than my own importance warrants. Any bitterness I might feel is secondary; my real aim is to denounce the system in all its barbarity and inhumanity.

I was arrested in the French Concession of Shanghai by two plainclothes-agents. They acted in complete disregard for all legal procedures, simply pointing a pistol at me, dragging me into a car parked nearby, and speeding off to the Special Service headquarters in the Chinese area of the city. Immediately on arrival, I was dragged off to the interrogation chamber, and subjected to non-stop 'hot and cold' treatment for more than forty hours. At first, I was 'welcomed' by a young man speaking with a Shaanxi accent, who said he was an old friend of mine and asked me if I recognised him. This was, of course, a lie, but it was clear that, at one time or another, he had been a member of the Communist Party. After some polite remarks, he produced pen and paper and told me to make a voluntary confession, adding that we were not in a prison but in a centre for making voluntary confessions. I told him that if I was not under arrest I did not have to do so and that, by rights, I should be free to go. He then said that he would dispense with the confession; all I had to do was give him the addresses of a few comrades. He would invite them to come and make voluntary confessions, and I myself would be set free. I replied that as all my friends were non-political there was no point in bringing them there. Just then two burly thugs rushed in from the next room shouting at the young man that there was no need to be polite with me. One of them grabbed me by the shoulders, while the other smashed a thick piece of wood on the back of my head. Everything turned black, and I fell unconscious. After a while I came to. I had a splitting headache. Several ferocious men were looking down at me, arms akimbo. They were just about to start on me again when two other men – these with kind, smiling faces – intervened to push them aside. They offered me a cup of tea and feigned 'concern' at the wound on the back of my head. One of them, who seemed to be the leader, even pretended to upbraid the others for beating me. Ordering them to leave the room, he sat down opposite me and 'sincerely apologised' for what had happened.

I was disgusted by the whole spectacle. Every one of them was an atrocious actor, but they were not in the least concerned with audience reaction, staging the same performance over and over again. Finally, they reduced their demands to only one: I should tell them the addresses of three comrades, and then I would be free to go. By this time, I could see there was no point in shamming ignorance or giving them misleading answers, so I told them directly that, do what they would, they would never get a single address out of me. The same afternoon, after seven or eight hours of the 'hot and cold' routine, the little drama reached its climax. I was dragged off into a special room by a gang of thugs. One of them gagged me and threw me down on the floor. I lay there flat on my face, with my legs tied tightly together, while men on either side of me jerked up my arms, and two others clubbed me on the back of the thighs and on the ankles. I am not sure how long this went on, for I lost consciousness after about thirty blows. By the time I came to, I was lying in an armchair in another room.

Once again it was time for the 'warm spell'. My 'old friend' asked me if I was hungry. I did not answer, but he went ahead and ordered me a meal of fried rice. I had eaten nothing all day, but I did not touch it, since I had completely lost my appetite. He then told me that I should 'look after my health', and think of my wife and daughter. Once again, he asked me to hand over the addresses, but I ignored him. The gentle approach having seemingly reached stalemate, the strong-arm men made another entrance, but the 'gentlemen' motioned them out again. I was now left alone in the room with just one man, who stood there looking at me. The atmosphere was very tense. The men in the next room were pretending to have an argument, just loud enough for me to catch the drift of it. The man who stayed behind with me pretended to be sympathetic, and said: 'Why go through it all again? You'll have to give in eventually, everyone does once they get in here. Use your brains. What's the point in resisting?' I was inwardly composed, having had ample experience by now of their torture, and knowing exactly what to expect. The worst they could do was kill me. The torturers came in again, and I braced myself for the onslaught. Two ordered me to get up and go with them. I could not stand, so each grabbed an arm and I was frog-marched out of the room. I thought I was in for another beating, but, to my surprise, I was deposited in a bare cell with wooden bars. They told me to get some rest. I lay down on the ground, my whole body racked with pain and bleeding from the head and ankles, but far too tired to feel depressed and wanting only to sleep. I closed my eyes, but, within five minutes, a group of men rushed into the cell and dragged me out. By now, I was completely incapable of supporting myself, and they had to carry me.

To my astonishment, I found a group of scholarly-looking gentlemen waiting for me. There were several armchairs in the room, grouped around a small circular table, on which were tea and cigarettes. I was told to help myself. As I was carried into the room the 'scholars' stood up and helped me to an armchair, with expressions of sympathy on their faces. After that, one began to speak, saying he wanted to exchange opinions with me and discuss a few questions: that they were entirely without any preconceived ideas and that all they were interested in was the truth. He also told me that if I managed to persuade them of my ideas they would join me, but if, as a result of our discussion, I decided they were right, then they hoped I would follow their example of open-mindedness and go over to their side. After he had outlined the aim of the meeting, another one of the 'scholars' suggested that we should discuss the 'nature of the Chinese Revolution'. Despite the horror of it all, I could see the humour in the situation and felt like laughing, but this impulse was immediately submerged by a wave of anger. The discussion continued, and one after another the 'scholars' stepped forward with 'brilliant arguments' in the service of the 'truth'. Gradually, my anger and hatred dissipated, and I began to see them as pathetic. The fact that such shameless cynics could exist on this earth made me want to weep. They spoke as if they had been wound up like gramophones beforehand, and what they called a 'discussion' was in fact the same old record played over and over again: all they had to do was open their mouths, and out it came. The argument went as follows: the Chinese Revolution was bourgeois in character – Lenin, Stalin, Trotsky, all were unanimous on this point – and, as 'scholars', they agreed with this view. It was therefore only natural that Generalissimo Chiang Kai-shek should lead the Revolution. Like Mao Zedong, we Trotskyists committed one absolutely unforgivable error: while we admitted that the Revolution was bourgeois in character, we refused to recognise that Chiang Kai-shek, the Guomindang, and the bourgeoisie were the leaders of the Revolution. As a result, we did nothing but cause trouble and disruption, thus preventing Chiang from completing the Revolution. Not only were we acting contrary to the needs of the Revolution, but we were violating the instructions of Lenin and Trotsky. Therefore, they concluded, if I wanted to be a true Marxist-Leninist, I should put my trust in the Guomindang.

At first, I said nothing in reply, but when they pressed me I told them that I was ignorant of theoretical questions. Finally, I could stand it no longer, and said that if they really wanted a discussion with me they should first restore my freedom, since between prisoner and jailer no discussion was possible. At this point some 'experts' of the other sort took over and ordered me to my feet, but by now I was incapable of standing. They again ordered me to get up, saying I could rest against the table if I needed to. When I collapsed they told me for a third time to get up, and one of them fired a single question at me: 'Where does Chen Qichang live?' All I had to do was answer that one question and I could go back to my cell and sleep. If they actually managed to catch him as a result of my tip-off, they would set me free immediately. I said nothing, and they started screaming at me like frenzied animals: 'Where does Chen Qichang live? Where does Chen Qichang live? Answer! Answer! Are you going to tell us?' They asked me the same question over and over again with monotonous regularity. Sometimes they shouted at the tops of their voices, sometimes they adopted a less aggressive tone. At the same time other men kept on walking round me in a circle, rolling up their sleeves in a threatening way, glowering at me and swearing constantly. Every now and then a 'friend' would intervene on my behalf and push them out of the way, at the same time earnestly advising me to co-operate. After a while, the exercise became pointless, and they once again changed tactics. Someone came in from the next room and whispered to the apparent leader of the team of interrogators, loud enough for me to hear: 'Do you want me to bring Chen Qichang in now?' The man pretended to think for a while, and then shook his head. Turning to me, he said: 'We have already got Chen Qichang here. We picked him up a long time ago. We were only asking you to tell us his address to give you a chance to prove that you're sincere about confessing'. It was a crude trick, which a child could have seen through. And so it went on, minute after minute and hour after hour, for almost two days and nights, during which time the only respite I got apart from a few visits to the toilet was the two or three hours I spent in my cell.

By the second night, I was half dead, lying in a daze on the floor of my cell. The thugs returned once again to drag me out, and my 'old friend' with the Shaanxi accent was waiting for me. He told me I was a great disappointment to them, and they had wasted a lot of time trying to save me from the pit into which I had fallen. There was nothing more they could do except send me to Nanjing. Just before I was to leave, he came up to give me some more 'friendly' advice, telling me that the new method of dealing with political offenders was to destroy them either politically or physically. The old days were now over, and I should harbour no illusions on that score. It was no longer a question of sitting out one's sentence at public expense, while studying in preparation for the day when one would return to the fight.

What he told me was true. The days of 'bourgeois democracy' were well and truly over, and the 'scientific' policing techniques perfected by Stalin and Hitler and adopted by Chiang Kai-shek were becoming more and more widely used. Any revolutionary arrested under such conditions had to be clear on this point, and face up to the stark choice between political and physical annihilation. Shortly before my arrest, I had pondered at length on the strange behaviour of the old Bolsheviks at the Moscow trials, little realising that I would very soon find the key to this apparent riddle in my own experience. Lying there in my cell, I suddenly remembered that Trotsky had once said: 'Even Bolsheviks are made of flesh and blood'. I shuddered involuntarily, resolving to increase my vigilance from then on.

I was put on the Shanghai-Nanjing night-train by two special agents. I fell asleep as soon as I got on the train, and only awoke when we drew into Xiaguan station in Nanjing. My first stop in Nanjing was a secret service centre housed in a luxury mansion surrounded by a big garden. I was led off to a beautifully furnished and decorated room where I flopped into an armchair, absolutely exhausted and racked with pain from the maltreatment I had suffered. The guards left me completely alone, so I managed to snatch a few hours' sleep. Later on, in the afternoon, a man dressed in the khaki uniform of a Guomindang officer came in to inspect me. I braced myself for yet another bout of torture, but he simply asked my name and place of birth, and then left. After a while, another man came in, also in officer's uniform. This time it really was an old friend of mine, an ex-Trotskyist I knew from Moscow. I prepared to resist his attempts to cajole me into surrender, but, to my surprise, all he did was offer me a cigarette and order the guards not to maltreat me. He then told me that if I wanted anything, I should send him a message, and left. Finally, a man in a Sun Yat-sen jacket came rushing in with a file of documents in his hand, saying that he had just finished reading the secret service reports on me from Shanghai and that in his opinion I had a 'feudal' sense of morality. 'Actually', he went on, 'it would be much more moral of you to tell us your friend's address, so that he can start a new life'. He told me I should think about what he had to say. When I said I knew of no addresses, he smiled knowingly and sighed. As he left the room I could hear him saying, 'Such a pity, such a pity!'

After that two guards and a special agent dragged me off into a car and drove me out through the Nanjing city gates and along a country road. I was sitting on the back seat, with a guard on one side and the special agent, who was holding a revolver, on the other. My hands were handcuffed together. No one said a word, and all three of my escorts had grim looks. The fields were absolutely deserted. We were racing along at high speed. I expected that at any moment the car would screech to a halt, and I would be pushed out and shot in the back of the head. The idea almost cheered me up, since at least it would have meant an end to the torture, and I was inwardly very composed.

My expectations proved to be unfounded. After an hour's drive, we arrived at a small town, where I was taken out of the car and into another secret service detention centre next to the Nanjing Metropolitan Reformatory.

Inside the detention centre was a small courtyard. The atmosphere was quiet and almost peaceful. Around the courtyard were ten newly built one-man cells, so tiny that there was only room in them for a bed and bucket. The distance from wall to wall was less than an arm's breadth, and from the door to the back wall less than five paces. The walls and the ceiling were whitewashed, so that, after a few hours, one's eyes began to ache. The bed was a bare wooden board. In other jails, the authorities would issue blankets or cotton-padded military overcoats, but here prisoners had to rely for warmth on the clothes they happened to be wearing at the time of their arrest, whatever the weather and whatever the time of day or night. It was early summer when I first got to the prison. Summer and autumn passed and winter set in, but, throughout this whole period, all I had to cover me was my thin western-style jacket.

I was totally cut off from all contact with the outside world, so there was no chance of getting my family to bring me in the things I needed. I was simply left to rot. I asked the jailer for a cotton-padded uniform, but was told: 'You can have whatever you want; all you have to do is to comply with the demands of the authorities'. In other words, I would have to betray my comrades. Clearly, their 'scientific' methods knew no limits: they were even prepared to exploit the changing seasons in their campaign of persecution. Here, unlike in normal prisons, there was no regular supervision of the cells every few minutes or so. The only time we ever saw the warders was when they came into the yard to make a quick inspection at the beginning of each new watch, but they always left again immediately. The chief jailer would then lock the outer gates and post a guard outside. This was all part of their 'scientific' method, intended to prevent prisoners from fraternising with the guards, so that there was none of the smuggling out of secret messages which had been a common feature of normal prison life.

For a long time, I never saw a soul, not even the grim faces of the prison-guards. Although the other nine cells were occupied, contact was impossible, and any attempt at establishing it would have been extremely dangerous, since one could never be sure whether the man in the cell next door was a genuine prisoner or not. Not only did I never see anyone, but I never heard a single sound either. The courtyard was absolutely silent and deserted. How I longed for some sign of life! Anyone who has never lived through such an experience could not possibly imagine the extent to which loneliness and isolation can eat into the soul. It is impossible to sleep all the time – for long periods of the day and night you must be awake, and, once awake, you cannot keep your eyes closed, however much you try. But, all the time you have them open, you are forced to look at that dazzling sheet of whiteness, at once menacing and monotonous. The bleak emptiness of it eventually makes you colour-blind, and even drives you mad. When awake, it is also impossible not to think. But, since you are without books to read, paper to write on, or contact with people or things, your thoughts wander aimlessly, like a small boat which has lost both rudder and sail. This seeming loneliness and isolation is in fact fraught with danger, for, at any moment, torturers may arrive to put an end to that terrible quiet. To die is not in itself a difficult thing – what is difficult to endure is the permanent threat of torture hanging over your head. There is a limit to the physical pain torture can cause; but the idea that the solitude may suddenly be interrupted by yet another bout of agony is enough to shatter your nerves.

I asked the prison authorities for a book to read – any book, on any subject. 'You shouldn't be reading', the guard answered politely, with just the trace of a smile. 'You should be doing some serious thinking. When you've thought matters through to a conclusion, you may request an interview with the prison authorities'.

I had been in the 'experimental' prison for over a month when I was summoned from my cell for the first time. Two armed guards escorted me along the corridor, and I was taken into an interrogation chamber. Inside were several agents in civilian clothes waiting for me. Some were standing up, others were seated. Each looked at me in a different way: some glared, others were smiling, some appeared to be totally indifferent, and some affected to show concern for me. My escort ordered me to sit down and wait, and told me that the chief interrogator had not yet arrived. I sat on the edge of my seat, bracing myself for the possibility of torture. After half an hour or so, a high-ranking official came into the room. The atmosphere became even more tense, and all the agents in the room seemed to be busy making preparations for some sort of sacrificial ceremony. The official sat down, and I was asked to sit down in front of him. Pretending to leaf through a file of documents, he proceeded to check my name, age, and place of birth against the report he had received from Shanghai. He asked me if I had anything new to say. I told him no. He then adjourned the sitting, ordering the guards to escort me back to my cell for 'another think '. It was not at all clear to me whether this little episode, which had started out so menacingly only to fizzle out, was a sign of the inefficiency of the secret service or part of a carefully conceived plan to break my will.

After an interval of two months, during which time I was ignored, another high-ranking officer of the secret service came to make an inspection of the courtyard. When he arrived at the door of my cell, I seized the opportunity to demand either to be handed over to the judiciary or to be transferred to the military police headquarters in Nanjing for a proper trial. He politely asked me my name, getting one of his aides to note it down for him, and then told me that I would receive an answer very soon. The same afternoon I was summoned from my cell and escorted to a room bare of all furniture. Two agents ripped off my coat, and while one of them held me by the arm, the other beat me on the back with a rubber truncheon until my shirt was in shreds and my blood was pouring down me. For days after this incident, I had to lie on my stomach because of the wounds. This was their way of answering my demand.

The next stage in the war of nerves against me was to move me into a bigger cell with two other men. One of them, called Kong, had been chief of staff to General Wang Delin, one of the commanders of guerrilla forces fighting the Japanese in Manchuria. Kong told me that he had been sent to Nanjing by his commander to receive instructions from the central government. Unaware of the antagonisms between the various factions in the capital, he had fallen foul of the Chen brothers by making contact with their rivals the Blueshirts, for which he had been arrested and thrown in jail. By the time I met him, he had been there for several months, during which time he had never once been contacted by the prison authorities.

Our other companion was a martial arts practitioner of the Shaolin School from Henan province. I later learned that he had been the bodyguard of one of the leaders of the 'Central Statistical Bureau' of the Guomindang intelligence services, and had been imprisoned as a punishment for some minor misdemeanour.

I had no idea why my conditions had suddenly improved, but, after spending such a long time in solitary confinement, I was glad of any human company. Kong was a pious Christian, and getting on in years. He was very sentimental and emotional, always worrying about his wife and family who were hiding out with the guerrillas on the wooded slopes of the Changbai Mountains in north-eastern China. He was deeply embittered, and, during his months of isolation, his one way of finding solace was through prayer. He prayed several times a day, but saved his longest and most moving prayers for the evening, just before going to bed. Sitting there in the darkness of the cell, he would invariably add a short prayer for his fellows in misfortune. Then he would break down, sobbing and choking with emotion. After he had said his final Amen, we would lie there in complete silence. I am a convinced atheist, and normally detest all forms of wallowing in emotion, but I must admit that his prayers disturbed my peace of mind.

At first, I suspected Kong was a plant and his prayers were part of the 'scientific' war of nerves against me, but I soon realised that he really was a leader of the North-East Volunteer Army and that his prayers were from the heart. The Shaolin boxer, on the other hand, was a plant. Every day, he was summoned out of the cell for an hour or two. Finally, in a bout of conscience, he confessed that he had been ordered by the authorities to spy on us, and told that he would be released from prison early if he found out the addresses of some of my comrades in Shanghai.

The tactic of improving my treatment had failed, and I was taken back to solitary confinement. It was like returning to the bleakness of the desert, with the never-ending isolation gnawing at the soul. And so it went on, day in, day out, until after the outbreak of hostilities in Shanghai on 13 August 1937. Even then, it was not until the Chinese forces had suffered repeated defeats that any change came about. During that period, the monotonous silence of the courtyard was broken only twice.

The first time was one midnight, when I heard the heavy tramp of jack-boots coming along the corridor, getting louder and louder. The heavy iron gate was clanked open, and a file of men marched into the courtyard. This was most unusual, since normally the change-over of sentries was much more relaxed. I sat up and braced myself for the worst, but, to my relief, the men marched past the door of my own cell and stopped at another at the end of the row. I heard them opening the lock and withdrawing the iron-bolt, and a voice ordering the prisoner to come out. This command was issued in a quiet but menacing voice. A terrible silence followed, and I could see in my mind's eye the tense confrontation that was taking place. I heard a distraught voice asking 'What for?' Once again the command was repeated. 'I'm not coming', answered the prisoner, terror and anger in his voice. 'Come out, nothing's going to happen to you, we just want to move you somewhere else'. They were obviously trying to coax him out. Another terrible silence followed. Then there was the sound of a struggle as the man was beaten and dragged from his cell. Once more, I heard the feet tramping past my cell door, marching out through the iron gate and disappearing along the corridor. Then the blanket of silence returned.

The second incident also took place at night. I suddenly heard noises coming from the cell to the left of me, where someone was hammering wildly on the cell door, screaming and crying at the top of his voice. The guards immediately rushed into the courtyard. First of all, they shouted at him to be quiet, and when this failed, threatened and finally beat him. Despite everything they did, the man continued to cry and shout. He had evidently gone mad. After all else failed, the guards tied him up and left him to calm down. He kept on shouting out a woman's name. At first, his voice was clear and loud, but later became very hoarse and began to crack and falter. He carried on like this until the afternoon of the next day, when the poor fellow was carried out, trussed up like a dead pig. Once again the silence returned.

I knew nothing of the outbreak of the war with Japan until the middle of August, when I saw three aircraft flying overhead and heard the sound of nearby anti-aircraft guns. Naturally, I was unaware of what precisely was happening, but it was obvious that the Japanese had declared war on China. I became very excited, since whatever happened in the real war, at least the war of nerves against me would almost certainly be called off. I would either end up being shot as a victim of Guomindang frustration in the case of a defeat, or else be released unharmed.

After the aerial battles over Nanjing started, the atmosphere in the courtyard changed. At first, the guards became less stern than usual, and sometimes even exchanged a few words with me. Previously, prisoners had been strictly forbidden to make contact with each other, but now the guards would occasionally open two cells at a time when bringing round food or taking away the night-soil buckets, and would allow us to chat together. After they had left the courtyard, we would even hold shouted conversations through the little holes in our cell doors.

I now learned for the first time that my neighbour to the right was no less than Wang Shaoao, a leading member of the Democratic-National Reconstruction Association, who became Vice-Minister of Finance in the People's Government after liberation. He had managed to keep his spirits up during his imprisonment, despite being an old man of nearly sixty. He used to practise shadow-boxing in his cell to while away the time, and through our 'telephone' conversations we got on very well together. When he was eventually released around the end of August, he delivered a letter to my wife for me, and we kept up our friendship long after our release from jail. I have met many of the leaders of the small so-called democratic parties that emerged after the Japanese surrender. Most were political careerists with talents more appropriate to an official than to a revolutionary, but Wang Shaoao was different. He was a man of backbone who always insisted on sticking to his own opinions, despite the fact that his politics were extremely confused, and he thought that the programme of the Chinese Revolution could be confined to demanding the right to education and the right to work.

One afternoon, something very strange happened. We heard the sound of slogans being shouted from the Nanjing Reformatory next door. One man took the lead and the others immediately echoed him, so that we could hear the words very clearly: 'Long live Generalissimo (or Chairman?) Chiang', 'Long live the Three People's Principles', 'Long live the Guomindang'. I could not imagine for the life of me what was happening. I also heard the same high-pitched voice that had been leading the shouting delivering some sort of speech. This went on for several hours, and. when the sentries came round the courtyard I asked them what was happening. They told me that the man making the speeches was the Communist representative Zhou Enlai, and that he had come to explain the CCP's new united front policy to the men working in the Reformatory, all of whom were members of the Party. I listened again, and sure enough it was the high-pitched voice of my old friend. I already knew that the CCP had changed its line and realised from my long experience as a revolutionary that tactical manoeuvres were often necessary and permissible; but, to a 'dogmatic' revolutionary like myself, this display was both absurd and incredible, and I could hardly believe what I had heard.

Shortly afterwards, all the prisoners in the Reformatory were released, and even those of us locked up in the little courtyard were being set free one by one, so that I too expected that a change would come about in my own situation. Towards the end of August, the authorities finally remembered my existence and sent two high-ranking officials down to talk with me. They told me that I could go free if I agreed to issue a statement supporting Chiang and the Guomindang, but I refused. I was prepared to declare my firm support for the War of Resistance to Japan under the leadership of the Guomindang, but not to give up my own approach to the various other questions involved. Our talk went on for several hours, and was rather like a haggling session in the marketplace, but no deal was struck. Just before I was escorted back to my cell one of the officials said to me: 'You can't blame us for keeping you here, you know. It's your own fault. You obviously don't want to be let out'.

September and October passed, and, half-way through November, I was still sitting there in my solitary cell. Other prisoners came and went, although as the months went by their political complexion gradually changed from anti- to pro-Japanese; but I, who 'didn't want to be let out', stayed behind bars throughout. It was clear from the growing number of Japanese aircraft over Nanjing, where they enjoyed unchallenged supremacy, that the War was going very badly for China. I think Yanziji (which was where the jail was) must have been on the Japanese warplanes' route to Nanjing, because we always heard them flying overhead just before the bombs fell on the city. At first, the Guomindang had regularly sent up a few planes to intercept the invaders and engage them in dogfights in the air space above us, but, after a while, they stopped coming, and the Japanese were free to come and go as they pleased, circling the city continuously from morning to night. Although splinters sometimes fell in the courtyard, and the prison was rocked by explosions, we were never allowed to go down into the air-raid shelters. As soon as the sirens sounded, the guards would lock the iron gates and hurry off to the shelters, leaving us to the mercies of the enemy aircraft. At first, I was scared by the attacks, but I soon got used to them. Since there was nothing I could do about them anyway, I used to climb up to the cell-window and watch the patterns traced out against the sky by the Japanese bombs and the anti-aircraft fire.

By late November, the repercussions of the disintegration of the Nanjing government could be felt even in our little courtyard, where none of the normal regulations seemed to apply any longer. Sometimes, guards would not turn up for sentry duty, and many had deserted their posts to escape the coming holocaust. Two days before I was finally released, I and another man called Jin, who had been arrested on suspicion of collaborating with the Japanese, were the only two prisoners left in the entire camp. We used to get our food sent in from a neighbouring village, since the prison kitchen had by then stopped functioning. There were no longer many aircraft around and the rumble of artillery-fire was getting louder and louder, indicating that the Japanese armies were by now very close to Nanjing. The next day, the collaborator was released, and I was the only one left in the courtyard. The day after that (I remember it was

28 November 1937, twelve days before Nanjing officially fell to the Japanese), I finally gained my freedom. The only remaining guard, a man called Wang Shunlin, unlocked my cell-door and said: 'Everyone else has gone. I want to go too. I want to get out before the Japanese get here. You're free to go now'. I told him that when I arrived at the prison a watch and a few dollars had been taken from me and locked up in the office, and asked him if he would go and get them for me. He smiled and told me that I was a 'frog at the bottom of the well', implying that I obviously knew nothing of the world outside. 'You must be mad if you think they're still there', he said. 'All the staff have fled already, and they've taken everything worth taking. Run for your life!' But that was easier said than done. I was friendless and penniless, the weather was freezing and all I had on was a ragged cotton shirt and a western-style jacket. If I didn't starve I would certainly freeze to death. To his credit, the guard put his hand in his pocket and gave me two dollars, so that I was able to make my way to Nanjing, where a friend of mine was living.

This was the last I saw of that 'scientific' hell. I was now about to start out on a new stage in my life.

But, before I finish this chapter, there is one more thing that I would like to mention. I learned later from friends that Ye Jianying, then CCP representative in Nanjing, spent two days scouring the capital trying to secure my release, apparently sometime in late September or early October. By then, all the other Trotskyists had been freed, Chen Duxiu and Peng Shuzhi from civilian prison, and Zheng Chaolin, He Zishen, and others from military prison. I was the only member of the organisation still imprisoned, and no one knew where I was. Chen Duxiu asked some of his friends in the government to make enquiries about me at the secret police headquarters, but they were told that there was no record of anyone of my name. Luo Han, who was at that time a pottery-teacher in Yixing county, also went to Nanjing, and, on hearing the news, decided to ask for Ye Jianying's help. This was typical of Luo Han's naivety, but to everyone's amazement Ye Jianying agreed to his request. The two of them then got into a car and drove round all the semi-secret special service sections in Nanjing for two days, but received the same reply wherever they went: 'Never heard of him'. My comrades therefore concluded I was dead, murdered by the secret police.

I am not trying to suggest that Ye Jianying spent so much of his time trying to track me down because I was in any way a 'big fish'. I am telling this story only to show once again that the attitude of CCP members towards us was neither consistently nor uniformly hostile. As Stalinists, they all opposed Trotskyism, but only a handful of them were clear about the issues involved and positively supported Stalin; and, of these, only Wang Ming and his friends used opposition to Trotskyism to bolster their own political position. Most people attached no importance to the struggle between the two factions, considering it an internal affair of the Soviet Party. The majority of the older generation of party members could never really take seriously the wild allegations levelled against us, and continued to look upon us as fellow-revolutionaries. The fact that Ye Jianying continued to treat Luo Han as an old friend and went to such lengths to help him gain my release can have no other possible explanation.

Chen Duxiu, the Chinese Trotskyists, and the War of Resistance

Wang Fanxi

Source: *Memoirs of a Chinese Revolutionary* (1957).

I walked all the way to Nanjing, where luckily I managed to borrow another twenty dollars from a friend of Lou Guohua. The whole area was devastated by war, and the weather freezing. Transport and communications had almost broken down completely. The story of how I got from Nanjing to Wuhan via Xuzhou and Zhengzhou on my twenty-two dollars is a very moving one. For the first time I experienced what it is like to be a beggar and a refugee. What I heard and saw in the course of my two-week journey completely revealed the reactionary way in which the Guomindang was leading the War of Resistance, and the tragic consequences that followed. Although such things are not without importance, this is not the place to talk about them, and, in any case, others with better qualifications to do so have already told the story of those tragic times.

When I arrived in Wuhan, after an absence of ten long years, it was already mid-December. Soon after getting there I read in the Wuhan press how General Tang Shengzhi had abandoned Nanjing after swearing that he would 'stand or fall' with it, and how Japanese soldiers had brutally put the city to the sword. Naturally these terrible events attracted my attention, but my most immediate problem was how to keep body and soul together. Even though I knew a number of my friends were living in Wuhan, I had no way of finding out their addresses. I walked the streets and hung around the ferry wharf in the hope that I might bump into someone I knew, but all to no avail. I slept two nights at the Dazhimen railway station in Hankou, without even the money for a crust of bread. On the morning of the third day, I sold my only remaining possession, a tooth-mug, to a stall-holder near the railway station. The sale brought me a few cents, which I used to pay for the ferry across the Yangtze to Lanka Hill in Wuchang. There I hoped to borrow some money from a professor at Wuhan University whom I knew from when we were at school together, although I would never have even thought of going to see him had I not been on the point of starving and freezing to death. After getting off the ferry, I went into a small restaurant to buy some noodles. Imagine my relief when in the restaurant I bumped into my old friend Li Zhongsan! Not only did he spare me the embarrassment of begging from someone I could not stand, but he brought my entire eight-month nightmare to a close – a period which I can describe without hesitation as the most difficult in my life.

After treating me to a hearty meal, Li Zhongsan bought me a cotton-padded jacket and some other clothes. In the afternoon, he took me to Chen Duxiu's home, where I stayed for nearly a fortnight. We talked together about many questions, some of which are worth recording in detail.

Chen Duxiu had been freed from jail three months earlier than I. Just before his release he had drafted some papers on the Anti-Japanese War.[1] After being set free, he had sent them to the comrades in Shanghai, who found that they did not completely agree with them. It was about this time that Luo Han arrived in Nanjing. As soon as he read Chen's papers he gave them his wholehearted support; he even argued that we should use them as a platform for gathering together a broadly-based movement encompassing both Trotskyists and others opposed to Japan and the Guomindang. The first step would be to propose to the CCP that they co-operate with us. Chen Duxiu knew of Luo Han's scheme, but did not encourage him in it. Luo Han, however, decided to take things into his own hands. He told Ye Jianying of his proposals, and Ye encouraged him to go to Yan'an to talk with Mao Zedong in person. Luo Han therefore left Nanjing for Xi'an, where he stayed at the house of Lin Boqu, also an old friend of his and the CCP representative in that city. Lin Boqu immediately transmitted Chen's papers and Luo Han's proposals for co-operation to Mao in Yan'an, by special messenger. Several days later, Mao's reply came through, saying that, if Chen Duxiu admitted his past mistakes and renounced Trotskyism, he could then work together with the CCP. Naïve though dear old Luo Han was, he was never so naïve as to think that Chen Duxiu would agree to such conditions. His hopes dashed, he left Xi'an. His actions not only angered Chen Duxiu but were roundly criticised by the provisional leadership of the Trotskyist movement in Shanghai, and he quietly returned to Yixing to resume teaching pottery.

At the time, Chen Duxiu was extremely dissatisfied with the Trotskyist leadership in Shanghai. Feeling that their narrow sectarian approach would never get anywhere, he had decided not to go east but to move on to Wuhan instead. After the main battles in the Shanghai area had been fought and lost and the Guomindang armies along the Nanjing-Shanghai railway had collapsed in disarray, Wuhan had temporarily become the political and military centre of China and the new hotbed of the mass movement. All the social forces and political groupings stirred into being by the War of Resistance had converged

---

[1] Since I no longer have these documents to hand, I cannot describe them in any detail.

on that city. Although Chen Duxiu had no organised force to back him up, he still enjoyed great prestige among the masses, and none of the existing political groupings could afford to ignore this old man of the Revolution. Before I arrived in Wuhan, Chen had been invited to give two public lectures at the YMCA headquarters, where he attracted capacity audiences. In his speech, he made it clear that in giving his views on the future of the resistance he was speaking only for himself and not for the Trotskyist movement as a whole. The contents of his speech were more or less the same as the papers he had drawn up earlier in Nanjing jail.

He let me read his papers and the text of his speech the day after I went to stay with him. The first day of my visit, he kept off more serious topics, to give me a chance to get over my recent experiences. We chatted about prison life in Nanjing, and that evening he even took the unusual step of getting his wife to cook some special dishes for me. This unexpectedly conventional gesture from so unconventional a man as Chen was a sign of his joy at meeting me again after the gap of six long years.

At that time, Chen was living in an old-fashioned, single-storey house with a garden, owned by a Guangxi officer who would only accept a nominal rent from his famous tenant. Chen was in excellent health, and used to get up very early in the morning. While in prison, he had got into the habit of pacing up and down his cell, and, even after his release, he would still walk round and round his garden every morning. On the second day of my visit, I joined him in this exercise, and it was then that we began our more 'formal' discussions. He immediately launched into a fierce tirade against the Trotskyist leadership in Shanghai. (The new provisional leadership had been chosen at a conference of activists shortly after Peng Shuzhi and other comrades had arrived back in Shanghai from Nanjing. Apart from Chen Qichang, Han Jun, and Lou Guohua, all three of whom were survivors from the old provisional leadership, the only newcomers to have been co-opted on to the Committee were Peng Shuzhi and Liu Jialiang.) He told me that, in his view, they were capable of nothing more than reciting Trotsky's old articles, and were useless when it came to real political struggles. He even went so far as to say that he no longer considered himself a member of any political party, and that, from now on, Chen Duxiu would represent Chen Duxiu and no one else. The question of who were his friends and who his enemies would have to be decided afresh in the course of the new struggles. I was at a loss to know what to say in answer to his attacks and complaints, having been separated from the movement for so many months and knowing little of the various points of view involved. I told him that I wanted to study both sides before giving my own opinion. He then took me back to his study, and gave me a copy of his papers on the War of Resistance and the texts of his two speeches. He told me that the Shanghai friends had sent him letters explaining their own point of view, but that he had not kept them – it occurred to me that he had probably thrown them into the waste-paper basket in a fit of rage. I read through what he had written, but did not agree with it completely. It seemed to me that, apart from a general expression of support for the War of Resistance, he had entirely failed to mention our own distinctive position as Trotskyists. However, we postponed further discussions until I had had a chance to acquaint myself with the views of the other comrades. That same morning, I asked him what he thought of the idea of starting up a journal in Wuhan. He rejected it out of hand, saying that it was not only impossible but unnecessary, and went on to argue that it was time to reject our old ways; if we really wanted to play a role in the political struggles of the day, we should adopt new methods.

After that, we spent every morning strolling around his untidy little garden, chatting freely about everything under the sun. We talked about his linguistic studies, Trotsky's *History of the Russian Revolution* (the only book in the English language which he ever bothered to take with him on his travels from one town to another), prison life in Nanjing and the Moscow trials, the Chinese Trotskyist movement and the Fourth International, the future of the War of Resistance and the coming World War, and many other things besides. Rather than argue, we simply expressed our respective points of view; in most cases, I did no more than listen to what he had to say. In this way, I gradually became acquainted with his opinions on the various fundamental questions of the day. Chen poured scorn on what he saw as the naïve notion that the War of Resistance could give birth to a revolution: 'if there was no skin, how could there be hairs?' He went on to point out that, because of the defeats suffered so far, the industrial cities had fallen to the enemy and the proletariat had been dispersed. Should the War be prolonged, a new industrial centre might grow up with American support in the south-western provinces. He therefore saw no chance of any revolution during the War of Resistance, let alone one along the lines that we imagined. It was true, of course, that the War would bring increasing suffering to the masses, especially the peasant masses, and this suffering could well give rise to riots and disturbances. But, as long as the Guomindang continued to resist the Japanese invasion, there was no possibility of that unrest growing into a revolution against the régime. In future years, many things would change, and discontent would grow both in the towns and in the villages. But the question was, who could lead these movements? Only those groups and parties which stood for democracy and freedom, and which, at the same time, commanded their own armed forces. It was therefore necessary to abandon the old idea of organising workers and winning them over to the revolution simply by publishing newspapers and journals. The only feasible method to adopt was first to unite all political tendencies independent both of the Guomindang and the CCP on the basis of a broad programme of freedom and democracy, and, second, to infiltrate the armed forces active in the resistance and thus create a means through which future developments in the situation could be exploited in favour of the revolution.

Chen Duxiu's dissatisfaction with the Shanghai organisation had two main causes. First, he bore a personal grudge against some of the individuals in the leadership, in particular Peng Shuzhi – relations between Chen and Peng had been very bad while they were in Nanjing jail together. Second, and more important, the comrades in Shanghai were, in his view, incapable of seeing what he had seen. In my opinion, the positions he was advancing had not yet reached the stage of a fundamental break with Trotskyism, and were even less in opposition to Lenin's ideas. On the contrary, Chen constantly talked about Lenin during this period of his life, arguing that the latter's greatness lay precisely in his refusal to be bound by ready-made Marxist formulae and in his courageous insistence on adopting new political slogans and methods of struggle to meet changing times and circumstances. His differences with the Shanghai comrades therefore involved questions of policy and tactics rather than fundamental beliefs of the socialist revolution. What particularly angered him was their refusal to engage in the slightest way in real practical activity, let alone plunge headlong into the political and military struggles of the day. Instead, they simply sat in their rented rooms in the International Settlement, commenting from the sidelines on the course of the War. Whatever the times and whatever the conditions, their conception of revolutionary work was invariably reduced to the production of a rather pathetic party paper. It was no wonder that Chen reacted so negatively when I suggested starting up a journal in Wuhan.

While I did not completely approve of Chen's arguments and criticisms, I felt that his proposals for practical activity were well worth considering. As Trotsky himself said (in a letter to the Chinese Oppositionists), Chen Duxiu was an 'astute observer' and could grasp political struggles in a concrete way – a quality he amply displayed in his conversations with me at that time. Even before Chen Duxiu had informed me of his views I felt that, in the swelling tide of resistance to Japan, it was out of the question to confine ourselves to reciting old dogmas and necessary to find ways of playing an active and positive role in the struggle. But I disagreed with his proposal to reduce our programme to the 'struggle for freedom and democracy', with his plans for an alliance with various so-called 'democratic groupings' and with his pessimistic assessment of the chances of a revolution developing during the War of Resistance. Although

I thought he was right to stress the need for new methods of struggle, I also considered that we needed a paper as a rallying point for the formation of the party. Since he himself was so fond of quoting Lenin, I reminded him that Lenin had called the party organ the 'organiser of the party', and went on to argue that, without a party, all our political and military work would be like a kite without a string. Our insignificant forces would be swallowed up without trace in the vast ocean of the resistance.

After several days of discussion, we got round to the question of how to start work in Wuhan. We tacitly agreed to leave on one side for the time being our fundamental disagreements on questions such as the relationship between the dictatorship of the proletariat and democracy (which we had already debated several years earlier in the pages of our theoretical journal *Huohua*). Chen carefully avoided raising issues of this sort, but, whenever our discussion drifted in that direction, it seemed to me that he had returned to a more classically Leninist stance. He maintained this position right up to the Hitler-Stalin pact of August 1939. When Chen Qichang went to visit the Old Man in Jiangjin in Sichuan sometime in the second half of 1938, he had still not publicly come out in opposition to any of the main postulates of Marxism or Leninism. As he himself later put it, he was still 'deeply pondering' his basic ideas. The point of view expressed in the formal statement which he asked Chen Qichang to send on to Trotsky in Mexico was the same as that which he had discussed with me in December 1937: that the Chinese Trotskyists should bend all their efforts to playing a real part in the resistance, and that outside such a framework it was pointless to talk of revolutionary activity. It was the Hitler-Stalin pact which precipitated the final change in Chen Duxiu's thinking, what one might broadly define as his retreat from Bolshevism to Kautskyism. But all this happened at a later date and I will therefore return to it in the following chapter.

After I had been living in Chen's house for about a fortnight, Pu Dezhi arrived in Wuhan from Anqing in Anhui province. The last time we had seen each other was in the Shanghai-Wusong Garrison Headquarters at Longhua in 1931. During the six intervening years, we had both been in and out of prison twice. The second time he had been arrested and released together with Chen Duxiu, and, for four long years, the two men had lived close to one another. I found that he had changed little during the six years of our separation, and still retained all his youthfulness. As a boy, he had been to Japan, where he had developed a love for the theatre, and he was a long-standing member of the famous Nanguo Dramatic Society that had been formed in the 1920s to spread new, Western styles of drama. He had what one might call an artistic temperament, and sometimes gave the impression of being rather flighty and superficial; but, on meeting him this time, I found that he had gained in depth, probably as a result of Chen Duxiu's influence. After his release from jail in August, he had gone home to Anqing to recuperate, but, as soon as his health had recovered, went straight to Wuhan to rejoin his old friend. Chen Duxiu was overjoyed to see him. His arrival added sparkle to our conversations, and put Chen Duxiu in an even better mood than usual. Pu Dezhi and I moved out of Chen's house and went to live in the home of an old friend of mine called Wu. Since Wu lived by himself, we could behave more freely than in Chen Duxiu's home. But we continued to spend most of the daylight hours together with Chen, and if, for any reason, we failed to visit him, he would come round to see us. Sometimes, we would eat out together at a small restaurant, or go for a stroll along the Yangtze River. We no longer talked about the more basic questions, where we continued to differ, but concentrated instead on how to penetrate the military forces of the resistance and how to make contact with other political groupings. On the fundamental questions, Pu Dezhi's positions were close to mine; he was rather dissatisfied with Chen's proposal to reduce our programme to the struggle for 'freedom and democracy'.[2] He called Chen's two speeches at the Wuhan YMCA 'shamelessly grey' (a term used to describe people who concealed their radical views and made concessions to bourgeois public opinion). But, like me, he was also deeply influenced by Chen's 'activist' approach to methods of work. Chen Duxiu was not the sort of man given to empty talk. Using his many connections, he soon began to take steps towards putting his plan into action. At that time, there was a general named He Jifeng convalescing in Wuhan from wounds he had received somewhere in north China. This same man had headed the brigade stationed at the Marco Polo Bridge outside Beijing when, in July 1937, the famous Incident[3] took place which was to lead directly to the full-scale Japanese invasion of north China; Ji Xingwen, who was known throughout the country as the heroic commander of the regiment which fired the first shot in the resistance, was in fact under the direct command of General He; and He himself was under the command of General Song Zheyuan. By the time that we came into contact with He, he had already been promoted to the post of commander of the 179th Division of the Twenty-Ninth Army. He was an extraordinary individual. According to Chen Duxiu, he had absolutely no vices; unlike most military men, he was gracious and urbane in manner, and very unassuming – he and his wife lived together in one room, without even a servant to look after them. When I first

---

2 Pu's differences with Chen, written under the pen name of Xiliu, can be found in Part VIII.
3 On 7 July 1937, the escalating Japanese invasion met with resistance for the first time in the Lugouqiao (Marco Polo Bridge) area near Beijing. This marked the beginning of the nationwide War of Resistance, which lasted from 1937 to 1945.

met him (through Chen Duxiu), his wounds had already healed and he was about to rejoin his division. I formed a good impression of him, during our conversation. He was staunchly anti-Japanese, and felt very bitter towards the Guomindang leadership. Six months of fighting in north China had taught him that, unless the political consciousness of the troops was raised, there could be no effective resistance to the Japanese invasion, let alone final victory. Consequently, he had spent his convalescence reading whatever books he could get his hands on about the resistance and about social science in general. As a result of his reading and thinking, he had decided to invite a number of young revolutionaries to carry out political education among his troops. It was during his search for suitable candidates for such a mission that he came into contact with Chen Duxiu. The two men got on well together, and General He looked up to Chen as a teacher. Needless to say, he already knew what Chen's political position was, and it must have been obvious to him that we had differences with the Communist Eighth Route Army. For his own part, Chen made no attempt to pretend that he had any great forces at his disposal. As I recall the conversations that the three of us had at that time, Chen was always absolutely frank, explaining that he had long since broken off all relations with the CCP and did not even represent the Chinese Trotskyist movement; he said that he was acting solely in a personal capacity, as were those of us working with him. During the conversations at which I was present, the only question under discussion was the future direction of our political work in the division under He's command. We finally arrived at the following important conclusion: we would strengthen our military forces by mobilising the masses through a limited agrarian reform programme, and thus prepare the way for victory in the resistance.

When Pu Dezhi met General He for the first time, he too received a very favourable impression of him. However, both Pu and I doubted whether Chen Duxiu's proposed measures would be of advantage to the revolution. During the period 1925–7, there had been many instances of revolutionaries working as 'concubines' (as we called those who did political work in the armed forces during the period of the Northern Expedition) at various levels of the military structure, and their tragic fate was still fresh in our minds. Even fresher was the memory of the ill-fated marriage between the CCP and Feng Yuxiang. While I was still in Beijing in 1926, I had personally witnessed the 'courtship' between Li Dazhao and General Feng, and had afterwards read the famous 'Wuyuan Manifesto' which Feng wrote on his return from Moscow early in 1927. We had spent a lot of time doing 'political work' for him among the masses, trying to persuade them that he really was the 'peasant soldier' he claimed to be. But a few months later, in Wuhan, I had also personally witnessed this same Feng reuniting with Chiang Kai-shek to cause the collapse of the Wuhan Government, and saw his political workers arriving in the city by special train after he had sacked them from their jobs in his army. Afterwards, many of these former political workers had joined the Opposition, and I was on good terms with a number of them, who had told me many stories of Feng's hypocrisy.

With these events in mind, but independently of each other, Pu Dezhi and I began to voice the same doubts: what was there to prevent He Jifeng from becoming another Feng Yuxiang, if on a smaller scale? Were we about to repeat the whole sad experience all over again? We expressed our reservations to Chen Duxiu on returning home from our visit to the General. Chen said it would be absolutely wrong to characterise our activities as military opportunism. 'The present situation is entirely different', he said. 'We are not the Third International, we have no resources of our own, nothing at all that He Jifeng could trick us out of. What is more, we are not joining his army with the aim of replacing him as commander, or of winning him over as a revolutionary. We have already had experience of dealing with military men. From now on, we must clearly understand that our most important task in the army is to educate the rank-and-file soldiers and bend all our efforts towards creating revolutionary conditions among the masses. This means that we must do all we can to launch agrarian reform in the area under our control, thus also speeding the revolutionisation of the troops themselves. Finally, it seems to me that He Jifeng is not as devious as Feng Yuxiang, and that there is even a chance of making a genuine revolutionary out of him. If he were to become one, then his not inconsiderable forces could easily come under our political leadership. If not, then the fact that we have never made any attempt to hide our aims or beliefs means that we would be free to withdraw at any time with no harmful consequences'.

I agreed with what the old man had said. However, our next step immediately led to a new dispute with him. Pu and I thought that, for the project to develop favourably, we should inform the provisional leadership in Shanghai and seek their approval, so that they could fit it in with our work nationally and send some reinforcements to Wuhan. But Chen Duxiu disliked the Shanghai comrades, and therefore opposed our proposals. He thought it would be better for us to wait until we had achieved some results and then if necessary pass on a request for extra forces. But we never resolved our differences, because, even before we had begun to carry our plan into practice, the whole venture came to a sudden and unexpected end. We had already completed all the necessary preparations: Pu Dezhi, myself, and another young comrade from Henan called Ma were about to follow He Jifeng to Neihuang, where his divisional headquarters were; I was to act as his chief political adviser and Pu Dezhi as his staff-officer. We had already bought our tickets for the Beijing train when suddenly, on the eve of our departure, He Jifeng was informed that he had been relieved of his command and instructed not to return to Neihuang. We guessed at the time that the Blueshirt secret agents must have found out about his relations with Chen Duxiu, and had taken this step to forestall the radicalisation of his forces.

The bubble had burst: our hopes of infiltrating the army had not materialised. After that, we never had another chance to put our plan into practice. During the whole period of the War of Resistance, the Chinese Trotskyist movement taken as a whole never engaged in military struggle. As far as I know, the only two exceptions were Wang Changyao and his wife Zhang Sanjie, who led a guerrilla column some two thousand strong in Shandong, which was eventually destroyed by a CCP attack from the rear during an engagement with the Japanese; and Chen Zhongxi, who led a guerrilla detachment in Zhongshan county in Guangdong and was killed in battle by the Japanese. In retrospect, our failure to participate in the military resistance was one of the main failures of the Chinese Trotskyist movement. We should have admitted that it was a big mistake to oppose all military activities and place ourselves outside the mainstream of the resistance simply for fear of committing a 'military opportunist' deviation.

One of the most important lessons of the mass movement that has emerged in most backward countries since the Second World war is that, when the ruling class is becoming more and more reactionary and the system more and more militarised, no revolutionary party can hope to seize power unless it engages in armed struggle. This is not a new discovery: one of the basic differences between Leninism and reformism in all its guises lies precisely in this recognition of the importance of military force. Today, as bourgeois democracy continues in its decline, it is increasingly important to recognise this principle.

Chen Duxiu's estimate of He Jifeng did not prove wrong. After this episode, none of us had any contact with him for many years and the next time I heard his name was in 1948, during the great Huaihai battle in which the Guomindang forces north of the Yangtze were destroyed. One of the main contributing factors to this brilliant and decisive victory of the People's Liberation Army was He Jifeng's active collaboration with them from within the Guomindang camp. It was as a direct result of the rebellion of the forces under his and Zhang Kexia's command that Huang Baitao's army group was surrounded and destroyed. He is at present a member of the CCP's National Defence Council.

At the same time as we were preparing our military venture, Chen Duxiu was making contacts with the Third Party (a small organisation led by Zhang Bojun), with the National Salvation Association (an anti-Japanese movement of intellectuals founded in 1936), and with some 'democratic personages' whose names I no longer recall. His aim was to set up a united front with them, and fight in the resistance camp for democracy and freedom under a banner independent of both the Guomindang and the CCP. There was a wide basis of support for such a programme in Wuhan at that time. The Guomindang government was so unpopular that not only the workers, the peasants, and the broad masses of the petty bourgeoisie but also a section of the traditionally pro-Guomindang bourgeoisie were moving rapidly into opposition, pinning their hopes more and more on the CCP in Yan'an. Naturally, the CCP did not allow such a situation to pass by, and either openly or secretly helped in the formation of a united front of the democratic parties. Chen Duxiu, with his sharp political instinct, considered that we (he always used the term 'we Trotskyists', although he denied that he was any longer a member of the organisation) should participate in this movement in order to extend our influence and break out of our isolation, which was in some ways self-imposed. Moreover, by participating in the movement, we could prevent it from being utilised by the Stalinists.

Pu Dezhi and I firmly rejected Chen's analysis and proposals. We considered that the so-called democratic parties were in reality nothing more than a handful of worthless politicians without any real mass following, and that we should therefore maintain our independence instead of entering into an alliance with them; our real task should be to win over any groups or individuals who might have illusions about them. I once again proposed that we should start up a paper of our own.

Chen Duxiu was furious at our attitude. He told me that I was a dogmatist with no idea of political reality, and that I and the Shanghai comrades were 'jackals of the same lair'. He asked me to attend a conference with the three democratic groups as his representative, but I refused; he then asked Pu Dezhi, and got the same reply. It was at that point that Luo Han turned up in the city, thus resolving the question.

After Luo Han's return from his fruitless mission to Xi'an, he had gone back to Yixing to resume his career as a pottery teacher. Yixing was soon engulfed by the war, and Luo Han, not prepared to leave his students behind, made his way to Nanjing with a group of twenty or thirty of them. (This was some time before I was released from prison.) When he got there, he found that the trains, buses and steamships were full to overflowing with rich men or high officials and their families, so he got hold of a pair of rafts, built cabins on them, lashed them together, stocked up with provisions and sailed slowly up the Yangtze to Wuhan. For security purposes, he also managed to get hold of two rifles. His little flotilla was a month or more on the water. After numerous dangers and adventures, he eventually reached Wuhan sometime in January 1938. The first thing he did when he set foot on dry land was to try to sell his two rifles at an inflated price to his old friend Ye Ting, one of the newly appointed commanders of the Communist forces. With the money from the sale, he hoped to help his students settle down in their new environment. Despite the fact that Luo Han was officially an 'enemy', Ye Ting found it hard to turn down his request. Although it was impossible for him to buy the rifles (which, in fact, he handed over to the Guomindang authorities) he managed to raise a small sum of money to enable his kind-hearted old friend to find accommodation for his pupils.

Most of the leaders of the democratic parties were old acquaintances of Luo Han, so he was in a better position to deal with them than I was. But, by nature, he was far from being a politician of that sort; he was too honest and straightforward, and completely unversed in the diplomatic arts. Therefore, after a few meetings with the members of the other groups involved, he tendered his resignation to Chen Duxiu. Chen then turned to the veteran Trotskyist Gao Yuhan, who was at that time living in Changsha, and asked him to take over as his representative; but, before Gao could get to Wuhan, the democratic parties suddenly broke with Chen. Thus the whole venture, like our military plans, came to nothing; this time, it was thwarted not by the Guomindang, but by the CCP. In order to contain the political influence of the Chinese Trotskyist movement, the CCP intimated to their 'democratic' allies that they should immediately break all links with us, at the same time launching a shameful and hysterical smear campaign against Chinese Trotskyism in general and Chen Duxiu in particular in the pages of the newly founded *Xinhua Daily*. The man who directed and master-minded this campaign was none other than our old friend Wang Ming, who had recently returned to China from Moscow and was in charge of CCP contacts with the Guomindang in Wuhan.

At this point, a short account of developments in the factional struggle in the CCP in the period before 1938 is needed. At the Zunyi meeting of the Central Committee in January 1935,[4] the Wang Ming group had lost its dominant position in the Party, and Mao Zedong, Liu Shaoqi, and their supporters took over the leadership – a position they maintained right up to Liberation and beyond. But Mao's victory over Wang Ming at Zunyi was neither complete nor decisive, and the latter's influence continued to linger on for a number of years; more-

---

4   Zunyi Conference. An enlarged Politburo conference held during the Long March in January 1935 at Zunyi, Guizhou province. At it, Mao won back his control of the military from the Wang Ming group.

over, this struggle is still not over yet, even as I write these lines.[5] The reason Wang Ming's group in China was defeated but not crushed is not hard to understand. Wang Ming was an authentic Stalinist, always looked upon by whoever happened to be in charge in the Kremlin (whether Stalin or Khrushchev) as the Soviet Union's most trustworthy agent. The CCP, despite the fact that it is led by a 'nationalist' like Mao and has grown strong roots of its own, is still forced to rely in many ways on Soviet aid, and is therefore obliged to tolerate Stalin's favourite Chinese son. This delicate relationship explains why Wang Ming was purged but not liquidated, and criticised but still awarded a seat (albeit the lowest ranking) on the Central Committee. After the Zunyi meeting, he continued to hold the top position in the Chinese community in the Soviet Union. Occupying a high position in the Comintern, he spun Stalin's instructions into 'theories', and wrote long articles in Russian for the press of the international Communist movement. He passed himself off as the chief spokesman of the CCP, prided himself on being a confidant of the 'great leader' and used Soviet aid to bolster his own position in the Chinese Party, all with the aim of maintaining remote control over the direction of the Chinese Revolution. After the outbreak of the war against Japan in China, he raised a number of proposals which diverged from Mao Zedong's line for the Party, and attempted to win back his old position in the leadership. Up to now, I have not been able to get hold of any of Wang Ming's basic documents of that period, but, according to Mao, the 'second Wang Ming line' was actually 'a revival in a new situation of Chen Duxiu's right opportunism during the period of the civil war'. According to party histories the lines of Mao Zedong and Wang Ming were clearly opposed to each other, but, in my opinion, it would be more accurate to say that this confrontation was in fact a protest by the revolutionary wing of the CCP (possibly including Mao Zedong himself) against the directives which Stalin was issuing from Moscow. Of course, Wang Ming invariably and unconditionally supported each and every position that Stalin adopted, unlike most of the other leaders of the Party in China.

When Hitler's Germany threatened the Soviet Union as a formidable new military power in the West, and the Japanese militarists were behaving more and more aggressively in the East, Stalin finally gave up hope of saving the Soviet Union through revolutions abroad and sneeringly described the world-revolution as a 'tragi-comic misunderstanding'. Communist parties outside the Soviet Union were treated as small change in the dealing that was going on between Moscow and the foreign powers, and their fate depended on whether or not Stalin could reach an agreement with the bourgeoisies in their coun-

---

5   [In 1957.]

tries. If any power, fascist or democratic, wanted reconciliation with the Soviet Union (reconciliation which was both temporary and unreliable), Stalin did not hesitate to order the Communist party in that country to submit to and support its ruling class. In the Far East, this policy was carried out in the most barefaced way. On the one hand, he 'demanded that the CCP make concessions to the Guomindang and its anti-popular policies, restrict its activities within the limits which the Guomindang and Chiang Kai-shek were prepared to tolerate, completely integrate the Eighth Route Army and the New Fourth Army into the Guomindang forces and carry out the line of unified command, unified organisation, unified armaments, unified discipline and unified military activities'. On the other hand, for fear of scaring Chiang Kai-shek and the Guomindang away from the anti-Japanese camp, he opposed going all out to mobilise the masses for the struggle, expanding the liberated areas, and arming the popular masses in the Japanese-occupied areas.[6] In short, Stalin wanted the CCP leaders to beg Chiang Kai-shek on their knees to tie down Japanese imperialism and prevent it from attacking the Soviet Union. At the same time, Stalin was flirting even more ardently with the Japanese themselves, in the hope of getting them to sign a mutual non-aggression pact. He finally achieved his aim in 1942, when he and Matsuoka Yosuke – a representative of Japanese militarism, but in Stalin's own assessment a 'moral Communist' – embraced in Moscow.

Stalin's shameful sell-out of his foreign comrades inevitably gave rise to protests among those people who were still to one degree or another true to the revolution. During the War of Resistance, the CCP by and large obeyed Stalin's directives, but made a number of revisions in their tactical implementation. I would argue that this is what is really meant by the 'two lines'.

The 'Wang Ming line' failed to succeed in the Party, and was denounced at the Sixth Plenum of the Central Committee in October 1938. Nevertheless, Wang Ming continued to play quite a role in the CCP as a Kremlin-appointed Inspector-General.[7] One manifestation of this was the smear campaign launched in Wuhan against the 'Trotsky-Chen Duxiu liquidationists'.

---

6   See Hu Qiaomu's comments on the 'Wang Ming line' – in reality Stalin's line for China – in the Chinese edition of *Thirty Years of the Chinese Communist Party*, p. 41, reprinted by People's Publishers, Guangzhou, July 1951.

7   I had indirect evidence of the authority which Wang Ming enjoyed after he arrived in Wuhan in early 1938. I was very close to a group of young refugees from Jiangsu and Zhejiang. They came from many different sorts of background: some were ex-members of the CCP, others were only just becoming involved in politics for the first time, and others still were members of the Guomindang's Three People's Principles Youth Corps, but the bulk of them were

When I first arrived in Wuhan, Wang Ming was still in Yan'an. The two men in charge of the Eighth Route Army office in the city and secretly directing the work of the CCP in that area were Dong Biwu and Qin Bangxian (Bo Gu). Dong's relations with us Trotskyists could be described as friendly. Luo Han was a frequent visitor to the Eighth Route Army-office and used to put all kinds of naïve proposals to Dong, Qin, and the others, which either embarrassed them or made them laugh. Dong Biwu even told my friend Peng Chesan that he would like to meet Chen Duxiu some time, and that, when Zhou Enlai came to Wuhan, he hoped that the two men could get together for a discussion. This was not just a typically Chinese polite remark; it also reflected, in some ways, the fact that, at that time, the CCP had not yet decided to attack the Trotskyists as enemies. But, when Wang Ming arrived in the city, the situation changed abruptly. All social contacts with the Trotskyists ceased at once. A vicious smear campaign was started up, at first secretly but later openly, against Trotskyism in general and Chen Duxiu in particular. Wang Ming was said to have launched this movement on the direct orders of Moscow, to co-ordinate with Stalin's world-wide offensive against all left-wing revolutionaries and, in particular, with his criminal policy of liquidating a whole generation of Old Bolsheviks within the Soviet Union. Under the influence of this campaign, the so-called democratic groups (which had all along followed the lead of the Communist Party) hastened to cut their links with us and swell the anti-Trotskyist choir.

Thus, Chen Duxiu's plans for joint activities with the democratic groups were thwarted, and he was forced to carry out a struggle against the growing slander campaign against him. When I left Wuhan in February 1938, however,

---

first-rate young men working in the resistance through the National Salvation Association. In order to find work and to stave off the threat of starvation, they spent most of their time chasing around after influential people in the Guomindang and the democratic groups. I found them an invaluable source of information. Once, when a group of them came back from an interview with the democratic leader Shen Junru, they told me how excited he had been after a meeting with Wang Ming. According to them, Shen Junru was greatly moved by that 'brilliant and capable man, with his deep theoretical understanding'. The democratic groups really did think that Wang Ming was the CCP's 'most outstanding talent'. On another occasion, I was told that Dr H. H. K'ung, at that time head of the Guomindang's Executive Yuan, had specially arranged for an interview with Wang Ming, since, according to my friends, 'he considered that it was Wang Ming who was the real representative, he was the direct representative of the Third International'. Hearing them, I could not help recalling an occasion in Longhua prison in Shanghai six years before, when I had learned from my fellow prisoners that Wang Ming had at last achieved his goal of controlling the Party. Now it was clear to me from what my young friends told me that Wang was 'down but not out'.

the campaign had still not formally begun. My main reason for leaving was that it seemed to me that there was nothing that could be done there, especially since all Chen's plans had fallen through. A second reason was that I had failed to arrive at any agreement with Chen on various questions relating to the War and the future course of the resistance. I found that, even though I agreed with him on some practical questions, my positions were generally much closer to those of the Shanghai comrades. Finally, after nearly a year of terrible hardship I wanted to see my wife and children again. For all these reasons, I decided to return to Shanghai and take part in the underground resistance there.

Chen Duxiu was strongly opposed to my going, mainly because he thought that—once I got to Shanghai—I would inevitably fall back into the old way of working which he described as 'three months' work, three years' jail'. But my mind was already made up, and there was no holding me back. Just before I left, he handed me thirty dollars for the journey and said he hoped I would return to the Guomindang rear in six months' time and work together with him again. By now, the Japanese armies were advancing along the Yangtze River towards Wuhan, and the Guomindang government had already pulled some of its offices back to Chongqing in Sichuan province in the south-west of China. At the same time, people were busy making plans to leave Wuhan. Chen Duxiu was preparing to leave for Sichuan, and Pu Dezhi and Luo Han intended to go to Yunnan and Hunan respectively. I was the first of us to leave: my journey took me through Hunan and Guangdong, and, in Hong Kong, I took a boat back to the International Settlement in Shanghai.

Soon after I got back there, Wang Ming's anti-Trotskyist and anti-Chen campaign hit the front page of the CCP's *Xinhua Daily* in Wuhan. On 15 March 1938, that same party organ republished an article by Kang Sheng (who had returned to Yan'an from Russia together with Wang Ming only a few months before) from the Yan'an *Liberation Weekly* titled 'Uproot the Trotskyist Gangsters – the Spies of the Japanese Bandits and the Common Enemy of Our Nation'. In support of the allegation that the Chinese Trotskyists were spies in the service of Japanese imperialism, Kang Sheng wrote:

> After the 18 September Incident of 1931, the Japanese imperialists occupied the three north-eastern provinces of China. At the same time, Japanese agents in Shanghai were negotiating with the Trotskyite gangster centre made up of Chen Duxiu, Peng Shuzhi, Luo Han, and others.... As a result, the Japanese agreed to give Chen Duxiu three hundred dollars a month through Tang Youren (a high-ranking official in the Foreign Ministry of

the Guomindang Government at that time). It was Luo Han who actually took the money on Chen's behalf.

The charges were so utterly absurd and contrary to common sense that, as soon as they were made public, not only Chen Duxiu's friends but also many people who had never before been involved in politics were outraged. A number of pro-Communist intellectuals also felt that these allegations went too far, and expressed their astonishment and disquiet. In reply to Wang Ming's deceitful campaign, Chen Duxiu compiled a pamphlet refuting all the charges made against him. It was published by the Oriental Book Company in Shanghai.

In acting in this way, Wang Ming appears to have confirmed the charge of 'dogmatism' which Mao Zedong had laid against him, for he had clearly failed to recognise that Wuhan in 1938 was not Moscow, that the *Xinhua Daily* could not play the same role as *Pravda*, and that Chinese public opinion would never accept such charges against a universally recognised revolutionary. Like all his other miscalculations, this could ultimately be traced back to Stalin. The year 1938 was the high point of the Moscow trials, when Bukharin, Rykov, and other Old Bolsheviks in Moscow were on trial for their lives as 'Trotskyists'. It was typical of Stalinism that whatever developments took place in the Soviet Union or the Soviet Communist Party were automatically transplanted to Communist parties throughout the world. Wang Ming was simply making a clumsy and foolish attempt to copy what was going on in Moscow.

But there was another, and hidden, motive behind Wang Ming's smear-campaign. At the time, we were only vaguely aware of the factional struggle that was going on in the CCP, and therefore interpreted Wang's campaign as an attempt to whip the leftist-inclined lower cadres into line at a time when the Party as a whole was moving rapidly to the right. There was some truth in this explanation; at the time of the CCP Guomindang 'remarriage', there was indeed widespread dissatisfaction and confusion in the party ranks, and, to stifle such dissent, the leadership decided to drag out the old Trotskyist bogey. But it is clear from material published since Liberation that another of the targets of the campaign was Mao Zedong himself, and that Wang Ming was using it as part of his attempt to regain power in the Party. History has shown that he failed in his aim, but had he and his friends succeeded in the intra-party struggle, and ousted Mao Zedong and Liu Shaoqi from the leadership, it is almost certain that the latter, like Zinoviev and Bukharin in the Soviet Union, would have gone down in Chinese history as members of the 'Trotsky-Chen gang'. From the time of the first Moscow trials in 1934 right up to Stalin's death in 1953, the victorious factions in the Communist parties have always claimed the mantle of Marxism-Leninism, while all the defeated factions have been denounced as

'Trotskyite gangsters', in confirmation of the adage known to Chinese in the form 'all victors become kings, all losers are bandits'. Wang Ming's aim was to kill two birds with one stone; but, unluckily for him, he missed his target and the stone fell back down on to his own head, in the shape of Mao's accusation that he was 'reviving Chen Duxiu's right-opportunist errors in a new setting'. The fact that Wang Ming was branded only as a 'Chen Duxiu' and not a 'Trotsky' confirms that he had been defeated but not yet routed.

The CCP also attempted to spread its anti-Trotskyist campaign to Shanghai, in an even more shameful way but with even less success. The course of events was as follows: Li Guojie, grandson of the famous Qing dynasty viceroy Li Hongzhang, became a collaborator with the Japanese and took up a post as general manager of the Japanese-controlled China Navigation Company in Shanghai; soon afterwards, he was assassinated by underground resistance-fighters. A few days later, the Communist-controlled newspaper *Yibao* carried a report that before his death Li Guojie had been seen in the company of the Trotskyist Peng Shuzhi. This scurrilous news-item was meant both to suggest that the Trotskyists and the collaborators were working together and also to prepare the ground for the assassination of Peng Shuzhi, either directly by Communist agents or indirectly by the Guomindang, and thus to 'prove' the original charge. We took the following countermeasures: Peng Shuzhi left home for a while and went to live elsewhere; at the same time, we asked a foreign lawyer by the name of Jowishoff (a German Jew who had fled the Nazis) to write to *Yibao* on Peng's behalf and demand a retraction of the defamatory statement. (We asked Jowishoff to represent us firstly because as a friend of the foreign comrade Li Furen [Frank Glass] he offered us his services free of charge, and, secondly, because the Chinese lawyers in Shanghai were afraid to touch the case.) As a result, *Yibao* published Jowishoff's letter and thus brought the whole sordid affair to an end.

On my way back to Shanghai I had stopped off in Hong Kong, where, for the first time, I met Liu Jialiang, a member of the provisional leadership of the organisation and chief organiser in the Hong Kong area. The first thing he asked me was what I thought of Chen Duxiu. He also fired a number of other questions at me, demanding that I answer yes or no. The atmosphere was so hostile that I felt as if I was back again in the old factional situation of the early 1930s. It was impossible under the circumstances to hold a real discussion, and, in addition, I had already bought my ticket for the journey by boat to Shanghai, so we discontinued our talks and hurriedly parted. Rather depressed, I walked back to my hotel on the Hong Kong waterfront with Chen Zhongxi. On the way, Chen unburdened himself to me. He told me that, in his view, Liu Jialiang's main aim seemed to be to create an artificial division between the young and old generations in the membership, and to rally the newer recruits under his own leadership. Chen went on to say that Liu took a very hostile attitude towards himself, Luo Xin, and other older comrades, and discriminated against them in the work of the organisation. I now realised that the reason Liu Jialiang had treated me so brusquely was because he regarded me too as 'old and worthless'. I advised Chen not to worry too much about being discriminated against. I had always considered that the best way of dealing with petty factionalism was to refuse to reciprocate, to avoid sterile classification into abstract categories such as young and old, and to concentrate instead on political questions and on the more long-term interests of the revolution, so that the problem would eventually disappear of its own accord. Chen Zhongxi had never received much of an education, but his nobility of character and his long experience of struggle enabled him to place himself above any narrow-minded considerations. He saw me to the ship and we said goodbye to each other. Unfortunately, we never had a chance to meet again. Six years later, Chen Zhongxi, by then the leader of a Trotskyist guerrilla unit, was killed by the Japanese during a battle somewhere in Zhongshan county.

On my return to Shanghai, I had a joyful reunion with my old friends Chen Qichang, Lou Guohua, and others. It was one of the happiest periods in my life. Only just under a year had elapsed between my arrest and enforced departure from Shanghai in May 1937 and my return to the city via a circuitous route in late February 1938, but it seemed to me that more things had changed in those few months than in the whole of the preceding half century. The International Settlement and French Concession of Shanghai had been turned into an island, cut off from the surrounding world by barbed wire beyond which demons and monsters danced fiendishly together, a world of ghosts and evil spirits. I myself had passed through numerous terrible hardships and had been within a hair's breadth of dying – it was a nightmare to think back on my experiences. But, here, I was back among old friends again – it was like being born a second time. Wang Mengzou, the publisher, was very pleased to see me back in Shanghai, and invited me and a few old friends round to his office for a meal. Among the other guests were Peng Shuzhi and his wife Chen Biyun (Bilan). A few days after I returned to the city, however, my one-year-old daughter, who had been born one month before my arrest, died of measles. I desperately needed money for my family, and every day our plight was worsening. In spite of the fact that my health had been badly damaged and I needed time to recuperate, the situation was so pressing that I immediately set about translating Malraux's *Les Conquérants* for a Shanghai publishing house. On top of this, I also had my political work to do. The functions of the old provisional committee had by now been taken over by the editorial board of *Struggle*, and I was asked to resume my position on it. Thus, a new period in my life began, in which my activities were mainly given over to translation and writing.

Ten years of working in the Opposition had left me with a hearty dislike for factional wrangling. During my long period of imprisonment, I had had the opportunity to reflect on many things. I regretted none of my past political activities, which, even to this day, I maintain were absolutely worthwhile; but there are certain things which, when I think back on them, sadden me, in particular the energy we wasted on factional struggle. While I was in Jail I often used to sigh and say to myself or my friends: 'If only we could have spent all our energies on deepening our theoretical understanding, and translating Trotsky's writings into Chinese, instead of wasting time winning people over to factional positions'. My sheer good fortune in getting out of Nanjing jail alive made me swear all the more firmly to put my remaining years to the best possible use and translate as many of Trotsky's writings as possible into Chinese. I used to think it was a paradox that, although Trotskyism had existed in China for ten years now, Trotsky's writings on the Chinese Revolution, which had been one of the main bases for the formation of the international Trotskyist movement after 1917, had still not all been translated into Chinese; and some of the translations that did exist were very poor. I promised myself that I would do my best to remedy this deficiency.

The period was one of swift and dramatic changes. Any serious revolutionary could not help but realise that whether or not one's projects and proposals became an active element in the situation would be determined not so much by literary activity as by political and especially military work. I entirely agreed with Chen Duxiu's emphasis on these points, and gave him my whole-hearted support. But, as our efforts in this direction never got off the ground, and I was back in Shanghai, where more active work was impossible, my interest once again turned to translation and writing.

Immediately after arriving back in the city, I received visits from Chen Qichang and Han Jun. From them I learned that in Shanghai too there was a division between 'old' and 'new' members, and that Han Jun, the leader of the 'young generation', had rallied support mainly on the basis of fighting against Chen Duxiu's opportunism. At the same time, this group discriminated against the whole of the 'older generation' in the organisation – those comrades, Peng Shuzhi among them, who had survived from the period of the unification of the four groups. Several days later, I discovered that this move to drive a wedge between the generations had been jointly initiated by Liu Jialiang and Han

Jun, the former from his base in Hong Kong and the latter in Shanghai. There was one comrade in particular in Shanghai, Jiang Zhendong (one of the leaders of the Shanghai insurrection in 1927), who thought, like Chen Zhongxi in Hong Kong, that Liu and Han's factionalist activities could only harm the organisation, and should therefore be exposed and halted. I advised Jiang Zhendong not to take these goings-on too seriously, and argued that no faction could last long or play a really active role in the revolution unless it was based on a clear political or organisational conception. To call all 'old men' corrupt and reactionary was just as meaningless as to say that 'new' equals 'good'. To oppose Chen Duxiu's political ideas was a very different thing from opposing all 'old men' who may for a longer or shorter period of time have had anything to do with him. Moreover, as I pointed out earlier, for the period from the autumn of 1937 to the spring of 1938, a clear distinction must be drawn between Chen Duxiu's political ideas and his more practical projects, and much of what he had to say was worthy of our consideration. Han Jun and Liu Jialiang were both promising revolutionaries. Han Jun in particular was an extremely hard-working comrade, in the excellent activist tradition of the CCP's middle and lower cadres. He was universally admired by all the younger comrades in the Opposition.

As for the 'old men', by the time the War of Resistance broke out, there were not very many of them left in the ranks of the Trotskyist movement, and those that were still there were, for the most part, apathetic, and given more to empty talk than to action. They would rather sit around reminiscing than work out the future prospects of the organisation. Others devoted themselves entirely to their wives and children, and their own individual interests and pursuits. Under the circumstances, it was understandable that those young people who had joined the organisation on the eve of the War of Resistance should want to brush aside such obstacles and move quickly forward. But the problem was that the really apathetic 'old men' had in fact left the movement of their own accord, and there was therefore no need to take active steps to exclude them from the organisation. As for that tiny handful of veteran Trotskyists who had remained members of the organisation and were nominally represented on its leading bodies, they were only too ready to make way for more active comrades and it was therefore pointless to talk of 'edging them out'.

Apart from these two categories, those veteran Trotskyists who – far from being an obstacle to the further development of the organisation – were actually one of its most valuable assets, numbered less than a dozen. Given this situation, it was not only unnecessary but positively harmful to want to set up an independent centre with the aim of squeezing out the 'old men'. Even though Han Jun and Liu Jialiang may have been acting from the best possible motives, their behaviour was clearly detrimental to the interests of the movement. Fortunately, the 'Liu-Han centre' was short-lived: by the summer of 1938, Liu Jialiang was forced by the British authorities to leave Hong Kong, and Han Jun took over in the colony from where Liu had left off; shortly afterwards, the two men fell out with one another, and the 'Liu-Han centre' ceased to function. As a result, this little episode of unprincipled factionalism did no lasting damage to the organisation.

But this is not to say that there were no differences of political principle within the Chinese Trotskyist movement at the outbreak of the War of Resistance to Japan. Broadly speaking, there were three main political divisions at the time: Chen Duxiu's position, which can be described as unconditional support for the War of Resistance; Zheng Chaolin's position, which opposed support for the War on the grounds that the Sino-Japanese conflict was from the very beginning an integral part of the imminent world war; and the position of the overwhelming majority of the Chinese Trotskyists, which can be summarised as support for the War, but criticism of the leadership. This third position drew support from 'young' and 'old' comrades alike, and was backed not only by Peng Shuzhi, but also by Chen Qichang and myself. These differences were serious, and could, by rights, have been expected to give rise to major confrontations within the movement, but, in fact, Chen Duxiu had already openly declared that his views were his own and not those of the Chinese Trotskyist movement, and there was no one in the organisation who completely supported his position; as for Zheng Chaolin, he lived in a remote part of the Anhui countryside, and had never seriously tried to put his views to the membership or to win influence. This meant that, from the failure of the attempt to divide the movement by age-groups, until the outbreak of the Pacific War in the winter of 1941, no ideological or factional struggles split the Trotskyist movement.

The period from the winter of 1937 to the winter of 1941, when Shanghai was cut off from the Chinese hinterland by the Japanese invasion, saw a boom in political publications by the various groups active in the city. During those years, the Japanese imperialists and their Chinese collaborators did not control the International Settlement and the French Concession, and the British and French authorities took advantage of their neutral status to give a certain protection to resistance activities. As long as a newspaper or journal was nominally published by a British or American citizen, it could be openly in favour of the resistance without fear of Japanese interference. At that time, all newspapers and magazines in Shanghai, whether run by the Communists or by the Guomindang, used to announce themselves as being either American or British concerns. Some of the Britons and Americans who acted as front-men for these publishing businesses only did so for the money, but most genuinely sympathised with the aims of the resistance.

It so happened that a young American photographer in Shanghai by the name of Alex Buchman was a sympathiser with the Trotskyist movement, and two or three relatively well-off Chinese sympathisers were willing to contribute a hundred dollars a month towards the cost of bringing out a Trotskyist journal; so the way was open for us to resume our public propaganda. With Buchman as our publisher, we launched a monthly journal in July 1939 under the name of *Dongxiang* (Tendency). Its main contributors were the poet Wang Duqing, Chen Qichang, Peng Shuzhi, Liu Jialiang, and myself. I edited the journal, and Lou Guohua looked after the technical side, including fund-raising and circulation. At two thousand copies a month, the circulation of *Dongxiang* was not particularly big, but – considering that it was confined to Shanghai – its influence was not inconsiderable. Even though we only managed to bring it out for a few months, it quickly got results: our correspondence was so large that we could dispense with the usual practice of writing our own 'readers' letters', and we made contact with many who shared our ideas.

Unfortunately, however, Japanese agents forced us to cease publication after only four issues. At that time, it was illegal for any publication to be printed unless it carried the name and address of its publisher. We had an arrangement with the Shanghai *Children's Newspaper* whereby we used their address and they used Buchman's name as their legal cover. Of course, the Japanese gendarmes were only too aware of the true meaning of 'American Limited Company', and, after a while, they began to put pressure on the publishers of *Children's Newspaper* through their Chinese collaborators in the Settlement, threatening them with bombs unless they stopped publishing *Dongxiang* from that address. Unwilling to run the risk, our 'hosts' immediately complied with the Japanese demands. The Japanese also began to put diplomatic pressure on the Settlement police and the American Consulate in Shanghai, with the result that Buchman was no longer able to act as our legal front-man. Though *Dongxiang* died an early death in October 1939, it had many mourners who wanted to see it resurrected somehow, including some who were willing to contribute money towards such a venture, so we decided to continue publication in pamphlet-form and thus avoid the need for registration. We brought out two pamphlets: *Poxiao* (Daybreak) that October, and *Xiliu* (Against the Stream) in January 1940.

During this same period, we managed to bring out a number of Trotsky's writings in Chinese, including *The Revolution Betrayed*, a collection of articles on the Hitler-Stalin Pact, and Victor Serge's *From Lenin to Stalin*. At the same time, we published fourteen pamphlets, some by Trotsky and others by Chinese comrades, through the Shanghai-based Oriental Book Company. These pamphlets achieved quite an impact, and circulated as legal publications throughout all those parts of China not under Japanese occupation. The most influential of these was Trotsky's *On the Eve of a New World War*, which sold over 10,000 copies and was the best selling publication we ever produced.

Shortly after the publication of *Poxiao*, Zheng Chaolin arrived back in Shanghai from south Anhui. His arrival was a great help in our publication-work. He was a brilliant linguist, although a poor speaker, and proficient in nearly all the main European languages, in particular French and German. It was he who translated Bukharin and Preobrazhensky's ABC *of Communism*, the earliest and most influential Marxist textbook in the Chinese language, in the 1920s. He had great stamina as a translator, and was both accurate and prolific. He had come to Shanghai partly because he had now recovered from his long imprisonment and was eager to get down to work again, and partly because we had asked him to share in translating Trotsky's monumental *History of the Russian Revolution* into Chinese. This was our most ambitious literary project ever, and took me and Zheng Chaolin a full year to complete. Ever since 1929, when I produced a full-length translation of Plekhanov's *From Idealism to Materialism*, I had earned my living as a translator of numerous books and articles. But, since my main aim had been to make money and most of the books I worked on were chosen for me by my publishers, I had come to look upon translating as forced labour and had taken neither pride nor interest in much of my work. But now things were different. Both Zheng Chaolin and I got down to work with all the creative zeal of writers. We worked with the utmost care and attention, referring not only to the Russian original but also to the French and English translations. Afterwards, we checked over each other's drafts, in order to reduce errors in the text to the very minimum if not to remove them altogether. The same sort of care was put into the proof-reading, and we eventually discovered fewer than ten printing errors in a book of over one million characters.

While the work was still in progress we informed Trotsky, who was by then in Mexico, and asked him to write a special preface for the Chinese edition. With great pleasure, Trotsky agreed. In order to fit in with our own publication deadline, he dropped everything he was doing and settled down to write a short introduction to our translation. But tragically, he was never able to complete the task, since soon afterwards his genius was struck down in its flower by a Stalinist assassin. When we came to print the *History*, we left four pages blank at the beginning of the first volume, to mark our deep sense of loss. But, just before we finished, something very unexpected happened: Trotsky's wife came across a part of the draft preface among her husband's posthumous papers, and immediately posted it on to us in Shanghai; with a mixture of grief and joy, we translated it into Chinese and included it as an appendix to the third volume.

We printed two thousand sets of the *History*, but had only sold two or three hundred of them when the Pacific War broke out and the Shanghai International Settlement was overrun by the Japanese, who immediately set about confiscating and destroying all anti-Japanese and other revolutionary literature. We did everything possible to prevent the remaining copies of the *History* from falling into their hands, but when the Japanese gendarmes finally threatened to search all the warehouses in Shanghai, the owner of the building where we were keeping the books lost his nerve and we were forced to burn them – nearly one thousand copies in all – in the courtyard. Even today, it hurts me to think of this enforced act of vandalism. After the War, we did a photographic reprint of the original and ran off two hundred sets of the three volumes, but the technical quality was far below that of the original.

Even the books we published seemed to be under the same curse as the Chinese Trotskyist movement as a whole. Despite all our efforts Trotsky's *History* was never able to achieve the influence we had hoped for. But, looked at in a broad perspective, we still had grounds for being satisfied with what we had achieved. Truth will prevail, and none of the many books that have been written on the October Revolution can hope to match Trotsky's *History*. Sooner or later, historians and Communists are bound to want to know the truth, and Chinese Communists will be no exception to this rule. In the course of their search, Trotsky's *History* will become a beacon to light up the ocean of darkness. We can console ourselves with this thought.

Just as I was checking through the final draft of the *History* I fell ill with tuberculosis. I was coughing up a lot of blood, and it was vital that I should get some rest. While I was on my sick-bed, the Pacific War broke out.

The Pacific War and a New Split in the Organisation

Wang Fanxi

Source: *Memoirs of a Chinese Revolutionary* (1957).

A new split came about in the Chinese Trotskyist organisation in 1941, on the eve of the Pacific War. It resulted mainly from two factors: a political dispute on how to characterise the War of Resistance and what attitude we should adopt towards it should China be drawn into the wider international conflict; and, later, organisational problems in relation to the status and rights of the minorities in the Party.

The War of Resistance was by now two and a half years old and the Guomindang government had fled to the south-west corner of China, where, but for the outbreak of the war in Europe, it would almost certainly have joined the Japanese-sponsored 'Greater East Asia Co-Prosperity Zone'. The European war gave Chiang Kai-shek a new lease of life, and the more complicated international situation increased his room for manoeuvre. In the early stages of the war, he had relied on Soviet aid (hence his co-operation with the CCP) to improve his bargaining position with the Japanese, but the course of the conflict, the balance of class forces at home, and the nature of China's relations with other countries prevented him from doing a deal with Japan and resulted in the prolongation of the resistance. When it became obvious in mid-1939 that the outbreak of a new world war was imminent, the Chinese bourgeoisie, headed by the Guomindang, made the fundamental change to an alliance with the democratic powers, linking its fortunes to the United States. The domestic policy of the government underwent a sudden and obvious change: it began to suppress all leftist groups, soon turning against its CCP allies – whose support it no longer needed – and partially destroying their New Fourth Army. This trend hardened after the Russo-Japanese pact of April 1941, the increasing tension between Japan and the United States, and the German invasion of the Soviet Union in June of the same year.

Early in 1940, one question was uppermost in our minds: once the War of Resistance to Japan became an integral part of the World war, would it undergo a change in character, and, if so, should our attitude towards it change accordingly? Sometime in the autumn of 1940, I wrote an article on this subject for *Struggle* under the title 'The Pacific War and the Chinese War of Resistance'. My main conclusions were as follows: once the Pacific War broke out, the Chinese resistance (insofar as it was controlled by the Guomindang) would have to be seen as an integral part of the wider imperialist war, since the Guomindang, as junior partner of American imperialism, would have to accommodate its plans to the grand strategy of the US Supreme Command; as a result, the aim of national liberation would of necessity become subordinate to American ambitions to take over from Japan as the dominant power in East Asia. As long as China's struggle against Japan was waged more or less independently of all imperialist powers, it would remain progressive, but, once it became enmeshed in the World war, its progressive aspect would dwindle away to insignificance or disappear entirely. After the Pacific War broke out, our attitude towards the Guomindang-led war should correspond more to the revolutionary policy advocated by Lenin during the First World war. We would lay more stress on the victory of the revolution than of the War.

Apart from Peng Shuzhi, who had just left Shanghai for Hong Kong, all the other members of the editorial board – Chen Qichang, Zheng Chaolin (who had been co-opted into it after his return from south Anhui, as a member of the original Central Committee elected at the unification conference in 1931), Lou Guohua, and Liu Jialiang – expressed their agreement with the article when it came up for discussion. At about this time, Peng Shuzhi adopted a completely different position in an article published in the Hong Kong Trotskyist organ *Huoxing* (Sparkle). He argued that the War of Resistance would remain progressive, regardless of whether it became caught up in the wider imperialist conflict, unless – and this was his sole reservation – British or American troops fought against Japanese troops on Chinese soil, in which case, that part of the War would not be progressive.

A fierce and long-drawn-out internal dispute therefore broke out as soon as Peng got back to Shanghai. At first, it was confined to the editorial board, but later it spread to the whole organisation. At first, the line-up in the leadership was five to one, but later Liu Jialiang went over to Peng's position to form a minority of two. In the course of the discussion in the branches of the organisation in Shanghai and Hong Kong, most of the rank and file at first sided with the majority on the editorial board; but, after the foreign comrade Li Furen arrived in Shanghai with a resolution drafted by himself, adopted by the Pacific Bureau of the Fourth International and broadly in keeping with the positions of Peng Shuzhi, the majority of the membership swung the other way, although the line-up on the editorial board remained unchanged. This controversy raged for several months, covering an ever wider area and delving more and more deeply into the various issues involved, so that it was not without a certain political and theoretical value. I presented my own positions on the ideological disputes of that period in my introduction (written in 1947) to our edition of Trotsky's *Problems of the Chinese Revolution*.

The subsequent split in the organisation, however, came about for other reasons. In the summer of 1941, Peng Shuzhi and his followers sponsored the so-called Second National Delegate Conference of the Chinese Trotskyist movement. I was too ill to attend, while Zheng Chaolin, Chen Qichang and Lou Guohua boycotted the meeting because of the way it had been prepared; as a result, the only participants were a small number of activists from the Shanghai area and four or five comrades from Hong Kong and Guangxi. The conference elected a new leadership made up of Peng's wife and other supporters of the pro-Peng majority, although, immediately afterwards, two of its five leading members came over to the minority. Naturally, we were not satisfied with the conference arrangements and the procedure adopted there, but we agreed to accept its outcome and to function as a minority within the organisation. At the same time, we demanded that a column should be set aside in our paper *Struggle* for a continuation of the discussion between the two tendencies, so that the issues at stake could be clarified. Our request was turned down, as was our later request for a continuation of the debate in the *Internal Bulletin*. We therefore decided to bring out our own bulletin, which we later called *Internationalist*, declaring that we would cease publication the moment the new Central Committee allowed us a discussion column in *Struggle*. Once again, Peng and the other members of the standing committee rejected our overtures, claiming our activities were in violation of organisational norms. They added that, if we continued to publish our bulletin, they would declare that we had left the Chinese Trotskyist movement of our own accord.

In this way the Chinese Trotskyist movement, which had united on 1 May 1931, split once again in May 1941, since when two separate organisations have continued in existence right down to the present day.

All this happened many years ago, and I have no intention of reckoning up old scores in the spirit of bitter or narrow-minded sectarianism. It seems to me, however, that the concept of the rights of factions and minorities within the party to exist and advance their views retains its force and is of enormous significance not only for Trotskyists but for the revolutionary-socialist movement as a whole.

Many of Stalin's worst crimes were committed under the spurious banner of 'Leninism'. Among the principles he most commonly abused was that of 'iron-unity', which, in his vocabulary, meant the prohibition of all factions within the Party and other parties outside it. It would be absurd to imagine, however, that a large organisation will be free from many differences of opinion; and it would be equally absurd to think that disagreements of this sort will not eventually result in opposing factions. The organisational principles elaborated by Lenin (including a part of his theory of the state) are not a crude negation of the traditions of bourgeois democracy, but a critique and further development of them. Although Lenin poured scorn on bourgeois parliamentarianism, the soviet system he advocated did not deny in principle the plurality of political parties. Immediately after the October Revolution, other socialist parties were active alongside the Bolsheviks in the Soviets. One-party rule was not a necessary feature of the system but a product of the unprecedented intensification of the class struggle during the Civil War. Leninist democratic centralism in the Party did not deprive minorities of their right to exist, or prevent their supporters from speaking up for themselves both within the Party and outside it. Lenin had often found himself in a minority in the Russian Social-Democratic Party, and always insisted on minority rights so that he could continue to struggle for his own positions.

The resolution which banned factions, passed at the Tenth Congress of the CPSU in March 1921 as an emergency measure at the time of the Kronstadt Uprising, was transformed by Stalin and his friends into an immutable and iron law of organisation. At first, it was a crime to start a faction in the Party, and, later, it became a capital offence to hold a different opinion from that of the General Secretary. Lenin's system of democratic centralism was transformed at the cost of innumerable lives into a despicable caricature of Hitler's 'one State, one Führer'. The perversion of Lenin's principles of organisation and the wiping out of a whole generation of revolutionaries by the bureaucracy was rooted in deeper historical causes than Stalin's personal inclination to abuse power, but it is undeniable that the Stalinist interpretation of 'Leninism' smoothed the way to Thermidorian reaction. Principles of this sort can lead to show-trials, bloodbaths and reaction in a country where the revolutionary party has already won state power, and to endless splits and organisational wrangles in a party which has not yet done so, as the tragic experiences of the Soviet Union and the Stalinist parties over the last thirty years show.

Although it is not my intention here to offer a full appraisal of Peng Shuzhi as a revolutionary, I feel that a few words are in order. Peng is undoubtedly a revolutionary, but his defects outweigh his virtues. His greatest defect was his acceptance of 'Leninism' in its Stalinist garb, in particular the Stalinist norms of organisation.

Shortly after the split in the movement, the Pacific War broke out. The entry of the Japanese army and gendarmerie into the International Settlement area made our work even harder. From December 1941 to the Japanese surrender in August 1945, it was hardly possible for us to develop any field of work, and difficult to maintain even a bare existence. Our links with other countries and other parts of China were severed and our activities restricted in scope. Since our organisation was small and weak, we made no attempt to engage as a group in any sort of direct armed confrontation against the Japanese oppressors. Faithful to our working-class orientation, we continued to devote ourselves to activities among the workers, with the aim of educating and organising them. In that respect, the recruitment of the lawyer Zhang Deze and his sister Zhang Dehan into the group is worthy of mention, since, with the help of their generous contributions, we were able to finance the running of the two schools in the workers' district in west Shanghai, and thus deepen our contacts with the working class. The workers in the silk-weaving factories in this area had long been in contact with the Chinese Trotskyist movement. Jiang Zhendong, one of the leaders of the famous Shanghai insurrections of 1927, assisted by my nephew Wang Songjiu, was in charge of these schools, which were staffed exclusively by Trotskyist teachers. Through them, we managed to extend our influence among these workers, whose children made up the majority of our pupils. Through the links we established, we succeeded in leading a number of struggles directly under the noses of the Japanese imperialists. We also built a base among the tram-workers in the French Concession during this period.

In spite of the priority we continued to give to the working-class struggle, various individual comrades joined anti-Japanese guerrilla detachments in north and south Jiangsu, and, unknown to us, played quite an important role in them. More significantly, two groups of Chinese Trotskyists, led by Chen Zhongxi in Guangdong, and by Wang Changyao and his wife Zhang Sanjie in Shandong, succeeded (again without the knowledge of the Shanghai centre) in organising guerrilla detachments several thousand strong and carrying on fighting against the Japanese for nearly two years. Unfortunately, as mentioned earlier, both were annihilated, either by the Japanese (in Guangdong) or by the combined forces of the Japanese and the CCP (in Shandong).

Taken as a whole, however, our guerrilla activities during the period of the Japanese occupation were of little account. Our efforts in Shanghai as usual centred on education, propaganda, writing, and publishing. Considering the unbearable conditions, this was not easy. At great risk to our lives and despite enormous difficulties, we managed to bring out some fifteen issues of *Internationalist* during this period. *Struggle*, which had first been published in 1936 and had the longest run of any Trotskyist journal in China, was taken over by Peng's new Central Committee after the split, but it folded during the occupation of the International Settlement of Shanghai. Apart from a short interval at the beginning, Peng's group published no organ whatsoever during the Japanese rule of the city. The pages of *Internationalist* carried commentaries on current political developments, anti-Japanese propaganda, and many theoretical analyses of the War and of the inevitability of revolution. Most of the important articles were written by Zheng Chaolin. Zheng had long been famous as a contributor to the CCP press but it was only now that his talents as a creative theoretician began to bloom. During those darkest years, he wrote his most brilliant and substantial pieces, including *Dialogue Between Three Travellers* (a theoretical treatise of revolution written in novel form), a book of memoirs (an inner history of the CCP from the early 1920s through to 1930), and the *ABC of the Theory of Permanent Revolution*.

But the one work to which he devoted most care and attention was his *Critical Biography of Chen Duxiu*, which – to judge from a reading of the manuscript – was the most brilliant history of modern Chinese thought to have been written to date. The pity of it was that apart from the ABC, none of his manuscripts from this period ever saw the light of day. When the Chinese Trotskyist movement was destroyed during the nation-wide round-up in December 1952, they were locked up by Mao's political police together with their author.

Chen Duxiu died on 27 May 1942 in Jiangjin, Sichuan province. His death was not unexpected, since we had known for a long time that he was suffering from incurable sclerosis, but it still saddened us immensely. Before the outbreak of the Pacific War, we had regularly received letters from him in which he kept us informed about his state of health, and, on the basis of these reports, a doctor we knew in Shanghai used to prescribe medicine which we then posted on to him via Hong Kong, since it was by that time unobtainable in the interior of the country. Those of us who had been on intimate terms with Chen Duxiu experienced the loss more keenly than those who had never known him. Chen Duxiu's thinking in the final years of his life was already far from Trotskyism, but I was not alone in thinking that, had he lived longer, he would almost certainly have progressed beyond these views and, under the pressure of events, returned to the Trotskyist camp, since he not only had all the attributes of a genuine revolutionary but also was a shrewd and brilliant observer. Even though we on the *Internationalist* editorial board were further from Chen's views – especially on the question of the War and the resistance – than Peng Shuzhi's group, we nevertheless looked upon him as a comrade and even a teacher, and published two articles (one by Zheng Chaolin, one by me) in mourning for the death of this giant of the modern Chinese Revolution. At the same time, Peng Shuzhi denounced Chen in a mimeographed issue of *Struggle* for 'failing to maintain his integrity in later life'.

Peng then attacked us for the 'non-political' attitude we had taken in going out of our way to sing the praises of a former comrade who ideologically had gone over to the enemy camp. We disagreed with him at the time, and today

I am even more firmly convinced that we were right in what we had done, since the very act of making an appraisal of Chen Duxiu as a person involved questions which were, primarily, not ideological but political. In assessing and mourning him, we had to bear in mind that, in their own narrow party interests, the CCP and the Guomindang combined to destroy his reputation – the former either by passing over his death in silence or by besmirching his memory, and the latter by paying him false compliments and distorting his ideas. Their aims were essentially the same: to deprive him of his rightful place in history, and in so doing to strike a mortal blow at Chinese Trotskyism.

In mourning Chen Duxiu, we had to do everything within our power to restore him to his rightful position as the most outstanding figure in the history of modern Chinese thought and the embodiment of the entire period of Western political thought from Rousseau to Marx, and point out that the adoption by such a man of Trotskyism showed that the historical role of our movement in China was to act as a link between the revolutionary traditions of the past and the promise of the future. We therefore had to stress his positive and progressive sides and his great contribution to cultural and political life over the previous thirty years. His later ideological differences with us (differences which, it should be added, never had any effect whatsoever on the actual political life of China) were of minor importance. In the face of our bitterest enemies, it was only right that we should screen the weaknesses of our old comrade-in-arms.

The struggle to restore Chen Duxiu to his rightful place in history, inseparable as it is from the struggle to rehabilitate the name of Chinese Trotskyism as a whole, will be even more important in future years. Mao Zedong understands this point well, which is why, to this very day, despite his own great victory and despite the fact that Chen died many years ago, he has never once relaxed the struggle against him.[1] The first Chinese translation of the autobiography Mao related to the American journalist Edgar Snow, published in Hankou in 1937, contains a frank acknowledgement of the influence Chen Duxiu had on him; and it would be no exaggeration to say that Mao, both ideologically and personally, sat at the feet of Chen. In the original interview, Mao deliberately played down this influence, but, after the launching of the Moscow-inspired campaign against Chen and Trotsky, even this small acknowledgement was enough to get the book withdrawn from circulation. From then on, intellectual circles in Yan'an and fellow-travellers in other parts of China systematically

---

1 During the last years of his life Mao himself never said anything about Chen Duxiu. Through the so-called 'Gang of Four', however, Chen was bitterly denounced during the Cultural Revolution as a 'traitor' and a 'Confucianist'.

began to falsify the history of modern Chinese thought, and, in particular, the history of the May Fourth Movement, with the main aim of playing down the role of Chen Duxiu. For Mao to pass over the role of Chen Duxiu in silence when listing the names of progressive thinkers in China in his 1949 article 'On the People's Democratic Dictatorship' was equivalent to the Bolsheviks' naming of only the Decembrists and the Narodniki as their forerunners, and their denial of the role of Plekhanov as their immediate predecessor. Chen Duxiu's position in the history of Chinese revolutionary thought can at least be put on a par with that of Plekhanov, and, even if we concede that he 'failed to maintain his integrity in old age', then this was, at worst, a failing he shared with his Russian counterpart. But, after the October Revolution, Lenin repeatedly expressed his admiration for that 'father of Russian Marxism' and urged young people to make a careful study of his philosophical writings, which he described as 'the best of their kind in international Marxism'. On one side of Red Square, there is a memorial dedicated to progressive forerunners of the revolution, on which Plekhanov's name figures as the last in line and direct predecessor of the Bolsheviks. Why then does not Mao Zedong treat China's Plekhanov – a comparison, if anything, flattering to the Russian – with similar justice? The answer is quite simply that Chen Duxiu's thought ties in with that of Trotsky, the most implacable enemy of Stalinism, the transmitter of the true values of Marxism and the October Revolution, and for that very reason the gravedigger of the Stalinist system.

A year or so after Chen Duxiu's death, we suffered another tragic loss: Chen Qichang died at the hands of the Japanese, after withstanding several months of the most terrible torture. Chen Qichang was a martyr of Chinese Trotskyism, and had been one of China's foremost revolutionary veterans. Born in Luoyang in Henan province, he joined the Chinese Communist Party while a student at Peking University in 1925, and carried out secret activities for the Party among students and workers. During the months and years after the defeat of 1927, he worked as a middle- and then a high-ranking member of the Party. On becoming a Trotskyist in 1929, he was expelled. He devoted the rest of his life to the activities of the Chinese Trotskyist movement. Like many other of my comrades, he earned his living by writing articles and editorials for various newspapers and magazines in Shanghai. Among the books and pamphlets published by the Oriental Book Company in Shanghai, he was responsible for editing and translating Trotsky's *I Stake My Life* and for writing and compiling *The Truth About the Moscow Trials* and *The Verdict of the John Dewey Commission*. He also wrote a book called *The Great Migration of the Chinese Nationalities*, and was one of the main contributors to *Struggle*: most of the articles on economic questions came from his pen. He had all the qualities of a first-rate revolutionary. He knew how to endure poverty and hardship, and was never interested in the luxuries of life; he hated evil in all its forms, and had a great compassion for all oppressed and downtrodden people; he could not stand pretentiousness, and had none of the affectations of a 'leader'. He always placed himself in the front line whenever danger threatened and was a strange mixture of new-style comradeship and the old-style loyalty to his friends of a Chinese knight errant; he was so concerned about the safety and welfare of his comrades that he was known to everyone as 'elder brother'. Between 1931 and 1937, when the Guomindang white terror was at its most intense and the organisations we had established in China were being destroyed one after the other, it was he who provided the continuity in our repeated attempts to re-establish the movement. He was extremely vigilant in underground work, never once relaxing his guard; more than once, his courage and alertness saved the organisation from destruction. I described in Chapter 9 of these *Memoirs* how he managed to shake off the two secret agents who were trailing him and make his way back to Han Jun's house to raise the alarm. He was the complete opposite of those 'revolutionaries' who are so obsessed with their own importance that they put personal safety above all else, fleeing and leaving their comrades to their fate at the slightest hint of danger. Chen Qichang was especially contemptuous of behaviour of this sort.

Chen was arrested not as a Trotskyist but as a participant in the anti-Japanese underground resistance. After his arrest, however, the Japanese gendarmes discovered a large quantity of Trotskyist literature in his home, and his 'crime' immediately became more serious. He was subjected to terrible torture by his captors and asked the names and addresses of the other members of the organisation, but refused to submit and was eventually secretly executed in the gendarmerie headquarters.

Early in 1945, Han Jun died in Hong Kong under the Japanese occupation. Although, as I explained above, we never got on very well, I must say that he was also a first-rate revolutionary, an able organiser, and a man of experience in leading the mass struggle. He had originally been a leading member of the trade union-based He Mengxiong faction of the CCP, and had an expert knowledge of the Chinese labour movement. As a Trotskyist, he served three years in jail under the Guomindang. When the Japanese army occupied Hong Kong, Han was the leader of the branch of our organisation there. Although all the other anti-Japanese activists (both Guomindang and CCP) fled the former British Colony, Han decided to stay with the Hong Kong workers to whom he was so closely linked, living as a labourer, suffering and struggling together with his friends and comrades, and finally dying of terrible poverty and starvation. He was the husband of the most outstanding woman revolutionary in the Chinese Trotskyist movement, Li Cailian.

Li Cailian, who had in fact died in 1936, was born into a poor working-class family in Hankou. Her father died while she was still a baby and her mother eked out a living by taking in laundry. When the Northern Expedition reached Wuhan in 1927, Li Cailian, although only a girl of fifteen, plunged headlong into revolutionary work and was active as a trade union organiser in the workers' district of Qiaokou. After the defeat of the Revolution, she was sent to study at Sun Yat-sen University in Moscow, where she had a wide circle of admirers and was known as the 'Beautiful Sparrow'. Though courted by the sons of high Guomindang officials (who, despite their fathers' break with the CCP, were still living in Moscow), she contemptuously spurned her suitors and ended up marrying a student called Lu, who had absolutely no links with the Guomindang bureaucracy. After the factional struggle in the CPSU spilled over into the Chinese community in Moscow, she became a member of the underground Left Opposition. She returned to China with my group in 1929, worked for a short period in the Party and was expelled at about the same time as I. During the period in which four separate Trotskyist organisations were in existence, she was a member of the October group.

After the destruction of the unified organisation in 1931, her husband Lu went over to the Nanjing government. At the time of his defection Li Cailian was giving birth to a son in a Red Cross hospital in Shanghai, but, when her husband told her of his decision, she secretly decided to break with him and fled the hospital soon after. To her great sorrow, she was forced to leave her child behind. It was a cruel choice to make, but she had no money to settle accounts with the hospital authorities and was afraid that, if she lingered a moment longer, she would be sent to Nanjing together with her husband. After this incident, she became even more firmly committed to the revolution, tirelessly throwing herself into the struggle at grass-roots level and diligently studying the writings of the great masters of Marxism. She had a frail constitution and lived in great poverty, but, as Confucius said of his disciple Yan Hui, 'others could not bear to see such suffering, but he himself was always happy'. At first, Cailian was loved mainly for her looks, but, after she became a fully-fledged revolutionary, this rather superficial love gave way to feelings of deep respect and honour. We were amazed that such a strong will could inhabit such a frail body. However, extreme poverty gradually took its toll of her health, and she was found to be suffering from pulmonary tuberculosis. Like the rest of us, she was penniless and had no chance of receiving treatment, so her condition gradually worsened.

When I saw her again in early 1935 (after four years of separation) she had already lost her voice, and had to lie on her bed all the time. But I was astonished by her high spirits, her continuing sense of fun and her complete confidence in our cause. We all fervently hoped that her strong will would enable her to overcome her physical exhaustion, and that she would recover her health, or at least survive to see Han Jun come out of jail. But will-power cannot hold back the laws of nature forever, and, one evening in the early summer of 1936, she died suddenly while staying at a comrade's house, at the age of twenty-four. The extent of our grief can be judged from a letter Chen Duxiu wrote at the time to Zhao Ji. It made a deep impression on me when I read it, and I believe I can quote correctly from memory: 'Cailian's death grieved me deeply. Although many of my closest comrades have met an early death, I have never before experienced such sorrow. Perhaps it is because I am getting old...'. But the key to Chen's sorrow must have lain elsewhere than in his age, for we younger comrades were no less grief-stricken than he. The untimely death of a loyal revolutionary is always hard to bear; all the more so, that of an outstanding woman comrade. Historical conditions have up to now meant that women militants are invariably outnumbered by men, so that they are all the more treasured, and their loss the more keenly felt.

I have described only a few of the Trotskyists who died and suffered during that period. Many, many more were oppressed, thrown into prison and even murdered for their beliefs, not only by the Japanese invaders but also by the Guomindang government and the CCP authorities. In the Guomindang areas, particularly Chongqing, Trotskyist workers in the arsenal and other factories were arrested and some, including Wang Shuben, one of the leaders of young Trotskyists, were imprisoned and murdered in the notorious Xifeng concentration camp in Guizhou province. In the areas controlled by the CCP, those Trotskyists who had gone there of their own accord (for example Wang Shiwei) were brutally persecuted and eventually murdered. All of these comrades equally deserve to be remembered, but, unfortunately, space does not permit me to do so. All I have done is to give some examples of how Chinese Trotskyists lived and struggled during these years.

From War to Revolution

Wang Fanxi

Source: *Memoirs of a Chinese Revolutionary* (1957).

When the Japanese surrendered in August 1945, there was a sudden surge of activity among the people of the occupied areas. I had never before seen such an abrupt and dramatic transformation in the mood of the masses after a long period of inactivity. Overnight, their mood changed from deep despair to exhilarated optimism, and, at the same speed, from optimism to angry dissatisfaction when they saw their hopes dashed by the Guomindang. Ever since the launching of the War of Resistance in 1937, we had been firmly convinced that a revolution was inevitable, that war was the mother of revolution. There was, therefore, an important difference between us and Chen Duxiu, and even between us and the 'majority' around Peng Shuzhi, since we stressed the need not only to prepare, but – even more importantly – to prepare ourselves for, the revolution. But, despite our firm conviction that the revolution was imminent, we found ourselves ideologically and organisationally unprepared for it when it actually broke out.

When the masses began to show their readiness to act, there was no strong revolutionary-Marxist party to give them shape and direction. The CCP had long since withdrawn its cadres from the cities of southeast China, and the various 'democratic parties' could do little more than show the flag. There was therefore a vacuum of revolutionary leadership. If the Chinese Trotskyist movement had had several hundred or, better still, several thousand basic cadres, I believe we would have been in a position to fill that vacuum. Even if the forces of the CCP had then re-entered the cities to dispute the leadership of the mass movement with us, we would not necessarily have suffered a smashing defeat; and even though they might still have ended up by winning control of the whole of China, at least the political situation in the Guomindang areas in the period from 1945 to 1949 would have gone down in history in a very different form.

But, although we were few, and weakened by the split, we successfully intervened with our small forces in the postwar movement, rapidly growing in strength and influence. This was mainly because the political situation in China favoured our position. Having suffered terribly during the eight years of war, everyone was eager for peace, but the 'victorious' Guomindang was actively preparing a new all-out war against the Communists which rapidly led to economic crisis and ruin. People in the Guomindang-controlled areas, especially the students and the working masses, angrily rose up against the government around the slogans 'no civil war', 'no dictatorship', and 'no starvation'. These slogans fitted in perfectly with the revolutionary-democratic programme for which the Chinese Trotskyist movement had been struggling for over fifteen years.

Shortly after the War, we in the Internationalist group began to edit a daily supplement to *Qianxian ribao* (Front-line Daily), a Shanghai newspaper whose chief editor was Huan Xiang (at the time of writing, Chinese Chargé d'Affaires in London). Everyone with any literary ability in our group was mobilised to write for it on militant themes. We achieved quite an impact among students and workers in Shanghai, and, for that reason, the Guomindang Department of Social Affairs in the city intervened after only a few weeks to silence us.

By this time, we were no longer publishing our mimeographed *Internationalist*. Now that new newspapers and periodicals were springing up on all sides, we decided to bring out a properly printed and openly distributed fortnightly of our own called *Xinqi* (New Banner). The first issue came out in July 1946. The main responsibility for writing and editing fell on Zheng Chaolin and myself. This meant that the two of us were under a great deal of strain. Just before the sixteenth issue appeared, the paper was banned by government-decree, so the news stands would not take it and our commercial printers refused to print it. Unwilling to bow to Guomindang pressure, we rigged up a printing press which though small (and similarly operated) was bigger than the one on which we had printed *Struggle*, and got two of our comrades to do the typesetting. We brought out a further six rather unattractive, hand-printed issues of *Xinqi*. Because of printing difficulties, the paper no longer appeared as regularly as before, so we switched our main efforts to books and pamphlets, publishing under the name *Xinqi Library*. As far as I remember, we brought out Zheng Chaolin's *ABC of the Theory of Permanent Revolution*, his translation of Trotsky's *The Permanent Revolution* and his abridged translation of Trotsky's *My Life*. I put together an edition of Trotsky's articles and letters on China, calling it *Problems of the Chinese Revolution*. We also brought out the photographic reprint, mentioned earlier, of the Chinese translation of Trotsky's *History of the Russian Revolution*.

During the same period, the members of the 'majority' also resumed their publishing activities. At first, they brought out an academic periodical called *Qiuzhen* (Seeking the Truth), later joined by a smaller magazine initially called *Qingnian yu funü* ('Youth and Women') and afterwards renamed *Xinsheng*

('New Voice'). These two publications also had a certain influence, particularly among students. They differed in their editorial policy from our own *Xinqi*. In order not to fall foul of the authorities, they blurred their true positions and concentrated their fire on the CCP rather than the Guomindang.

The organisational work of our group also developed during this period, partly because many old comrades who had lost touch with us during the War found their way back into our ranks, but mainly because, through our propaganda, we recruited many new members in the mass upsurge then taking place. Many old friends returned to Shanghai, among them He Zishen, whom I had last seen in Suzhou Jail fifteen years before. He brought with him Chen Duxiu's posthumous manuscripts and papers on philological and political subjects which he intended to publish in Shanghai. Many of our old friends scattered throughout the remote south-eastern provinces of China (Sichuan, Yunnan, and Guangxi) came to Shanghai for a short stay to re-establish links, and the rest resumed contact through correspondence.

They were inevitably rather discouraged to learn of the new split in the movement. Most of them looked forward to early re-unification, and they held discussions with both groups to probe the depth of the differences that separated us and the possibility of fusion. But, when they discovered that re-unification was out of the question (for the time being at least), they had to opt for one of the existing organisations. All the 'veteran cadres', apart from Yin Kuan, who sat on the fence, joined the 'minority'.

Through our postwar publishing activities, we made contact with a number of young revolutionaries. Although *Xinqi* had a print-run of only 2,000, we managed to distribute copies to readers in Shanghai and other parts of China, so that it had quite an influence among both people we knew and others we did not. During the Japanese occupation, a youth group had been set up in Shanghai called Yishe ('Society of Tomorrow'). Most of its members were university students, teachers in middle and primary schools, and shop and office workers; there were also several artisans and factory workers. Under the cover of being a centre for social and academic activities, it was an anti-Japanese political organisation, whose leaders at first inclined towards the CCP but were gradually won over to Trotskyism. By the end of the War, when we began to publish *Xinqi*, practically the whole group had come over to our side, living and working in close contact with the younger members of our own organisation. They also set up a correspondence society and published their letters in a weekly symposium. The discussion evolved informally, so everyone engaged in it could take part in a free exchange of opinions. This correspondence society was afterwards re-organised into a Marxist Youth League under our political guidance, and was one of the main forces behind the numerous mass protest-movements launched by Shanghai students in the years 1946 to 1948.

The 'majority' developed along more or less similar lines and engaged in similar work, but preferred Stalinist-style cultural and recreational activities, such as folk-dancing, singing, and picnics.

As they were growing in influence, each of the Trotskyist organisations began to move at about the same time towards founding a party. Neither of the rival leaderships really wanted re-unification, so, despite a strong wish for reconciliation among the rank and file, the two Chinese Trotskyist groups moved rapidly towards becoming two parties. The 'majority' held a national delegate conference in August of 1948 which adopted the name of Revolutionary Communist Party of China. We made similar preparations and held a national delegate conference six months later, on 27 and 28 April 1949, when we passed a number of resolutions on organisational and political questions, set up a Standing Committee composed of Zheng Chaolin, He Zishen, Lin Huanhua, comrade Y. (the leader of the Yishe group),[1] and myself, and adopted the name of Internationalist Workers' Party of China. Our membership was tiny: we had sixty-four comrades in Shanghai and a little over one hundred in China as a whole, although we had a rather larger number of sympathisers. The 'majority' party's membership was probably bigger than ours, but not by much. The two parties together had a membership roughly half the size of that registered at the Unification Conference in 1931, and less even than the number of Chinese Trotskyists active in the Soviet Union in 1929, But, despite its small resources, Chinese Trotskyism, then exactly twenty years old, was clearly heading for a revival, after suffering repeated blows from all sides. Had the rise of the revolutionary mass movement among the students and urban poor not been interrupted and brought under control by the unexpectedly rapid military victory of the CCP, the Chinese section of the Fourth International might have grown into a powerful political force.

But, unfortunately, events did not develop in the way we would have liked. The Guomindang régime emerged from the War much more corrupt than it had gone into it. The whole ruling class around the Guomindang had been transformed into a gigantic group of speculators, smugglers, parasites, and plunderers, alienating itself from nearly every other class of Chinese society. But just how rotten and isolated it had become was still not apparent. With the support of US imperialism, it looked very powerful. Only when it was put to the test of civil war was the awe-inspiring régime of the Guomindang revealed as a building riddled to the core with termites. The speed with which the whole Guomindang system collapsed not only shocked the Chiang Kai-shek clique and its patrons in Washington, but also took Stalin and, to some extent, even Mao Zedong by surprise. We Chinese Trotskyists, needless to say, were also caught unawares.

Thus, at the end of 1948, with the People's Liberation Army threatening Nanjing after their brilliant victory in the Xuzhou area, Peng Shuzhi continued to insist at the Emergency Conference of his party that the Chinese Stalinists could not and would not achieve victory on a national scale, although he and his followers resolved at the same time to transfer their central committee and other leading members from Shanghai to Hong Kong.

By the time we held the founding conference of our party in April 1949, the Communist armies had already crossed the Yangtze River and occupied Nanjing and were marching on Shanghai along the Nanjing-Shanghai railway line. The victory of the CCP was certain, and all our discussions of political and organisational questions took it as their starting point. As I lost all the relevant documents when I was arrested and expelled from my 'sanctuary' in 1949, I cannot say exactly what was in our political resolutions; but I do remember that we approved a series of guidelines, drawn up in a programmatic resolution by Zheng Chaolin, on our fundamental positions concerning the proletarian revolution, and also appointed a programme commission to work out their political content in more detail. I myself drew up the political resolution, but am unable to reproduce its contents from memory. The organisational resolution drawn up by Comrade Y. discussed the lessons of the split with Peng's group at some length, and, for the first time ever in the literature of the Chinese Communist movement, officially stated that, according to our interpretation of the Leninist principle of democratic centralism, minorities in the party have the right to form factions or tendencies on the basis of their different political positions; that minorities should subordinate themselves to the majority in action; and that the majority should respect the rights of all minorities.

The main question before the conference was how to continue our work under CCP rule. We decided not to move the organisation out of China. This was not because we had the slightest illusions about the 'magnanimity' of the CCP or were unaware how easily the CCP's system of mass-based political surveillance could crush our small organisation. It was based on the simple conviction that it was better for a revolutionary organisation of the working class to go down fighting than to quit the field without a contest. Although this conviction was widespread in the organisation and could not be attributed to any one individual, Zheng Chaolin was its staunchest upholder. Even if we leave aside Zheng Chaolin's other strengths, his Peter-like spirit of martyrdom alone will ensure him a lasting place in the history of the revolution. Our dilemma was similar in many ways to that of the early Christians under Nero – should we stay in the capital or flee to a safe place? Some approached the question mainly from the point of view of their own fate, others from the point of view of the future of the organisation as a whole; but Zheng Chaolin did not wait for a voice from the heavens to ask '*Quo vadis?*': his mind was made up from the very outset.

In no sense was our attitude one of collective suicide. After we had decided to stay, we turned to the problem of how to work in the changing circumstances. In brief, we decided to dissolve our organisation into a collection of discrete units, breaking off all horizontal links and establishing a co-ordinating centre in a safe place beyond the reach of the CCP. I was chosen to man the co-ordinating centre and therefore had to leave Shanghai. As I was no deserter, I must admit that I was moved by the spirit of St Peter and retreated to my 'safe place' only with extreme reluctance.

Ironically, the place to which I had gone [Hong Kong] proved in the space of a mere four months to be anything but 'safe'. The authorities there, hypersensitive as a result of the dramatic changes that were taking place in China, did not allow me to stay, while the comrades who had stayed behind in 'Rome' continued in operation until the night of 22 December 1952.

During the three and a half years between the Communist takeover of Shanghai late in May 1949 and the nation-wide round-up of Trotskyists in December 1952, our comrades worked in many varied fields. The younger members of the Internationalist Workers' Party continued to bring out a journal with the title *Marxist Youth*, never flinching to raise criticisms of the new régime wherever necessary. Many of our comrades took an active part in the agrarian reform movement, and not a few joined the PLA, to fight in its campaigns to liberate the rest of the country. Those in industry led many strikes against capitalist employers, thus challenging the new government's policy of collaboration between workers and capitalists. In many areas, they became leaders of the masses, not only because they acted as staunch champions of the workers' interests but also because the workers who came under their influence were deeply impressed, in a period where Marxism was much in vogue, by their command of revolutionary-Marxist politics. In Guangzhou, Lin Huanhua became one of the principal leaders of the Guangdong Print Workers' Union; in what had earlier been the French Concession in Shanghai, a group of comrades led a series of strikes; and other comrades also engaged in various struggles in the Shanghai textile industry. Some of our members were inevitably dazzled by the Communist success and either openly or secretly renounced their beliefs and went over to the government. A smaller number betrayed the organisation to the authorities, so that, from early 1950, a series of raids was carried out against our members, particularly in the Shanghai and Wenzhou areas, in which we suffered serious losses. For example, Lian Zhengxiang, a worker in Wenzhou, and two former members of the organisation in Guangxi province died in front of firing squads. But, generally speaking, the CCP did not yet appear to have taken a firm decision to destroy our organisation. In some cases they clearly knew the whereabouts of certain leading comrades, but refrained from any moves against them. In other cases, they even made approaches to some of our older comrades through intermediaries. For example, the head of the CCP's United Front Department, Li Weihan, sent the ex-Communist Shi Fuliang to try to persuade Zheng Chaolin to do some translations for the government. But we continued to grow both in numbers and in influence throughout those three and a half years, which is the main reason why the CCP's secret police finally carried out their nation-wide raid on the Trotskyists in December 1952.

Since my links with the movement were automatically severed by the raid, I do not know exactly how many were arrested. A conservative estimate would be two to three hundred, but, since many of our sympathisers and relatives of known Trotskyists were also taken into custody, the actual number was almost certainly much higher. To take my own case as an example, my two nephews and my brother-in-law, who – apart from occasionally reading our newspaper – had no connection with the Trotskyist movement, were taken off to jail; worse still, a number of their friends, who were not even readers of *Xinqi*, were rounded up by the police. My wife, a totally non-political person, was also detained for a short period.

The raid was carried out in great secrecy, and the CCP has never once publicly acknowledged that it took place. In the four and a half years since then, our comrades have not yet been publicly brought to trial. Nor have any been set free so far – they are in prison or labour camp, and some of them may have been executed. As 'counter-revolutionaries', they are forced to share their cells with genuine counter-revolutionaries and common criminals, so that, on top of their physical oppression, they have to endure an even more painful spiritual oppression. It cannot be often enough said that these men and women have done absolutely nothing to deserve such treatment, and that they are genuine communists who have given their best years to the cause of the emancipation of the working class. The reason for the CCP's fear to give them a fair and open trial is clearly that Mao Zedong, Liu Shaoqi, Zhou Enlai, Li Weihan, and others know their 'old friends' very well and realise that if their revolutionary life-histories once became public, they would win the sympathy of Chinese workers and revolutionaries everywhere.

The immediate effect of the CCP victory was to send a shock-wave through the ideological life of the Chinese Trotskyist movement. The period from late 1949 to early 1950 saw an unprecedented upsurge in the level of theoretical activity – there was hardly a comrade in China who was not pondering the problems raised by the new developments. Zheng Chaolin in Shanghai and I in a seaport off the south China coast [Macao] began at almost exactly the same time to carry out a re-examination of the nature of Stalinism and the Soviet Union and an assessment of the reasons for the CCP's victory and the nature of the newly established state. Both of us put down our conclusions in writing, and secretly distributed them throughout China and beyond as reference materials to further the discussion. Peng's group (the Revolutionary Communist Party of China) also underwent a period of intense ideological ferment and produced a number of articles on political themes, the first of which to appear in book-form was Liu Jialiang's *The Present and the Future of China*. Two years later, Peng Shuzhi wrote his lengthy 'Report to the International Secretariat of the Fourth International'.

Since then, more than six years have gone by. In the meantime, a whole series of colourful and complex events have taken place, both in China and on a world scale. The time has now come to make a comprehensive and thorough-going assessment of the various opinions each of us advanced in the period immediately following the CCP victory, to decide which of them have stood the test of time and which have failed. I hope to make such a study, which would be beyond the scope of this book, at some future date.

The Communist League of China

Frank Glass (Li Furen)

January 1940

The following account reproduces pp. 9–20 of a report by Frank Glass found in the Trotsky Archive in the Houghton Library of Harvard University, where it bears the number T2.16872. Thanks are due to that body for permission to publish and make it available. The Niel Sih mentioned in the report is the pseudonym of Liu Renjing, Frank Glass's main ally inside the Trotskyist movement, who was broken by torture in 1937 and joined the Guomindang, subsequently making his peace with Mao in 1949. The text was written after consultation with Harold Isaacs towards the end of 1939, and, according to the correspondence in the Houghton archive, was sent to Trotsky on 21 January. Source: Revolutionary History, *vol. 2, no. 4, spring 1990.*

And now to our movement in China. My information is valid only up to 1 September when I left Shanghai. Again, all factual information concerning our organisation is at best approximate. Even our own comrades vary considerably concerning such factual information as the number of comrades, and so on.

The Communist League of China was founded in 1931, about four years following the Shanghai coup d'état of Chiang Kai-shek in April 1927. Subsequent to the coup, revolutionaries who disassociated themselves from Stalinism formed several different groups. These groups were united and consolidated, thanks mainly to Comrade Graves [Frank Glass], who arrived from South Africa, in 1931 when the League was formally founded.

The present strength of our party is approximately 500 members throughout the country, of whom approximately half are active. The distribution is approximately as follows: 100 members at Shanghai, 100 members at Fuzhou, a port half-way between Shanghai and the British Crown Colony at Hong Kong, 100 members at Hong Kong and Kowloon, which are adjacent, 100 members in the Zhongshan district, which is in the Pearl River Delta in South China, and the balance scattered throughout China. Comrades differ in their estimation of our strength. Some put the figure at 500, others state that 200 is more accurate. The War has made it impossible to ascertain the correct picture.

The number of comrades does not give a precise indication of the influence of the movement. We have in China close sympathisers in many quarters, particularly in student and intellectual circles. This is reflected somewhat by references in various publications to the Communist League and to the Fourth International.

The leaders of our party are all veteran revolutionists, many of whom were in the movement in China since 1921. Save for one member, I believe all members of the Central Committee have been in Guomindang jails. Among outstanding active comrades one might mention Comrade Wang Mingyuan [Wang Fanxi], who was a Left Oppositionist from the very beginning in Moscow, Comrade Peng Shuzhi, a original member of the CC of the CP of China, Comrade Chen [Zheng Chaolin] another original member of the CC of the CCP, Comrades Chen Qichang, Luo, and Han.

About 60 per cent of all comrades are workers; others are intellectuals or white-collar workers.

With minor exceptions, all the work of the party is illegal. Prior to August 1937, some 50 of our comrades, including Comrade Chen Duxiu, were in jail. All were released at various intervals up to the fall of Nanjing in December 1937. Prior to the War, our comrades were arrested on sight; two Central Committees were arrested en masse. These arrests were all made by the Guomindang or with the cooperation of the British or French police, as the case might be. In general, the Guomindang at present takes no active steps against our comrades unless they are participating in legal activity. The Guomindang threat against our comrades has, for the time being, abated.

In the two foreign areas of Shanghai, our comrades now have relative safety, but the British or French police will turn them over to the Japanese hangmen upon the demand of the latter without trial. Up to the time I left, none of our comrades had been arrested in Shanghai since the two preceding years.

The greatest danger in Shanghai, and elsewhere in China for that matter, at present lies in the GPU and Stalinists. Several of our comrades, including Comrades Peng and Graves, have been sent black-hand letters and warnings of one kind or another showing beyond any doubt a Stalinist or a GPU source. By linking the names in their press of our comrades with Japanese puppets, the Stalinists have in reality invited their assassination. Naturally, in Shanghai, our comrades take the greatest of precautions. Several, through fear of being recognised by Stalinists, live in complete hiding.

Recently, the Stalinists in Shanghai published a leaflet in Chinese entitled *The Crimes of the Trotskyists*. These 'crimes' included the usual stock charges, which have been rather well discredited by our party in bourgeois papers friendly to us. Unable to find any 'crimes', the Stalinists have resorted to personal slander and the pamphlet states, for example, that 'almost all Trotskyites are homosexuals and hold orgies in bathhouses'. Another 'crime' is the accusation that

Comrade Graves wrote a favourable review of Comrade Isaacs's *Tragedy of the Chinese Revolution*.

These slanders appear from time to time in Stalinist papers as well. But the Stalinists have not been completely successful. In Chongqing, they stated that Comrade Chen Duxiu was working with the Japanese and was a 'counter-revolutionary Trotskyite'. About 30 leading Chinese liberals, many of them very well-known public figures, wrote a vigorous denunciation of this statement. This denunciation, with the signatures of the writers, was widely published. Since then the Stalinists have said nothing publicly about Chen Duxiu. Chen also answered the accusation in a statement, widely printed, exposing with devastation the Stalinist accusation.

In Shanghai, our party, through its sympathisers, forced a Stalinist-controlled sheet to publish a retraction that Comrade Peng Shuzhi was working with Japanese puppets. These two examples show that the Stalinists must tread carefully in their slander campaign against us in China.

In Hong Kong, up to the time that I left, the British government had given the Stalinists carte blanche to do whatsoever they wished. But not our comrades. Several of our comrades led a strike against work on a Japanese boat. They were arrested and spent several weeks in jail. The arrests, our comrades learned from the British police officers, came about as a result of betrayals of our comrades by Stalinists. Subsequently, and probably as a direct result, the Hong Kong government passed laws providing for the arrest, imprisonment, or banishment without trial of any Chinese. Several of our comrades were forced to leave Hong Kong.

In areas under Guomindang control, work is likewise difficult. The death-penalty has been decreed for strikes 'or any other activities prejudicial to the interests of the state'. Early in 1938, two of our comrades, assisted by Niel Sih, published a legal magazine entitled *The Path of Struggle*. This magazine was suppressed after the second issue. Comrade Chen Duxiu has written numerous articles on the War. The government has banned publication of at least half of them. One of these articles consisted of an appeal to Japanese troops. As far as is known, none of our comrades has been arrested in areas under Guomindang control since the start of the War. At least one of them, however – Comrade Luo Han, a veteran revolutionist – met his death in Chongqing during a Japanese air-raid.

Some time ago, in Hankou, students organised an anti-Japanese demonstration. Our comrades were active in this demonstration. The police, however, prohibited the demonstration while it was in progress. They succeeded in stopping the demonstration only by firing at the students, killing one of them. Enraged, the students attacked a guilty plainclothes man. Tearing his clothes away, the students found the man to be a member of the Blue Shirts, Chiang Kai-shek's terrorist gang. Not a word of this incident appeared in any papers in China, including the Stalinist press.

Partisan

In areas under Japanese control, there are but few of our comrades, with the exception of the Zhongshan district in South China near Guangzhou in the Pearl River Delta. Here, some five to twelve of our comrades have been leading a guerrilla partisan band of some 100 to 200 fighters under the flag of the Fourth International since the fall of Canton in the Autumn of 1938. Reportedly, our comrades have engaged in several skirmishes with the Japanese with success. These comrades are led by a veteran of the Hong Kong strike. In the Japanese-controlled areas, the Japanese usually kill any Chinese found engaged in what is termed anti-Japanese work, under which charge comes anything from not having a cigarette for a Japanese soldier, incorrect bowing to sentries, and possession of a Guomindang newspaper. In these areas, the Japanese terror is directed not only against revolutionists, but against the entire population. Countless villages thought by the Japanese to have been assisting guerrilla-forces have been wiped out by fire, the Japanese machine-gunning fleeing inhabitants. These stories are by no means fanciful. They have been corroborated time and time again. The result of this terror has been that the peasants who attempted to return to their farms in Japanese-occupied areas have, for the most part, sought the safety of foreign areas, or of cities, or have gone to the interior. It is estimated that the war in China has produced no less than 60 million refugees.

The work of the party, at the present stage, is centred upon translations and publications, in strengthening the leadership, in building up the membership. There is relatively little agitational work at present, as such attempts as have been made have proved fruitless because of the passivity of the workers. Leaflets, however, are issued with frequency as special occasions arise, in both Chinese and Japanese.

Our party publishes two newspapers regularly. *Douzheng* ('Struggle') is issued once or twice a month in 1,000 copies, in tabloid format, of four to eight pages, with a circulation nationwide. *Douzheng* is published in Shanghai, and has appeared regularly since 1936, though it appeared irregularly some two years previously. *Huohua* (Iskra, 'Spark') has been published regularly in Hong Kong since 1937. It is issued once or twice a month, of four to eight pages, in tabloid size, in 1,000 copies, with a circulation nationwide. These papers are printed on presses designed and built by our comrades, and the press work is done by our comrades. The presses are practically silent, and are very ingenious. Presses are also used for various pamphlets, leaflets, internal bulletins, and so on. All our material in China is printed; workers will not look at a mimeographed page.

Our comrades stole most of the type from newspaper offices, print-shops, and so on. Originally, our comrades had a sympathiser do the printing. This sympathiser gradually raised his prices. A crisis was reached. Finally, Comrade Graves and other comrades posed as foreign police officers and in a 'raid' seized the press and type. It was quite a task, but was successfully done. From then on, the organisation operated its own press.

The distribution of our papers presents numerous problems. But thanks to sympathisers in the post-office, numerous copies go successfully through the mails. Others are distributed by our comrades and sympathisers in factories, among refugees, and so on. Our comrades estimate that each copy of our paper has at least four readers.

With the disappearance of Guomindang influence in Shanghai in the past two years, our comrades have found it possible for the first time to publish legally, in the foreign areas of Shanghai, several Marxist and other books. In this, the comrades have been greatly assisted by a sympathiser who is a publisher, and by a foreign comrade enjoying foreign protection who has set up a publishing concern, especially for this purpose. Our comrades now edit and publish a legal monthly (though not in the name of the party) which is the first legal publication of our party other than books. This monthly, called *Dongxiang*, or in English, *Living Age*, had a first print of 1,000 copies, almost all of which were sold. The only magazine in China to predict the Moscow-Berlin Pact, the magazine has gained great prestige and, provided it is not banned, may be of great importance.... Sympathisers edit and publish a daily legal newspaper for children, with a circulation of 3,000 copies. Recently, numerous books by Marx, Engels, Lenin, and Trotsky have been published legally, in addition to numerous pamphlets. Other books include Victor Serge *From Lenin to Stalin*, André Gide's *Retour and Retouches*, Malraux's *Les Conquérants*, and Silone's *Fontamara*. These translations mean a tremendous amount of work, the average requiring two comrades working from three to six months full time. At present, our comrades are translating *The Stalin School of Falsification* and *The Tragedy of the Chinese Revolution*. Since relatively few know foreign languages well, translation work goes very slowly. These comrades must also support themselves by doing translations for bourgeois concerns.

Release

As far as is known, there have been no betrayals of any of our arrested or other comrades since the founding of our organisation. There have been about five defections, three prior to 1936. In March 1937, four months prior to his scheduled release from prison, Comrade Niel Sih (Liu Renjing) capitulated to the Guomindang, but did not betray. Niel Sih was expelled from the organisation, and claimed he was unfairly treated. For a time, he was in close touch with some of our comrades, and assisted them with some legal work, but later joined the Publicity Section of the National-Military Council of the Guomindang.... Comrade Si, an exceptionally capable and brilliant comrade, was released from prison in December 1937. He is now mentally deranged, and has become a Buddhist monk. He claims to have discovered a new theory, and insisted that I send to Comrade Trotsky several huge volumes of Buddhist literature – in Chinese – for Comrade Trotsky's perusal.

Comrade Chen Duxiu was released from prison in August 1937. He went subsequently to Hankou, where he wrote for several legal publications. When denounced as a Trotskyist by Stalinists, Chen stated publicly that he wrote in his own name only and was not associated with any party or group. Later, a correspondent of the *New York Times*, who is a close sympathiser, interviewed Comrade Chen. Perhaps because of language difficulties, the interview was very unfortunate and Comrade Chen is said to have expressed the opinion that it would be best if Japan succeed in conquering China, because only this would give any perspective to the revolutionary movement. Fortunately, the correspondent mentioned this interview to no one save our comrades. Comrade Chen's statement that he belonged to no group drew great fire from our younger comrades. Finally, a comrade was sent to visit Chen and reported as follows: Chen stands 100 per cent with the Fourth International, but publicly disavows any party allegiance. In essence, the comrades decide neither to avow nor disavow, publicly, Comrade Chen, as long as in the net balance he proved helpful to the movement as a whole. This is, I believe, the situation at present. At present, Chen, who is in his seventies, is exceedingly ill. He is now living near Chongqing, and is said to be too ill now even to write. Concerted attempts were made to persuade Comrade Chen to go to the United States. When, finally, he agreed, it was too late: permission to travel was refused by the Guomindang, and also, his health now makes travelling impossible. Both because of his relative inactivity and his tremendous prestige, I do not personally believe Comrade Chen is in any danger from the Guomindang or GPU. He does, however, take precautions.

Aside from the case of Chen Duxiu, there have been no serious factional disputes for the past three years. There have been some minor disputes. One, as to whether our comrades should play an active role in forming anti-Japanese organisations, disappeared with the onslaught of the War. The other, concerning Chen Duxiu, has been practically liquidated. Up to the time I left, there had been no differences whatsoever concerning 'unconditional' defence or 'conditional' defence of the Soviet Union. The party stood unanimously for unconditional defence. In general, one may say that the Chinese organisation is at present free from any serious factional disputes. It is a closely knit, well grounded organisation. There is an almost complete absence of petty jealousies and politics. From 1931 to 1937, there were indeed severe disputes and factional fights. These resulted mainly from carry-overs from Stalinism. In these years of dispute, the party was set on a firm basis, its leaders schooled, and its programme was made clear and firm.

Shanghai is a complex city, but consists, briefly, of two foreign areas surrounded by Chinese areas. These latter areas are now in the hands of the Japanese. At least half of the Chinese industries were situated in these Chinese districts. Both at Shanghai and throughout China where the Japanese have conquered, industry has been completely smashed and there has been no revival whatsoever. Industries are flourishing, however, within the foreign areas of Shanghai and at Hong Kong. The cost of living in the past two years has increased tremendously. Rents alone are 150 per cent up, while food is up at least 50 per cent. The depreciation of the Chinese currency has also severely lowered the standard of living. Wages have been raised about 15 per cent in big industries, but, in actuality, real wages are much less than before hostilities started. The average wage in a cotton-mill, for example, is 15 Shanghai dollars a month for a 12-hour day with one holiday per month. In American currency, this would be about $1.15. These conditions, plus the oversupply of labour caused by the War, plus the complete passivity of the workers and peasants towards the War, have made it exceedingly difficult for our organisation to gain new members. Nevertheless, there are several new comrades, most of them being workers and students, especially the latter. For the first time, there are several women comrades. It is significant that in the single city under Guomindang control which has enjoyed 'prosperity', that is, in Fuzhou, the only remaining open coastal port, our strength has grown tremendously. The same is true to a lesser extent in such cities in the Southwest as Guilin, Yunnanfu, and other now important transport and industrial centres.

PART 7

Chen Duxiu

Chen Duxiu, Founder of Chinese Communism

Wang Fanxi

This article first appeared in a slightly different form in Benton (ed.) 1982, pp. 157–67.

To many younger Chinese socialists, the name Chen Duxiu means little, and to most socialists outside China, it means nothing at all. Of China's main Communist leaders, only Mao, Zhou Enlai, Liu Shaoqi, and a handful of others have won fame in the outside world. How could Chen, a nonentity, stand alongside these great leaders? But, in truth, Chen was anything but a nonentity in the history of the Chinese Revolution. If judged not just by what he achieved directly but by his influence over an entire historical period, he ranks not only above Zhou and Liu, but even above Mao himself

In 1936, in conversation with Edgar Snow, Zhou and Mao frankly acknowledged Chen's influence on them, and Snow reported their remarks in his classic *Red Star Over China*. But Zhou and Mao apparently had second thoughts, for the Chinese translation of Snow's book was withdrawn from circulation in the spring of 1938. Zhou had told Snow: 'Before going to France, I read translations of the *Communist Manifesto*; Kautsky's *Class Struggle*; and *The October Revolution*. These books were published under the auspices of *Xin qingnian*, which was published by Ch'en Tu-hsiu [Chen Duxiu]. I also personally met Ch'en Tu-hsiu as well as Li Ta-chao [Li Dazhao] – who were to become founders of the CCP'. Mao Zedong said: 'I went to Shanghai for the second time in 1919. There once more I saw Ch'en Tu-hsi-u. I had first met him in Peking [Beijing], when I was at Peking National University, and he had influenced me perhaps more than anyone else'. So Mao was Chen's pupil, not just before the Party was founded, but for a long time afterwards, too.

Chen Duxiu was born on 8 October 1879, thirty-five years after the Opium War and fifteen years after the defeat of the Taiping Rebellion. Outer pressure and inner dissension had already shaken the Qing dynasty to its foundations. The corruption and incompetence of the imperial system and the growing Western threat had woken many Chinese intellectuals to the need for reform. So, when Chen Duxiu was born, China was already in the first stages of political ferment and change.

But Chen was brought up in a strictly traditional way. Born into an Anhui gentry family, he lost his father in the first months of his life, and was raised and educated by his grandfather and his elder brother. The latter were both classical Confucianists, and they set out to train the young Duxiu for the imperial examinations, which were the sole path to bureaucratic office under the Qing.

Chen had no liking for the Confucian classics and even less for the *bagu* or eight-legged essay, a form of composition in which examination candidates were required to excel. However, to please his grandfather and his mother, he took the first exam at the age of seventeen and came top of the list with a *xiucai* degree.[1] The following year, in 1897, he went to Nanjing to take part in the triennial examination for the degree *of juren*. As a result of his experiences there, he lost interest once and for all in the imperial examinations and, more importantly, began to question the soundness of China's basic institutions. He vividly described his feelings in his unfinished autobiography.[2] One candidate, a fat man from Xuzhou, who paced up and down the examination pen naked but for a pair of broken sandals, chanting his favourite *bagu*, made a particularly deep impression on Chen:

> I could not take my eyes off him. As I watched, I fell to thinking about the whole strange business of the examination system, and then I began to think about how much my country and its people would suffer once these brutes achieved positions of power. Finally, I began to doubt the whole system of selecting talent through examination. It was like a circus of monkeys and bears, repeated every so many years. But was the examination system an exception, or were not China's other institutions equally rotten? I ended up agreeing with the criticisms raised in the newspaper *Shiwu* ['Contemporary Events'], and I switched my allegiance from the examination system to the reformist party of Kang Youwei[3] and Liang Qichao. And, so, an hour or two of pondering decided the course of my life for the next dozen years.

The Kang-Liang reform movement was considered very radical when Chen Duxiu joined it. It called for the replacement of the absolute monarchy by a constitutional monarchy, and it proposed a series of reforms to change China.

---

1 The first degree, gained at county level, in the imperial examinations under the Ming and Qing dynasties.
2 See Part II.
3 Kang Youwei (K'ang Yu-wei) (1858–1927) was leader of the reform movement that culminated in the short-lived Hundred Days Reform of 1898 and was a prominent scholar of the New Text School of the Confucian classics.

But, just a year later, in 1898, the reformists suffered a crushing defeat, and, in 1900, the Qing rulers were humiliated by eight foreign powers during the Yihetuan (or Boxer) upheavals. Chen's outlook on life and politics became more and more radical under the impact of these events. In 1904, in Anhui, he published *Suhua bao* ('Vernacular Magazine'), a newspaper written in vernacular Chinese. In 1908, he went to Shanghai, where he joined an underground terrorist group and learned how to make bombs. By now, his political views had already left Kang and Liang way behind, and he was advocating the overthrow of the Qing dynasty by force.

Even before the fall of the Qing in 1911, Chen was arrested for his political activities in Anhui. After his release, he was driven into exile in Japan. There, he collaborated with Sun Yat-sen, founder of the Guomindang and chief-architect of the Qing's overthrow, but he did not join Sun's organisation. On his return to China during the 1911 Revolution, Chen became political director of the revolutionary army in Anhui. But, after the Nationalists compromised with Yuan Shikai, representative of the *ancien régime*, he was once again forced into exile in Japan, where he published a revolutionary newspaper. Returning to China in 1915, he founded the journal *Qingnian* ('Youth') in Shanghai, renamed *Xin qingnian* the following year. *Xin qingnian* played a major role in the further unfolding of the Chinese Revolution. In 1917, *Xin qingnian*'s editorial board moved north to Beijing, where Chen was invited to become Dean of Letters at Beijing National University, China's highest and most progressive institution. Here were gathered many of China's best scholars, including Li Dazhao, a founder and early martyr of the CCP; Dr Hu Shi, the philosopher; Lu Xun, the essayist; Qian Xuantong, the historian; and Zhou Zuoren,[4] the essayist. With their help, and that of some students, *Xin qingnian* quickly gained in circulation and influence.

In any case, circumstances favoured its rapid growth. The war in Europe had temporarily loosened the West's economic grip on China, so that a national bourgeoisie was born, and, with it, a modern working class. At the same time, revolution was brewing in Russia, and, in 1917, the Bolsheviks took power in a revolution that decisively influenced modern China's course. Many ideological and social movements sprang up throughout the world, and especially in Europe, at the end of the War. Thus encouraged, some Chinese intellectuals began to search more earnestly than ever for new solutions to the problems that China had faced ever since being dragged into the world's eddy by Western

---

4   Zhou Zuoren (Chou Tso-jen) (1885–1968), a main contributor to Chen Duxiu's *Xin qingnian*, introduced Japanese and Eastern European literature into China. He was the brother of Lu Xun.

businessmen and soldiers. At the same time, these social and political developments gave the intellectuals a ready-made audience of tens of thousands, and a firm social base on which to realise their ideals.

Xin qingnian did not begin as a directly political publication. In the early days, it campaigned on two main fronts: against China's traditional ethics and social practices; and against classical Chinese, which was still used for most written communication. The campaign against traditional ethics was known as the New Thought Movement, and the campaign against classical Chinese was known as the Literary Revolution. On the first front, *Xin qingnian,* especially Chen Duxiu, took Confucius as the main target. Confucianism had dominated China for over two millennia, and was the ideological mainstay of the whole reactionary system. For Chen and his comrades, China's backwardness was due above all to its ossification under Confucian teaching; they believed that there could be no social progress until the Chinese people was freed from the Confucian grip. The Literary Revolution was closely linked to this struggle against Confucianism. Classical Chinese, based on the spoken language of more than one thousand years ago, differed radically from modern spoken Chinese. So, until it was replaced by a written form based on modern spoken Chinese, mass illiteracy would remain and progressive intellectuals would never be able to awaken the people. This was not the first time that Chen had called for language reform. As early as 1904, he had published a newspaper with articles in the vernacular. But it was only now that the conditions for a literary revolution had fully ripened. Now, despite stiff opposition from the literati, daily speech finally won out, and living Chinese replaced dead Chinese as the official means of communication.

Yet Chen Duxiu's main contribution to the New Thought Movement and the Literary Revolution lay less in his constructive achievement than in his destructive energy: in his dauntless urge to discredit, criticise, and destroy everything traditional. He was among the greatest iconoclasts in the history of human thought; and, like all iconoclasts and pioneers, he worked not with a scalpel but with a bulldozer. For him, the main thing was to pull down the dilapidated house of the past, and this he did to devastating effect. But, for a long time, he had only the vaguest idea of what sort of house to put in its place, except that it must be in the Western style. So, during the first four years of *Xin qingnian,* Chen Duxiu should properly be called a Westerniser or a radical-bourgeois democrat. He admired almost everything Western, especially great events and people from the past three centuries of European history; he cited them enthusiastically in his writings, comparing them with events and people from the Chinese past. Great names like Francis Bacon, Jean-Jacques Rousseau, Auguste Comte, Charles Darwin, Louis Pasteur, Victor Hugo, Emile Zola, Kant,

Hegel, Goethe, Dickens, and even Oscar Wilde he introduced indiscriminately as models for Chinese youth to admire and emulate. But he did not know these people well, nor did he have a sound grasp of Western thought. He mastered no European language, so he acquired all his new knowledge through Japanese translations; and his Japanese was not good either. The result was that all he learned from the West were a few broad concepts such as humanism, democracy, individualism, and scientific method. From these, he singled out democracy and science as the two surgeons capable of saving China.

The October Revolution of 1917 had an enormous effect on Chen's thinking, but it was not until later that Chen definitively embraced Marxism and concluded that China would never become modernised unless the Chinese, like the Bolsheviks, carried out an economic as well as a political revolution.

It was above all May Fourth that precipitated this change in Chen's thinking. On 4 May 1919, a student movement broke out in Beijing and spread to all China's major cities. This movement was in protest against the decision of the Paris Peace Conference to transfer German concessions in China to Japan, and against the Beijing government for acting as Japan's tool. May Fourth happened under the direct influence of Chen's *Xin qingnian* journal. It was *Xin qingnian's* first victory, but also its first big test. May Fourth quickly split the *Xin qingnian* leaders into two competing camps. For some time, a process of differentiation had been going on among the journal's main supporters. Now, this process quickened. Chen Duxiu and Li Dazhao went further to the left and plunged into revolutionary work, while Hu Shi and others moved further to the right under the pretext of 'retreating to the study'.

As a leader of May Fourth and its chief inspirer, Chen Duxiu was the main target for government repression at the end of it. In June, he was seized and jailed for three months. After his release, he left Beijing University for good, and began a critical review of the doctrines he had earlier indiscriminately adopted. In September 1920, he declared himself a Marxist.

Now that he had committed himself wholly to the revolution, he began to work towards the establishment of a Communist party in China. In August 1920, he set up a Socialist Youth Corps in Shanghai. At the same time, Marxist Study Groups were organised in big cities throughout China. In July 1921, the CCP held its First National Congress in Shanghai. Chen was elected General Secretary, and, the following year, he represented the Party at the Fourth Congress of the Communist International in Moscow. He was re-elected leader at the following four party congresses; he led the Party during the Revolution of 1925–7.

The Revolution of 1925–7 has been called a tragedy by some historians, and it certainly ended in tragic defeats. What was Chen's role in that tragedy?

There are various answers to this question, which has been the subject of much heated controversy. The view of the Communist International and (until recently) of the CCP was that Chen was an opportunist and a bungler whose wrong policy led the Revolution to defeat. According to this view, the main if not the exclusive blame for the defeat was Chen Duxiu's. But not everyone agrees with this assessment. Some of Chen's fellow-revolutionaries and many scholars believe that Chen's mistake was to be too faithful to the directives of the Comintern, which was then controlled by Stalin and Bukharin, and that he was merely Stalin's scapegoat. My own experience of the events of 1925–7, and my later reflections on them, led me too to this conclusion.

Chen Duxiu was dismissed as party leader at the 7 August (1927) Emergency Conference of the Central Committee. He was succeeded by Qu Qiubai, who, under Moscow's orders, switched to an adventurist line culminating in the disastrous Guangzhou [Canton] Insurrection of December 1927. In retirement, Chen wrote several letters to the Party warning against putschism and demanding a critical review of policy, but this merely widened the gap between him and the new leaders.

In late 1929, Chen could acquaint himself with the Russian Left Opposition's views on China through documents brought back to China by Communists who had studied in Moscow. Until then, Chen had no true understanding of the differences between Trotsky and Stalin on the Chinese Revolution. These documents opened up a new field of vision for him, and helped dispel doubts that had vexed him for years. He soon went over to the positions of the Left Opposition, and wrote to the party leaders demanding that the issues in the Chinese Revolution should be put up for discussion in the Party and in the entire world communist movement. He was promptly expelled as a result; in response, he wrote his famous 'Open Letter to all Comrades' of 10 December 1929, and put his name to the statement 'Our Political Views' signed by eighty-one veteran party members. Needless to say, all these people were expelled from the Party. A few months later, in February 1930, Stalin tried to 'win Chen Duxiu back' by inviting him to Moscow. Chen turned down the invitation, thus severing all ties with the party he had founded nine years earlier.

Chen then organised his followers into a Left Opposition and published the newspaper *Wuchanzhe* ['Proletarian']. In May 1931, this organisation merged with three other Trotskyist groups to form the Chinese section of the International of Bolshevik-Leninists, of which Chen was elected General Secretary. But, in October 1932, Chen was arrested and put before the Nanjing Military Tribunal, where he faced the death sentence. In court, he behaved every inch like a revolutionary leader; from the dock, he denounced the Guomindang's régime of terror. His arrest and trial led to a nationwide campaign to free him. As a result, he was spared the death penalty and given a thirteen-year jail sentence instead.

Chen stayed in prison until shortly after the outbreak of the Sino-Japanese War in 1937, when he was freed along with other political prisoners, but he was still kept under strict watch, and this prevented him from doing revolutionary work. After a brief stay in Wuhan, he was compelled to stay in a small town near Chongqing in Sichuan province, where the Guomindang had its wartime capital. His health had worsened in prison, and on 27 May 1942, he died of heart sickness and phlebitis, aged sixty-four.

Chen spent his last years in great poverty, bad health, and isolation. Nevertheless, the Guomindang and the Communist Party persecuted him to the end. In the summer of 1938, the Communist Party began a strident slander campaign against him. This campaign was directed by Wang Ming, Stalin's chief representative in China. Wang Ming accused Chen of 'collaborating with the Japanese imperialists'. At the same time, the Guomindang prohibited Chen from resuming his literary activities. All he could do during those hard times was to think and to exchange opinions by letter with a few old friends. After his death, these letters and a few articles from the years 1940–2 were compiled by one of his former pupils, He Zishen, and published in Shanghai in 1948. In 1949, Dr Hu Shi, once an old friend of Chen's but later a staunch supporter of Chiang Kai-shek, reprinted this collection of writings in Taiwan, and wrote an introduction to it in which he welcomed Chen's ideas as those of a 'prodigal returned'.

As for the CCP, it regarded Chen as a renegade, and even some Trotskyists thought the same, although for different reasons. So what was Chen's new position, and did it represent his final reconciliation with bourgeois thought?

The main themes of Chen's last letters and articles were as follows. First, no revolutions would break out during the War, and only if the Allies defeated the Axis would revolutionary crises happen. Socialists throughout the world were therefore duty-bound to support the democratic Allies against the fascist Axis. Second, there is no essential difference between bourgeois and proletarian democracy, but only a difference of degree. Proletarian democracy is therefore an extension rather than a negation of bourgeois democracy, and it is wrong to say that bourgeois democracy is historically superseded. Third, capitalism is the root of war, which only world revolution can end. Fourth, the struggle for national liberation is interlinked with proletarian revolution in the advanced countries, and the forces behind these two struggles make socialist revolution together. Fifth, the Soviet Union under Lenin was qualitatively different from the Soviet Union under Stalin. The former was socialist, the latter was not. (Chen died before he could elaborate on what kind of régime the Soviet Union under Stalin had become.) Sixth, although Lenin's régime was not like Stalin's, Lenin was partly to blame for Stalin's crimes, since it was he who had counterposed proletarian dictatorship to democracy in general. Seventh, a true socialist revolution is one in which democracy – or, more exactly, democratic rights – are respected and extended.

Chen's thinking had changed greatly during the early war years, but his views, however muddled, still fell far short of a reconciliation with his old enemy, the bourgeoisie. Instead, they represented a return by Chen in his old age to the positions he had held as a young man. It is interesting to ask why this happened, especially since, in my experience, it is not uncommon for intellectuals in backward countries to revert in this way to the ideas of their youth.

China's isolation was broken down by guns and ships. China's 'modernisation' stemmed not from gradual change based on evolutions within its own society, but from outside pressures. Development of this sort is inevitably by leaps and bounds, and is condensed and telescoped. In China, the transition from democratic radicalism to the founding of a modern socialist movement took some twenty years. In Britain and France, the same process took several centuries, and in Russia it took several scores of years.

Moreover, China's progress from democratic agitation to full-blown communism took place in one and the same person: Chen Duxiu. Chen was China's Belinsky, Chernyshevsky, Plekhanov, and Lenin rolled into one. True, he reached the stature of none of these great Russians, but he traversed the entire gamut of their thinking, from the first awakening of individualism to the struggle for socialist collectivism. Thus, Chen embodies what Russian Marxists referred to as combined development. However, combined development is both a privilege and a curse. It explains not only Chen's merits but also his faults. Chen rapidly and boldly assimilated an impressive list of isms, but in none did he reach real depth. In his teens, he became a 'left-wing Confucianist'; in his twenties, he was intoxicated by Western democracy; in his thirties, he criticised Confucianism; and at 41, he became a Marxist. Inevitably, he retained elements of older ideologies among the new ones, as he raced from one ism to the next. And, by the time that he embraced Marxism, he had reached an age where new thinking rarely sinks deep into the soul. So it is understandable that, in the last years of his life, Chen returned in part to his intellectual first love, 'pure' democracy.

Other factors, too, disposed Chen to look favourably on democracy. Above all, he was appalled by the degeneration of the Stalinist régime in the Soviet Union. It was the Moscow trials that initially led him to rethink the Leninist view of bourgeois democracy.

How, then, should one appraise Chen's life? Despite his political failures and his intellectual limitations, Chen was not only modern China's bravest thinker but one of history's great revolutionaries, because of both his leading role in the Chinese Revolution and his personal indomitability. He did not hesitate to give up a brilliant career for the uncertain and hard life of a revolutionary. He heroically bore the loss of his family and his two sons (murdered by the Guomindang in 1927 and 1928). He stuck to his beliefs under the threat of imprisonment and death. And, during the last years of his life, when he was gravely ill and desperately poor, he refused to accept money offered him by the Guomindang through one of his old friends. All this shows that Chen was a man of revolutionary mettle; his memory remains that of a great revolutionary. Another appraisal of Chen is that he was 'an oppositionist for life to any established authority', and Chen himself liked this description of his career.

Chen Duxiu and the Trotskyists

Zheng Chaolin

Zheng Chaolin's memoirs, completed in 1945 but not at the time published, were unearthed from a government vault in 1979, shortly after Zheng's release (after twenty seven years) from jail under the CCP. Sometime in 1979 or 1980, several copies of the manuscript were mimeographed in Beijing under the title Zheng Chaolin 1945 nian huiyi lu ('Zheng Chaolin's 1945 Memoirs') for distribution as reference material among party historians. In 1986, after sitting for several years on the manuscript, Chinese Communist officials finally authorised its publication, in an edition restricted to privileged categories of officials and researchers. In 1986, Beijing's Xiandai shiliao biankan she ('The association to edit and publish materials on contemporary history') published a printed version under the title Zheng Chaolin huiyi lu ('Zheng Chaolin's Memoirs'), with this appendix commissioned by party historians and written by Zheng. The appendix comprises a special study on Chen Duxiu's relationship to Trotskyism. On 11 December 1987, Zheng explained in a postscript to the English translation of his memoirs the circumstances under which he had composed the study on Chen Duxiu: 'I wrote the appendix "Chen Duxiu and the Trotskyists" at the invitation of a certain research institute in 1980, shortly after I had regained my freedom. At the time, public opinion tended to make a distinction between Chen Duxiu and the Trotskyists. People said that Chen Duxiu was a good man whose good name should be restored, but they made no evaluation of the Trotskyists. So the aim of this long article is to show that Chen Duxiu and the Trotskyists cannot be dealt with separately'. This translation first appeared in Benton 1996.

1   From the Moscow Group to the Chen Duxiu Group

The Cadres Who Returned from Moscow in 1924
1924 was an important year in the history of the CCP. It was the first year of formal cooperation between it and the Guomindang. Early on in 1924, the Guomindang, with the Communist Party's help, convened the First Reorganisation Congress; several Communist Party leaders were elected onto the Guomindang's Central Executive Committee; the Huangpu (Whampoa) Military Academy was started up; Soviet political and military advisers started work; Guomindang branches in most places came under Communist control; the urban labour movement, which had become passive after the strike of 7

February 1923, livened up again; and Communist activity developed on an unprecedented scale. Even more cadres were needed to carry out party tasks. To meet the need, the Moscow branch of the CCP dispatched back to China a number of Chinese comrades studying at Moscow's KUTV. They returned in batches; all in all, they accounted for more than half the original number of Chinese students at KUTV. Of those who stayed behind, some switched to the Military Academy and others were preparing to return to China after a further six months.

The first batch returned before the 1924 summer holidays; the second set out from Moscow during the summer holidays; during and after the summer holidays, right through until the spring of the following year, people trickled back to China in smaller groups of two and three or four and five, or even singly.

All those who returned in 1924 or in the spring of 1925 took up high office in the Party. Peng Shuzhi sat in on the Central Committee as head of the Propaganda Department and attended all its meetings. Though he had not been elected onto it by the Third Congress, he assumed the same powers as one of its normal members: he interviewed cadres and issued directives; even Deng Zhongxia behaved respectfully in his presence, not to mention Zhuang Wengong, Secretary of the Shanghai District Committee. As for Chen Yannian, just a few days after arriving in Shanghai he was sent to Guangzhou to be Secretary of the Southern Regional Committee. Yin Kuan, who had returned before the summer holidays, had earlier gone to Shandong to be Provincial Secretary there. Zhao Shiyan, who had come to China on his own, took charge of the Northern Regional Committee in Beijing. This Committee was nominally under Li Dazhao, but Zhao Shiyan did the actual work. Wang Ruofei did not get back until early 1925, whereupon he was quickly appointed as Secretary to the Provincial Committee in Henan. Wang Zekai was sent to Anyuan to lead the Party there. Luo Yinong at first came to Shanghai but later went to Guangzhou and, later still, went to Beijing to run the party school and to train cadres; finally, in late 1925 or early 1926, he came back to Shanghai to become Secretary to the Jiangsu-Zhejiang Regional Committee. Chen Qiaonian, who got back in early 1925, helped Zhao Shiyan on the Northern Regional Committee. Ren Bishi, like Peng Shuzhi in the adult party, sat in on the Central Committee of the Youth League immediately after getting back to China, without having been elected to it. Xue Shilun at first worked as Treasurer and Secretary to the Central Committee in Shanghai, but he was not up to it, so he was sent to Hunan to help Li Weihan; Ren Zuomin took over his old jobs. Zheng Chaolin was appointed Secretary to the Central Committee's Propaganda Department, where Zhang Bojian, who had gone back from Moscow before the summer holidays, was already working. Many of the other people who returned from

Moscow were assigned to the labour movement; later Wang Yifei, Yan Changyi, and others returned to China after having studied military science in Moscow and some of them were assigned to the Party's Military Committee.

The students who returned to China from Moscow in 1924 (including the first half of 1925) were united as one and worked in close concert. They had received a common schooling, and just before returning they had received special training; their views on the theory of the Chinese Revolution and on methods of work were in close accord, as if printed from the same font. Party cadres and members from before 1924 looked askance on us and dubbed us the 'Moscow people'. At first sight, this was a neutral appellation, but, secretly, it reflected a mood of dissatisfaction among cadres and comrades from before 1924, who thought that these people had come to occupy a special position in the Party and formed a virtual clique. There had already been one such virtual clique in the Party – Zhang Guotao's 'National Trade Union group'. Li Longzhi (who later changed his name to Li Lisan), Liu Shaoqi, and Xiang Delong (who later called himself Xiang Ying), all three of whom had worked in the labour movement in the South, did not belong to the 'National Trade union group' so they were more prepared to cooperate with the 'Moscow people'. Li Weihan, the Provincial Secretary in Hunan, had returned to China directly from France, without passing through Moscow, but he, too, counted as one of the Moscow people. Zhang Tailei and Qu Qiubai, on the other hand, were not members even though they had been in Moscow. Later, they gradually became hostile to the Moscow people.

The 'National Trade Union group' and the Moscow group were virtual cliques. The former had united around Zhang Guotao and Luo Zhanglong, Zhang's right-hand man. It derived its solidarity from personal and working relationships; its solidarity could hardly be said to be grounded in theory or principle. Needless to say, the 'workerist' views that Zhang Guotao developed in the early period of the CCP were not entirely without relevance to his group's coherence. The Moscow group, however, was united mainly on the basis of theory and principle, though at the same time personal relationships also played a role in it.

The theory of the Moscow group was called 'the theory of national revolution'.

'The Theory of National Revolution'

In early 1924 – at the earliest in the fourth quarter of 1923 – comrades in the Comintern's Far Eastern Bureau and leaders of the CCP's Moscow branch met frequently to discuss the theory of national revolution. I knew about this, though I never attended any of the meetings, nor do I know who did. Naturally,

Luo Yinong and Peng Shuzhi attended, but whether anyone else did I do not know. The outcome of these meetings was the 'theory of national revolution'.

The content of the theory is set out in Peng Shuzhi's programmatic essay in *New Youth Quarterly* no. 4, which was specially devoted to 'national revolution', and in the political resolution passed by the Fourth Congress and drafted by the Comintern representative Voitinsky. The two documents are the same. That is not surprising, for the 'theory of national revolution' was worked out jointly by leaders of the Comintern's Far Eastern Bureau and of the Moscow branch; or, rather, it was worked out by the Comintern and embraced by the leaders of the Moscow branch.

I have not seen those two documents in fifty-five years, and for the moment there is no way in which I can borrow them to read, but I still recall their general drift. Basically, they promote two arguments: China cannot carry out proletarian-socialist revolution without first going through national revolution, that is, bourgeois-democratic revolution; and the proletariat must strive for the leadership of the national revolution.[1]

This was a new theory in the history of the CCP. We know that, before the CCP's First Congress, everyone viewed the Chinese Revolution as similar in character to Russia's October Revolution. I have to hand a copy of the 'Manifesto of the CCP', published in November 1920,[2] which says: 'The first

---

1   After finishing the first draft of this section, I managed to borrow the two documents concerned. Peng Shuzhi's article says: 'National revolution is the only way out'. Peng asks: 'Why does the Chinese working class not make this revolution its own class revolution – the proletarian revolution?' He gives three reasons, the second of which is that national revolution is 'the only road along which the Chinese proletariat can go forward to proletarian revolution'. After analysing China's bourgeoisie and China's proletariat, Peng concludes: 'So the Chinese working class is the natural leader of the Chinese Revolution'. The resolution that Voitinsky drafted for the Fourth Congress also stresses that there can be no talk of proletarian revolution without first going through national revolution, and that after the victory of national revolution the question 'whether or not there must first be a period of bourgeois democracy before going on to proletarian revolution' can only be answered in the light of the proletariat's level of preparation and the world political situation. The resolution also says: 'National revolution can only succeed if the most revolutionary proletariat is in the leading position'. In those days people stressed the proletariat's leading role in national revolution, but they denied that the Guomindang was a bourgeois party. Peng said: the Guomindang is 'built on the lumpenproletariat, for example bandit armies'. Voitinsky said: the Guomindang is a 'multi-class party'. [Note by Zheng Chaolin.]
2   Even before the First Congress, which met on 23 July 1921, a 'Manifesto' was drafted in November 1920 and published on 7 November in the inaugural issue of the underground monthly *Gongchan dang* ('Communist').

step towards realising our ideal society is to eradicate the present bourgeois system. That can only be done by forcefully overthrowing the capitalists' state'. It also says:

> The Communist Party will lead the revolutionary proletariat to struggle against the capitalists and seize political power from the hands of the capitalists, for it is that power that maintains the capitalist state; and it will place that power in the hands of the workers and peasants, just as the Russian Communists did in 1917.

I also have a copy of the programme approved by the First Congress, which describes its aim as 'to overthrow the bourgeoisie with the revolutionary army of the proletariat and to re-establish the state on the basis of the toiling classes, until class differences are extinguished'. In sum, before and at the First Congress there was no theory – not even a glimmering of one – about first having to complete bourgeois-democratic revolution before starting proletarian-socialist revolution. After the First Congress, the question of cooperating with the Guomindang was raised. It was discussed at the Second Congress and again at the West Lake Conference, and the Third Congress decided to join the Guomindang. But it was raised as a tactic, in terms of how can we even more quickly and effectively develop the revolutionary movement and party forces.

But, after the decision to cooperate with the Guomindang had been taken and implemented, and after the alliance between the Guomindang and Russia, when the Soviets sent advisers to China plus funds and weaponry to help the Guomindang, the old tactical formula was no longer enough and the question had to be reframed in strategic terms: the old line of 'Guomindang-Communist cooperation' had to be replaced by one grounded in principle and basic Marxist theory. Thus was born the 'theory of national revolution', with its emphasis on the need to complete bourgeois-democratic revolution before going on to proletarian-socialist revolution. Were there grounds for such a theory? Yes, people cited the theoretical disputes in Russia before the Revolution as a basis for it. But they avoided talking about the actual course of events in 1917, for that showed that the Russians had already carried out the proletarian-socialist revolution even before completing the bourgeois-democratic one, that bourgeois-democratic revolution in Russia was completed as a by-product of proletarian-socialist revolution.

The second main argument connected with the 'theory of national revolution', that is, that the proletariat must strive for leadership, is clearly subsidiary and, from a Marxist point of view, cosmetic. Before the Revolution, Lenin's idea that the proletariat must lead Russia's bourgeois revolution was premised in the belief that Russia's bourgeoisie had already forfeited its revolutionary role. How could the view that China's bourgeoisie still had a revolutionary role to play, that it should be richly aided with funds, weaponry, and advisers, and that the Communist Party should even be made to join the Guomindang as a wing of it – how could this view be reconciled with striving for proletarian hegemony in the revolution? Striving for proletarian hegemony was mere cosmetics, as the comments of senior members of the CCP clearly show. Peng Shuzhi, who imported the theory to China, said that hegemony over the revolution 'naturally' belonged to the proletariat so there was no need to strive for it; Qu Qiubai exposed this belief of Peng's in his pamphlet *Against Peng Shuzhi-ism*. According to Peng, there was no bourgeoisie in China, just the ghost of one. When Mao Zedong wrote his 'Analysis of the Classes in Chinese Society' in March 1926, more than a year after the proclamation at the Fourth Congress of the 'theory of national revolution', he did not say anything about the proletariat leading China's other classes. The present version of that article in Mao's *Selected Works* says that 'the proletariat is the leading force in the revolutionary movement', but the sentence was added later, when the *Selected Works* were edited for publication, and cannot be found in the 1926 text.

In late 1924 or early 1925, the CCP officially proclaimed 'national revolution' as the guiding theory for the entire revolutionary movement. The actual course of the Revolution of 1925 to 1927 showed this theory up as bankrupt. We who had been in Moscow studied this theory before returning home, and we all complied with it: it was the banner behind which we united. That it had been exposed as bankrupt implied the dissolution of the Moscow group.

The Central Force in the Party

The Moscow group was not tangible but it undeniably existed. The Moscow branch was originally led by three people, Luo Yinong, Peng Shuzhi, and Bu Shiqi. In early 1923, Bu Shiqi went back to China, leaving Luo and Peng in charge. After cooperation between the Guomindang and the CCP had been formally implemented, the 'theory of national revolution' formally launched, and the order sending comrades back to China formally issued, the Moscow branch decided that Luo Yinong would stay on to continue to lead it and that Peng Shuzhi would go back to China to join the Central Committee of the CCP and at the same time rally and lead the returning cadres, that is, the so-called Moscow people. Why did Luo not go instead of Peng? I do not know. I was never told the reasons for that decision.

In early 1925, not long after the Fourth Congress, Peng Shuzhi fell ill with typhoid fever after editing the 'Lenin' number of the first issue of *New Youth Monthly*. Luo Yinong, who had just got back from Moscow, came to the

Propaganda Department to see us. He was sitting beside Peng's bed. I happened to be standing there, and some of the things he said attracted my attention. I remember them to this day. The gist of his remarks was that we should form a central force in the Party so that we would be in a position to control the rest of it.

The actual situation in the Party at that time was like this. The batch of cadres who had returned to China from the Soviet Union all supported Peng Shuzhi and Luo Yinong. (The exception was Jiang Guangchi, who had opposed Luo and Peng in Moscow; after getting back to China he supported not them but Qu Qiubai, but the rest of the Moscow people opposed Jiang.) These cadres now occupied important positions in the Party. As long as they got on well with Chen Duxiu, they could control the feudal lords by using the emperor's name and so take over the Party's commanding heights. And that is more or less what happened.

Had Luo and Peng decided on such a plan before going back to China? Obviously not, or Luo would have had no need for his bedside talk with Peng. But the general tendency was there, even in Moscow.

It is worth noting that after Luo had spoken, Peng hummed and hawed and did not come out clearly in support of the proposal; but nor did he come out clearly against it. With the benefit of hindsight, I would judge Luo's comments as follows.

Peng Shuzhi was unlikely to oppose the idea of uniting the Moscow people around Chen Duxiu and using Chen's name to control the 'feudal lords': of setting up a central force in the CCP to control the rest of it. The reason he did not actively support Luo's proposal was certainly not because he was against it, and even less so because he supported the prohibition on factions passed at the Tenth Congress of the Russian Communist Party. It was simply that he planned to keep the leadership of the Moscow group for himself rather than share it with Luo Yinong. In Moscow, Luo played first fiddle and Peng second. On the surface, they cooperated well together, but I had already noticed that they had by no means completely merged. Luo invented for Peng the nickname Confucius, which caught on and still sticks. The nickname was meant to imply that Peng was a bookworm, that he had read a lot, that he knew lots of theory, but that he was no good at doing things. Peng hated his nickname so we never used it to his face, but we did use it behind his back. Peng saw himself as China's Lenin, but, in Moscow, he had to yield to Luo. Back in China, where he was elected onto the Central Committee at the Fourth Congress, he joined the Presidium (later called the Standing Committee) and simultaneously ran the Propaganda Department. By then, Peng's position was higher than Luo's. Luo was simply a cadre awaiting assignment. How did Peng manage to force

Luo to share the leadership of the Moscow people? After their bedside talk, Peng decided to enter Baolong Hospital and arranged for Luo to move into the Propaganda Department building, where Luo slept on Peng's bed. Before going to the hospital, Peng told me to lock his desk-drawer and not to let Luo rummage in it. I was surprised, but I did as he said. Later, on account of Chen Bilan,[3] Luo and Peng became enemies and stayed so. But that has nothing to do with what I am now discussing, so let us stop talking about it.

As far as I remember, Luo and Peng did not mention Chen Duxiu in their bedside talk. But they did not need to. In Moscow, if we were discussing the Central Committee of the CCP or the party leadership, we had only Chen Duxiu in mind. Li Dazhao followed Chen in everything. We never mentioned the names Zhang Guotao, Qu Qiubai, Cai Hesen, or Tang Pingshan. In those days, the leader cult had started up in the Soviet Union and the Soviet Central Committee was instilling it into the party membership and the people. We worshipped Lenin as the supreme leader of the Soviet Republic – and, in China, we worshipped Chen Duxiu. But, in Moscow, the cult of Chen Duxiu meant something other to Peng and Luo than to the rest of us. Peng in Moscow saw himself as the Chinese Lenin, but he had to yield to Luo. Back in China, in the autumn of 1924, he sneaked his way above Luo, but he still had to yield to Chen Duxiu. The only reason he clasped Chen's leg was so that one day he could replace him.

There were five members of the Standing Committee (or Presidium) after the Fourth Congress, namely Chen Duxiu, Cai Hesen, Zhang Guotao, Qu Qiubai, and Peng Shuzhi. At around the time of National Day[4] in 1925, after Cai had gone to Moscow to represent the CCP at the Comintern right up to the time when the Central Committee moved to Wuhan, it only had four members. I often sat in on its meetings. I used to hate Peng's performance at them. Almost every time, he would first wait for Chen Duxiu to say what he thought and then – at great length and with much pedantry – supply additional arguments to back Chen up. He used to speak at great length but no depth, so that the others in attendance became impatient at the loss of time, though Peng himself did not notice this. I must have betrayed my irritation and contempt, for Qu Qiubai – who was extremely sensitive – noticed it and told

---

3   Chen Bilan had been Luo Yinong's lover in Moscow, but she dropped him for Peng when they returned to China.
4   Then 10 October (the anniversary of the Revolution of 1911), now 1 October (the anniversary of the proclamation of the People's Republic in 1949).

Jiang Guangchi. Jiang wrote it up in his novel *Des sans-culottes*,[5] where I make a shadowy appearance.

Needless to say, on several occasions at these meetings, Peng expressed opinions that differed from those of Chen. He boasted to me once that, at the meetings, Qu Qiubai and Zhang Guotao used slavishly to follow the 'Old Man's' lead, and that only he, Peng, dared face up to Chen.

'Qiubai is simply a higher technician', he said. 'Guotao is simply a higher administrator'. What he meant was that only he, Peng, was a 'higher politician', that is, a politician of higher quality.

We Moscow people, later to become followers of Chen Duxiu, were early on against Peng: we did not wait until after the Fifth Congress to chime in with Qu Qiubai against him. Wang Ruofei, Chen Qiaonian, Ren Xu, He Zishen, and others all despised Peng Shuzhi. Perhaps Chen Yannian's opposition to Peng was a result of Borodin's influence. Luo Yinong had personal reasons to be against Peng. Ren Bishi and Xiao Zizhang, who worked for the Youth League, were probably swayed by Qu Qiubai and the Youth International, but that is another matter. We were opposed to Peng the man, not the 'theory of national revolution' he brought back from Moscow; and even less did we oppose Peng as a cover for attacking Chen Duxiu. Naturally, a minority, like Wang Zekai and Liu Bozhuang, supported Peng all along.

The Moscow Group Splits

After the Fourth Congress, the development of the Chinese Revolution was accompanied by splits in the Moscow group. Luo and Peng's plan was to use us as a central force with which to take over the entire party, but, as the Party grew, the Moscow group – contrary to general expectations – split apart and was defeated and destroyed.

The first people to split away were those in the group under Chen Yannian. Chen Yannian (Secretary of the Southern Regional Committee), Mu Qing (head of the Organisational Bureau), and Huang Guozuo (alias Huang Ping, head of the Propaganda Bureau) had all returned from Moscow, where they had studied and supported the 'theory of national revolution'. But, not long after Chen Yannian and others began working in Guangzhou, they became involved in the struggle between Borodin and Chen Duxiu, supporting the former against the latter. Borodin was a senior adviser to the National[6] Government; perhaps he also represented the Comintern. Whatever the case, he meddled in the affairs

---

5 Reprinted in Jiang Guangchi 1983, pp. 189–270.
6 That is, the government of the Guomindang in Guangzhou.

of the CCP. He directly led the Party's Southern Committee regardless of the opinion of the Central Committee of the CCP and did his best to control party work – at least where the 'national-revolutionary movement' was concerned – across the whole of China. In so doing, he encroached on the competencies of the official Comintern representative, Voitinsky. Before Chen Yannian took up his post in Guangzhou, in the summer of 1924, Borodin instigated Qu Qiubai (then staying in Guangzhou) to deal with the Guomindang in the name of the CCP, but many of Qu's speeches and actions did not tally with the Central Committee's position. Chen Duxiu and Cai Hesen in Shanghai were very angry about this, and, in the name of the Central Committee, ordered Qu to quit Guangzhou and return to Shanghai, which he did, leaving scars on his mind. Chen Yannian went to Guangzhou in the autumn, whereupon Borodin instigated Chen Yannian instead, regardless of whether the actions he encouraged Chen to undertake accorded with the wishes of the Central Committee. I know little about the struggle between Borodin and the Central Committee in Shanghai, for the issues in it were never publicly aired. All I know is that, on one occasion when Chen Yannian came to Shanghai to deliver a report to the Central Committee, he stayed at my place and told me that Borodin had told him that the Central Committee in Shanghai only knew the slogan 'Workers of the world, unite!' What Borodin meant was that the Central Committee in Shanghai only knew how to mouth principles, and was incapable of flexibly applying them. But Chen Yannian did not say exactly what principles were at stake. Borodin had arrived in China before the Comintern's Far Eastern Bureau had settled on the 'national revolution' formula, with which Voitinsky (who brought the idea to China) instructed the Fourth Congress. I am not saying that Borodin did not know about the theory, just that 'politicians' like Borodin put no price whatsoever on principle or theory and were only good at political conspiring. He behaved quite wilfully in Guangzhou, and paid not the slightest attention to the views of either the Shanghai Central Committee or Voitinsky, who was the official Comintern representative in China. Every time Borodin and Chen Duxiu clashed seriously, the Southern comrades led by Chen Yannian backed Borodin. In this way, the Moscow people in Southern China set up their own banner under the leadership of Chen Yannian.

The second group to split away from the Moscow group were leading members of the Youth League. The Youth League turned against Chen Duxiu much later than the Guangdong cadres. I cannot say for sure when the split began, but it was probably not until 1926. After the Fourth Congress of the CCP, the Youth League also held a Congress and changed its name from Socialist to Communist. At the same time, Ren Bishi took over as its General Secretary from Zhang Tailei. The plan stemmed originally from Moscow: Peng Shuzhi, too, knew about and agreed with it. By 1926, the Youth League had gradually turned against Chen Duxiu, chiefly under the influence of the internal struggle in the Soviet Party. The Soviet Youth League (or Komsomol) did not agree with the Comintern's China policy and was especially opposed to Voitinsky, the official Comintern representative in China. According to Komsomol leaders, Voitinsky was an 'opportunist' and a 'rightist'. I do not know too clearly on what actual grounds they opposed him. In 1923, the Trotsky opposition incited the Komsomol against the leading triumvirate in the Soviet Party, namely Zinoviev, Kamenev, and Stalin. But Trotsky was overthrown and the Komsomol, too, was purged. By 1926, it was apparently no longer in a position to oppose from a Trotskyist point of view the China policy of the Central Committee of the Soviet Communist Party and of the Comintern. But it is a fact that the Komsomol leaders opposed Voitinsky and through him Chen Duxiu, who was supposedly under his influence. After the controversy in the Chinese leadership about the Northern Expedition, Qu Qiubai joined the Komsomol in opposing Chen.

Qu Qiubai and Zhang Guotao both supported Chiang Kai-shek's Northern Expedition. Zhang was a well-known schemer and intriguer, but, even so, his skills as such fell short of Qu's. At the Central Committee meeting where the Northern Expedition was discussed, Zhang clashed frontally with Chen Duxiu but Qu – who supported the Northern Expedition no less than Zhang – pretended to comply with Chen. From then on, Qu plotted against Chen from behind the scenes. Whether Zhang did, too, I do not know, but I do know that Qu Qiubai did. In the second half of 1926, he said he was ill and stopped attending Central Committee meetings or working for the Party. Wang Ruofei, head of the Central Committee's Secretariat, early on became aware of what was happening. One morning in late autumn, while I was still asleep, he came to drag me from my lair and take me to Ximen Road where Qu lived. As we entered the upstairs room, Qu was sitting squarely at his desk working on an article. When he saw us he seemed a bit embarrassed. We exchanged a few words with him and then left. On the way back neither of us said anything about the incident, nor did we need to. It turned out that Qu was not ill but was working hard on an article that he did not want anyone else to know about. It remained a mystery until the spring of 1927 in Wuhan, when it became clear that he had been writing up his pamphlet *Against Peng Shuzhi-ism*. Apart from that, he had been inciting people against Chen Duxiu. These people included Ren Bishi and Xiao Zizhang, who had returned from Moscow to work in the Youth League, and others like He Chang and Lu Dingyi who had never been in Moscow. All this happened behind the backs of Chen Duxiu and Peng Shuzhi. Qu never argued his positions openly at a meeting of the Central Committee.

There must also have been a third group of Chen Duxiu supporters who turned against Chen because of mistakes they detected in the way the leadership conducted actual struggles, but I cannot say exactly who they were.

Those of us who continued to support Chen learned early on to despise Peng Shuzhi as mean, dull-witted, vain, and unable to work together with other people. I was not the only one who thought like this. So did Wang Ruofei, Chen Qiaonian, Zhao Shiyan, and above all Luo Yinong. Whenever Peng's name came up, none of us liked to continue talking. But we all clearly distinguished between Peng and Chen Duxiu; we thought it was unseemly the way Peng always clung to Chen's leg.

The struggle against Chen broke out at the Fifth Congress. After Wuhan had fallen to the Northern Expedition, many senior officials of the CCP began to congregate there. People like Zhang Guotao, Tan Pingshan, Zhang Tailei, Li Lisan, Liu Shaoqi, Mao Zedong, Qu Qiubai, Luo Zhanglong, and Cai Hesen all went there. I cannot say exactly when each arrived, or from where. All I remember is that Qu Qiubai left Shanghai for Wuhan after the defeat of the second Shanghai insurrection in February 1927. Chen Duxiu and Peng Shuzhi, who were on the Standing Affairs Committee, stayed in Shanghai. Chen was still the Party's General Secretary, but Qu Qiubai, Zhang Guotao, and Tan Pingshan re-established the Central Committee in Wuhan and started issuing directives.[7] For a while, there were two Central Committees: the one in Wuhan lacked a General Secretary, but it dealt with the Central Committee

---

7 Some people disagree with me on this. They say that the Wuhan Central Committee was set up on the basis of a resolution passed by a plenary session of the Central Committee and that it was merely an accident that Chen and Peng stayed behind in Shanghai; their presence there did not imply that there was still a Central Committee in Shanghai. But they have been unable to find this resolution. I, on the other hand, have found the necessary evidence to support my own contention. A recently published speech by Roy in Wuhan (not included by Roy in his book but published by Bakulin, the Russian minutes keeper) says quite clearly:
"When the Comintern Executive reached Hankou, there were actually two Communist centres in existence in China: one in Shanghai (representing the Central Committee) and another in Hankou (representing certain members of the Central Committee). The Hankou centre demanded the immediate convening of a congress of delegates on the grounds that there was a leadership crisis and the leadership had to be replaced. They expressed universal dissatisfaction with the Central Committee. (See *Guowai Zhongguo jindai shi yanjiu* ['Foreign Research on Modern Chinese History'], No. 6, 268.)"
This is definitely reliable, for Roy was leader of the Comintern delegation. He must have known whether the Central Committee had resolved to move from Shanghai to Hankou. His speech was made on 12 May 1927, that is, several days after the Fifth Congress. According to Roy, the Shanghai centre was the Central Committee; it was not simply that one or two of its members had been left behind. As for the Hankou centre, it merely represented 'certain

of the Guomindang in the name of the Central Committee of the CCP; Chen Duxiu, acting on behalf of the Central Committee in Shanghai, issued a joint declaration with Wang Jingwei, who had just got back from Moscow. It was not until just before 12 April 1927, at around the time of Peng and Chen's departure for Wuhan, that the Shanghai Central Committee went out of existence.

By the time that Chen and Peng arrived in Wuhan, Qu's pamphlet attacking Peng had already appeared, and so had Mao's 'Report on an Investigation of the Hunan Peasant Movement'. The mood against right-opportunism had already been manufactured in Wuhan. I delayed leaving Shanghai for Wuhan until late April; when I arrived, I went straight to the Central Committee offices to see them. The Central Committee was housed in a three-storey foreign-style building with the guard room and the canteen on the ground floor, the conference room on the first floor, and the living quarters of Chen Duxiu, Cai Hesen, and Peng Shuzhi on the second floor. After chatting for a bit, we went downstairs to eat. Present were Chen, Peng, Cai, Huang Wenrong, and I. I cannot remember whether Chen Bilan and Li Yichun attended. While we were still eating, Peng mentioned Qu's pamphlet. He addressed Chen Duxiu, probably with a request for support in a counter-attack against Qu, I cannot remember exactly. Cai Hesen merely smiled. Chen said sternly, 'You're you, I'm me'. Chen had no intention of cooperating with Peng in an inner-party struggle, so Peng had no choice but to fight alone. He stepped up work on his counterblast to Qu.

By that time, Qu Qiubai, Zhang Guotao, and Tan Pingshan controlled the Central Committee. They used to caucus before it met to harmonise their views. They distributed tasks and chimed in with one another at the meetings, so their views always ended up by winning out. Peng Shuzhi was like a pathetic daughter-in-law – whatever he did, he was in the wrong.[8] Chen Duxiu become a puppet of the Qu-Zhang-Tang troika and implemented its decisions. Needless to say, the members of the troika also harmonised their views in advance with Borodin.

The Comintern wanted to replace Chen Duxiu as General Secretary, but soundings showed that his prestige was too high for that to happen easily. What is more, it was hard to know who to replace him with. At one point, the Comintern leaders settled on Tan Pingshan, but Qu and Zhang also considered themselves in contention for the post. Chen Yannian's name came up too, but

---

members of the Central Committee', and moreover was opposed to the Central Committee. [Note added by Zheng Chaolin in the early 1980s.]

8   Daughters-in-law were commonly abused, especially by mothers-in-law, under the traditional Chinese family system.

he refused. Some people said that he was not against replacing Chen Duxiu, but that he simply did not want to succeed him personally.

So at the Fifth Congress the Comintern representative and the Qu-Zhang-Tan troika adopted the tactic of isolating Chen: they kept him on, but they got rid of all those who supported him. On the day the Congress opened, Luo Zhanglong, head of the Hubei delegation, proposed a slate of names for the Congress Presidium. Chen was on it, but none of his associates was. On the final day of the Congress, when the elections for the Central Committee were about to take place, this Presidium put forward another slate that like the first one had Chen Duxiu on it but none of his supporters. After the slate had been put forward, Roy stood up in the name of the Comintern and proposed adding the names of Peng Shuzhi and Luo Yinong to it. Congress agreed, but afterwards the new Central Committee immediately sent Peng to Beijing, Luo Yinong to Jiangxi, Wang Ruofei to Shanghai, Yin Kuan to Guangdong, and me to Hubei. In short, we were not allowed to remain on the Central Committee. The only exception was Chen Qiaonian, who became Secretary of the Central Committee's Organisational Bureau.

By the way, here's an interesting anecdote. Although Li Weihan wasn't among those people who had been in Moscow, like them he had in the past supported Chen Duxiu. During the Congress he at one point told Wang Ruofei that the other leaders were applying the trick known as 'removing the emperor's entourage'. It was not difficult for him to see what was really going on during the inner-Party struggle. I got this by hearsay, from Wang Ruofei. But after the Congress, Li resolutely opposed Chen.

By then the 'Moscow group' was no longer in existence. There were people who had returned from Moscow, but there was no 'Moscow group'. Those who stuck by Chen Duxiu, whether or not they'd been in Moscow, were known as the 'Chen Duxiu group'.

2   From the Chen Duxiu Group to the Trotsky Group

The Chen Duxiu Group after the 7 August Conference

Today everyone says with one voice that Chen Duxiu was removed as General Secretary at the 7 August Conference. But actually, he stepped down. I've always said so. Recently while re-reading Cai Hesen's *Dang de jihui zhuyi shi* ('History of opportunism in the Party'), I came across a passage that said that sometime early in July Borodin had passed on a Comintern directive ordering Chen Duxiu and Tan Pingshan to go to Moscow and Qu Qiubai and Cai Hesen to go to Vladivostok, and that 'the next day Duxiu stopped attending to his duties'. So Chen Duxiu himself relinquished the General Secretaryship a good month before the 7 August Conference.[9]

Perhaps the 7 August Conference formally removed Chen from his post? No, it didn't. I was at the 7 August Conference. I heard Qu Qiubai read out the 'Letter to Comrades' and I heard other people deliver speeches. They all criticised past opportunist errors. Doubtless their criticisms were aimed at Chen Duxiu, but from start to finish no one at the Conference so much as mentioned his name, let alone resolved to sack him. The recently published collection of essays by Cai Hesen[10] includes a transcript of his speech to the Conference. In it he declares his support for the new line and criticises the old opportunist line, but he, too, fails to mention the name Chen Duxiu.

In the two months or more between the Fifth Congress and the 7 August Conference, the balance of power on the Central Committee changed greatly. The Qu-Zhang-Tan alliance had already come apart. Qu Qiubai now occupied the leading role, Zhang and Tan had marched South with the Ye-He army, Borodin had gone back to Russia, Roy and Voitinsky had resigned, and the 'prodigy' Lominadze had arrived in China to replace them. Even more remarkably, the ex-Chen Duxiu-ite Luo Yinong, who had been transferred from his

---

9   It was not until after I had finished writing this draft that I came across a quotation from Zhang Guotao's *Memoirs* saying: 'On 14 July Mr Chen Duxiu was also in a secret hideout from which he did not emerge'. The person who quotes this added: On 15 July, Chen Duxiu sent a letter of resignation to the Central Committee. He said: 'On the one hand the Comintern wants us to carry out our own policy, on the other it won't let us withdraw from the Guomindang. There really is no way out, I really can't continue my work'. He asked the Central Committee of the CCP to relieve him of his post as General Secretary.

The author of this article gives no source for Chen's letter of resignation, so we don't know whether he or she is quoting directly from the letter or from some other document. If the quote is reliable, it proves even more surely that it is nonsense to claim – as people have been doing for decades now – that the 7 August Conference sacked Chen. Huang Jieran says that when Li Weihan went to Chen's secret hideout and told him that the Central Committee had already removed him as General Secretary, Chen was furious. That can't be true either. If he resigned himself, why would he get furious? It is clear from all this that Chen's resignation was mainly in protest at the Comintern's decision not to let the CCP withdraw from the Guomindang. [Note by Zheng Chaolin.] Here Zheng has obviously forgotten Chen Duxiu's 'Appeal to All Comrades of the Party'. In it Chen wrote: 'From the beginning I could not persistently maintain my opinion; but this time I could no longer bear it. I then tendered my resignation to the Central Committee. My chief reason for this was: The International wishes us to carry out our own policy on the one hand, and does not allow us to withdraw from the Kuomintang on the other. There is really no way out and I cannot continue with my work' (Evans and Block [eds.] 1976, p. 604).

10 *Cai Hesende shierpian wenjian* ('Twelve articles by Cai Hesen').

old post as Provincial Secretary in Jiangxi to do the same job in Hubei, rose on the eve of the 7 August Conference to become a member of the all-powerful Standing Committee[11] while simultaneously retaining his Hubei post. Luo was extremely capable, and in such critical times his support could hardly be dispensed with. But this is only an apparent explanation. I later heard that Luo had written to Zhang Guotao from Jiangxi saying that he would no longer back Chen Duxiu but would carry out the line of the Fifth Congress. This is hearsay and I have not yet been able to confirm it, let alone to see the letter. But I tend to think that it is the true reason for his sudden rise.

Luo Yinong lacked followers and in Shanghai he relied on the Chen Duxiu people. While he was Secretary in Hubei both Liu Bojian (the head of his Organisational Bureau) and Zheng Chaolin (who continued to run his Propaganda Department) were Chen Duxiu supporters; Ren Xu, the head of his Peasant Department, who had worked in Mao Zedong's Peasant Training Institute in Guangzhou, also became a Chen Duxiu-ite shortly after his transfer to Hubei. About one week after the 7 August Conference the Central Committee replaced Liu Bojian in Hubei with Chen Qiaonian and Zheng Chaolin with Hua Lin (also a Chen Duxiu supporter). Zheng Chaolin was switched back to the Central Committee, where he was assigned to revive the publication of *Guide Weekly*, which had been suspended for a long time.

Just imagine: at around the time of the Fifth Congress the Central Committee did everything in its power to exclude followers of Chen Duxiu, but after the 7 August Conference they had to be allowed back onto the same body that had campaigned against them. But it's not really so surprising. Chen Duxiu himself was no longer a member of the Central Committee, and Luo Yinong was no longer a Chen Duxiu-ite but a semi-Chen Duxiu-ite. Luo had no following, nor did Qu Qiubai; of the three members of the Standing Committee, only Li Weihan had a 'following' that had escaped with him to Wuhan from Hunan, but the Central Committee could not be kept going exclusively by Hunanese. For example, they couldn't revive *Guide Weekly*. In July Zhang Guotao had proposed getting Shen Yanbing to revive it, but Shen had a family to support. After the 7 August Conference it occurred to them that I could do it, for I was still a bachelor; what's more, I had experience in publishing. So they brought me

---

11   Before the 7 August Conference, Luo was simply a member of the Central Committee, but after the Conference he was promoted into the Politburo. When the Central Committee moved back to Shanghai, Luo was still a member of the Politburo. He became a member of the Standing Committee of the Politburo in late 1927 or early 1928. He had already attended meetings of it even before then. The Standing Committee consisted of Qu Qiubai, Li Weihan, and Su Zhaozheng. [Note added by Zheng Chaolin in 1990.]

back to work in the Central Committee. In late September, when the Central Committee transferred back to Shanghai, I was formally appointed editor of the Party journal.

In Shanghai the Central Committee had originally appointed Deng Zhongxia as Secretary of the Jiangsu Provincial Committee, but the cadres of the Committee were Chen Duxiu supporters who ignored Deng and listened only to Wang Ruofei. 'I'm only Deputy Secretary!' Deng complained to the Central Committee shortly after its transfer to Shanghai. What he meant was that real power in the Provincial Committee belonged to Wang Ruofei. Not long after that, he left the Jiangsu Provincial Committee.

Yin Kuan in Guangdong was unable to cooperate with Zhang Tailei, so he returned to Shanghai; the Central Committee made him Provincial Secretary in Anhui. He Zishen ran the Hunan Provincial Committee's Organisation Department and became its Secretary after Mao Zedong went up the mountains. The Hubei Committee was made up exclusively of Chen Duxiu supporters. In Beijing Peng Shuzhi took the post vacated by the death of Li Dazhao. And so on, and so forth.

Wang Ruofei worked out a plan to get Chen Duxiu back onto the Central Committee, but nothing came of it. The first obstacle was the Comintern. It was precisely the Comintern, precisely Stalin, that forced Chen Duxiu to 'throw away his official's hat' in early July, 1927; Chen had no choice but to resign as General Secretary (or, as Cai Hesen put it, to 'stop attending to his duties'). So the Comintern wouldn't have let Chen Duxiu return as General Secretary. In the summer of 1927, the Chen Duxiu people could never have been defeated in the inner-Party struggle but for the intervention of the Comintern. The second obstacle was the Guomindang's White terror, as a result of which Chen Qiaonian and Luo Yinong had been seized and martyred. Luo was a 'semi-Chen Duxiu-ite' who at the time was sitting on the fence. If conditions had been right, he might have approved of Chen Duxiu's return to power and backed him from his position on the Standing Committee as Director of the Organisation Bureau. The third obstacle was Chen Duxiu himself. He was completely passive, and had no wish to take up work again after having just given it up. Lots of people went to talk with him, but as soon as politics came up he'd change the subject. For example, when Luo Qiyuan tried to discuss inner-Party matters with him, he took out his scheme for spelling Chinese characters and started asking Luo how you said this character or that character in Cantonese. He later said that at the time he had been pondering basic questions in the Chinese Revolution, including how much responsibility he himself should take for the defeat. He weighed the issues over a long period of time, but was unable to resolve them. On occasions he raised criticisms of various policies then being pursued by the Central Committee. He recorded them in letters, but needless to say the Central Committee was not prepared to accept them.[12] He knew that Wang Ruofei and Chen Qiaonian were working hard on his behalf, but he did nothing to encourage them, nor did he forbid them to do what they were doing. Some people thought that he was only pretending to be passive, and that he was secretly masterminding Wang and Chen's campaign. I disagree, but I, too, find it hard to explain why Chen had become so passive. Facts show that he could again become active once he had finished pondering the issues. In the second half of 1929, he was helped to do so by Trotsky's articles. He then came out resolutely against Stalin, against the Communist International, and against the Central Committee of the CCP.

In the face of these three obstacles, the Chen Duxiu-ites under the leadership of Wang Ruofei were doomed to failure.

Under the Politburo Elected by the 7 August Conference

The Central Committee elected by the 7 August Conference moved back to Shanghai in late September. Qu Qiubai and Luo Yinong were still very respectful towards Chen Duxiu. Two or three days after arriving in Shanghai, Qu went to visit him; his attitude towards him was the same as it had ever been. I don't know what they talked about. At that time Huang Wenrong was still living in Chen's house as his private secretary; he, too, didn't tell me what they talked about. All I know is that Chen handed Huang back to the Central Committee, and Qu accepted him. A few days after that Luo Yinong also went to visit Chen; needless to say, he, too, behaved respectfully. Chen got Huang to make a record of his conversation with Luo, but I haven't seen it. Not long after that, Huang was assigned to help me set up the editorial office of the Central Committee

---

12   Chen's letters of 11 and 12 November and of 13 December, 1927, are still extant, together with two replies by the Standing Committee. Chen's correspondence with the Standing Committee was greater than just these few items. According to his letter of 5 August, 1929, to the Standing Committee, at around the time of the Guangzhou Insurrection he 'wrote several letters to the Central Committee that did not avoid taboo subjects'. 'The Central Committee not only paid no attention to the opinions I raised in my letters but spread them round as if they were jokes'. That reminds me of something that Chen once told me. The reason he stopped writing to the Central Committee born from the 7 August Conference was because Chen Qiaonian told him not to, on the grounds that the Central Committee was making jokes about his letters. It was not until 28 July, 1929, after he had basically become a Trotskyist, that he wrote three letters on the subject of the Chinese Eastern Railway. The Central Committee born of the 7 August Conference considered his letters to be a 'joke': the Central Committee elected by the Sixth Congress considered them to be 'counter-revolutionary'. [Note added by Zheng Chaolin in 1980.]

organ. In late December, Luo Yinong came and asked me to invite Chen to stay in my house (that is, in the editorial office) for three days so that he and Qu could have a discussion with the Old Man. On 24 December, Huang hired a car to bring Chen over. Chen slept in Huang's room. That evening I organised a dinner for Chen, Qu, Luo, Wang Ruofei, and some other guests. The next day Qu and Luo had their talk with Chen. I had some private business, so I did not attend. On the fourth day Huang took Chen back home.

One day while we were chatting, Qu told me that the Old Man had said that if we had decided earlier to quit the Guomindang and carry out land revolution, he would have acted on the decision. Qu went on to express strong opposition to Chen's statement. I seem to remember that he asked me what I thought, but I said nothing.

The Standing Committee appointed Qu Qiubai, Luo Yinong, Deng Zhongxia, Wang Ruofei, and Zheng Chaolin to the editorial board of the Central Committee organ, with Qu Qiubai as chairman. I only recently saw the document, dated 12 October, 1927, in which this decision was recorded. I'd always thought that I was editor and Qu was the bridge between us and the Standing Committee, that he represented the Standing Committee on the editorial board and told us what it thought and told it what we were doing. Clearly I remembered wrong. There's no mistake about the document. I must have known about it, but I'd completely forgotten. The editorial board was a fiction, it never met even once. Qu and Luo represented the Central Committee, Deng and Wang represented the Jiangsu Provincial Committee, and I did the actual work. Shortly after his appointment Deng left the Jiangsu Provincial Committee. He never once came to my house. Luo and Wang often used to come, but not for the editorial board.

The new organ no longer used the name *Guide Weekly* but called itself *Bolshevik*. I wrote an article for the founding issue titled 'What Next for the Chinese Revolution after the Betrayal of the Revolution by the Guomindang?' The article concluded that the revolution had already been defeated, and that we would have to start again. After it came out, no one discussed it with me, but I myself discovered that my own viewpoint directly contradicted that of the Central Committee, that is, of the Comintern. It turned out that the Central Committee, that is, the Comintern, not only did not recognise that the Chinese Revolution had already been defeated but concluded that it was still in spate, and that the tide had risen even further. I delivered myself a private warning: in future write fewer articles on policy. No one pointed out that my article ran counter to the Comintern line, and no one even noticed that it did. Wang Ruofei – not because he had noticed the article, but simply in the course of an idle conversation – once told me that he'd gone to see the Old Man with He Zishen and the Old Man said: Look, the British, US, and French troops stationed in Shanghai are withdrawing in batches, do you think that the imperialists would do that if the tide of the Chinese Revolution were still rising? Wang told me that it was as if Chen's comment had suddenly jolted him awake. I thought to myself, so the Old Man thinks the same as me, that the Chinese Revolution has already been defeated.

I invariably asked Qu Qiubai to write the *Bolshevik* editorials, for as a member of the Standing Committee he was familiar with Party policy. But for some reason he was too busy to attend the editorial conference that planned *Bolshevik* No. 11, so the task devolved on me. The Guangzhou Insurrection had just ended, so I called my editorial 'Long Live Soviet Power'. I said in it that China had only two possible futures: either a 'Great Dragon Empire' under the dictatorship of the warlord Zhang Zuolin and a Guomindang Republic under the dictatorship of the bourgeoisie, or a Soviet Republic under the dictatorship of the proletariat. There was no third way. The editorial got me into a lot of trouble. About a fortnight after it came out, at a meeting of the editorial board, Qu Qiubai reported that according to Li Weihan speaking at a meeting of the Standing Committee, Zheng Chaolin's editorial was at odds with Comintern policy; our slogan was 'workers and peasants' democratic dictatorship', not 'dictatorship of the proletariat'. So Qu wrote an editorial for *Bolshevik* No. 14 rectifying my mistake. He energetically explained that the Soviets set up during the Guangzhou Insurrection were a 'workers and peasants' democratic dictatorship', not a 'proletarian dictatorship'. After that I stopped writing editorials, and I generally did my best to write as little as possible. But my heresy as yet found no echo in the views of Chen Duxiu. Quite the contrary. Later, after we came into contact with Trotsky's writings, I immediately agreed with Trotsky's views on the nature of the future Chinese revolutionary state, but Chen Duxiu stood out against Trotsky on this point for quite some time.

After Qu Qiubai had returned to Shanghai from Wuhan, the first time he visited Chen Duxiu he asked him to write some articles for the forthcoming Party journal. Far from refusing, Chen sent me numerous items for his 'Inch of Iron' column, all of which I published, in issue after issue. They're in the recent reprint, you can read them for yourselves. He wrote them under the name Sa Weng, meaning 'Old Man Sa'.[13] I guess he wanted to say by using that name that he'd never again play any role in the leadership of the CCP. Apart from 'Inch of Iron', he also wrote some ballads satirising the Guomindang. Each issue of *Bolshevik* contained one or more of these space-fillers. They were omitted from the reprint series, but I still remember a few lines from one of them:

13 *Sashou* means to relinquish or let go one's hold.

The Three People's Principles are a muddle.
The Five Rights[14] are a mess.
Education that conforms to Party propaganda is tyranny.
Under military rule, only warlords have a say.
In the period of tutelage, the bureaucrats hold sway.
The period of constitutional rule is far, far away.[15]

Later, I can't remember when, he stopped writing 'Inch of Iron', and the verses stopped even earlier. I never learned what he thought of the various issues of *Bolshevik* that came out.

In the first six months after the move to Shanghai, three people were very friendly to me: Qu Qiubai, Luo Yinong, and Wang Ruofei. All of them wanted to win me over, but I kept a certain distance from them. I knew about Wang Ruofei and Chen Qiaonian's campaign, but I took no part in it. Wang never tried to force me to join them. He knew I'd never gang up with anyone against Chen Duxiu. Not long after the Central Committee elected by the Sixth Congress had returned to Shanghai from the Soviet Union and started work, Wang Maoting, Secretary of the Yunnan Provincial Committee, came to see me on his way back from Moscow and handed me a letter written in invisible ink. Wang Ruofei had asked him in Moscow to give it to me and to tell me how to make the characters appear. I got the two necessary chemicals and mixed them according to Wang Maoting's prescription. I made the characters appear and handed the letter to Chen Duxiu, for it was addressed to him. Wang Ruofei had asked the Central Committee to pass the letter on to Chen Duxiu through ordinary channels, but knowing that that would not happen, he had made an invisible copy of it and asked Wang Maoting to deliver it into my hands. All I remember about the letter is that it reported on the proceedings of the Sixth Congress and Wang Ruofei's own reactions to it, and that it mentioned Qu Qiubai's 'Zero International' and Cai Hesen's *History of Opportunism*, both of which it called 'shameful documents'. Wang Ruofei told Wang Maoting to ask me to send him Chen's reply written in the same invisible ink. I was prepared to do so, but after Chen had read the letter his face registered not the slightest reaction, and he did not reply. The reason I recount this incident is because it shows that Wang

---

14   Sun Yat-sen's 'Quintuple Constitution' was based on the five principles of administrative authority, that is, judicial authority, legislative authority, executive authority, authority for conducting civil service tests, and authority to censor.

15   Sun Yat-sen had predicted that the Nationalist Revolution would go through three stages: military rule; political tutelage, that is, rule by the party on behalf of the people; and, finally, democratic constitutional rule.

Ruofei trusted me completely, and it also shows that at that time Chen Duxiu was still not prepared to take an active part in the struggle.

Under the Central Committee Elected by the Sixth Congress

In September 1928, the Central Committee elected by the Sixth Congress took up its official duties in Shanghai. The General Secretary Xiang Zhongfa was a puppet: real power was in the hands of Cai Hesen, who ran the Propaganda Department. According to reports, before returning to China Cai had asked Qu Qiubai who should edit *Bolshevik*. Qu recommended that I be kept on to do so. I worked under Cai just as I had previously worked under Qu, but I got on with him less well than I had with Qu, though we still managed to push our way forward. That didn't last for long, however. Very soon Cai was toppled and replaced by Li Lisan. I was even less happy about working together with Li Lisan, for he was openly opposed to Chen Duxiu and knew I was a Chen supporter. We not only got on badly: we were downright hostile to one another. There were several instances of friction between us. At a meeting of the editorial board I asked Li to find someone more suited to the job. To my face he refused to let me go, but behind my back he sought the opinion of Qu Qiubai, then in Moscow. Qu decided to send Wu Jiyan back to replace me. As an interim measure Li appointed Pan Wenyu, who had already got back from Russia, to take over from me. So I quit work and lived idly. Chen Duxiu told Peng Shuzhi that if Qu Qiubai had been on the Central Committee in Shanghai, Zheng Chaolin would never have ended up in such a way.

While Li Lisan held power, that was exactly how followers of Chen were dealt with. Sharing my idleness were Yin Kuan, who resigned as Provincial Secretary in Anhui; Peng Shuzhi, who resigned as Provincial Secretary in Zhili;[16] Wang Zekai, who'd been active together with Wang Ruofei at the Sixth Congress and had been kept out of a job by the Central Committee; Liu Bojian, who had escaped from Hubei, where he had been Provincial Secretary, to Shanghai, but was kept idle by the Central Committee; and Ren Xu, who was in the same boat as Wang Zekai.

I and Jing moved out of the Central Committee office and went to stay with Cai Zhende. Zhang Yisen, the wife of He Zishen, was living in the small room with her baby daughter, not yet weaned. He Zishen himself had been sent to Shandong on Party business, though the Central Committee had at the same time warned the Provincial Committee in Shandong not to ask him to do any 'political work'. Not long afterwards something went wrong in the Provincial Committee and He Zishen was arrested and thrown in prison. Cai Zhende was

---

16   Present-day Hebei.

at that time a member of the Jiangsu Provincial Committee. Starting with the Jiangsu-Zhejiang Regional Committee, most cadre members of the committees at all the different levels in Shanghai were Chen Duxiu supporters. After the Sixth Congress, when Wang Ruofei was detained in Moscow, Li Fuchun took over from him as Secretary of the Provincial Committee in Jiangsu and his followers were gradually replaced by Li's friends; the only two to survive were Cai Zhende and Ma Yufu.

In early 1929, the Jiangsu Provincial Committee and the Central Committee clashed. There was a struggle, and the Jiangsu Committee even declared its 'independence'. I forget what the conflict was about, but it was personal rather than political. Li Lisan and Xiang Ying on the Politburo had both worked in the labour movement. In 1924, when I had first got back to China, Li was in charge of the labour movement in West Shanghai and Xiang in East Shanghai. They vied with one another to see who could achieve most. Li Lisan won, and became leader of the Shanghai General Labour Union. At some point, ill will grew up between them. By this time, after the Sixth Congress, Xiang was on the Politburo, but his power and status were below Li's. I seem to remember that after the Sixth Congress Xiang Ying at first took over as Provincial Secretary in Jiangsu and it was not until later that Li Fuchun got that job. Xiang Ying incited Li Fuchun and the Jiangsu Provincial Committee against Li Lisan. He Mengxiong, head of the Organisational Department of the Provincial Committee in Jiangsu, also joined in the campaign. They asked Cai Zhende and Ma Yufu to see if Chen Duxiu was willing to help them. They especially needed help on the propaganda side, for they lacked people who could write. He Mengxiong said: get Zheng Chaolin. Cai Zhende heard him say this, and told me. Li Fuchun came personally to visit me. At that time I was living in the house of Li Minzhi. Li Fuchun told me about the conflict and said he hoped that I would help the Jiangsu Committee. I said I would. But he added that later he wanted me to take over as head of the Propaganda Department on the Jiangsu Provincial Committee. I took unkindly to that, and did not respond. During those days we Chen Duxiu supporters (Peng Shuzhi, Liu Bozhuang, Wang Zekai, Zheng Chaolin, Cai Zhende, and Ma Yufu) gathered at Cai Zhende's place to hear Cai's report on the conflict and to draft some necessary documents. In the end, the Jiangsu Committee lost its struggle after Zhou Enlai took measures against it. He called together comrades from all over China then in Shanghai for a meeting that passed a resolution reproaching the Jiangsu Committee in the name of the entire Party throughout China; at the same time the Politburo met and a majority jointly attacked Xiang Ying. So Xiang and Li Fuchun had no choice but to abandon their positions. The Jiangsu Committee was reformed, whereupon Cai Zhende and Ma Yufu, the two Chen Duxiu supporters who were Wang Ruofei's friends on the Committee, withdrew from it.

During this conflict Chen Duxiu neither egged us on nor held us back. It is especially noteworthy that this time there was no choice but to allow Peng Shuzhi to join in the campaign. A year earlier, when Wang Ruofei and Chen Qiaonian were campaigning on behalf of Chen Duxiu, there was no question of letting Peng join them, and even less of letting him lead them. But now Chen Qiaonian was dead and Wang Ruofei was under detention in Moscow. Cai Zhende, Ma Yufu, and Zheng Chaolin despised Peng, but Wang Zekai and Liu Bojian supported him, so we had little choice but to let him join our campaign.

After Cai Zhende and Ma Yufu had withdrawn from the Jiangsu Provincial Committee, the Committee continued to provide for their livelihood and let Cai live in one of the furnished houses at the disposal of the Committee. Cai invited me and Jing to go and live with him. We moved there in mid February.

The Chen Duxiu Supporters' Leap to Trotskyism

Cai Zhende and his wife lived on the first floor of a three-storey building and Jing and I lived on the top floor. He Zishen's wife Zhang Yisen lived in the smallest room with her newborn daughter. Ma Yufu often used to drop in for a chat.

After the defeat of the Jiangsu Committee, the Chen Duxiu supporters' campaign against the Central Committee was exposed. Why were we against the Central Committee? From my own point of view there were four main reasons. First, the reproaches made at and after the 7 August Conference against the Central Committee represented by Chen Duxiu were unfair. The defeat of the revolution wasn't Chen's fault. Chen was simply carrying out the line of the Fourth Congress. Second, after the defeat had happened, the 7 August Conference denied it and claimed that the revolution was on the crest of an even higher wave, so the Central Committee called for insurrections and many lost their lives in vain in armed risings, without benefiting the revolution in the slightest. Third, there was no democracy in the Party, and senior cadres were split into numerous unprincipled warring cliques pursuing private ends. Fourth, the Party's various leaders were not acting in an upright way: they were base in character and morals. And so on, and so forth. Perhaps the other Chen Duxiu supporters saw things differently. In short, the issues we raised in the course of this struggle were all quite narrow and rarely touched on points of high principle. It's a fact that we failed to grasp those fundamental questions of the revolution; save for Chen Duxiu, we knew very little about the reality of China. If we'd carried on like that, then even if the Central Committee had tolerated us instead of attacking us our little group would soon have vanished.

On 18 March, less than a month after my wife and I went to live with Cai Zhende, officers of the Guomindang's Public Security Bureau came to arrest Zhang Yisen and in passing unearthed documents in the rooms of our two families, so we were all taken off to prison. Ma Yufu, who had just happened to drop in at that moment, was also seized.

The Military Committee of the Central Committee under Zhou Enlai did everything in its power to rescue us, and some social contacts of mine and Cai Zhende's helped too, so except for Zhang Yisen, who spent several months in jail, the rest of us left the Garrison Headquarters' detention centre at Longhua on 29 April.

After we'd moved and settled down, Yin Kuan dropped in on us one day. Yin was meant to have visited us on the day we were arrested, but for some reason he hadn't come, so he'd escaped the misfortune that befell the rest of us. Now he started coming regularly again. Probably in mid or late May 1929, he brought some unusual mimeographed documents for us to see, documents of the Trotskyist Opposition in the Soviet Union. They were poorly translated and poorly mimeographed, but still they were intelligible. Yin Kuan had obviously been affected by them. He excitedly introduced them to us. I can't remember which documents they were, and whether he brought them separately or in one go, but they immediately gripped me. I had known that there was a fierce struggle going on in the Soviet Party, and that at first the Trotskyist Opposition had opposed the faction in power, consisting of Zinoviev, Kamenev, Bukharin, and Stalin; and that later Zinoviev and Kamenev had somehow allied with the Trotskyist Opposition against Bukharin and Stalin, who in the meantime had taken over. But I didn't know what the issues were, or even that they extended to the question of the Chinese Revolution. But now I had the documents in my hands. It turned out that Trotsky had publicly pointed out long before the defeat of the revolution that the Comintern's basic line on the Chinese Revolution was wrong, and that after the defeat of the revolution he had publicly pointed out that Bukharin and Stalin should take the blame for it. It also turned out that Trotsky had pointed out even after the Wuhan debacle that the Chinese Revolution had already been defeated. This was exactly what Chen Duxiu and his followers thought. We immediately embraced Trotsky's system of thought and steeped ourselves in his writings in order to discover on what grounds he had arrived at these two standpoints. They were not simply derived from his basic theory of 'permanent revolution'. He had analysed and quoted a large number of documents, including a copy of the resolution of the Jiangsu Provincial Committee drafted by Wang Ruofei pointing out numerous errors committed by the Central Committee of the CCP. Wang Ruofei had published this document in Moscow and the Trotskyist students there had translated it into Russian for Trotsky. But it was very hard for us to achieve a thorough understanding of Trotsky's basic theory. In Moscow we (for almost of us who had now become Chen Duxiu supporters were Moscow people) had studied Marxism and Leninism, but not Trotskyism. We'd known for a long time that Trotsky had a 'theory of permanent revolution', but we had no idea what it said. In the past we'd also applied ourselves to questions like the nature of society, the nature of the revolution, the motive power of the revolution, the object of the revolution, the stages of the revolution, revolutionary strategy and tactics, the revolutionary state, and so on. But we'd studied them one by one, in isolation from one another: we were unable to assemble such a wide range of topics into a single whole, so the more we learned, the more muddled we became. Now, after studying the 'theory of permanent revolution', these topics suddenly sprang to life and became linked together in a coherent system, so they were no longer confusing. After that I dropped the question of who was to blame for the defeat of the revolution and whether the tide was high or low and went on to 'indulge myself in abstract thinking', that is, to study basic principles and the theoretical aspect of how these various issues hung together.

Another issue that attracted my attention while reading Trotsky was his consistent opposition to the CCP's entry into the Guomindang. In 1922, in France, when the branches of the Communist Youth Party had discussed this question, I'd been against it and got into an argument with Yin Kuan, who was for it. As for Peng Shuzhi, in Moscow in 1923, he enthusiastically supported entry.

We all quickly embraced Trotskyism. After discussing and exchanging ideas for just a week or two, we basically became Trotskyists. But Chen Duxiu held out for longer than the rest of us. At the same time as Yin Kuan gave Trotsky's mimeographed articles to us (Cai Zhende and his wife Wang Shaohua, Zheng Chaolin and his wife Wu Jingru, and Ma Yufu) to read, he also gave them to Peng Shuzhi and his wife Chen Bilan, to Wang Zekai and his wife Du Lin, and to Liu Bozhuang. The Peng and Wang families lived together in a house on Kunming Road opposite the high wall of Ward Road Jail where Chen Duxiu often used to visit them. It was there that he read Trotsky's documents. He discussed them with Peng Shuzhi, Yin Kuan, and Wang Zekai, and they convinced him. I personally did not take part in those discussions. We were not long out of jail, and Chen Duxiu did not come to visit me in that period, nor did I go to visit him in his new house. Yin Kuan used to pass between my place and Peng's, so it was mainly from Yin that I heard about the change in Chen's thinking.

After reading each of Trotsky's documents, Chen would raise a disagreement, and then they would argue with him; but by the next time he came he would have abandoned his previous disagreement and would raise a new one on the shoulders of their old argument. In the course of his gradual conversion to their point of view, he had never once yielded to them in their presence, but next time he came face to face with them he would raise new differences on the basis of what they had previously told him. And so it went on. The person who put the most effort into winning him was Yin Kuan. But in the end, when it came to the question of the revolutionary power (should it be a dictatorship of the proletariat?), Chen was not persuaded, or at least not wholly persuaded. After Liu Renjing came back to China, and even when we and the other three groups were holding talks, Chen still didn't wholly accept Trotsky's views on the nature of this power.

In the course of this debate Chen not only spoke his views but also wrote them down in articles that he took along with him for Peng, Yin, and Wang to read. There were probably seven or eight such articles, all of which I read. None was published or kept, which is a pity, nor was a record made of the discussions. Otherwise we could have used it and the articles to trace the entire process whereby one of China's major modern thinkers came round to Trotskyism.

All this probably happened between the second half of May and the first half of July 1929. The reason I'm paying so much attention to dates and times is in order to dispel some current myths.

The most common myth is that Chen was unaware of Trotsky's views until Liu Renjing got back to China with a number of documents written by Trotsky, and that it was only then that Chen came under Trotsky's influence and became his follower. Actually, by the time that Liu Renjing met Chen Duxiu, Chen had already embraced Trotskyism (save for his above-mentioned reservations on certain theoretical questions). We followers of Chen Duxiu were by then even more resolutely Trotskyist. Liu Renjing reached Shanghai in September. He knew from the Chinese Trotskyist organisation that had returned to China from Moscow – he even knew it while he was still abroad, probably because Trotsky told him – that Chen Duxiu and his followers had already embraced Trotskyism. That's why he got someone to bring a letter to Yin Kuan and me asking us to visit him in a hostel in the French Concession. We spoke a common Trotskyist language. Later, when I took Liu Renjing to my home (on East Youheng Road) to meet Chen Duxiu, they, too, spoke a common Trotskyist language. Liu Renjing brought three documents with him back to China: one was the Draft Programme of the Chinese Bolshevik-Leninists, which Trotsky had specially written while Liu was a guest in Trotsky's house in Turkey; another, called 'Results and Prospects of the Chinese Revolution', was Trotsky's criticism of the part relating to the Chinese Revolution in Bukharin's draft programme for the Communist International; another was an article by Trotsky, titled 'The Chinese Question after the Sixth Congress', written after the Sixth Congress of the Communist International. The two articles were very long and in Russian, as, too, was the draft programme of the Chinese Opposition.

Someone told me that Liu Renjing recently told a visitor from the Party History Department of one of the Beijing universities that the draft programme he brought back to China had already been translated into Chinese when it was handed over to Chen Duxiu, and that Zheng Chaolin later polished it for publication. That's possible, I can't remember. As for the two long articles, I remember clearly that we decided that Liu would translate 'Results and Prospects' and I would translate 'After the Sixth Congress'. The two translations formed the text of the second volume of *On the Question of the Chinese Revolution*. (The first volume consisted of the earlier articles by Trotsky that had come into our hands; it was published before Liu Renjing returned to China.)

Then there's Pu Qingquan's[17] theory. Pu says that Chen Duxiu first learned about Trotsky's views from his (Chen's) nephew Wu Jiyan. According to Pu, Wu came to see Chen Duxiu and us at the end of 1929, after he'd been unmasked as a Trotskyist, sacked from his post, and expelled from the Party. That was even longer after Liu's return to China. By then Chen Duxiu no longer needed a Wu Jiyan to show him Trotsky's writings. Before his expulsion Wu had been Secretary of the Central Committee's Propaganda Department and wouldn't have dared have dealings with his uncle or with us.

Then there's Peng Shuzhi's theory. Peng says that he got hold of 'Results and Prospects' and 'After the Sixth Congress' from some Trotskyist students who had returned from Moscow and showed them to Chen. What actually happened is that Yin Kuan got them from Wang Pingyi,[18] Yin gave them to Peng, and Peng gave them to Chen. Peng deliberately obscured Yin's link in the chain; what Peng showed Chen was not the two long articles but a number of shorter articles, that is, those collected in the first volume of the Chinese edition of *On the Question of the Chinese Revolution*. The two long articles were not translated into Chinese until after Liu got back from Europe. The story of how the two volumes were prepared and published is sufficient to refute Peng's theory.

Apart from this there are various other rumours, but what I've just said is the truth, and whatever does not accord with it should be rectified.

---

17   Alias Pu Dezhi, who was arrested together with Chen Duxiu and held in the same prison. In 1952, Pu was arrested by the CCP together with all the other Chinese Trotskyists, but he capitulated and was released. He wrote a long article called 'Chen Duxiu as I knew him' in *Wenshi ziliao xuanji*, no. 71, published by Zhongguo wenshi chubanshe for the National People's Political Consultative Conference.

18   A student returned from Moscow. See Sheng 1971, pp. 171–2.

All of us Chen Duxiu-ites became Trotskyists, but our motives, goals, and emphases were by no means identical. Roughly speaking, we were of two main sorts. One stressed the practical movement and recognised that given the defeat of the revolution, we should now conduct peaceful and legal campaigns, deeply enter into the masses, strike roots there, oppose the Central Committee's ill-omened armed struggle, and wait until the mass movement revived before preparing to take up arms again. Absolutely no one proposed disbanding the underground Party. So the charge of 'liquidationism' bandied about by the Comintern and the Central Committee was simply slander. The *liquidateurs* in Russian revolutionary history proposed disbanding the underground Party, for in French *liquider* means to disband or dissolve. It's a commercial term. If a company or an enterprise goes bankrupt and closes down, it 'goes into liquidation'. The words 'liquidate' and 'liquidator' entered our language through Japanese. What is it that's liquidated? The underground Party is liquidated, that is, disbanded. So if no one proposes disbanding the Party, then it's wrong to start calling people 'liquidators'. Some Trotskyists of this variety opposed discussing theoretical questions concerning the nature of society, the revolution, and the state, and wanted to confine discussion to questions concerning practical activity and the practical struggle. The second sort stressed theory; they wanted to discuss basic issues of the revolution. But like the first sort, they were not against practical activity. One of the biggest differences between the Chinese Revolution and the early Russian Revolution was that the Russians had only set up their Party after extensively debating and quarrelling about basic issues of the revolution, and continued to do so even afterwards. So the Russian revolutionaries had already clarified these issues in the course of their revolutionary activity, and they all had their own ways of looking at things. The Chinese Revolution was not like that. There was no clear and wide-ranging theoretical struggle before the founding of the Party, nor afterwards either, when we hurled ourselves into the raging fire. For theory we relied on foreign comrades and the Comintern: we trusted them to solve our problems for us. This may be why the CCP was repeatedly defeated. The emergence of Trotskyism in China might have provided an opportunity for steeling revolutionaries in polemic and increasing their knowledge of theory, but unfortunately by that time the Comintern and the CCP were in the rough grip of Stalinism, so the opportunity was missed and only a handful of revolutionaries got a thorough theoretical training.

The intellectual preparation for China's proletarian revolution was far inferior to that not only of Russia's proletarian revolution but also of China's own bourgeois revolution. The polemics waged between reformists and revolutionaries before the Revolution of 1911 shook the whole country, that goes without saying; before the Coup of 1898, there were even violent theoretical disputes between conservatives and reformists, between the Orthodox Confucianists and the Modern Text School. In the course of the polemic, both sides relied on their own resources to resolve the various theoretical issues in dispute, and certainly neither of them looked abroad for help, from organisations or individuals. The proletarian revolution is of course world-wide, unlike the bourgeois revolution, which is contained within national boundaries, so the theoretical struggle on a world scale can more or less be substituted for that in one country; but that by no means dispenses with the need for theoretical struggle within the state where the revolution is occurring.

In this theoretical struggle Chen Duxiu was active, conscientious, and persistent, quite the opposite of his previous self. Many people had misunderstood his previous apathy. They had thought that he was just pretending, that he was deliberately letting Wang Ruofei campaign on his behalf while he hid behind the screen and pulled the strings. Others thought that he was genuinely apathetic about the revolution and about politics, that he had completely lost heart and given up. But now it can be shown that both suppositions were wrong. Between July 1927, when he 'stopped attending to his duties', and May 1929, when he first came across Trotsky's writings, Chen was passive because he had not yet thought through to the end important questions of revolutionary theory; by himself he was not capable of resolving the weighty issues in the Chinese and world revolutions with which he was then wrestling. Those at his side, starting with Wang Ruofei, were unable to help him in this enterprise. Only Trotsky's articles could do that.

I don't have his 'Letter to All Party Comrades' to hand, nor do I have the statement 'Our Political Views' signed by 81 people. But I do have his 'Reply to the Comintern' dated 17 February 1930. In it he says:

> After the tragic and shameful defeat of the Chinese Revolution in 1927, for a while I was really at a loss as to what course of action to follow, since I myself bore a heavy responsibility for the defeat. So I spent almost a whole year personally reflecting on those events. Although I did not thoroughly grasp the lessons of the defeat in time, and failed to discover a new way forward, I am deeply aware on the basis of my own experience that this defeat was the inevitable outcome of the entire political line of the past period.

He also says:

> Because of your deceiving ways and your blockade on the free passage of information, it was not until half a year ago that some documents by Comrade Trotsky on the Chinese question and some questions relating to the Soviet Union came into our hands. It was only then that we thoroughly and systematically understood the true source of the opportunism and adventurism perpetrated in the course of the Chinese Revolution.

He also says:

> At present the main issues concerning the Chinese Revolution are: (1) Will the revolutionary power issuing from the future third revolution be a workers and peasants' democratic dictatorship or a proletarian dictatorship? (2) Should we now directly prepare an armed insurrection, or should we raise political slogans appropriate to a transitional period in the revolution (such as the call for a National Assembly), and struggle for democracy?

Trotsky's writings had a big impact not only on Chen Duxiu but on Communists and revolutionaries the world over. When Trotsky's 'Criticism of the Draft Programme of the Comintern' was handed over to the Sixth Congress of the Comintern, it was initially kept from delegates; it was only when some delegates demanded to see it that the Comintern, under the control of the Soviet Party, allowed three delegates from each country to read it, under the strict injunction to divulge its contents to no one. Many unprejudiced delegates – and even some prejudiced ones – were influenced by Trotsky's critique and changed their view of the man. According to what someone told me, the Chinese delegation appointed Qu Qiubai, Guan Xiangying, and another person (whose name I forget) to read it. As a result Qu wavered but soon steadied; Guan was even more strongly moved, but he, too, later steadied. As for delegates of other countries, I read in James P. Cannon's *History of American Trotskyism* that he and a number of other Americans at the Sixth Congress were swayed by what they read, stole a copy, smuggled it back to the US, and carried out Trotskyist activity inside the US Communist Party. When one of Cannon's comrades, a militant, heard that Cannon had gone Trotskyist, he travelled from the West Coast all the way to New York to win him back. When Cannon realised what the visit was about, he asked the man to sit down and read the English translation of Trotsky's 'Critique' for himself. He did so, and stood up beaming. He, too, had become a Trotskyist.

Let's now go from theory to action.

3   The trials of Chinese Trotskyism

Our Activities

The first thing we did was to get organised. We set up three branches and worked hard on our new Trotskyist thinking. Yin Kuan drafted a 'Propaganda Outline', which was very long and was mimeographed as a fat pamphlet that served as a basis for discussion in the branches and for outside propaganda. Doubtless Chen Duxiu and Peng Shuzhi read it and agreed to its contents before it was printed. I can't remember whether I did too. We also collected together the articles by Trotsky then in circulation and published them in a printed volume titled *On the Question of the Chinese Revolution*. It consisted of writings by Trotsky himself but included none of the unsigned articles by Trotsky's Soviet followers. It's possible that the Trotskyists who'd returned to China from Moscow asked us for the money to help them publish this book. Wang Pingyi and others read the proofs. I was an experienced proof-reader but they ignored me and gave the job to Wang Pingyi and others, who had no experience whatsoever. So the book was riddled with mistakes, which particularly saddened me. The articles were poorly translated, and some sentences were unreadable. If I'd been proof-reader I could at least have rendered the translation a little smoother, even though I had none of the original texts to hand. The book was not announced as 'Volume 1'. When Liu Renjing brought back the Russian texts of the two long articles to China, Liu and I translated them into Chinese from the originals, so the translation was far superior. We published it as the second volume of *On the Question of the Chinese Revolution*. When it was decided to go ahead with this second volume, I rather impolitely claimed the proof-reading for myself, so the result was also much better. Apart from that, we published a periodical that was mimeographed and had no name. I can't remember how many issues of it we brought out.

Chen Duxiu financed all these publications, both printed and mimeographed. At some point, the CCP had stopped paying Chen's living expenses, but he managed to raise some money from his social connections, including some to finance our political work. As for the rest of us, we, too, had to fend for ourselves. At first the organisation had kept me and Jing; but after we left prison in the spring of 1929, when I started translating for the Propaganda Department, I got paid by the word: if I translated nothing, I got nothing. Every time I delivered a translation to the Propaganda Department I was given something new to do. Later, either because I stopped translating or because they didn't need me anymore, this source of livelihood dried up. Fortunately the newly opened Hubin Bookshop, where Ma Renzhi worked as manager and

Yang Xianzhen as editor, gave me some translating work to do, so I solved my problem. Ma Renzhi was from the same county as Peng Shuzhi, who told him about Trotskyism and won him over. But Yang was impossible to win. Not long afterwards he went to Northern China, and the Bookshop fell completely into the hands of Ma Renzhi.

Apart from written propaganda, we were also active as an organisation, and we won over various Party comrades to our side. Ma Yufu was especially active in work of that sort. He had been the person on the Jiangsu Provincial Committee responsible for labour movement cadres. He knew lots of worker comrades and leaders of branches with a large working-class membership. Though he'd already withdrawn from the Jiangsu Provincial Committee, he still had connections in the Party. He won over a whole branch attached to the newspaper workers' union and another in a silk factory; he also won over a large number of individual workers, including railway workers, tram workers, mill workers, print workers, and building workers; apart from that, he won over several cadres who had been working for long periods in Shanghai. Peng Shuzhi and Wang Zekai won over some members of the Party and the Youth League who had come to Shanghai from other parts of China.

Ma Yufu let Yin Kuan, He Zishen, and Zheng Chaolin deal with these various individuals and branches. I personally was assigned the newspaper branch and two worker cadres. Tu Yangzhi, secretary of the newspaper branch, was full-square with us, and two of his branch cadres also generally supported us. Tu called a plenary branch meeting in the great hall of an old-style house within the area of the Little North Gate. I attended this meeting, and at it I opposed the policies of the Central Committee from the standpoint of the Trotskyist Opposition. Some activists backed me up, but by no means all of the twenty-odd people in attendance did so. To consolidate our influence, Ma Yufu and I decided to take Tu and the two cadres to meet Chen Duxiu. We borrowed the house of Dong Tiejian, a comrade, for the meeting. I also took advantage of my wife Liu Jingzhen's contacts among the Yunnanese in Shanghai to hold discussions with some Yunnanese comrades, including one sent to Shanghai by the Provincial Committee in Yunnan to make contact with the Party centre. I also met regularly with a cadre active among print workers and another active among railway workers, and gave classes in their homes on revolutionary theory and politics. From my own small effort you can gather the extent of our activities as a whole in those days.

Our Expulsion from the Party

Precisely because we were so active, Chen Duxiu and the rest of us were expelled from the Party. A few days before that, the Central Committee arranged for a car to fetch Chen and take him to a certain place to meet a representative of the Comintern. The representative, who was seated behind a desk, behaved extremely discourteously. He spoke a few sentences to Chen. His attitude was appalling. An interpreter, whose attitude was equally bad, stood by his side and translated all this into Chinese. It was not at all like a discussion among comrades – more like an exchange between a judge and a convict. Chen turned on his heels and walked out, and so the meeting ended. A few days later *Hongqi* ('Red Flag') carried a statement announcing Chen's expulsion from the Party. As I remembered it, at first only Chen and Peng were expelled. But recently I saw the record of the expulsions; actually, only Chen was expelled by the Central Committee: Peng's expulsion, which took place at the same time, was carried out by the Jiangsu Provincial Committee with the assent of the Central Committee, along with that of Wang Zekai, Cai Zhende, and Ma Yufu. I carried on attending Yang Xianjiang's branch meetings, and at them I protested as a member of the Communist Party at the Central Committee's expulsion of Chen and Peng, on the grounds that it violated inner-Party democracy. After that, when I turned up as usual for a meeting of the branch, Yang Xianjiang politely greeted me and Jing and told us that the branch would not meet that day. Soon someone told me that I and Jing had been expelled, and that the resolution expelling us had been published in *Red Flag*. The charge against me was that I had incited members of the newspaper branch against the Central Committee, and that I had talked at Liu Shaoyou's home with the Yunnan delegate about my criticisms of the Central Committee. To this day I have not seen the resolution expelling us. I remember that before we were expelled, the Jiangsu Provincial Committee sent someone to talk with me and Jing. Those who came were Wang Kequan and Li Chuli. Li took the notes but didn't utter a word throughout the meeting.

The others were similarly expelled. The last batch of expulsions took place after the publication of the Manifesto signed by eighty one people. First the Central Committee published a notice in *Red Flag* asking certain comrades whose names were among the signatories to the Manifesto to say within a given number of days whether they had signed it themselves or someone else had signed it for them. They, too, were expelled, for they failed to make the required statements.

According to a recent account, Chen Duxiu was expelled because he wrote three letters to the Central Committee attacking its position on the Chinese Eastern Railway Incident. I've not seen the resolution on Chen's expulsion, so the only thing I have to go on is my own memory. True, the Central Committee of the CCP published a pamphlet with a number of articles denouncing Chen and an appendix containing Chen's three letters on the Chinese Eastern

Railway question. True, in 1931, Cai Hesen published an article called 'On Chen Duxiu-ism' which said that these letters clearly showed that Chen had gone over to the counter-revolution. But in November 1929, Chen was expelled for 'anti-Party activity', not for expressing 'wrong opinions' on the Chinese Eastern Railway question.

Those of us who had been expelled denied the validity of the resolutions expelling us. We protested, and continued to view ourselves as members of the CCP. Chen Duxiu published his 'Letter to all Party Comrades'; we published 'Our Political Views', signed by eighty one people (about a third of them invented). The two documents are still extant, and recently someone quoted from them in a study. I myself haven't seen them in fifty years, so I forget what was in them. Recently I came across Chen Duxiu's letter to the Comintern written in 1930. On 8 February, 1930, the Politburo of the CCP told Chen Duxiu that the Comintern had telegraphed requesting him to go to Moscow to discuss the expulsions. On 17 February, Chen replied to the Comintern letter.

The main thing is that we set up a formal organisation. We set up branches, we set up several district committees, we elected leaders, and we published *Proletarian* in a properly printed edition.

Our first leadership consisted of Chen Duxiu, Peng Shuzhi, Yin Kuan, Ma Yufu, and Du Peizhi, who was secretary of a branch of the CCP in a silk-factory in Shanghai that Ma Yufu had won over. In those days we copied the Central Committee's practice of promoting workers into leadership positions, so there were workers at every level of our organisation. Du Peizhi, who had been elected on the recommendation of Ma Yufu, attended two meetings of the Central Committee, both of them at my place. Later he was arrested and held in Nanjing. Ma Yufu flew into a panic, fearing that Du would reveal where we held our meetings, for after one such gathering Du had joked that he could 'easily get rich, all I have to do is tell the detectives of the Guomindang that they can arrest Chen Duxiu at such-and-such a time at such-and-such a place and I'll get a big reward'. We were on the point of moving house when Ma rushed in to tell us that Du had been shot in Nanjing. It turned out that he'd been arrested not on political charges but for armed robbery in a city on the Nanjing-Shanghai railway line. He'd been delivered to Nanjing where they'd shot him shortly afterwards. He'd not breathed a word about his political activity: he'd not sold out Chen Duxiu.

Du Peilin, the elder brother of Du Peizhi, remained a member of our organisation. I met him on one or two occasions. But just before the First Congress of the united organisation in 1931, I heard that he, too, had been taken. Three weeks after the Congress, when the first batch of our Central Committee members were arrested, I bumped into Du Peilin in the detention centre run by the Longhua Garrison Headquarters. He'd changed his name to Wang Qichang. It turned out that he, too, had been arrested in Shanghai for an attempted armed robbery. He introduced to me his accomplice, a man called Zhou, who he said was a Trotskyist sympathiser. He'd been planning to introduce this man to our organisation. Du Peilin was politically quite knowledgeable, and a good speaker. Whenever we discussed political questions with Communist Party members in our prison, Du would occasionally interject a few sentences. Later he was sentenced to seven years in jail. After Wang Fanxi was released from prison, he met Du in Shanghai and had a talk with him in a tea-house. Wang tried to get Du to become politically active again, but he refused. In 1940 when I returned to Shanghai I once saw him walking along the pavement while I was riding in a tram.

After Du's exit from the leadership, Ma Yufu recommended that he be replaced by Luo Shifan. Wu Jiyan was in charge of our Secretariat.

Proletarian was published in thirty-two mo format. We brought out two or three issues of it. I never wrote for it, though I had thought up its name, and I was responsible for putting the name in French just below the main mast-head. I also used to read the proofs. The printing factory was at the junction of North Zhejiang Road and Haining Road. One of our print-worker comrades, a man called Wang, had introduced us to it. It was just an ordinary printing factory, but when I delivered the proofs some of the workers recognised me and said hello. It turned out that in the old days they'd worked in the printing factory that I'd run for the Central Committee, and for some reason or other had ended up here. Comrade Wang was one of the two worker cadres I mentioned for whom I used to hold classes. I'd been to his home. He didn't know my address, but he had enough clues to find it out had he wanted to. *Proletarian* was raided while the third or fourth issue was in the press. The police traced it back to Comrade Wang, who was jailed for six months. He didn't talk about us to his captors, but after his release he no longer sought us out.

We were active and organised in several factories and on several tram-lines in East and West Shanghai; and in the French Concession and Nantao we were active among some groups of intellectuals. We were also able to use our contacts with the Hubin Book Company. We had links with the Shenzhou Guoguang Society and produced a magazine for it called *Dongli* ('Motive Force'), which Wu Jiyan edited. On several occasions we mobilised the entire organisation to distribute leaflets.

But in that period we put most of our time and effort into campaigning to 'unite' with the other three Trotskyist organisations.

The Emergence of the Original Trotskyist Organisation and Its Later Schisms

We Trotskyists under Chen Duxiu were midway converts, the product of propaganda and activity by the original Chinese Trotskyist organisation, which had grown up in Moscow in 1927. I only know about its early period from hearsay, so there's not much that I can say about it. I can just talk generally about it, on the basis of what other people told me.

Moscow's Sun Yat-sen University was founded in the autumn of 1925. Its first principal was Radek, a leader of the Soviet Trotskyist Opposition; there were also a number of Oppositionists on its teaching staff. These people were active among Chinese students and helped them set up a Chinese Trotskyist organisation. That was in the heyday of the Chinese Revolution, when the eyes of revolutionaries all over the world were fixed on China and when the Chinese Revolution was one of the three main issues of controversy in the Soviet Party. The Oppositionists had pointed out early on that the China policy of the Comintern, under the leadership of the Soviet Communist Party led by Stalin, was wrong and would lead to the defeat of the Chinese Revolution. But the Stalinists persisted with their mistaken policy. The course of the Chinese Revolution vindicated the Opposition on all counts, which brought more and more members and supporters of the Soviet Party over to its side; among the Chinese students, too, it grew and grew, as did the self-confidence of its members. On 7 November 1927, the Soviet Opposition staged a demonstration against Stalin during the march-past on the occasion of the tenth anniversary of the October Revolution. There were demonstrations both in Moscow and in Leningrad, where Trotsky and Zinoviev personally participated. In Moscow some Chinese Trotskyists also took part in the demonstration.

After these demonstrations, Zinoviev and Trotsky were expelled from the Party one after the other. Probably at the same time, the Trotskyists at Sun Yat-sen University came further into the open and were deported back to China, where they organised along Trotskyist lines. Some continued to be active in branches of the CCP. The main Trotskyist activity was in Shanghai and Hong Kong. In Hong Kong some people were active in the Tai-ku Dockyards, where they succeeded in gathering a group of workers around them. In Shanghai they began bringing out a mimeographed publication called *Our Word*. (Before 1916, Trotsky had published a Russian-language journal in Paris called *Nashiye Slovo* ['Our Word'], which some people translated into China as *Womende yanlun* ['Our Views']. I don't know why the members of the original Trotskyist organisation in China insisted on using the same name as Trotsky.) They translated and mimeographed Oppositionist documents and they also controlled a small bookshop called New Universe. Apart from the comrades who'd come back from Moscow, quite a few comrades were recruited in Hong Kong and especially in Shanghai, most of them members of the CCP.

To lump together what I know from different periods, the best-known members of the Our Word group were Ou Fang, Shi Tang, Chen Yimou, Liang Ganqiao, Zhang Te, Lu Yiyuan, Zhang Shi, and Duan Ziliang.

These people still kept up secret links to the Chinese Trotskyists in the Soviet Union, using the New Universe Bookshop as their correspondence address.

After the first batch of Trotskyist students had been deported, the Chinese Trotskyist organisation in Moscow continued to exist and indeed to flourish. Apparently at one time nearly half the students there were Trotskyists, including at KUTV and other colleges. There was even a Trotskyist (that is, Liu Renjing) at the Lenin Institute. They carried out their clandestine work most professionally, and succeeded in maintaining their cover.

In 1929, word went round that a batch of students were to be sent back to China to work for the Party. When the Trotskyists heard this, they met secretly and discussed what their response should be. They decided that the comrades who went back would continue to work for the official Party, and moreover would strive to do so better than anyone else; but that they would do everything they could to avoid being discovered, and await the chance to reform the Party from within.

Quite a few of these people took up important jobs in the Party. Wu Jiyan became Secretary of the Central Committee's Propaganda Department, Wang Fanxi became an aide in the Organisation Department, Du Weizhi (that is, Tu Qingqi) took up some important post in the Central Committee, and Zhao Ji, Liu Yin, and Pu Dezhi also worked for the Party after attending a training school.

But Liu Renjing came out openly as a Trotskyist. He returned to China via Western Europe. He visited the Trotskyist organisations in Germany and France, and in Turkey he stayed in Trotsky's home[19] for several days. He discussed the Chinese Revolution with Trotsky, who wrote the 'Draft Programme of the Chinese Left Opposition' for Liu to take back to China with him and to present for use as an internal discussion document. Once Liu Renjing had got back to Shanghai, he started looking up old friends, for example Yun Daiying. He told Yun that the Central Committee was bureaucratic, but Yun denied this and demanded proof; he also said that if the Central Committee really was bureaucratic, then he (Yun) would join Liu in opposing it.

---

19 Trotsky was exiled to Alma Ata in Soviet Central Asia in January 1928 and deported to Turkey in January 1929.

Liu Renjing already knew that we Chen Duxiu-ites had gone over to Trotskyism. Through intermediaries he sent a letter to Yin Kuan and me asking us to go him and see in a hostel in the French Concession. He warmly greeted us. In 1926, when he was working in the Central Committee of Communist Youth, I'd been quite close to him, and in the spring and autumn we'd often gone for outings together if the weather was nice. I'd given him a quilt with cotton wadding on the eve of his departure for abroad, and I'd invited him for a meal at the East Asia Restaurant. It was quite natural that we should greet each other with such warmth. I forget what he told us that day. Obviously we talked about how we had become Trotskyists. He also told us about his meeting with Yun Daiying (described above).

I don't know if it was on that day or another day that he arranged to meet Chen Duxiu at my place. At the time I was living on East Youheng Road. I went to his hostel to fetch him, while Chen Duxiu waited for him in my home. I remember that when we had almost reached my house, Liu Renjing nodded to someone coming in the other direction. I asked him who it was. He said it was Li Mogeng.[20]

When he met with Chen Duxiu there was no longer any need to discuss who was right, Stalin or Trotsky. Liu took out Trotsky's 'Draft Programme' and his two long articles, typed in Russian. I've already described how Liu and I arranged between the two of us to translate these documents into Chinese, and how we Chen Duxiu-ites published them as Volume 2 of *On the Question of the Chinese Revolution*.

Sometime after Liu Renjing's return to China the Trotskyist organisation in Moscow was unearthed, a list of names was found, and two hundred-odd people came to grief. According to reports, after Liberation[21] two or three of them returned to China from places of exile in Siberia. As for the Trotskyists who had already returned home, if their names were on the list then the Comintern or the Soviet Party informed the Central Committee of the CCP, which expelled the lot of them. It's said that Zhou Enlai told the better-known ones that if they admitted their mistakes and criticised Trotsky, they could stay in. No one took up his offer.

In normal times these people still hidden in the Party had kept up secret ties to the original Trotskyist group. After their expulsion, the handful of people around Wu Jiyan came over to the Chen Duxiu group, but the rest joined

---

20   An ex-student of Beijing University, and briefly a member of the early CCP.
21   That is, after the proclamation of the People's Republic of China in 1949. Actually, these people managed to cross the border and return to China not after but before October 1949.

the original Trotskyist group. Wu and his people all signed the statement 'Our Political Views'.

Shortly after the Trotskyists from Moscow expelled while still working in the Party joined the original Trotskyist organisation, conflict broke out in its ranks and some people split away from it. This was mainly due to the activity of Liu Renjing.[22]

Liu Renjing prided himself on being a veteran who had met Trotsky in Turkey and had brought Trotsky's 'Draft Programme' back to China. He despised the young leaders of the original Trotskyist organisation. They in their turn despised him. So they got into a fight. Liu Renjing then wrote a long article listing some peccadillos committed by these young leaders and incited some members of their organisation against them. Most of them had only got back to China in 1929 and had only recently been discovered and expelled. The main one among them was Wang Fanxi, who in those days called himself Wang Wenyuan. They brought out a printed journal called *Shiyue* ('October') and set up a new organisation. After that a minority, actually, only four people, copied them and set up yet another organisation and yet another journal, called *Zhandou*. In those days we used to receive through the post copies of *Militant*, the newspaper of the Trotskyists in the USA. Actually, *Zhandou* is not the equivalent of this word in Chinese. *Zhandou* means 'combat', whereas the English word 'militant' means combatant or (in Party terms) cadre. (I'm too lazy to check whether this definition is actually given in the English dictionary.) Whatever the case, these four people – Zhao Ji, Liu Yin, Wang Pingyi, and Pock-Marked Xu – translated it as *Zhandou*, regardless of what it meant in English. I never saw any copies of *Zhandou*, so I don't know whether it was printed or mimeographed. Later some other people joined this small group, but it was not as big as the October group and certainly not as big as the Our Word group.

Though these three groups fought one another, they were unanimous in their attitude towards the Chen Duxiu-ite Trotskyists: they considered us as opportunists who had lost favour with Stalin and now wanted to climb back into prominence using Trotsky's name. All three groups wrote to Trotsky setting out their views on us. After we had formally set up an organisation, we, too, sent Trotsky a letter explaining our point of view and enclosing a translation into English of the 'Letter to All Party Comrades' put out by Chen Duxiu after his expulsion, together with the statement on 'Our Political Views' signed by eighty one people. As far as I remember, we didn't explain to Trotsky what our attitude was towards the original Trotskyist group in China. Not long after Liu Renjing and Wang Fanxi had organised the October group, for some reason or

---

22 See Wang Fan-hsi 1991, pp. 132, 140, and 141.

another Liu resigned from it and set up on his own. Later he published a journal called *Mingtian* ('Tomorrow'). He was Trotsky's 'correspondent' in China, so he often used to write to Trotsky and Trotsky to him. I don't know how he estimated us Chen Duxiu-ites in his correspondence with Trotsky, but I know at least a little about the exchange between the two men. In October 1929, still in the period before our expulsion, our branch secretary Yang Xianjiang ordered me to join a flying demonstration[23] in front of the General Post Office on North Sichuan Road. After I'd got rid of all my leaflets, I bumped into Liu Renjing, so the two of us pretended to be passers-by and watched what was going on. We saw several demonstrators being arrested, and some dustmen sweeping up our leaflets and stuffing them into rubbish-carts. I and Liu then went our separate ways. Liu wrote to Trotsky describing this demonstration. His aim was to denigrate it, and to show that it was not worth the sacrifice. But Trotsky wrote back disagreeing. He said that demonstrations of this sort served at least one purpose, which was to let people know that the CCP still lived.

Though we Chen Duxiu-ites and Liu Renjing were constantly in touch, we never discussed organisational questions. None of us thought of trying to draw him into our group, nor did he ever ask to join. Under the circumstances, it is easy to see why. Nevertheless, some people say that after Liu Renjing got back to China he asked to be allowed to join us and to lead our Propaganda Department but that Chen Duxiu said no, whereupon Liu joined the Our Word group and began opposing Chen. That is not in accordance with the facts.

I deliberately use the word 'group' (*jituan*) rather than 'society' (*she*) to describe the organisations formed around *Our Word*, *October*, *Combat*, and *Proletarian*, for 'society' was what others called us, whereas we ourselves never referred to our organisations in that way; and in any case 'group' is a better description of them.

The Negotiating Committee

There were four Trotskyist organisations in China. How did they become one?

At first the Our Word group put forward the following condition. The Chen Duxiu-ite opportunists, including Chen himself, would only be allowed to join their original Trotskyist organisation singly, after individual vetting. As far as I remember, Chen himself never expressed an opinion on this, but Peng Shuzhi did. In Peng's opinion there was only one conceivable way of achieving unity. These students who had come back to China from Moscow, being young and inexperienced, should join our organisation, which was built around a nucleus of old men steeled in the Great Revolution. Yin Kuan, on the other

---

23   See Wang Fan-hsi 1991, p. 118 for a description of a flying demonstration.

hand, proposed all along that it shouldn't be a question of either us joining their organisation or them joining ours, but of a merger of the various groups after a period of joint discussion. Yin Kuan had more contact than the rest of us with members of the other organisations, and at one time shared a house with Zhao Ji and Liu Yin. He knew that neither of the above proposals would work. The various concerned parties reported to Trotsky, who wrote back criticising the students from Moscow for their attitude towards Chen Duxiu and his supporters. He carefully examined the documents of the Chen Duxiu group and could find nothing wrong with them in principle: the arguments advanced by the returned students were mere nitpicking. Trotsky also said that Chen Duxiu knew what revolution meant, which is not necessarily true of you young people. He proposed that we should first unite and then deal with the outstanding issues, for differences in our theoretical approaches could best be resolved by discussion within the framework of a unified organisation.

This letter had a big impact. The Our Word group had no choice but to back down from its original proposal and to recognise that Chen Duxiu was also a Trotskyist, on a par with them. The other two groups were naturally happy to accept Trotsky's proposal. But the Chen Duxiu-ites (actually, Peng Shuzhi and his followers) became arrogant. On the surface they recognised that the four groups were equal, but in reality, they wanted the other three groups to unite around the Proletarian group.

Each organisation nominated two delegates to the Negotiating Committee. At first I had nothing to do with this body, so I can't say who represented the other three groups. All I remember is that initially, the Our Word group was represented by Ou Fang (I forget who the second delegate was), and that after Ou's arrest they were represented by Liang Ganqiao and Chen Yimou. The October group was represented by Wang Fanxi and Song Fengchun or Pu Dezhi. The Combat group was probably represented by Zhao Ji and Liu Yin. The Central Committee of the Proletarian group formally nominated Ma Yufu and Wu Jiyan.

The negotiations had been going on for a long time, but they were making no progress. On one occasion Wu Jiyan told me in the course of a private chat that the delegates had obviously studied the mores of bourgeois parliamentarians, arguing first about this, then about that, and making no headway whatsoever on the central issue, which was how to unite. Since I had nothing to do with these negotiations nor did I attend meetings of our Central Committee, I have no idea what the arguments were about. But for Yin Kuan's intervention, the wrangling might have gone on forever.

At this point, I shall return for a moment to discuss dealings between us Chen Duxiu-ites and Chen Duxiu himself. During the period of the Great

Revolution no one ever knew precisely where Chen lived. He always used to come to us, never the other way around. Even Ren Zuomin, who was Party Treasurer and Secretary to the Central Committee, didn't know where Chen lived, with the result that at the end of 1925 or the beginning of 1926, there was a big scare for a while when Chen Duxiu suddenly disappeared. Chen had not been to Ren's place to attend to Party affairs for quite some time, everyone began to panic. For the time being there was nothing for it but to wait and see. We waited and waited, but still Chen did not show up. We began to think that the imperialists or the warlords had secretly kidnapped him or even killed him. Chen Yannian, who happened to be passing through Shanghai, looked up Wang Mengzou, owner of the Oriental Book Company, and pleaded with tears in his eyes for news of his father. The Oriental Book Company people said that they, too, had not seen Chen for ages. Previously Chen had made a habit of going to look up Wang Mengzou at the Book Company's editorial office on Changsha Road, which was where he got most of his news about events in society and politics. The employees there were absolutely reliable, but they, too, had not seen him for what was already a long time. We sent Gao Erbo, a member of Communist Youth, back to Songjiang to make enquiries. Chen Taoyi, the then Governor of Jiangsu Province, was from Songjiang, where his family had been on friendly terms with Gao Erbo's family for several generations. If Chen had indeed been secretly arrested, some information might have leaked out about it. But there was not a whisper to be heard. Instead, Chen Taoyi was roundly denouncing various malpractices of the warlords, especially sex scandals. As far as I remember, Sun Chuanfang was then Commander-in-Chief in Nanjing of the Five Provinces.[24] On one occasion, in the course of a chat in the Central Committee's Peasant Department or some other Department, I seem to recall that Zhang Guotao said that the situation was quite hopeless. He began to talk with me about Chen's life, and he ended up by remarking that if Chen, with all his talents, had chosen a government career, he would have gone right to the top, but instead he'd become a revolutionary, and now look where he was. Everyone thought that Chen was already dead. Ren Zuomin put a missing-person notice in *Republic Daily*, but to no avail. One day, however, Chen Duxiu suddenly turned up at the liaison centre run by Ren Zuomin. Everyone rushed in all directions to spread the news. Chen Yannian had already boarded a ship to leave Shanghai, so we sent someone to fetch him back ashore. What had happened? It turned out that Chen Duxiu had contracted typhoid fever and gone to hospital, where his mysterious lover had looked after him. He hadn't

---

24   Sun Chuanfang appointed himself to this post after routing the Fengtian warlords in October 1925.

wanted us to know about his lover, who was still a secret. He told us that before going into hospital he'd already informed Ren Zuomin that he'd be absent for quite a while. He'd seen the notice in *Republic Daily* while in hospital, but he'd paid no attention to it, thinking that he would soon recover and be discharged. Everyone was very angry about this, though I don't know if anyone criticised him. After that he apparently allowed Ren Zuomin (but no one else) to visit him at home. I don't know if the same applied to Wang Ruofei after Ren quit his job and a Central Committee Secretariat was set up under Wang. Neither Ren nor Wang ever breathed a word about where Chen lived.

Before the three armed risings of 1927, Chen's home had apparently already broken up. A few days before the risings started, Chen went to stay in the Central Committee's Propaganda Department, where he held meetings and met cadres. He was there on the night of the rising too, receiving reports and issuing directives. I was among the people who transmitted messages for him. It was not until early April, after his joint declaration with Wang Jingwei, that he left the Propaganda Department and went to Wuhan.

In Wuhan he stayed on the second floor of the Central Committee office, with Huang Wenrong as his private secretary. After he had 'stopped attending to his duties' he went into hiding together with Huang somewhere in Hankou. After returning to Shanghai, he went to live in a three-storey house on Fusheng Road (to the North of Range Road). He lived on the middle floor, under Peng Lihe and his wife, who acted as his cover. Wang Ruofei had arranged the house for them. Lots of people used to go and see him there. After I'd returned to Shanghai and settled down, I, too, went to see him; after I'd got married I took Jing to meet him. I know for certain that the following people went to visit him: Wang Ruofei, Qu Qiubai, Luo Yinong, Chen Qiaonian, He Zishen, Peng Shuzhi, Wang Zekai, and Luo Qiyuan. Wang Mengzou was also a regular visitor.

In 1928, after the arrest of Luo Yinong, Peng Shuzhi urged Chen to move, but Chen stayed put. In 1929, after I and Jing had been arrested, Peng again urged Chen to move, and eventually he did, to a place still North of Range Road but nearer to North Sichuan Road. Afterwards, Peng explained to me that it wasn't because he didn't trust me, but because he feared that my wife would be unable to stand the test of prison. After my release I refrained from visiting Chen in case someone might be following me.

Actually, all this has nothing to do with my main present theme, but since it occurs to me I might as well say it, for in any case these anecdotes concern the life of Chen Duxiu.

After his relations with the Central Committee of the CCP had been disrupted, Chen Duxiu moved from his house on Range Road into a place in the Tilanqiao area, but without informing the Central Committee of his new address. As far as I know, in this period only Peng Shuzhi knew where he lived.

Probably sometime in the second half of 1930, Chen moved to the upper floor of a terrace house on Dent Road near Seward Road. By that time several people were able to visit him, in particular Peng Shuzhi, Ma Yufu, and Zheng Chaolin. Little Pan[25] was already living with him. I think it's here that they got to know each other. One day in 1931 while I was out walking near the Hongkou Market I bumped into him and we walked along together. I asked him how things were. He told me that there was a man living in the small room above his kitchen who had told Little Pan that he was in the Communist Party, so Chen intended to move out. I told him that he should do so without delay, but he said things weren't yet so serious. I said I'd help him move. After a while either he or I found an empty room above a tailor's shop at the end of a lane off Zhoujiazui Road near Alcock Road and rented it. I helped him hire a cart and move. After that, I was the only person who knew where he lived. Little Pan didn't even know my name, and used to call me 'Little Fatty'. After that I seem to recall that he moved to another room at the top of a house on the same lane.

Yin Kuan never once went to Chen's place. He was only able to meet Chen at Peng Shuzhi's place, with Peng invariably in attendance. Yin never dared say anything to which Peng would object. Peng was like Chen's 'manager'. On one occasion Yin apparently bumped into Chen on the street and arranged for him to go to Yin's home and meet some people who told him about what was going on in the Negotiating Committee. Chen learned for the first time that Peng Shuzhi and Ma Yufu had been keeping him in the dark. It turned out that on the question of unity Peng and Ma thought as one: that the other three groups should unite around the Proletarian group. Wu Jiyan, Secretary to the Central Committee, went along with them. They had stuck to their opinion, in complete violation of the principle that the four groups should be equal and kept the true facts to themselves whenever the Central Committee of the Proletarian group met.

Chen Duxiu could not agree with this. He clearly felt that we embodied lethargy and lifelessness, and he enjoyed the youthful spirits of the Moscow-returned students. Before this, he had met and talked with a group of these students. I forget whether he reported on this at a meeting of the branch or told me about it in private conversation, but whatever the case he described the emotions he had felt at the time. He said it was like meeting young people at the time of the May Fourth Movement in 1919 or at the time of the founding of the Communist Party. He'd felt that they were full of vigour and vitality,

---

25   Chen Duxiu's last 'secret lover'.

and full of hope. So I don't believe Pu Qingquan when he says[26] that Chen Duxiu denounced these young Trotskyists as 'monkey pups still smelling of their mother's milk'. Pu doesn't say whether he himself heard Chen say this or someone else told him that Chen said it. Judging by what Chen told me at the time about his feelings, I can hardly believe that he entertained such thoughts and even less that he expressed himself in such hostile terms.

What Yin Kuan said made Chen very angry. At the next meeting of the Central Committee he raised the issue. Peng argued back, and the Central Committee split into two factions. Chen and Yin proposed negotiating on the basis of equality: Peng Shuzhi and Ma Yufu stuck to their original proposal, which boiled down to uniting around the Proletarian group. I don't know what attitude Luo Shifan and Wu Jiyan took. The outcome was victory for Chen and Yin, whereupon Ma Yufu and Wu Jiyan were recalled as delegates to the Negotiating Committee and replaced by Chen and Yin. After that there was an argument – and a fierce one – every time the Central Committee met, right up to the time of the Unification Congress. Later Ma Yufu stopped attending meetings of the Central Committee and He Zishen took over from Wu Jiyan as Secretary. He Zishen stood full-square with Chen Duxiu.

After the Proletarian group had changed its representatives, the work of the Negotiating Committee progressed smoothly. It had discussed theoretical questions before too, but in a nitpicking way. Now, everyone put forward their points of view in a calm and measured way, so that it was quite easy to reach common conclusions. There was a serious and businesslike discussion about preparing the Congress. The Negotiating Committee became a Preparatory Committee for the Congress, which drafted a set of resolutions for the Congress and in the process hit some controversies, mainly on the question of proletarian dictatorship and the call for a National Assembly, which two issues were basically resolved by the Negotiating Committee. Either at the same time or later, the question of the number of delegates was raised, together with concrete arrangements for the holding of the Congress. It was decided that the Proletarian group would take charge of arrangements and funding, and that each group would elect its own delegates on the basis of the size of its membership. The Our Word group and the Proletarian group were allowed an equal number of delegates; the October group was allowed a much smaller number; and the Combat group was allowed one delegate.

Ma Yufu withdrew from the Central Committee and became inactive. Peng Shuzhi, on the other hand, held out in opposition to everything that the Negotiating Committee decided, and even called it 'a conference of robbers

---

26   In 'Chen Duxiu as I knew him'.

out to divide the spoils'. Those who supported Peng didn't dare oppose Chen Duxiu, so they concentrated their fire instead on Yin Kuan. Yin had fewer followers than Peng. So Chen Duxiu and He Zishen decided to drag out Zheng Chaolin.

After becoming a Trotskyist, I observed discipline, obeyed the order to attend the meetings of a Party branch, gave classes to new recruits from the Party, and discussed with various comrades how best to attack the Central Committee of the CCP, but I took no part in the internal activities of our own organisation. By trade I was a translator and publisher, so I volunteered to translate things for the organisation. But I wrote no articles, engaged in no diplomacy, and fought for no positions. Zhao Ji and Liu Yin, who lived in the same house as Yin Kuan, reproached Yin for sealing them off from people and for not letting them meet other Chen Duxiu-ites. They especially said that they wanted to meet Zheng Chaolin, Cai Zhende, and Ma Yufu. Yin Kuan told me about this on several occasions, but I never went. Someone once told me that one day while a number of comrades were chatting together at Peng Shuzhi's place, Chen Duxiu commented that Zheng Chaolin lacked the 'desire to be a leader'. Yin Kuan countered that it wasn't the 'desire to be a leader' that Zheng lacked, but a sense of duty to the cause. What Yin meant was that the reason he was always running about was not because he wanted to be leader but because of his sense of duty to the revolution. I still don't know to this day whether it's sense of duty that I lack, or 'desire to be a leader'.

When I was finally 'dragged out' to work for the organisation, at first I was Secretary of the East Shanghai District Committee, as successor to Liu Bozhuang. Liu Bozhuang was a Peng Shuzhi supporter. There should have been three people on the Committee, but I only remember the railway worker Wang Zhihuai helping me, I forget who the third person was. In those days most of our membership was concentrated in East Shanghai, and most of our branches were the Party's old Chen Duxiu-ite branches. As far as I remember, there was no workers' branch as such, just a certain number of workers we'd come into contact with on an individual basis. The Our Word group also had an East Shanghai District Committee. The Unification Congress had not yet taken place, but the work of the Negotiating Committee was proceeding smoothly and a decision had been taken to merge the district committees of the different groups forthwith. I accepted an invitation to go for talks on cooperation to a primary school run by the Our Word group in East Shanghai. There were three members of the Our Word group present, led by Shi Tang. I'd often heard his name, but this was the first time I'd actually met him. He knew me, however. It turned out that he'd worked as Ni Youtian's apprentice in the Central Committee's printing factory, where I'd often had to go on business. Many people worked there, and though I didn't know them, they knew me. Shi Tang had been sent to Moscow either before or after the defeat to study at Sun Yat-sen University. Within a short while this printing worker had excelled beyond all expectations and become a well-informed and well-read cadre of the revolution. After unification he went to Guangxi to teach in a middle school where he became very popular among the students, many of whom came to Trotskyism through him. But all that happened later.

Shi Tang asked me: 'Why did we not hear people talk about you more often?' But what was so strange about that? I had no dealings with the Moscow-returned students, I was not on the Negotiating Committee, I had not uttered an opinion on unification, and though I'd said what I thought on some theoretical questions that were raised in the branch, I'd not talked about them outside the branch. But now that I had become Secretary of the East Shanghai District Committee, and was trying to implement cooperation at branch level, my name was often in people's mouths.

I also ran the election of delegates to the Unification Congress for the East Shanghai District Committee of the Proletarian group, so I was inevitably drawn into the internal struggle. The person in charge of preparing wax stencils and running the mimeograph was Wang Zekai's nephew Wang Fusheng. At a meeting he opposed my arrangements for the election. His uncle, a Peng Shuzhi supporter, had put him up to this. Wang had come to my place and argued with me about unification, and we'd parted on bad terms. If the negotiations had gone on any longer, Peng's supporters might have switched their sights from Yin Kuan to me.

The violent conflict in the Proletarian group about unification and the election showed Peng, Yin Kuan, and Ma Yufu in their true colours. Their main ambition was to become 'leaders' of the Chinese Trotskyist movement.

The Unification Congress

He Zishen was in charge of Congress arrangements. We rented a newly built two-storey lane house in an alley to the North of Ward Road on Dalian Bay Road. Wang Zhihuai and his wife and daughter lived downstairs as landlords, and we pretended to rent the upper storey. We made a rule that from 1 May to 3 May, while the Congress was in session, no one save Chen Duxiu should be allowed to leave the building.

The Proletarian group was represented by Chen Duxiu, Zheng Chaolin, Wang Zhihuai, Jiang Zhendong, and Jiang Changshi; later, after a membership count, we were allowed one more delegate, that is, Peng Shuzhi. The Our Word group was represented by Liang Ganqiao, Chen Yimou, Song Jingxiu, and two workers from Hong Kong. The October group was represented by Wang Fanxi,

Song Fengchun, Pu Dezhi, and Luo Han. The Combat group had only one delegate, Lai Yantang.

There are two questions on which people's recollections differ. The first is whether Luo Han represented the October group or the Our Word group. I've always believed that he represented the October group, and so does Pu Dezhi in his recent memoir. But Wang Fanxi told me in a recent communication that Luo Han represented Our Word's Northern Region. If that's true, other things fall into place. The Proletarian group had six delegates, and the Our Word group should also have had six; but according to my list, it only had five. If Luo Han attended the Congress as a representative of the Our Word group, then that would make six.[27] As for the October group, it was much smaller than the other two, so it shouldn't have had four delegates; if Luo Han was actually an Our Word delegate, that would bring the October group down to three, which is more commensurate with their real size. The second question is whether or not Peng Shuzhi attended the Unification Congress. I've always thought he didn't, but other surviving attenders say he did.[28] It seems as though I must amend my opinion. My view that Peng did not attend is also influenced by another matter that I shall mention shortly, though this other matter does not necessarily prove that Peng was not at the Congress.

The Congress went on for three days. Apart from the elections at the end, it spent its whole time discussing resolutions, principally political ones, that had been drafted by the Negotiating Committee after a long and intense discussion. But this discussion had been quite different in character from that during the early stages of negotiations, which had been little more than an exercise in mutual fault-finding. This later discussion was premised in a sincere wish for unity. The Negotiating Committee had reached broad unanimity on the questions of proletarian dictatorship and the National Assembly. The same went for other resolutions on the labour movement, the peasant

---

27 Wang Fanxi recently wrote to me about Luo Han's status at the Unification Congress. According to Wang, Luo represented the October group but had been elected by the North China organisation of the Our Word group. The apparent contradiction here arises from the fact that the North China organisation of the Our Word group had already split away at the Second Congress in 1929 and later became a founding unit of the October group. I never knew this. It is now clear to me that it was not excessive to award four delegates to the October group. Another thing I must amend is that there were four, not two, Hong Kong workers represented at the Congress. [Note added by Zheng Chaolin in the early 1980s.]

28 Wang Fanxi, however, was convinced that Peng didn't attend the Unification Congress, although he was elected as an alternate member of the Trotskyist Central Committee that issued from it.

movement, women, youth, and so on, as well as on rules and regulations. The Congress did not only pass resolutions. When the political resolution came up for discussion, Chen Duxiu addressed the Congress about it in the name of the Negotiating Committee; others then got up and spoke or argued, but only about minor details that were easily resolved. The same thing happened when the other resolutions came up. All these resolutions fell into the hands of the Guomindang intelligence service and may be available in the Guomindang archives on Taiwan.

The Congress elected a Central Committee composed of members and alternate members. Everyone's agreed that there were nine members, but most people have forgotten about the two alternate members. Different people remember different names. For example, I remember the full members as being Chen Duxiu, Wang Fanxi, Zheng Chaolin, Chen Yimou, Song Fengchun, Pu Dezhi, Ou Fang, Wang Zhihuai, and a Hong Kong worker; and the alternate members as Song Jingxiu and Peng Shuzhi. They didn't include Luo Han.[29] So the following controversies arise. Was Luo Han elected to the Central Committee? Was Peng Shuzhi a full member or an alternate member? Was Ou Fang elected? I stick to my opinion that Luo Han was not elected; as for Peng, as far as I remember the two people (Peng and Liang Ganqiao) who came bottom got an equal number of votes, so there was a run-off that Peng won, as a result of which he was elected. Nine of the eleven successful candidates became full members and two (Song Jingxiu and Peng) became alternate members. Ou Fang was in Caohejing Jail at the time, still alive. He was elected as a gesture honouring him.

On 4 May, we rested for a day. On 5 May, we held our first Central Committee meeting, at the same place. Chen Duxiu was made General Secretary, Chen Yimou took charge of the Organisation Department, Zheng Chaolin became head of the Propaganda Department, Wang Fanxi was appointed editor of the Party organ, and Song Fengchun took over the Secretariat. The same five people constituted the Standing Committee.

An incident took place at this meeting that left a deep impression on those present, and that most survivors of the meeting still remember. I am referring to Peng's letter to Chen Duxiu. Peng, who had not originally been a delegate to the Unification Congress, had written a long letter to Chen Duxiu denouncing the Congress as a 'conference of robbers out to divide the spoils' and

---

29   After posting off this manuscript, I had second thoughts, so I'll mention my new theory just for reference. Seven full members and two alternate members were elected, that is, nine people were elected and the two who came bottom were made alternate members. Ou Fang and Wang Zhihuai weren't elected. [Note by Zheng Chaolin.]

making other similar unpleasant allegations. After we'd all gone to start the Congress, he took this letter to the home of He Zishen (who was in charge of the Proletarian group's Secretariat) and asked him to give to Chen Duxiu. Peng didn't know where Chen lived, so he had no choice but to deliver it in this way. I don't know when He Zishen actually handed it over to Chen, but at the first plenary session of the Central Committee on 5 May Chen produced it and as far as I remember someone read it out aloud. Chen then asked Peng if he still stood by the letter. All eyes turned to Peng, who sat there blushing violently and unable to utter a single word. If it had been Yin Kuan, he'd have bluffed his way out of it with some plausible-sounding argument. I suddenly began to feel sorry for Peng and said 'Let's not take this too far'. After all, it's no fun to watch someone speechless and squirming with embarrassment. Later Chen Duxiu told He Zishen what had happened, and He Zishen then told me off for being too soft: he said it could lead to bungles. He said that if Peng had won the upper hand, Peng would never have shown mercy. He Zishen was right, of course. I remember this incident clearly, but at the same time I have no clear recollection of Peng attending the Unification Congress, which is why I originally thought that Peng only came to Dalian Bay Road when the plenary session of the Central Committee was held on 5 May.

The plenary session instructed Chen Yimou (head of the Organisation Department) to merge the branches of the four organisations as soon as possible and assigned Wu Jiyan, Zhao Ji, and Yan Lingfeng to the Propaganda Department. A decision was taken to call the Party journal *Huahuo* ('Spark') and to rush out the first issue. Finally, the Central Committee sent a letter to Comrade Trotsky reporting on the Unification Congress. I remember that Wang Fanxi wrote the letter and the rest of us all signed it. Now that Harvard University has opened Trotsky's letters archive, one day someone will probably unearth it.

I can't remember what happened between 5 May and 21 May. I forget whether I stopped being Secretary of the East Shanghai District Committee, and if so, who replaced me. In those days my main visitors were Wang Zhihuai and Song Jingxiu. Song made a point of talking to me about Ou Fang, who he said should be promoted into the leadership as soon as he was released from prison. One day Wang told me that Ma Yufu wanted to know where Wang lived and where I'd moved to so that he could pay me a visit, and that he'd told him, which I said was all right. I wasn't the slightest bit vigilant at the time. Naturally, I didn't agree with Ma's attitude to unification and I disliked his inactivity, but it never occurred to me that he'd betray us. Peng Shuzhi moved from the house he'd been living for quite some time to a place on Route Père Robert in the French Concession and told lots of people, including Ma Yufu, his new address. Ma

Yufu, too, often used to visit him there. I was the only person Peng didn't tell. I didn't tell him when I moved, either.

Sometime between 5 May and 21 May, we held a meeting of the Standing Committee to assess the draft of the first issue of *Spark*. I remember I had written an article for it on the Spanish Revolution. We decided to hold a rather bigger meeting on the 22nd. On the 21st, I held a meeting at my place about propaganda work. That afternoon Wu Jiyan, Zhao Ji, and Yan Lingfeng were all there. Yan, who was from Fuzhou, wasn't in any group at the time, having declared that he'd only join after they united. I'd heard about him, but I'd never met him. He told me that before he'd left China for the Soviet Union, he'd heard me give a lecture at Shanghai University. In 1926, the Jiangsu-Zhejiang Regional Committee had frequently assigned me to give lectures at Shanghai University. These lectures weren't part of the formal curriculum, and took place in the evenings. Crowds of people used to attend them, including many who weren't students. I wasn't the only one who used to give them.

I forget what we decided at this meeting. I had a plan to make a study of actual issues in China and of Chinese history. It was easy to talk about Marxism, even though our knowledge of it was still quite limited, but whenever we got round to discussing China's 'national characteristics' we could only come up with commonplaces. At that meeting we could have done no more than talk about this plan, there was no discussion or decision.

We are Arrested

After the meeting Zhao left, but Wu and Yan stayed behind for a game of mahjong that our landlord came up to join. I'd been there less than a month, so with that many visitors it was wise to play a game of mahjong to allay any suspicions that my landlord may have entertained. He was called Zheng, like me, and was twenty-odd, from Ningbo. He worked for an insurance company and was a member of the Merchants' Volunteer Corps[30] that the police used to call out when necessary to help maintain public order.

Just as the game was underway, Peng Guiqiu came rushing up and asked me if Yu Mutao knew where I lived. I quickly steered him out onto the sun terrace and quietly asked him what had happened. He told me that Yu had turned informer, that that evening at ten o'clock people would be arrested, and that I should flee. I told him that Yu didn't know my address. Peng Guiqiu then left, and after we had finished playing mahjong Yan Lingfeng left too, but Wu Jiyan and his wife stayed. I told them what Peng Guiqiu had said. They agreed

---

30 The Merchant Volunteers were an armed organisation financed by wealthy businessmen and, reputedly, by foreign interests.

that since Yu Mutao didn't know my address, we were safe, so they stayed in my place while I went to tell other people what had happened. I first went to Chen Duxiu's place. I was the only one who knew where he lived. We decided to scrap the meeting planned for tomorrow, and that he wouldn't go to Dalian Bay Road. I then went to Peng Guiqiu's place, where I met Xie Depan. There I learned that Peng Shuzhi had told Xie to bring me the news of the impending raid, but that Xie had sent Peng Guiqiu instead. It turned out that the story about Yu Mutao had been guess-work on the part of Peng Shuzhi. That there would be a raid at ten o'clock that night was a fact, but the rest was inference. Peng Shuzhi knew that the only unreliable person among those who knew his address was Yu Mutao, for Yu had recently asked Cai Yuanpei to write a preface for a book that Yu was about to publish. I now realised that the matter was not as straightforward as I had originally thought. Perhaps the informer did know where I lived. Perhaps he even knew where the meeting was to take place.

I immediately went to see Liu Renjing, who lived close by. His wife, Lu Mengyi's younger sister, was already in bed, but Liu was still up. I told him what had happened, and he promised to get someone to go the following day to the meeting place and warn people. As I was walking home I had second thoughts, and went myself to the house where the meeting was to be held. The people inside were all asleep. They answered my knocking, and I told them what had happened. At the time I still thought that a raid was possible rather than certain, so I didn't insist that they vacate the building there and then. I told them that the meeting would not go through, but I failed to tell Song Fengchun to go that same night and warn Wang Fanxi and the others in West Shanghai. That was because of my general irresolution in the face of important events. I didn't think either to inform He Zishen, for very few people knew him, and all those who did were reliable. Had I done so, he was so vigilant and resolute that he would have proposed fleeing forthwith. When I got home it was already past midnight. Wu Jiyan and his wife were still there, but they, too, drew no new conclusions from the new information I gave them. They then went home. I thought to myself, since I had been emphatically instructed to flee, even though ten o'clock had long since come and gone, it would be best not to leave anything to chance. After a discussion, Jing and I started preparing to pack a few necessities into a small suitcase so that we could spend the night in a hotel. Just as we were packing, there came a knock at the door. It was a team of detectives from the Longhua Garrison Headquarters together with some Chinese and foreign policemen from Tilanqiao Police Station.

I and Jing, together with the maidservant who cooked for us, were taken by van to Tilanqiao Police Station, where we were put behind bars; the van then drove off again, to reappear not long afterwards with He Zishen and his wife. At that point, I realised that the informer was Ma Yufu. He knew where He Zishen lived, he knew where Peng Shuzhi lived, he'd recently found out where I lived from Wang Zhihuai, and he knew where the house was where the Congress had been held. Sure enough, the van soon reappeared with Wang Zhihuai and his wife and daughter, and with Song Fengchun and Jiang Changshi. None of us slept that night. The next morning sometime after nine the van took the whole lot of us to the Magistracy of the Settlement, where we were asked a few questions before being sent back to Tilanqiao. As we walked back in, we saw Chen Yimou, Wang Fanxi, and Pu Dezhi in the lock-up. It turned out that some policemen had stayed behind in the house where the meeting was to have been held, and when these people turned up as planned, they had been seized. Wang Fanxi had gone together with Zhang Te[31] (I don't know what the meeting was about). As soon as they entered, Zhang was snapped into handcuffs. Wang rushed out through the back door, and the policemen rushed out after him, so Zhang Te fled through the front door, still handcuffed. He took a rickshaw to Jiangwan, where he removed the handcuffs at a friend's house.

According to He Zishen, that very morning Chen Duxiu had gone to He's house, but at the mouth of the alley he had met the landlord, who informed him that He Zishen and his family had been arrested the previous night. That's more or less what did happen, but I don't know if He Zishen heard it from one of the other prisoners or just guessed it.

At Tilanqiao Police Station we were divided up into men and women. The men's lock-up was a big cell alongside a smaller one. One afternoon a lawyer came, accompanied by another person. A prisoner who some of us recognised as Lou Guohua was called out from the small cell. We understood from his conversation with the lawyer that on the 22nd he'd gone to visit friends on the Dalian Bay Road but unfortunately had knocked on the wrong door and been seized. He managed some firm for Yu Qiaqing; the man accompanying the lawyer was Yu's son. So he'd been locked up in a different place from us and handled differently. I realised that Liu Renjing must have told him to go to the place where he had been arrested and to tell the people there to flee. Later I found out that before doing so he'd shifted all the documents from his house and made preparations for the period after his arrest; only then had he gone to Dalian Bay Road to knock on that fateful door. He'd been a delegate for the Our Word group. His wife, also a comrade, had given birth on 1 May, so he hadn't been able to attend the Congress and Song Jingxiu had filled in for him.

---

31 According to Wang Fanxi, Wang did not go to this place together with Zhang Te. Zhang had already been arrested and handcuffed when Wang knocked at the door.

A few days later the entire case was sent for judgment to the courts in the International Settlement. Wang Zhihuai and his wife and daughter, my wife Liu Jingzhen, and He Zishen's wife Zhang Yisen were not extradited but kept in a lock-up attached to the courts (it was a month before they were released). Lou Guohua was remanded on bail of $10,000. The rest of us – seven in all, mostly under aliases – were extradited to the Shanghai Garrison Headquarters.

We were all bundled into a van and taken off to the White Cloud Temple at West Gate, where the detectives attached to the Garrison had their office. The boss, a man called Ma from Anhui, interrogated us individually. I told him I was Wang Jian from Ganzhou in Jiangxi.

'If you won't even tell me your right name, how do you expect me to do my job?' he said.

He kept on at me for quite some time and eventually began to threaten me with electric shocks, but still I refused to yield.

'Think of it from my point of view', he continued. 'All I want from you is your real name and an admission that you are a member of the Communist Party'.

As he said that, he dipped his finger in some tea and traced the name 'Zhongfu' on the table in front of him.

'Nor am I asking you about him',[32] he added. 'He's an old friend of mine'.

After that, I had no choice but to tell him my real name and that I was a member of the Communist Party.

Ma Yufu knew that only through me could Chen Duxiu be found. As soon as I had got through the door of Tilanqiao Police Station the Detective Sergeant there, a man called Wang Bin, had asked me to 'help out' by telling him where Chen lived. He asked the foreign police sergeant to use torture on me, but the man refused. The day we were extradited Wang Bin spread his hands and said that after so many days the bird would certainly have flown. Chief Detective Ma of the White Cloud Temple probably also calculated that even if I did tell them, Chen would by then have moved, so he might as well be kind to me.

None of the others save He Zishen had been arrested according to a special list of names, so the question did not arise whether the names they had given were true or false. The police at the White Cloud Temple took mug-shots of them and showed them to Ma Yufu. Naturally, he knew who they were, but the police didn't force him to put names to faces. He got He Zishen's family name wrong, and wrote it with another character that is pronounced similarly but in a different tone; and an official wrote the character *zi* as a *xian*, which looks quite similar. So Hé Zishen spent six years in jail as Hè Xianshen. And that was

---

32   Zhongfu was one of the names used by Chen Duxiu. Like this man Ma, Chen was from Anhui.

lucky for him, because earlier he'd escaped from court-house custody in Ji'nan, and the Guomindang had put out a warrant for his re-arrest. If they'd found out who he really was, they might have sent him back to Ji'nan to be dealt with. Wang Fanxi, Pu Dezhi, and Chen Yimou didn't even say where they lived. They frequently felt the end of Wang Bin's rattan cane, but in the end he gave up on them.

We probably spent a week to ten days in the White Cloud Temple before being handed over to Longhua. Just before that, a detective told Jiang Changshi: 'You've got Ma Yufu to thank for this'.

A little over a month after we had reached Longhua, Lou Guohua turned up. He'd been bailed out all right, on a surety of $10,000 paid in by his friend. By then he believed that he was in the clear, so he attended court for the hearing, meaning afterwards to retrieve the $10,000 bail. But unluckily for him, in the meantime Wang Bin's people had searched He Zishen's house and unearthed a form that Lou had filled out at the time of the Unification Congress.

During our time at Longhua we were active in various ways, we had our struggles, and a number of interesting things happened, but I don't intend to talk about them here. I'll mention just one thing. A rumour reached us from outside that He Zishen and I were to be shot, but the others would be spared. In late October or early November I was called out for a mug-shot. Prisoners who'd been in Longhua for a long time knew that two or three days after that happened, you were invariably taken out and shot. I myself had seen the same thing happen on several occasions. But what could you do? 'An earthen pot will inevitably be broken on the well'.[33] However, the second day went by without anything happening, and so did the third, and so did a whole week of days. Finally, all seven of us were told to pack our things and attend court, where an official stood on a platform and read out our sentences from a notebook. I got fifteen years, He Zishen got ten, Pu Dezhi got two and a half, and the rest got six.[34] We were then sent to Caohejing Model Prison.

According to what others have told me, the reason I escaped the firing squad was because Xiong Shihui, Commander of the Shanghai Garrison Headquarters, was replaced by Dai Ji. Dai Ji was a general of the Nineteenth Route Army, which had just arrived to garrison Shanghai and was far more enlightened than the armies of Chiang Kai-shek's military clique.[35]

---

33 That is, a revolutionary must expect to die for the revolution.
34 In the original text I mistakenly said they got five years. [Note added by Zheng Chaolin in 1990.]
35 In late 1933 and early 1934, this same army staged a rebellion in Fujian against Chiang Kai-shek and made friendly overtures to the Chinese Communists.

I don't intend to say anything about our odyssey through Chiang's prisons: how we went from Caohejing to Hangzhou, from Hangzhou to Suzhou, from Suzhou to Nanjing, and how we spent five years behind bars in Nanjing Jail.

Finally, I should explain how it was that we knew that we would be arrested on the night of 21 May. Our Comrade Ma Renzhi, manager of the Hubin Book Company, originally called Ma Shicai, had followed He Yingqin to Fuzhou at the time of the Northern Expedition. In Fuzhou he had carried out some revolutionary activities, and had worked together with Pan Gugong, a leader of the left-wing of the Guomindang in Fujian.[36] In 1929, when Pan escaped to Shanghai, the two met often. Most of the military judges at Longhua were Fujianese, and some were friends of Pan. Somehow or another Pan got wind of the arrests and informed Ma, who rushed by car to Peng Shuzhi's place on Route Père Robert to tell Peng. He then intended to drive over to my place to tell me, but Xie Depan happened to be at Peng's place, so Peng told Xie to take the news to East Shanghai. That's how things went wrong. Naturally, Ma didn't know that He Zishen and the people at the Congress building had also been targeted for arrest.

Things I Heard Said

I was in prison for the whole of the six years and three months between the night of 21 May 1931, when I was arrested, and the morning of 29 August 1937, when I was freed after the bombing of Nanjing.[37] I was not personally engaged in Trotskyist activity in that period, so I only know about it from hearsay. Some things I heard about while I was still in jail, other things I only learned of after my release. I can't vouch for the accuracy of what follows.

While we were at Longhua, news filtered in that four members of the former Our Word group had issued a declaration breaking from Trotskyism and capitulating to the Guomindang. They were Liang Ganqiao, Zhang Shi, Lu Mengyi, and a fourth person whose name I forget. They'd quite simply gone over from revolution to counter-revolution, but they didn't serve up any comrades to the Guomindang as a 'gift on the occasion of a first meeting', so in that respect they did not quite sink to the depths of Ma Yufu. (Later, however, Zhang Shi and Lu Mengyi became leading members of Guomindang intelligence, and Liang Ganqiao became a leading anti-Communist under Hu Zongnan.)

It was hardly surprising that these four turned traitor. The Our Word group had originally opposed unifying with the Chen Duxiu-ites, and though Trotsky's letter had forced their hand, a minority of them were still inwardly

---

36 Of which Fuzhou is the capital.
37 By the Japanese.

opposed to it. The people around Ou Fang in the Our Word group were all right, but those around Liang Ganqiao were not. After Ou disappeared into jail, Liang took over. His ambition was to become leader of the united Trotskyists, so that he could then indulge in his conspiratorial schemes. He planned to have Chen Duxiu elected General Secretary at the Unification Congress and then to send him to Turkey[38] so that he himself could take over, but things didn't turn out as he wished. He came bottom of the poll together with Peng Shuzhi in the election for the Central Committee, and he lost in the run-off. Peng's name stank in the nostrils of most delegates, but Liang's stank worse.

During the Congress, Wang Pingyi, a member of the Combat group, had to return to his home in Shandong after something came up. He returned to Shanghai after the Congress, and the people who were dissatisfied with its outcome disparaged it to him, so he declared that he would lead the opposition to it. I had heard about this even before our arrest. Sometime later Wang Pingyi, too, joined the Guomindang secret police and changed his name to Wang Boping.

After our arrest some people in the Our Word group, including Zhang Te and Shi Tang, left Shanghai for Guangxi. In those days Guangxi was under Li Zongren and Bai Chongxi,[39] who were busy recruiting talent and going on about autonomy, for they planned to resist Chiang Kai-shek's Nanjing Government. Zhang Te was from Guangxi, though the others probably weren't. Zhang Te returned to Guangxi to become an official and participate in the internal struggles of the Guangxi clique; not long afterwards he abandoned Trotskyism. But some people, led by Shi Tang, went to become not officials but middle-school teachers, and they continued to propagate Trotskyist ideas both in the classroom and outside. They influenced no few of their students, who played an important role in a whole series of student movements in Guangxi. But Shi Tang and his friends never developed a Trotskyist organisation in Guangxi; on the contrary, they left the Trotskyist organisation. I only mention this in connection with the defection of Liang Ganqiao and the three others.

At Longhua we met up with seven other new Trotskyist prisoners. They were: Yin Kuan, Jiang Zhendong, Liu Yi, Song Jingxiu, and three others; all were held on a different block from us. According to what others have told me, there are two theories about these people. Yin Kuan says that when they realised that they were without a leadership, a number of them met together in a hotel on Fuzhou Road to set up a new one, but unfortunately one of the people at the meeting was a spy who betrayed them. According to Song Jingxiu, however, there was already a new leadership and Yin Kuan's aim at this meeting was to

---

38   Where Trotsky was.
39   Li and Bai were leaders of the anti-Chiang Kai-shek Guangxi clique.

set up a faction. So when Song learned about it he went to the hotel and urged Yin against this course of action, but unfortunately they were all arrested. I don't know who's telling the truth.[40] Subsequently Yin Kuan and Song Jingxiu were both sent to prison, but Jiang Zhendong, Liu Yi, and the other three were freed on bail. Later Song died in jail, but Yin Kuan was bailed out when he fell ill, after which he failed to report back to prison.

I don't know when the leadership under Chen Duxiu was restored. After first we and then Song Jingxiu had been arrested, as far as I remember the only members – one full, the other alternate – left on the Central Committee were Chen Duxiu and Peng Shuzhi. Wang Zhihuai had gone to work as a labourer on the Zhejiang-Jiangxi Railway, Ou Fang had already died (in jail), the Hong Kong worker had gone back to Hong Kong after the Congress, and though Pu Dezhi and Song Fengchun were already out of jail, they were temporarily inactive. I don't know what activities this leadership engaged in. This was the period of the 18 September Incident[41] and the Battle of Shanghai,[42] so the country was in turmoil and conditions were ripe for revolutionary agitation.

In the late spring or early summer of 1932, Peng Shuzhi, Li Ji, Wu Jiyan, and Du Weizhi gathered briefly in Shanghai's Zhongshan Park for a meeting. After the meeting Peng and Li left by the back gate and Wu and Du by the front. Keeping watch at the front gate was Gu Shunzhang, who recognised Wu (though he didn't know his name) and arrested him and Du. They were handed over to the Nanjing Garrison Headquarters. Du Weizhi, a professor at Anhui University, phoned the principal of the University, Cheng Yansheng, and the Garrison Headquarters decided to send him to Anqing and hand him over to Cheng, whence he escaped back to Shanghai the same night. Wu Jiyan's cover eventually broke and he was sentenced to life imprisonment. A few years later his relatives got him out.

In October 1932, I was in Nanjing's Central Military Prison. The man in charge of the Education Section in this prison was Shen Bingquan, a student of Hangzhou Law College and originally a member of the Communist Party

---

40 When Jiang Zhendong read this passage, he came up with a third theory. He said that the meeting was to set up a West Shanghai District Committee and that Song Jingxiu – a member of the revived leadership organ – was there on Peng Shuzhi's instructions. [Note by Zheng Chaolin.]

41 The seizure of Shenyang in 1931 by the Japanese, as a step towards occupying the entire Northeast.

42 On 28 January 1932, the Nineteenth Route Army successfully held out for more than a month against a Japanese attack on land, on sea, and in the air before a truce was declared and the Shanghai area was demilitarised.

who had been arrested on 12 April 1927, at Hangzhou. Somehow or another he'd ended up working for the Guomindang in this prison. Politics are a complicated business. Most people would call this man a traitor, and so did I at the time, but it's not true. In the Central Military prison he showed special consideration to political prisoners, particularly the better-known ones. When I was first in the South block of the prison, he got the Second Section to transfer me after a few months to the preferential treatment unit, where there were already two other political prisoners, both students of Nanjing's Central University, one a man called Yang Jinhao from Pudong, the other a man from Suzhou called Wang Chubao, the half-brother of Wang Rongbao. After we'd settled in, Shen Bingquan came to see us. He told us that the prison authorities planned to teach illiterate prisoners to read and write, so the three of us had been assigned to prepare a text-book. The other two thanked him and agreed to do so, but I kept quiet. This preferential treatment unit was alongside the prison sports ground, you could see it whenever you were let out for exercise. People used to say that Noulens and his wife[43] were at first kept here, though they were later moved to another place. In the summer of 1932, when I was let out for exercise on one occasion, I saw two political prisoners who were living in this preferential treatment unit, both of them members of the CCP who'd studied abroad, one called Chen Jiakang and the other Jiang Zemin.[44] We'd already met them at Longhua. They'd mended Wang Zhennan's car for him, so Wang Zhennan (who was Minister of Military Justice at the time) had instructed the prison authorities to send them to the preferential treatment unit. I could tell from the way that other prisoners talked whenever we were let out onto the sports ground that they heartily despised people who lived in the preferential treatment unit. After Chen and Jiang had left, Shen Bingquan managed to get me and the other two prisoners transferred there.

During that period, one day a young political prisoner I knew came to see the doctor in the clinic on the other side of the sports ground. At the time I was taking a walk in front of the entrance to the preferential treatment unit. This

---

43   Hilaire Noulens and his wife Wandeli (a transliteration from the Chinese, perhaps representing her cover name, Marie Vandercruyssen) were said to be representatives in China of the Comintern's Far Eastern Bureau. They arrived in Shanghai in March and June respectively, and were arrested in the International Settlement in June 1931 and handed over to the Chinese authorities. They were tried by the High Court of Jiangsu Province and sentenced to life imprisonment, but were freed in September 1937, shortly after the Japanese invasion. Frederick S. Litten has written a manuscript titled 'The Noulens Affair'.
44   Jiang Zemin (written with the same characters) is also the name of the man who took over from Zhao Ziyang as General Secretary of the CCP after the 4 June Massacre in 1989, but this is a different Jiang Zemin.

young man told me, 'Chen Duxiu has been arrested'. His words struck me like a thunderbolt. On one occasion at Longhua I'd heard a rifle-shot from across the wall and realised that another political prisoner was dead. A few minutes later one of the guards, a man from Jiangxi, had stopped at the gate to our block to tell us that the man who had just died was an old man, a Communist Party leader. That, too, had given me a nasty shock, and it wasn't until later that I learned from another prisoner that the man they'd shot was Xiang Zhongfa. Now, in my preferential treatment unit, I hoped against hope that the rumour was not true. But the same day or the next, Shen Bingquan came to see us. He said with pretended nonchalance that Chen Duxiu was unlikely to die. I said instinctively that if he'd been arrested, I could see no reason why he wouldn't die. Shen Bingquan had thought that his words would startle me, and had never imagined that on the contrary my words would startle him. He asked me how I knew that Chen had been arrested. I can't remember how I answered. He must have thought that we political prisoners were extremely well informed. And so we were.

A few days later I wrote to Shen Bingquan requesting to be transferred back to the South block, and he had no choice but to accede.

While I'm on the subject, there's something else I ought to add about Shen Bingquan. In the summer of 1933, he again came to visit me in the South block. Without beating about the bush, he told me that he was responding to a request by my friend Hua Lin, who came from the same province as Shen, to show me special consideration. He told me that something had come up, and he asked me if I was interested. It turned out that the Military Court intended to appoint some people who knew foreign languages to translate foreign military law into Chinese for use as reference material in drafting a legal code for the Chinese military. The translators would be housed in the North block, and would spend their working day in the instruction rooms and return to their cells in the evening. Since I owed this chance to Hua Lin, I said I'd do it.

Later, my wife Liu Jingzhen came to see me and told me about Chen Duxiu's arrest. She said it was Xie Depan who had informed on him. I asked her whether he'd informed on him before or after his arrest. She said after.

At the time Jing was teaching in Shanghai. Each year during the summer and winter holidays she would visit me in Nanjing's Military Prison. She also visited me once or twice during term-time. Naturally, she also visited Chen Duxiu whenever she was in Nanjing. It wasn't until after my release that she told me that she had been in charge of liaison between Chen and the outside world. She used to smuggle letters and documents of the Shanghai organisation to Chen, and to smuggle out articles and documents by him. Each time she would hide these things in the bottom of a biscuit tin, underneath the biscuits.

She didn't necessarily read the documents, nor was she the only person who worked for the organisation in this way. Because she did this work, Chen Duxiu directed the organisation not to enrol her in any of its branches. I believe that some Shanghai Trotskyist leaders went in person to visit Chen in jail. The articles contained in the mimeographed publications that we brought out in that period, together with Chen's secret letters, which are still in existence, will probably throw light on the nature of this liaison, and on the extent to which Chen Duxiu had the Shanghai Trotskyist organisation under remote control in those days.

After her arrest in 1952, Liu Jingzhen told the Government about her role as link-woman in that period. She was freed in 1957. It's hard to believe that in 1968, while she was under criticism in the Cultural Revolution, she was asked once again to talk about the 'biscuit tin' episode, and her tricking of the Guomindang dictatorship was used against her as evidence of 'counter-revolutionary criminal activity'.

I don't know under what circumstances the Shanghai organisation was restored after Chen Duxiu's arrest. According to what I've heard, the main mover was Chen Qichang, later assisted by Yin Kuan after he had got out of jail; after Yin's second arrest, Wang Fanxi got out of jail and also helped. It was in this period that the organisation was rent by a serious conflict.

At some point, a South African Trotskyist came to Shanghai to work as a journalist. He was Deputy Editor of Shanghai's *China Weekly Review*, second only on that publication to Edgar Snow. His name was Frank Glass, and his Chinese name was Li Furen. Under his influence another left-wing newspaper man in Shanghai, Yi Luosheng (Harold R. Isaacs), came over from the Third International to the Fourth. These two both hoped to build the Chinese Trotskyist movement. They tracked down Chen Qichang, and at the same time they tracked down Liu Renjing. Frank Glass gave Chen Qichang $300 to set up a printing factory. It was a printing factory of a special sort: no machines but just lead type, which you formed into bars, clipped into place, and smeared with ink before printing.[45] At around this time Liu Renjing had brought some young students to Shanghai from Beijing and had usurped the leadership of the Trotskyist organisation. These people, having set up a Central Committee formed by Si Chaosheng, Liu Jialiang, Hu Wenzhang, and Wang Shuben, with Liu Renjing as General Secretary, got Frank Glass to support them. I believe he was even a member of this Central Committee. But Yin Kuan and Chen Qichang refused to recognise it, and were loath to hand over their 'printing factory'. A struggle ensued, on questions of both theory and organisation, and

---

45   Cf. Wang Fan-hsi 1991, p. 176.

also on matters concerning people's private lives. I know nothing of all that, save that Chen Duxiu supported Yin Kuan and Chen Qichang, and that when Liu Renjing's Central Committee expelled Yin Kuan and Chen Qichang they expelled Chen Duxiu as well. Frank Glass backed all this. Chen Duxiu didn't trust Frank Glass. He said that that foreigner is an agent of the Settlement police, and told comrades to pay no attention to him. Not long afterwards Liu Renjing's Central Committee was raided by the Guomindang and they were all arrested. From then on the only leadership in existence was that of Yin Kuan and Chen Qichang.[46]

The case of Liu Renjing and his supporters was handed over to the Nanjing Garrison Headquarters. Liu Renjing immediately turned traitor, so instead of going to jail he was sent to the Suzhou Reformatory for a period of self-examination. The others – Si, Liu, Hu, and Wang – were not prepared to capitulate, so they ended up in jail: Liu Jialiang got seven years, the rest got five. They were handed over to the Central Military Prison.

I met Si, Hu, and Wang there, but I never met Liu Jialiang, who was kept in the South block. Somehow they managed to persuade a fellow-prisoner who was a member of the CCP to explain about them to me. I didn't know this man, nor he me. He worked in the prison printing factory. The prisoners in the West block used to exercise in the area just in front of the printing factory windows. One day, I forget which year, but it was one or two years before the outbreak of the war with Japan, one of the prisoners working in the printing factory called me over to the window while I was out exercising. This man stood by the window and talked with me for a few minutes. He told me that there were four Trotskyists in the prison, that they had put up a good show while being held in the Nanjing Garrison Headquarters, and that they wanted to meet me but were afraid I wouldn't trust them, so they'd asked him to introduce them to me. Later, again while I was out exercising, a man came across and began walking alongside me. He told me that his name was Hu Wenwei (alias Hu Wenzhang); on another occasion, Wang Huating (alias Wang Shuben) also came across and started talking with me, and the same thing happened on several subsequent occasions. Hu and Wang told me about their struggle with Yin Kuan and Chen Qichang, and especially about the underground printing apparatus. At the time I thought it was a wrangle over a mimeograph. It never occurred to me that the so-called underground printing apparatus was in fact a 'printing

---

46 This paragraph is based on hearsay, and it may not all be true. At first Liu Renjing wasn't General Secretary. He was in Beijing, so the Central Committee was simply under his remote control. Some say that Si Chaosheng was General Secretary during this early period, others say Liu Jialiang was. [Note by Zheng Chaolin.]

factory'.⁴⁷ Wang Huating also told me about their analysis of the various classes in Chinese society. On one occasion when Si Chaosheng met me in the bathhouse he talked with me at great length, not (like Hu and Wang) about the past but about the future. They heard from somewhere that I would soon be released, so Si proposed that I set up a magazine to propagate Trotskyist ideas. In the course of my talks with these three men I avoided voicing my own opinion. None of them tried to disguise their detestation of Liu Renjing.

Later, after I had got out of jail, I heard that Liu Renjing had behaved quite shamelessly in the Reformatory, where he had become leader of the 'Students' Society' (or whatever the so-called autonomous organisation was called that the Guomindang political police set up for prisoners), with He Zizhen as his deputy. The two of them were one hundred per cent behind the Guomindang in its persecution of Communist prisoners. While I was in the Central Military Prison I came across an issue of the magazine put out by the Reformatory, in it an article by Liu Renjing praising Chen Lifu's theory of vitalism. (Another article by Peng Kang⁴⁸ was about Laozi. The magazine is probably available in some archive.)

Si, Liu, Hu, and Wang were also set free on 29 August 1937. They first stayed in a hotel in Nanjing for a while and only then went back to Shanghai. While they were in the hotel, Si said he didn't want to be a Trotskyist anymore, but the rest continued to be active in Shanghai. They kept up their struggle against Chen Duxiu, and even denounced him as a 'Fuzhou Road prostitute'. Later Hu Wenzhang went to Manchuria to join an anti-Japanese army, and nothing more was heard of him. Liu Jialiang was seized and martyred in Vietnam.⁴⁹ As for Wang Shuben, at the time of Liberation he died in the headquarters of the Sino-American Joint Mission⁵⁰ in Chongqing.

---

47 According to Wang Fanxi, the printing machine here referred to was left behind by Harold Isaacs when he stopped publishing *China Forum* and went to Beijing to write *The Tragedy of the Chinese Revolution*. This machine was eventually sold to get some money with which to run the organisation. One or two years later, a new Provisional Committee was elected including Wang Fanxi, Chen Qichang, Yin Kuan, and Frank Glass. This new leadership decided to bring out an underground journal called *Douzheng* ('Struggle'), so a new machine was put together. It was very primitive, consisting of just two wooden frames into which type was inserted. This story is told in Wang Fan-hsi 1991, p. 176.

48 One of the Creation Society writers.

49 He was trapped by the secret service of the Vietcong together with some Vietnamese Trotskyists in 1950, and died in prison shortly afterwards.

50 A collaborative effort, between the CIA and Guomindang intelligence, whereby the former advised the latter in the use of modern techniques of surveillance, interrogation, and torture. The Centre's real name was the Sino-American Centre for Cooperation in Special

The printing press led to quite a storm. Either before or after Liu Renjing's usurpation of the leadership, a comrade working in the printing factory decided that he would expropriate the equipment for his own private ends and open a shop. Frank Glass then disguised himself as a British policeman and went by car, with Shao Lu acting as his chauffeur, to steal it back, with Little Zhao [Zhicheng] from the Telephone Company pretending to be his interpreter.

Chen Duxiu and Peng Shuzhi finally split in Tiger Bridge Prison in Nanjing. Pu Dezhi and Luo Shifan stood by Chen. Outside the prison, Yin Kuan and Chen Qichang also opposed Peng.

Apart from Pu Dezhi and Luo Shifan, four other people were arrested at the same time as Chen Duxiu and Peng Shuzhi. They were: Zeng Meng, He Zizhen, Peng Daozhi, and Song Fengchun. Not long after entering jail, Zeng was freed through the intercession of former fellow-students of his from Huangpu Military Academy after writing a letter of repentance. The others considered him a traitor. He Zizhen also got out, but via the Reformatory, where he behaved despicably. Peng Daozhi, Peng Shuzhi's younger brother, died in jail of typhoid fever. Song Fengchun was also freed as a result of a campaign by people outside prison.

There's one other episode I'd like to recount concerning Chen Duxiu in jail. Sometime in 1935 (the exact time would have to be checked) Mao Dun was responsible for editing a book called *Zhongguo de yiri* ('One Day in China').[51] Through Wang Yuanfang he asked Chen Duxiu to record his activities, thoughts, and feelings on a given day. Chen agreed, and the ensuing record was published in *One Day in China*. Through some other person Mao Dun also asked Lou Shiyi, in the Central Military Prison, to do the same, which he did. I was one of the people he wrote about, though I'm not named as such. After the book came out, while I was still in prison, I saw it. Chen Duxiu's reflections brimmed with the spirit of internationalism, though he had usually spoken of

---

Techniques (see Shen Zui and Wen Qiang 1984, pp. 71 ff). Wang Shuben was killed by the Guomindang as part of its preparations to flee to Taiwan.

51   The advertisements calling for contributions to a record of one day – Thursday, 21 May 1936 – were in fact posted in the spring of 1936. The book was published in September 1936 in Shanghai by Shenghuo Shudian. The idea for the book came from the proposal by Maxim Gorky at the First Congress of Soviet Writers in 1934 for a book called *Den Mira* ('One day in the world'), eventually published (in Russian) in 1937. An English-language version of Mao Dun's book, one-fifth the size of the original and without Chen Duxiu's contribution, was published by Yale University Press in 1983 under the title *One Day in China: May 21, 1936*, translated and edited by Sherman Cochran, Andrew C.K. Hsieh, and Janis Cochran.

the Chinese Revolution from the standpoint of China as a single country. His essay made a deep impression on me.

A Talk on the Eve of our Separation in Nanjing

On 7 July 1937, the Lugouqiao or Marco Polo Bridge Incident took place,[52] marking the start of all-out war between Japan and China. By that time the Guomindang and the Communists had already formed their second united front. The Chinese Red Army had become the Eighth Route Army of the National Revolutionary Armed Forces and had set up an office in Nanjing. The Communists demanded the freeing of political prisoners and so did public opinion, but for a long time before that a number of celebrities – old friends of Chen Duxiu – had been demanding Chen's release.

Before the Marco Polo Bridge Incident but after the establishment of the Eighth Route Army's office in Nanjing, Pan Hannian, a member of the office staff, had visited the Central Military Prison to see his cousin Pan Zinian. He told Pan Zinian that the Guomindang was still not prepared to free all political prisoners, and that it would only consider freeing prisoners if the CCP made a list of those it wanted released. Pan Zinian came back and reported on this exchange; I only heard about it indirectly. After a while Pan Zinian, who was serving life, was freed early. Only then can the question of a 'list' have come up, for if all the prisoners had been freed, there'd have been no need for one.

Some people said that the CCP asked the Guomindang to free a list of people including Chen Duxiu. I've never heard such a theory before, and common sense tells me that it's not true. Chen Duxiu was freed as a result of the campaign by those celebrities. It had nothing to do with the CCP. The formal procedure was that Hu Shi and Zhang Bolin bailed him out. Some office of the Guomindang proclaimed that it had resolved to free Chen on bail because he 'loves his country deeply, and deeply regrets what he has done'. (Two days after his release, on 25 August, Chen protested at this statement in a letter to the editor of Shanghai's *Shenbao* newspaper: 'A sincere patriot would not venture to brag about his love of country, and I know of nothing that I should regret'; 'I have done no wrong, so regret would have no object'.) In short, Chen Duxiu's release was not connected in any way with the CCP.

Then there's the black propaganda of the Guomindang's dirty tricks department. According to one report, Zhou Enlai visited Chen Duxiu in jail; according to another, Chen Lifu and Tao Xisheng greeted Chen Duxiu as he left the prison, Chen went to stay in the Guomindang Central Committee's guest house, Chen Lifu invited Chen Duxiu to dinner on the evening of his release, and at the

---

52   This act of aggression was staged by the Japanese at Marco Polo Bridge near Beijing.

banquet Chen Duxiu made a tearful speech of thanks. This is all mischievous fabrication. Zhou Enlai never visited Chen Duxiu in jail and when Chen walked free it was his student Chen Zhongfan (then Director of Jinling University's Literature Department) who personally fetched him from jail and put him up in his house in Yinyangying. As for us Trotskyists in the Central Military Prison and Tiger Bridge Prison, our release, too, had nothing whatsoever to do with the CCP. By 13 August, the war had already reached Shanghai, and by 15 August, Nanjing was being bombarded from the air. The Guomindang was preparing to abandon Nanjing, so it put into operation a regulation commonly used in bourgeois countries whereby in times of war the jails are emptied and the prisoners dispersed. The great majority of the prisoners – political, common, and military – were released. Pu Dezhi, Luo Shifan, and Peng Shuzhi were freed in late August. Luo and Peng immediately went to Shanghai, Pu immediately returned to Anqing. He Zishen, whose original sentence had been shorter than mine, was freed about one week earlier than me and went to Tiger Bridge Prison to visit Chen Duxiu; he also met Pu, Luo, and Peng there. Chen Duxiu arranged for He Zishen and for me and my wife to go to Jixi in Anhui to stay for a while in the house of Wang Mengzou, owner of the Oriental Book Company. Without waiting for me to leave jail, He Zishen was taken by my wife Liu Jingzhen to the Science Book Company in Wuhu.[53] I wasn't released until 29 August, whereupon I immediately went with Jing to Chen Zhongfan's two-storey foreign-style house in Yinyangying. Downstairs was a guest-room and a dining room; upstairs was the main room, where Chen Duxiu and Little Pan were staying. Chen Zhongfan had already sent his dependants back to his native place in Yancheng, and he himself had moved into the upstairs side room. When I and Jing arrived, Chen Duxiu and Little Pan were temporarily away, so we waited for them in the main room. Pan came back first: Chen Duxiu didn't get back until the afternoon. Several groups of guests called in on him, and he received them in the downstairs guest-room. I and Jing went out to buy some bread and cakes for our supper. That night we slept on the floor in Chen Duxiu's room, and early next morning we set out for Wuhu.

When we went up or down the stairs, we often saw Chen Zhongfan come out of his room. Chen Duxiu hadn't introduced us to him by name, he'd simply said that we lived in East Nanjing and had fled here to escape the bombing. Whenever Chen Zhongfan met Chen Duxiu he would stand respectfully by, in the manner of an old-style student in the presence of his teacher. On Chen

---

53   The journey from Nanjing to Jixi passes through Wuhu. The Science Book Company was owned by Wang Mengzou. He Zishen went there to await Zheng Chaolin's release.

Duxiu's bedside table I saw a *wuyangufeng*[54] that Chen Zhongfan had newly written for his old teacher. Part of it used the story about the divine dragon, and how you could see its head but not its tail, to praise Chen Duxiu.

In the evening I chatted with Chen Duxiu, who already knew my views[55] on the war from He Zishen. Naturally, he disagreed, but that evening he deliberately avoiding mentioning them. He merely showed me the theses he had composed in jail. I studied them carefully, but I, too, disagreed with him. For the most part I can no longer remember what they said, but one still sticks in my mind. It said that for the time being we should have an 'armistice' with the Guomindang. I especially disagreed with that one, and read it but said nothing. He knew why. So we didn't talk any further about our estimate of the war and our attitude towards it. Instead we talked of other things, among them the question of the CCP. By then I opposed the CCP, not just generally but from a whole number of theoretical and practical angles. My opposition had been especially heightened by the recent Moscow trials, for in my opinion the CCP breathed out of the same set of nostrils as Stalin on this question.[56] I knew from Chen Duxiu's past attitude and from the tone of voice he adopted that evening that he, too, opposed the CCP. I crystallised my attitude to the CCP in the form of a question. I asked Chen Duxiu: Will the CCP disband wholesale and enter the Guomindang? No, he said, after a moment's thought: if they were to do that, they would no longer be in a position to play out their reactionary role to the end. He put special emphasis on the word 'reactionary'. It was completely obvious to me from his reply that he was even more opposed to the CCP than I was. So all the talk then by the Guomindang and the Communists about Chen wanting to start working again for the Communist Party was pure fabrication. Today people are still peddling the same rumours. Some people even claim that Chen said to Dong Biwu 'Of course I want to start working again for the Communist Party'. Others say that in 1938 in Wuhan every time he spoke Chen said that 'the Party's line and policy is completely correct' and that 'we resolutely support Party policy'. But in truth Chen opposed the CCP even more thoroughly than I, the only difference being that at that time he didn't oppose the proposal for an alliance against Japan between the Party and the Guomindang. He had his own view of this proposal, which by no means boiled down to the view that 'the Party's line and policy is completely correct'. Chen Duxiu's subsequent speeches and actions right through until his death

---

54 A classical poem with five words in each line.
55 According to Zheng Chaolin, the war between China and Japan was from the very beginning an integral part of the imminent world war, so he opposed supporting it.
56 Actually, Mao Zedong privately criticised the Moscow trials.

are all explicable in terms of what he told me that evening about his attitude towards the CCP.

We also talked of other things, but I only remember one of them, namely that I would take responsibility for finishing the translation that Pu Dezhi and Luo Shifan had begun in Tiger Bridge Prison of Trotsky's *Revolution Betrayed*.[57] The original text was in English. I took it and the draft translation with me to Jixi and after I'd completed it and checked it through, I posted it to Shanghai to be published. I believe that Chen Duxiu had given my wife the original book and the draft translation even before my release from jail. I still remember Chen's evaluation of the book. He said it was not only a book written in opposition to Stalin and to the Soviet Union as it had then become but one that further developed the Marxist theory of the state.

That was the last time that Chen Duxiu and I met and talked.

The next morning I and Jing left Chen Zhongfan's house and went to the Railway Station outside Nanjing's Zhonghua Gate to catch the train to Wuhu. Chen Duxiu escorted us to the door and waved goodbye as we disappeared in rickshaws.

We corresponded with Chen Duxiu a few times after reaching Jixi. Probably some of his replies are still in existence.

After I parted from him I heard only indirectly about his life and thought in Nanjing, Wuhan, Chongqing, and Jiangjin, so I'd best leave to others the job of describing it.

4   Trotsky's Theory of Permanent Revolution

It's impossible to write a memoir of the Chinese Trotskyist movement or of Chen Duxiu's relationship to that movement without talking about the theoretical debates within Chinese Trotskyism. And in the final analysis it's impossible to talk about those debates without going back to Trotsky's theory of permanent revolution.

Trotsky's Estimate of Chen Duxiu

I once heard Liu Renjing say that while he was staying with Trotsky in Turkey the two men talked about Chen Duxiu. Trotsky highly estimated Chen Duxiu's talents as a revolutionary, but he said that Chen was no theoretician. Later, when Liu Renjing turned against Chen, he told people what Trotsky had said.

---

57   Called in Chinese *Suliande xianzhuang yu qiantu* ('The Soviet Union now and in the future').

Naturally, he put the emphasis on Chen Duxiu not being a theoretician rather than on him being a revolutionary, thus making Trotsky's comment seem derogatory. But in my opinion it was simply a statement of fact. The crucial question is what Trotsky meant by 'theoretician'.

By it he meant people like Marx and Engels and like Lenin, or at the very least people who were well versed in the writings of Marx and Engels and of the thinkers whose ideas Marx and Engels borrowed in the course of elaborating their theoretical system. Such people were not only good at theory but were also good at embedding theory in real conditions and using it to explain real conditions, and also at supplementing and even revising it on the basis of practice whenever it broke down. Clearly Chen Duxiu did not meet the requirements for a 'theoretician' of that sort.

But that doesn't mean that he was in no sense a theoretician. In preparing and enacting the Revolution of 1911, in opposing Duan Qirui and leading the New Culture Movement, in setting up the CCP, and in leading the Revolution of 1925–7, he advanced original theories and wrote theoretical essays. Looking back on his life as a revolutionary, it is evident that during each of its successive periods his acute vision enabled him to grasp the main elements in the objective situation and to propose policies for dealing with it. Before the Revolution of 1911 he realised that 'reform and modernisation' were no longer enough and that what was needed was 'revolution', so he stopped supporting Kang Youwei and became a 'rebel'. After the defeat of the Revolution of 1911 and of the Second Revolution,[58] he realised that the New Army, the secret societies, and armed activity were no longer the way forward, and that it was necessary to launch a direct onslaught on traditional morality and culture. So he set up a youth journal and attacked the doctrines of Confucius and Mencius that for more than two thousand years had ruled China. Unlike Kang Youwei and Liang Qichao, who carried out reforms under the cover of the 'Late Texts School',

---

58   Although the Revolution of 1911 was started by members of the Guomindang (then called the Tongmenghui), power over the new government fell into the hands of Yuan Shikai. Yuan commanded strong armed forces and would not tolerate the armed forces – weak as they were – influenced by the Guomindang in the Southern provinces. So he threatened to eliminate them. When they became aware of his plans they took preemptive military action, in July 1913, but they were defeated by Yuan in September of the same year. These events were called the 'Second Revolution' to distinguish them from the 'First Revolution' of October 1911. At the time Chen Duxiu was very active in Anhui province, and played a small role in these events, as a result of which he almost lost his life. It was precisely from this 'Second Revolution' that Chen concluded that pure military actions without mass support were bound to fail. So he broke with China's traditional way of rebellion. [Note added by Zheng Chaolin in 1990.]

or Zhang Binlin, who did the same under the cover of the 'Old Texts School',[59] he preferred to assail Confucianism head-on. And he was right. The situation as it then was required precisely such an assault on the 'Confucian shop': neither the Confucius of the Late Texts School nor the Confucius of the Old Texts School were capable of mobilising young people. After the May Fourth Movement, Chen realised that cultural revolution by itself was not enough and that political revolution was called for, so he threw himself into building the Chinese Communist movement and gathered together like-minded people to found the CCP. From then on his views constantly diverged from those of the 'China experts' in the Comintern's Far Eastern section. In 1926, after the Zhongshan Gunboat Incident, he immediately proposed that the CCP withdraw from the Guomindang and cooperate with it from the outside, but those same 'China experts' disagreed. Constrained by discipline, he was unable to break completely and decisively from his opponents, as he had done from Hu Shi and his ilk in the later phases of the May Fourth Movement on whether or not to 'talk politics'.[60] After the defeat of the so-called 'Great Revolution' he clearly saw that the revolution had been defeated and that the blame for the defeat belonged to those self-same 'China experts' and ultimately to Stalin, who had usurped power in the Soviet Union. But he was unable to understand precisely why Stalin wanted to deny that the revolution had been defeated and why Stalin imputed to him the Party's past mistakes. He mulled these questions over in his mind for more than a year, but he was still unable to resolve them. It was not until mid–1929, when he read Trotsky's articles, that the scales finally fell from his eyes.

---

59 The Late Texts School and the Old Texts School were schools formed in the Western Han dynasty (206–23 BC) in annotating the Confucian classics. Qin Shihuangdi, the First Emperor of the Qin dynasty, banned and burned the Confucian classics, but the Han dynasty, which replaced the Qin, rehabilitated and patronised Confucianism. Some surviving scholars wrote down the classics from memory. These texts with their annotations were later called the 'Late Texts'. Sometime during the reign of Emperor Jing (156–141 BC) a whole set of Confucian classics was accidentally discovered in the walls of the Confucian Family Mansion in Qufu in Shandong. These texts generally coincided with those rewritten from memory but the annotations were different; they later became known as the 'Old Texts'. From then on two schools formed around the two lots of texts, each school calling the other texts forgeries. In the late nineteenth century some scholars of the Late Texts School (the best known being Kang Youwei) saw an implicit theory with various progressive and even revolutionary implications in the annotations to the *Spring and Autumn Annals* (the only book attributed to Confucius) and used them as the theoretical basis for their reform movement.

60 According to liberals like Hu Shi, the student movement of 1919 was not political, nor should it be. They agreed with the signs hanging in the tea-shops: 'Don't talk politics'.

Considering Chen Duxiu's life as a whole, the reason he could grasp the main elements in the situation, make a correct assessment of it, and settle on appropriate policies for dealing with it was because he had a clearer vision than his contemporaries, but it was also because objective conditions had by that time ripened so far that the main elements in the situation were starkly visible. Before then even the clearest vision would not have helped: only a systematic grasp of theory and of Marxism would have illuminated their hidden contours. But Chen Duxiu lacked such knowledge: he frequently understood things correctly and grasped the main elements in the situation, but he was unable to analyse them from the point of view of systematic theory or to discern them in a situation that had not yet ripened.

However, that does not give us the right to denigrate Chen Duxiu's standing as a revolutionary. Though never a theoretician to match Marx, Engels, Lenin, or Trotsky, he can still be considered an outstanding revolutionary. Karl Liebknecht was a brilliant revolutionary, but he didn't understand dialectical materialism and was even against it. Plekhanov, on the other hand, though completely familiar with the theories of Marx and Engels, was blind to the objective situation. In a revolution you don't want people who know lots of theory but are blind to what's going on around them: better someone who is not well versed in theory but is alive to real events. The final judgment on a person can only be passed when the last nail has been hammered into his coffin lid. Our judgment on Chen Duxiu should be that he was a Communist revolutionary of the first water, a Marxist, a Chinese revolutionary thinker, and a theoretician – even if not on a par with Marx, Engels, Lenin, and Trotsky.

Theoretical Disputes within Chinese Trotskyism

From the moment when they first embraced Trotskyist ideas, the Trotskyists in China have been divided by numerous theoretical disputes, and perhaps they still are even to this day.[61]

When we Chen Duxiu supporters first came across Trotsky's articles in May and June 1929, we did not become Trotskyists overnight. Our conversion must be considered as a process. The Chinese Revolution had already been defeated and the fault was Stalin's – we accepted these two points forthwith, for we thought the same. But there were other elements in Trotskyist theory that took longer to accept. One was the thesis that not feudal remnants but capitalist relations were predominant in China, that China had long been

---

61   Zheng Chaolin in Shanghai was not in a position in 1980 to follow developments in the Chinese Trotskyist movement outside China, but his surmise was correct. The Trotskyist movement in Hong Kong is still split, and the lines of the split have their origin in the disputes of the 1930s and 1940s.

capitalistic, that China's backward rural economy was dominated by urban capitalism, and that Chinese society was already bourgeois; so the job of the Chinese Revolution was to expropriate the bourgeoisie, set up a dictatorship of the proletariat, coordinate with the revolution in other countries, and found a socialist society – in short, China's revolution (or rather, China's third revolution) would be proletarian-socialist. Only after a rather long period of reflection and debate did we each in our own time come round to this and other theses of Trotskyism. The speed and depth of conversion differed from person to person. Chen Duxiu held out longest and raised a host of differences in the course of his discussions with us (mainly with Yin Kuan and Peng Shuzhi). The debate was not just verbal but written, in the form of articles. Unfortunately these writings of Chen Duxiu have all been lost. According to what Yin Kuan told me, at the end of each separate discussion the Old Man would stick to his own opinions and oppose ours; but by the next meeting he would already have accepted our position and would raise new issues on the basis of it.

Finally, Chen accepted the thesis that Chinese society was already capitalist, that the cities controlled the villages, and that capitalism benefited from feudal exploitation. He made these views his own: they became a constituent element in his thinking. Using his rich knowledge of Chinese history, he explained the special function of Chinese commercial capital. He even used his philological knowledge of ancient Chinese to show that China had never known a slave society. This reminds me of an incident in late 1929, when Zhou Enlai and Xiang Zhongfa went to visit Chen in his house on Range Road. Just at that moment Peng Shuzhi came in. Chen's two guests got up, shook hands with Peng, and said hello. Peng then joined in the conversation. I don't know what they talked about, nor do I know the purpose of Zhou and Xiang's visit, but I do know either from Peng or Chen that at one point, there was a discussion about whether the towns dominated the villages or vice versa. As soon as Chen raised this question, Xiang replied without thinking that the villages dominated the towns. Zhou Enlai intervened in a conciliatory way to say that things were not quite so simple. Zhou Enlai, who knew more about society than Xiang, realised that Xiang was making a fool of himself. This incident happened just at the time when Chen Duxiu was coming over to Trotskyism. I don't believe that this was an expression of Chen's acceptance of Trotsky's analysis of the nature of Chinese society, for it's a truism that towns dominate villages, you don't need to be a Trotskyist to think that.[62] It was simply a temporal coincidence. But right up to his death Chen never completely accepted the Trotskyist thesis on the

---

62 To my surprise, today I came across a document that confirms this incident. On 5 August 1929, Chen Duxiu wrote in a long letter to the Central Committee:

nature of the Chinese Revolution and of revolutionary state power. He broadly embraced it, but he did so reluctantly, and rather less than whole-heartedly. Even as late as 1939 in his reply to Trotsky's letter he still criticised some Trotskyist comrades for saying that China's third revolution would be socialist from the outset. Actually, the comrades who sustained this thesis had correctly grasped Trotsky's theory of permanent revolution, but Chen Duxiu failed to do so, right up to his death. There's a document (Chen's letter of 5 August 1929, to the Central Committee) in which Chen advances the thesis that the present Chinese Revolution is not bourgeois-democratic but what 'Lenin in Russia had called a "democratic revolution of the proletariat and peasantry"'. This shows that Chen had already embraced Trotsky's thinking but was still wavering on the question of the nature of the revolution. When on 17 February 1930 Chen replied to the Comintern's telegram inviting him to Moscow, he proposed a 'proletarian dictatorship' in opposition to the Central Committee's 'democratic dictatorship of the workers and peasants'. That means that he had already solved the problem of how to define state power and, consequently, the nature of Chinese society. Finally, by 1938, the only problem he had still not solved was whether or not China's third revolution would be socialist from the start.

Yin Kuan and Peng Shuzhi, Chen's interlocutors in those days, also failed ever to understand Trotsky's theory of permanent revolution.

Yin Kuan opposed our raising the question of the nature of Chinese society and its revolution in discussions with other comrades in the branch before we were expelled from it. In his view it was enough to discuss issues like whether

---

'You ignore these evident facts, so that today you still overestimate the position of the feudal forces. Even a leading comrade on the Central Committee said to me recently in the course of a discussion about the relative weight of the bourgeoisie and the feudal forces: "At present in the Chinese economy the villages dominate the towns"'.

This is a reference to the incident I described; the 'leading comrade on the Central Committee' was Xiang Zhongfa. But after this passage in Chen Duxiu's letter, the editor of *Zhongguo geming yu jihui zhuyi* ('The Chinese Revolution and opportunism') adds the following note:

"Yet another fabrication. The Central Committee merely said that China was a backward agricultural country in which rural production exceeds urban production; naturally, the trend of development was for the towns to dominate the villages, there were no differences of opinion on that. But there can be no doubt that the villages are more backward than the towns, and cannot be considered on a par with cities like Shanghai and Hankou." Probably Zhou Enlai didn't tell the Central Committee about Xiang Zhongfa's indiscretion, so this 'editor' arbitrarily accused Chen Duxiu of 'fabrication'. This document shows that Xiang and Zhou must have visited Chen before 5 August 1929. [Note by Zheng Chaolin.]

the revolution was in ebb or in spate, who was to blame for its defeat, and the need under present circumstances to conduct the struggle by peaceful and legal means. He thought that it was scholastic and harmful to discuss the nature of society and of the revolution. Yin Kuan was a good writer, but I forget whether he wrote any articles on systematic theory. His position suggests to me that he did not properly grasp what Trotsky's theory of permanent revolution meant.

I had an argument with Peng Shuzhi at one of our branch meetings at which Chen and Peng were both present. This is what I said. The Chinese Revolution is in essence proletarian-socialist. From a theoretical point of view, the past defeats happened because the Chinese Revolution was viewed as bourgeois. Actually, my remark was a mere commonplace. In June 1922 in Paris I had already held this opinion when I and many other comrades launched the Communist Youth Party. In 1921, the programme adopted by the CCP at its First Congress also embodied this thesis. It said:

> Our Party programme is as follows. (1) To overthrow the bourgeoisie with a revolutionary army of the proletariat and to rebuild the state with the toiling classes, until all class distinctions are abolished. (2) To introduce a dictatorship of the proletariat in order to achieve the goal of class struggle – an end to classes. (3) To destroy the system of bourgeois private property and to expropriate machines, land, factories, and the means of production, including semi-finished products. (4) To ally with the Third International.

Peng Shuzhi probably didn't know about this programme (I myself saw it for the first time only recently). At the meeting he argued against me, saying that China's third revolution would be socialist but that its second had still been bourgeois-democratic. He argued that the consciousness of the masses can decide the nature of a revolution, and that during the second revolution the masses had still not gone through this experience, so they lacked that consciousness. After the discussion, Chen Duxiu spoke. He chose his words cautiously, but their drift tended in the direction of Peng's position. We never resumed this discussion in the Proletarian group. Later, on the Negotiating Committee, Wang Fanxi drafted a document in which he said that 'the coming [third] Chinese revolution will be socialist in character from the very outset'.[63] This caused a commotion. Liu Renjing was the first to criticise this formulation, and apparently the *Proletarian* also published criticisms of it. I'd forgot-

---

63   See Wang Fan-hsi 1991, p. 143.

ten about this. Actually, Wang was quoting directly from Trotsky. In his article 'Summary and Perspectives of the Chinese Revolution' Trotsky said: China's third revolution will be forced from the very start to shake both the feudal and the bourgeois systems of ownership.[64] In short, Wang and I (at the time we still didn't know each other) at least had differences of a formal nature. Wang was only talking about the third revolution, whereas in my view the second revolution, that is, that of 1925 to 1927, also should have been proletarian-socialist.

In the internal controversies of the Chinese Trotskyist movement Liu Renjing certainly played an important role, but I could never make out exactly what he thought. He was renowned for his fickle opinions and for skipping from left to right and back again. I can't say whether he correctly understood Trotsky's theory of permanent revolution. The reason I haven't mentioned him in this context is not because he later degenerated into a counter-revolutionary, a turncoat, and an agent of Hu Zongnan and the CC Clique.[65]

Our 1942 split[66] was also about the question of the nature of the revolution (though other issues also entered into it). It turned out that Peng Shuzhi denied the socialist character not only of the second revolution but also of the first stage of the third revolution. In his opinion the first stage of the third revolution was still democratic. Only after it was over would the revolution 'permanently' develop along socialist lines. Fifty years later, I don't know whether today's Peng Shuzhi has acquired a sounder grasp of Trotsky's theory.

Trotsky's Theory of Permanent Revolution

I don't have to hand a copy of *Permanent Revolution*, which Trotsky finally wrote in 1928, nor of his 1905 version of the same thesis. These things are not

---

64   Trotsky actually said: '... [T]he third Chinese revolution, despite the great backwardness of China, or more correctly, because of this great backwardness as compared with Russia, will not have a "democratic" period, not even such a six-month period as the October revolution had (November 1917 to July 1918); but it will be compelled from the very outset to effect the most decisive shake-up and abolition of bourgeois property in the city and village': Evans and Block (eds) 1976, p. 305.

65   According to one version, the ultra-conservative CC clique got its name from the Chen brothers, Lifu and Guofu, who directed the investigation division and the organisation department of the Guomindang respectively; according to another, it stands for 'Central Club'.

66   In 1942, the Chinese Trotskyists split into two organisations, each with each own publication. The Peng Shuzhi group continued to bring out *Douzheng* ('Struggle'); the group around Zheng Chaolin and Wang Fanxi started bringing out *Guoji zhuyizhe* ('Internationalist').

available in China.[67] But I do have a 1922 version of it, quoted by Stalin in one of his attacks on Trotsky reprinted in Stalin's *Problems of Leninism*. My wife Liu Jingzhen gave me this book while I was still in jail in 1964. It didn't 'reform' my thought, but it delivered into my hands Trotsky's famous formula, so that whenever necessary in jail I could measure my ideas against it.

Here is the passage Stalin quoted in his article 'The October Revolution and the Tactics of the Russian Communists':

> It was precisely during the interval between 9 January and the general strike of October 1905 that the views on the character of the revolutionary development of Russia which came to be known as the theory of 'permanent revolution' crystallised in the author's mind. This abstruse term represented the idea that the Russian Revolution, whose immediate objectives were bourgeois in nature, would not, however, stop, when those objectives had been achieved. The revolution would not be able to solve its immediate bourgeois problems except by placing the proletariat in power. And the latter, upon assuming power, would not be able to confine itself to the bourgeois limits of the revolution. On the contrary, precisely in order to ensure its victory, the proletarian vanguard would be forced in the very early stages of its rule to make deep inroads not only into feudal property but into bourgeois property as well. In this it would come into *hostile collision* not only with all the bourgeois groupings which supported the proletariat during the first stages of its revolutionary struggle, *but also with the broad masses of the peasants* who had been instrumental in bringing it into power. The contradictions in the position of a workers' government in a backward country with an overwhelming majority of peasants can be solved *only* on an international scale, in the arena of the world proletarian revolution.[68]

Clearly the Russian Revolution of 1917 unfolded precisely in accordance with Trotsky's formula of permanent revolution.

Here I should add that the differences and disputes that arose between Lenin and Trotsky before the Revolution of 1917 evaporated after it, when the views of the two men tended to converge.

---

67 I am wrong here. Trotsky's *Permanent Revolution* was published in China while the Gang of Four was still in power. The volume included both Trotsky's 1928 book and his 1906 essay. But it was translated into Chinese as 'negative teaching material' and its circulation was restricted to senior Party members. [Note added by Zheng Chaolin in 1986.]

68 Stalin 1940, p. 92. The italics in this passage are Stalin's.

When Trotsky first advanced his theory of permanent revolution in 1905, he argued with Lenin on a whole series of questions. Trotsky thought that in a backward country like Russia the bourgeois-democratic revolution could only be completed if the proletariat controlled the state, but if the proletariat did control the state, then the bourgeois-democratic revolution in Russia would burst its historically prescribed bounds: proletarian state power would encroach deeply not only on the feudal but also on the bourgeois property system. Lenin, on the other hand, believed that Russia's bourgeois-democratic revolution could not exceed its historically prescribed bounds, and proletarian-socialist revolution could only begin after bourgeois-democratic revolution had been completed. These two revolutions could not become intertwined. So Lenin insisted on the slogan of workers and peasants' democratic dictatorship, and opposed the slogan of proletarian dictatorship. Lenin frequently wrote on this question. I shall quote just one or two instances.

In Chapter 10 of *Two Tactics* he said:

> Our slogan – a revolutionary democratic dictatorship of the proletariat and the peasantry – [recognises] the incontestably bourgeois nature of a revolution incapable of *directly* overstepping the bounds of a mere democratic revolution...[69]

In the same chapter he stressed that these two revolutions should not become confused and intertwined:

> To confuse the petty bourgeoisie's struggle for a complete democratic revolution with the proletariat's struggle for a socialist revolution threatens the socialist with political bankruptcy. Marx's warning to this effect is quite justified. The reason:
>
> In actual historical circumstances, the elements of the past become interwoven with those of the future; the two paths cross. Wage-labour with its struggle against private property exists under the autocracy as well; it arises even under serfdom. But this does not in the least prevent us from logically and historically distinguishing between the major stages of development. We all counterpose bourgeois revolution to socialist revolution; we all insist on the absolute necessity of strictly distinguishing between them; however, can it be denied that in the course of history individual, particular elements of the two revolutions become interwoven? Has the period of democratic revolutions in Europe not been

---

69   Lenin 1960–72 [1905], p. 87.

familiar with a number of socialist movements and attempts to establish socialism? And will not the future socialist revolution in Europe still have to complete a great deal left undone in the field of democratism?[70]

Here Lenin admitted that the 'the elements of the past become interwoven with those of the future', that 'their paths cross', but only in order to emphasise that their main and essential components should not be allowed to do so.

Lenin stuck to this opinion right through until 1917, on the eve of his return to Russia. On 20 March of that year, that is, after Russia's February Revolution had already broken out, while preparing to return to Russia Lenin wrote in 'Letters from Afar':

> With these two allies, the proletariat, *utilising the peculiarities* of the present transition situation, can and will proceed, first, to the achievement of a democratic republic and complete victory of the peasantry over the landlords, instead of the Guchkov and Milyukov semi-monarchy, and then to *socialism*, which alone can give the war-weary people *peace, bread* and *freedom*.[71]

Right up to that point, Lenin had insisted that socialist revolution could only start when bourgeois revolution ended. The two revolutions must not be confused. Their main and essential components must not become intertwined.

But after his return to Petrograd on 4 April, his views on the nature of the Russian Revolution changed. First, he abandoned the call for a 'democratic republic' and started calling for a 'commune state', meaning that power must be placed 'in the hands of the proletariat and the poorest sections of the peasants'. Next, he started calling for the 'confiscation of all landed estates' and for 'the immediate amalgamation of all banks in the country into a single national bank, and the institution of control over it by the Soviet of Workers' Deputies'.[72] This means that he wanted simultaneously to carry out bourgeois revolution and socialist revolution, simultaneously to encroach on the feudal and bourgeois property systems. 'The Threatening Catastrophe and How to Fight it', which he wrote five months later, put this same position even more clearly: 'We are living in the twentieth century, and power over the land *without power over the banks* is not capable of regenerating, rejuvenating the life of

---

70 Lenin 1960–72 [1905], pp. 85–7.
71 Lenin 1960–72 [1917a], p. 308.
72 Lenin 1960–72 [1917b].

the people'.[73] Here, the intertwining of the two revolutions is by no means just that of 'elements', but concerns components as important and fundamental as the expropriation of the land and of the banks.

Finally, a few months after the October Revolution, Lenin once again wrote (in 'New Times and Old Mistakes in an Old Guise'):[74]

> Was the revolution a bourgeois revolution at that time? Of course it was, insofar as our function was to complete the bourgeois-democratic revolution, insofar as there was as yet no class struggle among the 'peasantry'. But, at the same time, we accomplished a great deal *over and above* the bourgeois revolution *for* the socialist, proletarian revolution.

The revolution did not just go beyond its limit. Four years after the October Revolution Lenin said: The tasks of Russia's bourgeois revolution can only be resolved by proletarian-socialist revolution, and what's more the former will be resolved as a by-product of the latter. In 'Fourth Anniversary of the October Revolution' he said: 'We solved the problems of the bourgeois-democratic revolution in passing, as a "by-product" of our main and genuinely *proletarian-* revolutionary, socialist activities'.[75]

Trotsky had only said that at the same time as encroaching on the feudal property system the revolution will encroach on the bourgeois property system. Lenin went one step further. He said that encroaching on the bourgeois property system was the main revolution, and encroaching on the feudal property system was a 'by-product' of this main revolution, that it was achieved in passing.

In short, after Lenin's return to Russia in 1917, there were no longer any differences between him and Trotsky on how the Russian Revolution would develop.

After Lenin's death, Joffe (the same Joffe who signed the joint manifesto with Sun Yat-sen),[76] a leader of the Trotskyist Opposition, committed suicide in the course of an intense struggle within the Soviet Party. Before doing so he wrote Trotsky a letter in which he recalled a conversation he had once had with Lenin where they had discussed Lenin's pre–1917 dispute on how the Russian

---

73   Lenin n. d., p. 214.
74   Actually, this article was written in August 1921; see Lenin 1960–72 [1921a], p. 22.
75   Lenin 1960–72 [1921b], p. 54.
76   On 26 January 1923, Sun Yat-sen and the Soviet diplomat Adolf Joffe issued a joint manifesto which said that the Soviet system was not suitable for China and that the Soviet Union would help the Guomindang unify China.

Revolution would develop. Lenin had admitted that in the dispute Trotsky had been right and he himself had been wrong.

In 1917, Lenin and Trotsky jointly led the Russian Revolution to victory on the basis of the theory of permanent revolution. Thirteen years later, in 1930, Trotsky reflected on that revolution and elucidated its inner nature with the help of this same theory in his *History of the Russian Revolution*, which graphically explains the revolution. The book's main thesis is that the core of the Russian Revolution of 1917 was socialist but that it was wrapped in numerous democratic layers that first had to be peeled away before its true nature was bared.

Trotsky's theory of permanent revolution is inseparable from his 'law of combined development'. Lenin discovered the 'law of uneven development' and used it to explain a great many things. Trotsky invented his 'law of combined development' on the foundations of Lenin's discovery, and used it to explain even more things. Trotsky's law showed that a large number of so-called 'transitional' periods in history are not simply 'transitional' but constitute social systems in their own right. Past and future forms of development 'combine' their special characteristics and so develop into a system. For example, the system of 'autocratism' in modern European history produced by the 'combination' of certain special features of capitalism with others of feudalism can endure for a comparatively long time and sustain its own special politics, culture, and thought. 'Tsarism', the system that ruled Russia in the late nineteenth and early twentieth centuries, was not only 'transitional' but formed a rather integrated system in its own right, its special characteristic being that capitalism controlled the state by making use of feudal exploitation and feudal methods of rule. It's precisely because capitalism and feudalism developed in combination that the Russian Revolution could not first topple and expropriate the feudal system of ownership but had simultaneously to topple and expropriate the capitalist system of ownership. Many historical and practical problems are easily solved using Trotsky's law of combined development.

Why did some Chinese Trotskyists, led by Peng Shuzhi, find it so hard to understand the theory of permanent revolution? Were they too stupid? Or were they just pretending that they did not understand it? Certainly they frequently paid lip-service to the theory, piously intoning that the revolution will develop 'permanently', that it must not stop after completing the bourgeois-democratic revolution, and that as long as the bourgeois-democratic revolution has not been completed all efforts must be bent towards completing it, so that the revolution that happens afterwards will have an initial bourgeois-democratic stage; and so on. In *Hongqi* ('Red Flag') No. 16 (1980) there is an article criticising Kang Sheng that quotes Kang's interpretation of the Marxist-

Leninist theory of 'uninterrupted' revolution. Kang Sheng says that Marx' and Lenin's theory of uninterrupted revolution 'is mainly about the stage where democratic revolution turns into socialist revolution, and how it must not stop'. Peng Shuzhi's interpretation of Trotsky's theory of permanent revolution is the same.

There's an old saying that 'when a scholar returns after being away for three days, you will see a difference in him'. I've not seen Peng for more than thirty years: maybe he's changed his ideas in the meantime.

The 'National Assembly' Slogan

Another important dispute in the Chinese Trotskyist movement concerned the call for a National Assembly.

In 'The Chinese Question after the Sixth Congress' Trotsky said that a democratic movement should be carried out in China, around the call for a National Assembly; slogans calling for socialism, proletarian dictatorship, and soviets should be relegated to general propaganda. This proposal of Trotsky's is inseparable from his appraisal of the Chinese situation at the time. As a realist, he considered that the Chinese Revolution had already been defeated, that the revolution was at a low ebb, and that the tactics adopted by revolutionaries in such circumstances must differ from those used while the revolution is in flood.

In his reply to the Comintern dated 17 February 1930, Chen Duxiu quoted Lenin to the effect that in a period of reaction

> the revolutionary parties had to complete their education. They were learning how to attack. Now they had to realise that such knowledge must be supplemented with the knowledge of how to retreat in good order.[77]

It is sheer common sense that in a period of reaction, when the revolution is at a low ebb, revolutionaries should change their tactics. The tactics adopted by the Bolsheviks in the years between the defeat of the Revolution of 1905 and the relaunching of the revolution in 1917 are a case in point. But Trotsky's suggestion that Chinese revolutionaries should call for a National Assembly and employ the tactic of a democratic movement provoked a violent dispute among Chinese Trotskyists. The dispute, at first internal, gradually became public. Deng Yanda, who was just setting up his Third Party at that time, sent a car to fetch Gao Yuhan for talks, after which Gao reported back to Chen Duxiu. I, too, knew about it at the time, and though I've forgotten most of it,

---

77   Lenin 1960–72 [1920a], p. 28.

one things sticks in my mind. Deng asked Gao why the Trotskyists called for a National Assembly when they thought that the Chinese Revolution was proletarian-socialist. He didn't understand, just as he didn't understand why the CCP adopted the tactic of soviets and armed struggle when according to them the Chinese Revolution was bourgeois-democratic. Actually, if Deng was clever enough to pose the question in this way, a moment's reflection should have told him the answer to it.

At their Sixth Congress the Chinese Communists reluctantly admitted that the revolution had been defeated and that it was at a low ebb, but in their heart of hearts they still believed that it was in flood or at the very least soon would be. Various measures that the Party took were premised in this belief. Otherwise how can we explain the so-called 'Li Lisan line' of late 1930 or the 'third left line' that ruled the CCP for four long years?[78] The tactics that the CCP followed in those years were tactics appropriate to a period of revolutionary high tide.

Even some Chinese Trotskyists believed that the revolution was still in flood. They were convinced by Trotsky's ideas on basic issues in the Chinese Revolution, but they did not accept his estimate of the situation in China. Before the unification talks started, I came across a mimeographed copy of *Our Word* on a bookstall at the intersection of North Sichuan Road and Range Road. Flicking through it, I noticed that the lead article stressed that the revolution was at high tide. Needless to say, people who believed that could hardly accept Trotsky's proposal for a National Assembly, and even if they did, it would be contrary to their convictions. They would attach all sorts of bizarre interpretations to the slogan. As far as I know, this view was not represented in the Proletarian group.

Some other Chinese Trotskyists believed that the next revolutionary high tide was distant and uncertain, that China's bourgeois state would probably enjoy a long period of stability, and that the present system of military dictatorship would gradually give way to parliamentary democracy, which in their view would be long-lasting. Naturally, these people, whose main representative was said to be Liu Renjing, welcomed the call for a National Assembly.

Between these two extremes came a variety of nuances. In short, most people did not grasp the need to distinguish between strategy and tactics, between propaganda and agitation, between the revolution in flood and at ebb. They thought that the call for a National Assembly was incompatible with

---

78 The 'third left line' refers to the period from 1931 to 1934, when the leadership of the Party was in the hands of Wang Ming and Bo Gu; the Party's Maoist leaders consider this line to have been 'even more sectarian' than that of Li Lisan.

the socialist character of the Chinese Revolution, and that this slogan and the slogan calling for Soviet state power were mutually exclusive.

A large number of people wrote to Trotsky reporting on this controversy. I still remember one passage in Trotsky's reply where he warned against absolutely counterposing the two slogans. He said that generally speaking in a period of reflux we should use the National Assembly slogan to mobilise the masses and to bring on the high tide. But we can't rule out that with the masses on the rise and a National Assembly elected and leading the revolution, it might be possible in the name of the National Assembly to proclaim China a Soviet Republic!

Even today people still ask why Trotsky proposed calling for a National Assembly, and what role this slogan played in the history of the Chinese Revolution. I have already explained its active meaning; as for the actual role this slogan played in China's recent history, all I can say is that the Chinese Trotskyists, whose job it was to give full scope to the slogan in its positive sense, were in no position to do so, battered as they were from two directions at the same time: by the Guomindang, which was out to destroy their bodies, and by the CCP, which was out to destroy their souls. So the slogan was monopolised by the Guomindang, which employed it in its passive and counter-revolutionary sense.

5   Chen Duxiu and the Trotskyists

Was or was not Chen Duxiu a Trotskyist?

This is one of the hardest questions currently facing students of contemporary Chinese history and people who wish to study and grasp the present political situation in China. Chen's role in Chinese and world history can never be rubbed out. The old slanders against him cannot be upheld.

Just think of the picture of Chen Duxiu painted by several generations of political commentators! An opportunist who buried the Great Revolution, a renegade, a national traitor, a paid agent of the Guomindang, a counter-revolutionary, and so on. The founder of the CCP, elected its top leader at five successive congresses, was that sort of man? Some people even go so far as to claim that the leader of the May Fourth Movement of 1919 was not Chen Duxiu but someone else.[79]

---

79   For many years, the pretence was maintained in China that the May Fourth Movement was led by Li Dazhao and Lu Xun.

Things only began to change in 1979, which was Chen's hundredth birthday and the sixtieth anniversary of May Fourth, after which the press began to recognise Chen's role in leading it. Around 1 July and 1 October[80] of that year the press also started to recognise Chen's role in founding the CCP. The Museum of the Revolution in Beijing displayed his picture and the taboo on discussing the relationship between the Comintern and the CCP was broken. Historians began to reach new conclusions that were more in accordance with the facts. Articles began to appear in the open and the internal press[81] showing that when Chen Duxiu said in 1923 that China's bourgeois revolution would be led by the bourgeoisie, he was simply representing the Comintern's point of view; and that when in 1926 and 1927 the CCP was pursuing an opportunist line, it was also following Comintern directives. Later, during the War of Resistance to Japan, an article appeared in *Xinhua Ribao* ('New China Daily') accusing Chen Duxiu and Luo Han of coming to an agreement through Tang Youren with Japanese intelligence by which they would be paid $300 a month: but now evidence has been produced to reveal this as political calumny. In the past, people used to say that Chen's three letters to the Central Committee of the CCP about the Chinese Eastern Railway Incident proved that he had gone over to the counter-revolution, but now others are saying that in this controversy the Central Committee was wrong and Chen was right. As for the charge that he capitulated to the Guomindang, became an agent, and took money from Chiang Kai-shek, many, many people have now produced evidence to rebut it.

Finally, there is the question of the Trotskyists. The Comintern taboo has already been broken; but the taboo on Trotskyism remains, and people carry on repeating – as they have been doing for decades now – that the international Trotskyists and the Chinese Trotskyists are counter-revolutionaries. So how come Chen Duxiu, leader of May Fourth and founder of the CCP, got mixed up with this counter-revolutionary political organisation?

Some people say that he was only influenced intellectually by Trotsky, and that he didn't join the Trotskyist organisation.

Some people say that he joined the Trotskyist organisation but broke with it after the Guomindang arrested him.

Some people say that after his release from the Guomindang jail he declared that he was not a Trotskyist, that is, that he broke with the Trotskyist organisation, and that after that there is no evidence that he had anything more to do with the Trotskyists.

---

80 The anniversaries of the founding of the Party (in 1921) and the People's Republic (in 1949).

81 The internal or *neibu* press is accessible only to privileged categories of people.

Some people say that when he joined the Trotskyist organisation the Trotskyist question was still a contradiction among the people,[82] and that by the time the Trotskyists had become a bunch of murderers and foreign spies he had already broken with them.

Some people say that he gave up his Trotskyist ideas a few years before he died.

And so on.

Naturally, there are also people who know full well that the Trotskyists are anything but counter-revolutionary and that Chen Duxiu's conversion to Trotskyism and his membership of the Trotskyist organisation were an organic outcome of his entire intellectual development. But they still don't dare say so in public.

In my view, there is no longer any need for me today to defend Chen Duxiu against the charge that he was an 'opportunist', that he was to blame for the defeat of the revolution, or that he was a 'counter-revolutionary', a 'renegade', an 'agent', a 'running dog of the Guomindang', and a 'national traitor'. I simply wish to explain the facts and meaning of his relationship to the Trotskyists, and to say that any attempt to research his life and thought that tries to bypass this relationship is as self-deceiving as the stupid thief who in trying to steal a bell plugs his own ears in the hope that no one will hear it ringing.

There is no way that Chen's membership and leadership of the Chinese Trotskyist organisation can be denied, or of denying that while in jail he continued through secret channels to control that organisation. There are documents and articles to show that this is true. His declaration after leaving jail that he no longer had dealings with the Trotskyist organisation was mere diplomatic verbiage. At that time he wanted to unite in the war against Japan democratic personages beyond the influence of the Guomindang and the CCP, so he wanted to avoid getting entangled at the outset in the Trotskyist question; in any case, by then the leadership of the Trotskyist organisation had been taken over by Peng Shuzhi, so Chen was not inclined to submit his statements and actions to its disciplinary constraints. But it is clear from contemporary sources that he had by no means left the Chinese Trotskyist organisation. His 1938 letter to Chen Qichang *et al.*, which still exists, is enough to show that he still considered the Trotskyist organisation his own, that he looked upon Luo Shifan, Chen Qichang, Zhao Ji, and Han Jun as his own cadres, and that he only criticised them because he cared for them and for the Trotskyist organisation, even

---

82   A Maoist expression, used in opposition to a 'contradiction between the enemy and us [that is, the revolutionary people]'.

though he was not then working to revive Trotskyist organisation. In early 1939 or late 1938 the Trotskyist organisation sent Chen Qichang by devious routes from Shanghai to Jiangjin to meet Chen Duxiu, and to pass on Trotsky's advice to him to leave the country. Chen wrote a personal letter to Trotsky the tone of which showed quite clearly that he considered the Trotskyist organisation his own: the sharp criticisms he raised in it only showed that he still loved and cherished this body. Let's quote some passages from his letter.

> The membership of the CCP is far in excess of ours, but they're just armed forces with intellectuals but without any working-class base at all. We have fewer than fifty people in Shanghai and Hong Kong, plus probably more than one hundred stragglers in other parts of the country.
>
> Needless to say, we do not fool ourselves that we will grow quickly in this war, but if we had pursued more or less right tactics, we would not be in our present feeble state. From the very start our group tended towards ultra-left positions.... A small closed-door ultra-left organisation of this sort obviously stands no chance of winning members; and even if it did, it would be an obstacle to the further development of the Chinese Revolution....
>
> We should beware of perpetuating the illusion that we can only restart our activities after the recovery of territories now occupied by the Japanese. Even today, while Japan continues to occupy parts of our country, we should prepare forthwith to start work afresh, within the narrow space that remains open to us....
>
> If ultra-leftists who stay aloof from the masses and the real struggle ... continue to brag and pretend to be big leaders, to organise leadership bodies that lack all substance, and to found petty kingdoms for themselves behind closed doors and relying on the name of the Fourth International, they will achieve nothing beyond the tarnishing of the Fourth International's prestige in China.

Ask yourself, are those the words of someone who has placed himself outside the Chinese Trotskyist organisation?

At the time of the Hitler-Stalin Pact, Chen Duxiu became so angry that he said things in letters to his friends that went beyond the limit of what is permissible, but it would be wrong to take that as proof that he had broken with Trotskyism.

I have in my possession an article he wrote on 13 May 1942, a fortnight or so before his death. The article, called 'The Future of Oppressed Peoples', shows that he remained a Trotskyist to his dying day. Here are some excerpts from it.

> So in my opinion, in a capitalist-imperialist world, no small or weak people can hope for a future so long as it tries only behind closed doors, relying only on its own small forces, to remove the reality of imperialist aggression. Its only hope lies with oppressed toilers the world over. The national question will automatically be resolved if the oppressed, backward peoples unite, overthrow imperialism everywhere, and replace the old world of international capitalism based on commodity deals with a new world of international socialism based on mutual help and a division of labour.[83]

This passage shows that right up to his death Chen Duxiu continued to stand on the side of Trotsky's world revolution and rejected Stalin's idea of socialism in one country.

The article also says:

> Some people vilify the Soviet Union of the early period, whereas we support it; others flatter the Soviet Union of the later period, whereas we detest it. There's a very big difference between these two periods. In the former period the Soviet Union stood for world revolution; in the latter, for Russian national self-interest. Ever since the Soviet leaders first betrayed their own cause after the setback to the revolution in Western Europe and abandoned the policy of putting world revolution to the fore, replacing it instead with Russian national self-interest, clear-thinking people in all countries have gradually progressed from scepticism to disappointment; and though some still think that the hope for mankind lies with the Soviet Union, in reality they can only view it as one among a number of world powers. People who stubbornly insist on calling it socialist only besmirch the name of socialism.

This passage, too, supports Trotsky and opposes Stalin. The difference is that Trotsky still considered the 'Soviet Union of the later period' to be a 'degenerated workers' state', whereas Chen Duxiu denounced it point-blank as a one of the 'world powers'. It's a fact that the 'Soviet Union of the later period' had

---

83   See Part VIII.

already degenerated into 'social imperialism'; it had started to degenerate from the time of Stalin onwards.

So Chen Duxiu remained a Trotskyist till his dying day, from both an organisational and a theoretical point of view.

Looking back, the main 'injustices, frame-ups, and mistakes'[84] were the show-trials of the 1930s, which practically wiped out a generation of revolutionaries. Even today the victims of these trials are treated with contempt. First they must be rehabilitated.

Needless to say, I am not speaking from a juridical point of view. Only a Soviet court, under the control of the Communist Party, can judicially rehabilitate these victims – the so-called 'Trotskyites', 'Zinovievites', and 'Bukharinites'. I am speaking only from the point of view of historical fact. From the point of view of history, that is, from the point of view of the overwhelming majority of knowledgeable people in the world, these victims have long since been rehabilitated. Just a short time ago the new Pope John Paul II rehabilitated Galileo, but for the past several hundred years there can hardly have been anyone still convinced by the charges against Galileo. Today probably only a handful of people in the world still believe the Moscow verdicts against the 'Trotskyites'.

A footnote in Mao Zedong's *Selected Works* quotes Stalin as follows:

> In the past, seven or eight years ago, Trotskyism was one of such political trends in the working class, an anti-Leninist trend, it is true, and therefore profoundly mistaken, but nevertheless a political trend.... Present-day Trotskyism is not a political trend in the working class, but a gang without principle and without ideas, of wreckers and diversionists, intelligence service agents, spies, murderers, a gang of sworn enemies of the working class, working in the pay of the intelligence services of foreign states.[85]

Stalin said this in 1937, in the period of the Moscow show-trials. But on what grounds did Stalin claim that the Trotskyists were 'agents, spies, murderers'? True, Vishkinsky, who was in charge of investigations, came up with all sorts of 'criminal evidence', but this 'evidence' has already been systematically rebutted by the Dewey Committee. This Committee published two volumes of findings to show that the charges were groundless, and it declared Trotsky innocent.

---

84   A phrase often used in China in the wake of the Cultural Revolution to describe the 'fascist lawlessness' of the 'Gang of Four'.

85   Quoted in Mao Tse-tung 1967 [1935], p. 177, fn. 31. (This note has been removed from the current edition of Mao's *Selected Works*.)

Dewey apart, other evidence has accumulated over the past forty or more years that I would like to mention.

According to Stalin, Trotsky's two biggest crimes were to assassinate Kirov and to spy for the Gestapo in order to help plot Germany's invasion of the Soviet Union.

First the assassination of Kirov. Even at the time Trotsky came up with evidence to show that Stalin himself killed Kirov to frame the then Opposition, but this evidence did not have much impact. More than twenty years later, Stalin's successor Khrushchev, at the Twenty Second Congress of the Communist Party of the Soviet Union, proved that Kirov had indeed been killed by Stalin. Recently twenty letters by Stalin's daughter Svetlana were published in China. In one of them Svetlana denies Khrushchev's allegation and says that Kirov was killed not by Stalin but by Beria. Whatever the case, in today's world, including in the Soviet Union, no one – or at least hardly anyone – any longer believes that Kirov was killed by Zinoviev and Trotsky.

Stalin also killed Tukhashevski, Blücher, and two other Red Army generals on trumped-up charges of having secret dealings with the Nazis and plotting to betray the Soviet Union. But at the Twenty Second Congress Khrushchev declared these allegations, too, to be Stalin's fabrications. Stalin had first forged them and then surreptitiously leaked them to President Benes of Czechoslovakia. Benes, believing them to be true, secretly informed Stalin, who imposed death sentences on the basis of them.

This is just one piece of 'evidence' among many. After the Second World War, when the Allies tried the Nazis for war crimes at Nuremberg, some well-known people led by H. G. Wells wrote to the Tribunal asking it to produce from among its vast files evidence of Trotskyist collaboration with the Nazis. It couldn't.

For the time being I'll restrict myself to just these three points. There is a mountain of evidence to show that the charges levelled against the Trotskyists at the Moscow show trials were groundless, and another mountain of evidence produced by the Dewey Committee. Today researchers can investigate whether or not this evidence substantiates Stalin's charges against the Trotskyists.

As for the Trotskyist organisation in China, there is ample evidence to clear its name. It has already been shown that Chen Duxiu and Luo Han did not act via Tang Youren as paid agents for Japanese intelligence, but the strange thing is that people still believe that the Chinese Trotskyists did. It has been proved that Chen Duxiu was not a Guomindang agent or a running dog of Chiang Kai-shek, but people still think that the Chinese Trotskyists were. The charges against Chen Duxiu were unable to stand up under scrutiny. But what is the evidence against the organisation of the Chinese Trotskyists? Can it stand up under scrutiny?

We commemorate Chen Duxiu, this outstanding figure of modern Chinese and world politics. In commemorating him, we Trotskyists are stirred deeper than other people. We recall that for a while he was General Secretary of our organisation. We consider this an honour.[86]

---

86   This extra section was written thirty five years after the memoir proper. The two parts of this book frequently overlap and repeat one another; not surprisingly there are discrepancies between them, for an interval of so many years places an inevitable strain on human memory. I'll let them stand as they are. [Note added by Zheng Chaolin after reading the proofs of the Chinese edition of his memoirs, to which this study was a supplement.]

Chen Duxiu Had No Wish to Rejoin the CCP on Leaving Jail

Zheng Chaolin

This article was completed on 10 August 1981, two years after Zheng Chaolin himself had emerged from twenty-seven years in prison under the Chinese Communists and while he was under Party supervision and denied access to the archives. On the basis of the scant documentation available to him he builds a strong case for 'historical truth' and against received opinion regarding Chen Duxiu's view of the Communist Party in 1937. I translated the article from its unpublished manuscript version, titled 'Chen Duxiu chuyu hou jue wu fuhui Zhonggong de yuanwang' ('Chen Duxiu definitely did not wish to rejoin the CCP after leaving prison'); at some point, it was published under the same title in Zhongbao yuekan *(Hong Kong).*

Just as many people claim that Chen Duxiu was dismissed as General Secretary [of the Communist Party] by the 7 August Conference [of 1927],[1] so for several decades now people have been saying with one voice that after his release from a Guomindang jail in 1937, Chen expressed a wish to return to the Communist Party; but Mao Zedong raised three conditions and wanted Chen publicly to repent his errors, which Chen did not do, so Chen did not rejoin. Not only Communist Party members say this; so do some democrats, and they have even been joined by the ex-Trotskyist Pu Qingquan.[2] In his article 'Chen Duxiu as I knew him',[3] Pu ascribed the following words, told in reported speech, to Chen: 'I definitely want to return to Party work'. In this way, Pu 'proves' the groundless rumours of that period. But when he was a Trotskyist, Pu gave no credence to these rumours. I shall clarify this question by discussing a few facts.

I myself have never believed these rumours, and I always considered that they were not worth discussing. In recent years, however, more and more people have started doing research on Chen Duxiu, and nearly all of them believe the rumours to be true. The time has therefore come to clarify the matter and

---

1 According to Zheng Chaolin, Chen Duxiu resigned before the conference; see Zheng Chaolin, 'Chen Duxiu and the Trotskyists'. See also Wilbur 1983, p. 144.
2 That is, Pu Dezhi.
3 Pu Qingquan 1980. Pu's article was reprinted in four instalments in *Zhongbao yuekan* (Hong Kong), also in 1980.

save from further error those who now and in the future engage in research on Chen and on this period in Chinese history.

No, between leaving jail and dying, Chen never entertained the idea of rejoining the Communist Party. The idea never once occurred to him after he had embraced Trotsky's proposals and worked in the Trotskyist organisation.

Personally, I have not the slightest doubt of this. I do not need to consult a single document or fact; I base my conclusion solely on his usual conversations with us [before we went to prison]. On 29 September 1937,[4] the day I was released from prison, I went to stay at his residence and had a talk with him. Our talk proved to me that he had not changed; as a result, I am even more firmly convinced of my opinion on this matter.

But I cannot expect to convince others to share my firm belief simply by referring to conversations that Chen had with several of us before going to jail and to a talk he had with me on the first night after my release. Elsewhere, I have already explained on the basis of our conversation that evening that after leaving prison in 1937 he had not the slightest intention of rejoining the Communist Party.[5] Here, today, I do not intend to base my argument on that talk, because it can convince only me. Instead I shall provide more objective evidence.

The best proof that Chen Duxiu expressed no wish to rejoin the Communist Party after leaving jail in 1937 can be found in Chen's own words. In Hankou in [March] 1938 he wrote an open letter to *Xinhua ribao* in which he said: 'According to Luo Han, they still hope I will rejoin the Party'.[6] In other words, he himself did not hope to 'rejoin the Party', but the Communist Party hoped that he would, and moreover had dropped Luo Han a hint along these lines.

Let us see what light Luo Han's famous 'open letter'[7] throws on this question. In August [1937], after the start of the battle for Shanghai, Luo Han came to Nanjing. Chen Duxiu was still in jail at the time, and Luo did not visit him. He went directly to the Eighth Route Army office at Fuhougang in search of Ye Jianying.[8] At the time of the Northern Expedition, Luo had been 'Party representative' (or 'director of the political department') of the Fourth Army of the

---

4 Writing in 'Chen Duxiu and the Trotskyists', Zheng Chaolin recalls that he was freed from jail on 29 August (not September) 1937.
5 See Zheng Chaolin, 'Chen Duxiu and the Trotskyists'.
6 Chen Duxiu 1980 [1938].
7 On 24–25 April 1938, Luo Han published an open letter to Zhou Enlai and others in *Zhengbao* ('Upright Daily'). See Feigon 1983, p. 223, fn. 73.
8 The Eighth Route Army was formed in 1937 on the basis of the old Red Army. Ye Jianying was the Communist Party's representative in Nanjing.

[Guomindang's] National Revolutionary Armed Forces, at the same time that Ye Jianying (if my memory serves me rightly) was its chief of staff. The two men were naturally close to one another. Luo Han had two aims in going to the Eighth Route Army office: first, to ask the Communist Party to do what it could to get the Guomindang to release political prisoners, including Chen Duxiu and the other Trotskyists still in jail; and, second, to repeat the old proposal of 1932, when the Trotskyist organisation had formally suggested bilateral cooperation with the Communist Party against Japan. In 1932, the Communist Party had ignored the proposal, but now that it was working together with the Guomindang against Japan, Luo Han, acting in his personal capacity, revived the proposal. This shows that Luo Han's proposal referred to the question of the Trotskyists and the Communist Party working together against Japan, and not to the question of Chen Duxiu or other Trotskyists 'rejoining the Party'. Luo Han spoke very clearly about this to Ye Jianying in Nanjing and to Lin Boqu[9] in Xi'an, and Ye and Lin heard very clearly what he had to say. Luo Han declared several times that he represented only himself and not the Trotskyist organisation or Chen Duxiu. Lin Boqu said: 'Since you are only setting out your own views, in a personal capacity, and do not enter into discussions in a representative capacity, things could as well be settled by radio communication'.

Even so, [the Communist leaders in] Yan'an did not completely believe what Luo Han said, and still thought that he was representing Chen Duxiu. They therefore set three conditions for Chen's 'capitulation'. That is to say, even though the two sides would be merely cooperating, Chen would still have to repent his errors and oppose Trotskyism. It is also possible that Yan'an actually thought that Chen Duxiu had sent Luo Han, to discuss not just cooperation but 'rejoining the Party'. All these things passed through a series of lips and finally reached the conclusion that Chen Duxiu would repent his past errors and return to the Party ranks. (During a talk between Wang Ruofei and Luo Han, Wang said something about sections of the Third International not admitting members of the Fourth International; this remark was precisely a reference to this question of 'rejoining the Party'.) Chen Duxiu did not repent, whereupon the rumour-mill again began to grind: Chen Duxiu had been unable to accept the three conditions, so he had not been allowed to rejoin the Party.

From what I have said above, we can see that all this talk about Chen Duxiu wanting to rejoin the Party or go to Yan'an is Communist Party propaganda without any basis in fact.

Some people might, of course, object that I base my argument solely on letters of Chen Duxiu and Luo Han, that I have absolute faith in their veracity, and

---

9   Lin Boqu (1896–1960) was a veteran Party leader.

that I completely ignore Communist Party documents that provide evidence to the contrary.

Regarding such documents, I have access only to Ye Jianying, Bo Gu, and Dong Biwu's letter to *Xinhua ribao*.[10] I don't even have the other articles published in *Xinhua ribao* on this question. So I can quote only from Ye, Bo, and Dong's letter.

This letter was written in reply to Chen Duxiu's open letter to *Xinhua ribao*. It says: 'At the beginning of September, after his release from jail, Chen entrusted Luo Han to talk with us, and told us that he wanted to return to work under Party leadership'. This statement can, of course, be interpreted as meaning that 'Chen wished to rejoin the Party'. There is a difference between this statement and what Luo Han said in his 'open letter'. Luo Han declared that he was acting on his own account, whereas this letter says that he was representing Chen Duxiu; Luo Han said that he had gone to negotiate cooperation, this letter says that he transmitted Chen Duxiu's wish to return to work under Party leadership. So who is right and who is wrong? I believe Luo Han to be right, since he gives dates. He went to Nanjing to talk to Ye Jianying in August [1937], before Chen Duxiu had left prison; he left Nanjing for Xi'an on 30 August, arrived in Xi'an on 2 September, met Lin Boqu on 3 September, received Yan'an's three conditions on 10 September, and returned to Nanjing on 15 September, by which time Chen had already left for Wuhan. In the week from 23 August, when Chen left jail, and 30 August, Luo Han did not meet Chen Duxiu. This is understandable, since he did not know where Chen lived. I was at Chen's house the whole of 29 August, day and night; I did not meet Luo Han, nor did anyone else mention him.

Ye, Bo, and Dong's letter goes on to say:

> After Luo had left Nanjing, Chen also sent Mr Li xx [that is, Li Huaying][11] to hold talks: Mr Chen had already broken decisively with the Trotskyists, and urgently wanted to meet us. We took the view that this would be dif-

---

10 Bo Gu (1907–46), the alias of Qin Bangxian, had been acting General Secretary of the Chinese Communist Party from 1932 to 1935. Dong Biwu (1886–1975) was a veteran Communist, and became a Central Committee member after 1945. The two men were members at the start of the war of the Party's Changjiang Bureau, set up to represent the Party and lead its work in central and southern China. The letter by Ye, Bo, and Dong referred to here is reprinted in Zhang Yongtong and Liu Chuanxue (eds) 1980, pp. 235–6. See Feigon 1983, p. 223, fn. 73.

11 The given name was added by Zheng Chaolin; it is not clear who Li Huaying was.

ficult, since Chen had not publicly set out his political position. Mr Li xx said: what Mr Chen wants is precisely to explain his political position to us, so Bo Gu and Ye Jianying met Mr Chen. We requested him to explain his attitude to the anti-Japanese national united front and to leave the Trotskyists.... Afterwards, Chen again sent someone to say that because Li xx had been at the meeting, Chen had found it difficult to speak freely, so he asked to see [Ye] Jianying a second time. At the meeting, Jianying asked Mr Chen publicly to express to the entire nation his opinion on three points.... [Dong] Biwu too met Chen in Hankou to urge Mr Chen to fulfil these three conditions.

These three meetings all ended inconclusively. Even more noteworthy, in the course of them Chen Duxiu expressed no wish to 'rejoin the Party'. So apart from the opening sentence about Chen wanting to 'return to work under Party leadership', what other support does this letter provide for the claim that Chen wanted to 'rejoin the Party'? (As I have already explained, even this sentence is unreliable: Luo Han had not met Chen in Nanjing, so there was no way that he could have received a commission from him.)

What is more, the claim that Chen wanted to 'return to work under Party leadership' is open to another explanation: the 'united front' entailed various groups and parties working together with the Communist Party yet outside the Party, but it also entailed these groups and parties 'working under the leadership of the Party'. Ye, Bo, and Dong deliberately used this ambiguous formulation in their letter, and for the following reason: neither Chen Duxiu nor Luo Han had spoken of 'rejoining the Party', so if Ye, Bo, and Dong had said 'Chen wants to come back into the Party and work under the leadership of the Central Committee', their statement would have had no basis in fact.

If Zhang Guotao's memoirs are to be believed, Yan'an discussed Chen Duxiu's case in terms of 'cooperation' and not of 'rejoining the Party'.

Recalling the Politburo Conference of December 1937 in Yan'an, Zhang notes a speech by Wang Ming:

> We can cooperate against Japan with anyone except the Trotskyists. Internationally, we can cooperate with bourgeois politicians, warlords, and even anti-Communist executioners, but we cannot cooperate with the followers of Trotsky. In China, we can cooperate with Chiang Kai-shek and his anti-Communist special agents, but we cannot cooperate with Chen Duxiu.

Finally, I would like to mention the attitude of the Trotskyist cadres, who were concentrated in Shanghai. At that time, Peng Shuzhi's supporters and his opponents were equally dissatisfied with Chen Duxiu's activities in Wuhan.

But they only opposed Chen's wish to cooperate with the CCP and not his alleged wish to 'rejoin the Party'. They found it completely inconceivable that Chen would wish to 'rejoin the Party'. On 21 November 1937, Chen wrote to Luo Shifan, Chen Qichang, and Zhao Ji:

> About cooperating with the Stalinists, my view is that there's nothing wrong with it in principle, but at present its out of the question. To cooperate, both sides must have something to give; in addition, there must be some common activity that necessitates both sides getting in touch – yet at present such conditions do not obtain. Naturally it's crazy to talk of 'cooperation'; Luo [Han] didn't mention this matter to me, you have no cause to get oversensitive about it.[12]

In other words, Chen Duxiu was not opposed in principle to cooperating with the Communist Party against Japan, but saw such cooperation as conditional on our having a certain strength, and on the necessity of constant contacts with the Communist Party arising from the anti-Japanese activities. At the time, that condition was absent, so Chen opposed cooperating with the Communist Party. So he would have been even less likely to want to 'rejoin the Party'. If those 'oversensitive' individuals had suspected that Chen was inclined to 'rejoin the Party', rest assured that they would have raised a great hue and cry.

Chen Duxiu's letter proves even more conclusively that Luo Han's actions in Nanjing and Xi'an were his own personal initiative. After he had met with a rebuff and gone to see Chen, he 'never talked about' the cooperation.

Whether we are dealing with big matters or small, we should always stick to the historical truth. Anything that does not accord with historical truth should be pushed aside, even though people repeat it as if with one voice. Some may consider that it is a minor question, not worthy of detailed study, whether or not Chen Duxiu expressed a wish to 'return to Party work' after his release from jail. But in my opinion, from the point of view of the struggle of the Chinese Trotskyists, of Chen Duxiu's character, and of Chen's relationship with the Chinese Trotskyists, it is no minor matter, but one that requires thorough clarification on the basis of historical evidence.

---

12   See the 'Letter to Chen Qichang and Others' in this volume, p. 711.

Preface to the Collected Poems of Chen Duxiu

Xiao Ke

In August 1981, at an academic symposium, the veteran Communist General Xiao Ke praised Chen Duxiu's role in the Chinese Revolution and hinted at the possibility of a rehabilitation not only of Chen but of his previously reviled Trotskyist comrades. In his talk, Xiao Ke summarised various positive evaluations of Chen by Mao Zedong and Zhou Enlai. Source: Xiao Ke 1994.

Comrades Ren Jianshu, Li Yueshan, and Jin Shupeng have asked me to write a preface to their edition of Chen Duxiu's collected poems, and to write the title of the book in calligraphy. I know little about poetry, but the fact that the collection was by Chen Duxiu excited my interest.[1] Chen Duxiu was the early twentieth century's man of the hour. When I was young, I read many of his essays in *Duxiu wencun* ('Duxiu's writings'), in bound volumes of *Xin qingnian* ('New youth'), and in *Xiangdao* ('Guide weekly'). But I don't recall reading his poems, so I was pleasantly surprised to see this collection. I feel that in this nation where poems and songs are so highly valued, it is essential that Chen's poems are edited and published.

I would like to argue that Chen should be seriously studied. After the defeat of the Great Revolution, Chen split from the Party and I no longer trusted him politically, so my impression of him dimmed. But I continued to admire his essays and meritorious exploits in the struggle against feudal remnants and superstition and to promote science and democracy. I constantly followed the course of his life and his situation in the years between the defeat of the Great Revolution and his death. On 18 August 1981, at an academic symposium to mark the sixtieth anniversary of the founding of the CCP, I gave a speech a passage of which I shall now quote:

In the past, the Chen Duxiu question was taboo; today it is semi-taboo, by which I mean that although no few people have touched on some aspects of that question, their research is not yet all-sided or profound. Probably people still have apprehensions. Must this question be researched in a comprehensive fashion? Yes. Comrade Mao Zedong said, 'Chen Duxiu was the

---

1 We know of 140 poems written by Chen Duxiu over a span of nearly forty years, from 1903 to 1942. Only one of these poems was written in the 1920s, when Chen devoted almost his entire energy to revolutionary activity. He resumed his poetry writing in the early 1930s, in prison. Chen's poems were either published in journals or kept in manuscript by his old friends.

Commander-in-Chief of the May Fourth Movement', Chen Duxiu and Li Dazhao and others 'gathered together' progressive youth who had embraced Marxism and 'founded the Communist Party...', which was his merit. When we write China's history, we must note his merit in that regard'. Comrade Zhou Enlai said: 'Chen Duxiu performed a meritorious service in founding the Communist Party'. In my opinion, we should make an all-sided evaluation of this Commander-in-Chief of a glorious age, this distinguished founder of the Party, even though in his later period he committed the error of rightist capitulationism and became a Trotsky-Chen liquidationist after his expulsion from the Party. Comrade Mao Zedong also said, 'In various respects, Chen Duxiu resembled Russia's Plekhanov'. I completely agree with that assessment; unless we conscientiously research Chen Duxiu, our future writing of Party history could become lop-sided. Not long ago, I watched [the documentary film] *Xianquzhe de ge* ('Pioneers' song'), which said nothing about Chen Duxiu, Commander-in-Chief of the May Fourth Movement and the main figure in the founding of the Party. Only Li Dazhao appears in the lens of this film. But it is a universally recognised fact of history that 'Chen in the south and Li in the north' [played the main role in founding the Party]. Although Li Dazhao was a principal figure in the founding of the Party, the prime place [in that process] belonged to Chen Duxiu. We should not blame the comrades who wrote the script and directed the film for this error; it is a problem relevant to research into the history of our Party. In my opinion, in researching Chen Duxiu we cannot confine ourselves merely to his days in the Party or before the founding of the Party, but must also include the Trotsky-Chen liquidationist period. What were the differences between China's Trotsky-Chen liquidationist faction and foreign Trotskyists? How was their programme? What was their attitude to Chiang Kai-shek's Guomindang régime? What was their attitude to the Communist Party? What was their attitude to imperialism and in particular to Japanese imperialism? How did they acquit themselves in the jails of the Guomindang? What was [Chen's] political attitude between his release from prison [in 1937] and his death? All these issues need to be researched. As for our evaluation of Chen Duxiu, we should follow Comrade Mao Zedong's guidance and learn too from Lenin's critical view and standpoint. From 1903 until the period of the October Revolution [in 1917], Lenin repeatedly criticised Plekhanov's ideological and political errors. Especially during the period of the imperialist [First World] War, he criticised Plekhanov as a 'mediocrity', a 'social chauvinist', a 'Marxist renegade'. But after Plekhanov's death, at a joint conference of the All-Russia Executive of the Central Committee of Soviets and the Moscow City Soviet with the Trade Unions, he stood with the delegates in silent tribute to Plekhanov. Later, a memorial meeting in Leningrad was attended by

Lunacharsky and Zinoviev representing the Moscow Party and Government. Not long afterwards, Lenin ordered the publishing of Plekhanov's complete works, established the Plekhanov Institute, and called on everyone to study Plekhanov's philosophy. 'Unless we study Plekhanov's entire philosophical writings', he said, 'we will never become conscious, true communists'. Lenin made a concrete analysis of Plekhanov's political activity and attitudes in each of his periods. When Stalin at the time of the War of National Defence listed the twenty most outstanding people in Russian history, Plekhanov came top. Just because they criticised him, they did not rob him of his position in history, nor in commending his virtues did they conceal his vices. I do not say that we should use the same methods in relation to Chen Duxiu as the Russian Party in relation to Plekhanov. I simply mean we should approach that problem by adopting Lenin's view and standpoint (see 'Dangshi huiyi baogao ji' ['Reports at the meeting on Party history'], pp. 39–69).

In my opinion, in studying Chen Duxiu we should not confine ourselves to political questions but look at other relevant issues. Comrades Ren, Li, and Jin, in editing Chen Duxiu's collected poems, have provided us with material for such a study. Chen wrote his poems half a century ago. The reader needs to know the age in and the difficulties under which they were conceived, and the process of ideological development they reflect. 'Poetry speaks of lofty ambitions'. This statement is true too of the poetry of Chen Duxiu, and especially evident in the purposefulness of the poetry of his late period, for example the long poem *Jinfenlei* ('Tears alongside luxury and debauchery').[2] The study of Chen Duxiu's poetry helps understand other aspects of his career.

2 June 1993

---

2 This poem, of 56 stanzas, was written in Nanjing Jail in 1934. It satirised the corruption, debauchery, tyranny, and capitulation to Japan of the Chiang Kai-shek régime, and expressed sympathy for those suffering under it. *Liuchao jinfen di* usually denotes Nanjing, Chiang Kai-shek's capital, but *jinfen* also means 'gold' and 'women', that is, corruption and debauchery.

PART 8

Chen Duxiu's Last Articles and Letters (1937–42)

Editor's Introduction to Chen Duxiu's Last Articles and Letters

Gregor Benton

Source: Benton (ed.) 1998; here edited.

Chen Duxiu (1879–1942) is a surpassing presence in modern Chinese thought and politics. At the start of the century, he helped prepare the ground for the Revolution of 1911 that overthrew the Manchus and brought in the Republic. Between 1915 and 1919, he led the remarkable New Culture (or May Fourth) Movement that electrified Chinese student youth and laid the intellectual foundations for transforming China's politics and society. In 1921 he founded the Chinese Communist Party (CCP); he was elected General Secretary at its first five congresses. In 1929 he became a Trotskyist and in 1931 he helped found the Chinese Left Opposition, which he then led. In 1932 he was arrested (for the fifth and last time in his life[1]) and sent to prison on charges of seeking to overthrow the government and replace it with a proletarian dictatorship. Between his release from prison in 1937 and his death on 27 May 1942, he wrote the letters and articles collected in this volume.

Chen was a seminal and latitudinarian thinker, broad enough to encompass a multitude of contradictions. Some see in him the Lenin of the Chinese Revolution, but he lacked Lenin's knowledge of and gift for theory. Others view him as China's Plekhanov, because he inspired the rise of Communism in his country and served as a bridge between Marx and Mao, just as Plekhanov bridged Marx and Lenin; or as China's Lassalle, on account of his practical bent, his want of ideological polish, and his strong literary engagement. Another judgment, by Chen's American biographer Lee Feigon, is that Chen was more the Moses than the Trotsky or Plekhanov of the Chinese Revolution, for after introducing his people to the new doctrines he was left behind by them when they reached the promised land.[2] But Chen's friend Hu Shi, his fellow leader in the New Culture movement, thought of him as 'an oppositionist for life' to any established authority, and it is perhaps this epithet that fits him best.

'Chen Duxiu', wrote his pupil and follower Wang Fanxi, 'was best known as a revolutionary politician, but in fact he was a man of enormous versatility.

---

1 Qiang Zhonghua et al. (eds) 1982 documents Chen's various arrests.
2 Feigon 1983b, p. 236.

He was also a poet, a writer, an educator, and a linguist. Above all, he was a most audacious and independent-minded thinker. In his letter to Chen Qichang and others of 21 November 1937 [see Part VIII of this volume], he wrote:

> I have not the slightest compunction about inclining to the left or to the right, I shall always strive to be extreme, I view with contempt the doctrine of the golden mean, I absolutely detest parrotry, I refuse to utter commonplaces that neither hurt nor itch, I want to be absolutely right and absolutely wrong in all my utterances; the last thing I want is never to say anything wrong and at the same time never to say anything right.

'This unconventional and original spirit pervades all Chen's articles and letters'.[3]

Although a giant of modern Chinese politics and letters and trigger of one of the twentieth century's great revolutions, for several decades after his conversion to Trotskyism Chen Duxiu's name was blackened, his achievements were concealed, and his ideas were damned by his former Party comrades, especially after they took power in 1949. Chen Duxiu in China was subjected to the same revilement as Leon Trotsky at the hands of Stalin in the Soviet Union. Today in China, Chen's unpersoning has been largely reversed and most of the discredit heaped upon him has been removed. Young Chinese now are in a position to evaluate him more or less according to his merits; his writings have been published in new editions; friendly descriptions of his life and cause have begun to appear in the learned and popular presses. Yet in the West, Chen's name is barely known outside small circles, and the positions he developed between 1937 and 1942 are known even less.

The CCP that Chen Duxiu founded in 1921 was helped into the world by envoys of the Communist International, and owed much of its early success to Russian aid. But when in 1927 disaster overtook it, that disaster was due in large part to Russian interference.[4] On or around 13 July 1927, after having over a period of several years repeatedly but unsuccessfully advocated the Party's withdrawal from the Guomindang, Chen Duxiu resigned as its General Secretary.[5] The Comintern made him a scapegoat for the failure of policies implemented before the summer of 1927, including entering the Guomindang, that he had opposed (though never openly).

---

3   Wang Fanxi, personal communication, 13 July 1993.
4   See the introduction to this volume.
5   Wilbur 1983, p. 144.

The strategy of Communist immersion in the Guomindang was not the only issue in the 1920s on which Chen Duxiu's political project differed radically from that of the Comintern's Russian leaders. The role of democracy in the revolutionary movement was another important point of difference between him and them and remained so for the rest of his life, as his letters and articles in this volume show. Democracy ran a poor course in the Chinese Revolution, but Chen Duxiu, having found traditional strategies for social change wanting after the degeneration of China's Republican Revolution of 1911, fixed once for all on socialism with democracy as the appropriate remedy for his country's ills.

Chen Duxiu may have drawn his inspiration for the Party from the Bolsheviks, but his idea of it was quite different from theirs. He opposed the creation of a strong Party chief and even let non-Marxists and anarchists join the Party. Under his leadership, different points of view vied rather freely, and though the outcome of the discussion was settled largely in Moscow, it was several years before the Chinese Party was wholly transformed along Russian lines.[6] The young Chen Duxiu shared with the Chinese anarchists a libertarian suspicion of the state that partly explains his later anti-Stalinism. Other connections, too, can be made between Chen and the anarchists. Before the Revolution of 1911, when anarcho-socialist ideas were for a time highly popular among young Chinese revolutionaries, Chen's radical friends had included several anarchists and nihilists.

By 1920, Chen had emerged as one of the anarchists' sternest left-wing critics. Even so, similarities remained between his politics and theirs. He shared with them a commitment both to radical democracy and to internationalism and an opposition to militarism, even in its 'revolutionary' guise. Like the anarchist leader Li Shizeng, Chen believed that revolutions carried out by armies would create new forms of oppression and lead to a self-perpetuating militarist cycle. And like China's second generation of anarchists active after 1915, Chen was equally opposed to native capitalists and foreign imperialists, and put his main emphasis on the revolutionary role of urban culture and the proletariat (though not to the exclusion of the peasants).[7]

Before he became a Communist, Chen's project, as formulated by his journal *Xin qingnian* ('New Youth'), was to save China by learning from the West. Just as Europe's early Enlighteners had once looked to China for models of the

---

6 Ip 1994 discusses the democratic concerns of China's first Communist leaders. She says (p. 52) that Chen Duxiu and Li Dazhao's 'cosmopolitan–internationalist commitment to democracy strengthened their appreciation of socialism, a doctrine which contained a marked cosmopolitan–internationalist message'.

7 See Zarrow 1990, for an account of Chinese anarchism.

rational society, so China's Enlighteners of 1919 sought their light in Western thought and practice. But they learned them in artificially compressed time, unlike the *philosophes*, who had a century to prepare and spread their ideas. So even democracy was rather shallowly rooted in his thinking, and no match for the 'Bolshevisers'.

After his Trotskyist conversion, Chen Duxiu focussed his political energy on the struggle for an all-powerful National (or Constituent) Assembly elected by universal secret ballot, to bring together China's disparate economic and political struggles, and relegated the call for socialism, proletarian dictatorship, and soviets to the realm of general propaganda. Chen Duxiu had for a long time opposed calling for the 'dictatorship of the proletariat', and when – as a Trotskyist – he eventually accepted it, he did so reluctantly, believing it to be too radical in the Chinese context, and still preferred to talk of the 'democratic dictatorship of the proletariat and the poor peasantry'.

Chen Duxiu was a creative and independent-minded thinker, not the sort of man to toe the Party line, but a sceptic and an innovator. He had come to Marxism after a breathless rush through telescoped isms of centuries of European thought. Though his revolutionary commitment was total, his grasp of Marxism was quite shaky. Wang Fanxi has compared him in this respect to Mao:

> Both had their first love of learning in Confucianism; both built their ideological foundations in the Chinese classics; both acquired their knowledge of modern European thought, in particular Marxism-Leninism, ... by building a rough superstructure of foreign style on a solid Chinese foundation at a time when they were physically as well as intellectually fully matured.[8]

Unlike some of his more doctrinaire comrades, Chen was not afraid to challenge accepted policies and beliefs, even those that bore Trotsky's personal imprimatur. The Chinese and the Russian admired and appreciated one another; Trotsky even remarked that he 'should learn Chinese' so as to be able to read Chen's writings.[9] But whereas for most Trotskyists in China Trotsky was a fount of pure wisdom, for Chen Duxiu – who was Trotsky's age (the two men were born in the same year) and a veteran practical revolutionary in his own right – Trotsky was an equal, whose proposals were open to scrutiny and question.

---

8 Wang Fan-hsi 1991, p. 269.
9 Ren Jianshu and Tang Baolin 1989, Volume 2, p. 87.

Chen believed that the essence of the greatness of revolutionaries like Lenin was their 'refusal to be bound by ready-made Marxist formulae' and their 'insistence on adopting new political slogans and methods of struggle to meet changing times and circumstances'.[10] Chen was never prepared to accept uncritically the word of foreign Communists, for in general he had a poor opinion of them (wrote Wang Fanxi), 'all the more so after Moscow had shamelessly heaped the whole of the blame for the defeat of the 1927 revolution on his shoulders'. He had an even poorer view of Chinese 'red compradors' who 'kowtowed to foreign comrades'.[11]

Between 1936 and 1938 and again in late 1939 or early 1940, Chen Duxiu and his Trotskyist comrades had a vigorous exchange of views on the issue of democracy. Sometime in 1936 Chen, then in prison under Chiang Kai-shek, smuggled an article on democracy to the Trotskyists in Shanghai, where Wang Fanxi published it in *Huohua* ('Spark'), together with his own critical comments. Three or four years later, Wang and others again discussed democracy with Chen, by then in Sichuan, in letters that they sent him from Shanghai. A selection of Chen's letters and replies, together with some articles by him from this period, forms the main content of this book.

Chen first raised in a letter of 15 May 1934 his doubts about the Trotskyist belief that the Soviet Union was a workers' state that revolutionaries must defend against bourgeois aggressors. He wrote:

> We should not just organize a new party, but also fight the illusion that the Stalin régime can be reformed. We must replace the slogan 'Defend the USSR' with the slogan 'Recreate the Soviet Union of October!'

This letter shows that Chen's opposition to defending the Stalinist state preceded by several years the signing of the Hitler-Stalin Pact of 1939 (after which he began to express his opposition more forcefully). It also shows that Chen did not scruple to set aside orthodox formulations of Trotskyism when he felt they had outlived their usefulness. But it would be wrong to represent his proposal as a complete departure from Trotskyist theory. In the letter, he made clear his continuing commitment to the Oppositionist cause and to 'the movement for world revolution'. 'Our answer to Stalinist falsifications', he concluded, 'is class struggle'.[12]

---

10   Wang Fan-hsi 1991, p. 209.
11   Wang Fan-hsi 1991, p. 269.
12   This letter, here included in Part XI, is in Stanford University's Hoover Institution under the Subject File 'International Left Opposition and the Fourth International'. Unfortunately,

In the mid to late 1930s, the Moscow show-trials and Stalin's alliance with Hitler caused Chen to rethink even more deeply many of the basic views on democracy advanced by Lenin and by Trotsky. Chen concluded that Lenin's complete denial of the value of democracy was, in part, responsible for Stalin's bureaucratic crimes and that dictatorship of any sort, revolutionary or counter-revolutionary, is incompatible with democracy. Whereas in orthodox Leninist terms the dictatorship of the proletariat is simultaneously – at least for the workers – the most extensive form of democratic government, Chen no longer bothered to distinguish the various democratic rights from democracy as the bourgeois governing form, and saw 'pure' democracy as an indispensable part of the socialist society. After his move to Sichuan in 1938, it seemed to his comrades in Shanghai that he had gone back in his declining years to his original attachment to this 'pure' democracy: that at the end of his life he had returned to his intellectual 'first love'.

For Wang Fanxi and Chen's other Trotskyist correspondents, democracy was not abstract but bounded by class and time, whereas for Chen after 1937 it was a transcendental concept embodied in universal institutions. Even so, Wang did not dismiss out of hand Chen's formulations, and instead strove to develop along Marxist lines the elements in them that he found to be valuable;[13] just as Trotsky continued to admire Chen, and even mentioned him as a possible member of a special committee of the Fourth International he wished to form.[14] In their letters and articles of this period, Chen and his Trotskyist correspondents raised – decades in advance of the mainstream of Communist dissent – issues that bear directly on the vexed relationship between socialist government and democratic freedoms.

In the final years of his life, Chen wrote in the papers collected in this volume about democracy and dictatorship, war and revolution, and the future (in the light of his views) of China and the world. In these posthumous papers, Chen repeated some of the arguments that he had advanced in *Huohua* in 1936. He asserted that democracy is the content and form of each stage of human history, and must not be exclusively equated with the bourgeoisie. On the con-

---

its Chinese original is not available. Wang Fanxi translated the letter back into Chinese and introduced it in 'Chen Duxiu yuzhong zhi guoji zuopai fanduipai xin' ('Chen Duxiu's letter from jail to the International Left Opposition'), *Xinmiao* (Hong Kong), no. 21 (15 May 1992), pp. 68–71. Wang points out that the original English translation, probably made by Trotskyists in Shanghai, is not necessarily literal.

13 See Part VIII.

14 Van Heijenoort 1978 p. 143. This special committee, elsewhere called the General Council, was intended to be an honorary organisation; it never came into being.

trary, in the modern world, proletarians were the principal democrats. At the start of this new trend in his thinking, Chen simply counterposed democracy and bureaucratism, but he later ended up by counter-posing democracy and proletarian dictatorship in all its forms. He completely denied the progressive import not only of proletarian dictatorship but also of Bolshevism, which he described as the twin of Fascism and the father of Stalinism. However, he rejected proletarian dictatorship not in favour of capitalism but in the name of Marxism.

At times, for example in a letter of 23 December 1941, to Zheng Xuejia, a former Trotskyist sympathiser who had later become associated with the Guomindang, he even appeared to reject Marxism itself, as irrelevant not only to China but even to Russia and Western Europe.[15] On the whole, however, his final views are not irreconcilable with Marxism as Karl Kautsky and others understood it.[16]

In June 1940 and January 1941, the Peng Shuzhi faction of Trotskyists in Shanghai passed two resolutions in which they criticised Chen Duxiu for Plekhanov-style 'opportunism' and for failing to 'defend the Soviet Union's ... socialist system of property' or to call for world proletarian revolution'. According to Peng Shuzhi, the late Chen had not only abandoned his revolutionary ideas but had lost his integrity.

Other Trotskyists put a different interpretation on Chen's later evolution, and made a far more positive appraisal of him. Wang Fanxi, for example, believed that though Chen's thinking

> in the final years of his life was already far from Trotskyism, ... had he lived longer, he would almost certainly have ... returned to the Trotskyist camp, since he not only had all the attributes of a genuine revolutionary but also was a shrewd and brilliant observer.[17]

According to Zheng Chaolin, at the time of the Hitler-Stalin pact Chen got angry and went too far, 'but it would be wrong to take that as proof that he had broken with Trotskyism'.[18] Zheng goes on to quote an article Chen wrote on 13 May 1942, a fortnight before his death, that in Zheng's view shows that Chen 'remained a Trotskyist to his dying day'. The article called on 'oppressed toilers the world over' to unite against imperialism and to 'replace the old world

---

15   For Chen's letter to Zheng Xuejia, see Ren Jianshu and Tang Baolin 1989, Volume 2, p. 286.
16   Ren Jianshu and Tang Baolin 1989, Volume 2, pp. 287–8.
17   Wang Fan-hsi 1991, p. 239.
18   See Part VII.

of international capitalism based on commodity deals with a new world of international socialism'. The main difference between Chen and Trotsky (by then dead) was that by 1942 Chen no longer considered the Soviet Union a 'degenerated workers' state'.

Though Chen Duxiu was prepared after 1937 to support the Guomindang against the Japanese, he remained alert to Nationalist provocations. Despite his hostility to Stalinism, he was careful to avoid assisting the Guomindang's propaganda campaign against the CCP. When Guomindang leaders like Hu Zongnan and Dai Li tried in 1939 to extract from Chen views they could use as ammunition against the Communists, Chen stuck to political neutrality.[19] 'In 1935 the 'democratic upsurge' Chen had been predicting since the late 1920s finally began in China. Yet it was not the Trotskyists (at first mostly still in prison) but the Communists, with their 'second united front', freshly created in Moscow to chime with Stalin's new defence and foreign policy initiatives, who were best placed to take advantage of the new opening. 'For years they had constantly misrepresented and caricatured our democratic programme', wrote Wang Fanxi, 'but suddenly they took up positions identical with all the worst features of the caricatures they had made of us'.[20] The CCP's new turn foredoomed Chen's hopes of a revolutionary-democratic alliance in 1938, for the Communists, having occupied the space Chen planned to enter, warned their new friends in the democratic parties against dealing with Chen Duxiu. They even branded their former leader a 'national traitor' and accused him of taking money from the Japanese, just as Stalin had denounced Trotsky as a 'Hitler agent'.[21] But although their attempt to turn Chen into a political pariah met with general hostility in China's democratic circles, Chen's chances of finding allies were by now quite slim, for with Stalinists and Trotskyists apparently calling for the same thing, centrist politicians naturally sided with the bigger party.

The new literature on Chen Duxiu and the Trotskyists that has become available in recent years has attracted a considerable measure of attention and scrutiny in mainland China. This interest is hardly surprising, for layer after layer of the official leadership that slandered the Trotskyists in the 1930s and eventually jailed them in 1952 has been discredited in the public eye and the crisis of faith in Stalinism and Maoism is deep and general. At the same time,

---

19   Ren Jianshu and Tang Baolin 1989, Volume 2, pp. 289–90. Huang Yongsheng and Wang Yafei 1987 also describe Chen's reluctance to enter into dealings with pro-Guomindang politicians after his retreat to Jiangjin in August 1938.
20   Wang Fan-hsi 1991, p. 182.
21   See introduction.

many younger historians have taken seriously the régime's call for truthful and factual scholarship.

In the new, more liberal climate of the 1980s and early 1990s, even Chen's Trotskyism has no longer been wholly taboo, and some scholars have begun to study it objectively. Speaking at an academic symposium held in 1981 to mark the sixtieth anniversary of the founding of the CCP, the veteran Communist General Xiao Ke proposed a positive assessment of Chen's leadership of the Party, and suggested even his Trotskyist period deserved a truthful appraisal.[22] But Trotskyism remains a suspect ideology in China, so younger scholars anxious to rescue Chen Duxiu the champion of 'Science and Democracy' try to purge him of his Trotskyist commitment.

The Trotskyist Zheng Chaolin summed up the range of suggested formulas for this decontamination: Chen Duxiu was only influenced by Trotskyism, he didn't join the Trotskyist organisation; he joined it but broke with it after his arrest in 1932; he joined it but broke with it before it became a cover for murderers and spies; he gave up his Trotskyist beliefs a few years before he died. But it is impossible to stop the biography of Chen Duxiu short of his Trotskyism, so the new tolerance of and even enthusiasm for him has inevitably helped bring Chinese Trotskyism back into the public eye.

The rehabilitation of Chen Duxiu extended to his bones. At Chen's funeral in Jiangjin in Sichuan province in 1942, his comrade Gao Yuhan said in an oration that 'Mr Duxiu is at home everywhere', and naturally an adherent of the view that 'my bones may be buried no matter where among the green mountains'. In 1982, however, the authorities repatriated his physical remains to his birthplace in Anqing, Anhui province, for reburial. Ten years later, the provincial and municipal governments designated Chen's tomb 'a major tourist resource and site imbued with human and cultural meaning' and accorded it official protection. By 1995, a sort of Chen-mania seemed to be sweeping Anqing, and to have infected the official guardians of Chen's remains. The local authorities rebuilt the tomb as a *lingyuan* or 'garden tomb', enclosed in a park, of the sort built in the past for dead emperors or national heroes like the legendary General Yue Fei (1103–42) of the Southern Song; or, in recent times, for martyrs of the Communist revolution. The new tomb was modelled on Yue Fei's; just as Yue Fei was entombed (beside Hangzhou's West Lake) with one of his sons, so Chen Duxiu was joined in death by his two martyred sons, Qiaonian and Yannian.[23]

---

22   See Part VII.
23   Information about Chen's tomb was reported in *Zhongguo qingnian bao* on 26 October 1993.

At the same time, conferences were held to discuss Chen Duxiu's life and work, a journal *Chen Duxiu yanjiu* ('Chen Duxiu studies') was launched, and a group of scholars from Beijing, Shanghai, and Anhui province (where Chen Duxiu was born) met in the capital and, with the approval and support of the Association for Party History and its leader Zhang Jingru, founded a Society for Chen Duxiu Studies, which has grown in membership and held several conferences.

The students who occupied Tian'anmen Square in May and June 1989 drew their inspiration directly and explicitly from the May Fourth Movement of 1919, which Chen Duxiu led. They copied Chen's famous early slogan calling for science and democracy and echoed – consciously or unconsciously – many of his later anti-Stalinist proposals. 'My biography of Chen Duxiu, founder of the CCP, seemed especially relevant to the events of 1989', wrote the historian Lee Feigon in his analysis of the background to the Tian'anmen Square massacre.[24]

How Chen Duxiu's Last Letters and Articles First Came to Be Published

In the summer of 1946, the Trotskyist He Zhiyu (alias He Zishen) took Chen Duxiu's last articles and letters from Sichuan to Shanghai. He Zhiyu worked as a middle-school teacher in Jiangjin, Sichuan province, where Chen Duxiu lived between 1938 and his death in 1942, and acted as an intermediary between Chen and the outside world. After Chen's death, he was Chen's literary executor. He edited into a pamphlet the manuscripts of a number of what he considered to be the more important letters, together with four of the articles. None of these letters, and none save the first part of one of the articles, had previously been published.

Probably in 1948,[25] those Trotskyists (in Shanghai) well-disposed to Chen's memory produced a primitively printed edition of He Zhiyu's pamphlet, to which they added the title *Chen Duxiu de zuihou lunwen he shuxin* ('Chen Duxiu's last articles and letters'). Today, this pamphlet is not available outside China, but it is sometimes quoted by mainland historians, so it must still be in existence somewhere in a Chinese library or archive.

He Zhiyu sent a copy of the pamphlet to Dr Hu Shi, who read it aboard a steamship in the Pacific Ocean in April 1949, while leaving China for exile in

---

24   Feigon 1990, p. ix.
25   The text published in 1950 by Free China Press in Taiwan on the basis of the original edition is dated 28 January 1948.

the United States. Hu Shi wrote his own introduction to the articles and letters, and later sent the introduction and pamphlet to friends by then in Taiwan. They published the collection in Taibei at the Ziyou Zhongguo chuban she ('Free China Press'), under the title *Chen Duxiu zuihou duiyu minzhu zhengzhi de jianjie (lunwen he shuxin)* ('Chen Duxiu's last views on democracy [articles and letters]').[26] (There was a second printing of the Free China Press edition in Hong Kong in June 1950.[27]) The Taiwan edition dropped Chen Duxiu's letter to Chen Qichang and others, his letter to Trotsky, a short note by him to He Zhiyu (addressed as Y), and one of two letters to Pu Dezhi (Xiliu).

How do we know the original edition published by the Trotskyists in Shanghai contained these missing letters? Because Hu Shi quotes the letter to Chen Qichang in his introduction written in 1949; and because both the letter to Chen Qichang and the other three missing items appear in recent mainland collections of Chen Duxiu's last writings (published and unpublished, including texts not selected by He Zhiyu), where their source is given as the 1948 pamphlet. In 1967, the truncated version of the pamphlet, together with a selection of other writings by and about Chen Duxiu, was published in Taibei by Zhuanji wenxue chuban she under the title *Shi'an zizhuan* ('Shi'an's autobiography'), the contents of which are (1) the two chapters of Chen's (that is, Shi'an's) unfinished autobiography;[28] (2) Hu Shi's selection of Chen's letters and articles; (3) an obituary by Chen of Cai Yuanpei (retained in this present volume); (4) Hu Shi's 1949 introduction; and (5) an article titled 'Ji Duxiu' ('Recollections of [Chen] Duxiu') by Tao Xisheng.[29] This English-language collection of Chen's last articles and letters is, as far as can be ascertained, an exact reconstruction, made from texts scattered across several sources (identified in footnotes), of the original 1948 edition.

Chen was famous for his clear and elegant writing, but the available editions of these texts are marred by muddled constructions and unintelligible sentences many of which are probably due to poor type-setting and proof-reading.

---

26   According to Kagan 1969, p. 168, the title was 'changed for propaganda reasons'. Kagan was unaware of He Zhiyu's role in the pamphlet's editing, which he attributed to Hu Shi.

27   This edition was acquired for me by Alex Buchman from Julia Tung at the Hoover Institution on War, Revolution, and Peace (Stanford, California).

28   This work, which Chen wrote in prison, was first published in 1937 in Lin Yutang's *Yuzhou feng* ('Cosmic wind'), nos. 51–3 (September–October). It is in Part II.

29   'Ji Duxiu' was first published in Taibei's *Zhuanji wenxue* ('Biographical literature'), Volume 5, nos. 3–4. Tao Xisheng, who studied at Beijing University, was initially close to the Communist Party, but began working for the Guomindang in July 1927. During the war against Japan he was for a time a member of the pro-Japanese Wang Jingwei faction, but he soon reverted to supporting Chiang Kai-shek.

During the preparation of the writings for translation, the real or correct meaning of ambiguous sentences and misprints was, where possible, identified (principally by Wang Fanxi). The corrections are not explained in this translation; there would be little point in doing so, for each new edition has added new mistakes (though some old errors, once committed, were subsequently copied and thus perpetuated). In any case, the reconstructed Chinese text is available to anyone who needs it. Most of the annotation here is new, by the editor of this volume. Those few footnotes added to the original 1948 edition (probably by He Zhiyu) are identified as such.

Letter to Chen Qichang and Others

Chen Duxiu wrote this letter three months after leaving prison on 23 August 1937. In prison, he had fallen out irreparably with the Trotskyist Peng Shuzhi, and his relations with other Trotskyist leaders (who had expelled him for 'opportunism' in 1935) were also poor. Chen had no wish to join with these people, and indeed denounces them as Stalinists in this letter; but in 1937 and 1938 he did maintain good relations in Wuhan with a small number of his old comrades. Chen's political project in 1937 was quite the opposite of that of the Shanghai Trotskyists: they refused to engage in practical activity and confined themselves to commenting from the sidelines on the war against Japan; he believed that, for the duration of the war, the Trotskyists should put their main energy into building a united front of all democratic parties independent of the Guomindang and the CCP, including patriotic soldiers, on the basis of a broad programme of freedom and democracy. Chen was even prepared to cooperate with the Chinese Communists, but he was shrewd enough to see that they would only take him seriously if he represented real forces. In the event, nothing came of his attempt to foster a 'democratic upsurge'. Does Chen's assertion in this letter that 'I no longer belong to any party' represent a definitive break with the Trotskyists? Not according to Zheng Chaolin, whose arguments are contained in Part VII. Chen was given to making sweeping statements and categorical assertions that in reality were often far from immutable. The question of the late Chen's Trotskyism can best be judged on the basis of the other letters and articles in this volume, which suggest an enduring interest in Trotsky's Fourth International, if not in its Chinese section. Source: Shui Ru (ed.) 1987, pp. 472–4. This letter is not included in the Taiwan edition of Chen's last writings published by Zhuanji wenxue chuban she.

Dear [Luo] Shifan, [Chen] Qichang, and [Zhao] Ji,

I have received your letters of 14 and 17 October. I also received your letter of 16 October together with Monkey's[1] letter and his plan for the book (plus the

---

1 The nickname of Sun Xi, whose other name was Sun Xuelu, a left-wing writer who joined the Trotskyists and at around this time was planning to write a book on economics. After the outbreak of the Sino-Japanese War in July 1937, Sun (a Sichuanese) went to Yunnan with Zhao Ji. After the Communists came to power in 1949, Sun, Zhao Ji, and Pu Dezhi (see below) were arrested and interviewed in Kunming by Zhou Enlai, who urged them to 'reform'; Pu did so, and was freed immediately; Zhao and Sun stood firm, and were kept in jail, Zhao until 1979 and Sun too probably until 1979; shortly after his release, Sun died.

letter of 20 October). The book he envisages will not be easy to write. I can make no comment except to admire his perseverance in wanting to write such a book, for I am ignorant of the subject. My replying to him along these lines will dampen his ardour, but I'm afraid I can't reply in any other way. I was both pleased and concerned to hear about Shifan's marriage:[2] pleased because the news was so unexpected, and concerned because I'm not sure how he'll earn his living. [Pu] Dezhi has already been here for a week, in a couple of days he'll probably be going to Hunan to be a schoolteacher. I don't want to stay here for long, nor can I do so, but I've not yet been able to fix on anywhere to go,[3] there seem to be bad people everywhere. I understand nothing about theory, and I have not the slightest compunction about inclining to the left or to the right, I shall always strive to be extreme, I view with contempt the doctrine of the golden mean,[4] I absolutely detest parrotry, I refuse to utter commonplaces that neither hurt nor itch, I want to be absolutely right and absolutely wrong in all my utterances; the last thing I want is never to say anything wrong and at the same time never to say anything right. You're all Stalinists, you're Peng [Shuzhi]'s friends, you're not my steadfast confederates.[5] Yes, Luo Han may be a bit muddleheaded,[6] but your unbridled attack on him is

---

2   Luo Shifan married the sister of Zhao Ji's wife shortly after Luo's release from jail in Nanjing and his arrival in Shanghai.
3   Chen was probably worried about the Japanese military threat to Wuhan (which fell in October 1938).
4   The *Doctrine of the Mean* is one of the Four Books embodying Confucian teachings, and is commonly accepted as the work of Confucius. It enjoins restraint, tolerance, equanimity, and the pursuit of the golden mean: 'Let the states of equilibrium and harmony exist in perfection, and a happy order will prevail throughout Heaven and Earth, while all things will be nourished and prosper'.
5   In fact, none of those addressed in this letter was a Peng supporter; both before and after the time of this letter, all were and remained Chen's friends and had not sided with Peng, though on the question of collaboration with the Guomindang during the war against Japan they disagreed with Chen. All of them were very angry about Luo Han's trip to Xi'an referred to in the following sentence.
6   Regarding the incident referred to in this letter, after Chen Duxiu's release from jail on 8 August 1937, Chen, in Nanjing, drafted some papers on the anti-Japanese war. Luo Han, encouraged by the Communist leader Ye Jianying (1897–1986), headed off in the direction of Yan'an, the Communists' wartime capital, to discuss Chen's proposals with Mao Zedong and negotiate conditions for collaboration between the Trotskyists – Chen Duxiu in particular – and the Maoists. Before Luo could reach Yan'an, Mao contacted him indirectly in the nearby city of Xi'an to say Chen could only work together with the Communists if he admitted his past mistakes and renounced Trotskyism. Luo thereupon gave up his attempt, which had angered Chen and was roundly criticised by the other Trotskyists. On this question, see Part VII, 'Chen Duxiu and the Trotskyists'.

a thousand times more muddleheaded. You violently denounced the Stalinists and the Guomindang, and you particularly attacked the Stalinists; though such attacks are not wrong in principle, tactically they are extremely wrong. If you carry on making such mistakes, goodness knows where you'll end up! Shifan calls other people religious fanatics, but he doesn't seem to realise that he himself has been infected by religious dogmatism! I've received Zhao Ji's letter of November 2. Although there's a slight difference of views between Shifan and Zhao Ji on the one side and Han Jun[12] and Qichang on the other, they're basically identical, that is, they fail to grasp the meaning of this war.[7] [Zheng] Chaolin goes even further,[8] but basically he's the same as you, that is, he indiscriminately applies theories concerning the last inter-imperialist war to today, an excellent example of fitting horses' jaws to cows' heads. I still have some hopes of Qichang and Han Jun, not because their view of the present situation approaches mine but because they have a rather positive attitude to work; those who work actively among the masses might eventually wake up to reality. About cooperating with the Stalinists, my view is that there's nothing wrong with it in principle, but at present it's out of the question. To cooperate, both sides must have something to give; in addition, there must be some common activity that necessitates both sides getting in touch – yet at present such conditions do not obtain. Naturally it's crazy to talk of 'cooperation'; Luo [Han] didn't mention this matter to me, you have no cause to get oversensitive about it. The rumour mongering and vilification is clearly the work of scoundrels.[9] You're like members of religious sects: you can't see the common enemy. As for Peng [Shuzhi] and Tall Man,[10] I swear I'll never engage in any common activity with them even if they agree with me, and what's more, our fundamental views are far removed from one another. I've also received Xiang's[11] letter. And I received your letters of 29 October and 3 November, together with the letter in English.[12] There's no way of doing what he suggests, nor do I want to try

---

7   The overwhelming majority of Trotskyists, Chen Qichang included, maintained a position of support for the war but criticism of its leaders.

8   Zheng Chaolin opposed support for China's war against Japan on the grounds that it was from the very beginning an integral part of the imminent world war.

9   The scoundrels in question perhaps included both the Stalinists and the Trotskyists, who were attacking one another by rumour mongering and vilification; they may also have been those Trotskyists in Shanghai who attacked Luo Han without a full knowledge of what Luo Han had done when he tried to approach the Maoists with Chen's theses.

10 The nickname of Yin Kuan.

11 It is not clear who Xiang was.

12 Most probably a letter from Frank Glass, who conveyed to Chen Duxiu Trotsky's advice to him to leave the country for his own safety and go to America, where he could rally support for the anti-Japanese cause.

to find a way; I fear it would be a thankless task. Luo [Han]'s recent setback should serve as a lesson. What the press said was mostly at variance with the facts. I've not read the *Shenbao* interview, could you send me a copy?[13] There are too many instances of this sort, there's nothing you can do to stop them or even to rectify them. The only thing one can do is to let matters run their course, what puts my mind at ease is that I have written a large number of articles that will be material witness in the future to what I have done. Regarding the speeches and articles I made public recently here [in Wuhan], I've widely and openly made plain that they are merely my personal opinions. All I'm concerned about is my own independent thinking, I won't give up my own ideas in order to accommodate to someone else's. They're merely my personal opinion, they represent no one, I no longer belong to any party, I'm subject to no one's orders or instigation, I make my own proposals and personally take responsibility for them.[14] At present I have no idea who will be my future friends. I'm not in the least afraid of being isolated. I wish you good health.

Zhong[15]

21 November 1937

---

13   Having released Chen Duxiu from prison, the Guomindang issued and published a statement saying that Chen had been released due to his 'repentance', whereupon Chen sent a statement to *Shenbao* in Shanghai repudiating this claim. *Shenbao* did not dare to publish Chen's counter-statement. Perhaps the interview Chen mentions had to do with this matter.
14   According to Zheng Chaolin, Chen Duxiu's post-prison claim not to belong to any party was purely diplomatic verbiage. See Part VII.
15   The first syllable of Zhongfu, one of Chen Duxiu's names.

Letter to Leon Trotsky

This letter, which Hu Shi omitted from his selection of Chen's last writings, shows Chen concerned to protect the good name of Trotsky's Fourth International in China against the activities of the Chinese Trotskyist 'ultra-leftists', who at the time were denouncing Chen for wanting to 'put national interests above party interests' in the war against Japan, and thus for 'betraying the organisation and betraying himself'. Chen notes in his counterattack that the Trotskyists' passive and even negative attitude towards the war gives credence to the Communist Party's campaign to paint them as pro-Japanese traitors, a campaign of which Chen himself had been the principal victim. The letter correctly predicts that China will fail to expel the Japanese, yet it seriously underestimates the Communist Party's prospects under Mao, with his strategy of guerrilla warfare waged independently from rural bases. But though Chen believes that the Trotskyists will only grow when industry (and thus the working class) revives, he insists that abstention from activity is no option, and he urges the Trotskyists to act now, both under Japanese and Nationalist rule, in order to prepare for future political openings. The letter shows that Chen was opposed not to the Chinese Trotskyist organisation as such but to its then leaders; and not to basic Trotskyist theories but to the Chinese Trotskyists' ultra-left interpretation of them. Source: Shui Ru (ed.), 1987, pp. 477–80. This letter was not included in the Free China Press edition or the Taiwan edition of the letters published in 1967 by Zhuanji wenxue chuban she.

Before the start of agrarian China's war against industrial Japan, the Guomindang government had no intention of fighting. It was forced to resist in haste, with a woeful lack of preparation, and in some fields with a complete lack of any preparation whatsoever. Moreover, after going to war, it reverted to counter-revolutionary methods[1] to carry out the tasks of national revolution, so it is not surprising that it has suffered military defeats.

Now that first Guangzhou and then Hankou have fallen, all the country's large commercial and industrial cities are in Japanese hands. The Guomindang government has proclaimed its military defence line to be west of the Beijing-Hankou and Guangzhou-Hankou railways. Changsha and Xi'an will probably fall too. If the Japanese take Changsha, they can occupy the whole of the

---

1 After the fall of Wuhan in October 1938, Chiang Kai-shek stepped up his campaign of political repression against Communists in Guomindang-controlled areas and his military campaign against Communist-controlled areas.

Guangdong-Hankou line. If they take Xi'an, they will be in a position to sever communications between China and the Soviet Union.[2] So these two cities are military targets that they are determined to capture. Although China's armies did not collapse completely as a result of the fall of Hankou, the most they could do was retreat to garrison Sichuan, Guizhou, Yunnan, and Guangxi. Economically and culturally, all those provinces are more backward than the lower reaches of the Yangtse. It will not be easy to mobilise them quickly for the counteroffensive. If Chiang Kai-shek's government is unable to get Anglo-French material aid through Yunnan,[3] there is no guarantee that even Sichuan, Yunnan, and Guizhou can be held.

China today faces three possible prospects. (1) Through Anglo-French mediation, Chiang Kai-shek recognises Japan's demands and submits. (2) Chiang Kai-shek's government retreats to garrison Sichuan, Guizhou, and Yunnan but in reality abandons the war. (3) Japan invades Yunnan; Chiang Kai-shek flees abroad.[4] If (1), then China's future circumstances will depend on the degree of submission and the Guomindang government's domestic policy. If (2), then Japan will find it hard to rule such an enormous expanse of Chinese territory; hard but not impossible, for even though the state of Japan's economy is daily worsening and Japan lacks the strength to open up China, the large amount of natural resources in stock that it gets from China, together with *matériel* and extensive new markets, will probably enable the Japanese to scrape together enough resources to support the army they require to garrison China. In addition, they have occupied some major strongpoints and communications in China with new-style weapons and defence works. So, barring big changes in Japan or internationally, China lacks the strength to drive them out.

China's newborn proletariat, after the defeat of the last revolution and the massacre brought on by the CCP's adventurist policies, has been greatly weakened, in addition to which most factories and transport facilities throughout China have been destroyed in the present war. Numerically, materially, and spiritually, China's workers are back to where they were thirty or forty years ago.

The membership of the CCP is far in excess of ours,[5] but they're just armed forces with intellectuals and no working-class base at all. We have fewer than

---

2 Xi'an never fell. As for Changsha, Chinese under the Guomindang General Xue Yue successfully defended the city three times against the Japanese; Changsha (and the vital Guangzhou–Hankou Railway) did not fall to the Japanese until early 1945.
3 From Burma, along the Yunnan–Burma Highway.
4 In effect, the second of Chen's three prospects was realised.
5 In May 1937, the Chinese Communist Party had 50,000 members; by July 1940, 800,000.

fifty people in Shanghai and Hong Kong, plus probably one hundred-odd stragglers in other parts of the country.

Needless to say, we do not fool ourselves that we will grow quickly in this war, but if we had pursued more or less right policies, we would not be in our present feeble state. From the very start our group tended towards ultra-left positions.

For example, some people think that the democratic revolution in China is already over; some that the next revolution will be purely socialist in nature, with no democratic component; some that the next revolution will be socialist from the start; some that the call for a constituent assembly is void of class content, and thus suspect; some that the call for a constituent assembly is a slogan for periods of reaction and peaceful movements that cannot be used for seizing state power, for which only the slogan of soviets is applicable;[6] some that the national-democratic struggle is a bourgeois task, that the proletariat can participate in the movement but should not view it as its own task, and that those comrades who propose that the Chinese proletariat should take upon its own shoulders the resolution of national-democratic tasks are imbued with the consciousness of the left-wing of the bourgeoisie; some that, whatever the period, the incident, or the circumstances, to agree with the parties of other classes on joint action against foreign imperialists or domestic dictators is opportunism.[7] These ultra-left tendencies have played a big part in propaganda and education within the organisation and have consequently determined its entire attitude towards the Sino-Japanese War. There is no one

---

6 Soviet power was based on participation by workers, peasants, and soldiers in a pyramid of soviets (that is, councils) from the local to the national level. Its goal was to establish a dictatorship of the toiling classes.

7 In May 1931, at their Unification Conference, the Chinese Trotskyists decided to launch a nationwide campaign for a constituent assembly, in order to 'rally the revolutionary forces against the military dictatorship, and to prepare the way for a new revolutionary upsurge' (Wang Fan-hsi 1991, p. 150). At first, some Chinese Trotskyists opposed the campaign for a constituent assembly, on the grounds that it was not sufficiently revolutionary, and called instead for the establishment of soviet power. After a short period of doubt and confusion, none of them any longer opposed the campaign. The differences among the Chinese Trotskyists in this regard concerned the role and perspective of the constituent assembly slogan and the struggle for its realisation. Liu Renjing's position was that to fight for a constituent assembly was to fight for a parliamentary perspective in China; for most Chinese Trotskyists, however, it was chiefly a strategic means of reassembling the defeated revolutionary forces and of leading them to fight against and finally overthrow the Guomindang régime through democratic struggle. At the time, only the Stalinists opposed the call for a constituent assembly.

capable of rectifying this mistake; whoever tries to do so is denounced as an opportunist. As for the war, ultra-leftists of this sort say that they will join the resistance but at the same time they oppose rating its significance too highly. They believe that only the war against Guomindang rule is revolutionary, that the war against Japanese imperialism cannot be counted as such; some sneer at the word 'patriotism', and even consider that this war is between Chiang Kai-shek and the Mikado;[8] some think that if the workers join the war, they will be acting as cannon-fodder for the bourgeoisie, and that to try to negotiate with the Communist Party or the Guomindang for joint work against Japan means degeneration and capitulation; in the eyes of the masses, the 'Trotskyists', instead of resisting the Japanese, are filling their publications with articles bitterly denouncing the CCP and the Guomindang. The result is that the Stalinists' propaganda about the 'Trotskyist traitors' finds an echo in all layers of the population, and even those who sympathise with us are at a loss to understand precisely who it is that the 'Trotskyists' at present see as the main enemy. Ever since the start of the war, the 'Trotskyists' have continued to act in this same way. Not only is it impossible for them to win support, but it's impossible for them even to approach other people; as a result, their vision grows ever narrower, even to the point where some of them have invented the theory that the fewer the social relations a member of a revolutionary party has, the better.

A small closed-door ultra-left organisation of this sort (with only a very few exceptions among its members) obviously stands no chance of winning new adherents; and even if it did win new members, it would be an obstacle to the further development of the Chinese Revolution.

The Stalinists failed to understand the new situation in China after the defeat of the last revolution, so they fell into many errors; the changes that would happen if the present [resistance war] were defeated would be many times more serious and give even less cause for optimism. Today, if we fail to develop a profound understanding of possible future political developments and of the real strength of the Chinese proletariat and the condition of its political party,[9] and if we fail to determine on the basis of such an understanding the proper order in which feasible policies can be implemented, we are at best garret scribblers indulging in self-advertisement and self-consolation.

---

8 Here Chen caricatured Zheng Chaolin's position.
9 By 'political party of the proletariat', Chen probably meant the Trotskyists rather than the CCP.

After the fall of Hankou, further large-scale warfare is unlikely. The fragmentary resistance led by the CCP and the Guomindang in the villages and small towns will probably spread everywhere within a short period of time. In terms of modern warfare, that struggle is no more than an ebb wave, it cannot form into a centralised force capable of beating back the enemy. If the Guomindang government goes the way of the Czechs by submitting to the Japanese and ceding a large part of its territory to them, and with Anglo-American help retains several provinces in the Yangtse valley, it is quite likely under such conditions of rule that it would revert to its anti-Communist stance.[10] In that case, not only we but even the Communists would stand no chance of retaining even a semilegal status unless they reorganised and changed their party's name.

We should beware of perpetuating the illusion that we can only restart our activities after the recovery of territories now occupied by the Japanese. Even today, while Japan continues to occupy parts of our country, we should prepare forthwith to start work afresh, within the narrow space that remains open to us, though to develop our forces we must wait for a while; only when industry begins to recover, after the war (whether under foreign or Chinese rule), can our work develop relatively smoothly. When that time comes, Marxist groups, whether underground or semi-public, will inevitably crop up in a number of places; without a big movement and a central force, it will be difficult to unite them. Only a small group that, organisationally, has won the support of a large numbers of workers and, politically, has gone all out to engage in the democratic and national struggle, is qualified to be the central force that recreates a proletarian party. The initial and fundamental job of striving to form organisational links to the workers and making propaganda for the democratic and national struggle are the policies we should adopt in both Japanese-occupied and Guomindang-occupied territories, the only difference being that under the Japanese secrecy is even more essential. If the ultra-leftists who today stay aloof from the masses and the real struggle fail to realise that they were wrong to look down upon the national-democratic struggle, if they fail to change their attitude in all respects and to knuckle under to the hard work entailed in the policies I have just proposed, if they continue to brag and pretend to be big leaders, to organise leadership bodies that lack all substance, and to found petty kingdoms for themselves behind closed doors and relying on the name

---

10   After January 1941, the united front between Chiang Kai-shek and the Communists collapsed in all but name, and the Guomindang reverted to systematic repression of the Communists.

of the Fourth International, they will achieve nothing beyond the tarnishing of the Fourth International's prestige in China.

3 November 1938[11]

Somewhere in Sichuan

---

11 Shui Ru (ed.) 1987, p. 480, gives the date as 'X month, 1939', but this is unlikely, for Frank Glass was already in possession of this letter on 19 January 1939, when he forwarded it to Trotsky (see Appendix 2); and during the war, a letter would have needed at least one month to get from Sichuan (where Chen was) to Shanghai (where Glass was). According to *Cahiers Leon Trotsky* (Grenoble, September 1983, no. 15, p. 108), whose editor has consulted a version of Chen's letter in the archives of the Hoover Institution on War, Revolution, and Peace, it was written on 3 November 1938.

Letter to Xiliu and Others

Chen's concern in this letter is to maintain the necessary distinction between Fascism and democracy, which Trotskyists like Pu Dezhi tended to view as mere variant modes of bourgeois rule. Whereas Chen wants the Allies to defeat the Fascists, Pu was prepared to see either side defeated, in the firm expectation (based on Lenin's theories about the First World War) that a workers' rising would then follow. In this regard, there was no distinction between Pu and the Chinese Communists, who in the first stages of the war condemned both sides as predators. Chen has not yet gone so far as to equate Fascism and Stalinism, and he expresses his approval of Trotsky's old slogan of 'a united front of the international proletariat against Fascism'. Source: Zhuanji wenxue zazhi she (eds) 1967, pp. 63–5. Xiliu is an alias of Pu Dezhi. The 'others' to whom this letter is addressed are probably the Trotskyists, including Zhao Ji, living at the time in Yunnan.

In the past, the slogan of the Third International against Fascism was not wrong. Where the Third International went wrong was in its pipedream of allying with bourgeois governments on the basis of the absurd slogan of a 'popular front' and a 'front against aggression' rather than organising a united front of the international proletariat against Fascism.[1] When the British and French bourgeois governments declared war on the Hitlerite state, the leaders of the Third International actually sided with Hitler while at the same time proclaiming their opposition to an imperialist war and encouraging British and French workers to oppose such a war.[2] More than forty members of the

---

1 Between 1930 and 1933, Trotsky proposed a united front of working-class parties (Communist and Social Democrat) against Fascism, while Stalin saw the Social Democrats not as potential allies but as enemies. Subsequently, Trotsky condemned the popular (or people's) front launched by the Stalinists in 1934 as an unprincipled alliance between representatives of the proletariat and of the middle classes; this alliance, by subordinating workers to the 'anti-Fascist' bourgeoisie in the capitalist countries, would hold back their revolutionary potential. The popular front, which had no precedents in the history of the labour movement, was adopted to suit the needs not of the labour movement but of Soviet foreign policy.
2 In August 1939, in a stunning volte-face, the Kremlin signed a pact with the German Nazis and divided up Poland with them. This pact deceived and demoralised the anti-fascist movement and facilitated and even encouraged Hitler's conquest of Europe. Comintern manifestos of 1939 and 1940 disguised this appeasement of the Nazis by calling on Communists to take advantage of the war in order to bring about revolutions. But this seemingly orthodox Leninist line was directed not against the Nazis but against the bourgeois democrats, who (together with the Social Democrats) had by now taken over from Fascism as the main enemy

French Communist Party were expelled for favouring a war against Hitler. In effect their expulsion gave succour to Hitler in his campaign to defeat Britain and France. *Xinhua ribao* ['New China daily'],[3] which appears in Chongqing, has published numerous translations of articles by Lenin opposing the war of 1914; day after day it makes a great show of denouncing this war as a repeat performance of the last one, that is, as a war of two imperialist states for the right to enslave their own peoples and pillage the colonies. *Dongxiang yuebao* ['Living Age'][4] followed suit, as their yesmen; on the point of this theory, I can see no difference between the Chinese Trotskyists and the Stalinists. Why was Lenin's theory about the 1914 war right?[5] Because he was not prepared to parrot the ready-made theories developed by Marx and Engels to explain the Franco-Prussian war,[6] and instead applied his own mind to observing and analysing the circumstances and special nature of the imperialist war of his day; his slogan was effective because Tsarist Russia was practically vanquished, and moreover because of Russia's huge size, so that Germany was in no position to persecute it beyond the extortions visited on Russia under the provisions of the Brest-Litovsk Peace Treaty;[7] thus the October Revolution was preserved. Today, we, too, rather than borrow indiscriminately from Lenin's theories about the 1914 war, should apply our own minds to observing and analysing the circum-

---

in Stalin's eyes. After 22 June 1941, when Hitler invaded the Soviet Union, Stalin switched his support back to the 'anti-Fascist bourgeoisie'.

3   *Xinhua ribao* was the Chinese Communist Party's main newspaper during the war. Founded in Hankou on 11 January 1938, it moved to Chongqing, Chiang Kai-shek's wartime capital, in November 1938; it was closed down by the Guomindang on 28 February 1947.

4   *Dongxiang*, a monthly journal launched in July 1939, carried the English subtitle *Living Age*; Alexander Buchman, an American Trotskyist then working in Shanghai, was its nominal editor.

5   Lenin argued war is the inevitable product of the contradictions of the world capitalist system. Practically alone among Europe's main socialist leaders, he stuck to the line of revolutionary defeatism after the outbreak of the First World War, and called on the workers of each country to work for the military defeat of their own government and turn imperialist war into civil war.

6   Soon after the Franco-Prussian War had broken out on 19 July 1870, Marx and Engels argued that if France (under Louis Napoleon) won, Germany and its independent workers' movement would be '*kaputt* [broken] for years'. They therefore came out in support of the Germans, but on condition that the German war remained defensive. Later, Marx condemned the Prussians under Wilhelm I for turning the conflict into an offensive war.

7   In 1918 the Soviet Government was forced to accept a treaty with the Central Powers by which Russia lost Ukraine, its Polish and Baltic territories, and Finland, places inhabited by one-third of its population. The treaty was annulled later in the year, after the Allied defeat of Germany.

stances and special nature of this imperialist war, for all theories and slogans inhabit time and space and cannot be copied at will. Incapable of grasping the actual circumstances and special nature of a major event like the present European war, which they declare to be a mere repeat performance of past history and deal with by repeating from memory the experiences and theories of the last war, Marxists of this sort are plagiarists of the old eight-legged essay school.[8] History does not happen twice, though mistakes do. Some people have applied Lenin's theories and slogans about the 1914 war to [this] Sino-Japanese War, forgetting the special characteristics of opposition to imperialism by an oppressed people.[9] However left-wing these people may sound, in practice they can only aid Japan. Those who apply to this war Lenin's theories and slogans from past years lose sight of the special nature of anti-Fascism and can only aid Hitler, however left-wing they may sound. Though Britain and France are not oppressed nations like Prussia was [during the Franco-Prussian War], Hitler is nevertheless a Napoleon III riding roughshod over Europe rather than a Wilhelm II.[10] As a result, the parties of the proletariat in Britain and France as well as in Germany should adopt the slogan 'unite in struggle against the Fascist Hitler', not 'defend the motherland'. Today's weapons and communications are completely different from in the past. Even if a civil war in Britain and France could be won, if it happened before the overthrow of Hitler, the fate of the new revolutionary state would under no circumstances be akin to that [of the Soviet state] after signing the Brest-Litovsk Peace Treaty! You too have written to me to say: 'If Fascism wins, catastrophe will befall the human race, so we should do everything in our power to prevent its victory'. You are absolutely right. But how can we prevent the victory of Fascism? As I see it, only if Hitler loses his war against Britain and France and his defeat, like that of Napoleon the Third, provokes a national revolution, can Fascism be thwarted. To adopt a defeatist strategy in Britain and France can only facilitate catastrophe. Victory would definitely fall to Hitler, not to the governments of Britain or France, nor to the proletariats of Britain and France or that of Germany. To equate as imperialists both sides in the conflict and to say that the workers should resist them equally is to make exactly the same mistake as equating Hitler and Brüning,[11] Nazism and social democracy. A failure to distinguish

---

8   See p. 165, fn. 5.
9   According to the Leninist view, the national struggle of oppressed peoples against imperialism was an integral part of the overall struggle of the proletariat for liberation.
10   Actually, Wilhelm I, King of Prussia, who became emperor of all Germany on 18 January 1871.
11   Heinrich Brüning was a centrist party leader who became German Chancellor in March 1930. Trotsky denounced Stalin for proposing Brüning's downfall when the alternative

between opposites helped Hitler conquer Germany; a similar failure today may well help Hitler conquer the world. Naturally the proletariat must prepare for tomorrow, but what must it do today? Today it is already at war! In practice and in theory, there should be no ambiguity. Either support Hitler, or resist him. If you oppose Hitler, you should not at the same time overthrow his enemies. Otherwise all talk of resisting Hitler and preventing the victory of Fascism is empty. What do you think? I await your response.

1 March 1940

---

was Hitler.

Letter to Xiliu and Others

In this letter, Chen defines Fascism and Stalinism as one and the same thing, and describes their overthrow as a precondition for world progress. Chen's commitment to an internationalist politics drives him to subordinate every struggle to the universal struggle between democracy and Fascism, even to the point where he is ready to condemn the Indian nationalist leaders for rocking the anti-Fascist boat. Source: Zhuanji wenxue zazhi she (eds) 1967, pp. 63–5.

... In my previous letter I did not exhaust the subject, so I shall elucidate my ideas further as follows. I believe two things. (1) Until this war is concluded, and even for a short while thereafter, there is no possibility of realising the mass democratic revolution. (2) German Nazism and Russian GPU[1] politics (the Italians and Japanese are mere ancillaries) are the modern inquisition. If humankind is to advance, it must first overthrow this system, which is even more barbarous than the medieval inquisition. Every struggle (including the struggle against imperialism) must take second place to this struggle. Any struggle that harms this struggle is reactionary. In light of these views, I believe that not only the anti-war movement in Britain, France, and the United States of America but also the movement for Indian independence is reactionary. Once the national struggle is divorced from the interests of the world struggle, it inevitably becomes reactionary. In reality, once India breaks away from Britain, it will inevitably come under Japanese or Russian control, and Hitler will win a decisive victory over Britain. If that's not reactionary, what is it? This opinion will not only cause Liangen[2] to gasp with amazement: you will view it cautiously, for it sharply contradicts the formulae that we learned previously. I would be most grateful if you could copy this letter to Liangen and copy my previous letter to Mr X...[3]

24 April 1940

---

1. The GPU was one of the names of the Soviet political police, successor to the Cheka and forerunner of the NKVD and KGB, set up during the civil war after 1917 to direct revolutionary terror against anti-Bolshevik enemies of the revolution; in the 1920s, it turned into the Stalinist dictatorship's permanent arm of repression.
2. That is, Wang Fanxi, who briefly worked with Chen in Wuhan in 1938. Wang was more than once Chen's opponent on political and theoretical questions, but on the whole saw himself as Chen's pupil.
3. It is not clear who is meant by Mr X.

P.S. That the great struggle against Nazism and GPU politics is being carried out not by the common people but by Britain and France, in the form of a war against Germany, is something of which revolutionaries of the world should be ashamed. If now, by high-sounding words, we allow Nazism to win out, we should feel even more deeply ashamed and guilty.

Letter to Xiliu

In this letter, Chen argues that bourgeois democracy is more conducive to the emergence of socialist democracy than is Fascism or Stalinism, and that therefore revolutionaries cannot but side with democracy against Fascism and Stalinism. Lenin had proposed a defeatist policy for workers under capitalism everywhere, on the grounds that defeat would trigger and permit workers' revolutions. But, says Chen, Lenin was speaking before the birth of Fascism. Source: Zhang Yongtong and Liu Chuanxue (eds) 1980, pp. 189–91. The letter as reproduced in this source bears no date and is listed as one of three letters to 'Xiliu and others'; however, it is clear from the text that it was addressed to Xiliu alone. This letter is not included in the Free China Press edition or the Taiwan edition of the letters published in 1967 by Zhuanji wenxue chuban she.

... Regarding your views on the European war, I reply as follows. Basically speaking, you have turned the view you previously held of democracy and the Soviet Union on its head and inevitably fallen prisoner to current theories and formulas, that is, to Lenin's theories and formulas about the last war. You have proved incapable of using your own brains to ponder these questions, that is, you have committed the first of the two mistakes I mentioned in my last letter to you. Marx and Engels had never experienced the imperialism of Lenin's day, so Lenin was unable to take over the ready-made theories that Marx and Engels developed to deal with the Franco-Prussian War; [similarly,] Lenin never experienced Fascism and GPU politics, so we are unable to take over his theories about the last war. In the last world war, whoever lost, Britain or Germany, would have made little difference to human destiny; today, however, if Germany and Russia win, humankind will be cast for at least half a century into an even greater darkness – only if Britain, France, and America win and preserve bourgeois democracy will the road be open to popular democracy. Is it possible for us to consider that the victory of Fascism is capable of speeding the realisation of popular democracy? Your sort of thinking is a repeat of the absurd views propagated by the 'dead dogs'[1] before Hitler's rise to power. Can we really believe today that the way to deal with Fascism is to call for revolutions in Britain and France? If we view objective conditions, there is nothing that will support such a reckless hypothesis, the sole outcome of which would

---

1   That is, the Stalinists. *Sigou* ('Stalinist lackeys') sounds nearly the same in Chinese as the word for 'dead dogs' (*sigou*).

be to aid Hitler and the 'dead dogs'. In the past, many people[2] rejected the constituent assembly and wanted only soviets. I said to them, of course soviets are better than a constituent assembly, but what's the best way of achieving soviets? Now you tell me, 'We cannot forget popular democracy'. But I'd like to ask you, 'There's no use in simply not forgetting it, the question is, how to achieve it?' Formal and limited democracy aids the struggle for popular democracy; Fascism and GPU politics are a brake on popular democracy. From China's point of view, if Britain and France are defeated, China will have no choice but to come under the control of Japan and Russia; if Britain and France win, the Fascist movement throughout the world will collapse. Naturally, victory for Britain and France will lead to the restoration of the old East-West order, and it is easy to imagine its impact on China's domestic politics. [But] is there some better, more beautiful dream that we can dream? In the past, the Third International's slogan nationally was for a 'people's front', whereas internationally it was for 'peace fronts'; it rarely called for a 'democratic front', and even if Communist parties in some countries had raised such a [democratic] slogan, I could not but consider it improper, for the Soviet Union itself was not democratic and the democratic countries themselves had not yet expressed their readiness to fight against Hitler in a decisive war – at that time, to raise the [slogan of a] democratic front as a gift with which to court the favours of Britain and the USA would simply be to play the role of a brake on the massive popular struggles in those democratic countries. It would have been just as wrong as the policy of rejecting the democratic front now, when all the democratic countries have already opened fire against Hitler. Supporting democracy now cannot be equated with supporting democracy in the last world war, for in those days there was no Fascist problem. I have explained this in detail above [in this letter], and the rest I explained, also in detail, in my last letter to you, you can consult it. Please send this letter to XX and the previous letter to Old X, so that I don't have to repeat myself in a new letter.[3] You and I realised many years ago that the dead dogs are arch-criminals on a world scale (this time my opinions on these questions are not as OX said, they are not emotional and ill-considered), whoever overthrew such people, we would endorse. Have

---

2   This is probably a reference to those of Chen's old comrades who doubted the validity of the constituent assembly slogan before they decided to accept Trotskyism.

3   XX is probably Wang Fanxi; Old X is probably Zhao Ji. Chen usually got Pu Dezhi (Xiliu) to copy to Wang Fanxi Chen's letters to Pu. It is not clear who OX is; it too may be a reference to Wang Fanxi.

you forgotten so quickly what we agreed?[4] Today I say in all frankness: I will kowtow before whoever overthrows the dead dogs and Hitler, I will willingly be their slave....

---

4 In prison, Chen Duxiu had at first shared his cell with Peng Shuzhi, but after he broke off his relations with Peng, the prison authorities gave special permission to Pu Dezhi and Luo Shifan (also prisoners) to spend two days a week in the same ward as Chen, so that these two younger men could look after their elderly comrade. In prison, Chen convinced Pu of his opinion on the question of democracy, but after his release Pu was persuaded by the views of Wang Fanxi.

Letter to Liangen

Here, Chen states his theory that though over time democracy undergoes important changes, such changes are unlike those in the economic system, in that they concern not the fundamental content of democracy but only the extent of its realisation. Chen criticises Lenin and Trotsky for dismissing bourgeois democracy as a mere form of bourgeois political control and for counterposing it to proletarian democracy; and thus for paving the way not only for Stalinist dictatorship but also for the Fascists, who copied the Bolshevik example. He sketches an economic theory of Fascism in an attempt to explain the nature of its political system. Chen's defence of bourgeois democracy is not an end in itself but an intermediate stage – made necessary by the ubiquitous crosscurrent of dictatorship – in the struggle for a more extensive democracy. Source: Zhuanji wenxue zazhi she (eds) 1967, pp. 68–71.

... I have seen that you [and other friends in Shanghai] unanimously [disagree with my views], so in spite of my illness, I shall make a brief reply to you. The roots of your error are as follows. First, you fail (like Lenin and Trotsky) to understand the true value of bourgeois democracy. You see democracy simply as a mode of bourgeois rule, as hypocrisy, as deception. You fail to understand democracy's true content, which is: no institution apart from the courts has the right of arrest; there may be no taxation without representation; the government has no right to levy taxes unless they are agreed by parliament; opposition parties are free to organise, speak, and publish; workers have the right to strike; peasants have the right to till the land; there is freedom of thought and worship; and so on. These rights and freedoms are what the people wanted; they are the 'bourgeois democracy' that people today enjoy as a result of more than seven hundred years of bloody struggle, they are what Russia, Italy, and Germany want to overthrow. The only difference between 'proletarian democracy' and bourgeois democracy is in the extent of its realisation; it is not that proletarian democracy has a different content. Ever since October [1917], the vacant and abstract term 'proletarian democracy' has been used as a weapon to destroy actual bourgeois democracy, and it led to the emergence of today's Soviet Union under Stalin – Italy and Germany are only following suit. Now you too are employing this hollow phrase as a weapon with which to attack the bourgeois democracies of Britain and America on Hitler's behalf. Second, you fail to understand the different class functions of Fascism and of the British, US, and French imperialists. (Imperialism is the product of an alliance between the financial oligarchy and the middle classes; only up to a certain point does it tolerate the proletariat's organisation and propaganda. Fascism is the fusion of the financial oligarchy with the lumpenproletariat and the radical right-wing of the petty bourgeoisie; it wholly eradicates the proletariat's organisation and propaganda.) You fail to see that the economic system of Fascism, unlike that of British and American imperialism, rather than becoming with each passing day more and more international, has reverted to becoming more and more national, to a process of self-contained and self-supporting feudalisation; instead you think that the only difference is in the political system. Political systems are propelled by class-based economic motors, they're not born of nothing. Even if we only consider the political system as an abstraction, is the difference between the German, Italian, and Russian GPU system and the British, American, and French parliamentary system merely tiny? Third, you fail to understand the importance of 'intermediate struggles'. If we have our eyes only on the final battle and argue that Fascism can be destroyed forever only in the course of that last battle, that only then can the problem be resolved, then there is no point in intermediate struggles such as the anti-Fascist movement, the strike movement, the movement for the convocation of a national assembly, and so on. Instead, we can sit back and wait for the final struggle to drop from the sky. And there's a fourth point. It is an utter illusion and sheer fantasy to assume that after the defeat of Britain and France a revolution will arise to overthrow bourgeois rule everywhere. (I refer you to my letter to xx.)[1] These four errors are all founded in one general error, which can be summed up as 'Closing your eyes to the actual course of historical events, blindly resorting to abstract formulae'. Even the formulae of the natural sciences can sometimes be demolished: those of the social sciences are far more fragile. History does not repeat itself. To consider old prescriptions as a sort of panacea and to apply them to the complex and increasingly volatile events of today is like matching horses' jaws to cows' heads.

Since the start of the war, *Xinhua ribao* in Chongqing has made a great point on the basis of Lenin's theories about the last war of denouncing the hypocrisy of the democratic states of the British and French bourgeoisies, of opposing inter-imperialist wars, and of labelling both sides as aggressive bandits; but between the lines, it actually sides with Hitler. I have carefully studied your letter and come to the conclusion that it is identical with what the dead dogs are saying, not merely in its ideas but in its very words and phrases. Recently I read the pamphlet *Poxiao* ['Daybreak'],[2] which is of course based on the thinking of Leon Trotsky. It goes so far as to let Fascism off completely and to

---

1   xx is probably Xiliu.
2   Published in October 1939. See Wang Fan-hsi 1991, p. 230.

concentrate its attack exclusively on Britain and America. Moreover, it defends the Soviet attack on Finland.[3] Voluntarily to make propaganda of this sort for Stalin and Hitler is surely a clear enough statement of position. Having taken such a position, how can you still claim that you are supporting neither side? If you join together the three political positions of 'oppose the democratic states of Britain and America', 'don't attack Fascism', and 'support the Soviet Union', there is no reason why the Third International and the Fourth should not merge. So from now on, your further opposition to Stalin will simply be a contest for position between individuals; it will not involve political principle. Apart from organs of state rule such as the army, the police, and the courts, which are in Stalin's hands, is there some other Soviet Union suspended in mid-air that we can support? If there is no prospect of you changing your opinions, it is only a matter of time before you compromise with the dead dogs. And if, in accordance with your wishes (at least as expressed by the writer in *Daybreak*), the democratic states (including America) are defeated and Trotsky can no longer stay in Mexico, it is hard to see any way out for you other than coming to terms with the dead dogs!

31 July 1940

P.S. I'd like you to answer two questions. (1) How can the revolutionary parties in Britain and France under the menace of Nazism assemble forces more easily: by employing slogans against Nazism, or by employing slogans against their own governments? (2) If a democratic force in Germany were to start a civil war against the Nazis, would you propose overthrowing both it and the Nazis simultaneously or would you ally with the Nazis to overthrow the democrats? Or would you (like Yi Yin[4]) propose cold-shouldering both camps?

---

3 On 30 November 1939, Soviet troops attacked Finland. On March 6, 1940, Finland sued for peace, and admitted Soviet garrisons onto its territory.
4 A pen-name of Zheng Chaolin.

Letter to Xiliu

This letter argues there will be no revolutions after the war, mainly because of the destructive effect of Stalinism on the world workers' movement and the likely countermeasures of the bourgeoisie, which would sooner surrender power to foreign capitalists than to domestic revolutionaries; and that a defeatist policy in the bourgeois-democratic countries can only help the Nazis. Chen expounds at greater length his theory of democracy, which – he explains – cannot be reduced to the mere existence of a parliament; indeed, the history of humankind can be viewed as the history – still in progress – of democratisation, whose ultimate product will be not the class-based democracy of the bourgeoisie but mass democracy, that is, full democracy, a concept apparently coterminous for Chen with proletarian democracy. The Bolsheviks' failure to understand and appreciate the rich content of democracy has led them to slight democracy and even to reject it root and branch. Their attitude led ultimately to Stalin, who is a product, not the initiator, of the Stalinist system. Chen goes on to reject the orthodox Trotskyist view of the Soviet Union as a workers' state, albeit degenerated and bureaucratised, that revolutionaries must support against the bourgeois states. (Chen had first questioned in a letter dated 15 May 1934, to the International Secretariat of the Left Opposition, the theory that the Soviet Union was a workers' state.)[1] Stalin, Hitler, and Mussolini are the three main bulwarks of reaction, to the destruction of which all efforts should be bent. And the best prospect for proletarian revolution lies in the defeat of Germany, though even there liberal forces will rise before socialist ones. Source: Zhuanji wenxue zazhi she (eds) 1967, pp. 72–81.

Dear Xiliu,

I enclosed with yesterday's letter a letter from [Zheng] Chaolin; I trust you've already received it. I received your letter of 21 July and that of Shouyi,[2] and I have read them both, but ill health prevented me from replying to them, and still does. (It took me more than twenty days to finish the present letter; as you can imagine, I'm not in the best of spirits.) Please don't misinterpret my failure to reply.

Your letter says: 'His [Shouyi's] understanding of democracy and his view of the world situation is too optimistic, I'm afraid he's somewhat naive'. Our

---

1 See Chen's letter of 15 May 1934, to the International Secretariat, kept in Stanford University's Hoover Institution under the Subject File 'International Left Opposition and the Fourth International'.
2 A pen-name of Wang Fanxi.

discussion revolves precisely around the following two questions. (1) After the war, will there be a revolution in the defeated countries? (2) Should we support democracy? You call him naive (actually, it's reactionary) on the one hand and still claim that he's right on the other. Do you yourself realise that your position is self-contradictory?

Regarding the first question, all I can do is answer no, especially where Britain and America are concerned. On this point, [He] Zishen and Xizhi[3] have insisted even more vigorously than I that there will be no revolutionary situation in Britain and France, and for the following reasons. (1) The revolutionary forces in these countries have already been eradicated by Stalin. (2) The bourgeoisie in these countries has experienced [the revolutions of] 1871 and 1917; so in the event of defeat, they would sooner hand over their weapons to the foreign enemy than allow an internal enemy to profit from them. (3) Germany's armaments, military tactics, and methods of rule in the occupied territories are different from those used in 1871 [in the Franco-Prussian War] and in 1917. If the British and French governments fall,[4] for a while there is no possibility of sudden mutinies. (4) Germany has not yet achieved world hegemony; once Germany is defeated, the war will be over. If the Nazis fall, they are unlikely to be succeeded by another Fascist state. (The situation in Britain and France would be quite different.) When the time comes, the Social Democratic Party and the other liberal parties can raise their heads again; although such a turn could only benefit the emergence of a revolutionary movement, one could hardly say that Hitler's downfall would lead immediately to a revolution in Germany, since there is no revolutionary party there. For these reasons, our old formula about 'revolutions breaking out in the defeated countries in the wake of an imperialist war' has been invalidated. Only those who cling to shibboleths and close their eyes to the course of history can dream of 1917 and claim that this war is a repeat performance of the last one. Since there is no prospect of revolution in Britain or France, what (other than helping Hitler win the war) is the point of adopting a defeatist position in those countries? History does not repeat itself, but human error does. We used to think that the Brüning cabinet and Hitler were identical, and in so doing we helped the Nazis into power; today we equate German Nazism and British and French democracy and have helped Hitler to subdue France, with its democratic traditions. I can argue further that if people continue to despise democracy and worship dictatorship, then, as Shouyi says, 'Regardless of good and bad, humankind can choose only between Fascist dictatorship and socialist dictatorship'. In other words, the only choice is between the political system of Russia and that of

---

3 The pseudonym of Wu Jiyan.
4 The French government had already fallen by this time.

Germany: which means that even if the defeat of Britain and France provoked a revolution, it would, like a victory for Hitler, have the effect only of plunging the world even deeper into darkness and degeneracy. One GPU-style Soviet Russia is enough to stifle people: could you endure a whole series of new GPU states in France, America, and Britain? So we had better have a considered debate about the second question, which is (as Shouyi put it): 'The main difference between us concerns democracy'.

Regarding this second question, for the last six or seven years I have deeply pondered the experience of Soviet Russia over the last two decades before arriving at my present views. (1) Without a state in which the broad masses of the people participate there can be no broad democracy: in the absence of broad democracy, so-called popular state power or proletarian dictatorship will inevitably drift towards a Stalin-style GPU system controlled by a tiny minority of people. Such a system is the necessary outcome of such a situation; it is not because Stalin is particularly vicious. (2) To replace bourgeois democracy with a state in which the broad masses of the people participate is to go forward; to replace British, French, or American democracy with German or Russian dictatorship is to go backward. Those who (directly or indirectly, knowingly or unknowingly) assist in a retrogression are reactionary, however left-wing they may sound. (3) Democracy is not merely an abstract term: it has a specific content. The content of proletarian democracy is broadly similar to that of bourgeois democracy; the only difference is that it is broader in the scope of its implementation. (See my previous letter and the diagram in the latter part of this letter.) (4) Though the content of democracy includes the parliamentary system, such a system does not exhaust democracy's content. Many people have for years equated democracy with a parliamentary system, and in rejecting the one have also rejected the other; precisely this is the chief cause of the degeneration of Soviet Russia. Parliamentarism can expire, it can become a relic of the past, but the same is not true of democracy; a soviet system without democratic content remains a representative system that is democratic in form only or even resembles the soviets in Russia; it will be inferior even to bourgeois formal democracy. (5) Democracy is the standard beneath which the oppressed peoples of every age – in ancient Greece and Rome, now and tomorrow – resist the minority privileged class, it is not merely an historical phenomenon bound to a particular age, a mere form of bourgeois rule belonging to a period now past. If democratism is already past its time, gone never to return, then politics and the state too are already past their time, already dead and buried. To say that democracy is but a form of bourgeois rule while the sole form of proletarian state power is dictatorship and can under no circumstances be democratic is to justify Stalin's crimes and to render superfluous Lenin's description of democracy as 'an antitoxin to bureaucracy'. Leon

Trotsky's call to struggle for the restoration of democracy in the soviets, the trade unions, and the party also becomes a cry for the return of the past, a call for common people to shed blood for ghosts. To say that proletarian democracy and bourgeois democracy are different is to fail to grasp democracy's basic content (habeus corpus, the open existence of an opposition, freedom of thought and of the press, the right to strike and to vote, and so on.), which is the same whether it be proletarian or bourgeois. To say that there is no relationship between Stalin's crimes and the system of proletarian dictatorship is tantamount to saying that those crimes are not the product of violations committed ever since October (these violations of democracy did not start with Stalin) against the basic content of democracy by the Soviet Union, but are the product instead of Stalin's viciousness – a wholly idealist explanation. Stalin's crimes are a logical development of proletarian dictatorship. Are they not also the product of the power that has accrued since October to the secret police, and of a whole series of anti-democratic dictatorships that forbid parties, factions, freedom of thought and of the press, and freedom to strike and vote? Unless such democratic freedoms are restored, anyone who succeeds Stalin could become 'grand dictator'. So to ascribe to Stalin all the Soviet Union's evils rather than trace their source to the harmful nature of the Soviet dictatorship is tantamount to saying that by toppling Stalin all the Soviet Union's wrongs would be righted. Such prejudices, which fetishise the individual and neglect the system, are unworthy of any fair-minded politician. The experience of the Soviet Union over the last twenty and particularly the last ten years should cause us to reflect. If we fail to trace the origin of such defects to the system and to draw the appropriate lessons, if we simply screw up our eyes and oppose Stalin, we will never see the truth. With one Stalin gone, innumerable other Stalins will spring to life in Russia and other countries. In Soviet Russia after October, it was clearly the dictatorship that produced Stalin rather than the other way round. If we take the position that bourgeois democracy has already reached the point at which its social momentum is spent, that there is no longer any need to struggle for democracy, then we are saying that the proletarian state has no need for democracy, a point of view that spells ruin for all times! (6) The content of modern democracy is far richer than that of democracy in ancient Greece and Rome, its reach far wider. Because the modern age is the age of bourgeois rule, we call this democracy bourgeois. In reality, however, this system is not wholly welcome to the bourgeoisie, but is the accomplishment of the tens of millions of common people who over the last five to six hundred years have spilt their blood in struggle. Science, modern democracy, and socialism are three main inventions, precious beyond measure, of the genius of modern humankind; unfortunately, since the October Revolution democracy has been rejected together with bourgeois rule; dictatorship has been substituted for democracy, the basic content of democracy has been repudiated, and so-called 'proletarian democracy' or 'mass democracy' is nothing more than verbiage void of all real content, false colours under which to resist bourgeois democracy. Having seized state power, the proletariat will have at its disposal large-scale nationalised industry, armed forces, police, courts, and a soviet electoral law. With such useful weapons to hand, it will be strong enough to suppress bourgeois counter-revolution and will have no need to substitute dictatorship for democracy. Dictatorship is just a sharp knife, what it today does to its enemies it will tomorrow do to itself. Lenin in his time was aware that democracy is 'an antitoxin to bureaucracy' but did not conscientiously apply democratic norms, for example by abolishing the secret police, tolerating the open existence of opposition parties, and allowing people to think, publish, strike, and vote freely. Leon Trotsky only discovered after personally experiencing the dictator's knife that the party, the trade unions, and the soviets at all levels need democracy and free elections, but by then it was too late! The rest of the Bolsheviks, more ignorant, lauded dictatorship even more highly and cursed democracy as worse than dogshit. This preposterous idea swept the world in the wake of the authority of the October Revolution. Mussolini was the first to apply it and next came Hitler, while in the land of its birth – the Soviet Union – the dictatorship was intensified and all manner of crimes were committed, whereupon the hangers-on and their spawn of the cult of dictatorship spread across the entire planet, particularly in Europe, so that today three of the five powers are dictatorships. (So it's untrue that the East needs democracy whereas the West doesn't.) The first is Moscow, the second is Berlin, and the third is Rome.[5] These three bulwarks of reaction have turned the present into a new middle ages, and they now plan to turn thinking humans into unthinking mechanical beasts of burden who jump to the dictators' whip; if humankind is powerless to overthrow these three bulwarks of reaction, its fate is clear. So today all struggles throughout the world will have meaning only if they unite to overthrow these three bulwarks of reaction; otherwise, whatever sonorous names they may go under (proletarian revolution, national revolution), from an objective point of view they will unwittingly help to consolidate and extend the power of the three bulwarks. If we recognise that the overthrow of these bulwarks is the main objective, first we must concede that even the imperfect democracy of Britain, France, and America is worth defending; second, we must repudiate the bankrupt theory of Liu Renjing, which holds that whatever the time and whatever the event, the proletariat

---

5   Chen forgot to name Japan among the dictatorships.

cannot act jointly with other classes. This theory clearly could not be applied at the time of [Chiang Kai-shek's] Northern Expedition [of 1926–7], nor can it be applied in the War of Resistance against Japan or in today's world war; if applied, it could only play a reactionary role. [Chen Qi]chang says: 'Today, in the midst of war, the obvious distinction between democracy and Fascism has been lost, or is about to be lost'. I find this sentence baffling! (1) From the point of view of the political system, the absolute distinction between democracy and Fascism will persist forever. (2) If the author means that democracy in Britain, France, and America is turning more and more into Fascism, then even if that were true, it would be absolutely wrong to take it as a reason to welcome dictatorship and oppose democracy. (3) If Britain, France, and America go Fascist, it will be partly because the Third International and the Fourth International helped Hitler achieve complete victory: Hitler's army will bring Fascism to whichever territories it conquers; but for that army, the democratic traditions of Britain, France, and America could not so easily be crushed. To equate wartime strengthening of the cabinet with going Fascist is to fail to understand the first thing about Fascism. (4) I ask those who believe the distinction between democratic countries and Fascism has already been lost to look at this table of comparisons.

(i) Democracy in Britain, America, and pre-war France.
(ii) Fascism in Russia, Germany, and Italy. (Soviet Russia's political system was the model for Germany and Italy, so these three countries can be classed together.)
A (i) Parliamentary elections are contested by all parties (including opposition parties). Although each constituency is monopolised by a [particular] party, each party must publish an election programme and make election addresses in order to cater to the people's demands, for the electorate is, through suffrage, the final arbiter. Meetings are attended by lively discussion and debate.
A (ii) Elections to the soviets or to the national assembly are fixed by the government party. These bodies meet simply to raise their hands in assent, not to debate.

B (i) No one may be deprived of liberty or life without first coming before a court.
B (ii) The secret police may arrest and kill people at will.

C (i) Opposition parties, even the Communist Party, are openly permitted.
C (ii) The one-party state permits the existence of no other party.

D (i)   People are more or less free to think, say, and publish what they want.
D (ii) There is an absolute prohibition on freedom of thought, speech, and the press.

E (i)   To strike is not in itself a crime.
E (ii) Strikes are outlawed, that is, criminal.

Judging from this table, tell me when in Britain and America the distinction between the two systems was lost? And as for France, why was it lost? What Communist, having studied this table, is still prepared to condemn bourgeois democracy? Surely the age of religious superstition is of the past and it is time we came to our senses! If, in the future, revolutionaries continue to believe that 'democracy belongs to the past; proletarian state power can take the form only of a dictatorship, never that of a democracy', they will merely allow the GPU to trample underfoot the whole of humankind; moreover, since such a revolution cannot break out after the defeat of Britain and France, in whose ultimate interest is your proposal to adopt a defeatist slogan in those countries? Stalin's first ingenious move was to replace the slogan against Fascism with one against imperialism; his second step was to launch a sneak attack on Britain, France, and America in order to defend Fascism. You are going the same way: your second step is quite clear from *Daybreak* and from Shouyi's letter to me! Shouyi and his friends' attitude towards the world war is based on their view of the nature of the Soviet Union[6] and their attitude to democracy. My opinion is in all respects the opposite. Both positions are consistent. You, on the other hand, agree with Shouyi only in respect of your attitude to the world war; your attitude to the Soviet Union and democracy is apparently still close to mine, which I find truly incomprehensible. Please copy this letter to Zhao [Ji] and to Shouyi and the others. I hope that you will return to me the original, together with my earlier letters, for I plan at some future date to publish them. I enclose [Chen Qi]chang's letter. Greetings and good health,

Zhong

September 1940

---

6 That is, that although it was degenerate and bureaucratised, it was still fundamentally a workers' state, in the sense that the legacy of the October Revolution had not been completely squandered and the state that had resulted from it could still either go forward to real socialism by means of a political revolution or backwards to the restoration of capitalism; and that it must therefore be defended against the bourgeois states.

My Basic Views

This article summarises in thesis form the positions that Chen developed in his letters and articles before and after leaving prison: that the revolution is nowhere imminent; that war will merely simplify the structure of imperialism, not destroy it; that the bourgeoisie still has some progressive role to play; that Bolshevism has paved the way for Stalinism; that democracy is a universal mode of politics; and that the dictatorship of the proletariat is equal to the dictatorship of the Communist Party. Proletarian dictatorship is the very opposite of proletarian democracy, and thus of socialism, which is the economic complement of full democracy. Capitalism, in contrast, is the economic complement of limited, that is, bourgeois, democracy. Chen adds that colonial peoples cannot hope to win national liberation in the absence of social revolutions in the metropolitan countries. Source: Zhuanji wenxue zazhi she (eds) 1967, pp. 82–8.

1. Revolutionary situations do not arise at any time and any place. It is preposterous to talk of a period of reaction as if it were one of revolution; that is, to pretend that the ruling class is on the road to collapse when it is on the road to stabilisation after winning victory; to pretend that the middle classes are beginning to vacillate in their support for the ruling class when in reality they are vacillating in their support for the revolution, and starting to abandon its ranks; and to pretend that the revolutionary mood is rising when it has sunk into depression in the wake of a defeat. We must forget this nonsense about 'the poorer people are, the more revolutionary they become'. True, the law of physics that 'every force has a reaction that is equal and opposite to it' can also be applied to society, but only on condition that the oppressed are sufficiently resilient.
2. The proletarian masses are not at all times disposed to revolution, especially not in the wake of crushing defeats or at times of social or economic catastrophe.
3. Without the numerical strength to match its social importance and without economic and political organisation, the proletariat is not so very different from other strata of the people. In particular the experience over the last dozen or so years of bureaucratic rule in Soviet Russia and the experience of the Sino-Japanese War and of the present imperialist world war should caution us against overestimating the present strength of the proletariat in the world and lightly predicting the 'imminent end of capitalism'. Unless some world-shaking force intervenes, this world war will

under no circumstances mark the end of capitalism and imperialism but will mark instead the second stage of its development, namely, from a plurality of imperialist states to the beginnings of a simple opposition between two imperialist blocs.

4. We should strictly distinguish between the arbitrary 'concentration' and 'unity' of the petty bourgeoisie and the voluntary 'concentration' and 'unity' of the proletariat.

5. We should strictly distinguish between the empty radicalism of the petty bourgeoisie and the straightforward determination of the proletariat.

6. Now is definitely not the day of the final struggle, either in the backward countries or in the advanced countries of Europe and America. Those who arbitrarily proclaim that the bourgeoisie and the petty bourgeoisie are no longer in the slightest way progressive and have already absconded lock, stock, and barrel to the camp of reaction will simply capitulate in confusion when it becomes apparent that the bourgeois classes are still capable of playing a progressive role.

7. We must grasp without prejudice the lessons of the last two decades and more of Soviet Russia. We must re-evaluate in a spirit of scientific detachment, free from all religious passion, the Bolsheviks' theories and their qualities as leaders. It is quite wrong to blame every crime on Stalin, for example in relation to the question of democracy under the proletarian state.

8. Democracy is the banner under which in every age, ever since humans first developed political organisation, right down until the withering away of politics (in Greece, in Rome, today, tomorrow), the majority class opposes the privileges of the minority. 'Proletarian democracy' is no empty phrase. Its specific content, like that of bourgeois democracy, demands for every citizen the freedom to assemble, form associations, speak, publish, and strike; and above all the freedom to form a party of opposition. Without such freedoms, neither parliament nor soviet is worth a fig.

9. Democracy (from a political point of view) and socialism (from an economic point of view) are complements and not opposites. Democracy is not indissolubly bound to capitalism and the bourgeoisie. If in opposing the bourgeoisie and capitalism, the political party of the proletariat opposes democracy as well, then even if so-called 'proletarian revolution' were to break out in a number of countries, without democracy to act as an antitoxin to bureaucracy, they will be nothing more than Stalin-style bureaucratic states, brutal, corrupt, hypocritical, fraudulent, rotten, degenerate, and incapable of engendering any form of socialism. There is

no such thing as 'proletarian dictatorship' but only dictatorship of the party, which ends up as dictatorship of the leaders. All dictatorships are inseparable from brutality, fraudulence, corruption, and bureaucratic politics.

10. Yes, the present world war is a war for world hegemony between two imperialist blocs. Yes, the so-called 'war for democracy and freedom' is a facade. That does not mean, however, that there is not still a certain measure of democracy and freedom in Britain and America. In those two countries opposition parties, trade unions, and strikes are a reality and not a mere promise. Only a lackey of the Nazi fifth column would argue otherwise. It is even more unthinkable that America would use against the Isolationists[1] methods like those used by the Nazis against the Jews. Hitler's Nazis are out to rule the world with the same barbaric and reactionary methods with which they now rule Germany. In other words, they aim by means of a new and even more terrible Inquisition to impose everywhere one doctrine, one party, and one leader. They will not permit the slightest dissent, not even the existence of indigenous Nazi or Fascist movements in the countries they conquer. A Hitlerite victory will mean the stifling of all humankind, it will transform humans everywhere from thinking people endowed with free consciousness into unthinking mechanical beasts of burden void of free consciousness; so ever since the start of this world war and in future, too, progressive people of good intent in every country (including, of course, Germany) should make the destruction of Hitler's Nazis the general goal of a common offensive of all peoples; all other battles can only be deemed progressive insofar as they serve that general end. For once Hitler's Nazis win, all talk of socialism, democracy, and national liberation will be meaningless.

11. In the present imperialist world war, to adopt a defeatist line in the democratic countries, a policy of turning the imperialist war into a revolutionary civil war, may sound left-wing but in reality it can only speed the Nazis' victory. For example, if the British government were toppled in a revolution by its own people, the British army, navy, and air force would inevitably split and become enfeebled, and the new revolutionary government would be in no position to nurture strong forces quickly enough to prevent a Nazi invasion of England. (Some people might object that 'the defeat of one's own imperialist government is a lesser evil', in which case the Czechs and the French are indeed fortunate to be under Nazi

---

1 The Isolationists were Americans opposed to the US playing a central role in world politics; they believed that US resources could be better spent on solving domestic problems.

occupation!) If you neglect the time factor, what might under other circumstances be true becomes preposterous. People rightly observe that the Sino-Japanese War has changed in nature as a result of the imperialist world war, but even so it would be wrong because of that to propose a defeatist policy in China and to work for the destruction of [Chiang Kai-shek's] Chongqing government. Under the conditions of today, such a policy would only hasten the victory of the Axis[2] – any other view is an illusion. For the same reason, we don't propose adopting a defeatist position in the Soviet Union, even though we have no reason to think that in the matter of human freedom Stalin's followers are any better than Hitler's.

12. There is no reason to believe that preparing the revolution, that is, uniting the masses, would be even more difficult in a state endowed with a certain measure of democracy than under the centralised rule of the Nazis; or that a Nazi victory would be more useful to the German revolutionary movement than a Nazi defeat. No one can foresee how long Nazi hegemony will last in Europe. To predict the inevitable collapse of Nazism in the wake of its victory and take such a prediction as a justification for helping Hitler win whatever the cost in human sacrifice is a strategy of farce. It is on the same level as Stalin's policy at the time of the German coup of 'letting Hitler take power', 'he will soon lose power'. In today's Europe, as in China during the Warring States period [475–221 BC] and Europe at the start of the modern era, economic development requires unity, and since there is no revolutionary unity, objective conditions may allow the Nazis to realise their reactionary unity. But such reactionary unity will not be able to shake off capitalism's economic constraints on productivity (the system of private property) in the way that feudal constraints on productivity (serfdom and the guild system) were shaken off during Europe's monarchical period; it will lack this progressive function. From a political point of view, the destruction of democracy and the restoration (for however short a time) of medieval reaction will be a terrible disaster for humankind and an incalculable loss.

13. Only in countries inclined towards progress are war and revolution the product of the development of production and can become in their turn a cause of its further development; in declining countries, war and revolution weaken production even further, cause the national character and morals to become even more degenerate, grotesque, corrupt, wasteful,

---

2 In September 1940, Germany, Italy, and Japan signed the Tripartite Pact, which brought the Axis into being; the signatories promised to go to war against any nation attacking one of their number, save those already at war when the pact was signed.

and unjust, and turn the political system into a reactionary military dictatorship.

14. Only when two nations are equal in respect of weaponry and military techniques do the number of the armed forces, the degree of popular support, and the morale of the combatants count decisively towards who wins and who loses an international war. Even in civil wars the invention in the nineteenth century of new weapons obliged Engels to take a second look at the value of barricade fighting;[3] the invention of new weapons and techniques in the twentieth century will reduce even further the possibility of mass risings and barricades, unless splits occur in the ruling camp.

15. Colonies or semi-colonies are a *sine qua non* of imperialism, as private ownership of property is of capitalism. It would be illusory to think that the system of private ownership of property will collapse without the collapse of capitalism, just as it would be illusory to expect the war for national independence in the colonies to win victory without first linking up with social revolution in the imperialist countries (the metropolitan states and their enemies). Today, with the Anglo-American and the German imperialists locked in a struggle to enslave the entire planet, an isolated national [liberation] war, no matter which class leads it, will either collapse altogether or will simply work a change (possibly for the worse) of master; even were the oppressed people to acquire a more enlightened master, one prepared to help stimulate political and economic development, it would work no fundamental change in its original slave status as a colony or semi-colony.

28 November 1940

---

[3] In his preface to the new German edition, published in 1895, of Karl Marx, *The Class Struggles in France,* Engels noted that after 1848, 'rebellion in the old style, the street fight with barricades, which up to 1848 gave everywhere the final decision, was to a considerable extent obsolete'.

Letter to Y

In this letter, Chen seems to wish to reassure He Zhiyu that his letter to Hu Qiuyuan and Sun Jiyi (the next text in this volume) did not represent a break with Marxism. Source: Shui Ru (ed.) 1987, p. 513. This letter is not included in the Free China Press edition or in the Taiwan edition published by Zhuanji wenxue chuban she. Y is He Zhiyu.

Dear Y,

I enclose my letter to H and S,[1] please forward it when you next correspond with them.... H and his ilk hope that I will quit the Marxist fold (so does Tao Menghe),[2] there's nothing strange about that, it's what they've always wished for. Our best policy is to discuss real issues (both historical and contemporary) with them so that they have no refuge. In order to avoid possible confusion, it's best not to enter the sphere of abstract theories and isms. Tao Menghe understood it rather well, while [Deng] Zhongchun[3] simply misunderstood.... I hope you are in good health.

Duxiu

19 January [1941]

---

1 The next letter.
2 Tao Menghe (T'ao Meng-ho) was a non-Marxist professor of sociology at Beijing University and a contributor to Chen Duxiu's *Xin qingnian* ('New Youth').
3 Deng Zhongchun, a medical doctor, was one of Chen's non-political admirers; Deng helped Chen greatly after Chen moved to Jiangjin.

Letter to H and S

In this letter, Chen informs his non-Trotskyist friends of his new view of Lenin and Trotsky, and appears to abandon Marxist theory for a pragmatic approach to political questions. See too his letter (not included in this volume) of 23 December 1941, to Zheng Xuejia, a former Trotskyist sympathiser who had later become associated with the Guomindang, in which he rejects Marxism as irrelevant not only to China but even to Russia and Western Europe. On the whole, however, his final views are not irreconcilable with Marxism as Karl Kautsky and others understood it.[1] Source: Zhuanji wenxue zazhi she (eds) 1967, pp. 89–90.

Dear Messrs H and S,

Three years have passed since I and Mr H parted, and it is more than twenty years since I last saw Mr S. When I think back on my Beijing days [spent with Mr S], I cannot but feel nostalgic.[2]

I have seen your letters to Y and your comments on my latest works, I thank you warmly for them. In formulating my opinions, I prefer to base myself on the historical and contemporary process of events rather than on vacuous isms, and I am even more loath to quote as a foundation for my thinking what others may have said in the past. This method of 'measuring by saints' words' is a weapon drawn from the armoury of religion, not of science.[3]

In 'My Basic Views', which I completed recently, I have also avoided bringing in any sort of ism. My seventh thesis [in that essay] proposes re-evaluating the Bolsheviks' theories and leaders (including both Lenin and Trotsky) not by some Marxist measure but on the basis of the lessons of more than two decades of Soviet history. If the Soviet Union had rational grounds for exis-

---

1 For Chen's letter to Zheng Xuejia, see Ren Jianshu and Tang Baolin 1989, Volume 2, p. 286.
2 H and S are Hu Qiuyuan and Sun Jiyi. Hu Qiuyuan was among the Chinese students who returned to China sometime in the early to mid-1930s, after studying in Japan. The majority of these returned students supported the Chinese Communist Party, but a few (notably Hu and Zheng Xuejia) showed some sympathy for Trotskyism and borrowed weapons from the Trotskyist armoury to attack the Chinese Stalinists. The leaders of the Communist Party were extremely hostile to Hu, Zheng, and the other members of their group, and attacked them in an effort to discredit Chen Duxiu and the real Trotskyists. Hu and his friends very quickly became associated with the Guomindang. Hu earned his living by writing for the Shenzhou Publishing Company.
3 A Buddhist term, meaning to take saints' words as the sole judgment and measure of truth or falsehood, right or wrong.

tence (no matter whether it succeeds or fails), no one could repudiate it, even if its existence were not in conformity with Marxism. To confine oneself to a definite 'circle' is to be 'sectarian'. The so-called 'orthodox' is the equivalent of what the Confucianists of the Song dynasty called *daotong*.[4] None of these things were ever to my liking. That's why I came out against Confucianism when I found it to be wrong, and against the Third International when I found its policies to be wrong. And I'll take the same stance towards the Fourth, Fifth, and ... th Internationals. Shizhi[5] has called me 'an oppositionist for life', and it's true, though not by my design; facts forced me along this road. Figuratively speaking, if meat tastes good, no one cares about which butcher sold it. But if it tastes bad and one still likes it simply because it was sold by Lugaojian,[6] that would be an exercise in superstition. Superstition and prejudice cannot withstand the test of events or the passage of time; I'll have nothing to do with either of them. That's all for now. Even from this [short letter], I trust you can discern my attitude in searching for the truth.

If I write new articles, I'll certainly send them to you for comments. I've a lot more to say, but unfortunately my poor health prevents me from writing. Moreover, even if I do write, it's very hard to get things mimeographed.

Best wishes,

Duxiu

19 January [1941]

---

4 The legitimate legacy of Confucianism.
5 Hu Shi (Hu Shih) (1891–1962), a philosopher, writer, advocate of the vernacular literature, and one of modern China's most influential liberal scholars. Hu taught at Beijing University from 1917 to 1927; between 1918 and 1920, he helped edit Chen Duxiu's *Xin qingnian*, After May Fourth, 1919, Hu split from Chen Duxiu and was strongly criticised by the Communists. He was a supporter of the Guomindang, and pro-American.
6 Suzhou's best-known cooked pork shop, established several hundred years ago.

A Sketch of the Post-War World

Here, Chen is at his most pessimistic, He doubts if the democratic countries can win the war, and predicts new world wars soon after the end of the present one; there will be no lasting peace, no justice, and no equality, either within nations or between them, whichever side emerges victorious. Imperialism will not weaken but grow stronger and bipolar: the post-war world will be divided between the hostile powers of America and Germany or of America and Britain; the two victors will attack one another and act as magnets for the lesser powers. Unless the 'leading' countries go socialist (which Chen thinks unlikely, though he clearly hopes that it will happen), there will be no new independent states, for the Soviet example has shown that imperialism will not fall merely because its weakest link has snapped. Perhaps imperialism's resilience is in some ways a good thing, for economic unification is progressive even when achieved by counter-revolutionary force, and will inevitably pave the way to socialism. The Chinese people should resist imperialism, but they should at the same time learn from the West. They should seek to expand their industry in order to create the conditions for chiming in with future revolutions in the industrial countries. If the interests of nation and world democracy collide, the latter must take precedence. During his last years in Sichuan, Chen generally made his views known not in public but through letters. This 'Sketch of the Post-War World' is an exception. It was published in Dagong bao *on 21 March 1942, just two months before Chen's death. The Guomindang refused to allow it to be published in Chengdu, apparently for fear of offending the Soviet Union, which Chen denounces in the article, and suppressed its sequel ('Once Again on the World Situation', the next text below) (see Ren Jianshu and Tang Baolin 1989, vol. 2, p. 298). Source: Zhuanji wenxue zazhi she (eds) 1967, pp. 91–103.*

History does not repeat itself, and this present war has already caused huge changes throughout the world, or laid the basis for such changes. It is pointless to try to depict the future with theories drawn from the past.

There are only three possible outcomes to this war: neither Britain and America nor Germany and Japan will prevail, but both sides will talk peace; Britain and America will win; Germany and Japan will win. Least likely is the first outcome, so there is no need to speculate on it here. Of the second and third outcomes, which is the more likely? To judge by present conditions, it seems clear that Germany and Japan have the upper hand. The war has already been going on for more than two years. Having now acquired the support of the Soviet Union, for the last six months Britain has enjoyed a lull in the war, yet even with its entire forces it cannot block the advance of the numerically smaller German army in North Africa. It is hard to see how in the near future Britain can defeat the main German army. If one accepts that Britain's defeats in the various battle theatres have been due to the outnumbering of its army and its air force, then within a year or eighteen months, after the British and Americans have had a chance to expand their arms production, there may well be a change in the overall situation. But today, although some people are calling for a 'wholesale reorientation of factory production', to judge by the past and present behaviour of government officials – which was characterised by inertia – and factory owners, who care only about their own interests, it is doubtful whether Britain and America can succeed in beating Germany and the neighbours under its control in the arms race. And even if we do assume that at some future date they will be in a position to do so, are we also to assume that for some mysterious reason Hitler and his partners win simply bide their time and refrain from launching offensives in that year to eighteen months while Britain and America increase their armaments? Yes, Germany's internal crisis surpasses that of Britain and America, but it will only reach explosive proportions once war-weariness sets in or the German army is defeated. Germany's only weakness is its lack of oil. That is why Germany cannot sustain a long war unless it succeeds in capturing the Caucasus or Iran. For that reason, Germany needs a quick victory. The interest of Britain and America, on the other hand, lies in a protracted war. The main aim of both sides is to fix the time for action in their favour. So in Germany's imminent spring offensive, whether it happens in the Mediterranean or in European Russia, whoever is victorious along the line between Malta, Gibraltar, the Suez Canal, and Singapore or that between Moscow, the Caucasus, Iran, Iraq, Syria, and Singapore will have won the key to overall victory in the war. If the Axis powers win, Britain and America will be incapable of sustaining a protracted war. Throughout the history of warfare, space, numbers, and resources have never been the main factor in deciding victory.

If Britain and America win and the Axis powers are finished, new oppositions will arise at the peace table or the international conference to deal with the war's aftermath. It will not be easy for post-war Britain to clear up the situation in Europe, North Africa, the Near East, and the Middle East, and for a while its strength will not stretch to the Far East. The Far East, including Southeast Asia and Australasia, is likely to become an American sphere of influence. Under such circumstances, the friendship of Soviet Russia will be a prize for which Britain and America compete; their fate will hang on the next world war.

If Hitler wins the war, Britain will be finished, and America too will for the time being be forced to withdraw to safety behind the Atlantic and the Pacific.

Even if Hitler does win, his guns will continue to point West, for he lacks the military might to extend directly into the region to the east of the Urals, Iran, and India. If such a time comes, then regardless of whether America and Japan hold peace talks, America and Germany will vie for the friendship of Japan. America will not necessarily continue to fight Japan, so until Hitler subjugates America, he too is unlikely to risk offending Japan on account of the Far Eastern question and driving his valued ally into the hands of the Americans, thereby severing the right prong of his two-pronged offensive against America from the Atlantic and the Pacific. Hitler knows that if, with Britain's strength in the Far East destroyed, he were to threaten Japan, there would be the danger of Japan and America cooperating, on condition that America withdraws from the Far East. In that case, America and Germany's fate would hang on the next world war.

It is still impossible to say how many more world wars there will be: all we can say is that as long as the cause of war is not eliminated, wars will inevitably happen, and that if Germany wins, the next war will come more quickly. Evidently there will be no formal peace talks between America and Germany, yet the actual fighting is bound to come to a temporary halt. And even though Germany needs a respite from war so that it can set up its New Order, pluck the fruits of victory, and (even more importantly) build sufficient numbers of warships and cargo ships capable of crossing the Atlantic, once it had done so, it would then restart the war against America, probably from South America. Actually, every world war is nothing but a continuation of the previous world war. We should under no circumstances allow ourselves to be befuddled by high-sounding propaganda about 'perpetual peace', 'national self-determination', 'the equality of nations', and 'the destruction of the capitalist system'; under no circumstances should we believe that after the war these ideals are likely to be realised.

The European and American project to reform capitalism is nothing new; however, it has resulted in the imposing emergence of the trusts alongside joint-stock companies and cooperatives; with labour legislation extended to half the world, in the so-called 'socialist state' people have to restore the system of piece work. If reforming the system is not easy, destroying capitalism is even harder, and certainly not as effortless as some people imagine. When this war is over, not only Britain and America but also the Axis powers will inevitably try to reform the capitalist system, to make it more amenable to their rule. No one should be taken in by Hitler's denunciations of capitalism, they are simply his private joke. The reform project of all these states is simply to reduce barriers within each bloc by means of tariff agreements and even of economic unions, to diminish the role of currency by means of barter, and to nationalise some private firms. While tariff barriers within each bloc go down, those between the blocs will become intensified; not everything is barterable, and those goods that can be bartered are still valued in terms of currency, so it is still a sort of commodity transaction, not a form of division of labour. Even in the nineteenth century some industries were nationalised; wholesale nationalisation, that is, so-called state capitalism, seems to be conceivable in theory but not in practice. If the cliques that control the means of production are not expropriated by revolution, there is no chance of them voluntarily handing over their private property to the state. Some people imagine that a 'supra-class' government will peacefully expropriate private property, but any such government would itself be expropriated in double-quick time. So the three above-mentioned projects for reform are incapable of shaking the fundament of the capitalist system. Ever since capitalism first arose, its weals and woes have intensified in accordance with the logic of its internal development. Since reforms are incapable of disturbing its foundations, any measures to control it can only hasten the decline of the entire society and economy; to imagine that you can draw on its weals and avoid its woes is wishful thinking, it will get you nowhere. Private property and the commodity system are the basis of capitalism, and the root source of all capitalism's evils. The aim of the capitalist system of production is to augment the private wealth of those who own the productive means by selling its products as commodities, not in any direct way to satisfy the needs of the whole people. The more the productive forces develop, the more the laws of supply and demand – productive power and purchasing power – get out of kilter. The result is a crisis of overproduction, falling prices, factory closures, unemployment, and economic panic. After a while, the productive forces are restored to strength, and because they might now be even stronger than before, they lurch towards an even deeper crisis; hence the periodic law of cyclical crises. Usually there are two ways of coping with overproduction. One is the self-imposed reduction of the volume of production and even the destruction of products, a foolish and ridiculous method; the other is to conquer colonies, win markets overseas, and go to war, an insane and terrifying method. Because of the need to peddle surplus commodities on foreign markets and to stop foreigners invading the domestic market, tariff barriers are inevitably raised, armaments are increased, preparations are made for war, and in some cases hostilities begin. This chain of cause and effect inevitably binds present-day state authorities. For since they are incapable of destroying the capitalist system and instead allow it to lead them by the nose (any other response on their part would be defeated), this sequence of events is unavoidable – it cannot be changed by any ideology or moral principle. In an age when a number of strong states across the globe must vie for markets, prepare for war, and go to war, when they do everything in their power to extend their spheres of influence, when they are packed so tightly against one another that not a drop of water could trickle down between them, what point is there in talking about national self-determination or national liberation? At the end of the last war, [Woodrow] Wilson's Fourteen Points shook the entire planet;[1] the reason they disappeared from the scene was not because [David] Lloyd George and Georges Clemenceau hoodwinked Wilson but because Wilson hoodwinked himself;[2] moreover, the deception led France to ruin, and England and America were prevented from taking a strong stand towards Japan. After the present war, those who flaunt pacifist illusions in the capitalist world will be vanquished in the next war.

Will imperialist rule remain unchanged after the present war, no matter who ends up victor? As long as capitalism exists, imperialism, which is capitalism's natural product, will surely not reject itself. However, the actual form of imperialist rule will inevitably change. Take, for example, the change from nation states to international blocs. Such changes by no means signal the end of the imperialist system; on the contrary, they show that imperialism is spreading and growing stronger. From now on, the pre-nineteenth century movement towards nation states will decline in the wake of the spread of imperialism, and the early twentieth-century opposition between seven or eight imperialist powers will also end. The Axis powers have belatedly completed the transition from nation state to imperialist state, Japan most recently of all. The imperialists are vying to grab the markets of the colonial and backward countries before anyone else gets hold of them. That is the sole reason they are prepared to take such risks, even to the point of trying to change the old imperialist world order by military means. This war will leave only two leading nations capable of complete independence and free from all alien controls, and those two nations – America and Germany or Britain and America – will be locked in opposition

---

1 Wilson's Fourteen Points embodied the principles that he regarded as essential for a just and lasting peace after the First World War and his wish for a world government that would prevent future wars. The Fourteen Points included the right to self-determination, which coincided with the aspirations of China's nationalist movement at the time. At the Paris Peace Conference in 1919, Wilson bargained away the Fourteen Points in deals with Lloyd George and Clemenceau, his wartime allies, who favoured a policy of peace-for-revenge, and disappointed the Chinese, thus triggering the events in China of 4 May 1919. People in China at the time felt that Wilson was a naive and idealistic scholar, ignorant of real politics, who deceived even himself.

2 That is, France was defeated and occupied by Germany.

A SKETCH OF THE POST-WAR WORLD (10 FEBRUARY 1942)

to one another. The peoples of all other countries will be subordinate to one or other of the resulting blocs, either as allies or as full-scale collaborators. Naturally Japan and Soviet Russia also aspire to lead their own blocs, but their fate will depend in the last resort on the level of their productive forces. As for the other colonial and backward countries, the age in which they might have hoped through the national struggle to form new independent states is already over. Within the blocs, countries can be roughly grouped into four categories, according to their strengths and weaknesses. The first category consists of relatively prestigious 'allies', as Japan is for example to Germany and Soviet Russia is to Britain and America. The second consists of semi-colonies, for example Italy (in relation to Germany) and Holland, Belgium, and France (in relation to Britain and America); although these countries have their own governments, politically and (even more so) economically they are all more or less under the control of the leading nations. The third consists of dependent countries[3] like France and Belgium (in relation to Germany), Denmark and Italy (in relation to Britain),[4] and the Philippines (in relation to America); although they have their own governments, they are incapable of independent diplomacy. The fourth consists of the colonies, which lack even their own government and are controlled by governors from the metropolitan countries. There are none worse off than the colonies, unless it be the indigenous peoples of the Americas or of Australia. Though not all the nations and peoples in the two main blocs are alike in status, they have one thing in common, namely their political and economic systems are to a greater or lesser degree remade on the model of the leading nations. Systems that are absolutely contrary in character [to those of the leading nations] are inconceivable: in the German bloc, they are all modelled more or less closely on the Nazi system; in the Anglo-American bloc, on the democratic system. And the socialist system? Such a system can only be realised after the victory of the revolution in the leading countries, only then can socialism influence all the countries of the bloc. The experience of the Russian Revolution suggests that breaking the weakest link in the chain of world imperialism cannot eventually lead to the disintegration of imperialism as a whole. As for Soviet Russia today, it is not entitled to be a leading country, not only because of its low productivity but also because it has long since abandoned socialism.

---

3 I translate *bei baohu guo* as 'dependent countries'; literally, it suggests 'protectorates', a term that in this context carries the wrong connotations.

4 This passage is confusing: Italy belonged to the Axis and was not invaded by the Allies until July 1943; Denmark was occupied by the Nazis, like France and Belgium.

At the start of this world war, some dreamers imagined that the chance had come for small, weak nations to achieve their independence. In reality, however, the colonies of Asia traded Anglo-American for Japanese control; and the colonies of Africa traded British for German and Italian control. Some people even imagined that the war would speed socialist revolution, but, to their great sorrow, things turned out differently; when they now discover that even the national struggle is labouring under constraints and that the Nazis are probably about to take over nearly half the world, they will plunge from their imaginary paradise into the deepest abysses, they will begin to believe that history is destined to go downhill. In reality, the history of human progress continues along its usual disinterested track, bound neither for paradise nor for the abysses of destruction; it bears not the slightest responsibility for the disappointment and sorrow that results from the destruction of the illusory hopes and joys of these people. Even if, by some tragic course of events, victory in this war were to go to the Nazis and half the world's population came under their domination, though politically this would result in a long period of catastrophic suffocation, it would have the same economic consequences as an Anglo-American victory. The Nazis would naturally be in no position to shake off the restraints imposed on productivity by the capitalist system, but a great step forward would be made within the capitalist system. For example, due to the unification of various currencies, the lowering of customs barriers, the concentration of resources, and so on, the number of the world's smaller economic units would be gradually reduced, thus removing some of the obstacles that have hitherto prevented economic development, and society's productivity would be increased much more rapidly than before the war. Objectively, this process would increase the material basis for broadening the road towards a socialist world, and is nothing more than capitalism's usual practice of creating progress by means of its bloody crimes: only a narrow-minded dogmatist would fail to see that. Human history is in this sense no different from the planet earth: it continues relentlessly on its path, whether at noontime or at midnight.

To be serious, genuine national liberation can only be realised in conjunction with socialist revolution in the imperialist countries. In a capitalist-imperialist world, 'national self-determination' and 'national liberation' for the backward countries and the weak nations is an illusion. The national struggle is even more likely to be restricted in an age like the present, when two rival imperialist camps compete through wars to force the backward countries and weak nations all over the world into war. Only a dreamer would be startled by such a comment. Looked at from the point of view of the progressive unification of the world economy, such constraints on the national struggle are not necessarily wholly bad. In the absence of revolutionary unity, even counter-revolutionary unity has a progressive significance, whether on a world scale or within a single country. For example, Wu Peifu's unity was better than the separatist warlord régimes, and Liu Xiang's was better than the age of 'protection areas'.[5] Moreover, to say that the national struggle will probably be to a certain extent restricted does not mean that nations led hitherto by other people will become as a flock of sheep, incapable of initiative. It simply means that the national struggle will meet with certain restrictions, the recognition of which is a precondition for effective action of the following sorts. (1) To work hard for the democratisation of the political system and the development of national industry, in order to increase the nation's weight within the bloc to which it belongs. Today is no longer the age of Li Hongzhang.[6] One should stop dreaming the pleasant dream that [China] could become a rich, strong country at a single leap – that it could become an independent nation state like those achieved in the eighteenth or nineteenth centuries and become a first-class power in the twentieth century. (2) To create the forces (industry and national organisation) necessary for coordinating with the revolutionary struggle in the leading nations in order to achieve true national liberation and progress. It is wrong to dream of slamming the door shut, of eliminating imperialist might from a single country by the efforts of a single people in order to achieve independence for a national bourgeois state. (3) As for the struggle overseas, it should start out from the point of view of the interests not of nationalism but of democracy, regardless of whether this struggle is conducted against Axis or non-Axis powers, for the despotisms of Germany, Italy, and Japan, rampaging across the world hand in hand, have already broken through the last defences of the nations of the various countries. We are no longer talking about the fate of this or that nation but of the survival of freedom and democracy throughout the world. If we continue to fight our battles on national grounds, India's present enemy is Britain, and China will at some future point be forced once again to wage resistance, this time against America. (4) We must do all in our power to resist imperialist aggression, which threatens our survival as a nation, but we should not reject foreign culture. The conservative tendency to reject

---

5 Liu Xiang (1890–1938) was the most powerful of the Sichuan warlords in the 1920s and 1930s; while he (sporadically) held supreme power in the province, numerous smaller warlords each occupied and controlled a certain territory and designated it a 'protection area'.

6 Li Hongzhang (Li Hung-chang) (1823–1901) was a member of the faction that argued that China would have to achieve parity in industry and technology with the West if it was to remain independent and united under the monarchy. He and other members of his faction ran nearly all China's modern state-owned industries between 1860 and 1895.

foreign culture can have only one effect: to cause one's own national culture, now stagnating, to decline. True, Chinese culture has its strong points, but taken too far, it would look down on other branches of culture and even exclude from the notion of culture those technical-material achievements upon which the people's livelihood and national defence depend. As a result, there are people who even go so far as to exclude from the notion of culture glorious Chinese inventions such as printing and gunpowder, and instead reduce culture to art and literature. The baleful effect of this misunderstanding of the meaning of culture in the present Sino-Japanese War has been twofold. On the one hand, it has gratuitously transformed rhymers and scribblers into 'people of culture'. This is scarcely different from Japan's ironical remark that China is a country of words. On the other hand, by trying to resist warplanes, artillery, and tanks with the chanting of slogans and the singing of songs, it continues to promote the old Boxer idea that magic incantations can stop bullets; this is the impasse to which the lop-sided development of Chinese culture ultimately leads. Zhang Zhidong's harmful idea about 'using Chinese learning for essentials and Western learning for application' has already held us back for half a century.[7] By shouting about 'our own culture' and 'Oriental culture', we will similarly harm future generations of our people.

Some may consider that this war is a war between the imperialists of the Axis and the anti-Axis, with each side out to extend its own power and influence; it is not a struggle for national liberation; there is no point in small and weak peoples participating in it. This view is due to a failure to understand that although small and weak peoples cannot achieve their liberation by relying on imperialist assistance, they cannot resolve problems by their own efforts either. Moreover, at the present stage in the history of war, 'neutrality' has become a thing of the past. If the people of Burma say, 'Better the devil we know than the angel we don't know', we must reply: 'We know of no angels in today's world, all we know is that the devil you know is ten times worse than the devil you don't'.[8] If some people in China say, 'To help America defeat Japan is like chasing a tiger away from the front door and letting a wolf in at the back', we must reply: 'If America wins the war, then we stand a chance of restoring our old

---

7 Zhang Zhidong (Chang Chih-tung) (1837–1909) was a leading official who favoured reform, but warned against changes that would threaten Confucian culture, a position summed up in the slogan 'Chinese values, Western means'.

8 By 'the devil you know', Chen means Japan. Some anti-colonialist Burmese leaders of the Dobama Asiayone or Thakin Party fell for Japan's 'Asia for the Asiatics' propaganda and assisted the Japanese at the time of their overrunning of Burma in 1942. They were soon alienated by the behaviour of the Japanese occupiers.

semi-colonial status if we work hard to renew ourselves and stop conniving at corruption. But if the Axis wins the war, we will surely become a colony from which before long even the puppet government in Nanjing will be expunged!'

Some people may think that what I have written is too low-key: future events will teach them otherwise.

10 February 1942

Once Again on the World Situation

In this article, Chen insists that the probability of a victory by Germany and Japan must not prevent the Chinese people from working for a British-American victory, if only to inspire the next generation of youth. To ensure collective security after the war, democrats must work towards a world federation, not an Asian federation that would exclude the rich countries. Source: Zhuanji wenxue zazhi she (eds) 1967, pp. 104–12.

Some people say that the international situation as I described it in 'A Sketch of the Post-War World', namely the possible prospect of a world wholly under imperialist rule, is too pessimistic. It seems to me that in assessing objective circumstances, important is whether or not you are realistic, not whether or not you are pessimistic. Ever since the late nineteenth century, finance capital has broken through national barriers and the world has been an imperialist world. That's exactly what imperialism is about. This is not something that relates to the future: the only thing that will happen in the future is that today's seven or eight imperialist powers will fight each other and consequently be reduced to two imperialist blocs. In the absence of a great revolution to shake the entire world, this state of affairs will continue and may even become worse than we have estimated. For should victory in the war go to Hitler, Britain will be finished, [Franklin D.] Roosevelt will fall to a Hitler of the Americas, and the next world war (between Germany and America) will be between two Fascist blocs rather than between democracy and Nazism. Then what Roosevelt said will have been proved right: democracy and freedom will die out for several hundred years. In that case, the course of human progress could be plotted as follows.

> *Pre-Historic Antiquity*
> Clan democracy.
>
> *The Ancient World (Greece and Rome)*
> Democracy of the townspeople.
> Autocracy of the great landlords, grand priests, and military leaders.
>
> *The Modern World*
> Bourgeois democracy.
> The feudal lords and (in the last phase) absolute monarchy.

The Future World
From proletarian democracy onwards to democracy of the whole people. Fascist dictatorship.

According to this chart, Fascism, like other previous systems of dictatorship, would develop universally and come to constitute an entire historical stage, and democratic systems throughout history have always passed and will pass through a period of dark dictatorship. If people are content to sit back in their easy chairs and dream their optimistic dreams and thereby let Nazism grow, we must be prepared to admit the possibility of such an age of darkness.

Although there should not be too great a discrepancy between objective evaluations and subjective efforts, they need not always head in the same direction. For example, even though we may believe that Germany and Japan are more likely to win the present war, that should not stop us in advance of the outcome from proposing that we do everything in our power to help Britain and America win; at the same time, our duty to work hard for the victory of our democratic allies should not lead us to believe that the Axis powers face inevitable defeat. We may pursue ideals, but we should not pursue completely unrealistic illusions; we should strive to advance ideals that are not absolutely unattainable, even though attaining them may still take many years, but we should beware of consoling ourselves with pipedreams. It is by no means a bad idea, when others set up comforting mirages and even abandon all vigilance, to paint the bleakest possible picture of events in the real world, in order to remind oneself of, and rouse others to, the need for even greater efforts. Rather than close one's eyes to the possibility of a world where imperialism reigns supreme, it is far better to stare hard at the tragic course of events and to admit that the danger exists that Fascist imperialist dictatorship might be universally established for an entire historic period. So in this present war we should do everything within our subjective might to rout Hitler and his accomplices and to penalise them with the utmost severity; we should inundate Fascist ideology with a great tide of democracy and freedom, so that after the war it is incapable of reviving under new guises in the victorious countries and of diverting the modern history of human progress along another path, in other words, so that we are not forced to live through an entire period of Fascist dictatorship and instead can pass directly into a world of extensive democracy; even if that is beyond the realm of the possible, we must still do everything we can, in the spirit of the old saying, 'To do it even though we know it is impossible',[1] to influ-

---

[1] A Confucian saying.

ence the next generation of young people to continue to fight to end Fascist reaction within the shortest period possible. That is the only ideal that we can possibly now pursue. To imagine that the present war can be transformed from an imperialist war into a war to overthrow imperialism everywhere is in all respects illusory. That is why I have braved the ridicule of old friends and backed the anti-Nazi alliance with Britain and America. Worst of all is to substitute an optimistic assessment of the objective world for subjective hard work; if before the present war [Prime Minister Neville] Chamberlain, Voroshilov, and Knox[2] had not chosen to view the enemy through rose-coloured spectacles, as not warranting an attack, and had instead made full military preparations rather than simply talking big, the war today would be going far better. For today's enemy is not like the stupid high officials of the Chancery of the Qing dynasty, who simply capitulated before the foreigners' braggadocio, nor can he be deceived by the passing [in parliament or Congress] of an empty bill for increased armaments or by the revelation of figures showing a rapid increase in arms production. The age of winning victories through sheer intimidation and deception is now past!

Litvinov's speech at a dinner party in the New York Club of Economists on 16 March [1942] was right on several points: 'In my opinion the time factor is an unreliable and treacherous ally for both warring sides. We are on the one hand engaged in a prolonged war and on the other hand we are preparing military provisions and reserve forces to an extent surpassing that of the enemy. Yes, we are on the right track in so doing; but such a plan can only serve its purpose if during the same period the enemy does nothing. You gentlemen know, however, that our enemies are not like that. They will build on their existing achievements to continue their advance, to continue to occupy territories, to gobble up new sources of raw materials, to enslave hundreds of millions of people, and even to acquire new allies. These advantages will inevitably far outstrip the advantages that our side acquires in terms of military preparations during this one-sided ceasefire'. 'If we console each other with empty talk about the impossibility of defeat, we will be even further from victory; this prospect causes us great anxiety'.[3] This is a salutary if painful antidote to the frivolous optimism of those Americans and their allies who believe that 'final

---

2 Marshall Kliment Yefremovich Voroshilov was Defence Commissar of the Soviet Union before and at the outbreak of the Second World War. Colonel Frank Knox became US Secretary of the Navy on 19 June 1940. Actually, before his appointment Knox was known in the US as an internationalist, an opponent of the Neutrality Act, and a champion of compulsory universal military conscription.

3 This speech by Litvinov has been retranslated into English from Chinese.

victory will inevitably be ours' and 'the Axis powers can only end in defeat'. Let bygones be bygones, but we cannot afford to let the opportunity slip time and time again. If we wish to achieve final victory, we must strictly guard against empty optimism. Compare, for instance, the speech delivered at the same New York Club of Economists by [Viscount] Halifax (identified by British public opinion after the Battle of Dunkirk as one of the appeasers in the cabinet of Chamberlain) with that of Litvinov.[4] [In the light of such attitudes], we must even more surely root out [excessively] optimistic opinion, treat it as an enemy, and make doubly sure that we substitute for it the following theses.

(1) Britain and America should not be suspicious of Russia, but should provide large-scale aid to the Russian army so that it can hold on to Moscow. They should not (to quote Litvinov) 'deploy their best-equipped forces in places where there is no fighting'. Nor should they believe the nonsense about Russia having already demonstrated in the course of the war that its forces outstrip those of Britain and America, that it is in a position to rout Hitler. Least of all should they delude themselves into thinking that the successful defence of Moscow is in only Russia's interests. Higher arms production is vital for an Allied victory, and time is needed to produce arms. Halifax said optimistically: 'Militarily and industrially, America still has latent potential'. He forgets that we cannot magically transform that latent power overnight into weapons. Hitler has postponed his spring offensive until the summer. His target is probably still Moscow. Only if Moscow can be defended for a year or eighteen months, so that Hitler is unable to switch his forces to the south, will America and Britain have enough time to increase the level of their arms production above that of their enemies. Otherwise, the fall of Moscow and the routing of Russia's crack troops in accordance with Hitler's plans will enable Hitler to take advantage of his victory to move his troops south towards the Caucasus, Iran, and Iraq and to join forces with Japan at Suez in order to blockade the Mediterranean. If by then Britain and America have still not increased their arms production, the game will be as good as lost!

(2) Arms production cannot be raised by empty words. There are not at present enough arms factories to match and outstrip the enemy in this regard, nor is there enough time to build new ones. The only solution is 'compulsory reassignment', that is, switching other factories as far as possible to producing armaments. There can be no final victory until our arms production outstrips that of the enemy. At this point I fear that some people will object that I am

---

4 Maksim Maksimovich Litvinov (1876–1951) was Soviet Ambassador to the USA from November 1941 to August 1943.

a proponent of the theory that 'weapons alone decide the outcome of war'. Actually, ever since the invention of flint arrowheads, victory or defeat in war has depended increasingly on arms, to the point where today it is virtually true to say that war is a competition of arms. The heroic yet tragic defeat of France at Sedan and of Britain at Dunkirk and in Malaya and Singapore proves the truth of this axiom. Opponents of the theory that 'weapons alone decide the outcome of war'[5] are no less vociferous than others in demanding tanks and planes of the Americans; they too prove my point.

(3) The experience of the League of Nations shows that both to win victory in a war and to ensure collective security after it one must organise an international bloc capable of leadership and endowed with an economy and armed forces that are strong enough [to carry out its decisions]. The passage from the growth of nationalism to that of a new international collective is not only inevitable but is a prerequisite of human progress, a prerequisite – we must do all in our power to replace Fascism with a democratic bloc – of the transition to a world federation. [Jawaharlal] Nehru's proposal for an Asian bloc[6] without Britain and America sounds nice, but its only real effect would be to prolong Asia's backwardness; and like the Burmese theory of 'sooner the devil you know', it's a racialist prejudice that can only help boost Japan's 'Greater East Asian Co-Prosperity Sphere'.[7] We must dispel such noxious illusions! For to imagine, in a world bent on war, that there might happen a rising of armed masses independent of the two imperialist blocs is either an illusion or conscious fraud. Nehru's proposal for Asian independence does not share the same motive as Subhas [Chandra] Bose's[8] call for Indian independence, but its effect will be the same: to give succour to Germany and Japan.

---

5 Evidently a reference to the Chinese Communists, in their wartime capital of Yan'an.
6 Nehru's strong pan-Asian feeling found expression at around this time in his call for an Eastern Federation, in which India and China would be the senior partners. Nehru had earlier argued that India should play a crucial role in the Afro-Asian world. Nehru's attitude towards the war (when he was imprisoned by the British) was that if India were to participate enthusiastically in the anti-Fascist struggle, it would first have to be granted freedom.
7 The 'Greater East Asian Co-Prosperity Sphere', an extension of Japan's anti-Communist 'New Order in East Asia' proclaimed in November 1938, envisaged in 1940–1 including China, the mandated Pacific islands, all of Southeast Asia, and even Australia and New Zealand in a self-sufficient economic system free from Western exploitation and under Japanese political hegemony.
8 Subhas Chandra Bose (1897–1945) was a leader of the Indian Congress Party who broke with the majority of the Congress leaders and tried to achieve India's independence with the help of Japanese imperialism. He led an Indian national force against the West during the Second World War.

(4) Since we are participating in the anti-Nazi struggle led by the democratic arsenal of America and in an Allied bloc battling to protect democracy and freedom throughout the world, naturally we must make democracy and freedom the central thought of our compatriots so that all concentrate on the same militant goal: China's economic backwardness, its [undemocratic] tradition, and the war situation we are now in must not prevent us from creating an ideal system of democracy and freedom. That fact is obvious, but we must at the very least express the determination to carry on down the road towards democracy and freedom. We should not be like those people who oppose democracy and freedom root and branch, who denounce democracy and freedom as clichés, and who say that those of us who favour democracy and freedom are living anachronists; or who, a little less bluntly, oppose Chinese-style 'democracy and freedom' to the basic principle of democracy that underlies the world's democratic countries; they share in common the belief that democracy is no longer appropriate to the modern state, by which they indisputably mean Germany, Italy, and Japan (with or without Russia), definitely not Britain and America. By adopting such an attitude [towards democracy and freedom], will the progressive Chinese in general fail to understand to what end we make our War of Resistance against Japan a part of the war against Germany, Italy, and Japan? Will they succeed in dissipating China's determination to see this war through to the end? Will they manage to assist our enemies' sinister and contemptuous denunciation of America for 'aiding non-democratic nations with democratic goods and materials'? And, finally, will they succeed in causing our allies to distrust the sincerity of our adherence to the democratic alliance? These are questions that we should deeply ponder. Perhaps some people believe that the only conceivable future is a Fascist world, and not just for a limited period of time; that democracy and freedom will be dead forever. This is simply speculation, without any basis in facts or history. It is simply an ideology; it cannot be designated either as pessimistic or as optimistic.

19 April 1942

The Future of the Oppressed Nations

In this article, Chen retreats somewhat from the reservations he seemed to express in 'Once Again on the World Situation' about the usefulness of uniting oppressed nations. Though he continues to insist that some imperialists are worse than others, he also says that all movements of oppressed peoples against imperialism must be supported and oppressed workers and peoples everywhere must unite to that end, in order to bring about world socialism. But only a revolution encompassing 'advanced' as well as 'backward' countries can lead to the development of the economies of the poor countries; in the absence of world revolution, imperialism will help forge the links that create such unity. National liberation will follow from world socialist revolution, just as the abolition of unequal treaties in China followed on the October Revolution in the years before it degenerated. Struggles for national liberation can no longer proceed in separation and isolation from one another: people everywhere will have to become free together, in an international socialist federation. This argument is the late Chen's clearest and most trenchant restatement of his commitment to Marxist internationalism and the Trotskyist theory of permanent revolution, and of his undying hostility to capitalism and imperialism. Source: Zhuanji wenxue zazhi she (eds) 1967, pp. 113–20.

The oppressed nations are the product of capitalist imperialism. The oppressed toilers produce commodities for imperialism; the oppressed peoples of the backward nations buy commodities from the imperialists and produce raw materials for them. These are capitalist imperialism's two props. It is only natural that oppressed peoples should resist oppression by capitalist imperialism even to the point of going to war against it. There can be no blame in such conduct. Every progressive member of the nation should support such struggles for national freedom, regardless of who leads them. For even a national liberation struggle led by the bourgeoisie, even one led by the feudal nobility, is progressive insofar as it strikes a blow at capitalist imperialism. But what will be the future of such a struggle if it stays confined within the bounds of a national struggle?

(1) From a national angle, experience suggests that war is not only incapable of making a nation less backward but will even make it more so. Quite apart from setting back political and academic thought, a protracted war will lead to a blockading of the economy and to inflation. In the absence of social sanctions, and given the weakness of our political organisation, it is easy for corrupt officials, unscrupulous merchants, and landowners to use the sheer chance cre-

ated by national hardships to collect windfalls by engaging in the hoarding and cornering of goods; and owing to their crimes, our resistance fighters are dying in pools of blood at the front and our common toiling people starving and suffering in the rear. Should you propose applying more or less unpeaceful methods to change this state of affairs, people will scream at you that you are exceeding the bounds of national struggle and sabotaging the national front against the invader. And in fact these methods do exceed the bounds of national struggle. Yet to let things go on as at present is precisely to deal a fatal blow to the war of national liberation. At the same time, these awful things cannot be done away with by resorting to propaganda and persuasion or to decrees issued by the government. What is to be done?

(2) From an international point of view, today, when the imperialists are competing for colonies and the market in the backward countries is greatly intensified, according to Gandhi one nation cannot gain freedom by depending on aid from an [imperialist] power; and he is one hundred per cent right. Yet nor can it without the assistance of one of the powers free itself from the present oppression of another power. What's more, some powers will come to your assistance whether or not you depend on them to do so; that too is an incontrovertible fact. At this point Nehru has no way out. Perhaps there is a slight difference between him and Gandhi, in the sense that he is not suggesting that American aid be rejected. Should America enter India, we know that its stance on the colonies is better than that not only of the Axis powers but even of Britain; the Philippines are a case in point, although they cannot be considered an independent nation-state. For the Indians to exchange British for Japanese rule on the grounds of national independence would be an even greater disaster. However much Gandhi and Nehru stress in their propaganda that the age when Indians will acquiesce in foreign oppression has now passed, they must know in their heart of hearts that they cannot simultaneously expel the British and repulse Japan and Germany. The outcome would simply be to languish under the rule of a new master and to [have to] continue with the campaign of civil disobedience. Well, what is to be done?

In my opinion, therefore, in the present world of capitalist imperialism, no small or weak nation is in a position to close itself off or to rely on its own national resources to expel all imperialist invaders in order to realise an independence of this sort. The only real way forward is to unite with the oppressed toilers and the oppressed and backward peoples of the entire world to overthrow imperialism everywhere, and in so doing to replace the old world of international capitalist commodity exchange with a new world of international socialism based on a division of labour and mutual aid. When that happens, the national question will solve itself.

There are two conceivable objections to such an opinion. Some may ask how a backward nation can speak of socialism, and how it can unite with the toilers of other nations and with small or weak nations; others, whether socialism implies national liberation.

Those who raise the first objection are blinkered by the old nationalist viewpoint. They are unable to see the future trend towards ever-greater internationalisation. It is, of course, self-evident that the backward countries themselves, given their economic state, are in no position to speak of socialism, or even of capitalist development. Today the backward countries, whether out to develop capitalism or socialism, can do so only in reliance on the advanced countries. Only an obsessive nationalist would believe otherwise. Over the last hundred years, capitalism's colonial policy has already breached the Great Wall that surrounded backward nations everywhere. After this war, the form of imperialist rule will in all cases change from a policy of colonialism to one of an even more concentrated and organic international bloc. Talks about the so-called Atlantic Charter, Pacific Charter,[1] and the like mark the start of that process towards a reconstitution into blocs. If, after the defeat of the Nazis, Germany were to emerge as a socialist state leading an international bloc, some advanced countries would before long fuse with the backward countries in a socialist federation. Even in an international bloc led by capitalist imperialist countries into which backward countries are absorbed and where they are forced to cooperate in every respect with the leading countries, even under that sort of unequal cooperation, the working people of the backward countries and the leading countries would get the chance to unite with one another, leading to a huge concentration of the oppressed, a force brought into being by the imperialist robbers that will lead eventually to their own downfall. No nationalist hero will be capable of holding up this new trend towards the formation of international blocs. As for the oppressed peoples, only if they know how best to accommodate to this new trend will they have a future.

Those who raise the second sort of objection have been befuddled by the theories of the Second International.[2] The project of the Second International

---

1 The Atlantic Charter was drawn up by Franklin ID. Roosevelt and Winston Churchill in August 1941 as a joint statement of principles for which to fight the war and on which to base the peace; it was a first step towards founding the United Nations. The Pacific Charter was either a projected Pacific version of the same thing, thought up in Chongqing or Washington, or Chen's rhetorical invention.

2 The Second International (1889–1914), though never a uniform, centralised organisation like the Third, was dominated by the figure of Karl Kautsky, who transformed Social Democracy into a movement of reform on which revolutionary slogans were mere ornaments. At first

is to pursue a reform campaign within the confines of bourgeois rule; being one of the props of imperialism, it has paid no attention to the question of the liberation of the oppressed nations. A true socialist movement wishes to overthrow international capitalist imperialism root and branch. That is why, ever since the First International, 'the liberation of the oppressed toiling peoples' and 'the liberation of the oppressed nations' have been the two banners of this movement.[3] Once socialist revolution succeeds, as long as it does not change colour in mid path it will be unable to coexist for long with the system of commodity and money. When such a time arrives, will there still be oppressed peoples? This is not just a theory, but was the actual experience of Russia's October Revolution. The October Revolution was the achievement of the overwhelming majority of the Russian people united under the three great banners of the Communist Party: 'liberate the toilers', 'liberate the peasants', and 'liberate small nations'. After the victory of the revolution, each of these three slogans was realised: they were not just dud cheques issued by the Russian Communists. What's more, the voluntary abolition was proclaimed of all unequal treaties forced on other countries during the Tsarist period. One by one the Communists announced the relinquishment in oppressed countries of Tsarist privileges such as settlements and consular jurisdiction.[4] As a result, working people and oppressed nations throughout the world came to see Moscow as a beacon for the oppressed peoples of the world, and as the general headquarters of the world revolutionary movement. If some people, on the basis of recent Soviet policies towards the Sino-Japanese War and, at the start of the conflict, towards Poland and Hitler, are sceptical about the attitude of socialist countries to the liberation struggle of oppressed peoples, that's because they are confused! There is a world of difference between the Soviet Union of the early days, which we support and others defame, and that of the latter period, which they flatter and we deplore. The Soviet Union of the early period stood on the side of world revolution; of the latter period, on that of Russian national interest. Since then, the Soviet leaders, in view of the

---

the Second International opposed militarism and espoused internationalism, but when war came in 1914, most socialist parties obeyed the call of the fatherland; the Second International collapsed, and Lenin decided that the time had come to found the Third.

3 'The problem of the liberation of the oppressed nations' was raised by Lenin and the Third International. Marx' slogan was 'Workers of all countries, unite!' Lenin's was 'Workers of all countries and oppressed nations of the world, unite!'

4 That is, of extraterritoriality. On 25 July 1919, the Soviet Government in Russia declared the abolition of the unequal treaties signed between Tsarist Russia and China and the privileges enjoyed by Russia in China (though in practice it hung on for a while to some of them).

setback of the revolution in Western Europe, have turned their coats when midway towards their goal and switched their main focus from world revolution to defending Russia's national interest; as a result, perceptive people everywhere have gradually become sceptical and finally disillusioned, so that by now, although people in their heart of hearts still cherish some measure of hope for the Soviet Union, in reality they have no choice but to admit that it is simply one among the world powers. Anyone who continues to insist that the Soviet Union is a socialist country can only do so by perverting the very meaning of socialism! Were Russia today still abiding by its old position of international socialism, then once war broke out between China and Japan, it would have supported China with all its might, that is, not like Britain and America, who back China in a detached sort of way, but as if the responsibility for leading China's resistance against Japan were Russia's own, by committing troops to take part in the war, by living or dying together with the Chinese people. This would be the only truly internationalist standpoint; no other standpoint would befit a truly leading nation! Had that happened, Japan would have found it harder to occupy Shanghai and Nanjing. If Moscow had stopped appeasing Japan at the very start of the Sino-Japanese War or, at the very least, after the outbreak of clashes between the Red Army and the [Japanese-backed Chinese army] at Zhanggufeng,[5] Wuhan would not have fallen. And had China and Russia continued to resist shoulder to shoulder to this day, Japan would have been in no position to rampage through Southeast Asia and to devastate a whole number of small, weak nations such as the Philippines, Malaya, Java, and Burma! When the Nazis invaded Poland, if the Soviet Union had still stood on an international socialist position it would not have compromised with Hitler and would not have described the role of representative democracy and the great cause of leading all oppressed and invaded nations to fight against the Fascist offensive as pulling the chest-nuts from the fire for someone else, and it would have been even less likely to gang up with the Fascists to divide Poland! At that time, the British, French, and Belgian allied army had not yet disintegrated, and Hitler had not yet convinced himself that he was capable of simultaneously winning victory on the Eastern and the Western fronts. Only

---

5   In late July and early August 1938, Japanese troops provoked Soviet troops at Zhanggufeng on the border between China, Korea, and the Soviet Union. The Japanese were defeated, and sued for peace. On 11 August in Moscow, both sides agreed that a mixed commission of two Soviets and two representatives of Japan and the Japanese puppet régime of 'Manchukuo' would investigate and settle the border question in the region. The Zhanggufeng Incident at first gave heart to some Chinese, who thought that a Soviet-Japanese War would break out and enable China to go onto the counter-offensive against Japan.

after the defeat of isolated Poland and the absence of any further problems in the Eastern battle theatre did Hitler have the strength to rout the British, French, and Belgians and to vanquish a host of small nations such as Norway, Holland, Denmark, Yugoslavia, and Greece.

These historical stories alone, which show how the different positions taken by Russia in its earlier and later days brought different results, are quite enough for us to understand the relationship between international socialism and the oppressed nations.

Given that, in European terms, Russia is itself after all a relatively backward nation, what will be the outcome of its whole policy on the national problem? In order to protect itself, Russia substituted a policy of compromising with Fascism for one of attacking it; as a result, the war in Russia began not when Hitler was isolated in Europe but after Hitler had routed the European nations. Hitler has occupied not only half of Poland and the three Baltic countries, which had been offered to Russia as the price of Russian compromise with Fascism, but also most of European Russia. But for the help of Britain and America, even Moscow might by now have fallen. In the interests of its own security, Russia has all along avoided going to war against Japan, so that even the CCP has been accused of 'roving around without fighting.[6] The result is, despite Russia's standby attitude, that Japan will still help Hitler attack Russia tomorrow, thus plunging the Russian people into a state of great insecurity. When that time comes, Russia will miss the support of China, having sat back and watched while Japan crippled China. So any backward nation that confines its policy entirely to one of the pursuit of national interest will inevitably become isolated and bereft of any future, for a national policy is in reality a policy of isolation. This goes for Soviet Russia too.

13 May 1942[7]

---

6   A pun, directed by the Guomindang against the Communists, on *youji*, 'guerrilla warfare', literally 'to rove and attack'.
7   Fourteen days before Chen's death.

My Feelings on the Death of Mr Cai Jiemin

Chen Duxiu

This obituary was added by Hu Shi or his friends in Taiwan to the Free China Press edition of Chen Duxiu's last writings; it is absent from the original Shanghai edition. Cai Jiemin is another name of Cai Yuanpei (Ts'ai Yuan-p'ei) (1868–1940), who was a member of the Shanghai group of terrorist assassins (which Chen Duxiu briefly joined) and a supporter of Russian nihilism before he joined the Guomindang, of which he became a veteran leader. Cai was China's most outstanding liberal educationalist. He sponsored the May Fourth (or New Culture Movement) around 1919 in his capacity (between 1916 and 1926) as Chancellor of Beijing University. He founded and became President of the Academia Sinica. Source: Zhuanji wenxue zazhi she (eds), 1967, pp. 123–7.

'Who since ancient times has not died?'[1] Life is short, and death counts for little, yet I cannot help but grieve the death of Cai Jiemin, not only because of his contribution to the public weal, but also on account of the personal relationship between us! Thoughts and feelings about society and politics over the last forty years!

The first time I collaborated with Mr Cai was in the last years of the Guangxu reign [1875–1908] of the Qing dynasty. In those days, Yang Dusheng, He Haiqiao, Zhang Xingyan,[2] and others in Shanghai launched an organisation committed to studying the use of explosives in a projected campaign of assassination. Xingyan wrote a letter inviting me to join, and once I had reached Shanghai from Anhui, I did so. I stayed in Shanghai for more than a month, and each day I experimented together with Yang Dusheng and Zhong Xianchang[3] in manufacturing explosives. Mr Cai too used to attend frequently in order to conduct experiments and get together for a chat. The second time I collaborated with

---

1 A line from a poem by Wen Tianxiang, a national hero and poet captured by the Mongol army and finally put to death because he refused to serve the new Yuan dynasty. The following line says, 'Let my red heart glitter in history'.
2 Zhang Xingyan (1872–1973) (another name of Zhang Shizhao) achieved fame as a journalist, writer, and politician. He was one of Chen Duxiu's old friends, but his politics were extremely unstable. He changed from a radical into a conservative, and from a cabinet minister in a warlord's government into an admirer and supporter of Mao Zedong.
3 A member of the Shanghai terrorist group.

Mr Cai was from 1916 to 1918, at Beijing University. That period of joint activity lasted relatively long, and I got to know him much better.

Generally speaking, Mr Cai was a benign and uncontentious person, a lovable man who would offend no one. Sometimes, however, when his moral integrity or some matter of principle was at stake or when he had already resolved on a certain course of action, he became stubborn and unbending and was no longer prepared to accommodate others, even though he continued to adopt a mild and gentle attitude. That was the first thing that caused people to admire the old gentleman. After the Reform Movement of 1898,[4] Mr Cai himself often inclined towards the new progressive movement, but while he was President of Beijing University, he employed all sorts of people whose scholarship he admired: not only [radicals like] Hu Shi, Qian Xuantong,[5] and Chen Duxiu, but conservatives like Chen Hanzhang and Huang Kan[6] and even people such as Gu Hongming[7] (who wanted to restore the Qing) and Liu Shipei[8] (who participated in the Hongxian movement[9]). Such magnanimous toleration of dissident and alien viewpoints and respect for academic freedom

---

4 The Reform Movement, inaugurated by Kang Youwei in 1895 and supported by Liang Qichao, Tan Sitong, and other leading thinkers, advocated the transformation of Confucianism into a religious movement, to provide the basis for modernising the state and the education system and for establishing representative institutions. It came to an abrupt end in 1898, when the reactionary Empress Dowager, Cixi, carried out a coup against Kang and his supporters.

5 Qian Xuantong (Ch'ien Hsüan-t'ung) (1887–1939) became an anti-Manchu revolutionary in 1903 and later leaned to anarchism. He taught linguistics at Beijing University. During and after the May Fourth period, he played an important role in reforming written Chinese and in propagating the new culture in general. In some respects he went even further than Chen Duxiu and Hu Shi. Later on, however, he devoted himself entirely to the study of ancient Chinese history.

6 Huang Kan (Huang K'an) (1886–1935) was a leading disciple of Zhang Binglin (1868–1936), the famous classical scholar and revolutionary; in 1915 he recommended Qian Xuantong to Beijing University.

7 Gu Hongming (Ku Hung-ming) (1857–1928), born of Chinese ancestors in Penang, Malaya, was known as an 'imitation Western man'; he was fluent in several European languages but not in Chinese. He wore a queue and hated both foreign colonialism and Chinese republicanism.

8 Liu Shipei (Liu Shih-p'ei) (1884–1919) was an early Chinese advocate (in Japan) of socialism. At first he was an anti-Manchu revolutionary. Later he became a conservative literary man and favoured the restoration of the monarchy in China.

9 In August 1915, Yuan Shikai, president of the newly established Chinese Republic, launched a movement to restore the monarchy, with himself as emperor. He announced as his reign title 'Grand Constitutional Era' (*hongxian*), which was to begin with 1916. Within six months, Yuan was discountenanced and dead; his Hongxian dynasty lasted a mere one hundred days.

of thought is rare among Oriental people, who are accustomed to despotism and respect only what is orthodox. That is the second thing that caused people to admire the old gentleman even more.

Now that Mr Cai is no longer with us, his friends, his students, and all those who recall him should bear in mind these two virtues!

After Mr Cai passed away, an old fellow-student of mine at Beijing University wrote asking me to compose an obituary for Cai, to be published in a special issue dedicated to Cai's death, and added: 'Ever since May Fourth,[10] some people have recommended the casting aside of national essence and morality. Perhaps in your essay you can show how that is wrong and indicate the right path'.

On this question, my opinion is as follows. All peoples worthy of the name have their culture, or their national essence; in the great furnace of world cultures, the culture of each people, insofar as it is of value, that is, insofar as it can be called national 'essence' rather than national 'dregs', is not easy to melt down. Even if a people becomes extinct, its culture may live on. The question is whether a national culture is preserved in the hands of the nation itself. If a people becomes extinct, or even if it is not yet extinct, and its culture or national essence is preserved by the people of another nation, that is truly catastrophic. Only in this sense does 'preserving the national essence' have meaning. If some people view national culture in isolation from world culture and national essence in isolation from world learning, and with closed eyes extol themselves and deprecate everything foreign, shutting the city gates to keep out foreign science, even to the point of refusing to use foreign scientific methods as a tool for sorting out Chinese knowledge, then all our learning will have lost the advantage of comparative study; it will be impossible to choose the best of it and expound it comprehensively. Those who embrace as national 'essence' what are in effect national 'dregs' and who advocate reading aloud

---

10   In 1914, Japan seized German-controlled territory in Shandong. In 1917, Britain, France, and Italy secretly agreed to support Japan's claim to this territory, and in 1918 the Government in Beijing secretly acquiesced in this decision; in 1919, the Paris Peace Conference agreed to transfer German rights in China to Japan. On 4 May 1919, three thousand students demonstrated in Beijing against this 'national betrayal', and in the course of the demonstration beat a pro-Japanese official. There followed a nationwide movement of strikes, lecture-strikes, and anti-Japanese boycotts. On 28 June, the Beijing Government gave in to the protest movement and refused to sign the Peace Treaty with Germany. So the May Fourth Movement in its narrowest sense had been brought to a successful end. In its broadest sense, May Fourth was a movement of cultural renewal and revolution that lasted roughly from 1917 to 1921.

from the Confucian classics while remaining wholly ignorant of the textual knowledge and real meaning contained in them are truly frightful!

In human society, besides law, morality is an indispensable cement. Those who fundamentally deny morality, whatever class or party they belong to, are shamelessly wicked and base-minded. However, morals, unlike truth, were formed to meet social needs, and are bounded by time and space. What this person sees as moral, that person may not; what people in the past saw as moral, people today may not. For example, widow burning was considered moral in old India, but not in China, where widows were expected to live chastely after the death of their husband. A widow who remarried was considered immoral in China but not in the West, and even in China today it is no longer considered as something extremely bad. To kill a person is the most immoral thing of all, but in battle he who kills or wounds the greatest number of people is a hero. Stories about burying the living along with the dead and cutting off pieces of one's own flesh[11] as an act of loyalty or filial piety used to be told with approval. The idea, imported to China from the West, of equal rights for men and women was naturally highly incompatible with China's ancient morality, that is, the ethical code of Confucianism; even so, members of today's Chinese gentry no longer publicly defend to the death the old system of morality. As a matter of fact, to practise equal rights between men and women, the virtue of self-restraint is necessary on the part of the men. In short, morals change according to the age and the social system; they are not immutable and frozen. Morality is a form of self-discipline and not an obligation that you simply impose on others. It requires that you practise what you preach; it should not be empty verbiage designed for the purposes of self-glorification. The louder people shout about morality in a society, the more backward and degenerate that society will be. On the other hand, the personal conduct of the great scientists of the West is no worse than that of the sanctimonious priests and pastors, while that of the philologists[12] of the Qing dynasty was much better and more honest than the ethical intentions of moralists like Tang Bin[13] and Li Guangdi.[14] As for Mr Cai, he proposed replacing religion with aesthetic education. He opposed

---

11 A so-called 'filial son' would cut small pieces of flesh from his arm or leg, mix them with medicinal herbs, boil the mixture, and serve it to his ailing parents as a drink.

12 *Puxue*, a scholastic tendency devoted to philological research, mainly into the Chinese classics, and spurning speculative philosophy supposedly based on those classics.

13 Tang Bin (T'ang Pin) (1627–87) was an orthodox early Qing Confucian.

14 Li Guangdi (Li Kuang-ti) (1642–1718) aspired to be known as a follower of the Song philosophers, though he was accused of paying more attention in practice to his career than to the Confucian dictate of filial piety.

the worship of Confucius and he never preached morality, but his moral quality far surpassed that of many of those who constantly go on about morality.

This is not just my personal opinion. I daresay that on these two questions my position is more or less identical with that of Mr Cai and Mr Hu Shizhi. Shizhi is still alive. If you don't believe that our views are more or less identical, you can go and ask him. And anyone intimately acquainted with Mr Cai's words and actions will know that what I have said about him is not mere rubbish.

The May Fourth Movement was an inevitable product of the contemporary development of Chinese society. Whether one views it as an achievement or as cause for blame, it should not simply be attributed to those few people. However, Mr Cai, Shizhi, and I were principally responsible in those days for articulating intellectual opinion, and since the public has raised doubts about important questions, in the absence of Shizhi (who is abroad),[15] I – as the sole survivor still resident in China – have no choice but to venture a few passing comments in this brief essay for the public of today and of tomorrow, and in commemoration of Mr Cai![16]

---

15   Hu Shi was Chinese Ambassador to the USA from 1938 to 1942.
16   The original text can be found in *Central Daily News,* Chongqing, 24 March 1940 (note by Hu Shi).

On Chen Duxiu's Last Views

Shuang (Wang Fanxi) Shan

Between 1936 and 1938 and again in late 1939 or early 1940, the Trotskyist Wang Fanxi had a vigorous exchange of views with Chen Duxiu on the issue of democracy. Sometime in 1936, Chen Duxiu, then in prison, smuggled out an article on democracy to the Trotskyists in Shanghai, where Wang published it in Huohua ('Spark') together with his own critical comments. Three or four years later, Wang again discussed this same question with Chen, by then in Sichuan, in letters that he wrote to him from Shanghai. Chen's view, expressed in his last letters and articles, that Lenin had fathered Stalinism, and Chen's rejection of dictatorship of any sort, revolutionary or counter-revolutionary, alienated his Trotskyist comrades, who believed (as orthodox Leninists) in a dictatorship of the workers. Wang's replies to Chen in Spark and the letters he wrote to him before Chen died have apparently been lost, but in an article written in Macao in 1957, Wang summarised in seven points positions derived from those that he had developed in his last exchanges with Chen. Wang's seven theses show that far from rejecting Chen's criticism outright, he strove to incorporate its insights into his own political thinking and to reconcile the idea of checks and balances, political pluralism, and democratic rights with the need for violent revolution and proletarian dictatorship. Source: Shuang Shan 1957.

1. Under present historical conditions, if the proletariat through its political party aims to overthrow the political and economic rule of the bourgeoisie, it must carry out a violent revolution and set up a dictatorship to expropriate the expropriators. So in nine cases out of ten it is bound to destroy the bourgeoisie's traditional means of rule – the parliamentary system. To complete such a transformation 'peacefully', through parliament, is practically if not absolutely impossible.
2. A proletarian dictatorship set up in such a way neither must nor should destroy the various democratic rights – including habeus corpus; freedom of speech, the press, assembly, and association; the right to strike; and so on and so forth – already won by the people under the bourgeois democratic system.
3. The organs of the dictatorship elected by the entire toiling people should be under the thorough-going supervision of the electors and recallable by them at all times; and the power of the dictatorship should not be concentrated in one body but should be spread across several structures so

that there is a system of checks and balances to prevent the emergence of an autocracy or monocracy.
4. Opposition parties should be allowed to exist under the dictatorship as long as they support the revolution. Whether they meet this condition should be decided by the workers and peasants in free ballot.
5. Opposition factions must be tolerated within the party of the proletariat. Under no circumstances must organisational sanctions, secret service measures, or incriminatory sanctions be used to deal with dissidents; under no circumstances must thought be made a crime.
6. Under no circumstances must proletarian dictatorship become the dictatorship of a single party. Workers' parties organised by part of the working class and the intelligentsia must under no circumstances replace the political power democratically elected by the toilers as a whole. There must be an end to the present system in the Communist countries, where government is a facade behind which secretaries of the party branches assume direct command. The ruling party's strategic policies must first be discussed and approved by an empowered parliament (or soviet) that includes opposition parties and factions, and only then should they be implemented by government; and their implementation must continue to be supervised by parliament.
7. Finally, ... since political democracy is actually a reflection of economic democracy and no political democracy is possible under a system of absolutely centralised economic control, ... to create the material base for socialist democracy a system of divided power and self-management within the overall planned economy is essential.

All these points are not in themselves enough to save a revolutionary power from bureaucratic degeneration; but since they are not plucked from the void but rooted in bloody experience, they should – if formulated with sufficient clarity – (a) help workers and peasants in countries that have had revolutions to win their anti-bureaucratic struggle when the conditions for the democratisation of the dictatorial state have further ripened; and (b) enable new revolutionary states from the very outset to avoid bureaucratic poisoning.

PART 9

*Peng Shuzhi and Wang Fanxi
on Leon Trotsky*

∴

Introduction to *Leon Trotsky on China*

Peng Shuzhi

(26 April 1974)

This is Peng Shuzhi's introduction to Leon Trotsky on China, *published in 1976 by Monad Press in New York and edited by Les Evans and Russell Block. The introduction was translated by Joseph T. Miller and Hui-fang Miller. It has here been slightly shortened.*

It is hard to overestimate Trotsky's contribution to understanding the revolution in China. Even though the second Chinese revolution was defeated as a result of Stalin's opportunistic leadership, Trotsky's views on it were proved correct. In this way, Trotsky expanded upon the lessons of the October revolution. Just as in 1917 in Russia, there were two irreconcilable political lines in the second Chinese revolution. Trotsky represented the Bolshevik line, Stalin the Menshevik. In Russia, the Bolshevik line triumphed, bringing about the victory of October 1917: in China, the Menshevik line of the Stalinist bureaucracy brought defeat. This defeat, no less than the success in Russia, served as a lesson for China, the colonial and semi-colonial countries, and the advanced capitalist countries. As Trotsky wrote:

> A study of the Chinese revolution is a most important and urgent matter for every communist and every advanced worker. It is not possible to talk seriously in any country about the struggle of the proletariat for power without a study by the proletarian vanguard of the fundamental events, motive forces, and strategic methods of the Chinese revolution. It is not possible to understand what day is without knowing what night is; to understand what summer is without experiencing winter. *In the same way, it is not possible to understand the meaning of the methods of the October uprising without a study of the methods of the Chinese catastrophe* ['A History of the Second Chinese Revolution Is Needed' (published September 1930), emphasis added].

1   The Bolshevism of the Early CCP

Trotsky's systematic presentation of his views on the Chinese revolution did not begin until 30 August 1926, in a letter to Karl Radek. Even though he stated that in 1923 he was 'resolutely opposed to the Communist Party joining the Guomindang' and in 1926 he 'once more presented the formal proposal that the Communist Party leave the Guomindang instantly' (letter to Max Shachtman, 10 December 1930), we have no copy of his 'formal proposal'. So it is difficult to discuss Trotsky's views about China before August 1926, especially regarding the CCP's response to Comintern policies. It is necessary to look deeper into the historical background of the Chinese communist movement to gain a better understanding of Trotsky's contribution.

The first Communist group (CG) in China was established in Shanghai in May 1920 with the help of Grigori Voitinsky, the first representative sent to China by the Comintern. It faced three urgent tasks: to recruit and train cadres, organise unions, and spread communist ideas. Communist parties in the West were established by people who left Social Democratic parties. China was different. China had to start from scratch, having no Marxist tradition or modern unions. Two months after the Shanghai group, a Socialist Youth Corps (SYC) was founded and recruited communists to study in Moscow. Beginning in August 1920, the CG published *The Labourer*, to spread communist ideas and develop unions. *New Youth*, edited by Chen Duxiu, became its organ. In November, the CG published a clandestine monthly, *The Communist*, which introduced Bolshevik ideas and writings about communist movements in other countries. Both *New Youth* and *The Communist* criticised anarchist thought (quite widespread among radical youth) and the opportunism of the Second International, while advocating proletarian dictatorship. Other communist groups were set up in Beijing, Wuhan, Changsha, Guangzhou, and Jinan. This was the foundation upon which the CCP was established in July 1921.

Chen Duxiu was unable to attend this inaugural congress of the CCP, so only a resolution setting up a Bolshevik-style party was passed. There were no other definite decisions on political matters. However, a secretariat for organising the labour movement was established. Plans were made to further the workers' movement in the industrial centres, mines, and railroads by organising unions and leading struggles. In 1921–2, the CCP led strikes and won some victories. The Secretariat called the First National Labour Congress in May 1922 in Guangzhou. Those attending represented 230,000 organised workers. In one short year the CCP had become the centre of the working-class movement At the same time, the CCP leadership, headed by Chen Duxiu, received help from Voitinsky, the Comintern representative. (Voitinsky introduced the CCP to the fundamentals of Bolshevism and Lenin's views on national democratic revolution.) In the spring of 1922, the CCP determined its strategic line towards China's national democratic revolution. It was expressed in the 'Manifesto of the Second Congress':

> The proletariat's support of the democratic revolution is not (equivalent to) its surrender to the capitalists. Not to prolong the life of the feudal system is absolutely necessary in order to raise the power of the proletariat. This is the proletariat's own class interest.... The CCP is the party of the proletariat. Its aims are to organise the proletariat and to struggle for the dictatorship of the workers and peasants, the abolition of private property, and the gradual attainment of a Communist society. *At present the CCP must, in the interest of the workers and poor peasants, lead the workers to support the democratic revolution and forge a democratic united front of workers, poor peasants, and petty bourgeoisie* [Brandt, Schwartz and Fairbank (eds), 1967, pp. 63–4, emphasis added].

The CCP's objectives included 'the overthrow of military cliques, and the establishment of internal peace ..., the removal of oppression by international imperialism and the complete independence of the Chinese nation ..., a free federation [of China proper with Tibet, Mongolia, and Xinjiang, and] ... legislation for workers, peasants, and women'. The manifesto pointed out that the objectives

> are all in the interests of the workers, peasants, and petty bourgeoisie and are prerequisites for their liberation.... The workers and poor peasants will flock to the banner of (our) Party and the petty bourgeoisie will also link up with us. However, *the workers must not become the appendage of the petty bourgeoisie within this democratic united front, but must fight for their own class interests. Therefore it is imperative that the workers be organised in the Party as well as in labour unions. Ever mindful of their class independence, the workers must develop the strength of their fighting organisation (in order to) prepare for the establishment of soviets in conjunction with the poor peasantry and in order to achieve (the goal of) complete liberation.... The Party calls on the Chinese workers and peasants to rush to its banner....* Only an alliance of the world proletariat and oppressed peoples can liberate the world [Brandt, Schwartz and Fairbank, eds, 1967, p. 65, emphasis added].

This was the CCP's first programmatic document regarding the Chinese revolution. It points out that workers must be 'mindful of their class independence' and 'prepare for the establishment of soviets in conjunction with the poor peasantry ... to achieve complete liberation'. This is the same as Lenin's 'Draft Theses on the National and Colonial Questions' at the Second Comintern Congress in July 1920.... At the close of the Second Congress of the CCP, the

Central Committee issued the 'First Manifesto of the CCP on the Current Situation':

> The CP takes the initiative in calling a conference, to be participated in by the revolutionary elements of the Guomindang and revolutionary socialists, to discuss the question of creating a united front for struggle against warlords of the feudal type and against all relics of feudalism. This struggle along a broad united front is a war to liberate the Chinese people from a dual yoke – the yoke of foreigners and the yoke of powerful militarists in our country – a war which is just as urgently needed as it is inevitable [Brandt, Schwartz and Fairbank (eds) 1967, p. 63].

This call for 'a united front' of 'revolutionary elements of the Guomindang and revolutionary socialists' did not deviate from Lenin's idea of 'a temporary alliance with bourgeois democracy'. Through this strategy, the CCP could maintain its independence and 'develop the strength of their fighting organisation to prepare for the establishment of soviets in conjunction with the poor peasantry and to achieve complete liberation'. This was the early CCP's policy.

2   Repression of the CCP and the Turn Towards Menshevism

Just as the CCP was determining its policy, the Comintern made an about turn, reflected in the instructions brought by its representative Maring (alias Sneevliet). In August 1922, after meeting with Sun Yat-sen, Maring told the CCP Central Committee that members should join the Guomindang as individuals and collaborate with it to advance the national revolutionary movement. Those at the meeting opposed this proposal, for the Guomindang represents the bourgeoisie and the CCP represents the proletariat, so a merger was out of the question; and this type of multiclass organisation could only obstruct the CCP's independence. Maring, however, raised the question of Comintern discipline. So the Central Committee agreed to the proposal, but on condition that it was discussed by the party and a decision was made at the Third Congress.

The branches debated whether or not to join the Guomindang. The strongest opposition came from the workers' movement. According to Chen Duxiu, before he went to Moscow in 1922 for the Fourth Comintern Congress, he still had doubts about requiring members to join the Guomindang. Because of this, the Comintern leaders watched him closely. Radek even made a public criticism, saying the CCP's task was to 'bring the workers into a rational relationship with the objectively revolutionary elements of the bourgeoisie' (Brandt, Schwartz and Fairbank, eds, 1967, p. 53).

Given the opposition by CCP cadres to joining the Guomindang, the chairman of the Comintern, Zinoviev, formally raised the question for discussion in the Russian Communist Party (RCP) Politburo in January 1923. Except for Trotsky, all the others, such as Stalin, Zinoviev, and Bukharin, approved CCP members joining the Guomindang. Zinoviev wrote a resolution on CCP Guomindang collaboration, dated 12 January 1923, and adopted by the Executive Committee of the Comintern (ECCI):

> 1. The only serious national-revolutionary group in China is the Guomindang, which is based partly on the liberal-democratic bourgeoisie and petty bourgeoisie, partly on the intelligentsia and workers.
> 2. Since the independent workers' movement in the country is still weak, and since the central task for China is the national revolution against the imperialists and their feudal agents within the country, and since, moreover, the working class is directly interested in the solution of this national-revolutionary problem, while still being insufficiently differentiated as a wholly independent social force, the ECCI considers that action between the Guomindang and the young CCP should be co-ordinated.
> 3. Consequently in present conditions it is expedient for members of the CCP to remain in the Guomindang [Degras 1960, pp. 5–6].

The Comintern recognised the Guomindang as 'the only serious national-revolutionary group in China' and ordered 'members of the CCP to remain in the Guomindang' with its base in 'the liberal-democratic bourgeoisie'. The party of the proletariat was thus placed under the control of the party of the bourgeoisie, in direct opposition to the stand of the Bolsheviks towards the 'liberal-democratic bourgeoisie' and Lenin's views as expressed in the 'Draft Theses on the National and Colonial Questions'. This Menshevik line led to the tragedy of the Chinese revolution.

The Soviet government sent Adolf Joffe to negotiate directly with Sun Yat-sen regarding cooperation and Soviet aid to the Guomindang. On 26 January 1923, a 'Joint Manifesto of Sun Yat-sen and A. A. Joffe' said:

> Dr Sun is of the opinion that, because of the non-existence of conditions favourable to their successful application in China, it is not possible to carry out either Communism or even the soviet system in China. M. Joffe agrees entirely with this view; he is further of the opinion that China's most important and most pressing problems are the completion

of national unification and the attainment of full national independence. With regard to these great tasks, M. Joffe has assured Dr Sun of the Russian people's warmest sympathy for China, and of (their) willingness to lend support [Brandt, Schwartz and Fairbank (eds) 1967, p. 70].

Sun's feelings that 'it is not possible to carry out either Communism or even the soviet system in China' are a candid expression of his bourgeois views. Joffe, the Soviet representative, openly 'agrees entirely with this view' and promised Soviet 'support' for Sun to complete 'national unification' and full 'national independence'. The CCP was left with one task: follow the lead of Soviet policy in support of the Guomindang efforts to attain 'national unification' and 'national independence'. This was the concrete manifestation of the 12 January 1923 Comintern resolution, and, it goes without saying, it was carried out in accordance with Stalin's directions.

Following the Comintern resolution and the Joint Manifesto of 26 January 1923, the CCP called its Third Congress in June 1923. The Comintern representative was, again, Maring. Even though there was sharp debate at this congress, the authority of the Soviet government and the Comintern caused most delegates to approve the resolution calling for CCP members to join the Guomindang. Its main points were:

> *The Guomindang should be the central force of the national revolution and should assume its leadership.* Unfortunately, however, the Guomindang often suffers from two erroneous notions. Firstly, it relies on foreign powers for help.... Secondly, it concentrates all its efforts on military action, neglecting propaganda work.... We *still hope that all the revolutionary elements in our society will rally to the Guomindang, speeding the completion of the national revolutionary movement* [and] the Guomindang will discard reliance on foreign powers and concentration on military action and *will pay attention to political propaganda among the people – never missing an opportunity for (such) propaganda in order to create a true central force for the national welfare and a true leadership for the national revolution* [Brandt, Schwartz and Fairbank, eds, 1967, pp. 71–72, emphasis added].

The CCP had gone from Bolshevism into the mire of Menshevism. It was even worse off than the Russian Mensheviks: at least they retained their independence and did not have to join the Constitutional Democrats, whereas the CCP had to join the party of the Chinese bourgeoisie. The source of this change was the degeneration of the Soviet Communist Party and Comintern leadership. Following Lenin's illness in May 1922, Stalin, together with Zinoviev and Kamenev, formed a small group within the Politburo whose main objective was to get rid of Trotsky (they feared his assuming a leadership position following Lenin's death). Their foreign policy in China was based on maintaining cooperation with the 'democratic faction' of the bourgeoisie. Because of this, the Comintern ordered the CCP to join the Guomindang in August 1922 (not yet three months after Lenin fell ill).

Following the approval of this policy at the CCP's Third Congress, some CCP leaders, to find 'theoretical' justification for joining the Guomindang, exaggerated the bourgeoisie's revolutionary character. The initial advocate of this work was Mao Zedong. Newly elected to the Central Committee at the Third Congress, he submitted an article to *Xiangdao* (Guide Weekly) that argued:

> The present political problem in China is none other than the problem of the national revolution. To use the strength of the people to overthrow the militarists and foreign imperialism, with which the former are in collusion to accomplish their treasonable acts, is the historic mission of the Chinese people. This revolution is the task of the people as a whole. The merchants, workers, peasants, students, and teachers should all come forward to take on the responsibility for a portion of the revolutionary work; but *because of historical necessity and current tendencies, the work for which the merchants should be responsible in the national revolution is more urgent and important than the work the rest of the people should take upon themselves.* We know that the politics of semi-colonial China is characterised by the fact that the militarists and the foreign powers have banded together to impose a twofold oppression on the people of the whole country. The people of the whole country suffer profoundly under this twofold oppression. *Nevertheless the merchants are the ones who feel these sufferings most acutely and most urgently* [Schram, ed., 1963, pp. 206–7, emphasis added].

'The merchants feel these sufferings most acutely', so their work in the national revolution 'is both more urgent and more important'. Mao concluded:

> The Shanghai merchants have risen and begun to act. We hope the merchants outside Shanghai will rise up and act together.... The broader the organisation of merchants, the greater will be their influence, *the greater*

will be their ability to lead the people of the whole country, and the more rapid the success of the revolution! [Schram (ed.) 1963, p. 208, emphasis added].

Mao's 'hope' that the 'success of the revolution' lay in the merchants' 'ability to lead the people of the whole country' was the basest form of Menshevism.

After Chen Duxiu received notice of the resolution approved by the Comintern on 12 January 1923 calling for CCP members to join the Guomindang, and due to the 'February Seventh Incident', when railroad workers were attacked, he started to retrench on his original opposition to uniting with the bourgeoisie. He argued that 'co-operation with the revolutionary bourgeoisie is the necessary road for the Chinese proletariat' (Isaacs 1961, p. 59; *Xiangdao*, 23 April 1923). On 1 December 1923, he said the bourgeoisie had the greatest influence and the working class had little power in numbers and was poor and ignorant, so it was impossible to expect workers to lead the national revolution. This revolution was bourgeois, so the workers must cooperate with the bourgeoisie to successfully complete the national revolution.

Chen Duxiu said 'the working class cannot lead the revolution, but must cooperate with the bourgeoisie. Only then can they complete the national revolution'. Mao said the merchants 'feel these sufferings most acutely and most urgently', and, thus have the 'ability to lead the people of the whole country' to a quicker 'success of the revolution'. These are manifestations of the same Menshevik thinking.

Another new Central Committee member, Qu Qiubai, wrote an article titled 'Reform of the Guomindang and the National Revolutionary Movement', which appeared in the 19 December 1923 issue of *Xiangdao*. It said:

> The author of the 1911 revolution was the Guomindang, and it has been working hard for many years despite hardships and criticisms. It was the Guomindang that fought for the rights of the common people in opposition to the Beiyang militarists.... (1) Since then, the political movement of the common people and military revolutionary activity have both advanced; (2) a mass, democratic party has been organised and corrupt elements have been purged; (3) strict discipline has been established, along with an organised, systematic national movement which always represents the common people.... *At present the Guomindang is the centre of power. The only way we can throw off oppression by the great powers and the militarists and establish our own true, common people's republic, a truly independent nation, is to develop the common people's own party.... This is our Guomindang. We must participate, merchants, peasants, workers, students, and teachers, all who belong to the common people should join the Guomindang.*

Concretising Mao's and Chen's illusions, Qu Qiubai expressed his own petty-bourgeois mentality. These views were shared by all CCP leaders. The Guomindang 'is the common people's own party' and 'the centre of power', so through this 'centre' it is possible to 'throw off oppression by the great powers and the militarists and establish our own true common people's republic'. Qu concluded that 'all work should go towards building the Guomindang'.

From the Third Congress on, the Central Committee made all party and SYC members join the Guomindang, help reorganise the Guomindang, and participate in Guomindang work. Mao Zedong put all his time into propaganda work for the Guomindang and abandoned work for his own party. Tan Pingshan specialised in working for the Guomindang's organisational department in its Central Committee. In Hunan, Hubei, Sichuan, Beijing, and Tianjin, CCP cadres worked hard to reorganise the Guomindang. Li Lisan, Xiang Ying, Deng Zhongxia, and others, originally cadres in the labour movement, left to 'reorganise' the Guomindang. The labour movement was forgotten, even to the point of disbanding the CCP's labour secretariat!

The RCP sent Mikhail Borodin to Guangzhou in the autumn of 1923 to act as Sun Yat-sen's adviser and help reorganise the Guomindang. Borodin introduced the Guomindang to RCP-style party organisation to turn it into 'the centre of power', a party in which 'strict discipline has been established'. He developed a programme for it utilising abstract phrases like 'equalisation of land rights' and 'restriction of private capital' to prettify its reactionary nature. In January 1924, the Guomindang held its First Reorganisation Congress and adopted Borodin's platform and system. This congress elected some CCP leaders to the Guomindang's Central Committee (Li Dazhao, Tan Pingshan, Lin Boqu) and some as alternates (Qu Qiubai, Mao Zedong, Zhang Guotao, and others). The Guomindang, originally corrupt and disorganised, put on a new mask and became Qu Qiubai's 'common people's party', under the influence of Soviet aid and using CCP skills.

In the spring of 1924, the Soviet Union sent General Galen (Vassily Blücher) to Guangzhou to act as military adviser to the Guomindang. He brought military experts and weapons to help reorganise Guomindang military units and introduced the Soviet Red Army's political commissar system to them. He helped Chiang Kai-shek establish the Huangpu Military Academy, trained military cadres, and made preparations for a new army. This was the foundation for all later developments. Because of it, the Guomindang was 'armed' both politically and militarily.

The old cadres in the Guomindang felt that uniting with Soviet Russia and taking in the Communist Party was dangerous. They said: 'Since the Communist Party joined the Guomindang... all its propaganda against British, American,

French, and Japanese imperialism has served to undermine the Guomindang's international image ... and that against militarism has destroyed any chance of cooperation between the Guomindang and powerful internal forces. Their plan is to destroy the Guomindang' (Zhang Ji et al., 'Bill of Impeachment', *Geming wenxian* IX, pp. 72–80). Sun Yat-sen gave the following explanation to these old cadres:

> If Russia wants to co-operate with China, she must co-operate with our Party and not with Chen Duxiu. If Chen disobeys our Party, he will be ousted. The Chinese revolution has never been welcomed by the foreign powers, which have often helped our [warlord] opponents in attempts to destroy our Party.... Sympathy can only be expected from Russia.... It was not Chen Duxiu's but Russia's idea to befriend us [Brandt, Schwartz and Fairbank (eds) 1967, p. 73].

Sun's explanation is clear: all he needed was Russia's 'sympathy', that is, Soviet military and financial aid. This foreshadowed the later moves by Chiang Kai-shek and Wang Jingwei to purge the Guomindang of CCP members.

To soothe the opposition, Sun initiated further controls on CCP members. In August 1924 he called on the Guomindang Central Committee to review Comintern resolutions and orders to the CCP. Qu Qiubai said he agreed with Sun's motion but that he must ask the opinion of the CCP Central Committee.

3 The CCP Turns to the Left – Towards the Working Class

When I returned to Shanghai from Moscow in August 1924, Cai Hesen told me about Sun's motion regarding Guomindang review of Comintern resolutions and orders. 'Has the Central Committee accepted this demand?' I asked. Cai replied, 'They are thinking it over'. 'The Central Committee must refuse Sun's demand', I said, 'or, our party will become a mere appendage to the Guomindang'. Cai talked this over with Chen Duxiu (Chen and Cai were the only standing members of the Central Committee left in Shanghai), and they sent a telegram ordering Qu Qiubai to refuse Sun's demand. This was the turning point in the CCP attitude towards the Guomindang.

I presented three resolutions to the Central Committee: we should (1) take a critical attitude towards the Guomindang; (2) renew our local party organisations; call on comrades who had returned from the University of the Toilers of the East in Moscow to take responsibility for this renewal of party organisations and the workers' movement; and (3) establish a Labour movement Committee to lead the national workers' movement. The Central Committee adopted these resolutions and directed Li Lisan, Xiang Ying, Li Qihan, and myself to form the Labour movement Committee. This committee established workers' evening schools and clubs in Shanghai. This was the foundation for the strike in Shanghai's Japanese cotton mills in February 1925.

On the seventh anniversary of the October revolution, in an article for the 7 November 1924 issue of *Xiangdao*, I pointed out, 'The October revolution is the model for the world revolution; China's revolution must follow this path'. In other words, China's national revolution, under the leadership of the proletariat, would turn into a socialist revolution. Chen Duxiu and I carried on a serious discussion about which class should lead the national revolution. Even though, throughout this discussion, Chen maintained his view that the bourgeoisie should lead the national revolution, he modified it somewhat. The Central Committee appointed me editor of *New Youth*. I planned to devote the December 1924 to 'The National Revolution'. Besides translation of those resolutions from the Second Comintern Congress on national and colonial questions and Lenin's remarks, this issue also contained my article 'Who Is the Leader of the National Revolution?' Before the issue was published, I gave the draft to Chen Duxiu and asked him to write something on the question. The idea was to further public discussion on the issue if he disagreed with my views and wished to criticise me.

My article was in answer to Chen's article on 'The National Revolution and Social Classes'. After analysing the material advantages and mutual relations of each class in Chinese society, I pointed out that the bourgeoisie, due to its close ties with the warlords and imperialists, could never lead the national revolution against them. Because of its fear of the proletariat, it would inevitably be reactionary. I concluded:

> After analysing all the classes... we may affirm that from the standpoint of their material basis, revolutionary consciousness, and the conditions of the international revolution... *only the working class can become the leader of the national revolution* [emphasis in original].

Chen Duxiu's article for *New Youth*, titled 'The Lessons of the National Movement over the Past Twenty-Seven Years', concluded that only with proletarian leadership could the national revolution win; he had given up on the idea of bourgeois leadership. So Chen and I agreed on which class would lead the national revolution.

In January 1925, the CCP held its Fourth Congress. A resolution called for proletarian leadership and plans were made to develop the workers' movement. The Second Congress of the National General Union of Railway Workers was called. Plans were made for a Second National Labour Congress. Whereas the Third Congress said the 'leader of the national revolution' was the bourgeois Guomindang, this Fourth Congress resolved that the proletariat was the leader of the national revolution and all work should be concentrated on developing the labour movement. This congress marked the return of the CCP to Bolshevism.

The Second Congress of the National General Union of Railway Workers opened on 7 February 1925 in Zhengzhou, Henan (where the union's First Congress had been closed down). Forty-five delegates representing twelve branches of the union passed resolutions concerning workers' economic interests and political rights. This lent great impetus to the future struggles of the railway workers.

At about the same time, the strike in Shanghai's Japanese cotton mills was going on. Seventy thousand were involved, under the leadership of the 'workers' clubs' in West Shanghai. Wages rose and working conditions improved, and the legal right to organise unions was established. This was the first great accomplishment in the history of the Shanghai workers' movement.

The Second National Labour Congress met on May Day 1925, in Guangzhou, with 281 delegates representing 166 unions and a membership of more than 570,000. The congress pointed out that the working class should participate in the national democratic liberation struggles and be the leading force in them.

Following the Congress, the workers in Shanghai's Japanese cotton mills again went on strike as a result of a counterattack by the Japanese capitalists, who forbade union activity and carried out bloody repression. On 15 May, Gu Zhenghong, a workers' leader, was killed. This led to protests by students and workers. This anti-imperialist movement peaked on 30 May, when thousands gathered on Nanjing Road and demanded the release of arrested demonstrators. British police raised their guns and killed seven and wounded dozens of demonstrators. This was the 'May Thirtieth Incident', which shook China and started the second Chinese revolution.

4 The Revolution Begins – The Conflict Between Comintern and CCP Policies

Following the May Thirtieth Incident, all Shanghai's students, workers, and merchants went on strike in a great wave of anti-imperialism. The CCP mobilised all its members and the SYC to organise the Shanghai Student Federation. With the cotton mill unions as a foundation, the Shanghai General Labour Union was established in less than a week. It became the general headquarters in the later struggles of the Shanghai workers' movement.

Under the influence of the anti-imperialist movement in Shanghai, every major city saw students, workers, and the general public rise in strikes and demonstrations and a flood of anti-imperialist sentiment.

In Guangzhou, students and workers held a demonstration on 23 June to protest the butchery carried out by the British in Shanghai. As the demonstration approached Shamian, the imperialist concession area, the British and French military police strafed it with machine guns. Fifty-seven people were killed and one hundred and seventeen injured in the 'Shaji Incident'. Workers in Hong Kong called a general strike, and many travelled to Guangzhou. A Guangzhou-Hong Kong Strike Committee was established. It became the bastion for the anti-imperialist movement in South China, initiating the blockade of Hong Kong.

The bourgeoisie quickly came to terms with the imperialists to stop the movement. The first move was made by the Shanghai General Merchants Association, which ordered merchants to open their stores. The bourgeoisie had discovered that its fundamental conflict with the working class overrode its conflict with imperialism. This situation was reflected in the party of the bourgeoisie, the Guomindang, and became a struggle against the working class and the CCP. In July 1925, Dai Jitao, a theoretician for the Guomindang, published 'The Fundamentals of Sun Yat-senism' with emphasis on 'national interest and unification' and attacking the concept of class struggle, especially workers' struggles under the leadership of the CCP. This article expressed the views of the bourgeoisie. Soon after it appeared, Chiang Kai-shek organised the Society for the Study of Sun Yat-senism at the Huangpu Military Academy and the units under his direct command. This organisation spread and specialised in opposing the communists. The Shanghai bourgeoisie, seeing this public expression by Dai Jitao, moved to ally itself with the local warlords and initiate a policy of repression. On 20 September 1925, they closed down the Shanghai General Labour Union, hoping to defuse the workers' struggle. The fact of being 'closed down' did not keep the Shanghai General Labour Union from leading the workers' movement. It merely went underground.

I wrote in an article for *Xiangdao* (5 October 1925) on 'The Closing of the Shanghai General Labour Union and the Present Responsibilities of the Workers':

> The success of the Chinese national revolution is possible only on condition that the Chinese workers rise and fight. Shanghai...is the equivalent of Russia's Petrograd – the February revolution and the October revolution in Russia were under the leadership of the workers in Petrograd.... The hundreds of thousands of workers in Shanghai have gained much experience in the May Thirtieth Movement under the

leadership of the General Labour Union, and have become familiar with a number of the elementary methods of carrying out a revolution. *In future they will advance further along the road of armed insurrection... following the example set by the workers of Petrograd from the February revolution to the October revolution* [emphasis in original].

When I stressed the decisive function of the workers in the May Thirtieth Movement and foresaw the need for an armed insurrection to take power, I was in direct contradiction with the official policy of the Comintern.

Chen Duxiu had personally seen the working class demonstrate its leadership role in the May Thirtieth Movement. He felt strongly that the CCP should base itself in the working class, and he made a public statement in *Xiangdao* calling on workers to join the CCP. This was a fundamental change from Qu Qiubai, who called on workers, merchants, and students to join 'our common people's Guomindang'.

When Chen Duxiu criticised Dai Jitao's 'Fundamentals of Sun Yat-senism' in an August 1925 issue of *Xiangdao*, he could not publicly criticise the reactionary views of Sun Yat-sen because of the 'Guomindang-CCP collaboration'. Chen witnessed those members of the Society for the Study of Sun Yat-senism moving closer to the right wing of the Guomindang. This led him to believe that a policy that required the CCP to remain within the Guomindang only served to restrain the CCP's independence in leading the masses. So he proposed that the CCP quit the Guomindang and cooperate with it outside. This proposal was made at a plenum of the CCP Central Committee in October 1925. The Comintern representative felt that the most immediate task for the CCP was to try to use the Guomindang's upcoming Second Congress to push the party to the left, and thus take over leadership of the national revolutionary movement. Chen's proposal to leave the Guomindang was defeated. This was the first instance of conflict between the CCP and the Comintern over the collaboration policy.

The Second Congress of the Guomindang was in Guangzhou in January 1926. 'Leftist leader' Wang Jingwei expressed his apparent sincerity towards the revolution and collaboration with the CCP. In the Central Executive Committee elections, many Guomindang left-wingers and CCP members were added, while some rightists were removed. Chiang Kai-shek, a 'leftist, was elected. The new heads of the Central Headquarters, Organisational Section, and Peasant Section were all CCP members. The Propaganda Section, Workers' Section, Youth Section, Women's Section, and so on, all had CCP secretaries. Mao Zedong was a secretary in the Propaganda Section under Wang Jingwei. 'The whole Guomindang' became the 'left wing'. CCP members held 'leadership positions' in the Central Committee of the Guomindang; however, in less than two months this 'left wing Guomindang' failed in the face of Chiang Kai-shek's coup of 20 March 1926.

This anticommunist coup was plotted and carried out under the direction of Chiang Kai-shek. More than fifty CCP members in military units under Chiang were arrested on the day of the coup. Weapons were taken from Strike Committee pickets and Soviet Russian guard units, and Chiang established his own personal dictatorship after chasing out Wang Jingwei, chairman of the national government.

The CCP Central Committee hoped for guidance from Moscow, but after three weeks there was no word (Stalin simply sat on the sidelines watching the situation develop). It became necessary to determine our own policy. The important points were: unite with the left wing of the Guomindang and their military forces to oppose Chiang; expand the troops under Ye Ting, a CCP member (close to 3,000 men); and arm the workers and peasants as the basic force of the revolution. I went to Guangzhou to organise a committee (consisting of CC members Tan Pingshan and Zhang Guotao and Guangdong Provincial Committee members Chen Yannian, Zhou Enlai, and Zhang Tailei) to discuss with Borodin how to deal with Chiang Kai-shek.

I arrived in Guangzhou in late April 1926. Borodin had returned from the Soviet Union with directives from Stalin. I called a meeting of the special committee and invited Borodin. I reported on the resolutions of the CCP Central Committee regarding Chiang Kai-shek. Borodin emphasised the 'extreme danger inherent in the present situation' and used this to oppose discussion. When I proposed that CCP members leave the Guomindang and cooperate from outside, Borodin said 'the question of leaving the Guomindang must be agreed upon by the left wing of the Guomindang'. Borodin voiced Stalin's orders that no matter how serious the results of Chiang's March coup, 'Guomindang-CCP collaboration' must be maintained. He said the CCP should accept the situation that resulted from the March coup, recognise Chiang's military dictatorship, and accept his 'Resolution Adjusting Party Affairs', while assisting him in the leadership of the Northern Expedition. Borodin soothed the other comrades: 'The advancement of the Northern Expedition will have advantages for us in the future'. Except for me, everyone agreed. The policy of opposing Chiang Kai-shek became a policy of surrender. This smoothed the way for Chiang's next coup. This was the turning point that led the second Chinese revolution to defeat.

Chen Duxiu and I saw the danger in this policy of surrender, but there was no way to publicly oppose it. All we could do was call a plenum of the CC. This plenum was held in mid-July 1926, a week after Chiang Kai-shek took command of the Northern Expedition. The situation had become more intense. Chen Duxiu and I proposed that all CCP members should leave the Guomindang, cooperate only from outside, and establish a united front with its left wing. We explained that only by throwing off control of the CCP by the Guomindang could we carry out a truly independent policy. Under pressure from the Comintern representative, a majority of the CC, led by Qu Qiubai, turned down our resolution but agreed to forward it to the Comintern. The Comintern refused to consider it, and Bukharin published an article in *Pravda* saying those who advocated withdrawal from the Guomindang were as wrong as those in the Soviet Opposition who advocated Soviet withdrawal from the Anglo-Russian Committee. Trotsky, however, said later:

> It is necessary to approve as unconditionally correct the resolution of the June plenum of the CC of the Chinese CP, which demands that the party withdraw from the Guomindang and conclude a bloc with that organisation through its left wing ['Class Relations in the Chinese Revolution' (3 April 1927)].

5 Collaboration with the Guomindang Leads the CCP into a Blind Alley

The resolution by Chen Duxiu and Peng Shuzhi called for 'CCP members [to] leave the Guomindang, only to cooperate with the Guomindang from outside party ranks, and to establish a united front with the left wing of the Guomindang' – this 'unconditionally correct' resolution was rejected by the Comintern. After this, the CCP could only remain active within the restraints of the policy of 'Guomindang-CCP collaboration'.

Thus the CCP was restrained from criticising the Three People's Principles of Sun Yat-sen and the reactionary behaviour of Chiang Kai-shek. An even more serious restriction was the prohibition on advocating agrarian revolution, calling on the peasants to struggle for the land, organising workers', peasants', and soldiers' soviets, and pulling soldiers into revolutionary units. All of this would have been in direct opposition to the Comintern policy of 'Guomindang-CCP collaboration'. The CCP's mission, according to the Comintern, was to 'bend all efforts towards mobilising the workers and peasants into support for the Northern Expedition'.

The CCP mobilised all party members and Youth Corps members on every front against the Northern militarists and in favour of the Northern Expedition.

They organised workers and peasants into commando units to handle reconnaissance, spying, and scouting. These units sabotaged communications behind enemy lines and collected weapons when the enemy retreated. Dozens of CCP members acted as company commanders, battalion commanders, and regimental commanders in the National Revolutionary Army. Some died in battle. In less than four months (July to October 1926), and with few serious battles, the Western Route of the Northern Expedition reached the Yangtze and secured Wuhan. The Central Route, under Chiang Kai-shek, occupied Nanchang in November 1926. The Eastern Route occupied Hangzhou in February 1927. All these victories were the result of aid rendered by the worker and peasant masses mobilised by the CCP.

At the time the workers and peasants mobilised to aid the Northern Expedition were organising unions and associations. Hunan peasant associations had a membership of more than four million. The Hunan General Union had a membership of about 500,000. In October 1926, after the Northern Expedition had occupied Wuhan, 300,000 workers organised the Hubei General Union. The peasant movement in Hubei also developed rapidly. The working class in Shanghai, under the influence of victories of the Northern Expedition, turned from economic strikes to political strikes and demonstrations, while preparing for armed insurrection. The masses in Hankou and Jiujiang took over the concession areas under the control of British imperialism in January 1927. From the time these forces entered the Yangtze valley, the worker-peasant movement in Hunan and Hubei was an angry tide, overturning all social relations. The workers were on the verge of attacking the system of private ownership itself. The peasants, especially in Hunan, went from struggles aimed at lowering rents and interest rates to revolutionary activity to get rid of the landlords and gentry and take over the land. Peasant associations became ruling organisations in most villages.

However, Chiang Kai-shek repressed the workers and peasants who had helped the Northern Expedition, and through whom so many victories were won. He closed down the unions, abolished the peasant associations, and assassinated leaders of the workers and peasants. He disbanded provincial branches of the left wing of the Guomindang. He began talks with warlords in an attempt to establish an 'anti-Red united front'. In Shanghai, his henchmen got together with reactionary politicians and gangster leaders and approved their collaboration with the imperialist concessions in developing schemes to oppose the workers and the Communist Party. I wrote an article titled 'The Present Revolutionary Crisis of the Rightward Tendency' (published in *Xiangdao* on 6 March 1927), which said:

> *The whole situation of the Chinese revolution is already apparent.... On the one hand, the power of the revolution, especially the power of the National Revolutionary Army, the workers, and the peasants, is developing with exceptional rapidity. The tide of revolution is swelling and deepening.... On the other hand... a compromising and reactionary tendency among the leaders of the National Revolutionary Army has become apparent.... They have attempted, publicly or secretly, to compromise with the enemy against the masses. This is the most dangerous phenomenon in the revolution at present, and may well destroy the whole revolution* [emphasis in original].

Besides pointing out these grave dangers, I also revealed the counter-revolutionary tendency of Chiang Kai-shek (at the time, both the Northern warlords and the imperialists called Chiang's faction the 'moderate group'):

> The so-called moderate group in the Guomindang has fully disclosed its bourgeois tendency; *they... have seen the workers and peasants rising to fight not only for general revolutionary interests but in the interests of the workers and peasants themselves.* They have also noted the concessions granted by the imperialists and the warlords. Hence this group aims at stopping the revolutionary process... to unify all the compradors, bureaucrats, and landlords, the rotten gentry and those enemies of the revolution, the imperialists and the warlords, *for the purpose of striking back at the worker and peasant masses* [emphasis in original].

Chiang Kai-shek's group plotted the attack on the worker-peasant masses and the Communist Party. They had already begun the work of repression in Jiangxi and Anhui. Faced with such danger, what policy should the CCP have adopted? There was no other route than to carry out an armed uprising and establish a revolutionary dictatorship. The CCP was already preparing the uprising in Shanghai. Since it was a matter of tactics, I could not initiate a public discussion. However, in the same article I did say what the régime following the victory of the armed uprising should be like:

> *The Chinese revolution should create a régime of revolutionary democracy, and, above all, should not create a personal military dictatorship* (Chiang Kai-shek).... The present revolution is urgently in need of a revolutionary régime of democratic dictatorship. That means a régime for the masses in their majority, composed of workers, peasants, and petty bourgeois, in which they participate directly, thus controlling the government in order to carry out their interest in *striking down all the elements of the*

counter-revolution and in enforcing a revolutionary dictatorship over them [emphasis in original].

I concentrated on exposing the counter-revolutionary plans of the bourgeoisie represented by Chiang Kai-shek's group. On 18 March 1927, I published 'After Reading Chiang Kai-shek's Speech of 21 February' (in *Xiangdao*). In it, I exposed Chiang's counter-revolutionary activities, including his '20 March coup', his personal military dictatorship, his unification of reactionary forces and alignment with imperialism, and the repression of the worker-peasant movement and persecution of the CCP. I voiced the following warning: 'The coming struggle in China is a life and death struggle between the forces of the revolution and the anti-revolutionary forces represented by Chiang Kai-shek'. The revolutionary democratic dictatorship was in opposition to the bourgeois dictatorship Chiang represented.

What was the Comintern's view? What was its estimate of Chiang Kai-shek's Northern Expedition, or his national government in Guangzhou? For an answer, one need only look at Stalin's remarks to the Seventh Plenum of the ECCI, which met in Moscow in November-December 1926. Two sections should help clarify the problem. When Stalin mentioned the Northern Expedition led by Chiang, he said:

> The advance of the Guangzhou troops meant a blow aimed at imperialism, a blow aimed at its agents in China. It meant the freedom of assembly, freedom to strike, freedom of the press, freedom of coalition for all the revolutionary elements in China and for the workers in particular [Isaacs 1961, p. 119].

As a matter of fact, as soon as the Northern Expedition began, under Chiang's leadership, it imposed severe limitations on the freedom of assembly, press, and especially the freedom strike. The 'advance' of the 'Guangzhou troops' under his leadership was not 'a blow aimed at imperialism' but a method by which he could advantageously come to an agreement with imperialism. When Stalin spoke of Chiang's national government, he emphasised:

> What is important is not the bourgeois-democratic character of the Guangzhou government, which forms the nucleus of the future all-Chinese revolutionary power. The most important thing is that this power is an anti-militarist power, and can be nothing else, that every advance of this power is a blow aimed at world imperialism and is therefore a stroke in favour of the world revolutionary movement [Isaacs 1961, p. 119].

This was the opposite of the facts. 'The Guangzhou government ... forms the nucleus of the future all-Chinese *counter-revolutionary* power'. 'Every advance of this power is *a blow aimed at* the world revolutionary movement'.

The policies of the Comintern's Seventh Plenum regarding the Chinese revolution were decided by the attitude of Stalin towards Chiang Kai-shek's Northern Expedition and national government. The plenum invited Chiang's representative, Shao Lizi, to attend, recognised the Guomindang as a 'sympathising party', determined that the Chinese communists should participate in his government, and assigned to the Northern Expedition the role of expelling imperialism, defeating the warlords, and gaining national independence and unification. The CCP could not launch any effective opposition to Chiang Kai-shek's counter-revolutionary activities and plots, let alone prepare to overthrow him. *The CCP was forced into a blind alley.*

Thus, even though the CCP led the Shanghai workers in an armed insurrection on 21 March 1927, they could not establish a revolutionary régime. Such a régime would have initiated a dictatorship against the bourgeoisie and have opposed and defeated Chiang Kai-shek's coup. They could not do this because it would destroy 'Guomindang-CCP collaboration', obstruct the 'bloc of four classes', and disrupt Chiang Kai-shek's Northern Expedition. Even though the CCP had taken Shanghai and gained the support of the entire working class and most of the lower petty bourgeoisie, along with the sympathy of a section of the soldiers, it could do nothing but establish a Shanghai provisional government in collaboration with the bourgeoisie. Those representatives of the bourgeoisie 'elected' to serve in the provisional government used sabotage and opposition, under Chiang Kai-shek's direction, to paralyse the government and prepare the way for Chiang's next coup.

Under these circumstances, the CCP slipped into a period of distress and dilemma. The only members of the Central Committee left in Shanghai were Chen Duxiu and myself, since Qu Qiubai had gone to Wuhan a few days after the Shanghai workers' victory, without obtaining the permission of the Central Committee.[1] Chen and I had discussed many times how to get out of the critical

---

1   Qu Qiubai went to Wuhan to organise the takeover of the leadership and get rid of Chen and me, because he always defended Comintern policies. He defended Stalin's theory of revolution by stages as against Trotsky's theory of permanent revolution. He wrote a pamphlet titled *The Problem of the Chinese Revolution* to attack me and my position on 'permanent revolution'. This was in answer to an article I wrote titled 'Is Leninism Applicable to the National Peculiarities of China?', which appeared in *Xiangdao* on 21 January 1927. In it I analysed the similarities between China and Russia before the October revolution. I concluded Leninism was applicable to China. I suggested the slogan of 'permanent revolution' and pointed out:

situation the party had fallen into. We felt that without extensively arming the workers and building an alliance with units of the National Revolutionary Army sympathetic to the workers' movement, there was no way to defend ourselves against the coup planned by Chiang Kai-shek (nearly everyone was aware of Chiang's plans; only Moscow denied they existed). Our plans for armed struggle against Chiang ran up against a fundamental problem in the relationship between the CCP and the Comintern, that of discipline. To go ahead would have been to oppose the Comintern's policy; it would have meant a complete break with the Comintern. Both Chen Duxiu and I were undecided on what to do, so we asked the Shanghai regional secretary, Luo Yinong, and Zhou Enlai, then directing the Shanghai insurrection. They completely agreed with us: there was no other way than armed struggle against Chiang. However, they also agreed with Chen that it was not possible to go against Comintern policy. Chen Duxiu asked me to go to Wuhan and discuss the problem of armed struggle against Chiang with the Comintern representatives and the rest of the Central Committee. Then we would decide.

At the end of March 1927, I left Shanghai and went to Nanjing, where the Second and Sixth armies of the National Revolutionary Army were based. These two units were part of the Guomindang left wing and opposed Chiang Kai-shek. The political commissars were Communists; there were many Communists in these units responsible for other political and military work. After I arrived, an emergency meeting was called with cadres in the Second and Sixth armies, along with the Russian advisers. I reported that the CCP Central Committee advocated the use of armed struggle against the anticommunist coup being prepared by Chiang Kai-shek. The discussion resulted in total approval of the CC plan, especially by the Russian advisers. According to units based in Shanghai, Nanjing, and Wuxi, victory over Chiang Kai-shek could be gained through the use of military force. They requested the CC representative to order military action against Chiang. I told them that armed struggle against Chiang would be in opposition to Moscow's official policy, so the Central Committee was sending me to Wuhan to discuss the problem with Comintern representatives and other CC members. They urged me to hurry; they would wait for the results of the discussion before initiating any action.

I arrived in Wuhan on 10 April 1927, but on 12 April Chiang Kai-shek began his coup in Shanghai. Thousands were massacred. Workers' organisations were destroyed. All of the industries in Shanghai and the southeast were taken over by Chiang's forces. This was Stalin's final reward for his policy of collaboration, his

---

'China's revolution will move directly from a national revolution to a proletarian revolution'. Qu retorted that this was 'copying Trotskyism', thus maintaining his good relations with Stalin.

support for the Northern Expedition, his concealment and defence of Chiang's counter-revolutionary activity, and his hopes for Chiang's success in destroying imperialism and the warlords and completing the struggle for independence.

6 The Turn from Chiang Kai-shek to Wang Jingwei

Two weeks after Chiang Kai-shek's coup, the CCP held its Fifth Congress (27 April 1927, to the beginning of May). It would have been reasonable to submit the coup to a thorough discussion, so lessons could be learned and a new political line developed. However, M. N. Roy didn't even mention Chiang's coup. He merely said:

> The differentiation of the classes within the Guomindang has strengthened the bonds between its Left Wing and the Communist Party. The departure of the big bourgeoisie has permitted the transformation of the Guomindang into a revolutionary bloc composed of the industrial proletariat, the peasants, and the petty bourgeoisie.... The Chinese revolution continues to develop on the basis of a class coalition and cannot yet be submitted to the exclusive leadership of the proletariat.... The leading members of the Guomindang participated in the opening meeting of the Congress and declared that they were ready to fortify the bloc with the Communist Party [Isaacs 1961, p. 218].

Translated into concrete language, this meant that Chiang Kai-shek's anti-communist coup 'has strengthened the bonds between the Guomindang's left wing and the Communist Party'. The 'bloc of four classes' remained; it merely became necessary to get rid of that part of the big bourgeoisie represented by Chiang Kai-shek. The policy of 'Guomindang-CCP collaboration' remained; it was only necessary to get rid of the 'Guomindang right wing' Chiang represented, and replace it with the 'Guomindang left wing' led by Wang Jingwei.

In my own speech, I concentrated on analysing the connection between Chiang's first coup (20 March 1926) and his second coup (12 April 1927). I pointed out the latest coup was a logical development of the earlier one. Since our party adopted a policy of extreme compromise following Chiang's first coup, we failed to adopt any effective method to stop this latest coup. I called upon this congress to carry out a thorough discussion of this experience. During a break, M. N. Roy told me: 'Your analysis of events is Marxist'. But he said nothing about my proposal to discuss the coup. He had received orders from the Comintern and a draft of Stalin's article on 'Questions of the Chinese Revolution'. This article declared: 'The line adopted was the only correct line'. Since 'the line adopted was the only correct line', it was impermissible to discuss its mistakes, especially the coup of Chiang Kai-shek.

According to that 'only correct line', Stalin made the following elucidation:

> Chiang Kai-shek's coup means that from now on there will be in South China two camps, two governments, two armies, two centres, *the centre of revolution in Wuhan* and the centre of counter-revolution in Nanjing.... *This means that the revolutionary Guomindang in Wuhan, by a determined fight against militarism and imperialism, will in fact be converted into an organ of the revolutionary-democratic dictatorship of the proletariat and the peasantry.*... [We must adopt] the *policy of concentrating the whole power in the country in the hands of the revolutionary Guomindang*.... It further follows that *the policy of close co-operation between the Lefts and the Communists within the Guomindang in this stage acquires special force and special significance... and that without such co-operation the victory of the revolution is impossible* [*International Press Correspondence*, 28 April 1927, emphasis added].

Roy's report and Stalin's article placed the Fifth Congress of the CCP in a straitjacket. All questions discussed by the congress were limited to how to 'strengthen the bonds between the Guomindang's left wing and the Communist Party'; how to push forward the day when 'the revolutionary Guomindang in Wuhan... will in fact be converted into an organ of the revolutionary-democratic dictatorship of the proletariat and the peasantry'; and how to strengthen 'the centre of revolution in Wuhan'. To complete these tasks, the CCP could not have its own independent stance. Everything must accommodate the intentions of the Guomindang left wing. Regarding the urgent problem of land, the resolution completely surrendered to Wang Jingwei's views: 'no confiscation of the land of small landlords and Revolutionary Army officers'. This was equivalent to giving up on land reform, since the 'Revolutionary Army officers' were either landlords or closely related to landlords.

To 'strengthen the centre of revolution in Wuhan', the Fifth Congress sent Tan Pingshan and Su Zhaozheng to join the Guomindang government in Wuhan as heads of the Agriculture and Labour ministries. Officially, they were to protect the interests of the workers and peasants, but in fact, they were sent to contain any revolutionary activity by workers and peasants, any 'worker-peasant excesses'.

During and immediately after the Fifth Congress, the revolutionary movement in Hunan and Hubei reached its height. Currency devaluation and rising prices made life unbearable for the workers. The closing of factories and stores resulted in many unemployed. The workers and clerks demanded that the factories and stores be turned over to them to run. The peasants, especially in Hunan, chased out the landlords and took over the land and organised armed units to battle against the armed landlords and gentry. This indicated the urgent need for the unification of workers and peasants in soviets. Soldiers influenced by the worker and peasant masses had no way to develop an organised connection with them since they were under the control of reactionary officers. *The only way to attain this kind of connection was through soviets.*

The unions in Hunan and Hubei had a membership of over one million. The Hunan Peasant Association had close to ten million members, while that in Hubei had close to three million. This was a great organised mass force. If the CCP had followed Trotsky's advice[2] and relied upon them, while calling for the organisation of worker-peasant-soldier soviets to become the central revolutionary organisation, and, through these armed soviets, carried out the agrarian revolution, giving land to the peasants and revolutionary soldiers, they not only could have assembled all the poor masses of Hunan and Hubei into soviets, but they could have destroyed the foundation of the reactionary officers and destabilised Chiang's army. The revolution could have advanced along the road of proletarian dictatorship.

Unfortunately, however, the CCP not only failed to organise soviets and initiate the agrarian revolution, but also failed to warn the worker-peasant masses and help them plan self-defence measures. The CCP leadership put all its hope in the leader of the Guomindang left wing, Wang Jingwei. They sought 'close cooperation' with him and asked him to improve the conditions of the workers and initiate land reform, while they made every effort to contain 'worker-peasant excesses'. They forbade the takeover of factories and stores and of land by the peasants, to avoid undermining the Guomindang left wing, which might push the 'revolutionary officers' on the road to reaction. *The revolutionary activity of the workers and peasants was paralysed, while the officers had sufficient time to prepare their attack. The result was a counter-revolutionary rebellion by Xia Douyin on 17 May 1927. Four days later, Xu Kexiang (Tang Shengzhi's subordinate) carried out a counter-revolutionary coup in Changsha.* Xia Douyin's rebellion was destroyed by military units under Ye Ting, a CCP member, but the coup by Xu Kexiang met with no resistance, and he took control of Changsha.

---

2   See 'Letter to Alsky' (29 March 1927) and 'Class Relations in the Chinese Revolution' (3 April 1927).

What policy did the CCP leadership adopt towards Xu Kexiang's coup? The same as that following Chiang's Shanghai coup: the Guomindang in Wuhan was requested to send units to punish Xu. Wuhan, however, asked Xu's superior, Tang Shengzhi, to go to Changsha to handle the situation. Tang reported:

> I have found that the workers' and peasants' movement, under the misguidance of their leaders, has broken loose from control and precipitated a reign of terror against the people.... Although Xu Kexiang's actions were animated by a passion for justice, he has overstepped the limits of law and discipline. He should receive a light punishment in the form of a demerit but should be retained in the army service [Isaacs 1961, p. 250].

Xu Kexiang 'should be retained in the army service', that is, allowed to destroy all workers' and peasants' organisations and get rid of all communists. In the following few months, Hunan, originally a centre of revolutionary power, became the strongest counter-revolutionary bastion.

Two days after Xu Kexiang's coup in Changsha (23 May 1927), the Eighth Plenum of the Executive Committee of the Communist International began in Moscow. It reacted to Xu's coup in the same way as to Chiang's; it made every effort to cover it up. In Stalin's speech on 24 May not one word was said about Xu's counter-revolutionary coup. All he did was attack the Trotskyist Opposition and their advocacy of soviets:

> Does the Opposition understand that the creation of soviets of workers' and peasants' deputies now is tantamount to the creation of a dual government, shared by the soviets and the Hankou government, and leads to calling for the overthrow of the Hankou Government?... It would be quite another matter were there no popular, revolutionary democratic organisation such as the Left Guomindang in China. But since there is such a specific revolutionary organisation, adapted to the peculiarities of Chinese conditions and demonstrating its value for the further development of the bourgeois democratic revolution in China – *it would be stupid and unwise to destroy this organisation*, which it has taken so many years to build, at a moment when the bourgeois democratic revolution has just begun, has not yet conquered, and cannot be victorious for some time [Isaacs 1961, p. 241, emphasis added].

This passage, besides exposing Stalin's illusions regarding the Guomindang left wing, reveals his own reactionary thinking about the establishment of soviets.

He was afraid that they would lead to calling for the overthrow of the Hankou Government'. Here is Stalin's appraisal of the 'Hankou Government':

> Since *China is experiencing an agrarian revolution, ... it is necessary to support the Guomindang in Wuhan....* Is the present Hankou government an organ of the revolutionary dictatorship of the proletariat and the peasantry? No. So far it is not, nor will it be so very soon, *but it has all the chances of developing into such an organ in the further development of the revolution* [Isaacs 1961, p. 241, emphasis added].

Stalin said the 'Hankou Government ... has all the chances of developing into [an organ of the revolutionary dictatorship of the proletariat and the peasantry] in the further development of the revolution', so it could take the place of soviets in completing the 'agrarian revolution'. One only need look at Xu Kexiang's coup to realise that Stalin was spouting nonsense. During the plenary session, Trotsky attacked Stalin's disastrous policy and appealed to the Chinese peasants and workers:

> Stalin has again declared himself here against workers' and peasants' soviets with the argument that the Guomindang and the Wuhan government are sufficient means and instruments for the agrarian revolution. Thereby Stalin assumes, and wants the International to assume, the responsibility for the policy of the Guomindang and the Wuhan government, as he repeatedly assumed the responsibility for the policy of the former 'national government' of Chiang Kai-shek.... We do not want to assume even a shadow of responsibility for the policy of the Wuhan government and the leadership of the Guomindang, and we urgently advise the Comintern to reject this responsibility. We say directly to the Chinese peasants: The leaders of the left Guomindang of the type of Wang Jingwei and Company will inevitably betray you if you follow the Wuhan heads instead of forming your own independent soviets. The agrarian revolution is a serious thing. Politicians of the Wang Jingwei type, under difficult conditions, will unite ten times with Chiang Kai-shek against the workers and peasants. Under such conditions, two communists in a bourgeois government become impotent hostages, if not a direct mask for the preparation of a new blow against the working masses. We say to the workers of China: The peasants will not carry out the agrarian revolution to the end if they let themselves be led by petty-bourgeois radicals instead of by you, the revolutionary proletarians. Therefore, build up your workers' soviets, ally them with the peasant soviets, arm yourselves

through the soviets, draw soldiers' representatives into the soviets, shoot the generals who do not recognise the soviets, shoot the bureaucrats and bourgeois liberals who will organise uprisings against the soviets. Only through peasants' and soldiers' soviets will you win over the majority of Chiang Kai-shek's soldiers to your side.... *The Chinese bourgeois democratic revolution will go forward and be victorious either in the soviet form or not at all* ['Second Speech on the Chinese Question' (May 24, 1927), emphasis in original].

If the Comintern had adopted Trotsky's proposals, the revolution might have been saved. However, because of Stalin's control of the Comintern and suppression of Opposition documents, Trotsky's call to the workers and peasants never reached China and was never published in the Comintern's internal bulletins. So Trotsky's final proposal to save the Chinese revolution only served to prophesy the tragedy of the second Chinese revolution.

The Eighth Plenum of the Comintern was completely under Stalin's control, and the resolution regarding the China question was Stalin's resolution. For example:

> No matter what the political situation, the Communist Party must never become merged with any other political organisation. It must represent an independent force.... The Communist Party must never allow restrictions to be imposed on it in advocating its views and mobilising the masses under its own banner.... The independence of the CCP must not, however, be interpreted to mean that it must become exclusive and isolated from the non-proletarian toiling strata and particularly from the peasantry. On these grounds, the ECCI resolutely rejects all demands for the Communist Party to leave the Guomindang, or that it should take up a position which would actually lead to its leaving the Guomindang.... It is impossible to claim the role of leader for the proletariat *unless* the Communist Party, as the Party of the working class, claims the role of leader *within* the Guomindang. The ECCI regards as incorrect the view which underestimates the Hankou Government and which in fact denies its great revolutionary role. The Hankou Government and the leaders of the Left Guomindang by their class composition represent not only the peasants, workers and artisans, but also a section of the middle bourgeoisie. Therefore, the Hankou Government, being the government of the Left Guomindang, is not yet the dictatorship of the proletariat and the peasantry, but is on the road to it and will inevitably, in the course of the victorious class struggle of the proletariat and in discarding its

radical bourgeois camp followers, develop in the direction of such dictatorship ['Resolution on the Chinese Question', *International Press Correspondence*, 16 June 1927. Emphasis in original].

It seems Stalin had already discovered that the 'revolutionary left Guomindang' did not correspond with his ideals. He felt that the generals controlling the 'Hankou government' were 'unreliable'. So at the closing of the Comintern plenary session, on 1 June 1927, he sent a telegram to the CCP. It contained five important points, of which the most outstanding were:

> A large number of new peasant and working class leaders... will stiffen the backs of the old leaders or throw them into the discard.... It is necessary to liquidate the unreliable generals. Mobilise about 20,000 Communists and about 50,000 revolutionary workers and peasants from Hunan and Hubei, form several new army corps [North and Eudin (eds) 1963, p. 107].

But how were the 'new peasant and working class leaders' to be placed on the Guomindang Central Executive Committee? How to 'liquidate the unreliable generals'? And where to obtain the weapons to 'organise our own reliable army'? Stalin did not deal with these problems. It was as if Wuhan were under his direct control and he could use bureaucratic directives to obtain whatever he wanted. When the Politburo of the CCP received Stalin's directive, they were frightened and didn't know how to deal with it. All they could do was meet with Comintern representatives to discuss the matter. Everyone felt there was no way to carry out Stalin's directive. But Roy decided to turn the directive over to Wang Jingwei, hoping that he would agree to it. By that time, Wang had already decided to drive out the Communist Party. When he saw Stalin's telegram, it speeded his plans.

On 12 June 1927, Wang Jingwei and other anti-communist officials went to Zhengzhou, Henan, for a secret meeting with General Feng Yuxiang. The main problem was how to oppose the CCP and Chiang Kai-shek. Feng advocated the immediate expulsion of the CCP and the suppression of the workers' and peasants' movement in Hunan and Hubei, followed by negotiations with Chiang. A week after his meeting with Wang in Zhengzhou, Feng met with Chiang in Suzhou. Following this meeting, Feng told reporters of his 'sincere desire to cooperate with the Nationalists and extirpate militarism and Communism'. This was the man Moscow had called the 'son of a labourer' and a 'most reliable ally'.

Following the Zhengzhou meeting, the atmosphere in Wuhan suddenly became very tense. The leaders of the CCP and the Comintern representatives felt a shadow resting on their heads. On 20 June 1927, the CCP met to try to ward off calamity. The meeting issued a statement which expressed the CCP attitude towards the left wing Guomindang, following a discussion between Qu Qiubai and the Comintern representatives. Its important points were:

> The Guomindang... is naturally in the leading position of the national revolution.... The workers' and peasants' mass organisations should accept the leadership and control of the Guomindang.... According to Guomindang principles, the masses must be armed. But the armed groups of the workers and peasants should submit to the regulation and training of the government. In order to avoid political troubles, the present armed pickets at Wuhan can be reduced or incorporated into the army [Isaacs 1961, pp. 262–3].

This statement was the final surrender by the CCP to the Guomindang. A week later, the General Trades Union of Hubei disbanded its pickets and turned its weapons over to the military guard in Wuhan. Two days later (30 June), the CCP ordered Tan Pingshan and Su Zhaozheng to resign from the Wuhan government.

In mid June, Chen Duxiu felt the collaboration with the Guomindang left wing had reached a dead end and proposed that the CCP quit the Guomindang and determine its own independent policy. The Comintern rejected Chen's proposal, arguing that to quit the Guomindang would be to give up the Guomindang's revolutionary banner to the reactionary right wing. Chen resigned as CCP general secretary in July 1927. Qu Qiubai became the acting general secretary. Qu's only task was to wait to see how the CCP would be treated by the left Guomindang.

On 15 June 1927, the Central Executive Committee of the left Guomindang issued an order requiring all CCP members in the Guomindang and the Revolutionary Army to withdraw from the CCP. Stalin's policy of 'Guomindang-CCP collaboration' thus came to a shameful conclusion. Trotsky had said:

> Politicians of the Wang Jingwei type, under difficult conditions, will unite ten times with Chiang Kai-shek against the workers and peasants.... *The Chinese bourgeois-democratic revolution will go forward and be victorious either in the soviet form or not at all.*

In less than seven weeks, his prediction had been fulfilled.

7 The Leap from Ultra-Right Opportunism to Ultra-Left Adventurism

Stalin reacted in the same manner to Wang Jingwei's expulsion of the Communists as to Chiang's coup. He refused to consider the situation and called the defeat a 'development of the revolution to a higher stage'. This produced a chain of adventurist insurrections through the next few months:

1. *The Nanchang uprising.* After Wang Jingwei announced the expulsion of the communists, Stalin sent Lominadze to Wuhan. Without so much as investigating the revolution's defeat or assembling those CCP cadres still in Wuhan to discuss the situation, he conveyed Stalin's new directive calling for armed struggle, for Qu Qiubai to carry out. Those military forces participating in the Nanchang uprising on 1 August 1927 included He Long's independent Fifteenth Division, Ye Ting's Twenty-Fourth Division in the Eleventh Army, and Zhu De's model unit (formerly belonging to Zhu Peide's Third Army), a total of some 30,000 men. After these units took over the city of Nanchang, Jiangxi, they announced the establishment of a 'Revolutionary Committee'. Included among its members were Song Qingling (Sun Yat-sen's widow), and the head of the National Revolutionary Army's Fourth Army, Zhang Fakui. The committee had no programme and carried out no revolutionary measures. The insurrection was carried out under the banner of the Guomindang, so in the eyes of the public it was a coup of the left Guomindang against the right.

The forces led by He Long and Ye Ting were forced to retreat from the city when they were attacked by Zhang Fakui. They fled south and took the towns of Chaozhou and Shantou. They were again dispersed by reactionary units in the Guomindang army. He and Ye escaped; Zhu De brought a small unit composed of remnants out of Guangdong and into the Jinggang Mountains, where they converged with Mao Zedong's forces, later to become the basic cadre for the 'Red Army'.

Two days after the defeat, on 7 August, Qu Qiubai, under Lominadze's direction, called an emergency conference of the Central Committee, the '7 August Emergency Conference'. This conference approved the 'Circular Letter of the CC to All Party Members', in which the responsibility for the revolution's defeat was placed on Chen Duxiu and Tan Pingshan. This relieved Stalin and Bukharin of responsibility for the defeat. The 'Emergency Conference' failed to discuss the lessons of Nanchang and even decided to initiate Autumn Harvest uprisings in Hunan and Hubei.

2. *The Hunan-Hubei Autumn Harvest uprisings.* After Xu Kexiang's revolt in Changsha, Hunan became a world of 'white terror'. Almost all the unions and peasant associations were destroyed. All that was left were worker and peasant cadres hiding in mines, factories, and smaller villages. The situation in

Hubei was even worse. To carry out armed insurrections to take power would be insane. Some 3,000 people took part in the insurrection in Hunan. Miners and peasants in Pingxiang and Anyuan took over the bigger towns in these counties, but were defeated by the Guomindang army in a few days. Most of the insurrectionists were dispersed, but a few followed Mao Zedong to the Jinggang Mountains. In Hubei, only a minority of peasants from a few southern counties participated, and were quickly suppressed. The so-called Hunan-Hubei Autumn Harvest uprising led to many cadres being killed or wounded. Those concealed in the mines and villages were now exposed. The CCP lost its contacts with the workers and peasants.

3. *The Hailufeng soviet movement.* China's peasant associations originated in Haifeng and Lufeng (known jointly as Hailufeng) in Guangdong. They were built up from 1922 by Peng Pai. The peasant associations in these two counties had about 200,000 members and a strong organisation. They became models for the movement elsewhere in Guangdong. Even after Li Jishen carried out his '15 April coup', the Hailufeng peasant association was able to retain power. Following the defeat of the Nanchang uprising and the Autumn Harvest uprising, the adventurists in the CCP chose Hailufeng as the experimental ground for a soviet movement. This was in line with Stalin's instruction of 30 September 1927, that 'the propaganda slogan of soviets must become a slogan of action!'

The Hailufeng insurrection began in late October, and by 1 November the towns of Haifeng and Lufeng had fallen. Soviets were established, a peasant army was organised, and it was announced that land would be distributed to the peasants. Two or three hundred thousand peasants and handicraft workers took part. However, it received no leadership or support from the working class in Guangzhou, Hong Kong, or other large cities (the working class in both Guangzhou and Hong Kong was in the midst of a period of extreme oppression and exploitation due to the defeat it suffered as a result of opportunist policies), so it became isolated and was destroyed. The number of peasant fighters killed or wounded was never recorded.

4. *The Guangzhou insurrection.* After the Nanchang uprising and the Autumn Harvest uprising were defeated, Stalin ordered Lominadze to prepare a new insurrection, and sent Heinz Neumann to China to assist in planning it. From a report delivered by Qu Qiubai, the leader of the Central Committee, Lominadze learned that there was part of a military force (under Zhang Fakui) in Guangzhou, which took orders from CCP members. Even though the Guangzhou-Hong Kong Strike Committee had been dispersed, there were many cadres left, including former pickets. So Lominadze chose Guangzhou as the base for the final insurrection. In mid November 1927, a civil war broke out in Guangdong between Zhang Fakui (representing the Guangdong clique)

and Li Jishen (representing the Guangxi clique). Lominadze took advantage of this situation, and ordered the Guangdong CCP to carry out an insurrection in Guangzhou. He sent Neumann to control it. The Guangzhou insurrection began on 11 December 1927. Its main force was model units and workers' pickets of the Guangzhou-Hong Kong Strike Committee, plus thousands of party members and workers. A 'Soviet Government' (delegates were appointed by the party) was announced, along with decrees of a socialist nature: nationalisation of large industries and banks; confiscation of land for the use of the peasants; confiscation of the houses of the bourgeoisie for the use of the common people, and so on. The insurrection lasted three days, before being destroyed by the combined forces of Zhang Fakui and Li Jishen. According to official reports, more than 5,700 people died.

8 Trotsky's Contribution to the Study of the Problems of the Chinese Revolution

... Here, I present a simple explanation of the most important problems Trotsky wrote about, especially those he debated with Stalin.

1. *The attitude of each class towards the anti-imperialist revolution.* Stalin felt that, under imperialist oppression, each class, from the bourgeoisie, petty bourgeoisie, and peasantry to the proletariat, would equally feel the need for a united struggle. Inter-class struggles would become less significant. So he advocated the 'bloc of four classes' as the foundation for the fight against imperialism.

Trotsky believed that imperialist aggression would not weaken class struggle, especially between the bourgeoisie and the proletariat, but sharpen it. He pointed out:

> It is a gross mistake to think that imperialism mechanically welds together all the classes of China from without.... The revolutionary struggle against imperialism does not weaken, but rather strengthens the political differentiation of the classes. Imperialism is a highly powerful force in the internal relationships of China. The main source of this force is not the warships in the waters of the Yangtze... but the economic and political bond between foreign capital and the native bourgeoisie....
> [E]verything that brings the oppressed and exploited masses of the toilers to their feet inevitably pushes the national bourgeoisie into an open bloc with the imperialists. The class struggle between the bourgeoisie and the masses of workers and peasants is not weakened, but on the con-

trary, it is sharpened by imperialist oppression, to the point of bloody civil war at every serious conflict ['The Chinese Revolution and the Theses of Comrade Stalin' (7 May 1927)].

Trotsky therefore said Stalin's policy of a 'bloc of four classes' was the most effective way of destroying the national revolution. The only hope was for the proletariat, along with the peasants and the poor from urban and rural areas, to crush the bourgeoisie's attempts to compromise with imperialism.

2. *Independence for the Communist Party.* Stalin thought the Guomindang was a party of all classes, a 'bloc of four classes', so he ordered the CCP to enter the Guomindang and carry out 'inner-party collaboration'. Through this kind of collaboration, Stalin believed it could lead the national revolution.

Trotsky's attitude towards the Guomindang was completely different. It did not matter how many petty bourgeois, workers, or peasants were in the Guomindang, it was still a party of the bourgeoisie led by bourgeois representatives. If the CCP joined the Guomindang, it would become a tool to cheat the workers and the peasants. Trotsky opposed the policy in the Politburo of the Russian Communist Party in 1923. In 1926, he 'advocated that the Communist Party immediately withdraw from the Guomindang'. On 4 March 1927, in a letter to Radek, he again stressed the absolute necessity for the CCP to quit the Guomindang. He predicted: 'For the Communist Party to remain in the Guomindang any longer threatens to have dire consequences for the proletariat and for the revolution'. This prediction was quickly verified.

On 10 May 1927, in 'The Communist Party and the Guomindang', Trotsky refuted the arguments used to oppose withdrawal from the Guomindang. He warned: 'By remaining in the same organisation with the Wang Jingweis, we are sharing the responsibility for their waverings and betrayals'.

According to Marxist theory, the independence of the party of the proletariat is indispensable. Its historical mission is to unite the vanguard of that class, become the leader of the revolution, expose frauds by bourgeois and petty-bourgeois politicians, organise the exploited and oppressed, and prepare for armed struggle to destroy the bourgeois state and establish its own régime. Stalin, however, renounced Marxist theory and Bolshevik experience by turning over all hopes for leadership of the revolution and social change to Chiang Kai-shek and Wang Jingwei.

From the beginning, Trotsky opposed the CCP's entering the Guomindang. He unceasingly called for its withdrawal and for an independent proletarian policy. He remained true to the Bolshevik tradition. If the CCP had followed his thinking, the possibilities for victory would have been great, because by March–April 1927 the CCP had become a mass party. Even though the party, including the members of the Communist Youth Corps, numbered only about 100,000, it led three million organised workers and fifteen million peasants in peasant associations.

3. *The problem of soviets.* If the Communist Party is the proletariat's revolutionary staff, soviets are the instrument through which the workers, peasants, and soldiers are united, the organisational centre of the revolution. They are the command posts through which the masses are armed, carry out the insurrection, and take power. After taking power, they become the basic organ of the state. Lenin, in the founding documents of the Communist International, emphasised soviets as a fundamental part of the political programme. Stalin, however, forgot about this programme, and placed all hopes for the organisation of the masses and the taking of power in the Guomindang. He saw the Guomindang as a 'revolutionary parliament', and opposed the establishment of soviets. After Chiang Kai-shek's 12 April coup took away this 'revolutionary parliament', Stalin thought the left-wing Guomindang could take the place of soviets. Since 'the revolutionary Guomindang in Wuhan...will in fact be converted into an organ of the revolutionary-democratic dictatorship of the proletariat and peasantry', it would decide the democratic tasks, such as national independence and the land problem. However, 'the revolutionary Guomindang' 'converted' into an executioner of the Communist Party and the workers and peasants.

Trotsky felt that no other organisational form except workers', peasants', and soldiers' soviets could prepare for armed insurrection and the taking of power. From the very start, he advocated soviets. On 29 March 1927, he wrote:

> It is precisely through soviets that the crystallisation of the class forces can keep pace with the new stage of the revolution instead of conforming to the organisational-political traditions of a bygone day, of the kind being offered by the Guomindang.... The indispensable condition is an independent proletarian party. The form for its closest collaboration with the rural and urban petty bourgeoisie is the soviets as organs of the struggle for power or as organs of power. Large sections of the Chinese National Revolutionary Army are still green, and bourgeois landowners' sons wield great influence within the ranks of the commanding staff. Because of this the future of the revolution is in danger. Once more, I do not see any other way to oppose this danger than soldiers' deputies joining workers' deputies, and so on.

This passage speaks clearly about the basic functions and capabilities of the soviets. It points to the great danger of the National Revolutionary Army and the fact that he did 'not see any other way to oppose this danger than soldiers' deputies joining workers' deputies' in united soviets. Had the CCP had the benefit of Trotsky's guidance, the situation would have changed. Most soldiers in Shanghai were sympathetic to the working masses. Even a division commander, Xue Yue, was sympathetic to the Communist Party. Troops in Wuxi and Suzhou were also against Chiang. If the CCP had called for workers' and soldiers' soviets, Chiang's troops could have been dispersed and his April coup overturned.

Following Chiang Kai-shek's coup, Trotsky called even more urgently for soviets. He explained the decisive significance of soviets in a revolutionary situation (see 'The Chinese Revolution and the Theses of Comrade Stalin'). He pointed out that only soviets can extend the horizons of the revolution. A 'critical point' was about to be reached in Hunan and Hubei. The workers and peasants had already been organised by the Communist Party. The workers were demanding better living conditions, the peasants were demanding land. The soldiers remained under the control of officers related to the landlords and the bourgeoisie. This became a barrier of mutual opposition between workers and soldiers. To avert this danger, it was necessary to establish workers', peasants', and soldiers' soviets. Then workers' and peasants' deputies could have cooperated with the soldiers, throwing off the control of bourgeois officers. But Stalin opposed soviets. His reason was that if soviets were established it would push the officers into the reactionary camp. The facts, however, were the opposite. Only soviets could have stopped the reactionary officers....

4. *The problem of strategy following the defeat of the revolution.* After the second Chinese revolution was defeated, Stalin initiated armed insurrections that destroyed the remaining revolutionary forces and deepened the defeat. After helping Chiang Kai-shek stabilise his dictatorship, Stalin suddenly discovered the philosophy of the 'Third Period'. According to this philosophy, world revolution was growing daily, and the proletariat urgently needed to prepare insurrections to take power. So, the 'Theses on the Revolutionary Movement in the Colonies and Semi-colonies' passed by the Sixth Comintern Congress set up the following line for the CCP:

> The Party must everywhere propagate the idea of soviets, the idea of the dictatorship of the proletariat and peasantry, and the inevitability of the coming revolutionary mass armed uprising. It must already

now emphasise in its agitation the necessity of overthrow of the ruling bloc and the mobilisation of the masses for revolutionary demonstrations,... it must consistently and undeviatingly follow the line of seizure of State power, organisation of soviets as organs of the insurrection, expropriation of the landlords and big property-owners, expulsion of the foreign imperialists and the confiscation of their property.... In China, the future growth of the revolution will place before the Party as an immediate practical task the preparation for and carrying through of armed insurrection as the sole path to the completion of the bourgeois-democratic revolution and to the overthrow... of the Guomindang [*International Press Correspondence*, 12 December 1928].

Protracted guerrilla war, the organisation of the 'Red Army', and the establishment of 'soviets' were all in accordance with the line set down at the Sixth Comintern Congress. Following Wang Jingwei's 'July Communist expulsion', Trotsky pointed out that the CCP should adopt a defensive policy. He argued that armed insurrection would only serve to destroy the remaining revolutionary forces. However, Stalin called Trotsky's defensive policy 'liquidationism' because it would 'liquidate' Stalinist adventurism. When Trotsky saw the adventurist strategic line set down for the CCP at the Sixth Comintern Congress, he wrote:

Bolshevik policy is characterised not only by its revolutionary scope, but also by its political realism. These two aspects of Bolshevism are inseparable. The greatest task is to know how to recognise in time a revolutionary situation and to exploit it to the end. But it is no less important to understand when this situation is exhausted and is converted, from the political point of view, into its antithesis. Nothing is more fruitless and worthless than to show one's fist after the battle.... It must be distinctly understood that there is not, at the present time, a revolutionary situation in China. It is rather a counter-revolutionary situation that has been substituted there, transforming itself into an inter-revolutionary period of indefinite duration ['The Chinese Question After the Sixth Congress' (4 October 1928)].

Since 'a counter-revolutionary situation.... has been substituted there, transforming itself into an inter-revolutionary period of indefinite duration', Trotsky proposed a transitional programme of democratic demands, in place of Stalin's adventurist line. Trotsky demanded an eight-hour day; freedom of speech, press, assembly, and association; and the right to strike. These demands were contained in one general slogan: convene a constituent assembly with full powers, elected by universal, equal, and direct suffrage. While propagandising for a constituent assembly, the party should also call for the expropriation of the landlords and national independence. The aim was to renew the confidence of the masses through a political struggle for everyday demands, while helping them unite in opposition to the Guomindang dictatorship. The party would gradually go from the defensive onto the offensive. When that happened, soviets would be established and the proletariat would prepare to lead the peasants in a struggle for power. The Left Opposition in the CCP, formed in 1929, based its propaganda and activity on this programme.

The CCP did not see Trotsky's proposals, since it was under Stalin's control. It could only honour the resolution of the Sixth Comintern Congress in 'the preparation for and carrying through of armed insurrection as the sole path to the completion of the bourgeois-democratic revolution and to the overthrow... of the Guomindang'. Starting in the autumn of 1928, in Jiangxi, Fujian, Hubei, and Anhui, the CCP initiated small-scale guerrilla wars and organised the 'Red Army' and 'soviets', including a 'Chinese Soviet Republic'. Between 1930 and 1934, the guerrilla movement spread widely. Chiang Kai-shek had to concentrate his forces in an encircling attack. In the autumn of 1934, the CCP leaders finally gave up the 'soviet' in southern Jiangxi and began the 'Long March' to the Northwest. In the autumn of 1935, they reached Yan'an, in northern Shaanxi. Millions of peasants in Jiangxi, Fujian, Anhui, and Hubei were left to the mercy of Chiang Kai-shek. Hundreds of thousands were killed, and 90 per cent of the Long Marchers were lost.

Chiang Kai-shek sent Zhang Xueliang's army to surround Yan'an, and prepared to destroy the CCP. In Moscow in the summer of 1935, the Seventh Congress of the Comintern adopted Stalin's Popular Front line of offering support to friendly bourgeois governments. Carrying out Stalin's line and trying to extricate itself from the military trap in which it found itself, the CCP reversed its previous policy. It switched from trying to overthrow the Guomindang to proposing a 'national united front' to resist Japan. However, in Chiang Kai-shek's view, before they could resist the Japanese, the CCP's army must be destroyed.

In December 1936, he personally went to Xi'an to inspect Zhang Xueliang's troops and prepare the attack on Yan'an. After his arrival, a group of Zhang's officers threatened to kill him because of his failure to resist Japan. When Stalin heard about the incident, he saw it as an opportunity to renew collaboration with Chiang Kai-shek. He ordered the CCP to find a way to 'save Chiang'. The CCP, already in great danger, sent Zhou Enlai to Xi'an to talk with Chiang. The CCP guaranteed Chiang's safety if he would consent to lead the struggle against

Japan, and it agreed to abolish the 'Red Army' and the 'soviets' and give up agrarian revolution. Its armed forces would participate in the war against Japan under Chiang's command. This was the outcome of 'armed insurrection ... to overthrow ... the Guomindang' and ten years of bloody struggle, sacrificing hundreds of thousands of lives. Trotsky drew a lesson from this outcome and wrote in the Fourth International's Transitional Programme:

> Following the inevitable collapse of the Guangzhou uprising, the Comintern took the road of guerrilla warfare and peasant soviets with complete passivity on the part of the industrial proletariat. Landing thus in a blind alley, the Comintern took advantage of the Sino-Japanese War to liquidate 'Soviet China' with a stroke of the pen, subordinating not only the peasant 'Red Army' but also the so-called 'Communist' Party to the identical Guomindang, that is, the bourgeoisie ['The Death Agony of Capitalism and the Tasks of the Fourth International' (1938) in *The Transitional Programme for Socialist Revolution* (New York: Pathfinder Press, 1974), p. 98].

5. *The problem of the nature of the Chinese revolution.* While the second Chinese revolution was unfolding, Trotsky did not explicitly advocate permanent revolution as a strategic line for the Chinese revolution, but his articles, especially those criticising Stalin, were all in accordance with that theory.

The line Stalin adopted was a Menshevik line of revolution by stages. He argued for the completion of the democratic tasks of the bourgeois revolution (national independence and land reform) and then socialist revolution (when the proletariat takes power). To complete the democratic tasks, he argued the proletariat must 'collaborate' with the bourgeoisie in a 'bloc of four classes'. To maintain 'collaboration', Stalin forced the CCP to carry out Guomindang policies. Stalin supported Chiang Kai-shek, even after Chiang's 'March coup' (1926). He hoped that Chiang would defeat imperialism and the warlords and achieve national independence and unification. Not until after Chiang's 'April coup' (1927) did Stalin give up his hopes for Chiang. However, he continued to look for completion of the democratic revolution to the Guomindang, the left Guomindang of Wang Jingwei. Only after Wang Jingwei copied Chiang's 'April coup' did Stalin give up his illusion that the Guomindang would carry out the bourgeois-democratic revolution.

Stalin's opposition to the CCP quitting the Guomindang to carry out an independent policy and organise workers', peasants', and soldiers' soviets was in keeping with his basic attitude of revolution by stages. In Stalin's view, these actions would go beyond his 'stage of the democratic revolution'. Thus, the second Chinese revolution was strangled with the rope of Stalin's theory of revolution by stages.

Trotsky's stand was the opposite. He believed that the bourgeoisie not only could not complete the tasks of the democratic revolution but could not avoid coming to terms with imperialism in opposition to the democratic demands of the worker and peasant masses. He consistently opposed Stalin's 'bloc of four classes' and 'Guomindang-CCP collaboration'. He felt this would 'have dire consequences for the proletariat and for the revolution'. So he opposed the CCP joining the Guomindang from the beginning, and later advocated its withdrawal. During the rising tide of revolution, he unceasingly promoted the organisation of soviets to oppose the Guomindang of Chiang Kai-shek and Wang Jingwei and to prepare to take power when the opportunity presented itself.

Why didn't Trotsky publicly promote permanent revolution during the second Chinese revolution? The main reason was that some the important leaders in the Left Opposition, such as Radek, Preobrazhensky, and Smilga, also disagreed with the theory. To obtain their cooperation, Trotsky had to refrain from using the term 'permanent revolution'; but actually, the outlook of permanent revolution permeated all his analyses and proposals. His analysis of the reactionary nature of the Chinese bourgeoisie, his criticism of the bloc of four classes and the Guomindang-CCP coalition government, and his promotion of complete independence for the CCP and the establishment of soviets were all practical manifestations of a concrete programme grounded in the theory of permanent revolution.

The first time Trotsky openly pointed out the permanent nature of the Chinese revolution was after the defeat of the Guangzhou insurrection. After analysing the soviet régime that resulted from this insurrection and its socialist policies, he concluded that in the coming third Chinese revolution, the dictatorship of the proletariat would settle the democratic tasks and follow the socialist road:

> [T]he class dialectics of the revolution, having spent all its other resources, clearly and conclusively put on the order of the day the *dictatorship of the proletariat*, leading the countless millions of oppressed and disinherited.... The Guangzhou insurrection, with all its prematurity, with all the adventurism of its leadership, raised the curtain of a new stage, or, more correctly, of the coming *third* Chinese revolution.... The workers of Guangzhou outlawed the Guomindang, *declaring all of its tendencies illegal.* This means that for the solution of the basic national tasks, not only the big bourgeoisie but also the petty bourgeoisie was

incapable of producing a political force, a party, or a faction, in conjunction with which the party of the proletariat might be able to solve the tasks of the bourgeois-democratic revolution. The key to the situation lies precisely in the fact that *the task of winning the movement of the poor peasants already fell entirely upon the shoulders of the proletariat*, and directly upon the Communist Party; and that the approach to a genuine solution of the bourgeois-democratic tasks of the revolution necessitated the concentration of all power in the hands of the proletariat.... These fundamental and, at the same time, incontrovertible social and political prerequisites of the third Chinese revolution demonstrate not only that the formula of the democratic dictatorship has *hopelessly outlived its usefulness*, but also that the revolution ... will not have a 'democratic' period ... but will be compelled from the very outset to effect the most decisive shake-up and abolition of bourgeois property in city and village ['Summary and Perspectives of the Chinese Revolution' (June 1928), emphasis in original].

The third Chinese revolution, led by the CCP, won under the exceptional conditions created by the Japanese War and Second World War. However, the CCP still upheld the theory of revolution by stages, established an alliance with the bourgeoisie and petty bourgeoisie (the 'Consultative Conference'), and organised a 'coalition government of four classes'. They protected bourgeois and imperialist property and postponed land reform, to realise Mao Zedong's 'New Democracy'. Still, under the pressure of the dialectical logic of the class struggle and the grave threats from hostile classes inside and outside China (especially after the outbreak of the Korean War in 1950 and the counterattack on the part of the internal bourgeoisie), the CCP could not but adopt some socialist measures, such as a planned economy and monopolisation of foreign trade, to limit the activities of the bourgeoisie. They also used the method of 'state and private joint ownership' (1955) to gradually take away bourgeois property rights. In 1956, at the Eighth Congress, Liu Shaoqi announced the 'dictatorship of the proletariat', to show that the 'coalition government of four classes' had come to an end. Under the pressure of objective conditions the CCP, to protect itself, was forced to yield to the laws of permanent revolution and nationalise the property of the bourgeoisie, making China a workers' state. So Trotsky's prediction about the permanent development of the Chinese revolution was basically correct.

However, the CCP was forced to yield to the permanent revolution; it did so unconsciously and empirically, thus greatly distorting the natural development of permanent revolution. This distortion can be seen in the substitution of an all-inclusive 'People's Congress' for workers' and peasants' soviets, and the substitution of a *bureaucratic dictatorship* for the dictatorship of the proletariat. This became an irreconcilable contradiction between society's economic foundation and its political superstructure. The only way to get rid of this kind of contradiction, allow the revolution to develop, destroy all internal exploitative relations, and push forward the world revolution is for China (as well as the Soviet Union, Eastern Europe, North Korea, and North Vietnam) to undergo a political revolution, which would get rid of the bureaucratic dictatorship and establish a proletarian democratic system.

6. *The Sino-Japanese War.* The Sino-Japanese War, which began in July 1937, was the most important event in modern Chinese history. It not only had decisive significance for Chinese national independence but was one of the most explosive factors in the world situation at the time. Hitler, who initiated the Second World War, utilised the Sino-Japanese War to obtain a military alliance with Japan. The Japanese war was one of aggression, and thus reactionary. The Chinese resistance was just and progressive, but its leader, Chiang Kai-shek, was reactionary. He was the butcher of the second Chinese revolution and after September 1931, when Japan invaded Manchuria, let Japanese imperialism initiate its war of aggression.

The CCP abolished the 'Red Army' and the 'soviets', gave up demands for democratic reforms and unconditionally supported Chiang Kai-shek, placing itself under his direction in the war. This was a repetition of the policy carried out by Stalin in the second Chinese revolution. Others felt that, since Chiang Kai-shek was a counter-revolutionary, the war of resistance under him could not be progressive; that 'the Sino-Japanese War was a war between the Japanese emperor and Chiang Kai-shek', and both sides were reactionary. They advocated a defeatist policy. One representative of this tendency was Zheng Chaolin. In the early period of the war, it did not have much influence. But about the time of American involvement in the war, Wang Fanxi felt that if war broke out between Japan and the United States, the Chinese war would become subsumed in an imperialist war, thus losing its progressive nature and becoming reactionary. He then used this 'theory of the changing nature of the war of resistance' to support defeatism. The Chinese Trotskyist organisation entered a period of confusion and debate, and finally split. ...

Trotsky made a precise analysis of the war and pointed out a strategic direction for it: 'In participation in the military struggle under the orders of Chiang Kai-shek ... to prepare politically the overthrow of Chiang Kai-shek'. This strategic line was not just 'the only revolutionary policy' for that period but could be utilised by any oppressed nation in the struggle against aggression (the oppressed nation's struggles against aggression are frequently forced upon the ruling class for its own protection). This strategic direction can also be used in workers' states under Stalinist parties confronted with armed aggression by imperialists. 'In participation in the military struggle under the orders of the bureaucracy... to prepare politically the overthrow of the bureaucracy'....

9   Conclusion

We can divide CCP history (up to Trotsky's assassination) into seven periods:

1. Under the influence of the ideas of Lenin and Trotsky, it follows the Bolshevik line (1920 to July 1922).
2. As a result of Stalin's ordering the CCP to join the Guomindang, it turns from a Bolshevik line to Menshevik opportunism (August 1922 to August 1924).
3. One part of the CCP leadership, in accordance with basic principles of Bolshevism, participates in the leadership of the working class movement (August 1924 to December 1925).
4. Because of the problem of 'Guomindang-CCP collaboration', the CCP and the Comintern develop a disagreement (December 1925 to July 1926).
5. The CCP, forced to follow Stalin's Menshevik line, is defeated. The debate over China between Trotsky and Stalin became fiercest (1926 to July 1927).
6. Under the control of Stalin, the CCP jumps from ultra-rightist opportunism to ultra-leftist adventurism; Trotsky, having opposed Stalin's opportunism, now opposes his adventurism (July 1927 to July 1937).
7. Following the defeats of the adventurist armed insurrections initiated under Stalin's direction, the CCP returns to an opportunist line and carries out, for the second time, a policy of 'Guomindang-CCP collaboration'; having opposed Stalin's adventurism, Trotsky now opposes his opportunism (1937 to 1940).

After the defeat of the revolution, the CCP became Stalinist, politically and organisationally. Its leadership became a tool for carrying out Stalin's policies. On the other hand, part of the CCP leadership and some cadres, learning the lesson of the defeat of the revolution, organised a Left Opposition....

Introduction: Leon Trotsky and Chinese Communism

Wang Fanxi

(October 1980)

This is a previously unpublished English version of Wang Fanxi's introduction ('Einleitung: Trotzki und der chinesische Kommunismus') to the two China volumes (Schriften über China) that formed part of the definitive ten-volume German edition of Trotsky's works (Leo Trotzki, Schriften), edited by Helmut Dahmer and published in Hamburg by Rasch and Röhring in 1990. Source: a manuscript in the editor's possession.

This book is a collection of Leon Trotsky's articles, speeches, and letters on China – on the Chinese revolution of 1925–7 and the Sino-Japanese war that broke out in 1937. The pieces cover a period of sixteen years, from 1924 to 1940, when the author was assassinated.

The main writings were published in Chinese by Chinese Trotskyists, first in 1930 and then in an enlarged edition in 1947. This German edition, based on the 1976 American edition, larger than the Chinese one, adds to that edition material from Trotsky's Exile Papers and other unpublished documents. It is the most complete presentation of Trotsky's work on China to date.

It would be superfluous to commend these writings, which are basic for an understanding of the history of the communist movement in China and the Soviet Union and of the tactics and strategy of world socialist revolution. That said, there remains a need to link these separate pieces and make more intelligible certain aspects of various fiercely contested problems. Having participated in the events described, I can claim some qualification for writing these notes.

The Chinese Communist Party (CCP) was an offspring of Russia's October Revolution. Ideologically and materially, it owed its birth and growth to the aid of Soviet Communists, who had already achieved victory in their own revolution. Without this aid, a Communist organisation might still have emerged in China in the early 1920s, but it is unlikely to have grown at the same speed; nor could it have played as powerful a role in the revolution of 1925–7.

This outside aid not only promoted the emergence and growth of the CCP and sped the development of the revolution; it also, ironically, became a main cause of its tragic defeats. To explain this paradox, we must look at the nature of the aid, particularly the Comintern's directives.

No strategy for the countries of the East was advanced by the Comintern until its Second Congress, in July–August 1920, when leaders of the world Communist movement, through Lenin, worked out their theses on the national and colonial questions. These recommended 'support [for] bourgeois-democratic national movement in the colonial and backward countries only on the condition that, in these countries, the elements of future proletarian parties, which will be communist not only in name, are brought together and trained to understand their special tasks, that is, those of the struggle against the bourgeois-democratic movements within their own nations. The Communist International must establish temporary relations and even unions with the revolutionary movements in the colonies and backward countries without amalgamation with them, but preserving the independent character of the proletarian movement, even though it be still in its embryonic form' (Lenin, *Collected Works*, vol. 31, p. 149).

These Leninist principles could not be carried out under Lenin's personal guidance because of his illness and death. When revolution broke out in China in 1925 (and even during its brewing), the leadership of the Comintern and the Soviet Communist Party had fallen into other hands (first the Stalin-Zinoviev bloc, then the Stalin and Bukharin faction). A new chapter had begun in the history of the Russian revolution, in which conservatism replaced revolutionary enthusiasm, 'socialism in one country' replaced 'world revolution', and arbitrary bureaucracy emerged and consolidated itself. The new leaders monopolised the direction of the Chinese revolution, adopting a line opposite to Lenin's. In defence of the October tradition and of Lenin's strategy for China, Trotsky and his co-thinkers tried to secure a change of course, but failed.

The defeats of the Russian Opposition and the Chinese revolution were closely linked. The clearer the bankruptcy of Stalin's China policy, the more violent the suppression of the Opposition. When the revolution was brought to catastrophe in the autumn of 1927, the Trotskyist Oppositionists were annihilated – first politically and then physically. Their views – confirmed by events in China – were suppressed, distorted, and tabooed. But the documents survived Stalinist censorship, and the truth can be established.

The first controversy that arose before the outbreak of the revolution and continued until its defeat was whether the CCP should retain its independence. This first and perhaps most important controversy on a fundamental question of the Chinese revolution initially broke out not in the Russian or Comintern leadership but between leaders of the young CCP and the Comintern, immediately after the CCP's Second Congress in July 1922.

INTRODUCTION: LEON TROTSKY AND CHINESE COMMUNISM (1980)

The Founding Congress of the CCP, in July 1921, did no more than proclaim a series of principles. It declared that the Chinese Communists had determined to follow the Russian example, to struggle establish a proletarian dictatorship in order to realise Communist aims in China, and to set up a Communist Party based on the organisational principles of the Bolsheviks to achieve that aim. No attempt was made to link the ultimate goal of communism to the realities of contemporary China except for a decision by the CCP to devote itself to education and organising the working class.

After a year of practical work, the Second Congress (July 1922) took a different approach. For the first time, it proposed tackling questions of the anti-imperialist, anti-feudal, and national-democratic revolution, and the relationship between the CCP and the Guomindang. On 10 June, the CCP issued its 'First Manifesto on the Current Situation', which declared 'the urgent task of the proletariat is to act jointly with the democratic party to establish a united front of democratic revolution to struggle for the overthrow of the military and for the organisation of a real democratic government.... Of all the political parties existing in China, only the Guomindang can be characterised as a revolutionary party'.[1] The Congress described the CCP's attitude towards the 'national revolution': 'We believe the national revolution is advantageous not only to the bourgeoisie but also to the proletariat. We should unite with all revolutionary parties and form a united front with the Guomindang.... At the same time we must tell [the workers and peasants] that such a united front is not to make sacrifice for the sake of the Guomindang but for the sake of securing a temporary freedom. The proletariat must not forget, in the course of the struggle, to maintain its independent organisation'.[2]

This complied with Lenin's theses. However, the Comintern leaders did not approve it. By then the Russian government and the Comintern's main concern was the Soviet Union's diplomatic isolation in East Asia. After the Russians helped establish a communist party, they sent a series of representatives to Sun Yat-sen to discuss the possibility of friendly relations with China and cooperation between the CCP and the Guomindang. Voitinsky went in the autumn of 1920, Maring in the winter of 1921, and Dalin during the CCP's Second Congress, to propose a united front of revolutionary groups. Sun instead proposed that members of the CCP and the Communist League of Youth join the Guomindang as individuals and obey its programme and discipline.

Underestimating the CCP's potential strength and overestimating the Guomindang's, Moscow accepted Sun Yat-sen's demands and told the CCP to

---

1 Brandt, Conrad, Benjamin Schwartz and John K. Fairbank (eds) 1967, pp. 58 and 62.
2 Guo Hualun 1969–71, Volume 1, p. 82.

do as Sun wished. Maring went to China to push for such a decision. The CCP had already passed a resolution calling for a different form of co-operation, so Maring demanded an emergency conference. The five members of the Central Committee refused to reconsider. To join the Guomindang, argued Chen Duxiu, would confuse class organisations and reduce the Party's independence. Only by resorting to Comintern discipline and playing on the Comintern's prestige did Maring succeed in persuading them to yield.

Whether or not the CCP should have joined the Guomindang was among the first major differences between Trotsky and Stalin. Trotsky opposed entry in 1923 ('Letter to Shachtman', 1930), but he did not made his position public until 1926, because of concessions (which he later admitted were a mistake) to the Left Opposition (chiefly Radek) and to the Zinovievists in 1926. Not until 27 September 1926 did he openly reveal his opinion, in his article 'The CCP and the Guomindang'. Even then his arguments were mild, for he was still bound by the discipline of the United Opposition. On 7 May 1927, however, under the impact of Chiang Kai-shek's 12 April coup, he launched a thunderous attack on the abandoning of the CCP's independence. On 2 July 1927, on the eve of the 'betrayal' by the 'left' Guomindang in Wuhan, Zinoviev and his followers issued a common document with Trotsky ('The New Stage of the Chinese Revolution') calling for withdrawal, but by then it was too late. It was no longer a question of whether to stay in or withdraw, but how to survive under Guomindang terror and organise the resistance.

The Stalin-Bukharin faction took a far worse position. Even after Wang Jingwei, the 'left' Guomindang leader, assassinated communists on a mass scale, the CCP was still not allowed to drop the Guomindang banner and had to continue 'cooperating' with a party that had completely turned against it and was killing its followers. The policy of 'fighting the Guomindang under the banner of the Guomindang' was not abandoned until the tragic defeat of the Guangzhou insurrection of 11 December 1927.

The difference between Trotsky on the one hand and Stalin and Bukharin (and to some extent Zinoviev and Radek) on the other on relations with the Guomindang was an extension of their views on the Guomindang as a party. The majority saw it as 'a bloc of proletariat, peasantry, urban petty bourgeoisie, and the national bourgeoisie' (Resolution of the Seventh Plenum of the Comintern Executive [ECCI]). Stalin at first (1925) called it a 'workers' and peasants' party' ('Problems of Leninism', p. 264), and in May 1927 he called it a 'party of a bloc of several oppressed classes'('Talk with Students of Sun Yat-sen University'). If it was a bloc in which workers and peasants predominated, the

CCP's entry into it would not (according to the Stalinists) prevent the CCP from maintaining its independence but would enable it to win more allies.

Trotsky pointed out as early as 1924 that Sun Yat-sen's ideology was bourgeois (see 'Perspectives and Tasks in the East'). He believed that defining the Guomindang as a workers' and peasants' party 'has nothing in common with Marxism' ('The Chinese Revolution and the Theses of Comrade Stalin', p. 178). He argued that 'to depict the Guomindang as a formless organisation committed to no one is to distort the very meaning of the question. No matter how formless the Guomindang is at its periphery, its central apparatus has the revolutionary dictatorship firmly in hand' (p. 202). So he asserted that '[t]he Guomindang is *a party*, and in the time of revolution it can be understood as a party. In the past period, this party has not embodied the "bloc of four classes" but the leading role of the bourgeoisie over the masses of the people, the proletariat and the Communist Party included' (p. 227, emphasis in the original).

The CCP leaders knew little about this difference of opinion. Ever since being forced to abandon their independence and join the Guomindang, they had worked hard to implement the policy of entry. However, on several occasions they (or some of them) proposed a change in policy to the Comintern, as the official line became increasingly difficult to follow. After Chiang Kai-shek's pre-emptive strike against the communists on 20 March 1926, and the CCP's capitulation to Chiang under Comintern pressure, Chen Duxiu (who had opposed entry at and after the CCP's Second Congress) again raised his opposition and said in a personal report to the Comintern 'that cooperation with the Guomindang by means of joint work within it should be changed to cooperation from outside the Guomindang' ('Appeal to All Comrades of the CCP'). Chen's proposal was bitterly attacked by Bukharin in *Pravda*.

Nearly four months later, the CCP's Fourth Central Committee passed a resolution at its Second Plenum titled 'On the Relations between the CCP and the Guomindang'. While not demanding immediate withdrawal from the Guomindang, it proposed five concrete measures to guarantee the CCP's independent activity. These measures were sharply criticised in an editorial in *Communist International* that called for a thorough reversal of these wrong decisions.[3]

---

3 The Resolution was sent to Moscow but there was no reaction to it from the Comintern until the following year, when an editorial in *Communist International* (no. 11, 16 March 1927) titled 'The Fifth Congress of the CCP and the Guomindang' criticised it severely and demanded that the CCP's forthcoming Congress revise all the decisions taken at the July 1926 Plenum.

So the CCP revolted a second time on the question of the Guomindang. A third revolt took place after the anti-communist coup in Changsha on 21 May 1927. Twice Chen Duxiu proposed withdrawing at a meeting of the CCP's Politburo. His proposals were rejected by the majority and by the representatives in attendance (ibid.).

Finally, on 15 July 1927, Chen Duxiu tendered his resignation as general secretary on the grounds that the 'International wishes us to carry out our own policy on the one hand, and does not allow us to withdraw from the Guomindang on the other. There is really no way out and I cannot continue my work' (ibid.).

Although unfamiliar with each other's views, Chen Duxiu and Trotsky had the same attitude towards the relationship between the CCP and the Guomindang. This was a main reason why Chen Duxiu and his close friends became Trotskyists when they got access to Oppositionist writings in the autumn of 1929.

Trotsky's article 'Class Relations in the Chinese Revolution' was a direct criticism of the editorial. He said: 'It is necessary to approve as unconditionally correct the Resolution of the June [actually July] Plenum of the CC of the CCP, which demands that the party withdraw from the Guomindang'. Trotsky had already seen the Resolution six months earlier and had criticised it in his article 'The CCP and the Guomindang', where he wrote: 'We have taken the above-mentioned arguments from the 14 July 1926 resolution of the CCP Central Committee Plenum. This resolution, along with other documents of the Plenum, testifies to the extremely contradictory policies of the CCP and to the dangers flowing from that' (p. 115).

Stalin's Guomindang policy was based on the idea of the 'bloc of four classes', which, in turn, was supported by the fact of imperialist oppression in China. While this oppression had not, according to Stalin, eliminated class antagonisms, it had greatly weakened and modified them; it made necessary and possible the formation of an 'all-national united front'; and the Guomindang was the political expression of that united front.

To support his assertion that the Chinese bourgeoisie could and should occupy an important position in the united front, Stalin stressed the division

---

The editorial distorted the Resolution, claiming it proposed to 'substitute an alliance as separate bodies for the policy of alliance by affiliation... which logically pre-supposes the CP's exit from the Guomindang'. Actually it said 'it is entirely wrong to advocate as some comrades do that the CCP should sever all organisational relations with the Guomindang, to liquidate right now this party of the bloc of all classes' (Guo Hualun 1969–71, Volume 1, p. 190).

of the Chinese big bourgeoisie into two uncompromising opposites: national bourgeoisie and comprador bourgeoisie. 'The former was anti-imperialist, and the founder of the Guomindang, while the latter was pro-imperialist, and it was and remains a sworn enemy of the Guomindang' ('The Third Question in Stalin's Talk with Students of Sun Yat-sen University').

As if anticipating this conception of the national bourgeoisie, in July 1920, in his Report of the Commission on the National and Colonial Question, at the Second Congress of the Comintern, Lenin pointed out 'A certain rapprochement has been brought about between the bourgeoisie of the exploiting countries and those of the colonial countries so that very often, even in the majority of cases, perhaps, where the bourgeoisie of the oppressed countries does support the national movement, it simultaneously works in harmony with the imperialist bourgeoisie, that is, it joins the latter in fighting against the revolutionary movements and revolutionary classes'.

In conformity with Lenin's ideas, Trotsky repeatedly expressed his opinions on the same question after 1925 and elaborated them in his criticism of Stalin's Theses on the Chinese Revolution. 'It would further be profound naivety to believe that an abyss lies between the so-called comprador bourgeoisie, that is, the economic and political agency of foreign capital in China, and the so-called national bourgeoisie', he wrote. 'No, these two sections stand incomparably closer to each other than the bourgeoisie and the masses of workers and peasants. The bourgeoisie participated in the national war as an internal brake, looking upon the worker and peasant masses with growing hostility and becoming even readier to conclude a compromise with imperialism' (pp. 160–1).

These lines were written on 7 May 1927, twenty-five days after Chiang Kai-shek, leader of the 'national bourgeoisie', had 'capitulated to the comprador bourgeoisie' and massacred the workers. Now Stalin offered the title of 'national bourgeoisie' to another Guomindang leader, Wang Jingwei (head of the Wuhan government), declaring he would carry on the anti-comprador campaign. Two months later, Wang Jingwei also capitulated to the 'comprador bourgeoisie' and began massacring workers and peasants in Wuhan.

Closely linked with the above was the dispute around the question of soviets. If, judging from arguments alone, Stalin and company were also of the opinion that the national bourgeoisie was weak-willed in its fight against imperialism, that it might compromise with imperialism, and that the CCP should act to prevent the possible betrayal of the revolution by the bourgeoisie, then the vital difference between Trotsky and Stalin lay in the following: How could the

CCP and the workers and peasants prevent and launch a counterattack against the national bourgeoisie's possible betrayal? According to Trotsky, the only reliable way was to call for soviets, carry on propaganda for them, and organise them when millions of peasants and workers in Hunan and Hubei were aroused in response to the advance of the Nationalist armies.[4]

The Stalinists bitterly opposed this slogan throughout the revolution. Their reasons: 1) to call for soviets would damage the united front with the bourgeoisie; 2) it would give imperialists a new excuse to fight against the Chinese revolution by saying that the Chinese revolution was an 'artificially transplanted Moscow sovietisation'; 3) soviets could only be organised as an organ for insurrection and for socialist proletarian revolution; 4) the Left Guomindang had already been a sort of soviet.

According to Trotsky, Stalin's 'entire logic represents a flagrant distortion of the meaning of our entire revolutionary experience, illuminated theoretically by Lenin' (p. 150). The further development of the Chinese revolution proved Trotsky right. Without soviets, the Chinese workers and peasant masses were impotent and at the mercy of their butchers, in the face of repeated betrayals by the bourgeoisie.

The CCP leadership did not participate in the discussion. Although the Hong Kong-Guangzhou Strike Committee (1925–6) was the 'Chinese version of workers' deputies'; although the peasant associations organised in Hunan during the Northern Expedition to some extent played the role of peasant soviets (cf. Isaacs 1961, pp. 112–13); and although the Shanghai workers organised their own 'soviets' after their armed insurrection of 22 February 1927, the CCP leaders paid no attention to this question. However, Qu Qiubai, a so-called left-wing leader of the CCP at the time, wrote that he 'proposed to call on workers of different factories and trade unions to elect representatives, and to agitate among the small merchants to do the same so that "a provincial soviet of deputies of the townspeople" could be created'.[5] But it was a passing thought; he did not raise the suggestion again, probably because he had been told of the position adopted by the CPSU's dominant faction and submitted to it.

A further charge was that Trotsky overlooked the role the petty bourgeoisie and peasantry could play in the revolution. As a matter of fact, Trotsky was

---

[4] The earliest published call for soviets so far traced is in his letter to Alsky, 29 March 1927. However, in 'Summary and Perspectives of the Chinese Revolution' he writes: '[F]rom 1926 on the Opposition advanced the slogan of soviets in China' (p. 321).

[5] Such as the 'District Soviet of Workers of Yangshupu' (see Qu Qiubai, 'Controversial Problems of the Chinese Revolution', Appendix 1, pp. 194–6).

more discriminating. For him the questions were: 1) with what part of the petty bourgeoisie should the proletariat ally and 2) how could they thus unite? To the first question, Trotsky replied as follows:

> When we, the Opposition, spoke of the necessity for the revolutionary alliance of the proletariat and the petty bourgeoisie we had in mind the oppressed masses, the tens and hundreds of millions of poor of town and countryside. The Comintern leadership understood and understands by the petty bourgeoisie those petty bourgeois summits, overwhelmingly intellectuals, who, under the form of democratic parties and organisations, exploit the rural and urban poor, selling them out at the decisive moment to the big bourgeoisie ('The Political Situation in China and the Tasks of the Bolshevik-Leninists Opposition', p. 404).

To the second question, Trotsky's answer was: the petty bourgeoisie must be won over to the alliance through the struggle of the proletariat.

According to Stalin and that part of the left opposition represented by M. Alsky, China was then divided into two camps: in one were the imperialists and militarists and layers of the Chinese bourgeoisie; in the other were the workers, artisans, petty bourgeois, students, intellectuals, and middle bourgeois with a nationalist orientation. They represented a reactionary alliance on the one hand, and a revolutionary front on the other. This division was definite and clear-cut. The former was manipulated by the imperialists, while the latter was 'by right' under the hegemony of the proletariat. Most policies adopted by the Stalinists during that period were based on this theory of two camps.

Trotsky considered such a view not only mechanistic but false and dangerous. 'In fact', he said, 'there are three camps in China – the reactionary, the liberal bourgeoisie and the proletariat – fighting for hegemony over the lower strata of the petty bourgeoisie and the peasantry' ('Letter to Alsky', p. 128, in *Leon Trotsky on China*).

Historical experiences and socio-economic analysis show that neither the urban petty bourgeoisie nor the peasantry will join the revolutionary camp and follow the leadership of the working class 'by nature', simply because of their class position. The opposite is true: the petty bourgeoisie, particularly its upper layers, were apt to be deceived and dominated by the national bourgeoisie and even by the reactionaries, and to be directed against the working class. To prevent this, Trotsky based almost all his policies in the Chinese revolution on the theory of three camps. The question that concerned him above all was: how could the party of the working class win the tens and hundreds of millions of poor in town and village to the camp of the proletariat in order to fight the two other camps, the reactionaries and the liberal bourgeoisie.

On the character of Chinese society and the Chinese revolution, Stalin levelled two charges against his opponent: he failed to understand that 'survivals of feudalism are the predominating factor in the oppression in China at the moment' ('The Revolution in China and the Tasks of the Comintern'); and he tried 'mechanically to implant certain general formulas, regardless of the concrete conditions of the movement in different countries' ('Notes on Contemporary Themes').

But what Trotsky wrote between April 1924 and March–April 1927 shows both charges are unfounded. Unlike Radek, who thought that in China feudal remnants were insignificant (he said so in his book on the Chinese revolution, originally given as lectures at Sun Yat-sen University in Moscow), Trotsky recognised not only the existence of 'survivals of feudalism' in China but their 'undeniable strength'. But he strongly opposed Stalin-Bukharin's argument that the 'survivals of feudalism dominated in Chinese economic life', and he opposed even more strongly the idea that this dominance determined the bourgeois character of the revolution and the revolutionary character of the bourgeoisie. In his view, feudal and capitalist relations in China were interlaced in a complex and tortuous way. 'There is no caste of feudal landlords in China in opposition to the bourgeoisie.... The agrarian revolution is therefore just as much anti-bourgeois as it is anti-feudal in character' ('Summary and Perspectives of the Chinese Revolution').

Trotsky did not deduce his views from a priori definition or historical analogies but from the living structure of Chinese society and its inner dynamics. Only by closely following the developments of the revolution, and through a series of successive approximations, did Trotsky reach his final 'formula' about the character of the Chinese revolution and its revolutionary power.

On 21 April 1924, Trotsky spoke for the first time about the Chinese revolution's character and perspectives. He said: 'There is no doubt that if the Chinese Guomindang party manages to unify China under a national-democratic régime then the capitalist development of China will go ahead with seven-mile strides. Yet all this will prepare the mobilisation of the countless proletarian masses who will at once burst out of prehistoric, semi-barbaric state and cast themselves into industry's melting-pot, the factory'.

In 1925 and 1926, Trotsky did not, as far we can see, discuss the character of the Chinese revolution in particular. He concentrated on the independence of the CCP. He was angry because the Comintern, while forbidding the CCP to withdraw from the Guomindang, which he thought a fundamental condition for the victory of the revolution, simultaneously comforted itself and the

Chinese workers with the promise of a 'non-capitalist perspective of China'. This perspective, he believed, could only be decided by a number of international factors.

In March 1927, Trotsky returned to the question in his letter to Alsky (29 March):

> Only an ignoramus of the socialist-reactionary variety could think that *present-day* China, with its *current* technological and economic foundations, can through its *own* efforts jump over the capitalist phase (emphasis in the original).

Two days later, on 31 March, 1927, in a letter to the Politburo of the CPSU(B), he again raised this question in connection with the slogan of soviets:

> A system of soviets in China would not be, at least not in the coming period, an instrument of proletarian dictatorship, but one of revolutionary national liberation and democratic unification of the country.... In China, what is occurring is a national-democratic revolution, not a socialist revolution (p. 135).

On 3 April 1927, eight days before Chiang Kai-shek's coup, in his article 'Class Relations in the Chinese Revolution', he further elaborated his ideas on this question:

> Above all it must be made clear to the vanguard of the Chinese proletariat that China has no prerequisites whatsoever economically for an independent transition to socialism; that the revolution now unfolding under the leadership of the Guomindang is a bourgeois-national revolution, that it can have as its consequence, even in the event of complete victory, only the further development of productive forces on the basis of capitalism. But it is necessary to develop no less forcefully before the Chinese proletariat the converse side of the question as well: The belated bourgeois-national revolution is unfolding in China in conditions of the imperialist decay of capitalism. As the Russian experience had already shown – in contrast, say, to the English – politics does not at all develop in parity with economics. China's further development must be taken in an international perspective. Despite the backwardness of Chinese economy, and in part precisely because of this backwardness, the Chinese revolution is wholly capable of bringing to political power an alliance of workers and peasants, under the

leadership of the proletariat. This régime will be China's political link with the world revolution (p. 142).

So Trotsky concluded that the permanent revolution 'formula' might, even should, be applied to China. But with one reservation: the revolutionary power established by the worker-peasant alliance would be a sort of democratic dictatorship of workers and peasants, not a dictatorship of the proletariat. It took him another year, during which he saw how the 'revolutionary' bourgeoisie and leaders of the petty bourgeoisie betrayed the revolution and broke the 'democratic alliance of workers and peasants'. Now for the first time he declared: 'We must understand that after the experience with the Guomindang in general and with the left Guomindang in particular, *a historically overdue slogan will become a weapon of the forces working against the revolution*. And for us it is no longer a question of the democratic dictatorship of the proletariat and the peasantry, but of the dictatorship of the proletariat supported by the inexhaustible masses of urban and rural poor' ('New Opportunities for the Chinese Revolution, New Tasks, and New Mistakes', 19 September 1927, emphasis in the original, p. 266).

Finally, in December 1927, from the defeat of the Guangzhou insurrection ('a laboratory experiment of a gigantic scale'), Trotsky drew the following conclusion:

> These fundamental and, at the same time, incontrovertible social and political prerequisites of the third Chinese revolution demonstrate not only that the formula of the democratic dictatorship had *hopelessly outlived its usefulness*, but also that the third revolution ... will not have a 'democratic' period, ... but it will be compelled from the very outset to effect the most decisive shake-up and abolition of bourgeois property in city and village (p. 305, emphasis in the original).

That is to say, the revolution in China will be socialist from the beginning.

Such was the progress of Trotsky's thinking on the character of the Chinese revolution, set out in his three letters to Preobrazhensky (March–April 1928). People might dispute his views, but they cannot accuse him of applying his 'theory of permanent revolution' to China regardless of the concrete condition of the Chinese movement.

Did the third Chinese revolution[6] confirm Trotsky's views on the character of the revolution? Leading members of the CCP, including Mao Zedong, who

---

6 Marxists in China and the Soviet Union called the 1911 revolution the first revolution, the 1925–7 revolution the second, and the 1949 revolution the third.

all along followed Stalin's formulas of 'bourgeois democratic revolution' and 'dictatorship of people's democracy' (a variation of the democratic dictatorship of workers and peasants), were finally compelled to declare under the pressure of actual developments that the 'dictatorship of the people's democracy' was in essence a dictatorship of the proletariat (Liu Shaoqi, Political Report to the Eighth Congress of the CCP, 1956).

After the defeat of the revolution in 1927, disagreements between Trotskyists and Stalinists concerned three problems:

1. How to assess the new situation and what slogan to adopt for it;
2. what relationship to expect between peasant war and the next upsurge of revolution;
3. what attitude to take towards China's war of resistance against Japan.

When did the second Chinese revolution end? In retrospect, the answer is easy: in July 1927, when the Wuhan government turned against the Communists and workers' organisations throughout China were smashed. At the time, however, it was rather a complicated and difficult question. Even Trotsky did not reach a conclusion immediately.[7] In 'New Opportunities for the Chinese Revolution, New Tasks, and New Mistakes', written in September 1927 in connection with He Long and Ye Ting's 'Southern Expedition' and the peasant uprisings in Hunan, Trotsky posed the question as follows: 'Is it the epilogue common enough after great historic defeats... or is it the spontaneous beginning of a great new chapter in the Chinese revolution?' (p. 258). His answer: 'Neither of these possibilities is excluded' (p. 259).

As a revolutionary, Trotsky at first took a cautious and hopeful view of the situation created after the Wuhan debacle. However, the defeat of the 'Southern Expedition' and the tragedy of the Guangzhou insurrection showed that profound changes had occurred in class relationships in China, so he declared in June 1928 that the Chinese revolution had been defeated and was 'entering a period of reflux' (p. 313).

In October 1928, he put it more trenchantly: 'It must be distinctly understood there is not, at the present time, a revolutionary situation in China. It is rather a counter-revolutionary situation that has been substituted there, transforming itself into an inter-revolutionary period of indefinite duration. Turn with contempt from those who would tell you that this is pessimism and lack

---

7 Until I read 'New Opportunities for the Chinese Revolution, New Tasks, and New Mistakes', published in English for the first time in 1976, I thought Trotsky had declared the Chinese revolution defeated immediately after Wang Jingwei's betrayal in July 1927.

of faith. To shut one's eyes to facts is the most infamous form of lack of faith' (p. 357).

This 'infamous' attitude well describes that struck by Stalin and Bukharin. It was neither cautious nor responsible. They were concerned above all to conceal the disasters caused by their treacherous policies, so they not only refused to admit the defeat of the revolution but said it had 'entered a higher phase'. To 'confirm' this, they ordered the CCP, already on the brink of disintegration, to launch armed struggle throughout the country. One defeat followed another, culminating in the Guangzhou bloodbath. Stalin was compelled to call the Guangzhou insurrection a 'rearguard battle', yet at the same time he and Bukharin described it as the 'standard of the new soviet phase of the revolution' (p. 351). Had the revolution been defeated? They never gave a clear answer. In the summer of 1928, at the CCP's Sixth Congress, Stalin and Bukharin's assessment of the situation in China was still ambiguous and treacherous. While declaring the 'passing of the revolutionary rising tide', they said 'a new, extensive revolutionary tide is inevitable' (Section 11, Political Resolution of the CCP's Sixth National Congress).

Different assessments of the situation led to different slogans and policies. Aware that the revolutionary situation had turned into a counter-revolutionary one, Trotsky made a timely estimate of possible developments in China's politics and economy: 'There are sufficient grounds for assuming that the smashing of the Chinese revolution, directly due to the false leadership, will permit the Chinese and foreign bourgeoisie to overcome to a lesser or greater degree the frightful economic crisis now raging in the country' ('Summary and Perspectives'). In 'The Chinese Question after the Sixth Congress' (4 October 1928), he said that in the period of 'very lame stabilisation', with the reawakening of its class consciousness, the Chinese bourgeoisie would try to reap the fruits of its triumph by 'compelling the military cliques of the Guomindang to submit to the centralised apparatus of the bourgeois state' in order to 'obtain an all the more favourable compromise' with the imperialists; 'the aspiration of the most "progressive" elements of the bourgeoisie and of the democratic petty bourgeoisie are now being directed' to a constitutional development, and even the agrarian problem will revert to the foreground and be posed on the parliamentary field. So Trotsky formulated as his central slogan the call for a constituent assembly with full powers, elected by universal, equal, direct, and secret suffrage. Only though an all-out struggle for a constituent assembly and its programme (an eight-hour day, confiscation of the land, and China's complete independence) could the CCP re-assemble and strengthen its own forces, re-emerge from underground, make a bloc with the masses, win their confidence, and prepare for the creation of soviets and the direct struggle for power. To call for soviets in such a situation and to embark on armed struggle under that slogan was, in Trotsky's opinion, 'doctrinaire, lifeless, or what is just bad, it will be the slogan of adventurists' (p. 379).

Arguing that the revolution was in a 'trough between two waves', Stalin and co. opposed the call for a national assembly and ordered the CCP to carry out armed struggle under the slogan of soviets, which they had condemned during the previous two years, when the revolution was rising. They accused Trotsky of 'liquidationism' because of his sober estimate of the situation and his democratic slogan. The result is well-known: by 1934, the CCP had been eradicated from the cities.[8]

When the left-wing Guomindang (said by Stalin to be the petty bourgeoisie) betrayed the revolution in the wake of the right-wing Guomindang (national bourgeoisie) and the urban working class suffered crushing defeats, the Stalinists, clinging to their theory of the 'bloc of four revolutionary classes', claimed that all this meant was that three classes had withdrawn from the bloc, leaving just one – the peasantry, which no longer needed to worry about a 'united front' and was free to carry on the agrarian revolution. So the revolution had entered a deeper as well as a higher phase.

Substituting arithmetic for Marxism, the leaders of the Comintern and the CCP called for armed struggle throughout the country, relying entirely on the peasantry. Although they never put this theory into any official resolution, CCP leaders repeatedly said: 'We lost tens of thousands of workers, but in compensation we got millions, even tens of millions, of peasants'. (This was a mantra of Xiang Zhongfa, elected General Secretary of the CCP at the Sixth Congress.)

When Trotsky read that a Chinese delegate at the Comintern's Sixth Congress declared that after the defeat of the Guangzhou insurrection 'the membership of the party did not decrease but grew' by tens of thousands of new members among the peasants, he wrote: 'It seems incredible that such monstrous information could have been presented to a world congress without immediately encountering an indignant refutation'. He added:

> After the decisive defeat suffered by the revolution in the cities, the party, for a certain time, can still draw tens of thousands of new members from the awakening peasantry. This fact is important as a precursory sign of the great possibility in the future. But in the period under consideration it is only one form of the dissolution and the liquidation of the CCP, for

---

8 According to Liu Shaoqi's report to the Eighth Congress (September 1956), after 1933 the underground organisation in the cities was one hundred per cent eradicated.

by losing its proletarian nucleus, it ceases to be in conformity with its historical destination' (p. 347).

An immediate result of the defeat of the Chinese revolution was to heighten Japanese ambition. To reduce China to the status of a colony, Japan was putting increasing pressure, diplomatic and military, on the Guomindang. The latter, because of its hostility towards the workers and peasants, stuck to its policy of non-resistance and made one concession after another. Demonstrations and protests by students and others (including Zhang Xueliang's capture of Chiang Kai-shek in Xi'an in December 1936) against the Japanese invaders and the Guomindang were supported by workers, urban petty bourgeois, and even army groups not directly connected with Chiang Kai-shek. Under this pressure, and supported by the US, Britain, and the USSR, Chiang finally began to resist Japan in July 1937. The attitude Chinese communists should take towards the war led to a new dispute between Stalin and the exiled Trotsky, and between their followers in China and the world.

In line with the switch by international Stalinism from the ultra-left policy of the 'third period' to an ultra-right 'popular front policy', in August 1935 the CCP called on the Guomindang to stop the civil war and form an anti-Japanese united front. In the autumn of 1937, the CCP accepted that it would: 1) strive to realise Sun Yat-sen-ism; 2) abandon its policy of overthrowing the Guomindang and confiscating the landlords' land; 3) abolish soviet government in the areas under its control; and 4) integrate the Red Army into the Guomindang army under the command of the Guomindang government.

Trotsky denounced this as 'a crime all the more horrible because it is being committed for the second time' (p. 573), following the first capitulation in 1925–7. He supported China's struggle against Japan as that of a semi-colonial country fighting for independence against imperialist invasion. 'The duty of all the workers' organisations of China', he declared, 'was to participate actively in the front line of the present war against Japan'. But they should not 'abandon, for a single moment, their own programme and independent activity' (p. 567). Because the war was directed by the arch-reactionary Chiang Kai-shek, there was no assurance of victory and there was always the possibility of a rotten compromise with the invaders. So in the interests both of the war and of the revolution, Trotsky believed 'the vanguard of the proletariat remains during the time of war in irreconcilable opposition to the bourgeoisie. The task of the vanguard consists in that, basing itself on the experience of the war, it is to weld the workers around the revolutionary vanguard, to rally the peasants around the workers, and by that to prepare for the genuine worker-peasant government, that is, the dictatorship of the proletariat, leading behind it millions of peasants' (p. 565).

The strategic course he proposed was the same as in the revolution of 1925–7. Hence: '[D]uring the civil war against the internal agents of imperialism, as in the national war against the foreign imperialism, the working class, while remaining in the front line of *military* struggle, prepare the *political* overthrow of the bourgeoisie' (p. 570, emphasis in the original).

But if the 'second Guomindang-CCP alliance' was a criminal repetition of the 'first alliance' of 1925–7, why did it not again bring disaster to the CCP? Why, on the contrary, did it apparently help China win the war and help the CCP win the revolution? I shall discuss this in more detail later on.

The exodus of tens of thousands of revolutionaries from the cities after the defeat was not a new strategy adopted by the Comintern or the CCP but a result of objective circumstances. No one at the time advocated replacing urban workers with peasants as the main force in the revolution. For example, in July 1928 Bukharin condemned 'another proposal intending to seek another special kind of revolutionary class as the basis of the party, viz. to leave the proletariat and go to the peasantry' (Section 6, 'The Chinese Revolution and the Tasks of the Chinese Communists'). He even insisted on the need to 'emphasise work in major cities'. He said: 'The entire peasant uprising without the aid of the cities, or, more accurately, without urban leadership, inevitably will result in defeat. Uprisings involving no cities cannot achieve victory' (Section 9).

The CCP's Sixth Congress accepted Bukharin's line. It declared in the Political Resolution: '[T]he bases in the Soviet régime preserved until the present time (in the Southern provinces) and their few revolutionary armies of workers and peasants will become an ever more important element in the new rising tide'. On the other hand it warned that 'the signs mentioned above *should not be overestimated*, because ... at present the urban working class has not yet overcome its setbacks' (Political Resolution, section 2, point 3, emphasis added).

In January 1928, in 'A Single Spark Can Start a Prairie Fire', Mao Zedong advocated peasant guerrilla war but also said that 'proletarian leadership is the key to victory in the revolution. Building a proletarian foundation for the Party and setting up Party branches in industrial enterprises in key districts are important organisational tasks for the Party.... Therefore it would be wrong to abandon the struggle in the cities' (Mao Zedong, *Selected Works*, vol. 1, pp. 122–3).

So from 1928 to 1930, neither Stalin-Bukharin nor Mao had any differences with the traditional Marxist position on which class should be the leading force in the coming Chinese revolution. There was no difference (at least on the surface) between Stalinists and Trotskyists. The real difference was about tactics: how and under what slogan should the CCP direct the peasant struggle then developing in southern China?

Having concluded that the situation in China was 'inter-revolutionary and counter-revolutionary', Trotsky called for a national assembly to unify politically the scattered peasant uprisings, coordinate the peasants' armed struggle with that of the working class, and link these outbursts of agrarian revolution to a possible revival of the urban struggle for democracy and national independence. Only in this way, Trotsky thought, could the peasant uprisings continue to grow and finally help precipitate a new revolution and bring it to victory.

Since Stalin and co. had no consistent assessment of the situation in China until long after the defeat of the revolution, their tactical line for the peasant struggle was also inconsistent and ambivalent. They kept declaring up until 1934 that the priority should be among industrial workers. Yet at the same time, CCP members were being dragged into the peasant armed struggle. Like gamblers, they bet on the armed struggle of the peasants, in which they had no great confidence, in the hope that fortune might deliver a 'revolutionary tide' and even lead to victory in the revolution. So they opposed a democratic campaign and condemned the call for a national assembly as 'opportunism'.

Which of the two lines concerning peasant struggle in that period was proved correct? In his report to the Central Committee of the CCP, titled 'The Struggle in the Jinggang Mountains', (November 1928), Mao wrote:

> In the past year we have fought in many places and are keenly aware that the revolutionary tide is on the ebb in the country as a whole. While Red political power has been established in a few small areas, in the country as a whole the people lack the ordinary democratic rights, the workers, the peasants and even the bourgeois democrats do not have freedom of speech or assembly, and the worst crime is to join the Communist Party. Wherever the Red Army goes, the masses are cold and aloof, and only after our propaganda do they slowly move to action.... We have an acute sense of isolation which we keep hoping will end. Only by launching a political and economic struggle for democracy, which will also involve the urban petty bourgeoisie, can we turn the revolution into a seething tide that will surge through the country (*Selected Works*, vol. 3, pp. 97–8).

There could not be a better testimony!

From the initial difference on tactics, the disagreements between the Stalinists and Trotskyists on peasant war moved on to more fundamental questions. Could the peasantry replace the working class as the main force of the revolution? Was the leadership that the communists, separated from the urban working class, gave peasant war the same as leadership by the working class? What were the prospects for armed peasant forces led by communists? What attitude should Chinese revolutionaries take towards the peasant 'Red Army' and rural 'soviets'?

Trotsky was the first to raise these questions, and he gave unequivocal answers, but his opponents never openly entered the debate. Stalin and his followers never attempted a serious theoretical analysis of the problems or gave formal directives regarding the peasant struggles led by the CCP, which after 1930 was to some extent left to its own fate and had to grope its way forward.

All Stalin had to say about the Chinese Red Army and the soviet movement were, to my knowledge, five sentences in a speech to the CPSU's Sixteenth Congress:

> It would be ridiculous to think this misconduct of imperialists will pass unpunished. The Chinese workers and peasants have already replied by creating soviets and a Red Army. It is said that a soviet government has already been created there. I think if this is true there is nothing surprising in it. There is no doubt that only soviets can save China from complete dismemberment and impoverishment (*Pravda*, 29 June 1930).

This was, as Trotsky said, simply 'administrative argumentation in all its power and splendour!' It had nothing to do with theory or responsibility. It was equivocal and treacherous. Its sole aim was to blame the Chinese communists if things went wrong and to win Stalin a reputation for wisdom if things went right.

D. Manuilsky, Stalin's spokesperson at the Comintern, fared no better in his attempt to justify peasant armed struggle in China theoretically. He wrote in *Pravda* on 7 November 1930:

> The Chinese revolution has at its disposal a Red Army, is in possession of a considerable territory, at this very movement it is creating on this territory a soviet system of workers' and peasants' power in whose government the communists are in majority. And this condition permits the proletariat to realise not only an ideological but also state hegemony over the peasantry.

Manuilsky merely revealed the ideological background to Stalin's 'administrative argumentation', the bureaucratic ideology that had already formed in the CPSU, which ordained that 'cadres decide everything'. '[C]ommunists [being] in majority' was a self-sufficient guarantee for the realisation of ideological and state hegemony over the peasants. Having discovered that guarantee, Stalin and Manuilsky rested from further thinking. They did not ask how the Chinese revolution could have a Red Army at its disposal not long after its crushing defeats. In what kind of areas and in what way was the soviet system created? What was the relationship between the communists at the head of the government and the proletariat? If the communists were separated from the urban proletariat, how could they realise working-class hegemony over the peasantry? Without answers to these questions, it was impossible to formulate a political line on the Red Army and the soviet movement in China. So one cannot say whether further developments confirmed the Stalinist line, for there was no line.

Trotsky, on the other hand, formulated a clear-cut strategic line and proposed tactical measures when the Red Army and the soviet movement in China began to attract world attention. In September 1930 he declared: 'The peasantry, even the most revolutionary, cannot create an independent government'. *'Only the predominance of the proletariat in the decisive industrial and political centre of the country* creates the necessary basis for the organisation of a Red Army and for the extension of a soviet system into the countryside'. He said 'the heart of the Chinese revolution consists in political coordination and the organisational combination of the proletarian and peasant uprisings. Those who talk about the victory of the soviet revolution in China, although confined to separate provinces in the South and confronted with passivity in the industrial North, ignore the dual problem of the Chinese revolution: the problem of an alliance between the workers and peasants and the problem of the leading role of the workers in this alliance' (p. 480, emphasis in the original).

Proceeding to practical measures, Trotsky advised the Chinese communists not 'to scatter their forces among the isolated flames of the peasant revolt' but to 'concentrate their forces in the factories and the shops and in the workers' districts in order to explain to the workers the meaning of what is happening in the provinces, to lift the spirits of the tired and discouraged, to organise groups of workers for a struggle to defend their economic interests, and to raise the slogan of the democratic-agrarian revolution' (p. 481).

In a reply to Stalin-Manuilsky's 'administrative argumentation', he wrote: 'In what way can the proletariat realise "state hegemony" over the peasantry when state power is not in its hands? It is absolutely impossible to understand this. The leading role of the isolated communists and the isolated communist groups in the peasant war does not decide the question of power. Classes decide and not parties' (p. 486). Trotsky repeated the same line of argument in

September 1932 in a letter to his Chinese comrades titled 'Peasant War in China and the Proletariat'.

Trotsky's position was in line with the Marxist view on peasant war and was formulated on the basis of the experience of the Russian revolution and the long history of peasant rebellions in China. However, the road taken by the third Chinese revolution was at variance with Trotsky's prognoses, which events 'revised' and supplemented.

Trotsky was assassinated in 1940. He did not live to see the outcome of developments in China, so the new generation of Trotskyists must resolve the problems arising from the CCP's victory. How could CCP-led peasant war achieve victory?

First, I should point out that Trotsky and most Chinese Trotskyists differed on two points regarding peasant war. One was how to defend the peasants' armed detachments; the other was how to assess the class nature of the CCP after it transferred to the countryside. In his letter to the Chinese Opposition of 8 January 1931, Trotsky wrote:

> [W]ithout abandoning our own methods and tasks, we must persistently and courageously defend these detachments.... We cannot throw our own forces into the partisan struggle at present. We have another field of endeavour and other tasks. Nevertheless, it is very desirable to have our people, Oppositionists, at least in the large divisions of the 'Red Army', to share the fate of these detachments, to observe attentively the relations between these detachments and the peasantry, and to keep the organisation of the Left Opposition informed (p. 494).

This the Chinese Trotskyists failed to do. The main reason was the severe repression by the counter-revolutionary régime, which weakened and destabilised us. But this is no excuse for our lack of preparedness and determination. Some of us even opposed it in principle, and condemned any attempt to participate in the armed detachments as 'military putschism'. Trotsky cannot be held responsible for this passivity.

The same goes for how to assess the class nature of the CCP after it had left the cities. From 1930 onwards, Trotsky warned that the CCP might degenerate into a petty-bourgeois peasant party and armed detachments under its command might antagonise the poor peasantry. However, he never said such a possibility had become a reality. In January 1931 he said that precisely because of this danger, 'it is all the more necessary for us to keep an eye on these detachments, in order to be able to adjust our position as necessary' (p. 494). Two years later he repeated: 'On the basis of our observations, reports, and other documents we must painstakingly study the life and development of the peasant armies and the régime established in the regions occupied by them; we must discover the true nature of the contradictory class tendencies and clearly point out to the workers the tendencies we support and those we oppose' (p. 528).

But we were far from careful and painstaking. Basing ourselves on ideological propositions, we declared that the CCP had become a petty-bourgeois peasant party since around the mid-thirties.[9] So we fell into confusion at the victory of the third Chinese revolution, for according to the theory of the permanent revolution a peasant party was incapable of leading a revolution to victory. This error was also ours, not Trotsky's.

As for the relationship between class and the party, Lenin said in *What Is to Be Done* that 'Socialism and class struggle arise side by side and not one from the other; each arises under different conditions', quoting Kautsky. The relationship between the party and the working class is not as direct and simple as that between fish and water. They are both inseparable and separable. Without the proletariat there can be no proletarian party, they are inseparable. But they come into being under different conditions and the proletarian vanguard is not so linked with the workers that it can tolerate no moment of separation. For example, when the party undergoes repression and some or most of its members are forced to leave the cities and the workers to continue their

---

9 Peng Shuzhi said in his Report to the Third World Congress of the Fourth International (August 1951): 'Concerning the class character of the CCP, almost all Chinese comrades are of the opinion that [the CCP] is a petty-bourgeois party based on the peasantry. This had been the traditional assessment of the CCP held by the Chinese Trotskyists for twenty years' (Peng Shuzhi, *Selected Works*, Chinese edition, p. 65). In the same report, Peng attributed this assessment to Trotsky: 'This traditional assessment was first established by Trotsky' (ibid.). But this is wrong. In his letter to the Chinese Left Opposition (22 September 1932) titled 'Peasant War in China and the Proletariat', Trotsky did say that '[i]n the years of the counter-revolution, [the Stalinists] passed over from the proletariat to the peasantry, that is, they undertook that role which was fulfilled in our country by the [Social Revolutionaries] when they were still a revolutionary party'. He also said: 'The [CCP] actually tore itself away from its class'. But we Chinese Trotskyists, Peng Shuzhi in particular, wrongly took this to mean that the CCP had become a peasant party and no longer represented the historical interests of the working class. Trotsky's letter was written a year and ten months before he called for preparations for a new international. In the letter he called the struggle between Stalinists and Bolshevik-Leninists 'the struggle between the two communist fractions'. It would have been inconsistent to insist that the Left Opposition should remain a faction of a party that had already degenerated into a peasant party.

struggle by relying on oppressed classes other than the proletariat, it will not necessarily degenerate into a non-working class party. If it sticks to its socialist programme, continues to struggle against the exploiters, and maintains a united and disciplined organisation for a relatively long time, it is *not impossible* for it to remain a workers' party. . . .

Between 1928 and 1949, we Chinese Trotskyists read the CCP's policy proclamations and followed its practices. However, we set too much store by what it said and too little by what it did. So as soon as we saw its appeals for a 'cessation of civil war' in the mid 1930s, we concluded it had finally degenerated into a petty-bourgeois party. But what the CCP said was mostly manoeuvring; while what it did, no matter how treacherous it seemed, kept basically within a class approach. It retained its socialist programme, and both in the 'ten years of civil war' (1928–37) and the 'Second United Front' (1937–47) it recruited its members and soldiers strictly along 'class lines', that is, from among poor peasants, farm labourers, and craftsmen. The party was dominated by Stalinist centralism, but there was still some democracy in the ranks, necessitated by the intensity of the struggle. So the CCP retained its working class nature, regardless of its separation from the class for more than two decades, and it was eventually able to defeat the Guomindang, accomplish the revolution's national and democratic tasks, and embark on the road of socialist revolution.

Why did the peasant war of the 1930s and 1940s achieve an outcome different from China's earlier peasant uprisings? Why did it not end in defeat or under a new feudal dynasty? Chiefly because it was not led by peasants, not even by a modern peasant party, but by revolutionary socialists committed to the interests of the working class.

And how was the CCP able retain its working-class nature in peasant surroundings? Because international capitalism was in its death agony and because the Soviet Union, despite its degeneration, still represents an alternative to dying capitalism. So the existence and activities of a working class party in a particular country are no longer pre-conditioned by the conditions of the working class in that country alone, but by those of the working classes of the whole world.

That is why Trotsky never said the CCP changed in nature when it left the cities. Nor did he say that a peasant-based CCP must lose its working-class nature. The CCP's experience was new in the history of revolution, so the special road it took could be said to represent a supplement to, or even a 'revision' of, Marxist revolutionary strategy. And what a supplement! Since then, revolutionaries in Cuba, Vietnam, Laos, Kampuchea, and, most recently, Nicaragua have followed the road of guerrilla warfare, and others in Asia, Africa, and Latin America will surely follow.

So is Trotsky's position on Chinese peasant war outdated, invalid? No. It remains fundamentally true, as an inquiry into the positive and negative aspects of Maoism shows.

As far as its strategic line was concerned, Stalin had nothing to do with the development of the third Chinese revolution. The road Chinese revolutionaries took was forced on them by the counter-revolution, before they consciously adopted it in the course of a long struggle. It was not 'invented' by Mao but was the collective product of tens of thousands of fighters. Nevertheless, Mao played a key role in the search for a policy and its systematic exposition. In 1938, ten years after the start of rural guerrilla war, he said:

> Because of these characteristics, it is the task of the party of the proletariat in the capitalist countries to educate the workers and build up strength through a long period of legal struggle, and thus prepare for the final overthrow of capitalism.... All this has been done by CPs in capitalist countries, and it has been proved correct by the October revolution in Russia. China is different however. The characteristics of China are that she is not independent and democratic but semi-colonial and semi-feudal, that internally she has no democracy but is under feudal oppression and is oppressed by imperialism. It follows that we have no parliament to make use of and no legal right to organise the workers to strike. Basically, the task of the CP here is not to go through a long period of legal struggle before launching insurrection and war, and not to seize the big cities first and then the countryside, but the reverse (Mao Zedong, Selected Works, vol. 1, pp. 219–20).

Here Mao expounded the strategic line of encircling the cities from the countryside and 'liberating the working class by means of the peasantry'. However, he failed to link it to fundamental postulates of Marxism on peasant war. He never pondered questions such as: the contradiction of interests between the proletariat and the peasantry, the incompatibility of the victory of peasant armies with the democratic orientation of socialism, and so forth. Pragmatically, he separated the proletarian party from the proletariat: ideologically, he had no idea in what sense they could be separated and in what sense they were inseparable. So after achieving victory, Mao and his comrades were unprepared to meet the problems they faced.

Trotsky foresaw nearly all these problems. In his Letter to the Chinese Left Opposition (22 September 1932), he talked about the 'living dialectic of the class interrelations of the proletariat, the peasantry and the bourgeoisie'. He warned: 'the fact that individual communists are in the leadership of the peasant armies does not at all transform the social character of the armies'. He said 'the commanding stratum of the Chinese "Red Army" has no doubt succeeded in inculcating itself with the habit of issuing commands. The absence of a strong revolutionary party and of mass organisations of the proletariat renders control over the commanding stratum virtually impossible'. He continued: 'The peasant movement...in the event of further successes...will become linked up with the urban industrial centres and...will come face to face with the working class. What will be the nature of this encounter? Is it certain that its character will be peaceful and friendly?' His answer: there might be 'civil war between the peasant army...and the proletarian vanguard'.

Trotsky's prophecies and warnings were confirmed – if not literally then essentially – in China after 1949. After nearly three decades, the CCP returned to meet the class it represented as 'liberator' and 'saviour'. It did not consider the reunion an opportunity to put party, government, and army back into the hands of the working class. Instead, it behaved like a conqueror. The workers had no say in deciding the new government's policies. The military-bureaucratic stratum formed during more than twenty years of peasant war ruled arbitrarily and justified this by claiming to be building communism (not socialism!) in a single country, by means of a Great Leap Forward.

If Mao and co. had understood Trotsky's strictures,...they would surely have done everything possible to rely on the toilers and to foster democracy in their own ranks in order to replace the backward consciousness of the peasantry with the consciousness and discipline of the working class, both during the years of struggle in the countryside and after nationwide victory. Then the period of armed struggle would have been shortened, the sufferings of the people greatly alleviated, the CCP's 'feudal-fascist despotic rule' avoided, and the bureaucratism that has infected the new régime mitigated.

As for the Sino-Japanese war, why did the Stalin-dictated Second United Front between the Guomindang and the CCP not end in disaster, like the first? Japan's defeat in China followed its defeat in the world war. It cannot be attributed either to the Guomindang or to the CCP, that is, Stalin's policy. But did the CCP win the revolution by making use of the 'unearned' victory in the Sino-Japanese war? Yes, but not because of Stalin's policy. On the contrary, it won only because it rejected, or at least partly rejected, Stalin's policy.

The CCP leadership was divided on how to implement the Second United Front. Wang Ming, representing the Soviet bureaucracy, insisted on sincere collaboration with Chiang Kai-shek, while Mao's 'indigenous communists' were 'outwardly compliant, inwardly unsubmissive', both to Stalin and to Chiang

Kai-shek.... Mao's approach was a combination of guns and Machiavellianism. Strategically, he remained within the framework of Stalin's 'popular frontism', but his efforts to maintain the CCP's independence and take the initiative by manoeuvring were closer to Trotsky's position and in defiance of Stalin's policy. Mainly because of their 'semi-Trotskyism', the Maoists were able to turn the wartime victory into a victory of the revolution.

But if a semi-Trotskyist line helped the CCP defeat the Guomindang, why did the Trotskyists themselves play no significant role in the post-war upsurge?[10] ... Trotsky's position on China's resistance to the Japanese invasion was that it was progressive and revolutionaries should support and participate in it, even though it was commanded by Chiang Kai-shek; but that they should 'not abandon, for a single moment, their own programme and independent activity', so that 'at a certain point, which we cannot fix in advance, this political opposition can and must be transformed into armed conflict', with the aim of replacing Chiang Kai-shek's régime ('On the Sino-Japanese War', p. 567).

This line was new in Marxism. Before the First World War, Marxists distinguished wars between nations as progressive or reactionary, according to the states engaged in them, their war aims, and their possible furtherance or hindrance of revolution. Marxists supported progressive wars and opposed reactionary ones. 'Support' meant helping people to win, 'opposition' meant helping their defeat. In progressive wars, revolutionaries remained in opposition to the ruling class, but confined themselves to constructive criticism and did not make revolution.... Not so in reactionary wars. Here one continued the class struggle and tried to stop the war or turn it into revolution.

Lenin's strategy in the First World War was based on the premise that both camps were imperialist and reactionary. Trotsky for the first time argued that in a progressive war, revolutionaries should not discontinue the class struggle and should try to turn 'political opposition into military conflict', to replace the reactionary government with revolutionary power, so as to win the war as well as the revolution.

Was this in conflict with Marx and Lenin's teaching? No. It was a logical development of the traditional attitude, necessitated by changes between the First World War and the Sino-Japanese war. These changes, which need not be listed here, meant two things. First, 'if there is no socialist revolution in

---

10   For a fuller discussion: 'Thinking in Solitude' [in this volume], Shuang Shan 1957; and 'On the Causes of the CCP's Victory and the Failure of the Chinese Trotskyists' [also in this volume].

the next historical epoch, a disaster will certainly threaten the whole civilisation of humankind', and 'the objective pre-requisites for the proletarian revolution have not only ripened, but somewhat decayed' (Transitional Programme, section 1). Second, the backward and colonial countries were also ripe, not economically but politically, for proletarian revolution. The Chinese revolution and its consequences showed that even to achieve national and democratic tasks it was necessary in a backward county to fight for the dictatorship of the proletariat supported by the poor peasants. So revolutionaries and workers in all countries should fight for proletarian power in any possible situation and by all means. On the question of the attitude towards war, Trotsky therefore went beyond Lenin, who did not live to see these developments.

In substance, Trotsky extended Lenin's strategy towards imperialist war to objectively progressive and just wars. This did not mean revolutionary policy should be applied in the same way to progressive wars as to imperialist wars. If our attitude towards reactionary wars can be called 'revolutionary defeatism', that towards progressive wars can be called 'revolutionary victoryism'. In the case of progressive wars, one cannot say that 'the defeat of one's own country is the lesser evil'. The reason we must continue the class struggle and even prepare revolution is precisely to win the war, which cannot be done under the incompetent command of a reactionary bourgeois government.

In carrying out such a policy, revolutionaries will face many difficulties. The two parts of the formula 'support the war but oppose its leadership' are seemingly in opposition yet are in fact complementary. How to combine and coordinate them in different conditions and at different times in the right proportion so that our policy is accepted by the masses and we can then lead them further onto the road of opposing the reactionary leadership of the war is a complex and difficult task. Unless you master it, you will at best end up either a sectarian or an opportunist.

Trotsky knew this, and stressed the importance of keeping a realistic proportion between the two parts. In August 1937, the International Secretariat of the Movement for the Fourth International adopted a resolution on the Sino-Japanese war that said:

> The urgent task of the Chinese proletariat is to fight to mobilise and arm the broadest masses with the aim of defeating the invaders and bringing revolution to Japan, while at the same time causing the Guomindang – the lackey of imperialism – to be defeated by the Chinese proletariat (Appendix to the Chinese edition of Trotsky's 'Problems of the Chinese Revolution', retranslated from Chinese).

The resolution might be used by 'ultra-leftists, neutralists, doubters and quibblers' as a 'second-line trench' to defend their wrong positions on the Sino-Japanese war, so Trotsky wrote a letter (27 October 1937) commenting on it as follows:

> I cannot object to any part of your document[11] and even to any sentence of it. Every assertion in itself is correct, but the proportion between different parts seems to me not sufficiently realistic (English edition, p. 574).

The 'different parts' of the document are the two parts I discussed above. The disagreements among the Chinese Trotskyists on the Sino-Japanese war can be reduced to the proportions fixed by the two tendencies between the two component parts of Trotsky's new policy towards an objectively progressive war.

Those under Peng Shuzhi (later the Revolutionary Communist Party of China) stressed the progressiveness of the war and support for it, concentrated on opposing a compromise between Chiang and Japan, and stuck to the slogan of 'continuing the war to the very end'. For them, it was if Trotsky's idea of 'transforming the political opposition into armed conflict', replacing Chiang Kai-shek during the war, and preparing for a worker-peasant government did not exist. I and others (later the Internationalist Workers Party of China) stressed the other part of Trotsky's position, winning the war through revolution, and thought that revolutionaries supported and participated in the war not only because it was progressive but to gain influence and authority among workers, peasants, and soldiers, so that 'at a certain point, which we cannot fix in advance', they might transform political opposition to the ruling class into armed conflict. The heat of revolution would demoralise and disintegrate the invading armies and spark a revolution in Japan. If revolution in China resulted in temporary defeats against Japan, still the revolution should not stop, for its victory would remedy such temporary defeats.

The Chinese Trotskyist organisation remained propagandist[12] throughout the war, so these disagreements were not tested in practice. Neither position was confirmed or refuted. Even so, Trotsky's criticism of the policies pursued

---

11   Trotsky's comments ('Concerning the Resolution on the War') were included in *Leon Trotsky on China* (p. 574), whose editors said nothing about the Resolution. A translation of it was appended to the Chinese edition of Trotsky's *Writings on the Problems of the Chinese Revolution* (1947). Officially adopted by the International Secretariat of the Movement for the Fourth International in August 1937, it is probably in the FI archives.

12   My faction had sixty comrades in Shanghai and more than one hundred altogether in April 1949. The Peng group was probably bigger, but not by much.

by the Spanish communists, socialists and POUMists in the civil war against Franco showed what side he would have been on. In an epoch in which revolutions and wars are closely intertwined, revolutionaries, especially in backward countries, will be more and more involved in 'objectively progressive' wars. They will face the same question: how to support a war against an external foe without abandoning one's revolutionary programme and activities against the internal enemy. They will have to choose, as we had to, between 'victory first, revolution later' and 'support and win the progressive war by deepening the revolution'.

Many will accept (a) that the Stalinist strategy and tactics applied to the Chinese revolution of 1925–7 were responsible for its defeat; (b) that the policies adopted after the defeat were the main reason the counter-revolutionary period in China lasted so long and brought so much suffering to the workers and peasants; and (c) that the victory of the revolution in 1949, as far as its subjective causes go, was due to the partial rejection of Stalinism by Chinese communists, who adopted a more revolutionary policy. Many would also agree that Trotsky was right and his warnings were borne out.

After 1949, however, people argued that what matters for revolutionaries is victory, and now it has been won by the CCP despite its errors, why do the Chinese Trotskyists insist because of old controversies on continuing as an organised opposition?

My answer is that we should continue our activities not so much because of past controversies but because of future differences.[13] The CCP's victory in 1949 was of great historical significance, but it did not mean the accomplishment of the Chinese revolution. It was merely the start of a new 'long march', far longer and harder than that in the 1930s.

---

13 The CCP victory in 1949 plunged Chinese Trotskyists into ideological and political confusion. Some old, tired members capitulated to Maoism and denounced Trotskyism. But this crisis soon passed, as the new régime's anti-working-class attitude (such as the ban on strikes) became clear. The great majority remained faithful to their convictions and continued their underground struggle. Their activities bore some fruit. Their views and criticisms appealed to urban youth. This alarmed the CCP rulers, who arrested and jailed two to three hundred Trotskyists in December 1952. The survivors were released in June 1979. Today there is no Trotskyist organisation in China, but individual Trotskyists are attracting more and more people as a result of their commitment to socialist internationalism and proletarian democracy and their opposition to the CCP bureaucracy. The experience of the Cultural Revolution and the policy of restoring capitalism have created fertile grounds for the revival and growth of genuine Marxism in China.

The Cultural Revolution, described as a 'disaster unprecedented in history' by Mao's successors, was the most tragic illustration of Maoism's inadequacy. Socialism can only be built on an international scale and never in a single country, especially one as backward as China. Socialist revolution in China, achieved thanks to a combination of favourable circumstances, does not guarantee its own smooth progress, still less the success of socialist construction. Only as an integral part of world revolution can victory be secured. And only if it is attuned to the perspectives of international socialism will socialist construction in a single country attain its final goal. But Maoism, a variant of Stalinism, is characterised above all by its narrow national vision.

Mao's successors and critics – Deng Xiaoping and his supporters – are even more narrow-minded and have considerably less revolutionary verve and courage than Mao. Although their reforms have to some extent eased the terrible tensions resulting from Mao's 'revolutionary' measures and improved economic and social life in China, the post-Mao leadership will, in the long run, lead China into the bosom of world capitalism unless it can be replaced in time by a genuine Marxist-internationalist policy.

In China as elsewhere in the world, only the Trotskyists are upholding the revolutionary programme of internationalism. Only they fight for world revolution and proletarian democracy. That is why the main hope of rescuing new China from its spiral of crises and degeneration lies in the fostering and materialisation of Trotskyism.

PART 10

*Peng Shuzhi and Wang Fanxi:
A Confrontation*

Trotskyism in China

Peng Shuzhi

After the attack on Pearl Harbor in 1941, the Chinese Trotskyist movement split over what attitude to take towards the war between Japan and China now that it had become part of the world war. The group led by Peng Shuzhi started publishing a theoretical magazine, Qiuzhen *('Seeking the truth'), in May 1946, and in August 1948 they changed their name from Communist League of China to the Chinese Revolutionary Communist Party. This report represents the views of this organisation on Chinese Trotskyism in the war and the post-war years. Wang Fanxi's riposte follows. First published in* Fourth International, *vol. 9, no. 7, July–August 1947, pp. 211–15, it is here copied from* Revolutionary History, *vol. 2, no. 4, spring 1990.*

Our organisation in China was put to the serious test of a long war for the first time since its formation. When several old comrades were released from Nanjing prisons and arrived at Shanghai at the end of August 1937, they found that the organisation was plunged in chaos. Our organisation had been isolated from the masses for too long and, what is more, it suffered heavily under the terrorism of the Guomindang. Almost the whole old generation of Trotskyists were in prisons. So it was not surprising that the handful of inexperienced comrades that remained did not know how to meet the war. Only after the comrades who returned from the Nanjing prisons provided the organisation with a new impetus, only after a serious ideological re-education, was the movement put in order. We convoked a conference of the Shanghai organisation at the end of 1937, where we unanimously adopted our guiding political resolution. It can be said without exaggeration that our League was rebuilt only after the 1937 Conference, that only on the sound basis of our political resolution were we able to combat all the ideological deviations.

Struggles

We have gone through two big ideological struggles under the pressure of war. The defensive war against Japanese imperialism began with the inauguration of the new Guomindang-Stalinist bloc. It was an ill omen for the Chinese workers and peasants. But, in the absence of a genuine revolutionary party, the petty bourgeoisie and even the workers pinned their hopes on the new bloc. They had suffocated in the big concentration camp of the Guomindang's terrorist rule too long and were longing for a new turn. The radical intellectuals controlled and collectively reflected the public opinion of the petty bourgeoisie. They sang the new chorus of Mao Zedong's opportunism. They misrepresented the shameful capitulation of the Communist Party as a big leap in human history. They flew to Yan'an as the Moscow of China. Their optimism was unlimited. It was from the almost uncontrollable delirium of the petty bourgeoisie that Chen Duxiu's opportunism emerged. It was the echo of the Stalinist chorus. We want to point out that Chen Duxiu's degeneration is not accidental. He turned his back on our League almost immediately after he left prison. He completely isolated himself from the proletarian environment and dissolved himself in the vulgar atmosphere of petty bourgeois politicians. We tried to help him out by every possible means, but he lost his head and went so far as to declare in a letter to one of our old comrades in Shanghai that he decided to combat damned Bolshevism to the very end of his life! His degeneration was not a personal matter. It was a question of the complete retreat and disillusionment of the old Bolsheviks. Because almost all the comrades who belonged to the 1925–7 generation were grouped around him, Chen's retreat exercised a decisive influence over them. That was the main reason why we had to conduct a stubborn, uncompromising struggle against this 'old man'. Thus we hoped to save as many of our old co-thinkers as possible and, furthermore, to give our young comrades a thorough education. We did succeed in the second instance although we could not collect too much fruit on the first.

Trotsky often said that sectarianism is a big obstacle in our ranks. It existed too in the movement of Chinese Trotskyism. Almost at the same time that Trotsky was relentlessly denouncing the absurd politics of the Mexican ultra-leftists, Comrade C [Zheng Chaolin], one of our old comrades, put forward the same infantile theory that the Sino-Japanese war was merely a war between Chiang Kai-shek and the Mikado. On the basis of this naive conception, he preached defeatism in the defensive war of China, even at its very beginning. But his politics were too far out of line with his surroundings. At that time, the strong opportunist illusion nourished by the delirious petty bourgeoisie proved fertile only for the growth of Stalinist and Chen Duxiu's thoughts.

Line

Because his line called forth no response, C retired to a small town for a long time. Only after the world war broke out in Europe did he return here [to Shanghai]. The outburst of the world war coincided with a great military debacle on all Chinese fronts. Wuhan was occupied after an ineffective resistance. Guangzhou was shamefully betrayed by the impotent and corrupt Guomindang officials and generals. The Guomindang leadership, the Guomindang-Stalinist bloc and the war itself appeared hopeless. Dark clouds gathered on the horizon once again. Disappointment, disillusionment, and demoralisation gradually spread among the masses, especially the intellectuals, who just yesterday proclaimed themselves the pioneers of the 'new era'. The general mood of the Chinese petty bourgeoisie changed rapidly from extreme optimism to extreme pessimism. And this petty bourgeois pessimism coincided with the Stalinists' new turn.

In view of the coming Japanese-Russian Pact, the Chinese Stalinists cynically played a new tune: 'China should take a neutral position in the coming imperialist war between America and Japan'. 'If our war against Japan be mixed up with the imperialist war, its character will change from progressive to reactionary', and so on. That is the original version of the theory of the 'changing character of the war'. The influence of petty-bourgeois pessimism and Stalinist demagogy found an echo in our ranks too. Not long ago when we had to conduct a fight against Chen Duxiu's opportunism, we had come up against a harmful eclectic tendency that obstructed our way. This tendency was represented by some old comrades who tried to bridge the wide abyss between Chen Duxiu and us by rotten compromise. Now, after 24 hours, the same eclectic tendency represented by the same comrades suddenly moved from right to left. They simply repeated the Stalinist line, because they preached the same theory of the 'changing character of the war', and, furthermore, they drew the logical conclusion of 'defeatism' from Stalinist 'neutrality'. The eclecticism in our ranks was a reflection of the petty-bourgeois mood. Only thus can we understand these seemingly absurd swings. Just as they clung to Chen Duxiu yesterday, so now they found their ideal leader in C. This time, they tried to bridge the abyss between sectarianism and Marxism. Encouraged by our eclectics, C, the hitherto isolated defeatist, bravely took the road of rebellion against us. He openly attacked our Transitional Programme. He stated that under present twentieth century conditions, we had only the alternative of imperialism or socialism. He denounced the movement of colonial emancipation as reactionary and adopted a neutral or defeatist position in the Chinese war. He proposed that the colonial programme of the Fourth International be revised. We gnashed our teeth upon learning of this light-minded and absurd revisionist argument. The shameful capitulation of the eclectics caused much anger in our ranks. Only a short time ago, when they chased after Chen Duxiu's shadow, these people labelled us 'hopeless sectarians' or 'ultra-leftists'. Now, they themselves capitulated before the genuine ultra-leftist, C, and called us 'hopeless opportunists'! We had to wage a new battle in defence of our Marxist programme. After a thorough discussion lasting six months, we defeated and isolated them completely. We convoked a national convention to decide the issue on the eve of the Pacific War. The convention of 1941 condemned the ultra-leftist politics and adopted a political resolution to meet the coming Pacific War. The new resolution not only reaffirmed our political line adopted in 1937 at the beginning of the Chinese war, but also fully harmonised with the spirit of the International resolution adopted in 1941.

Victory

Our struggle was obviously the continuation of the struggle of the American [Trotskyist] Party in 1940. Our victory was so complete that the minority was reduced to a tiny group of four generals without soldiers.

In the first four years of the Chinese war, almost a whole generation of the old Bolsheviks left us. Headed by Chen Duxiu, they abandoned our small organisation with an air of contempt. Now, with the outburst of the Pacific war, came the split of the minority led by C. We stubbornly pointed out from the first that, under cover of their radical phrases, the minority represented a petty-bourgeois tendency of pessimism and desertion. Our minority had the same class basis as the Shachtmanites.[1] They deserted our ranks under the pressure and threat of the same imperialist war, and what was more significant, they unexpectedly met in a same political camp – the well-known 'third camp' – as soon as the Pacific war broke out. (Now we know that the Shachtmanites held the same theory of the 'changing character of the Chinese war'. What a coincidence!) It is therefore no surprise that they drew the same conclusion on the plane of organisation. They trampled underfoot the principle of democratic centralism, and virtually under the same pretext. The only difference between them was this: the Chinese minority was a miniature of the Shachtmanites.

The split was no fatal blow to our movement. We had to meet the more serious blows of the war. The year after the historical attack on Pearl Harbor, our

---

1   On Max Shachtman, see p. 864.

organisation was cut to pieces. Every local unit had to rely on its own initiative and courage to meet the emergencies. Only common ideas and traditions continued to bind us together. No news, no communications could be exchanged. Even after the war, we had to wait another one-and-a-half years to get a complete picture of our organisation on a national scale. Wherever we had a group of comrades or a unit, we had a glorious epic to record. We say that without any exaggeration. Let us give you some brief sketches.

1) Our comrades in Shanghai maintained the official organ, *Douzheng* (Struggle), even under the most difficult conditions. They continued revolutionary activities among workers and students. Our young student comrades went to work in the factories. They successfully penetrated the ranks of the Communist Party and won over some militants. One of our comrades led numerous strikes in the textile factories and was finally put under arrest by Japanese policemen. A girl student comrade paid a careless visit to the prisoner and was taken into custody at once. Completely terrorised by the brutal torture, she went mad and betrayed everything she knew. A group of young comrades were immediately arrested. Comrade L, who just left the hospital after a serious operation, had a narrow escape. Comrade P also escaped from the hands of the Japanese butchers. We have to make a deep reverence to this old Bolshevik who not only showed his great abilities and courage in the face of emergencies, but went hand in hand with us even under the most dangerous wartime conditions.

In spite of the fact that our enemies knew his name very well, he bravely lectured in two universities under a pseudonym and converted a group of Stalinist students to our cause. After the wholesale arrests and raids, our Shanghai organisation almost broke down. Other responsible comrades were forced to hide and Comrade L was paralysed in his sick bed again. Yet Comrade P boldly and calmly continued to fight. Not long before the Mikado's surrender, our comrades in prison were set free. They went through a heroic struggle in the iron grip of Japanese policemen. They could and did stand up to the cruellest torture. Without their heroism and self-sacrifices, we could not even dream of the revival of the Trotskyist movement in post-war China.

2) Our comrades in Shandong became the best fighters in the guerrilla war. Some comrades fought in the Stalinist Eighth Route Army. As soon as they were discovered, they were shamefully shot, one after another. One of our young comrades died a very heroic death. Before the first Stalinist bullet killed his voice, he made a revolutionary speech attacking Stalinism among his fellow fighters and cried out the revolutionary slogans to his last breath. How many comrades lost their lives at the criminal bloody hands of the Stalinist murderers? We cannot yet give an exact account.

Fate

We met the same fate in Guomindang-controlled areas. For instance, Comrade Cheong Tzi Ching, one of our leading comrades in North China, was brutally killed by the Guomindang. Comrade Cheong formed a guerrilla detachment in his native county in Shandong immediately after he was released from Nanjing prison in August 1937. But the guerrilla detachment was no sooner formed than it was disarmed and imprisoned wholesale in a special concentration camp. Cheong tried to escape, but was unfortunately recaptured and shot. He also 'drank the bullets with a smile'.

Another group of Shandong comrades, headed by a brave young comrade Cheong Li Ming, set up a small guerrilla detachment on the border of Jiangsu and Anhui. They had to conduct their guerrilla war not only against the Japanese but also resisting the murderous attacks of the Guomindang and Stalinist armies. However, they successfully overcame all obstacles and slipped through to eastern Zhejiang. There their small detachment rapidly swelled to an army of 2000 fighters. Comrade Cheong Li Ming was elected commander. Even the native Stalinists held a mass meeting to welcome 'the most loyal anti-Japanese fighter Commander Cheong'. Comrade Cheong's army attacked the Japanese armies frequently. Its dynamic quality made a deep impression on the peasants. And its popularity was the cause of great envy in the top Stalinist ranks. Only the Stalinists' weakness held back their murderous hands. When Cheong's guerrilla army suffered a bad defeat in the battle of Jinhua, the Stalinists grasped their golden opportunity. Comrade Cheong and his wife were captured in the Stalinist-controlled zone. Together with them, a wife and a small son of another comrade, a Taiwanese revolutionist, just converted to Trotskyism, and several women, were all placed under arrest. At first, the Stalinists tried to get a denunciation of Trotskyism out of Cheong. When they found it impossible to bend his will, they mercilessly beheaded him. His wife and all other captives were shot. Even the six-year-old innocent boy was not spared by the Stalinist beasts. He was thrown into the sea and drowned! Comrades! We, Chinese Trotskyists – our knowledge of Stalinism has nothing abstract in it.

3) In South China, our comrades stubbornly maintained the party nuclei in the Japanese-controlled factories and docks. They worked hard and led a 'life even worse than that of an ox or a horse' in Hong Kong and Guangzhou. It is with pride that we point to the fact that our Guangzhou base was established only after the beginning of the Pacific War. And the emergence of our organisation in Guangzhou meant that the Communist movement began to take root again

in traditional revolutionary soil, after a lapse of 15 years, since the Guangzhou putsch. We are indebted for this significant initiative to Comrade Fun, one of our leading comrades in Southern China, who sadly was killed by an American bomb on his way from Hong Kong to Shanghai.

Comrade S, a leading member of the southern organisation, carried on courageous work among his fellow workers. Once he led a strike in defiance of the Japanese authority. A Japanese agent threatened him in such a terrible manner that he had to choose either death or signing an order to stop the strike. Some friendly workers advised him to give in. But Comrade S said calmly before the strikers and the Japanese agent: 'I prefer death to an order of surrender'. All the strikers admired and supported him. The enemy was dumbfounded by this proletarian heroism, and finally conceded. From then Comrade S won great popularity among the workers of Guangzhou and Hong Kong. It should not be forgotten that our comrades were working under the most brutal rule of the Japanese occupation army. Only Trotskyists could stand it.

Suffered

In southwestern China, especially in Chongqing, the stronghold of 'free China' [during the war against Japan], our comrades suffered no less persecution under Chiang's régime, because they alone had the courage to conduct strikes and criticise the treacherous policy of the Guomindang government. There were repeated raids and arrests. A great number of our comrades in the interior went through hardship in concentration or hard labour camps. Even now, we still have several comrades in the camps.

This is the true picture of the movement of Chinese Trotskyism in the war. Numerically, it seemed small. But a group of tested cadres emerged. That was the most valuable and significant thing in our eyes. And that is enough for unlimited optimism. In post-war China a movement was actually revived by their efforts. And a new party will surely emerge from this foundation.

With the war ended the iron discipline of war-time. All conflicts and contradictions accumulated in the process of the war were let loose. The Guomindang régime not only discredited itself completely in 'free China' but rapidly evoked bitter hostility and disappointment among the people of the 'recovered area'. Chiang's régime had never been so helpless and isolated. On the other hand, the Stalinists militarily controlled North China and enjoyed an incontestable prestige and popularity among the masses. In the great industrial centres, the working class plunged into a rising tide of strikes, and won the 'rising scale of wages'. The general strike of Kunming students inspired the entire nation. The bourgeoisie and its government lost their self-confidence and had to make a number of concessions. All looked to Yan'an. The Stalinists held the key. It was an unmistakably pre-revolutionary situation. What was lacking was a revolutionary party. Therein lay the tragedy of the Chinese revolution. Instead of an audacious political offensive came the rotten compromise of Mao Zedong. The prolonged negotiations served only as a smoke screen covering the military manoeuvre of the Guomindang. Stalinists lost one position after another, and gradually Chiang's régime recovered a partial equilibrium, at least militarily. A series of defeats suffered by the Stalinists were crowned with the abandonment of Yan'an. The strike wave of the workers and students ebbed, demoralisation and confusion once again seized hold of the Chinese masses. They became sceptical and were disappointed. They hated the Guomindang bitterly, but they also began to mistrust the Stalinists. In the chaos, they began groping for a 'third road'.

All our work in the past one and a half years was based on a correct diagnosis of the evolution of the above-described situation. Taking the place of Japan, Yankee imperialism with its Guomindang agent became our main enemy. Down with American imperialism and the Guomindang! The entire Transitional Programme and tactical tasks had to be readjusted around this main task. We joined and set up united fronts in all mass movements against our main enemy. We showed deepest sympathy to the war conducted by the Stalinist peasant armies, although we never ceased to point out that their defeat was, is, and will be caused by the treacherous policies of the party and the Kremlin. We also took a more careful yet realistic and bold attitude towards the anti-Kremlin demonstrations. We did not consider that they were merely an expression of the reactionary anti-Soviet sentiment of the Chinese ruling class and its master. The extremely isolated Guomindang régime could not conduct and never had conducted a serious mass movement. If it did now, the mass movement itself necessarily reflected some profound mood of the masses. We opposed the arch-reactionary leadership of the Guomindang, yet it was our duty to pay closer attention to the justified dissatisfaction and revulsion of the Chinese people towards the Kremlin bureaucracy. In this sense, it was not wise to take an abstentionist attitude towards this movement. On the contrary, we boldly plunged into it to expose all the evil intentions of the Guomindang, expand and deepen it, and try finally to convert its leadership. Only Trotskyist leadership can give full and correct expression to the feelings and needs of the Chinese masses. The Stalinists, as you would expect, cynically denounced the anti-Kremlin mass movement as a reactionary trick of the Guomindang, and consequently boycotted it.

Tasks

In the past one-and-a-half years, we concentrated our efforts on three big organisational tasks: (1) to make the greatest use possible of the concessions of the ruling class; (2) to make contact with the rank-and-file Stalinists and channel the movement into the riverbed of genuine Marxism; and (3) to revive our organisational work on a national scale.

We began our work in Shanghai with bare hands. The great current of the war carried away many from our ranks. Only a handful of cadres with superhuman will remained to swim against the current. Yet with the help of our sympathisers we were able to publish two periodicals. One is a big theoretical magazine, the other a semi-monthly organ whose purpose is to popularise our programme among the youth and women. The Guomindang was obliged to register our periodicals along with other 'democratic' publications. We had two periodicals for the first time. We knew very well that it was mass pressure that made the rulers yield a little. Without illusions, we grasped the opportunity. The distribution of our periodicals gained steadily. They could be bought in all the big industrial and cultural centres. We received an enthusiastic response from even the remotest parts. Everywhere we have a traditional influence and an organisational presence, our magazines have won a wide circulation. Our literary efforts produced two valuable results. First, through them we made contact again with comrades who for a long time had lost track of us. Second, we drove an ideological wedge into the rank and file Stalinists. For instance, in Wenzhou (a commercial centre of eastern Zhejiang), the radical students were for long under strong Stalinist influence. But after our publications arrived in this city, the authority of Stalinism rapidly broke down. Our slogan 'For a national assembly elected by universal suffrage' was carried into the street for the first time.

In Nanjing and Guangzhou, our publications also produced great ferment among the rank and file Stalinists. A group of Stalinist students passed over to us in Nanjing. Among the workers of Shanghai and Hong Kong, our publications received a no less enthusiastic response.

As a result of these activities we have made significant progress among the workers and students and built up effective groups in the main industrial centres. We did not come out of the war with empty hands. We have created the rudiments of a proletarian party with a true Marxist tradition.

The objective conditions are favourable to the growth of our movement. We see unlimited possibilities for our expansion in future political and economic developments. It seems the Guomindang has gradually regained an equilibrium by military means in the past year. But after the unlimited destruction of eight years of war and the threat of an unceasing guerrilla war by the Stalinists, the material basis of the Chinese ruling class is so weakened that the whole upper structure of its rule is tottering. Even a slight push can send it down. The Chinese bourgeoisie was never so nervous and isolated. It lost confidence and split into several groups, each savagely fighting the other. Its future is dark. It is significant that this February, when Chiang Kai-shek celebrated his military victory over the Stalinist armies, the gold market crashed – symbolising incurable social and economic bankruptcy – and a general uprising of the Taiwanese people exposed the true nature and instability of his régime. Chiang dreams of surviving by a series of emergency decrees and brutal military suppressions. He is wrong!

Shock

The final suppression of the rising peasant movement could not save the feudal ruling class of the Qing Dynasty from the revolutionary tide of 1911. The bourgeois rule represented by Chiang will be even more helpless to withstand a great shock even if it successfully downs the Stalinist peasant armies. Under Chiang's dictatorship, the conditions of the Chinese people can only go from bad to worse. He is doomed. But he will never go down automatically. Only the perfidious Stalinists still believe that through a peaceful democratic process, a new People's Front will be able to reform the bureaucratic rule of the Nanjing government. They attempted this many times. Yet Chiang never was and never will be reformed or removed in this way. We firmly believe that pre-revolutionary conditions will not be lacking. What we do lack is a revolutionary party, without which Chiang's dead hands will not be removed. We have a long revolutionary period before us. We take it as a starting point of our struggle.

After the split, the minority headed by C retreated into their small room instead of keeping their promise to go directly to the masses over our head. They deserted our ranks. After Chen Qichang, a minorityite, was arrested by the Japanese police, they severed all relations with us. Chen Qichang's death caused deep mourning in our ranks, yet it did not cancel our right of criticism. On the contrary, his case should serve as an object lessons for the unprincipled hair-splitters. He secretly served in an underground radio station of the Chongqing government in Shanghai purely for personal purposes. This was not only dangerous and harmful for our work, but politically inconsistent with his 'defeatism' – 'our main enemy Chiang Kai-shek!' Yet he risked his head for his 'main enemy', and he kept this matter secret even from his political friends.

The latter issued several issues of the so-called *Internationalist* to preach 'defeatism' in the war. After the war, when they saw our work rapidly reviving, they awoke from their long sleep and published a small periodical called *Xinqi* (New flag). We thought perhaps they wanted to do some serious work now. We tried to contact them and proposed united action as the first step towards unity. But their attitude was disloyal. While we distributed their publications, they kept ours in their drawers. What is most intolerable is their incurable infantilism. While we put forth our democratic slogans and demanded the immediate realisation of all basic transitional demands, they attacked us because we were allegedly forgetting the proletarian revolution. While we preached the elementary ideas of Permanent Revolution, as a revolution starting from the democratic struggle to the goal of socialism, they condemned us as opportunists, because, according to their conceptions, the Chinese revolution will be socialist from the beginning. 'Either socialism or imperialism', they proclaimed. Yesterday in a colonial war resisting imperialism they took the position of defeatism – because the war was under the leadership of the Guomindang. Today when the Chinese people are only beginning to fight for elementary democratic demands, they take a passive position – nothing less than socialism! As if the promised socialism would drop from the sky and does not grow out of the dirty ground of daily struggles! Everything is oversimplified and transformed into a lifeless abstraction.

On the plane of tactics, the gap between us and the radical phrase-mongers is even wider. While we attempted to accelerate the progressive ferment of the masses by a systematic criticism of Stalinist policy, they misrepresented our position as 'neutral'. While we audaciously took a part in the anti-Kremlin mass demonstration for the purpose of exposing the reactionary motives of Chiang's régime and to redirect the movement into a revolutionary struggle against imperialism, they condemned us as 'a tail of the Guomindang', and took a position of neutrality and abstentionism. They yield to the pressure of Stalinist-controlled public opinion to such a degree that they portray some pro-Stalinist petty-bourgeois politicians as genuine revolutionists. Abstentionism and opportunism are organically linked with sectarianism.

Small

As for their work, we cannot expect much from these phrasemongers. They do not want to find a way to the masses. They want only to write as they please. We tried to get them out of their small room, but in vain! For instance, last year when we invited them to attend a Trotsky memorial meeting, they rejected the invitation without explanation. They are contented with their small *Xinqi*, which has a very poor circulation. They do not represent a serious and responsible faction. They represent the past of our movement. They have not enough courage to break with the bad traditions of a small propaganda circle. That is why they isolate themselves completely, not only from the masses but also from our ranks. It is significant that all they could recruit from our ranks was a handful of intellectuals who had lost mental equilibrium and long ago morally discredited themselves. Those who want to do something serious go hand in hand with us.

Our comrades have a strong argument: they want to finish with childish tricks of split and unity. They want a completely new type of leader who possesses not just a fluent pen but a capacity for conducting small and big struggles, and for organising the masses.

We had never resorted to expulsions or splits because of political differences; yet the minority split in contempt of the tradition of Bolshevik organisation, because of political differences. Now, since the political differences still exist and even deepen, we have decided that, until the *Xinqi* group gives an unambiguous explanation of their split during the war, we will not consider their proposal of unity as serious and loyal. No democratic centralism – no unity.

Problems of Chinese Trotskyism

Wang Fanxi

When the Chinese Trotskyists split in May 1941, the group led by Zheng Chaolin and Wang Fanxi started publishing Guoji zhuyizhe *('Internationalist') and then, from June 1946,* Xinqi *('New banner'). When* Fourth International, *the organ of James Cannon's Socialist Workers Party, published Peng Shuzhi's 'Trotskyism in China' in 1947, the Internationalist group was 'surprised and embittered'. They described Peng's article as a 'combination of slanders, distortions, black lies and irresponsible boasts' and said it had 'aroused no little indignation in our ranks'. This rejoinder to Peng by Wang Fanxi was sent to the editorial board of Fourth International as well as to the Workers Party of Max Shachtman, who published it in condensed form in his journal* New International. *Max Shachtman was a polemicist and agitator who split with Cannon in 1940, when he concluded (after Stalin's invasions of Poland and Finland) that the Soviet Union was no longer a workers' state, not even a degenerated one. This shows that the disagreements among Chinese Trotskyists about the war were not confined to them alone. The document deals mainly with the problem of policy in the Sino-Japanese War and the subsequent civil war between the Guomindang and the Communist Party, but it begins with a review of the politics of Chen Duxiu at his life's end. From* Revolutionary History, *vol. 2, no. 4, spring 1990. Originally published in* New International, *vol. 14, no. 2, February 1948, pp. 58–62, and no. 3, March 1948, pp. 90–2.*

The Struggle with Chen Duxiu

The *Report* begins with a description of the struggle carried on between the Chinese Trotskyist organisation and Chen Duxiu. It attempts to describe the relations which existed between the Chinese Old Man and the old revolutionists of the 1925–7 generation. The *Report* says of Chen Duxiu: 'He turned his back upon our League almost immediately after he left prison' and 'declared in a letter to one of our old comrades in Shanghai that he had decided to combat damned Bolshevism to the very end of his life!'

Such a description is oversimplified, therefore incorrect. Chen Duxiu, 'the father of Chinese Communism', the General Secretary of the Chinese Communist Party from its very inception until August 1927, the No. 1 leader of the Chinese Revolution of 1925–7, who became a Trotskyist after the debacle of the revolution, became one of the founders and leaders of the Chinese

Trotskyist movement, served four years in a Guomindang prison while remaining a staunch Trotskyist – Chen Duxiu did break with Bolshevism during the Second World War. But this break did not take place 'immediately' and was not final.

During the period from the beginning of the anti-Japanese war down to the outbreak of the Second World War, he held the position that the Chinese Trotskyists could do nothing else than support the anti-Japanese war unconditionally. In his opinion it was quite out of the question to speak of revolution during the war or of transforming the war into a revolution. But as usual with him, Chen Duxiu did not present this position as a matter of principle but rather empirically and tactically. He justified his position in the following manner: we must at present support the war; as for this revolution, let's speak of it later. You can see from this that Chen Duxiu's position was false; but it was neither final nor systematic.

In 1939, one year after the beginning of the Sino-Japanese War, in order to acquaint himself with the position of the Chinese Old Man, Trotsky asked Comrade Li Furen [Frank Glass] to make an inquiry of him. Chen Duxiu wrote a statement in answer that was given to Trotsky by Li Furen. After reading Chen Duxiu's statement Trotsky wrote to Comrade Li as follows:

I am extremely glad to know that our friend remained our friend politically, although there are some *possible* divergences existing between us; but right now I cannot judge these *possible* divergences with necessary precision.... However, I consider that what he expressed is essentially correct.[1]

Chen Duxiu's position moved further away from that of the Trotskyists after the signing of the German-Soviet pact and the outbreak of war in Europe. He held that we should support the democracies against the Fascist and Russian 'imperialisms'. He was of the opinion that in order to facilitate the victory of the democracies in the war, the Indians should for the time being put a stop to their nationalist movement.

It goes without saying that this is the same as the position held by Plekhanov, Guesde, and Co during the First World War and by the Third International after the outbreak of the German-Soviet war, during the last slaughter of mankind. Needless to say, such a position meant a complete break with Trotskyism.

But, as we have said and as Trotsky had correctly observed, Chen Duxiu was not a theoretician of Plekhanov's type but a revolutionist *à la* Lassalle. Lacking profound theoretical training, his action was always directed by impressions, his opinions were changeable and fallible; but at the same time and for the same reason he was often able to make bold corrections of his mistakes.

---

1 Trotsky's letter to Li Furen, 11 March 1939, retranslated from the Chinese.

The history of Chen Duxiu's revolutionary activity, which lasted more than thirty years, was replete with such conflicts and mistakes. One's defects sometimes become one's merit. It was partially because of this 'defect', we believe, that Chen Duxiu was able to complete his evolution from a democrat to a Communist and from a Communist in general to a Trotskyist, in the brief period of seven or eight years.

We may speculate whether, if Chen had not died, he would have devoted the remaining years of his life to the cause of the Fourth International. We cannot give a definite answer to this question. That is why we also said that his break with Trotskyism would not be considered as final.

What attitude did we, the so-called 'old comrades of the 1925–7 generation, take towards Chen's false ideas? Comrade Li Furen gave very good testimony on this point in the August 1942 issue of the *Fourth International*:

> This polemic, which was carried on by correspondence between the remote Sichuan town where Chen lived and the Central Committee in Shanghai, left Chen in a minority of *one* [our emphasis].

How far the Chinese revolutionary movement has advanced beyond the political level which Chen represented is evidenced most strikingly in the fact that he could not find in the Chinese organisation a single supporter for his later political ideas.

Comrade Li Furen is an old friend of the Chinese Trotskyists. He lived in China during the period 1935 to 1941. He was a member of the Chinese organisation and more than that, he was once elected a member of the provisional Central Committee. Since he is quite conversant with the ideological groupings of Chinese Trotskyism, his testimony is trustworthy.

But the *Report* claimed to the contrary: 'Almost all the comrades who belong to the 1925–7 generation were grouped around him; Chen's retreat exercised a decisive influence over them'. What a black lie!

We, whom the *Report* calls the 'old generation', not only did not support Chen's ideas but carried on a most uncompromising struggle with him; so much so that finally the 'Old Man' became very angry with us and broke off all relations.

In attempting to describe the 'old generation' the *Report* fell into a gross self-contradiction. In the first paragraph it said: 'Only after the comrades who returned from the Nanjing prisons provided the organisation with a new impetus, only after a serious ideological re-education was the movement put in order', while in the second paragraph it said: 'It was a question of the complete retreat and disillusionment of the Old Bolsheviks'.

Neither the first nor the second paragraph is correct. The former exaggerated the role of the 'old comrades', while the latter derogated from them.

The Traditional Ideological Differences within Chinese Trotskyism

The inception of the Chinese Trotskyist movement dates back to 1928. There were serious divergences, political as well as theoretical, in its ranks almost from its very birth.

During the 19 years of Chinese Trotskyist organisation there have been two main issues on which there were great differences of opinion. These were: (1) the relation between the democratic revolution and the socialist revolution; and (2) tactical questions regarding our attitude towards the Guomindang, centring around the slogan of the constituent assembly.

On the first question there were many comrades who showed Stalinist leanings, headed by Comrade Peng Shuzhi, the present leader of the Struggle group, and the traitor Liu Renjing, known in the foreign press as Niel Sih. The latter took and the former still takes the position that the democratic and socialist revolutions constitute two different and successive stages, if not two different historical epochs. In their opinion the future Chinese revolution will begin with the democratic revolution, during which power will be conquered, while the socialist revolution will begin only after the establishment of workers' power.

The *Report* clearly describes this idea when it says: 'We preach the elementary ideas of the permanent revolution, as a revolution starting from the democratic struggle to the goal of socialism'.

Another group of comrades, the present leading elements of the Internationalist group, opposed this idea from the very beginning. They considered that such an explanation of the idea of Permanent Revolution has nothing in common with Trotskyist theory, since the idea of 'starting from the democratic struggle to the goal of socialism' can be accepted not only by Stalin but also even by Leon Blum and Clement Attlee. We hold a different position, one which really follows Trotsky's analysis of the character of China's future revolution.

According to Trotsky the character of the future Chinese revolution will be socialist from the very beginning owing to the following considerations: (1) the class struggle, especially the struggle between bourgeoisie and working class, has become extremely sharp; (2) the agrarian revolution in China is anti-capitalist; and (3) the struggle for the expropriation of the factories has become imperative.[2]

---

2 Trotsky 1957 [1928], p. 184.

In accordance with his ideas we are of the opinion that the democratic and socialist tasks of the Chinese revolution are interlaced with each other, not that they successively follow each other. Thus we held and still hold that the democratic tasks can only be solved, in passing, by the socialist revolution; that the scope of the democratic movement can be widened and deepened into a revolution; and that the revolution can have a perspective of development only when the democratic struggle is waged as a factor of socialist revolution. If, on the contrary, we make socialism a 'goal' and limit ourselves to staying within the circle of 'democratic struggle' in the first stages of revolution, then the 'goal' would become (as we Chinese put it) the 'flower in the looking glass' that will never be reached.

There were also two positions opposed to each other from the very beginning on the second question – that is, on the tactical question of our attitude towards the Guomindang, with the constituent assembly as the central slogan. One group, again headed by Peng Shuzhi and the traitor Liu Renjing, saw in the constituent assembly slogan mainly a 'historical driving force'. They hoped there would be a parliamentary perspective of long duration in China, and that the Chinese proletariat would carry their socialist revolution onto a 'higher historical plane'.

Starting from this elementary idea, they always leaned towards maintaining a 'united front' with the 'democratic' bourgeoisie and towards believing in the possibility of the solution (at least the partial solution) of the democratic and national tasks through 'democratic means', through the constituent assembly, and so on. The traitor Liu Renjing gave a famous formulation on this point: 'The constituent assembly is the popular formula for the proletarian dictatorship'.

This group of comrades, of course, invested too much hope in the bourgeois 'national and democratic struggles'.

Another group, represented by the leading comrades of the present Internationalists, has always taken the position that the importance of the constituent assembly slogan lies mainly in the fact that it is a means of consolidating the proletariat and helping them to re-enter the political scene. Starting from this position the attitude of this group on other tactical questions naturally emphasised the problem of how to mobilise the masses in opposition to the bourgeoisie.

In essence the many rich discussions within the Chinese Trotskyist movement during the past 19 years can be reduced to the above-mentioned two questions. They revolved around these two questions as a permanent axis. Chen Duxiu's position on the two fundamental questions coincided with that of Peng Shuzhi & Co. except at the beginning of the 1930s, when his ideas on the character of the future Chinese revolution were very close to ours. We are therefore justified in saying that Chen Duxiu's eventual break with Trotskyism was due largely to his position on the fundamental disputed questions within the Chinese Trotskyist organisation.

It goes without saying that the two traditional divergences in Chinese Trotskyism reflected different social bases: the 'democrats' represent the petty-bourgeois wing of our ranks, while the 'socialist revolutionists' represent the proletarian tendency. But we are not ready to resort to this 'class analysis' since the cause of our ideological division is in no small degree due to infantilism and theoretical backwardness. In the case of only a few of the old leaders, such as Peng Shuzhi, is their opportunism systematic and obstinate.

Issues in the Split of 1942

The *Report* told you that the internal struggle among the Chinese Trotskyists in 1942 was 'the continuation of the struggle in the American party in 1940'. This statement is false to the core, made with the obvious aim of winning your sympathy and support. In reality it was a continuation of the traditional struggle within the Chinese Trotskyists. It was merely the old divergences reflected in the new question of the Sino-Japanese war.

Even before 1940 there were differences of opinion among the Chinese comrades with respect to China's anti-Japanese war, although they were still minor and episodic. Although they could already be considered divergences of principle, not all participants in the discussion had yet fully developed their arguments on the plane of principle. This was mainly due to the weakness of the Chinese organisation. As a result of it, its position did not have the opportunity to be matched against the real development of events.

Among the potential and episodic disputes the following facts are important:

(1) After the outbreak of the Sino-Japanese war, Comrade Peng Shuzhi insisted on the withdrawal of our central slogan, 'Down with the Guomindang', while the late Comrade Chen Qichang fought with equal persistence to keep the slogan in our programme. Peng's proposal finally won out, when Comrade Yvon Zheng [Zheng Chaolin] was out of Shanghai and Comrade Wang Mingyuan [Wang Fanxi] was still in a Guomindang prison; the traditional slogan of Chinese Trotskyism, 'Down with the Guomindang', was thus withdrawn.

(2) Comrade Chen Duxiu looked upon the anti-Japanese war as a higher development of the national struggle of the Chinese people, while other comrades preferred to point out that China's anti-Japanese war was a result of the defeat of the Chinese revolution.

(3) The conference in November 1937 under the leadership of Peng Shuzhi decided that we should centre our attack on the compromising tendencies of the Guomindang in the anti-Japanese war, and called for a workers' and peasants' uprising to support the war with the aim of *prolonging* it. On the other hand, other comrades, first Chen Qichang and then Wang Mingyuan, took the position of *deepening* the social basis of the war, above all, of 'supporting' the war with agrarian revolution.

(4) Comrade Yvon Zheng was of the opinion that the Sino-Japanese war could only be considered as a part of the imperialist war; consequently, he opposed the war itself from the very beginning and wanted to apply the Leninist policy of revolutionary defeatism to the war. His position did not win a single supporter at that time.

If we ignore the tactical side of these questions, there were evidently two opposing fundamental tendencies behind the above-mentioned 'episodic' divergences: on the one hand, a tendency that emphasised the meaning of the war itself and consequently considered it the means through which the national tasks of China might be solved; on the other hand, a tendency that looked at the anti-Japanese war from the point of view of proletarian revolution and consequently considered it mainly as a road along which one might or might not achieve the workers' and peasants' revolution.

The former is a position of pure democratism (national emancipation is only one of the democratic tasks), while the latter is the position of socialist revolution, namely, the position of permanent revolution. The former was represented by Chen Duxiu and Peng Shuzhi, while the latter was represented by the leading comrades of the present Internationalist group (Comrades Chen Qichang, Yvon Cheng, Wang Mingyuan, and others). Such a line-up was not accidental but rather quite faithful to the traditional ideological groupment within the Chinese Trotskyists over the past nearly twenty years.

But the different views on the anti-Japanese war were not fundamentally and finally formulated until 1940, when the war between the imperialists and the Sino-Japanese war began to intertwine. At the end of 1940 the international situation posed a new problem to the Chinese Trotskyists, namely, the fast-approaching Japanese-American war in the Pacific was sure to make China's anti-Japanese war a phase of the imperialist war. Should the Chinese Trotskyists then reconsider their attitude and policy on the war?

With this question as a starting point there broke out a very sharp internal struggle that caused the traditional divergences of Chinese Trotskyism to again erupt deeply and extensively on the question of policy on the anti-Japanese war in particular and the national question in general.

What were the Different Views? How did the Discussion Take Place?

The first question discussed at that time was formulated in the following manner: did the Sino-Japanese war become an integral part of the imperialist war in the autumn of 1940, when the so-called 'ABCD front' in the Pacific was formed?[3] To this question nearly all the Chinese Trotskyists answered in the affirmative. They had some differences only on the question of timing. Peng said: the Sino-Japanese war will become a part of the imperialist war only after the outbreak of the war in the Pacific. Wang Mingyuan said: the Sino-Japanese war has already been intertwined with the undeclared and not-yet-shooting war between Japan and the US. Yvon Zheng said: 'It was part of the imperialist war from the very beginning'.

The second question was: is there any difference in the character of China's anti-Japanese war now that China is fighting as the junior partner of an imperialist power as compared with the time when it was fighting independently? In answering this question Comrade Peng said: the character of China's anti-Japanese war will not be changed in the least regardless of how it is fought. Other comrades[4] – that is, all members of the Political Committee except Peng Shuzhi – were of the opinion that the anti-Japanese war was progressive when fought by China more or less independently but that it was reactionary when fought as part of the imperialist war. In different cases the character of the same anti-Japanese war was different as well. In the course of discussion, however, Comrade Liu Jialiang changed his view and went over to Peng Shuzhi's position.

The third question: if the character of the war has changed, should our attitude towards it change accordingly? Comrade Wang Mingyuan, the sponsor of the 'changing-character theory', insisted that once the character of the war had changed from progressive to reactionary, our attitude must be changed from defencism to defeatism. Comrade Yvon Zheng, who had been a defeatist from the very beginning, naturally supported Comrade Wang's position, while Comrade Peng, and later on also Liu, fought desperately against the defeatist position.

The fourth question: what is defeatism? Is Trotsky's position on the Chinese war defencist or defeatist? This question, as you may easily see, is merely a

---

3 'ABCD': The American-British-Chinese-Dutch encirclement.
4 The leading body of the Communist League of China was the editorial board of *Struggle*, corresponding to the Political Committee of your party. Six comrades constituted the board, Chen Qichang, Kou Woo [?], Wang Mingyuan, Yvon Cheng, Peng Shuzhi, and Liu Jialiang.

continuation of the third question. We, four out of six of the then editorial board of *Douzheng* (Struggle), were of the opinion that especially in the case of China's anti-Japanese war, the meaning of defeatism should be understood as a policy of prosecuting the class struggle during the war with the aim of developing this struggle into a civil war. To take a historical analogy, the 'defeatism' of the Chinese Trotskyists may be compared, in a not very exact manner, to the 'defeatism' of the Russian Bolsheviks after the February revolution when they 'supported' Kerensky in the fight against the Germans and Kornilovists.

Peng Shuzhi & Co., either out of simple ignorance or as an intentional distortion, declared that revolutionary defeatism with respect to China's side of the war meant favouring the victory of Japanese imperialism and, even worse, 'sabotage and other destructive activities in the Guomindang area'. . . .

Tactical

What position did Comrade Trotsky adopt on China's anti-Japanese war? In his letter to Diego Rivera (published in *La Lutte Ouvrière*, organ of the Belgian PSR, No.43, 23 October 1937), he repudiated 'defeatism'; but in the same letter he outlined the following tactical line for us Chinese Trotskyists:

> It is necessary to win influence and prestige in the course of the military struggle against the foreign enemy's invasion, and in the political struggle against the weakness, failures, and betrayals within. At a certain point which we cannot fix in advance, this political opposition can and must be transformed into armed struggle, for civil war like any other war is nothing else than the continuation of politics.
>
> To fight against the internal enemy politically, and more than that, to transform this political opposition into armed struggle – that is, to transform the national war into civil war – is a thoroughly revolutionary policy. In our opinion, this policy, no matter on what position we stand when we carry it out, is essentially different from traditional defencism and even from defencism *à la* Clemenceau, but quite close to the Leninist policy of revolutionary defeatism.

It goes without saying that defeatism, as applied to China, cannot be fully equal to the defeatism maintained by Lenin in 1914–18 in relation to the Russo-German war. But this does not prevent us from considering Trotsky's position on the Chinese war as defeatist in essence, just as the defeatism adopted by the French, English, and American revolutionists during the Second World War was also somewhat different in application and implication from that of the Russian revolutionists in the First World War.

The victory of Hitler was not a 'lesser evil' for the French, British, and American working classes. So during the Second World War, in the democratic imperialist countries, the defeatist position could and should be understood merely as a policy of prosecuting the class struggle during the war and transforming the national war into civil war. These two fundamental ideas were obviously implied in Trotsky's position on China's anti-Japanese war from the very beginning.

Thus, in the course of the discussion the attitudes of Comrade Wang Mingyuan and Comrade Yvon Zheng on the anti-Japanese war became identical. The former also granted that the attitude which we adopted towards the war should be 'defeatist' or nearly 'defeatist' in essence from the very beginning, although he still insisted that China's anti-Japanese war was objectively progressive in its first period.

With the deepening of the questions in dispute, the comrades who later organised the Internationalist Group came to the conclusion that the Leninist defeatist line was less concerned with the character of the war than with the task imposed upon a revolutionary party of conquering power during the war. They believe that if the task of the revolutionary conquest of power by the proletariat is put before the world working class in general, then once war breaks out, no matter in what country and no matter what character it may assume, the fundamental attitude towards the war that a revolutionist should take must be one that is nearer to 'defeatism' and farther from 'defencism'. It cannot be otherwise if the revolutionists wish to seize power during the war. In other words, to transform the war into civil war is the strategic line of 'defeatism', no matter on what tactical basis one puts this line into effect.

On the other hand, Peng Shuzhi and his supporters had an opportunistic and obstinate attitude on this question. They were not willing to move a single step from their interpretation of 'defeatism' on the basis of their ridiculous definition, namely, 'to explode bridges for the enemy'. From Trotsky's position on the Sino-Japanese war they remembered only the term 'defencism'. Its content – that is, 'to transform political opposition into armed struggle', 'to overthrow the Guomindang during the war' – was forgotten by them completely.

Their essentially compromising attitude towards the Guomindang thus became clearer as a result of the discussion. They openly declared that 'so long as the Guomindang fights against the Japanese we cannot change our attitude towards the war and towards the Guomindang government, we cannot put the slogan "Down with the Guomindang" back into our programme'. In their opinion, it is therefore absurd and false to subordinate the interests of war to those of revolution.

Thus the Peng Shuzhi group supported Chiang Kai-shek's war up to V-J Day. Before V-J Day they invariably declared that 'in spite of the intertwining of the

Sino-Japanese and Japanese-American wars, China's war of resistance will never lose its great historical significance of regaining national independence from the hands of Japanese imperialism'. But after 'victory', they had to admit in a resolution, as if suddenly awakened out of a dream, that 'China is going to be a second Philippines'! They did not even bother to ask themselves the following question: were not Peng Shuzhi & Co among those supporters of the war to the 'victorious end' that had helped to make China 'a second Philippines'?

The fifth question was on the possibility of an independent bourgeois China. We said and still say that *while struggling for the independence of China we must make clear the following truth to ourselves as well as to the advanced workers: in the present stage of imperialism there are only two alternatives for China* – either an independent soviet socialist China (an integral part of a world socialist union), or a colony under the control of American imperialism. There is not and cannot be a middle way.

An independent capitalist China is an illusion. Peng and his followers, however, opposed this position of ours with all their might, declaring that the 'imperialism or socialism' formula is false, a sort of 'ultra-leftism'. For them a non-capitalist and non-socialist perspective for China is possible. But you know no less than we that outside of the formula 'imperialism or socialism' there are only Shachtman's 'socialism or bureaucratism or barbarism'[5] or Mao Zedong's 'new democratism' left for Peng Shuzhi to support.

---

5   Comrade Wang here gives sad evidence of the effects of the systematic slander and misrepresentation campaign against the Workers Party carried on by the Cannonite agents abroad, especially among those Trotskyist groups not yet in close contact with us. He is the undoubtedly honest victim of these slanders, having not yet learned to distrust their purveyors. There are only two things wrong with his reference here to Shachtman's 'socialism or bureaucratism or barbarism'. (1) Neither Shachtman nor the Workers Party has ever, anywhere, put forward such a triple formula. We accept as ours only Trotsky's and the Fourth International's 'socialism or barbarism' as the historic alternatives before society. We do add that the 'barbarism' here counterposed to socialism can mean a form of totalitarian bureaucratic statism or bureaucratic collectivism – but that much even Trotsky said already in his *In Defence of Marxism*. The only place where this absurd triple-alternative formula can be read written down in print is, to be sure, in an SWP attack upon us (see Shachtman's *The Nature of the Russian State, New International*, April 1947). (2) In any case, neither the use of 'socialism or barbarism' by us or Trotsky, nor our view that Russia is a totalitarian bureaucratic-collectivist society has anything to do with the more immediate alternatives of 'imperialism or socialism' for China today. It is undoubtedly correct that either China breaks with all imperialism through a revolutionary socialist workers' government or it remains under the direct or indirect control of imperialism. We urge the Chinese comrades to remember that the same Cannon who prints what they call Peng Shuzhi's slanders against *them* is the master workman in that field, Peng at worst only an apprentice [note by Max Shachtman].

The difference on this question clearly reveals two opposing tendencies: Permanent Revolution, and the theory of a purely democratic revolution.

Meaning

The sixth question is on the meaning of the theory of Permanent Revolution. This is simply a revival of an old divergence. As we said above, Peng and his followers 'preached the elementary ideas of the Permanent Revolution as a revolution starting from the democratic struggle to the goal of socialism'. Dear comrades, are you satisfied with such an explanation of Permanent Revolution? What is meant by 'to the goal of socialism'? Do not Attlee and Leon Blum also take socialism as their 'goal'? Are we not right to condemn this position as 'opportunism'? We said that, to speak more exactly, we only followed Trotsky in saying that the future Chinese revolution will be socialist from the very start. This is so, first of all, because we, together with the proletariat, in the future revolution will orient ourselves on the road of struggle for power at the first revolutionary tide, regardless of whether the immediate cause of revolution is democratic or nationalist.

Secondly, because the democratic and nationalist tasks of the Chinese revolution – that is, the agrarian revolution and the anti-imperialist struggle, just as Trotsky analysed them – themselves have an anti-capitalist character. Therefore, he said:

> The third Chinese revolution ... will not have a 'democratic' period ... but will be compelled from the very outset to effect the most decisive shake-up and abolition of bourgeois property in city and village.[6]

Is it not clear from this that according to Trotsky, 'socialism' in the future Chinese revolution will be the means of carrying on the revolution, not a 'goal' to be reached? If we believe that the third Chinese revolution 'will be compelled from the very outset to effect the most decisive shake-up and abolition of bourgeois property in city and village', then we are justified in asserting that the future revolution will be socialist from the very beginning.

In 'A Review and Some Perspectives', after quoting Ferdinand Lassalle, Trotsky wrote in 1906 that 'the future Russian revolution must be declared socialist from the very beginning'. The same view must be held by us on the character of the Chinese revolution. Trotsky has dealt with the same question in great detail in his *Letters to Preobrazhensky, A Criticism of the Draft Programme of the Communist International, Retreat in Disorder*, and other works. His ideas constitute a flat refutation of the theory of 'socialism as a goal'.

---

6 Trotsky 1957 [1928], pp. 184–5.

It is our hope, therefore, that international Trotskyism will return to the old fundamental platform, Trotsky's ideas on the character of the Chinese revolution, which as you well know has been one of the few most important questions marking the division between Stalinism and Trotskyism.

Conclusion

Our tactical divergences at the present stage are centred on the question of the civil war now being waged between the Guomindang and the Chinese Stalinists. In January 1946 the Struggle group adopted a resolution on the civil war that declared the war to be 'meaningless strife between selfish gangs'. They ostensibly took the position of the 'third camp', but in reality they took the side of the Guomindang by branding the armed struggle led by the Chinese Stalinists a manifestation of the 'particularism of new warlords', as 'military adventurism', and by demanding that the CCP 'give up their arms in order to fight for the constituent assembly'.

We reject and oppose this bankrupt position. We maintain that the Guomindang and the Chinese Communist Party represent different class forces in Chinese society. The former represents the landlords and bourgeoisie, while the latter represents mainly the poor peasants. So if we take only its national factor into consideration, the present civil war in China is a peasant war against the landlords and rural capitalists. As a peasant war, the civil war has a progressive character on the side of the peasants; but, as a peasant war only, the civil war is devoid of any perspective, and is even doomed to failure because of its Stalinist domination.

Basing ourselves on this estimate of the civil war, our attitude towards it is to defend the peasant forces against the oppression of the Wall Street-Guomindang alliance on the one hand, and attack the treacherous Stalinist leadership on the other.

In defending the peasant forces we not only fight side by side with the masses, but also call for unconditional peace. This is not a self-contradictory policy. This is so because the slogan 'immediate cessation of the war without disarming the Stalinist armies' at the present time would constitute a blow against the Guomindang warlords, and with the progress of events it would also mean a blow against the Stalinists. In war-weary China today no other slogan can play as great a revolutionary role as the slogan of peace.

In a word, our position on the civil war is: for the immediate and unconditional cessation of the war; in favour of participation in the *de facto* civil war on the side of the peasant forces; and at the same time to point out that the victorious outcome of the civil war can only be secured through the revolutionary leadership of the urban proletariat and the removal of the Stalinists from control of the peasant armed forces.

The position taken by the Struggle group on the civil war is quite close to that of the Shachtmanites, but worse than that, they even openly take the side of the Guomindang. Their participation in the Guomindang-sponsored 'Sovereignty Protection Movement' was an example of this position. In the *Report* they accused us of 'boycottism' and 'abstentionism' with respect to the 'mass anti-Kremlin demonstrations', while they, as they put it, 'boldly plunged into it to expose all the evil intentions of the Guomindang, expand and deepen it, and try finally to convert its leadership'.

But these 'anti-Kremlin demonstrations' were not really supported by large masses. Three such demonstrations have taken place since V-J Day, instigated by the most reactionary clique of the Guomindang, organised as anti-Russian demonstrations but really intended only to counterbalance pro-Russian feeling and support the failing prestige of the Guomindang and American imperialism. The first, in February 1946, drew large mass support, and we did not boycott it. We did not stand aside but participated, in order the better to expose and fight its reactionary sponsors and to distinguish our policy from that of the Stalinists. Our participation also produced good organisational gains for us.

The second anti-Soviet demonstration, in March 1947, was a great failure. Nobody came out in support and no demonstrations of any size took place. Peng Shuzhi and the Struggle Group were in favour of 'boldly plunging into it' but we considered that it was merely the affair of a few professional red-baiters and advocated boycotting it.

The third, in June, organised with an equally reactionary motive though ostensibly directed against the invasion of the Mongolian army into Xinjiang province, was abortive and even more miserable in scope than the second. Under the influence of our criticism, Peng Shuzhi and his followers also took the stand of 'abstentionism' in this case.

This mistake of the Struggle group was not accidental either. Here we believe it fitting to tell you of an old difference of opinion among the Chinese Trotskyists. In 1939, when Stalin waged war against Finland, Peng Shuzhi was the only one in the leadership of the Chinese section of the Fourth International who stood for the 'defence of poor little Finland'. He stood on the position of national independence of Finland, and favoured the adoption of defeatism in the USSR.

In spite of this, however, Peng Shuzhi now has the courage to tell you that he and his followers are simply 'continuing the internal struggle in the American party' in China. What cheap flattery this is! Peng Shuzhi followed in the footsteps of the American minority and was converted to Trotsky's point of view only after he read the latter's article; but on fundamental points he has not changed his opinion – it reappeared on the question of the civil war and also on the question of 'plunging into' an 'anti-Kremlin' demonstration.

Since the Struggle group takes a neutral, even pro-Guomindang, attitude on the question of the civil war; since they identify the left mass movement partially led by Stalinists with the quite isolated 'patriotic' movement completely conducted by Guomindang agents, it is quite natural that Peng Shuzhi cannot have correct views on party work.

A sort of liquidationist tendency has invariably decided the direction of the leadership of the Peng Shuzhi group. Their 'general line' of activity is to 'utilise the antagonism' between the Guomindang and the Stalinists in order to seek a full legal existence under the Guomindang régime. In order to attain this goal they are ready to pay, and have paid, no small price; until now, they did not dare to revive *Struggle*, which had been suspended for five years; they preferred the publication of 'theoretical' magazines and 'popular' periodicals with bourgeois scholars to the introduction and publication of any book or document of the Fourth International or of Trotsky; they discounted our slogans and adapted them to Guomindang policy; they echoed the Guomindang publicity ministry in branding the Chinese Communists 'new warlords' and demanding 'the voluntary disarmament' of the Stalinist army.

All this was done in the name of the struggle for legalisation and in the belief that this was the shortest road for the Trotskyists to reach the 'masses'. The direction of their policy can be justifiably called one of 'legislation at any cost'.

Can the present Guomindang régime grant the Chinese Trotskyists the right to legal activity? If this is possible then it is only on the following condition: that the Trotskyists will fight against the Stalinist party only, and put this 'fight' under the direction of the Guomindang. If the Chinese Trotskyists were ready to accept this condition, the Guomindang government would grant us not only legal status but 'protection' and 'subsidies' as well....

With respect to party work and the party paper, our attitude is precisely contrary to that of the Peng Shuzhi group. We maintained and still maintain that, no matter how bad the circumstances of our organs (*Internationalist* from 1942 to October 1945 and *New Banner* from June 1946 until now), we would rather translate and publish Trotsky's books and the documents of the Fourth International than cooperate with bourgeois scholars in issuing legal magazines. We would rather *New Banner* were banned by the Guomindang (October 1946) than change our attitude towards the government; we would rather assemble a handful of worker revolutionaries under the programme of the Fourth International than recruit more petty-bourgeois sympathisers under the 'democratic banner' of a third party.

Price

Needless to say, we are not fetishists on the question of 'underground work' and we know no less than they the significance of the struggle for legality. But at the same time we firmly believe that it would be a betrayal of our cause if we were ready to pay the price of legality: suspension of our party organ, refraining from propaganda for the ideas of the Fourth International and Trotskyism, cessation of the fight against the Guomindang, and, finally, supporting the Guomindang and conducting a one-sided attack against the Stalinists. We believe that a revolutionary party's struggle for legal existence is an uncompromising fight, not an adaptation to the reactionary laws, still less to the reactionary policy, of the ruling class. But the 'struggle for legality' by the Struggle group in recent years has consisted precisely of political concessions. That is why we could do nothing else but criticise and oppose them mercilessly.

The favourite accusation the Struggle group directs against us is that we 'attacked the *Transitional Programme*', 'revised the colonial programme of the Fourth International'. According to them, it is absolutely impermissible to 'attack' or 'revise' the *Transitional Programme*, regardless of *how* the programme is revised and whether the revision is right or wrong. The demand for, or attempt at, revision is in itself in their opinion a sort of 'betrayal' or 'crime'. We consider this attitude far from healthy and contrary to the spirit of Trotskyism. In this respect Trotsky said correctly: '[A] platform is not created so as not to part from it, but rather to apply and develop it'.[7]

The Struggle group attacks Comrade Wang and others as 'eclectics'. According to these 'eclectics', the anti-imperialist war of a colonial or semi-colonial country is progressive, even if it is under the leadership of the bourgeoisie. This is, of course, the traditional Leninist position and also the position of the *Transitional Programme*. But, these comrades say, if the leadership of the emancipation movement of a colonial country remains in the hands of the bourgeoisie for long, then the progressive movement will sooner or later degenerate into a kind of counter-revolution, serving the interests of the imperialists and against the interests of the native workers and peasants. In addition these comrades hold the opinion that, once the anti-imperialist war of a colonial country intermeshes with a war waged between rival imperialist powers, it is in no circumstances progressive but becomes reactionary in character. So according to them, China's anti-Japanese war was no longer progressive since it had become intermeshed with the anti-Japanese war of American imperialism.

---

7   *Fourth International*, September–October 1947, p. 254.

This position cannot be found in the *Transitional Programme* of the Fourth International, because at the time the programme was drafted such a situation did not exist, and there was no need for a corresponding answer. Here, quite clearly, it is not a question of revision or non-revision of the programme; in this respect there is nothing to be revised. But if we consider the question in the light of the fundamental ideas as well as the writings of Lenin and Trotsky, we can easily see that such a position coincides with the tradition of revolutionary Marxism.

In his *History of the Russian Revolution* Trotsky said: the participation of China in the First World War was 'the interference of a slave in the fight of the masters' (p. 38). 'The interference of a slave in the fight of the masters' is, of course, not progressive. As for Lenin, it is well known that he had two different views on the first and later stages of Serbia's war of resistance against Austria in the First World War in 1916. In a polemic against Rosa Luxemburg, Lenin also admitted, in *The Military Programme of Proletarian Revolution*, that 'national wars may be swallowed up by the war between rival imperialists and become imperialist in character'. On this question we believe that we have not revised the programme but have supplemented it with something not said previously.

However, the Struggle Group's fiercest criticism has been levelled against Comrade Yvon Zheng. They attack him for 'revising' the programme but do not bother to criticise the content of his 'revision'. There are two points to Comrade Zheng's view. At first, he said only that China's war had been a part of the imperialist war from the beginning; that it was reactionary from the beginning; but he still agreed that the anti-imperialist war of a colonial country alone is progressive.

Doomed

Secondly – that is, later on – having studied Lenin's theses on the national and colonial question, Comrade Zheng arrived at the conclusion that in the imperialist epoch all emancipation movements or national warsled by the colonial bourgeoisie are doomed to be impotent and devoid of progressive significance. He developed this idea in a pamphlet called *The Permanent Revolution and the Chinese Revolution*. It found some supporters in our organisation.

This position of Comrade Zheng's is, of course, a revision of a point in our *Transitional Programme*. But, whether we support or oppose his ideas, the fact of 'revision' itself is not a 'crime'. Instead of calling it so, we should rather call for its consideration and discussion. Now, there are not a few comrades in the Fourth International who propose giving up the slogan 'unconditional defence of the Soviet Union'. This is also a revision of a very important part of the *Transitional Programme*. We can and should discuss such revisions in the field of theory, fight against or for them; but we cannot simply attack them and refuse to discuss with their proponents on the sole ground that our programme is 'not to be parted from'.

Positions resembling Comrade Zheng's were held 30 years ago by Rosa Luxemburg, and during the first years of the Communist International they were held by some Italian Communists. Yet we never heard Lenin or Trotsky refuse to cooperate with, or refuse to make attempts to unite with, Luxemburg or Serrati because of this difference – or call them 'traitors'. Twenty or thirty years have elapsed since then; during these stormy years there have been revolutions and counter-revolutions in Turkey, Iran, and China. Many colonial wars took place during and after the Second World War. History has provided us with much experience and many lessons that are worth careful study and attention. So we hope that the Fourth International and its sections will carry out an unprejudiced consideration and decision on the colonial question. Only then can we decide what should be preserved of our traditional positions, what should be revised, and what should be developed.

To refute the Struggle Group's accusations that we are 'opportunist', 'sectarian', and 'ultra-leftist' we cite our programme. You can clearly see whether we have 'abandoned the transitional demands', 'want no democratic struggles but only socialism', or 'yield to the pressure of Stalinist-controlled public opinion'.

1. For the immediate cessation of the civil war.
2. For workers' security and the improvement of their livelihood.
3. Land to the poor peasants.
4. For the democratisation of the army (Guomindang and Communist).
5. Defend the standard of living of the urban poor.
6. Equality in education and job security for youth.
7. Freedom of speech, press, assembly, association, demonstration, appeal, strike, and picketing.
8. For the national independence of China and self-determination for minorities.
9. Defend the USSR. Down with the policy of the Stalinist bureaucracy! Against the Guomindang as the cat's-paw of American imperialism to attack the Soviet Union.
10. Solidarity with the working class and oppressed peoples of the world.
11. For the immediate convocation of an all-powerful constituent assembly elected on the basis of universal suffrage.... For a workers' and peasants' government.

At the end of this long letter we wish to say a few words about the publication of the Struggle Group's *Reports* in your magazine. The writer of that *Report* repeated the following many times:

> Our struggle was obviously the continuation of the struggle in the American party in 1940.
> Our minority had the same class basis as the Shachtmanites.
> The Chinese minority was a miniature of the Shachtmanites.

In publishing their *Report*, you did not express your opinion of it. That was cautious. But readers of your magazine were naturally impressed by the fact that you were satisfied with the declarations in the *Report*, and that you had thus taken sides in the internal polemics of the Chinese organisation. We admit that the ideological regroupment in the ranks of Trotskyism will take place on an international scale; but we do not think that such regroupment has taken place definitively in the national sections or in the International as a whole.

For example, on questions like the character of the USSR, the estimation of the international situation, the civil war in China, and national questions in Europe, our position still coincides with yours; while on the question of the attitude towards China's anti-Japanese war after it had been merged with the imperialist war, the Shachtmanites took, after the Pearl Harbour debacle, the same position we held before that event. On the other hand, the Struggle group, especially its leader Peng Shuzhi, took the same attitude towards the Soviet-Finnish war as the Shachtmanites, and their position on the present Chinese civil war was and is quite close to that of the Workers Party of the US. But on the question of China's war, their position coincides with yours.

In such circumstances, which group in the Chinese organisation shall be labelled the 'petty-bourgeois wing', and which group the 'proletarian tendency'? Again: the Bolshevik-Leninist Party of India, for example, took the same point of view on the colonial anti-imperialist war, during the World War, as we; should it be called the Indian 'miniature of the Shachtmanites'? Of course not!

A sharp process of ideological regroupment is taking place in the world Trotskyist movement. This is a result of the development of the world situation. We are not pessimistic about it. On the contrary, we consider it quite natural. But instead of weakening or destroying world Trotskyism, the artificial generation of factional prejudices must be avoided in order to strengthen and consolidate it. To reach that goal, we hope that Trotskyists of all countries will take the trouble to learn and study the polemics arising in the various national sections before taking sides on them.

We agreed completely with Comrade Li Furen when he said in his last letter to us that 'it was an error to print the article [the *Report*] as it was written', although we also agreed with him when he said in the same letter that you 'cannot be blamed for it as you are not conversant with the affairs of China'.

12 November 1947

PART 11

Some Articles and Speeches by Trotsky about the Chinese Trotskyists and Some Correspondence between Him and Them

The Speech of Comrade Chen Duxiu on the Tasks of the Chinese Communist Party

Leon Trotsky

17 May 1927

Epilogue to 'The Chinese Revolution and the Theses of Comrade Stalin', Problems of the Chinese Revolution, *written 1927–31, edited by Max Shachtman, New York: Pioneer Publishers, 1932. Online Version by Marxists Internet Archive, 2002, transcribed by Robert Barrois,* HTML *Markup by D. Walters.*

What purpose does Marxism serve in politics? To understand that which is and to foresee that which will be. Foresight must be the foundation of action. We already know what has happened to the predictions of comrade Stalin: one week before the coup d'état of Chiang Kai-shek, he defended him and blew the trumpet for him by calling for the utilisation of the right wing, its experiences, its connections (speech to the Moscow functionaries on 5 April). In the theses analysed by us, Stalin gives another example of foresight which has also been tested by life. The central question of our criticism of Stalin's theses was formulated by us above as follows: 'Does there already exist a new centre of the revolution or must one first be created?' Stalin contended that after the coup d'état of Chiang Kai-shek there were '*two governments, two armies, two centres: the revolutionary centre in Wuhan and the counter-revolutionary centre in Nanjing*'. Stalin contended that no soviets can be built because that would signify an uprising against the Wuhan centre, against the '*only government*' in Southern China. We called this characterisation of the situation 'false, superficial, vulgar'. We called this so-called Wuhan government the '*leaders of Wuhan*' and showed that in Southern China, after the abrupt veering of the civil war to another class line, there is no government as yet, that one must be first created.

In *Pravda* of 15 May the speech of comrade Chen Duxiu at the convention of the Chinese Communist Party (29 April) is reprinted.

Neither Stalin nor we had this speech when Stalin wrote his theses and we wrote a criticism of them. Chen Duxiu characterises the situation not on the basis of a general analysis of the circumstances but on the basis of his direct observations. Now, what does Chen Duxiu say of the new revolutionary movement? He declares plainly that 'it would be a mistake' to consider the Wuhan government an organ of the revolutionary democratic dictatorship: 'It is *not yet a government of the worker and peasant masses but solely a bloc of leaders*'. But is this not word for word what we said against Stalin?

Stalin wrote: 'There is now no other governmental power than the government of the revolutionary Guomindang'. We answered him on that: 'These words fairly reek with the apparatus-like and bureaucratic conception of revolutionary authority. The classes come and go but the continuity of the Guomindang government goes on forever [allegedly]. But it is not enough to call Wuhan the centre of the revolution for it really to be that' (cf. above). Instead of making it clear to the Chinese revolutionists, to the Communists primarily, that the Wuhan government will break its head against a wall if it imagines that it is itself already the only government in China; instead of turning relentlessly against the decorative hypocrisy of the petty-bourgeois revolutionists who have already destroyed so many revolutions; instead of shouting right into the ear of the uncertain, faltering, vacillating centre of Wuhan: 'Do not be misled by outward appearances, do not be dazzled by the glitter of our own titles and manifestos, begin to perform the hard daily work, set masses in motion, build up workers', soldiers' and peasants' soviets, build up a revolutionary governmental power' – instead of all this, Stalin hurls himself against the slogan of the soviets and supports the worst, the most provincial and bureaucratic prejudices and superstitious views of those ill-fated revolutionists who fear people's soviets, and instead have faith in the sacred ink-blots on the notepaper of the Guomindang.

Comrade Chen Duxiu characterises the situation on the basis of his own observations with exactly the same words with which we characterised the situation on the basis of theoretical consideration. No revolutionary government but only a bloc of leaders. But this does not at all mean that comrade Chen Duxiu himself draws correct conclusions from the circumstances correctly characterised by him. Since he is bound hand and foot by false directives, Chen Duxiu draws conclusions which radically contradict his own analysis. He says: 'We have before us the task of beginning to build up a genuinely revolutionary and democratic government *as soon as the situation in the sphere of the national government has changed and the threat of foreign intervention and the offensive of the militarists have disappeared*'.

Here we must say directly and openly: put the question this way and you adopt the surest and shortest road to ruin. The creation of a genuinely revolutionary government basing itself on the popular masses is relegated to the moment when the dangers have disappeared. But the central danger consists precisely of the fact that instead of a revolutionary government in Southern

China, there is for the time being only a bloc of leaders. Through this principal evil, all the other dangers are increased tenfold, including also the military danger. If we are to be guarded to the highest possible degree against the foreign and our 'own' militarist bands, we must become strong, consolidate ourselves, organise, and arm ourselves. There are no other roads. We should not stick our heads in the sand. No artifice will help us here. The enthusiasm of the masses must be aroused, their readiness to fight and to die for their own cause. But for this the masses must be gripped as deeply as possible, politically and organisationally. Without losing even an hour, they must be given a revolutionary programme of action and the organisational form of the soviets. There are no other roads. Postpone the creation of a revolutionary government until somebody has eliminated the danger of war in some way or other, and you take the surest and shortest road to ruin.

With regard to the agrarian movement, comrade Chen Duxiu admits honestly that the agrarian programme of the Party (reduction of rent payments) is completely insufficient. The peasant movement, he says, 'is being transformed into the struggle for land. The peasantry arises spontaneously and wants to settle the land question itself'. Further on, comrade Chen Duxiu declares openly: '*We followed a too pacific policy*. Now it is necessary to confiscate the large estates'. If the content of these words is developed in a Marxian manner, it constitutes the harshest condemnation of the whole past line of the Communist Party of China, and the Comintern as well, in the agrarian question of the Chinese revolution. Instead of anticipating the course of the agrarian movement, of establishing the slogans in time and throwing them among the peasant masses through the workers, the revolutionary soldiers and the advanced peasants, the Chinese Communist Party remained a vast distance behind the spontaneous agrarian movement. Can there be a more monstrous form of *chvostism* [tailism]? '*We followed a too pacific policy*'. But what does a pacific policy of a revolutionary party mean in the period of a spontaneous agrarian revolution? It signifies the most grievous historical mistake that a party of the proletariat can possibly commit. A pacific policy (the reduction of rent payments), while the peasant is already fighting spontaneously for land, is not a policy of Menshevik compromise but of liberal compromise. Only a philistine corrupted by alleged statecraft can fail to understand this, but never a revolutionist.

But from his correct, and therefore deadly, characterisation of the relations of the party to the agrarian movement, comrade Chen Duxiu draws not only false but positively disastrous conclusions. 'It is now necessary', he says, 'to confiscate the large estates, but at the same time to make concessions to the small landowners who must be reckoned with'. In principle, such a way of posing the question cannot be assailed. It must be clearly determined who and in what part of China is to be considered a small landowner, how and to what limits he must be reckoned with. But Chen Duxiu says further:

'Nevertheless, it is necessary to await *the further development of the military actions* even for the confiscation of the large estates. The only correct decision at the present moment is the principle of deepening the revolution *only after its extension*'.

This road is the surest, the most positive, the shortest road to ruin. The peasant has already risen to seize the property of the large landowners. Our party, in monstrous contradiction to its programme, to its name, pursues a pacific-liberal agrarian policy. Chen Duxiu himself declares that it is 'now [?] necessary to confiscate the large estates', but he immediately recalls that we 'must not fall into left extremism' (Chen Duxiu's own words) and he adds that we must 'await the further development of the military actions' for the confiscation of the property of the large landowners, that the revolution must first be extended and only later deepened.

But this is simply a blind repetition of the old, well-known and outworn formula of national-liberal deception of the masses: First the victory, then the reform. First we will 'extend' the country – for whom: for the large landowner? – and then, after the victory, we will concern ourselves very tranquilly with the 'deepening'. To this, every intelligent and half-way sensible peasant will answer comrade Chen Duxiu: 'If the Wuhan government today, when it finds itself encircled by foes and needs our peasant support for life and death – if this government does not dare now to give us the land of the large landowners or does not want to do it, then after it has extricated itself from its encirclement, after it has vanquished the enemy with our help, it will give us just as much land as Chiang Kai-shek gave the workers of Shanghai'. It must be said quite clearly: The agrarian formula of comrade Chen Duxiu, who is bound hand and foot by the false leadership of the representatives of the Comintern, is objectively nothing else than the formula of the severance of the Chinese Communist Party from the real agrarian movement which is now proceeding in China and which is producing a new wave of the Chinese revolution.

To strengthen this wave and to deepen it we need peasants' soviets with the unfurled banner of the agrarian revolution, not after the victory but immediately, in order to guarantee the victory.

If we do not want to permit the peasant wave to come to nought and be splattered into froth, the peasants' soviets must be united through workers' soviets in the cities and the industrial centres, and to the workers' soviets must be added the soviets of the poor population from the urban trade and handwork districts.

If we do not want to permit the bourgeoisie to drive a wedge between the revolutionary masses and the army, then soldiers' soviets must be fitted into the revolutionary chain.

As quickly as possible, as boldly as possible, as energetically as possible, the revolution must be deepened, not after the victory but immediately, or else there will be no victory.

The deepening of the agrarian revolution, the immediate seizure of the land by the peasants, will weaken Chiang Kai-shek on the spot, bring confusion into the ranks of his soldiers, and set the peasant hinterland in motion. There is no other road to victory and there can be none.

Have we really carried through three revolutions within two decades only to forget the ABC of the first of them? Whoever carries on a *pacific* policy during the agrarian revolution, is lost. Whoever postpones matters, vacillates, temporises, loses time, is lost. The formula of Chen Duxiu is the surest road to the destruction of the revolution.

Slanderers will be found who will say that our words are dictated by a hatred of the Chinese Communist Party and its leaders. Was it not once said that our position on the Anglo-Russian Committee signified a hostile attitude towards the British Communist Party? The events confirmed the fact that it was we who acted as loyal revolutionists towards the British Communists, and not as bureaucratic sycophants. Events will confirm the fact – they confirm it every day – that our criticism of the Chinese Communists was dictated by a more serious, more Marxist, revolutionary attitude towards the Chinese revolution than was the attitude of the bureaucratic sycophants who approve of everything after the fact, provided that they do not have to foresee for the future.

The fact that the speech of comrade Chen Duxiu is reprinted in *Pravda* without a single word of commentary, that no article revealing the ruinous course of this speech is devoted to it – this fact by itself must fill every revolutionist with the greatest misgivings, for it is the central organ of Lenin's party that is involved!

Let not the pacifiers and flatterers tell us about 'the unavoidable mistakes of a young Communist Party'. It is not a question of isolated mistakes. It is a question of the false basic line, the consummate expression of which is the theses of comrade Stalin.

The Necessary Final Accord

In the 9 May number of *Sotsialisticheski Vestnik*, it says in the article devoted to the theses of comrade Stalin:

If we strip the envelope of words that is obligatory for the theses of a Communist leader, then very little can be said against the essence of the 'line' traced there. As much as possible to remain in the Guomindang, and to cling to its left wing and to the Wuhan government to the last possible moment: 'to avoid a decisive struggle under unfavourable conditions'; not to issue the slogan 'all power to the soviets' so as not 'to give new weapons into the hands of the enemies of the Chinese people for the struggle against the revolution, for creating new legends that it is not a national revolution that is taking place in China, but an artificial transplanting of Moscow sovietisation' – what can actually be more sensible for the Bolsheviks now, after the 'united front' has obviously been irremediably destroyed, and so much porcelain has been smashed under the 'most unfavourable conditions'?[1]

Thus, after *Sotsialisticheski Vestnik*, in its 23 April number, acknowledged that Martynov analysed the tasks of the Chinese revolution in *Pravda* 'very impressively' and 'entirely in the Menshevik manner', the leading article in the central organ of the Mensheviks declares in its latest number that 'very little can be said against the essence of the 'line' traced' in the theses of comrade Stalin. This harmony of political lines hardly requires special elucidation.

But still more: The same article in *Sotsialisticheski Vestnik* speaks further on in a mocking tone – we quote literally! – of *'the line of Radek which, covered with extreme "left" slogans (withdrawal from Guomindang, "propaganda of the soviet system" and so on), simply desires in reality to give up the game and to step aside'*.[2] The line of Radek is characterised here with the words of the leading articles and the feuilletons of *Pravda*. After all, it cannot be otherwise: Radek cannot say anything openly in the press about his line, for otherwise the Party would learn that Radek's line is being confirmed by the whole course of events. The editors of *Sotsialisticheski Vestnik* not only describe 'the line of Radek' with the words of *Pravda* but also evaluate them in full accord with the articles of *Pravda*: The line of the Opposition, according to Dan, gives the possibility, 'covered with extreme "left" slogans', in reality 'to give up the game and to step aside'. We have already read in the articles of *Pravda* that 'a mass for the dead must be read' for the Chinese revolution, that the Chinese Communists must 'retire within themselves', that they must renounce 'great deeds and great plans', and that all this is the 'sermon of the liquidation of the Chinese revolution' – if the line of the Opposition is adopted. This was said literally, for exam-

---

1 *Sotsialisticheski Vestnik*, no. 9, p. 1.
2 *Sotsialisticheski Vestnik*, no. 9, p. 2.

ple, in the leading article in *Pravda* of 16 May 1927. As we see, it is word for word the same thing that Dan says, or more correctly, Dan says of the Opposition word for word what *Pravda* has said in a series of its articles. Dan approves the theses of Stalin and derides the 'liquidator' Radek, who covers his liquidation with extremely left phrases. Everything is clear now: The liquidationism of Radek is the same liquidationism which is evaluated as such by the renowned revolutionist Dan. That is the lesson that the leading articles in *Sotsialisticheski Vestnik* presents to those who are still capable of learning anything.

It is surely portentous that the quoted number of *Sotsialisticheski Vestnik* should arrive in Moscow on the eve of the opening of the session of the Executive Committee of the Communist International, which must consider the problem of the Chinese revolution in its full scope.

A Remarkable Document on the Policy and the Régime of the Communist International

Leon Trotsky

4 October 1928 (the Jiangsu Committee resolution is dated 7 May 1928)

Appendix to 'The Chinese Question After the Sixth Congress', Problems of the Chinese Revolution, written 1927–31, edited by Max Shachtman, New York: Pioneer Publishers, 1932. Online Version by Marxists Internet Archive, 2002, transcribed by Robert Barrois, HTML Markup by D. Walters.

We referred above several times to the remarkable resolution of the Plenum of the Central Committee of the CCP (November 1927), precisely the one which the Ninth Plenum of the Executive Committee of the Communist International (CI) charged with 'Trotskyism', and about which Lominadze justified himself in such a variegated manner while Stalin very monotonously slunk off in silence. In reality, this resolution is a combination of opportunism and adventurism, reflecting with perfect precision the policy of the Executive Committee of the Communist International before and after July 1927. In condemning this resolution *after the defeat of the Guangzhou insurrection*, the leaders of the Communist International not only did not publish it but did not even quote from it. It was too embarrassing for them to show themselves in the Chinese mirror. This resolution was published in a special *Documentation*, accessible to very few, printed by the Chinese Sun Yat-sen University (no. 10).

No. 14 of the same publication, which reached our hands when our work (*The Chinese Question After the Sixth Congress*) was already completed, contains a no less remarkable document, even though of a different, that is, of a critical character: it is a resolution adopted by the Jiangsu District Committee of the Chinese Communist Party on 7 May 1928, in connection with the decisions of the Ninth Plenum of the Executive Committee of the Comintern. Remember that Shanghai and Guangzhou are part of the province of Jiangsu.[1]

This resolution, as has already been said, constitutes a truly remarkable document, in spite of the errors in principle and the political misunderstandings it contains. The essence of the resolution amounts to a deadly condemnation not only of the decisions of the Ninth Plenum of the Executive Committee of

---

1 Guangzhou is actually in Guangdong, not Jiangsu.

the Communist International, but, in general, of the whole leadership of the Comintern in the questions of the Chinese revolution. Naturally, in conformity with the whole régime existing in the Comintern, the criticism directed against the Executive Committee of the CI bears a camouflaged and conventionally diplomatic character. The immediate point of the resolution is directed against the Central Committee itself as against a responsible ministry under an irresponsible monarch who, as is known, 'can do no wrong'. There are even polite eulogies for certain parts of the resolution of the ECCI. This whole way of approaching the question by 'manoeuvring' is in itself a harsh criticism of the régime of the Communist International; hypocrisy is inseparable from bureaucratism. But what the resolution says in essence about the political leadership and its methods has a much more damning character.

'After the 7 August (1927) conference', the Jiangsu Committee relates, 'the Central Committee formulated a judgement on the situation which was tantamount to saying that even though the revolution had suffered a triple defeat, it is nevertheless going through a rising phase'.

This appreciation is entirely in conformity with the caricature Bukharin makes of the theory of the permanent revolution, a caricature he applied first to Russia, then to Europe and finally to Asia. The actual events of the struggle, that is, the three defeats, are one thing and the permanent 'rise' is another.

The Central Committee of the Chinese party draws the following conclusion from the resolution adopted by the Eighth Plenum of the Executive Committee of the Communist International (in May):

'Wherever this is objectively possible, we must *immediately* prepare and organise armed insurrections'.

What are the political premises for this? The Jiangsu Committee declares that in August 1927 'the political report of the Central Committee pointed out that the *workers* of Hunan, after the cruel *defeat, are abandoning the leadership of the Party*, that we are not confronted with an objectively revolutionary situation ... but in spite of this ... the Central Committee says plainly that the general situation, from the economic, political and social [precisely! – *L.T.*] point of view is favourable to the insurrection. Since *it is already no longer possible to launch revolts in the cities*, the armed struggle must be transferred to the villages. That is where the centres of the uprising must be, while the town must be an auxiliary force'.

Let us recall that immediately after the May Plenum of the Executive Committee of the Communist International, which entrusted the leadership of the agrarian revolution to the Left Guomindang, the latter began to exterminate the workers and peasants. The position of the ECCI became completely untenable. At all costs, there had to be, and that without delay, 'left' actions in

China to refute the 'calumny' of the Opposition, that is, its irreproachable prognosis. That is why the Chinese Central Committee, which found itself between the hammer and the anvil, was obliged, in August 1927, to turn the proletarian policy topsy-turvy all over again. Even though there was no revolutionary situation and the working masses were abandoning the Party, this Committee declared that the economic and social situation was, in its opinion, 'favourable to the insurrection'. In any case, a triumphant uprising would have been very 'favourable' to the prestige of the Executive Committee of the Comintern. Given the fact that the workers were abandoning the revolution, it was necessary to turn one's back to the towns and endeavour to launch isolated uprisings in the villages.

Already at the May Plenum (1927) of the ECCI, we pointed out that the adventurist uprisings of He Long and Ye Ting were doomed to defeat because of insufficient political preparation and because they were bound up with no movement of the masses. That is just what happened. The resolution of the Jiangsu Committee says on this subject:

'In spite of the defeat of the armies of He Long and Ye Ting in Guangdong, even after the November Plenum the Central Committee persists in clinging to the tactic of immediate uprisings and takes as its point of departure an estimation leading to the direct ascent of the revolution'.

For understandable reasons, the Jiangsu Committee passes in silence over the fact that this appreciation was also that of the Executive Committee of the Comintern itself, which treated as 'liquidators' those who correctly estimated the situation, and the fact that the Chinese Central Committee was forced, in November 1927, on pain of being immediately overthrown and expelled from the Party, to present the decline of the revolution as its rise.

The Guangzhou insurrection sprang up by basing itself upon this tip-tilted manner of approaching the question; manifestly, this uprising was not regarded as a rearguard battle (only raging madmen could have urged passing over to the insurrection and to the conquest of power through a 'rearguard battle'); no, this uprising was conceived as part of a general coup d'état. The Jiangsu resolution says on this point:

> During the Guangzhou insurrection of December, the Central Committee decided once more to launch an immediate uprising in Hunan, Hubei, and Jiangsu in order to defend Guangdong, in order to extend the framework of the movement all over China (this can be verified from the information letters of the Central Committee, nos. 16 and 22). These measures flowed

from a subjective estimation of the situation and did not correspond to the objective circumstances. Obviously, under such conditions defeats will be inevitable.

The Guangzhou experience frightened the leaders not only of China but also of Moscow. A warning was issued against putschism, but in essence the political line did not change. The orientation remained the same: towards insurrection. The Central Committee of the Chinese Communist Party transmitted this ambiguous instruction to the lower bodies; it also warned against the tactic of skirmishes, while setting down in its circulars academic definitions of adventurism.

'But given that the Central Committee based its estimation of the revolutionary movement upon an uninterrupted advance', as the Jiangsu resolution says correctly and pointedly, 'no modifications were brought into this question at the bottom. The forces of the enemy are far too greatly underrated and at the same time, no attention is paid to the fact that our organisations have lost contact with the masses. Therefore, in spite of the fact that the Central Committee had sent its information letter no. 28 (on putschism) everywhere, it did not at the same time correct its mistakes'.

Once more, it is not a question of the Central Committee of the Chinese party. The February Plenum of the Executive Committee of the Communist International introduced no modifications into its policy either. While warning against the tactics of skirmishes in general (in order to insure itself against all eventualities), the resolution of this Plenum pounced furiously upon the Opposition which spoke of the necessity of a resolute change in the whole orientation. In February 1928, the course continued as before to lead towards insurrection. The Central Committee of the Chinese Communist Party only served as a mechanism to transmit this instruction. The Jiangsu Committee says:

> The Central Committee circular no. 38, of 6 March [take careful note: 6 March 1928! – *L.T.*], shows very clearly that the Central Committee still finds itself under the influence of illusions about a favourable situation for general insurrection in Hunan, Hubei, and Jiangsu, and the possibility of conquering power throughout the province of Guangdong. The radical quarrel over the choice of Changsha or Hankou as the centre of insurrection still continued between – the Political Bureau of the Central Committee and the instructor of the Central Committee in Hunan and Hubei.

Such was the disastrous significance of the resolution of the February Plenum, not only false in principle but deliberately ambiguous from the practical point of view. The thought concealed behind this resolution was always the same: if, contrary to expectations, the uprising extends itself, we shall refer to that part which speaks against the liquidators; if the insurrection goes no further than partisan affrays, we will point a finger at that part of the resolution which warns against putschism.

Even though the Jiangsu resolution nowhere dares criticise the Executive Committee of the Communist International (everybody knows what this costs), nevertheless, in none of its documents has the Opposition dealt such deadly blows to the leadership of the Comintern as does the Jiangsu Committee in its arraignment, aimed formally at the Central Committee of the Chinese Communist Party. After listing chronologically the policies of adventurism month after month, the resolution turns to the general causes for the disastrous course.

'How is one to explain', asks the resolution, 'this erroneous estimation of the situation established by the Central Committee which influenced the practical struggle and contained serious errors? It is to be explained as follows:

1. The revolutionary movement was estimated as an uninterrupted ascent [the 'permanent revolution' à la Bukharin-Lominadze! – L.T.].
2. No attention was paid to the loss of contact between our party and the masses, nor to the decomposition of the mass organisations at the turning point of the revolution.
3. No account was taken of the new regrouping of class forces inside the enemy camp during this turn.
4. No consideration was given to leading the movement in the cities.
5. No attention was paid to the importance of the anti-imperialist movement in a semicolonial country.
6. During the insurrection, no account was taken of the objective conditions, nor of the necessity of applying different methods of struggle in conformity with them.
7. A peasant deviation made itself felt.
8. The Central Committee, in its estimation of the situation, was guided by a subjective point of view.

It is doubtful if the Jiangsu Committee has read what the Opposition wrote and said on all these questions. One can even say with certainty that it did not read it. As a matter of fact, if it had, it would have feared to formulate with such precision its considerations, coinciding entirely in this part with ours. The Jiangsu Committee repeated our words without suspecting it.

The eight points enumerated above, characterising the false line of the Central Committee (that is, the Executive Committee of the Communist International), are equally important. If we wish to say a few words on the fifth point, it is simply because we have here a particularly striking confirmation 'by facts' of the justice of our criticism in its most essential features. The Jiangsu resolution charges the policy of the Central Committee with neglecting the problems of the anti-imperialist movement in a semicolonial country. How could this happen? By the force of the dialectic of the false political line; mistakes have their dialectic like everything else in the world. The point of departure of official opportunism was that the Chinese revolution is essentially an anti-imperialist revolution, and that the yoke of imperialism welds together all the classes or at the very least 'all the living forces of the country'. We objected that a successful struggle against imperialism is possible only by means of an audacious extension of the class struggle, and, consequently, of the agrarian revolution. We rose up intransigently against the attempt to subordinate the class struggle to the abstract criterion of the struggle against imperialism (substitution of arbitration commissions for the strike movement, telegraphic advice not to stir up the agrarian revolution, prohibiting the formation of soviets, and so on). This was the first stage of the question. After Chiang Kai-shek's coup d'état, and especially after the 'treason' of the 'friend' Wang Jingwei, there was an about face of 180 degrees. Now, it turns out that the question of customs independence, that is, of the economic '(and consequently, the political)' sovereignty of China is a secondary 'bureaucratic' problem (Stalin).

The essence of the Chinese revolution was supposed to consist of the agrarian upheaval. The concentration of power in the hands of the bourgeoisie, the abandonment of the revolution by the workers, the schism between the Party and the masses, were appraised as secondary phenomena in comparison with the peasant revolts. Instead of a genuine hegemony of the proletariat, in the anti-imperialist as well as in the agrarian struggle, that is, in the democratic revolution as a whole, there took place a wretched capitulation before the primitive peasant forces, with 'secondary' adventures in the cities. However, such a capitulation is the fundamental premise of putschism. The whole history of the revolutionary movement in Russia, as well as in other countries, is witness to that. The events in China of the past year have confirmed it.

In its estimation and its warnings, the Opposition took as its point of departure general theoretical considerations, basing itself upon official information, very incomplete and sometimes deliberately distorted. The Jiangsu Committee has as its point of departure facts it observed directly at the centre of the revolutionary movement; from the theoretical point of view this Committee still writhes in the toils of Bukharinist scholasticism. The fact that its empirical conclusions coincide completely with our own has, in politics, the same significance as, for example, the discovery in laboratories of a new element whose existence was predicted in advance on the basis of theoretical deductions has in chemistry. Unfortunately, the triumph from the theoretical point of view of our Marxian analysis, in the case before us, has as its political foundation mortal defeats for the revolution.

The abrupt and essentially adventurist turn in the policy of the Executive Committee of the Communist International in the middle of 1927 could not but provoke painful shocks in the Chinese Communist Party, which was taken off its guard by it. Here we pass from the political line of the Executive Committee of the Communist International to the régime of the Comintern and to the organisational methods of the leadership. Here is what the Jiangsu Committee resolution says on this point:

> After the conference of August 7 (1927), the Central Committee should have assumed the responsibility for the putschist tendencies, for it demanded rigorously of the local committees that the *new political line* be applied; if anybody was not in agreement with *the new line*, without further ceremony he was not permitted to renew his party card and even comrades who had already carried out this operation were expelled At this time, the putschist mood was making headway throughout the Party; if anybody expressed doubts about the policy of uprisings, he was immediately called an opportunist and pitilessly attacked. This circumstance provoked great friction within the Party organisations.

All this took place to the accompaniment of pious academic warnings against the dangers of putschism 'in general'.

The policy of the sudden, hastily improvised armed insurrection demanded a speedy overhauling and a regrouping of the entire Party. The Central Committee tolerated in the Party only those who silently acknowledged the course of armed insurrection in the face of an obvious decline of the revolution. It would be well to publish the instructions furnished by the Executive Committee of the Communist International during this period. They could be reduced to one: an instruction for the organisation of defeat. The Jiangsu resolution sets forth that

'The Central Committee continues not to take notice of the defeats and the depressed mood of the workers; it does not see that this situation is the result of the mistakes of its leadership'.

But that is not all:

> The Central Committee accuses someone or other [just so! – *L.T.*] for the fact that:
>
> *a*) the local committees have not sufficiently well checked up on the reorganisation;
>
> *b*) the worker and peasant elements are not *pushed ahead*;
>
> *c*) the local organisations are not purged of opportunist elements, and so on.

All this happens abruptly, by telegraph: somehow or other, the mouth of the Opposition must be closed. But nevertheless since matters are in a bad way, the Central Committee asserts that: 'the disposition of the masses would be entirely different if the signal for revolt had been given at least in one single province. Does not this last indication bespeak a one hundred per cent putschism of the Central Committee itself?' (page 6) asks the Jiangsu Committee with full justice, passing prudently over in silence the fact that the Central Committee only executed the instructions of the Executive Committee of the Communist International.

For five years the Party was led and educated in an opportunist spirit. At the present moment, it is demanded of it that it be ultra-radical and 'immediately put forward' worker-leaders. How?... Very simply: by fixing a certain percentage of them. The Jiangsu Committee complains:

1. No account is taken of the fact that the ones who are to supplement the leading cadres should be advanced in the course of the struggle. Whereas the Central Committee confines itself to a formal establishment of a percentage fixed in advance of workers and peasants in the leading organs of the various organisations.
2. In spite of the numerous failures, they do not examine the point to which our party is already restored, but they simply say formally that it is necessary to reorganise.
3. The Central Committee simply says dictatorially that the local organisations do not put forward new elements, that they do not rid themselves of opportunism; at the same time, the Central Committee makes baseless

attacks upon the militants of the cadres and replaces them light-mindedly.
4. Without paying attention to the mistakes of its own leadership, the Central Committee nevertheless demands the most severe party discipline from the rank-and-file militants.

Does it not seem as though all these paragraphs are copied from the *Platform of the Opposition*? No, they are copied from life. But since the *Platform* is also copied from life, there is no coincidence. Where then is the 'peculiarity' of Chinese conditions? Bureaucratism levels down each and every peculiarity. The policy as well as the régime are determined by the Executive Committee of the Communist International, more exactly by the Central Committee of the Communist Party of the Soviet Union. The Central Committee of the Chinese Communist Party drives both down into the lower organs. Here is how this takes place according to the Jiangsu resolution:

> The following declaration made by a comrade of a district committee is very characteristic: 'At present it is very difficult to work; but the Central Committee shows that it has a very subjective manner of regarding the problem. It pounces down with accusations and says that the Provincial Committee is no good; the latter in its turn accuses the rank-and-file organisations and asserts that the district committee is bad. The latter also begins to accuse and asserts that it is the comrades working on the spot who are no good. And the comrades declare that the masses are not revolutionary'.

There you really have a striking picture. Only, there is nothing peculiarly Chinese about it. Every resolution of the Executive Committee of the Communist International, in registering new defeats, declares that on the one hand all had been foreseen and that on the other it is the 'executors' who are the cause of the defeats because they did not understand the line that had been pointed out to them from above. It remains unexplained how the perspicacious leadership was able to foresee everything save that the executors did not measure up to its instructions. The essential thing in the leadership does not consist of presenting an abstract line, of writing a letter without an address, but of selecting and educating the executors. The correctness of the leadership is tested precisely in execution. The reliability and perspicacity of the leadership are confirmed only when words and deeds harmonise. But if, chronically, from one stage to the other, over the course of many years, the leadership is obliged *post factum* to complain at every turn that it has not been understood, that its ideas have been deformed, that the executors have ruined its plan, that is a sure sign that the fault devolves entirely upon the leadership. This 'self-criticism' is all the more murderous by the fact that it is involuntary and unconscious. According to the Sixth Congress, the leadership of the Opposition must be held responsible for every group of turncoats; but *per contra* the leadership of the Communist International should in no wise have to answer for the Central Committee of all the national parties in the most decisive historical moments. But a leadership which is answerable for nothing is an irresponsible leadership. In that is to be found the root of all the evils.

In protecting itself against the criticism of the ranks, the Central Committee of the Chinese Communist Party bases itself on the Executive Committee of the Communist International, that is, it draws a chalk line on the floor which cannot be stepped over. Nor does the Jiangsu Committee overstep it. But within the confines of this chalk line, it tells some bitter truths to its Central Committee which automatically extend to the Executive Committee of the Communist International. We are once more forced to quote an extract from the remarkable document of Jiangsu:

> The Central Committee says that the whole past leadership was exercised in accordance with the instructions of the Communist International. As if all these hesitations and errors depended only upon the rank-and-file militants. If one adopts such a manner of regarding the question, the Central Committee will itself be unable either to repair the mistakes or to educate the comrades to study this experience. It will not be able to strengthen its ties with the lower Party apparatus. The Central Committee always says that its leadership was right; it charges the rank-and-file comrades with all the mistakes, always especially underscoring the hesitations of the rank-and-file Party committees.

A little further on:

> If the leadership only attacks light-mindedly the local leading comrades or organs by pointing out their errors, but without actually analysing the source of these mistakes, this only produces friction within the Party; such an attitude is disloyal ['rude and disloyal' – *L.T.*] and can do no good to the revolution and to the Party. If the leadership itself covers up its errors and throws the blame on others, such conduct will do no good to the Party or to the revolution.

A simple but classic characterisation of bureaucratic centrism's work of decaying and devastating the consciousness.

The Jiangsu resolution shows in an entirely exemplary manner how and by what methods the Chinese revolution was led to numerous defeats, and the Chinese party to the brink of catastrophe. For the imaginary hundred thousand members who figure on paper in the Chinese Communist Party only represent a gross self-deception. They would then constitute one-sixth of the total membership of the Communist parties of all the capitalist countries. The payments which Chinese Communism must make for the crime of the leadership are still far from completed.

Further decline is ahead. There will be great difficulty in rising again. Every false step will fling the Party into a deeper ditch. The resolution of the Sixth Congress dooms the Chinese Communist Party to errors and false steps. With the present course of the Communist International, under its present régime, victory is impossible. The course must be changed. This is what the resolution of the Jiangsu Provincial Committee says once more.

Peasant War in China and the Proletariat

Leon Trotsky

22 September 1932

Source: The Militant, *15 October 1932, pp. 2–3; transcribed and* HTML *markup by David Walters, copyleft Leon Trotsky Internet Archive (www.marxists.org) 2003.*

Dear Comrades,

After a long delay, we received your letter of 15 June. Needless to say we were overjoyed by the revival and the renascence of the Chinese Left Opposition, despite the most ferocious police persecutions it had endured.

Our irreconcilable attitude towards the vulgar democratic Stalinist position on the peasant movement has, of course, nothing in common with a careless or passive attitude towards the peasant movement itself. The manifesto of the International Left Opposition that was issued two years ago and that evaluated the peasant movement in the southern provinces of China declared: 'The Chinese revolution, betrayed, defeated, exhausted, shows that it is still alive. Let us hope that the time when it will again lift its proletarian head is not far off'. Further on it says: 'The vast flood of peasant revolts can unquestionably provide the impulse for the revival of political struggle in the industrial centres. We firmly count on it'.

Your letter testifies that under the influence of the crisis and the Japanese intervention, against the background of the peasant war, the struggle of the city workers is burgeoning once again. In the manifesto we wrote about this possibility with necessary caution: 'Nobody can foretell now whether the hearths of the peasant revolt can keep a fire burning through the whole long period of time which the proletarian vanguard will need to gather its own strength, bring the working class into the fight, and co-ordinate its struggle for power with the general offensive of the peasants against their most immediate enemies'.

At the present time it is evident that there are substantial grounds for expressing the hope that, through a correct policy, it will be possible to unite the workers' movement, and the urban movement in general, with the peasant war; and this would constitute the beginning of the third Chinese revolution. But in the meantime this still remains only a hope, not a certainty. The most important work lies ahead.

In this letter I want to pose only one question which seems to me, at least from afar, to be the most important and acute. Once again I must remind you that the information at my disposal is altogether insufficient, accidental, and disjointed. I would indeed welcome any amplification and correction.

The peasant movement has created its own armies, has seized great territories, and has installed its own institutions. In the event of further successes – and all of us, of course, passionately desire such successes – the movement will become linked up with the urban and industrial centres and, through that very fact it will come face to face with the working class. What will be the nature of this encounter? Is it certain that its character will be peaceful and friendly?

At first glance the question might appear to be superfluous. The peasant movement is headed by Communists or sympathisers. Isn't it self-evident that in the event of their coming together the workers and the peasants must unanimously unite under the Communist banner?

Unfortunately the question is not at all so simple. Let me refer to the experience of Russia. During the years of the civil war the peasantry in various parts of the country created its own guerrilla detachments, which sometimes grew into full-fledged armies. Some of these detachments considered themselves Bolshevik, and were often led by workers. Others remained non-party and most often were led by former non-commissioned officers from among the peasantry. There was also an 'anarchist' army under the command of Makhno.

So long as the guerrilla armies operated in the rear of the White Guards, they served the cause of the revolution. Some of them were distinguished by exceptional heroism and fortitude. But within the cities these armies often came into conflict with the workers and with the local party organisations. Conflicts also arose during encounters of the partisans with the regular Red Army, and in some instances they took an extremely painful and sharp character.

The grim experience of the civil war demonstrated to us the necessity of disarming peasant detachments immediately after the Red Army occupied provinces which had been cleared of the White Guards. In these cases the best, the most class-conscious and disciplined elements were absorbed into the ranks of the Red Army. But a considerable portion of the partisans strived to maintain an independent existence and often came into direct armed conflict with the Soviet power. Such was the case with the anarchist army of Makhno, entirely kulak in spirit. But that was not the sole instance; many peasant detachments, which fought splendidly enough against the restoration of the landlords, became transformed after victory into instruments of counter-revolution.

Regardless of their origin in each isolated instance – whether caused by conscious provocation of the White Guards, or by tactlessness of the Communists, or by an unfavourable combination of circumstances – the conflicts between armed peasants and workers were rooted in one and the same social soil: the difference between the class position and training of the workers and of the peasants. The worker approaches questions from the socialist standpoint; the peasant's viewpoint is petty bourgeois. The worker strives to socialise the property that is taken away from the exploiters; the peasant seeks to divide it up. The worker desires to put palaces and parks to common use; the peasant, insofar as he cannot divide them, inclines to burning the palaces and cutting down the parks. The worker strives to solve problems on a national scale and in accordance with a plan; the peasant, on the other hand, approaches all problems on a local scale and takes a hostile attitude to centralised planning, and so on.

It is understood that a peasant also is capable of raising himself to the socialist viewpoint. Under a proletarian régime more and more masses of peasants become re-educated in the socialist spirit. But this requires time, years, even decades. It should be borne in mind that in the initial stages of revolution, contradictions between proletarian socialism and peasant individualism often take on an extremely acute character.

But after all aren't there Communists at the head of the Chinese Red armies? Doesn't this by itself exclude the possibility of conflicts between the peasant detachments and the workers' organisations? No, that does not exclude it. The fact that individual Communists are in the leadership of the present armies does not at all transform the social character of these armies, even if their Communist leaders bear a definite proletarian stamp. And how do matters stand in China?

Among the Communist leaders of Red detachments there indubitably are many declassed intellectuals and semi-intellectuals who have not gone through the school of proletarian struggle. For two or three years they live the lives of partisan commanders and commissars; they wage battles, seize territories, and so on. They absorb the spirit of their environment. Meanwhile the majority of the rank-and-file Communists in the Red detachments unquestionably consists of peasants, who assume the name Communist in all honesty and sincerity but who in actuality remain revolutionary paupers or revolutionary petty proprietors. In politics he who judges by denominations and labels and not by social facts is lost. All the more so when the politics concerned is carried out arms in hand.

The true Communist party is the organisation of the proletarian vanguard. But we must not forget that the working class of China has been kept in an oppressed and amorphous condition during the last four years, and only recently has it evinced signs of revival. It is one thing when a Communist party, firmly resting on the flower of the urban proletariat, strives through the workers to lead a peasant war. It is an altogether different thing when a few thousand or even tens of thousands of revolutionists, who are truly Communists or only take the name, assume the leadership of a peasant war without having serious support from the proletariat. This is precisely the situation in China. This acts to augment to an extreme the danger of conflicts between the workers and the armed peasants. In any event, one may rest assured there will be no dearth of bourgeois provocateurs.

In Russia, in the period of civil war, the proletariat was already in power in the greater part of the country, the leadership of the struggle was in the hands of a strong and tempered party, the entire commanding apparatus of the centralised Red Army was in the hands of the workers. Notwithstanding all this, the peasant detachments, incomparably weaker than the Red Army, often came into conflict with it after it victoriously moved into peasant guerrilla sectors.

In China the situation is radically different and moreover completely to the disadvantage of the workers. In the most important regions of China the power is in the hands of bourgeois militarists; in other regions, in the hands of leaders of armed peasants. Nowhere is there any proletarian power as yet. The trade unions are weak. The influence of the party among the workers is insignificant. The peasant detachments, flushed with victories they have achieved, stand under the wing of the Comintern. They call themselves 'the Red Army', that is, they identify themselves with the armed forces of the Soviets. What results consequently is that the revolutionary peasantry of China, in the person of its ruling stratum, seems to have appropriated to itself beforehand the political and moral capital which should by the nature of things belong to the Chinese workers. Isn't it possible that things may turn out so that all this capital will be directed at a certain moment *against* the workers?

Naturally the peasant poor, and in China they constitute the overwhelming majority, to the extent they think politically, and these comprise a small minority, sincerely and passionately desire alliance and friendship with the workers. But the peasantry, even when armed, is incapable of conducting an independent policy.

Occupying in daily life an intermediate, indeterminate, and vacillating position, the peasantry at decisive moments can follow either the proletariat or the bourgeoisie. The peasantry does not find the road to the proletariat easily but only after a series of mistakes and defeats. The bridge between the peasantry and the bourgeoisie is provided by the urban petty bourgeoisie, chiefly by the intellectuals, who commonly come forward under the banner of socialism and even communism.

The commanding stratum of the Chinese 'Red Army' has no doubt succeeded in inculcating itself with the habit of issuing commands. The absence of a strong revolutionary party and of mass organisations of the proletariat renders control over the commanding stratum virtually impossible. The commanders and commissars appear in the guise of absolute masters of the situation and upon occupying cities will be rather apt to look down from above upon the workers. The demands of the workers might often appear to them either inopportune or ill-advised.

Nor should one forget such 'trifles' as the fact that within cities the staffs and offices of the victorious armies are established not in the proletarian huts but in the finest city buildings, in the houses and apartments of the bourgeoisie; and all this facilitates the inclination of the upper stratum of the peasant armies to feel itself part of the 'cultured' and 'educated' classes, in no way part of the proletariat.

Thus in China the causes and grounds for conflicts between the army, which is peasant in composition and petty bourgeois in leadership, and the workers not only are not eliminated but on the contrary, all the circumstances are such as to greatly increase the possibility and even the inevitability of such conflicts; and in addition the chances of the proletariat are far less favourable to begin with than was the case in Russia.

From the theoretical and political side the danger is increased many times because the Stalinist bureaucracy covers up the contradictory situation by its slogan of 'democratic dictatorship' of workers and peasants. Is it possible to conceive of a snare more attractive in appearance and more perfidious in essence? The epigones do their thinking not by means of social concepts, but by means of stereotyped phrases; formalism is the basic trait of bureaucracy.

The Russian Narodniks used to accuse the Russian Marxists of 'ignoring' the peasantry, of not carrying on work in the villages, and so on. To this, the Marxists replied: 'We will arouse and organise the advanced workers and through the workers we shall arouse the peasants'. Such in general is the only conceivable road for the proletarian party.

The Chinese Stalinists have acted otherwise. During the revolution of 1925–7 they subordinated directly and immediately the interests of the workers and the peasants to the interests of the national bourgeoisie. In the years of the counter-revolution they passed over from the proletariat to the peasantry, that is, they undertook that role which was fulfilled in our country by the [Social Revolutionaries]when they were still a revolutionary party. Had the Chinese Communist Party concentrated its efforts for the last few years in the cities, in industry, on the railroads; had it sustained the trade unions, the educational clubs and circles; had it, without breaking off from the workers, taught them to understand what was occurring in the villages – the share of the proletariat in the general correlation of forces would have been incomparably more favourable today.

The party actually tore itself away from its class. Thereby in the last analysis it can cause injury to the peasantry as well. For should the proletariat continue to remain on the sidelines, without organisation, without leadership, then the peasant war even if fully victorious will inevitably arrive in a blind alley.

In old China every victorious peasant revolution was concluded by the creation of a new dynasty, and subsequently also by a new group of large proprietors; the movement was caught in a vicious circle. Under present conditions the peasant war by itself, without the direct leadership of the proletarian vanguard, can only pass on the power to a new bourgeois clique, some 'left' Guomindang or other, a 'third party', and such like, which in practice will differ very little from the Guomindang of Chiang Kai-shek. And this would signify in turn a new massacre of the workers with the weapons of 'democratic dictatorship'.

What then are the conclusions that follow from all this? The first conclusion is that one must boldly and openly face the facts as they are. The peasant movement is a mighty revolutionary factor insofar as it is directed against the large landowners, militarists, feudalists, and usurers. But in the peasant movement itself are very powerful proprietary and reactionary tendencies, and at a certain stage it can become hostile to the workers and sustain that hostility already equipped with arms. He who forgets about the dual nature of the peasantry is not a Marxist. The advanced workers must be taught to distinguish from among 'communist' labels and banners the actual social processes.

The activities of the 'Red armies' must be attentively followed, and the workers must be given a detailed explanation of the course, significance, and perspectives of the peasant war; and the immediate demands and the tasks of the proletariat must be tied up with the slogans for the liberation of the peasantry.

On the bases of our own observations, reports, and other documents we must painstakingly study the life processes of the peasant armies and the régime established in the regions occupied by them; we must discover in living facts the contradictory class tendencies and clearly point out to the workers the tendencies we support and those we oppose.

We must follow the interrelations between the Red armies and the local workers with special care, without overlooking even the minor misunderstandings between them. Within the framework of isolated cities and regions, conflicts, even if acute, might appear to be insignificant local episodes. But with the development of events, class conflicts may take on a national scope and lead the revolution to a catastrophe, that is, to a new massacre of the workers by the peasants, hoodwinked by the bourgeoisie. The history of revolutions is full of such examples.

The more clearly the advanced workers understand the living dialectic of the class interrelations of the proletariat, the peasantry, and the bourgeoisie, the more confidently will they seek unity with the peasant strata closest to them, and the more successfully will they counteract the counter-revolutionary provocateurs within the peasant armies themselves as well as within the cities.

The trade union and the party units must be built up; the advanced workers must be educated, the proletarian vanguard must be brought together and drawn into the battle.

We must turn to all the members of the official Communist Party with words of explanation and challenge. It is quite probable that the rank-and-file Communists who have been led astray by the Stalinist faction will not understand us at once. The bureaucrats will set up a howl about our 'underestimation' of the peasantry, perhaps even about our 'hostility' to the peasantry. (Chernov always accused Lenin of being hostile to the peasantry.) Naturally such howling will not confuse the Bolshevik-Leninists. When prior to April 1927 we warned against the inevitable coup d'état of Chiang Kai-shek, the Stalinists accused us of hostility to the Chinese national revolution. Events have demonstrated who was right. Events will provide a confirmation this time as well.

The Left Opposition may turn out to be too weak to direct events in the interests of the proletariat at the present stage. But we are sufficiently strong right now to point out to the workers the correct road and, in the development of the class struggle, to demonstrate to the workers our correctness and political insight. Only in this way can a revolutionary party gain the confidence of the workers, only in this way will it grow, become strong, and take its place at the head of the popular masses.

Postscript, 26 September 1932

In order to express my ideas as clearly as possible, let me sketch the following variant which is theoretically quite possible.

Let us assume that the Chinese Left Opposition carries on in the near future widespread and successful work among the industrial proletariat and attains the preponderant influence over it. The official party, in the meantime, continues to concentrate all its forces on the 'Red armies' and in the peasant regions. The moment arrives when the peasant troops occupy the industrial centres and are brought face to face with the workers. In such a situation, in what manner will the Chinese Stalinists act?

It is not difficult to foresee that they will counterpose the peasant army to the 'counter-revolutionary Trotskyists' in a hostile manner. In other words, they will incite the armed peasants against the advanced workers. This is what the Russian SRs and the Mensheviks did in 1917; having lost the workers, they fought might and main for support among the soldiers, inciting the barracks against the factory, the armed peasant against the worker Bolshevik. Kerensky, Tsereteli, and Dan, if they did not label the Bolsheviks outright as counter-revolutionists, called them either 'unconscious aides' or 'involuntary agents' of counter-revolution. The Stalinists are less choice in their application of political terminology. But the tendency is the same: malicious incitement of the peasant, and generally petty-bourgeois, elements against the vanguard of the working class.

Bureaucratic centrism, as centrism, cannot have an independent class support. But in its struggle against the Bolshevik-Leninists it is compelled to seek support from the right, that is, from the peasantry and the petty bourgeoisie, counterposing them to the proletariat. The struggle between the two Communist factions, the Stalinists and the Bolshevik-Leninists, thus bears in itself an inner *tendency* towards transformation into a class struggle. The revolutionary development of events in China may draw this tendency to its conclusion, that is, to a civil war between the peasant army led by the Stalinists and the proletarian vanguard led by the Leninists.

Were such a tragic conflict to arise, due entirely to the Chinese Stalinists, it would signify that the Left Opposition and the Stalinists ceased to be Communist factions and had become hostile political parties, each having a different class base.

However is such a perspective inevitable? No, I don't think so at all. Within the Stalinist faction (the official Chinese Communist Party) there are not only peasant, that is, petty-bourgeois tendencies but also proletarian tendencies. It is extremely important for the Left Opposition to seek to establish connections with the proletarian wing of the Stalinists by presenting to them the Marxist evaluation of 'Red armies' and the interrelations between the proletariat and the peasantry in general.

While maintaining its political independence, the proletarian vanguard must be ready always to assure united action with revolutionary democracy. While we refuse to identify the armed peasant detachment with the Red Army as the armed power of the proletariat and have no inclination to shut our eyes to the fact that the Communist banner hides the petty-bourgeois content of the peasant movement, we, on the other hand, take an absolutely clear view of the tremendous revolutionary-democratic significance of the peasant war. We teach the workers to appreciate its significance and we are ready to do all in our power in order to achieve the necessary military alliance with the peasant organisations.

Consequently our task consists not only in preventing the political-military command over the proletariat by the petty-bourgeois democracy that leans upon the armed peasant, but in preparing and ensuring the proletarian leadership of the peasant movement, its 'Red armies' in particular.

The more clearly the Chinese Bolshevik-Leninists comprehend the political events and the tasks that spring from them, the more successfully will they extend their base within the proletariat. The more persistently they carry out the policy of the united front in relation to the official party and the peasant movement led by it, the more surely will they succeed not only in shielding the revolution from a terribly dangerous conflict between the proletariat and the peasantry and in ensuring the necessary united action between the two revolutionary classes, but also in transforming their united front into the historical step towards the dictatorship of the proletariat.

A Strategy of Action and Not of Speculation: Letter to Beijing Friends. What are, at Present, the Chief Elements of the Political Situation in China?

Leon Trotsky

Prinkipo, 3 October, 1932

Source: Class Struggle, Official Organ of the Communist League of Struggle (Adhering to the International Left Opposition), *vol. 3, no. 6, June 1933. Edited from the online version in the Vera Buch and Albert Weisbord Internet Archive, transcribed/HTML Markup by Albert Weisbord, Internet Archive by David Walters.*

The two most important revolutionary problems, the national problem and the agrarian problem, have again become aggravated. The pace of the peasant war, slow and crawling but generally victorious, is evidence that the dictatorship of the Guomindang has proved incapable of satisfying the countryside or of intimidating it further. The Japanese intervention in Shanghai and the effective annexation of Manchuria have placed in relief the military bankruptcy of Guomindang dictatorship. The crisis of power which, at bottom, has not stopped for a single moment during these last years had to grow fatally worse. The struggle between the militarist cliques is destroying what remains of the unity of the country.

If the peasant war has radicalised the intellectuals who have connections in the countryside, the Japanese intervention, on the contrary, gave a political stimulation to the petty bourgeoisie of the cities. This has only again aggravated the crises of power. There is not a single section of the bourgeoisie called 'Nationalists' which does not tend to arrive at the conclusion that the Guomindang régime devours much and gives little. To demand an end of the period of 'education' of the Guomindang is to demand that the military dictatorship give way to parliamentarism.

The Left Opposition press has sometimes labelled as fascist the régime of Chiang Kai-shek. This definition was formed from the fact that in China as in Italy, the military-police power is concentrated in the hands of one bourgeois party alone to the exclusion of all other parties and, notably, of the workers' organisations. But after the experience of the last years, an experience complicated by the confusion the Stalinists brought to the question of fascism, it would not be very correct, nevertheless, to identify the dictatorship of the

Guomindang with fascism. Hitler, as in his time Mussolini, supports himself, before all, on the counter-revolutionary petty bourgeoisie; there is the essence of fascism. The Guomindang has not this point of support. Thus in Germany the peasants march behind Hitler and by this fact indirectly support Von Papen; in China the peasants carry on the raging struggle against Chiang Kai-shek.

The régime of the Guomindang contains more of Bonapartist traits than of fascism: Not possessing a social base, no matter how small, the Guomindang, is half between the pressure of the imperialists and compradors on the one hand, and the revolutionary movement on the other. But Bonapartism can pretend to stability only when the land hunger of the peasants is satisfied. This is not true in the case of China. Hence the impotence of the military dictatorship which maintains itself thanks only to the dispersion of its enemies. But under their growing attack even this begins to be unhinged.

It is the proletariat which in the revolution of 1925–7 morally and physically suffered the most. That is why at the present time it is the workers who are in the rear of the other classes and in fact not only of the petty bourgeoisie, beginning with the students, but also, in a certain sense, of the peasants. On the other hand it is just this which proves that the third Chinese revolution not only will not win but will not even be produced as long as the working class has not again entered into the lists.

The slogans of the revolutionary democracy correspond in the best possible way to the political pre-revolutionary situation in China.

That the peasants, whatever their banner, fight for the aims of agrarian petty bourgeois democracy is what, for a Marxist, does not have to be demonstrated. The slogan of independence of China, raised to a white heat by the Japanese intervention, is a slogan of the national democracy. The powerlessness of the military dictatorship and the partition of the country among the militarist dictatorship and the partition of the country among the militarist cliques put on the end of the day the slogan of political democracy.

The students cry: 'Down with the Guomindang government'. The groups of workers' vanguard support this slogan. The 'national' bourgeoisie demands they go on to a constitutional régime. The peasants revolt against the dearth of land, the yoke of the militarists, government officials, and usurious loans. Under these circumstances the party of the proletariat cannot favour any other political central slogan than that of the NATIONAL ASSEMBLY (Constituent).

Does this mean, it will be asked, that we demand from the present government the convocation of the National Assembly or that we should strive to convoke it ourselves? This way of posing the question, at least at the present stage, is too formalistic. For a certain number of years, the Russian

Revolution coordinated two slogans: 'Down with Absolutism' and 'Long Live the Constituent Assembly'. To the question who will convoke the Constituent Assembly for a long time we answered: the future will show, that is to say, the relation of forces, as they are established in the process of the revolution itself. This manner of approaching the question remains equally correct for China. Will the government of the Guomindang try, at the moment of its disappearance, to convoke such or such a representative assembly, what will be the attitude that we shall adopt in regard to this, that is to say how shall we utilise it in the interests of the revolution, whether we should boycott the elections or whether we should participate in them; will the revolutionary masses succeed in giving rise to an independent government organism which will take upon itself the convocation of the National Assembly; will the proletariat succeed, in the course of the struggle for the slogans of democracy, in creating the soviets; will the latter not render superfluous the convocation of the National Assembly? This is what is actually impossible to foretell. After all, the task consists not in making prognostications from the calendar but in mobilising the workers around the slogans flowing from the political situation. Our strategy is a strategy of revolutionary action and not of abstract speculations.

Today, by the force of events, the revolutionary agitation is directed above all against the government of the Guomindang. We explain to the masses that the dictatorship of Chiang Kai-shek is the main obstacle in the way of the National Assembly and that we can clean China of the militarist cliques only by means of an armed insurrection. Agitation, spoken and written, strikes, meetings, demonstrations, boycotts whatever may be the concrete questions to which they are consecrated, must have as a corollary the slogans: 'Down with the Guomindang, long live the Constituent Assembly!'

In order to arrive at real national liberation it is necessary to overthrow the Guomindang. But this does not mean that we postpone the struggle until the time when the Guomindang is overthrown. The more the struggle against foreign oppression spreads, the more difficulties the Guomindang will have. The more we line up the masses against the Guomindang the more the struggle against imperialism will develop.

At the acute moment of Japanese intervention the workers and the students called for arms. From whom? Again from the Guomindang. It would be a sectarian absurdity to abandon this demand under the pretext that we wish to overthrow the Guomindang. We wish to overthrow it but we have not yet reached that point. The more energetically we demand the arming of the workers, the sooner we shall reach it.

The official Communist Party, in spite of its ultra-leftism, favours 'the resumption of Russian-Chinese diplomatic relations'. Now this slogan is addressed directly against the Guomindang. To formulate it does not at all mean that one has 'confidence' in the Guomindang. On the contrary, this slogan has for object to render more difficult the situation of the latter before the masses. Certain Guomindang leaders have already had to take up on their own account the slogan of the re-establishment of relations with the USSR. We know that with these gentlemen it is a long way between works and acts. But here, as in all the other questions, everything depends on the force that the pressure of the masses will attain.

If, under the whip of the revolution, the Guomindang government begins to make petty concessions on the agrarian question, tries to call a semblance of a National Assembly, sees itself obliged to give arms to the workers or to take up relations with the USSR, it goes without saying that we will at once exploit these concessions, that we will cling to them firmly at the same time that we show with perfect correctness their insufficiency so as to make of the concessions by the Guomindang a weapon to overthrow it. Such is in general the reciprocal relation of reforms and of revolution in Marxist politics.

Does not the scope the peasant war is reaching mean that there is no longer time nor place for the slogans and problems of parliamentary democracy in China? Let us go back to that question.

If the revolutionary Chinese peasants today call their fighting organisations 'soviets' we have no reason to give up the name. We must simply not get intoxicated with words. To believe that soviet power in essentially rural regions can be an important, stable revolutionary power is to give proof of great frivolity. It is not possible to be ignorant of the experience offered by the only country where soviet power has effectively won. Although in Petrograd, Moscow, and other industrial centres and basins of Russia, soviet power has held firmly and constantly since November 1917, in all the immense periphery (Ukraine, Northern Caucasus, Transcaucasia, Urals, Siberia, Central Asia, Archangel Murmansk) this power has appeared and disappeared several times not only because of foreign interventions, but also as a consequence of internal revolts. Chinese soviet power has an essential rural, peripheral character, and still entirely lacks a point of support in the industrial proletariat. The less stable and sure this power is, the less of a soviet power it is.

Ko-Lin's article in the German paper *Der rote Aufbau* claims that in the red armies the workers represent 36 per cent, the peasants 57 per cent, the intellectuals 7 per cent. I confess that these figures arouse in me serious doubts. If the percentages apply to all the armed forces of the insurrection, forces which according to the author reach 350,000 men, the result is that the army includes about 125,000 workers. If the 36 per cent only applies to the red armies, it appears that of 150,000 soldiers, there are more than 50,000 workers. Is this really so? Did they belong to the unions before, to the party, and did they take part in the revolutionary struggle? But even that does clinch the question. On account of the absence of strong, independent proletarian organisations in the industrial centres, the revolutionary workers, inexperienced or too little experienced, become fatally lost in the peasant, petty-bourgeois environment.

Wang Ming's article, which appeared at the beginning of the year in the CI press, singularly exaggerates, as far as I can judge, the scope of the movement in the cities, the degree of independence of the workers in the movement and the importance of the influence of the Communist Party. The misfortune of the present official press is that its mercilessly deforms facts in the name of its factional interest. Hence it is not hard to realise, even by Wang Ming's article, that the leading place in the movement which began in the autumn of last year (1931) belonged to the students or in general to the school youth. The university strikes had an appreciable importance, greater than the factory strikes.

To arouse the workers, to group them, to give them the possibility of leaning on the national and agrarian movements in order to take the head of both: such is the task that falls to us. The immediate demands of the proletariat as such (length of work day, wages, right to organise, and such like) must form the basis of our agitation. But that alone is not sufficient. Only three slogans can raise the proletariat to the role of head of the nation: the independence of China, land to the poor peasants, the National Assembly.

The Stalinists imagine that the minute the insurgent peasants call their organisations soviets, the stage of revolutionary parliamentarism has already passed. This is a serious mistake. The rebel peasants can serve as a point of support to the soviets of the proletariat only if the latter shows practically its ability to lead. Hence, without the leadership of the proletariat, the peasant movement can only assure the advantage of one bourgeois clique over another in order to break up finally into provincial fractions. The National Assembly, thanks to its centralising importance, would constitute a serious stage in the development of the agrarian revolution. The existence of rural 'soviets' and 'red armies' would help the peasants elect revolutionary representatives. This is the only way at the present stage to link up the peasant movement politically with the national and proletarian movements.

The official Chinese Communist Party declares that its 'principal slogan' is at present that of national revolutionary war against Japanese imperialism (see Wang Ming's article in the *Communist International*, no. 1, 1932). That is a one-sided and even adventurist way to pose the question. It is certain that the struggle against imperialism, which is the essential task of the Chinese proletariat, cannot be carried through to the end except by insurrection and revolutionary war. But it does not in the least follow that the struggle against

Japanese imperialism constitutes the central slogan of the present moment. The question must be solved from the international angle.

At the beginning of this year, they thought in CI circles that Japan had entered upon its military action against China in order to push things immediately to war against the Soviet Union. I wrote then that the Tokyo government would have to be completely out of its head to run the risk of a war with the Soviet Union without having beforehand at least somewhat consolidated the military base which Manchuria constitutes for it. In reply to this estimation of the situation, the American Stalinists, the most vulgar and stupid of all, declared that I worked in the interest of the Japanese general staff. – And yet, what have the events of these last months shown? The fear of Japan's leading circles for the consequences of a military adventure was so great that the military clique had to send from life to death a certain number of Japanese statesmen in order to arouse the Mikado's government to follow up the annexation of Manchuria to the end. That even today the war against the Soviet Union remains a very real perspective there is no doubt, but in politics time has great value.

If the Soviet government considered war with Japan to be inevitable right now, it would have neither the right nor the possibility of carrying out a peace policy, that is, an ostrich policy. In reality, in the course of the year, the Soviet government has concluded an arrangement with Japan to furnish Soviet naphtha to the Japanese war fleet. If war is right now inevitable, to furnish naphtha to Japan is equivalent to committing a real treason towards the proletarian revolution. We will not discuss here the question of knowing to what extent this or that declaration or step of the Soviet government is correct. One thing is clear: contrary to the American Stalinists whose zeal is beyond measure, the Moscow Stalinists have been oriented towards peace with Japan and not towards war.

Pravda of 24 September writes: 'With vast impatience the world bourgeoisie was expecting a Nippo-Soviet war. But the fact that the USSR has rigorously abstained from mixing in the Sino-Japanese conflict and the firm peace policy she is following, has forestalled war' – admitting that the attitude of the American and other windbags has any political meaning at all, it had only one meaning: they pushed soviet power on the same road where the world bourgeoisie pushed it. We do mean that they consciously served the Japanese general staff. Suffice it to state they are incapable of consciously serving the proletarian revolution.

The Chinese proletariat inscribes on its banner not only resumption of diplomatic relations with the Soviet Union but the conclusion of a close offensive and defensive alliance with it. This implies that the policy of the Chinese proletariat must be in conformity with the whole of the international situation and above all with the policy of the Soviet Union. If Japan were today to thrust war upon the Soviet Union, the fact of drawing China into that war would be a question of life or death for the Chinese proletariat and its party. The war would open up boundless horizons before the Chinese revolution. But to the extent that the international situation and internal conditions oblige the Soviet Union to make serious concessions in the Far East in order to avoid war, that is, to defer it as far as possible, and to the extent that Japan does not find itself strong enough to begin hostilities, the war against Japanese imperialism cannot constitute, in any case at the present time, the central fighting slogan of the Chinese Communist Party.

Wang Ming quotes the following slogans of the Left Opposition in China: 'Reconstitution of the mass movement', 'Convocation of the National Assembly' and 'Resumption of diplomatic relations between China and the Soviet Union'. Under the simple pretext that these slogans are, it seems, poorly motivated, in an article in the legal organ of the opposition, Wang Ming calls the Left Opposition in China a 'counter-revolutionary Trotskyist-Chen Duxiu group'.

Now, even if we admit that the motivation of the revolutionary slogans was not fortunate, this does not give them, nor the organisation that formulated them, a counter-revolutionary character. But Wang Ming and his like are obliged to speak of the counter-revolutionary spirit of the 'Trotskyists' if they do not wish their posts and emoluments withdrawn.

At the same time they declare themselves so severe against the Bolshevik Leninists who have been proved right in the course of the events that have taken place in China from 1932, the Stalinists show themselves as indulgent as possible towards themselves, that is, towards the uninterrupted chain of their errors.

In the days when Japan was attacking Shanghai, the Guomindang supported 'the united front of the workers, peasants, soldiers, merchants and students to combat imperialism'. But this is the famous 'bloc of four classes' of Stalin-Martinov! Since the second revolution, foreign oppression in China has not weakened, but on the contrary has grown. The antagonism between the needs of the country's evolution and the régime of imperialism has likewise sharpened. Since then, all the old Stalinist arguments in favour of the bloc of four classes have acquired double strength. This time, the Stalinists have interpreted the Guomindang's proposal as a new attempt to deceive the masses. Very well! But they have forgotten to explain why from 1924 to 1927 the CI leadership helped the Chinese bourgeoisie deceive to the end, and why the philosophy that consisted in being at the Guomindang's beck and call has found expression in the programme of the CI.

It is evident that we can and must support the slogan of democratic self-government of the election of functionaries by the people, and so on. The programme of democracy constitutes a great step forward in relation to the régime of military dictatorship. We must just bring together each time the isolated, partial democratic slogans with the essential slogans and attach them to the problems of revolutionary grouping and the arming of the workers.

The question of 'patriotism' and 'nationalism', like certain other questions contained in your letter, deals with terminology rather than with the essence of things. The Bolsheviks, favouring the national liberation of oppressed peoples by revolutionary means, support by all means the movement of the masses of the people for national liberation not only against foreign imperialists but also against the bourgeois exploiters inside the national movement, in the nature of the Guomindang.

Must we still introduce the term 'patriotism', discredited and soiled enough? I doubt it. Must we not see in this attempt a tendency to want to adapt oneself to petty-bourgeois ideology and terminology? If this tendency were to really appear in our ranks, we would have to fight it mercilessly.

Many questions of a tactical and strategical character will appear insoluble if approached in a formalistic way. But they will fall into their right place if we pose them dialectically, that is, in the perspective of the living struggle of classes and parties. It is in real action that revolutionary dialectic is best assimilated. I do not doubt that our comrades in ideas and our Chinese friends the Bolshevik Leninists not only discuss passionately the complex problems of the Chinese revolution, but also participate no less passionately in the developing struggle. We are for a strategy of action – not for speculation.

Excerpts from Letters from China Written or Copied to Trotsky (1934)

Leon Trotsky

Source: *A manuscript in the editor's possession*

1   Letter from Comrade Frank Glass, 30 August 1934

The organisation was unable to maintain *China Forum*. Chen Duxiu, who is a loyal and courageous comrade, but one who has been unable to complete the break from his Stalinist formation and who has no capacity to play a leading role, has written a letter to the IS [International Secretariat] on the Soviet state and the relation of the Bolshevik-Leninists to it. Niel Sih has taken a position against 'Chen Duxiu-ism'. The Nanjing government's dependence on Japan continues to become more obvious.

2   Letter from H. R. Isaacs to the Central Committee of the
           Communist Party of China (CCP) concerning *China Forum*

The Communist Party has obliged the journal, which had not only been maintained under the most difficult conditions from January 1932 to January 1934 but also considerably expanded – there were Readers' Circles of *China Forum* in 5 provinces – to cease publication. Aside from slight financial support the CP never did anything for the journal and has forced it to stop publication because internal party considerations are more important to it than the fight for the revolution and against imperialism. The methods of the CCP are characterised by the fact that propaganda and truth are counterposed concepts for it. It falsifies facts in order to manufacture great successes, although in fact the movement has been forced onto the defensive and is still poorly organised, despite the heroism and endurance of the communist minded workers. The mass movement of 1925–7 has disintegrated due to the fault of the leaders of the CCP. One example: in 1926 there were 257 strikes in greater Shanghai, in 1932 there were only 32, in which only a minimal number of workers participated – and they were only defensive strikes against wage reductions, and so on. The January 1932 massacre by the Japanese of tens of thousands of workers in the International Settlement in Shanghai did not give rise to any strikes that could disrupt normal life in the Settlement. It is false that nothing could have been done to oppose the white terror and the reactionary Guomindang; but to do anything would have required the well-planned education and organisation of the masses. Isolated peasant uprisings and the heroic deeds of the red army in Jiangxi won't bring down the Guomindang. It is also wrong to withdraw the best working class elements from their factories to participate in the movement in the red areas: in this way the most active forces are lost to the cities. The tactics of the party have not taken the real necessities into account. So it turns out that the oppression of the working masses has not developed into a struggle against the imperialists: the leaders are lacking. This is the same wrong policy of the communists as in other countries. For the sake of our common goals the *Forum* never took up these questions. In only one case did the journal passively resist the instructions of the CCP: when Chen Duxiu was sentenced to thirteen years in jail, we were told not to write about how he developed from a leader of the CCP in 1927 to a leader of the left opposition in 1933. We were told to make disparaging comments to the effect that the Guomindang persecuted even the leader of the left opposition. Of course we didn't do that. When Isaacs returned from Fujian in December 1933, the CCP demanded that he write that the left opposition was linked to the Fuzhou régime, even though from his own personal experience he knew the opposite to be true. Of course he refused, but, for the sake of peace with the CCP, he passed the question over in silence. Despite this conciliatory attitude, which went as far as humanly possible, Isaacs was given an ultimatum in January 1934: the *Forum* had to refrain from any criticism whatever of communist policies in China, Germany, USSR, and so on, and instead attack 'counter-revolutionary' Trotskyism. In the discussions Isaacs was told: 'A certain degree of exaggeration is necessary for propaganda purposes, but we know the real facts and base our policy on these alone, not on the exaggerations'. Isaacs offered to publish all official communications of the CP, reserving the possibility of commenting on or criticising them. This was rejected. Since Isaacs could not maintain the *Forum* out of his own pocket, but under these circumstances also didn't want to transfer it to the CCP, he had to cease publication. But he will continue the true and honourable revolutionary struggle.

Beijing, 20 May 1934.

3   **Letter from Frank Glass to the International Secretariat**

The Chinese Left Opposition is stagnating. That can be explained by the general situation, but above all by its own deficiencies. Concrete political perspectives are lacking, time is wasted on routine organisational work. We have about 300 members: 60 in Shanghai; 100 in Hong Kong and Guangzhou; 40 in Beijing; 70 in Qingdao and Jinan; 20 in Fuzhou; and about 12 individual members. The Chinese organisation publishes *Iskra* in Shanghai and *Vanguard* in Beijing.

These are mimeographed sheets which appear irregularly and have a very small readership. According to statements by the leading committee the political level of the comrades, especially outside Shanghai, is very low, the basic principles of the left opposition are not well known. The majority of the comrades feel that given counter-revolution triumphant that we should now limit ourselves to the fight for democratic demands, yet this fight is waged without perspectives.

They don't recognise the relationship between political and economic struggles; don't see the danger that in the event the economic situation worsens, the Chinese proletariat will be even more exploited. They put all their hopes in 'great world historical events' (Russo-Japanese War and such like). Niel Sih and G. [Glass?] believe that such a policy, with its Ifs and Buts, will lead to complete passivity; that reality will be lost sight of, and that events will be viewed empirically and not on the basis of Marxist principles. Niel Sih now belongs only formally to the Chinese left opposition, which he thinks is dying, and he hopes for a new organisation of Chinese Bolshevik-Leninists.

We used some of the money I administer – the contribution for printing the *Forum*, which Isaacs gave us – to print Trotsky's 'Soviet Union and the Fourth International'. Niel Sih is in favour of using the remaining money to begin publishing a legal newspaper, criticising the events in China from a Marxist perspective, and which he would control. Since the other comrades don't agree with that, and I don't want to decide the question, I place this question before the IS.

According to Niel Sih's letters, there is not much possibility that Trotsky's and the IS's instructions will be followed if they take a position against Chen Duxiu-ism. I myself don't know whether that is true; the comrades on the standing committee seem serious and honourable to me. Despite the fact that I don't entirely agree with Niel Sih in this matter, I have to say that I consider him the most talented and clear-thinking of the comrades; his voice is the voice of Marxism in China.

We ask that Trotsky and the IS express their position at length, especially above all in regard to the following questions:

1. The question of the National Assembly with particular reference to the line the left opposition should take with respect to a National Convention, which the Guomindang seems to be planning to call for March 1935;

2. the question of an economic upturn as a perspective for democratic struggles in China;
3. the question of founding a legal newspaper and using our funds for this purpose.

Either our organisation here will get out of the swamp or, if not, it would be better to die rapidly. The healthy elements will then come together under the banner of Marxism, together with new comrades.

Shanghai, 26 August 1934.

4   On Peasant War and Economic Upturn. By Niel Sih

Without a movement in the cities the peasant uprisings will have no future. But while we condemn the Stalinists for abandoning work among the urban proletariat, and deny that the peasant army is a Red Army and its organisation that of a soviet, we must nevertheless recognise that peasant war has its own logic. The Guomindang's incapacity to institute reforms that will lighten the burden of the peasants means that the peasant movement will spread to other provinces. In Sichuan, Guizhou, West Hunan, and West Hubei the movement will have greater success because the peasants there really have nothing to lose but their chains. The influence of imperialism is slight in these areas and the army of oppression is divided and poorly armed. On the other hand, the red armies are greatly loved by the peasants because they call mass meetings, free them from taxes and reorganise the economy. The fact that Chiang Kai-shek needed harvesting brigades which could penetrate into red areas only under military protection proves how much better agrarian economic relationships there are than in the Guomindang-controlled areas. The two questions that are raised are: Will the unceasing peasant war grind the Chiang Kai-shek régime down to the point of collapse? Can the red armies implant themselves in large areas, for example in Sichuan in West China, to an extent that they will have a positive influence on industrial cities and give new impetus to the workers' movement? We must hope that the red army succeeds and we must penetrate the workers movement in the cities so that in the future we can establish the link with the peasant armies. If the peasant revolution has even a few successes, China can still develop economically. If it is destroyed by the Guomindang, such a chaos will emerge that – however paradoxical it may seem – it is doubtful that the Guomindang will survive.

Beijing, 21 September 1934.

5 Letter from Chen Duxiu to the International Secretariat

When I read in the newspapers about the tribulations Comrade Trotsky suffers from French imperialism, and how reactionary are the deeds of the Stalinists, I am very deeply grieved. Stalin has destroyed the living capacities and spirit of the communist parties by a bureaucratic party system. He has replaced the real leaders of these parties by his lackeys. The 'leaders' who have been installed in China are not even his lackeys, just his [Pavel] Mifs. The proletariat in the West probably doesn't even know that these 'leaders' are merely fighting over control of the party apparatus. Stalin serves the world bourgeoisie. In the Soviet Union Stalin's personal dictatorship is replacing that of the proletariat and the proletarian vanguard. The so-called 'workers' state' and soviet power exist only in name. The Soviet Union is ruled by the petty bourgeoisie, on the back of the proletariat, and it is opening the door to bourgeois counter-revolution. The imperialists don't need weapons to fight the Soviet Union anymore, they can reach their goals via the Stalinists. The final suppression of proletarian power, which now exists only formally, by reactionary forces in the Soviet Union, does not necessarily lead to a Thermidor. In any event it will be brought about by the Stalinists. Stalin's position is similar to that of Dollfuss in Austria. Stalin has delivered the leaders of the October Revolution to the West European bourgeoisie and the White Russian émigré parties. We must be vigilant. We should not just organise a new party, but also fight the illusion that the Stalin régime can be reformed. We must replace the slogan 'Defend the USSR' with the slogan 'Recreate the Soviet Union of October!' That is my suggestion to the IS. The Guomindang, which imprisons our dear ones, cannot prevent our spirit from being at one with the world proletariat. What encourages us in our barbaric dungeon is news of the movement for world revolution. Our answer to Stalinist falsifications is class struggle!

Nanjing Prison, 15 May 1934

Chen Duxiu and the General Council

Leon Trotsky

10 August 1935

This is a letter to Frank Glass, based on oral reports on the Chinese section and dictated in English. Source: Cannon archives, Library of Social History. From microfilm provided by the Holt Labor Library. Transcribed by Andrew Pollack. Copyleft: Leon Trotsky Internet Archive (www.marxists.org) 2005.

Dear Comrade,

With the help of Comrades H. and V. [Harold Isaacs and Viola Robinson] I have plunged once more into the Chinese question. I am only at the beginning. I must in the next several days study the more important documents and you will understand that I cannot now give my opinion on the differences within the Chinese section. But I am exceedingly anxious to write to you at once on the more immediate and burning question of Comrade CTH [Chen Duxiu].

He is an international figure. He is in prison. He remains faithful not only to the revolution but to our tendency in particular. We are now creating the Fourth International and the General Council [GC] as its guiding theoretical and consultative body. In principle, the GC will be composed of two kinds of members: (1) direct representatives of the sections of the International Communist League (ICL) and other adhering organisations and (2) individuals who by their past and present are fit to contribute to the elaboration of our programme, strategic principles, and so on. It is my conviction that Comrade CTH undoubtedly belongs on the GC, despite his important differences with the Chinese section, whose direct representative, in my opinion, should be Comrade NS [Niel Sih, that is, Liu Renjing].

You must take into consideration the fact that the composition of the GC must be impeccable, in the sense that it will guarantee us against unfortunate crises, capitulations, treasons, and so on. That is why it is necessary to recommend for the GC only comrades who are known, proved, and absolutely dependable.

It may be replied – and some Chinese comrades will certainly reply – that on a number of important questions CTH has opinions which appear to them to be absolutely false. For the time being I express no opinion on differences whose content I have not yet sufficiently studied. But the Chinese comrades, like all others, must clearly understand that the creation of groupings for the

Fourth International has changed the situation, in that we, the Bolshevik-Leninists, represent only one faction among these groupings. Thus the GC must reflect not only the Bolshevik-Leninist sections, but *all* the revolutionary forces moving in the direction of the Fourth International. I will give you an example: The well-known German comrades, Maslow and Ruth Fischer, who led the German party in 1923–5, adhere to the organisation of forces for the Fourth International without adhering to the German section of the ICL, with which they have serious differences. Nevertheless, the IS has unanimously proposed Maslow as a member of the GC. There is an analogous case in Czechoslovakia, and so on. Thus you see that it is not a question of making an exception for China.

I draw your attention to another aspect of the same matter. Because of its extremely difficult situation, the Chinese section remains quite weak. Arrests and persecution deprive it of organisational stability. We are all absolutely sure that the Chinese section, which has devoted and courageous comrades, will grow in the nearest future. But for the moment, to introduce into the GC a young, entirely new comrade, unknown internationally, would be imprudent. This is my personal opinion only, but I believe that the arguments I have advanced here are dictated by the whole situation. I have no need to tell you that the Chinese section has the full right to propose other candidates, just as all other sections have, but I am sure that the candidacy of Comrade CTH will be supported by all our sections, because it would be a serious blow to the authority of the Fourth International to renounce the collaboration of CTH while the possibility still remains of settling the existing differences through international organisational procedure.

The Chinese section has not formally broken with CTH and for that I sincerely rejoice. At the same time the Chinese section has formed its own Central Committee entirely independently of CTH and his partisans. This is naturally the full right of the Chinese section. The introduction of CTH into the GC need not in any way, of itself, change the situation in China, the composition of the Chinese Central Committee, its political leadership, and so on. On the other hand, the GC will be able to intervene in an amicable fashion, to clarify the differences, soften the conflict and improve relations.

With the creation of groupings for the Fourth International, I again emphasise, we dispose of larger organisational cadres and of new possibilities of action. I will give you a recent example: In Belgium our section, as you know, has become a faction of Vandervelde's opportunist party, the Parti Ouvrier Belge (Belgian Labour Party, POB) (wherein, incidentally, they have made great progress). The Vereecken group in Brussels separated from our section and thus remains outside our international organisation. But after the launching of the Open Letter for the Fourth International, Vereecken declared solidarity with it, and it is quite possible that he will be admitted as a sympathising organisation. The adherence of his group to the Fourth International will give us the possibility of drawing him once more into our section and in any event to impose upon him a loyal and friendly attitude towards our section. You see by this example that we are far from considering the Fourth International as a simple reproduction of the International Communist League and this fact alone can serve to demonstrate to the Chinese comrades that CTH can and must have his place in the cadres of the Fourth International.

I do not mean by this that every group which will proclaim itself in favour of the Fourth International will be automatically admitted. I named Vereecken because his attitude towards the Bolshevik-Leninists after the split provoked by him remains loyal. He sees, besides, the great success of our section and in the last number of his journal he advocated support for the Action Socialiste faction in the POB. There is thus a vast difference between the attitude of Vereecken and that of a Weisbord or a Field, who attack our international organisation and the WPUS [Workers' Party of the United States] in a venomous and disloyal fashion and who attack in the same manner our French section which today marches at the head of our whole international organisation.

I regret very much that you did not come with Comrades H. and V. and that I have not had a chance to meet you. I regret it the more since I should have liked to discuss with you not only the Chinese questions but also and especially the South African question. I will ask our IS to send you all the documents thereon and we will await with interest your assessments, comments, and advice.

I ask you to transmit my most fraternal greetings to all the Chinese comrades. Yours fraternally,

Leon Trotsky

Introduction to Harold R. Isaacs, *The Tragedy of the Chinese Revolution*

Leon Trotsky

The Tragedy of the Chinese Revolution *was published in London by Seeker and Warburg in 1938. The source of this introduction is* Fourth International (*New York*), *vol. 6, no. 10* (*whole no. 59*), *October 1945, pp. 312–16.*

First of all, the mere fact that the author of this book belongs to the school of historical materialism would be entirely insufficient in our eyes to win approval for his work. In present day conditions the Marxist label would predispose us to mistrust rather than to acceptance. In close connection with the degeneration of the Soviet State, Marxism has in the past fifteen years passed through an unprecedented period of decline and debasement. From an instrument of analysis and criticism, it has been turned into an instrument of cheap apologetics. Instead of analysing facts, it occupies itself with selecting sophisms in the interests of exalted clients.

In the Chinese Revolution of 1925–7 the Communist International played a very great role, depicted in this book quite comprehensively. We would, however, seek in vain in the library of the Communist International for a single book which attempts in any way to give a rounded picture of the Chinese Revolution. Instead, we find scores of 'conjunctural' works which docilely reflect each zigzag in the politics of the Communist International, or, more correctly, of Soviet diplomacy in China, and subordinating to each zigzag facts as well as general treatment. In contrast to this literature, which cannot arouse anything but mental revulsion, Isaacs' book represents a scientific work from beginning to end. It is based on a conscientious study of a vast number of original sources and supplementary material. Isaacs spent more than three years on this work. It should be added that he had previously passed about five years in China as a journalist and observer of Chinese life.

The author of this book approaches the revolution as a revolutionist, and he sees no reason for concealing it. In the eyes of a philistine a revolutionary point of view is virtually equivalent to an absence of scientific objectivity. We think just the opposite: only a revolutionist – provided, of course, that he is equipped with the scientific method – is capable of laying bare the objective dynamics of the revolution. Apprehending thought in general is not contemplative, but active. The element of will is indispensable for penetrating the secrets of nature and society. Just as a surgeon, on whose scalpel a human life depends, distinguishes with extreme care between the various tissues of an organism, so a revolutionist, if he has a serious attitude towards his task, is obliged with strict conscientiousness to analyse the structure of society, its functions and reflexes.

To understand the present war between Japan and China one must take the Second Chinese Revolution as a point of departure. In both cases we meet not only identical social forces, but frequently the same personalities. Suffice it to say that the person of Chiang Kai-shek occupies the central place in this book. As these lines are being written it is still difficult to forecast when and in what manner the Sino-Japanese war will end. But the outcome of the present conflict in the Far East will in any case have a provisional character. The world war which is approaching with irresistible force will review the Chinese problem together with all other problems of colonial domination. For it is in this that the real task of the second world war will consist: to divide the planet anew in accord with the new relationship of imperialist forces. The principal arena of struggle will, of course, not be that Lilliputian bath-tub, the Mediterranean, nor even the Atlantic Ocean, but the basin of the Pacific. The most important object of struggle will be China, embracing about one-fourth of the human race. The fate of the Soviet Union – the other big stake in the coming war – will also to a certain degree be decided in the Far East. Preparing for this clash of Titans, Tokyo is attempting today to assure itself of the broadest possible drill-ground on the continent of Asia. Great Britain and the United States are likewise losing no time. It can, however, be predicted with certainty – and this is in essence acknowledged by the present makers of destiny – that the world war will not produce the final decision: it will be followed by a new series of revolutions which will review not only the decisions of the war but all those property conditions which give rise to war.

History is No Pacifist

This prospect, it must be confessed, is very far from being an idyll, but Clio, the muse of history, was never a member of a Ladies' Peace Society. The older generation which passed through the war of 1914–18 did not discharge a single one of its tasks. It leaves to the new generation as heritage the burden of wars and revolutions. These most important and tragic events in human history have often marched side by side. They will definitely form the background of the coming decades. It remains only to hope that the new generation, which cannot arbitrarily cut loose from the conditions it has inherited, has learned at least to understand better the laws of its epoch. For acquainting itself with the Chinese Revolution of 1925–7 it will not find today a better guide than this book.

Despite the unquestionable greatness of the Anglo-Saxon genius, it is impossible not to see that the laws of revolutions are least understood precisely in the Anglo-Saxon countries. The explanation for this lies, on the one hand, in the fact that the very appearance of revolution in these countries relates to a long-distant past, and evokes in official 'sociologists' a condescending smile, as would childish pranks. On the other hand, pragmatism, so characteristic of Anglo-Saxon thinking, is least of all useful for understanding revolutionary crises.

The English Revolution of the seventeenth century, like the French Revolution of the eighteenth, had the task of 'rationalising' the structure of society, that is, cleansing it of feudal stalactites and stalagmites, and subjecting it to the laws of free competition, which in that epoch seemed to be the laws of 'common sense'. In doing this, the Puritan revolution draped itself in Biblical dress, thereby revealing a purely infantile incapacity to understand its own significance. The French Revolution, which had considerable influence on progressive thought in the United States, was guided by formulas of pure rationalism. Common sense, which is still afraid of itself and resorts to the mask of Biblical prophets, or secularised common sense, which looks upon society as the product of a rational 'contract', remain to this day the fundamental forms of Anglo-Saxon thinking in the domains of philosophy and sociology.

Yet the real society of history has not been constructed, following Rousseau, upon a rational 'contract', nor, as according to Bentham, upon the principle of the 'greatest good', but has unfolded 'irrationally', on the basis of contradictions and antagonisms. For revolution to become inevitable class contradictions have to be strained to the breaking point. It is precisely this historically inescapable necessity for conflict, which depends neither on good nor ill will but on the objective interrelationship of classes, that makes revolution, together with war, the most dramatic expression of the 'irrational' foundation of the historic process.

'Irrational' does not, however, mean arbitrary. On the contrary, in the molecular preparation of revolution, in its explosion, in its ascent and decline, there is lodged a profound inner lawfulness which can be apprehended and, in the main, foreseen. Revolutions, as has been said more than once, have a logic of their own. But this is not the logic of Aristotle, and even less the pragmatic demi-logic of 'common sense'. It is the higher function of thought: the logic of development and its contradictions, that is, the dialectic.

The obstinacy of Anglo-Saxon pragmatism and its hostility to dialectical thinking thus have their material causes. Just as a poet cannot attain to the dialectic through books without his own personal experiences, so a well-to-do society, unused to convulsions and habituated to uninterrupted 'progress', is incapable of understanding the dialectic of its own development. However, it is only too obvious that this privilege of the Anglo-Saxon world has receded into the past. History is preparing to give Great Britain as well as the United States serious lessons in the dialectic.

Character of Chinese Revolution

The author of this book tries to deduce the character of the Chinese Revolution not from *a priori* definitions and not from historical analogies, but from the living structure of Chinese society and from the dynamics of its inner forces. In this lies the chief methodological value of the book. The reader will carry away not only a better-knit picture of the march of events but – what is more important – will learn to understand their social mainsprings. Only on this basis is it possible correctly to appraise political programmes and the slogans of struggling parties – which, even if neither independent nor in the final analysis the decisive factors in the process, are nevertheless its most manifest signs.

In its immediate aims the uncompleted Chinese Revolution is 'bourgeois'. This term, however, which is used as a mere echo of the bourgeois revolutions of the past, actually helps us very little. Lest the historical analogy turn into a trap for the mind, it is necessary to check it in the light of a concrete sociological analysis. What are the classes which are struggling in China? What are the interrelationships of these classes? How, and in what direction, are these relations being transformed? What are the objective tasks of the Chinese Revolution, that is, those tasks dictated by the course of development? On the shoulders of which classes rests the solution of these tasks? With what methods can they be solved? Isaacs' book gives the answers to precisely these questions.

Colonial and semi-colonial – and therefore backward – countries, which embrace by far the greater part of mankind, differ extraordinarily from one another in their degree of backwardness, representing an historical ladder reaching from nomadry, and even cannibalism, up to the most modern industrial culture. The combination of extremes in one degree or another characterises all of the backward countries. However, the hierarchy of backwardness, if one may employ such an expression, is determined by the specific weight of the elements of barbarism and culture in the life of each colonial country. Equatorial Africa lags far behind Algeria, Paraguay behind Mexico, Abyssinia behind India or China. With their common economic dependence upon the imperialist metropolis, their political dependence bears in some instances the character of open colonial slavery (India, Equatorial Africa), while in others it is concealed by the fiction of State independence (China, Latin America).

In agrarian relations backwardness finds its most organic and cruel expression. Not one of these countries has carried its democratic revolution through to any real extent. Half-way agrarian reforms are absorbed by semi-serf relations, and these are inescapably reproduced in the soil of poverty and oppression. Agrarian barbarism always goes hand-in-hand with the absence of roads, with the isolation of provinces, with 'medieval' particularism, and absence of national consciousness. The purging of social relations of the remnants of ancient and the encrustations of modern feudalism is the most important task in all these countries.

The achievement of the agrarian revolution is unthinkable, however, with the preservation of dependence upon foreign imperialism, which with one hand implants capitalist relations while supporting and re-creating with the other all the forms of slavery and serfdom. The struggle for the democratisation of social relations and the creation of a national state thus uninterruptedly passes into an open uprising against foreign domination.

Historical backwardness does not imply a simple reproduction of the development of advanced countries, England or France, with a delay of one, two, or three centuries. It engenders an entirely new 'combined' social formation in which the latest conquests of capitalist technique and structure root themselves into relations of feudal or pre-feudal barbarism, transforming and subjecting them and creating peculiar relations of classes.

Bourgeoisie Hostile to People

Not a single one of the tasks of the 'bourgeois' revolution can be solved in these backward countries under the leadership of the 'national' bourgeoisie, because the latter emerges at once with foreign support as a class alien or hostile to the people. Every stage in its development binds it only the more closely to the foreign finance capital of which it is essentially the agency. The petty bourgeoisie of the colonies, that of handicrafts and trade, is the first to fall victim in the unequal struggle with foreign capital, declining into economic insignificance, becoming declassed and pauperised. It cannot even conceive of playing an independent political role. The peasantry, the largest numerically and the most atomised, backward, and oppressed class, is capable of local uprisings and partisan warfare, but requires the leadership of a more advanced and centralised class in order for this struggle to be elevated to an all-national level. The task of such leadership falls in the nature of things upon the colonial proletariat, which, from its very first steps, stands opposed not only to the foreign but also to its own national bourgeoisie.

Out of the conglomeration of provinces and tribes, bound together by geographical proximity and the bureaucratic apparatus, capitalist development has transformed China into the semblance of an economic entity. The revolutionary movement of the masses translated this growing unity for the first time into the language of national consciousness. In the strikes, agrarian uprisings, and military expeditions of 1925–7 a new China was born. While the generals, tied to their own and the foreign bourgeoisie, could only tear the country to pieces, the Chinese workers became the standard-bearers of an irresistible urge to national unity. This movement provides an incontestable analogy with the struggle of the French Third Estate against particularism, or with the later struggle of the Germans and Italians for national unification. But in contrast to the first-born countries of capitalism, where the problem of achieving national unity fell to the petty bourgeoisie, in part under the leadership of the bourgeoisie and even of the landlords (Prussia!), in China it was the proletariat that emerged as the primary motive force and potential leader of this movement. But precisely thereby, the proletariat confronted the bourgeoisie with the danger that the leadership of the unified fatherland would not remain in the latter's hands. Patriotism has been throughout all history inseparably bound up with power and property. In the face of danger the ruling classes have never stopped short of dismembering their own country so long as they were able in this way to preserve power over one part of it. It is not at all surprising, therefore, if the Chinese bourgeoisie, represented by Chiang Kai-shek, turned its weapons in 1927 against the proletariat, the standard-bearer of national unity. The exposition and explanation of this turn, which occupies the central place in Isaacs' book, provides the key to the understanding of the fundamental problems of the Chinese Revolution as well as of the present Sino-Japanese war.

The so-called 'national' bourgeoisie tolerates all forms of national degradation so long as it can hope to maintain its own privileged existence. But at the moment when foreign capital sets out to assume undivided domination of the entire wealth of the country, the colonial bourgeoisie is forced to remind itself of its 'national' obligations. Under pressure of the masses it may even find itself plunged into a war. But this will be a war waged against one of the imperialist powers, the one least amenable to negotiations, with the hope of passing into the service of some other, more magnanimous power. Chiang Kai-shek struggles against the Japanese violators only within the limits indicated to him by his British or American patrons. Only that class which has nothing to lose but its chains can conduct to the very end the war against imperialism for national emancipation.

Grandiose Historical Test

The above developed views regarding the special character of the 'bourgeois' revolutions in historically belated countries are by no means the product of theoretical analysis alone. Before the second Chinese Revolution (1925–7) they had already been submitted to a grandiose historical test. The experience of the three Russian Revolutions (1905, February and October 1917) bears no less significance for the twentieth century than the French Revolution bore for the nineteenth. To understand the destinies of modern China readers must have before their eyes the struggle of conceptions in the Russian revolutionary movement, because these conceptions exerted, and still exert, a direct and, moreover, powerful influence upon the politics of the Chinese proletariat and an indirect influence upon the politics of the Chinese bourgeoisie.

It was precisely because of its historical backwardness that Czarist Russia turned out to be the only European country where Marxism as a doctrine and the Social Democracy as a party attained powerful development before the bourgeois revolution. It was in Russia, quite naturally, that the problem of the correlation between the struggle for democracy and the struggle for socialism, or between the bourgeois revolution and the socialist, was submitted to theoretical analysis. The first to pose this problem in the early eighties of the last century was the founder of the Russian Social Democracy, Plekhanov. In the struggle against so-called Populism (Narodnikism), a variety of socialist Utopianism, Plekhanov established that Russia had no reason whatever to expect a privileged path of development, that like the 'profane' nations, it would have to pass through the stage of capitalism and that along this path it would acquire the régime of bourgeois democracy indispensable for the further struggle of the proletariat for socialism. Plekhanov not only separated the bourgeois revolution as a task distinct from the socialist revolution – which he postponed to the indefinite future – but he depicted entirely different combinations of forces. The bourgeois revolution was to be achieved by the proletariat in alliance with the liberal bourgeoisie, and thus clear the path for capitalist progress; after a number of decades and on a higher level of capitalist development, the proletariat would carry out the socialist revolution in direct struggle against the bourgeoisie.

Lenin – not immediately, to be sure – reviewed this doctrine. At the beginning of the present century, with much greater force and consistency than Plekhanov, he posed the agrarian problem as the central problem of the bourgeois revolution in Russia. With this he came to the conclusion that the liberal bourgeoisie was hostile to the expropriation of the landlords' estates, and precisely for this reason would seek a compromise with the monarchy on the basis of a constitution on the Prussian pattern. To Plekhanov's idea of an alliance between the proletariat and the liberal bourgeoisie, Lenin opposed the idea of an alliance between the proletariat and the peasantry. The aim of the revolutionary collaboration of these two classes he proclaimed to be the establishment of the 'bourgeois-democratic dictatorship of the proletariat and the peasantry' as the only means of cleansing the Czarist empire of its feudal-police refuse, of creating a free farmers' system, and of clearing the road for the development of capitalism along American lines. Lenin's formula represented a gigantic step forward in that, in contrast to Plekhanov's, it correctly indicated the central task of the revolution, namely, the democratic overturn of agrarian relations, and equally correctly sketched out the only realistic combination of class forces capable of solving this task. But up to 1917 the thought of Lenin himself remained bound to the traditional concept of the 'bourgeois' revolution. Like Plekhanov, Lenin proceeded from the premise that only after the 'completion of the bourgeois democratic revolution' would the tasks of the socialist revolution come on the order of the day. Lenin, however, contrary to the legend later manufactured by the epigones, considered that after the completion of the democratic overturn, the peasantry, as peasantry, could not remain the ally of the proletariat. Lenin based his socialist hopes on the agricultural labourers and the semi-proletarianised peasants who sell their labour power.

An Internal Contradiction

The weak point in Lenin's conception was the internally contradictory idea of the 'bourgeois-democratic dictatorship of the proletariat and the peasantry'. A political bloc of two classes whose interests only partially coincide excludes a dictatorship. Lenin himself emphasised the fundamental limitation of the 'dictatorship of the proletariat and the peasantry' when he openly called it bourgeois. By this he meant to say that for the sake of maintaining the alliance with the peasantry the proletariat would, in the coming revolution, have to forego the direct posing of the socialist tasks. But this would signify, to be precise, that the proletariat would have to give up the dictatorship. In that event, in whose hands would the revolutionary power be concentrated? In the hands of the peasantry? But it is least capable of such a role.

Lenin left these questions unanswered up to his famous Theses of 4 April 1917. Only here did he break for the first time with the traditional understanding of the 'bourgeois' revolution and with the formula of the 'bourgeois-democratic dictatorship of the proletariat and the peasantry'. He declared the struggle for the dictatorship of the proletariat to be the sole means of carrying out the agrarian revolution to the end and of securing the freedom of the oppressed nationalities. The régime of the proletarian dictatorship, by its very nature, however, could not limit itself to the framework of bourgeois property. The rule of the proletariat automatically placed on the agenda the socialist revolution, which in this case was not separated from the democratic revolution by any historical period, but was uninterruptedly connected with it, or, to put it more accurately, was an organic outgrowth of it. At what tempo the socialist transformation of society would occur and what limits it would attain in the nearest future would depend not only upon internal but upon external conditions. The Russian revolution was only a link in the international revolution. Such was, in broad outline, the essence of the conception of the permanent (uninterrupted) revolution. It was precisely this conception that guaranteed the victory of the proletariat in October.

But such is the bitter irony of history: the experience of the Russian Revolution not only did not help the Chinese proletariat but, on the contrary, it became, in its reactionary, distorted form, one of the chief obstacles in its path. The Comintern of the epigones began by canonising for all countries of the Orient the formula of the 'democratic dictatorship of the proletariat and peasantry' which Lenin, influenced by historical experience, had acknowledged to be without value. As always in history, a formula that had outlived itself served to cover a political content which was the direct opposite of that which the formula had served in its day. The mass plebeian, revolutionary alliance of the workers and peasants, sealed through freely elected soviets as the direct organs of action, the Comintern replaced by a bureaucratic bloc of party centres. The right to represent the peasantry in this bloc was unexpectedly given to the Guomindang, that is, a thoroughly bourgeois party vitally interested in the preservation of capitalist property, not only in the means of production but in land. The alliance of the proletariat and the peasantry was broadened into a 'bloc of four classes'; workers, peasants, urban petty bourgeoisie, and the so-called 'national' bourgeoisie. In other words, the Comintern picked up a formula discarded by Lenin only in order to open the road to the politics of Plekhanov and, moreover, in a masked and therefore more harmful form.

To justify the political subordination of the proletariat to the bourgeoisie, the theoreticians of the Comintern (Stalin, Bukharin) adduced the fact of imperialist oppression which supposedly impelled 'all the progressive forces in the country' to an alliance. But this was precisely in its day the argument of the Russian Mensheviks, with the difference that in their case the place of imperialism was occupied by Czarism. In reality, the subjection of the Chinese Communist Party to the Guomindang signified its break with the mass movement and a direct betrayal of its historical interests. In this way the catastrophe of the second Chinese revolution was prepared under the direct leadership of Moscow.

Significance of Russian Marxism

To many political philistines who in politics are inclined to substitute 'common sense' guesses for scientific analysis, the controversy among the Russian Marxists over the nature of the revolution and the dynamics of its class forces seemed to be sheer scholasticism. Historical experience revealed, however, the profoundly vital significance of the 'doctrinaire formulas' of Russian Marxism. Those who have not understood this up to today can learn a great deal from Isaacs' book. The politics of the Communist International in China showed convincingly what the Russian Revolution would have been converted into if the Mensheviks and the Social Revolutionaries had not been thrust aside in time by the Bolsheviks. In China the conception of the permanent revolution was confirmed once more, this time not in the form of a victory, but of a catastrophe.

It would, of course, be impermissible to identify Russia and China. With all their important common traits, the differences are all too obvious. But it is not hard to convince oneself that these differences do not weaken but, on the contrary, strengthen the fundamental conclusions of Bolshevism. In one sense Czarist Russia was also a colonial country, and this found its expression in the predominant role of foreign capital. But the Russian bourgeoisie enjoyed the benefits of an immeasurably greater independence from foreign imperialism than the Chinese bourgeoisie. Russia itself was an imperialist country. With all its meagreness, Russian liberalism had far more serious traditions and more of a basis of support than the Chinese. To the left of the liberals stood powerful petty bourgeois parties, revolutionary or semi-revolutionary in relation to Czarism. The party of the Social Revolutionaries managed to find considerable support among the peasantry, chiefly from its upper layers. The Social

Democratic (Menshevik) Party led behind it broad circles of the urban petty bourgeoisie and labour aristocracy. It was precisely these three parties – the Liberals, the Social Revolutionaries, and the Mensheviks – who for a long time prepared, and in 1917 definitely formed, a coalition which was not yet then called the People's Front but which had all of its traits. In contrast to this the Bolsheviks, from the eve of the revolution in 1905, took up an irreconcilable position in relation to the liberal bourgeoisie. Only this policy, which achieved its highest expression in the 'defeatism' of 1914–1917, enabled the Bolshevik Party to conquer power.

The differences between China and Russia, the incomparably greater dependence of the Chinese bourgeoisie on foreign capital, the absence of independent revolutionary traditions among the petty bourgeoisie, the mass gravitation of the workers and peasants to the banner of the Comintern – demanded a still more irreconcilable policy – if such were possible, than that pursued in Russia. Yet the Chinese section of the Comintern, at Moscow's command, renounced Marxism, accepted the reactionary scholastic 'principles of Sun Yat-sen', and entered the ranks of the Guomindang, submitting to its discipline. In other words, it went much further along the road of submission to the bourgeoisie than the Russian Mensheviks or Social Revolutionaries ever did. The same fatal policy is now being repeated in the conditions of the war with Japan.

New Methods of Bureaucracy

How could the bureaucracy emerging from the Bolshevik Revolution apply in China, as throughout the world, methods fundamentally opposed to those of Bolshevism? It would be far too superficial to answer this question with a reference to the incapacity or ignorance of this or that individual. The gist of the matter lies in this: together with the new conditions of existence the bureaucracy acquired new methods of thinking. The Bolshevik Party led the masses. The bureaucracy began to order them about. The Bolsheviks won the possibility of leadership by correctly expressing the interests of the masses. The bureaucracy was compelled to resort to command in order to secure its own interests against those of the masses. The method of command was naturally extended to the Communist International as well. The Moscow leaders began quite seriously to imagine that they could compel the Chinese bourgeoisie to move to the left of its interests and the Chinese workers and peasants to the right of theirs, along the diagonals drawn in the Kremlin. Yet it is the very essence of revolution that the exploited as well as the exploiters invest their interests with the most extreme expression. If hostile classes would move along diagonals, there would be no need for a civil war. Armed by the authority of the October Revolution and the Communist International, not to mention inexhaustible financial resources, the bureaucracy transformed the young Chinese Communist Party from a motive force into a brake at the most important moment of the revolution. In contrast to Germany and Austria, where the bureaucracy could shift part of the responsibility for defeat to the Social Democracy, there was no Social Democracy in China. The Comintern had the monopoly in ruining the Chinese Revolution.

The present domination of the Guomindang over a considerable section of Chinese territory would have been impossible without the powerful national revolutionary movement of the masses in 1925–7. The massacre of this movement on the one hand concentrated power in the hands of Chiang Kai-shek, and on the other doomed Chiang Kai-shek to half-measures in the struggle against imperialism. The understanding of the course of the Chinese Revolution has in this way the most direct significance for an understanding of the course of the Sino-Japanese war. This historical work acquires thereby the most actual political significance.

War and revolution will be interlaced in the nearest future history of China. Japan's aim, to enslave forever, or at least for a long time to come, a gigantic country by dominating its strategic centres, is characterised not only by greediness but by wooden-headedness. Japan has arrived much too late. Torn by internal contradictions, the empire of the Mikado cannot reproduce the history of Britain's ascent. On the other hand, China has advanced far beyond the India of the seventeenth and eighteenth centuries. Old colonial countries are nowadays waging with ever greater success a struggle for their national independence. In these historic conditions, even if the present war in the Far East were to end with Japan's victory, and even if the victor himself could escape an internal catastrophe during the next few years – and neither the former nor the latter is in the least assured – Japan's domination over China would be measured by a very brief period, perhaps only the few years required to give a new impulse to the economic life of China and to mobilise its labouring masses once more.

The big Japanese trusts and concerns are already following in the wake of the army to divide the still unsecured booty. The Tokyo Government is seeking to regulate the appetites of the financial cliques that would tear North China to pieces. If Japan were to succeed in maintaining its conquered positions for an interval of some ten years, this would mean, above all, the intensive industrialisation of North China in the military interests of Japanese imperialism. New railways, mines, power stations, mining and metallurgical enterprises, and cotton plantations would rapidly spring up. The polarisation of the Chinese nation would receive a feverish impulse. New hundreds of thousands and millions of Chinese proletarians would be mobilised in the briefest possible space of time. On the other hand, the Chinese bourgeoisie would fall into an ever greater dependence on Japanese capital. Even less than in the past would it be capable of standing at the head of a national war, no less a national revolution. Face to face with the foreign violator would stand the numerically larger, socially strengthened, politically matured Chinese proletariat, called to lead the Chinese village. Hatred of the foreign enslaver is a mighty revolutionary cement. The new national revolution will, one must think, be placed on the agenda still in the lifetime of the present generation. To solve the tasks imposed upon it, the vanguard of the Chinese proletariat must thoroughly assimilate the lessons of the Chinese Revolution. Isaacs' book can serve it in this sense as an irreplaceable aid. It remains to be hoped that the book will be translated into Chinese as well as other foreign languages.

Coyoacán, D. F., 1938

Letter to Frank Glass

Leon Trotsky

Trotsky's letter to Frank Glass (Li Furen) in Shanghai is by way of a reply to Chen Duxiu's letter to Trotsky (contained in this volume) of 3 November 1938, which Glass had forwarded on Chen's behalf on 19 January 1939. Trotsky had expressed worries about Chen's physical security as early as 1937, and had become even more worried after April 1938, when Wang Ming and Kang Sheng started up a campaign in China to slander Chen as a 'paid agent of Japan'. He was therefore keen to get Chen to America, where he would be both safe and able (so Trotsky hoped) to play the same role in the Fourth International as the Japanese Katayama Sen had played in the Third. In a letter accompanying Chen's, Glass, commenting on Trotsky's efforts to persuade Chen to seek sanctuary in the United States, had said that Chen 'does not believe as Crux [Trotsky] did that he is in imminent personal danger from the Stalinists or the Kuomintang [Guomindang]' (since, as he says, the numbers and present influence of the Fourth Internationalists in China 'are not such as to invite strong attack'). According to one source, Chen did not rule out a sojourn in the United States and even tried to obtain a passport; he desisted only because his health deteriorated and, moreover, because it soon became clear to him that the Guomindang would under no circumstances let him leave China.[1] But Wang Fanxi, Chen's collaborator and correspondent in those years, believes this assertion to be untrue. Trotsky died in Mexico, at the hands of an assassin, on 20 August 1940. The original of this letter, written in English, is held in the China files of the 'Exile Papers of Leon Trotsky', deposited at Harvard University and made accessible in 1980. The full text of Frank Glass' letter to Trotsky is translated into French in Cahiers Leon Trotsky (Grenoble), September 1983, no. 15, pp. 113–18.

Coyoacán, D. F.

11 March 1939

Dear Friend,
It was with the greatest interest that I read your letter from Shanghai of 19 January and the statement [by Chen Duxiu] from Szechwan [Sichuan]. At last we have the information we lacked until now. I am very glad that our old

---

1 Peter Kuhfus 1985, pp. 273–4.

friend remains a friend politically in spite of some *possible* divergences which I cannot appreciate now with the necessary precision.

Of course, it is very difficult for me to form a definite opinion on the politics of our comrades or the degree of their ultra-leftism, and thus on the correctness of the sharp condemnation on the part of our old friend. However, the essence of his statement seems to me to be correct, and I hope that on this basis a permanent collaboration will be possible.

I continue to believe that the best thing for him would be his sojourn in the [United] States for a period. Do you not believe that it would be feasible even without the approval of the high authorities?

I cannot share his optimistic view that no danger threatens him now. Yes, for a period our Chinese comrades are protected to a small degree by their own weakness. However, we are becoming stronger and stronger internationally. Our party[2] has begun to play a serious role in the States. It is a tremendous warning to the Stalinists and they will try to prevent a similar danger in the other countries. They will begin with the most prominent figures of our movement.

My warmest greetings and good wishes.

Comradely,

T[rotsky]

---

2 A reference to the Socialist Workers Party, the US section of the Fourth International.

China and the Russian Revolution

Leon Trotsky

July 1940

Source: Fourth International, *New York, vol. 2, no. 3, March 1941, pp. 75–6. Online Version: Marxists' Internet Archive, 2003, transcribed/HTML Markup by David Walters, copyleft by Leon Trotsky Internet Archive 2003.*

Note by Natalia Trotsky: This was written by Comrade Trotsky in the early part of July 1940, as a first draft. Events prevented him from continuing the work and it was unfinished when Comrade Trotsky was murdered by a GPU assassin the following month. It was to have been the introduction to the Chinese translation of his History of the Russian Revolution.)

The day I learned that my *History of the Russian Revolution* was to be published in the Chinese language was a holiday for me. Now I have received word that the work of translation has been speeded up and that the first volume will be issued next year.

Let me express the firm hope that the book will prove profitable to Chinese readers. Whatever may be the shortcomings of my work, one thing I can say with assurance: facts are there presented with complete conscientiousness, that is, on the basis of verification with original sources; and in any case, not a single fact is altered or distorted in the interests of this or that preconceived theory or, what is worse yet, in the interests of this or that personal reputation.

The misfortune of the present young generation in all countries, among them China, consists in this: that there has been created under the label of Marxism a gigantic factory of historical, theoretical, and all other kinds of falsifications. This factory bears the name 'Communist International'. The totalitarian régime, that is, the régime of bureaucratic command in all spheres of life, inescapably seeks to extend its rule also over the past. History becomes transformed into raw material for whatever constructions are required by the ruling totalitarian clique. This fate was suffered by the October Revolution and by the History of the Bolshevik Party. The latest and to date most finished document of falsification and frame-up is the *History of the Communist Party of the Soviet Union*, issued some time ago under the personal direction of Stalin. In the entire library of humankind I do not know, and hardly anyone else knows, of a book in which facts, documents – and furthermore facts known to everybody – are so dishonestly altered, mangled, or simply deleted from the march of events in the interests of glorifying a single human being, namely Stalin.

Thanks to unlimited material resources at the disposal of the falsifiers, the rude and untalented falsification has been translated into all the languages of civilized mankind and circulated by compulsion in millions and tens of millions of copies.

We have at our disposal neither such financial resources nor such a colossal apparatus. But we do dispose of something greater: concern for historical truth and a correct scientific method. A falsification, even one compiled by a mighty state apparatus, cannot withstand the test of time and in the long run is blown up owing to the internal contradictions. On the contrary, historical truth, established through a scientific method, has its own internal persuasiveness and in the long run gains mastery over minds. The very necessity of reviewing, that is, recasting and altering – still more precisely, falsifying – the history of the revolution, arose from this: that the bureaucracy found itself compelled to sever the umbilical cord binding it to the Bolshevik Party. To recast, that is, to falsify the history of the revolution, became an urgent necessity for the bureaucracy which usurped the revolution and found itself compelled to cut short the tradition of Bolshevism.

The essence of Bolshevism was the class policy of the proletariat, which alone could bring about the conquest of power in October. In the course of its entire history, Bolshevism came out irreconcilably against the policy of collaboration with the bourgeoisie. Precisely in this consisted the fundamental contradiction between Bolshevism and Menshevism. Still more, the struggle within the labour movement, which preceded the rise of Bolshevism and Menshevism, always in the last analysis revolved around the central question, the central alternative: either collaboration with the bourgeoisie or irreconcilable class struggle. The policy of 'People's Fronts' does not include an iota of novelty, if we discount the solemn and essentially charlatan name. The matter at issue in all cases concerns the political subordination of the proletariat to the left wing of the exploiters, regardless of whether this practice bears the name of coalition or left bloc (as in France) or 'People's Front' in the language of the Comintern.

The policy of the 'People's Front' bore especially malignant fruit because it was applied in the epoch of the imperialist decay of the bourgeoisie. Stalin succeeded in conducting to the end, in the Chinese revolution, the policy which the Mensheviks tried to realize in the revolution of 1917. The same thing was repeated in Spain. Two grandiose revolutions suffered catastrophe owing to this: that the methods of the leadership were the methods of Stalinism, the most malignant form of Menshevism.

In the course of five years, the policy of the 'People's Front', by subjecting the proletariat to the bourgeoisie, made impossible the class struggle against war. If the defeat of the Chinese revolution, conditioned by the leadership of the Comintern, prepared the conditions for Japanese occupation, then the defeat of the Spanish revolution and the ignominious capitulation of the 'People's Front' in France prepared the conditions for the aggression and unprecedented military successes of Hitler.

The victories of Japan, like the victories of Hitler, are not the last word of history. War this time, too, will turn out to be the mother of revolutions. Revolution will once again pose and review all the questions of the history of humankind in advanced as well as in backward countries, and make a beginning for overcoming the very distinction between advanced and backward countries.

Reformists, opportunists, routine men will be flung aside by the course of events. Only revolutionists, tempered revolutionists enriched by the experience of the past, will be able to rise to the level of great events. The Chinese people are destined to occupy the first place in the future destinies of humankind. I shall be happy if the advanced Chinese revolutionists will assimilate from this history certain fundamental rules of class politics which will help them to avoid fatal mistakes in the future, mistakes which led to the shipwreck of the revolution of 1925–7.

PART 12

Chinese Trotskyist Reflections on Mao Zedong's Revolution

The Causes of the Victory of the Chinese Communist Party over Chiang Kai-shek, and the CCP's Perspectives. Report on the Chinese Situation to the Third World Congress of the Fourth International, August–September 1951

Peng Shuzhi

In this report and its supplement, Peng Shuzhi explains the causes of Mao's victory and of its radical turn in 1950. He attributes the victory chiefly to 'exceptional' circumstances: the Japanese invasion, Chiang Kai-shek's collapse, Washington's decision to abandon him, and Russian aid to the CCP. In the supplement, he explains Mao's anti-capitalist turn in 1950 by the influx of workers into the CCP. Excerpted from International Information Bulletin, *Socialist Workers Party, February 1952.*

The victory of the Chinese Communist Party over the reactionary power of Chiang Kai-shek, its occupation of the entire Chinese mainland, and the establishment of the 'People's Republic' (or the 'People's Democratic Dictatorship') has marked a great and even a monumental change in modern Chinese history, and has also caused profound changes in the Far East and in international relations.

These events were unexpected both among bourgeois ruling circles and the petty-bourgeois politicians, the former being stunned and panic-stricken; the latter, perplexed or dazzled. But these events were likewise far from being anticipated by us Trotskyists (including Trotsky himself), owing to the fact that the CCP came to its current victory through its extremely reactionary Menshevik programme of 'revolution by stages', coupled with the fact that the peasant armed forces were completely isolated from the urban working class.

As a result, a considerable amount of confusion has been raised in our ranks regarding Mao's victory, and serious differences of opinion have occurred over its causes and significance, the nature of the new power and its perspectives.... We must, therefore, very prudently and seriously examine Mao's victory and the extraordinary situation emerging from it.

First of all, we should not overlook the reactionary role of Stalinism independently of the CCP victory, and not reconcile ourselves or, even worse, surrender to it. We must still insist on the basic position of the permanent revolution, which is the only compass to guide China and all backward countries to genuine liberation; we must judge any further events from this position. But, in proceeding with the discussion, it is necessary not only to discard all subjective prejudices, desires, or mechanical analogies, but to free ourselves from traditional formulas (not, of course, principles)....

The Diverse Causes of the CCP Victory Over the Guomindang

One of the traditional concepts that Trotsky repeatedly put forward, and that the Chinese Trotskyists upheld for the past twenty years, was a strategy that ran counter to the Stalinist strategy of conquering the cities through peasant armed forces alone. The Trotskyists maintained that the overthrow of the bourgeois Guomindang régime was possible only if the urban working class stood up and led all the oppressed and exploited in the country, especially the peasant masses, carried forward a persistent struggle, and eventually brought about an armed insurrection. It was not possible to overthrow the bourgeois régime by relying exclusively on the peasant armed forces because, under the present conditions of society, the countryside is subordinated to the cities and the peasants can play a decisive role only under the leadership of the working class. But the fact now confronting us is exactly the contrary: it was a Stalinist party relying exclusively on the peasant armed forces that destroyed the old régime and seized power.

This extreme contradiction between the 'facts' and the 'traditional conception' first of all led to confusion and disputes among the Chinese comrades. Meanwhile, some comrades in the International, because of their inadequate understanding of Trotsky's traditional conception of the Chinese question and the specific causes of Mao's victory, emphasise the factor of 'mass pressure' to account for this victory. So I think that an accurate and detailed explanation of the causes of this victory is necessary, not only in order to overcome the differences of opinion among the Chinese comrades, but also in order to correct the deviations of some comrades in the International....

The Complete Rottenness and Collapse of Chiang's Régime
It is known to everyone that Chiang Kai-shek's régime was born amid the bloodshed of the defeat of the second Chinese revolution. Naturally it was extremely afraid of and hostile to the people. It oppressed the people and sustained itself on the exploitation of the masses (especially the peasant masses) by the most barbaric Asiatic methods. At the same time, since by its very nature this régime represented the bourgeoisie of the Orient (characterised in the saying that 'the

farther East the bourgeoisie goes, the more cowardly and the more incompetent it becomes'), Chiang's régime could only support itself on the imperialist powers (one of them, at least).

It united all reactionary influences, including feudal survivals, to resist the masses and to suppress them. It was consequently unable to fulfil any of the bourgeois-democratic tasks, not even such a slight reform as a 25 percent reduction in [land] rents. It was mainly characterised by consummate Asiatic despotism, corruption, and inefficiency. These characteristics were completely disclosed during the Resistance War. On one hand, after its policy of 'non-defencism' failed and the long period of concessions to the Japanese imperialists ended with the Chiang government forced to fight, it revealed its complete incompetence by losing one city after another. On the other hand, it clamped an iron grip over any spontaneous activity by the masses, while its bureaucrats and warlords, profiting from this rare opportunity, exploited and plundered the blood and flesh of the people by hoarding and smuggling goods and other extortions, and thus enriched themselves through the national disaster. These deeds stirred up great dissatisfaction and bitterness among the common people – which was reflected in the student demonstrations and the peasant unrest in certain regions during the closing period of the war.

After the surrender of Japanese imperialism, Chiang Kai-shek's tyranny, corruption, and inefficiency reached a climax.... The financial base of Chiang's government had already been exhausted in the course of the war. Chiang's sole prop was his military force and so he continued the fight to the end and would never compromise with Mao Zedong. He hoped to exterminate the CCP's peasant armed forces through his superior military equipment and prevent his doomed régime from being swept away. In fact, Chiang Kai-shek's army far surpassed the CCP's, not only in numbers but also in equipment. A considerable part of his army (about six to seven hundred thousand soldiers) was armed with the most modern American weapons. But this army had two fatal defects: First, most of the soldiers were recruited from the countryside by compulsory conscription, some of them even by kidnapping, so they naturally more or less reflected the dissatisfaction and hatred of the peasants. Second, all the generals and officers of high rank were rotten to the core; they mistreated the soldiers and steadily reduced rations. This oppression inflicted much suffering upon the soldiers and deepened their discontent and hatred. Once this hatred found a suitable outlet, it would be transformed into a deluge of flight and surrender. Mao Zedong's 'general counteroffensive' furnished this outlet.

All the above-stated facts demonstrate that Chiang's government was not only isolated from the people, who were hostile to it, but was also deserted by the majority of the bourgeoisie. Even those who formerly supported it turned bitter against it and were ready to sacrifice it in exchange for their own lives. This situation resulted in the appearance of various kinds of anti-Chiang factions and cliques within the Guomindang itself, which was thus involved in complete decomposition....

Chiang Finally Deserted by American Imperialism

Before the Second World War, the most powerful and decisive influences in Chinese economy and politics were the Japanese, British, and American imperialists. With the end of the war, the influence of Japanese imperialism vanished. British imperialism, because of its extreme decline, although still maintaining its rule in Hong Kong, has since completely left the political stage in China. The last one to attempt to control the country was American imperialism....

On the one hand, Washington tried to 'prevail upon' Chiang Kai-shek to make 'reforms', such as eliminating a few of the most corrupt and incompetent officials and generals, inviting some more able 'democratic' figures into the administration, and curtailing some of the more excessive forms of despotic oppression and exploitation. On the other hand, it manoeuvred for a temporary compromise between Chiang and Mao, in order to gain time to destroy Mao. This was the purpose of Gen. Marshall's special mission in China.

But Chiang not only refused to make any 'reforms'; he also obstinately balked at any compromise with Mao's party. Ultimately, the Marshall mission was a complete failure. The only alternative left for American imperialism was to engage in a direct military offensive against the CCP in Chiang's place (as one group of Republicans demanded at that time), and to extend its direct control over the administrative and military power of the government. It was very clear, however, that the situation emerging from the Second World War would never permit this headstrong action....

The result was that the US was finally compelled to abandon its aid to Chiang's government and adopt a wait-and-see attitude towards the CCP, pending a more favourable opportunity. This final decision by American imperialism came as a death blow to Chiang Kai-shek's régime....

The CCP's Subjective Strength

The CCP's basic strength lies in its peasant armed forces. These originated in the successive peasant revolts that exploded in China's southern provinces after the defeat of the second revolution. While these revolts had no real hope of victory, the armed forces they assembled were able to maintain their existence, develop, and carry on a durable peasant war. This was possible because of the CCP's deep involvement in organising and training the peasants, as well as the economic backwardness and other specific geographic conditions (the vastness of the country and the extreme lack of means of communication). Other factors included the utter despair of the peasants and the incompetence of the bourgeois government.

Later, when Chiang Kai-shek obtained enormous quantities of military aid from imperialism, the CCP's peasant army was forced to flee from South to North China, and even capitulated to Chiang's government by cancelling its agrarian policy and dissolving the 'Red Army' and the soviets.

However, as a result of the outbreak of the war against Japanese imperialism this armed force secured the opportunity for an unusual development. In particular, at the end of the war and right after it, the army made great progress in both numbers and in quality, becoming far stronger than in the Jiangxi period. This army thus grew into a strong military force.

Politically, the CCP always oscillated between adventurism and opportunism: it cancelled its agrarian revolution and dissolved the 'Red Army' and the soviets on the eve of the Resistance War; it collaborated servilely with the Guomindang and supported Chiang Kai-shek's leadership during the war. But despite all these things, it also carried on a long period of resistance against Chiang's government. It made certain criticisms of the political, economic, and military measures of the latter during the war, and had put forward a number of demands for democratic reform. It carried out agrarian reform, particularly in some regions of North China. Furthermore it was backed by the prestige of the tradition of the October revolution in the USSR, as well as by the amazing record of the Soviet Union in the recent world war and the powerful position it has held since the war's end.

On the other hand, the common people had become desperate and deeply resentful under the intolerable oppression and exploitation of Chiang's utterly despotic, rotten, and inefficient régime. The petty-bourgeois intellectuals and peasant masses in particular, in the absence of a powerful and really revolutionary party to lead them, lodged all their hopes in the CCP. This was the source of the CCP's political capital. This political capital, plus the peasant armed forces, constituted the party's subjective strength. But without aid from the Soviet Union, this victory would still not have been assured.

The Aid from the Soviet Union

Despite the Soviet bureaucracy's fear of the victory of a genuine revolution of the working class at the head of the peasant masses in China, and despite its foreign policy of seeking a compromise with American imperialism, in order to preserve its own privileges and resist the threat of American imperialism it would not refuse to give the CCP a certain amount of help, within the confines of its attempt to preserve control over the CCP. Therefore, in addition to its support in political agitation, the Soviet Union actually gave the CCP decisive material aid. The Soviet occupation of Manchuria (one of the greatest centres of heavy industry in China, built up during the several decades of Japanese occupation, and the area of the highest rural production), with its population of thirty million, objectively dealt a mortal blow to Chiang's government.

Despite the fact that the Soviet Union had recognised Chiang's régime as the official government, and had handed over to it the majority of the cities and mines in Manchuria, the Soviet bureaucracy had destroyed almost all the most important factories and mining machinery. (It also took away a part of them.) Thus industry was brought almost to a complete halt. Meanwhile, through its control over the two ports – Dalian and Lushun – it blocked the Chiang government's main lines of sea communication with Manchuria and barred its trade and commerce, especially its transportation of supplies to the army stationed in Manchuria.

On the other hand, it armed the CCP's troops with huge amounts of light and heavy weapons taken from the Japanese soldiers. (It is estimated that these weapons could be used to rearm a million soldiers.) This enabled the CCP to occupy the villages, smaller cities, and towns, and to besiege the great cities and mining districts where Chiang's army was stationed. Thus the cities and mines restored to Chiang Kai-shek did not benefit him, but, on the contrary, became an insupportable burden, and finally turned into a trap. To begin with, Chiang had to send a huge army (around half a million soldiers) with the best equipment, that is, armed with American weapons, to stand guard. At the same time, the Guomindang had to provide for the enormous expenditures in the big cities and in the mines. Consequently, this greatly limited and scattered Chiang Kai-shek's military force and accelerated the financial bankruptcy of his régime.

The weapons taken from the Japanese captives by the Soviet Union served to build up the CCP's army and produced a decisive effect upon Mao Zedong's military apparatus and strategy. (For example, Lin Biao's well-known and powerful Fourth Division was armed entirely with these weapons.) We must understand that the CCP's original peasant army, despite its preponderant size, was not only very backward but also had extremely scanty equipment, especially in heavy weapons. Having obtained this gigantic quantity of light and heavy weapons through the medium of the Soviet Union (in addition to numerous Soviet and Japanese military technicians), part of the originally very backward peasant troops were modernised overnight.

The bravery of the peasants and the military adroitness of the Communist generals, together with these modern weapons, then enabled the Communist army to transform guerrilla warfare into positional warfare. This was fully manifested in the battles where the Communist troops gained complete victory in conquering the great cities and mines in Manchuria during the changing season between autumn and winter of 1948. (These included Changchun, Shenyang, Jinzhou, and the big mining districts, Tieling, Fushun, and Anshan.) This victory won for the Communist army an ample economic base. Moreover, in the military field, since the best-equipped of Chiang's troops (about 80 per cent of those with American equipment) were destroyed, that meant that the greatest part of this American equipment was no longer effective.

...Henceforth the strategic attitude of the Communist army fundamentally changed, shifting over from guerrilla warfare to positional warfare and an offensive towards the big cities. This change was undoubtedly a decisive factor in the victory of the CCP inasmuch as it depended on the peasant army alone to conquer the cities.

Chiang Kai-shek's bourgeois-landlord régime collapsed in toto, both on the economic and political planes and in its military organisation. Its only supporter, American imperialism, deserted it in the end. The CCP's peasant army, having won the support of the peasants and the petty bourgeoisie in general, and especially having obtained military aid from the Soviet Union, had become a colossal and more or less modernised army. The combination of all these objective and subjective factors paved the way for this extraordinary victory....

The whole capitalist world – of which China is the weakest link – tended to an unparalleled decline and decay. The internal disintegration of the bourgeois Chiang Kai-shek régime was only the most consummate manifestation of the deterioration of the whole capitalist system. On the other hand, the Soviet bureaucracy, resting on the socialised property relations of the October revolution and exploiting the contradictions among the imperialist powers, was able to achieve an unprecedented expansion of its influence during the Second World War. This expansion greatly attracted the masses, especially of the backward Asian countries, who were deprived of hope under the extreme decline and decomposition of the capitalist system. This facilitated the explosive growth of the Stalinist parties in these countries. The CCP is precisely a perfected model of these Stalinist parties.

Meanwhile, placed in an unfavourable position in the international situation created by the Second World War, American imperialism was obliged to abandon its aid to Chiang and its interference with Mao. At the same time, the Soviet Union, which had secured a superior position in Manchuria at the end of the war, inflicted serious damage on Chiang's government and offered direct aid to the CCP. This enabled the latter to modernise its backward peasant army. Without this combination of circumstances, the victory of a party like the CCP, which relied purely on peasant forces, would be inconceivable....

Trotsky and the Chinese Trotskyists insisted that the overturn of the Guomindang régime could not be achieved by relying solely on the peasant armed forces, but could only be accomplished by the urban working class leading the peasant masses in a series of revolts. Even today, this conception is still entirely valid. It is derived from the fundamental Marxist theory that under the modern capitalist system – including that in the backward countries – it is the urban class that leads the rural masses. This is also the conclusion drawn from numerous experiences, especially that of the October Revolution. This is precisely one of the fundamental conceptions of permanent revolution, which we must firmly hold onto despite the present CCP victory....

We were unable to foresee the current victory of the CCP for the same reason that Trotsky and we Trotskyists were unable to predict in advance the unusual expansion that Stalinism underwent after the Second World War. In both cases our mistake was not one of principle. Rather, because we concentrated so much on principle, we more or less ignored the specific conditions involved in the unfolding of events and were unable to modify our tactics in time. Of course there is a lesson in this, a lesson we should assimilate and apply to the analysis of future developments in those Asian countries where the Stalinist parties maintain strong influence (such as Vietnam, Burma, and so on). That should help us to formulate a correct strategy in advance.

At the same time, we must understand that the victory gained by a party such as the CCP, which detached itself from the working class and relied entirely on the peasant armed forces, is not only abnormal in itself. It has also laid down many obstacles in the path of the future development of the Chinese revolutionary movement. To understand this is, in my opinion, of great importance in our judgment and estimation of the whole movement led by the CCP as well as in determining our strategy and tactics.

Is the CCP's Seizure of Power the Result of 'Mass Pressure', and in Opposition to the Kremlin's Objectives?

Some comrades of the International, not being very familiar with the concrete process and specific conditions of the events in China, have stressed the role of 'mass pressure', or interpreted the victory of the CCP by making an analogy with the Yugoslav events.... [They argue that] the CCP succeeded in conquering power, like the Yugoslav CP, under pressure from the masses, and in conflict with the objectives of the Kremlin. Unfortunately, this 'traditionally conceived' analogy can hardly be justified by the facts of the Chinese events. Let us first of all begin with these facts....

The period from September 1945 to the end of 1946 saw a considerable revival and growth of the mass movement in China. In this period the working masses in all the great cities, with Shanghai in the forefront, first brought forward their demands for a sliding-scale increase in wages, for the right to organise trade unions, against freezing of wages, and so on. They universally and continuously engaged in strikes and demonstrations.... Among the peasants, under the unbearable weight of compulsory contributions, taxes in kind, conscription, and the threat of starvation, the ferment of resentment was boiling.... The students played a notable role, representing the petty bourgeoisie in general, in large-scale protests, strikes, and demonstrations in the big cities. These took place in Chongqing, Kunming, Nanjing, Shanghai, Guangzhou, Beijing, and so on, under banners and slogans demanding democracy and peace, against the Guomindang dictatorship, against mobilisation for the civil war, and against the persecutions conducted by the Guomindang agents.

When Chiang's government returned to the 'recovered areas', it revealed its own extreme corruption and inefficiency in administration and stirred up strong resentment among the people. It already appeared to be tottering....

During this same period the CCP's military strength and its political influence among the masses were growing rapidly. The workers' struggles, the ferment of resentment and rebellion among the peasants, and widespread demonstrations by the students, accompanied by the corruption and insecurity of Chiang's régime and the strengthening of the CCP, plainly created a prerevolutionary situation.

If the CCP had then been able to stay in step with the situation, that is, to accept the 'pressure of the masses', it would have raised slogans for the overthrow of the Chiang Kai-shek government (that is, the slogan for the seizure of power). It would have joined this slogan to other demands for democratic reforms, especially the demand for agrarian revolution. And it would have been able to swiftly transform this prerevolutionary situation, to carry through the insurrection, and thereby arrive at the conquest of power in the most propitious way. Unfortunately, however,... it kowtowed to Chiang Kai-shek and pleaded for the establishment of a 'coalition government'. (For this purpose Mao flew to Chongqing to negotiate directly with Chiang, and even openly expressed his support to the latter in mass meetings.)...

As for the workers' economic struggles, the CCP offered no positive lead to transform them into political struggles; which was quite possible at that time, but on the contrary persuaded the working masses not to go to 'extremes' in their conflicts. Moreover, it dealt obsequiously with the leaders of the 'yellow trade unions' in order to check the 'excessive' demands of the workers.

The CCP's activities in the countryside were limited solely to organising guerrillas, while it avoided broad mass movements that would have encouraged and unified the peasant masses. The great student movement in the cities was handled as a simple instrument for exerting pressure on the Guomindang government to accept peace talks. It was never linked with the workers' strikes in a common struggle against Chiang Kai-shek's rule.

However, in May 1946, in response to the Guomindang's continuing military offensive, the CCP announced that it had begun agrarian reform in certain areas under its control. This served to strengthen the CCP's military position. Even then, this land reform was by no means thoroughgoing. It consisted largely of a compromise with the landlords and rich peasants, preserving all of their 'industrial and commercial properties' and allowing them to get the best and most of the land. It was also quite limited in its scope....

Chiang Kai-shek, for his part, made full use of the time during the peace conference to transport his army, with the aid of American planes and warships, from the interior to the great cities and the strategic bases in the 'recovered areas'. He solidified his position and prepared for armed attack on the CCP. In the meantime, he suppressed all the newly arising mass movements, especially the student movement. At the end of 1946, when all preparations were completed, Chiang's government openly barred all doors to compromise and peace talks by holding its own 'national assembly' and organising its own 'constituent government', which showed its determination to reject the establishment of any coalition government with the CCP....

Not until later, when Chiang Kai-shek drove away the CCP's peace delegation (March 1947) and succeeded in occupying Yan'an, its capital and stronghold (April 1947), did the CCP begin to realise the hopelessness of this attempt and only then did it muster its forces to engage in a military defence. But even at that time, it still did not dare to raise the slogan of the overthrow of the Guomindang government. Nor did it offer a programme of agrarian reform to mobilise the masses.

Even when Chiang's government published its 'warrant' for Mao Zedong's arrest (on 25 June 1947) and promulgated its 'mobilisation decree for suppressing revolts' (on 4 July), the CCP responded with several months of hesitation (during which it seemed to be waiting for instructions from Moscow). Finally on 10 October, it published its manifesto in the name of the 'People's Liberation Army' that openly called for Chiang Kai-shek's overthrow and the building of a 'New China'. It was also at this time that it once again revived its 'agrarian law', ordering the expropriation of the land of landlords and rich peasants and its redistribution to peasants with no land or whose land was inadequate. ('Industrial and commercial enterprises', however, remained untouched.)

This policy shift marked a fundamental change in the CCP's relations with Chiang's government. Was it the result of mass pressure? No, obviously not. The mass movement had already been brutally trampled by Chiang's régime and was at a low ebb. With Guomindang agents active everywhere, thousands of young students were arrested, tortured, and assassinated, and worker militants were constantly being arrested or hunted. The CCP was compelled to make this change solely because Chiang had burned all bridges leading towards compromise and because it was confronted with the mortal threat of a violent attack designed to annihilate its influence once and for all. So the shift was more the result of Chiang's pressure than of mass pressure.

To arm itself for a counteroffensive, the CCP began to make a 'left turn' on the political plane. Only then did it begin to make concessions to the demands of the masses, or to bend before 'mass pressure'. In particular it gave in to the demands of the peasant masses in areas it controlled, with the aim of regaining and strengthening its military power.

Hence, from November 1947 to the next spring, it initiated a universal struggle to 'correct the Right deviation' in areas where land reform was set into motion. In the course of this struggle, the CCP liquidated all the privileges previously granted to the landlords and kulaks, and re-expropriated and distributed the land among the poor peasants. It also deprived the landlords and kulaks of the posts they held in the local administration, the party, and the army. 'Poor Peasants' Committees' were created and given a few democratic rights, to allow them to directly fight the landlords and kulaks. They were even permitted to criticise lower-ranking party cadres, some of whom were removed from their posts and punished. These actions as a whole were quite successful in winning considerable support from the peasant masses and greatly strengthened the CCP's anti-Chiang military forces. But we should not forget that all these 'leftward' policies were taken in reaction to pressure from Chiang.

As regards the CCP's relations with the Kremlin, I can only offer as illustrations some important historical turns. After the disastrous defeat of the second Chinese revolution, when the Kremlin switched its policy from ultraright opportunism to ultraleft adventurism (the so-called third period in its general international line), the CCP leadership followed at the Kremlin's heels without hesitation. Closing their eyes to the most grave injuries the party suffered because of this turn, and deaf to the unremitting and sharp criticisms from Trotsky and the Chinese Left Opposition, the leading bodies carried out these adventurist policies and engaged in a desperate struggle to 'build up soviets and the Red Army' in the desolate and isolated villages. This was done without any connection with the urban workers' movement, and in the general counter-revolutionary climate of bourgeois victory and relative stability.

Threatened by Hitler's triumph, the Kremlin turned away from the 'third period' and back towards ultraright opportunism and the so-called Democratic Front and Peace Front. Just as before, adjusting to this turn of the Kremlin, the CCP unreservedly advocated the People's Front or the Front of National Defence, and renewed its appeal to the Guomindang for collaboration....

Later, the CCP's turn from compromise with Chiang to urging his overthrow was also in line with the Kremlin's foreign policy. Having failed in its attempt to achieve a compromise with American imperialism, Moscow turned to a defensive strategy as a result of the cold war. The timing of the CCP's 'big turn' in October 1947 followed the formation of the Cominform on the Kremlin's orders in September. This was not merely a coincidence and should suffice to prove that the CCP's turn, far from violating the Kremlin's objectives, was completed precisely under Moscow's direction.

Some comrades of the International have cited certain facts regarding the isolation of the CCP from Moscow during the Resistance War, in order to justify the theory that the latest turn in CCP policy was a result of violating the Kremlin's objectives. But these 'facts' are just the opposite of the real facts. Before the war, the Kremlin's agents stayed permanently in Yan'an (not openly), and there was regular radio communication between Yan'an and Moscow. After the war, the Soviet Union sent its ambassador to Chongqing, accompanied by its secret agents, so that it could openly and legally establish regular contact with the Chinese Communist delegation and its special agents in Chongqing, to dispatch news and instructions. Therefore we have sufficient reason to say that during the war the relations between the CCP and the Kremlin not only were not cut off, but on the contrary became closer than ever. In the postwar period, since the Soviet occupation of Manchuria, and with so many Soviet representatives working in the CCP and the army, the intimacy between Moscow and the CCP has been too evident to need further clarification.

So to put the Chinese and Yugoslav parties on the same plane and to consider the former's conquest of power as the result of similar 'mass pressure' and as overstepping the Kremlin's objectives is both mechanical and misleading.

...

8 November 1951

Supplementary Remarks on the Problem of the Character of the Chinese CP

When after the defeat of the second Chinese revolution the CCP abandoned the workers' movement in the cities, turned towards the countryside, absorbed a great number of peasants into the party, and concentrated on the peasant guerrillas, Trotsky and the Chinese Trotskyists declared that it had gradually degenerated and become a petty-bourgeois party based on the peasantry. But some comrades say that even if Trotsky expressed this opinion he was wrong.

In judging the character of a party, we base ourselves on two fundamental factors: the party's composition and its political tendency. If workers comprise the majority of the Party, and the Party truthfully represents the fundamental interests of the working class, this party can be called a healthy or revolutionary workers' party. If the workers comprise the majority of the party and its political leadership is of a petty-bourgeois or opportunist reformist type, we still call it a workers' party, but it is a deformed or degenerated workers' party. If the petty bourgeoisie predominates in its social composition and if the leadership is also opportunist, even if it pretends to be a workers' party, we can only designate it a petty-bourgeois party.

Regarding the evolution and the composition of the CCP, in the last period of the second Chinese revolution it had approximately 60,000 members, according to the report to the Party's Fifth Congress, in April 1927. Industrial workers accounted for 58 per cent of the membership. But after the disastrous defeats of this revolution and several adventuristic insurrections, particularly after the great defeat of the Guangzhou uprising, most of the workers were sacrificed or left the party. Proletarian membership declined to 10 per cent in 1928 and to 3 per cent in 1929 (see Zhou Enlai, 'On the Organisational Question'). It fell to 2.5 per cent in March 1930 (*Red Flag*, 26 March 1930), and to 1.6 per cent in September of the same year (Zhou Enlai, 'Report to the Third Plenum of the CC of the Party').

The 10 October 1931 issue of *Bolshevik* admitted 'the percentage of workers had already fallen to less than 1 per cent'. After most of the workers' branches of Shanghai were won over to the Left Opposition 'Trotskyist Group', *Red Flag* complained on 23 October 1933 that in Shanghai, the largest industrial city of the country, 'There is not a single real workers' branch'. But in the same period they said that the number of members had risen to over 300,000. This is proof that the CCP had an almost exclusively peasant composition. Precisely because of that, Trotsky concluded that 'The Chinese Stalinists... in the years of the counter-revolution... passed over from the proletariat to the peasantry, that is, they undertook that role which was fulfilled in our country by the SRs

[Social Revolutionary Party] when they were still a revolutionary party.... The party actually tore itself away from its class.... The causes and grounds for conflicts between the army, which is peasant in composition and petty bourgeois in leadership, and the workers not only are not eliminated but, on the contrary, all the circumstances are such as to greatly increase the possibility and even the inevitability of such conflicts.... Consequently our task consists not only in preventing the political-military command over the proletariat by the petty-bourgeois democracy that leans upon the armed peasant, but in preparing and ensuring the proletarian leadership of the peasant movement, its "Red armies" in particular'.[1]

When the CCP was obliged to flee from the South to the North, to Yan'an, the number of its worker members dropped still further because the conditions there were still more primitive. The only possible recruitment of worker elements came from village artisans. Consequently the petty-bourgeois peasant atmosphere enveloped the entire party and was formally crystallised in the 'theory of the revolutionary peasantry'....

The CCP, by supporting the Guomindang's leadership, not only insisted on class collaboration in its propaganda but showed openly in its practice that 'the workers should increase production to aid the government in the common resistance against Japan'. It rejected the 'exorbitant demands' presented by the workers to the national bourgeoisie, charging that the Trotskyist policy of class struggle was a 'policy of betrayal to aid the enemy', thus slandering the Trotskyists as 'traitors'. Naturally, in the workers' real struggles the CCP was always on the side of the national bourgeoisie and against the workers' reasonable demands, even sabotaging these struggles.

At the same time, the CCP did everything possible to encourage the most active elements of the working class to leave the struggle in the cities and join the peasants in the countryside. It was for precisely this reason that while the CCP considerably increased its armed peasant forces during the Resistance War, its influence remained extremely weak among the worker masses of the cities.

After the Anti-Japanese War it is true that the CCP once again joined the workers' movement in the cities, recruiting cadres among the workers and building an organisation. But its main aim was to obtain the workers' support to pressure Chiang Kai-shek into accepting the CCP's compromise with him in a 'coalition government'. So in that period the CCP's policy towards the workers was always to lead the mass of the workers into a compromise with the

---

1 Trotsky, in a letter to the Chinese Left Opposition and postscript to this letter, 22 and 26 September 1932.

national bourgeoisie, hoping through the national bourgeoisie to put pressure on Chiang Kai-shek to successfully conclude its negotiations with him. As a result, the CCP's influence among the workers was very feeble.

Finally, when the CCP was obliged to carry on a general counteroffensive against the Chiang government and to occupy the big cities, not only did it not make any appeal to the mass of the workers to carry on some form of struggle, but it did its best to curb their activities. Its only appeal was to call upon them to 'protect production and watch Chiang Kai-shek's bandits who are sabotaging it'. When the CCP occupied the cities it imposed severe restrictions on all activity or spontaneous organisation of the working class.

When the workers went on strike to demand wage increases or to resist oppressive conditions, it was brutal in its repressions, going to the point of massacres. For example, the strikers in several factories in Tianjin were arrested and executed. The workers of Shenxin Factory No. 9 (which employed 8,000 workers) were attacked with machine guns because they refused to leave the city with the factory; there were more than 300 casualties. At coal mines in Hebei Province, when the workers revolted against the cruelty and arrogance of the Soviet advisers and specialists, the CCP sent a large number of troops to suppress the revolt. There were more than 200 dead or wounded workers and more than a thousand were expelled and exiled to Manchuria or Siberia (this happened in May 1950).

All of this demonstrates this petty-bourgeois party's attitude towards the working class, an attitude of distrust, hostility, and even murderous rage. That partially confirms the prediction and the warning made by Trotsky nineteen years ago. If the worker masses of the cities had been more united under the leadership of another revolutionary force (the Trotskyists), the CCP would probably have had recourse to civil war to beat the workers down. As Trotsky said, 'they will incite the armed peasants against the advanced workers'.

Whether Trotsky and the Chinese Trotskyists were right in their estimation of the nature of the CCP can be left to the re-examination of those comrades who have doubts on the matter. If the comrades have adequate facts and correct theoretical reasons to demonstrate that the estimation of the CCP made by Trotsky and the Chinese Trotskyists was incorrect, we are ready to abandon our estimation and adopt the new one.

The CCP, through its change in composition, gradually degenerated into a petty-bourgeois party based on the peasantry. It adopted as its ideology Mao Zedong's theory that 'the Chinese revolution is essentially a peasant revolution.... The politics of New Democracy means giving the peasants their rights'. But because of its historical origin as a section of the Communist International, because of some working-class traditions remaining from the second revolution, because of its close relations with the international Stalinist party (which, although degenerate, remains a workers' party), and because of its general support for Marxism-Leninism, the dictatorship of the proletariat and the perspective of communism, and so on, we must admit that even after it had degenerated into a peasant party there remained a certain inclination in it towards the workers. But this tendency was curbed and repressed during the long years of peasant guerrilla war.

When this party entered the cities and came into contact with the mass of the workers, and especially when it needed working-class support to resist the threats of the bourgeoisie and imperialism, the worker tendency, long hidden and repressed, had the opportunity to emerge and to place some pressure on the leadership of the party. It demanded the transfer of the party's base from the peasantry to the working class and called for certain concessions to the demands of the worker masses. The events of the last two years, and particularly of the last six months, have clearly reflected this tendency.

The CCP decided to stop the recruitment of peasants into the party and emphasised the need for rapid recruitment of workers. The *People's Daily* editorial of 1 July 1950, stressed a reform in party composition, that is, the absorption of workers into the party. It said that in the recent period, among the 6,648 new members in Tianjin, 73 per cent were workers, and out of 3,350 in Beijing, more than 50 per cent were workers.

So a considerable number of workers have been recruited by the CCP in the last two years in the large industrial cities and in the mines in the Northeast, in Shanghai, and in Wuhan. Of course, if consideration is given to the composition of the entire party (according to the same editorial in the *People's Daily*, there are some 5 million members in the party), the number of workers is still very small. (Gao Gang, secretary for the Northeast Region, admitted in a 10 January speech to party heads that 'working-class elements are still not very numerous in our party'. This was given as the principal reason for the emergence of a right-wing tendency in the party and widespread party corruption.)

But the CCP's turn towards insisting on working-class recruitment in order to change its composition has unquestionably had an important effect on the class nature of the Party.

This turn is more or less reflected in the process of agrarian reform. According to the plan for agrarian reform adopted by the Political Consultative Conference of the CCP and other organisations and parties in May 1950, special emphasis is placed on 'the protection of the commercial and industrial property of the landlords and the rich peasants'. The decree of the minister of the interior severely prohibits 'excessive actions' by the poor peasants against the landed proprietors and rich peasants. When this project was first implemented, not only were the industrial and commercial properties of the landlords and the rich peasants generally protected, but in numerous areas they obtained the best and the largest share of the land, and even preserved local power (such as head of the Peasants' Association or of the village, and so on). But then, when the masses of the poor peasantry gradually awakened in the course of the movement, the lower cadres, under the demands and pressure of the poor peasants, considerably altered the agrarian reform project and even upset it. That is to say, a great number of industrial and commercial properties of the landlords and rich peasants were subjected to severe penalties by the poor peasantry. (Recent reports on the agrarian reform in Chinese newspapers reveal these facts.)

In face of the 'left' tendency of lower cadres to upset the party's guidelines and defend the interests of the masses, the CCP leadership not only has not retaliated for these expropriations but on the contrary has generally acquiesced in them. Although the CCP has not fundamentally changed its policy of protecting the industrial and commercial properties of the landlords and rich peasants, there is nevertheless a tendency to defend the interests of the poor peasants, which manifests itself strongly among lower cadres and in the party ranks. This is particularly worthy of our attention.

In the campaign of recent months against corruption, waste, and bureaucratism, an anti-bourgeois, working-class tendency is clearly revealed in the CCP ranks. The main reason for this campaign is corruption, waste, and bureaucracy among CCP officials in the state apparatus, the army, and mass organisations, and in particular in the industrial and commercial sector.

These cadres fatten themselves by pilfering state funds under their control and wasting public funds. They also associate with bourgeois elements 'to sell commercial information, state resources, and raw materials, cut the working force and raise production costs in order to profit the capitalists. The capitalists do not hesitate to provide the necessary sums to corrupt these corrupted elements' (see Gao Gang's report).

This has caused enormous financial and economic loss to the state and aroused mass discontent, especially among workers in the party. (See Comrade Fang Xing's report on this campaign.)

So the CCP leadership is obliged to organise this campaign to expel rotten cadres and attack bourgeois elements as a means of appeasing discontent in the party ranks and among the workers.

The corruption and degeneration at various levels of the CCP is due primarily to the opportunist policy of class collaboration and bureaucratic practices that violate workers' democracy. This campaign against corruption, waste, and bureaucratism does not fundamentally alter the CCP's opportunism and bureaucratism; it is carried out by bureaucratic methods. The tendency towards corruption will not be eliminated in this way. Nevertheless, the anti-bourgeois, working-class tendency within the CCP is strengthened by this campaign.

The CCP leadership talks about 'the need to recognise the corrosive influence of bourgeois ideology on the party and the harm caused by the right-wing tendency in the party'. They say that 'to base oneself on the bourgeoisie means abandoning the working class, the popular masses, and the role of the party and the country' (see Gao Gang's report). In fact, they have more or less accepted the demands of the working masses.

They now publish descriptions of the oppression and exploitation of workers in state enterprises in recent years by CCP cadres, as well as 'violations' involving exploitation and oppression by private capitalists. Such things were rarely mentioned in the past.

Although peasants and other petty-bourgeois elements still predominate in the CCP (more than 90 per cent of the 5 million members), the worker elements have increased in the last two years. The working-class tendency has been strengthened during agrarian reform and the campaign against corruption. That is why up to now the CCP has had a dual character. From the point of view of its composition, given the acceleration in the recruitment of workers and the halting of peasant recruitment, it is in transition towards a workers' party.

From the point of view of ideology, the right wing in the CCP represents the upper strata of the petty bourgeoisie of the cities and the rich peasants; the left wing represents the workers and the poor peasants; and the centrists represent the top leadership. These three tendencies, in particular the right and left, have not yet crystallised, but ... when the international and national situation reaches a serious, decisive stage, the party will inevitably split. ... But at present it is moving in the direction of a deformed dictatorship of the proletariat.

10 May 1952

Thinking in Solitude (1957)

Wang Fanxi

Source: Memoirs of a Chinese Revolutionary (1957). *This chapter, omitted from the 1980 Oxford University Press edition, was reinstated in 1991 by Columbia University Press.*

At the time of writing these lines, in July 1957, I am fifty years old. For the past eight years I have been living on a tiny island off the south China coast [Macao], with more than a little time to think. To earn my living I have had to devote much of my energy to writing plays, but this has in no way changed my basic calling. I have remained a revolutionary, keeping a close watch on the changes that have taken place in the world at large and particularly in China. Since December 1952, when my comrades inside China were rounded up by the CCP's secret police, I have no longer been able to play an active part in political life, but this has not prevented me from thinking. In absolute isolation and solitude a person's thinking usually gains in intensity, and so it was with me. The pity is that so much of my time has been taken up with the problem of earning a bare living that up to now I have never had the chance to record all my thoughts over these last few years.

Although I have no intention in what is essentially a book of memoirs of making a detailed examination of the recent development of my thinking, still a short account of some of the problems I have engaged will not be altogether out of place here, particularly since thinking has been more or less my sole political activity in recent times. In an epoch such as ours, however few people may actually share my positions, there must be many addressing similar questions and searching just as anxiously for answers. To such people, I hope my opinions will be of some value.

My thinking over the last few years has focused mainly on two questions. Why, if in terms of overall strategy the Chinese Stalinists were wrong and the Chinese Trotskyists were right, did they end up victorious and we in defeat? And what are the main lessons for the world socialist movement of their victory and our failure?

'Ah-Q-ism'[1] is a harmful affliction, particularly in a revolutionary, but revolutionaries are particularly prey to it, for the very qualities that mark them out – perseverance, tenacity, and an unbounded confidence in one's cause –

---

1   Ah-Q is the antihero of Lu Xun's *The True Story of Ah-Q*. The usual meaning of Ah-Q-ism is to seek consolation by fantasising defeat into victory.

often prevent them from recognising their own defeats and admitting their enemies' successes. It is hard, of course, to draw a clear distinction between self-confidence of this sort and revolutionary firmness, for the one is an essential ingredient of the other. But carried to excess, what may originally have been a virtue ends up as 'Ah-Q-ism' of the worst sort. To defend one's beliefs blindly and to dress up others' victories as defeats and our defeats as victories is positively harmful to the revolution. A fact remains a fact whether or not we recognise it as one. People who deliberately close their eyes to reality sooner or later end up bumping their heads against it, whereupon they usually surrender unconditionally to the very facts that only yesterday they so stubbornly denied.

True revolutionary confidence comes only on the basis of a cool assessment of how things really are. To recognise defeat is not at all the same as to surrender to the enemy: there is no reason why it should automatically lead to demoralisation. In all social struggles – particularly the bitter and complex struggles of modern class society – victories and defeats invariably alternate, so the path to socialism is never straight but zigzag and uneven. Those who travel it must be able to draw the lessons of the defeats through which it inevitably passes.

'What is known as calamity is often good fortune in disguise. What is called good fortune is often a cause of calamity'. This is Mao Zedong's favourite quotation from the ancient Chinese philosopher Laozi [Lao Tzu]; he often took heart from it in his darkest hours. Perhaps we too can profit from an examination of the 'good fortune' of the Chinese Stalinists and the 'calamity' of the Chinese Trotskyists in the light of Laozi's teaching. But good fortune is only bestowed on those capable of grasping reality. Here Laozi reminds us of Spinoza's 'not to laugh, not to cry, but to understand', advice we would do well to bear in mind in attempting any such assessment.

As I said earlier, the Chinese Trotskyist movement entered a period of intellectual ferment in late 1949 and early 1950. Shaken to the core by the unexpectedness of what had happened (for none of us had ever reckoned with the possibility of a CCP victory), we began in the light of the new situation to reconsider our fundamental positions and beliefs. In this atmosphere of intense turmoil and in the heat of events, I made my own attempt to come to grips with the causes of the CCP victory, and noted some of my conclusions in a booklet published in early 1950.[2] In it I said that the Soviet Union had turned into a bureaucratic collectivist state, and the Stalinist party into a party of collectivist bureaucrats. From this I concluded that the victory of the CCP was

---

2 Yi De 1950.

merely the victory of a collectivist bureaucratic party and in no way the victory of a Chinese proletarian party, that is, of proletarian revolution.

This analysis seemed to me to explain many features of the Stalinist parties and to solve the riddle of the CCP victory. Gradually, however, I discovered that for all its advantages and its theoretical consistency, once applied to revolutionary practice (such as which side to take in the civil war between the CCP and the Guomindang) it proved to be wholly inappropriate and plainly wrong. Armed with this discovery, I returned again from the realm of politics to sociology and from practicalities to theoretical research, and eventually I arrived at the conclusion that among the numerous theoretical analyses of the Soviet Union and Stalinism advanced both inside and outside the Fourth International, Trotsky's was by far the strongest and in the best interests of socialist revolution. I had launched my soul onto unknown seas only to land again at the port where I had embarked. Some may mock me for this. Let them. All that matters to me is the search for truth, and for the key to the completion of the revolution.

To tell the whole story of how I travelled this ideological circuit, with its various periods and stages, would require more lines than I have room for here, and in any case I intend to devote a special study to this question.[3]

So I will confine myself here to a brief discussion of the class nature of the CCP and the historical role of Stalinist parties in general, for it was on these two questions that we Chinese Trotskyists developed a number of positions from which flowed our wrong analysis in and around 1949. Perhaps this discussion will serve as a warning example of how easy it is for revolutionaries to fall captive to their own prescriptions if they do not continually check them against events.

For many years up to and even after 1949 we Chinese Trotskyists had believed that the CCP represented the interests of the petty bourgeoisie (mainly peasants and intellectuals) and was no longer a party of the working class. None of us had ever considered why – we simply took it as self-evident. That the CCP had withdrawn from the big cities, lived in and drawn its forces from the countryside, and abandoned class struggle in favour of class peace was more than enough to confirm us in our opinion.

It is impossible to say who first advanced this analysis. In his report to the International Secretariat of the Fourth International in November 1951,

---

3 This study, titled *Sixiang wenti* ('Some ideological questions'), was mimeographed in 1962 and printed in Hong Kong in 1982. It comprises three articles: 'On Chen Duxiu's Opinions Expressed in His Last Years' (1957); 'On the Twentieth Anniversary of the Transitional Programme' (1958); and 'A Letter to Friends' (1958).

Peng Shuzhi tried to attribute it to Trotsky, arguing that 'beginning with 1930, Trotsky repeatedly pointed out that the CCP had gradually degenerated from a workers' party into a peasant party'.[4] But this assertion is quite groundless. In the letter to the Chinese Left Opposition that Peng quotes ('Peasant War in China and the Proletariat'), Trotsky never once argued that the CCP had 'gradually degenerated from a workers' party into a peasant party'. Instead he simply talked about the possible outcome of the struggle between the two factions of the CCP, that is, if a civil war were to break out between a peasant army led by Stalinists and a proletarian vanguard led by Leninists 'the Left Opposition and the Stalinists would have ceased to be communist factions and would have become hostile parties, each with a different class basis'. But he went straight on from this theoretical hypothesis to ask if such a perspective was inevitable. His answer was unequivocal: 'No, I don't think so at all. Within the Stalinist faction (the official Chinese Communist Party) there are not only peasant, that is, petty bourgeois tendencies, but also proletarian tendencies'.[5]

Trotsky's letter was written on 22 September 1932, nearly a whole year before he decided to call for new communist parties and a new International. So at a time when we still considered ourselves a faction of the CCP, Trotsky was allegedly arguing that this same CCP had degenerated from a workers' into a peasants' party!

It was precisely our wrong understanding of the class nature of the CCP that to a large extent determined our positions on it – in particular the significance of its eventual victory over the Guomindang – both before and after 1949. Having once established that it was a petty bourgeois party, we were logically driven to conclude that it could never lead a genuine revolution, still less lead to victory: for it is a fundamental theorem of Marxism (and of Trotsky's theory of permanent revolution in particular) that in the modern age and in a backward country even the bourgeois-democratic tasks of the revolution can only be solved by a thoroughgoing revolution led by the proletariat and its party. Even during the civil war between the CCP and the Guomindang from 1946 to 1949 we invariably argued that a peasant army led by a petty bourgeois party was almost bound to lose, and that even if by some remote chance it won, it would inevitably end up in a blind alley. When facts proved otherwise and the revolution led by the CCP not only triumphed but deepened, we remained tightly bound by our old preconceptions. Instead of promptly recognising the revolution for what it was, we continued to cling to our old assessment and to look for theoretical supports to bridge the growing gap between what had

---

4 P'eng Shu-tse 1980b, p. 108.
5 P'eng Shu-tse 1980a, p. 530.

really happened and what we thought had happened. We now argued not only that the CCP was no longer a proletarian party but that it was not even a petty bourgeois party; instead, it represented the interests of an entirely new class – a class Zheng Chaolin called state capitalist and I called bureaucratic collectivist. We believed that such classes were the product of a whole series of defeats of the revolution on a world scale and of the overgrowth of the capitalist system, so they were powerful but reactionary. Unlike the petty bourgeoisie, they were strong enough to overthrow the old bourgeois régimes – in China, the Guomindang – and to turn society on its head. But unlike the proletariat, they were incapable of moving onward in the direction of socialism, and would at best establish a régime of state capitalism or bureaucratic collectivism.

In this way, Zheng Chaolin and I built further on our old assessment of the CCP.

Peng Shuzhi and a number of his followers responded to the situation in a different way, clinging to the same old formula and flatly denying that China had had a revolution. For two years, right up to November 1951, Peng argued that the new régime was 'actually a naked Bonapartist military dictatorship of the petty bourgeoisie and bourgeoisie, based on the armed peasantry', and that 'such a military dictatorship will never change its bourgeois character'.[6] In May 1952, however, he suddenly discovered that it had lost its bourgeois character and acquired a 'dual character' because 'the worker elements have increased in number in the last two years ... (during the agrarian reform and the campaign against corruption)'.[7] However, he continued to insist that the party up to then had been a party of peasants, and that its earlier seizure of power had been not a revolution but an accident resulting from a conjuncture of exceptional historical circumstances.

Like Zheng Chaolin and me, Peng was unable to wrench himself free from the old formula, but unlike us he continues to insist to this day that we Chinese Trotskyists were absolutely right to apply it to the theory and practice of the Chinese revolution at each stage in its development. I am not concerned here with whether Peng's claim to infallibility is valid, and will return to it in a future study.[8]

---

6   Quoted from 'The Political Resolution', written by Peng on 17 January 1950, and adopted at a meeting of Peng's group in Hong Kong. In his report to the Third Congress of the Fourth International, Peng formulated the same idea in a slightly different form. See P'eng Shu-tse 1980b, p. 110.
7   This volume, p. 966.
8   Wang Fanxi 1973.

I said earlier that we had based our assessment of the CCP on the observation that it had (a) withdrawn from the cities into the countryside and recruited its forces almost exclusively from the peasantry rather than the working class and (b) capitulated in 1937 to the Guomindang in the name of unity against Japan, by declaring its conversion to Sun Yat-senism, accepting the reorganisation of its armed forces into the armed forces of the Guomindang, and promising to give up class struggle. On the face of it, this was decisive enough proof of the charges we were making: a party that had torn itself away from the working class, left the main battleground, and given up its revolutionary platform could no longer be called working class.

So when we first declared in the mid-1930s that the CCP had degenerated into a party of the petty bourgeoisie, we were acting on entirely reasonable assumptions. Where we went wrong was in failing to check our assessment against reality, and in closing our eyes to developments that might falsify our analysis. Looking back, I can now see we ignored four key facts. First, the CCP withdrawal from the cities was neither voluntary nor deliberate, but mainly the result of Guomindang persecution and repression, so it could not be taken as proof that the CCP had committed itself to a new strategic orientation to peasant war rather than proletarian revolution. Second, after withdrawing into the countryside the CCP did not forsake, in either words or deeds, the platform of 'a revolutionary united front under the leadership of the proletariat'. Third, while it is true that the CCP abandoned class struggle during the second united front, that is, it called off land revolution and submitted to the leadership of Chiang Kai-shek in a decisive turn that we rightly denounced at the time as a final capitulation, by and large the turn was at the level of tactical manoeuvre rather than of strategy and was never carried to its logical conclusion, the main reason being that there were still revolutionary tendencies in the CCP that opposed Stalin's policy of capitulation. Fourth, during both the 'soviet and Red Army' period and the 'united front and Eighth Route Army' period, the CCP all along remained an organisation of highly disciplined revolutionaries and carried out its recruitment (both political and military) on a class basis. If we Chinese Trotskyists had kept a closer eye on these developments and constantly checked our assessment of the CCP against them, we would have understood the true meaning of the victory of the CCP and would have made fewer mistakes in developing our own work and ideas. Lenin once said something of relevance in this connection. Discussing the problem of British Communists joining the Labour Party, he said: 'Of course, most of the Labour Party's members are working men. However, whether or not a party is really a political Party of workers does not depend solely upon a membership of workers but also upon the men that lead it, and the content of its actions and its political tactics. Only this latter determines whether we really have before us a political party of the proletariat. Regarded from this, the only correct, point of view, the Labour Party is a thoroughly bourgeois party...'.[9]

Following Lenin's method, we Chinese Trotskyists should have paid more attention to the 'men [and women] that led' the CCP. We should have kept a close eye on the struggle between the various tendencies (particularly the Maoists and the Wang Mingites) in its leadership and tirelessly analysed the 'content of its actions and political tactics'. But instead we put too much emphasis on its social composition, which was overwhelmingly peasant, and so concluded that it was a petty bourgeois party; which later led me to adopt the theory of bureaucratic collectivism. So we were unable to foresee a great many of the developments in the Third Chinese Revolution or to understand them even after they had happened. Had we followed Lenin's method, we would early on have developed a different view of the CCP. We would have admitted that in spite of its massive bureaucratic degeneration and its oppressive internal régime, its overwhelmingly peasant composition, its unprincipled manoeuvres, and its distortions of Marxism, it was still a working class party of sorts, though it was more so in some periods than in others and it acquired a number of grotesque and repellent features.

It is precisely because we failed to follow this procedure that we fell so wide of the mark in our criticism of the CCP in the 1940s and immediately after the establishment of the new régime.

The extreme confusion sown in the ranks of the Trotskyist movement in both China and the world by the victory of the CCP in 1949 was due not only to our wrong analysis of the class nature of that party but also to one crucial mistake in our view of the historical role of Stalinism in general.

Ever since the task of creating a new International was first broached in 1933, we had analysed the Third International as historically spent and no longer capable of playing the role of headquarters of the world revolution. The parties affiliated to it, organisationally and ideologically rotted by the Stalin canker, could no longer be renovated or revitalised into revolutionary parties. They never led a revolution to victory, and they would go out of their way to sabotage, betray, and suppress any revolutionary upsurge not under their direct control. However incredible it might seem, they not only could not but would not take victory for themselves, for any victorious revolution outside the USSR would in the long run weaken and destroy Moscow's bureaucratic control over its 'vassals and dependencies' in the Third International.

---

9   Lenin 1960–72 [1920b], p. 257.

This analysis is fundamentally sound and was in the main borne out by a number of events of world importance between 1934 and 1945. However, in our exaggerated and mechanical interpretation of it, the view that Stalinist parties will refuse to make revolution even if to do so puts the helm of state into their hands developed into a sheer prejudice, and explains our utter confusion in the face of the CCP victory in 1949.

This is not the place for a detailed account of the overall evolution of Trotskyism on a world scale – how it grew from a faction of the Communist Party into an independent organisation, and how it broke from the Third International and launched the Fourth. Suffice it to say that in the summer and autumn of 1933, after Stalin's 'Third Period' policy had paved the way for Hitler's triumph in Germany and the whole of the Third International had supported his positions, Trotsky's decision to call for new communist parties and a new International was just as necessary and had the same historic significance as Lenin's call for a new (Third) International in 1914, when the parties of the Second International came out in support of their respective ruling classes in the imperialist war.

In making the analogy, however, we should note that the history of the past twenty years has shown that the actions of the Third International (which we declared dead in 1933) have differed in significant ways from those of the Second International after 1914. There are a number of fundamental differences between the parties of Stalinism and of social democracy. Even today the former are actually still not reconcilable with capitalism, for they fight to maintain and consolidate state property in the Soviet Union and at the same time work for the creation of a similar system in the capitalist countries. To judge by what they say and write, they are scarcely distinguishable from classical Menshevism, but whereas classical Menshevism is a position of principle and strategy, 'Menshevism' of the Stalinist variety has (at least since 1930) been little more than a series of tactical measures, a smokescreen behind which to carry out political manoeuvres. We Trotskyists have never taken this difference seriously, so we have tended to overlook or underestimate the anti-capitalist aspect of Stalinist parties and have been taken unawares by at least three important developments over the past ten years: first, instead of reverting to capitalism (as we had predicted), the system of state property in the Soviet Union emerged from the Second World War stronger than ever; second, the economic and political system of the Soviet Union was exported (at bayonet point) to Eastern Europe; third, the Chinese Communist Party defeated the Guomindang and began to reconstruct the Chinese economy on the model of the Soviet Union.

So we must admit that we have underestimated the anti-capitalist potential of these parties, which even now is still not entirely exhausted. What then of Trotsky's decision to establish a new International?

Judged from the point of view of the long-term interests of world socialist revolution, we were right to argue that the Third International no longer had any positive role to play, that its thinking, politics, and organisation had degenerated to the point where it would never again complete a revolution like the one in Russia or establish a workers' government like in the early days of the Soviet Union. The path of internal reform had been blocked: a new revolutionary International had become necessary.

This was the only conceivable solution to the problems posed by historical circumstance, and we must continue to defend it now and in the future as stubbornly as we ever did in the past.

But the way in which we understood and interpreted the 1933 decision must be judged separately. Our contention that the Stalinist parties would do no more than serve the Kremlin directly and the world bourgeoisie indirectly, squander the fruits of revolution (especially state-owned property) in the Soviet Union, and betray or crush revolutions that might break out elsewhere in the world even where this would place state power in their hands was demonstrably wrong.

Perhaps one or two of these views can be ascribed to Trotsky, but most of them are mechanistic derivatives from or even caricatures of Trotsky's original positions. Here I am not interested in who authored these mistakes. What does concern me is that over the last twenty years or more, precisely these views have decided our attitude as Trotskyists towards Stalinism throughout the world; and we Chinese Trotskyists were at the very least among their most stubborn proponents.

This is why, even after the CCP's stunning victories around Xuzhou and Bengbu in late 1948, Trotskyists like Liu Jialiang argued that the Chinese Stalinists would never inflict a nationwide defeat on the Guomindang; why, even after the fall of Guangzhou in the autumn of 1949, they declared that the CCP would decline to reap the fruit of victory; and why, even after the new régime had been established in Beijing and land revolution had been extended throughout China, they asserted that the CCP was not only unable but unwilling to retain state power, and that agrarian reform would (for some unspecified reason) stop at the northern bank of the Yangtze.[10]

---

10   Liu Jialiang 1949.

But if we renounce such seemingly essential parts of our analysis of Stalinism, how can we continue to argue that the 1933 decision to create a new International was and remains correct and necessary? Should we not admit that since the analysis upon which this decision was based has been undermined, the International should disband and surrender to the Stalinists?

No few Chinese Trotskyists have done so, including veterans like Li Ji and Liu Renjing. A few surrendered under pressure, but most did so from conviction. Before they finally went over to the CCP in the early 1950s I had a chance to discuss this with a number of them, either face to face or through letters. My arguments can be more or less reduced to the following two points.

First, while it is true that Stalinist parties are far less easily reconciled to capitalism than are the social democratic parties, there is still no reason to believe they can adopt a strategy and tactics of the sort necessary for socialist revolution.

Second, even if Stalinist parties can under certain circumstances fight capitalism and carry out a revolution, we should not neglect the equally fundamental question of how they do so, and what sort of régimes they form. As the newly established Stalinist states multiply, this aspect of the problem will increasingly eclipse the other in importance.

Revolutions cannot be made to order and along a predetermined path, but we should still recognise that goal and means are interdependent and that means to no small extent determine goals. The difference between one means and another can amount to hundreds of thousands of human lives, so the choice between them is crucially important and deserves our closest consideration. Moreover, bureaucratic rule will never create a truly socialist society. In the absence (however unlikely) of a successful anti-bureaucratic upsurge by the workers, bureaucratic rule, with its inevitable inter-state wars and conflicts, will spell the collapse into barbarism of human society as a whole.

Needless to say, I did not succeed in convincing my old friends or in preventing them from going over (some from Hong Kong) to the new régime in China. To their great misfortune and disappointment, the authorities doubted the sincerity of their conversion, so few of them got jobs and some were even arrested and cast into jail. In the light of their own experience and of recent developments in the Soviet Union, Poland, and Hungary, most must now realise that their decision to surrender to the Stalinists was wrong.

The Yugoslavian experience, Khrushchev's exposure of Stalin's crimes at the Twentieth Congress of the CPSU, and the tragic events in Poland and Hungary have posed in all its immediacy the problem of how to establish and maintain genuine workers' power.

In his famous speech of 7 December 1956, E. Kardelj, Vice-President of the Federal People's Assembly of Yugoslavia, said: 'It should be noted that since the progressive socialist forces have thus far lacked experience in combating bureaucratism, to induce a form of true democracy from experience is out of the question. Before the Twentieth Congress of the CPSU only the Yugoslavian party had ever seriously searched for and eventually found a series of political measures to resolve the contradictions of the period of transition and established institutions of mass self-management in various areas of social activity, thereby enabling our society to get rid of those political forms and measures used by bureaucratic elements in their attempt to reduce the whole of society to stagnation'.[11]

Kardelj rightly emphasised the importance of combating bureaucratism (though it is another question whether Yugoslavia itself has succeeded in doing so). But he forgot to say that Trotskyism was born from precisely such a struggle and has accumulated valuable experience from the fight for a 'form of true democracy'. For although the Fourth International has so far achieved little of real significance in practical politics, it has contributed richly to theoretical research into the problems of the transition to socialism, in which sense it represents the pinnacle of contemporary Marxism.

Recent experience in the Soviet Union and Eastern Europe shows that there has been no serious or successful attempt to resolve the problems of bureaucratic rule, although the struggles that have broken out there have in general been against bureaucracy. This suggests that without the programme advocated over the years by the Fourth International, the efforts of those currently raising a hue and cry against bureaucratism will surely fail. But although such people have still not broken in practice with Stalinism, what they say is still encouraging. It proves that we Trotskyists have not been fighting in vain over the last thirty years, that our ranks will swell, and that Stalinist domination of the world communist movement is coming to an end. In coming years whether we actually achieve anything will depend in part on how far we succeed in integrating our programme and membership with the anti-bureaucratic mass movement in countries under communist rule. But we must never forget to check our positions in the light of events, to hold firm to those that are right, and to right or discard those that are wrong. A Fourth International full of life and energy is more necessary now than it ever was, and must be strengthened and expanded. We have no reason to be pessimistic, still less to desert our organisation.

---

11   This quotation is retranslated from the Chinese.

We first launched the campaign for a new International in 1933, mainly because of our political appraisal of Stalinism but also because of the internal structure of Stalinist parties, which brook no opposition. Now, however, we have begun to notice for the first time (beyond the isolated example of Yugoslavia) that a general process of differentiation is taking place within the Stalinist parties and the countries under their rule, so there is a slight prospect of some degree of internal reform. Should we change our attitude towards them accordingly? Should the world Trotskyist movement return to its old pre-1933 position, which looked to reform existing communist parties rather than set up new ones? I think not. The events in Hungary in 1956 showed how stubbornly those in power in the party and the state will fight to defend themselves and that they will not make the slightest concessions except under the direct revolutionary pressure of the mass movement. So we should continue to propagate unwaveringly the necessity of anti-bureaucratic political revolution in these countries. But at the same time we should avoid interpreting and applying this position mechanistically. The various communist parties and the states they control are no longer Stalinist to an identical degree, and conflicts and struggles are breaking out among them. We should not stand aside from these fights, like passive onlookers. Rather than indiscriminately attack each side with equal force, we should distinguish between them and tirelessly pay attention to the conflicts and struggles, no matter how small, that divide them; and we should give critical support to those that prove the more progressive. In so doing, our revolutionary attitude towards the faction or party concerned should be fairly flexible in its tactical application.

In sum, with our fundamental tenets unrevised, that is, sticking firmly to the position of preparing political revolution in all degenerated or deformed workers' states (whether Stalinist, semi-Stalinist, or 'de-Stalinised') by siding with the toiling people in their fight for democracy and against privilege, we should at the same time pay more attention to the specific application to different circumstances of our basically identical position. A right policy is not enough – it must be supplemented by elastic and flexible tactics.

Is the CCP a Stalinist party, to what extent has it been Stalinised, and what position does it occupy within Stalinism as a world system? Is Mao a Chinese Tito, or will he become one? What is the nature of the People's Republic of China and what stance should we adopt towards it?

These questions have haunted me in recent years, so I will briefly deal with them. I pointed out in an earlier chapter that it is clear from the history of the factional struggle in the CCP ever since the mid-1950s that Mao has never been a Stalinist in terms of faction. The Stalinists would never have recruited anyone as opinionated as Mao into their inner circle, and he is in any case by nature incapable of acting like a Wang Ming. I have never had the chance to work closely with Mao, but we have no few mutual friends, among them Xu Zhixing (Mao's childhood friend) and He Zishen (who worked closely with Mao for many years and has been in prison under him since 1952). From them I learned many things about Mao's character, his learning, and his way of thinking and working. Combining these indirect impressions with my own knowledge of Mao's life and writings, I conclude that as a man he has many traits in common with Chen Duxiu, the founding father of Chinese communism. Both had their first love of learning in Confucianism; both built their ideological foundations in the Chinese classics; both acquired their knowledge of modern European thought, in particular Marxism-Leninism, in the same way, by building a rough superstructure of foreign style on a solid Chinese foundation at a time when they were physically as well as intellectually fully matured. So both Chen and Mao take 'Chinese learning as substance, western learning for practical application' (to quote the words of the Qing dynasty reformer Zhang Zhidong). They can never become 'thoroughly Europeanised', nor will they ever cast aside that self-conceited pride peculiar to old-style Chinese scholars. I pointed out in an earlier chapter that Chen Duxiu had a poor opinion of foreign Communists, all the more so after Moscow had shamelessly heaped the whole of the blame for the defeat of 1927 on his shoulders. He always spoke with hatred and contempt of those Chinese Communists who kowtowed to foreign comrades, and dismissed them as 'red compradors'. Mao, being more diplomatic, substituted the word 'dogmatist' for 'comprador', but he looked down just as deeply on men like Wang Ming who could only quote from the works of Marx, Lenin, and Stalin and from resolutions of the Comintern. He Zishen once told me an interesting anecdote in this connection. While he and Mao were carrying out underground work for the Hunan Provincial Committee of the CCP in Changsha in the autumn of 1927, at a time when the revolution was in chaotic retreat and hundreds of communists were being sent to Moscow to study, Mao once said to him: 'I won't go to Moscow until the revolution triumphs'.

Even at that early date Stalin must have been aware of the recalcitrance of this leader of equal ambition, desperately struggling for survival in the faraway mountains of Jiangxi. That is why he unfalteringly placed his confidence in Wang Ming and finally planted him as leader of the CCP and the Red Army in 1931. But this 'red comprador' proved unequal to the job, so Mao and other 'indigenous' leaders squeezed his followers out of the leadership at the Zunyi conference in 1935. After that, Mao (in the words of Zheng Chaolin) was a 'Titoist before Tito'.

Mao has all along remained outside the clique transplanted into the CCP from Moscow, but that has not prevented him from being a staunch Stalinist, just as it has not prevented the CCP from becoming Stalinised and the People's Republic of China from being organised and constituted after an essentially Stalinist model. Historical and social factors are incomparably stronger than individual likes and dislikes in determining the character of states and institutions. The extreme backwardness of Chinese economy and society, the peasant environment in which the CCP was forced to live and grow, its protracted involvement in a predominantly military struggle, the ebb of the world revolution, the ever-deepening bureaucratic involution of the Soviet state between 1930 and 1945, and (last but not least) Mao's undemocratic disposition and training – all these factors combined to force the Chinese Communist Party and its leading figure onto the Stalinist road. In fundamental ideological terms Stalinism means the substitution of nationalism for internationalism, of tactical inter-class manoeuvres for class struggle, and of bureaucratic dictatorship for the democracy of the toiling people. In practical terms, it means that all initiatives from lower levels of party and government organisations are stifled, that everything is done according to instruction, that political and social life is dominated by a frantic personality cult and a hierarchy of privilege, that all forms of thinking are controlled by the secret police, that all oppositions are purged, that all factions and parties are forbidden, and so on ad nauseam – all these measures have already been copied from Stalin and the CPSU by Mao and the CCP.

I am told that some Marxists in the Fourth International believe that since the victory of the CCP was due mainly to its having broken successfully from Stalinism, or to its freedom from Stalinist influence and domination, the CCP can no longer be regarded as a Stalinist party. Such a view is one-sided and unsound. True, under the direct impact of class struggle the CCP, with Mao Zedong at its head, tactically violated Stalin's directives and at crucial junctures took an opposite path to that of Stalin by going all out to mobilise the masses, giving a bold leadership to their struggles, and finally achieving revolution. In that sense, although the CCP remained a fundamentally Stalinist party, one of the main reasons it triumphed was because it failed to follow the line of Stalinism.

So Maoism and Stalinism are not direct equivalents. The different conditions of time and space in which the Russian and Chinese revolutions occurred, the different cultural backgrounds and traditions of those who made them, and the different personal qualities of a Stalin and a Mao have led to important differences in both the outlook and the practice of the two men. The elements of identity and difference between them make an interesting and important subject for investigation, from both an historical and a political point of view, to which I shall return in a separate study.¹² But for my present purposes I must insist: checked off against my earlier list of the basic characteristics of Stalinism as a political force and a political system, the CCP is still fundamentally a Stalinist party and Maoism is still fundamentally a variant of Stalinism.

One question that is worth discussing is what will become of the CCP now that Stalin and Stalinism are coming under fire in the Soviet Union and Eastern Europe and the Stalinist camp is beginning to differentiate.

Immediately after the victory of the revolution in China many people were inclined to think that Stalinism in the CCP would be shaken off much earlier and much more easily than in other Stalinised parties, and that in some branches of the new-born state machine Stalinist methods of rule and institutions would never be systematically established. Later developments showed this view to be naive. Judging from its reaction to 'de-Stalinisation' in the CPSU and its hostile attitude to the Hungarian Revolution, the leadership of the CCP sticks faster to Stalinism than many of us thought. It has not actively facilitated the breakdown of Stalinism, and in some ways it has even turned out to be a bulwark of this obnoxious doctrine and its reactionary practice.

But this is hardly surprising, for the CCP set out to construct socialism from a socio-economic level lower even than that of the Soviet Union in the early 1920s and based its policies on the Stalinist principle of nationalist autarchy. So Stalinism will persist and even grow in China, at least in the short term. However, there is an important difference between now and when Stalinism first emerged and consolidated itself as a system. Then the curve of world revolutions was downward, now it is upward. What's more, even though the Chinese Revolution is artificially confined by its leaders to within strict national boundaries, it is impossible to prevent it from coming under the influence of revolutionary movements elsewhere in the world. The most obvious example was the tragicomic 'Hundred Flowers' campaign, unimaginable but for the Hungarian Revolution of 1956. It would be naive to think that campaign was in any way a real attempt to grapple with the actual problems of Stalinism, but even so there was a strong link between it and the events in Hungary.

The 'Hundred Flowers' campaign showed that most top-level intellectuals in China and many students and workers and practically the whole of the peasantry are deeply dissatisfied with the CCP's Stalinist régime. But their demands were ruthlessly suppressed during the subsequent 'anti-rightist' campaign, and those called upon by the party to speak out were mercilessly persecuted. The result of this act of treachery will be (as Mao Zedong himself said in another

---

12   San Yuan 1972 and Shuang Shan 1973 deal with this question in more detail.

context) to 'make such a mess of things that it can never be cleaned up'. If through the current anti-rightist campaign the CCP further strengthens the Stalinist system in all its aspects, the anti-Stalinist indignation of China's intellectual youth and of its workers and peasants will explode all the sooner and with all the more serious and wide-ranging consequences. Impelled by events both in China and in the world, a genuine and powerful left wing may come into being within the CCP, perhaps linking up with the forces of Chinese Trotskyism to channel all anti-Stalinist (that is, anti-Maoist) movements in the direction of a new anti-bureaucratic revolution. Such a revolution would aim to establish a real government of workers and peasants and to ally with the world proletariat to speed the advance to socialism.

I believe that history will show that such a prospect, far from being a mere pipedream, is entirely realistic.

PART 13

Chinese Trotskyism and Guerrilla Warfare

∴

The Real Lesson of China on Guerrilla Warfare: Reply to a 'Letter from a Chinese Trotskyist'

Chen Bilan

10 January 1971

Source: International Internal Discussion Bulletin, *vol. X, no. 2, February 1973. Published as a fraternal courtesy to the United Secretariat of the Fourth International by the* (US) *Socialist Workers Party.* HTML *Markup/Transcription/ Proofing: Andrew Pollack. Public Domain: Ch'en Pi-lan Internet Archive 2005.*

On reading 'Guerrilla Warfare: The Lesson of China',[1] I was surprised that the author did not put his name to it. Nonetheless I know that the author of the article was Wang [Fanxi], inasmuch as we received a copy of the original in Chinese. In order to help readers to understand better what the letter is about, I should like to say a few words about Wang.

He was the leader of a small group that split from the Communist League of China, the Chinese section of the Fourth International, early in 1942. Prior to the outbreak of the Japanese-American war in December 1941, Wang advanced the theory that if such a war were to occur, China would become involved in an inter-imperialist conflict and this would lead to a qualitative change in the character of the 'anti-Japanese war', so the Chinese national war of resistance against Japanese imperialism would lose its progressive nature. According to Wang's reasoning, this would require us to adopt a defeatist attitude towards the war of resistance conducted under the leadership of Chiang Kai-shek.

Peng Shuzhi argued against this, holding that the war of resistance against Japanese imperialism would retain its progressive character even if war broke out between Japan and the United States. So long as Japanese troops occupied China on a large scale it would be necessary to continue fighting Japanese imperialism in order to win freedom for China. Peng held that Wang's proposed defeatist policy would objectively serve the interests of Japanese imperialism.

At the national convention of the Communist League of China in August 1941, Wang's position was rejected and Peng's proposed resolution was adopted

---

1 [Wang Fanxi] 1970. The arguments in this letter are more fully expounded in Wang Fanxi 1973 (the following document), so Wang's letter is not reproduced here.

by an overwhelming majority. Wang, however, not only insisted on his defeatist position; he also violated the norms of democratic centralism by having his group (at that time consisting of only four members) publish an internal bulletin that continued to attack the resolution adopted by the convention. He followed this up by publishing a public journal that openly propagated a defeatist position. In this way the group led by Wang split from the Communist League of China shortly after hostilities opened between Japan and the United States. The split, as can be seen, took place not long after the Shachtmanite split from the Socialist Workers Party in 1940.

It is worth observing in addition that in June 1950 Wang published a pamphlet titled *The Soviet Union and Socialism* in which he argued for the theory of bureaucratic collectivism. Analysing the social layers and their relationship in the Soviet Union in detail, he held that the bureaucracy in the Soviet Union represented not a caste but a social class (he called it the 'collective bureaucratic class'), since it controlled all the means of production in the country and had succeeded in expropriating the workers and peasants. His conclusion in accordance with this was that the character of the state in the Soviet Union had to be defined not as a degenerated workers state but as a collective bureaucratic class state; that is, essentially a capitalist state. He proposed therefore that 'the old position held by the Fourth International on the degenerated workers state, which was based upon the nationalisation of property, should be abandoned'. And he called on the Fourth International to take the following stand: 'If a third world war cannot be prevented and breaks out, our position will be, of course, to take a defeatist attitude towards both sides. Defence of a bureaucratic collectivist Soviet Union is just as reactionary as defence of an imperialist United States' (*The Soviet Union and Socialism*, p. 70.) Wang's position on the Soviet Union, it is quite clear, reflected that held by Shachtman.

Confronted with the 1956 Hungarian revolution, Wang said that the new events could not be explained on the basis of his position on the Soviet Union. This position therefore had to be dropped. While he returned to Trotsky's position of defence of the Soviet Union, he maintained the correctness of his theory concerning the existence of social classes in the Soviet Union.

Finally, in my judgment, Wang was impressionistic. He often changed positions under the influence of passing events. Sometimes he shifted to the right, supporting opportunism, sometimes he shifted in favour of ultra-left adventurism. In the organisation he was an advocate of democracy to the n*th* degree, a stand that often led to splits.

Let me now turn to Wang's article, 'Guerrilla Warfare: The Lesson of China'.

According to Wang, 'Comrade Peng's opinions about guerrilla warfare are absurd'. This is a reference to the article by Peng, 'Return to the Road of Trotskyism', in the *International Information Bulletin*, no. 5, March 1969. Unfortunately, Wang did not specify what part of Peng's article was absurd. Wang claimed that Peng did not understand the lessons of the Chinese revolution or the experiences of the Chinese Trotskyists. Again unfortunately, he did not specify what lessons. Instead, he cited two paragraphs written by Trotsky.

The first one reads as follows:

> Of course, we shall not ourselves be engaged in the guerrilla war (against the Guomindang). We have another field of action, other tasks to perform. Yet we very earnestly hope that at least we should have our own men in some of the most powerful armed detachments of the Red Army. The Oppositionists should live and die together with these armed detachments. They should help maintain contact between the detachments and the peasants and should have the (guidance of the) organisation of the Left Opposition when carrying on this kind of work ('Letter to the Left Opposition of China', 8 January 1931.) (See *International Information Bulletin*, September 1970, p. 4.)[2]

Wang quoted only the latter part of the paragraph. The complete paragraph reads as follows:

> In some letters, complaints have been made about some groups or individual comrades taking a wrong position with regard to the Chinese 'Red Army' by likening its detachments to bandits. If that is true, then a stop must be put to it. Of course lumpenproletarian elements and professional bandits are joining the revolutionary peasant detachments. Yet the movement as a whole arises from wellsprings deep in the conditions of the Chinese village, and these are the same sources from which the dictatorship of the proletariat will have to nourish itself, later on. *The policy of the Stalinists towards these detachments is a policy of criminal bureaucratic adventurism. This policy must be mercilessly exposed.* We must not

---

2 The English translation from the original Russian reads somewhat differently from the above translation from the Chinese version: 'Naturally, we cannot throw our own forces into the partisan struggle – at present we have another field of endeavour and other tasks. Nevertheless, it is very desirable to have our people, Oppositionists, at least in the larger divisions of the "Red Army", to share the fate of these detachments, to observe attentively the relations between these detachments and the peasantry and to keep the Left Opposition informed'. The full text of the letter has been published by *Intercontinental Press* (6 November 1972, pp. 1217–20). – Translator.

share or encourage the illusions of the leaders and the participants of the partisan detachments. We must explain to them that without a proletarian revolution and the seizure of power by the workers the partisan detachments of the peasantry cannot lead the way to victory. [Emphasis added.] However, we must conduct this work of clarification as real friends, not detached onlookers and – especially – not as enemies. Without abandoning our own methods and tasks, we must persistently and courageously defend these detachments against the Guomindang repression and bourgeois slander and persecution. We must explain to the workers the enormous *symptomatic* [emphasis in original] significance of these detachments. *Naturally, we cannot throw our own forces into the partisan struggle – at present we have another field of endeavour and other tasks.* [Emphasis added.] Nevertheless, it is very desirable to have our people, Oppositionists, at least in the larger divisions of the 'Red Army', to share the fate of these detachments, to observe attentively the relations between these detachments and the peasantry and to keep the Left Opposition informed (Chinese edition of *Problems of the Chinese Revolution*, p. 285, 'A Letter to the Chinese Left Oppositionists' by Leon Trotsky, dated 8 January 1931.)

It is clear that Wang took a section out of context to suit his own purpose, thereby grossly distorting Trotsky's views. He presented a small excerpt, not Trotsky's fundamental views on the question of guerrilla warfare. Trotsky's basic position was: 'The policy of the Stalinists towards these detachments is a policy of criminal bureaucratic adventurism. This policy must be mercilessly exposed. We must not share or encourage the illusions of the leaders and the participants of the partisan detachments. We must explain to them that without a proletarian revolution and the seizure of power by the workers the partisan detachments of the peasantry cannot lead the way to victory.... Naturally, we cannot throw our own forces into the partisan struggle – at present we have another field of endeavour and other tasks'.

In this letter, Trotsky did not specify what our field of endeavour should be or name our tasks. However, he had covered these in other documents. In his article 'The Chinese Question After the Sixth Congress', he advanced the following programme of democratic demands for the period lying ahead; namely, the eight-hour working day; complete freedom of speech and of the press, and the right to strike; confiscation of the land; full national independence for China; a Constituent Assembly with full powers, elected by universal, equal, direct suffrage exercised through a secret ballot. Equipped with these slogans, the Left Oppositionists in China would be able to reorganise the workers and peasants in their fight against the military dictatorship of Chiang Kai-shek. These were the tasks we persisted in carrying out.

Wang does not grasp Trotsky's fundamental views concerning Stalin's adventurist policy. Nor does he grasp the import of the slogans that Trotsky worked out for the Chinese Left Oppositionists. He cites but a few sentences from Trotsky's paragraph and asserts that 'Trotsky repeatedly counselled his Chinese followers (circumstances permitting) to support and where possible participate in armed struggles against the Guomindang...'. If Wang's assertion were correct, how to explain Trotsky's insistence on attacking the 'policy of the Stalinists towards these detachments' as a 'policy of criminal bureaucratic adventurism' and his insistence that 'without a proletarian revolution and the seizure of power by the workers the partisan detachments of the peasantry cannot lead the way to victory'? And Trotsky's comment, 'Naturally, we cannot throw our own forces into the partisan struggle – at present we have another field of endeavour and other tasks'?

The truth is that Trotsky was in fundamental opposition to the policy of the Stalinist bureaucracy towards these detachments. He sought to replace that policy with a policy based on a programme of democratic demands. Numerous documents written by him in that period testify to this. Why then did he say: 'Nevertheless, it is very desirable to have our people, Oppositionists, at least in the larger divisions of the "Red Army", to share the fate of these detachments...'? Had the Left Opposition in China possessed a strong organisation with a large membership at that time, this 'hope' or opinion of Trotsky would have been acceptable to us. We could even have had our own people in the armies of the Guomindang carrying out revolutionary work, not to mention the Stalinist guerrilla forces which by their nature were anti-Guomindang and revolutionary minded. Unfortunately, we were too weak then.

I should point out that when Trotsky wrote his letter of 8 January 1931, the Left Oppositionists were split and had just begun unity negotiations. In that situation it was impossible to send people into the 'Red Army'. Within two weeks after the Left Oppositionists achieved unity in May 1931, a number of cadres were arrested by the Guomindang. Not long after that, another layer of cadres was arrested. These repeated arrests greatly depleted the newly unified Left Opposition.

After the Japanese invaded Manchuria on 18 September 1931, a great movement against Japanese imperialism swept China. The Left Oppositionists gained some strength then. But a year later, a bigger disaster struck us. On 15 October 1932, Chen Duxiu, Peng Shuzhi, and a number of other cadres were arrested. These arrests almost completely disrupted and paralysed the Left Opposition. The paralysis lasted five years until Chen, Peng, and other cadres were released from prison in August 1937. In the desperate situation we faced from 1931 to 1937 it was impossible to send people into the Stalinist 'Red Army'.

On the other hand, beginning in 1931 Chiang Kai-shek repeatedly sought to encircle and destroy the Stalinist 'Red Army'. It finally had to give up its guerrilla bastion in Jiangxi Province in central east China and start the 'long march' in 1934. By the time the 'Red Army' reached Yan'an in northwest China towards the end of 1935, it had lost over 90 per cent of its initial 300,000 men, and was still constantly under threat of being encircled and wiped out by Chiang Kai-shek's armies.

The Japanese imperialist armies then opened up fresh savage attacks in north China. Most of Chiang's forces deployed against Yan'an consisted of the 'Northeast Army' which had withdrawn from its home base in Manchuria after the Japanese occupied this area in 1931. These soldiers were very indignant at Chiang's policy of not resisting the Japanese – it had cost them the loss of their homeland, Manchuria. When Chiang went to the Xi'an base of the 'Northeast Army' to order an attack on the 'Red Army', a group of lower-ranking officers rebelled and forced their commander, Zhang Xueliang, to kidnap Chiang. Their idea was to execute him. This became known as the Xi'an Incident of December 1936.

Stalin exploited the kidnapping of Chiang in his own way. He ordered the Chinese Communist Party to make peace with Chiang so as to fight jointly against Japanese imperialism. The CCP sent Zhou Enlai to Xi'an to negotiate directly with Chiang. A deal was made: (1) The CCP guaranteed Chiang Kai-shek's safety if he agreed to lead the fight against the Japanese. (2) The CCP agreed to liquidate the 'soviets' and the 'Red Army' and to give up the agrarian revolution. This was the conclusion of the guerrilla warfare conducted by the CCP from 1928 to 1937. Trotsky referred to it as follows in the Transitional Programme:

> Following the inevitable collapse of the Guangzhou uprising, the Comintern took the road of guerrilla warfare and peasant soviets with complete passivity on the part of the industrial proletariat. Landing thus in a blind alley, the Comintern took advantage of the Sino-Japanese War to liquidate 'Soviet China' with a stroke of the pen, subordinating not only the peasant 'Red Army' but also the so-called 'Communist' Party to the identical Guomindang, that is, the bourgeoisie.

That is Trotsky's summary of the CCP's ten years of guerrilla warfare (1928–37). This is the real 'lesson of China'. But Wang did not mention this in his article.

Clearly he is either ignorant or is deliberately distorting the real lesson of guerrilla warfare in China.

The second paragraph Wang cited from Trotsky was: 'I said all workers' organisations in China should participate in the present war against the Japanese invasion. They should put themselves in the front lines. At the same time, they should not give up their programme and their independent activities'.[3]

According to Wang this advice was never followed: 'We did not participate in the anti-Japanese war, except by manifestoes and articles, although the conditions for such participation were excellent. For this false attitude towards armed struggle, Comrade Peng is not, of course, alone responsible. I, as one of the leading members of the organisation, bear a share of the responsibility, although I did once attempt to enter the armed struggle and Comrade Peng condemned it. However, it was Comrade Peng who insisted most stubbornly on the false line of the Chinese Trotskyists in the question of armed struggle. He has not examined his attitude in retrospect and still clings to it'.

Not only is Wang's condemnation of Peng false; his boast about himself is contrary to the facts. Because of this it is necessary to take it up in detail by going back to those times.

After the outbreak of the Sino-Japanese war in August 1937, three tendencies formed in the Communist League of China [CLC], the Chinese Trotskyist organisation.

The first tendency, represented by Peng, held a position that was adopted by the majority of the CLC. In the military field we supported the war against Japanese imperialism being waged under Chiang; but politically we remained independent, criticising Chiang's reactionary policy of passive resistance and continual repression of the popular movement against the Japanese.

The second tendency, represented by Chen Duxiu, was completely opportunistic. Chen supported the war against Japanese imperialism but in an uncritical way. He opposed publishing in our party press any criticism of the Chiang régime's reactionary policy towards the popular movement.

The third tendency, led by Zheng Chaolin, was ultra-leftist. Zheng considered the Sino-Japanese conflict to be a 'war between the Chiang government and the imperialist Hirohito'. Consequently he advocated a policy of defeatism.

---

3 The text of the letter was published by Pathfinder Press in *Writings of Leon Trotsky* (1937–8), p. 107. There the sentence in question reads: 'In my declaration to the bourgeois press, I said that the duty of all the workers' organisations of China was to participate actively and in the front lines of the present war against Japan, without abandoning, for a single moment, their own programme and independent activity'.

In addition to his uncritical support of Chiang's conduct of the war against Japan and his opposition to our criticising Chiang's political acrobatics, Chen Duxiu was firmly against rebuilding our political organisation and developing its programme. Following his release from prison in August 1937, he stated publicly that he no longer belonged to the Trotskyist organisation. He was ready to cooperate with a petty-bourgeois 'third party' in publishing a journal. Furthermore, through this group he made connections with a small Guomindang warlord, and was prepared to send Wang and others to do 'political work' in his army. This is the truth about what Wang claims to be his 'attempt to enter the armed struggle'. He and his group did not need a Trotskyist organisation and programme. They wanted only to send a few men into Chiang's army to do 'political work' and to 'propagate' uncritical support to Chiang's leadership. Was this not a military gamble? Although Chen and Wang and company did not succeed in carrying out their plan of taking a gamble in the military field, they did clearly reveal their opportunist tendency. It was this military opportunism that Peng harshly criticised.

After being criticised by Peng and in response to the pressure from the great majority of comrades, Wang moved a little closer to Peng's position. But just before the outbreak of the war in the Pacific between Japan and the United States, Wang started to move 'leftwards', finally landing in Zheng Chaolin's camp of ultra-leftist 'defeatism'. Here I should like to ask him a question. Since he supported Zheng's 'defeatism', how could he have participated in the 'armed struggle' against the Japanese under the banner of his defeatism; would he not have sought to defeat the war led by Chiang Kai-shek? Is this not a gross contradiction?

The position of the Communist League of China, which Peng represented, was on the one hand to support Chiang's anti-Japanese war militarily, while on the other hand to criticise his reactionary policy politically. The CLC called on 'all the workers' organisations in China to participate in the present war against the Japanese invasion'. This call was clearly stated in the political resolution passed at the emergency meeting of the CLC in November 1937. Yet Wang holds Peng responsible for the organisation's not actually participating in the anti-Japanese war 'except by manifestoes and articles'.

The fact is that the Chinese Trotskyist organisation fell into a state of complete paralysis after Chen and Peng and a number of other cadres were imprisoned in 1932. These comrades were not released until after the outbreak of the Sino-Japanese war in July 1937. After they were released, their most urgent and fundamental tasks were to restore the Trotskyist organisation, to re-establish a leadership, to design a programme for participating in the anti-Japanese war, to publish a party organ, to restore connections with local branches, and to re-establish our connections with the masses, and so on. In such a situation, where everything had to be started anew, how could we have had sufficient strength to send people to participate in 'armed struggle'?

In 1940, with the expansion of the organisation and the development of new opportunities, Peng consulted with a branch in Zhejiang Province about the possibility of their organising a peasant guerrilla force in the villages to participate in the anti-Japanese 'armed struggle'. Because of the limited number of cadres and the weakness of our relations with the peasants, it was not possible to organise the peasants on sufficient scale to begin armed struggle immediately. We had to prepare. It was just at that time that Wang announced his theory of a possible qualitative change occurring in the anti-Japanese war (August 1940). He proposed that as soon as the Japanese-American war broke out, we should adopt a policy of defeatism towards Chiang's anti-Japanese war. This touched off a stormy dispute and caused considerable confusion in the Chinese Trotskyist organisation. Under such circumstances we had to give up preparations for 'armed struggle'.

After the outbreak of the 'Japanese-American' war in December 1941, the Japanese army occupied Shanghai and the entire area of southeast China. Our party now suffered the heaviest blows of all. Connections with almost all the local branches were cut off. A number of cadres were arrested by the Japanese military police. A large number of our books and documents were confiscated. The minority group led by Wang split away. That was the difficult situation we faced in which Wang, in retrospect, now condemns Peng for not having sent comrades to participate in the armed struggle. This not only reveals Wang's complete blindness with regard to the difficult and even disastrous situation in which the Chinese Trotskyists found themselves, it also exposes his ill will towards a political opponent. Let me ask him again: Why didn't he and his 'defeatist' followers engage in an armed struggle to help defeat Chiang in the anti-Japanese war?

Wang said: 'The Chinese Trotskyists formally organised themselves into a unified political group in 1931. When the Chinese Communist Party seized power, [the Trotskyists] had existed as a political tendency, if not as a party, for twenty years. Yet they had carried out no significant action or any work of great significance. One could advance many reasons, whether real or imaginary, to explain this regrettable fact. The most important, or one of the most important, however, was our erroneous position towards armed struggles.... Hence we never thought of sending some of our comrades to work in the anti-Guomindang armed detachments.... We did not participate in the anti-Japanese war'.

I have pointed out above that from 1931 to 1945 the Chinese Trotskyist organisation was under double repression – from Chiang Kai-shek and from the Japanese imperialists. It had suffered severe damage. This fact alone is sufficient to expose the fallaciousness of Wang's reasoning and to show that he is either blind to the facts or is deliberately spinning tales to deceive comrades abroad.

I should point out one thing: If it is true that for twenty years the Chinese Trotskyists, because of various setbacks, 'had carried out no significant action', they did consistently uphold the concepts and tradition of Trotskyism and did take a correct stand on the Stalinist 'policy of criminal bureaucratic adventurism'. After the outbreak of the Sino-Japanese war they waged an uncompromising struggle against Chen Duxiu's rightist opportunism and Zheng Chaolin's ultra-leftist 'defeatism'. In particular in 1940, on the eve of the Japanese-American war, they conducted a serious struggle against Wang's defeatism as embodied in his theory of a qualitative change in the character of the anti-Japanese war, and his petty-bourgeois democratism that threatened to destroy democratic centralism in the party. The Chinese organisation consistently upheld Trotsky's correct position on the anti-Japanese war in China, the Second World War, and the class nature of the Soviet Union, as well as upholding the principle of democratic centralism. These were the contributions of the Chinese Trotskyists during that period, and we should always remain proud of them....

Wang spent a good part of his 'letter' dealing with the cause of the victory of the Chinese Communist Party in 1949. He charged Peng with inability to comprehend the cause of the CCP's victory. He claimed that the victory of the CCP resulted from guerrilla war and armed struggle waged against the Guomindang after the defeat of the second Chinese revolution in 1925–7. If Wang thinks his view is correct, he should first of all blame Trotsky, because Trotsky clearly stated that the 'policy of the Stalinists towards these detachments is a policy of criminal bureaucratic adventurism.... [W]*ithout a proletarian revolution and the seizure of power by the workers the partisan detachments of the peasantry cannot lead the way to victory*'(emphasis added). Why doesn't Wang criticise Trotsky?

I have pointed out that the policy of waging guerrilla war against the Guomindang, which the CCP started in 1928, ended in bankruptcy in 1937 when it capitulated to Chiang Kai-shek. Trotsky summarised the main lesson in the Transitional Programme. Does Wang propose to erase this disastrous and bloody chapter in history and revise the 'lesson of China' which Trotsky included in the Transitional Programme?

As to how the CCP entered the anti-Japanese war in 1937, at first under the (nominal) command of Chiang Kai-shek, how the CCP escalated its conflict with him during the anti-Japanese war, and how the CCP at last overthrew the Chiang Kai-shek government in 1949, we can only explain this process in the light of the 'exceptional historical circumstances created as a result of the Japanese invasion of China and the Second World War'. Peng has given a most detailed explanation of the various causes of this victory in his 'Report on the Chinese situation'. (See 'The Chinese Revolution', Education for Socialists, published by the Socialist Workers Party, Part I.) Here is an excerpt:

> From the facts illustrated above, we are able to make out a clear picture as follows: the bourgeois-landlord régime of Chiang Kai-shek collapsed automatically in toto, both on the economic and political planes and in its military organisation. Its only supporter, American imperialism, forsook it at last. The peasant army of the CCP, having won the support of the peasants and the petty bourgeoisie in general and especially having obtained military aid from the Soviet Union, had become a colossal and more or less modernised army. The combination of these objective and subjective factors paved the way for this extraordinary victory....
>
> Now we can comprehend that it was under the specific conditions of a definite historical stage – the combination of various intricate and exceptional conditions emerging from the Second World War – that the CCP which relied on the peasant army isolated from the urban working class could win power from the bourgeois-landlord rule of Chiang Kai-shek. The essential features of these exceptional conditions are as follows: the whole capitalist world wherein China is the weakest link tended to an unparalleled decline and decay; the automatic disintegration of the bourgeois Chiang Kai-shek régime was only the most consummate manifestation of the deterioration of the whole capitalist system. While on the other hand, resting on the socialised property relations of the October Revolution and exploiting the contradictions among the imperialist powers, the Soviet bureaucracy was able to achieve an unprecedented expansion of its influence during the Second World War, and this expansion greatly attracted the masses, who were deprived of hope under the extreme decline and decomposition of the capitalist system, especially the masses of the backward oriental countries. This facilitated the hypertrophy of the Stalinist parties in these countries. The CCP is precisely a perfected model of these Stalinist parties.
>
> Meanwhile, placed in an unfavourable position in the international situation – the situation brought forth by the Second World War – American imperialism was obliged to abandon its aid to Chiang and its interference with Mao. While the Soviet Union, which had secured a superior position in Manchuria at the end of the war, inflicted serious

damage upon Chiang's government and provided direct aid to the CCP on this basis, enabling the latter to modernise its backward peasant army. Without the combination of these conditions, the victory of a party like the CCP which relied purely on peasant forces would be inconceivable. For example, if Manchuria had not been occupied by the Soviet Union but had fallen entirely under Chiang's control, Chiang Kai-shek would have utilised the economic resources and the Japanese arms in Manchuria to cut off direct connection between the CCP and the Soviet Union, and block the armed support by the latter to the former. Similarly: if the situation at that time had permitted direct intervention by American imperialism in relation to the military activities of the CCP – under either of these two conditions – the victory of Mao Zedong would have been very doubtful. Or on the other hand, if we recall the defeat which the peasant army of the CCP suffered during the Jiangxi period of 1930–1935 when the power of the bourgeois Guomindang was considerably stabilised, owing to the incessant aid from imperialism and the isolation of the CCP from the Soviet Union, we can also derive sufficient reason to justify the conclusion that today's victory of the CCP is entirely the result of the specific conditions created by the Second World War.

This quotation confirms Peng's judgment made by Peng as quoted by Wang: 'The taking of power in 1949 by the CCP, however, was in no way a result of the guerrilla warfare strategy itself, but rather, a result of the exceptional historical circumstances created as a result of the Japanese invasion of China and Second World War'. Wang closed his eyes to the historical fact of the CCP's surrender to Chiang Kai-shek in 1937, and to the 'exceptional historical circumstances created as a result of the Japanese invasion of China and the Second World War'. Yet he has the audacity to say of Peng that 'if he has not forgotten anything, he has learned nothing either'!

Continuing his argument, Wang asks: 'If the Chinese Communist Party had not engaged in armed struggle against the Guomindang during the preceding twenty years, how would they have been able to take advantage of the "exceptional historical circumstances" created as a result of the Second World War?'

But one could ask him: If there had been no such 'exceptional historical circumstances', what would the CCP have achieved even if they had 'engaged in armed struggle against the Guomindang during the preceding twenty years'? Didn't they in 1937 abolish the 'soviets' and the 'Red Army', abandon the agrarian revolution, and surrender to Chiang Kai-shek? Had there been no such 'exceptional historical circumstances' created as a result of the Japanese invasion of China and Second World War, the CCP would not only have been unable to take power – its military forces would have been crushed by Chiang Kai-shek.

Wang thinks that the reason why the CCP was in position to take advantage of the 'exceptional historical circumstances' was owing to their having 'engaged in armed struggle... during the preceding twenty years'. This is equivalent to admitting that it was correct of Stalin to engage in an adventurist policy of armed struggle which he ordered the CCP to carry out after the defeat of the second Chinese revolution. It follows logically from this that Trotsky's criticism of Stalin's policy was erroneous. See what a trap Wang has fallen into! Under the impact of the CCP's victory, he so completely lost his bearings that he entirely forgot the teachings of Trotsky and fell into a position where – if he were logical – he would revise his position on the Stalinist policy of 'criminal bureaucratic adventurism' and become its defender!

I should like to remind him: Despite the CCP's taking power in 1949, its Stalinist adventurist policy of 'armed struggle' after the defeat of the second Chinese revolution in 1927 was fundamentally wrong. This policy led to great disasters. More than 30,000 fighters were lost when the CCP ordered He Long and Ye Ting to stage the Nanchang uprising on 1 August 1927. In the Autumn Harvest uprising in the provinces of Henan and Hebei in the fall of 1927, the bases of peasant organisations extending over wide areas were destroyed. In the peasant revolt and ensuing soviet movement in the Haifeng and Lufeng counties in the province of Guangdong, the powerful peasant organisation in that region was destroyed. In the Guangzhou uprising on 11 December 1927, entire organisations of the workers in that city were destroyed and more than 5,000 party members and workers lost their lives. In the guerrilla war during the ensuing ten years (1928–37), more than 10,000 party members and more than 1,000,000 workers and peasants were killed. In short, the CCP's adventurist policy of 'armed struggle' cost the lives of the great majority of the most militant cadres and party members and the complete liquidation of strong bases among the workers and peasants. The CCP then transformed itself from a proletarian party into a petty-bourgeois party based mainly on the peasantry. Its guerrilla war (or 'armed struggle') was defeated in 1934. It escaped from Jiangxi in central-east China to Yan'an in northwest China in 1935 and surrendered politically to Chiang Kai-shek in 1937. In the eyes of Wang, all these grim historical facts and man-made disasters either did not occur or lacked any significance! He sees only the fact that the CCP came to power; he has forgotten the great disaster brought on by that adventurist policy.

To this it should be added that if the CCP had carried out Trotsky's defensive policy instead of Stalin's adventurist policy of 'armed struggle' after the defeat of the second Chinese revolution – in other words, if the CCP had followed the process proposed by Trotsky of reorganising the workers' and peasants' organisations and mobilising the masses to wage a struggle against the military dictatorship of Chiang Kai-shek – the aftermath would have been entirely different.

First of all, the CCP could have retained its strong organisational bases among the revolutionary workers and peasants and could have avoided the unnecessary sacrifice of the lives of more than 10,000 of the most militant members of the party and the Young Communists. On this huge mass base, the CCP could have turned to account the conflicts between Chiang Kai-shek and the various warlords, the factional struggle within the Guomindang, and the anti-Japanese and anti-Chiang Kai-shek sentiments of the masses to topple the government. This held especially true in the period following the Japanese occupation of Manchuria on 18 September 1931, and the Japanese invasion of Shanghai on 28 January 1932, when opposition to Japanese imperialism swept like a tide over all of China. In protest against Chiang Kai-shek's policy of non-resistance, the student masses from Beijing and Shanghai marched to Nanjing, then the capital of the Chiang Kai-shek government, occupied the headquarters of the Central Committee of the Guomindang, and beat up high-ranking Guomindang officials. Chiang Kai-shek fled the capital, and his military dictatorship stood on the verge of collapse. Had the CCP followed Trotsky's policy of maintaining strong party and mass bases in the cities instead of turning to guerrilla warfare in the remote countryside, it could at a certain point have turned from the defence and taken the offensive, calling upon the people of the entire country to fight against the Japanese invasion of China and the non-resistance policy of Chiang Kai-shek. In this way the CCP could have become the leader of the countrywide anti-Japanese and anti-Chiang Kai-shek movement. The third Chinese revolution could have occurred in the thirties, enabling the CCP to take power and establish the dictatorship of the proletariat and poor peasants before the Second World War. This would have had tremendous repercussions internationally, above all in the Soviet Union, where it would have shaken Stalin's bureaucratic dictatorship. It could even have prevented the outbreak of the Second World War.

Unfortunately, the path followed by the CCP after the defeat of the second Chinese revolution was not that pointed to by Trotsky but the one ordered by Stalin – the adventurist policy of guerrilla war that Wang calls 'armed struggle'. This erroneous policy of 'armed struggle' not only destroyed a great majority of the party's cadres, its entire organisational bases in the cities, the huge workers' and peasants' mass organisation, and its clandestine forces in the Guomindang army (such as the forces of He Long and Ye Ting and a number of sympathisers of the Guomindang army), but also drove the various Guomindang warlords into a united front in pursuit of the common aim of defeating the guerrillas of the CCP. As a result of all this, Chiang Kai-shek was able to stabilise and strengthen his military dictatorship and concentrate his entire military force on the objective of encircling and attacking the CCP guerrillas, driving them from central-east China to northwest China, and forcing their eventual political capitulation in 1937.

Even more absurd is the following question asked by Wang: 'If the Chinese Communists had not trained themselves as "soldier-revolutionaries", how could they have utilised the modern weapons given them by the Russians?' We could ask him in return: if the Russians had not occupied Manchuria at the end of the Second World War, had not captured the modern weapons from the Japanese armies, and had not given these weapons to the CCP, how could the 'soldier-revolutionaries' have utilised their training? Did not the CCP train several hundred thousand 'soldier-revolutionaries' in central-east China when they started to engage in 'armed struggle' in 1928? Were they not driven by Chiang Kai-shek from central-east China to northwest China in 1934–5? Did they not capitulate to Chiang Kai-shek in 1937?

Still another theoretical question might be asked: In order to organise and lead the working class to power, should the proletarian vanguard party in its initial stage begin to engage in 'armed struggle' so as to provide some training for its 'soldier-revolutionaries'? If Wang's position were correct, it would be very difficult for the proletarian vanguard party to take power, inasmuch as the proletarian vanguard party in the advanced capitalist countries (and even in the backward ones) cannot arbitrarily engage in 'armed struggle' to train its 'soldier-revolutionaries'. Before 1917, the Bolsheviks did not train its 'soldier-revolutionaries' by such means. What made it possible, then, for them to win power in October through armed struggle of a different kind?

Wang should understand that a Marxist revolutionary party cannot and should not attempt to wage 'armed struggle' in the initial stages of preparing for the revolution in order to provide the military training required for its 'soldier-revolutionaries' in the process of leading the working class towards the conquest of power. It is not that easy. The primary task for the party in the beginning is to patiently conduct propaganda work among the working class and other poor people, to organise them, and to bring them to an understanding of the irreconcilability of their interests with preservation of the capitalist system. Furthermore, the vanguard party needs to convince the working class that its emancipation depends on doing away with the capitalist system completely and constructing a socialist society. With this aim in mind, the vanguard party must organise the working class, win their support, and become a truly revolutionary mass party. Then it will be in position to stage an 'armed uprising' to seize power and establish the dictatorship of the proletariat.

The timing of the 'armed uprising' is very important. It should take place at the height of the revolutionary tide, when the bourgeoisie has become completely shaken and demoralised, when the lower layer of the petty bourgeoisie is utterly disillusioned with the rule of the big bourgeoisie and wants a radical change, and when a serious differentiation has eroded the bourgeois army so that a large section of it has become sympathetic to the revolution or is turning towards it. Only under these conditions is it possible for the proletarian vanguard party to project without adventurism an 'armed uprising' to seize power from the bourgeoisie. The October revolution constitutes a model for this. . . .

On the Causes of the CCP's Victory and the Failure of the Chinese Trotskyists in the Third Chinese Revolution: A Reply to Peng Shuzhi

Wang Fanxi

August 1973

Source: A manuscript in the editor's possession

In the twenty-four years since the triumph of the third Chinese revolution, there have been uninterrupted discussions in our world movement about that great historical event, which created numerous theoretical puzzles for revolutionary Marxists. Upon these problems, we Chinese Trotskyists have also pondered and written, especially about the reasons why the CCP triumphed and we failed. Yet most of the opinions we expressed are unknown to our foreign comrades because of the language barrier. As a result, the international discussion on China has gone on without the participation of the Chinese Trotskyists. The only exception is Peng Shuzhi, who, thanks to his favourable circumstances and to the help he has received from foreign friends, has been able to make his opinions available to the whole of the Fourth International.

However, this has brought negative rather than positive results. Peng's positions has been consistently on the right, and, worse still, the account he has given of himself, of Chinese comrades and of the Chinese organisation in his articles, and especially in his wife's articles,[1] is invariably self-centred and prejudiced. There are so many falsifications of facts and misrepresentations of the views of Peng's opponents that the readers may be led to believe that the history of the Chinese Trotskyist movement is no more than a history of Peng alone and of his 'infallibility'. Thus we are compelled to break through the barrier of language and hold a direct discussion with Trotskyists all over the world on important questions regarding the revolution in general and the truth of our movement in China in particular, so as to draw correct revolutionary lessons and acquaint our comrades in other countries with the true history of our activities before and during the revolution.

For the time being, however, I will not deal with the distortion of facts and misrepresentations in Peng Shuzhi and Chen Bilan's articles but will confine

---

1 Ch'en Pi-lan (Chen Bilan) 1980 [1970].

my comments to a criticism of Peng's opinions about the Chinese revolution as expressed in his own writings.

To Begin with a Fact

To draw the right lessons from the third Chinese revolution, we must first know that between 1946 and 1949, when the revolution began to develop mainly under the leadership or control of the CCP and in the form of a military struggle (civil war), going from the military defensive onto the offensive, and finally triumphing over the Guomindang armies, we Chinese Trotskyists, without exception, did not understand what was happening. Not only before and during that time, but long after that, we could not and would not admit that what had been accomplished in China was a revolution, to say nothing of a revolution of great historical importance.

This may be difficult to believe. A political organisation that had all along been struggling to prepare the third Chinese revolution, expecting its approach every day, and doing everything to accelerate its coming, did not even recognise it when it finally arrived came.

How could such a strange thing happen? In a nutshell, it was because our thinking as revolutionaries lagged far behind the actual development of the revolution.

In the combination of the social forces it represented and the form in which it developed, as well as in the process it passed through, the actual third Chinese revolution clearly contradicted many of the views and forecasts of international Trotskyists, especially the Chinese Trotskyists. According to our traditional view, the main force of the third Chinese revolution had to be the urban working class. The form in which the revolutionary struggles would develop would be as follows: the working class and the urban poor, under the leadership of a revolutionary workers' party, would carry on day-to-day economic and political struggles in coordination with the agrarian struggle of the poor peasants in order to converge with them later in a tremendous revolutionary nationwide movement for democratic demands. And the course of the revolutionary struggle would probably be as follows: first it would triumph in big cities (especially economic and political centres like Shanghai and Nanjing) by overthrowing the Guomindang government and establishing a central revolutionary power, and then it would mobilise the poor peasants and have them armed or unite with and take the leadership of armed peasant forces already in existence, with the aim of waging a long or brief civil war against the old governing classes that, though defeated, were not yet destroyed. Such a perspective had been deeply embedded for a long time in the minds of Chinese Trotskyists.

But in fact the third Chinese revolution began, developed and triumphed in quite a different way: first, the main force that defeated the Guomindang's political and military forces was not the working class but the peasantry; the working class remained politically inactive and organisationally dispersed during the whole period of the civil war. Second, the party that led the peasant army to victory was, as we saw it at the time, not a revolutionary party of the proletariat but of the reformist petty bourgeoisie. Third, there had been a prolonged civil war between two regions – a civil war between a local revolutionary government and the national reactionary government. So it was not a central revolutionary government that started the civil war. Instead, a military victory on the part of the rebellious side in the civil war set up the new national government. So the actual course of the revolution was in blatant disaccord with our forecasts.

Since the developments of the revolution and the form in which it had achieved success were so different from our conceptions, we were naturally caught in a profound contradiction. We were confronted with the following alternatives: either continue to insist that our traditional position was the only correct one and thus refuse to admit that what had happened was, objectively, a revolution; or admit that the CCP's victory was the victory of a revolution, which would require us to make an overhaul of our long-held views.

During the period in which the CCP triumphed and for quite a long time after that, all Chinese Trotskyists chose the first alternative. Insisting firmly on the traditional view, all without exception refused to admit that what had happened in China was a revolution. In the sameness, however, there was also difference. We were identical in our denial that what had happened was a revolution; but on the question of how to understand the actual character of the 'non-revolution', our opinions diverged. Roughly speaking, there were two positions and three views. The first position was: not to admit that CCP's triumph was a triumph of revolution, but even so to recognise that the triumph had brought about a *qualitative* change in China's politico-economical structure (this was Zheng Chaolin and my position). The second was that the military victory of the CCP over the Guomindang had not produced any sort of *qualitative* change (this was Peng Shuzhi's position). As for the three views, they were:

1. The CCP régime was a form of state capitalism (Zheng Chaolin).
2. The CCP régime was giving birth to a new class – a class of collectivist bureaucracy (Wang Fanxi).
3. The transfer of power from the Guomindang to the CCP was simply the substitution of a new tyrant for an old one, both representing the bourgeoisie (Peng Shuzhi).

Zheng Chaolin later elaborated his views in a pamphlet and did not change them before his arrest by Mao's secret police in December 1952. But as early as October 1950 he agreed with a platform drafted by me at the time and also agreed with 'An Open Letter to the CC of the CCP' drafted by me in November 1952, neither of which argued the state capitalism or collectivist bureaucratism thesis and both of which accepted that the struggle to overthrow the Guomindang was a revolution and declared our fundamental support for that revolution.

Personally, I did not maintain the position of collectivist bureaucratism for long. While drafting the two documents I just mentioned, I became dissatisfied with the new position I took. First through practice and later as a result of theoretical considerations, I discovered where I had gone wrong, and once I did so, I openly admitted my mistake and openly abandoned my erroneous position. I openly described how and why I had initially adopted it and then given it up. At the same time, I openly reassessed our traditional position, pointing out which part of it was still correct and which part of it had been proved incorrect, and I therefore openly proposed what we as Chinese Trotskyists should stick to and what we should give up. All of these ideas were set out in a pamphlet titled 'Some Ideological Questions Concerning the Chinese Revolution',[2] which I will not repeat here.

Under the pressure of facts, Peng Shuzhi too could not but change his views about the new régime. The process of his change was as follows:

1. In January 1950, when the Communist army, in spite of Peng's forecast to the contrary, had not only scored victory after victory but dealt a final and fatal blow to the Guomindang army on the Chinese mainland, Peng declared that the civil war between the Guomindang and the CCP had already reached a 'decisive stage'. On the character of the new régime installed by the CCP he wrote a resolution that said: 'The so-called "people's democratic dictatorship" or "coalition Government" of workers, peasants, petty bourgeoisie and bourgeoisie is actually a Bonapartist military dictatorship of the petty bourgeoisie and bourgeoisie based on armed peasants. Such a military dictatorship will never change its bourgeois character, no matter what "people's representative congress" might give it a disguise in the future'.[3]

2. In November 1951 Peng saw the CCP's victory for the first time as 'a great and even a monumental change in modern Chinese history, and [one that] has also caused profound changes in the Far East and in international relations'. He also admitted that the victory represented 'a deformed revolution'

---

2 Shuang Shan 1957.
3 Peng Shuzhi, 'Political Resolution on the Situation in China after the CCP Seized Power'.

and confessed that we had been 'unable to foresee the current victory of the CCP'; but at the same time, he stressed that 'during the civil war between the Guomindang and the CCP, our basic line and our position towards the CCP have been correct'. He particularly stressed the 'consistent correctness' of his position concerning the character of the CCP and the new communist régime: the former was 'petty-bourgeois peasant', while the latter was 'bourgeois'.

3. In May 1952, Peng was of the opinion that 'new facts' enabled him to believe that the CCP had been transformed from a petty-bourgeois peasant party to a party of a 'dual character', and that meanwhile the Communist régime too had been transformed from a power of 'unchangeable bourgeois character' to one of 'dual character'.

4. Since then Peng has never taken any further trouble to tell us how the party and the state of 'dual character' were transformed into one of 'single character'. In his articles written after that time, Peng simply called the CCP a bureaucratically degenerated workers' party and the People's Republic of China a bureaucratically degenerated workers' state, without any explanation. Clearly, Peng's attitude towards the changes he has made concerning the nature of the third Chinese revolution has been entirely different from ours. What he cares about above all is his own 'face'. What he most anxiously sought to do is distort facts in order to confirm his own 'infallibility'. So even when he changes his views, one can never learn anything from him.

To effect a real change in our view of what has happened in China, and to rectify rather than justify our mistakes on this question, we should first of all admit frankly and honestly what mistakes we have made. As far as our ideological understanding is concerned, we must first admit that our assessment of the character of the CCP was wrong. We failed to see that the CCP was still a workers' party and we took it for a petty-bourgeois peasant party. This led to a series of other mistakes. Taking this wrong assessment as our point of departure, we were unable to explain: how the CCP, a party of peasants and other layers of the petty bourgeoisie, could resolutely lead a peasant army; how it could overthrow the bourgeois government through resolute armed struggle in a revolutionary situation; how it could carry out agrarian revolution after overthrowing bourgeois rule; and how it could carry out revolutionary measures of a socialist character, including nationalisation of the means of production, and so on.

Why did we arrive at such an assessment of the CCP long before and even long after its victory? And in what ways was that assessment wrong?

According to Peng Shuzhi, Leon Trotsky made the assessment first, and we simply followed suit. As for the assessment itself, it had according to Peng been correct and still was correct unless somebody could give him 'sufficient facts and correct arguments' to the contrary.

Let us consider a number of facts and arguments.

In attributing the assessment of the CCP as a peasant party to Trotsky, Peng referred to Trotsky's letter to the Chinese Left-Opposition, 'Peasant War in China and the Proletariat' (22 September 1932). In it, Trotsky said: 'In the years of the counter-revolution they [the Stalinists] passed over from the proletariat to the peasantry, that is, they undertook that role which was fulfilled in our country by the SRs when they were still a revolutionary party'. He also said: 'The party actually tore itself away from its class'.[4] However, to argue that Party A undertook the same role as Party B is not necessarily to say that A and B represent the same class interests, and to say that a party tore itself away from its class is also not necessarily to say that it no longer represents its class, still less that it will never again represent it. In fact, the letter deals with the prospect of peasant struggle and studies beforehand the relationship that may develop between the peasant struggle and the working class. Its main point was to consider possible developments, not accomplished facts. The same is true of Trotsky's assessment of the Chinese Stalinists. This is what he said in the letter:

> Bureaucratic centrism, as centrism, cannot have an independent class support. But in its struggle against the Bolshevik-Leninists it is compelled to seek support from the right, that is, from the peasantry and the petty-bourgeoisie, counterposing them to the proletariat. The struggle between the two Communist factions, the Stalinists and the Bolshevik-Leninists, thus bears in itself an inner *tendency* towards transformation into a class struggle. The revolutionary development of events in China may draw this tendency to its conclusion, that is, to a civil war between the peasant army led by the Stalinists and the proletarian vanguard led by the Leninists. Were such a tragic conflict to arise, due entirely to the Chinese Stalinists, it would signify that the Left Opposition and the Stalinists ceased to be Communist factions and had become hostile parties, each having a different class base.[5]

Clearly Trotsky did not assert that the CCP had already become 'a party of peasantry and petty bourgeoisie'. '[S]uch a tragic conflict ... would signify that the Left Opposition and the Stalinists ceased to be Communist factions and had become hostile parties, each having a different class base'. So he was discussing a hypothetical situation. Thus he continued: 'However, is such a perspective inevitable? No, I don't think so at all'.[6] Yet Peng Shuzhi misinterprets Trotsky's

---

4 This volume, p. 908.
5 This volume, p. 910.
6 This volume, p. 910.

words about what might happen under certain conditions for what actually happened.

One should also note that this letter was written in September 1932. Anybody familiar with the history of the Fourth International knows that it was not until July 1933 that Trotsky called for the first time for preparations for the building of a new party and a new International. Up to that time, Trotskyists throughout the world (whether expelled from the Communist Party or not) had considered themselves a faction of the Communist Party, which they still considered to be a proletarian organisation capable of reform, no matter how degenerate. So how could Trotsky have assessed the CCP in September 1932 as an organisation already transformed into a 'party of peasantry and petty bourgeoisie'?

Peng's attempt to shift the responsibility for the wrong assessment of the CCP onto Trotsky's shoulders is pointless. It does not accord with the facts.

The next question is: Is it true that from 1933 (at least) until 1952 the CCP had become a party representing peasantry, as all the Chinese Trotskyists then believed? On second thoughts, I think not. I have dealt with this question in great detail in my article 'Some Ideological Questions'.[7] Here I'll simply quote a few passages:

> Two circumstances caused us to deny that the CCP was a working class party. 1. Since 1934 the CCP had completely passed over from the proletariat to the peasantry, from the cities to the countryside. 2. Starting in 1937, the CCP, in the name of a joint resistance against the Japanese invasion, capitulated to the Guomindang by declaring its conversion to Sun Yat-sen-ism, accepting the reorganisation of the Red Army and promising to give up class struggle. These two circumstances were of course important enough for serious Marxist revolutionaries to pass a judgement on a party. A party that tears itself from the working class, leaves its proper scene of battle, and gives up its revolutionary platform of class struggle would no longer appear to be a working-class party.
>
> So we were not wrong in prin ciple when we first declared that the CCP had become a peasant party in the mid-1930s. Where we went wrong is in not checking the CCP's actual doings. Still worse, we refused to see facts that might have refuted us.
>
> In retrospect, we should acknowledge that we ignored the following: 1. The CCP's withdrawal from the cities did not take place of its own will, nor was it in accordance with a plan: it was the result of Guomindang persecution and repression. So it should not be seen as the implementation

---

7 Shuang Shan 1957.

of a new orientation towards peasant war rather than proletarian revolution. 2. Having withdrawn to the countryside, the CCP did not forsake, either in words or in deeds, the platform of a revolutionary united front under the leadership of the working class, and in reality (though not on a grand scale) continued class struggle in villages even during the honeymoon period of its 'second marriage' with the Guomindang. 3. During the Second United with the Guomindang starting in 1937, it is true that the CCP dropped the policy of class struggle not only in words but also in deeds: it discontinued the struggle against the landlords, placed itself under the leadership of Chiang Kai-shek, and declared its acceptance of Sun Yet-sen-ism. It was indeed a turn of decisive importance that we rightly denounced at the time as a final capitulation. In retrospect, however, we should still admit that the shameful betrayal of the CCP, thanks to multiple objective and subjective reasons that I won't go into for the time being, never reached its logical end. By and large it was a matter of tactical manoeuvre rather than a strategic turn. 4. Both during the 'soviet and Red Army' period and the period of the 'Second United Front and the Eighth Route Army', the CCP all along remained an organisation of highly disciplined revolutionary professionals and the recruitment of its members and soldiers was carried out on class basis.

If we had paid close attention to such facts, we would have managed much earlier to rectify our assessment of the CCP as a peasant party and to conclude that in spite of its complete separation from the working class and even its conversion to Sun Yat-sen-ism, it remained to a lesser or greater extent a party inclined towards the working class.

This reassessment of the nature of the CCP is quite different from Peng Shuzhi's. I recognised that we were wrong to call the CCP a party representing the interests of peasants and other petty-bourgeois layers. We were wrong because our assessment was based on abstract principles that did not take the facts into account. So we should now admit that the CCP 'remained to a lesser or greater extent a party inclined towards the of working class', that it can still be considered as a party representing, although in very bureaucratic way, the historical interests of the working class, and that for that reason it was able to make use of favourable circumstances during the third Chinese revolution to achieve a series of victories.

According to Peng Shuzhi, we were right to see the CCP as a peasant party, and so we were also right when we refused to recognise the victory of the CCP as the victory of the Chinese revolution and labelled the new government a 'bourgeois state'. But under the pressure of events, Peng could not but admit that the CCP was in substance a workers' party and the People's Republic of China a kind of workers' state. So how could he explain this change in his view? How could he 'mend' his mistakes on the one hand and maintain his 'infallibility' on the other? By resorting to the magic of 'facts'. To this end, Peng pointed to the following facts: 'Although peasants and other petty-bourgeois elements still predominate in the CCP (more than 90 per cent of the 5 million members), the worker elements have increased in the last two years. The working-class tendency has been strengthened during agrarian reform and the campaign against corruption'.[8] According to Peng, this fact, and this fact alone, showed that the CCP, 'a party of peasants and other petty-bourgeois layers', had 'progressed towards a workers' party' through an intermediate stage of 'dual character' and that the 'bourgeois' régime set up by the CCP had also thereby become a 'dual power' first and a 'degenerated workers' state' a little later on.

But unfortunately Peng never asks why the same CCP that had overthrown bourgeois rule two years earlier did not qualify for a reassessment of its class nature. Was not the problem of power the most important of any revolution? Was not the seizure of power from the ruling class a fact of much more decisive importance than any other in the course of the revolution? Simply to pose these questions shows how untenable Peng's 'facts' and 'arguments' are.

Like all Chinese Trotskyists, Peng had wrongly assessed the class character of the CCP; but unlike other Chinese comrades, he lacked the courage to admit his mistakes. Instead of mending them, he tried to cover them up, and consequently created an even bigger mental confusion that brought good neither to himself nor to other comrades.

The Triumph of the CCP and Its Causes

Our misjudgement of the social character of the CCP prevented us from not only understanding the victory of the Chinese revolution but also from foreseeing the possibility of the Communist army's military triumph. During the civil war, we categorically declared that 'the defeat of the Communist army is inevitable' on the grounds that peasant guerrilla units led by a 'peasant party' could never defeat a regular army led by the bourgeoisie. Such forecasts were commonplace among us, but in this respect too Peng went furthest. Here is a random example, from an editorial in *Truth*, which Peng edited:

---

8   This volume, p. 966.

As for the CCP, it has undoubtedly suffered a severe and irrecoverable military blow; it lost many cities and lines of communication to the Guomindang in the Northeast, and its military strength has been greatly weakened. Although it still occupies vast areas of countryside, still carries on guerrilla warfare with the aim of cutting the lines of communication of the Guomindang army, and still threatens the cities and towns occupied by the Guomindang army in order to eat up the latter's strength, yet all this cannot solve the serious problems posed at the present time. The successive defeats suffered by the CCP army have not only greatly lowered the CCP's political standing but have deeply shaken its internal foundations as a party.... If such a situation continues, it is inevitable that all kinds of differentiation and acts of betrayal will happen in the CCP and its army and catastrophe will follow. Few have pointed out this perspective, but it is very well understood by those who have sufficient courage to face the facts and who understand the logical consequences of a defeat of the mass movement of the peasants.[9]

Since Peng failed to see and stubbornly refused to recognise the indisputable fact of the CCP's military victory, he can hardly be expected to make a study of its causes.

In November 1951, two years after the CCP's complete triumph, Peng for the first (and last) time enquired into the causes of Chinese Stalinists' victory. Here are the results of his study:

> Relying on a peasant army, which was kept apart from the urban working class, the CCP achieved victory over the Chiang Kai-shek régime of the landlord-bourgeoisie. This victory was brought about entirely under the specific conditions of a certain historical phase, that is, under a combination of various complicated specific conditions which were created by the Second World War.[10]

What are these 'specific conditions'? They are, according to Peng: 1. 'The absolute corruption and self-disintegration of the Chiang Kai-shek régime'; 2. 'The abandonment of Chiang Kai-shek by the US imperialists'; 3. 'The subjective strength of the CCP'; 4. 'The aid given by the USSR to the CCP'. Such an enumeration of the causes of the victory of the CCP would be adequate for the

---

9   *Truth*, Volume 1, nos. 2 and 3, January 1947.
10 Peng Shuzhi, 'Report on the Chinese Situation', November 1951, pp. 11–12, Chinese edition.

purposes of a middle school history teacher, but not for a participant in the revolution, especially for one of the leaders of a party competing with the CCP to win during the revolution.

A responsible revolutionary who has participated in a revolution and failed to win cannot just fatalistically point to the objective reasons for his rival's victory and then lie back on his couch and continue to give 'directions to the revolution'.

Having lighted on these causes, Peng should first of all have asked himself why, under the same 'specific conditions', the party that succeeded in making use of them and thereby overthrowing the Guomindang was not the Trotskyists, who had always pursued a correct revolutionary strategy, but the CCP, which had always pursued a wrong political line? Second, he should ask himself why the US imperialists 'abandoned' Chiang Kai-shek (although in fact they have not yet done so even now)? Was it the objective situation of the Chinese revolution, especially the powerful advance of the Communist army, that persuaded the US imperialists that it would be useless to continue to aid Chiang, or did they abandon Chiang for some unknown reason and thus help the CCP gain the upper hand in the civil war? Third, he should ask himself how, if the CCP had (as we believed) capitulated of its own accord to the Guomindang, and thus become both organisationally and politically a petty-bourgeois party – how then could it suddenly become a powerful force on the battlefield? Had the CCP not been tempered and organised in armed struggle for many years, could it still have seized the chance to vanquish Chiang Kai-shek's army? Finally, he should ask himself whether the Guomindang propaganda was true, whether the USSR really did hand over to the CCP all the weapons it took from the Japanese army and whether it really was true that a great number of Soviet experts and Japanese prisoners-of-war helped the Communist army direct its modern war? And even if it was true (and we know that it was not), could the CCP have made use of this assistance (the weapons and the expertise) to achieve victory in the war as well as in the revolution if it had not been in a position to make use them?

None of these questions was ever asked by Peng, still less answered. He simply pointed to the four exceptional conditions to show that the CCP's victory was 'exceptional', and thus beyond the 'forecast' of an 'orthodox Marxist'. Since it was an exceptional case in history, it was not in accordance with the 'prognoses of traditional Marxism'. And since exceptions do not necessarily invalidate rules, the traditional position of Chinese Trotskyism (and of Peng Shuzhi in particular) needs no revision. But such an attitude is, in my opinion, absurd.

True, at another point in his 'Report' he says the following:

> Just as we and Trotsky did not foresee the extraordinary expansion of Stalinism during the period after the Second World War, so we did not foresee the triumph of the CCP today. Our mistake is neither of principle, nor of methodology. It is rather a result of our clinging too stubbornly to the principle, so that we had to a certain extent ignored the specific conditions created by the development of events and this prevented us from changing our tactics in time. We should accept the lesson in this respect.[11]

Here he finally recognises a mistake, albeit (as usual) under the cover of Trotsky and in a very limited way. 'We had to a certain extent ignored the specific conditions created by the development of events and this prevented us from changing our tactics in time'. Well said, and surely valuable lessons might be drawn from it if only one went more deeply into questions such as which precisely of the 'specific conditions' was ignored and which tactics exactly did we 'fail to change in time'. Unfortunately, Peng did not try to answer the former question, nor did he try to answer the latter. So the only point in Peng's article with meaning lost that meaning.

On the 'Specific Condition' We Ignored and the 'Tactic We Failed to Change in Good Time'

Among the four 'specific conditions' pointed out by Peng, only the CCP's 'subjective strength really deserves special attention, yet we have completely (not 'to certain extent', but completely) ignored it. All the tactical mistakes we made during the third Chinese revolution can be traced to this 'neglect'. So the lesson we must 'accept' has to gained on the basis of a close study of this 'subjective strength'. In Peng's article, however, this 'specific condition' was least elaborated, as if it was not worth dealing with. According to Peng, the specific character of this condition consisted simply in the fact that the CCP as a 'peasant party' and the peasant army under its command, which should have been liquidated and in fact had been liquidated in 1937, was fortunate enough to witness the outbreak of the anti-Japanese war and thus 'gained a tremendous growth and built up for themselves a formidable military strength'.[12] From such an explanation, of course, one can draw no lesson. Chinese Trotskyists can learn little from Peng's research, just as revolutionaries of other underdeveloped countries can gain no enlightenment from it. Since these 'specific

---

11   Peng Shuzhi, 'Report on the Chinese Situation', November 1951, p. 13.
12   Peng Shuzhi, 'Report on the Chinese Situation', November 1951, p. 8.

CAUSES OF THE CCP'S VICTORY: A REPLY TO PENG SHUZHI (1973)

conditions' are a result of luck, they cannot be sought, for they are 'accidents' independent of one's subjective efforts.

A serious study of the subjective strength of the CCP requires first of all an enquiry into the class character of the party. This I have already discussed above, so I will not repeat my argument here. What I will now discuss is the most 'specific' of the 'specifics', the relationship between the triumph of the CCP and armed struggle, one of the most important tactics that we had failed to change in time.

Let us look back briefly at the two lines on the Chinese revolution represented by Stalinists and Trotskyists. In the fall of 1927, when the second Chinese revolution failed definitively, Stalin and his followers declared that it had not been defeated but on the contrary had entered its 'highest stage', the stage of establishing Chinese soviet power by means of armed struggle. The outcome is well known: the putschist policy executed first by Qu Qiubai and then by Li Lisan succeeded only in squandering the revolutionary forces that had survived the defeat and deepened the counter-revolutionary crisis throughout the country (especially in the cities).

Trotsky gave a warning just in time, and in October 1928 he provided Chinese revolutionaries with an entirely different platform for their future struggle, in which he said the Chinese revolution had been defeated because of the Stalin-Bukharin opportunist leadership and China now was not in 'an epoch of ever growing revolutionary upsurge' but in 'an intermediate epoch between two revolutions'. According to Trotsky, the counter-revolution had triumphed but the democratic and national tasks of the revolution had not been resolved; and would be raised again during the counter-revolutionary period in the form of a democratic struggle.

So the revolutionary party urgently needed to propose a comprehensive revolutionary democratic platform, by calling for the convocation of an all-powerful constituent assembly elected by secret ballot and based on universal suffrage. We should struggle for this platform with all our strength in order to reassemble our cadres, re-establish connections with the toiling masses, and gradually transform the counter-revolutionary situation into a revolutionary one.

Of the two different assessments made during that period of the Chinese revolution and the two different lines adopted as a result, which was right and which was wrong has been proved conclusively by history, and further comment is unnecessary.

Later, because of the profound potential of the Chinese revolution, that is, China's complicated internal contradictions and its politico-economic and geographic specificities, the peasants, especially those in southern China baptised by the revolution, rose up under the leadership of Communists, opening a new scene of battle that was tremendous in scale and great in influence. Meanwhile, in the cities, and in particular in the big industrial cities, the reactionary rule of the bourgeoisie achieved a relative stability both economic and political, which helped the Guomindang's 'scientifically organised' secret police to repress the working class and its party more and more effectively.

Under the new circumstances, the CCP was gradually forced out of the big cities and the working class and sank ever deeper roots in the peasantry. In regard to revolutionary tactics and strategy, it gradually and pragmatically adapted to the point where in the end it delineated a line of long-term armed struggle against the reactionary central government by establishing revolutionary power in certain regions of the country and encircling the cities with the countryside.

Trotsky closely watched the situation develop, analysing it incessantly, and provided us with timely advice. He was delighted by the 'revolutionary revival in the countryside', voiced his joy at each and every victory of the poor peasants, and sincerely hoped that 'the dusk of the second Chinese revolution' would be immediately followed by 'the dawn of the third revolution'. At the same time he severely criticised 'the criminal policy of bureaucratic putschism' pursued by the Stalinists and trenchantly exposed the illusion that revolution could be made by peasant guerrilla warfare alone. Towards the 'Red Army', which had already grown into a considerable force, Trotsky formulated the following approach:

> While we refuse to identify the armed peasant detachment with the Red Army as the armed power of the proletariat and have no inclination to shut our eyes to the fact that the Communist banner hides the petty-bourgeois content of the peasant movement, we on the other hand take an absolutely clear view of the tremendous revolutionary-democratic significance of the peasant war. We teach the workers to appreciate its significance and we are ready to do all in our power in order to achieve the necessary military alliance with the peasant organisations.[13]

Looking back upon the two lines of that period from the point of view of Marxism, we can conclude that the position taken by Trotsky was right. But in retrospect, we should reconsider one point as far as the activities of the Chinese Trotskyists are concerned. In the years 1931 to 1937, when our organisation was successively crushed by the Guomindang secret police and our strength was progressively reduced almost to nil, would it not have been better for us, while

---

13   'Peasant War in China and the Proletariat', pp. 903–11 of the present volume.

continuing to maintain our strictly clandestine organisation in cities, if we had at the same time gone to open up a new battlefield in the countryside, where the masses were more minded to struggle and the repression by reaction was less harsh, with the aim of preserving our cadres and recruiting new militants? Should we not have done as Trotsky once advised: 'To have our people, Oppositionists, at least in the larger divisions of the "Red Army", to share the fate of these detachments, to observe attentively the relations between these detachments and the peasantry and to keep the Left Opposition informed'?[14] If we had actually done so, would our strength not have been much greater than it was on the eve of the outbreak of the Sino-Japanese war in 1937? To all these questions I have to answer in the affirmative.

But if we had sent our comrades into the 'Red Army', according to a plan and under the leadership of our organisation, or if (circumstances permitting) we had gained the leadership of an independent peasant detachment, would that have been a capitulation to Stalinist strategy? At the time we thought it would have been. Now, I believe we were wrong to think that. If we had done as I just said, we would and could have acted quite differently from the Stalinists. First, we would have insisted on the priority of work in the urban working class and would have spared no effort to restore and strengthen underground work in the cities even if Guomindang white terror had partially or completely destroyed our organisation there. We would all along have viewed the peasant struggle as a roundabout way through which to stimulate and develop the struggle of the urban toiling masses. Second, we would have participated in the armed struggle of the peasantry as a component part of our overall revolutionary-democratic struggle, of our struggle for a constituent assembly, that is to say, we would not done so like the Stalinists, to establish soviet power using peasant armed forces, but we would have used such struggles as a powerful means of realising our revolutionary-democratic programme, to convoke an all-powerful, universally elected constituent assembly. So if we had adopted a more positive attitude, and one more consonant with the spirit of Trotsky's letters, towards the peasants' armed struggle in the period 1932–7, we would have been better equipped to deal with the new situation created by China's resistance war against the Japanese invasion.

The Resistance War that broke out in the autumn of 1937 not only created an entirely new political situation but altered the relationship between the classes of Chinese society and changed many forms of struggle. One of the most remarkable changes was that the life of the entire nation and its antagonisms

---

14   Leon Trotsky, 'Letter to Chinese Left Oppositionists', reprinted in *Intercontinental Press*, 6 November 1972.

became directly involved in the war. All questions were settled more directly by armed force. China's Stalinist party, notwithstanding its absurdity, shamelessness and hypocrisy, realised this, and made full use of the war to increase the number of its guns. Even Peng Shuzhi said in his 'Report' that

> as a result of the outbreak of the war against Japanese imperialism this armed force secured the opportunity for an unusual development. In particular, at the end of the war and right after it, the army made great progress in both numbers and in quality, becoming far stronger than in the Jiangxi period. This army thus grew into a strong military force.[15]

Now let us suppose that our support for the Resistance War had not been confined to paper but had stretched to actual and planned participation in the anti-Japanese armed forces; or that we had at least given ideological encouragement and political leadership to those comrades who participated in armed struggles or even led independent detachments (for example in Shandong and Guangdong provinces). We would then have found ourselves in a different situation at the end of war and thereafter. Naturally we can't say for certain that we would have built up a force strong enough to compete with the CCP, but at least we would not have ended up as we did: during the war, our organisation practically collapsed, some cadres even starved to death, and we made no contribution in action to the anti-Japanese effort, while in the post-war period, despite the favourable pre-revolutionary situation, our revived organisation (or rather, two organisations) was too weak to profit from it, and we adopted an entirely passive attitude towards the civil war between the CCP and the Guomindang, in which we played the role of bystanders.

Peng said: 'We more or less overlooked the specific conditions of the development of the events, and consequently it prevented us from making tactical changes in good time'. If this statement is to mean anything, he has to point out precisely which 'specific condition' of the armed struggle of the CCP we 'overlooked'. At the same time, he should openly admit that at least and as late as in 1937, after the outbreak of the Resistance War, we should have made a timely change in respect of our tactics regarding armed struggle. Unfortunately, Peng did not and would not do this. Basing himself on 'Chinese experience', he gave the following advice to revolutionaries in backward countries who were in the same situation as we Chinese Trotskyists had been: 'The tactic of guerrilla warfare can and should be used in the countryside to aid the armed insurrection of the working class in the cities when the conditions are ripe for an insurrection

---

15   This volume, p. 953.

in the main cities. The tactic of guerrilla warfare or "armed struggle" should not be used when the conditions for an insurrection by the working class in the cities do not exist'.[16]

If these lines had been written before the Second World War, when people had not yet witnessed the revolutions in Yugoslavia, Vietnam, China, North Korea, and Cuba, they would probably not have met with any objection. But if we recognise these to be real revolutions, and revolutions of a socialist character, we cannot fail to admit that a peasant insurrection under the leadership of a workers' party did happen before the insurrection of the working class in the cities, and triumphed as genuine revolutions. True, they did not start and proceed completely in accordance with 'the three conditions' of insurrection posed by Lenin, nor did they accord with Trotsky's teachings on peasant uprisings. But what makes the theory of revolution valuable? That it is incessantly induced from the experience of revolutionary struggles and thus gives direction to further struggles, or that it can serve as a fixed formula not verifiable against new experiences and thereby a limit on future struggles? I would argue thus: 'Revolutionary theory is no dogma, but a direction for revolutionary action'. Why is it able to direct action? Because it has been incessantly proved and is continuously verified in action. This also applies to the theory of armed struggle.

Trotsky's views on the relation between peasant guerrilla war and workers' insurrections were correct and remain so. However, in the light of revolutionary experience since the Second World War, we must add that while Trotsky was right, there are other correct ways too. For objective historical reasons, under certain 'specific conditions', peasant guerrilla war (led by a party imbued with the class consciousness of urban workers) can break out and proceed in colonial and semi-colonial countries before the workers' insurrection in the cities. Here, a statement by the US Socialist Workers' Party is worth citing:

> Along the road of a revolution beginning with simple democratic demands and ending in the rupture of capitalist property relations, guerrilla warfare conducted by landless and semi-proletarian forces, under a leadership that becomes committed to carrying the revolution through to a conclusion, can play a decisive role in undermining and precipitating the downfall of a colonial or semi-colonial power. This is one of the main lessons to be drawn from experiences since the Second World War.

---

16   In fact this is quoted from an article by Chen Bilan, Peng Shuzhi's wife (Ch'en Pi-lan 1973).

It must be consciously incorporated into the strategy of building revolutionary parties in colonial countries.[17]

This supplements Trotsky's ideas. If Trotsky were alive today, he would agree. But Peng condemns any supplement of this kind as a departure from Trotskyism, and therefore raised the call for a 'Return to the road of Trotskyism!' ...

On the 'Specific' and 'Normal' Conditions of a Revolution

The main reason Peng cannot draw any lesson from the victory of the CCP is his conviction that it resulted from exceptional historical circumstances and bears no relation to the CCP's policy and tactics or to its armed struggle. According to Peng, the CCP's armed struggle suffered a crushing defeat in 1937. Only accidentally, as a result of the 'specific conditions' of the Japanese invasion, the Second World War, the Guomindang's postwar corruption, the Guomindang's abandonment by US imperialism, and the readiness of the USSR to assist the CCP, did the CCP's 'irrecoverable' armed forces succeed in 'resurrecting themselves from death' and overthrowing the Guomindang. All this, according to Peng, was accidental and in no way attributable to CCP policy, still less to its policy of the armed struggle, which in Peng's opinion should not be incorporated into the strategy of building revolutionary parties in colonial countries....

The only kind of revolution Peng recognises is one made neither 'on a certain specific historical phase' nor 'under specific conditions'. But was there ever such a revolution? ...

Some Marxists believe proletarian revolution can only break out when a nation's productive force can no longer co-exist with its productive relations. Proletarian socialist revolution is, according to them, as natural as the birth of a child. There is no need for artificial intervention, which would make the conditions 'exceptional' and the revolution 'impure'.

Such 'Marxists' refused to recognise Russia's October Revolution. They argued it was not natural and normal, but an 'abnormal' result produced by 'exceptional conditions on a certain specific historical phase'. It broke out during world war; it happened at the time when the Tsarist government had 'self-disintegrated'; it was accidentally facilitated by the Anglo-French imperialists' abandonment of the Kerensky régime and it was made easier by the Germen imperialists' helping Lenin and others to go home. So according to them it

---

17   'For Early Reunification of the World Trotskyist Movement', 1 March 1963.

was not a proletarian socialist revolution but a mere 'revolution of soldiers', 'an armed uprising of peasants'.

According to them, a real proletarian revolution must first break out in the advanced capitalist countries. It must be carried out by normal and legal methods. If a revolution was not won through parliamentary struggle, it would have resorted to 'exceptional conditions' and therefore could not be considered genuine.

Needless to say, Peng is a Trotskyist who believes in the theory of permanent revolution.... But he shares with Karl Kautsky his view on the role played by democratic parliaments. Both make a fetish of this democratic institution.

After the defeat of the second Chinese revolution in 1927,... Trotsky raised the slogan of 'an all-powerful and universally elected constituent assembly' in his criticism of the line adopted on China at the Sixth Congress of the Comintern.... This slogan was a standard around which the first generation of Chinese Trotskyists rallied. But it was on this question that the first and most heated theoretical dispute broke out among the Chinese Trotskyists.

Some accepted the slogan from the left, others from the right. Some considered that the aim was to realise a parliamentary perspective in China, for a parliamentary system was better than the Guomindang military dictatorship and would be much more advantageous to the revolution. Others thought the aim was not so much the realisation of a parliament as to reassemble the masses, rebuild the party, re-inspire the masses, and enter the road of the third Chinese revolution on the basis of the struggle for democratic (and national) demands....

The main representative of the former view was Liu Renjing, supported by some older comrades; while the latter position was mainly advocated by young Trotskyists (including me). Peng, as far as I know, did not take part in this discussion. However, judging from the way in which he has since applied the slogan, I can safely say that he embraced it from the right. In the postwar years and during the civil war, Peng's editorials in *Truth* centred on the two parallel demands: convocation of a constituent assembly and immediate cessation of the civil war. Peng condemned both the Guomindang and the CCP equally for 'continuing the extremely cruel civil war regardless of the damage it might cause'. He demanded an immediate cessation of 'the meaningless war... and called for a constituent assembly to settle all the issues.[18] Such was Peng's attitude towards the civil war and to the constituent assembly slogan. He did not recognise the different class interests represented by the warring parties and saw the constituent assembly as a panacea. Both positions rendered

---

18   Peng Shuzhi, 'On the Constituent Assembly', *Truth*, Volume 1, no. 7.

help (objectively, of course) to the Guomindang and its fraudulent constitutional plan.

To be fair, not only Peng made this mistake. Nearly all the Chinese Trotskyists did, of the majority and the minority, including me. But Peng made the mistake most glaringly....

In January 1950, in the political resolution quoted above, the call for a constituent assembly still figured among the 'ten demands of the political programme'. This shows Peng believed even then that the revolution had not yet begun (according to him, the third Chinese revolution started in November 1951); and that a genuine revolution could only be achieved through the struggle for a constituent assembly, not through armed struggle – not through a 'meaningless' civil war.

Here, Peng contradicted Trotsky. In raising the slogan of the constituent assembly, Trotsky did not intend to counterpose illegal armed struggle with legal peaceful struggle. He envisaged a central political slogan under which all kinds of struggles, including the armed struggle of the poor peasants, could be unified at the political level. Yet in Peng's and other rightwing Trotskyists' opinion, the struggle for the constituent assembly was a legal and peaceful substitute for the illegal armed struggle. When an internal discussion about the slogan took place among Chinese Trotskyists in the late 1920s, Trotsky wrote in a letter to Chinese comrades:

> The struggle for democracy is precisely an indispensable condition for building the party. The slogan of the constituent assembly can unify politically *the scattered movements and insurrections in various provinces* and provide a basis for the solidarity of the CP, so that it can become the national leader of the proletariat and all the toiling masses.[19]

This passage clarifies the relationship between the slogan of the constituent assembly and the 'scattered movements and insurrections in various provinces'. Unfortunately the Chinese Trotskyists ignored this directive, and Peng and his co-thinkers turned the struggle for a constituent assembly into a policy diametrically opposed to armed struggle.... This view, which originated in a wrong interpretation of the struggle for the constituent assembly, meant that Chinese Trotskyists (especially Peng Shuzhi) failed to recognise the third Chinese revolution when it happened and adopted an absurd attitude towards it even long after it had triumphed.

---

19   Leon Trotsky, 'Letter to Chinese oppositionists', 2 April 1930, retranslated from Wang's Chinese translation; Wang's emphasis.

The Stalinists and Maoists' gravest mistake lay not in carrying on a long-term armed struggle (this was actually their merit, and Mao Zedong's in particular) but in their refusal to launch a struggle for democratic demands around the call for a constituent assembly. As a result, the CCP was for many years deprived of a central political slogan and suffered what Mao called 'an acute sense of isolation'[20] and a series of heavy defeats for the Red Army, which at one point threatened both the party and its armed forces with extinction.

... In Peng's opinion, the gravest mistake the CCP ever made was to embark on and persevere in long-term armed struggle. If the Chinese Communist had not taken up arms and had instead launched a struggle for a constituent assembly, then, according to his wife, Chen Bilan,

> the third Chinese revolution could have occurred in the thirties, enabling the CCP to take power and establish the dictatorship of the proletariat and poor peasants before the Second World War. ... It could have avoided the unnecessary sacrifice of the lives of more than 10,000 of the most militant members of the party and the young communists. ... Unfortunately, the path followed by the CCP after the defeat of the second Chinese revolution was not that pointed to by Trotsky but the one ordered by Stalin – the adventurist policy or guerrilla war that Wang [Fanxi] called 'armed struggle'. This erroneous policy of 'armed struggle' not only destroyed a great majority of the party's cadres, its entire organisational bases in the cities, the huge workers and peasants' mass organisations, and its clandestine forces in the Guomindang army (such as the forces of He Long and Ye Ting and a number of sympathisers of the Guomindang army), but drove the various Guomindang warlords into a united front in pursuit of the common aim of defeating the guerrillas of the CCP.[21]

Anyone who knows something of the history of the Chinese revolution will realise the absurdity of the argument that 'the clandestine forces of He Long and Ye Ting' would not have been destroyed and the 'various warlords' would

---

20   In his report to the CC of the CCP (25 November 1928) on 'The Struggle in the Jinggang Mountains', Mao wrote: 'We have an acute sense of isolation which we keep hoping will end. Only by launching a political and economic struggle for democracy, which will also involve the urban petty bourgeoisie, can we turn the revolution into a seething tide that will surge through the country' (*Selected Works*, vol. 1, pp. 97–8).
21   Ch'en Pi-lan (Chen Bilan) 1973, p. 8.

not have been 'driven into a united front' against the CCP guerrillas if the CCP had not engaged in armed struggle....

Peng and other comrades had the chance to carry out exactly the same line they would have liked the CCP to adopt. What was the result of our endeavours? Our organisation and its cadres were brought to the brink of extinction (not to say utterly extinguished). Although we did not engage in guerrilla warfare, we were suppressed and destroyed no less severely than the CCP by the Guomindang secret police [in the 1930s]. Even worse, unlike the CCP during the counter-revolutionary period, the Japanese invasion, and the civil war after the Second World War, we played no political role of any importance. Yes, we worked in accordance with 'the line pointed to by Trotsky' and struggled for a revolutionary-democratic programme, but we were unable to overthrow the Guomindang in the 1930s in the way Peng thought the CCP could have done had it followed Trotsky's instead of Stalin's line.... How can we explain this paradox?

The explanation is that the Chinese Trotskyists wrongly counterposed the democratic struggle for the constituent assembly to the armed struggle of the poor peasants and did not make the latter a component part of the former. We failed because we did not integrate the two struggles, because we rejected, in deeds though not in words, the armed struggle of the poor peasants. Trotsky cannot be held responsible for this mistake, for he pointed out that we should 'unify politically the dispersed movements and insurrections in various provinces' with a struggle for a constituent assembly.

So in colonial and semi-colonial countries, a revolutionary party representing the working class must first struggle for a revolutionary-democratic programme (with the call for an all-powerful constituent assembly as its centre) to mobilise, unify, and lead the masses of the cities and the villages to overthrow the ruling class. Yet in this struggle, they must avoid the illusion of a 'peaceful parliamentary road' and watch out for 'fascist' armed repression by reactionaries. They must use every opportunity to get access to arms with which to arm themselves and the masses; and when objective conditions necessitate and permit, they should lead proletarians, semi-proletarians, and peasants in armed struggle, as part of a nationwide struggle for a revolutionary democratic programme, to seize power and start the socialist revolution.

'Revolutionary Defeatism' and Other Things

... In her article, Chen Bilan accuses me of having given 'uncritical support to the leadership of Chiang Kai-shek' at the start of the Resistance War against

Japan and taken a position of 'defeatism' in its final stage. The first charge is a groundless lie, so I will ignore it for now. Regarding the different views on 'defeatism' held by Peng and me, it is common knowledge that there were two prerequisites for Lenin's slogan of revolutionary defeatism: both sides in a war must be imperialists; and the proletariat in all warring countries must be confronted with the historical task of making socialist revolution. The two main contents of Lenin's 'defeatism' were (a) that the main enemy is in one's own country and the defeat of one's 'own' ruling class is a lesser evil and (b) that the external war must be transformed into a civil war, even at the risk of temporary defeats at the hands of the foreign imperialists. Lenin formulated his idea of revolutionary defeatism during the First World War, when it was absolutely correct and fully applicable.

In the Second World War, Trotskyists remained in principle committed to revolutionary defeatism in fascist imperialist countries, as well as in democratic ones. However, in its concrete application, especially after the defeat of France, we made some significant changes. In fascist countries we continued to apply revolutionary defeatism in the same way as in the First World War, but not in the democratic countries. The defeat in France at the start of the war was in no sense a 'lesser evil'. The anti-fascist sentiments of the toiling masses throughout the world were progressive and even revolutionary. Revolutionary defeatism in the democratic imperialist countries retained its validity, but it had to be understood and applied in a somewhat different way: as the continuation of class struggle regardless of the war against fascism in the not yet defeated countries, and as a revolutionary liberation war under the leadership of the working class against the fascist occupiers in the defeated countries.

... China in the 1930s was a semi-colonial country ruled by a reactionary bourgeois-landlord government. It had just experienced a revolution that had been defeated, with none of its tasks solved. Class antagonisms were intense when the Japanese set out to turn China into a complete colony.... The war on China's part was progressive and just, because it was against imperialism and in defence of national independence. Chinese workers and peasants had to support the war even though it was under the leadership of Chiang Kai-shek. But support for the Resistance War was not equivalent to support for the leadership of Chiang Kai-shek. The Chiang Kai-shek government, which was linked to the imperialists and antagonistic to the interests of the workers and poor peasants, was unable to lead the war to final victory. Only a revolutionary government could do that. So our attitude was to support the Resistance War but not the Guomindang leadership; to participate in the war against the external enemy, but not to abandon the revolution against the internal enemy.

Was this defencism or defeatism? True, it was not the same as the defeatist position Lenin took in the First World War, but nor was it defencism in the proper sense of the term. In a sense, it resembled the 'defeatism' of European revolutionaries in the democratic imperialist countries after Hitler had defeated their governments and occupied their countries.

To support and fight in a progressive war (whether against external enemies or internal ones, like during the Spanish civil war in the 1930s) cannot but be 'revolutionary defeatist' in essence if the revolutionaries remain committed to their revolutionary tasks, but it would be more exact to call it 'revolutionary victoryism' (in the sense that the war cannot be won except through revolution). The only alternative would be a position of 'victory first, then revolution', which leads not only to the betrayal of the revolution but to the defeat of the progressive war.

The 'revolutionary defeatism' (which we called 'revolutionary victoryism') defended by Zheng Chaolin and me during the Resistance War was precisely this kind of revolutionary victoryism. For Peng, the question was very simple: in imperialist wars, we are defeatist; in progressive wars, we are defensist. As for how to continue the class struggle in the progressive war; how to apply the 'arms of criticism' to the reactionary leadership of the progressive war; how to transform the 'arms of criticism' into the 'criticism of arms', such questions probably never entered his head. Instead he simply repeated the cliché 'Support the war, criticise the leadership'. Fortunately for Peng, the Chinese Trotskyists never played a serious role in the Resistance War and there was no strong revolutionary movement in the cities in the unoccupied areas against the Guomindang government, so he could safely stick to his hackneyed views. Otherwise he would have been exposed like most of the communist and socialist leaders in the Spanish civil war, who insisted on 'victory first and revolution second' and condemned as 'national traitors' or 'defeatists' those who put revolution first. . . .

PART 14

Chinese Trotskyism and Literature

Chinese Trotskyism and the World of Letters

Gregor Benton

Source: Benton 1996.

The Chinese Trotskyists' influence on literature and scholarship before 1949, particularly at the end of the 1920s and in the early 1930s, was far greater than their political influence and in some respects could match the CCP's. Whereas many of the CCP's early generation of writers and scholars either died or retired from the revolution (or became Trotskyists), China's leading Oppositionists continued to publish large numbers of books and articles on political and other subjects after the birth in 1929 of Shanghai's socialist cultural movement.

The main trend in the literary movement sponsored by the CCP in Shanghai at around the same time as the emergence of the broader movement was proletarian literature or 'proletkult', a futurist import from the Soviet Union that rejected 'intellectualism' and the bourgeois literary tradition in favour of a 'pure' literature of the working class. 'Proletkult', defined by Philip Rahv as 'an internationally uniform literature ... whose main service was the carrying out of party assignments',[1] found little sympathy with Lenin or with Trotsky, who criticised it harshly in *Literature and Revolution*[2] and insisted that the arts must be a sphere unto themselves rather than an artificial product of official decrees.[3] According to literary critics, proletarian literature as practised in China after 1929 was a hollow, stilted, clichéd, and mediocre form of writing. According to Wang Fanxi, its practitioners 'lagged a long way behind us in their publishing.... They achieved nothing of note, just like similar "proletarian literature" movements elsewhere in the world, and it was not until after 1933 ... that their cultural movement began to show any real sign of life'.[4]

It was partly the thinning after 1927 of the CCP's critical intelligence through the death or defection of its writers and scholars that permitted the rise to power in the Party of a man like Wang Ming, whose fluency in Soviet-style Marxism-Leninism was one of his main assets in an organisation otherwise devoid of 'theoreticians'; and of Mao Zedong, who recruited the

---

1 Quoted in C.T. Hsia 1971, p. 272.
2 For an English translation, see Trotsky 1960.
3 For Trotsky's views on 'proletarian culture', see Knei-Paz 1978, pp. 289–301.
4 Wang Fan-hsi 1991, pp. 159–61.

hack-philosopher Ai Siqi to lend himself a semblance of Marxist learning by plagiarising Soviet 'dialectical materialism'.[5]

The Chinese Trotskyists' greatest and most influential literary figure was Chen Duxiu, who in *New Youth* in January 1917 published and enthusiastically supported Hu Shi's famous article on literary reform. In a fiery manifesto titled 'On the Literary Revolution', he wrote:

> Overthrow the painted, powdered, and obsequious literature of the aristocratic few, ... the stereotyped and over-ornamental literature of classicism, ... [and] the pedantic, unintelligible, and obscurantist literature of the hermit and recluse, [and] create the plain, simple and expressive literature of the people, ... the fresh and sincere literature of realism, ... and ... the plain-speaking and popular literature of society in general.[6]

Chen was a pioneer of the movement to abolish classical Chinese from the contemporary press and spread the vernacular; in 1904, in his native Anhui province, he published *Suhua bao* ('Vernacular speech journal'), a newspaper written in vernacular Chinese. During the May Fourth period, through *New Youth* he played a major part in introducing modern Western literature to China. The discussion in 1916 by Chen Duxiu and others of Western and Chinese literary trends was, says Chow Tse-tsung, 'probably the first manifestation of the new intellectuals' intention to reform Chinese literature in accordance with Western theories and foreshadowed trends of Chinese literary thought in later years'.[7]

During his Communist and Trotskyist period, Chen mainly concerned himself with social and political movements, but he did occasionally return to his philological studies. He did so as part of his project to alphabetise the Chinese script, in pursuit of his dream of universal literacy.

Chen hoped eventually to replace China's many dialects with a single national language that would promote unity and patriotism,[8] but in the meantime he put great emphasis on the need for a proper study of dialects, on the grounds that the national language as conceived in the 1920s was 'too artificial, too removed from the real language'. Until such a time as a truly national language arises, he said in 1929, we should manage the transition by taking

---

5 On this question, see Fogel 1987.
6 Chow Tse-tsung 1960, p. 276.
7 Chow Tse-tsung 1960, p. 273.
8 Feigon 1983b, p. 71.

as our standard the most influential local languages, namely, those of Beijing, Shanghai, Hankou, and Guangzhou, for these are 'the biggest metropolitan centres of production and politics'. Chen sent his dialect study to the publishers but it was not accepted, due to Chen's 'wanted' status. Nonetheless, his linguistic research was well regarded, and among those who contributed towards his living in the difficult years of his Trotskyist period was the linguist Zhao Yuanren.[9]

After Chen Duxiu, China's best-known literary 'Trotskyists' were Wang Duqing and Wang Shiwei, who though never actually members of any Trotskyist organisation were very close to the Trotskyists on many questions and completely agreed with Trotsky's polemic against the idea of 'proletarian literature'.

Wang Duqing was a French-returned student of fine art, a poet, and one of the four founders of the Creation Society, a Communist literary group in the 1920s. Wang became a Trotskyist in 1929, together with Chen Duxiu, after serving as dean first of the liberal arts college of Sun Yat-sen University in Guangzhou and then of the Shanghai College of Fine Arts. After the disbanding of the Creation Society, Wang founded his own journal, *Zhankai* ('Unfurled'), in 1930. In it he accused the other Creationists, particularly the pro-Comintern Guo Moruo, of being Stalin's lackeys and selling out the revolution.[10]

As for Wang Shiwei, today he has become a main symbol of libertarian dissent for critical Chinese youth, who have access to his 'counter-revolutionary' writings in various collections of 'negative teaching materials' put out by the Party;[11] and, increasingly, for critical historians of Chinese Communism in the West.[12]

Wang Shiwei, who joined the CCP in 1926, was a gifted writer and translator, and one of many city intellectuals who, as patriots and socialists, went by secret and dangerous paths to the Communist headquarters at Yan'an after 1937. The relationship between the Party and the writers who went to Yan'an

---

9   Ren Jianshu and Tang Baolin 1989, Vol. 2, pp. 5–7.
10 C.T. Hsia 1971, p. 120; Kagan 1969, p. 164.
11 In 1989, Dai Qing, one of China's best-known investigative journalists, arrested after the June massacre in Tian'anmen Square on suspicion of 'taking part in the turmoil', published a major study on three writers, including Wang Shiwei, that defended Wang's libertarian stand and denounced his murder (Dai Qing 1989). Some months earlier, these three studies had appeared as separate articles in Shanghai's *Wenhui yuebao*. Dai's writings on Wang Shiwei are translated together with some documents concerning Wang's case in Dai Qing 1994.
12 The following discussion of the Wang Shiwei incident is based on Benton 1982.

to assist in the Communists' war against Japan was a difficult one; eventually, Mao cracked down on some of the writers' leaders.

The conflict between the Party and the writers began in 1942, shortly after Mao had launched his Rectification Campaign against 'bureaucratic tendencies' in the Party, when Wang Shiwei and others (including the well-known feminist writer Ding Ling, the short-story writer Luo Feng, the novelist Xiao Jun, and the poet Ai Qing) published essays voicing their disquiet about the existence in Yan'an of a privileged elite.[13] They also dealt in their essays with the role of literature in a revolutionary society. Wang Shiwei said that writing should be free of political control, that it should be allowed to monitor privilege and bureaucracy, and that it should be free to treat questions of human spirit, to which politics has no answer.[14]

At first Wang Shiwei and the writers were widely applauded, particularly by young people in Yan'an. Many spectators at Wang Shiwei's later trial initially dissented from the official condemnation of him. Wang Shiwei alone among the writers was put on show-trial for his views. He was the scapegoat, first, because he was the least known of the writers, so he would attract the least outside attention; second, because he took his criticisms of Yan'an society further than the others; third, because of his past Trotskyist associations; and, last, because he refused to eat his words.

Such was the depth of support for the Yan'an writers that in May 1942 they became the main target of Mao's famous Talks on Art and Literature, in which he advanced the thesis that the task of literature was not to expose the 'dark side' of revolutionary society, but to reflect its 'bright side' and to extol the masses. He also attacked the Trotskyist view that literature should be pluralist and free of political restrictions. 'Party work in literature and art', said Mao

> occupies a definite and assigned position in Party revolutionary work as a whole and is subordinated to the revolutionary tasks set by the Party.... Opposition to this arrangement is certain to lead to dualism or pluralism, and in essence amounts to 'politics – Marxist, art – bourgeois', as with Trotsky.[15]

Wang Shiwei's insistence on the separation of politics from art was incompatible with this centralist and manipulative Maoist view of the role of art and

---

13   For writings by Wang Shiwei and the Yan'an group, see Benton 1975 and Benton and Hunter (eds) 1995.
14   See Wang Shiwei 1982 [1942].
15   Mao Tse-tung 1955 [1942], p. 86.

literature. Wang Shiwei and the Trotskyists represented 'a model for cultural freedom', wrote Richard Kagan, that had as its goal 'the combination of polity with culture, of social justice with personal development, of equality with individuality'.[16] Because of their libertarian stand, Mao made them a principal target of his campaign to 'ensure that literature and art fit well into the whole revolutionary machine as a component part'.[17]

But despite the writers' initial popularity and the obvious impact of their criticisms, the authorities' campaign against them quickly took effect. The Trotskyists' apparent failure from the point of view of Communists in Yan'an to join wholeheartedly in the Resistance had not made them popular, and Wang Ming had smeared them as agents of Japan. So the charge of 'Trotskyism' levelled against Wang Shiwei was extremely damaging, and helped swing public opinion against him.

Was Wang Shiwei a Trotskyist? It is not clear what his relationship to the CCP was at this time. His biographer Dai Qing says that he had quit the Party after it criticised him in 1927 for falling unhappily in love with a woman Communist. But his friend Wang Fanxi believes that he lost his membership later, when Chiang Kai-shek's White terror reached Beijing in 1928 and Communist organisation in the city was automatically dissolved. That would mean he neither left nor was expelled, but was simply cut adrift like many thousands of other Party members during the crisis years after 1927.

In 1930, he tried, unsuccessfully, to get back into touch with the Party in Shanghai. While he was living in extreme poverty in Shanghai, his closest friends (in particular Wang Fanxi) were driven from the CCP as Oppositionists, and he, too, became an Oppositionist of sorts. He was against their expulsion, and he translated various political writings for them. But he passionately believed that social revolution was never so radical as revolution in the soul, since unreformed human nature – the source, as he saw it, of Stalinism – would taint any future revolution that failed to deal with it. So his Trotskyist friends considered him an emotional revolutionary rather than a hardened Bolshevik, and he never joined their ranks. He probably rejoined the CCP after going to Yan'an in 1937.[18]

Evidence of various sorts was offered at Wang Shiwei's 'trial' to 'prove' that he was indeed a Trotskyist: he had described Stalin as boorish and unattractive; he had condemned the Moscow purges and the sentencing of Zinoviev; he had refused to brand the Russian Oppositionists as fascists, and continued to

---

16   Kagan 1969, pp. 166–7.
17   Mao Tse-tung 1955 [1942], p. 70.
18   This biographical sketch of Wang Shiwei is based on materials provided by Wang Fanxi.

insist that Trotskyists like Wang Fanxi and Chen Qichang were 'Communists of humanity'; he had made a distinction between a political party of the workers and a peasant party with proletarian leaders; and he was allegedly negative about the wartime united front with the Guomindang. But Wang's article 'Wild Lily' suggests that his position on the united front was in fact quite orthodox. As for Wang Shiwei's other views, Mao Zedong himself is reported to have said similar things about the Moscow purges and the Trotskyists, just as the Stalinist envoy Wang Ming had criticised the CCP's overwhelmingly peasant composition after his return from Moscow in late 1937.

Wang Shiwei stuck to his views even though he was attacked and humiliated in front of an audience that at times numbered more than one thousand. Eventually, he was dismissed from his translating job and sent to work in a matchbox factory. In 1947, he was hacked to death with a sword. In 1962, Mao said that it had been wrong to kill him, though he approved of the other penal sanctions against Wang. Curiously, Mao then remembered Wang as a 'Guomindang agent'. In the 1980s, however, all the slanders against Wang were openly retracted; and finally, in 1991, he was officially rehabilitated.[19]

Probably the first and certainly the finest Chinese writer to be strongly influenced by Trotsky's theory of art and literature was Lu Xun, the universally acknowledged giant of modern Chinese writing and a George Orwell of the Chinese left. Yet literary historians have paid scant attention to this intellectual link between Lu Xun and Trotsky;[20] and in China, where for many years the safely dead Lu Xun has served as an icon of political orthodoxy, knowledge of his link to the Third International's worst bugbear has been systematically suppressed.

Lu Xun has even been portrayed by the Chinese authorities as an implacable opponent of the Trotskyists, whom he allegedly held in deepest political contempt. In 1993, however, new evidence emerged that would seem to discredit this view of him, and at the same time to right a great wrong committed against the Trotskyists more than half a century ago by their enemies in the Chinese Communist Party (CCP).

Lu Xun read *Literature and Revolution*, a key text that contains the essence of Trotsky's thought on literature, in Japanese translation; he sponsored its translation into Chinese by Wei Shuyuan (from Russian) and Li Qiye (from English),

---

19   Lin Cuifen 1991. At the time of Wang's rehabilitation, two members of the Public Security Bureau tried to give Wang's widow ten thousand yuan 'as an expression of sympathy', but she refused to accept the money for herself and instead donated it to endow a literary prize. See *Wenhuibao* (Shanghai), 22 February 1993.
20   A connection between the two thinkers is briefly noted in Pickowicz 1977, p. 368.

but Wei died of tuberculosis, so the translation was done by Li alone, and published in 1926. Lu Xun himself translated (from Japanese) Trotsky's long speech delivered at the meeting on literary policy organised by the Central Committee of the CPSU on 9 May 1924,[21] and in 1926 he translated (also from Japanese) the third chapter, on Alexander Blok, of *Literature and Revolution* for an appendix to a translation published by Weiming congshu ('Unnamed Library'), under Lu Xun's editorship, of Blok's famous poem 'The Twelve'.[22] In April 1927, Lu Xun, echoing Trotsky, said of 'people's literature' that it 'is nothing of the sort, for the people have not yet opened their mouths. These works voice the sentiments of onlookers'.[23]

It is interesting to note that Lu Xun's sponsorship in 1926 of the translation of Trotsky's writings clearly postdated Trotsky's break with Stalin. On 22 May 1929, three months after Trotsky's final deportation from the Soviet Union, Lu Xun (in a talk to Yanjing University's Chinese Literature Society) was still openly expressing the same point of view as Trotsky on the relationship between politics and literature.[24] He stopped referring to Trotsky's theory after 1929, probably for diplomatic reasons, but its rejection as vulgar and ignorant of the idea that culture merely mirrors economic interest continued to inform his lifetime's work.[25]

Lu Xun's continuing respect for the Chinese Trotskyist leader Chen Duxiu also set him apart from orthodox Stalinist opinion. A study by the Hong Kong scholar Chen Shengchang on Trotsky's literary influence on Lu Xun presents an interesting theory about Lu Xun's attitude in early 1933 to Chen Duxiu. In February 1933, Lu Xun's Communist or fellow-travelling literary opponents attacked the 'realist' writer Hu Qiuyuan[26] for indiscriminately '"admiring"

---

21   I have this information about the translation into Chinese of Trotsky's writings on literature from Wang Fanxi, in a personal communication. See also Hui Quan 1971, pp. 1–3. According to Pickowicz 1977, p. 367, 'Lu Xun and other members of the Unnamed Society translated Trotsky's *Literature and Revolution*'. The most recent Chinese translation, in this case from the Russian, of *Literature and Revolution* is Tuoluociji 1992.
22   Yi Ding 1978, p. 307. See also Lee 1982, pp. 166–7; and Chen Shengchang 1990, pp. 285–311.
23   Lu Xun 1956–60 [1927], p. 340.
24   Lu Xun 1956–60 [1929], particularly the last paragraph on p. 52.
25   Yi Ding 1978, pp. 284–7.
26   Hu Qiuyuan was among the Chinese students who returned to China sometime in the early to mid-1930s, after studying in Japan. The majority of these returned students supported the Chinese Communist Party, but a few (notably Hu and Zheng Xuejia) showed some sympathy for Trotskyism and borrowed weapons from the Trotskyist armoury to attack the Chinese Stalinists. The leaders of the Communist Party were extremely hostile to Hu, Zheng, and the other members of their group, and attacked them in an effort to

Stalin, "sympathizing" with Trotsky, "greatly respecting" Kropotkin, and even "regretting [the fate of] Chen Duxiu and Deng Yanda".[27] According to Chen Shengchang, Lu Xun interpreted this criticism as an oblique attack on his own politics, and answered it (also obliquely) on 5 March 1933, in an essay titled 'How I started writing novels'. This essay contained the sentence: 'Here I must commemorate Mr Chen Duxiu, who was among those who put most effort into encouraging me to write novels'.[28] Chen Shengchang explains this statement by recalling Lu Xun's words on another occasion: 'In China there are very few who show sympathy to a defeated hero, ... and very few who weep over a defeated rebel's cause'.[29] Chen Shengchang concludes: 'In my opinion, when the League of Left-Wing Writers recklessly attacked the so-called "Trotskyists" in the literary world, Lu Xun used the chance to commemorate Chen Duxiu and at the same time to show sympathy to [the defeated] Trotsky'.[30]

Lu Xun's propagation of Trotsky's libertarian and pluralist theory of art and literature directly or indirectly inspired the left-wing writers Wang Shiwei, Ding Ling, Luo Feng, Xiao Jun, and Ai Qing, persecuted by the Maoists in Yan'an in 1942. It also appears to have swayed the literary thinking of Hu Feng, a poet and maverick literary theorist who – though himself a Stalinist – was rarely out of trouble with the Party and in 1955 became the object of a nationwide ideological campaign because of his opposition to literary dictation by the Party leadership.[31]

The overt Trotskyist connections of Wang Shiwei are well known, but the apparent origin of what we might call Hu Feng's literary Trotskyism, implied but never plainly stated, was only recently revealed, in his posthumous papers published in Beijing in 1993. Hu Feng's acquaintance with future Trotskyist thinkers began as early as the summer of 1925, when (as Zhang Guangren) he studied for a year in the same class as Wang Shiwei and the future Trotskyist leader Wang Fanxi at Beijing University's Department of Letters. Though this coincidence had no immediate political issue, it is interesting to note that one small class in 1925 thus harboured the two men who would become Chinese

---

    discredit Chen Duxiu and the real Trotskyists. Hu and his friends very quickly became associated with the Guomindang. Hu earned his living by writing for the Shenzhou Publishing Company.

27   Chen had been jailed and Deng had been shot, both by Chiang Kai-shek.
28   Lu Xun 1963 [1933], p. 393.
29   Lu Xun 1963 [1926], p. 107.
30   Chen Shengchang 1990, p. 311.
31   Goldman 1967, pp. 129–57; Mei Zhi 2013.

Communism's best-known literary dissidents and martyrs, and another who would be among its fiercest left-wing critics.[32]

In an article written in Beijing in 1984, but not published until 1993, after his death, Hu Feng recalled some of the writings that had influenced his thinking about literature in the 1920s, and, in so doing, incidentally revealed what was probably the primary source of the dissidence that stubbornly informed his view on literature for the rest of his life.[33] In an extremely condensed passage at the beginning of his article, he mentioned the translation made under Lu Xun's direction of Blok's poem 'The Twelve' and went on to praise Lu Xun's postscript to the publication, which he said had helped him to understand the relationship between literature and revolution and 'further freed him from a vulgar sociological [understanding] of the creative process'. He added that the postscript had even allowed him to appreciate (Lu Xun's translation of) the theoretical work *Kumô no shôchô* ('Symbols of agony') by Kuriyagawa Hakuson, an 'idealist' Japanese literary critic who put forward the quite un-Marxist view (which Hu Feng would otherwise have felt duty-bound to damn) that 'agony or frustration arising from the suppression of human vitality is the foundation of literature and art, and the way to express it is symbolism in its broadest sense'.[34]

Hu Feng, like many young left-wing Chinese scholars and writers in 1926, had fallen under the spell of *Symbols of Agony*, but had been puzzled by how an 'idealist' like Kuriyagawa Hakuson could explain so convincingly the process of artistic creation, which according to 'sociologists' only materialists could grasp. After reading Lu Xun's publication of 'The Twelve', however, Hu Feng realised that not all Marxists believed that everything in the creative process has a 'material' or 'economic' base that can be discerned only by those schooled in the so-called 'laws of sociology'.[35]

Though, for obvious reasons, Hu Feng did not explicitly mention the chapter from Trotsky's *Literature and Revolution* that Lu Xun had used to illuminate the literary genius of the 'bourgeois' Blok, it is quite clear that this chapter (together with Lu Xun's brief postscript, which is deeply imbued with the

---

32 See Wang Fan-hsi 1991, p. 16. Also among Wang Fanxi's friends in Beijing's 'Montmartre' of the 1920s was Feng Xuefeng, who together with Hu Feng became a main actor in the story of Lu Xun and the Trotskyists; but according to Wang Fanxi, Feng was probably unacquainted at the time with either Hu Feng or Wang Shiwei (personal communication).

33 Hu Feng 1993a.

34 For Lu Xun's postscript to 'The Twelve', see Lu Xun, *Collected Works*, Volume 7, pp. 397–401. On the little-known Kuriyagawa Hakuson (1880–1923), see Ching-mao Cheng 1977, pp. 84–6.

35 For an elaboration of this point and a detailed analysis of the relevant passage in Hu Feng's article, see Wang Fanxi 1993.

spirit of Trotsky's style of literary appreciation and with a profound respect for Trotsky's theory of literary creation) was the early mainspring of his later (fateful) opposition to Party decreed 'mechanicalism' and Mao's 'cultural desert'.[36]

In 1936, about a year before China went to war against Japan, Lu Xun criticised calls by some pro-Communist writers for a 'literature of national defence', which in his view smacked of class collaboration. Instead, he proposed a 'literature of the masses for national revolutionary war'.[37] (Though this slogan is usually attributed to Lu Xun, his disciple and associate Hu Feng claimed in a recently published article to have been the one who actually coined it;[38] at the time, however, Lu Xun took responsibility for it.)[39] The rival slogans can be seen in retrospect to have roughly mirrored two positions in the CCP: Mao's position, which advocated struggle as well as unity in the united front with the Guomindang against Japan; and Wang Ming's, which advocated unity without friction.

But Lu Xun's favoured slogan also had some points in common with the Trotskyist position on the war, that is, support for the resistance but class-based criticism of the Chinese government. After the publication of the slogan, the Trotskyist Chen Qichang, impressed by its radical content and persuaded of the 'unbending morality' of Lu Xun (whom he idolised), sent the writer some Trotskyist literature. In an accompanying letter, Chen told Lu Xun that the only result of the new united front ordered by the 'Moscow bureaucrats' would be 'to deliver the revolutionary masses into the hands of the [Guomindang] executioners for further slaughter'.[40] Chen Qichang was not alone in sensing a Trotskyist dimension to the slogan promoted by Lu Xun, whose Party critics did their best to slap a 'Trotskyist' hat on him on account of it. Hu Feng's posthumous papers revealed that even Communist leaders in Yan'an had suspected him of Trotskyist sympathies for authoring it;[41] Tian Han and Zhou Yang, two

---

36 Hu Feng 1993a, p. 5.
37 On Lu Xun's resistance to the new line, see Tsi-an Hsia 1968, pp. 101–45.
38 Hu Feng 1993b, p. 143.
39 Lu Xun 1956–60 [1936b], p. 291.
40 For Chen Qichang's letter, see this volume, pp. 103–4. See also Wang Fan-hsi in this volume, pp. 513–5, where he points out that Chen had not discussed the contents of his letter with any other of the Trotskyists before sending it; as a result, they criticised him for his action.
41 Hu Feng 1993b, p. 143. Tsi-an Hsia 1968, p. 132, also noted that Lu Xun's policy in this period amounted to 'an eclecticism of Trotskyism and the current line of the Communist Party. This was perhaps the only compromise he could make to satisfy the demands of Mao Tsetung and Stalin without sacrificing the principle of class struggle'. But Hsia wrongly characterised the Trotskyist policy as one of 'proletarian revolution as against the national interest'. As Chen Qichang made clear in his letter to Lu Xun, the Trotskyists had been

leading supporters of the 'literature of national defence' slogan, even tried to convince Lu Xun that Hu Feng 'was a traitor sent by the authorities'.[42]

Shortly before Lu Xun's death, in 1936, a document appeared that was purportedly his reply to the 'Letter from the Trotskyites'. This document, which created quite a stir at the time of its publication, defended Stalin against Chen Qichang's criticism. It went on to imply that the Trotskyists were in the pay of the Japanese; it drew a fat political line between Lu Xun and his Trotskyist correspondent:

> Your 'theory' [that the anti-Japanese united front is a betrayal of the revolution] is certainly much loftier than that of Mao Zedong: yours is high in the sky, while his is simply on the ground. But admirable as is such loftiness, it will unfortunately be just the thing welcomed by the Japanese aggressors.... Since the Japanese welcome your lofty theories, I cannot help feeling concern for you when I see your well-printed publications. If someone deliberately spreads a malicious rumour to discredit you, accusing you of accepting money for these publications from the Japanese, how are you to clear yourselves? I say this not to retaliate because some of you formerly joined certain others to accuse me of accepting Russian roubles.[43] No, I would not stoop so low, and I do not believe that you could stoop so low as to take money from the Japanese.... But I want to warn you that your lofty theory will not be welcomed by the Chinese people, and that your behaviour runs counter to present-day Chinese people's standards of morality. This is all I have to say about your views. In conclusion, this sudden receipt of a letter and periodicals from you has made me rather uncomfortable.... It must be because some of my 'comrades-in-arms' have been accusing me of certain faults. But whatever my faults, I am convinced that my views are quite different from yours.[44]

---

calling since the late 1920s for a 'revolutionary democratic struggle' (Chen [Zhongshan] 1956–60, p. 280).

42 Lu Xun 1956–60 [1936b], p. 294.

43 I questioned Wang Fanxi about this claim; Wang denies that Trotskyist ever made such an allegation, and although he accepts people associated with the Guomindang may have included Lu Xun on their list of recipients of 'Kremlin gold', he personally doubts even they would have been so stupid. He interprets the charge as an instance of the familiar tactic of pretending to have been attacked first when you yourself go onto the offensive.

44 The purported reply by Lu Xun is translated in Lu Xun, *Selected Works*, Volume 4, pp. 281–2; the passage cited is on p. 282.

Ironically, the letter's implication that the Trotskyists were traitors was later made explicit by Wang Ming, whose policies Lu Xun had – knowingly or unknowingly – been attacking.[45] Also ironically, and tragically, Chen Qichang, the man smeared in the letter as Japan's hireling, was seized, tortured, and killed by Japanese gendarmes while working for the anti-Japanese resistance in Shanghai in 1942.[46]

The Shanghai Trotskyists responded to Lu Xun's letter with a brief 'Special Declaration' written by Wang Fanxi in the name of the 'Communist League of China (Bolshevik-Leninists)' and published in *Huohua* ('Spark'), the League's theoretical journal. The declaration pointed out that although Lu Xun had titled his letter 'Reply to a letter from the Chinese Trotskyists', in fact Chen Qichang had been the sole author of the initial correspondence, for which Chen bore the complete responsibility. The declaration linked Lu Xun's letter to Stalin's general campaign against Trotsky, and concluded:

> We disdain to expend valuable time and energy on profitless disputation with Lu Xun. We simply call on all proletarian fighters and all revolutionaries to protest at the Stalinist Party's campaign to unite the enemy classes of the entire world against us, and in particular at the shameless vilification of Comrade Trotsky. For Lu Xun's slanders are merely one slender thread floating in a great torrent of venom.[47]

Chen Qichang, in contrast, was clearly wounded by Lu Xun's insinuations, and wrote him a second private letter even longer than the first. In this second letter, he returned to the theme of the united front and bitterly reproached Lu Xun for having replied to his political arguments with cheap mudslinging. 'You sneakily spread rumours that the Japanese pay us to produce our journals, and such like', he wrote.

> You really have a nerve to twist things so utterly! The Bolshevik-Leninists' [Trotskyists'] *Douzheng* ['Struggle'] and *Huohua* ['Spark'] only exist because comrades who skimp on food and clothes and live in tiny garret rooms are prepared to drip sweat in order to bring them to the light of day. Precisely because we have no financial resources, *Struggle*, previously weekly, has already gone fortnightly, and according to reports will

---

45   See Yi Ding 1978 for the case that Lu Xun knew his target was Wang Ming.
46   Wang Fan-hsi 1991, pp. 159–61.
47   'Tebie shengming' ('Special declaration'), *Huohua*, Volume 3, no. 3, 25 September 1936. The text of this declaration can also be found in Yi Ding 1976.

soon have to go monthly. If the Bolshevik-Leninists really were paid by the Japanese to produce their publications, then no doubt they would be in the same position as you people, who openly bring out book after book and journal after journal, and have them displayed for sale along the main roads... instead of printing and distributing them yourselves.

Chen Qichang waited in vain for a reply to this second letter. The letter remained hidden in Lu Xun's archive for more than forty years, until January 1976 or 1977, when it was published in Beijing by *Lu Xun yanjiu ziliao* ('Research materials on Lu Xun'), no. 4.[48]

Today, evidence has finally emerged to show that the hostile and sarcastic reply to Chen Qichang's first letter was written not by Lu Xun but by the Communist Feng Xuefeng, using his friend's name but not necessarily with his conscious consent (at the time Lu Xun was bed-ridden and soon to die). As early as 1978, in his book about Lu Xun published in Paris by the Centre de publication Asie orientale, the Trotskyist writer Lou Guohua (then living in Hong Kong) had named several arguments to back his suspicion that the letter strongly reflected Feng's influence. Its slanderous tone was inconsonant with Lu Xun's high standards of moral integrity; in particular, Lu Xun detested the 'rouble theory', and would hardly have used a new variant of it against his political opponents.[49] What's more, during the brief recovery from illness that preceded his eventual death (on 19 October 1936), Lu Xun never once returned to the question of Chen's letter. He did, however, say something in a subsequent letter to Xu Maoyong (his Communist opponent in the battle of the slogans, and administrative secretary at the time of the League of Left-Wing Writers) that sharply called into question the intended shaming of Chen Qichang. '[J]udging by my own experience', he wrote, 'those who pose as "revolutionaries" are prone to slander others as "renegades," "counter-revolutionaries," "Trotskyites" or even "traitors" and are usually up to no good'. He also wrote, 'What we should first get rid of are those despots who use a great banner as a tiger-skin to disguise themselves and intimidate others; when they feel the

---

48 Chen Qichang's second letter to Lu Xun, dated 4 July 1936, was republished as an appendix to Yi Ding 1976, pp. 25–6.
49 Although famous for his scathing polemics, Lu Xun distinguished between sarcasm and calumny, slander, or rumour mongering. In 'Abuse and Threats are not Fighting' (Lu Xun, *Selected Works*, Volume 3, 197–199), he said (see p. 199) that 'slander, rumour, threats and abuse... should be made over to the lap-dog writers.... [M]ilitant writers... must stop at ridicule or at heated denunciation'.

least offended they use their "authority" (!) to pass sentence on others, and the charges are fearfully heavy'.[50]

During his recovery, in some 'jottings' published in *Zuojia* ('Writer') in October 1936, Lu Xun reiterated the need for left-wingers to retain their independence in the projected anti-Japanese united front; his arguments, though elliptic, were similar in spirit to those in the letter sent him by Chen Qichang. The second and third 'jottings' were:

> Naturally it is good to proclaim by the written and spoken word the sufferings of those who are slaves under a foreign yoke. But we must take great care lest people reach this conclusion: 'Then it is better after all to be slaves to our own compatriots'.
>
> Since a 'united front' was proposed, those 'revolutionary writers' who went over to the enemy have reappeared, posing as pioneers of the 'united front'. Their contemptible surrender to and collusion with the enemy is now made out to be 'progressive' and glorious.[51]

'Jotting' number two, which apparently referred to the Japanese occupation of 'Manchuria', warned against those who would prefer the rule of Chiang Kai-shek to that of the Mikado. 'Jotting' number three referred to leftists like the playwright Tian Han and the novelist Mu Mutian, who in Lu Xun's opinion had made their 'peace' with the Nationalists too early, either by recanting or by involuntary submission.[52]

As for the stout defence of Stalin made in the letter to Chen Qichang, Lou Guohua pointed out that Lu Xun had by no means unconditionally supported the dictator, and quoted as evidence a story told him by his cousin Lou Shiyi,

---

50 Lu Xun 1956–60 [1936b], p. 298.
51 Lu Xun 1956–60 [1936a], pp. 480–1.
52 An error in the English translation (by Yang Xianyi and Gladys Yang) of Lu Xun's 'Mid-Summer Jottings' may, unintentionally, have added credence to the belief that Lu Xun readily attributed venal motives to his political opponents; for those who read Lu Xun in English, the mistake seemed to legitimise (by making commonplace) the implication in the letter to Chen Qichang that the Chinese Trotskyists were paid agents of the Japanese. In the article, Lu Xun criticised '"revolutionary writers"' who practised '*nakuan*', an unfamiliar archaism that literally seems to mean 'receiving sums of money' or, in the Yangs' rendering, 'the acceptance of bribes' (Lu Xun 1956–60 [1936a], p. 302). However, *nakuan* means not 'to take bribes' but 'to submit' (and, in the original sense, 'pay tribute'). In using it, Lu Xun was therefore criticising those leftists who had surrendered to the Guomindang authorities after 1927, and were now posing as precursors of the newly hatched united front.

a senior editor in Beijing under the Communists. Lou Shiyi's story concerned the publication of André Gide's *Retour de l'URSS*, which had earned Gide the label in Stalinist circles of 'fascist running dog' because of its criticism of the Stalin cult and its defence of the Trotskyists; Gide's book had gone straight onto the Chinese Communists' blacklist after Zheng Chaolin translated it in 1936.[53] According to Lou Shiyi, Lu Xun, who thought extremely highly of Gide, had opposed the denunciation of him, and had even said that if he had seen what Gide had seen in the Soviet Union, he would probably have written the same thing. Here, said Lou Guohua, was the real Lu Xun, a man quite different from the author of the infamous letter.[54]

Lou Guohua also knew that in his personal relations, even with political unpersons routinely coldshouldered by his Party friends, Lu Xun was completely lacking in the sectarian spite that the letter to Chen Qichang epitomised. An example of Lu Xun's principled refusal to live by Stalinist political proscriptions was his friendship with the US Trotskyist Harold Isaacs, in whose honour he gave a farewell dinner on the eve of Isaacs' departure from Shanghai in 1934.[55]

In his recently published 1984 article, Hu Feng told the whole story behind the 'Lu Xun letter', and in so doing bore out Lou Guohua's early hunches.[56] Hu Feng's account revealed that Lu Xun had been in no position to discuss the reply to Chen Qichang's letter, or even to sit up or speak. It also showed that part of Feng Xuefeng's motivation for smearing the Trotskyists was to defend himself, Lu Xun, and other supporters of the radical slogan against the charge

---

53   Lou Shiyi 1989, p. 5. Zheng's was one of three translations of *Retour de l'URSS* that appeared in Shanghai.
54   Yi Ding 1987, pp. 246–9.
55   Isaacs 1985, pp. 111–17; Yi Ding 1987, pp. 310–12. According to Wang Fanxi, Lu Xun did not necessarily know that Isaacs had become a Trotskyist; though Isaacs had fallen out with the CCP's underground workers, he remained a friend of Soong Ching-ling and was, like Lu Xun, a member of Soong's China League for Civil Rights. (In 1976, Xinhua News Agency published a group photograph of Soong Ching-ling, Lu Xun, and others from which Isaacs had been painted out.) Isaacs, however, was convinced that the dinner had a special meaning: 'what looked like a simple friendly act was in fact a political and personal act of considerable weight' (Isaacs 1985, p. 115).
56   The article in question is Hu Feng 1993a. Lou Guohua responded (under the pseudonym Yi Ding) to the publication of this article with an as yet unpublished essay titled 'Changda ban shijide yijian lishi gongan' ('An historical case unsettled for as long as half a century') (30 September 1993); Zheng Chaolin also responded, with an essay (also as yet unpublished) titled 'Tan Hu Feng 'Lu Xun xiansheng' yougan' ('A reaction to Hu Feng's 'Mr Lu Xun'') (23 August 1993) (listed in the References as Zheng Chaolin 1993).

of Trotskyism that their opponents in the Party were levelling at them; and that Feng did not scruple at subjecting Lu Xun to the most cynical manipulation. Hu Feng's complete lack of Trotskyist sympathies would seem to put beyond dispute the sincerity of his story about the letter.

'[*Xianshi wenxue* ("Realistic Literature")] published Lu Xun's "Letter to the Trotskyites" and "On Our Current Literary Movement"', wrote Hu Feng.

> The two articles both made it appear that they had been dictated by him [Lu Xun] and transcribed by O. V. Actually, both were drafted by Feng Xuefeng. O. V. was an attempt at rendering my name,[57] so that no one would guess that it was actually he [Feng Xuefeng]. He was a Party leader, so I felt it was my duty to do all I could to shield him.
>
> After the question of the slogans had arisen, the literature of national defence faction went onto the all-out offensive. Feng Xuefeng flew into something of a panic, and wanted to take steps to stem the offensive. At the time, Lu Xun was seriously ill and could neither sit up nor speak, it was not even possible to discuss with him. Just then the foolish Trotskyists, believing the rumours, thought that they might be able to profit from the situation, and wrote a letter hoping to 'draw' Lu Xun over to their side. Lu Xun was angry when he read the letter, and Feng Xuefeng drafted this reply after he himself had read it. The 'literature of national defence' faction were spreading rumours to the effect that 'literature of the masses for national revolutionary war' was a Trotskyist slogan. Feng Xuefeng's reply was intended as a rebuttal of this slander. He arranged for us to go together with his draft [letter] to see Lu Xun and read it out to him. Lu Xun listened with his eyes closed and said nothing, but simply nodded to indicate agreement.
>
> After Feng Xuefeng had gone back, he felt that he ought to provide some theoretical basis for the slogan [of 'literature for the masses'], so he drafted 'On Our Current Literary Movement', and again arranged to go with me to read it to Lu Xun.[58] Lu Xun was clearly weaker than the previous evening and was even less capable of speaking, all he did was nod to

---

57   According to both Tsi-an Hsia 1968, p. 132, fn. 81, and Yi Ding 1987, pp. 246–8, O. V. stood for Feng Xuefeng, but as Hu Feng himself pointed out, actually, it stood for Hu Feng (probably written something like Oo Vung). The mistake probably derived from the annotation to Volume 6 of the Chinese edition of Lu Xun's *Collected Works* (p. 616, fn. 16).

58   'Lun xianzai womende wenxue yundong: Bingzhong da fangwenzhe, O. V. bilu' ('On our current literary movement: Answers given while ill to a visitor, recorded in writing by O. V.') is in Lu Xun, *Collected Works*, Volume 6, pp. 475–7; it is dated June 6, 1936.

indicate agreement, but he also showed some slight signs of impatience. After we had left, Xuefeng suddenly said to me: I hadn't expected Lu Xun to be so difficult, he's not as good as Gorki; Gorki's political comments are all written by the secretary assigned to him by the Party, all Gorki does is sign them.[59]

This passage shows that Lu Xun did not initiate the letter to Chen Qichang; and Hu Feng's comment that Lu Xun betrayed 'slight signs of impatience' at the end of the second meeting, when the article was read to him, suggests that the ailing writer was by no means wholly convinced of the political point that either the letter or the article embodied (for the two documents were of a piece, and cannot be considered separately).[60] In his article, Hu Feng went on to say that 'where ideological questions were concerned, Lu Xun was exceptionally serious and principled; if you expected him to take responsibility for ideological viewpoints that he had not deeply reflected (and in that period he was incapable of doing so), he would feel extremely uneasy'.[61]

Lu Xun's failure to distance himself from Feng Xuefeng's letter after recovering from his illness is no evidence that he approved of its insinuations. Lu Xun, like Romain Rolland, Bernard Shaw, and other so-called 'friends of the Soviet Union', was a man of letters, not a politician, and belonged to a political type quite common in the 1930s. He would not and could not openly break with Stalinism and the CCP, which, in the political circumstances of the mid 1930s, seemed to him to represent the only progressive force in the world. If he had disowned the letter, he would certainly have had to break with the CCP's front groups. And why did he not reply to Chen Qichang's second letter? Probably because he preferred the whole affair to end rather than go further, for if he had decided to pursue it, he would have had to voice his own opinion, which might have constituted a refutation, or partial refutation, of the letter drafted by Feng Xuefeng. Several months later, however, in his elliptical 'Mid-Summer Jottings', he made the same criticism of the CCP's new policy as had Chen Qichang in his two letters.

---

59   Hu Feng 1993a, p. 28.
60   This point is made in Zheng Chaolin 1993. In his 'Reply to Xu Maoyong' (Lu Xun 1956–60 [1936b], p. 295), Lu Xun seemed to take responsibility for the document (that is, 'On Our Current Literary Movement') 'dictated to O. V.'; but in a letter that was central to his campaign against literary and political dictation by his opponents in the League of Left-Wing Writers, he could hardly have dissociated himself from his two young supporters by revealing the document's true origin.
61   Hu Feng 1993a, p. 29.

After 1949, the 'Lu Xun letter' was used as a powerful weapon in the Maoist régime's campaign to brand the Trotskyists as quislings and class traitors, and (more generally) to warn young Chinese against dabbling in dissidence of any sort. For decades the letter was included in a Chinese language textbook used in senior-middle schools throughout the country, both because it allegedly exemplified Lu Xun's superior writing and because of the political message that it carried. Ironically, its style was no less pinchbeck than its message. During Lu Xun's brief recovery from his illness, Hu Feng remarked to him that Feng Xuefeng had aped his tone well, whereupon Lu Xun 'laughed drily and said, "in my opinion there's no similarity whatsoever"'.[62]

For years the Party had been proud to publish the 'Lu Xun letter', but after the Third Plenum of its Eleventh Central Committee, when Chen Duxiu was partly rehabilitated and historians were finally free to rebut the charge (levelled by Kang Sheng on behalf of Wang Ming in 1938) that Chen Duxiu had taken a monthly subsidy from the Japanese, the letter suddenly became a grave embarrassment. (The abashment no doubt grew when the description of the Trotskyists as 'Japanese agents' was excised from the notes to the 1991 edition of Mao's *Selected Works*.) In his essay on the Hu Feng article, Zheng Chaolin analyses the attempts by various writers to defend the 'Lu Xun letter' in the new, more truthful climate of the 1980s. Their principal defence had been that the letter did not actually call the Trotskyists traitors but simply warned them that they were in danger of becoming traitors unless they mended their ways. Zheng Chaolin dismisses this defence as untenable, for Mao Zedong himself had used the letter as 'proof' that the Trotskyists were indeed traitors; in any case, the Trotskyists had brushed aside the warning in it and refused to 'mend their ways'. Today, however, the intellectual acrobats of the régime's literary establishment have tumbled into a clownish heap, 'for the implication that the Trotskyists were traitors was not Lu Xun's own idea; there is no evidence that if Lu Xun had been able to ponder the matter deeply, he would have agreed with an insinuation, made on his behalf by Feng Xuefeng, that violated his own principles'.[63]

Apart from an indirect influence on writers like Lu Xun through translations of Trotsky's *Literature and Revolution* and, more directly, on Wang Shiwei and other critical intellectuals who hovered between the orthodox Party and the Opposition, the Chinese Trotskyists contributed vast reams of copy to the 'cultural enterprises' that mushroomed in Shanghai after 1929. The scholars and writers who opted for Trotskyism in the late 1920s gave up writing as a

---

62   Ibid.
63   Zheng Chaolin 1993.

permanent career, but to earn a living and to finance their political work they formed close links to a number of these publishers, who specialised mainly in social science books.

Until the crackdown in 1931, the Chinese Trotskyists published far more Marxist writings, including translations of the Marxist classics, than did the official Party. They also translated numerous histories (including Trotsky's and Kropotkin's) of the European revolutionary movement.[64] 'In the early 1930s', according to a CCP ideologue,

> the Trotskyists published a great many articles and books to spread their fallacious 'theories' about the nature of Chinese society and the Chinese revolution, which forced Chinese Marxists and Communist Party members into serious and vigorous polemics to counter their demagoguery and eliminate its negative influence.[65]

The early Chinese Communists knew little or nothing about Marxist theory. It was not until 1937 that the Party's China-based leaders became acquainted with descriptions of it sent to them from the Soviet Union. But by then Soviet Marxism was no longer a critical philosophy with competing schools but a closed state ideology whose main purpose was to justify Stalin's bureaucratic dictatorship. This was the 'Marxism' that Mao, through Ai Siqi, appropriated and used as a weapon to beat off the challenge to his leadership by Wang Ming in the early years of the war against Japan and, subsequently, as a tool with which to shape his tyrannical régime.[66]

Insofar as Marxism in its classical form reached China in the 1930s, it was mainly through the endeavour of the Chinese Trotskyists. To write independently in China in those years, authors needed capital to tide them over the period of writing; if they did translations, however, they could calculate exactly how much effort was necessary to secure a living. So the Trotskyists worked mainly on translations in this period. But they also wrote novels, short stories, biographies, political and social studies, and histories. 'Our "rice-bowl" literary activities during that period played no small part in popularizing and deepening socialist thinking in China', wrote Wang Fanxi.[67]

---

64 Wang Fan-hsi 1991, p. 161.
65 Wang Hongmo 1985, p. 30.
66 This process is described in Ladany 1988; for an outstanding early analysis of the invention of 'Mao Zedong Thought' see Shuang Shan 1973, pp. 65–90.
67 This volume, p. 502. For an early account of the literary activities of the Chinese Trotskyists, see Glass 1990 [1939].

Both Trotskyists and Stalinists wrote for a large number of publishing houses, most of them run on behalf of wealthy former bureaucrats and soldiers who had fallen out with Chiang Kai-shek and decided for the time being to invest their money in publishing.[68] The main exception to this pattern of commercially motivated book-selling was the Oriental Book Company, a radical publishing house that had supported progressive movements in China ever since its foundation in 1903 and was proudly described by its owner Wang Mengzou as 'a product of reform and revolution'.[69] In 1983, introducing a memoir written in 1953 by Wang Yuanfang, an old employee of the company, the CCP's former publishing chief Wang Ziye summed up the company's history as follows:

> You could roughly say that from the Revolution of 1911 to May Fourth [1919] was its pioneering period, from May Fourth to the Great Revolution was its golden age, and after the defeat of the Great Revolution it entered on a downward path. Although in its latter period it produced some [politically] bad books that exercised a bad influence,... it still brought out a large number of good books.[70]

Wang Ziye, like Wang Mengzou a native of Anhui, had served the Oriental Book Company as an apprentice between 1930 and 1934 and in 1938 had gone to Yan'an, where he worked for the CCP; after 1949, he was appointed head of the Party's Publishing Bureau. Why did he distance himself so categorically from the company's later evolution? Mainly because starting in 1929, it published several dozen books written or translated by Chinese Trotskyists. Of some 140 books brought out by the company between 1929 and 1949, at least 61 were written or translated by Trotskyists; they included histories of various foreign revolutionary movements; economic studies; studies on dialectics, the philosophy of Kant, women's liberation, Japanese imperialism, the war in Europe, Darwinism, and science and social science; translations of works by Marx, Engels, Trotsky, André Gide, and John Dewey; and several books by Chen Duxiu.[71] Because of Wang Mengzou's resolute commitment to publishing dangerous dissident and *avant-garde* literature, he was rarely out of trouble, even under the Communists, and he died in 1953, shortly after the Maoists had

---

68   Wang Fan-hsi 1991, pp. 159–60.
69   Quoted in Wang Ziye 1983, p. 1.
70   Wang Ziye 1983, p. 1.
71   The list of books published by the Oriental Book Company up to 1952 is contained in an appendix to Wang Yuanfang 1983, pp. 216–28.

closed down his company because of its history of subversive publishing, and after their political police had confiscated its stock of 'reactionary literature'.[72]

The Trotskyists played an important role, too, in the famous academic debate in the 1930s on the nature of Chinese society. *Dongli* ('Motive Force'), founded in July 1930 and renamed *Dushu zazhi* ('Readers' Magazine') in 1931, was an important Trotskyist forum on social, political, and philosophical issues of the day.[73] Whereas writers influenced by the Stalinists believed that Chinese society was basically feudal, the Trotskyists thought that it combined features of both feudalism and capitalism, and that capitalist relations were dominant in both town and countryside. But for most of the duration of the debate the main Trotskyist thinkers were in prison, and those – including Yan Lingfeng and Ren Shu – who argued the Trotskyist theses were either ex-Trotskyists or Trotskyists of the second rank, most of whom later went over to the Guomindang and brought Trotskyism into discredit.[74]

---

72 Wang Yuanfang 1983, pp. 211–13.
73 For a discussion of the Trotskyist contribution to the polemic on the nature of Chinese society, see Douw 1991, pp. 92–95.
74 Wang Fan-hsi 1991, p. 161; Ch'en Pi-lan 1980, p. 34.

Wild Lily

Wang Shiwei (1942)

This and the following article appeared in the journal of the Yan'an Literary Resistance Association in February 1942. In June of that year, they were cited in a condemnation of Wang Shiwei by the Yan'an Forum on Literature and Art: 'We unanimously agree that Wang Shiwei's fundamental thought and activities are Trotskyite. They are anti-proletarian and harmful to the Communist Party and the revolutionary cause.... Wang Shiwei's 'Wild Lily' and 'Politicians, Artists' are propaganda reflecting his incorrect thought. It is inappropriate for the Literature and Art column of Jiefang ribao (Liberation daily) *and* Guyu (Spring rain) *to print them instead of exposing and criticising them.'*[1]

While I was walking alone along the riverbank, I saw a comrade wearing a pair of old-style padded cotton shoes. I immediately fell to thinking of Comrade Li Fen, who also wore such shoes. Li Fen, my dearest and very first friend. As usual my blood began to race. Li Fen was a student in 1926 on the preparatory course in literature at Beijing University. In the same year she joined the Party. In the spring of 1928 she sacrificed her life in her home district of Baoqing in Hunan Province. Her own uncle tied her up and sent her to the local garrison – a good illustration of the barbarity of old China. Before going to her death, she put on all her three sets of underclothes and sewed them tightly together at the top and the bottom. This was because the troops in Baoqing often incited riff-raff to defile the corpses of the young women Communists they had shot – yet another example of the brutality, evil, filth, and darkness of the old society. When I got news of her death, I was consumed with feelings of deep love and hatred. Whenever I think of her, I have a vision of her pure, sacred martyrdom, with her three layers of underclothes sewn tightly together, tied up and sent by her very own uncle to meet her death with dignity. (It seems rather out of place to talk of such things in tranquil Yan'an, against the warbled background of 'Yu tang chun' and the swirling steps of the golden lotus dance;[2] but the whole atmosphere in Yan'an does not seem particularly appropriate to

---

1　Dai Qing 1994, p. 114.
2　'Yu tang chun' ('Spring in the Jade Hall') was a well-known Beijing opera aria. The phrase may simply be a sarcastic comment on living conditions in Yan'an. Dai Qing reports that it may also be a veiled attack on Mao, who married the actress Jiang Qing in 1939. See Dai Qing 1994, p. 36.

the conditions of the day – close your eyes and think for a moment of our dear comrades dying every minute in a sea of carnage.)

In the interest of the nation, I will not reckon up old scores of class hatred. We are genuinely selfless. With all our might we are dragging the representatives of old China along the road with us towards the light. But in the process the filth and dirt is rubbing off on us, spreading its diseases.

On scores of occasions I have drawn strength from the memory of Li Fen – vital and militant strength. Thinking back on her on this occasion, I was moved to write a *zawen* under the title 'Wild Lily'. This name has a twofold significance. First, the wild lily is the most beautiful of the wild flowers in the hills and countryside around Yan'an, and therefore a fitting dedication to her memory. Second, although its bulbs are similar to those of other lilies, they are said to be slightly bitter to the taste and of greater medicinal value, but I myself am not sure of this.

What is Lacking in Our Lives?

Recently young people here in Yan'an seem to have lost some of their enthusiasm, and to have become inwardly ill at ease.

Why is this? What is lacking in our lives? Some would answer that it is because we are badly nourished and short of vitamins. Others, that it is because the ratio of men to women is eighteen to one, and many young men are unable to find girlfriends. Or because life in Yan'an is dreary and lacks amusements.

There is some truth in all these answers. It is true there is need for better food, more partners of the opposite sex, and more interest in life. That is only natural. But one must also recognise that young people here in Yan'an came with a spirit of sacrifice to make revolution, and not for food, sex, and an enjoyable life. I cannot agree with those who say that their lack of enthusiasm, their inward disquiet even, are a result of our inability to resolve these problems. So what is lacking in our lives? Perhaps the following conversation holds some clues.

During the New Year holiday I was walking home in the dark one evening from a friend's place. Ahead of me were two women comrades talking in animated whispers. We were some way apart so I quietly moved closer to hear what they were saying.

'He keeps on talking about other people's petty-bourgeois egalitarianism; but the truth is that he thinks he is something special. He always looks after his own interests. As for the comrades underneath him, he doesn't care whether they're sick or well, he doesn't even care if they die, he hardly gives a damn!... Crows are black wherever they are. Even Comrade xxx acts like that'.

'You're right! All this bullshit about loving your own class. They don't even show ordinary human sympathy! You often see people pretending to smile and be friendly, but it's all on the surface, it doesn't mean anything. And if you offend them, they glare at you, pull their rank, and start lecturing you'.

'It's not only the big shots who act like that, the small fry are just the same. Our section leader xxx crawls when he's talking to his superiors, but he behaves very arrogantly towards us. Often comrades have been ill and he hasn't even dropped in to see how they are. But when an eagle stole one of his chickens, you should have seen the fuss he made! After that, every time he saw an eagle he'd start screaming and throwing clods of earth at it – the self-seeking bastard!'

There was a long silence. In one way, I admired the comrade's sharp tongue. But I also suddenly felt depressed.

'It's sad that so many comrades are falling ill. Nobody wants people like that to visit them when they fall ill, they just make you feel worse. Their tone of voice, their whole attitude – they don't make you feel they care about you'.

'Right. They don't care about others, and others don't care about them. If they did mass work, they'd be bound to fail'.

They carried on their conversation in animated whispers. At this point our ways parted, and I heard no more of what they had to say. In many ways their views were one-sided and exaggerated. Perhaps the picture they drew does not apply widely; but there is no denying that it is useful as a mirror.

Running into 'Running into Difficulties'

On 'Youth Page' no. 12 of this paper [*Liberation Daily*, the paper in which Wang Shiwei's article first appeared], I read an article titled 'Running into Difficulties' that aroused my interest. Here are two passages from that article.

> Recently a middle-aged friend arrived from the Guomindang rear. When he saw that young people in Yan'an were incapable of putting up with anything and were constantly grumbling, he raised his voice:
>
> 'What's all this about? We people in the outside world have run into countless difficulties and suffered constant ill-treatment...'.
>
> He was right. Life in Yan'an may anger or offend you. But in the eyes of someone who has run up against countless difficulties and who has

experienced the hardships of life, they are mere trifles. But it is an entirely different matter in the case of immature young people, especially those of student origin. Their parents and teachers coddle them into adulthood, whispering to them about life with love and warmth and teaching them to imitate pure and beautiful emotions. The ugliness and bleakness of their present situation is entirely new to them, and it is not surprising that as soon as they come up against difficulty they begin to bawl and to feel upset.

I have no idea what sort of person this author's 'middle-aged friend' is, but in my view his sort of philosophy, which is based on the principle of being contented with one's lot, is positively harmful. Young people should be treasured for their purity, their perceptiveness, their ardour, their courage, and their energy. They experience the darkness before others experience it, they see the filth before others see it; what others do not wish or dare to say, they say. Because of this they are more critical, but this is by no means 'grumbling'. What they say is not always well balanced, but it is by no means 'bawling'. We should inquire into problems that give rise to 'grumbling', 'bawling', and 'disquiet', and set about removing their causes in a rational way. (Yes, rational! It is completely untrue that young people are always engaged in 'thoughtless clamour'.) To say that Yan'an is superior to the 'outside world', to tell young people not to 'grumble', to describe Yan'an's dark side as some 'slight disappointment' will solve no problems. Yes, Yan'an is superior to the 'outside world', but it should and can be better still.

Of course, young people are often hot-headed and impatient – an observation that appears to be the main theme of 'Running into Difficulties'. But if all young people were to be mature before their time, how desolate this world would be! In reality, young people in Yan'an have already seen a great deal of the world – after all, the grumbling conversation between the two women comrades that I quoted earlier was held in whispers in the dark. So far from resenting 'grumbling' of this sort, we should use it as a mirror in which to inspect ourselves. To say that youth 'of student origin' are 'coddled into adulthood, whispered to about life with love and warmth, and taught to imitate pure and beautiful emotions' is very subjectivist. Even though most Yan'an youth come from 'a student background', are 'inexperienced', and have not 'seen more than enough of life's hardships', most arrived in Yan'an after a whole series of struggles and it is not true to say they experienced nothing but 'love and warmth'; on the contrary, it was precisely because they knew all about 'hatred and cold' that they joined the revolutionary camp in the first place. From what the author of

'Running into Difficulties' says, all the young people in Yan'an were brought up pampered, and only 'grumble' because they miss their candied fruit. But it was because of 'evil and coldness' that they came to Yan'an in search of 'beauty and warmth', that they identified the 'evil and coldness' here in Yan'an and insisted on 'grumbling' about it in the hope of alerting people's attention and reducing it to a minimum.

In the winter of 1938 our Party carried out a large-scale investigation of our work and summoned comrades to 'unfold a lively criticism' and to 'give full vent to their criticisms, no matter whether they were right or wrong'. I hope we have another such investigation, and listen to the 'grumbles' of the youth. 'Our camp exists amidst the darkness of the old society, and therefore there is inevitably darkness in it too'. Of course, that's 'Marxism'! But that is only one-sided Marxism. There is an even more important side which the 'masters of subjectivist factionalism' have forgotten, that is, the need, after having recognised the inevitability of such darkness, to prevent its emergence through Bolshevik activism, to reduce its growth, and to give full play to the ability of consciousness to transform objective reality. Given present conditions, to clean out all traces of darkness from our camp is impossible. But to destroy as much of it as we can is not only possible but necessary. The 'great masters', however, have not only failed to emphasise this point, but have scarcely even mentioned it. All they do is point out that it is 'inevitable' and then doze off to sleep. They use 'inevitability' as an excuse for self-indulgence. In their dreams they tell themselves: 'Comrade, you are a product of the old society, and there is a tiny spot of darkness in your soul. But that is inevitable, no need to get embarrassed about it'.

After the 'theory' of 'inevitability' comes the 'national form theory' known as 'the heavens won't fall in'. Yes, it is impossible for the heavens to fall in. But what of our work and our cause? Will they suffer as a result? The 'great masters' have given little or no thought to this problem. If this 'inevitability' is 'inevitably' allowed to pursue its course, then the heavens – the heavens of our revolutionary cause – will 'inevitably' fall in. I suggest we should not be so complacent.

The so-called 'small things' theory is linked with this. A criticises B. B tells A he shouldn't waste his time on 'small things'. Some 'great masters' even say: 'Damn it! It's bad enough with the women comrades, now the men are spending all their time on trivia too!' It is true that there is probably no danger in Yan'an of such big problems as treason against the Party or the nation. But each individual, through the small things they do in the course of their everyday lives, either helps the light or helps the darkness. And the 'small things' in the lives of 'great people' are even more capable of calling forth warmth or desolation.

Egalitarianism and the System of Ranks

According to what I heard, one comrade wrote an article with a similar title for his departmental wall newspaper, and as a result was criticised and attacked by his department 'head' and driven half-mad. I hope this story is untrue. But since there have been genuine cases of madness even among the 'little devils' [orphan children who acted as personal assistants to the Communist cadres], I fear there may be some madness among adults. Even though the state of my nerves is not as 'healthy' as some people's, I still have enough life in me not to go mad under any circumstances. I therefore intend to follow in the footsteps of that comrade and discuss the question of equality and the ranking system.

Communism is not the same as egalitarianism, and we are not at present at the stage of Communist revolution. There is no need for me to write an eight-legged essay on that question, since there is no cook crazy enough to want to live in the same style as one of the 'heads'. (I don't dare write 'kitchen operative', since it sounds like a caricature; but whenever I speak to cooks I always address them in the warmest possible way as 'comrade kitchen-operatives' – what a pitiful example of warmth!) The question of a system of ranks is rather more difficult.

Those who say that a system of ranks is reasonable use roughly the following arguments: (1) they base themselves on the principle of 'from each according to their ability, to each according to their worth', which means that those with more responsibilities should consume more; (2) in the near future the three-thirds government [the 'tripartite system' under which the Communists nominally shared power with the 'petty bourgeoisie and the enlightened gentry' in the areas under their control] intends to carry out a new salary system, and naturally there will be pay differentials; and (3) the Soviet Union also has a system of ranks.

In my opinion all these arguments are open to debate. As for (1), we are still in the midst of the revolution, with all its hardships and difficulties; all of us, despite fatigue, are labouring to surmount the present crisis, and many comrades have ruined their precious health. Because of this it does not yet seem the right time for anyone, no matter who, to start talking about 'to each according to their worth'. On the contrary, all the more reason why those with greater responsibilities should show themselves willing to share weal and woe with the rank and file. (This is a national virtue that should be encouraged.) In so doing, they would win the profound love of the lower ranks. Only then would it be possible to create iron-like unity. It goes without saying that it is not only reasonable but necessary that those with big responsibilities who need special treatment for their health should get such treatment. The same goes for those with positions of medium responsibility. As for (2), the pay system of the three-thirds government should also avoid excessive differentials;³ it is right that non-Party officials should get slightly better treatment, but those officials who are Party members should uphold our excellent traditions of frugal struggle so that we are in a position to mobilise even more non-Party people to join us and cooperate with us. As for (3), excuse my rudeness, but I would beg those 'great masters' who can't open their mouths without talking about 'Ancient Greece' to hold their tongues.⁴

I am not an egalitarian, but to divide clothing into three and food into five grades is neither necessary nor rational, especially with regard to clothes. (I myself am graded as 'cadres' clothes and private kitchen', so this is not just a case of sour grapes.) All such problems should be resolved on the basis of need and reason. At present there is no noodle soup for sick comrades to eat and young students only get two meals of thin congee a day (when they are asked whether they have had enough to eat, Party members are expected to lead the rest in a chorus of 'Yes, we're full'). Relatively healthy 'big shots' get far more than they need to eat and drink, with the result that their subordinates look upon them as a race apart, and not only do not love them, but even.... This makes me most uneasy. But perhaps it is a 'petty bourgeois emotion' to always be talking about 'love' and 'warmth'? I await your verdict.

---

3 The Communists' wartime version of the united front, comprising Communists, members of other parties, and members of no party.
4 A dig at Wang Ming-style dogmatists who can't talk about China except in terms derived from European history.

Politicians, Artists

Wang Shiwei (1942)

THERE are two sides to the revolution: changing the social system, and changing people. Politicians are the revolution's strategists and tacticians; they unite, organise, and lead the revolution. Their main task is to transform the social system. Artists are the 'engineers of the soul', and their main task is to transform people's heart, spirit, thinking, and consciousness. The filth and darkness in people's souls are the product of an irrational social system, and the soul's fundamental transformation is impossible until the social system has been fundamentally transformed. In the process of transforming the social system the soul too is transformed.... The tasks of the politician and the artist are complementary. The politicians command the revolution's material forces; the artists arouse the revolution's spiritual forces. The politicians are generally cool, collected people, good at waging practical struggles to eliminate filth and darkness, and to bring about cleanliness and light. The artists are generally more emotional and more sensitive, good at exposing filth and darkness, and at pointing out cleanliness and light....

The politicians understand that during the revolution the people in their own camp will be less than perfect, and things will rarely be done ideally. They take the broad view, making sure that the wheel of history advances and the light wins. The artists, more passionate and more sensitive, long for people to be more lovable and things to be more splendid. When they write they take small things as their starting points: they hope to eliminate the darkness as far as they can so that the wheel of history can advance as fast as possible. As the practical transformers of the social system, the politicians take things more seriously; the artists, as the soul's engineers, go even further in demanding perfection of people. In uniting, organising, and leading the revolution and waging practical struggles, the politicians are superior. But the artists are better at plunging into the depths of the soul to change it – transforming our side in order to strengthen it, and transforming the enemies so as to undermine them.

The politicians and the artists each have their weak points. If the politicians are to attack the enemy successfully, establish links with allied forces, and strengthen our side, they must understand human nature and the ways of the world, be masters of tricks and devices, and be skilled in making and breaking alliances. Their weakness springs from these very strengths. When they use them for the revolutionary cause they become the most beautiful and exquisite 'revolutionary art', but unless they are truly great politicians they are bound to make use of them for their own fame, position, and interest, thus harming the revolution. In this respect we must insist that cat's claws be used only for catching rats and not for seizing chickens. Here we must distinguish politicians from artists; and we must be ever on our guard against cats that are good not at catching rats but at taking chickens. The main weaknesses of most artists are pride, narrowness, isolation, inability to unite with others, and mutual suspicion and exclusion. Here we must ask the engineers of the soul to start by making their own souls clean and bright. This is hard and painful, but it is the only way to greatness.

The Chinese revolution is especially hard. The difficulties of changing the social system are well known, but few realise that changing people's souls is even harder. 'The further east you go, the darker society becomes'. Old China is full of gore and pus, darkness and filth, all of which have inevitably stained the Chinese who grew up in it. Even we, the revolutionary fighters creating a new China, cannot escape this cruel fact. Only if we have the courage to look it in the face can we understand why we must be even more rigorous in our efforts to transform souls, so as to accelerate and win the struggle to change the social system.

Lu Xun was a fighter all his life, but anyone who understands him will know that at heart he was lonely. He struggled because he recognised the laws of social development and believed that the future was bound to be better than the present; he was lonely because he saw that even in the souls of his own comrades there was filth and darkness. He knew that the task of transforming old China could only be carried out by the sons and daughters of old China, despite their filth and darkness. But his great heart could not help yearning for his comrades to be more lovable.

The revolutionary camp exists in old China, and the revolution's fighters have grown up in old China, which means that our souls are inevitably stained. The present revolution requires that we ally not only with the peasants and the urban petty bourgeoisie but with even more backward classes and strata, and that we make concessions to them, thus becoming contaminated with yet more filth and darkness. This makes the artist's task of transforming the soul even more important, difficult, and urgent. To boldly expose and wash away all that is filthy and dark is as important as praising the light, if not more important. Exposing and cleansing is not merely negative, because when darkness is eliminated the light can shine even brighter. Some people think revolutionary artists must 'direct their fire outside', and that if we expose our weaknesses we give the enemy easy targets. This is a short-sighted view. Though our camp is now strong enough for us to have no fears about exposing our shortcomings, it is not yet fully consolidated; self-criticism is the best way of consolidating it.

As for the maggots and traitors in anti-Communist secret service organs, they would concoct rumours and slanders even if we were flawless; they even hope that we will hush up our faults and shun those who might cure them, so that the darkness grows.

Some who think highly of themselves as politicians smile sarcastically when they speak of artists. Others who pride themselves on being artists shrug their shoulders when they mention politicians. But there is always some truth in objective reflections: each would do well to use the other as a mirror. They should not forget that they are both children of old China.

A truly great politician must have a soul great enough to move the souls of others and cleanse them; thus a great politician is a great artist. An artist who has a truly great soul is bound to have a part to play in uniting, organising, and leading the forces of revolution; thus a great artist is also a great politician.

Finally I would like to appeal warmly to artist comrades: be even more effective in transforming the soul, and aim in the first place at ourselves and our own camp. In China transforming the soul will have an even greater effect on transforming society. It will determine not only how soon but even whether the revolution succeeds.

PART 15

Prefaces and Introductions to Chinese Trotskyist Memoirs and Biographies

∴

Editor's Introduction to Zheng Chaolin's *Memoirs*

Gregor Benton

Zheng Chaolin started this book in 1944 and finished it in February 1945, but at the time, he never got round to publishing it. In 1986, after sitting on the manuscript (newly unearthed from a government vault) for several years, Chinese Communist officials finally authorised its publication minus the chapter 'Love and Politics', and recently they ordered a second printing. Access to these editions is restricted to privileged categories of officials and researchers. Sometime in the 1980s, that is, before it was eventually printed, a few copies of the manuscript were mimeographed for Party history workers, but I do not know in what form. This translation is probably the fullest published version of the book to date, for it includes the 'Love and Politics' chapter that for reasons of prudery was cut from the 1986 Chinese edition.

The text of the original manuscript broke off rather abruptly, and for two reasons. One was the death early in 1945 of Zheng's son Frei, which broke Zheng's heart. The other was the end of the war, which brought Shanghai into a lively ferment and opened up new opportunities for Zheng's Trotskyists, who switched into a higher gear, so that Zheng's attention was soon commanded by more urgent matters. Then, in December 1952, Zheng, his comrades, and his manuscript were swept behind bars by Mao's political police. When on 5 June 1979 Zheng, his surviving friends, and his book were finally released – all of them into restricted circulation –, some researchers from a Party history institute got Zheng to round out his story with a special study, completed in 1980, of Chen Duxiu's relationship to Trotskyism, which they appended to the 1986 edition.[1]

This present volume [Benton, ed., 1997] concludes with a brief autobiographical sketch in which Zheng in 1990, at the age of ninety, brings up to date the remarkable story of his life; and an interview, published in 1993, in which he tells the story of his imprisonment under the Chinese Communist Party (CCP) between 1952 and 1979.

What sort of a man is Zheng Chaolin? His book is, essentially, a reflection on the politics of China's revolution and on the people in it among whom Zheng spent his early manhood. But even a memoir announces the quality of its

---

1 See Part VII.

author, so what manner of person does this book reveal Zheng to be? It shows him to be modest, frank, argus eyed, compassionate, broad-minded, humorous, playful, stubborn, inquisitive, inventive, creative, loyal, free from all vanity and pretensions, and with the memory of an elephant. Born in another age, he would have shone as an academician, a philosopher, or a poet. But instead, he was born with the twentieth century, and into eventual martyrdom. His great contribution to the Chinese Revolution – both in the official Party before 1929 and, after that, in its Trotskyist offshoot – was in the realm of theory and propaganda. He evinces little interest in practical affairs; he despises the power struggles that punctuate political life and on which others thrive. Above all, he is an 'oppositionist for life'[2] to all forms of established authority. This description, originally made by Hu Shi of Zheng's mentor Chen Duxiu, fits Zheng to the letter, which is why he has spent more than one third of his days as a prisoner of conscience under repressive régimes of different colours.

Zheng's writing is scrupulously truthful, accurate, and stringent. He tells us what he knows, how he came to know it, and what remained unknown to him, so his testimony is a perfect source for history writers; and it is free from the self-exculpation and ideological axe-grinding that distorts most political memoirs of this sort. Chinese memoirs since 1949 have all the usual drawbacks of the genre, together with several more. They are winners' history written in a society where 'the loser is a thief'. They cleave closely to the dominant political line. They are rarely designed to stand alone as records of integral, independent lives, but are meant to furnish 'concrete' illustrations of the general truths of Party history that dictate their framework and their setting. To quarry the few hard truths from cultic biography of this sort, the historian must first hack through a dense layer of political shibboleths, editorial embellishment, and edifying anecdotes; even then, what remains is not necessarily the unvarnished truth. So Zheng's book is a lonely beacon that lights up a small patch on the great dark plain of China's recent past,[3] and will be seen by fair-minded observers everywhere as something rare and precious.

In his book Zheng frequently reviews the character, motives, and behaviour of his friends and enemies, but he rarely says much about himself. So it is interesting to look at what other people have said about him over the years.

---

2   Hu Shi used this phrase in his preface to *Chen Duxiu zuihou lunwen he shuxin* ('Chen Duxiu's last articles and letters'), first published posthumously by Chen's friends and later republished on Taiwan with Hu Shi's preface (see Part VIII).

3   In recent years Chinese historians and archivists have produced a flood of valuable studies on and collections of documents from the 1920s.

Wang Fanxi, Zheng's close collaborator in the Trotskyist enterprise, was struck above all by his formidable staunchness and his total disregard, like a Buddhist monk who has attained the Way, for his own personal fate. 'Even if we leave aside Zheng Chaolin's other strengths', wrote Wang in 1957, in reference to the Trotskyists' decision not to flee China in 1949, 'his Peter-like spirit of martyrdom alone will ensure him a lasting place in the history of the Revolution. Our dilemma was similar in many ways to that of the early Christians under Nero – should we stay in the capital or flee to a safe place? Some approached the question mainly from the point of view of their own fate, others from the point of view of the future of the organisation as a whole; but Zheng Chaolin did not wait for a voice from the heavens to ask "*Quo vadis*?": his mind was made up from the very outset'.[4]

Lou Shiyi, who knew Zheng Chaolin in the 1920s and visited him again in the 1980s, wrote a long appreciation of him in a preface to a volume of Zheng's poems,[5] most of them written while Zheng was in jail under the Communists. Lou, a veteran and orthodox member of the CCP, was for many years a senior literary editor in Beijing. So his view of Zheng is not coloured by sympathy for Zheng's Trotskyist politics, and is therefore all the more remarkable and reliable.

> The old man Yu Yin, Comrade Zheng Chaolin, is my teacher. He is also my old friend – one of those with whom I shared many trials and who today number very few, as few as the disappearing stars in the early morning sky. It would be presumptuous of me to add mere tittle-tattle to my teacher's book. However, as his old friend, and in order to express my delight on this occasion, I shall venture to recall some events that happened during our long friendship and that younger readers may enjoy hearing about.
>
> I remember that several months after the end of the May Thirtieth movement of 1925 – winter had already set in – I and a few other young people attended night school several times a week in the home of a friend on Baotong Road in Shanghai's Zhabei. We were not many, but a group of people took turns at lecturing to us. We studied current affairs and the rudiments of Marxism. Our teachers included pioneers of the revolution like Qu Qiubai, Yun Daiying, Yin Kuan, and Zhao Shiyan; they also included Comrade Zheng Chaolin. In those days, he was still a young

---

4 This volume, p. 573.
5 The volume, called *Yu Yin canji* ('Surviving poems by Yu Yin'), was edited by Zhu Zheng and published by Hunan renmin chuban she in 1989. Yu Yin is similar in pronunciation to two other Chinese characters meaning 'prison' and 'hermit' – a hermit in prison; it is also a Chinese rendering of Zheng Chaolin's French name, Yvon.

man, with a full head of black hair and an elegant bearing. He had probably not long been back in China. He had squeezed his plump body into a neat Western-style suit; a bright watch-chain protruded from his left-hand pocket and disappeared into his waistcoat button-hole. As far as I remember, his subject was 'The Meaning for the Chinese Revolution of the May Thirtieth Movement'. He was not a very fluent speaker and he had a slight Fujian accent, but he was very kind and approachable and left a deep impression on those of us who studied under him; in my mind's eye I can still see him to this day.

The night school was abandoned before very long, and after that, I had no further occasion to meet Zheng. But fate is a strange thing, and ten or so years later, we renewed our acquaintance under remarkable circumstances – in the Guomindang's Central Military Prison in Nanjing. His solitary cell was on the same block as mine, just eight or nine doors away, but we rarely caught a glimpse of one another. One day, I was escorted to the Education Section, where a short thin man who was in charge talked cordially with me and allocated me to 'penal labour', after which I was taken to a big room that had originally been part of the Education Section. It was bright and clean, with a row of ping-pong tables along the windows, each capable of accommodating six or seven people, who sat there doing literary work. I was allocated the German Military Code to translate. This threw me into confusion, for my German was quite elementary; I could remember little more than how to say the alphabet in it. How on earth was I to translate such a book? But when I lifted my head and looked around, I noticed several familiar faces. The first to greet me was Pan Zinian, who told me that I should accept the assignment, that everything would be all right. The person in charge of the Education Section was a man called Shen Bingquan. In order to make life easier for some cultural figures (I guess today you would call them 'higher intellectuals'), he had specially requested this cushy job [for us] from the Ministry of Military Administration. So we had a reason to leave our cells each day, we could get some exercise, and we got the chance to do some reading and writing. At my table were four other fellow inmates. All but one – even Pan Zinian – had only beginners' German. The exception, seated opposite Pan, was none other than Comrade Zheng Chaolin, whom I had not seen for a decade. He had aged somewhat in the meantime, and had lost his hair. He was the only true translator among us. All the rest of us learned German from him. In front of each of us was a German text, a dictionary, an exercise book, and a pile of loose writing paper. We spent our time reading and writing and called it translating, but in effect, all we did was learn from our teacher. A semi-literate warder on guard in the hall used to wander round the tables to see how conscientious and diligent we were; he thought that we were working hard and was very satisfied with us. We could get up and stretch our legs at will, or take time off for a quiet chat; no one ever interfered with us. Section Director Shen often used to visit us, and would sit down and talk with us about what was in the newspapers. We were not allowed to read the dailies, but we were allowed to receive large quantities of books and periodicals, so there was nothing that we did not know. Chaolin was of a different political persuasion from the rest of us, so we rarely discussed politics with him. Nevertheless, we viewed his big bald skull as a living encyclopaedia. He was never averse to answering our questions. At all times, he sincerely and tirelessly helped us. He not only taught us German; he also taught two youngsters French. At the same time, he helped us all with our translations. He was extraordinarily assiduous. He read and translated non-stop. I remember that he translated Thomas Mann's *Buddenbrooks* from German and D. Merezhkovsky's *Resurrection of the Gods* from Russian. We all vied to read this translation of Merezhkovsky's book, which was a fictional biography of Leonardo da Vinci. At one time, he translated from the French André Gide's *Retour de l'URSS*. Some of the people with us said that this book was anti-Soviet and told us to ignore it. But surreptitiously, I became the first reader of Zheng's Chinese translation, for which I was roundly criticised by my prison-mates. I was not convinced by their strictures.

The rest of us attended to our own research and translation. Section Director Shen helped us by posting our manuscripts to our friends in Shanghai, so they quickly appeared in print and we earned quite a lot of money. Some of us were even able to maintain our families. Chaolin, being the fastest and the most productive translator, naturally earned most. His wife Liu Jingzhen, who had stayed behind in Shanghai, came regularly and often to visit him in prison in Nanjing, and brought him large amounts of food, winter clothing, medicine, and nutriments. His own needs were few, and he often used to give away the larger part to prisoners whose distress was greater and who received no assistance from outside. He did this regardless of their political views, and did not even know some of the people he helped. There was one prisoner, a long-term inmate of the sick-ward stricken by tuberculosis of the lymphous gland, whom he met by accident only once in the clinic, while visiting the doctor. When Chaolin learned that this man was poor as well as sick, he got Jingzhen to bring a big bottle of cod-liver oil with her every time she came to the prison, and passed it on to this man through one of the prison guards.

We lived together in the same prison right through until 1937, when we were released after the outbreak in China of the full-scale War of Resistance against Japan. Actually, Chaolin had lost his freedom as early as 1931, and had been kept in various prisons before finally being moved to Nanjing's Military Prison, where he was an old lag. After our release, war beacons filled the sky all over China, and each went his own way. I heard nothing more of Chaolin after that. And so forty years passed. In the spring of 1979, I made a special trip to Shanghai to attend the service in memory of Fu Lei and his wife.[6] A friend in Shanghai told me that Chaolin had in the meantime spent another twenty years behind bars, and that he had just been freed; but he warned me not to visit him, for he was still under strict supervision. Not until a year or so later did I discover that Chaolin had already been restored to complete liberty, and that even though he still maintained his old political position, he had been invited to become a member of Shanghai's People's Political Consultative Conference. Just at that time, I was going to Shanghai on an official mission, so I visited my old teacher from half a century earlier, my prison-mate from forty years earlier. Being the same age as the century, he was already an old man, but even so, he was warmly hospitable, tirelessly talkative, and overflowing with high spirits. It was as if he had sustained not the slightest damage from his trials and tribulations. But on the day[7] that he was restored to complete freedom, his wife Liu Jingzhen, who for twenty seven years had done everything possible from the other side of prison walls to alleviate his sufferings, who had defended him, and who had waited loyally for him, quietly left this world, after seemingly having completed her appointed task. And his only child, born during the War against Japan, has also left behind nothing but a precious wide-eyed photographic image pinned to the wall of Zheng's lonely study. Zheng lives a life of great calm and great intensity. He reads, he writes, and he receives and instructs an endless flow of comrades researching special issues in the history of the Chinese Communist Party.

---

6 The parents of the famous pianist Fu Ts'ong. Fu Lei, who translated R. Rolland and H. Balzac into Chinese, committed suicide in the Cultural Revolution and was rehabilitated in 1979.
7 Actually, Liu Jingzhen died on 14 October 1979, four months and ten days after the release of her husband.

Another brief pen-picture of Zheng can be found in the first volume of the memoirs of the Trotskyist Peng Shuzhi. There was no love lost between Zheng and Peng, but even so, Peng draws a rather affectionate picture of Zheng in the 1920s. 'Zheng Chaolin was a strapping young fellow with a broad forehead, always smiling and extremely kind-hearted. There is no denying that he was something of a pedant. He had a stammer. And politically, he was rather uninventive. But in his way, he was a linguistic genius, in the very special sense that he could learn at high speed to decipher, read, and render into decent Chinese any language whatsoever, provided that it was at the level of political discourse and provided, above all, that he was never expected to articulate a single sentence or to understand it *orally*. For example, it only took him a few months in Moscow to disentangle Russian, just as it had taken him only a few months in France to familiarise himself – also at the level of political discourse – with French. To the knowledge – political and bookish – of these two languages he soon added English, German, Italian, and Esperanto'.[8]

Traditionally, Auguste Blanqui, the French revolutionary who spent thirty three of his seventy five years in prison (and so became known in France as *l'enfermé*), has been regarded as the record holder for political imprisonment. But Zheng Chaolin had beaten Blanqui's record by one year when he stepped free in June 1979 after being locked up as a 'counter-revolutionary' for twenty seven years, to add to the seven he had already served as a revolutionary under Chiang Kai-shek. With him were eleven other Trotskyist survivors, together with his wife Liu Jingzhen, who had voluntarily shared the last seven years of his detention. A photograph taken on the eve of Zheng and Liu's release shows them smiling serenely and beatifically.

After the death of Mao and the fall of his 'Gang of Four' in 1976, tens of thousands of political prisoners were released; the freeing of Zheng and his comrades happened in that context. In May 1979, shortly before their release, Zheng had been named prisoner of the month by Amnesty International, which campaigned on his behalf, though no one knew whether he was alive or dead. Perhaps this naming jogged the memory and conscience of some official who in the 1920s had been Zheng's friend in Europe or in China, before he became a Trotskyist.

Zheng's revolutionary career had begun in the early 1920s in Paris, where he and other young Chinese students set up what was to become the European

---

8   Claude Cadart and Cheng Yingxiang 1983, p. 321. Actually, Zheng learned Esperanto in France.

branch of the Chinese Communist Party. Among Zheng's comrades in those days were Zhou Enlai, Li Weihan (later head of the United Front Department of the Chinese Communist Party), and the seventeen-year old Deng Xiaoping. From Paris, Zheng went on to Moscow, where he was one of the first students at the new Communist University for the Toilers of the East. In 1924, he went back to China and was appointed Secretary of the Party's Propaganda Department. He also translated Bukharin's *ABC of Communism*, which became the standard work for generations of Chinese revolutionaries.

The strategy imposed on the Chinese Communist Party by Moscow in the 1920s led to catastrophic defeat in 1927, after which Zheng continued for a while to work underground for the Party. During this time, he came into contact with the views of Leon Trotsky, and he soon became Trotsky's follower.

The origins of the Chinese Trotskyist group are to be found in an earlier faction that had formed in China in the mid 1920s: the so-called Moscow faction, comprising Chinese students like Zheng Chaolin sent back from Moscow to China in 1924 to staff the infant Chinese Communist Party. These Russia-returned students – the first of several generations of such – became important leaders of the Party back in China; they were united as one and worked in close concert as a 'virtual clique', according to Zheng Chaolin.

The group's core was formed by Peng Shuzhi, Wang Ruofei, Yin Kuan, Zheng Chaolin, and Chen Qiaonian. Three of these people later became Trotskyists, while Chen Qiaonian died and Wang Ruofei became a secret sympathiser of the Trotskyists, though he remained within the official Party. All save Peng Shuzhi had spent some time working and studying in France before going to Moscow in the early 1920s. They had joined the revolution more or less simultaneously and gone through a long period of shared experiences at a most formative time of their lives. This naturally inclined them to group together. In France they had lived a hard and taxing life, as wage-slaves in capitalist industry; and Zheng Chaolin in particular had learned libertarian ways of being and thinking that were alien to those Chinese students like Peng Shuzhi who had gone straight from China to Russia. Zheng knew that there could not be just one idea, one leader; his experience inclined him towards scepticism, intellectual curiosity, democracy, and internationalism. In Moscow, Zheng and some of his old comrades from France suffocated under the régime of stifling orthodoxy over which Peng and others presided. Zheng's habit of questioning accepted beliefs and values inclined him to an affinity with Chen Duxiu, Chinese Communism's founder, its most critical, free-thinking, and iconoclastic leader, and its most prominent Trotskyist.

While this opposition was growing up in China, Trotskyists were also becoming active among the several hundred young Communist survivors who had gone to Moscow to study after the 1927 defeat. Though these students knew next to nothing about the Soviet Union or the world Communist movement when they first arrived in Moscow, within a matter of weeks they were 'more or less acquainted with the substance of the controversy' between Stalin and Trotsky.[9] What they lacked in theoretical grounding before going to Russia they made up for in direct experience of the events in China, which formed one of the main battlegrounds on which Stalin and Trotsky fought.

Even before the end of their first year in Moscow, the seeds of sympathy with Russia's Left Opposition had been sown in the minds of some of the new Chinese arrivals, who quickly progressed through sceptical neutrality to active support for the Opposition. Earlier, they had swallowed the official explanation that the policies followed in 1926 and 1927 were 'mistakes committed by Chen Duxiu in defiance of Comintern instructions'. Now, the truth dawned on them: the policies ascribed to Chen Duxiu were Stalin's. Nor was Stalin's policy for China the sole issue that exercised their indignation. They had arrived in Moscow fresh from battle. They were bursting with restless, frustrated energy, moral courage, and a strong antipathy towards the high-handed ways of the Moscow leaders. By the winter of 1928, Trotskyists were everywhere among Moscow's Chinese students.

In late 1929, some two hundred of the Chinese Trotskyists in Moscow were seized by the Soviet political police. Some were imprisoned for a while, expelled from the Party after recanting, and then deported (these numbered fewer than ten). Others were sent to labour camps in Siberia or the Arctic Circle, whence two escaped back to China sometime before 1949 to tell the tale. Some were shot. The number of those who made it back to China from Moscow just before this crackdown, with their beliefs intact, was fewer than twenty.[10]

In early 1929, the two currents of opposition, one formed in Moscow, tight and highly ideological, the other – looser and vaguer – in China, started out on the long and difficult journey that would eventually join them for a brief moment in Shanghai, under the leadership of Chen Duxiu, before catastrophe overtook them.

Together with most of the other Trotskyist leaders, Zheng and his wife Liu were arrested in May 1931 by the Guomindang in cooperation with the British police, less than three weeks after they had unified their forces in a single body. Liu was freed soon afterwards by the Magistrate of the International Settlement, but Zheng was handed over to the Chinese authorities after a formal hearing and sent to prison for fifteen years as 'ringleader' of the group. He

---

9   Wang Fan-hsi 1991, p. 48.
10 Wang Fan-hsi 1991, p. 105.

was released in 1937, after the outbreak of war with Japan and the adoption by the Guomindang of 'special measures for disposing of prisoners during times of war', having served seven of the fifteen. His health had worsened in jail, so he went with Liu to a small town in Anhui to get better. There, their only child was born. They called the boy Frei (German for 'Free') in an internationalist gesture to celebrate Zheng's regained freedom. Frei died aged eight, of tuberculosis.

In 1940, the couple returned to Shanghai, where Liu taught in one of two workers' schools that the Trotskyists set up under the noses of the Japanese occupiers. During the war, Zheng's main activity was writing and translating. 'Most of the important articles [in *Internationalist* in the war years] were written by Zheng Chaolin', wrote Wang Fanxi. 'Zheng had long been famous as a contributor to the CCP press but it was only now that his talents as a creative theoretician began to bloom. During those darkest years he wrote his most brilliant and substantial pieces, including *Dialogue Between Three Travellers* (a theoretical treatise of revolution written in novel form), a book of memoirs (an inner history of the CCP from the early 1920s through to 1930),[11] and the *ABC of the Theory of Permanent Revolution*. But the one work to which he devoted most care and attention was his *Critical Biography of Ch'en Tu-hsiu* [Chen Duxiu], which – to judge from a reading of the manuscript – was the most brilliant history of modern Chinese thought to have been written to date. The pity of it was that apart from the *ABC*, none of his manuscripts from this period ever saw the light of day. When the Chinese Trotskyist movement was destroyed during the nation-wide round-up in December 1952, they were locked up by Mao's political police together with their author'.[12]

After the war, Zheng continued to work for the Trotskyist movement in Shanghai. In 1949, just a few months before Chiang Kai-shek's rule on the Chinese mainland ended, he helped found the Internationalist Workers' Party, which never had more than a few hundred members.

At first, Zheng's old friends in the new régime set up in 1949 tried to talk him into joining them. Li Weihan, acting through the intermediacy of Shi Fuliang, sought a reconciliation, but Zheng refused to accept his offer. Finally, on the night of 22 December 1952, Zheng and two to three hundred other Trotskyists disappeared into prison. Liu Jingzhen was sentenced after a secret trial to ten years in jail but was released in 1957, due to illness. By then, her old lameness had worsened. Her rich family was afraid to keep up relations with her so she had become roofless, but fortunately her earlier neighbours helped her find a room, and friends in Hong Kong were able to send her sums of money. In

---

11   Benton, ed., 1997.
12   This book, p. 562.

the Cultural Revolution of the late 1960s, Liu, by then half-blind, was interrogated several times by Red Guards, though she was not maltreated. One of the charges against her was that in the 1930s, she had smuggled messages to and from the Trotskyist leader Chen Duxiu, at a time when Chen Duxiu had been in jail under Chiang Kai-shek as a revolutionary. In 1972, when Zheng was transferred from prison to the reform-through-labour glass works in Shanghai's Pudong, Liu was allowed to join him. In Pudong Zheng's life eased slightly.

In prison under the Communists, Zheng wrote a number of books on political themes and hundreds of poems, but as he explains in 'A Self-Description at the Age of Ninety' and 'A Brief Account of My Third Spell in Prison', these writings were destroyed in the Cultural Revolution. Fortunately, he was able to reproduce a number of the poems from memory, and in 1989, Hunan People's Press published them in a slim volume. Like Mao Zedong, Zheng combines in his character a belief in radical revolution with a love for poetry in the classical style. In a letter to Lou Shiyi, Zheng – whose prose style is plain and demotic even to the point of bluntness – explained why he is averse to writing poems in the modern idiom:

> For prose, the literary reform of May Fourth 1919 worked. Today no one writes in classical Chinese any more. But for poetry, it failed. The first generation of literary reformers like Chen Duxiu and Lu Xun all wrote poetry in the old style. Poetry needs rules and forms. This is true of poetry (excluding free verse) in all the Western languages. I know of no new-style poetry in Chinese that is broadly read, like Lu Xun's old-style poems. So I take a very serious attitude to old-style poetry and would never stoop to writing doggerel.[13]

Did Zheng stay true to his Trotskyist beliefs after 1952? To anyone who knows even a little about the man, the question is ridiculous. That fact has not stopped Zheng's detractors from insinuating, wickedly and outrageously, that he traded his principles for his freedom in 1979 and 'is now happy to render dubious services to ... die-hard Stalinists'.[14] Fortunately, there is ample evidence that Zheng's convictions, and his integrity, were one hundred per cent intact when

---

13   Yu Yin 1989, p. 8.
14   Cheng and Cadart 1986, p. 534. Cheng and Cadart are the daughter and son-in-law of Peng Shuzhi, Zheng's old adversary in the Chinese Trotskyist movement.

he walked free in 1979, having stayed in China thirty years earlier to hold the Trotskyist flag. Even in jail he secretly celebrated his admiration for Trotsky in a poetic rebus that he wrote after reading in a Chinese newspaper that at the Twenty Second Congress of the Soviet Communist Party in 1961 Khrushchev had proposed building a memorial in Moscow to the victims of Stalin's terror; and that the Trotskyist Fourth International had sent a telegram to Moscow saying that when the memorial was built, Trotsky's name should be carved on it 'in gold letters'. 'At the time, I was still in prison waiting to be dealt with', wrote Zheng in 1988. 'That is to say, I could be taken out at any time and shot. I thought to myself, if there is life after death, where will my spirit go? First, it will go to Moscow to put a bouquet of flowers on that memorial'.[15] The Chinese character *ding* 丁 is close in shape to the Western letter T, and in his prison poem Zheng uses it to stand for Trotsky. The prison authorities failed to see through this thin disguise and took the poem as a piece of nonsense.

Memorial to Ding

The north wind gusts, the snowflakes dance,
vast buildings tower by the way.
Red flags on rooftops dapple white,
crowds surge like tides from subway gates.[16]
This stubborn shade, this wisp of smoke,
will face God with its granite brain:[17]
clutching fresh blooms it treads the snow,
enquiring of each passer-by,
'Where is the grand memorial?'

---

15 This comment and the poem are translated from Yu Yin 1989, pp. 88–91. Zheng also wrote in 1988: 'Not until after I was released from jail in 1979 did I learn that the memorial proposed by Khrushchev had not been built. So even if the disembodied soul in my poem really had taken flowers to Moscow, it would have had to lay them before a disembodied stone. Today, there is every chance that the memorial of my dreams will finally be built, whether or not Trotsky's name appears on it in gold. As for myself, I am still not yet a wandering ghost. Now, I do not need to write about my dreams in ways that will fool the censor, for it is no longer a crime to speak out against Stalin. But I have no wish to write a new poem to voice my feelings, so I shall let the poem I wrote twenty-odd years ago stand, under its original title "Memorial to Ding", as a record of the events of those days'.

16 Zheng Chaolin imagines a new Moscow, different from the one he left in 1924.

17 Mao once said of his opponents who refused to give up their positions: 'Let them go to see their God with their granite brains'.

When last here, I was very young.
Bullet scars could still be seen
around the university.
Yet people rose above the mean
and narrow streets to dwarf the gods.
Now poverty has given way
to affluence, unlettered night
to dawning of the lettered day.
Sapling of my youth, you've grown
into a tree where people take
shade from the sun and pick fresh fruit;
those who planted it are dead,
the earth beneath is stained jade green.[18]
See, the marble comes in sight
clean and white as frozen fat.
Flowers bedeck the steps and plinth.
With spinning eyes I scan the stone
line by line for words of gold.
Framed in the blurred names' giddy ring,
whichever way I look I see
nothing but *ding, ding, ding,* and *ding*.

Nor can the publication and republication of Zheng's memoirs by the Chinese Communist authorities be taken to imply that he in any way compromised with the régime in Beijing. This truth is evident from the comment with which Zheng's official publishers in China prefaced their edition of his book. 'Zheng Chaolin is currently a member, aged eighty two, of the People's Political Consultative Conference of the Municipality of Shanghai', they wrote in August 1982. 'He was an early member of the Chinese Communist Party. As he himself says, after the second half of 1927, he gradually departed from the line of the Communist International and the Chinese Communist Party and, after 1929, went over completely to Trotskyist positions; moreover, he became a main leader of the Chinese Trotskyist organisation.... To this day, the author fully upholds Trotskyist positions on various important issues in the Chinese

---

18 The philosopher Zhuangzi (c. 370–300 BC) told a story about Chang Hong, a high official wrongly killed by a prince in Shu (now Sichuan). Chang Hong's blood, after being stored for three years, changed colour from red to emerald, whence the popular saying that the blood of those wrongly killed turns green, and even becomes green jade.

Revolution and the Russian Revolution, and still supports various of Trotsky's and of Chen Duxiu's opinions. We are now publishing this book in a limited edition, restricted to internal circulation, as reference material for leading cadres in relevant departments and for scientific workers in the field of contemporary history'.

In China, where by traditional reckoning a person reaches the age of one sooner than in the West,[19] Zheng Chaolin, though born in 1901, celebrated his ninetieth birthday in 1990. At a birthday reception given in his honour, he reported on his life to elders of his native Zhangping in Fujian province. He told them: 'Seventy one of my ninety years were spent outside Zhangping, but I have certainly not forgotten that I am a son of Zhangping. I was born in Zhangping, I grew up in Zhangping, and I had my schooling in Zhangping. My forebears moved to Zhangping 756 years ago.... How should I report to the elders of Zhangping? What have I, who for seventy one years have lived far from home, done in that time? And what do I still want to do? There is so much to say and so little time to say it, so I will be brief: there is nothing in my life that I feel unable to report on to the elders of Zhangping'.

The publication of this translation of Zheng's book, which describes and explains the birth of Stalinism in the Chinese Communist Party, is timely, for Stalinism everywhere has either died or passed into a general crisis the nature of which is best explained historically. How will Zheng greet this volume? When he heard the news that his book of poems was to be published, he wrote to a friend: 'People value their old brooms, even though they're broken and of little value. When the book comes out and I have a copy in my hands, when I see that it's well published and can smell the ink, I shall pat and feel it for several minutes. And my joy at the age of ninety will be no less than the joy of a nine-year old boy who has been given a new toy'.[20]

---

19 In China, a person traditionally counts as one-year old at birth and becomes a year older when the New Year starts. For example, a person born on the last day of the last month of the lunar year will become two years old the following day.

20 Yu Yin 1989, p. 9.

Peng Shuzhi and the Chinese Revolution: Notes Towards a Political Biography[1]

Joseph T. Miller

Originally published in Historical Materialism, *no. 8 (summer 2001); here revised.*

Who was Peng Shuzhi? How influential was he, and in what ways, in the early development of Chinese communism and the Trotskyist movement in China? Revolutionaries are products of their background, their experiences, and the general conditions of their existence. Any analysis must include the context in which such individuals act, and must allow for, even expect, transformation through changing circumstances.

This work is an introduction to the life and early political activism of Peng Shuzhi, up to his role in the formation of the Communist League of China (CLC) in 1931. Obviously, this cannot be the complete story of the Chinese Trotskyist movement, with all the variants and differing perceptions that term encompasses.[2] Rather, it is a small effort to place Peng's life in the context of a period of revolutionary possibility for China and to question some perceptions about his role in the development of Chinese communism.

Peng's roles as a party theorist and chief of the CCP's propaganda department during the period of the second Chinese revolution (1924–7) attest to his centrality in the history of the communist movement. Then, as he and hundreds of others helped form the Left Opposition inside the CCP in the late

---

1 Much of original source material is from research first done in the late 1970s for my doctoral dissertation. It includes interviews and archival materials obtained at Taiwan's Institute for International Relations and the Bureau of Investigation, as well as material from the Hoover Institute. In addition to primary documents obtained from Peng Shuzhi between 1974 and 1983, there are materials provided by Peng's daughter and activists in Hong Kong. Newly available documents from the CCP have also been utilised. I can only read English and Chinese, so Russian documents in the Comintern archives are not included. I express my appreciation to the anonymous reviewers of the original draft. Their comments and research suggestions were very helpful and have been incorporated where feasible, though I remain responsible for errors or omissions. I am deeply grateful to Ms Cheung Ching Choy for her support and guidance.

2 See Kagan 1969, Miller 1979, and Benton 1996 for extensive material on this movement. Readers will find many areas of continuing dispute in the treatments of Chinese Trotskyism, some reflected in this article. For a note on the term 'Trotskyism', see Mandel 1994, pp. 9–10.

1920s, Peng remained on a revolutionary path against overwhelming obstacles, leading ultimately to exile, first in Hong Kong and Vietnam, then to Paris, and, finally, in the United States. During this forced exile with his wife and life-partner in revolution, Chen Bilan, both served as a leaders and teachers to other revolutionaries, young and old, in the Fourth International, especially its Chinese section, the Revolutionary Communist Party of China (RCPC), until Peng's death in California in November 1983 and Chen's death in Hong Kong in 1987.

On my first meeting with Peng and Chen Bilan in August 1974, they were clearly still active partners in revolutionary struggle and fully engaged in the day to day operations of the Fourth International. They spent days and weeks meeting with young people from around the world, educating them and learning from them. They assisted the RCPC in Hong Kong in starting up the journal *Shiyue pinglun* (October Review), a periodical that continues more than twenty-five years later. They were not tired or demoralised, but rather, energetic and hopeful about the future.

Over the next nine years, we met for interviews and updates, exchanged letters, and shared notes on political struggles in which we were involved. During our very first meeting he wrote a Chinese couplet in my notebook, expressing his advice for me and reflecting his and Bilan's own life story:

Kangkai shashen yi;
to go nobly to one's death is easy;
Changqi fendou nan.
to struggle for the long term is difficult.

It is in this spirit that one should view the life and work of this 'constant dissident'.[3]

The Early Years (1895–1921)

Peng Shuzhi was born in the village of Tongle, in Baoqing (or Shaoyang) *xian*, on 24 November 1895. Peng's family was one of the few better-off peasant families in this poor village. He viewed his family as part of the 'small landlord' class, though still farmers. 'They lived a simple frugal life and saved their money', according to Peng, 'which they used to buy more land. Thus the life

---

3 Cheng 1998, p. 16. Remarks by the daughter of Peng and Chen at their final burial ceremony in France, 31 March 1998.

of a peasant, though a small landlord, could still be hard and bitter. My family was like this'.[4]

The family was also more educated, with the traditional emphasis placed on education of the male children. At age seven, Peng Shuzhi was placed in a school where the youth of several families were taught by a hired instructor. After five years, his education was brought to a temporary halt due to the illness of his grandmother.[5]

One early influence on Peng's thinking and developing worldview was Chen Tianhua's 1903 volume *Xingshi zhong* (Alarm to Rouse the World), an early reflection of a nascent Chinese nationalism. This was Peng's first window on the arena of world politics and China's place in it. Whereas previously, his 'world' consisted only of his village, Peng now learned that 'China was a big country and that it was in danger.... It was then that I thought of the need for China to develop a sense of nationalism'.[6]

Eventually, Peng was able to return to school, where he began to question an educational system which put a premium on rote learning of the Chinese classics, and taught nothing about the real world or the outside world. A newly-hired science teacher took a special interest in this young student, and, recognising the limitations of a small village school, encouraged Peng to go elsewhere for a modern education.[7]

During the autumn of 1912, Peng and some others from his village travelled to the larger town of Changsha, the capital of Hunan province, where they enrolled in Shaoyang Middle School. According to Peng, this school was staffed 'from top to bottom' with 'Japan returned students' who had been members of the national revolutionary group known as the Tongmeng hui (the predecessor to the Guomindang or Nationalist Party). The principal of this school, He Yanwu, was also a member of the Tongmeng hui, and he encouraged new forms of learning, which included debates on political issues.[8]

This was Peng's further introduction to politics and revolution. Since the Qing Dynasty had been overthrown in 1911–12, young people like himself were easily drawn to the national revolutionary spirit of the times. Clearly, China

---

4 Peng Shuzhi, interviewed by Miller, Tape 1, Side A (Hereafter, Miller interviews). These interviews were conducted in Chinese, while Peng and Chen were living in California. For those who read French, see Claude Cadart and Cheng Yingxiang, *Mémoirs de Peng Shuzhi. L'Envol du communisme en Chine* (Paris: Gallimard, 1983). This volume covers Peng's life up to 1925.
5 Miller interviews, Tape 1, Side A.
6 Ibid.
7 Ibid.
8 Ibid.

was still in the grip of Western and Japanese imperialism. Qing efforts to break or weaken this hold had been pitiful against the overwhelming impact of this exploitative world system. Of course, this situation moved many to action – from the Taiping Rebellion in the 1850s and 1860s to the Boxers of 1900 to the 1911 Revolution. All had their roots in nationalistic, anti-foreign attitudes largely resulting from these imperialist pressures and the concomitant internal problems.[9]

As for Peng's home province of Hunan, it was one of those most affected by Kang Youwei's progressive reform movement of the late nineteenth century. Furthermore, according to Zhang Guotao, 'It was always on Hunan that the North-South wars converged. The Hunanese had suffered from war for a very long time, and, generally speaking, their young people inclined to the Left ideologically and were politically highly sensitive. Indeed, to each modern Chinese revolutionary movement, Hunan contributed a number of outstanding figures'.[10]

Peng finally finished his high school education in the autumn of 1916. Since his family could not afford to send him to college, he began teaching in an upper level elementary school in Shaoyang. He followed national and international events through any newspapers or magazines he could find, including Chen Duxiu's *Xin qingnian* (New Youth), which greatly impressed him. Gradually, he learned more about radical political theories and movements through such reading and through events taking place around him.[11]

Eventually, at the end of the school term in 1919, he quit teaching. He was confused about his future direction, though he knew he wanted to be politically active. He later recalled that 'At that time, my thinking on socialism was very vague, just at its embryonic stage. It was also mixed with Marxism and anarchism'.[12]

Early in 1920, Peng finally decided to leave his home village, with the hopes of getting to Beijing, the centre of Chinese radicalism since the May Fourth Movement of the previous year. Due to warlord activity, however, he never made it. He stayed with relatives in Guizhou for a time before finally returning to Changsha in September, where he linked up with a major influence, Principal He Minfan.[13]

---

9   Marx and Engels 1972, pp. 213–20; Esherick 1972.
10 Chang 1971, p. 129.
11 Miller interviews, Tape 1, Side B.
12 Ibid.
13 Ibid.

He Minfan was in his sixties, but he had a very youthful demeanour and was always interested in new things, so he called himself 'Old Youth' (*lao shaonian*). He was organising a socialist youth group in Changsha, and he had already collected a small group of young people around him. Peng was soon encouraged by He to travel to Shanghai, where he could work directly with Chen Duxiu in a more advanced communist organisation. As Peng has reported, He Minfan suggested that Peng should go to Shanghai as one from among the 'founders of the Changsha communist organisation'. Since Chen and He Minfan had corresponded for some time, He provided a letter of introduction for Peng to Chen Duxiu.[14]

By 1920, small Marxist study groups were established in some of the major cities of China, inspired by the success of the Bolshevik revolution in Russia in 1917. The Shanghai group, called the Marxist Research Society (*Makesi zhuyi yanjiu hui*), was established by Chen Duxiu and others in May 1920. According to Arif Dirlik, Comintern emissary Gregory Voitinsky 'seems to have engaged [Chen's group] in considering the possibilities for founding a Communist party'.[15] While this first effort failed, the group did actually become the nucleus for the CCP. Also that summer, the Foreign Language Institute (*Waiguoyu xueshe*) had been established, led by Voitinsky's wife and Yang Mingzhai to train Chinese activists in Russian as part of their Marxist studies.[16]

On his arrival in Shanghai, Peng joined the Socialist Youth League (SYL) and Chen's study group, thus joining the CCP nucleus. He was also among some twenty students who were studying Russian at Yang's school. According to Peng, 'Of course, my main purpose for going to Shanghai was to go to Russia to study'.[17]

During this period, Voitinsky urged Chen Duxiu to send people to Moscow to attend the soon-to-be-established Communist University for the Toilers of the East (KUTV), an institution meant to provide trained communist revolutionaries to further the struggles in their home countries. According to Peng Shuzhi, he, along with about thirty others, was selected to attend. Separate

---

14 Peng Shuzhi 1983a, pp. 68–72; also Miller interviews, Tape 1, Side B; Peng letter to this author, 22 May 1976.
15 Dirlik 1989, p. 203; Feigon 1983b, pp. 162–5.
16 Dirlik 1989, p. 206; Peng 1983a; Miller interviews, Tape 1, Side B; see Smith 2000, pp. 13–17. For a very detailed description of the influence of the Bolshevik revolution on early Chinese Communists, see Pantsov 2000, Chapter 2.
17 Peng 1980, pp. 13–15; Miller interviews, Tape 1, Side B; Miller interviews, Tape 2, side A.

groups of two's and three's began to leave China unobtrusively during February 1921 so as not to attract attention.[18]

Peng travelled with Ren Zuomin on this rather harrowing journey. They carried with them a pass signed by Voitinsky to ease their way into Russia, but due to concerns about being searched by the Japanese in Vladivostok, they tore it up and tossed it into the sea:

> Leaving Japanese-controlled territory was no trouble. But after crossing the bridge over the Amur and getting into Russia, without a pass or ID, trouble developed at Khabarovsk station. Authorities would not take our word that we were travelling to Moscow to study. They did not accept our story about tearing up the pass.... Our problem was compounded by the fact that we could not explain ourselves in Russian, even after six months of studying the language.[19]

Peng and Ren soon solved their identification problem. However, they were prevailed upon to stay behind in Khabarovsk to write and edit a Chinese-language newspaper for a group of Chinese trade unionists. They were then transferred to the Red Army to do educational work for a group of Chinese and Koreans in a Siberian unit until it was disbanded in late July or early August 1921. Peng and Ren were finally allowed to finish their travels to Moscow, arriving in late August or early September, ready to settle in for their studies.[20]

The Moscow Years (1921–4)

Soviet Russia, surrounded by hostile forces, was in the midst of a struggle for stability in 1921. Though the Bolsheviks were victorious in the civil war against the forces of counter-revolution, they now faced a new enemy: economic and social reality in their devastated nation, surrounded by hostile forces.[21]

Some of the effects of these domestic instabilities and international controversies reached deep into the halls of the KUTV. When Peng Shuzhi finally

---

18 According to a memoir by Xiao Jingguang, one of these students, there were only fourteen in this first group. See Pantsov, 2000, pp. 166–7.
19 Miller interviews, Tape 1, Side B; Robert A. Burton interviews with Peng and Chen Bilan, in Brussels, 11–13 August 1966 (hereafter, Burton interviews). Copy of Burton interview transcript obtained from Richard Kagan in 1973.
20 Miller interviews, Tape 1, Side B.
21 Lenin 1966, pp. 21–9; Lenin 1971, p. 675.

arrived in Moscow, he was informed by Liu Shaoqi that factional disputes had developed among some of the earlier arrivals. As Peng explained in 1976, 'One of the factions consisted of about five students, centring around a man named Bu Shiqi, who spoke good Russian. He thus was able to speak to the school authorities'.[22]

This was a period of severe economic restrictions in Russia, due to the civil war and international isolation. There were bread rations, but still not enough to go around. Bu was able to secure extra rations due to his fluency in Russian, and he would distribute these only to the students in his faction. Such corrupt practices, often found in times of extreme scarcity, produced bitterness among the other Chinese students. As Peng described it, 'When a man is hungry, he does not mind his manners'.[23]

In an attempt to resolve the disputes, a meeting was called of all the Chinese students, where Bu's faction was required to admit its mistake and the other, larger faction was able to air its grievances. Eventually, with approval of the Comintern, a Moscow Branch of the Chinese Communist Party (CCP) was formed, since it was felt that the Chinese students needed more formal organisation. This was an unusual step, but it was certainly understandable in the context of language and other barriers. Peng was chosen to be secretary of this Moscow branch, a post he was to maintain until his departure from Moscow in 1924.[24]

During January and February of 1922, Peng was a delegate to the Congress of the Toilers of the Far East in Moscow and Petrograd. As the Congress proceeded, conflict developed over support for bourgeois liberation movements in the colonies and the less developed world. For China, the conflict centred on the efficacy of an alliance, or a bloc, with the Guomindang in China. The Chinese Communist delegates, including Peng Shuzhi, were very much aware of the fundamental class nature of the Guomindang, based as it was on merchants, rich peasants, and the military.[25] They were also aware of Lenin's statements concerning support for bourgeois liberation movements.[26]

---

22   Miller interviews, Tape 2, Side A. See biographical note on Bu in Pantsov, 2000, p. 280.
23   Ibid.
24   Ibid.; Zheng Chaolin, who arrived in Moscow two years later (in 1923), has a different take on the factional situation at Toilers University and what he viewed as Peng's authoritarian behaviour. See Benton, ed., 1997, pp. 47–51.
25   Whiting 1968, pp. 82–83; Chang 1971, pp. 204–5; see Chen 1922 for Chen Duxiu's early opposition to the alliance with the Guomindang.
26   Lenin 1971, pp. 603–4.

The issue was even further clarified by the remarks to this Congress of Georgi Safarov, head of the Eastern Department of the Comintern. In reference to the Chinese situation, he said:

> We support any national revolutionary movement, but only in so far as it is not directed against the proletarian movement. We must say: he is a traitor to the cause of the Communist proletarian revolution who does not support the national revolutionary movement. On the other hand we say: he is a traitor to the national cause who fights against the awakening of the proletarian movement, he is a traitor to his people and to his national cause who hinders the Chinese working class in its efforts to stand up on its own feet and speak its own language.[27]

This question arose once again at the Fourth Comintern Congress at the end of 1922. Chen Duxiu, head of the CCP's secretariat,[28] and Liu Renjing attended as representatives of the Chinese movement. Liu reported on the general political situation in China. He chided the Guomindang for scheming to make what he called a 'military revolution', while totally ignoring the necessity for 'mass propaganda in the country'. He also pointed to the numerous strikes which had recently taken place in China as some proof of the 'awakening of the labouring masses'. He declared that 'the mass movement is not a dream of the Socialists, but that it has already come into being'. In his later remarks to the Congress, however, Liu still argued that it was necessary for the CCP to join with the Nationalist Party.[29]

When measured against the strongly anti-bourgeois speeches made at this same Congress by Karl Radek, Leon Trotsky, and Gregory Zinoviev, Liu's presentation would seem to prepare the ground for even deeper confusion among the Chinese students then in Moscow. How could they be expected to return to China as effective fighters in the revolutionary struggle with such mixed signals?[30]

---

27 Communist International 1922, pp. 166–7.
28 Chen, 1991, p. 35; van de Ven 1991, p. 88.
29 Communist International 1923, pp. 216–17; Whiting 1968, pp. 92, 95; In 1976 Peng said that during this Congress he and Chen Duxiu established the Moscow Branch of the CCP as the liaison office for Europe in order to bring more Chinese students to KUTV. He acted on this immediately, bringing people like Zheng Chaolin to Moscow at the start of 1923 and significantly increasing the number of Chinese students. Miller interviews, Tape 2, Side A.
30 See Pantsov 2000, Chapter 3, for an extended discussion of Lenin's views.

By 1923, Peng Shuzhi gained an appointment as an instructor at KUTV. For the next year he taught courses such as the 'History of the Development of Social Formations', and he lectured on Marxist philosophy.[31] He was also admitted to membership of the Soviet Communist Party, due to his increasing fluency in the Russian language.

Peng's attendance at cadre meetings during 1923, at the time of the failure of the German revolution, also exposed him to some aspects in the developing political struggle between Stalin, by this time General Secretary of the Soviet Communist Party, and Leon Trotsky. He found it relatively easy to support the Lenin-Trotsky stance on economic questions, but he had to look deeper into the party question, that is, the relationship between democratic centralism and inner party democracy, before he was able to support them on this issue as well.[32]

'At the time', Peng said in 1976, 'I felt there was a division between the old guard and the young. I often thought about this problem among the Russians. Many among us worshipped Trotsky. Coming from China, we knew of only Trotsky and Lenin....

> But the problem of Trotsky versus Stalin was very difficult to understand. Among others, it was a problem between the old Bolsheviks and the young revolutionaries.... Trotsky in 'The New Course' said that the old fell behind; we couldn't understand. Later, of course, we did. In this situation, we were alone, with no one to help us. We knew that things were not good. We studied to find out why things were the way they were.[33]

During this period, the CCP in China was experiencing its own difficulties with party questions. The official Comintern policy of collaboration between the CCP and Guomindang had begun when the Sun-Joffe memorandum of 26 January 1923 declared China to be unripe for communism 'or even the Soviet system', and that 'China's most important and most pressing problems are the completion of national unification and the attainment of full national independence'.[34]

In spite of his early opposition to this policy, Chen Duxiu and the rest of the CCP leadership had finally acquiesced to the Comintern representative's push for CCP collaboration with the Guomindang and China's bourgeoisie.

31　Burton interviews, 11 August 1966; Price 1976, p. 34.
32　Miller interviews, Tape 2, Side B.
33　Miller interviews, Tape 2, Side B; See Trotsky 1975, pp. 50–62, for the basic issues involved.
34　Brandt, Schwartz, and Fairbank, eds, 1967, p. 70.

For example, in the 23 April 1923 issue of *Xiangdao zhoubao* (Guide Weekly), while Chen recognised the historic importance of the working class, he argued for an alliance between the 'revolutionary bourgeoisie' and the Chinese working class. Only with this type of leadership, he wrote, could the national revolution succeed.[35]

Later that same year, in *Qianfeng* (Vanguard), Chen argued that, while the working class was necessary for a successful proletarian revolution, it could not function as an independent force in China's national revolution. Only through a 'melting of class distinctions' could this national revolution succeed. Then the Chinese working class would follow with its own socialist revolution later.[36]

While still in Moscow, Peng Shuzhi claims to have developed very serious doubts about the efficacy of such a policy. As he described it to an interviewer in 1966, when friends tried to convince Peng this was analogous to communists joining the British Labour Party, he pointed out that the Labour Party was essentially a workers' party, whereas the Guomindang was fundamentally a party of the bourgeoisie.[37] Peng read Chen's articles and determined to challenge this attitude and the policies which grew from it on his return to China.

In April 1924, Trotsky spoke on the occasion of KUTV's third anniversary. It is likely that Peng Shuzhi attended this event, along with other instructors and students. Trotsky warned the audience about various attempts by the bourgeoisie to exploit Marxism and Marxist movements for their own purposes. Specifically on the question of China, he said:

> We approve of Communist support to the Guomindang Party in China, which we are endeavouring to revolutionise. This is inevitable, but here too there is a risk of national-democratic revival.... the young Marxists of the East run the risk of being torn out of the 'Emancipation of Labour' group and of becoming permeated with nationalist ideology.[38]

We see in Peng's later writings the apparent impact of these comments, since similar ideas appear quite clearly in many of his articles after his return to China. In particular, Peng generally makes the distinction between 'support' for the Guomindang and an outright alliance with the Guomindang, always warning about the capture of the movement by the Chinese bourgeoisie.

---

35 Chen 1923a.
36 Chen 1923b.
37 Burton interviews, 12 August 1966.
38 Trotsky 1969, p. 8.

Later that same year, Peng took part in the Fifth Comintern Congress, where Chen Duxiu was elected (in absentia) to the ECCI. It was this Congress, according to Isaac Deutscher, which 'put its seal on the excommunication of Trotsky'. By this time, he was so isolated that 'in the course of the full three weeks the congress heard nothing but foul-mouthed vituperation against the man to whom the previous four congresses had listened with deep respect and adoration'.[39]

There is no record of any voices raised in Trotsky's defence. Of course, since Trotsky decided not to defend himself, this should not be surprising. Also, Stalin, utilising his position in the Soviet party, had gradually increased the attacks on Trotsky after the 1923 disputes, especially following Lenin's death in 1924. As Peng recalled this Congress,

> we didn't understand then what was taking place. Trotsky didn't speak before the Congress.... We could sense then that Trotsky was being held down by Stalin.... I wanted to return to China. Thus, when the CCP Central Committee wanted me to return, I was pleased. Since I got nothing out of the Fifth Comintern Congress, I wanted to return to China and see what could be done.[40]

The Second Chinese Revolution (1924–7)

By the time Peng Shuzhi returned to China in August 1924, the CCP had already held three party congresses. The party had become a mere appendage to the Guomindang. Its mission now was to 'help strengthen the KMT's influence among workers and peasants',[41] since the Guomindang apparently was unsuccessful in this work by itself. Even Mao Zedong, a member of the CCP Central Committee, joined the Guomindang and supported the call for bourgeois leadership of the Chinese national revolution in 1923.[42]

Soon after Peng's return, he was appointed editor of *Xin qingnian*, now an official organ of the CCP. This gave him his first opportunity to challenge the policy of class collaboration then being followed by the CCP under Comintern directives. He planned a special issue for December 1924, on the theme of problems of the national revolution, a subject he had touched on earlier.

---

39   Deutscher 1959, p. 146; also see *International Press Correspondence*, 12 August 1924, p. 612.
40   Miller interviews, Tape 2, Side B.
41   Wilbur and How 1956, p. 66.
42   Mao 1923.

Peng's lead article in the special issue asked 'Who is the leader of the Chinese national revolution?' He provided a careful analysis of the classes in Chinese society, their respective strengths and weaknesses, and their probable attitudes towards the revolution. He argued that even though China's national revolution may be bourgeois-democratic in character, this did not preclude the 'necessity of having the most progressive class in the position of leadership'. Because of the 'unclear separation of classes in China', however, it was difficult to establish which class was the 'most progressive'. This was Peng's task.[43]

Through his analysis of the Chinese bourgeoisie, sector by sector, Peng determined that because of its 'intimate relationship' with both imperialism and feudal warlords, this class could not be expected to lead a successful national revolution.[44]

The Chinese working class, on the other hand, had sufficient numbers and consciousness to take leadership, since it was 'directly under the oppression of imperialism and the foreign capitalists'.[45] With working class leadership of the revolution, the peasants and the handicraft workers would become effective allies, and they would follow the working class 'even into the proletarian revolution'.[46]

Peng provided three answers to the question, 'If the working class is the only possible leader of the national revolution, why doesn't it change this revolution into one of the proletariat?' First of all, the Chinese bourgeoisie was not the only enemy to be dealt with; there was also imperialism and warlordism. Second, defeat of these two enemies would just be the 'first step' towards the proletarian revolution. Third, a premature revolution of proletarian nature might force friends of the national revolution into a counter-revolutionary stance. However, these concerns do not relieve the Chinese working class of its historic task, according to Peng. While it fights for the national revolution, the Chinese working class must at the same time prepare for its own proletarian revolution unfettered.[47]

According to Peng, upon his return from Moscow, he shared with Chen a draft of the above article, asking him to also write something on the question.[48] Chen's article was titled 'Lessons of the National Movement over

---

43 Zhongguo geming wenti lunwen ji 1948, pp. 4–5; reprinted in *Peng Shuzhi xuanji* 1983b, Vol. 1, pp. 177–93.
44 Zhongguo geming wenti lunwen ji 1948, p. 15.
45 Zhongguo geming wenti lunwen ji 1948, pp. 16–17.
46 Zhongguo geming wenti lunwen ji 1948, pp. 24–5.
47 Zhongguo geming wenti lunwen ji 1948, pp. 29–30.
48 Evans and Block 1976, p. 47.

the past 27 years'. He reviewed four earlier movements in modern Chinese history: the 1898 Reforms, the Boxer Rebellion of 1900, the 1911 Revolution, and the May Fourth Movement of 1919. Chen concluded that all of these efforts were 'defeated' because they were simply based on 'petty-bourgeois leadership'. He also credited the May Fourth Movement for being the first in which the proletariat began to show its social force. Finally, Chen made an obvious bow towards Peng's position when he wrote:

> The lesson we have learned from the last 27 years of the national movement is: of all social classes, only mankind's final class – the proletariat, is the most uncompromising revolutionary class. Furthermore, it is the natural enemy of the international capitalist imperialists. ... In the national revolutions of those countries oppressed by imperialism, the proletariat must assume leadership.[49]

In January 1925, the CCP held its Fourth National Congress in Shanghai. By this time the party had more than one thousand members, with a youth group of over nine thousand members.[50] Peng Shuzhi participated as the delegate from the Moscow Branch of the CCP, and he was elected to the Central Committee and the Political Bureau, taking charge of the party's propaganda department. His role at this congress continues to be a source of some controversy among participants in, and historians of, the Chinese Communist movement.

First, there is a dispute between Peng and Zheng Chaolin as to whether or not Voitinsky attended this Congress. According to Zheng's memoirs, the 'Comintern representative Voitinsky attended once, and Qu Qiubai interpreted his speech. Voitinsky drafted the political resolution and other important documents. ... On theoretical and political questions, the congress simply accepted Comintern instructions'.[51] The importance for Zheng of Voitinsky's appearance relates to an argument over the source for the political resolution at this congress. Zheng implies that Peng Shuzhi claimed responsibility for this resolution that, in Peng's words, 'marked the return of the CCP to Bolshevism and the setting of conditions for the second Chinese revolution'.[52]

Without access to all the sources, it seems to me that Peng Shuzhi simply denied that Voitinsky and Qu Qiubai attended the congress, and never claimed to have actually penned any resolution. One scholar argues that Peng wished

---

49   Isaacs Collection 1948, pp. 224–5, 229.
50   Wu Min and Xiao Feng 1951, p. 46; Zheng 1989, p. 549.
51   Zheng 1997, p. 78
52   Peng 1976, p. 48; also, see Zheng 1989, pp. 550–2; Smith 2000, p. 57.

to deny Qu's role in accepting the new line, though Zheng points out that Qu still favoured the CCP Guomindang alliance.[53] From the 'Resolution on the National Revolutionary Movement', however, it seems quite clear that the policies which Peng and Chen now opposed together were being revised, even if mildly. There was now a recognition that the Chinese working class should lead this revolution, even if some 'support' is given to the Guomindang, particularly its left wing. Unfortunately, this new shift did not actually end the period of 'entry' into the Guomindang.[54] While the 'setting of conditions' took place, more would have to happen to show the need for a final break, it seemed.

On this latter point, Zheng raised issue with a letter which Peng Shuzhi wrote to comrades back in Moscow just after the end of the Fourth Congress. This letter is actually a rather detailed report on the Fourth CCP Congress, which points out that the mistakes of the Third Congress (mistakes that Qu Qiubai supported), were now being corrected. Reporting on various debates which took place, Peng wrote:

> As to the workers' movement, should workers join the Guomindang? On this point, there were a few comrades who reflected a little infantile leftism, arguing that workers should not enter the Guomindang. In fact, if the working class thinks about how to actually lead the national revolutionary movement, entry into the Guomindang, in whatever scope, by workers is necessary.[55]

Is this in contradiction with Peng's views about CCP members being required to enter the Guomindang and accept its discipline? Perhaps, on the surface, but it may also be read in the spirit of Trotsky's 1924 comments concerning the effort to 'revolutionise' the Nationalist Party. Clearly, the leading role of the bourgeoisie is not the question here. Rather, it signals an attempt to assert the leading role of the working class, even in a party dominated by the bourgeoisie. In the context of the rising militancy of labour in 1925 China, this would seem to be a correct tactic.[56]

Another area of criticism of Peng's role at the Fourth Congress relates to a resolution 'attacking' Trotsky, according to Zheng. This was 'unscheduled'; it

---

53 Benton 1985, p. 324; Zheng 1997, p. 79; van de Ven 1991, pp. 211, 216–19, for more on Peng and Qu.
54 Zhongyang dang'an guan bian 1988, pp. 329–41.
55 Zhonggong zhongyang dangshi yanjiu shi 1982, pp. 17–18; see Benton 1985 for his full critique of Peng.
56 Smith 2000, Chapter 4.

had not been prepared in advance and handed out. As Zheng recalled, 'After the draft had been read, it was a long time before anyone spoke. Finally, Peng Shuzhi got up and made a speech along the lines that Trotsky was wrong on this or that point and must be opposed. The result was that the resolution was passed unanimously'.[57]

So Peng Shuzhi, who claimed in more recent materials to be among those who 'worshipped' Trotsky while in Moscow, now seems to have supported a resolution 'attacking' him. Of course, we are dependent on Zheng's memory for this, though he claimed to 'clearly remember some minor details' of the congress. According to Zheng, Peng apparently denied that such a resolution ever came up.[58]

However, a 'Resolution on the Attitude of Comrade Trotsky' does show up in more recently released archives of the Fourth CCP Congress. It cannot be appropriately labelled an 'attack', but rather, a mild critique in the early stages of the Stalin-Trotsky conflict. Trotsky was still a 'comrade', though he was criticised for his attitude towards the leadership of the Soviet party and the Comintern. The resolution stated that his statements may be used by the enemies of the world communist movement in a reactionary period, and it accepted the Soviet party's analysis of 'Trotskyism' as 'defeatist'. Finally, it called upon Trotsky to accept 'Leninism', at least as it was now being constructed by Stalin and his followers.[59]

Peng Shuzhi's denial may also be the result of faulty memory, though he did mention in his 1925 letter to Moscow comrades a 'report on Leninism and Trotskyism' at the congress.[60] If Peng saw this as a major issue for the congress, wouldn't he be expected to elaborate, especially if, as Benton constantly argues, he was a self-promoter? Wouldn't his strong support for such a resolution raise his status with the Comintern and within the CCP? Why didn't he say more about this in his letter to Moscow? We are still left with more questions than answers on this issue. Of course, Peng was elected to the Central Committee at this congress and put in charge of the Political Bureau's propaganda department, so he certainly was not seen as an outsider or a threat to 'established authority' at this point.

Following this congress, the CCP experienced rapid growth, due to its leadership in the growing and highly militant Chinese labour movement. These developments naturally met with great satisfaction in the Comintern. This did

---

57   Zheng 1997, p. 79.
58   Zheng 1997, pp. 78–9; Benton 1985, p. 325.
59   Zhongyang dang'an guan bian 1988, p. 325.
60   Zhonggong zhongyang dangshi yanjiu shi 1982, p. 17.

not result in acceptance of independent leadership by the Chinese working class, however. Rather, the Comintern remained committed to the 'powerful bloc between the proletariat and the urban middle classes'.[61]

In July 1925, just as the Chinese labour movement was growing in strength and a few months after the death of party founder Sun Yat-sen, Dai Jitao, the Guomindang's leading theoretician, called on all those in the Guomindang to dissolve any outside attachments 'and become "pure" Guomindang members'. Those Communists who joined the Guomindang under Comintern directives were now faced with a dilemma. Either stay in the Guomindang and give up their membership in the CCP, or leave the Guomindang and 'work openly in the name of the Chinese Communist Party'.[62]

According to Chen Duxiu, at a plenum in October 1925, he warned that Dai's pamphlet was 'an indication of the bourgeoisie's attempt to strengthen its power for the purpose of checking the proletariat and going over to the counter-revolution. We should prepare ourselves immediately to withdraw from the Guomindang and become independent'. Chen's proposal was rejected by a majority of the Central Committee and the Comintern representative, Voitinsky.[63]

Then, on 20 March 1926, Chiang Kai-shek carried out a coup in Guangzhou, arresting many CCP activists there. Within two months, the Guomindang announced its 'party adjusted programme', which included such things as exclusion of Communists from 'all higher posts in the Guomindang', cessation of any criticisms of the Three People's Principles, and the required registration of any CCP members.[64]

Immediately following the March coup, the CCP regional committee at Shanghai called a meeting at which it was decided that the policy of collaboration must be reconsidered. According to Zhang Guotao, then head of the CCP's military affairs department, the Central Committee decided to send him to Guangzhou to 'investigate the true facts of the incident' and implement a 'delaying policy of compromise' with Chiang's forces.[65]

On the other hand, Peng Shuzhi has argued that there was no 'policy of compromise'. Rather, the policy was one of preparation of an 'independent military force to oppose Chiang Kai-shek'. Furthermore, according to Peng, it was he who was sent to Guangzhou as the Central Committee representative to

---

61 Heller 1925, p. 16.
62 Wilbur and How, p. 206.
63 Evans and Block 1976, p. 600.
64 Brandt 1958, p. 75.
65 Chang 1971, p. 494.

demand from Michael Borodin, the new Comintern representative, a policy of opposition to Chiang. Peng pointed out the dangers of an imminent rightist counter-revolution in Guangdong province, and he proposed that all CCP members withdraw from the Guomindang in order to protect themselves.[66]

Borodin suggested a meeting with some of the leaders of the so-called 'left wing' of the Guomindang. Of the four Guomindang representatives, only one expressed disgust with Chiang's March coup, but he was still opposed to the Communists leaving the Nationalist Party, claiming that would only 'weaken the left wing's position'. In this way, Borodin was able to garner opposition to Peng's proposal, and that was the end of it.[67]

Peng left Guangzhou in June and returned to Shanghai. The Central Committee held another plenum in July, at which Chen Duxiu and Peng again advocated total withdrawal from the Guomindang. Their proposal was not adopted, according to Peng, but the Central Committee decided to send it on to Moscow, where it was later rejected as 'adventurist'.[68]

In September, Peng wrote that, although the Northern Expedition might be might be useful in ending warlordism and unifying China, its leadership (read Chiang Kai-shek) must be held accountable at every turn. It must not be allowed to turn this potentially useful tool for the good of China into an instrument of bourgeois power enrichment. This 'back door' criticism of Comintern policy seemed the only way left open to Peng and Chen Duxiu.[69]

By late 1926, the Nationalist Party was accepted into the Comintern as a 'sympathising party'. The CCP was ordered to restrain the peasant movement so as not to 'drive away the generals leading the victorious northward march' against the warlords.[70] Possibly responding to pressure from the Left Opposition led by Trotsky, however, the ECCI was still giving lip service to the 'independence' of the Communists inside the Guomindang.[71]

In January 1927, Peng Shuzhi asked the question, 'Is Leninism Applicable to the So-called "National Peculiarities" of China?' Answering in the affirmative, Peng did not stop there. After quoting Stalin's writings on Leninism, he proceeded to challenge the very foundation of Stalin's policies in China, though

---

66 Peng 1968, pp. 14–15; this is supported by Chen Duxiu's 1929 letter in Evans and Block 1976, p. 601.
67 Peng 1968, p. 16.
68 Burton interviews, August 12, 1966.
69 Peng 1926; reprinted in Peng Shuzhi 1982–3, Volume 1, pp. 205–18.
70 Isaacs 1961, p. 117.
71 Degras 1960, pp. 345–6.

indirectly. He enumerated five principles which he termed the 'basis' for the national revolution:

(1) the national revolution is one part of the world revolution;
(2) China's working class is the vanguard of the revolution;
(3) China's revolution must protect the interests of the peasants to the end;
(4) completely recognise the equality of all nationalities; and,
(5) permanent revolution.[72]

Elaborating on the second principle, Peng argued that 'if the interests of the working class are sacrificed, then the revolution has been sacrificed'. As for the fifth principle, Peng discussed this without even mentioning Trotsky. He merely pointed out that 'the national revolution is not the last revolutionary stage for China. It must go the way of socialist revolution'.[73]

In early March, reflecting growing concerns within the CCP Central Committee, Peng warned against the 'rightist dangers' which existed for the Chinese revolution. The fact that the revolution began to show signs of 'bourgeois compromise, and even reaction', led him to the belief that there was a real danger of defeat.[74]

Then, in what was to be his final article for *Xiangdao*, Peng analysed the 'anti-communist, anti-labour, and anti-Soviet' tendencies represented by Chiang Kai-shek. He argued that future struggles will necessarily be of a 'life or death' nature between the revolutionary forces of China's working class and Chiang's 'counter-revolutionary forces'.[75]

The CCP Central Committee could see the growing strength of Chiang's right wing in the Guomindang, yet, the Comintern still directed the workers of Shanghai not to come into conflict with Chiang's forces as they moved towards the city in late March. This directive was received after the armed insurrection of 21 March had placed workers in charge of the entire city, except for the foreign concessions.[76]

---

72 Peng 1927a; reprinted in Peng Shuzhi 1982–3, Volume 1, pp. 219–26. In fact, the term *yongxu geming* seems closer to the meaning of 'permanent revolution' that is generally discussed in the Trotskyist lexicon. This was later replaced by the term *buduan geming*, which is actually closer in meaning to 'continuous revolution' or 'revolution without stages'. I would agree that Peng was probably not writing in accord with Trotsky, but rather, in accord with how he (Peng) saw the Chinese events unfolding on the ground.
73 Peng 1927a; see footnote on Qu Qiubai's response to this in Evans and Block 1976, p. 61.
74 Peng 1927b; reprinted in Peng Shuzhi 1982–3, Volume 1, pp. 234–42.
75 Peng 1927c; reprinted in Peng Shuzhi 1982–3, Volume 1, pp. 250–7.
76 Isaacs 1961, p. 163.

On 12 April, Chiang Kai-shek, in collaboration with the Shanghai underworld, began a massacre which decimated the ranks of Shanghai's militant workers and CCP activists and soon spread to other areas of China. As the most famous chronicler of these events expressed it, 'the workers had died on the cross of Guomindang "unity". Under it, militarists and the bankers now gambled and bargained for the spoils'.[77] Now, according to Stalin, the Guomindang right wing had fully exposed itself, and the CCP could focus its efforts on the left wing, led by Wang Jingwei.

On 24 April 1927, in the midst of what became known as the 'white terror', the Fifth Congress of the CCP began far to the West of the Guomindang power centres. Over one hundred delegates arrived to represent the more than 50,000 members of the party.[78] The 'opportunism' of the party leadership was heavily criticised, but Chen Duxiu was re-elected to the post of General Secretary. Peng Shuzhi took part in this Congress as a delegate from Shanghai, and while he was re-elected to the Central Committee, he was removed from the Political Bureau position as propaganda chief and replaced by Cai Hesen, who had just returned from Moscow. This possibly reflected the conflict between Qu Qiubai and Peng over Peng's 'Trotskyism'.[79]

Peng was then transferred to the post of Secretary of the Northern Regional Committee, then vacant as a result of party co-founder Li Dazhao's arrest and execution by Chiang's Guomindang. Peng stayed there until Wang Jingwei of the Guomindang left wing initiated his own purge of the Communists in July. Following this, Peng and other party activists were required to go underground.[80]

During this critical and confusing period, an 'emergency conference' of the CCP Central Committee was called for 7 August 1927, in Hangzhou. This followed by only a couple of days the abortive Nanchang uprising led by Zhou Enlai and others in an effort to hold on to some base of operations for the CCP.

This emergency meeting was convened by Qu Qiubai, then head of the party's peasant department and a political opponent of Chen Duxiu and Peng Shuzhi. With only a few Central Committee members in attendance, this meeting officially removed Chen Duxiu as General Secretary, even though Chen

---

[77] Isaacs 1961, p. 185; see Evans and Block 1976, pp. 61–3 for Chen and Peng's plans for armed struggle.
[78] Wu Min and Xiao Feng 1951, p. 73.
[79] Zheng 1989, pp. 682–8; also Chang 1971, p. 621; Harrison 1972, p. 100; Schwartz 1951, pp. 68–71; see Peng 1928, a series of lectures presented by Peng in the immediate aftermath of the 1927 Guomindang coup in which he counters Qu's analysis of the revolution.
[80] Peng 1968.

had already resigned after Wang Jingwei's purge the month before. Chen, Tan Pingshan, and their so-called 'opportunism' were blamed for the defeat of the revolution, letting Stalin off the hook.[81]

After Qu 'unwillingly'[82] took control of the party, he proceeded to initiate, under directives brought to China by Stalin's protégé Lominadze, a policy of insurrection, even in the face of disastrous failures such as Nanchang. Peng Shuzhi, then still in the North, refused to take part in these efforts, believing its timing would only result in further decimation of the revolutionary forces. Ultimately, towards the end of 1927, Peng was removed from all major party responsibilities.[83]

As a result of this insurrectionary policy, many thousands of workers, peasants, and CCP organisers lost their lives or were imprisoned by Guomindang forces. By the end of 1927, CCP membership dropped from nearly 60,000 to 10,000. Rigor mortis had begun to set in on the Second Chinese Revolution.

Peng Shuzhi and the Origins of Chinese Trotskyism

Peng Shuzhi argued that 'the single most important reason for the beginning of the Trotskyist movement in China was the failure of the Chinese revolution of 1925–7'.[84] While this is surely true, the Chinese Left Opposition, or Chinese Trotskyist movement, had it earliest beginnings at Sun Yat-sen University in Moscow, not in China. Sun Yat-sen University was established in the autumn of 1925, following the death of Sun Yat-sen that March. Its purpose was to train revolutionary cadres for China who were not necessarily members of the Communist Party.

This group of early oppositionists consisted mainly of younger activists who were sent to Moscow during the years of revolution. According to Peng, 'they were won over to Trotskyism solely on the basis of Trotsky's writings and the influence of Karl Radek, who was the rector of Sun Yat-sen University at the time'.[85]

These supporters of Trotsky in Moscow were organised in secret around August 1928, just after the Sixth Comintern Congress and the Sixth CCP Congress, both of which were held in Moscow in order that they could develop

---

81 Evans and Block 1976, pp. 74–5; Zheng 1989, pp. 725–7.
82 Sima Lu 1962, p. 131.
83 P'eng 1980, pp. 28–9.
84 Miller interviews, Tape 3, Side A.
85 Ibid.

what became known as the 'Li Lisan Line' for the Chinese revolution.[86] Though Chen Duxiu and Peng Shuzhi were invited to attend these congresses, they declined, sensing a trap and realising that the party and the Comintern would not be open to criticism.[87]

As a direct result of the failure of the Russian Opposition, Stalin appointed Pavel Mif the new rector of Sun Yat-sen University, replacing Oppositionist Karl Radek. Mif and his protégé, a Chinese student named Wang Ming, then began to exercise tight control over the Chinese students. This fuelled the fires of opposition, and the secret organisations continued to grow.[88]

In an effort to keep the oppositionists from contaminating other students, they were generally sent back to China as they were discovered. During the spring of 1929, two of these returning students brought two major documents written by Trotsky to Peng Shuzhi. Upon reading them and finding himself in full agreement with the criticisms of Stalin's policies in China, Peng passed them on to Chen Duxiu, who also agreed with Trotsky's analysis. Chen and Peng then decided to organise a formal left opposition within the CCP.[89] Trotskyism in China now gained a new life and a very important audience: cadres and party branch secretaries who had not paid much attention to the earlier efforts to organise Trotskyist sympathisers.

In September 1929, five months after the formal organisation of the Chinese Left Opposition, Peng Shuzhi was called before a Communist Party Joint Conference to defend himself and Chen Duxiu against charges of 'opportunism'. He turned this conference into an argument for open discussion with the CCP on various political questions, including the opposition, as well as 'opportunism' and the 'nature of the future Chinese revolution'. The party defended repression of open discussion by referring to the 'tense situation' in China. Peng countered by arguing that this 'tense situation' could only be relieved through open discussion of important political questions.[90]

In general, Peng argued for a complete reappraisal of the Central Committee's political line, full freedom for party members to express and disseminate opinions within the party, the publication of Chen Duxiu's writings and the documents of the Opposition in order that 'all party comrades might freely discuss and criticise them', the abolition of 'iron discipline' within the

---

86   Sheng 1971, p. 166; also *International Press Correspondence,* October 4, 1928.
87   Miller interviews, Tape 3, Side A.
88   Kagan 1969, p. 61.
89   Miller interviews, Tape 3, Side A; Evans and Block 1976, pp. 291–341, 345–97.
90   Peng 1929, p. 2a; reprinted in Peng Shuzhi 1982–3, Volume 1, pp. 258–87.

party, and a return to the democratic practices which should be found in all Bolshevik parties.[91]

The joint conference was just one small part of the party leadership's campaign against the Chinese Left Opposition. Not surprisingly, the official criticisms of the Opposition in China were quite similar to those levied against Trotsky and the Opposition by Stalin only a few years earlier.

Eventually, these attacks won the day, for on 15 November 1929, Chen Duxiu, Peng Shuzhi, Wang Zekai, Ma Yufu, and Cai Zhende were all expelled from the CCP on charges of 'Trotskyism', factionalism, anti-party, and anti-International activities. Soon after, other sympathisers and adherents of the Left Opposition were expelled, including Chen Bilan, Yin Kuan, Zheng Chaolin, and others.[92]

In December, a document generally considered to be the single most important in the early history of the Chinese Trotskyist movement was released over the signatures of eighty-one former party members. This political platform, titled '*Women de zhengzhi yijian shu*' (Our Political Views), was co-authored by Chen Duxiu, Peng Shuzhi, and Yin Kuan. According to Peng, some twenty-eight of the signatories were workers (printers from many of the papers in Shanghai), while more than ten were 'returned students' from Moscow, some of whom had participated in party work during the 1925–7 revolution. The others were party cadres and branch secretaries who had been convinced of the correctness of Trotsky's position over the months since the establishment of the Left Opposition inside the party.[93]

Ultimately, it was this group which was to form the organisational nucleus of the unified Trotskyist movement. Its strength was found in its members' political experience and organisational abilities. According to Peng Shuzhi, when the document of the 'eighty-one' appeared, 'all of China was affected by it. After all, this was a split in the Chinese Communist Party'.[94]

With the expulsion of the Opposition group led by Chen and Peng, Chinese Trotskyism, at least its strongest section, was now transferred outside the 'mainstream' of CCP politics and activities.

---

91 Peng 1929, p. 26.
92 Zhongyang dang'an guan bian 1990, pp. 549–55.
93 Miller interviews, Tape 3, Side A; P'eng 1980, p. 14; Peng letter to Kagan, 12 January 1972. The complete text of *Women de zhengzhi yijian shu* may be found in Peng Shuzhi 1982–3, Vol. 1, pp. 305–35.
94 Miller interviews, Tape 3, Side A.

The Struggle for Unity and the Uncertain Future (1929–31)

The Chinese Trotskyist movement, which by 1930 consisted of four separate groups, was eventually unified for only about a year and a half, from May 1931 to October 1932, before a series of crises arose. In 1929 there were only two Trotskyist organisations.

The Our Word (*Women de hua*) faction was made up of Chinese students who had organised themselves while in Moscow and were sent back to China upon their exposure. Founded in China in late 1928, it took its name from its periodical.

The situation in China was very limited regarding the activities of the Our Word group. They had their first organisational meeting in January 1929, when a skeletal structure of responsibilities was established. They had only nine members in China at this time, and according to Peng Shuzhi, 'They had no position in the party. They could do no work within the ranks of the party'. The publication of *Women de hua* was about the extent of their activity at this early period. After a while, they managed to set up a 'branch with a fair amount of influence among the workers', according to Peng. Even so, their membership probably did not surpass twenty or thirty.[95]

Since most people in the Our Word group had no experience or position inside the CCP, according to Peng, they did not really understand the full substance of Trotsky's position on China. This was also the source of a sectarian attitude towards Chen Duxiu and other experienced revolutionaries. Chen was criticised by this group for maintaining his 'Stalinist opportunism and adventurism', and his group's advocacy of a 'workers' and peasants' dictatorship' was denounced as 'anti-Marxist'.[96]

The second organisation operating inside of China at this time was that of Chen Duxiu and Peng Shuzhi, along with important cadres and workers from within the CCP. Following their expulsion from the party, they began to publish, in March 1930, a periodical titled *Wuchanzhe* (Proletarian), thus becoming the Proletarian faction.

Sympathisers of this group began to appear inside the CCP. They were referred to in party documents as the 'conciliators', since they were pushing towards a conciliation between the current party leadership and the Left Opposition. Finally, the 'conciliators' were repressed, but not before large groups of cadres from all over China had been won to the perspective of

---

95   Miller interviews, Tape 3, side A.
96   Peng letter to Kagan, 12 January 1972.

the Left Opposition. According to Richard Kagan, the Proletarian group had attained a membership of some five hundred by 1931.[97]

Ironically, the third group grew out of the first two. This group, known as the October Society (*Shiyue she*), was led by Liu Renjing and Wang Fanxi, a member of the CCP since 1925 and someone who worked with the Our Word group. The October Society was actually the organisational result of factional activities carried on by Liu while he was also tenuously connected with the Our Word group.[98]

Liu was a sympathiser of the Trotskyist movement, and on his way back to China from Moscow in 1929, he stopped in Turkey to visit Trotsky, then in exile. He was given a programmatic document written by Trotsky for the Chinese Left Opposition. Liu carried this document back to China, where he gave it to Peng Shuzhi in September, just about the time that the Left Opposition was meeting with the Our Word group to discuss political differences.[99]

According to Peng, Liu discussed the issue of unification with him. He argued that members of the Left Opposition (they were still in the party at this time) should break with the party and openly join the Our Word group. Peng responded that he and Chen Duxiu had discovered serious organisational and political differences with Our Word. Furthermore, any unification which might take place must be a merger of two small groups, not just some individuals joining a group outside the party. Principled unification, Peng argued, required a full discussion of differences in order to develop a common standpoint, otherwise the unification would soon be followed by splits.[100]

Ultimately, Liu joined Our Word, where he conducted his own factional activities, gradually drawing some members from Beijing and Shanghai, including Wang Fanxi, around him. By the summer of 1930, they organised their own faction and set up the October Society.

Peng Shuzhi recalled that in the first issue of their short-lived journal, *Shiyue bao* (October), Liu attacked Chen Duxiu, referring to his 'Letter to All Comrades in the Party' as a 'shameful document'. This only served to reinforce the already negative attitudes of members of Our Word and the October Society towards Chen and the other old revolutionaries. Wang Fanxi described his own attitude in the following manner:

---

[97] Kagan 1969, p. 132.
[98] Wang 1991, pp. 133–6.
[99] Evans and Block 1976, p. 640; Peng letter to Kagan, 12 January 1972.
[100] Kagan 1969, p. 137; Peng letter to Kagan, 12 January 1972; also Tang Baolin 1994, pp. 117–19.

> As I, like all young Trotskyists of that time, did not quite believe the sincerity of the conversion of Chen Duxiu and his followers to Trotskyism, I did not want to join Chen's group. After some discussion with the Beijing comrades and Liu, I decided to work with them by organising ourselves into a separate group and publishing an organ called *October*.[101]

The establishment of the fourth Trotskyist group in China apparently followed fast on the heels of the October Society. This group called itself the Struggle Society (*Zhandou she*), and it also included some returned students from Moscow. They also organised sometime in the summer of 1930, with seven members, including the two students who had given Trotsky's articles to Peng Shuzhi in the spring of 1929. According to Peng, these individuals 'were rather petty-bourgeois in outlook, not really very good revolutionaries'.[102] Wang Fanxi has referred to the Struggle Society as the 'least important' of the four factions, and Kagan claimed that it 'did not exceed thirty members, and it was the least powerful and influential'.[103]

Thus, by the autumn of 1930, there were four Trotskyist factions, all with differing degrees of influence and involvement, and all with their own periodicals. As Wang Fanxi said, 'we all recognised that this was a bad state of affairs, and that it was essential to create a unified Trotskyist organisation in China'.[104]

A stumbling block to the establishment of a unified Trotskyist organisation was the mistrust which the younger Trotskyists had towards older revolutionaries who had been in CCP leadership positions. This was reflected in published attacks in the periodicals of Our Word, the October Society, and the Struggle Society. On the other hand, some of the statements made by Peng Shuzhi, for example, in interviews and in earlier writings, seem to express a certain attitude of superiority towards the younger activists, and this may only have exacerbated the differences which already existed. It is difficult, however, to dispute the fact, reported by Peng and by those who did not necessarily agree with him on other issues, that the Proletarian group was more effective in gaining adherents simply because of the seasoned revolutionaries found there.

A major source for the eventual unification of the movement, outside of the situational imperative (the CCP was using disputes between Trotskyist groups to undermine further efforts at recruitment), was the person of Leon Trotsky.

---

101   Wang 1976, p. 61.
102   Miller interviews, Tape 3, Side A.
103   Wang 1976, p. 61; Kagan 1969, p. 139.
104   Wang 1974, p. 28.

Since late 1929, he had been in regular correspondence with the various groups. Each organisation presented its case as the true reflection of Chinese Trotskyism.

Trotsky soon came to realise that some of the disputes between the factions were 'merely academic' or 'tactical questions', while others seemed to be purely personal. He could see no valid reason for the expressed negative views towards Chen Duxiu and the older revolutionaries.[105]

Early efforts at unification were already taking place in China. A Negotiating Council for Unification was organised, which consisted of representatives from each faction, and they worked on an agenda throughout the late summer and early autumn of 1930. According to Wang Fanxi, 'the negotiations took a very long time. Each group expressed different opinions at every meeting of the council'. The split between the old and young revolutionaries continued to be a central obstacle.[106]

Eventually, the Proletarian faction found it necessary to write an open letter to the members of the other three factions in an attempt to explain what was holding up the unification process. This letter pointed out that, during the meetings of the council, there were charges that the Proletarian group and some of its members were not engaged in sincere negotiation. It also pointed out that those involved in various splits admitted that these were not based on any particular principles. Basically, the Proletarian group made a final pitch for greater efforts at unification without the petty disputes which hindered the process up to that time. There was no question, however, that certain political questions still had to be worked out between the participants, and that the only successful unification would need to be a principled one.[107]

Peng Shuzhi admitted in 1976 that he felt more time was needed before a truly principled unification could be effected. Wang Fanxi has charged Peng with being totally opposed to the unification and required all other factions to dissolve into the Proletarian faction. Peng disputed this version, admitting that he was just a bit more reticent about a speedy unification than was Chen Duxiu.[108]

Finally, in a letter 'To the Chinese Left Opposition' dated 8 January 1931, Leon Trotsky made what was apparently the convincing case for quick unification. He then elaborated upon his own analysis of some of the 'controversial and semi-controversial questions' concerning the Chinese Opposition. After

---

105 Evans and Block 1976, p. 439.
106 Wang 1974, p. 28.
107 *Wuchanzhe*, Number 6, 25 November 1930.
108 Wang 1974, pp. 28–9; Miller interviews, Tape 3, Side A.

a review of these issues and the various opinions which were reflected in the different groups, he stated emphatically, 'Dear friends, fuse your organisations and your press definitively this very day! We must not drag out the preparations for the unification a long time, because in that way, without wanting to, we can create artificial differences'.[109]

Ultimately, as a result of Trotsky's intervention and guidance, some of the disputes between groups were muted (at least temporarily), rendering any continued division insupportable. The Unification Conference opened on 1 May 1931, and stretched over three days, with the final day devoted to the adoption of resolutions.

This united movement took on a new name, the Communist League of China. Trotsky's 1929 document, 'The Political Situation in China and the Tasks of the Bolshevik-Leninist Opposition', was adopted by the Communist League (CLC) as its programmatic foundation. Organisationally, a Central Committee was elected, with Chen Duxiu as the General Secretary. Other members were: Peng Shuzhi, Wang Fanxi, Song Fengchun, Chen Yimou, Song Jingxiu, Zhang Jiu, Zheng Chaolin, Liu Hanyi, and Pu Yifan.

The League began to work in China's urban centres. From the various estimates of strength during this period, it seems that a figure of five to six hundred CLC members throughout China is the most accurate. While on the surface, the League was small, its size did not mirror its capabilities for effective action given the high number of seasoned cadres in the organisation.

Almost immediately, however, the CLC came under constant harassment, from both the official CCP and Chiang's Guomindang. Within three weeks of the League's formal establishment, its members began to be arrested by the Nationalist Government. By late 1932, the main leaders of the League, including Chen Duxiu and Peng Shuzhi, were on trial and soon imprisoned. This seriously limited any further effective work on the part of these 'urban revolutionaries', but their odyssey continued in China for the next twenty years, in spite of these obstacles.

Reflections and Concluding Remarks

How to evaluate the role played by Peng Shuzhi in these years of turmoil for the Chinese revolution? His early days in chaotic post-Qing China seem to have awakened in him this revolutionary spirit; he was a man of his times. With each new experience he is drawn further into the fight for a new China. As a

---

109   Evans and Block 1976, p. 498.

'founding member' of the Changsha communist organisation and one of the earliest communist activists to study in Moscow, we see Peng develop quickly into a serious Bolshevik, in the truest sense of that term, one committed to revolutionary struggle and clear, critical thinking.

Why, as early as 1924, does Peng apparently break with the Comintern's policies towards the CCP and the Chinese revolution? This would not endear him to the Moscow centre, and it doesn't bode well for his so-called 'careerism' in the movement. Clearly, while Peng accepted the notion of party authority and Comintern authority, this did not mean unquestioned authority.

Perhaps in these internal debates, Peng thought the arguments presented by himself and Chen Duxiu would be enough to win concessions. Perhaps he still believed that democratic centralism actually operated in the Comintern. If so, he was obviously wrong, and he, along with others, paid a terrible price for this miscalculation.

In the end, with the failure of the second Chinese revolution, Peng Shuzhi was not afraid to continue on his revolutionary path, even with all the twists and turns that entailed. His work in the foundation of the Chinese Left Opposition and later the Communist League of China reflected this commitment, and it was not about career or privileged position, it was about the fight for a new China.

Preface to the Unpublished Manuscript of his *Memoirs* (1945)

Zheng Chaolin

Ten of these twelve chapters are about the 1920s, a glorious era in modern Chinese history. Few people recognise the significance of those years. But they point a way out for our country. In the 1920s, the workers became conscious of their mission; the Communist Party – their political representative – was born, grew strong, and almost took state power; between 1925 and 1927, the revolution was defeated, but still the 1920s hold crucial lessons for China's coming third revolution. In sum, the 1920s were a revolutionary epoch, more so than 1911, which brought about the Republic.[1]

In the late 1860s, several studies were published in Paris on the French Revolution of 1848. These studies revived interest in France on the forgotten events of the 1840s. Marx noticed this interest, and wrote to friends in Germany arguing that it portended a revival of the French Revolution. Not long after, the Paris Commune was established. I hope more books of memoirs and more studies about China in the 1920s will appear, so that we can conclude – like Marx in his day – that the Chinese Revolution is about to revive.

China still has a Communist Party today, but its view on the 1920s has not been set out for all to see. Generally speaking, Communist Party leaders fear memoirs about that period, for both its positive and its negative aspects throw light on their present errors. I have not been a member of the Party for many years, but I am honoured to have belonged to it in the 1920s and to have worked, struggled, and committed my own due share of errors alongside many revolutionaries whose names have gone down in history. The Chinese Communist Party can also boast its classical age. By 'classical' I do not mean that we should take it as a model. On the contrary, we did many wrong things in the 1920s, and the future party of the revolution would do well to avoid our mistakes. The 1920s were classical only by comparison with what came later. The Party in the 1920s, whatever its mistakes, was a party of the workers, who had mounted the political stage and united around the Communists. In the late 1920s, workers gradually left the Party. Communists abandoned the workers' movement and turned towards the peasants and the petty-bourgeois

---

1 The first revolution was that of 1911, the second that of 1925–7.

movement, to the point where now, it has become the political representative of patriotism.[2]

These twelve chapters are my personal reminiscences of political life in the 1920s. The views developed in them are my personal views. Memory can err. Unfortunately, I am not in a position to check my conclusions against historical evidence. Luckily, no one is likely to take my memoirs as a history of the revolution or the Communist Party.

I originally intended to scrap the chapter 'Love and Politics' because it might be deemed too close in content to the gossip columns of the Shanghai yellow press and might attract adverse comment. My aim in writing it was to describe different sorts of love among revolutionaries of that period and to throw light on the character of certain revolutionaries; it was in no way to pass moral judgments. Love of any sort is permissible in a revolutionary party so long as it does not cause political damage. Most of the men and women I write about in that chapter lost their lives in the White terror and some survivors have abandoned the revolution for a genteel life. They will probably think my descriptions of their youthful love affairs slanderous. All I can do is apologise. Unfortunately, the events described in 'Love and Politics' have broader implications; otherwise I would have left them out. Readers should not forget that I, too, was implicated in them. Now as then, I am completely without feudal or bourgeois prejudice concerning relations between the sexes.

20 February 1945

Postscript. Chapter 10 was completed under extremely difficult circumstances while my son Frei lay dying. Frei was born in the second year after my release from jail in 1937. The war began while he was still in his mother's womb. He was conceived, he was born, and he died in the war years. His place of birth was in the countryside, where we had taken refuge from the Japanese. So he was poorly nurtured and often feverish. He finally died of TB, three weeks after I wrote the above preface. He was a clever, lovable child. His death was the greatest blow to me. Over the last six months, I have been unable to drum up sufficient enthusiasm to write the final two chapters of this book. Now, I am busy with more important things, so I must let the book stand as it is.

29 August 1945

---

2   When Zheng Chaolin wrote this memoir in 1945, the Chinese Communist Party was still nominally in a united front with the Guomindang (or Nationalist Party) against the Japanese; it had abandoned land revolution for the duration of the war and had become the most active champion of the patriotic resistance to Japan. To the Chinese Trotskyists, it no longer seemed to be a party of class struggle.

Postscript to the English Edition of his *Memoirs* (1987)

Zheng Chaolin

I remember that a famous Westerner once said that when someone writes a book, that book starts to live independently. That statement is certainly true of this book. In late 1944, the Japanese army of aggression was a spent force, like a strong-bow shot at the end of its flight, and the Shanghai economy was languishing in deep depression. Publishers were no longer accepting manuscripts for publication, so I devoted the time I normally spent each month writing for publishers to recording what I had seen and heard in past years. I wrote ten chapters and then was unable to continue. The war ended. I circulated the manuscript among friends and asked someone to make a copy of it. Then I bundled it up and put it on the top shelf. In late 1952, after 'liberation', during the 'campaign to eliminate Trotskyism', when Trotskyists all over China were 'rounded up at one fell swoop', this manuscript together with the copy and the entire Trotskyist archive was inventoried and confiscated as 'criminal' evidence. No doubt the official in charge of the case scoured the manuscript for clues about the organisation and its members. After the case was closed, the Shanghai Public Security Bureau cleared out duplicate documents – a dozen or so sack-fulls according to reports – and sent them to the Ministry of Public Security in Beijing. As luck would have it, there were two copies of my memoir, so one was kept in Shanghai, and the other was stuffed into a Beijing-bound sack. My book, like my person, disappeared into captivity: I behind bars, it into the archive of the Public Security organs.

During the 'Great Cultural Revolution' of 1966–1969, it was decided – either by Red Guards who stormed the Ministry of Public Security or by the Ministry itself, in the course of sorting out its archives – to consign these sacks to the paper factory for reprocessing, but someone with a conscience secretly carried away two of the sacks and hid them. He took the sacks at random and had no idea what documents they contained.

After the Third Plenum of the Eleventh Central Committee of the Communist Party [in 1978], the situation changed, and some historians were instructed to carry out research on Chen Duxiu and the Trotskyists. Materials on Chen Duxiu before his expulsion and after his release from prison were easily available, but there were no materials on the Trotskyists or on the Trotskyist Chen Duxiu. Just as they were about to admit defeat, the fore-mentioned man of conscience remembered the two sacks and the problem was partly solved. The researchers discovered the manuscript of my book of memoirs. At first, they had no way of knowing who had written it, but when they reached the account of the May Thirtieth massacre, they found my name, and knew that the memoir was by me.

They then began to think of publishing the book. I had already been completely restored to liberty, so they sent someone to Shanghai to ask me if I agreed to their plan. At the same time, they mimeographed several copies of the manuscript under the title *Zheng Chaolin's 1945 Memoirs* and distributed them as reference material to important organisations concerned with Party history. I have seen only references to this mimeographed edition in articles by experts on Party history, and not the publication itself. I don't know if it is the complete text, or excerpts from the text, or summaries of it.

The publication of the printed version went less smoothly than that of the mimeographed edition. Agreement to publish was reached in 1980, but only in 1986 did the book actually see the light of day. In the meantime, its fortunes fluctuated with the ever-changing political tide. Before 1983, the question was whether or not to send it to the compositor. In 1983, after the final proofs had been read and the text had been made into a plate, the question was whether or not to send it to the printer, and whether or not to send it to the distributor. Only in 1986 did the book finally appear.

At that point, the book was finally delivered from the fate of 'humble prisoner', but it was certainly not yet an 'honoured guest': it had merely regained its 'civil rights'; I, the author, received my payment at the going rate. The book, published as 'internal reference material' by the Association to Edit and Publish Materials on Contemporary History,[1] was unobtainable in the shops. It was what Chinese readers called a 'grey book'. Fewer than ten such 'grey books' have been published. What unites them is that their contents are valuable as reference sources for students of the history of the Communist Party, though their standpoint is quite dissimilar to that of the Party. Needless to say, the standpoints of the books themselves also differ one from the other.

When, in 1980, the publishers asked me for permission to publish, they also asked me if I would agree to cut the chapter titled 'Love and Politics'. In my 1945 'Preface' I had already envisaged cutting this chapter, so I said yes. But I still think it's a pity. In those days, very many of the conflicts and fights among Chinese Communist officials were explicable only in terms of quarrels about love. So without that chapter, they could no longer be explained. Quite apart from this consideration, to cut an entire chapter from a book inevitably creates

---

1 The Xiandai shiliao biankan she.

discontinuities. Unfortunately, I have never set eyes on the manuscript since it 'went to jail', so there is no way that I can control its fate. Luckily, both the original manuscript and the copy are still around, one in Beijing and the other in Shanghai, and one day, they will surface. When that day comes, not only the chapter 'Love and Politics' but words and sentences excised from other chapters can be restored.

I wrote the appendix 'Chen Duxiu and the Trotskyists'[2] at the invitation of a certain research institute in 1980, shortly after I had regained my freedom. At the time, public opinion tended to distinguish between Chen Duxiu and the Trotskyists. People said Chen Duxiu was a good man, his good name should be restored, but they made no evaluation of the Trotskyists. So the aim of this long article is to show that Chen Duxiu and the Trotskyists cannot be dealt with separately. Today, however, public opinion no longer insists on this distinction, so the chapter may appear redundant.

When I learned that my book was to appear in English, I joyfully wrote these few lines to describe its independent life: how it grew from manuscript to printed page regardless of my intentions.

Shanghai, 11 December 1987

---

[2] Part VII.

A Self-Description at the Age of Ninety

Zheng Chaolin

Source: Appendix to An Oppositionist for Life (1989).

My name is Zheng Chaolin. I was born in 1901, so according to the old Chinese way of counting, this year I am ninety.

I was born in Zhangping, a small mountainous county in the south of Fujian province. My family was an old-established landlord family already in decline, but it still maintained the ancient trappings of culture and education. When I was a child, a 'foreign-style school' had already started up in my home town, but I still acquired my schooling at the old-style private academy, until, finally, I was inserted into the graduation class of the foreign-style school, to get my certificate of primary education. I graduated under the old-style system of middle school, that is, after a course in traditional Chinese culture lasting only four years.

I graduated from middle school in the same year as the May Fourth Movement broke out. In our small county high up in the mountains, we heard only about the student movement to boycott Japanese goods and knew nothing about the 'new culture movement'.

In the spring of that year, while I was preparing to take my graduation exams, some Guomindang troops under Chen Jiongming invaded Fujian from Guangdong and occupied the southern corner of the province, including my home town. Chen Jiongming ordered each county under his control to select two students to go to France under the work-study scheme. Each student would get an annual subsidy of $300 from his local authority. That is how I ended up in France. Those who went from Fujian were work-study students like the rest of the Chinese in France; the only difference being that they received these local subsidies.

I experienced my 'new culture movement' on the boat from China to France. The first time I saw *New Youth* and found out about the 'new culture movement' was on board the boat. Only then did I go through the struggle between the old culture in which I had received my schooling and the new culture that I learned about at sea.

In France, I got close to the progressive students on the work-study programme. I studied together with them, I struggled with them, and together with them, I organised the 'Communist Youth Party' and embarked on the road of revolution.

In 1923, the Communist Youth Party chose its first batch of members – twelve people in all, including me – to go to study at the Communist University for the Toilers of the East in Moscow. In the summer of 1924, the Moscow branch of the Chinese Communist Party chose its second batch of students to send back to China. I was among them.

As soon as I got back to Shanghai, I was allocated to work as secretary in the Party's newly founded Propaganda Department. My job was to write, translate, edit, and publish the Central Committee organ and its various publications, and at the same time to teach 'sociology' (that is, historical materialism) at Shanghai University. I participated in the May Thirtieth Movement and in Shanghai's second and third workers' insurrections.

In the spring of 1927, when the Central Committee moved to Wuhan, I, too, went to Wuhan and took part in the Fifth Congress there. After the Congress, I was allocated to the Hubei Provincial Committee to take charge of its Propaganda Department. I experienced the defeat of the revolution and attended the 7 August Conference. After that, I returned to do propaganda work in the Central Committee. In late September, the Central Committee moved back to Shanghai and so did I, to take charge of the Central Committee's Publishing Bureau and to edit *Bolshevik*. In the summer of 1928, I was sent to Xiamen to sort out organisational work in the Fujian Provincial Committee. In late September I returned to Shanghai to continue editing *Bolshevik*.

At the end of 1928, I resigned from *Bolshevik* and from various other propaganda tasks because of differences of opinion with Li Lisan, then in charge of the Central Committee's propaganda work. After that, I had nothing to do save wait for the Central Committee to assign me new work.

This period marked the end of the first stage of my work in the Party.

During it, my main activity was literary propaganda, though I also did some oral propaganda, teaching, and organising. Everything I did was in line with the Central Committee's policy; that in its turn was based on the line set for China by the Communist International, which you were not allowed to doubt. So during this stage, I scarcely needed to do any thinking of my own about basic questions of line. After the 7 August Conference, I began to question the line of the Communist International and to consider wrong some of the Central Committee's policies, but whenever I made propaganda outside the Party, I stuck to its line.

Factions had already started fighting one another inside the Party. The main struggle was between the Chen Duxiu supporters around Wang Ruofei and the Central Committee faction of Comintern loyalists around Qu Qiubai; the General Labour Union faction, previously under Zhang Guotao and now under Luo Zhanglong, vacillated between these two groups.

I personally inclined, for ideological and historical reasons, towards the Chen Duxiu group.

While editing *Bolshevik*, I went through the motions of propagating the policies of the Central Committee, but gradually, I exposed my own thinking. Because the revolution had been defeated, I could not but ponder certain fundamental questions of the Chinese Revolution, and in the course of this thinking, I gradually began to doubt the Comintern's position on the Chinese Revolution, both past and future. In the articles I wrote, I consciously or unconsciously betrayed my own ideas. The clearest instance of this was an unsigned editorial I wrote for the eleventh issue of *Bolshevik*, after the defeat of the Guangzhou insurrection, in which I clearly proposed that the Chinese Revolution had no choice but to institute a dictatorship of the proletariat, even though the Central Committee was proposing a democratic dictatorship of workers and peasants, in accordance with the Comintern line. The Central Committee then got Qu Qiubai to write another unsigned editorial for the fourteenth issue of *Bolshevik* correcting my previous editorial. But I had only just begun to develop my own ideas, which had not yet grown into a systematic vision of the Chinese and world revolutions.

After I had withdrawn from the Central Committee's Propaganda Department in early 1929, I continued my independent reflections.

It was then that I was first arrested. I had already married, and my wife Liu Jingzhen – from Kunming, a member of the Communist Party – worked together with me on *Bolshevik* and left the Central Propaganda Department together with me. We lived with other comrades in a Party building. When one of our number was arrested, the others, too, were implicated and seized. Through the intercession of the Central Committee, those of us who had got drawn into the incident were bailed out after spending forty-odd days at Longhua Garrison Headquarters.

Not long after that, we Chen Duxiu supporters set eyes for the first time on documents of the Soviet Trotskyist Opposition. We discussed them among ourselves and with Chen Duxiu; finally, we accepted Trotsky's proposals for the Chinese Revolution and for the world revolution. After that, we Chen Duxiu supporters and Chen Duxiu himself became Trotskyists and joined the international Trotskyist organisation.

This was a big event in my political life. It was of no less consequence than organising the Communist Youth Party in 1922.

On 1 May 1931, I was a delegate at the Chinese Trotskyists' Unification Congress, and was elected onto its Central Committee and put in charge of its Propaganda Department. Before three weeks had passed, our leadership was uncovered by the Guomindang, after we had been betrayed from within. The majority of the Central Committee members was arrested. I was among them, and was described as the ringleader. The death sentence was said to have been passed on me, but as a result of personnel changes in the Guomindang government, there was a new appointment to the Shanghai garrison and my death sentence was commuted to fifteen years.

The minority of Central Committee members who had escaped arrest, among them Chen Duxiu, restored the leadership and carried on the struggle, but in October 1932, they, too, were unearthed and arrested.

In jail, I continued to reflect independently on basic questions of the revolution and on other actual political questions.

Those of us arrested by the Guomindang during these two waves were not freed until late 1937, after the start of all-out war with Japan, the aerial bombing of Nanjing, and the Guomindang decision to move its capital east to Wuhan.

After my release, I decided that because communications with Shanghai were broken, I would go for a while to southern Anhui to escape the turmoil, recover my health, and await the opportunity to return to Shanghai. I never guessed that I would spend three years in Anhui, that my son would be born there, and that I and my wife would earn our living as schoolteachers. Not until 1940 did we leave Anhui through Zhejiang and sail to Shanghai via Ningbo.

Back in Shanghai, I joined the leadership of the Chinese Trotskyist organisation. At the same time, I translated into Chinese Trotsky's *History of the Russian Revolution* (vols 2 and 3).

There was a controversy in the Trotskyist leadership about what attitude to adopt towards the war against Japan. There were three different points of view: that the war itself had a progressive meaning, and that we should support the Guomindang's resistance; that the war itself had a progressive meaning, and we should resist independently; and that the war was part of the Second World War and we should prepare to carry out proletarian socialist revolution during it, like Lenin in the First World War. I supported the third position. As a result of the dispute, the Chinese Trotskyists split.

During the dispute and the split, my group independently brought out a mimeographed journal that was at first nameless and was later officially published under the name *Guoji zhuyizhe* ('Internationalist'). After the Japanese surrender, we started to bring out *Xinqi* ('New Banner'), in lead type. I wrote numerous articles for the nameless publication, for *Internationalist*, and for *New Banner*. Apart from that, I also wrote some books: *Buduan geming lun ABC* ('ABC of Permanent Revolution'), *San ren xing* ('Three Travellers'), and *Guojia ziben zhuyi lun* ('On State Capitalism').

These articles and books are products of my second stage, that is, they represent conclusions that I arrived at in the course of using my own brain and reflecting independently. Unfortunately, today I am no longer in a position to gather together my writings of that period. I myself value them above the writings of my first period, which were written according to a set line and cost me no great effort. Since *New Youth* (later period), *Guide Weekly, Bolshevik*, and other publications are still available, my articles must also have been preserved.

After 'liberation', I had no wish to flee abroad. I had devoted my entire life to proletarian socialist revolution, in the world and in China. I was fully aware that the Stalinist system could not tolerate the existence of the likes of me in this world – we had already learned that from the Moscow trials of the 1930s. But I still wanted to stay in China. Sure enough, three and a half years after the 'liberation' of Shanghai, on 22 December 1952, 'like a thunderclap the net fell', and all the Chinese Trotskyists were arrested. Again, I was singled out as the ringleader. Someone like me, who never sought the limelight, arrested three times and twice named as ringleader!

This time, I (together with four others) was locked up for twenty seven years (from 22 December 1952 to 5 June 1979). We were never sentenced, and never even charged. Strange? People told us that there were not many prisoners like us, but there were a few.

Starting in 1964, I was allowed openly to express opinions in jail, to write books, and to criticise current policies and theories. For from then on, I was allowed to form a study group with other prisoners arrested in connection with the same case, Trotskyists who, like me, had not yet been sentenced (at first, there were three of us, then there were two). (In 1956, we were all brought together to study, but at that time, there were as many as a dozen in a study group and the sessions never lasted long, so it was impossible to speak out freely.) We studied so-called 'anti-revisionist documents', that is, the theoretical dispute between the Chinese and Soviet Communists. Afterwards, we each had to write a 'summary'. Although no one told us 'you may write whatever you like', I used the occasion to develop a comprehensive critique of the Stalinist system on the basis of the ideas that I had formed in the course of my isolated prison reflections. I decided to disregard any possible consequences. Finally, I wrote up my 'study summaries' into a book of eighty five thousand characters, which I called *Ganbu zhuyi lun* ('On Cadreism').

In 1965, each of us got a set of Mao's *Selected Works* (volumes 1 to 4) and was told to study 'Mao Zedong Thought'. Needless to say, after studying it, we were expected to write summaries. So I wrote another book, of one hundred and thirty five thousand characters, called *Yuzhong du Mao Zedong xuanji*

('Reading Mao Zedong's Selected Works in Jail'). Apart from this, after reading Stalin's *Problems of Leninism*, I wrote a further book of criticism, and at the same time, I wrote a great many articles on current affairs as reported in the press. During the Cultural Revolution, after the prison came under military administration, the army representative ordered all these political and non-political writings to be confiscated and destroyed.

But the ideas that I developed in jail were indestructible. In 1972, the serious offenders in our case (including those not yet sentenced), having spent twenty years in jail, were no longer kept behind bars but released into a régime of strict supervision; and in 1979, we were released from strict supervision and had our civil rights restored. At last we were as if restored to freedom. I myself was co-opted onto the Shanghai Municipal People's Consultative Committee. But the Chinese Trotskyists arrested in December 1952 had still not been rehabilitated, and were still categorised as 'counter-revolutionaries'. In 1988, the Soviet Union completely reversed the verdicts on the three great wrongs perpetrated by the Moscow show trials of the 1930s: the 1936 trial of the 'Trotsky-Zinoviev anti-Soviet coalition', the 1937 Pyatkov-Radek trial, and the 1937 trial of Bukharin, Rykov, and others. In the same year, I wrote three letters to the Standing Committee of the Politburo of the Central Committee of the Chinese Communist Party demanding a reversal of the 1952 case against the Chinese Trotskyists, but like a stone dropping into the vast ocean, it disappeared without a trace.

In the eleven years between the restoration of my civil rights in 1979 and now, I have written no few articles and a number of books, and some of my letters are worth publishing and preserving. All in all, my output amounts to some eight hundred thousand characters. These are the works of my third period. Like my second period, they are the product of independent reflection, but the conclusions are not wholly the same as those of my second period. Only a small proportion of them has been published; the overwhelming majority has been copied or photocopied and circulated among a small number of readers.

During this third period, three books of mine have been published in China, but none of them was written in this period. One is my book of memoirs, written in the second half of 1944, during my second period. The manuscript, taken as evidence of my 'counter-revolutionary crimes', followed me into jail. After my civil rights were restored, it, too, became Party history material and was internally circulated, in an edition printed by the state publishers. The supplement, on Chen Duxiu and the Trotskyists, was newly written in 1980. The second book is *Yu Yin canji* ('Surviving Poems of Yu Yin'), which comprises the remnants of the poems I wrote in jail. The third is Merezhkovsky's *Resurrection of the Gods*, a novel that I translated and was published in the 1940s. As for what I have written in the last eleven years, I have no idea when it can be published.

It is a matter for rejoicing that now that I am celebrating my ninetieth birthday, important events are taking place in the world, and show who was right and who was wrong in the greatest debate of the century.

I mean the great debate about whether or not socialism can be built in a single country.

In early 1924, Lenin died. In the autumn of that year, the contours of the internal struggle in the Soviet Communist Party gradually became visible. It was not a debate about styles of work but a difference of opinion about what basic line to follow. Stalin proposed the theory that socialism can be built in a single country. This theory was incompatible with the Marxist tradition, and also with what Stalin himself wrote in early 1924, in the *Foundations of Leninism*. Thereupon, those old Bolsheviks like Zinoviev and Kamenev, who had previously sided with Stalin against Trotsky, gradually left Stalin and began to ally with Trotsky. The united opposition upheld the old view that socialism is only possible within the framework of world revolution, and opposed the Stalinists.

For sixty years now, Stalin and the Stalinists have used the reality of the Soviet Union, and later the reality of the 'socialist states' of Eastern Europe and elsewhere, to prove that socialism can indeed be built in one or a few relatively backward countries.

But what do the events of last year and this year in those countries show?

Seventy years ago, when I was around twenty, the socialist or social-democratic parties in various countries changed their names into communist parties (though, naturally, some did not change and continued to maintain their old positions). But this year and last year, we have seen the opposite happen: communist parties in various countries have changed their names into socialist or social-democratic parties (though, naturally, some have not changed and continue to maintain their old positions).

Seventy years ago, one process took place; now, seventy years later, the opposite process has taken place. What does this fact signify? Most say that it is an expression of the bankruptcy of socialism.

But that is wrong. It is merely an expression of the bankruptcy of Stalinism, of the doctrine of socialism in one country. We Trotskyists alone in the world have dared – and with justification – to reach this conclusion, for we alone over the last several decades have maintained that socialism cannot be built in one or a few countries. We have never conceded that the system realised in the Soviet Union or the other 'socialist states' is socialist.

Socialism cannot be built in a single country.

The greatest dispute in twentieth century history, which has been going on now for almost seventy years, has finally been settled: Trotsky was right, Stalin was wrong.

It is good that I lived to the age of ninety to see the end of this dispute.

Will I live long enough to see the outbreak of the second high tide of world revolution?

1 May 1990

Postscript to the 1980 Oxford Edition of *Memoirs of a Chinese Revolutionary*

Wang Fanxi

This work was completed in 1957, and the events it recounts came to an end in 1949. Almost a quarter of a century has elapsed between its completion and its publication in English. Since it is not an autobiography in the strict sense of the word, it does not cover the entire life-span of the author. But since it is also not an objective history, the reader naturally has the right to ask what has now become of its author. It seems that a few words are therefore in order.

After I was forced to leave Hong Kong in late November 1949, I lived in a peninsula of seven square miles extent on the south China coast [Macao] until March 1975, when through the help of friends I managed to find my way to Europe. I spent the first three years after 1949 pondering and reassessing the ideological positions of our movement. During that time I kept close contact with my friends in China. After December 1952, when they were all arrested and imprisoned by the secret police of the CCP, my political activities came to an end in practical terms. I managed to eke out a living by teaching and by writing plays, but this in no way stopped me thinking or changed my basic calling. I kept a close watch on the changes that were taking place in the world and more particularly in China. I kept a critical eye on each of the major events in China, including the Hundred Flowers campaign, the Great Leap Forward, the People's Communes movement, the Sino-Soviet debate, and the Cultural Revolution, my aim being both to formulate and clarify my own ideas and to exchange opinions with like-minded observers. My writings during this period, which were published and distributed with the help of some of my old friends, took the form of articles, pamphlets and even a book-length study of Mao Zedong's thought.[1]

But it was not until 1968 that our ideas and publications drew any real response. The glittering victories of the CCP and the unprecedented prosperity of the post-war western world combined to consign to the margins of major world developments what remained of revolutionary Marxism outside China, and – ideologically – to send it off course. The Red Guard movement launched in 1966 did provide a certain stimulus for overseas Chinese youth and partly shook off their political apathy. But it was only in 1968 that a fundamental change in the mood of a large number of young people became apparent. It

---

1 Shuang Shan 1973.

was in that year that Hong Kong youth in particular, influenced by the powerful wave of radical thinking that shook the world as a result of the Vietnam war, began seriously to raise their efforts for personal success to the level of a struggle for the betterment of society as a whole, of China, and of mankind. They began both to feel a deep hatred for the capitalist world and to deplore the bureaucratic régime of the CCP. Not surprisingly, many of them tended towards anarchism. Before long, however, as a result both of their own experience and of the influence of other ideological tendencies, they began to differentiate among themselves, so that a majority of them eventually turned towards revolutionary Marxism.

During the next four or five years they grew greatly in influence, gaining new support not only in Hong Kong but also in Europe and north America. Now we are able to see quite a powerful movement springing up among Chinese youth, workers as well as students, all over the world, with the aim of redirecting the new China into channels which will genuinely benefit the interests of the toiling masses; and in June 1979 Zheng Chaolin and eleven other old friends of mine were released from jail (though not rehabilitated) after twenty-seven years, as a result of the new turn in the policy of the CCP.

My role in preparing for this process of change was not particularly worthy of note, but neither was it entirely lacking. Now that I am approaching the end of my life's journey, I cannot but feel happy to find that what appears before me is not the darkness after sunset, but the bright glimmering of daybreak.

Leeds, 1980

Preface to the 1987 French Edition of *Memoirs of a Chinese Revolutionary*

Wang Fanxi

When I wrote these memoirs thirty years ago in Macao, without even the most elementary research facilities to help my memory, I never guessed that what first saw life as a rough mimeograph would not only be pirated in China but would be translated into Japanese, English, German, and now French. Of course I am delighted and there is much that I would like to say. I wrote no specific preface for any of the three previous translations, save for a short postscript to the English one. I did not plan to write a preface for the French translation either, until it occurred to me that I could use the opportunity to reply to some of my reviewers.

Their criticisms and comments have mainly been friendly and appreciative, but a few have been hostile, and it is these that I shall address.

One critic called my book a sort of dirge to Chinese Trotskyism.

Another called it a mere footnote to the history of the Chinese Revolution. A third said that it described a tragedy in which a small number of fanatics battled desperately for a lost cause.

Whether or not a cause is lost cannot be judged by short-term considerations or by this or that victory or defeat. Political movements must be judged above all by their programme. If the programme of a political movement meets objective needs and withstands the test of time, its cause is not lost; on the contrary, if the programme is wisely implemented, the cause will prosper.

The programme from which the world Trotskyist movement emerged, and for which it has been fighting, derives from the theory of permanent revolution. This theory has been proved right by past revolutions and shown by current events to be as indispensable today as it ever was.

The two great revolutions of this century – the Russian and the Chinese – won power by implementing the strategy of permanent revolution. In Russia the Bolsheviks did so with their eyes open, in China the Maoists did so blindly, and against their own declared intentions. Both parties seized power in the course of 'bourgeois-democratic revolutions' and established 'dictatorships of the workers and peasants': workers' states, but in a specifically conditioned sense, for these states are ruled by tyrannical bureaucracies (in Russia as a result of the defeat of the revolution after the death of Lenin, in China from the very beginning of the new régime). However, the founding of these states laid the basis for a future development, through political revolution, towards socialism.

Trotskyists everywhere have tirelessly advocated that working-class revolutionary parties can and should seize power in economically backward countries in the course of bourgeois-democratic revolutions; that the states thus formed can only be consolidated and developed by democracy and internationalism; and that socialism cannot be built unless the new state furthers the cause of world revolution and its leaders see their struggle as part of a future system of world socialism, that is, see that socialism cannot be built in just one country.

So the betrayal of the revolution in Russia and the monstrous perversion of socialism in China do not prove that it is wrong to take power in poor countries in line with the strategy of permanent revolution. On the contrary, they prove the theory of permanent revolution right, by showing that socialism cannot be built in a single country, especially if that country is economically backward. They also show that régimes in post-capitalist societies that lack democracy and internationalism cannot consolidate even a relatively progressive state, let alone a socialist state. On the contrary, such régimes will fall prey to Stalinist and Maoist 'new feudalism' or, even worse, to 'communism' of the Pol Pot sort, that is, a society crushed by mass murder.

So the cause of Trotskyism is by no means lost, nor need it be.

Only the programme of the Trotskyists, with its commitment to socialist democracy and internationalism, can lead China, the Soviet Union, and other 'socialist' countries from the blind alley they are now in (and from which they are vainly trying to extricate themselves by superficial reforms).

So I see no reason to regret my life. I am proud of my small role in what some would call a tragedy. I will not guess about the future. Are my memoirs a dirge? Or are they a short overture to the symphony of true socialism throughout the world? Only history will tell.

Leeds, August 1987

Preface to the 1991 Morningside Edition of *Memoirs of a Chinese Revolutionary*

Wang Fanxi

I was overjoyed to learn that Columbia University Press is preparing to make available for American readers a new edition of the English translation of my memoirs, first published by Oxford University Press in 1980.

The news could hardly have come at a better time, now that we are witnessing the general collapse of Stalinism. Starting in the late spring and early summer of 1989, earthshaking changes have taken place and are continuing to take place in countries of the 'socialist' camp: changes so sudden and dramatic that everyone – Stalinist and anti-Stalinist alike – has tried hard to find an explanation for them.

To understand Stalinism's present collapse, in my opinion we must first grasp how the Stalinist system came into being. The main content and central story of this book tells how a Chinese revolutionary and his comrades set out after 1927 to oppose both the theory and the practice of Stalinism, at first in the Soviet Union and then in China. Needless to say, it does not give a rounded and comprehensive picture of its subject, but even so it shows graphically how Stalinism and its Maoist variant were born, began to flourish, and eventually triumphed both in the Soviet Union and in China. What's more, it might in some degree help predict the future of the system of Stalinism.

I would like to use this preface to review a number of new issues, as well as some old issues that were once thought to have been settled but have now been raised afresh by the new developments in the 'socialist' camp. Is Stalinism really the equivalent of socialism? Does its collapse prove the bankruptcy of socialism and communism? Can and will it be capitalism that replaces Stalinism? Is capitalism from now on inviolable and irreplaceable? Will socialism and communism go down in history as reactionary illusions? Let me start by saying that my answer to these questions is in all cases no. I have spent the greater part of my life and effort in the struggle for socialism and against Stalinism, but that is not the main reason why I answer as I do. Under the new circumstances, even old questions must be freshly pondered and answered in the light of new facts. I have spent much energy considering these questions, and considering the answers that others have given to them. And my conclusion has not changed: I still believe that the bankruptcy of Stalinism is in no way equivalent to the bankruptcy of socialism. Nor do I believe that capitalism is 'immortal and unending'. On the contrary, I see no reason to change my view that the future of humankind depends on the realization of true, that is, non-Stalinist socialism.

Unfortunately I am too old and tired to deal with these ideas in any detail, and in any case a short preface is not the right place to deal with such weighty issues. So to compensate a little, I would like to quote a passage written fifty-two years ago by George Orwell while reviewing *The Communist International*, by Franz Borkenau:

> Dr Borkenau thinks that the root cause of the vagaries of the Comintern policy is the fact that revolution as Marx and Lenin predicted it and as it happened, more or less, in Russia, is not thinkable in the advanced western countries, at any rate at present. Here I believe he is right. Where I part company from him is when he says that for the western democracies the choice lies between Fascism and an orderly reconstruction through the co-operation of all classes. I do not believe in the second possibility, because I do not believe that a man with £50,000 a year and a man with fifteen shillings a week either can, or will, co-operate. The nature of their relationship is quite simply, that the one is robbing the other, and there is no reason to think that the robber will suddenly turn over a new leaf It would seem, therefore, that if the problems of western capitalism are to be solved, it will have to be through a third alternative, a movement which is genuinely revolutionary, that is, willing to make drastic changes and to use violence if necessary, but which does not lose touch, as Communism and Fascism have done, with the essential values of democracy. Such a thing is by no means unthinkable. The germs of such a movement exist in numerous countries, and they are capable of growing. At any rate, if they don't, there is no real exit from the pigsty we are in.[1]

I am not an Orwellite, but apart from where he agrees with Borkenau that the revolution predicted by Marx and Lenin cannot break out in the western democratic countries, I agree with most of what he says here and moreover applaud it, though naturally where he says 'communism' I would say Stalinism. It's a fact that society consists of different classes, and it is illusory to expect the robbers and the robbed to cooperate freely and even more so to expect the robbers to 'turn over a new leaf' of their own free will. Orwell's third road between fascism and Stalinism – a radical and if necessary violent class revolution to overthrow the robbers and at the same time to preserve by all means possible

---

1   Orwell and Angus (eds) 1970, pp. 387–8.

the democratic rights won across centuries of struggle – is indeed a way from the 'pigsty' and the only path to equality, freedom, and democracy, and to the realization of a socialist future.

But what relevance do Orwell's comments have for the proposals made over the years by the Trotskyists? It is commonly believed that the difference between Trotskyists and Stalinists is that the former are not only more radical than the latter but even more frightful, even more dictatorial and centralist, even less interested in democracy. This point of view is not only wrong but even a deliberate perversion of the truth. Though I would not presume to claim that what Orwell in his essay calls 'the germs of a movement' is a reference to Trotskyism or to a trend of opinion including Trotskyists, I must point out that Trotskyism does represent such a force. In my story I describe something of the Trotskyists' thinking and activity between 1927 and 1949. Readers can decide for themselves – at least where China is concerned – whether we fit the ugly picture drawn of us. Here I wish to say only one thing more: It was none other than Trotsky and his comrades who first (starting in 1923) and (through the proposals advanced and the criticisms made in Trotsky's *New Course*) most consistently came out against the degeneration of the Soviet state; it was they who all along exposed as an illusion the idea of 'building socialism in one country'; it was they who first and most implacably called for a struggle against bureaucratic dictatorship, who demanded a workers' and peasants' democracy, and who called for a multiparty system in the Soviet councils and the right to form factions in the Communist Party; and it was they who consistently fought against bureaucracy and for democracy, right through until they were dismissed from office, expelled from the Party, and jailed, deported, executed or assassinated. In short, over the past seventy years the Trotskyists – and only the Trotskyists – have been the group that struggled without regard to the cost for Orwell's 'third way'.

Could it be that in the world today, no matter whether it be the existing and now disintegrating 'socialist' countries, standing blindfolded on the brink of an uncertain future, or the superficially prosperous capitalist countries, which in reality are host to all sorts of irresolvable contradictions – that in the world today the only way forward is in the policies already mapped out for us in documents of the Trotskyists? Probably not, for human affairs are too complex and 'Old Man History' is too cunning for any individual or group to be able in advance to formulate an exit from crises that have not yet happened; new policies must constantly be developed to suit reality's ever-changing needs. I am deeply convinced, however, that as long as construction of our society continues to rest on an opposition of robbers and robbed, repressers and repressed,

PREFACE TO THE MORNINGSIDE EDITION OF MEMOIRS (1990)

the basic programmatic strategies laid down by the Trotskyists and by Marx cannot go out of date.

In the main, this new edition follows the old one, save for a few minor corrections of typographical and other errors. Apart from that, the translator has rewritten some passages in his original introduction and added others to it. The main difference between this and the Oxford edition is the reinstatement of the final chapter, 'Thinking in Solitude', dropped in 1980 to save space. And I have appended a translation of the preface to the French translation of this book.

Here I would like to say a special word of thanks to Alexander H. Buchman, but for whose tireless efforts over more than two years this edition of my book would never have seen the light of day. Alex Buchman is my old friend from more than fifty years ago in Shanghai, where we worked together in opposition to the Japanese imperialists who were then committing aggression against China.

I would also like to take the chance to express my long overdue thanks to Gregor Benton, whose faithful and creative translation of my memoirs not only made them available for the English-speaking world but allowed them to be rendered into German and French, so that they could make the acquaintance of an even wider circle of new friends. Gregor Benton is not only my literary collaborator but a support in my life without whose help I would have encountered even more difficulties during my fifteen years of exile in Western Europe.

Leeds, April 1990

PART 16

The Chinese Trotskyists' Imprisonment and Release From Prison

Statement by Chinese Trotskyists Overseas on the CCP's Release of Zheng Chaolin and Other Trotskyist Political Prisoners (24 July 1979)

Source: A document in the editor's possession

According to reliable and confirmed reports, on 5 June of this year [1979] eight Chinese Trotskyists, among them Zheng Chaolin, were released by the Chinese Communist authorities and restored to full citizenship. These eight people (apart from Zheng, the only other names we know for sure are those of Wu Jingru, Zheng's wife, and Jiang Zhendong, a leader of the Shanghai workers' insurrection in 1927) were arrested alongside more than two hundred others on the night of 22 December 1952, twenty seven years ago, by the CCP secret police. They have spent the entire period since then in prisons and labour camps, despite the fact that they were never publicly tried or sentenced.

As far as we know, over the last twenty seven years some of those arrested have been released under strict surveillance and returned to their places of origin, where they were forced under conditions of great hardship to participate in unpaid or badly paid manual labour, after spending five or more years in detention. Others died as a result of their sufferings in prison. Zheng Chaolin and the other seven released probably represent the last batch of those fortunate enough to have survived this experience.

Why did the CCP decide to arrest these people in the first place?

Their crime was said to have been that they engaged in counter-revolutionary activity. And why have they now been released? The ostensible reason is that a new régime of 'socialist legality' has been inaugurated. In our view the crime originally imputed to them was not only groundless but moreover slanderous. The conditions under which their release has taken place are not such as to inspire confidence. Hence this statement.

Chinese Trotskyists, like Trotskyists throughout the world, far from being counter-revolutionaries, are on the contrary the most loyal and sincere socialist revolutionaries. The Chinese Trotskyists originally constituted, and for many years remained, the Left Opposition of the Chinese Communist Party. This left Opposition was originally formed around Chen Duxiu, founder of the CCP, who was elected or re-elected General Secretary at each of the first five Congresses of the Party. The Chinese Left Opposition, basing itself on the experience of the Chinese Revolution of 1925–7 and the theories of internationalism and permanent revolution, directed its energies towards freeing the CCP from the grip of Stalinist nationalism and bureaucratism. After the defeat of the revolution, we advanced a revolutionary democratic programme and actively opposed the CCP's Moscow-inspired adventurist line. During the Sino-Japanese war of 1937–45, we resolved to support and actively participated in the Anti-Japanese Resistance, but we did not abandon our revolutionary position, and after the victory of the Resistance we called for immediate implementation of agrarian revolution as a means of countering Guomindang repression, and eventually of completely overthrowing the reactionary rule of the Guomindang. During the period of the civil war (1946–9) we participated in the struggle on all fronts, and played a special role in the big cities of east and south China, where we led struggles in workers' districts. After the victory of the revolution our main contribution was in the struggle for the democratisation of the new organs of government and for further advances along the road of socialist revolution. All this, far from being a crime, was positively in the interests both of the Chinese workers and peasants and of the revolution itself.

However, the CCP leaders, especially the Moscow-controlled Wang Ming faction, all along saw us as their main enemy, and attacked us mercilessly. Their first step was to expel us from the Party. Later they slandered and persecuted our supporters. They heaped the most ridiculous charges on us: for example they accused us of being 'pro-Japanese collaborators' and 'special agents of the Guomindang'. They took all sorts of unscrupulous measures against us, not stopping short of murder. In Changsha in 1930, they shot Lu Yucai, a Red Army divisional commander [accused of Trotskyism]; in the same year they killed Li Su in the Eastern River area of Guangdong Province; during the anti-Japanese War of Resistance, they ambushed and killed Wang Changyao, leader of a guerrilla column in Shandong Province; in 1947 or 1948 they killed the writer Wang Shiwei in north Shaanxi Province; and in 1950 they shot Lian Zhengxiang, a worker, in Wenzhou, together with several other comrades. Finally, in December 1952, they crushed our entire organisation by arresting all our comrades throughout China.

The CCP's treatment of the Chinese Trotskyists over the past fifty years is the most flagrant of the 'false charges', 'frame-ups', and 'mistaken verdicts' currently being denounced by the Beijing leaders. If the latter are sincere in their resolve to 'rectify' such abuses, then they should start by reversing the verdicts wrongfully passed on the Trotskyists, and completely rehabilitate them. They should not only restore them their freedom and their right to work, declare them innocent of any crime, and restore their good name as revolutionaries, but also grant the Chinese Trotskyist tendency full legal rights. Does the release of the final batch (assuming there are no others left in jails or labour camps) of

Chinese Trotskyists represent such a 'reversal of verdicts'? We think the answer is no.

It is true that among the several hundred thousand lower, middle and even upper-level reinstated cadres who suffered maltreatment and humiliation at the hands of the 'Gang of Four' there are no few who experienced this 'state of lawlessness' as intolerable, and who sought to put end to it and to prevent its repetition. Hence a so-called democratic tendency has emerged in the top hierarchy of the CCP since 1977, and over the past two years has taken several democratic measures, of which the release of the Chinese Trotskyists is one. At the same time, however, we are deeply convinced that the emergence of this tendency in the CCP leadership can be ascribed only to a very small extent to any lessons those top leaders might have drawn from their own bitter experience. More importantly and fundamentally it is a reflection of the dissatisfaction and anger of workers, peasants and intellectuals (of which the Tian'anmen Incident of 5 April 1976 was the most unmistakable expression) at the CCP's bureaucratic misrule. The anger of the masses accumulated over more than twenty years has created a widespread movement for democracy and legality, which, if things are allowed to run their course, would threaten the whole bureaucratic system of the CCP. In order to divert and control this movement, a more 'pragmatic' and sensitive faction of the leaders of the CCP emerged at the top. It diverted the movement into exclusive opposition to the 'Gang of Four' and their supporters. Thus the antagonism between the masses and the whole bureaucratic régime has been moderated.

It is not surprising that such a tendency for democracy and legality is incapable of sustaining its momentum. It will bring no fundamental changes in the nature of the CCP rule, which will remain totalitarian and bureaucratic. Rehabilitated top leaders who were only recently acclaimed by naive peasants as 'saviours' as a result of their pledges of democracy are now loudly clamouring for an end to 'relaxation' and an immediate clamp-down. Where once the whole world spoke admiringly of a 'Beijing spring' now a new autumn has set in.

In such a context the release of the Chinese Trotskyists by no means implies a 'reversal of verdicts'. Moreover, in the present situation in China a rather dangerous feature becomes immediately apparent: just as the new leadership of the CCP has tried to convince the masses that the 'Gang of Four' are alone responsible for all the evils happened of the last few years and that the 'fascist tyranny' of the 'Gang' is simply a sort of 'evil legacy of feudalism', that is, simply the recrudescence of China's age-old system of feudal rule under new conditions, so there are many among the masses who have come to the conclusion that Western democracy is the model to be followed. They idealize the capitalist system, seeing it as a prerequisite for such democracy. Consciously or unconsciously, they desire to push China back into the world capitalist system, which would in reality involve restoring China to the status of a colony of world capitalism. This is an extremely dangerous conclusion which may lead China onto an extremely reactionary path.

We should make clear to the masses (and also, where appropriate, to some of the leaders) that the CCP's system of bureaucratic totalitarianism is in even greater measure the result of the transplantation of Stalinist bureaucratic tyranny to China. Therefore in order to definitely remove this 'evil legacy of feudalism', from a political point of view, we must first eradicate the political system copied from the Soviet Union of Stalin's era, so that all workers and other toilers can genuinely take political power into their own hands by directly participating in the organs of the state, supervising the state, and controlling it, thus preventing the emergence of bureaucracy in any form whatsoever. At the same time, we must naturally take into account the whole experience, both positive and negative, of workers and peasants' government over the last fifty or more years, so that a state based on workers and peasants' councils establishes a healthy system of democracy and human rights, backed up by full legal guarantees. Only in this way can the re-emergence of 'fascist tyranny' be prevented without at the same time running the risk of restoring capitalism under the guise of a movement for democracy and legality.

Such are our first reactions to the CCP's decision to release our comrades. On the basis of these ideas we will advance shoulder to shoulder with the masses struggling for socialist democracy and legality in China.

Finally, we demand these measures from the CCP authorities with regard to our comrades:

a   Lift all restrictions on Trotskyists released from prison over the entire period since the early 1950s, and restore all their liberties and rights of citizenship.
b   Cease all discrimination against Trotskyist ex-prisoners and their dependants in relation to employment and other living conditions.
c   Formally proclaim the innocence of all Trotskyists (whether arrested or not, and whether within China or overseas), and guarantee their immunity from persecution.
d   Officially make public a list of those Trotskyists who died in jail over the past twenty seven years, and restore their good name.

e   Officially restore the good name of Chen Duxiu and other vilified Trotskyists (including Luo Han, Lu Yucai, Wang Shiwei and others), and thus correct the falsification of history.
f   Grant full legal rights to the Trotskyist organisation in China, and guarantee its members the right to engage in political activity and security of person.

Will the CCP authorities grant these demands? This depends on the struggle carried on by socialist revolutionaries both inside and outside China. In the past, not only did Trotskyists on a world scale protest on behalf of their comrades in China, but even the human rights organisation Amnesty International expressed its concern. These protests and expressions of concern played at least some role in the recent release of Zheng Chaolin and other comrades. We are grateful to these people for their past help, and hope that they will continue to give us support in our future struggles.

A Brief Account of My Third Spell in Prison

Zheng Chaolin

This article appeared in the Hong Kong Trotskyist journal Xinmiao *('New Sprouts'), August 1993, pp. 41–7, under the title 'Di san ci ruyu genggai' ('A brief account of my third spell in prison'). The same article appeared, with many deletions, in Hong Kong's* Kaifang. *Source: Appendix to* An Oppositionist for Life *(1989).*

Question: Would you please tell me about the case against the Trotskyists in 1952?

Answer: In my *Memoirs*, I wrote a chapter titled 'My First Spell in Prison'; I drafted a further chapter titled 'My Second Spell in Prison', but I never actually wrote it, and now it's unlikely that I ever will. If I had the chance and the opportunity to work further on my *Memoirs*, they would naturally include a chapter specially devoted to 'My Third Spell in Prison', but I'm afraid that's impossible, for even if I had the chance and the opportunity, my great age and [lack of] energy would prevent me from doing so. However, since you are kind enough to ask, I will do my best to sum up in a few thousand words what happened in the course of those twenty seven years.

The case went down in history as the movement to 'purge Trotskyism'. The case was prepared over a long period of time with great thoroughness, and executed most successfully. Later, the official in charge of the case, who was extremely proud of himself, told me: 'With the suddenness of a thunderbolt we netted you up in one fell swoop and invited you to this place'. I still remember to this day his choice of words. Actually, I knew in advance about the raid, but there was no way I could escape; I had no choice but to let things take their course. I had never imagined that they would take our case so seriously, 'using so many human, financial, and material resources'. (Again, I'm quoting the official in charge of our case.)

Just after ten o'clock at night on 22 December 1952, I was seized on my way home and taken directly to be locked up in No. 1 Detention Centre. No one asked me any questions. I was simply placed in an empty cell on the second floor; a card bearing my name had already been attached to the cell door. The cell was some sixteen square metres large and could have housed a dozen or so people, but I was its only occupant. I asked myself whether only I had been arrested, or whether the entire group had been rounded up. And surely my wife had not been arrested too?

The next day, no one came to question me, and the next day, too, and the next, right through until the new year. But my question had in the meantime been answered. On the third or fourth day of my arrest, I suddenly heard large numbers of people on the floors above and below me singing the Internationale. At first, I thought it was the prison guards, but when the singing finished, people started shouting slogans. Then I heard cell doors opening, and large numbers of people being taken away. Only then did it dawn on me that those singing and shouting were our people. It later transpired that a large group of comrades had been arrested.[1] But it was all over. I could no longer join in the singing and shouting, in solidarity with them.

I could understand them arresting just me, or arresting a few of us, but I was unprepared for arrests on such a scale. The entire organisation was finished; our movement of twenty-odd years was at an end.[2]

Nevertheless, the case would be easier to fight. I could tell the whole truth, and not just part of it. I would not need to hide anything.

So on 31 January 1953, twelve days after my arrest, when I was first fetched for interrogation, I promptly admitted to being 'Zheng Chaolin' and expressed my willingness to submit to questioning, to provide answers, and to write to my fellow detainees urging them to abandon their boycott.

I was then interrogated for several days in succession. I gave them information that they already knew or could easily discover. But I kept one piece of knowledge back. It seemed to me that they were unlikely to know where the Trotskyist archive was being held. We had sorted it out into two wooden boxes and hidden it in a place known only to a handful of people. The interrogation was exceedingly hostile. Normally, there would be two interrogators, but on this occasion, there was only one person present in the room, with another outside, listening through the hatch in the cell door. The interrogator wanted me to tell him about the entire structure of our organisation, its entire

---

1   For an estimate of the number of Trotskyists and their sympathisers arrested on 22 December 1952, see the letter from Zheng Chaolin appended to this article.
2   According to Wang Fanxi (personal communication), the raid was coordinated at national level and carried out more or less simultaneously in Guangxi, Guangdong, Fujian, Anhui, Zhejiang, Yunnan, the northeast, Beijing, and Shanghai. Some of those arrested were removed to other places to serve their sentences. For example, those arrested in Guangdong were taken to Wuhan, those in north and northeast China to Beijing, and those in Wenzhou and Anhui to Shanghai; but those arrested in Yunnan were detained locally.

membership, and all our archives. He particularly emphasised the word 'archives'; I pricked up my ears. 'I've already told you everything', I replied. He went on with his questions. One question in particular alarmed me. (I can no longer remember exactly what the question was.) If they had not yet found the two secret boxes containing our archive, he would have been unlikely to raise this question. It was clear to me that they had unearthed our two boxes, so I told him of their hiding-place. The air of tension immediately dissipated, the man behind the desk smiled, and the other man at the cell door came in and offered me his congratulations. 'If you had not told us this', he said, 'we would have interrogated you no further'. (That was a coded way of saying that I would immediately have been executed.)

One evening following this experience, I was again summoned for interrogation. However, I was taken not to the interrogation chamber but to one of the offices in the Detention Centre. I sat down on a sofa. Three or four other people sat on chairs beside a table. The conversation was informal and relaxed. It was in the course of this meeting that the official I quoted earlier made his comments. The official asked me, 'What do you think of this case?' I replied, 'It's simply a political difference between us and you'. After I had said that, they all burst out laughing – real laughter, not feigned laughter.

After many years of propaganda and education, they considered Trotskyists to be even greater 'war criminals' than the 'war criminals', and even more 'counter-revolutionary' than the 'counter-revolutionaries'. It was just as Wang Ming and Kang Sheng had said: 'We can cooperate with the special agents of the Guomindang, but not with the Trotskyists'. So it was hardly surprising that my answer roused them to such hilarity. Later, in the course of interrogations or conversations, they often mocked me on account of that comment, but I stuck to the truth of it. Such was my conviction during my twenty seven years in prison; such, too, is my conviction now that I have been restored to freedom.

Today, most people see the Trotskyists as 'political dissidents'. Within the Chinese Communist Party, too, more and more people are of that opinion. In the new annotation to the second edition of Mao Zedong's *Xuanji* ('Selected works') published a year ago, this point of view found formal expression.

According to note 33 on page 168 of volume one,[3] 'The Chinese Trotskyists considered that the Chinese bourgeoisie had already vanquished imperialism and the feudal forces, that the Chinese bourgeois-democratic revolution had already been concluded, that the Chinese proletariat had no choice but to wait until some future date to carry out socialist revolution, and that for the time being, it could simply wage a legal struggle around the call for a "National

---

3   Mao Zedong 1991, Volume 1, p. 168, fn. 33.

[that is, Constituent] Assembly"'. Whether or not this note can be regarded as accurate, the reference in the original annotation to Stalin's description of the Trotskyists as 'a gang without principles and without ideas, of wreckers and diversionists, intelligence service agents, spies, murderers, a gang of sworn enemies of the working class, working in the pay of the intelligence services of foreign states' had been completely excised. The new annotation simply made the point that the Trotskyists had different political ideas.

Note 9 on page 516 of volume two says: 'During the Anti-Japanese War of Resistance, in their propaganda the Trotskyists proposed resisting Japan, but they attacked the Chinese Communist Party's policy of an Anti-Japanese National United Front. The equation of the Trotskyists with national traitors was a product of the mistaken conclusion commonplace at the time in publications of the Communist International that the Chinese Trotskyists had links to Japanese imperialist intelligence organisations'. This passage states even more clearly that the Chinese Trotskyists were not 'national traitors'! During the war against Japan, the Chinese Communist Party and the Chinese Trotskyists were separated by mere political differences.

If my interrogators of those days read these two notes to the second edition of Mao Zedong's *Selected Works*, they should realise in retrospect that the answer I gave them at the time was by no means so ridiculous.

In 1955, when the case against the Trotskyists was concluded, the result was not a death sentence but prison sentences of life, fifteen years, twelve years, ten years, five years, and three years. The sentences were to be served in Shanghai's Tilanqiao Jail. I myself had not yet been sentenced. I remained locked up in No. 1 Detention Centre, in my lonely cell (though I was by now in a new, smaller cell).[4] I was no longer interrogated, and I was allowed to read *Jiefang ribao* ('Liberation daily'), though the copies I received were always several days old.

In 1956, I read in my newspaper that the Communist Party of the Soviet Union had held its Twentieth Congress. I was puzzled: why during the opening ceremonies had the delegates not stood in silent tribute to Stalin (who I knew from the wireless had died in 1953)? Also, Mikoyan's speech showed that he was dissatisfied with Stalin.[5] In June 1957, I received some pamphlets along

---

4 More important prisoners were usually kept alone.
5 Anastas Ivanovich Mikoyan, an Armenian revolutionary who was on the Politburo after 1939, supported Khrushchev's criticism of Stalin.

with my newspapers. I remember only that they included the text of a speech on intellectuals by Zhou Enlai.

On 29 June 1956, I was suddenly summoned to collect some things. I went down from the third floor to the second where I met Yin Kuan, who had also been summoned. We sat side by side in a jeep and drove out through the prison gate. No one had informed us of our destination, nor dared we ask, but we knew that we were not headed for the execution place. We ended up at Tilanqiao Jail. That day and the next, we saw people from far and wide who had been convicted in connection with our case and transferred [to Tilanqiao]. There were some forty of us in all; it turned out that we had been brought together for the purposes of studying [documents or books supplied by the officials]. We were divided into three small groups, and after a few days of studying, we were taken out on a series of trips [to see the achievements of the government]. After that, we again studied for a while, and at the end of our study, we wrote 'summary reports'. These events were not wholly without value, but it would take too many pages to write about them, so I prefer not to.

Our 'summary reports' were submitted to higher levels. On 11 August those of us that had not been sentenced were sent back to the Detention Centre. I imagined that we would be sent to No. 1 Detention Centre, but instead, we ended up in No. 2 Detention Centre, where the atmosphere was considerably more relaxed.

In No. 1 Detention Centre, the guards had fetched our food, brought up our nightsoil buckets, and cut our hair; we had been segregated not only from prisoners involved in our case but also from people involved in other cases and prisoners in penal servitude. In No. 2 Detention Centre, I still had a cell to myself and did not participate in study, but I could observe other prisoners studying outside my cell and converse with my neighbours; I was even less segregated from prisoners in penal servitude. I was even allowed to go downstairs with other prisoners to 'take air' in the open space.

Even more important, I had my own subscription to *Liberation Daily*: I could read the news every day, as it was reported. I was even allowed to buy pen, paper, and ink with which to comment on my reading, and to purchase publications advertised in my newspaper. I could do research.

After the Mid-Autumn Festival[6] in 1959, I was able to restore contact with my wife. She came each month to visit me or bring things. After receiving a sentence of ten years in prison, she had been released early in 1957 on health grounds.

---

6   On the fifteenth day of the eighth lunar month.

I spent six years in No. 2 Detention Centre, during which period I went several times to Tilanqiao Jail for joint outings [with other Trotskyist prisoners]. We watched the contingents of paraders on People's Square, but after returning, I did not take part in the subsequent study sessions. The director, political instructors, and guards at No. 2 Detention Centre were all very good to me, and treated me politely. Had I ever received a sentence, I would have asked to serve it in No. 2 Detention Centre rather than go to Tilanqiao Jail.

In October 1962, however, I was escorted [anyway] to Tilanqiao. This time, it was not to join up with the other Trotskyist prisoners. I had to take all my clothes and belongings with me. The people escorting me told me that even my census register was being transferred to Tilanqiao. It turned out that after the end of the 'three years of natural disasters', the government considered that I was malnourished, and had decided to transfer me to a certain floor of Prison No. 5 to enjoy a 'nutritious diet'. At the place to which I had been sent, there were already a dozen or so malnourished prisoners, but not one of them was a Trotskyist. I was still kept in a single cell and did not take part in the study sessions attended by the other prisoners. Each day, I received my newspaper. The 'nutritious food' consisted of a few slices of pork two or three times a week with the midday meal, alongside the usual diet of rice and vegetables. Gradually, pork appeared daily on our menu, and the number of prisoners on the nutritious diet doubled.

In Prison No. 5 (I was later transferred to Prison No. 3), where I spent a year and a half on the nutritious diet, I did not take part in the prisoners' study sessions. I continued to do what I had done in No. 2 Detention Centre, that is, study phonology and grammar, translate foreign texts, and write poetry. Every month, I received food or other things sent by my wife; sometimes, I was allowed to see and talk with her. Generally speaking, I was left alone [that is, without interference], but the authorities did not treat me with the same regard as in No. 2 Detention Centre.

In May 1964, the government took new measures regarding the Trotskyists. It concentrated in Shanghai those Trotskyist prisoners throughout China still serving their sentences; those Trotskyist prisoners scattered across Shanghai's various reform-through-labour groups and prisons were concentrated on the third floor of Prison No. 1. I, too, was taken there from Prison No. 3. This time, the transfer was not temporary but permanent; the aim was to 'reform' us more effectively.

Those of us who were brought together on the third floor of Prison No. 1 included four prisoners whose sentences had not yet been settled (Zheng

Chaolin, Yin Kuan, Yu Shouyi,[7] and Huang Jiantong), eight who had been given life sentences, three who had been given fifteen years, and four who had been given ten years (those who had been sentenced to fewer than ten years had already left prison). Apart from these people, there was still a woman prisoner who had been sentenced to twelve years and had not yet participated in study;[8] Du Weizhi did not participate in study because he had been transferred to Beijing after his arrest.

Those whose sentences had not yet been settled were still kept apart from the rest. The fifteen prisoners who had already received their sentences were kept on the third floor of the west wing, and were formed into a study group. They lived three to a cell, whereas I still had a cell to myself. We could only see these people during exercise periods. But they were at the front of the exercising column whereas we were at the rear, so we were not able to have any actual contact with them.

What did we study? We studied 'anti-revisionist documents'. The contradiction between the Soviet and Chinese Communist Parties had become public knowledge. The Central Committee of the Communist Party of the Soviet Union had published its 'open letter' to all Party comrades and the Chinese Communist Party had publicly criticised this 'open letter'. The criticism had gradually escalated into open ideological warfare. (The extreme criticism had been made public when we were gathered together in one place for the purposes of joint study.)

I decided at this study session to explain without any attempt at concealment the systematic views that I had developed over my previous few years of reflection. All that was expected of us was that we 'study', no one had ever explained to us that we were free to 'speak our minds' (that is, that even if we said the wrong things, we would not be found guilty). However, I demanded no such guarantee; I intended to speak out freely, just as we had done when we edited *Guoji zhuyizhe* ('Internationalist') and *Xinqi* ('New banner').[9] I paid no attention whatsoever to any possible consequences of my action.

Those of us in the small group of prisoners who had not yet been sentenced paid a visit to Shanghai municipality after nine preparatory meetings. In the

---

7 Yu Shouyi, alias Mai (or Mei) Erduan, was a Trotskyist activist in Beijing who spent a short period in 1950 in Hong Kong.
8 This woman, surnamed Cao, was a leader of the Trotskyists' Wenzhou Youth League. Her younger brother, also Cao, escaped from prison in Wenzhou together with his warder, Wang Guoquan, whom he converted to Trotskyism and who masterminded the escape; Wang later worked as a seaman from Hong Kong and was eventually blacklisted for leading strikes.
9 Two pre-1949 Trotskyist journals.

course of the visit, the two small groups [those who had been sentenced and those who had not yet been sentenced] could not avoid contact with one another. As a result of this contact, I learned for the first time that that we Trotskyist prisoners in Tilanqiao Jail were in a different position from other prisoners: not only could we be locked up together and formed into one study group, but one of the guards inadvertently let slip that we were enjoying something of a 'guest status'. Our study was still under the control of the unit that had so far dealt with our case, and the prison authorities had nothing to do with it – if we violated prison regulations, the violation would be dealt with by that unit.

After the visit but before the start of formal study, one day, Yin Kuan shouted to me from the neighbouring cell: 'Chaolin, I'm dying'. I said, 'Don't talk nonsense!' But I still reported the matter to the guards and got them to request a physician-prisoner[10] to take him to the hospital to be examined. I saw him pass by my cell door, after which, I received no further news of him. Three days later, the hospital sent some people to disinfect his cell, so I concluded that he must have died. I wrote two poems in the classical style in memory of him. (I have long forgotten how they went). I had been very sad not to hear him voice his opinions at our study session, but I knew what his attitude was, for when the two of us had been transferred from No. 2 Detention Centre on 29 June 1956, we had been put in the same cell and talked together until late at night. The next day, we were moved apart, but we had the chance to exchange a few comments during visits and study meetings. I realised that his admissions of guilt and expressions of contrition were feigned. He had been arrested in 1950 in his hometown of Tongcheng [in Anhui], and had been held in Hefei. At first, he had refused to admit his guilt, and as a result, he had suffered considerable hardship. His wrists had been handcuffed behind his back, someone else had had to feed him, someone else had had to wipe his backside when he went to the toilet, and so on. He had no choice but to admit his guilt. After his transfer to Shanghai, he was sometimes kept in a cell by himself and sometimes shared a cell with another; the government did not take his admission of guilt at face value.

By the time that we formally started studying the anti-revisionist texts, our small group had only three members left. I 'spoke out freely', and was therefore refuted by the other two. Every 'criticism' took a very long time to study. While studying, we had to take notes, and at the end of the period of study, I wrote up [my contribution to] the entire discussion in a systematic 'summary report' of some 85,000 characters. I read out my 'summary report' at

---

10   A medical doctor who, though a prisoner, served as a physician in the prison.

a meeting of the small group, and then handed it over to the head of the small group for forwarding to higher authorities (while keeping a copy for myself). This pamphlet was titled *Ganbu zhuyi lun* ('On cadreism').

Either before or after I wrote my summary, the unit dealing with our case supplied each member of our small group with volumes one to four of Mao Zedong's *Selected Works*. I believe that this was our next study task. After completing our study of these four volumes, we had to write a summary. I conscientiously read every article in them, and simultaneously took notes. But we no longer studied as we had, either because one of our number fell ill and went to hospital and the remaining two of us could no longer meet, or because both groups stopped studying Mao's *Selected Works*. Nevertheless, I still edited my notes into a book of 135,000 characters under the title *Yuzhong du Mao Zedong xuanji* ('Reading Mao Zedong's *Selected Works* in prison'). By the time that I had made a copy of the notes to keep for myself, the Cultural Revolution had already started; just as before, I handed the text to my guards.

During the same period, my wife sent me Stalin's *Problems of Leninism*, which a good friend had specially bought on my behalf. I read this book, too, from start to finish and took notes on it that I wrote up into a volume, but I failed to submit the volume to the authorities. I forget what I called it.

I kept the manuscripts of these three books by my side, but in 1968, when the prison came under military control, they were burned along with other manuscripts when the army representative ordered that the cells be searched and all the property in them confiscated. I do not know whether any copies of the first two studies, which were submitted to the authorities, have been preserved.

In mid-1965, I was still alone in a cell, and did not take part in study. The only other member of my small group had been assigned to the small group of those whose sentences had already been passed, and he had started studying in his new group. Two memorable things happened in that year.

In my *Yinyu canji* ('Surviving poems by Yu Yin'), there is a poem that goes as follows:

> You kindly advise me to follow others' suit.
> Though I would love to make concessions,
> there is a gulf that I can never cross.
> Though seemingly just inches wide,
> in fact, it reaches for a thousand miles.
> It is the gulf between a human and a beast.
> Should I drink the sweet and not the bitter cup,
> I would disgrace my father and my mother!

> And even if I crossed this gulf,
> my mind would be forever dissident.
> Do you not see some old acquaintances of mine
> bending their heads low
> and saying yes whenever yes is wanted,
> but all to no avail?
> Like me, they spent these thirteen years in jail,
> hungrily looking upwards at the goose
> that wings its way across the sky[11] –
> where is the leniency?

The line 'Like me, they spent these thirteen years in jail' shows that I wrote the poem in 1965. On one occasion, when my wife came on a special prison visit, three stools had been set out. A prison guard had sat to one side to supervise our conversation. Before the start of such meetings, the guard would inform relatives of the prisoner that it was their duty to persuade the prisoner to admit his or her guilt and undergo reform. So at the start of such visits, relatives would deliver some such 'exhortation'. I replied to the 'exhortation' in the presence of the guard. I said that I, too, wanted to compromise out of consideration for the general interest, but there were limits beyond which I would not go. And even if I did go beyond those limits, it would be to no avail. No few of those involved in our case had admitted their guilt but had still received no leniency, and, like me, had spent the previous thirteen years in jail.

After the special prison visit, that same evening, I wrote the above poem and posted it together with the next letter to my relatives, but it was returned to me.

As if to rebut my supposition, not long after this incident something else happened that seemed to say: if you admit your guilt and undergo reform, you definitely will receive lenient treatment.

One afternoon in early autumn, Section Chief Li of the unit dealing with our case suddenly turned up at the prison and had all the Trotskyists assemble on the ground floor of Prison No. 1. It turned out that the government had decided to let Yin Kuan go home, and wanted him to address a few words to us. A prisoner pushed Yin Kuan in a wheelchair to Prison No. 1. For a long time, I had thought that Yin Kuan was dead, yet there he was in the wheelchair. But though he saw us, he no longer recognised us. He spoke a few sentences to us, the gist of which was that we should admit our guilt and undergo reform, in which case, we would be released before our time, as he had been. His daughter had come to visit him from Tongcheng, and the next day, he would return

---

11   Cherishing an illusion that cannot be realised.

together with her. After he had finished speaking, the prisoner undergoing penal servitude helped him back into his wheelchair and returned him to the hospital. Section Chief Li then asked each of us to say what we felt. I deliberately kept my remarks to the end.

I said: 'Yin Kuan was ill in prison for a long time. Several years ago, I asked the government to let Yin Kuan and another prisoner who had been ill for a long time go home, since both of them had loving families to look after them, and, once home, their illness could be cured. My request was ignored for several years. It's wonderful that Yin Kuan is now to be released. We've seen the state that Yin Kuan is now in. Naturally, it's unlikely that Yin Kuan's release had anything to do with the request I made several years ago'.

Section Chief Li stood to one side and listened while I spoke. He made no attempt to silence me, and after I had finished speaking, he did not upbraid me. But sighing loudly, he said: 'Hum! You made the request! Hum! And you made it several years ago!'[12]

But there were no consequences.

The following year, 1966, was an 'unprecedented year in history'.[13] We knew from press reports or prison rumours that there was a 'craze for struggle' in the outside world. Some people[14] were 'encircled and suppressed' on the highways, and were 'struggled to death'.[15] Rumour had it that there would be a 'struggle' within the prison too.

The 'struggle' had already started among the prison officials and guards. In the western wing of Prison No. 1, people could be heard shouting slogans in the offices. According to reports, the prison walls and the surrounding streets were plastered with wall-newspapers. A 'struggle' was evidently being prepared among the prisoners. One day, Section Chief Li of the unit in charge of our case turned up at the prison for a meeting with me and several other Trotskyists. It turned out that I was to be the target of a 'struggle'. On 24 October 1966, my 'struggle meeting' started. On the first day, the guards told me to prepare a speech explaining the situation regarding my reform. Thirty-odd people

---

12   The Section Chief probably meant to imply that Yin Kuan's release had had nothing to do with Zheng's request.
13   The year in which the Cultural Revolution started.
14   Prisoners working outside the prison.
15   'Encircled and suppressed' is a term ironically borrowed from Chiang Kai-shek's policy of surrounding and destroying the Communists in southern China in the early 1930s.

turned up at the meeting; they had been mobilised by the prison authorities, who had secretly infiltrated among these people a number of others charged with saving my life. There was no obvious hatred between me and the [common] prisoners, so why would they want to beat me to death? Because they were keen to show they were activists who would stop at nothing, and hoped thereby to gain lenient treatment. But because of the measures taken by the authorities, though I was wounded at the struggle meeting, the wounding was not serious.

After the start of the struggle meeting, I read out my speech, the gist of which was as follows. The Trotskyists were not counter-revolutionaries, Trotsky was not a counter-revolutionary, Chen Duxiu was not a counter-revolutionary, I myself was not a counter-revolutionary, and none of the Trotskyists was a counter-revolutionary. Even before I had finished reading my speech, the meeting erupted into violence. I was dragged out and forced to my knees. I was cursed, I was beaten, my ears were pulled, my cheeks were pinched, and I was ordered to retract what I had said. On the day itself, the violence was without effect. Thereafter, however, I was subjected to new struggles lasting for two or three days, after which the number of participants diminished. Those seated at the long table no longer used violence but relied simply on verbal intimidation. After a week or so of this sort of treatment, I was forced to admit that I was a 'counter-revolutionary'. The struggle against me ceased only after a record of the proceedings had been made and I had been allowed to thumb-print and sign it.

From then on, my life-style changed. I lived no longer alone but in a cell shared with two other people, like other prisoners. I studied no longer by myself but in a small group with other Trotskyists. At first, I was instructed to listen to the views of others and not to utter my own opinions, but later, things gradually loosened up and I was expected to air my opinions; even so, I restricted myself to a few innocuous comments. I no longer wrote any books, did any translations, or wrote any articles. If I read any books or articles and was required to write notes on them, I did not dare to express myself freely in the notes. I wrote hardly any poetry, and I was much more careful about what I said in the course of everyday conversations. One guard who had recently been promoted to the office came to seek me out for a chat after the struggle meeting. He told me, 'This struggle meeting was aimed at curtailing your arrogance, just think how arrogant you were when you were first transferred to Prison No. 1!' Some people said that that guard was representing the unit in charge of our case, and that he knew that struggle was incapable of achieving its aim of 'reforming' me. But if the intention was to beat the arrogance out of me, it succeeded.

From the time of the struggle meeting until when I left Tilanqiao Jail six years later, there is nothing worth noting, save for the military administration of the prison in 1968. At that time, the entire prison was put in the hands of the People's Liberation Army. Not only did three representatives of the People's Liberation Army control the whole prison, including its director and administrators, but each prison, each floor, was placed under the control of three representatives of the army, and the original guards had to obey the orders of these people. The main consequence of this development for me personally was the order given by the army representatives for the cells to be searched and all publications save Mao Zedong's *Selected Works* and [the Communist Party journal] *Hongqi* ('Red flag') to be confiscated. The order applied even more surely to manuscripts; my books and manuscripts of more than one million characters were taken from me. When I left the prison, my books were returned to me, but not a single page of manuscript was given back. Later, after repeatedly enquiring about the matter, I was informed that all the manuscripts had been burned on army orders. The army continued to administer the prison until the rebellion and subsequent flight [in September 1971] of [People's Liberation Army Commander] Lin Biao. Only then was the administration put back into the hands of the prison authorities.

We left the prison on 28 September 1972. The Public Security Bureau sent someone to tell us that we were to be released, and to give us certificates of release. We affixed our thumb-prints to the certificates, but the unit concerned with our case immediately took the certificates back, for we were not allowed to return to our homes but could live only in a reform-through-labour factory (a glass-works) or on a reform-through-labour farm (Qingdong Farm), under administrative surveillance. I went to the glass-works, where I lived with five other people in one courtyard, one person to a room. The entrance to the courtyard was open, but we were not allowed to leave through it. Sometimes, when we did leave, we were required to go in pairs. If we left the factory gate, we had to be escorted by someone from the factory security force. This person, too, lived in the courtyard. He was responsible for our supervision. He took us shopping in Zhoupuzhen once a fortnight.

In December 1972, my wife moved in with me, so my monthly living allowance rose to eighty yuan. (The others received sixty yuan a month.) According to what I heard, eighty yuan was more than the salary of the factory director. Our three daily meals were brought to us from the canteen. We participated in manual labour, by helping the factory clinic to grow and harvest medicinal herbs. But our main activity was study. I continued to speak my mind freely at study meetings, even though I did not retract my admission that I was a 'counter-revolutionary'.[16]

We spent seven years under supervision in the glass-works, during which time, in 1976, Zhou Enlai, Zhu De, and Mao Zedong died, Hua Guofeng took over the succession, the 'Gang of Four' was smashed, Deng Xiaoping rose to power, and, finally, the Third Plenum of the Eleventh Central Committee inaugurated the reforms.

On 5 June 1979, we attended a sort of ceremony in a small assembly hall on Qingdong Farm together with six other people being held there who were implicated in our case. On the platform was a representative of the courts and another of the Public Security Bureau, from whose hands we received certificates restoring our civil rights. Afterwards, we were put up in the Oriental Hotel. We discussed our impressions, received information, attended a banquet given by Jing Renqiu, Deputy Head of the United Front Department, in the Hengshan Hotel, and went on a tour of Nanjing and Suzhou (which I didn't join). We then returned to the factory or farm to await allocation of housing.

In late June, apart from four of our number who had relatives outside Shanghai, eight of us were moved to new accommodation, where we started a new life.

---

16 After the struggle meeting, I did not retract my statement that I was a 'counter-revolutionary'. Sometimes, government workers would ask me, 'Does that amount to an admission of guilt?' I would then answer, 'I am a counter-revolutionary'. If they then asked, 'Why are you a counter-revolutionary?', I would reply, 'Because I oppose the Communist Party'. On one occasion, this answer proved insufficient, and my interlocutor said, 'Opposing the Communist Party is not [the same as being a] counter-revolutionary'. I was thrown aback, and retorted: 'Isn't opposing the Communist Party counter-revolutionary?' He said no, it isn't. I suddenly hit on a way out of my predicament. 'The Communist Party represents the people', I said. 'By opposing the Communist Party, I oppose the people'. Only then did he give up. After the Third Plenum of the Eleventh Central Committee [of the Party held in December 1978], when my citizenship was about to be restored, the authorities arranged for each of us to write a summary report, which we discussed and passed at a meeting. I made sure that I was the last to read out my report. In it, I said that 'I had not been successfully reformed' as a way of pointing out that I had never been guilty of any crime.[Note by Zheng Chaolin.]

Appendix

On 30 December 1993, Zheng Chaolin wrote a short reply to various questions put to him concerning this article. On the number of Trotskyists and their sympathisers arrested on 22 December 1952, he wrote as follows:

It's impossible to put an exact figure on the number of alleged Trotskyists arrested in 1952. According to my estimate, the number of both those who were arrested and imprisoned and those who were merely put under surveillance (whose freedom was restricted), like Wang Mengzou, Wang Yuanfang,[17] and such like, if not one thousand, must have been very close to that figure. Some of our young people were sent on courses for surveillance and training, where they were ordered to 'disclose' each other's (and other people's) [crimes]. The courses lasted for six months. In Shanghai, there were two such courses. Of those [sent on such courses], only a few were finally sentenced on account of their bad 'attitude', while most were freed after completing the course. (Deng Shuzhen[18] and Fang Xiong were among those freed. In fact, both had already surrendered [to the Chinese Communist authorities] before the national raid took place.)

In a subsequent letter, he said that seven of the twelve survivors released in 1979 were supporters of the group of Trotskyists led by Wang Fanxi and Zheng Chaolin, and five were Pengites. He was unable to say what had been the ratio between Peng's followers and followers of the Zheng-Wang group among those arrested in 1952.[19]

---

17 The Wangs, who were not Trotskyists themselves but were considered sympathisers of the Trotskyists, ran Shanghai's leftist Oriental Book Company.
18 Deng, a female, had been a student leader at Shanghai's Jiaotong University.
19 Wang Fanxi, letter, 9 February 1994.

PART 17

Wang Fanxi Reviews Tang Baolin's
History of Chinese Trotskyism

∴

Interviews with Wang Fanxi on Tang Baolin's *Zhongguo Tuopai shi* ('History of Chinese Trotskyism')

Gregor Benton

One of the only two people still alive in a position to correct and refute on the basis of personal knowledge and experience the various mistakes and unfair allegations in Tang's book is Wang Fanxi. The following comments by Wang, divided into nine separate points, are based on interviews with him held on 29 and 31 May 1995. The only other person in a position to respond knowledgeably to all Tang's claims and charges is the Trotskyist Zheng Chaolin. Unfortunately, Zheng, born in 1901, can no longer see well enough to subject Tang's book to thorough-going critical scrutiny, but he was able, with the help of a tape-recording, a magnifying glass, and an enlarged photocopy of the text, to read chapters 5 and 6. Through Wang Fanxi, I obtained a copy of the resulting review, which runs to some 16 pages, transcribed on Zheng's behalf by a copyist.[1] In the most recent issue of the Japanese journal Torotsukii kenkyû *('Trotsky Studies'), Tang Baolin is quoted as describing himself as Zheng's '[literary] agent' and 'firm friend'.[2] Such 'friendship', one can surmise, could hardly have outlived a reading of Tang's book, whose smears and jibes Zheng angrily repudiates in his review of it. 'This is a bad book', he writes, summarising the 'unanimous' opinion of other veteran Trotskyist survivors in Shanghai. 'It is an anti-Trotskyist screed that turns facts upside down and concocts untruths in order to vilify the Trotskyists. It should be severely criticised and rebutted'. It is, he concludes, 'the final repercussion of the anti-Trotskyist movement brought back to China from Moscow by [the arch-Stalinists] Kang Sheng and Wang Ming [in 1937]'. Zheng Chaolin's indignation is most fired by his 'friend's' practice of using as 'evidence' depositions made during the Cultural Revolution by Mao's Trotskyist prisoners. He points out that on the basis of similar 'confessions' by some of China's best-known writers jailed in the 1960s, all sorts of discreditable theories could be mounted; and that many of those (like Fu Lei, father of the pianist Fu Ts'ong) who refused to incriminate themselves or others by means of such depositions were driven to commit suicide. He describes the book as 'an arrogant manifestation of the contempt with which "victors" view the*

---

1 Zheng Chaolin, review (in Chinese), Tang Baolin, *Zhongguo Tuopai shi*, manuscript.
2 Ogata 1995.

"vanquished"'. Hardly any of its allegations, he says, are supported by convincing evidence; many are 'laughable'. Source: Benton 1996.

Permanent Revolution

Leon Trotsky's idea of permanent revolution can be understood in two related senses: 'vertically', meaning that in economically backward countries, the bourgeoisie is incapable of carrying out bourgeois revolution, so the bourgeois and socialist stages of revolution are telescoped and carried out under the leadership of the proletariat; and 'horizontally', meaning that 'the completion of the socialist revolution within national limits is unthinkable.... The socialist revolution begins on the national arena, unfolds on the international arena, and is completed on the world arena'.

Tang Baolin in his book does not elaborate much on permanent revolution in its vertical aspect, and he completely misunderstands it in its horizontal sense. He confuses permanent revolution with the export of revolution through military intervention, an idea wholly at odds with Trotsky's theory.

Trotsky was not in principle opposed to assisting revolutions that might break out in other countries, even by sending troops to help the revolutionaries. But he was prepared to do so only under strict conditions. In a famous article on military doctrine published in 1921, he wrote:

> In the gigantic class struggle unfolding today, the role of military intervention from the outside can acquire only a supplementary, contributory, auxiliary significance. Military intervention can hasten the culmination and facilitate the victory. But this cannot occur unless the revolution is mature not only with regard to social relations – and this condition is already fulfilled – but also with regard to political consciousness. Military intervention may be likened to the forceps of an obstetrician, which if applied in time can reduce the birth pangs, but if brought into play prematurely can produce only a miscarriage.[3]

Tang Baolin gives two alleged examples of permanent revolution in the sense of the export of revolution through military intervention. In 1919, he says, Trotsky personally proposed leading thirty or forty thousand cavalry to India; and in 1923, he wanted to 'send the regular Red Army to Germany under his

---

3 Trotsky 1971 [1921], p. 53.

personal command to ignite the fire of proletarian revolution in Europe'. Both examples are groundless.

In fact, in early 1919, no real Red Army yet existed in Russia. The old Tsarist army had been dissolved, and the Red Army had to be created on the basis of armed workers and peasants. Trotsky set up the Red Army from scratch, and commanded it in Russia's civil war. 1919 was the most dangerous year in that war. How could Trotsky have sent thirty or forty thousand cavalry to India? Furthermore, in 1919 there was no revolution in India to support.

The story about Germany is equally far-fetched. True, there were revolutionary crises in Germany in 1923, and controversies about the German Revolution took place, mainly among Zinoviev, Bukharin, and Trotsky. However, none of these people proposed 'sending the Red Army to Germany to ignite the revolution in Europe'.

Tang Baolin gives no source for his claims about Trotsky's proposals for military intervention. On the whole, they ape or echo the alarmist anti-Soviet propaganda of the bourgeois press in the late 1910s and early 1920s. The story about India may be based on a passage in Isaac Deutscher's study on Trotsky, in which Trotsky is said to have mentioned 'a serious military man' who had 'suggested to him a plan for the formation of an expeditionary cavalry corps to be used in India'.[4] The passage does not support Tang's assertion; Tang does not refer to it in his book.

Common Action and the United Front

For Stalin and the Stalinists, there was no difference between the 'united front' (sometimes called 'popular front') and common action. On the relationship between communists and bourgeois, petty-bourgeois, and other working-class parties, the Stalinists knew only two attitudes: join them uncritically and slavishly subordinate yourself to them; or indiscriminately attack, denounce, and persecute them. They never understood the tactic of common action by means of which a revolutionary party could, might, and even had to maintain a certain relationship with petty-bourgeois (and in special cases even bourgeois) parties and working-class organisations, in order to achieve some specific progressive purpose, while at the same time preserving its organisational and political independence.

In the early 1930s in Germany, the Stalinists called the German social-democrats 'social-fascists' and considered them (rather than the rising Nazis)

---

4 Deutscher 1954, p. 457.

to be the main enemy; they refused to enter into common action with the social democrats, as Trotsky was then urging them to do. Their refusal greatly helped the triumph of the Hitlerites. After the Nazis came to power, the Stalinists executed a 180 degree turn, in order to fight Nazism and fascism. At this point, they formed the 'popular front', which in fact represented a capitulation, both ideologically and organisationally, not only to the reformist parties, which they had only yesterday considered the 'main enemy', but also to bourgeois parties.

Trotskyists everywhere, including in China, always opposed the united front in its Stalinist sense, for example between 1924 and 1927 and, again, during the Sino-Japanese War of 1937–45. But they did not oppose common action with petty-bourgeois parties and politicians, as long as such action was undertaken for a specific, progressive purpose and for a limited period of time. In the course of such common action, the workers' party had to retain its independence of operation, plan, and idea. (It is true, though, as Chen Duxiu himself pointed out, that Chinese Trotskyists committed some sectarian errors while carrying out this sort of common action.)

Even though Tang Baolin seems to understand the distinction between united front and common action, he still argues that because we Trotskyists opposed the united front, we also opposed common action. However, Trotskyists did join and support the anti-Japanese resistance, though we did so under our own banner and while retaining our own programme and the right to criticise other political parties.

On this very point, Trotsky defended Chen Duxiu against Liu Renjing in 1932, when Liu, adopting an ultra-left position, accused Chen of opportunism for favouring common action with the Guomindang's Nineteenth Route Army in the defence of Shanghai against the Japanese.

In a discussion with Harold Isaacs held on 8 August 1935, Trotsky's position, as recorded by Isaacs, was as follows:

> On the problem of the united front with the bourgeoisie: Trotsky did not believe Liu Jen-ching's [Liu Renjing's] conclusion that Ch'en Tu-hsiu [Chen Duxiu] has become an opportunist. He thinks that Liu's argument was undialectical and that it tended to throw around ambiguous terminology. For instance, Trotsky thinks there should be a distinction between 'united fronts' and 'common action' ...

On 9 August Isaacs' record continues:

> To resume yesterday's discussion, Trotsky read my draft and pointed out a few weaknesses on the first page. He felt that my analysis of the different

layers of the bourgeoisie and their subjective and objective viewpoints was insufficient and undialectical. He said that if we used such a pat formula, we would tend to be dogmatic and opportunist. He emphasised:

'Common action, especially a short-term common action, is one thing, but capitulation to the bourgeoisie in the form of a permanent "united front" such as the French Popular Front is another. They are entirely different. It is good to keep our organisation completely independent; but the heart of the matter is how to use this independence. *We should continually carry out "common action" with the students' and peasants' organisations*'. [Emphasis added.][5]

Chen Duxiu's 'Mistake'

According to Tang Baolin, Chen Duxiu came to Trotskyism 'by mistake'. In reality, however, Chen's Trotskyism was the logical culmination of his thinking about democracy, imperialism, and socialism, and grew from his own bitter experience of the defeat, as a result of Stalin's misdirection, of the Revolution of 1925–7. Tang's theory is a Maoist rehash of the liberal philosopher Hu Shi's argument that Chen Duxiu became a communist by mistake, after leaving Beijing University and the company of his old friends. Chen Duxiu's last four articles, written shortly before he died, in 1942, are socialist and internationalist in content; in essence, they are still Trotskyist. So it is wrong to say that Chen Duxiu went over to Trotskyism by mistake and later reawakened to bourgeois democracy.

Double Standards

Tang Baolin neither sympathises with nor approves of the persecution of Stalin's critics and opponents in the Moscow trials. In China, too, the accusation of Trotskyism was, according to Tang, wrongly levelled at a number of innocent people, including Yu Xiusong[6] and Wang Shiwei.[7] However, Tang

---

5 Trotsky 1976 [1935], p. 541.
6 Yu, a veteran Communist, was arrested and put on trial together with the other veterans Dong Yixiang and Zhou Dawen by Wang Ming when Wang and Kang Sheng were on their way back to China via Xinjiang in 1937. Yu, Dong, and Zhou were sent to Russia and killed by Stalin in 1938.
7 See Part XIV.

goes on to give credence to confessions extracted by compulsion and under 'scientific interrogation' from young Trotskyists arrested in China in 1952; these confessions were then used to convict the deponents and their comrades of political crimes. (On the basis of analogous confessions obtained in the 1930s by the Soviet GPU, one could, of course, conclude that Zinoviev, Bukharin, and company were Hitler agents – but only at the cost of being thought insane.)

Much of the evidence that Tang selects from these confessions is quite bizarre, and concerns various alleged instances (of a sort originally imputed to us by the Moscow-trained Stalinists Wang Ming and Kang Sheng in the 1930s and long since discounted by serious historians even in China) of Trotskyist collusion with Guomindang politicians, police agents, and the Japanese. For example, on the basis of depositions made in 1973 (six years before the Trotskyists' release from jail, and twenty-one years after their arrest) by the imprisoned Ye Chunhua, the Trotskyist Peng Shuzhi is said to have colluded with the senior Nationalist politician Sun Ke (that is, Sun Fo), the son of Sun Yat-sen, who was supposedly particularly interested after the war in the fortunes of Peng's journal *Qiuzhen* ('Seek the truth'); Peng is also said to have tried to meet Sun Ke in Guangzhou while leaving China for Hong Kong in 1949; Zhang Shu, a Trotskyist renegade who became a senior police officer in Shanghai, is said to have protected us; and it is suggested (with scandalous implications) that I and Zheng Chaolin felt safe under the Japanese in occupied Shanghai at the time of the arrest of the Trotskyist martyr Chen Qichang.[8]

Regarding the 'evidence' provided by Ye Chunhua about Peng Shuzhi's alleged collusion with Sun Ke, Zhang Shu's alleged protection of us, and my and Zheng Chaolin's supposed sense of security under the Japanese, Ye admitted to Zheng Chaolin after his and Zheng's release from prison in 1979 that he had simply told his inquisitors what they wanted to hear; he had been a mere boy of thirteen in Wenzhou at the time of the events, and could not have known what he claimed to know.[9]

---

8 According to Tang Baolin, at the time of Chen's arrest by the Japanese gendarmerie, Wang Fanxi and Zheng Chaolin 'did not even bother to take the elementary precaution of moving house'. However, according to Zheng Chaolin's review, Wang and Zheng abandoned their homes straight after the arrest; Wang took his wife and daughter back to the couple's hometown, in Haining, while Zheng himself took his wife and baby son Frei to live with peasants in a village outside Shanghai (where Frei, their only child, caught the tuberculosis from which he died in 1945, aged seven). Both Wang and Zheng then returned to Shanghai, where they went to stay with friends.

9 Zheng Chaolin, letter to Wang Fanxi. According to Zheng's review, Ye Chunhua was simply recording the views expressed by prisoners anxious to be shown 'leniency' in the course of a meeting designed to 'expose the Trotskyists'.

As for the claim (by the ex-Trotskyist Song Fengchun) that Zhang Te[10] (whom I knew well) maintained long-standing relations with the Japanese after being caught by a Japanese agent in the act of mailing a package addressed to Trotsky, I know from personal experience that for reasons of security, mail was never addressed to Trotsky, but to 'Mr Sedov, Post Restante, Constantinople'. Regarding Tang Baolin's inference that Zhang Te was allowed because of this Japanese connection to escape from police custody after his arrest in 1931, I myself was present at the time of the arrest; Zhang Te managed to escape (still wearing handcuffs) only because I turned up at the scene and inadvertently created a diversion (by getting myself arrested).[11]

'Defeatism' and 'National Betrayal'

Tang Baolin does not accept Wang Ming and Kang Sheng's accusation that Chen Duxiu and the Chinese Trotskyists acted as paid agents of Japanese imperialism. However, he does appear to believe that the Chinese Trotskyists (though not Chen Duxiu) objectively, if not subjectively, played into the hands of the Japanese invaders. He accuses the Chinese Trotskyists of adopting a defeatist policy towards the Chinese side in the Sino-Japanese War. He also accuses them of adopting a defeatist policy towards the Chinese Communist Party during the civil war between it and the Guomindang.

He labels the Chinese Trotskyists as 'ultra-leftist and reactionary'. In fact, he fails to understand (or deliberately misunderstands) the Chinese Trotskyist view on the Sino-Japanese War; in particular, he misrepresents the meaning of revolutionary defeatism.

The policy of the Chinese Trotskyists on the Sino-Japanese War was based on Trotsky's analysis, which was stated as follows:

> In my declaration to the bourgeois press, I said that the duty of all the workers' organisations of China was to participate actively and in the front lines of the present war against Japan, without abandoning, for a single moment, their own programme and independent activity....
>
> But can Chiang Kai-shek assure the victory? I do not believe so. It is he, however, who began the war and who today directs it. To be able to replace him it is necessary to gain decisive influence among the proletariat

---

10   Zhang Te joined the Trotskyist movement in Moscow in 1927, left it in 1931, and became a high-ranking official under General Li Zongren's neo-Gui clique.

11   This story is told in Benton, ed., 1997, p. 323.

and in the army, and to do this it is necessary not to remain suspended in the air but to place oneself in the midst of the struggle. We must win influence and prestige in the *military* struggle against the foreign invasion and in the *political* struggle against the weaknesses, the deficiencies, and the internal betrayal. At a certain point, which we cannot fix in advance, this political opposition can and must be transformed into armed conflict, since the civil war, like war generally, is nothing more than the continuation of the political struggle. It is necessary, however, to know when and how to transform political opposition into armed insurrection. [Emphasis in the original.][12]

Is this policy defeatist or defencist? There is no simple answer to such a question. In Marxist politics, and in the vocabulary of Marxism, this policy of Trotsky's was completely new. It was not simply a form of traditional defencism, nor was it an example of revolutionary defeatism as formulated by Lenin in the First World War. Aiming to transform the war against the foreign invaders into a revolution to replace the leadership of the resistance war and thereby to assure the victory of the war against the foreign enemy – this policy was much nearer to revolutionary defeatism than to defencism.

Yet there is a big difference between Lenin's revolutionary defeatism and Trotsky's position on China's resistance war against Japanese imperialism, for the latter was not indifferent to the fate of the war, but regarded the revolution within as a guarantee (though not a prerequisite) of victory in the war without.

So in retrospect, I wrote that the position on the Sino-Japanese War taken by Trotsky and followed by us can more properly be called 'revolutionary victoryism' than defeatism.

(Here I won't touch on the differences among Chinese Trotskyists on this question.)[13]

What I have said should, I think, be enough to disprove Tang Baolin's charge that the Chinese Trotskyists objectively served the interests of Japanese imperialism.

Trotsky and the Chinese Trotskyists' policy of victoryism was thought out from the fact that the Sino-Japanese War was part of the aftermath of the defeat of the Revolution of 1925–7; it was premised in the assumption that the corrupted and compromising Guomindang régime could not really defeat

---

12   Trotsky 1976 [1937], pp. 567 and 569–70.
13   For a discussion of this issue, see Wang Fan-hsi 1991, Chapter 11.

the Japanese, and that the surest, safest way of doing so was to organise the workers and peasants under their own political banner. (After all, that part of the Guomindang led by Wang Jingwei had stopped resisting and become Japanese puppets, while the wing led by Chiang Kai-shek had all along vacillated and sought better conditions under which to surrender.)

Tang Baolin's other charge, that the Chinese Trotskyists adopted a defeatist policy towards the Chinese Communist Party during the civil war of 1945–1949, is wholly without substance.

The National Assembly

Tang Baolin fails to grasp why the Chinese Trotskyists called for a National Assembly after 1927. According to him, we Trotskyists from the very beginning suffered under the illusion that the Chinese Communist Party could conquer power by mobilising the urban workers in a movement for a National Assembly. The truth is, however, that the Trotskyists raised the call for a National Assembly only in the wake of the defeat of the revolution in 1927, at a time when Stalin (contending that the revolution was still in the ascendant) was calling for soviets and armed risings.

According to Tang Baolin, the Chinese Trotskyists' concentration on the urban proletariat and the call for a National Assembly led them to ignore the struggle of the peasants; as a result, their project was doomed. Mao Zedong, in contrast, succeeded because he led the peasants in armed struggle under the banner of the Chinese Soviet. Tang seems not to know that in 1928, Mao complained that because the Chinese Communist Party lacked democratic slogans, he was unable to rouse the peasants. He also forgets that in 1937, at the time of the Second United Front, the Party started campaigning for a National Assembly.

'Slaves of a Foreign Master'

Tang Baolin, conveniently forgetting the role played in the fortunes of the official Party by 'Moscow gold' and foreigners like Sneevliet, Borodin, Voitinski, Roy, Pavel Mif, and Otto Braun, attempts to smear the Chinese Trotskyists as 'slaves of a foreign master' on the grounds that, in December 1935, they elected the British-born Frank Glass (alias Li Furen) as secretary-cum-treasurer of their organisation. According to Tang Baolin,

A political party that receives foreign subsidies, and furthermore elects a foreigner as its leader, will scarcely find general acceptance and may even be denounced as 'national traitors', 'capitulationists', 'slaves', 'tools', and the like. Yet the Trotskyists, who see internationalism as their highest principle and world revolution as their mission, consider such behaviour appropriate.

Tang can sustain his thesis that Frank Glass 'led' the Chinese Trotskyists only by ignoring and suppressing my comment, recorded in the conference minutes (which Tang was able to consult), that the job given to Frank Glass should be considered 'technical', not political. The minutes (in English) are quite explicit on this point:

> Chen Chi-chang [Chen Qichang] – During this time it is important that the Secretary[-Treasurer][14] of the Standing Committee should be able to bring about unity between all the members of the committee. Therefore it is better that CFG [Frank Glass] should be the secretary.
>
> Discussion on the character of the secretary – that is whether the secretary is really the political spokesman or whether his tasks are primarily of a technical nature such as writing letters, keeping minutes, and so on.
>
> Wang Ming-yuen [Wang Fanxi] says the position of secretary should be regarded as one for performing technical tasks, and not as one which carries with it the deciding of the political line of the party.[15]

My proposal regarding the position of secretary was approved by all those in attendance at the conference.[16]

We Chinese Trotskyists viewed the post of secretary in much the same way as had the Bolsheviks under Lenin. For the Bolsheviks, it was a position to which no one attached any great importance; it 'could have only a technical character, never political'.[17] The view of the secretaryship as political was a post-Leninist invention of Stalin (the post's first 'political' occupant) and the

---

14 It is clear from the minutes that the post was in fact that of 'secretary-treasurer'. A suggestion by Glass that the two posts be separated was not taken up.
15 Minutes of Meeting of Provisional Committee of the Communist League of China (Bolshevik-Leninists), first meeting of Reconstituted Committee, Tuesday night, 3 December 1935, p. 7.
16 The minutes bear out this statement.
17 Trotsky 1970 [1930], p. 467.

Stalinists. Far from being the Chinese Trotskyists' political leader, Glass was our technical administrator.[18]

In effect, Glass' role during his fifteen months as administrator of the Chinese Trotskyist organisation was twofold. He was our de facto treasurer, a sensible 'technical' appointment, given that he was the main source of our income at the time; and he was our correspondent with, and letter box for, foreign Trotskyists overseas.[19] After Glass left Shanghai, for a short time Jack Belden (who was not himself a Trotskyist but a friend of Glass) took over from Glass this role as letter box. (As far as I remember, I received mail on only one occasion through Belden.)

What would Have Happened if the Revolution of 1925–7 Had Followed the Trotskyist Line?

According to Tang Baolin, the Chinese Revolution of 1925–7 would have been defeated under whatever leadership, even if it had followed the advice of Trotsky. The reaction, including the right wing of the Guomindang (says Tang Baolin), was too strong, the Chinese Communist Party was too immature, and the revolution as a whole had not yet ripened. So the disputes between Stalin and Trotsky regarding the Chinese Revolution were a tragi-comedy, or a farce; and the child of those disputes – the Chinese Trotskyist movement – was disfigured and disabled.

Neither I nor Tang Baolin has any way of knowing how the revolution would have ended if its leaders had pursued other policies. However, even if the Party had suffered a defeat under Trotsky's political line, the perspective before it after the defeat would have been quite different. Its members are unlikely to have felt disillusioned and deceived, as did many after the events of 1927; and the Party might have effected the switch to independence and opposition more quickly, more smoothly, more confidently, and at less cost in human life. (How many excellent revolutionaries died in the period of adventurism!) The re-entry into politics of the working class might have been sooner; under new revolutionary democratic slogans, the Party might have been able more easily to rebuild its organisation in the cities.

---

18   In a letter to Wang Fanxi dated 9 April 1995, Tang Baolin concedes that Glass' function was 'technical', not political, and that he, Tang, had failed to take account of Wang's comment in 1936 to that effect.

19   Cf. Hirson 2003.

In the case of a Japanese invasion, and Chinese involvement in world war, the workers, peasants, and urban toilers might have played a more independent role and brought about the Third Chinese Revolution with less pain and sacrifice.

Most important of all, the new régime that issued from such a revolution would not have been despotic and bureaucratic, but would have been genuinely internationalist, more inclined towards the proletariat, less influenced by peasant prejudice, and prepared to tolerate freedom of thought and creative activity of all sorts.

China would have been spared preposterous, whimsical, and highly destructive schemes like the People's Communes and the Great Proletarian Cultural Revolution.

In a word, there would have been greater democracy and freedom both in the building of a new China and in people's individual lives.

'Magnanimity' and 'Ingratitude'

On 22 December 1952, all the Trotskyists in China were arrested and put in prison. Tang Baolin says, 'The People's Government of China adopted a different policy towards those that it arrested from that followed by the Government of the USSR. It did not physically destroy them, but educated and reformed them, and treated them humanely'. He singles out the cases of Yin Kuan and Zheng Chaolin, who were (he says) frequently sent by the prison authorities for health check-ups and given better food – one or two shreds of meat three times a week.

Yet, says Tang, those Trotskyists who fled to Hong Kong before and after the Chinese Communist Party took over the whole of the country continued their anti-communist counter-revolutionary activities. As examples of such activities, Tang specifically mentions my memoirs and my study on Mao Zedong thought.[20] 'These two books', he writes, 'summed up Wang's and the Chinese Trotskyists' knowledge about Trotskyism and the Chinese Revolution; they also represent the consummation of the attack on Mao thought and the Chinese Communist Party'. Of the revolutionary optimism expressed in my memoirs, Tang writes: 'It would seem that history will continue to play jokes on the Chinese Trotskyists until the very end'.

It is true that Mao and the Maoists dealt with the Trotskyists in a different way from Stalin and his Chinese disciples Wang Ming and Kang Sheng. But the

---

20   Shuang Shan 1973.

difference is of degree, not principle. To persecute political oppositionists is incompatible with bourgeois democracy, let alone socialist democracy. To put political oppositionists in prison for twenty-seven years can never be called 'humane', however well they are treated.

I don't know how many Chinese Trotskyists died in jail, but many did, either by execution or owing to the intolerable conditions under which they were forced to live. I do know that my two nephews committed suicide, one in prison, the other immediately after his release, and that the young Trotskyist Lian Zhengyan was shot in Wenzhou.

But Tang Baolin is spellbound by the magnanimity of the oppressor and aghast at the ingratitude of the victims.

PART 18

Obituaries

Obituaries

All these obituaries were published in newspapers, in either a Western language or Chinese (or both). They are here reproduced from manuscripts in the editor's personal archive, except where stated otherwise.

Oration at the Funeral of Mr [Chen] Duxiu (1879–1942) by Gao Yuhan[1]

Place: School in Jiangjin,[2] Deng's villa

Time: Noon, 1 June, Year 31 of the Republic [1942]

Source: Wang Shudi et al., eds, 1982, vol. 2, pp. 406–10. This memorial address was first published in Dagong bao, Chongqing, 4 June 1942.

I would like to express on behalf of [my dead friend] Mr Duxiu and his family and relatives sincere thanks to the venerable Mr Deng Chanqiu, a leader of the Jiangjin gentry, and his respectable nephew Mr [Deng] Xiekang [for all that they have done for Mr Duxiu]. At the same time, and in the same way, let me thank Mr Sun Maochi, Chairman of the Board of Directors of Jiangjin's Yucai Middle School, and other gentlemen. When news that Mr Chen had fallen ill reached town, Mr Deng Xiekang, together with Mr Zhou Puling and me, went down to the village to pay Mr Chen a visit. After that, Mr Xiekang discussed with me what to do with Mr Chen's remains; he resolutely assumed responsibility, without waiting for anyone to ask him to do so. After returning to Jiangjin, he rushed around attending to Mr Chen's affairs, leaving himself little time to eat or sleep. He arranged the funeral vestments and the coffin to everyone's perfect satisfaction. In the meantime, some difficulties that arose concerning the procurement of the coffin were solved only after Mr Deng's tireless pleading and persuasion. The venerable Chan[qiu] is already more than seventy years old and living in retirement at Baisha Village, but as soon as he heard the sad news

---

1 Gao Yuhan (Kao Yü-han), an old friend of Chen's who had studied in Germany, was a writer and author of *Baihua shuxin* ('Letters in the vernacular'), a veteran revolutionary, and a political instructor at the Whampoa (Huangpu) Military Academy. (See also Biographical List.)
2 Jiangjin is a town near Chongqing, Sichuan province; Chen Duxiu lived in the countryside outside Jiangjin between 1938 and his death in 1942.

of the death of Mr Chen, he hurried to Jiangjin, and, after setting foot ashore, rushed without resting to Mr Chen's death bed at Heshanping to express his condolences. Regarding the grave, Mr Xiekang had already generously decided to turn his newly built villa – Kang Garden, situated at the side of Peach Tree Forest outside the Great West Gate – into Mr Chen's graveyard, and the venerable Chan has readily assented. At the same time, Mr Sun Maochi, Chairman of the Board of Directors of Yucai Middle School, representing the Middle School, generously offered to reserve a suitable plot of land in the school grounds in which to bury Mr Chen's coffin and remains; and to erect in the vicinity of the grave several buildings in which to display items left behind by the deceased, in order to give people an impression of what he was like while alive. These acts of friendship are born of simple and unaffected sensibility of a kind that cannot be won by force; in the modern age, such noble acts and feelings are as rare as the feather of a phoenix or the horn of a unicorn, and would have been rare too even in antiquity. Now that it has finally been settled that Mr Chen's grave will be in the grounds of Mr Xiekang's villa, things have happened as if predetermined: Mr Chen lived for four years in Jiangjin, during which time, the two Messrs Deng – uncle and nephew – of all the gentlemen in Jiangjin became his most intimate friends. Mr Chen several times went walking with the venerable Chan in the Peach Tree Forest; last spring, Mr and Mrs Chen, together with Mr [Zhou] Fuling and me, came to inspect the blossom and to gaze down at the great Yangtse River; we were captivated by both trees and water – so great was our delight that we lingered on, forgetting to return. Who could have guessed that the place where Mr Chen came to delight his eyes would also be the place where he closed them in eternal sleep? Were Mr Chen conscious in his grave, he would experience complete satisfaction. And the noble and generous example of uncle and nephew Deng will last forever!

But it is my belief, shared, I am sure, by all, that Mr Chen, by lying here, will at the very least not sully the worthy owner's pure soil, or fail to live up to the majesty of the mountains and rivers of this place. Mr Duxiu is at home everywhere, and naturally an adherent of the view that 'my bones may be buried no matter where among the green mountains'. Now that he sleeps peacefully here, it can truly be said that he rests in the right place. Considering the [grandiose] outlook he ever held, the [miserable] conditions he was recently forced to live in, and his perspective on the [present national and international] situation, we might console ourselves with the thought that he left the world at the proper time. In the moment before he passed away, I am sure that his conscience was completely clear. At this point, friends present will naturally turn their thoughts to the question of how to appraise Mr Chen's life. In regard to his learning, his cause [as a revolutionary], and his entire personality, and on the basis of his posthumous works and the inerasable imprint that he has left on the history of Chinese politics, culture, thought, and social movements over nearly forty years, people in the future will certainly make a fair appraisal of him. As for me, I want to raise three points that, as a crude sketch, will perhaps help Mr Duxiu's mourners here today understand what made him the man he was.

First, I wish to look at Mr Duxiu's position in the history of culture and thought. We must absolutely avoid [approaching any historical figure by distorting – not to say fabricating – his or her achievements, by either] exaggerating or belittling [them]. However, one thing is undeniable, namely, that during the May Fourth period it was he who solemnly raised the two slogans:

> Support Mr De (Democracy);
> Support Mr Sai (Science).

In those days, when Liang Qichao,[3] Zhang Junmai [Carsun Chang],[4] and others were zealously advocating metaphysics and the Beiyang warlord government[5] was fighting its last struggles, Mr Duxiu's sharp eyes had already seen what China's people and China's cultural and intellectual world urgently required; that is, he had already fully realised that if China was to free itself from the two heavy weights of warlordism and colonialism and to build an independent and free nation, politically it required democracy, while culturally he urgently called for science so that the country could be industrialised. Ever since, everything that we have struggled for, including the war of resistance that the government is urging us to wage, take as their guiding principle these two slogans. So Mr Duxiu's position in the history of culture and of thought is not difficult to understand.

---

3 Liang Qichao (Liang Ch'i-ch'ao) (1873–1929), a journalist, historian, and constitutional monarchist, became leader of the so-called Study Clique after the downfall of the Qing dynasty. In 1919, during the May Fourth Movement, he questioned 'the dream of the omnipotence of science'. In 1923, he supported the conservative view that China should value its own spiritual civilisation.

4 Carsun Chang, a student of Henri Bergson and Rudolf Eucken and founder (in 1934) of the Chinese National Socialist Party (which became the Democratic Socialist Party in 1946), felt that after May Fourth, too many Chinese believed that science could solve all problems. He argued in 1923 that science, being applicable only to dead matter, 'is not able to solve the problem of a view of life', and he questioned the value of a material civilisation achieved by science.

5 During the warlord era (1916–28), Beijing was in the hands of a succession of rival militarist cliques.

Second, I wish to look at Mr Duxiu's position in China's new literary movement. Naturally, the new literary movement was part of the cultural movement, but since the present generation of Chinese young people has not yet completely understood the emergence and development of this movement and its enormous influence on new China, it is worth dwelling on it for a moment. Everyone knows that Messrs Chen Duxiu and Hu Shi were pioneer advocates of the new literary movement, but it is not generally known that Mr Duxiu championed the new literature long before the May Fourth Movement, and even long before the 1911 Revolution.[6] While running the *Anhui baihua bao* ['Anhui vernacular magazine'] in Wuhu,[7] he already made clear his determination to reform Chinese literature. So literary reform was the precursor of the cultural movement, the political movement, and the social movement. At the time of Germany's fifteenth-century religious movement (actually, a minor part of Europe's great social and political movement, which borrowed the outer clothing of religion), Martin Luther's translation of the Bible into spoken German paved the way for Germany's new literary movement. The same thing happened after the importation into China of Buddhist culture in the Wei [220–65] and Jin [265–420] dynasties, when a group of intelligent monks headed by Kumarajiva[8] pioneered translation literature and, by their unprecedented endeavour, cleared away the fog of the classical written language. In the May Fourth Movement, Mr Duxiu and others resolutely took upon themselves the task of reforming written Chinese, and thereby simply met the new demands that had arisen in China at that time. Although some people in those days considered it somewhat extreme to wield one's pen furiously and declare war on the old literature, actually and ideologically this sort of reform was a movement for revolution. When revolutionaries storm the imperial palace to destroy the *ancien régime*, audacity and ruthlessness are indispensable. Of course, one must not forget in discussing China's new literary movement the pioneering achievements of Mr Liang Rengong,[9] who after the Reform Movement of 1898 courageously wrote articles using Europeanised sentence constructions, strove to import the whole range of Japanese and Western

---

6 The revolution under Sun Yat-sen that overthrew the Qing dynasty and inaugurated the Chinese Republic.
7 The actual name of this journal was *Anhui suhua bao* (also meaning 'Anhui vernacular magazine'), not *Anhui baihua bao*; it was published in 1904.
8 Kumarajiva, born in Central Asia to an Indian Lather, was captured by a Chinese expedition around 382 AD and taken to China, where he headed a major project to translate Buddhist scriptures into Chinese.
9 That is, Liang Qichao.

scientific and cultural names and technical terms, and transplanted Japanese and Western style into Chinese literature; in the initial stages of China's new literary movement, he played an undeniably enlightening and pioneering role. But only Chen Duxiu and Hu Shizhi laid the foundations on a grand scale for the founding of a new literary universe. Moreover, Hu Shizhi received his professorial appointment at Beijing University due to the strenuous efforts of Chen Duxiu. That gives us some idea of Mr Duxiu's position in China's new literary movement.

Third, I wish to look at Mr Duxiu the man. It is well-known that thinkers or writers who want in the course of their life's struggle to maintain an absolute balance between academic creation and moral integrity must have the determination and courage to sacrifice themselves for the truth, a spirit that manifests itself above all in the ability to endure poverty and hardship. Thirty years ago, Mr Duxiu, baggage and umbrella slung across his shoulder, scoured north and south of the rivers Yangtse and Huai in search of revolutionary comrades to prepare to overthrow the Qing and establish a republic. Wang Mengzou,[10] an old and lifelong friend of Mr Duxiu, had opened a bookshop in Wuhu and secretly maintained relations with the revolutionaries. One day, Mr Duxiu turned up, bag in one hand and umbrella in the other. Mr Wang said, 'All I have to eat here are two meals of gruel a day, life's really hard'. 'Two meals of gruel a day? That's great', replied Mr Duxiu, drily. So he stayed on, and spent every day in the room above the bookshop editing the *Anhui Vernacular Magazine* and making propaganda for the revolution; that was in the thirtieth year [that is, 1904] of the Guangxu reign [1875–1908]. After the defeat of the second revolution (against Yuan [Shikai]),[11] Mr Bo Liewu[12] withdrew from Anqing,[13] so Mr Duxiu fled to Shanghai, where he lived in Yuyang Terrace, in the French Settlement; there he edited the early *Qingnian* ['Youth'] (the forerunner of *Xin qingnian*). He was still eating two meals of gruel a day, but he never once tried to borrow money from his friends; for in matters of taking money from or giving it to others, he was extremely circumspect and stringent. As for Mr Duxiu's second virtue, I would say that he was wholly indifferent

---

10 For Wang Mengzou, see the Biographical List.
11 In 1913, Sun Yat-sen, leader of the Guomindang and architect of the destruction of the Qing dynasty, tried to regroup his revolutionary supporters to overthrow the increasingly dictatorial régime of Yuan Shikai, president of the new republic. This 'second revolution' was quickly defeated.
12 Another name of Bo Wenwei, the first revolutionary governor of Anhui province.
13 The capital at the time of Anhui province, where Bo Liewu was governor.

to death. I remember that after the defeat of the second revolution, when he was fleeing from Anqing to Wuhu, he was captured by troops of the Wuhu garrison. This military man [the commander of the garrison] had originally stood alongside Bo Liewu under the banner of opposition to Yuan Shikai, but for some reason he'd fallen out with Bo; now he was venting his anger on Mr Duxiu. He'd already issued a notice announcing that Mr Duxiu would be shot. Mr Duxiu coolly urged him, 'If you're going to shoot me, then get on with it'. The execution was averted at the last moment through the strenuous efforts of Mr Duxiu's friends Liu Shuya, Fan Hongyan, and Zhang Zigang,[14] who intervened to secure his release. Later, [in 1932,] after Mr Duxiu had been arrested in Shanghai by the Guomindang government, he fell soundly asleep while under police escort on the way to Nanjing, and did not wake until the train arrived in Nanjing the following morning, as if it were simply a day like any other.[15] This calm composure and fearlessness in the face of mortal danger were typical of the man. Unless one understands this moral essence of Mr Duxiu, one will fail to understand his entire personality and the worth of his legacy to us in the field of Chinese cultural history. Finally, I solemnly repeat: We must absolutely avoid [distorting a person's achievements, by either] exaggerating or belittling [them].

Wu Jingru (1907–79) by *Wang Fanxi*

Wu Jingru died in Shanghai on 15 October 1979, just three months and ten days after being moved out from a labour reform camp. She was first arrested by the CCP authorities in December 1952, together with her husband Zheng Chaolin and two to three hundred other Chinese Trotskyists. After serving five years in prison, she was released in 1957. She was crippled as a result of severe rheuma-

---

14 A group of influential people in Wuhu at that time.
15 Chen had been arrested on 15 October 1932, together with the entire Trotskyist leadership then still at large, in Shanghai's International Settlement, whence he was extradited to the Chinese authorities; this was his fourth (and last) arrest. It was widely believed at the time that he would be sentenced to death by the court in Nanjing, where he was sent to stand trial. The Guomindang organised a big propaganda campaign to call for his execution. At his trial, Chen calmly justified working for the overthrow of the Guomindang Government, on the grounds that the government had failed to defend China against Japanese aggression and had suppressed basic rights and freedoms. 'I rebelled not against the nation but against the Guomindang', he told the court. Liberals and other non-Communist radicals flocked to Chen's support. Probably as a result, he was sentenced not to death but to thirteen years in prison.

tism and malnutrition, and found herself entirely severed from relatives and friends. With nowhere to go she would have died of cold and starvation in the street had her old landlady not given her shelter and had old friends in Hong Kong not remitted a small sum of money so she could maintain her miserable living.

In the so-called Cultural Revolution she was once again thrown into distress. A convicted and imprisoned 'counter-revolutionary' and wife of a leader of a 'counter-revolutionary gang', she was the target of repeated 'criticism and struggle' by vicious Maoists and ignorant and deceived Red Guards. By that time, she was paralysed and nearly blind, yet these 'heroes' of the CCP showed no 'soft-heartedness' towards the disabled old woman. From time to time, they dragged her from the attic of a dilapidated building down to the street, where they insulted, scolded, and beat her. After each 'criticism', according to a witness, Wu Jingru was carried back to her room by a young boy, the son of her landlady, who knew her and, having been under her education since childhood, reverently called her granny and was deeply convinced that she was a good person, a revolutionary, not at all a 'counter-revolutionary', as accused.

In 1972, when the Cultural Revolution had reached its finale, a change came about in Jingru's ordeal. By that time, Zheng Chaolin and some other Trotskyists were transferred from ordinary prison to a labour camp in Shanghai's Pudong district, and Wu Jingru was ordered to move in with her husband. She remained there for seven years until 5 June this year [1979], when Zheng Chaolin and twelve other Trotskyists were allowed to move into a civilian house in a suburb of Shanghai and restored to 'full citizenship'. For the first time in twenty seven years, Jingru could hope to lead a more or less normal life, for example to resume correspondence with friends and re-establish contact with relatives. We were hoping that from now on this long-suffering old revolutionary would have the chance to taste some belated warmth, as an ordinary human being. Yet alas, the cruel vicissitude of fate deprived her of that chance.

As her comrades, we felt unlimited distress. To Comrade Zheng Chaolin, her lifelong companion, we send our unbounded sympathy and condolence.

But more important than simply expressing condolence, we must introduce Wu Jingru's noble, unspotted life of to our young comrades and friends.

She joined the Chinese Communist Party in 1927, while participating in the surging struggle of the working masses in Wuhan during the second Chinese revolution. She worked shoulder to shoulder with Zheng Chaolin. They fell in love during this joint struggle and later married. After the defeat of the revolution, she secretly went to Shanghai to engage in clandestine revolutionary activities. When the CCP split in 1930 into a right wing (the Stalinists) and a left wing (the Trotskyists), she joined the latter. In 1931, she was arrested for the first time in her life by the Guomindang together with Chaolin, but was released after a short period of imprisonment. After that, as a Trotskyist, she devoted herself to revolutionary educational work, in particular to the education of women and working-class children, until her arrest by the CCP's secret police in 1952.

As a revolutionary, such a life may seem ordinary. No important exploits or famous writings can be ascribed to her. Neither in the CCP nor in the Left Opposition, neither while working within the organisation nor among ordinary Chinese, did she acquire any title or hold any office from which to give direction. For several decades, she worked and fought as a rank-and-file soldier of the revolution. However, she was born with certain leadership skills, for she was a good administrator, as she showed by running schools as a schoolmistress. (Comrades always referred to her, half-jokingly, as 'teacher', without mentioning her name.) Nearly everybody who was close to her or worked with her saw her as an elder sister or mother and looked to her for direction. Yet she preferred to remain within the rank-and-file. This was because she disliked the way that even revolutionaries, especially when the Wang Ming group dominated the CCP, tried to climb the hierarchy of the party by any means available and were active only when they could occupy leading posts. Like her companion Zheng Chaolin, she was completely free of all personal ambition and uncompromisingly opposed to bureaucratism and careerism.

Wu Jingru never behaved like a heroine, nor did she show off as a militant. She was extremely gentle, yet she was endowed with extraordinary perseverance and bravery. Having fixed on her course and chosen her road in life, she went her way unfalteringly, despite hardships and difficulties. Since first meeting her in 1931, I have never once seen her determination waver, nor did I ever see her regret a decision. All along she walked the road she had chosen, until exhaustion and until the very end of her life.

In fact, such an ordinary life is quite unordinary, and is even extraordinary.

The perseverance and faithfulness with which Wu Jingru devoted herself to the revolution were also characteristic of her private life. (These two sides of her life were indivisible). She was born into a very rich family in Yunnan, so she was not without a place to retreat to. She could have returned to a comfortable life any time she wished. When the revolution was defeated in 1927, innumerable young men and women who had joined the revolution went home as 'returned prodigals' to compromise with their non-revolutionary or counter-revolutionary parents, but Jingru was not among them. She chose to risk her life by continuing her revolutionary activities in Shanghai, under Chiang Kai-shek's white terror. After 1931, the Chinese Trotskyists lived and worked under terrible repression. Quite a few, no longer able bear the misery and hardship, deserted. If Jingru had put her personal comfort and safety above the interests of the cause, she too would have gone home. After her release from prison and Zheng Chaolin's sentencing to fifteen years, she had reason enough to return to a life of luxury and security. But again, she made an unselfish decision. She decided to remain in Shanghai to serve as an intermediary between those comrades in prison and those still free to carry on their revolutionary activities. Finally, in 1952 and the years that followed, when the Chinese Trotskyists were rounded up and put in prison, she could have alleviated her misery by complying with the authorities and divorcing her 'counter-revolutionary' husband and coming to terms with her family. But she refused all these temptations and preferred to live a life of poverty and suffer the insults and beatings. Thus she stuck unswervingly to the revolutionary cause and awaited the return of the companion she loved so deeply.

It is quite natural that her death caused profound grief among those who knew her. It is impossible to imagine what a blow it was to Zheng Chaolin, her lifelong companion and comrade. We can only hope that this bravest of men, who emerged from numberless physical and moral tortures with a triumphant smile, will also bear up against this blow, which was undoubtedly the heaviest.

The older generation of Chinese Trotskyists have scarcely anything to leave to their younger comrades that could be proudly regarded as a legacy. However, the revolutionary spirit that was comparatively common among our comrades and outstandingly represented by Wu Jingru – the spirit of consistency, perseverance, contentment with personal poverty, and satisfaction with the status of a rank-and-file soldier of the revolution – such a spirit is, I think, worth preserving and copying. It is a guarantee of the final triumph of revolutionary Marxism both in China and throughout the world. In mourning Comrade Wu Jingru, I would therefore like to commend this tradition of Chinese Trotskyism to the younger generation of revolutionary Marxists in the world.

Frank Glass (Li Furen) (1901–88) by *Wang Fanxi*

After a long illness, Frank Glass (better known in the world Trotskyist movement as Li Furen) passed away on 21 March 1988, in Los Angeles.

Frank Glass was a true internationalist and a revolutionary Communist. During his long life he played important roles at different times in various countries – South Africa, China, and the US – and in the Fourth International.

Frank hardly ever spoke of himself. He was too modest to talk about his contributions and too honest to exaggerate his own importance. So it is not easy, even for someone like me, who knew Frank for half a century and worked together with him for nearly a decade, to describe his long and honourable life in detail.

He was born in Birmingham, England, in 1901. He spent his boyhood in London and went to South Africa in his late teens. As far as I know, he did not enjoy a good schooling. However, he educated himself to become a brilliant journalist. He served briefly in the British army at the end of the First World War and was influenced by the Russian Revolution. Back in South Africa, he joined the Social Democratic Federation, but before long he and other comrades broke away to found the Industrial Socialist League. In 1921, together with many other supporters of the Third International, he became a founder of the Communist Party of South Africa (CPSA). He attended the Party's Inauguration Congress (21 July to 1 August). According to Henry R. Pike's *History of Communism in South Africa*, the twenty-year-old delegate 'C. Frank Glass told a reporter present that the moves in South Africa to stop the Communist organisation are doomed to failure and the doom of the capitalist class is sealed'.

At the Second Congress of the CPSA (which opened on 28 April 1923), Frank was elected as organiser of the Party. In December 1924, at the Third Congress, he led an opposition group fighting against the Party's opportunist right wing. Thereafter he spent most of his time and energy leading the South African Association of Employees' Organisations (later renamed the South African Trades Union Congress). He had long sympathised with the Soviet Union's Left Opposition and became South Africa's first Trotskyist in 1928.

In 1929 or 1930, Frank left for the US, where he met J. Cannon, M. Shachtman, Arne Swabeck, and other pioneers of American Trotskyism. Then he proceeded to the Far East. He was denied entry to Japan and he finally settled down in Shanghai, probably in 1931.

Frank did not immediately get into contact with the Chinese Trotskyists. By that time the Chinese Trotskyists, having achieved unification at their First National Congress (1–3 May 1931), had plunged from the heights into the abyss as a result of Guomindang repression. Successive arrests of their leaders led them into panic and confusion. Frank earned his living in Shanghai as a journalist. He independently continued his revolutionary activity, mainly among Western intellectuals sympathetic to the Chinese Revolution. He won some to Trotskyism, including Harold Isaacs (who later wrote *The Tragedy of the Chinese Revolution*) and Alex Buchman, who served as one of Leon Trotsky's security guards in Mexico ten years later.

Frank's direct participation in the activities of the Chinese Trotskyists began in 1933. Frank played a rather important role in restoring and maintaining our underground organisation. He was elected to the Provisional Central Committee (as Secretary-Treasurer) at a conference of representatives of

Shanghai comrades in the winter of 1935. As a foreigner working under conditions of Guomindang repression, Frank's contribution to the movement was inevitably restricted. Financially, he and his wife Grace supplied nearly all the needs of our printing plant and the living expenses of the two comrades who operated it. Politically, it was through Frank that the Chinese comrades maintained relations with Trotsky in Norway (and later in Mexico) and with the centre of our world movement in Paris.

In May 1937, Frank left China to visit Trotsky in Mexico and discuss the Chinese situation with him on the eve of the Sino-Japanese War. He took with him a resolution drafted by me and adopted by the Provisional Central Committee. On the basis of Frank's report and this revolution, Trotsky and Frank held a long and important talk on 11 August 1937. (The record of this discussion is published in *Leon Trotsky on China*.) After several months in New York, where he worked with American comrades, Frank returned to China in the summer of 1938. His main concern was to achieve Trotsky's wish to get Chen Duxiu (then facing a smear campaign by the CCP and under constant threat of assassination by the Stalinists) out of China and into safety overseas. Trotsky wanted Chen Duxiu to play the same role for the Fourth International as the veteran Japanese socialist Katayama had once played for the Third International. But for various reasons, Trotsky's and Frank's plan to 'save Chen Duxiu' came to nothing.

Frank finally left China on the eve of the attack on Pearl Harbor that started the Pacific War between China and the US. He spent the next few years in New York. As far as I know, he helped run the affairs of the Fourth International, which had moved from Europe to the US as a result of the Nazi occupation of France. He wrote much, particularly about China. We resumed our correspondence after the Japanese surrender in 1945. Frank would very much have liked to return to China and rejoin his old friends, but his dream was never realised. He moved from New York to Los Angeles. He continued to watch developments in the Chinese Revolution, but he paid more and more attention to the problems of the Philippines – for a long time he edited a magazine for Filipinos.

After the victory of the CCP and the persecution of the Trotskyists in China, I restored contact with Frank. We exchanged opinions on nearly every turn in CCP policy. We saw eye to eye on most issues and disagreed on some. We remained very good comrades and friends.

Among Frank's virtues as a Communist internationalist and revolutionary, first and foremost was his complete lack of personal ambition. He was man of conviction: he had his own opinion on nearly every major political question. Once he had formed an opinion, he fought for it stubbornly. However, he was never opinionated and still less self-serving. He fought only on issues, never on personalities. In internal struggles he was magnanimous in victory and graceful in defeat. For example, when he and Arne Swabeck formed a bloc against the majority in the US Socialist Workers Party (SWP) on the question of China's 'People's Communes' and were defeated, Swabeck went over to Maoism but Frank remained a principled opponent of Stalinism-Maoism.

Because of old age and illness, Frank never wrote to me about his attitude to developments in the SWP (to which he belonged) over the years. But one thing I know for sure: he would never have agreed with the position that the theory of permanent revolution has been proved 'out of date' by new developments.

Frank's last wish, according to a friend who attended him during his illness, was to live to see Trotsky restored to a place of honour in the Soviet Union. Sadly, his wish was not granted. Sooner or later, however, not only Trotsky but all Trotskyists will be rehabilitated, not just in the Soviet Union but in China too, and in all those 'socialist' countries where Trotskyists have been persecuted.

Lou Guohua (1906–95) by *Wang Fanxi*

Lou Guohua was born in 1906 in Yuyao, Zhejiang province. He joined the CCP, via the Communist Youth League, in 1927. He accepted Trotskyism in 1929 and joined Our Word, China's first Trotskyist organisation, in 1929. He was elected one of the six delegates of the Our Word group to the Founding Conference of the Left Opposition of the CCP in May 1931, but failed to attend the conference because his wife gave birth to a daughter on the day that the conference opened. He was arrested by Chiang Kai-shek's political police together with all the members of the newly elected Executive Committee (save Chen Duxiu) nineteen days after the end of the conference, and sent to prison for six years.

Freed from prison in 1935, he continued his revolutionary work in the Trotskyist movement in Shanghai: from 1935 to 1937, under Chiang Kai-shek's Guomindang; from 1937 to 1945, under the Japanese; and from 1945 to 1949, again under the Guomindang. In Shanghai, he founded Chunye chuban she ('Spring Swallow Publishers'), which published Trotskyist books, including translations of *The Revolution Betrayed, Problems of the Chinese Revolution*, and *History of the Russian Revolution* as well as a journal called *Dongxiang* ('Living Age') of which the American Trotskyist Alexander Buchman was the official publisher. In 1949, he left for Hong Kong, shortly before the Maoist army entered Shanghai.

Lou Guohua was forced to spend the rest of his life in Hong Kong, where his main activity was to publish the literature of our movement. In the late 1950s, when Trotskyists were deported from the colony and Trotskyist literature was suppressed, he ventured to establish Xinda chuban she ('Sincere Press'), which subsequently published a dozen or so books, some of them translations. He contributed to various legally published magazines in the colony articles criticising the policies of the Maoists. It was mainly through his contacts and influence that those Hong Kong youth who in the 1970s inclined to anarchism (and gathered around Qiling niandai, 'the Society of Seventies') were won to Trotskyism and launched the Revolutionary Marxist League, of which he was a leading member.

Throughout his adult life, Lou was a professional revolutionary, but at the same time he was a revolutionary with a profession. That is not to say that he was an amateur or part-time revolutionary. It simply means that he always had a job at the same time as working for the revolution and, in particular, helping other, full-time revolutionaries financially. All genuinely revolutionary organisations in poor countries, and especially the Chinese Trotskyist organisation, have known financial hardship of a sort that comrades in the developed countries, and even young Chinese radicals in present-day Hong Kong, can hardly imagine. There were no donations, no dues, and no contributions whatsoever. Lou Guohua acted as a one-man MOPR[16] for the Chinese Trotskyists. He usually worked as a salaried accountant. He was exceedingly frugal, and saved from his income to help other comrades. For example, when the woman comrade Li Cailian died in the winter of 1936, Lou buried her. Almost every member of the earlier generations of our comrades was in one way or another his beneficiary.

Lou Guohua's elder cousin, Lou Shiyi, came to Communism at around the same time as Guohua. Shiyi remained a Stalinist and Maoist, but his relations with Guohua stayed cordial. In recent years, Shiyi, who became a senior editor in Beijing under the CCP, greatly appreciated Guohua's writings about Lu Xun, a giant of Chinese twentieth-century literature.

For apart from being the publisher of the Chinese Trotskyist movement, Lou Guohua was a brilliant author in his own right. Born in Yuyao, adjacent to Shaoxing, the birthplace of Lu Xun, he was a distinguished authority on Lu Xun's work, about which he wrote numerous articles and an important book.[17] In these writings, he exposed how China's Maoist authorities puffed up Lu Xun in order to obscure the founding role in China's New Culture Movement of 1915–21 played by Chen Duxiu. For though Lu Xun was modern China's best-known essayist and writer, he actually played only a supporting role in

---

16   MOPR is the Russian acronym for the International Organisation for Assisting Revolutionaries set up in the 1920s by the Third International.
17   Yi Ding 1978.

that seminal movement; while Chen Duxiu was renowned as its 'Commander-in-Chief'. But Chen, who went on in 1921 to found the CCP, has been a nonperson since 1931, when he fathered Chinese Trotskyism; so the myth of Lu Xun's role in the movement had to be invented to fill the resulting gap. Lou in his book exposed the falsification by quoting all the relevant evidence. In it, he also exposed the Maoists' slandering of Chen Duxiu in 1938 as an agent of Japan (to match Stalin's slandering of Trotsky as a Hitler agent); and advanced the hypothesis that Lu Xun's supposed 'Letter to the Trotskyists' of 1936, in which the Trotskyist Chen Qichang and his comrades were accused of treacherously taking money from the Japanese, was not dictated, as the Maoists claimed, by Lu Xun (who was above such mud-slinging) but written by the Stalinist Feng Xuefeng. Today, both Lou's theses have been confirmed by new materials published in China. Lou's hunch about the 'Lu Xun letter to the Trotskyists' was recently vindicated by the posthumous publication of an article by Hu Feng, Lu Xun's main disciple and the first victim after 1949 of the Maoists' policy on literature and art.

In Hong Kong, Lou also published *Zhiyanji* ('Speaking frankly'), a book of essays criticising Maoism from a Trotskyist standpoint, and numerous articles on many subjects.

Lou Guohua's death agony lasted two years. Before his final stroke, he lost the power of hearing. After it, he lost the power of speech. Finally, he lost the power of sight. He lapsed into unconsciousness ten days before his death. He is survived by his wife, a daughter, and three sons.

Lou Guohua was the publisher and 'philanthropist' of the Chinese Trotskyist movement. He remained a Trotskyist and a supporter of the Fourth International until his death. He died loved and respected by the younger generation of Hong Kong radicals.

Zheng Chaolin (1901–98) by *Wang Fanxi*

Zheng Chaolin, a veteran of the Chinese Communist Party (CCP) and of the Chinese Trotskyist movement, died on 1 August 1998, in Shanghai. He devoted his entire life to the cause of the liberation of the Chinese workers and peasants, and yet his achievement was far from restricted to the revolution.

Zheng was extremely versatile; his talents were numerous and many sided. He was at once a writer, a poet, an historian and linguist, and a translator. His achievements were not only numerous but exemplary. In all respects he avoided a superficial approach and probed deeply into the essence of things, assiduously perfecting his skills and knowledge.

Naturally, he was first and foremost a faithful and unyielding revolutionary. His efforts and achievements in other fields took as their keynote his revolutionary thinking, and were imbued with his revolutionary spirit. Therefore I shall restrict myself in this obituary to writing a brief introduction to his life as a revolutionary.

Zheng Chaolin was born in Zhangping in Fujian Province in 1901, and as a boy received a traditional Chinese education. In 1919 he went to France as part of the Work-Study Programme (under which young Chinese students financed their studies by working part-time in French industry), and came under the influence of Western thought, particularly the Russian Revolution.

As a result, he gradually abandoned his attachment to the philosophy of Confucius and Mencius and even of Laozi and Zhuangzi and embraced the ideas propagated by Chen Duxiu and his co-thinkers, who advocated democracy and science. Shortly afterwards he embraced Marxism, and very soon progressed from thought to action.

In June 1922, when some young Chinese Marxists living in Europe held a meeting in Paris at which they set up the Youth Communist Party, Zheng Chaolin was among the eighteen delegates, who included Zhou Enlai, Zhao Shiyan, and Yin Kuan. In 1923, he was selected to go to Russia to study at Moscow's University for the Toilers of the East.

In July 1924, when the CCP urgently needed cadres as a result of the rapid development of the revolutionary situation in China, he was sent back to China together with Chen Yannian and others. He worked in the Propaganda Department of the Central Committee, edited party journals, drafted internal educational materials and external propaganda materials, and translated Bukharin's *ABC of Communism* while at the same time teaching at the party school, that is, Shanghai University.

From 1925 to 1927, when the Chinese Revolution grew apace, he participated in the famous May Thirtieth Movement and in the second and third Shanghai workers' risings. After Chiang Kai-shek's bloody coup of 12 April 1927, Zheng went with the Central Committee of the CCP to the Wuhan, where he took part in the party's Fifth Congress. After the Congress, he was appointed head of Propaganda Department of the Hubei Provincial Committee.

After the final defeat of the revolution, he took part in the party's famous 7 August Conference, and soon afterward secretly moved back to Shanghai with the new Central Committee and took charge of the new party organ *Bolshevik*, as its chief editor.

In 1928, he went to Fujian to reorganise party affairs in the province. In 1929, he married comrade Liu Jingzhen. Not long afterwards, he was arrested for the first time by the Guomindang. Fortunately, his identity was not discovered, and after just forty days he was freed from prison as a result of the secret intervention of the party.

Between 1929 and 1930, he began to come into contact with Leon Trotsky's writings on the Chinese Revolution. Deeply impressed, he turned towards Trotskyism, together with Chen Duxiu and more than eighty veteran party members.

In May 1931, Zheng, Chen Duxiu and three other comrades represented the Proletariat group at the unification conference of the four Trotskyist groups. He was elected to the Central Committee of the new Trotskyist organisation and took charge of its Propaganda Department.

Not long afterwards, he was arrested by the Guomindang authorities and sentenced to fifteen years in prison, though he was freed after just seven years, when the Japanese War broke out.

After his release from prison, he rested and recuperated for a while in a village in Anhui Province together with his wife, and proofread and translated the remaining part of Trotsky's *The Revolution Betrayed* (one third of which had already been translated by two other Trotskyists in Nanjing Prison).

In 1940 he returned to Shanghai, where he joined the leadership of the Chinese Trotskyist organisation and the editorial board of its underground paper, *Struggle*. At the same time, he translated Volumes II and III of Trotsky's *History of the Russian Revolution*.

After the outbreak of a new World War in Western Europe in 1939, differences of opinion grew up in the Chinese Trotskyist leadership, principally in regard to what attitude to adopt to the Chinese resistance once the Anti-Japanese War in China became caught up in the wider war. A protracted dispute ensued, and spread from political to organisational split in 1942.

Chaolin was a leading member of the group later known as the International Workers' Party of China (IWP).

On 7 December 1941 the Japanese army occupied Shanghai's foreign settlements and revolutionary activity directed against the Japanese became extremely difficult. From then until the Japanese defeat in August 1945, Chaolin put his main effort into writing. Apart from editing *Internationalist*, the underground Trotskyist journal, he wrote his memoirs and *Three Travellers*, a collection of political debates in the form of imaginary dialogues.

He also wrote the ABC *of Permanent Revolution* and *A Critical Biography of Chen Duxiu* (uncompleted). To earn a living, he translated some literary works, among them Ignazio Silone's *Fontamara* and a book by André Gide.

From August 1945 to May 1949, from the Japanese surrender and the civil war between the Guomindang and the CCP through to the Communist victory in China, he wrote numerous articles for *New Banner*, a publicly declared

Trotskyist biweekly, which was banned by the Guomindang Government after twenty-one issues.

On the eve of the Communist occupation of Shanghai, the group to which he belonged reorganised as the IWP, which he helped lead. In the meantime, Chaolin systemically researched the social nature of the new China and wrote a pamphlet on the subject, *On State Capitalism*.

In the next two to three years, the IWP continued its activities under Communist rule and extended its influence. As a result, on 22 December 1952, its entire membership, together with all the other Chinese Trotskyists and even sympathisers, were netted up by the Maoist political police.

This development had naturally been foreseen. As a precaution, the other Trotskyist organisation, under Peng Shuzhi, had already transferred its leadership to Hong Kong. The group to which Zheng Chaolin belonged also decided to send someone to set up a liaison station in Hong Kong.

Chaolin himself, however, refused to go and insisted on staying behind in Shanghai, although he was fully aware of the great danger that he faced there. His St Peter-like spirit of self-sacrifice led him not to a martyr's grave but to a further twenty-seven years in prison, including physical and spiritual abuse.

In June 1979, as a result of changes in the leadership of the CCP and in response to calls by people both inside and outside China (in 1979 he was declared a Prisoner of Conscience by Amnesty International), Chaolin and eleven other Trotskyist survivors of Mao's prisons were restored to liberty.

In all, Chaolin spent a total of thirty-four years behind bars under first the Guomindang and then the CCP, thus equalling the record for political imprisonment set by the nineteenth-century French revolutionary Louis Auguste Blanqui.

In the nineteen years between his release in 1979 and his death in August 1998, Chaolin suffered from poor health as a result of his long years in prison, but he refused to live the sort of life that most retired people live, and put enormous effort into reflecting on or writing about events in the world around him.

In those years, he achieved three main things,

First, he helped various historians write true accounts of the Chinese Revolution and the CCP (including Chinese Trotskyism), to correct distortions made, consciously or unconsciously, by official historians, and in particular to refute past slanders and distortions directed by the CCP against Chen Duxiu.

Second, he reflected independently and systematically on fundamental questions in the Chinese and the World Revolution, and put the process and outcome of those reflections into writing in his long essay 'On Cadreism'.

Third, he repeatedly demanded of successive Congresses of the CCP that they rehabilitate the Chinese Trotskyists, formally declare Trotskyists (in China and throughout the world) not to be counter-revolutionaries, and admit that the past suppression of the Chinese Trotskyists had been wrong.

He recorded his efforts in these three regards in writings of more than one million Chinese characters. Unfortunately, so far it has been possible to publish only a small part of them. Even though Chaolin enjoyed personal freedom after 1979 and was even named as a member of the Shanghai Municipal Political Consultative Committee, he continued to be labelled a 'counter-revolutionary' and to suffer discrimination.

In recent years, his memoirs were twice allowed to be published 'internally' (that is, for a restricted readership) and his translation of D. Merezhkovski's *Resurrection of the Gods* was republished, but none of his main works dealing with ideological and political questions, whether written in prison or after his release, has received permission to be published.

Because Chaolin all along resolutely maintained his opposition to Stalinism and Maoism, he has continued to be viewed as a 'counter-revolutionary'. Of his main writings, only his memoirs have appeared in English, in a volume titled *An Oppositionist for Life: Memoirs of the Chinese Revolutionary Zheng Chaolin*, published in the USA in 1997 by Humanities Press. His memoirs were also published in German in 1991 by ISP Verlag Frankfurt, in a translation by Rudolf Segall under the title *Siebzig Jahre Rebell: Erinnerungen eines chinesischen Oppositionellen* ('Seventy years a rebel: Memoirs of a Chinese Oppositionist'). From these writings, foreign friends can get some idea of the life of this remarkable Chinese Marxist-Trotskyist.

Chaolin's wife Liu Jingzhen [alias Wu Jingru] died less than half a year after her and Chaolin's release from a labour camp in June 1979. Their son Frei, born in 1938, died in 1945. In his final years, Chaolin was cared for by his great niece.

Peng Shuzhi (1895–1983) and Chen Bilan (1902–87) by *Cheng Yingxiang and Claude Cadart*

This essay, here slightly adapted, was published in China Perspectives, *no. 17 (1998), by the French Centre for Research on Contemporary China (CEFC).*

Once prominent figures of the Chinese communist movement in its heroic early period (1927–8); of the Chinese Trotskyist movement (1928–47); and then later, in the 1950s, 1960s and 1970s, of international Trotskyism, Peng Shuzhi and Chen Bilan died some years ago – Peng on 28 November 1983, in Los Angeles, aged 88; Chen on 6 September 1987, in Hong Kong, aged 85. Yet it was only recently that we were able to build a tomb worthy of their names in

Montparnasse cemetery. On 31 March 1998, the tomb, a single slab of white stone, was unveiled in the presence of forty guests; on 22 April the two urns containing their ashes were placed inside.

It would have been more natural and desirable for them to have been interred in Shanghai, the city which had brought them together and where their love for each other had begun towards the end of 1925, as they threw themselves into their work. In Shanghai, side by side, they struggled the longest, right up to 1948, to change China's fate and, by extension, that of the world. Up to the end of 1994 we had thought this might be possible. For obvious reasons, we put our plans on hold after the massacre of 6 June 1989, in Beijing, but then the nature of political developments in China in the years which followed brought so much disappointment, anger, and despair that we abandoned any thought of returning their ashes to Shanghai.

Most of their long years of exile in the West had been spent in France, whose cultural traditions, way of life, and turbulent history they especially appreciated. They lived for twenty-two years in France, from 1951 to 1973, before moving to California. So Paris, their favourite city after Shanghai, was chosen as their final resting place.

Peng Shuzhi, Chen Bilan – two names erased from the record or dragged ignominiously through the mud by Stalinists and Maoists worldwide, for years on end; hence the widespread ignorance (although there are other contributing factors) about their lives among contemporary China specialists and popularisers, journalists, and others. This ignorance prompted us, as historians and individuals closely involved with them, to give this account.

Both came from the heart of China. Peng was born in Hunan in 1895 into a family of relatively well-off and well educated peasants in Tonglucun, a village in Shaoyang (then Baoqing). Chen was born in 1902 in Huangpi (near Hankou) in Hubei, into a family of mandarins and local scholars. Politically, they were of the same generation, despite the difference in age.

They were both receptive people, with lively minds, from the earliest age anxious to change the world and themselves by freeing China from its dependence and backwardness and saving themselves from the same fate. Even before they met, they had made names for themselves (although this was far from their intention) in their home provinces, and even nationally, caught up as they were in the powerful currents sweeping China after the trauma of the 1911 Revolution, and even more so by the May Fourth Movement, the patriotic, cultural and ideological process of national self-examination which started in 1915 and ended in 1925. They were 'children of May Fourth', which made its greatest impact on them at the moment it burst like an exploding firework, its most moderate components (who were, let us not forget, the most numerous) joining the Guomindang or shunning politics completely, while its most brilliant and radical constituents opted for Marxism, communism, and Russo-tropism, under the influence of people like Chen Duxiu and Li Dazhao.

In Peng Shuzhi's case, the watershed was 1920: in April, in Wuhan (where five and a half years later he was to meet Chen Bilan), he became a Marxist and communist, shocked by the appalling conditions of modern industry and the living conditions of the workers; in September, in Changsha, he was among the first to join the Hunan communist group (led by He Minfan – still a non-person in official history); and in October, in Shanghai, he entered the Central Group of the Chinese Communists' School of Foreign Languages for a three-month stint studying Russian before leaving for the Soviet Union. For Chen the crucial years were the autumn of 1921 to the summer of 1923. During this period, while still in her early twenties, she was attracted to the more radical expressions of new ideas, helped by a teacher at her school, a member of the Hunan communist group; there she became the leader of a cultural, feminist, and anti-'feudal' movement which scandalised Wuhan and led the school authorities to expel her; there her strengths as a skilled and courageous agitator and propagandist began to show; then she joined the Communist Party, and made trips to Beijing and Shanghai in preparation for her own stay in the Soviet Union.

Peng entered the 'Red Far East' at the beginning of March 1921 and arrived in Moscow in September, after numerous delays and setbacks. He stayed in the Soviet capital, which was also the capital of the Comintern-led world revolution, for almost three years, as a student (1921–3) and teacher (1923–4) in the Chinese section of the University of the Toilers of the East. In these three years (as we shall see), his destiny took shape – all the vicissitudes of his later life, and almost all those of his future companion, Chen Bilan, can be traced back to his prolonged stay in Moscow. He himself later understood this, as we realised in the late sixties in Paris when, barely containing his emotions and sucking on his pipe with more than his usual vigour, he recounted at length, 'objectively', this episode.

After a disappointing year in Beijing and Shanghai doing little, Chen set off for Moscow in the autumn of 1924 just a few weeks after Peng had come back, although the two had yet to meet. In the University of the Toilers of the East and elsewhere she again revealed her leadership qualities, as a feminist for whom feminism was one aspect of liberation, and grew in political maturity. But she stayed only one year rather than the planned three. In the autumn of 1925, along with other young Chinese in Moscow, she was called back to Shanghai by the 'Centre' in the aftermath of the May Thirtieth Movement in 1925. This created the conditions for the Chinese Communist Party (CCP) to assert itself. Peng Shuzhi, number two in the Centre's hierarchy, had played a decisive role in preparing the groundwork for the movement, from the autumn of 1924 to the spring of 1925. Lacking cadres who were both keen and competent, the Centre lost no time in appointing Chen to the Party executive for Jiangsu, Zhejiang, and Anhui, with responsibility for women and workers. In this setting Peng Shuzhi and Chen Bilan got to know each other. An enthusiastic revolutionary, Chen was also an attractive, sensitive, clever woman of remarkable vivacity (which she retained until her death). Peng was good-looking, a young man who exuded intelligence and drive, and whose prestige in the Party soared after 1922.

From then on they remained inseparable except when circumstances kept them apart. They followed the same path, to the end, without compromising their different personalities and sometimes different ideas. They had three children. The last two, both boys, are now dead; their elder sister, Cheng Yingxiang, is a writer of this article.

If we disregard the early years, the lives of Peng Shuzhi and Chen Bilan can be divided into two distinct periods, the communist years (1921–9) and the Trotskyist years (1929–83). In the first period Peng, later backed by Chen, played a leading role in the preparation and conduct of the 1925–7 Revolution. This Second Chinese Revolution, as Peng called it, to distinguish it from the First Chinese Revolution of 1911, failed (although he was not to blame). Throughout this period Peng steadfastly opposed the communists' line of organic collaboration with the Guomindang, which required communists to join Sun Yat-sen's Nationalist Party in its new Moscow-restructured format – that the party of the working class submit to the party of the 'national' bourgeoisie. Peng was outraged when the Comintern imposed this line on the CCP in the summer of 1922. He vigorously opposed it, right up to 12 April 1927, when disaster struck.

Four periods stand out in particular in these first eight years of Peng's political life. The first was his time in Moscow, where he was secretary to the group of young Chinese studying at the University of the Toilers of the East. He used his position – with their enthusiastic support – to advocate a return to an 'orthodox' line that would allow the CCP to develop independently of the Guomindang, and free itself from the demands and constraints of collaboration.

The second was the six months he spent in Shanghai from the beginning of August 1924 to the end of January 1925, when he managed to bring Chen Duxiu and Cai Hesen round to his way of thinking. With them, and at breakneck speed, he revamped the Party's line on all fronts and engineered its approval by the Fourth Party Congress in Shanghai in January 1925, paving the way for the May Thirtieth Movement.

The third was his trip to Guangzhou in May 1926 after Chiang Kai-shek's coup against the communists on 20 March 1926. His mission, as representative of the Centre and the communists in Shanghai, was to demand of Borodin, the

Comintern representative, and the Party's Guangdong Provincial Committee that they punish Chiang for his actions, abandon organic collaboration with the Guomindang, and arm the workers with the thousands of rifles they would need to defend themselves against Chiang's ill-disciplined troops if there was another coup. The mission was a failure, but while Peng emerged with his honour intact the same cannot be said of those comrades who made it a failure.

The fourth is when Peng and Chen Bilan did their highly effective groundwork for the workers' insurrection in Shanghai from 20 to 22 March 1927. But victory was short-lived – no one foresaw that Chiang, preparing to enter the city, would order his National Revolutionary Army to slaughter the insurrectionists and, from 12 April onwards, hunt down the communists. Between the end of March and 10 April the principal Party leaders and the communist leaders of 'fortress' Shanghai, suspecting nothing, began leaving for Wuhan to attend the Fifth Party Congress. Peng left at the beginning of April, Chen eight days later. Only on arrival in Wuhan did he learn of Chiang's treachery and the beginning of the end of the Revolution.

The Stalinists in Moscow, in control of the Comintern since 1924, had made up their minds before the Second Revolution collapsed to rid themselves of the Chen Duxiu-Peng Shuzhi duo, whose refusal to toe the line they found intolerable. This they intended to do with the help of a group of troublemakers in the Party headed by their henchman, Qu Qiubai. The collapse of the revolution set in train by Chiang's coup (and not completed until December) provided an opportunity to do this quickly, and with minimal fuss. They shifted the blame for the collapse of the revolution onto Chen and Peng while covering up the fact that they were the real culprits – in the time-honoured tradition of leaders who blame those who carry out their orders. The Stalinists in Moscow were past masters in the use of sacrificial scapegoats and lost no time in getting the CCP to sacrifice Chen Duxiu and Peng Shuzhi at the Fifth Party Congress in Wuhan in April 1927, at the 'extraordinary' meeting in Jiujiang in Jiangxi, on 7 August 1927, and at the Sixth Party Congress in Moscow in June 1928.

Peng Shuzhi and Chen Duxiu had no intention of being scapegoats. Initially thrown by the turn of events, all the more so because (unlike Qu Qiubai and co.) they knew nothing of the fierce struggle in Moscow in which 'the Chinese question' had become a major issue in the confrontation between Trotsky and Stalin, they quickly recovered and went on the offensive. They refused to accept blame for mistakes not of their own making, rejecting the charges laid against them and the putschist line that the CCP, at Moscow's behest, was putting into practice and that had no effect other than to accelerate the defeat of the Revolution. They shook off the bonds that had tied them to the Comintern and began to think for themselves. Hence their refusal to attend the CCP's

Sixth Party Congress in Moscow at the invitation of the Comintern. But they remained unsettled and not a little demoralised by what had happened and found it difficult to articulate clearly their thinking about events since 1920.

Thus it was with immense relief that in the summer of 1929 they came across key texts Trotsky had written on 'the Chinese question'. These had been brought back from Moscow by young Chinese communists who had sided with the Left Opposition. They expressed, in clearer language than they themselves could have found, what was on their minds. Reading these texts they realised that in some ways they had unwittingly been practising Trotskyism for two years already. They were converted. Immediately they set themselves up as champions of the Left Opposition in China and demanded that the new leadership of the CCP (since 1928, Li Lisan, replacing Qu Qiubai), and the Party in its entirety, undertake a critical enquiry into the causes of the defeat of the Second Revolution. On 15 November 1929, they were expelled by the leadership, followed a fortnight later by Chen Bilan – their Trotskyist years had begun. 15 December 1929 marked the starting point of this second period in their lives with the publication by Peng and Chen Duxiu of a solemn declaration of adherence to the Left Opposition, signed by 81 party activists.

A complete account of the lives of Peng Shuzhi and Chen Bilan would fill more pages than a novel and be no less rich; here we will focus on eight episodes from this second period in their political careers.

1. From the end of 1929 to the autumn of 1932, Peng, aided by Chen Bilan and in collaboration with Chen Duxiu and militants from other Trotskyist groups, won over a huge number of communist cells from Stalinist control and ensured support for the Left Opposition in Shanghai's working class districts. This rebirth of social and political resistance was a clandestine operation carried out under the nose of the Guomindang dictatorship. It was underpinned by a resurgence of anti-imperialist patriotism in the aftermath of Japanese aggression against China, including in Shanghai from September 1931 to January 1932.

2. In Shanghai and elsewhere, the Guomindang's police were on the alert. They made no distinction between Stalinists and Trotskyists. Repression was made easier by the CCP's leadership's continued adherence to a suicidal putschist strategy dictated by Moscow, which bred despair among the remaining party militants and encouraged informers. These were difficult times for Peng and Chen Bilan. On his way to a meeting on the night of 15 October 1932, Peng walked into a trap set by a comrade working for the enemy. Chen Duxiu and other comrades were also taken, the work of the same traitor.

3. For five years, from the autumn of 1932 to 1937, circumstances kept Peng and Chen Bilan apart. Peng and Chen Duxiu were in jail in Nanjing, saved from

death by the prestige they enjoyed, much though Chiang Kai-shek would have liked to eliminate them. They were sentenced to eight years. In prison they quarrelled – Peng remaining a convinced Trotskyist, Chen Duxiu turning his back on all forms of communism.

For Chen Bilan the problem was not only keeping herself out of the hands of the Guomindang's police but making a living to support herself and her two children. Old friends came to her rescue and helped her start her life again in the publications section of the YMCA, controlled by the Shanghai branch of the party. Almost every month she wrote articles for the major Shanghai periodicals, especially *Dongfang zazhi* ('Oriental magazine'), on a wide range of social issues. Signing herself Chen Biyun, she wrote about the problems of women and children and education.

4. The entry of Japanese troops into China's eastern provinces after 7 July 1937, and the realisation that the Chinese army was incapable of withstanding the invasion, caused such confusion and disorder in Nanjing that the authorities had no option other than to release first Chen Duxiu and then Peng Shuzhi. With Japanese bombs raining down on the roads and railways, Peng made his way back to Shanghai.

As soon as he had located Chen Bilan, he tried to start up a Trotskyist workers' movement in the International Concession, which the Japanese had yet to occupy. Pearl Harbor, which brought America and Britain into the war against Japan in December 1941, put paid to that initiative. He had had little success in any case, so stacked against him were the objective conditions.

The situation got worse when the Japanese occupied the International Concession. From 1942 to the end of the war they did everything they could to lay their hands on him. They accused him of sabotaging the Japanese war effort by instigating strikes, yet these were few and far between and, when they did occur, were savagely put down. Several times he just missed being captured and certain death before a firing squad. But with the help of the ingenious Chen Bilan and her sixth sense for danger, and his own long experience of surviving in the worst conditions, he always managed to slip through the net.

5. During the war against the Japanese Peng found a teaching post in a private university. This in the end became his principal activity. He had read widely and the solid intellectual foundation he gained in prison made him a brilliant teacher of the history of Chinese thought. He taught it in relation to the history of ideas worldwide. This novel contextualisation of Chinese ideas slowly attracted a large number of young left-wing disciples and when liberation came it was among them, from the autumn of 1945, that he found the supporters for his latest and now quasi-public attempt to create a Trotskyist movement.

Between 1937 and 1945 he had quietly built up a dense network of adult sympathisers who now helped fund the publication of two Trotskyist magazines, both quite successful. One was *Youth and Woman*, edited by Chen Bilan, the other was *The Search for Truth*, edited by Peng. They began publishing in early 1946 and folded at the end of 1948. When it became obvious that they would have to leave Shanghai for good to seek refuge in Guangzhou in the autumn of 1948, the organisation they had set up had hundreds of members. It did not survive the arrival of the Maoists.

When they took the boat from Shanghai to Guangzhou, Peng and Chen had no intention of leaving China. They were simply relocating to maintain their two-pronged struggle against the party of Mao Zedong and the party of Chiang Kai-shek, as their leadership roles required. They kept up the fight when they had to flee Guangzhou for Hong Kong in 1949 and again when they had to move on to Saigon after the British police forced them out of the colony. They remained in Saigon until their remaining comrades were murdered by the Vietminh along with the last surviving Vietnamese Trotskyists. At this point they decided to go to Europe. They arrived in Marseilles in June 1951 where they stayed a short while before leaving for Paris, the headquarters of the Fourth International.

7. Peng and Chen were now more or less part of the leadership of the Fourth International, but their foreign comrades, for whom Mao's victory was a cause for celebration, were loath to listen to their attempts to expose the true nature of this victory, an 'oriental' national revolution led by the urban petty bourgeoisie with the support of the peasantry, and not an authentically socialist, non-Stalinist revolution of a new type. Also, they had rejected the 'entryist' line – that Trotskyists should join the Stalinist parties – advocated by Michel Raptis, alias Pablo, which he had persuaded all sections of the Fourth International to adopt.

Justification for this line was provided by the theory that war between the USSR and the United States was inevitable. Perhaps this suicidal policy reminded Peng and Chen of the CCP's fateful collaboration with the Guomindang.

8. In their years of exile, first in Paris and then in Los Angeles, Peng and Chen were unremitting in their efforts to promote or resuscitate the international Trotskyist movement. All their time was spent trying to bring its diverse components together and to stop it breaking up into endless fractions, as it tended to do. They closely followed international affairs, discussing the latest developments with their comrades from all over the world and writing numerous commentaries.

They also kept a close watch on what was happening in China and were frequently disappointed by developments there. From 1976 there was more cause for hope. There were the events of 5 April 1976, and then, in 1978–9, Democracy Wall. Peng Shuzhi told us he was now sure that he had plenty of successors in China.

What is the significance of Peng Shuzhi and Chen Bilan for us? The cause they served so nobly – a worldwide Leninist-Trotskyist revolution – has been doubly defeated: because in eastern Europe, China, Korea, Vietnam, and Cuba and nearly all of the world's communist parties, the Stalinists triumphed over their ideological competitors; and because communism and even socialism in every corner of the world, including China, Vietnam, Korea, and Cuba, have fallen victim to global ultra-liberalism flying the American flag. Are Peng and Chen worthy of our attention as anything else but historical relics? We give five reasons to show why they are.

1. Peng and Chen always looked to the future with the conviction that it could be made a better place. They never lost hope. While they can be criticised for believing that the international Trotskyist movement still had a future after the distortions wreaked upon it by 'entryism' and the endless petty squabbling between factions and individuals, they cannot be reproached for remaining loyal to it in order to work for a better future. Even in old age they remained as energetic as ever, avidly following the news and monitoring the struggle of all the world's people against exploitation and oppression.

2. Their idealism was always tempered by a critical turn of mind – a rare combination, which one finds in the great Marxist thinkers, the early communists, whether or not one agrees with their views or their philosophy. They knew when to yield before the facts and modify their thinking, when to question their own certainties. The reserves of idealism in today's society are not unlimited. But neither were they in yesterday's societies. Idealism today tends to concentrate on causes other than those that concern revolutionary political movements. Idealism is still there – it has not disappeared. But what is rare is this combination of idealism and independence of mind – an aptitude to defend what one believes to be true and just, whatever the consequences.

3. They were true patriots who never lost sight of the need to put the defence of China, enslaved by imperialist powers, in the context of the interests of humanity. Their national conscience and their conscience as part of the human family mutually enhanced each other. Such notions are rare, even in Europe, where the conflict between patriotism and internationalism has supposedly been resolved by eliminating the former. We cannot know what Peng and Chen would have thought of the homogenising globalisation of the 'Global Village' and the financial markets. We suspect they would have made a distinc-

tion between it and internationalist globalisation that respects the diversity of nations. They would not have appreciated the hegemonic aspirations with which China has been infected for several years.

4. They realised violence was often the only way to bring about the future, but they did not like it. They distrusted revolutions that used bayonets and then killed off their generals. They detested militarism. For them a revolution was a mass movement, led by the workers and beginning in the cities. They were communists, but they also sought to be democrats. In the Second Chinese Revolution, Peng Shuzhi never came into open conflict with Mao Zedong, but if Mao represented the peasantry, rural China, narrow nationalism, the gun, violence, and despotism, Peng was his antithesis.

5. They made respect for the individual and an all-pervading humanism – two notions that inform the noblest currents of Chinese thought as well as that of old Europe – central to their thinking and actions. This humanism illuminated their vision of world revolution, including the Chinese revolution. At the end of the twentieth century, when bureaucrats and plutocrats the world over are devising ever new ways for people to exploit and oppress each other, comfort can be found in the ideas and example of Peng Shuzhi and Chen Bilan.

Wang Fanxi (1907–2002) by *Gregor Benton*

This obituary appeared in different forms in several newspapers, including The Guardian, *21 April 2003.*

On 30 December 2002, the Chinese Trotskyist leader Wang Fanxi died of heart failure in Leeds, Britain, aged 95. Born in Xiashi near Hangzhou in 1907, he joined the Chinese Communist Party (CCP) in 1925, abandoning his literature studies at Beijing University for the revolution. In 1931, he was expelled from the CCP and helped set up the Left Opposition led by Chen Duxiu, the CCP's founder and a giant of modern Chinese thought and letters.

He and the Trotskyists spent much of the 1930s in Chiang Kai-shek's jails. In 1949, when the Communists set up their régime in Beijing, his comrades sent him (much against his will) to Hong Kong, to act as their external link while they continued the fight in China for workers' democracy and socialism worldwide. The colonial authorities evicted him from his 'safe place' even before his comrades' arrest on the mainland in 1952. (Some stayed locked up for the next 27 years.) In 1975, he fled his second sanctuary in Macao, where Communist agents were plotting to spirit him across the border. He went on invitation to Leeds, where he lived until his death.

Wang was one of hundreds of young Chinese borne into radical politics by the New Culture movement, which peaked on 4 May 1919, in a campaign of protest against China's betrayal by the Versailles Peace Conference. Like May Fourth's leader Chen Duxiu, he continued to view internationalism and democracy as indispensable ingredients of Communist society, even after their extinction in the Stalinised CCP. An accomplished author who contributed to the seminal literary journal *Yusi* ('Threads of talk') before committing himself to a life of revolution, he was also a virtuoso linguist, fluent in English, Russian and several Chinese dialects and able to read Japanese, French and German. His university class in 1925 was unusually distinguished. Besides him, it contained the party's two best-known literary dissentients, his close friend Wang Shiwei (executed by the Communists in 1947) and Hu Feng. After his expulsion from the party, Wang resumed writing and translating in time snatched from politics, to help fund the impoverished Trotskyists and feed his family. In lonely exile in Macao, he had more time to write than he would have wished. His books in Chinese include *Mao Zedong sixiang lungao* ('Study of Mao Zedong Thought') and studies on the Cultural Revolution and many other subjects. His memoirs were published in English translation by Oxford University Press in 1980 and in an expanded edition by Columbia University Press in 1991.

Wang was imprisoned for the first time (of three) in Wuhan in 1927, after boldly criticising the CCP's senior Nationalist allies. Following the bloody collapse of the alliance, he went to Moscow for military training. There he rallied to Trotsky's criticism of the Chinese united front, which had ended in massacres of Red supporters. Back in Shanghai, he worked under Zhou Enlai as an undercover oppositionist until his exposure and expulsion in 1931, as a prelude to his second and third spells in jail. When not behind bars, Wang and the other Trotskyists strove in the early and mid 1930s to revive the revolution's shattered urban base by campaigning for a democratically elected constituent assembly. The campaign failed miserably, if only because most Trotskyists were in jail, but so did the rural strategy favoured by the CCP, which sacrificed its forces in futile warfare. In 1937, the start of the Japanese War radically altered the nature of Chinese politics.

Quixotically, Wang and Chen Duxiu tried to win armed forces to a policy of resistance combined with rural revolution. The CCP, hundreds of times bigger and with a decade of military experience and some Soviet support, effortlessly eclipsed them. After the war, the Trotskyists resumed their campaign for radical democracy and class struggle in the cities. They were as if blind to Mao's peasant armies, poised by 1949 to seize power everywhere on the mainland.

Wang spent the first years of his exile reflecting on the causes of the Maoist victory and the Trotskyist defeat. In a departure from Trotskyist orthodoxy, he found that a real revolution had indeed taken place under Mao. He criticised his own group's failure to develop armed forces and mobilise the peasants as one part of their activities. Yet he continued to question the overwhelmingly military thrust of Maoist strategy, which he feared in some ways was just another link in China's endless chain of wars followed by tyrannical restorations. Instead, he argued for the centrality of the industrial workers and the intelligentsia, new urban classes that offered a way of unlocking the cycle with an experiment in democratic communism.

Other Trotskyists around Peng Shuzhi, in exile in the United States, denounced Wang for 'capitulating' to Stalinism. The row was symptomatic of the Trotskyists' fractiousness, which left them even more vulnerable to their many enemies.

Relegated to the role of a mere observer of Chinese politics in later life, Wang could offer little more than commentary, but even in his early nineties he kept up a lively interest in developments in China and the world. He closely followed the CCP's evolution and predicted a new opposition would emerge from it. Communist officials tried to tempt him home, but he demanded in return the rehabilitation of Chen Duxiu and the others, a condition that stayed unmet. He kept up a voluminous three-way correspondence with the veteran oppositionist Zheng Chaolin in Shanghai (freed from prison in 1979) and the Trotskyist writer Lou Guohua in Hong Kong. The death of Lou in 1995 and of Zheng in 1998 shut down his sounding boards and sources of inspiration, at a time when ill health (caused partly by Nationalist torture) and massive exhaustion anyway made it hard for him to read let alone to comment.

The Trotskyists' main contribution to the Chinese Revolution was by the pen. The Maoists paid scant heed to Marxism until the late 1930s. By then, Stalin had reduced Marxist theory to a self-serving state ideology, which Mao plagiarised to boost his 'theoretical' credentials. Wang and his comrades, in contrast, published Marxist writings in Chinese by the shelf-full, including their own creative studies and translations of the classics. In the 1970s, Wang's memoirs were published in Beijing in a restricted edition. More recently, his study on Maoism also appeared. Before Mao's death, the very word Trotskyism was enough to trigger a violent shock in most old cadres, but bolder thinkers took a friendlier approach after official ideology began to lose its grip in an increasingly polarised and corrupt society. Among well-known thinkers who have shown sympathy for Wang's ideas are the former political prisoner Wang Xizhe, the party critic Liu Binyan, the philosopher Wang Ruoshui, and the woman dissident Dai Qing. Although this list of Wang's Chinese admirers is still short, their writings roused him to a state of high excitement.

In Britain, Wang did not directly engage in politics. However, he influenced students from China, Taiwan, Hong Kong, and Southeast Asia and was revered by radical leaders of the local Chinese community, who sought his advice on their campaigns for social equity in Chinatown and against white racism.

He was unswervingly radical but departed in almost all respects from the stereotype of the hard, narrow, unrelenting revolutionary. Friends knew him as deeply cultured, sensitive, modest, gentle, courteous, enlightened, approachable, open-minded, and absolutely true, to individuals as well as to the cause. His extreme selflessness and the fortitude with which he bore numerous personal tragedies and losses lent him an almost saintly aura. He is survived by his wife in Shanghai and by two children, three grandchildren, and two great grandchildren. Dora, a sort of adopted daughter, cared for him in his old age.

Bibliographical Note

Works on Chinese Trotskyism and by Chinese Trotskyists began to appear in China and the West in the 1980s, and studies on Chen Duxiu were completed in the 1960s. Three Trotskyist leaders published memoirs in the West, in translation, and the same and other memoirs have been published in Chinese in China (not necessarily with the authors' permission) and Hong Kong. Those published in the West are Wang Fan-hsi (Wang Fanxi), *Memoirs of a Chinese Revolutionary*, translated and with an introduction by Gregor Benton, New York: University of Columbia Press, 1991 (a revised and enlarged edition of *Chinese Revolutionary, Memoirs, 1919–1949*, Oxford: Oxford University Press, 1980), which also appeared in German, French, and Japanese; *An Oppositionist for Life: Memoirs of the Chinese Revolutionary Zheng Chaolin*, edited and translated by Gregor Benton, Atlantic Highlands, NJ: Humanities Press., which also appeared in German; and *Mémoires de Peng Shuzhi: L'Envol du communisme en Chine*, authored by Claude Cadart and Cheng Yingxiang and published in Paris by Gallimard in 1983. Peng's memoirs were described at the time of publication as the first of three volumes, but the second and third volumes have yet to appear. Both Wang Fanxi's and Zheng Chaolin's memoirs are excerpted in this sourcebook.

Wang's memoirs were first published in mimeograph in Hong Kong in 1957 as *Shuang Shan huiyi lu* ('Shuang Shan's memoirs'); they were published in a properly printed edition in 1977 in Hong Kong by Zhouji hang (Chow's Company) as Wang Fanxi, *Shuang Shan huiyi lu*, and were pirated in Beijing by Xiandai shiliao biankan she in 1981. In 1994, Shilin shudian in Hong Kong published an enlarged edition of this text. Zheng Chaolin's memoirs were written in 1945, but not at the time published; sometime in 1979 or 1980, several copies of the manuscript were mimeographed under the title *Zheng Chaolin 1945 nian huiyi lu* ('Zheng Chaolin's 1945 memoirs') for distribution as reference material among Party historians. In 1986 in Beijing, Xiandai shiliao biankan she ('The association to edit and publish materials on contemporary history') published a properly printed version under the title *Zheng Chaolin huiyi lu* ('Zheng Chaolin's memoirs'), with an appendix on 'Chen Duxiu and the Trotskyists' written by Zheng in 1980. Other editions have been published since, both in China and Hong Kong. For example, in 2004 Beijing's Dongfang chuban she published an edition in two volumes edited by Fan Yong. In 1998, Zheng Chaolin's memoirs and other writings were published in three volumes in Hong Kong under the title *Shishi yu huiyi: Zheng Chaolin wannian wenxuan* ('History and Recollections: A selection of Zheng Chaolin's late writings') by Tiandi tushu. Also in Hong Kong, the Trotskyist seafarer and writer Sun Liangsi completed his memoirs in 1986 (Bo Chen [Liang Si], *Huigu, 1918–1948* ['Recollections, 1918–1948'], an unpublished manuscript).

Between 1982 and 1984, Peng Shuzhi's writings were published in Chinese in three volumes (*Peng Shuzhi xuanji*) by Shiyue chuban she in Hong Kong. A fourth volume was published in 2010.

P'eng Shu-tse (Peng Shuzhi), *The Chinese Communist Party in Power* (New York: Monad, 1980), is a selection of essays by Peng Shuzhi on the Mao régime. It is prefaced by an article titled 'Looking Back Over My Years With P'eng Shu-tse' by Chen Bilan, first published in *Intercontinental Press* (New York) on 2, 9 and 16 November 1970 (under the name Peng Pi-lan). Chen Bilan was an activist in the early CCP and Peng's wife. She went to Moscow as a student and later joined the Trotskyists together with her husband.

In 1992, a memoir by Chen Bilan titled *Wo de huiyi: Yige Zhongguo gemingzhe de huigu* ('My memoirs: Recollections of a Chinese revolutionary') was published in Hong Kong by Shiyue shuju, and was republished as *Zaoqi Zhonggong yu Tuopai: Wo de geming shengya huiyi* ('The early CCP and the Trotskyists: Memoirs of my revolutionary career') by Hong Kong's Tiandi Press in 2010. The book has a preface by Cheng Yingxiang, the daughter of Peng Shuzhi and Chen Bilan. According to a note, the manuscript was completed in 1954. Its concluding chapters constitute the most substantial published memoir by a member of the Peng group of the history of the group between 1929 and 1952. Chapters 1–20 (pp. 17–329) describe Chen Bilan's family background, girlhood, and schooling, as well as her initiation into the CCP, her time in Moscow, and her work for the Party in Shanghai and other places in the mid to late 1920s, including after the start of the White Terror in 1927. Chapters 20–30 (pp. 330–526) cover the Trotskyist period in China and Peng and Chen's escape to Europe by way of Vietnam in 1950 and 1951. They describe Peng and Chen's expulsion from the CCP in 1929, their cultural activities, the betrayal of the Trotskyists in 1931, Peng's arrest in 1932, and Chen's five years without Peng during the period of his imprisonment. Chapters 25–27 tell the story of Peng's split with Chen Duxiu after the two men's release from prison in 1937, the split in the Chinese Trotskyist movement during the Japanese War, and the Peng group's underground work after the start of the Pacific War. The volume ends with a brief description of the group's emergence into the open in 1945, after the Japanese surrender, and Peng and Chen's subsequent flight south and then to Paris by way of Vietnam. It concludes, unacceptably in the view of many, with an appendix attacking the CCP martyr Qu Qiubai, shot by the Guomindang in 1935, and opposing a campaign by Ding Ling and others for Qu Qiubai's rehabilitation.

In 1995, Dai Qing, known in China and the world as a brilliant and fearless journalist, began publishing excerpts from her own new study on Chinese Trotskyism. Herself a dissident, she was naturally drawn to the story of the Chinese Trotskyists, and dedicates her book to Zheng Chaolin, Wang Fanxi, and Lou Guohua, whom she describes as champions of liberty and prophets before their time.[1]

---

1 Dai Qing's study is called *Zhonggong Tuopai he 'Tuopai'* ('The Chinese Communist Party's Trotskyists and its [alleged] "Trotskyists" '). Extracts were published in Hong Kong's *Xinbao*

Ever since the late 1950s, the veteran Trotskyists in Hong Kong have supported a lively press. After the CCP came to power in 1949, and especially after the arrest of the Trotskyists in China in 1952, Hong Kong was for a long time the sole place where the movement's few surviving members could make their voices heard. At first, the British colonial government in Hong Kong adopted a hostile attitude towards the Trotskyists, and in early 1950 it expelled nearly all the prominent Trotskyists active in Hong Kong. The few that remained were forced into complete inactivity and silence. In the late 1950s, Lou Guohua made the first break-through when he set up Xinda chuban she ('Sincere Press'), which published a number of books written or translated by Wang Fanxi. Lou was later joined by Sun Liangsi, who set up Zhouji hang ('Chow's Company'), another Trotskyist publishing enterprise.[2] In January 1974, supporters of Peng Shuzhi in Hong Kong began publishing *Shiyue pinglun* ('October Review'), which continues to appear. Other Trotskyist journals published in Hong Kong in the late twentieth century include *Xin sichao* ('New Tide of Thought'), *Zhanxun* ('Combat Bulletin') (founded in 1975), and *Xinmiao* ('New Sprouts'), plus a number of more ephemeral titles. All these publications are a source of information on Trotskyist activities before 1949, as well as on contemporary Trotskyism.

Research on Chen Duxiu progressed rapidly in China in the 1980s and the 1990s. No fewer than three book-length biographical studies on Chen Duxiu or chronologies of his life were published in China between 1987 and 1989, and a major new study was published in Taiwan. Three mainland biographies are Wang Guangyuan, ed., *Chen Duxiu nianpu* ('A chronology of the life of Chen Duxiu'), Chongqing: Chongqing chuban she, 1987; Tang Baolin and Lin Maosheng, *Chen Duxiu nianpu* ('A chronology of the life of Chen Duxiu'), Shanghai: Shanghai renmin chuban she, 1988; and Ren Jianshu and Tang Baolin, *Chen Duxiu zhuan* ('A biography of Chen Duxiu'), 2 vols, Shanghai: Shanghai renmin chuban she, 1989. Ren Jianshu wrote the first volume, subtitled *Cong xiucai dao zong shuji* ('From scholar to General Secretary'), and Tang Baolin wrote the second, subtitled *Cong zong shuji dao fanduipai* ('From General Secretary to oppositionist'). The Taiwan study is Zheng Xuejia, *Chen Duxiu zhuan* ('A biography of Chen Duxiu'),

---

on 16–17 March 1995, under the titles 'Kua shiji de zhuiqiu: Zhonggong Tuopai he "Tuopai"' ('A pursuit ahead of its time: The Chinese Communist Party's Trotskyists and its [alleged] "Trotskyists"') and 'Zhongguo Tuopai zouzai shehui biange zhi qian' ('The Chinese Trotskyists marching ahead of social transformations').

2 Publications by Xinda include Wang Fanxi's translations of Peter Fryer's *The Hungarian Tragedy*, Trotsky's *Literature and Revolution* and *The Revolution Betrayed*, Yevtushenko's *Precocious Autobiography and Poems*, Machiavelli's *The Prince*, and other works; Shuang Shan (Wang Fanxi), *Mao Zedong sixiang lungao* ('Studies on Mao Zedong thought') (1973), *Qishi niandai wang hechu qu?* ('Where is *Seventies* going?') (1972), and several other studies; Yi Yin (Zheng Chaolin), *Buduan geming lun ABC* ('An ABC of permanent revolution') (1958); and many other books and pamphlets. Sun Liangsi's company published Shuang Shan, *Huiyi lu* ('Memoirs').

2 vols, Taibei: Shiba wenhua chuban qiye youxian gongsi, 1989. Later, in 1992, Thomas Kuo's book on Chen (*Ch'en Tu-hsiu (1879–1942) and the Chinese Communist Movement*, South Orange, New Jersey: Seton Hall University Press, 1975, based on his 1969 PhD thesis of the same title) was published in Chinese translation by Taibei's Lianjing chuban shiye gongsi as Guo Chengtang (Thomas Kuo), *Chen Duxiu yu Zhongguo gongchan zhuyi yundong* ('Chen Duxiu and the Chinese Communist Movement'). An early (and probably the best available) Chinese-language chronology of Chen's life is Zhi Yuru (Chih Yuju), *Chen Duxiu nianpu* ('A chronology of the life of Chen Duxiu'), Hong Kong: Longmen shudian, 1974. An excellent Western study is Lee Feigon, *Chen Duxiu, Founder of the Chinese Communist Party*, Princeton: Princeton University Press, 1983.

For a sympathetic history of Chinese Trotskyism, see Gregor Benton, *China's Urban Revolutionaries: Explorations in the History of Chinese Trotskyism, 1921–1952*, New Jersey and London: Humanities Press, 1996. In August 1994, Tang Baolin, a mainland Chinese specialist on Chen Duxiu and Chinese Trotskyism working in the Institute of Modern History at the Chinese Academy of Social Sciences in Beijing, published *Zhongguo Tuopai shi* ('A history of Chinese Trotskyism') in the series Zhongguo xiandai shi congshu (Contemporary Chinese history library) under the general editorship of Zhang Yufa, at Taibei's Dongda tushu gongsi. This book, though partly based on primary sources, displays many of the same flaws and shortcomings as much other mainland Chinese writing on Chen Duxiu and Trotskyism. It resorts habitually to a double standard, one – harsh and cynical – for the Trotskyists, who can do little right, and another – fawning and indulgent – for the official Party, which can do nothing wrong. It peddles a familiar mixture of misunderstandings, crude misrepresentations, mindless copying of familiar Stalinist and Maoist smears, and mutually contradictory assertions alongside a substantial but erratic complement of truthful investigation and reporting that lends spurious credence to the lies. Its contents and the angle from which it views its subject can be gleaned from its chapter titles: (1) A bizarre baby conceived amid wind and storm; (2) Chen Duxiu went astray by error; (3) From a hotchpotch of grouplets to unification; (4) Stumbling and struggling under attacks from both the Guomindang and the Chinese Communist Party; (5) Striking wrong chords during the War against Japan; (6) In the end, the flower inevitably fades. An appendix contains various source materials on Chinese Trotskyism. (For a critical review of Tang Baolin's book, see pp. 1149–63 of the present volume).

PhD dissertations that discuss Chen Duxiu and the Chinese Trotskyists include Yu-ju Chih (Zhi Yuru), The Political Thought of Ch'en Tu-hsiu, Indiana University, 1965; Richard Kagan, The Chinese Trotskyist Movement and Ch'en Tu-hsiu: Culture, Revolution, and Polity, University of Pennsylvania, 1969; Thomas C. T. Kuo, Ch'en Tu-hsiu (1879–1942) and the Chinese Communist Movement, University of Pittsburgh, 1969; and Joseph T. Miller, The Politics of Chinese Trotskyism: The Role of a Permanent Opposition in Communism, University of Illinois at Urbana-Champaign, 1979.

BIBLIOGRAPHICAL NOTE

In 2003 Baruch Hirson's life of Frank Glass, at one time a leader of the Chinese Trotskyists (Chinese name Li Furen) was published in London by Porcupine Press under the title *Frank Glass, the Restless Revolutionary*. This volume is also an important source of information on the movement.

Papers relating to Peng Shuzhi and Chen Bilan are held by the Hoover Institution Archives at Stanford University. They were donated by the Anchor Foundation in 1992. Papers of Wang Fanxi are held by the Brotherton Library at Leeds University. Leon Trotsky's 'Exile Papers' at Harvard University has some primary documentation on the Chinese Trotskyist movement in the 1930s and the early 1940s. The wartime Japanese intelligence journal *Jôhô*, a classified bimonthly publication of the Political Affairs Bureau of Tokyo's Asia Development Board (Kôain Seimubu), carried reports on the Trotskyists and documents produced by them.[3] The opening of some Soviet archives (particularly the Comintern archive) after 1989 permitted new research on the origins and fate of Chinese Trotskyism in Russia.[4]

Relevant online archives include:

In English:

marxists.anu.edu.au/archive/trotsky/1932/pcr/13.htm (for Trotsky on China)
marxists.org/archive/peng/index.htm (for Peng Shuzhi)
marxists.org/history/etol/document/china/zheng.htm (for Zheng Chaolin)
marxists.org/archive/chen/index.htm (for Chen Bilan)

In Chinese:

marxists.org/chinese/ (has writings in Chinese by Chen Duxiu, Peng Shuzhi, Chen Bilan, Zheng Chaolin, Wang Fanxi, and Lou Guohua)
marxists.org/chinese/reference-books/marxist.org-chinese-shaolu.htm
marxists.org/chinese/liupingmei/index.htm
marxists.org/chinese/xieshan/index.htm
marxists.org/chinese/reference-books/index-class-struggling.htm
marxists.org/chinese/reference-books/new-voice/index.htm
marxists.org/chinese/404.htm
xinmiao.com.hk/trad/index.html
worker-democracy.com.tw/
youth-sparks.com/bbs/index.php

---

3   Kagan 1969, pp. 168 and 170.
4   This research has been done by Alexander Pantsov and Daria A. Spichak (see this volume).

Biographical List

The Chinese names in this list of Chinese Trotskyists and their supporters and other relevant people are in Hanyu Pinyin transcription; the Wade-Giles transcription is added in brackets where it differs from the Hanyu Pinyin transcription.

An Fu.
A leader of the Chinese Trotskyists in Moscow. Arrested in 1930 and executed by the GPU. Alias: Vitin.

Buchman, Alexander H. (1911–2003).
A US engineer who worked as a photographer and journalist in Shanghai between 1933 and 1939. Edited *What War Means: The Japanese Terror in China – A Documentary Record* (London: Gollancz, 1938). Worked together with the Trotskyists in Shanghai in opposition to the Japanese invasion of China, and later served briefly as a bodyguard for Trotsky. His motion pictures and stills taken in Shanghai and at Coyoacán are held by Stanford's Hoover Institute, among other institutions.

Cai Hesen 蔡和森 (Ts'ai Ho-sen) (1895–1931).
A leader and martyr of the CCP. Author of *The History of Opportunism in the CCP*.

Cai Yuanpei 蔡元培 (Ts'ai Yüan-p'ei) (1868–1940).
A veteran Guomindang leader and important liberal educationalist. Sponsored the New Culture Movement around 1919 in his capacity (between 1916 and 1926) as Chancellor of Beijing University. Founded and became President of the Academia Sinica.

Chen Bilan 陈碧兰 (Ch'en Pi-lan) (1902–87).
Joined the League of Socialist Youth in 1922 and the Communist Party in 1923. Sent to Moscow to study in 1924, and returned to China one year later. Active in the women's movement. Became a Trotskyist together with Chen Duxiu in 1929. Self-exiled at the end of 1948, first to Hong Kong, then to Vietnam, France, and the US; finally, she went to Hong Kong, where she died. The wife of Peng Shuzhi. Alias: Bi Yun.

Chen Duxiu 陈独秀 (Ch'en Tu-hsiu) (1879–1942).
Editor of *New Youth*, leader of the New Culture Movement, founder of the CCP, and its General Secretary until 1927. In 1931, became a Trotskyist and helped found the Chinese Left Opposition, which he then led. In 1932, went to prison on charges of seeking to overthrow the government and replace it with a proletarian dictatorship. Aliases: Shi An; Sa Weng; Xue Yi; Kong Jia; Zhong Fu; San Ai; Zhi Mian.

Chen Qiaonian 陈乔年 (Ch'en Ch'iao-nien) (1902–28).
Chen Duxiu's second son. Joined the Party in 1922 in France, and studied in Moscow. Elected onto the Central Committee in 1927. Arrested and executed by Chiang Kai-

shek in the spring of 1928, by which time he had become head of the Organisational Department of the Jiangsu Provincial Committee.

Chen Qichang 陈其长 (Ch'en Ch'i-ch'ang) (1901–43).

A Beijing student leader, and a member of the middle-ranking cadre of the CCP after 1925. Turned to Trotskyism in 1929, and became a leader of the Chinese Trotskyist movement. Arrested and executed by Japanese gendarmerie. Aliases: Chen Qingchen; Jiang Weiliang; Chen Zhongshan.

Chen Yannian 陈延年 (Ch'en Yen-nien) (1899–1927).

The eldest son of Chen Duxiu and a founder of the European Branch of the CCP. Secretary of the Southern China Regional Committee of the Party until 1926. Then Secretary of the Jiangsu Provincial Committee. Executed by Chiang Kai-shek in Shanghai in May 1927.

Chen Yimou 陈逸谋 (Ch'en I-mou) (1907–31).

See under Ou Fang.

Chen Zhongxi (Ch'en Chung-hsi) (1908–43).

A Hong Kong worker, who joined the Trotskyists in 1930. As a Communist, led an armed peasant struggle in Zhongshan county, Guangdong, towards the end of 1927. Was organiser of the Hong Kong Trotskyists in the mid-1930s and led an anti-Japanese guerrilla unit in Zhongshan during the War of Resistance. Died in battle around 1943.

Deng Yanda 邓演达 (Teng Yen-ta) (1895–1931).

Director of the General Political Department of the Northern Expedition, a leader of the left Guomindang, and an opponent of Chiang Kai-shek. In July 1927, resigned from the Wuhan Government in protest against its decision to expel the Communists. Arrested and executed by Chiang Kai-shek in 1931 for launching the Third Party and because of his activities against Chiang's Nanjing Government.

Dong Biwu 董必武 (Tung Pi-wu) (1886–1975).

Veteran Communist and Central Committee member after 1945. Vice-head of state. Member of the Politburo after 1966.

Dong Yixiang 董亦湘 (Tung I-hsiang).

Writer and veteran Communist. Framed by Wang Ming in Xinjiang in 1927 together with Yu Xiusong 俞秀松 and others as a 'Trotskyist' and sent back to the USSR, where he was executed.

Du Weizhi 杜畏之 (Tu Wei-chih) (?–1992).

Joined the Socialist Youth League and went to Moscow in 1925. Became a Trotskyist in 1931. Arrested in 1952 and sentenced to life, even though by that time he had left the movement. Translated Engels' *Dialectics of Nature*, Plekhanov's *Militant Materialism*, and other Marxist writings.

Fan Jinbiao 范金标 (Fan Chin-piao) (1904–?).

A leader of the Zhejiang student movement, he participated in the Northern Expedition as a political commissar and afterwards as a leader of the peasant movement in Zhejiang. Became a leader of the Chinese Trotskyists in Moscow, and was arrested there and sent to Siberia. Had been rehabilitated by 1955, when he returned to China. Aliases: Fan Wenhui; Alexei Makarovich Forel; Fang Tsing-lu.

Feng Xuefeng 冯雪峰 (Feng Hsüeh-feng) (1902–74).

Poet and critic. Joined the CCP in 1927. A leader of the National Association of Writers and Artists after 1949. Purged in the Cultural Revolution.

Gao Yuhan 高语罕 (Kao Yü-han).

Veteran revolutionary and a political instructor at the Huangpu Military Academy. The first Communist openly to attack Chiang Kai-shek, as 'the Southern Duan' (Duan Qirui 段祺瑞 was a leader of the Beiyang warlords in the north.) Became a Trotskyist in 1929. Alias: Wang Linggao.

Ge Chonge (Ko Ch'ung-o) (?–1931).

Became a Trotskyist in 1927 in Moscow and was sent back to China and expelled from the CCP at the end of the same year. A founder of the Trotskyist movement in northern China. Arrested by the Guomindang in 1931, and died in a Shanghai prison.

Glass, Frank 李福仁 (1901–88).

British-born Cecil Frank Glass arrived in China from South Africa in 1930 and worked in Shanghai as a journalist on various English-language newspapers. A radio commentator in Shanghai; his last job there was as an assistant editor on J. B. Powell's *China Weekly Review*. Aliases: Li Furen (Li Fu-jen); Frank Graves; John Liang.

Gu Shunzhang 顾顺章 (Ku Shun-chang) (1895–1935).

A worker and leader of the Shanghai insurrections in 1927. Chief of the CCP's 'special service' and member of the Politburo of the Central Committee. Arrested by the Guomindang, and became one of its most vicious anti-Communist agents. Finally executed by Chiang Kai-shek despite his defection to the Nationalists.

Guan Xiangying 关向应 (Kuan Hsiang-ying) (1904–46).

A printer, who joined the CCP in 1925. A member of the Central Committee until 1928. He Long's 贺龙 political commissar during the anti-Japanese war.

Han Jun 寒君 (Han Chün) (?–1945).

A leader of the younger generation of Chinese Trotskyists. Active among Hong Kong workers throughout the period of the Japanese occupation of the colony until his death in 1945.

He Mengxiong 何孟雄 (Ho Meng-hsiung) (1898–1931).

A labour leader in North China during the 1925–7 revolution. Head of the Organisational Department of the Jiangsu Provincial Committee of the CCP after 1927. Leader of those Communists who opposed Wang Ming's Central Committee. Arrested and executed by the Guomindang.

He Zishen 何资深 (Ho Tzu-shen) (1898–1961).

A Beijing student in the early 1920s. Participated in the Northern Expedition. Active in Hunan and succeeded Mao as Secretary of the Hunan Provincial Committee. Became a Trotskyist in 1929, and spent several years in jail under the Guomindang. Arrested by the Maoist secret police in 1952. According to his prison-mate Zheng Chaolin, he had collapsed in both body and spirit before he died of a stroke in prison in 1960. Aliases: Zhang Hongdu; He Zhiyu.

Hu Feng 胡风 (1906–85).

Alias Zhang Guangren 张光人, a disciple of Lu Xun and a well-known independent left-wing leader of the so-called Hu Feng clique. Purged in 1955 by Mao.

Hu Qiuyuan 胡秋原 (Hu Ch'iu-yuan) (1910–2004).

One of the Chinese students who returned to China sometime in the early to mid 1930s, after studying in Japan. The majority of these returned students supported the CCP, but a few (notably Hu and Zheng Xuejia 郑学稼) showed some sympathy for Trotskyism. However, Hu and his friends very quickly became associated with the Guomindang.

Hu Shi 胡适 (Hu Shih) (1891–1962).

Philosopher and writer. Advocate of the vernacular literature. Collaborator with Chen Duxiu on *New Youth*. After May Fourth, Hu split with Chen Duxiu and was strongly criticised by the Communists. A supporter of the Guomindang, and pro-American.

Hu Zongnan 胡宗南 (Hu Tsung-nan) (1895–1962).

A Guomindang military leader who became known as the 'King of the Northwest'.

Huang Jiantong 黄鑑銅 (Huang Chien-t'ung) (1918–87).

A leader of the Guangxi Trotskyists. Released from prison together with Zheng Chaolin in 1979, and died in 1991.

Isaacs, Harold Robert 伊罗生 (1910–86).

A US journalist who published *China Forum* in Shanghai in the early 1930s. Influenced by Frank Glass, he became sympathetic to Trotskyism and in Beijing he wrote *The Tragedy of the Chinese Revolution* with the help of Liu Renjing as his translator; he discussed the text with Trotsky, who wrote an introduction to it. The first (1938) edition was followed by several reprintings with Trotsky's introduction deleted. After Trotsky's assassination in 1940, Isaacs left the Trotskyist movement. Worked for the Columbia Broadcasting Company and *Newsweek* before entering academic life in 1950; in 1965, became Professor of Political Science at the Massachusetts Institute of Technology. Aliases: Yi Luosheng; Harold Roberts.

Jiang Zhendong 蒋振东 (Chiang Chen-tung) (1906–82).

A textile worker and veteran Communist. One of the leaders of the Shanghai insurrections of 1927. Became a Trotskyist in 1929. Arrested by the Maoist police in 1952 for his dissident activities. Released from prison in 1979.

Kang Sheng 康生 (K'ang Sheng) (1898–1975).

An intelligence and security specialist. Trained in Moscow as a henchman for Wang Ming by the NKVD, he became a Mao supporter after getting back to China. Mao's main inquisitor in the Cultural Revolution, and depicted as an 'ultra-leftist' by the rehabilitated 'moderate' Chinese Communist leaders who were his victims.

Kang Youwei 康有为 (K'ang Yu-wei) (1858–1927).

Leader of the reform movement that culminated in the short-lived Hundred Days Reform of 1898 and a prominent scholar of the New Text School of the Confucian classics.

Katayama Sen 片山潜 (1860–1933).

Founded the Japanese Socialist Party in 1906 and later became a Communist. Worked for the Comintern in Moscow from 1921 until death.

Kautsky, Karl (1854–1938).

Leader of the German Social Democratic Party. Best known before 1914 as a Marxist theoretician. Opposed the Bolshevik revolution in 1917 on the grounds that a genuine socialist proletarian revolution could only be achieved by democratic means, that is, by universal suffrage and not by the insurrection of a minority of the nation. Opposed Lenin's theory and practice of the dictatorship of the proletariat.

Kirov, Sergei Mironovich (1886–1934).

An old Bolshevik, elected to the Soviet Party's Central Committee in 1923 and to its Politburo in 1930. A staunch supporter of Stalin. His assassination in 1934 was followed by the Moscow trials. Actually, it was Stalin himself who masterminded the assassination when he discovered that Kirov was starting to become estranged from him. Stalin then used the assassination as an excuse to persecute his opponents.

Li Dazhao 李大钊 (Li Ta-chao) (1889–1927).

One of the founders of the CCP, second only to Chen Duxiu. Executed in Beijing in 1927.

Li Ji 李季 (Li Chi).

Known as the first Marxist scholar in China. Author of *A Biography of Karl Marx*. Became a Trotskyist in 1929. Recanted after 1949.

Li Lisan 李立三 (Li Li-san) (1899–1967).

A veteran Communist and labour organiser, was elected onto the Politburo in 1927. The chief executor of Stalin's ultra-left line in China during the period 1929–30; removed from the leadership in 1931 as a scapegoat for its failure. Detained in Russia until 1945. Attacked during the Cultural Revolution, he reportedly committed suicide.

Li Ping 李萍 (Li P'ing).

Became a Trotskyist in Moscow. Alias: Lektorov.

Li Weihan 李维汉 (Li Wei-han) (1896–1984).

Alias Luo Mai. He joined the CCP in France in 1922, and was head of the Orgburo in 1936. After 1949, mainly in charge of the Party's United Front work. Accused of 'anti-Party' activity in December 1966 and purged in June 1967.

BIOGRAPHICAL LIST   1205

Li Zhongsan 李仲三 (Li Chung-san).
A veteran Guomindang revolutionary, active in northwest China. Work-studied in France and became a Trotskyist in 1929.

Lian Zhengyan (Lien Cheng-yen) (1928–51).
A young Trotskyist student in Wenzhou, Zhejiang, shot by the Maoists in 1951.

Liang Ganqiao 梁干乔 (Liang Kan-ch'iao).
Studied in Moscow after graduating from the Huangpu Military Academy. Active in the Chinese Trotskyist movement for a few years, but became a leader of Chiang Kai-shek's 'Blueshirt Clique'.

Liang Qichao 梁启超 (Liang Ch'i-ch'ao) (1873–1929).
A journalist and historian, and a constitutional monarchist who became leader of the so-called 'Study Clique' after the downfall of the Qing dynasty.

Liang Si 梁贻 (Liang Ssu) (1912–87).
Joined the Trotskyists in 1932 and organised their branch in Shandong, his native province. Later worked underground with the Trotskyists in Beijing and Shanghai. Successively a peasant, a soldier (in the war against Japan), a worker (in the Chongqing arsenal, whence he was forced to flee after his arrest by the secret police), and, starting in 1946, a seafarer; in exile and retirement in Hong Kong, he became a writer, a businessman, and a publisher of Trotskyist literature. Killed in a road accident. Aliases: Sun Liangsi 孙梁泗; Bo Chen 波臣.

Lin Huanhua 林焕华.
A leader of the student Trotskyists in Guangxi province in the early 1930s. In charge of printing for the Trotskyist centre in the mid-1930s and a member of the Executive of the Printworkers' Trade Union in Guangzhou until his arrest in December 1952.

Liu Bozhuang 刘伯莊 (Liu Po-chuang).
A 'Frugal Study' student who turned to Trotskyism in 1929, but became a professor soon afterwards and left the movement.

Liu Jialiang 刘家良 (Liu Chia-liang) (?–1950).
Liu Jialiang, Si Chaosheng, and Wang Shuben were three of the leaders of the second generation of Chinese Trotskyists. Liu died in a Vietnamese prison in 1950, Si left the movement long before that, and Wang was executed by the Guomindang in a concentration camp on the eve of their military debacle. Aliases: Yao Ru; Liu Haisheng; Liu Shaoyan.

Liu Jingzhen 刘静贞 (Liu Ching-chen) (1902–79).
Joined the Party and took part in the Revolution of 1925–7. Married Zheng Chaolin and became a Trotskyist together with Chen Duxiu. When Chen was in prison she acted as a link between him and the surviving underground Trotskyist organisation. Arrested by the Communists in 1952, freed five years later, and rejoined her husband Zheng in a labour camp during the Cultural Revolution. Released in June 1979 and died in October of the same year. Alias: Wu Jingru.

Liu Renjing 刘仁静 (Liu Jen-ching) (1902–87).

A founding member of the CCP and General Secretary of the Socialist League of Youth, joined the Left Opposition in Moscow and visited Trotsky in Turkey in 1929. Played a part in organising the Trotskyist organisation in China and helped Harold Isaacs write *The Tragedy of the Chinese Revolution*. Arrested in 1934, and recanted in prison. After 1949, recanted again, to the Maoists. Died in a car accident in 1987. Aliases: Nelsi; Niel Sih; Liu Jingyuan; Lieershi; Xu Yong.

Liu Shaoqi 刘少奇 (Liu Shao-ch'i) (1898–1969).

A veteran Communist and prominent Chinese labour leader of the CCP from the mid-1940s on. Head of State of the People's Republic of China after 1959, purged in the Cultural Revolution, but rehabilitated in 1979.

Liu Yin 刘胤, alias Li Maimai.

A leader of the Wuhan student movement during the 1925–7 revolution. Studied in Moscow. Active for a while in the Chinese Trotskyist movement, then became a publicist for the Guomindang.

Lominadze, Vissarion (1898–1934).

Known as 'Stalin's prodigy'. Comintern representative in China from July to December 1927. He masterminded the 7 August (1927) Emergency Conference and, together with Heinz Neumann, directed the December 1927 Guangzhou Insurrection. Fell into disfavour after 1930 and committed suicide in 1934.

Long Yun 龙云 (Lung Yün) (1884–1962).

Governor of Yunnan from 1928 to 1945.

Lou Guohua 楼国华 (Lou Kuo-hua) (1906–95).

A Communist since 1925, he became a Trotskyist in 1928. One of the few late survivors of the first generation of Chinese Trotskyists, and in Hong Kong the chief publisher of Trotskyist literature in Chinese. Aliases: Zi Chun; Yi Ding; Shao Yuan; Ze Cheng.

Lou Shiyi 楼适夷 (Lou Shih-i) (1905–2001).

A veteran Communist, left-wing writer, translator into Chinese of several novels (including *Mother*) by Maxim Gorky, and cousin of the Trotskyist Lou Guohua. Sentenced to life imprisonment under the Guomindang. Became a leading official in Beijing's People's Press after 1949.

Lu Xun 鲁迅 (Lu Hsün) (1881–1936).

Modern China's best-known novelist, essayist, and critic, known as 'China's Gorky'. His original name was Zhou Shuren 周树人.

Luo Han 罗汉 (Lo Han) (1898–1941?).

Expelled from France in 1921 and joined the CCP in 1922. Active in the Guomindang army until the 20 March Incident (1926). Became a Trotskyist in 1928 in Moscow and a leader of the Chinese Left Opposition. Died in Chongqing in a Japanese air raid.

Luo Qiyuan 罗綺园 (Lo Ch'i-yüan) (1893–1931).

Leader of the peasant movement in Guangdong, was arrested in Shanghai in 1931 and executed despite recanting.

Luo Shifan 罗世藩 (Lo Shih-fan).
An old Communist who turned to Trotskyism in 1929 together with Chen Duxiu. An activist among the workers, at one time close to the 'Conciliationists' headed by He Mengxiong. Arrested together with Chen (under the false name Wang Zhaoqun) and sentenced to five years in jail, but freed early due to the outbreak of the Sino-Japanese War. Died of illness in Hunan, probably in 1939.

Luo Xin (Lo Hsin).
A Hong Kong worker who became a Trotskyist together with Chen Duxiu.

Luo Zhanglong 罗章龙 (Lo Chang-lung) (1897–?).
A student leader at Beijing University during the May Fourth Movement of 1919. Joined the CCP when it was formed and became very active in the workers' movement. The leader in 1929–30 of the so-called 'conciliators'. Retired from active politics after his arrest by the Guomindang and was released, probably on condition.

Ma Yufu 马玉夫 (Ma Yü-fu).
A CCP labour activist who became a Trotskyist in 1929 and defected to the Guomindang two years later.

Mao Hongjian 毛鸿鑑 (Mao Hung-chien).
A leader of the Guangxi Trotskyists in the early 1930s. A member of the Central Committee of the Internationalist Workers' Party after 1949. Left the movement in 1951.

Mif, Pavel (1901–38).
Patron of the so-called Twenty Eight Bolsheviks at Sun Yat-sen University in Moscow. Arrested in 1937 and disappeared during the purges.

Ou Fang 区芳 (?–1931).
With Chen Yimou, Song Fengchun, and Shi Tang, one of the main founders of the first Trotskyist group in China. Returned from Moscow in early 1928. Active among workers in Hong Kong. Arrested in 1930 in Shanghai and imprisoned by the Guomindang. Ou and Chen died in prison, while Song and Shi left the movement after their release. In 1931, Chen was elected head of the Organisational Department of the unified Chinese Trotskyist organisation.

Pan Wenyu 潘文郁 (P'an Wen-yü).
A returned student from Moscow and collaborator with Li Lisan, later purged by the Wang Ming group.

Peng Pai 彭湃 (P'eng P'ai) (1896–1929).
Leader of the peasant associations in Hailufeng, Guangdong, after 1922. In October 1927, organised a peasant insurrection and led the armed peasant struggle in that area. After the defeat fled to Shanghai, where he was arrested and executed by the Guomindang.

Peng Shuzhi 彭述之 (P'eng Shu-chih, also written P'eng Shu-tse) (1896–1983).
A returned student from Moscow and a member of the Central Committee of the CCP after 1925. Chief editor of the Party organ during the 1925–7 revolution. Expelled

together with Chen Duxiu in November 1929, for supporting Trotskyism. Lived for several years in Los Angeles, California, before his death there. Aliases: Ivan Petrov; Xi Zhao; Nan Guan; Tao Bo; Ou Bo.

Pu Dezhi 濮德志 (P'u Teh-chih) (1905–?).

Joined the CCP in 1926, and was active in literature and the theatre. Became a Trotskyist in Moscow in 1928. Arrested for the second time together with Chen Duxiu in 1932 and released from prison in 1937. See also under Sun Xi. Aliases: Xi Liu; Pu Qingquan.

Qu Qiubai 瞿秋白 (Ch'ü Ch'iu-pai) (1899–1935).

A writer, translator, veteran Communist, and *de facto* General Secretary of the CCP from August 1927 to July 1928. Executed by Chiang Kai-shek.

Radek, Karl (1885–1939).

Went over to Stalin in 1929 and was defendant at the second Moscow trial. Died in prison.

Roy, M. N. (1887–1954).

An Indian nationalist and Communist, went to China in May 1927 as a representative of the Comintern.

Shen Yanbing 沈雁冰 (Shen Yen-ping) (1896–1981).

The pen-name of Mao Dun 矛盾. A veteran Communist and a participant in the revolution of 1925–7. A famous writer, second only to Lu Xun. The first Minister of Culture in the post-1949 Communist Government.

Shi Tang 史唐 (Shih T'ang).

See under Ou Fang.

Si Chaosheng (Ssu Ch'ao-sheng).

See under Liu Jialiang.

Snow, Edgar (1905–72).

Author of *Red Star over China*, the classic study on the Chinese Soviet movement.

Song Fengchun 宋逢春 (Sung Feng-ch'un).

See under Ou Fang.

Song Qingling 宋庆龄 (Soong Ch'ing-ling) (1892–1981).

The widow of Sun Yat-sen, and a member of the State Council of the Wuhan Government. Continued to favour collaboration with the CCP even after the left wing of the Guomindang split with the Communists.

Sun Xi 孙熙 (Sun Hsi).

A left-wing writer who joined the Trotskyists. After the outbreak of the Sino-Japanese War in 1937, Sun went to Yunnan with Zhao Ji. After 1949, Sun, Zhao Ji, and Pu Dezhi were arrested and interviewed in Kunming by Zhou Enlai, who urged them to 'reform'; Pu did so, and was freed immediately; Zhao and Sun stood firm, and were kept in jail, Zhao until 1979 and Sun, too, probably until 1979. Shortly after his release, Sun died. Alias: Sun Xuelu 孙雪庐.

Tan Pingshan 谭平山 (T'an P'ing-shan) (1887–1956).
An early leader of the CCP, expelled in 1927. Joined the Guomindang in 1937 and later became a supporter of the Revolutionary Committee of the Guomindang, which backed the Beijing Government after 1949.

Tao Xisheng 陶希圣 (T'ao Hsi-sheng) (1893–1988).
A writer, responsible for Chiang Kai-shek's *China's Destiny*. A member of the National Defence Council under Wang Jingwei in 1937. Briefly supported Wang's attempt to conclude a peaceful settlement of the war against Japan.

Wang Changyao (Wang Ch'ang-yao).
A returned student from Moscow who became a Trotskyist in the early 1930s. Active in the Beijing student movement before he returned to his native province of Shandong, together with his wife, Zhang Sanjie, to organise an anti-Japanese guerrilla detachment that was destroyed by the CCP.

Wang Delin 王德林 (Wang Teh-lin).
A leader of the anti-Japanese guerrilla forces in Manchuria after 1931. Wang's units were chiefly active in the southern part of Jilin province.

Wang Duqing 王独清 (Wang Tu-ch'ing) (1898–1940).
A poet and one of the four founders of the Creation Society. A professor at Sun Yat-sen University in Guangzhou. Went over to Trotskyism in 1929 together with Chen Duxiu. Died of typhoid.

Wang Fanxi 王凡西 (Wang Fan-hsi) (1907–2002).
Joined the Party in 1925 while a student at Beijing University. Became a Trotskyist in Moscow in 1928. Returned to China in 1929 and worked for a while as an aide to Zhou Enlai. Worked as a Trotskyist with Chen Duxiu in 1930–1, after being expelled from the Party. Was arrested for the first time in 1931 and again in 1937. Spent most of the intervening years in jail. Lived in exile after 1949. Aliases: Vasilii Pavlovich Kletkin; Wang Wenyuan 王文元; Wang Mingyuan; Lian Gen; Shuang Shan; San Nan; Feng Gang; Shou Yi; Yi De; San Yuan; Hui Quan; Liu Shuxun.

Wang Guolong 王国龙 (Wang Kuo-lung) (1914–2010).
Became a Trotskyist in 1929. A leader of the Wenzhou Trotskyists. Arrested in 1952 and sentenced to life.

Wang Jingwei 汪精卫 (Wang Ching-wei) (1883–1944).
A veteran member of the Guomindang and at first leader of its left wing. Later compromised with Chiang Kai-shek and ended up a Japanese puppet.

Wang Kequan 王克全 (Wang K'o-ch'üan) (1906–39).
A Shanghai labour leader and member of the Central Committee of the CCP, purged by the Wang Ming group in 1931 for belonging to the 'Conciliationist' grouping. Became an agent of the Guomindang and was murdered by other agents.

Wang Mengzou 王孟邹 (Wang Meng-tsou) (1877–1953).
A publisher friend of Chen Duxiu and supporter of all progressive movements in China since the beginning of the century.

Wang Ming 王明 (1904–74).

The pseudonym of Chen Shaoyu 陈绍禹, who was Stalin's main supporter in the CCP. His group dominated the Party after 1931, but was defeated after the Long March. His influence was finally eliminated at the Seventh Congress of the CCP in 1945.

Wang Ruofei 王若飞 (Wang Jo-fei) (1896–1946).

He joined the CCP in 1922, and was a member of its Central Committee until 1945. While in Moscow in 1928 as a member of the Chinese delegation to the Comintern, secretly expressed sympathy for the Trotskyist Opposition.

Wang Shiwei 王实味 (Wang Shih-wei) (1907–47).

A writer and translator, author of the well-known article 'The Wild Lily', and a Trotskyist sympathiser. The first victim (in Yan'an) of the CCP's repressive literary policy. Rehabilitated in 1990.

Wang Shuben (Wang Shu-pen) (?–1949).

See under Liu Jialiang.

Wang Songjiu (Wang Sung-chiu) (1922–52).

A young Trotskyist educator and organiser in Japanese-occupied Shanghai. Arrested by the Maoist secret police in 1952 and committed suicide in prison.

Wu Jiyan 吴季严 (Wu Chi-yen) (1904–52).

A returned student from Moscow, and nephew of Chen Duxiu. Joined the Northern Expedition under Ye Ting in 1926. Became a Trotskyist in 1929. Imprisoned in 1932, he accompanied Chen Duxiu to Jiangjin in 1938. Died of illness in July 1952.

Xiang Ying 项英 (Hsiang Ying) (1898–1941).

An early labour leader, member of the Politburo, and leader of the remnant military forces in Jiangxi after the Long March. Vice-commander of the New Fourth Army in 1938. Killed by a traitor after the Wannan Incident of January 1941.

Xiang Zhongfa 向忠发 (Hsiang Zhongfa) (1880–1931).

General Secretary of the CCP from 1928 to 1931, he was a workers' leader, promoted because of his record in the labour movement and his proletarian credentials at a time when the 1927 defeat was being blamed on the shortage of workers in the Party leadership. But lacked political ability and was largely ignorant of Marxist theory. Executed by Chiang Kai-shek in spite of capitulating after his arrest.

Xiao Changbin (Hsiao Ch'ang-pin).

Became a Trotskyist in Moscow in 1927, and was a founder of the Chinese Trotskyist organisation. Active in North China, he left the movement in 1931.

Ye Jianying 叶剑英 (Yeh Chien-ying) (1898–1986).

A professional military man who participated in the Northern Expedition and the Guangzhou Insurrection of December 1927. Chief of Staff of the CCP's Eighth Route Army after 1937. Became Defence Minister in the Beijing Government and was a member of the Politburo's Standing Committee.

Yin Kuan 尹宽 (Yin K'uan) (1897–1967).

A veteran Communist who joined the CCP in France, was active in its Shandong Provincial Committee, its Anhui Provincial Committee, and its Jiangsu-Zhejiang Regional Committee in 1925–7, and became a Trotskyist in 1929. Twice arrested by the Guomindang for his revolutionary activities, and arrested by the Maoists in 1952.

Yu Qiaqing 虞洽卿 (Yü Ch'ia-ch'ing) (1867–1945).

A famous Shanghai capitalist, Chairman of the Chamber of Commerce, and a benefactor of Chiang Kai-shek.

Yu Shuoyi 俞硕逌(Yü Shuo-i).

A leader of the Shanghai young Trotskyists who was the first to be arrested after 1949 and died in an asylum where he had been sent after developing schizophrenia. Alias: Yu Shouyi.

Yu Xiusong 俞秀松 (Yü Hsiu-sung) (1899–1938).

A veteran Communist and early leader of the Chinese students in Moscow before Wang Ming. Framed by Wang Ming in Xinjiang in 1937 as a 'Trotskyist' and sent back to the USSR, where he was executed.

Yun Daiying 恽代英 (Yün Tai-ying) (1895–1931).

A political instructor at the Huangpu Military Academy, and a member of the Central Committee of the CCP, he was one of the most respected leaders of the Party among revolutionary youth during the revolution of 1925–7. Executed by the Guomindang in 1931.

Zeng Meng 曾猛 (Tseng Meng) (1904–58?).

Introduced to the Communist Party by Deng Zhongxia 邓中夏 and Li Qihan 李启汉 in Guangzhou. Became a Trotskyist in Moscow. Worked under Zhou Enlai on return to China before his discovery and expulsion. Arrested in 1932 with Chen Duxiu and Peng Shuzhi, but bailed by a Guomindang agent. Returned to Wenzhou, where he worked as a Trotskyist. Arrested after 1949 but never sentenced. Died in prison sometime between 1958 and 1960.

Zhang Bolin 张柏林 (Chang Po-lin) (1876–1951).

The liberal founder and President of Tianjin's Nankai University, and a prominent Christian educator.

Zhang Dehan (Chang Teh-han) (1918–87).

Joined the underground Trotskyist organisation in 1939 and carried out educational work among the workers in Shanghai. Arrested by the Maoist secret police in 1952, released from a labour camp in 1979, and died of illness in 1987.

Zhang Deze (Chang Teh-tse) (1915–44).

A lawyer, who rendered valuable help to resistance fighters under the Japanese occupation in Shanghai. Joined the underground Trotskyist movement in 1939, and died of tuberculosis.

Zhang Guotao 张国焘 (Chang Kuo-t'ao) (1897–1979).

A founder of the CCP and one of the main leaders of the Communist-sponsored labour movement in the 1920s, he directed the Secretariat of the Chinese Labour Unions set up in July 1921. Leader of the Party's Fourth Front Army during the Long March, when he clashed with Mao. Left the Party in 1938 and ceased political activity thereafter.

Zhang Shizhao 章士钊 (Chang Shih-chao) (1882–1973).

A journalist, educator, government official, and lawyer. Opposed to the New Culture Movement and a bitter enemy of Lu Xun, but died a supporter of Maoism.

Zhang Te (Chang T'e).

Joined the Trotskyist movement in Moscow in 1927, left it in 1931, and was thereafter a supporter of the Guangxi warlords.

Zhang Yisen 张以森 (Chang I-sen) (1909–1980).

The wife of He Zishen, she participated in the Revolution of 1925–7. After its defeat, remained in the Party. Twice arrested by the Guomindang and served short prison terms. Became a Trotskyist in 1929, and remained so until she was arrested and persecuted in 1952 by the Mao régime. Died in a fit of schizophrenia.

Zhang Zuolin 张作霖 (Chang Tso-lin) (1873–1928).

The fiercely anti-Communist warlord leader of Manchuria, known as the Old Marshal.

Zhao Ji 赵济 (Chao Chi) (1902–94).

A veteran Communist who participated in the Northern Expedition as a political commissar and became a Trotskyist in Moscow in 1928. Active in the early stages of the Trotskyist movement in China.

Zhao Yuanren 赵元任 (Chao Yüan-jen, known as Y. R. Chao or Chao Yuen-ren) (1892–1982).

An internationally known Chinese linguist.

Zheng Chaolin 郑超麟 (Cheng Ch'ao-lin) (1901–98).

A writer and translator, joined the CCP in Paris in 1922. Returned to China in 1924 to edit the Party organ *Xiangdao* ('Guide Weekly'). A member of the Party's Hubei Provincial Committee during the Revolution of 1925–7, and a participant in the Emergency Conference of 7 August 1927. Became a Trotskyist in 1929, and a founder and leader of the Chinese Trotskyist organisation. Served seven years in prison under Chiang Kai-shek. Arrested by the Maoist secret police in 1952 and kept in prison without trial until 1979. His memoirs were published in China in 1986. Aliases: Yvon; Marlotov; Lin Chaozhen; Yi Wen; Wang Jian; Shuyan; Lin Yiwen; Jue Min; Yi Yin; Lan Yin; Tang Yushi; Ze Lian.

Zhou Enlai 周恩来 (Chou En-lai) (1898–1976).

Joined the CCP in France in 1922, and became its most prominent organiser, negotiator, and administrator. Survived all the CCP's internal factional struggles, and was premier of the People's Republic of China from 1949 until his death.

BIOGRAPHICAL LIST

Zhou Lüqiang 周履鏘 (Chou Lü-ch'iang) (1927–).
The youngest of the known Trotskyists, he was born in Wenzhou and joined the movement in 1947. Arrested in 1952 and sentenced to seven years, but did not return to Shanghai from Inner Mongolia until 1987.

Zhou Rensheng 周仁生 (Chou Jen-sheng) (1922–2004).
Became a Trotskyist in 1940. Active in Wenzhou. Arrested in 1952 and sentenced to life. Together with Wang Guolong, translated Deutscher's *Trotsky* trilogy while in prison.

Characters for Additional Chinese Names in Pantsov's and Spichak's Articles

Bu Shiji 卜世畸
Cai Chang 蔡畅
Cao Li 曹力
Chen Gang 陈刚
Chen Tanqiu 陈潭秋
Chen Yu 陈郁
Chen Yun 陈云
Chiang Ching-kuo 蒋经国
Deng Yisheng 邓宜生
Deng Zhongxia 邓中夏
Dong Yixiang 董亦湘
Fan Wenhui 范文惠
Fu Qinghua 傅清华
Gao Zili 高自立
Gu Rongyi 雇容宜
Guo Miaogen 郭妙跟
Guo Zhaotang 郭肇堂
He Zizhen 贺子珍
Huang Ping 黄平
Jiang Yuanqing 江元青
Jin Weiying 金维映
Kong Yuan 孔原
Li Guangti 李光悌
Li Guoxuan 李国瑄
Li Ming 李叩
Li Peize 李沛泽
Li Sha 李莎
Li Ting 李廷

Lin Biao 林彪
Liu Changsheng 刘长胜
Lu Yeshen 鲁也参
Lu Yongquan 鲁湧泉
Luo Mai 罗迈
Ma Huizhi 马辉之
Ma Yuansheng 马员生
Meng Qingshu 孟庆树
Pan Kelu 潘克鲁
Sheng Yue 盛岳
Shi Zhe 师哲
Song Yiping 宋一平
Tang Youzhang 唐有章
Wang Guanlan 王观澜
Wang Jueyuan 王觉源
Wang Shiyuan 汪士元
Wen Yun 文云
Wu Kejian 吴克坚
Wu Xingcai 吴幸才
Xu Jie 徐杰
Yan Hongyan 阎红颜
Yang Xingfu 杨醒夫
Yang Xiufeng 杨秀峰
Yang Zhihua 杨之华
Yang Zhongyi 杨仲义
Zhang Hesheng 张和生
Zhou Dawen 周达文
Zhou Hesen 周和森
Zhu Daijie 朱代杰

References

Adibekov, G. M., E. M. Shakhnazarova, and K. K. Shirinia 1997, *Organizatsionnaia struktura Kominterna. 1919–1943* ('Organisational structure of the Comintern. 1919–1943'), Moscow: Rosspen.

Babichenko, Leonid G. 1989, 'Rol shkol Kominterna v ideino-teoreticheskom obuchenii kadrov kompartii' ('The role of the Comintern schools in the ideological and theoretical training of the communist parties' cadres'), in *Komintern: Opyt, traditsii, uroki: Materialy nauchnoi konferentsii, posviashchennoi 70-letiyu Kommunisticheskogo Internationala* ('The Comintern: Its experience, traditions, and lessons: Materials of the scientific conference dedicated to the Seventieth Anniversary of the Communist International'), Moscow.

Banac, Ivo (ed.) 2003, *The Diary of Georgi Dimitrov, 1933–1949*, New Haven: Yale University Press.

Benton, Gregor 1975, 'The Yenan Literary Opposition', *New Left Review*, I/92.

——— 1977, 'Teng's Comrade Still Behind Bars', International Edition of *The Guardian, Le Monde*, and *The Washington Post*, November 9.

——— 1979, 'Zheng Chaolin Released', *Intercontinental Press* (New York), 17, 35: 926–7.

——— 1982, 'Writers and the Party: The Ordeal of Wang Shiwei, Yan'an, 1942', in Benton (ed.) 1982.

——— 1985, 'Two Purged Leaders of Early Chinese Communism', *China Quarterly*, 102: 317–28.

——— 1991a, 'Introduction', in Wang Fan-hsi 1991.

——— 1991b, 'Zhang's Hat on Li's Head: Chronic Case of Quid Pro Quo in the History Books', *China Quarterly* 126: 364–6.

——— 1992, *Mountain Fires: The Red Army's Three-Year War in South China, 1934–1938*, Berkeley, CA: University of California Press.

——— 1996, *China's Urban Revolutionaries: Explorations in the History of Chinese Trotskyism, 1921–1952*, Atlantic Highlands, NJ: Humanities Press.

Benton, Gregor, and Alan Hunter (eds) 1995, *Wild Lily, Prairie Fire: China's Movement for Democracy, Yan'an to Tian'anmen, 1942–1989*, Princeton: Princeton University Press.

Benton, Gregor (ed.) 1982, *Wild Lilies, Poisonous Weeds: Dissident Voices from People's China*, London: Pluto.

——— 1997, *An Oppositionist for Life: Memoirs of the Chinese Revolutionary Zheng Chaolin*, translated by Gregor Benton, Atlantic Highlands, NJ: Humanities Press.

——— 1998, *Chen Duxiu's Last Articles and Letters, 1937–1942*, Honolulu: University of Hawaii Press.

Bo Chen (Liang Si) 1986, *Huigu, 1918–1948* ('Recollections, 1918–1948'), unpublished manuscript.

Brandt, Conrad 1958, *Stalin's Failure in China*, New York: W. W. Norton.

Brandt, Conrad, Benjamin Schwartz and John K. Fairbank (eds) 1967, *A Documentary History of Chinese Communism*, New York: Atheneum.

Burton, Robert A. 1966, Interviews with Peng Shuzhi and Chen Bilan, August 11–13.

Cadart, Claude, and Cheng Yingxiang 1983, *Mémoires de Peng Shuzhi: L'Envol du communisme en Chine*, Paris: Gallimard.

Cai Hesen 1961, 'Jihui zhuyi shi' ('A history of opportunism'), reprinted in *Gongfei huoguo shiliao huibian* ('Historical materials on the Communist bandits' ruining of China'), Vol. 1, Taibei.

Chang Kuo-t'ao (Zhang Guotao) 1971–2, *The Rise of the Chinese Communist Party, 1921–1938*, 2 vols, Lawrence, KA: The University Press of Kansas.

Chen [Zhongshan] 1956–60, 'The Letter', in Lu Xun 1956–60, Vol. 4.

Chen Bilan 1992, *Wo de huiyi: Yige Zhongguo gemingzhe de huigu* ('My memoirs: Recollections of a Chinese revolutionary'), Hong Kong: Shiyue shuju.

Chen Bilan 2010, *Zaoqi Zhonggong yu Tuopai: Wo de geming shengya huiyi* ('The early CCP and the Trotskyists: Memoirs of my revolutionary career'), Hong Kong: Tiandi.

Chen Bilan n.d. [1961], 'Gei Liu Yi tongzhi de xin' ('Letter to Comrade Liu Yi'), 29 April, in Peng Shuzhi 2010.

Chen Duxiu 1922, 'Chen Duxiu zhi Weitingkang de xin' ('Chen Duxiu's letter to Voitinsky'), in *Zhonggong zhongyang wenjian xuanji* ('Selected documents of the CCP Central Committee'), Vol. 1, Beijing: CCP Central Committee Party School.

———— 1923a, 'Zichan jieji de geming yu geming de zichan jieji' ('Bourgeois revolution and the revolutionary bourgeoisie'), *Xiangdao*, no. 22, Tokyo reprint 1963.

———— 1923b, 'Zhongguo guomin geming yu shehui ge jieji' ('The Chinese national revolution and all social classes'), *Qianfeng*, 1, 2.

———— 1980 [1938], 'Gei *Xinhua ribao* de xin' ('Letter to *New China Daily*'), reprinted in Zhang Yongtong and Liu Chuanxue (eds) 1980, pp. 112–33.

———— 1982–3 [1933], 'Fuyan' ('Appendix'), in Peng Shuzhi 1982–3, Vol. 2.

———— 1987 [1929], 'Zhi Zhonggong zhongyang (guanyu Zhongguo geming wenti)' ('To the Central Committee of the CCP [on the question of the Chinese Revolution]'), in Shui Ru (ed.) 1987.

Ch'en Pi-lan (Chen Bilan) 1973, 'The Real Lesson of China on Guerrilla Warfare: Reply to a "Letter from a Chinese Trotskyist"', *International Internal Discussion Bulletin*, x, 2, February.

Ch'en Pi-lan 1980 [1970], 'Introduction: Looking Back Over My Years With P'eng Shutse', in P'eng Shu-tse 1980. (This article was first published in English in three consecutive issues of *Intercontinental Press* [New York] on 2, 9 and 16 November 1970, under the name Peng Pi-lan.)

Chen Shengchang 1990, 'Tuoluociji de wenyi lilun dui Lu Xun de yingxiang' ('The influence on Lu Xun of Trotsky's literary theory'), *Xianggang Zhongwen daxue Zhongguo wenhua yanjiu suo xuebao*, 21: 285–311.

Chen Zhili 1991, *Zhongguo gongchandang jianshe shi* ('The founding of the Chinese Communist Party'), Shanghai: Shanghai renmin chuban she.

Cheng Yingxiang 1998, 'Xinji huanzhu, zhisi buxiu' ('Struggle until death in a painful world'), *Shiyue pinglun*, 191: 16–17.

Cheng Yingxiang and Claude Cadart 1986, 'Remarks on a Review of Peng Shuzhi's Memoirs', *China Quarterly*, 197: 530–4.

Cheng, Ching-mao 1977, 'The Impact of Japanese Literary Trends on Modern Chinese Writers', in Goldman (ed.) 1977.

Chiang Ching-kuo 1963, *My Days in Soviet Russia*, Taibei.

Chow Tse-tsung 1960, *The May Fourth Movement: Intellectual Revolution in Modern China*, Cambridge, MA: Harvard University Press.

Cohen, Steven 1973, *Bukharin and the Bolshevik Revolution: A Political Biography, 1888–1938*, New York: A. A. Knopf.

Communist International 1922, *The First Congress of the Toilers of the Far East*, Petrograd: The Communist International.

——— 1923, *Fourth World Congress of the Communist International, November 5–December 3, 1922*, Moscow and Petrograd: The Communist International.

Dai Qing 1989, *Xiandai Zhongguo zhishi fenzi qun: Liang Shuming, Wang Shiwei, Chu Anping* ('Contemporary Chinese intellectuals: Liang Shuming, Wang Shiwei, and Chu Anping'), Nanjing: Jiangsu wenyi chuban she.

——— 1994, *Wang Shiwei and 'Wild Lilies': Rectification and Purges in the Chinese Communist Party, 1942–1944*, edited by David E. Apter and Timothy Cheek, translated by Nancy Liu and Lawrence R. Sullivan, documents compiled by Song Jinshou, Armonk, NY: M. E. Sharpe.

Degras, Jane 1960, *The Communist International, 1919–1943*, Vol. 2, Oxford: Oxford University Press.

Deutscher, Isaac 1954, *The Prophet Armed. Trotsky: 1879–1921*, Oxford: Oxford University Press.

——— 1959, *The Prophet Unarmed, 1921–1929*, New York: Vintage Books.

Din-Savva, Lena 2000, *Iz Moskvy da v Pekin. Vospominaniya* (From Moscow to Beijing: Memoirs), Tenafly, NJ: Hermitage Publishers.

Dirlik, Arif 1989, *The Origins of Chinese Communism*, Oxford: Oxford University Press.

Douw, Leo 1991, The Representation of China's Rural Backwardness, 1932–1937, PhD thesis, University of Leiden.

Durand, Damien 1990, 'The Birth of the Chinese Left Opposition', *Revolutionary History*, 2, 4: 7–15.

Esherick, Joseph 1972, 'Harvard on China: The Apologetics of Imperialism', *Bulletin of Concerned Asian Scholars*, 4, 4: 9–16.

Evans, Les, and Russell Block (eds) 1976, *Leon Trotsky on China*, New York: Monad Press.

Feigon, Lee 1983a, book review, *Theory and Society*, 2: 259–65.

——— 1983b, *Chen Duxiu, Founder of the Chinese Communist Party*, Princeton: Princeton University Press.

——— 1990, *China Rising: The Meaning of Tiananmen*, Chicago: Ivan R. Dee.

Fogel, Joshua A. 1987, *Ai Ssu-ch'i's Contribution to the Development of Chinese Marxism*, Cambridge, MA: The Council on East Asian Studies/Harvard University, Harvard Contemporary China Series.

Franklin, Benjamin 1953, *The Autobiography*, New York: Liberal Arts Press.

Fu Shangwen 1983, 'Zhonggong "Sida" tichu wuchan jieji lingdaoquan wenti tantao' ('On the raising of the issue of proletarian hegemony at the Fourth Congress of the Chinese Communist Party'), *Lishi jiaoxue*, 12 (quoted in Zhen Yan n.d.).

Galitskii, Vladimir P. 2003, *Jiang Jingguo: Tragediya i triumf syna Chiang Kai-shek* ('Chiang Ching-kuo: A tragedy and triumph of Chiang Kai-shek's son'), Moscow: RAU-Universitet.

Gao Jun and Fan Yinzheng 1983, 'Ren Bishi', in Hu Hua (ed.) 1980–, Vol. 8.

Garver, John W. 1988, *Chinese-Soviet Relations, 1937–1945: The Diplomacy of Chinese Nationalism*, Oxford: Oxford University Press.

Glass, Frank 1990 [1939], 'The Communist League of China', *Revolutionary History*, 2, 4: 26–8.

Goldman, Merle 1967, *Literary Dissent in Communist China*, Cambridge, MA: Harvard University Press.

Goldman, Merle (ed.) 1977, *Modern Chinese Literature in the May Fourth Era*, Cambridge, MA: Harvard University Press.

Griffin, Nicholas John 1973, *The Use of Chinese Labor by the British Army, 1916–1920: The 'Raw Importation', Its Scope and Problems*, PhD thesis, University of Oklahoma.

Guo Chengtang (Thomas Kuo) 1992, *Chen Duxiu yu Zhongguo gongchan zhuyi yundong* ('Chen Duxiu and the Chinese Communist Movement'), Taibei: Lianjing chuban shiye gongsi.

Guo Hualun 1969–71, *Zhonggong shilun* ('Analytical history of the Chinese Communist Party'), 4 vols, Taibei: Zhonghua minguo guoji guanxi yanjiu suo.

Harrison, James P. 1972, *The Long March to Power: A History of the Chinese Communist Party, 1921–72*, New York: Macmillan.

Heller, I. 1925, 'The Labour movement in China', *The Communist International*, 17.

Hirson, Baruch 1988, 'Death of a Revolutionary: Frank Glass/Li Fu-jen/John Liang', *Searchlight South Africa*, 1: 28–41.

——— 2003, *Frank Glass, the Restless Revolutionary*, with an introduction by Gregor Benton, London: Porcupine Press.

Hsia, C. T. 1971, *A History of Modern Chinese Fiction*, second edition, New Haven: Yale University Press.

Hsia, Tsi-an 1968, 'Lu Hsün [Lu Xun] and the League of Leftist Writers', in *The Gate of Darkness: Studies on the Leftist Literary Movement in China*, Seattle: University of Washington Press.

Hsu, U. T. (Xu Enzeng) n.d., *The Invisible Conflict: The Behind-the-Scenes Battle in Pre-'49 China*, Hong Kong: Dragonfly Books.

Hu Feng 1993a, 'Lu Xun xiansheng' ('Mr Lu Xun'), *Xin wenxue shiliao* ('New historical materials on literature'), 1: 4–36.

────── 1993b, 'Guanyu sanshi niandai qianqi he Lu Xun youguan de ershier tiao tiwen' ('Twenty-two questions regarding Lu Xun in the early 1930s'), *Xinhua wenzhai*, 3: 135–46.

Hu Hua (ed.) 1980–, *Zhonggong dangshi renwu zhuan* ('Chinese Communist Party biographies'), Xi'an: Shaanxi renmin chuban she.

Huang Houheng 1981, 'Zhenjing chuxian baixi bunao' ('Keep calm in times of danger, be indomitable'), in *Huiyi Ye Ting* ('In memory of Ye Ting'), Beijing: Renmin chuban she.

Huang Yongsheng and Wang Yafei 1987, 'Chen Duxiu zai Jiangjin de zuihou suiyue' ('Chen Duxiu's last years at Jiangjin'), *Geming shi ziliao* ('Materials on revolutionary history'), no. 6, pp. 46–52.

Hui Quan (Wang Fanxi) 1971, 'Zhongyi ben chuban xiaoxu' ('Translator's preface to the Chinese edition'), Tuoluociji (Leon Trotsky), *Wenxue yu geming* ('Literature and Revolution'), translated by Hui Quan, Hong Kong: Xinda chuban she.

Hume, David 1854, 'My Own Life', in *Philosophical Works*, Vol. 1, Boston: Little, Brown & Co.

Ip, Hung-yok 1994, 'The Origins of Chinese Communism: A New Interpretation', *Modern China*, 20, 1: 34–63.

Isaacs, Harold R. 1961, *The Tragedy of the Chinese Revolution*, Stanford, CA: Stanford University Press.

────── 1985, *Re-encounters in China: Notes of a Journey in a Time Capsule*, Armonk, NY: M. E. Sharpe.

Jiang Guangchi 1983, *Xuanji* ('Selected works'), Beijing: Renmin wenxue chuban she.

Jiang Qi and Shou Shangwen 1980, 'Ruhe quanmian pingjia Tuoluociji de yisheng' ('How to make a rounded assessment of Trotsky's life'), *Shijie yanjiu dongtai*, 11.

Jiang Qi and Zhang Yueming 1980, 'Tuoluosiji "buduan geming lun" pingxi' ('Trotsky's "theory of permanent revolution"'), *Shijie yanjiu dongtai*, 11.

Jie Ya 1984, ' "Gongchan zhuyi zai Zhongguo de faren" – Faguo baokan dui Peng Shuzhi huiyi lu de pingjia' (' "Communism takes off in China" – Reviews in French periodicals of Peng Shuzhi's memoirs'), *Shiyue pinglun*, 1: 44–5.

Jin Shupeng 1993, ' "Lao Tuopai" Zheng Chaolin kanke yisheng' ('The lifetime of frustrations of the "old Trotskyist" Zheng Chaolin'), *Yanhuang chunqiu*, 16: 68–75.

Jin Zhao 1983, 'Chen Duxiu pingfan de qianqian houhou' ('Before and after the rehabilitation of Chen Duxiu'), *Zhongbao yuekan*, 7: 34–5.

Kagan, Richard 1969, *The Chinese Trotskyist Movement and Ch'en Tu-hsiu [Chen Duxiu]: Culture, Revolution, and Polity*, PhD thesis, University of Pennsylvania.

Kang Sheng 1938, 'Chanchu Rikou zhentan minzu gongdi de Tuoluociji feibang' ('Root out the Trotskyist criminals, who are spies for Japan and public enemies of the nation'), *Jiefang zhoukan*, 29 and 30 (28 January and 8 February).

Kipnis, S. Ye. 1998, *Novodevichii memorial. Nekropol monastyria i kladbishcha* ('The Novodevichii memorial: Necropolis of the monastery and the cemetery'), Moscow: Art-Biznes Tsentr.

Knei-Paz, Baruch 1978, *The Social and Political Thought of Leon Trotsky*, Oxford: Clarendon Press.

Krymov, Afanasii G. (Guo Shaotang) 1989, *Istoriko-memuarnyie zapiski kitaiskogo revoliutsionera* ('Historical and memoir notes of the Chinese revolutionary'), Moscow: Nauka.

Kuhfus, Peter 1985, 'Chen Duxiu and Leon Trotsky', *China Quarterly* 102: 253–76.

Kuo, Thomas 1975, *Ch'en Tu-hsiu (1879–1942) and the Chinese Communist Movement*, South Orange, NJ: Seton Hall University Press.

'La lettre du Shanghai, par trois membres de la mission de I.C. en Chine' 1965 [1927], in Pierre Broué (ed.) *La question chinoise dans l'Internationale Communiste (1926–1927)*, Paris: EDI.

Ladany, Laszlo 1988, *The Communist Party of China and Marxism, 1921–1985: A Self-Portrait*, London: Hurst.

Larin, Alexander G. 2003, *Kitaitsy v Rossii vchera i segodnia* ('The Chinese in Russia yesterday and today'), Moscow: IDV RAN.

Lau Sanching (Liu Shanqing) 1992, *Wuhui de zhengcheng* ('Journey without regrets'), Hong Kong: Mingbao chuban she.

Lee, Mabel 1982, 'Suicide of the Creative Self: The Case of Lu Hsün', in *Austrina: Essays in Commemoration of the 25th Anniversary of the Founding of the Oriental Society of Australia*, edited by A. R. Davis and A. D. Stefanowska, Sydney: Oriental Society of Australia.

Lenin, V. I. 1960–72 [1905], 'Two Tactics of Social-Democracy in the Democratic Revolution', *Collected Works*, Vol. 9, Moscow: Progress Publishers.

——— 1960–72 [1917a], 'Letters from Afar', *Collected Works*, Vol. 23, Moscow: Progress Publishers.

——— 1960–72 [1917b], 'The Tasks of the Proletariat in the Present Situation', *Collected Works*, Vol. 24, Moscow: Progress Publishers.

——— 1960–72 [1917c], 'Letter on Tactics', *Collected Works*, Vol. 24, Moscow: Progress Publishers.

——— 1960–72 [1920a], '"Left-Wing" Communism – An Infantile Disorder', *Collected Works*, Vol. 31, Moscow: Progress Publishers.

——— 1960–72 [1920b], 'Speech on Affiliation to the British Labour Party', 6 August, *Collected Works*, Vol. 31, Moscow: Progress Publishers.

——— 1960–72 [1921a], 'Fourth Anniversary of the October Revolution', *Collected Works*, Vol. 33, Moscow: Progress Publishers.

——— 1960–72 [1921b], 'New Times and Old Mistakes in an Old Guise', *Collected Works*, Vol. 33, Moscow: Progress Publishers.

Li Weihan 1981, 'Huainian Qiubai' ('In memory of Qiubai'), in 'Yi Qiubai' bianji xiaozu (eds), *Yi Qiubai* ('Remembering Qiubai'), Beijing: Renmin wenxue chuban she.

Lian Gen (Wang Fanxi) and Gu He (Lou Guohua) 1978, *Zuzhi zhangcheng (caoan)* ('Organisational statutes [draft]'), Hong Kong.

Lin Cuifen 1991, 'Zhonggong rencuo, Wang Shiwei pingfan' ('The CCP admits its error, Wang Shiwei is rehabilitated'), *Mingbao* (Hong Kong), 25 May.

Liu Jialiang 1949, *Zhongguo de xianzhuang yu qiantu* (China's present and future), Hong Kong.

Liu Qifa and Qian Feng 1981, 'Diyi ci guogong hezuo de celüe wenti' ('On the tactics of the first co-operation between the Guomindang and the Chinese Communist Party'), *Jiang Han luntan*, 4.

'Liu Renjing tan Tuoluociji pai zai Zhongguo' ('Liu Renjing on the Trotskyist group in China') 1982, *Zhonggong dangshi ziliao* ('CCP historical materials'), 1, February: 238–55.

Liu Shaoqi tongzhi shengping huodong nianbiao, 1898–1969 ('A Chronicle of the Activities of Comrade Liu Shaoqi, 1898–1969') 1980, Zhongguo geming bowuguan, April.

Liu Yiyu and Liu Jingchun 1983, 'Luo Yinong', in Hua Hua (ed.) 1980–, Vol. 8.

Lou Shiyi 1989, 'Xu' ('Preface'), in Zheng Chaolin, *Yu Yin canji* ('Surviving poems by Yu Yin [Zheng Chaolin]'), edited by Zhu Zheng, Changsha: Hunan renmin chuban she.

Lu Xun 1956–60, *Selected Works*, translated by Yang Xianyi and Gladys Yang, 4 Vols, Beijing: Foreign Languages Press.

——— 1956–60 [1927], 'Literature of a Revolutionary Period', in Lu Xun 1956–60, Vol. 2.

——— 1956–60 [1929], 'Some Thoughts on Our New Literature', in Lu Xun 1956–60, Vol. 3.

——— 1956–60 [1936a], 'Jottings in Mid-Summer', in Lu Xun 1956–60, Vol. 4.

——— 1956–60 [1936b], 'Reply to Xu Maoyong and on the Question of the United Front against Japanese Aggression', in Lu Xun 1956–60, Vol. 4.

——— 1963, *Quanji* ('Complete works'), Beijing: Renmin wenxue chuban she, 9 Vols.

——— 1963 [1933], 'Wo zenmo zuoqi xiaoshuo lai' ('How I started writing novels'), in Lu Xun 1963, vol. 4.

―――― 1991, *Quanji* ('Collected works'), 18 Vols, Beijing: Renmin wenxue chuban she.

―――― 1991 [1926], 'Zhege yu nege' ('This and that'), in Lu Xun 1991.

Ma Yuansheng 1987, *Liu Su jishi* ('Notes on my life in the USSR'), Beijing: Qunzhong chuban she.

Mandel, Ernest 1994, *Revolutionary Marxism and Social Reality in the Twentieth Century*, New Jersey: Humanities Press.

Mao Mao 1993, *Wo de fuqin Deng Xiaoping* ['My father Deng Xiaoping'], Vol. 1, Beijing: Zhongguo wenzang chuban she.

Mao Tse-tung (Mao Zedong) 1967 [1935], 'On Tactics Against Japanese Imperialism', *Selected Works*, Vol. 1, Beijing: Foreign Languages Press.

―――― 1955 [1942], 'Talks at the Yenan [Yan'an] Forum on Literature and Art', in *Selected Works of Mao Tse-tung*, Vol. 3, Beijing: Foreign Languages Press.

Mao Zedong 1923, 'Beijing zhengbian yu shangren' ('The Beijing coup and the merchants'), *Xiangdao*, 31–2, Tokyo reprint 1963.

―――― 1969 [1958], 'Zai Chengdu huiyishang de jianghua (1958 nian 3 yue), sanyue shiri de jianghua' ('Speeches at the Chengdu conference [March 1958], speech of 10 March'), in *Mao Zedong sixiang wansui* ('Long Live Mao Zedong Thought'), reprint, Taibei.

―――― 1970–2 [1926], 'Zhongguo shehui ge jieji de fenxi' ('An analysis of the classes in Chinese society') (1 February), in Mao Zedong, *Mao Zedong ji* (Collected writings of Mao Zedong), Vol. 1, Tokyo: Hokubosha.

―――― 1991, *Xuanji* (Selected works'), 4 Vols, Beijing: Renmin chuban she.

Marx, Karl, and Frederick Engels 1972, *On Colonialism*, New York: International Publishers.

Mathiez, Albert 1922–7, *La révolution française* ('The French Revolution'), 3 vols, Paris: Max Leclerc et Cie.

MacKinnon, Janice R., and Stephen R. MacKinnon 1988, *Agnes Smedley: The Life and Times of an American Radical*, Berkeley, CA: University of California Press.

McLoughlin, Barry 1997, 'Proletarian Academics or Party Functionaries? Irish Communists at the International Lenin School, Moscow, 1927–1937', in *Saothar (Yearbook of the Irish Labour History Society)*, 22.

Mei Zhi 2013, *F: Hu Feng's Prison Years*, edited and translated by Gregor Benton, London and New York: Verso.

Meng Qingshu n. d., *Vospominaniya o Wang Ming* (Memoirs of Wang Ming), manuscript, Moscow.

Miller, Joseph T. 1976, Interviews with Peng Shuzhi and Chen Bilan, January 9–16.

―――― 1979, *The Politics of Chinese Trotskyism: The Role of a Permanent Opposition in Communism*, PhD thesis, University of Illinois at Urbana-Champaign.

―――― 2001, 'Peng Shuzhi and the Chinese Revolution: Notes Towards a Political Biography', *Historical Materialism*, 8.

Ngo Van 1995, *Revolutionaries They Could Not Break: The Fight for the Fourth International in Indochina, 1930–1945*, London: Index Books.

―――― 2010, *In the Crossfire: Adventures of a Vietnamese Revolutionary*, edited by Ken Knabb and Hélène Fleury, translated by Hélène Fleury, Hilary Horrocks, Ken Knabb, and Naomi Sager, Edinburgh: AK Press.

Niel Sih [Liu Renjing] 1934, *Five Years of the Left Opposition: An Attempt to Explain its Failure to Make Progress*, unpublished manuscript, Peiping (Beijing), 7 July.

Nikiforov, Vladimir N. 1962, *Sovetskiye istoriki o problemakh Kitaia* ('Soviet historians on China issues'), Moscow: Nauka.

Ogata Yasushi 1995, 'Shohyô *Chûgoku Torotsukiha-shi*' ('Review of *A History of Chinese Trotskyism*'), *Torotsukii kenkyû* ('Trotsky Studies'), 15: 148–53.

Orwell, Sonia, and Ian Angus (eds) 1970, *The Collected Essays, Journalism and Letters of George Orwell*, Vol. 1, *An Age Like This, 1920–1940*, Harmondsworth: Penguin Books.

Pantsov, Alexander 1998, 'The Fate of a Chinese Trotskyist', *Problemy Dal'nego Vostoka* ('Problems of the Far East'), 3–4.

―――― 2000, *The Bolsheviks and the Chinese Revolution, 1919–1927*, Honolulu: University of Hawai'i Press.

―――― 2005, 'How Stalin Helped Mao Zedong Become the Leader: New Archival Documents On Moscow's Role in the Rise of Mao', *Issues and Studies*, 41, 3: 181–207.

―――― 2007, *Mao Zedong*, Moscow: Molodaya Gvardiya.

Pantsov, Alexander, and Gregor Benton 1994, 'Did Leon Trotsky Oppose the CCP Joining the Guomindang "From the First"?' *Republican China* 19: 52–66.

Pantsov, Alexander, and Steven I. Levine n.d., *Chinese Comintern Activists: An Analytic Biographic Dictionary*, unpublished manuscript.

Peng Shu-tse (Peng Shuzhi) 1976, 'Introduction', in Evans and Block (eds) 1976, translated from the Chinese by Joseph T. Miller and Huifang Li.

―――― 1980a, *The Chinese Communist Party in Power*, New York: Monad.

―――― 1980b, 'The Causes of the Victory of the Chinese Communist Party over Chiang Kai-shek, and the CCP's Perspectives', in P'eng Shu-tse (Peng Shuzhi) 1980a.

―――― 1980c, 'The Relationship and Differences Between Mao Tse-tung and Liu Shao-ch'i', in P'eng Shu-tse (Peng Shuzhi) 1980a.

Peng Shuzhi 1925, Letter, in Zhongyang dangshi ziliao zhengji weiyuan hui, Zhongyang dangshi yanjiu hui, eds, *Zhonggong dangshi ziliao*, Vol. 3, Zhongyang dangxiao chuban she.

―――― 1926, 'Womende beifa guan' ('Our views on the Northern Expedition'), *Xiangdao*, 170, Tokyo reprint 1963.

―――― 1927a, 'Liening zhuyi shifou bu shihe yu Zhongguo de suowei "guoqing"?' ('Is Leninism applicable to the so-called "national peculiarities" of China?'), *Xiangdao*, 184, Tokyo reprint 1963.

―――― 1927b, 'Muqian geming youqing weixian' ('Present rightist dangers to the revolution'), *Xiangdao*, 190, Tokyo reprint 1963.

———— 1927c, 'Dule Jiang Jieshi er yue ershiyi ri de jiangyan yihou' ('After reading Jiang Jieshi's February 21 speech'), *Xiangdao*, 192, Tokyo reprint 1963.

———— 1928, *Zhongguo geming zhong zhi genben wenti* ('Fundamental problems of the Chinese Revolution'), CCP Central Committee Publications Committee. Copy obtained from Peng Shuzhi in 1976.

———— 1929, *Gongdang lianxi huiyi tanhua* ('Talks to the Communist Party joint conference'), microfilm, University of Illinois Library.

———— 1948 [1924], *Zhongguo geming wenti lunwen ji* ('Documents on problems of the Chinese Revolution'), 1948, microfilm, Isaacs Collection.

———— 1968, 'Rang lishi de wenjian zuo zheng' ('Let historical documents show proof'), *Mingbao*, June.

———— 1972, letter to Richard Kagan, 12 January.

———— 1976, letter to Joseph T. Miller, 22 May.

———— 1980, 'Zhongguo di yige gongchan zhuyi xiaozu shi zenyang xingcheng de?' ('How did China's first Communist group form?'), *Shiyue pinglun*, 46: 13–15.

———— 1982–3, *Xuanji* ('Selected works'), 3 Vols, Hong Kong: Shiyue chuban she.

———— 1982–3 [1933], 'Lun lingxiu wenti' ('On the question of leadership'), in Peng Shuzhi 1982–3, Vol. 2.

———— 1982–3 [1942], 'Wei changwei dafu shaoshupai tongzhi shu' ('Reply on behalf of the standing committee to the minority comrades') (March 7), in Peng Shuzhi 1982–3, Vol. 2.

———— 1982–3 [1951], 'Guanyu Zhongguo jushi de baogao' ('Report on the situation in China'), in Peng Shuzhi 1982–3, Vol. 3.

———— 1983a, '*Peng Shuzhi huiyi lu* xuanyan: Bei yiwangle de Zhonggong jiandang renwu' ('From the *Memoirs of Peng Shuzhi*: A forgotten person in the establishment of the CCP'), translated by Cheng Yingxiang, *Zhengming*, 68: 68–72.

———— 1984, 'Dui Zheng Chaolin xugou gushi de jielu' ('Exposing Zheng Chaolin's fantastic stories'), *Zhongbao yuekan*, 1: 62–71.

———— 2010, *Xuanji* ('Selected Works'), Vol. 4, Hong Kong: Shiyue chuban she.

Pickowicz, Paul G. 1977, 'Qu Qiubai's Critique of the May Fourth Generation: Early Chinese Marxist Literary Criticism', in *Modern Chinese Literature in the May Fourth Era*, edited by Merle Goldman, Cambridge, MA: Harvard University Press.

Poeze, Harry Albert 1976, *Tan Malaka, Strijder voor Indonesië's Vrijheid: Levensloop van 1897 tot 1945*, The Hague: B. V. de Nederlandsche Boek-en Steen-drukkerij v/h H. L. Smits.

Price, Jane L. 1976, *Cadres, Commanders, and Commissars: The Training of the Chinese Communist Leadership, 1920–45*, Boulder, CO: Westview Press.

Price, Ruth 2005, *The Lives of Agnes Smedley*, Oxford: Oxford University Press.

Pu Qingquan 1980, 'Wo suo zhidao de Chen Duxiu' ('Chen Duxiu as I knew him'), *Wenshi ziliao xuanji* ('Selected materials on literature and history') (Beijing), no. 71.

Qian Jun 1985, ' "Suluyu bianqu" de gongfei "Su Tuo shijian" ' ('The Communist bandits' "purge of Trotskyists" in the "border region between Jiangsu, Shandong, and Henan" '), *Gongdang wenti yanjiu* (Taibei) 11, 4: 102–13.

Qiang Zhonghua et al. (eds) 1982, *Chen Duxiu beibu ziliao huibian* ('A compilation of materials concerning the times when Chen Duxiu was arrested'), Henan renmin chuban she.

Qin Yanshi et al. 1982, 'Liu Bojian', in Hu Hua (ed.) 1980–, Vol. 4.

Ren Jianshu and Tang Baolin 1989, *Chen Duxiu zhuan* ('A biography of Chen Duxiu'), 2 Vols, Shanghai: Shanghai renmin chuban she. (Ren wrote the first volume, subtitled *Cong xiucai dao zong shuji* ['From scholar to General Secretary'], and Tang the second, subtitled *Cong zong shuji dao fanduipai* ['From General Secretary to Oppositionist']).

Saich, Tony (ed.) 1991, *The Origins of the First United Front in China: The Role of Sneevliet (Alias Maring)*, 2 Vols, Leiden: Brill.

Saich, Tony and Hans van de Ven 1995, *New Perspectives on the Chinese Communist Revolution*, Armonk, New York: M. E. Sharpe.

San Yuan (Wang Fanxi) 1972, *Mao Zedong sixiang yu Zhong Su guanxi* ('Maoism and Sino-Soviet relations'), Hong Kong: Xinda chuban she.

Schram, Stuart R. (ed.) 1963, *The Political Thought of Mao Tse-tung*, Harmondsworth: Penguin.

Schwartz, Benjamin I. 1951, *Chinese Communism and the Rise of Mao*, Cambridge, MA: Harvard University Press.

Shachtman, Max 1969 [1931], 'Introduction to Leon Trotsky's *Problems of the Chinese Revolution*', in Trotsky 1969 [1931].

Shen Zui and Wen Qiang 1984, *Dai Li qi ren* ('Dai Li the man'), Beijing: Wenshi ziliao chuban she.

Sheng, Yueh 1971, *Sun Yat-sen University in Moscow and the Chinese Revolution: A Personal Account*, New York: Center for East Asian Studies, The University of Kansas.

Shi Zhe and Shi Qiulang 2001, *Wo de yisheng: Shi Zhe zishu* ('My life: The autobiography of Shi Zhe'), Beijing: Renmin chuban she.

Shuang Shan (Wang Fanxi) 1973, *Mao Zedong sixiang lungao* ('Studies on Mao Zedong Thought'), Hong Kong: Xinda chuban she.

——— 1978, *Lüeping 'Zuzhi yuanze yu fangfa'* ('A brief critique of "Organisational principles and methods" '), Hong Kong.

Shuang Shan 1957, 'Cong Chen Duxiu de "zuihou yijian" shuoqi' ('On Chen Duxiu's "last views" '), in *Sixiang wenti* ('Some ideological questions'), Hong Kong.

Shuang Shan (ed.) 1981, *Tuoluociji dang'an zhong zhi Zhongguo tongzhi de xin, 1929–1939* ('Letters in the Trotsky archives to Chinese comrades, 1929–1939'), Hong Kong.

Shui Ru (ed.) 1987, *Chen Duxiu shuxin ji* ('Collection of Chen Duxiu's letters'), Beijing: Xinhua chuban she.

Sima Lu 1962, *Qu Qiubai zhuan* ('A biography of Qu Qiubai'), Hong Kong.
Smith, S. A. 2000, *A Road is Made: Communism in Shanghai, 1920–1927*, Richmond: Curzon Press.
Stalin, Joseph 1940, *Leninism*, London: Lawrence and Wishart.
Summerskill, Michael 1982, *China on the Western Front: Britain's Chinese Work Force in the First World War*, London: Michael Summerskill.
Sun Qiming 1980, 'Chen Duxiu shifou Hanjian wenti de tantao' ('On whether or not Chen Duxiu was a traitor'), *Anhui daxue xuebao*, 2.
Tamás, G. M. 1993, 'The Legacy of Dissent', *Times Literary Supplement*, 14 May, 14–19.
Tang Baolin 1980, 'Jiu an xin kao: Guanyu Wang Ming Kang Sheng wuxian Chen Duxiu wei "Hanjian" de wenti', ('New research on an old case: On Wang Ming and Kang Sheng's framing of Chen Duxiu as a "national traitor" '), *Dangshi yanjiu*, 16.
——— 1994, *Zhongguo Tuopai shi* ('A history of Chinese Trotskyism'), Taibei: Dongda tushu gongsi.
Tang Baolin and Lin Maosheng 1988, *Chen Duxiu nianpu* ('A Chronology of the Life of Chen Duxiu'), Shanghai: Shanghai renmin chuban she.
Tang Baolin (ed.) 1993, *Chen Duxiu yucui* ('A compilation of Chen Duxiu's utterances'), Beijing: Huaxia chuban she.
Tang Youzhang 1988, *Geming yu liufang* ('Revolution and exile'), Changsha: Hunan renmin chuban she.
Thatcher, Ian 2002, *Trotsky*, London: Routledge.
Timofeeva, N. N. 1976, 'Kommunisticheskii universitet trudiashchikhsia Vostoka (KUTV) (1921–1925)' ('The Communist University of the Toilers of the East [KUTV] [1921–1925])', *Narody Azii i Afriki* ('Peoples of Asia and Africa'), 2: 47–57.
——— 1979, 'Kommunisticheskii universitet trudiashchikhsia Vostoka (KUTV) v 1926–1938 gg'. ('The Communist University of the Toilers of the East [KUTV] in 1926–1938'), *Narody Azii i Afriki* ('Peoples of Asia and Africa'), 5: 30–42.
Titarenko, M. L. et al. (eds) 1999, *VKP(B), Komintern i Kitai. Dokumenty* ('The AUCP[B], the Comintern and China. Documents'), Vols 3–4, Moscow: AO 'Buklet'.
Tőkés, Rudolf L. 1974, 'Dissent: The Politics for Change in the USSR', in *Soviet Politics and Society in the 1970's*, edited by Henry W. Morton, Rudolf L. Tőkés and J. N. Hazard, New York: The Free Press.
Torchinov, V. A., and A. M. Leontyuk 2000, *Vokrug Stalina. Istoriko-bibliograficheskii slovar* ('Around Stalin. A historical biographical dictionary'), St Petersburg: Filologicheskii fakul'tet Sankt-Peterburgskogo gosudarstvennogo universiteta.
Tripp, Ted n.d., *Moscow in the 1930s: How the Comintern was Stalinised*, available at <http://www.members.optushome.com.au/spainter/Tedtripp.html>.
Trotsky, Leon 1957 [1928], *The Third International after Lenin*, translated by John G. Wright, second edition, New York: Pioneer Publishers.

———— 1960, *Literature and Revolution*, translated by Rose Strunsky, Ann Arbor: University of Michigan Press.
———— 1967 [1932], *Problems of the Chinese Revolution*, edited by Max Shachtman, Ann Arbor: University of Michigan Press.
———— 1969 [1928], 'The Chinese Question after the Sixth Congress', in Trotsky 1969 [1931].
———— 1969 [1931], *Problems of the Chinese Revolution*, London: New Park.
———— 1970 [1930], *My Life: An Attempt at an Autobiography*, New York: Pathfinder Press.
———— 1971, 'Military Doctrine or Pseudo-Military Doctrinairism', in *Military Writings by Leon Trotsky*, New York: Pathfinder Press.
———— 1973 [1924], *Perspectives and Tasks in the East (Speech on the Third Anniversary of the Communist University for Toilers of the East, April 21, 1924)*, translated by R. Chappell, London: New Park Publications.
———— 1973 [1927], *The Platform of the Joint Opposition*, London: New Park.
———— 1975, *The Challenge of the Left Opposition (1923–25)*, New York: Pathfinder Press.
———— 1976 [1927], 'Summary and Perspective of the Chinese Revolution', in Evans and Block (eds) 1976.
———— 1976 [1935], 'Discussions with Harold Isaacs, August 1935', in Evans and Block (eds) 1976.
———— 1976 [1937], 'On the Sino-Japanese War', in Evans and Block (eds) 1976.
———— 1985 [1941], *Stalin*, 2 Vols, Benson, VT: Chalidze Press.
———— 1993, *Kommunisticheskii International posle Lenina. Velikii organizator porazhenii* ('The Comintern after Lenin. A great organiser of defeats'), Moscow: Spartakovets, Printima.
Trotzki, Leo (Leon Trotsky) 1990, *Schriften über China*, 2 vols, published as vols 2.1 and 2.2 of Leo Trotzki, *Schriften*, 10 Vols, edited by Helmut Dahmer, 1988-, Hamburg: Rasch and Röhring.
Tuoluociji (Leon Trotsky) 1947 [1927], 'Zhongguo geming de xin jieduan' ('The new stage in the Chinese Revolution'), in *Zhongguo geming wenti* ('Problems of the Chinese Revolution'), Shanghai: Chunyan chuban she.
———— 1992, *Wenxue yu geming* ('Literature and revolution'), translated by Liu Wenfei et al., Beijing: Waiguo wenxue chuban she.
Usov, Victor N. 1987, 'Internatsional'naia pomoshch' SSSR v dele podgotovki kitaiskikh partiinykh i revoliutsionnykh kadrov v 20–30-ie gody' ('Soviet international aid in the training of the Chinese party and revolutionary cadres in the 1920s–1930s'), *Problemy Dal'nego Vostoka* ('Far Eastern Affairs'), 5: 79–85.
Van de Ven, Hans 1991, *From Friend to Comrade: The Founding of the Chinese Communist Party, 1920–1927*, Berkeley, CA: University of California Press.

Van Goudoever, Albert Peter 1983, *Angst voor het verleden: Politieke rehabilitaties in de Sovjet Unie na 1953*, Utrecht: HES (translated as *The Limits of Destalinization in the Soviet Union: Political Rehabilitations in the Soviet Union since Stalin*, New York: St Martin's Press).

Van Heijenoort, Jean 1978, *With Trotsky in Exile: From Prinkipo to Coyoacán*, Cambridge, MA: Harvard University Press.

Wakeman, Jr, Frederic 1995, *Policing Shanghai, 1927–1937*, Berkeley, CA: University of California Press.

Wang F. (Wang Fanxi) 1974, 'Memoirs of a Chinese Trotskyist', *International*, 2, 3.

——— 1976, 'Corrections to "Memoirs of a Chinese Trotskyist"', *International*, 3, 2.

Wang Fan-hsi (Wang Fanxi) 1980, *Chinese Revolutionary: Memoirs, 1919–1949*, translated and with an introduction by Gregor Benton, Oxford: Oxford University Press.

Wang Fan-hsi 1991, *Memoirs of a Chinese Revolutionary*, translated and with an introduction by Gregor Benton, second revised edition, New York: Columbia University Press.

[Wang Fanxi] 1970, 'Guerrilla Warfare: The Lesson of China: Letter from a Chinese Trotskyist', *International Information Bulletin*, 7, September.

Wang Fanxi 1973, *On the Causes of the CCP's Victory and the Failure of the Chinese Trotskyists in the Third Chinese Revolution*, unpublished manuscript.

——— 1977, *Shuang Shan huiyi lu* ('Shuang Shan's memoirs'), Hong Kong: Zhouji hang.

——— 1980, *Shuang Shan huiyi lu* ('Shang Shan's memoirs'), Beijing: Xiandai shiliao biankan she (pirated from Wang Fanxi 1977).

——— 1982, 'Chen Duxiu, Father of Chinese Communism', in *Wild Lilies, Poisonous Weeds: Dissident Voices from People's China*, edited by Gregor Benton, London: Pluto.

——— 1990, 'Einleitung: Trotzki und der chinesische Kommunismus', in Trotzki 1990, Vol. 2, Part 1.

——— 1993, *Hu Feng yizhu duhou gan* ('A reaction to reading Hu Feng's posthumous writings'), unpublished manuscript, 1 November.

Wang Guangyuan (ed.) 1987, *Chen Duxiu nianpu* ('A Chronology of the Life of Chen Duxiu'), Chongqing: Chongqing chuban she.

Wang Hongmo 1985, 'Chen Duxiu: An Evaluation of His Life's Work', *Social Sciences in China*, 4, December: 9–38.

Wang Jueyuan 1969, *Liu E huiyi lu* ('Memoirs about my life in Russia'), Taibei: Sanmin shuju.

Wang Ruowang 1989, 'Yige "Tuopai fenzi" de gushi: Zizhuanzhi yizhang' ('The story of a "Trotskyist": A chapter of my autobiography'), *Wenhui yuekan*, 3 (Shanghai).

Wang Shiwei 1982 [1942], 'Politicians, Artists', in Benton (ed.) 1982.

Wang Shudi et al. (eds) 1982, *Chen Duxiu pinglun xuanbian* ('Selected appraisals of Chen Duxiu'), 2 Vols, Henan: Henan renmin chuban she.

Wang Yuanfang 1983, *Huiyi Yadong tushuguan* ('Remembering the Oriental Book Company'), Shanghai: Xinhua shudian.

Wang Ziye 1983, 'Xu' ('Preface'), in Wang Yuanfang 1983.

'Weijingsiji fu Shanghai mishi' ('Voitinsky's secret trip to Shanghai') 1981, in *Zhongguo geming yu Sulian guwen* ('The Chinese Revolution and Soviet advisors'), Beijing: Zhongguo shehui kexue chuban she.

Whiting, Alan S. 1968, *Soviet Policies in China, 1917–1924*, Stanford, CA: Stanford University Press.

Wilbur, C. Martin 1983, *The Nationalist Revolution in China, 1923–1928*, Cambridge: Cambridge University Press.

Wilbur, C. Martin and Julie Lien-ying How 1956, *Documents on Communism, Nationalism, and Soviet Advisers in China, 1918–1927*, New York: Columbia University Press.

Wilbur, C. Martin, and Julie Lien-ying How (eds) 1989, *Missionaries of Revolution: Soviet Advisers and Nationalist China, 1920–1927*, Cambridge, MA: Harvard University Press.

Wu Jimin 2008, *Lianyu: Zhongguo Tuopai de kunan yu fendou* ('Purgatory: The Chinese Trotskyists' ordeal and struggle'), Singapore: Bafang wenhua chuangzuo shi.

Wu K'un-jung 1974, 'The Left Opposition in the Chinese Communist Party', *Issues and Studies*, 10, 6.

Wu Min and Xiao Feng 1951, *Cong wusi dao Zhonghua renmin gonghe guo de dansheng* ('From May Fourth to the birth of the People's Republic of China'), Beijing: New Wave Bookstore.

Xiang Qing 1980, 'Guanyu gongchan guoji he Zhongguo wenti' ('On the Comintern and China'), *Xinhua yuebao*, 4: 75–9.

Xiao Jingguang 1980, 'Yi zaoqi fu Su xuexi shi de Shaoqi tongzhi' ('Memories of Comrade Shaoqi's early study in the Soviet Union'), in *Huainian Liu Shaoqi tongzhi* ('In commemoration of Comrade Liu Shaoqi'), Changsha: Hunan renmin chuban she.

―――― 1981, 'Fu Su xuexi qianhou' ('Before and after going to the Soviet Union to study'), in Zhongguo renmin zhengzhi xieshangyi quanguo weiyuan hui, wenshi ziliao yanjiu weiyuan hui, eds, *Geming shi ziliao* ('Materials on the history of the revolution'), 3, Beijing: Wenshi ziliao chuban she.

Xiao Ke 1994, 'Chen Duxiu shiji xu' ('Preface to the collected poems of Chen Duxiu'), in *Xin wenxue shiliao*, 1.

Xu Tian 2013, 'Tuoluociji zhuzuo cengshi jinshu, 1988 nian Sugong zhongyang wei qi pingfan' ('Trotsky's writings used to be forbidden, in 1988 they were rehabilitated by the Central Committee of the Soviet Communist Party'), *Zhongguo xinwen zhoukan* [Chinese news weekly], 14 November 2013.

Yang Xingfu 1985, 'Wo de huiyi: Fu Su jishi' ('My Memoirs: Notes on my trip to the USSR'), *Sulian wenti yanjiu ziliao* ('Materials on Soviet studies'), 1: 57–64.

Ye Qinhe 1981, 'Fengyu choumou yu xiongying' ('Amid storms to raise a great falcon'), in *Huiyi Ye Ting* ('In memory of Ye Ting'), Beijing: Renmin chuban she.

Yefimov, Gerontii V. 1977, 'Iz istorii Kommunisticheskogo universiteta trudiashchikhsia Kitaia' ('On the history of the Communist University of the Toilers of China'), *Problemy Dal'nego Vostoka* ('Far Eastern Affairs'), 2: 169–75.

Yi De (Wang Fanxi) 1950, *Sulian yanjiu* ('A study on the Soviet Union'), Hong Kong.

Yi Ding (Lou Guohua) 1976/77, 'Lu Xun yu Tuopai wenti de yixie xin ziliao' ('Some new materials regarding the question of Lu Xun and the Trotskyists'), *Xin guancha* (Hong Kong), pp. 24–6.

Yi Ding (Lou Guohua) 1976/77, *Lu Xun: Qi ren, qi shi, jiqi shidai* ('Lu Xun: The man, the works, and the age'), Paris: Centre de publication Asie orientale.

Yu Min-ling 1995, *Sun Yat-sen University in Moscow, 1925–1930*, PhD, New York University.

Yu Yin (Zheng Chaolin) 1989, *Yu Yin canji* ('Surviving poems by Yu Yin'), edited by Zhu Zheng, Hunan: Hunan renmin chuban she, 1989.

Yu-Ju Chih 1965, *The Political Thought of Ch'en Tu-hsiu*, PhD thesis, Indiana University.

Zarrow, Peter 1990, *Anarchism and Chinese Political Culture*, New York: Columbia University Press.

Zeng Yanxiu 2005, 'Dui Chen Duxiu jieshou Zhu Jiahua zengkuan shi jieyi' ('Clearing up doubts in regard to Chen Duxiu's acceptance of financial assistance from Zhu Jiahua'), *Yanhuang chunqiu*, 6.

Zhang Guotao 1973, 'Wo de huiyi ('My memoirs'), 3 vols, Hong Kong: Mingbao yuekan chuban she.

Zhang Yongtong and Liu Chuanxue, eds, 1980, *Houqi de Chen Duxiu jiqi wenzhang xuanbian* ('The later Chen Duxiu and a selection of his essays'), Sichuan: Renmin chuban she.

Zhen Yan n.d., *Dui ruogan zhengyixing lishi wenti de tantao* ('On some historical controversies'), unpublished manuscript.

[Zheng Chaolin] 1950, *Guojia ziben zhuyi lun* ('On state capitalism'), Hong Kong.

Zheng Chaolin 1979 or 1980, *Zheng Chaolin 1945 nian huiyi lu* ('Zheng Chaolin's 1945 memoirs'), mimeograph.

―――― 1983, 'Guanyu Muluhuosika (Mlokhoska) diming de shuoming' ('On the place-name Mlokhoska'), *Dangshi yanjiu ziliao*, 3.

―――― 1984a, 'Yiben gei ziji tuzhi mofen de huiyi lu' ('A self-whitewashing memoir'), 2 pts, *Zhongbao yuekan*, 4.

―――― 1984b, 'Peng Shuzhi biyan xiashuo' ('Peng Shuzhi's blind ramblings'), *Zhongbao yuekan*, 1: 62–71.

―――― 1986, *Zheng Chaolin huiyi lu* ('Zheng Chaolin's memoirs'), Beijing: Xiandai shiliao biankan she.

——— 1991, 'Xinban Maoxuan yu Tuopai yuan'an' ('The new edition of Mao's *Selected Works* and the injustice done to the Trotskyists'), *Kaifang zazhi*, 9 (Hong Kong): 47–9.
——— 1993, Tan Hu Feng 'Lu Xun xiansheng' yougan ('A reaction to Hu Feng's "Mr Lu Xun" ') (23 August), unpublished manuscript.
——— 1998, *Shishi yu huiyi: Zheng Chaolin wannian wenxuan* ('History and recollections: A selection of Zheng Chaolin's late writings'), Hong Kong: Tiandi tushu.
——— 2004, *Zheng Chaolin huiyi lu* ('Zheng Chaolin's memoirs'), 2 vols, edited by Fan Yong, Beijing: Dongfang chuban she.
Zheng Chaolin and Zhou Yongxiang 1983, 'Wo dui Qu Qiubai de yixie huiyi' ('Some recollections of Qu Qiubai'), *Shanghai wenshi ziliao xuanji*, 42: 42–52.
Zheng Xuejia 1989, *Chen Duxiu zhuan* ('A biography of Chen Duxiu'), 2 Vols, Taibei: Shibao wenhua chuban qiye youxian gongsi.
Zhi Yuru (Chih Yu-ju) 1974, *Chen Duxiu nianpu* ('A chronology of the life of Chen Duxiu'), Hong Kong: Longmen shudian.
Zhonggong liujie erzhong quanhui de 'zuzhi jueyian' (' "Resolutions on Organisational Issues," Second Plenary Session, Sixth Central Committee of the CCP') 1985 [1929], quoted in Wang Hongmo 1985.
Zhonggong zhongyang dangshi yanjiu shi (eds) 1982, *Zhonggong dangshi ziliao* ('Materials on CCP history'), Vol. 3, Beijing: CCP Central Committee Party School.
Zhonggong zhongyang dangxiao dangshi jiaoyan shi ziliao zu (eds) 1982, *Zhongguo gongchan dang lici zhongyao huiyiji* ('Important meetings of the Chinese Communist Party'), 2 Vols, Shanghai: Renmin chuban she.
Zhongguo geming bowuguan dangshi chenlie yanjiu bu (eds) 1982, *Zhonggong dangshi zhuyao shijian jianjie* ('Important events in the history of the Chinese Communist Party'), Chengdu: Sichuan renmin chuban she.
Zhongguo gongchandang zhongyang weiyuan hui 1991 [1936], 'Wei chuangli quanguo gedang gepai de kang Ri renmin zhenxian xuanyan' ('Manifesto for the setting up of an all-China anti-Japanese people's front of all parties and factions'), in Zhongyang dang'an guan (eds), *Zhonggong zhongyang wenjian xuanji* ('Selected documents of the Central Committee of the CCP'), Beijing: Zhonggong zhongyang dangxiao chuban she, 11, 25 April 1991: 17–19.
Zhongguo jiefang jun zhengzhi xueyuan shijiao yanshi (eds) n.d., *Zhonggong dangshi cankao ziliao* ('Reference materials on Chinese Communist Party history'), Vol. 3.
Zhongguo shehui kexue yuan jindai shi yanjiu suo fanyi shi (eds) 1981, *Gongchan guoji youguan Zhongguo geming de wenxian ziliao* ('Documentary materials of the Comintern relating to the Chinese Revolution'), Beijing: Zhongguo shehui kexue chuban she.
Zhongshan daxue 'Ye Ting' bianxie zu (eds) 1979, *Ye Ting*, Shaoguan: Guangdong renmin chuban she.

Zhongyang dang'an guan (eds) 1988, *Zhonggong zhongyang wenjian xuanji* ('Selected documents of the CCP Central Committee'), Beijing: CCP Central Committee Party School.

Zhongyang dangshi ziliao zhengji weiyuan hui, Zhongyang dangshi yanjiu hui (eds) n.d., *Zhonggong dangshi ziliao* ('Materials on Chinese Communist Party history'), Vol. 3, Zhongyang dangxiao chuban she.

Zhou Enlai 1981 [1929], 'On the Causes of the Emergence of a Trotskyite Opposition Faction in China and Its Prospects', October 1929, *Selected Works of Zhou Enlai*, Vol. 1, Beijing: Foreign Languages Press.

Zhou Meisen 1997, *Zhong'e* ('Hames'), Wuhan: Changjiang wen yi chuban she.

Zhou Yongxiang (ed.) 1983, *Qu Qiubai nianpu* ('Chronology of the life of Qu Qiubai'), Guangdong renmin chuban she.

Zhuanji wenxue zazhi she (eds) 1967, *Shi'an zizhuan* ('Autobiography of Shi'an [Chen Duxiu]'), Taibei: Zhuanji wenxue chuban she.

Zuo Shuangwen 2005, 'Guomindang dui wannian Chen Duxiu de zizhu yu Chen Duxiu de taidu' ('The Guomindang's assistance to Chen Duxiu in his later years and Chen Duxiu's attitude'), *Zhonggong dangshi yanjiu*, 2.

Index

ABC of Communism (Bukharin and Preobrazhensky), 255, 288; Zheng Chaolin translation of, 111, 254, 555, 1068, 1179
An Fu, 338–9, 341, 1200
anarchism and anarchists, 174, 192, 198, 304, 699
Anglo-Russian Trade Union Unity Committee, 403, 453, 792, 889
Anqing, 131, 168, 22a8, 652, 660, 705
anti-imperialist movement, 217, 220, 431, 788–9, 793
Anyuan, 226, 240, 248, 326, 429, 595, 807
Autumn Harvest uprising (1927), 341, 806–7, 997

Bai Chongxi, 118, 262, 651
Bao Pu, 310, 312, 314, 315, 318
Beijing, 5, 289, 778, 1167; literary groups in, 275–6; March Eighteenth Incident in, 276–7, 428; Peng Shuzhi in, 607, 610; political situation in, 273–4, 286, 1078; as publication centre, 274–5; Trotskyists in, 8, 357, 509, 922; Wang Fanxi in, 272–80, 286–91
Beijing-Hankou rail strike (1923), 228–9, 230
Beijing University, 272–3, 275, 1034; CCP at, 277–9, 286; Chen Duxiu and, 273, 303
'bloc of four classes', 796, 798, 808, 809, 814, 816, 822, 824, 833, 918, 936; Trotsky criticism of, 4, 808–9, 815, 823
Bo Gu (Qin Bangxian), 61, 64, 131, 493, 546; appointed leader of Central Committee, 61, 63; biographical sketch, 348, 688n; and Chen Duxiu, 97, 688–9; in Moscow, 59, 335
Bolshevik (*Buersaiweike*), 436, 446, 612, 1112; Chen Duxiu column in, 420, 613–14; Zheng Chaolin articles in, 422, 424, 612–13; Zheng Chaolin as editor of, 111, 417–18, 615, 1109, 1110, 1179
Bolshevik-Leninists. *See* Communist League of China; Left Opposition, Chinese
Bolshevik Party (Russia), 872, 919, 944
'Bolshevisation', 17, 20, 369, 495, 497
Borodin, Mikhail, 285, 602–3, 608, 1157; biographical sketch, 81; on CCP as 'Guomindang coolies', 69, 82, 402–3; Chen Duxiu struggle with, 83, 404, 602–3, 607; Peng Shuzhi meeting with, 402, 404, 791, 1090–1, 1185–6; shot by Stalin, 84; as Sun Yat-sen University advisor, 49–50, 128; support to Guomindang by, 48, 81–2, 198n, 229, 401, 785
bourgeoisie, Chinese, 401, 412, 454, 784, 789, 1083–4; during civil war, 860; and Guomindang, 246, 412; and landlordism, 454; Mao Zedong on, 783–4; and May Thirtieth Movement, 246–7, 401; Peng Shuzhi on, 787; Stalin on, 824–5, 827; subordination of proletariat to, 907–8, 937, 944
bourgeoisie, colonial: Lenin and Trotsky on, 825, 933–4, 1152–3
Bu Shiqi, 306, 599, 1081
Buchman, Alexander H., 554, 720n, 1123, 1174, 1176, 1200
Buersaiweike. *See Bolshevik*
Bukharin, Nikolai Ivanovich, 79–80, 251, 322, 323, 893; Chen Duxiu on, 399–400; and Chinese Revolution, 81, 336, 337, 433, 443, 832, 835; Moscow Trial of, 548, 1113, 1154; opposition to Guomindang withdrawal by, 403, 792, 822, 823; as rector of International Lenin School, 368, 388; rehabilitation of, 37; Stalin break with, 353, 356, 361, 368; Trotsky disagreements with, 4, 618; writings: *ABC of Communism*, 111, 254, 255, 288, 555, 562, 1068, 1179; *Lenin as a Marxist*, 255; *The Peasant Problem*, 255
bureaucratic centrism, 901–2, 910, 1006
bureaucratic collectivism, 968, 971, 973, 986, 1003, 1004

Cai Chang, 78, 387
Cai Hesen, 227, 228, 234, 250, 605, 606, 607; becomes Marxist, 194–5; biographical sketch, 78–9, 1200; capture and execution of, 66, 79; at CCP 7 August Emergency Conference, 266n, 608; as CCP central leader, 267, 446, 615; writings: at CCP Fourth Congress, 78, 236, 238, 601; and

Cai Hesen (*cont.*)
  CCP Propaganda Department, 78, 442, 444, 1093; in France, 192, 193, 194–5, 238; and *Guide Weekly*, 227, 234, 241; on Guomindang entry, 227, 401, 786; living arrangements of, 225, 233, 253; Peng Shuzhi and, 78–9, 786, 1185; and Qu Qiubai, 422, 603; and Xiang Jingyu, 78, 192, 227, 253; and Zheng Chaolin, 244, 444–5
  writings: *A History of the Development of Society*, 279; *History of Opportunism in the Party*, 607–8, 614; 'On Chen Duxiu-ism', 628
Cai Yuanpei (Cai Jiemin), 182n, 187, 214, 273, 502, 646; biographical sketch, 1200; Chen Duxiu on death of, 768–72
Cai Zhende, 6, 449, 465; expelled from CCP, 72, 627, 1096; given Trotskyist documents, 452, 619; Left Opposition work of, 464, 466–7, 473; as member of Jiangsu Provincial Committee, 615–17; and Peng Shuzhi, 617; and Zheng Chaolin, 450, 452, 615, 617
Cannon, James P., 864, 875n, 1174; *History of American Trotskyism*, 624
Cao Kun, 238, 241, 273n
Caohejing Model Prison, 474, 643, 649
capitalism: in China, 69, 210, 214, 336, 665–6, 874–5, 933, 1047; crises in, 749–50; and democracy, 739; economic constraints of, 741; prospects of, 747–50, 752
Changsha, 713–14, 806; Communist movement in, 5, 429, 778; counter-revolutionary coup in, 66, 405, 406, 800–1, 824; Mao Zedong in, 214, 304, 979; Peng Shuzhi in, 1077, 1078–9, 1102, 1184; Red Army and, 131, 494, 1128
Chen Bilan, 6, 10n, 74, 83, 550; archives of, 1199; and arrests of 1931, 91, 110; biographical sketch, 79–80, 1183, 1200; on CCP armed struggle, 990, 994–9, 1021; in exile, 112, 1183, 1189; expulsion from CCP of, 1096, 1187; joins CCP, 1184; as leader of CCP's women's work, 80, 122, 239, 1185, 1189; obituary of, 1182–91; and Peng Shuzhi, 73–4, 80, 87, 601; during Second Chinese Revolution, 81, 82; on Sino-Japanese War, 1022–3; as student in Moscow, 79–80, 619, 1184; Trotskyist leadership committee member, 122, 559; underground work of, 110, 1188
  — writings: 'The Real Lesson of China on Guerrilla Warfare', 985–1000; *Recollections of a Chinese Revolutionary*, 22, 73–4, 87, 112, 1196
Chen Boda (Chen Shangyou), 65, 134–5
Chen Daotong, 102, 108–9, 150
Chen Duxiu: and armed struggle, 637, 797; arrest and imprisonment of, 2, 11, 93, 94–5, 509, 534, 577, 590–1, 654–5, 921, 989, 1101, 1170, 1170n, 1187; becomes Marxist and communist, 214, 218, 230, 500, 588–9, 700, 866; at Beijing University, 273, 303; biographical sketch, 1165–70, 1200; *Bolshevik* column by, 420, 613–14; and Borodin, 83, 404, 602–3, 607; break with Bolshevism and Trotskyism by, 517, 537, 865, 869, 992; calls for withdrawal from Guomindang, 81, 82, 401–2, 403, 405, 407, 459, 612, 664, 790, 792, 805, 824, 1090, 1091; and CCP 7 August Emergency conference, 266–7, 590, 608, 1093–4; and CCP Fifth Congress, 83, 605–7, 1186; at CCP Fourth Congress, 78, 236; as CCP General Secretary, 238, 589, 687, 1093; CCP later overtures to, 97–8, 533; and CCP Sixth Congress, 68, 434–5, 446–7, 1095, 1186–7; and Chiang Kai-shek, 69, 97, 100, 463; childhood and youth, 160–3, 215, 585–6; as China's Plekhanov, 692, 697; at Comintern Fourth Congress, 211, 1082; and Communist Youth League, 603–4; compared to Lenin, 697; contemporary study of, 34–5, 678, 691–3, 704–5, 1197–8; death of, 101, 562, 591; dissatisfaction with Trotskyist organisation, 96–7, 533, 534, 536, 1152; education of, 163–6; efforts for united front in Resistance War, 96, 533, 536, 539–42, 543, 690, 704, 709, 711, 1192; examinations taken by, 166–71; expulsion from CCP, 9, 72, 394, 408–11, 416, 465–6, 590, 626–8, 1096; family of, 160, 161–3, 164–5; finances of, 139, 234, 625; and formation of Chinese Left Opposition, 71, 420–2, 467, 476, 1127; and founding of CCP, 218, 238, 589, 692, 697; Gao Yuhan on, 705, 1165–70; and Glass, 656, 866; *Guide*

Chen Duxiu (*cont.*)
  Weekly articles by, 234–5, 250, 691, 790, 1084; Guomindang overtures toward, 96, 97, 100; historical taboos about, 678, 691, 692, 698; illnesses of, 258, 636–7; and Kang-Liang reform movement, 586; as Left Opposition General Secretary, 87, 476, 493, 590, 643, 1101 and Li Lisan, 399, 421; and literary reform movement, 1028, 1168–9; and literature, 253–4, 1028; and Liu Renjing, 11, 25, 96, 452, 468–9, 483, 632, 920, 1152; and Lu Xun, 514, 1033; and Mao Zedong, 69, 97, 98, 461, 533, 563–4, 685, 700, 710n, 979; Mao Zedong on, 16, 101, 585, 691–2; Marxism reevaluated by, 703, 744–5; and May Fourth Movement, 101, 238, 589, 664, 677, 697, 772, 1087, 1165; member of CCP leadership committees, 78, 228, 238, 239, 601; member of Comintern Executive Committee, 1085; member of Trotskyist leadership committees, 10, 87, 475, 476, 492, 643, 1101; mentioned, 79, 137, 380, 442, 784, 853–4; military scheme of, 538–41, 992; and *New Youth*, 208, 218, 324, 500, 585, 587, 691, 699, 1028; on Northern Expedition, 82–3, 459; opposition to Guomindang entry by, 3, 68–9, 231, 401, 780–1, 790, 822, 823; as 'oppositionist for life', 593, 697, 745, 1062; and Our Word group, 8–9, 73–4, 472, 478–9; passivity toward fight in CCP, 446–8, 610–11, 623; Peng Shuzhi criticisms of, 11, 18, 448, 562–3, 703, 852; Peng Shuzhi discussions with, 637, 638, 1079, 1185; Peng Shuzhi relations with, 21, 472, 473, 536, 658, 709, 710, 711; Peng Shuzhi seeks to use, 471–2, 600, 605, 638; Peng Shuzhi support of, 6, 77, 404, 421, 617; personal appearance and qualities; 228, 296, 1169–70; poetry by, 691; and Proletarian group, 394, 469, 473, 486, 628, 1097; and Pu Dezhi, 538, 542, 621, 639, 658, 685, 727n; and Qu Qiubai, 68, 79, 267, 399, 405, 420, 435, 604, 606, 609, 611–12, 637, 805, 1109–10, 1186; rehabilitation of, 4, 35, 705–6, 1044, 1193; relationship to Trotskyism of, 581, 594, 678–84, 864–7, 1107; release from prison, 96, 530, 581, 659–60, 712; and reorganisation of Trotskyist leadership, 92, 132, 652; resigns from CCP leadership, 58, 67–8, 405, 419–20, 607–8, 610, 805, 824, 1093–4; scapegoated for revolution's defeat, 6–7, 45, 67–8, 70, 267, 337, 338, 419, 590, 698, 806, 1094, 1186; self-criticism by, 400, 407–8, 414; and Shanghai insurrection and massacre, 259, 263, 404; on Sino-Japanese War, 24–5, 26, 96, 533, 535–7, 539–42, 553, 591, 661, 713–14, 717, 721, 741, 765–6, 865, 870, 991, 1192; sons murdered, 6, 66, 97, 705; Stalin and, 495, 590, 610; Stalinist slander campaign against, 16, 36, 43–5, 92, 99–100, 543, 545–8, 578, 591, 678, 683, 941, 1044; and Sun Yat-sen, 587; support for enlighteners and modernisers by, 699–700; support for Trotskyist unification by, 86, 470–1, 473, 490, 638–9; supposed wish to rejoin CCP, 16, 685–90; sympathy toward within CCP, 13–14, 611–12; Tang Baolin on, 1153; and theory, 663–5, 866; tomb of, 705; Trotsky on, 9, 85, 469, 478, 484, 489, 536, 633, 635, 662–5, 700, 865, 885–89, 925–7, 941–2, 1175; at Unification Congress, 86, 474, 475, 491, 492, 641, 643–4; Wang Fanxi appraisal of, 542, 562–4, 585–93, 697–8, 700, 773–4; Wang Fanxi meetings with, 489–90, 515–16, 534–7, 538, 540; and Wang Jingwei, 83, 404, 606; and Wang Ming, 330; and Wang Ruofei, 68, 239, 423, 434–5, 610, 611, 612–13, 637, 687; won to Trotskyism, 6, 9, 70–1, 74–5, 304, 411, 416, 451–2, 459, 590, 619–20, 624–5, 664, 824; and working class, 31, 243, 790, 1084; Wu Jimin on, 73–6, 94–101; in Wuhan, 533, 606, 637–8; Zheng Chaolin as supporter of, 6, 9, 21, 97, 181, 423, 466, 609, 1062, 1109–10; Zheng Chaolin contact with, 74–5, 612, 638, 660–2; Zheng Chaolin on, 16, 68, 70, 594–684, 685–90, 703, 705; and Zhou Enlai, 68, 100, 101, 463, 546, 660, 666, 667n; Zhou Enlai on, 267, 585, 692
  — views: on character of Chinese Revolution, 488, 665–6, 667, 668, 717, 787, 869; on Chinese linguistics, 447, 610, 1028–9, 1168; on Chinese Red Army, 25, 26n, 459–60, 463–4, 483; on colonial and semi-colonial countries,

Chen Duxiu (*cont.*)
742, 751–2, 762–7; on Confucianism, 176–7, 588, 592, 664–5, 771; on constituent assembly, 24, 409–10, 412–13, 675–6, 700, 715; on culture, 31, 753–4, 770–1; on defeat of Chinese Revolution, 69, 613; on democracy, 9–10, 16, 18, 23, 34–5, 516–17, 591, 699, 701, 702–3, 725–6, 728, 733–7, 739, 761; on democratic dictatorship of workers and peasants, 9, 412, 700; on dictatorship of proletariat, 412, 483–4, 700, 702, 703, 734, 735, 739–40, 773–4; on fascism, 703, 719, 721–2, 723, 724, 725–6, 728–9, 730, 736, 757; as father, 296–7; on human history, 756–7; on Lenin, 23, 416, 536, 591–2, 702, 728; on morality, 771–2; on national liberation, 591, 752–3, 762; on October group, 468–9, 1098–9; on party organisation, 18, 699; on peasants, 31–2, 887–89; on Peng Shuzhi, 476, 644; on Soviet Union, 516–17, 591–2, 681, 701, 704, 733–5, 739, 759, 765–6, 767, 924; on soviets slogan, 412–13, 715, 726; on Stalin, 399–400, 734, 737, 924; on Trotsky, 70–1, 408, 411, 704, 728; on World War II, 591, 723–4, 726, 728, 730, 732–3, 735–6, 738–9, 740–1, 754–5, 757–9, 761; on Wuhan government, 404–5, 885–7, 888; on Zheng Chaolin, 711, 730

— writings: 'Appeal to All Comrades of the Chinese Communist Party', 92, 399–416, 480, 481, 590, 608, 628, 633, 1138; *Chen Duxiu's Last Articles and letters*, 706–8; *Duxiu's Writings*, 691; *Etymological Studies*, 100; 'The Future of the Oppressed Nations', 681, 762–7; 'The Lessons of the National Movement over the Past Twenty-seven Years', 787; 'Lessons of the National Movement over the Past 27 Years', 1086–7; letter to Chen Qichang and others, 679, 690, 698, 707, 709–12; letter to Comintern, 623–4, 628; letter to He Zhiyu, 743; letter to Hu Qiuyan and Sun Jiyi, 744–5; letter to International Secretariat, 924; 'letter to the Central Committee of the Chinese Communist Party on the Chinese Revolution, 70–1; letter to Wang Fanxi, 728–30; letters to Pu Dezhi, 719–22, 723–4, 725–7, 731–7; letters to Trotsky, 96, 680–1, 713–18; letters to Xiliu, 723–4, 725–7, 731–7; 'My Basic Views', 738–42, 744; 'My Feelings on the Death of Mr Cai Jiemin', 768–72; 'The National Revolution and Social Classes', 787; 'Once Again on the World Situation', 100, 756–61; open letter to *Xinhua ribao*, 686; 'Our Political Views', 75, 483–4, 1096; *A Philological Study of Chinese Characters*, 447; posthumous manuscripts of, 570; *Recollections of a Chinese Revolutionary*, 113; 'Reply to the Comintern', 623–4, 628; A Sketch of the Postwar World Situation', 100, 746–55; unfinished autobiography, 159–71

Chen Duxiu-ites (1927–9), 6; embrace of Trotskyism by, 7, 9, 618–22; and fight in CCP, 608–11, 615, 616–17; younger Trotskyists' suspicions about, 8–9, 73–4, 472, 478–9, 552, 633

Chen Fu, 33, 50

Chen Jiongming, 111, 159, 174–5, 182, 195, 297, 402, 1108

Chen Jiuding, 298, 302, 309, 310

Chen Lifu, 442, 657

Chen Lu, 197, 198, 299

Chen Qiaonian, 78, 79, 202, 434, 1068; arrest and execution of, 66, 302, 434, 610; biographical sketch, 1200–01; as CCP oppositionist, 6, 447; CCP responsibilities of, 267, 418, 595, 607, 609; and Chen Duxiu, 421, 611, 637, 705; and Peng Shuzhi, 421, 471, 602, 604, 617; personal qualities of, 296–7; as student in Moscow, 302, 316

Chen Qichang, 75, 95, 339, 517–18, 554, 577; biographical sketch, 102, 564, 1201; books authored by, 516, 564; and Chen Duxiu, 537, 679, 736; Chen Duxiu letter to, 679, 690, 698, 707, 709–12; and Communist League Provisional Committee, 12, 534, 657n, 872n; and Communist League split, 559; fight with Liu Renjing, 11–12, 25, 96, 655–7; and Lu Xun letter, 106, 513–14, 1036–39, 1178; and Peng Shuzhi, 658;

INDEX 1237

Chen Qichang (*cont.*)
  personal qualities of, 565; reestablishment of Trotskyist organisation by, 12, 102, 655; on Sino-Japanese War, 553, 870; torture and murder of, 107, 108, 278, 514, 565, 860, 1038; and Wang Fanxi, 108, 490, 550, 551; Wang Shiwei defence of, 35, 1031–2; Wu Jimin on, 102–9
Chen Tanqiu, 113, 236, 373–4
Chen Wangdao, 232, 251
Chen Yannian: arrest and execution of, 66, 302; biographical sketch, 1201; CCP responsibilities of, 80, 81, 326, 595, 791; and Chen Duxiu, 602, 637, 705; and Communist Youth organisation, 200, 201, 202, 204, 212; in France, 111, 200; personal qualities of, 296–7; pseudonyms of, 203, 302; return from Soviet Union by, 324, 325, 326, 1179; and Shanghai massacre, 264, 265; as student in Moscow, 302, 313, 316; support for Comintern line by, 83, 602, 606–7; won to communism, 240, 316
Chen Yi, 64, 170
Chen Yimou, 59, 1201; arrest and imprisonment of, 90, 499, 647, 649, 1207; Left Opposition organisational responsibilities of, 476, 493, 643, 644; member of Trotskyist leadership bodies, 10, 87, 476, 492, 643, 1101; in Our Word group, 486, 631; as Trotskyist martyr, 486, 508, 1207; at Unification Congress, 86, 475, 476, 492, 641; in unification negotiations, 487, 635
Chen Yun, 61, 99, 372
Chen Zhongfan, 96, 660–1
Chen Zhongxi, 508; as leader of guerrilla unit, 550, 561, 1201
Cheng Fangwu, 437, 439, 440, 441
Cheng Yingxiang, 22, 1196; obituary of Peng Shuzhi and Chen Bilan by, 1182–91
Chiang Ching-kuo, 367; and Chiang Kai-shek, 50, 57–8, 120–1; *My Life in the Soviet Union*, 51–2; as student in Moscow, 50, 57, 120, 380; as Trotskyist, 58, 120
Chiang Kai-shek: April 1927 coup by, 57, 60, 66, 264, 391, 797, 798, 810, 822, 1179; attacks on CCP armed forces by, 813, 990; and Chen Duxiu, 69, 97, 100, 463; and Chiang Ching-kuo, 50, 57–8, 120–1; and Guomindang, 82, 790; and Huangpu Military Academy, 229, 785, 789; and imperialism, 290, 952; and Japanese, 61, 80, 286, 834, 998; as leader of counter-revolution, 56–7, 431, 501, 939; Mao Zedong negotiations with, 957; March 1926 coup by, 80, 402, 403, 791, 795, 798, 1090; mentioned, 5, 48, 63, 146, 289, 929; and Northern Expedition, 55, 793; as self-proclaimed revolutionary, 60, 411; and Shanghai massacre, 4, 56, 66, 262, 263–5, 404, 797–8, 1093; Stalinist illusions in, 283, 521, 814; and Sun Yat-sen University, 50; trip to Soviet Union by, 49, 120, 319; Zhang Xueliang kidnapping of, 813–14, 834, 990; Zhou Enlai negotiations with, 528, 813–14, 990
China characteristics: capitalism, 69, 210, 214, 336, 665–6, 874–5, 933, 1047; feudal remnants, 214, 411–12, 455, 665–6, 1047; imperialist oppression, 824, 918, 989; industry, 60; modernisation, 210, 589, 592, 663, 769n; public education, 61; semi-colonial status, 453–4
China Forum, 395, 920–1
China Weekly Review, 515, 655
Chinese Civil War: anti-Kremlin demonstrations during, 858, 878; casualties in, 997, 998; CCP policy during Civil War, 857–8, 957, 958–9, 960, 963; Chen Bilan on, 995–6; Guomindang and, 557, 860, 923, 952, 958–9; Long March during, 17, 64, 433, 511, 813, 990; Peng Shuzhi on, 572, 857–8, 860, 877–8, 879, 954–5, 1018, 1019–20; Soviet support to CCP in, 953–4, 955; Trotskyist participation in, 27, 550, 561, 579, 651, 839, 855–7, 987, 988, 989, 992–4, 1015, 1016, 1128, 1209; US imperialism and, 952, 955; Wang Fanxi on, 877–9, 994, 997, 1009–12. *See also* Chinese Revolution, Third
Chinese Communist Party (CCP): adventurist line of, 14, 130–1, 336, 341, 413, 414, 498, 511–12, 590, 806–8, 811–12, 832, 894–99, 916–17, 997–8, 1013, 1094–5; anti-Trotskyist slander campaign of, 15–16, 25, 43–4, 48, 100, 396, 543, 545–9, 577–8, 591, 678, 716, 918, 941, 962, 1038, 1044, 1128, 1134–5, 1154; armed struggle line of, 462–3, 833, 952–3, 998, 1021–2; at Beijing University, 277–9,

Chinese Communist Party (CCP) (*cont.*)
286; 'Bolshevisation' of, 17, 20, 369, 495, 497; Borodin and, 81–2, 83, 229, 602–3, 606; bureaucratic totalitarianism of, 1129, 1130; cadres of, 240, 281–2, 287, 288, 500–1, 595–6; Cai Hesen leadership of, 267, 615; campaign against Trotskyism by, 38, 71–2, 394, 396, 543; Chang Jiang Bureau of, 418, 421; chaos and disarray in, 14, 443; Chen Duxiu as founding leader of, 218, 589, 692, 697; Chen Duxiu expulsion from, 9, 72, 394, 408–11, 416, 465–6, 590, 626–8, 1096; Chen Duxiu-ites within, 418–19, 420–2, 434–5, 448, 626–8, 1109–10; Chen Duxiu relations with, 13–14, 16, 97–8, 591, 661–2, 685–90, 710; and Chiang Kai-shek, 80–1, 350, 860, 958–9, 960, 990; and *China Forum*, 920–1; class character of, 29–30, 839–41, 907–8, 910, 956, 961, 962, 963–4, 966, 969–73, 997, 1005–09, 1013; class composition of, 961, 964, 966, 1103; Comintern and Soviet financing of, 49, 139, 366; Comintern as source of opportunism of, 43, 406–7, 408, 790, 938, 1091; 'conciliationist' faction of, 349, 463, 497–9, 596, 1109–10; contempt for theory in, 287–8, 500–1; controversy over independence of, 820–2; corruption within, 965–6; discussion on Northern Expedition by, 82–3; early Bolshevism of, 777–80; exodus from cities of, 833–4, 835, 962–3, 972, 1014; expenses of, 234; expulsion of Trotskyists from, 9, 72, 339, 467–8, 626–9, 632, 1095–6; factionalism in, 418–22, 543–6, 548–9; failure to recognize revolutionary defeat, 17, 423; founding of, 195, 218, 500, 778; and Guomindang 'left', 4–5, 290–1, 797–805, 880; Guomindang relations with, 69, 82, 229, 276, 287–8, 402–3, 594–5, 792–805, 1083–4; historical phases of, 818; Jiangsu Provincial Committee of, 6, 62, 421, 423, 438, 448, 449, 465, 498, 610, 616, 618–19, 627, 892–902; lack of democracy in, 17, 18, 617; and land reform, 958, 959, 964–5, 972, 990; left turn of (1925), 787–8, 1087, 1185; Li Lisan leadership of, 446, 494, 615, 616–17, 1187; line during Sino-Japanese War, 23, 24–5, 528, 817; and literature, art, and culture, 35, 275, 436–7, 438, 442, 503, 1027, 1029–30; Mao Zedong leadership of, 18, 388, 511, 543–4; membership of, 58, 66–7, 130, 240, 287, 714n, 809–10, 961, 966, 1087, 1089, 1093, 1094; and membership 'transference', 352–3; Menshevik turn of, 782–4; Military Committee of, 83, 256–7, 258–9, 468, 618; Moscow branch of, 212, 312, 315, 319, 323–4, 327–9, 330, 595, 599, 1081; 'Moscow group' of, 6, 21, 240, 596, 599, 600, 602–7; murder of Trotskyists by, 32, 514, 567, 574, 855–7, 1128, 1137, 1161; national revolution line of, 230, 231–2, 428, 597–9, 603, 778–9; Northern Bureau of, 83–4, 267n, 278, 283; and organisation of soviets, 350, 779, 826; Party History establishment of, 3, 152, 153, 154; and peasants, 428, 833, 952–3, 965, 969–73, 997, 1005–6, 1008–09; and personality cult, 362, 601, 980; policy during Civil War, 858, 957, 958–9, 960, 963; political education in, 278–9; popular front line of, 511, 512–13, 960; popular opinion toward, 443, 858; Presidium of, 228, 238, 239, 607; as product of Russian Revolution, 427, 819; recruitment to, 277–8, 287, 964; and Second United Front, 3, 17, 23, 29–30, 97, 433n, 511, 659, 704, 813–14, 834, 843–4, 851, 972; sectarianism in, 24–5, 512, 676n; in Shanghai, 5, 83, 243, 250–1, 418, 419, 421, 503, 518, 549, 778; and Socialist Youth League, 304; as Stalinist party, 955, 980–1; and Stalin's directives, 545, 843–4, 959–60, 972, 980; stance toward World War II, 853; and Sun Yat-sen, 241–2, 938; and Third Chinese Revolution, 29, 816, 952–3, 961–6, 1001–24; Trotsky on class nature of, 833–4, 839–40, 961–2, 963, 970, 1006–7; Trotskyist calls for cooperation with, 26, 92, 96, 533, 539–42, 1192; Trotskyist work within, 143, 631; Trotskyists consider themselves faction of, 357–8, 970, 1007; Wang Ming leadership of, 61, 339, 494, 495–6, 497–8, 1027; Women's Department of, 80, 122, 239, 1185, 1189; work in labour movement by, 229, 230, 233, 242–4, 594–5, 778, 786–7; workers' movement abandoned by, 961, 962–3, 1103–4; in Wuhan, 5, 605–6, 778; and

INDEX 1239

Chinese Communist Party (CCP) (*cont.*)
  Xu Kexiang coup, 801. *See also*
  Guomindang entry by CCP
Chinese Communist Party Central
  Committee plenums: Fourth CC enlarged
  plenum (Oct. 1925), 401–2; Fourth CC
  Second Plenum (July 1926), 82, 823; Sixth
  CC Second Plenum (June 1929), 394; Sixth
  CC Fourth Plenum (Jan. 1931), 61, 62, 494,
  495, 496; Sixth CC, Sixth Plenum (1938),
  545; Eleventh CC Third Plenum (1978),
  1105, 1145
Chinese Communist Party congresses and
  conferences:
  — First Congress (1921), 195, 230–1, 778,
    821; programme adopted by, 598, 668
  — Second Congress (1922), 67; Manifesto
    of, 5–6, 779–80, 821; on national-
    democratic revolution, 400, 821
  — Third Congress (1923), 427; debate on
    Guomindang entry at, 231, 320, 782
  — Fourth Congress (1925), 77–8, 601;
    Central Committee elected by, 238;
    Comintern representative's speech
    at, 236–7; debates at, 236–8, 1087–91;
    delegates at, 236; on national revolu-
    tion, 603, 1088; revamping of party line
    by, 787–8, 1087, 1185; on Trotsky, 237,
    1088–9; venue of, 235–6
  — Fifth Congress (April 1927), 1093, 1109,
    1179; Chen Duxiu and Peng Shuzhi
    ousted by, 83, 607, 1186; discussion on
    state of Chinese Revolution at, 798–800
  — Emergency Conference (7 August
    1927), 61, 255, 267–8, 608–9, 617; adven-
    turist line adopted by, 336, 414; Chen
    Duxiu as target of, 6, 67–8, 266–7, 590,
    806, 1093–4, 1186; resolutions adopted
    by, 266, 419–20; Zheng Chaolin atten-
    dance at, 265–9, 1179
  — Sixth Congress (1928), 129–30; Chen
    Duxiu and, 68, 413, 434–5, 614, 1186–7;
    discussion of Trotskyism at, 333, 445;
    discussion on Chinese Revolution at,
    333, 337, 350, 433, 676, 832, 835; new
    leadership chosen by, 331, 444, 446,
    615–17; political struggle at, 445, 446
Chinese Eastern Railroad Incident (1929), 410,
  627–8, 678

Chinese Revolution, First (1911), 229, 273, 434,
  622–33, 663, 860, 1077–78, 1183; Lenin on,
  47–8
Chinese Revolution, Second (1925–7):
  anti-imperialist upsurge during, 217, 220,
  431, 788–9, 793; bourgeoisie in, 789; CCP
  discussion on failure of, 337, 407–8; CCP
  Menshevik line during, 403–8, 501, 792–8,
  907–8; class struggle as feature of, 431–2,
  789; Comintern and, 336, 415, 928; and
  emergence of Chinese Trotskyism, 3–6;
  Guangzhou-Hong Kong general strike, 273,
  280, 284, 789, 826; honeymoon period of,
  276–7; impact at Sun Yat-sen University of,
  54–8, 129; internal contradictions within,
  283; as issue in Stalin-Trotsky struggle,
  6, 58, 68, 81, 129, 332, 426, 630, 1186; Mao
  Zedong during, 80, 605, 806; May Thirtieth
  Incident as spark for, 217, 426–7, 500,
  788–9; Northern Expedition and, 428–9,
  430–1, 432–3; peasant movement during,
  429–30, 793; Peng Shuzhi on, 81, 82, 402,
  789–90, 792–805, 806–8, 1085–94, 1185;
  proletariat and, 790, 793, 913; recognition
  of defeat of, 17, 423, 612–13, 676, 831–2,
  1013; scapegoating of Chen Duxiu for
  defeat of, 6–7, 45, 67–8, 70, 267, 337, 338,
  419, 590, 698, 806, 1094, 1186; Shanghai
  insurrection, 55, 129, 256–62, 796, 1092,
  1186; Shanghai massacre, 4, 56, 66, 129,
  262, 263–5, 289, 404, 428, 797–8, 1093; Tang
  Baolin on, 1159–60; Trotsky on, 811–14,
  831–2, 913, 939, 1013; Zheng Chaolin on,
  256–64, 417–50, 612–13, 1109
Chinese Revolution, Third (1949):
  approaching victory of, 145–6; CCP and,
  29, 816, 952–3, 961–6, 1001–24; Chinese
  Trotskyists' mistakes and failures during,
  30–3, 816, 830–1, 839, 840, 844, 956, 975–6,
  1002, 1003, 1019–20, 1022; and creation of
  workers' state, 816, 1009; and Guomindang
  rottenness, 571–2; 950–2; Liu Jialiang on,
  575, 975; and 'mass pressure' question,
  950, 956–59, 960; Peng Shuzhi on reasons
  for victory of, 29, 575, 950–5, 995–6, 1003,
  1004–5, 1009–12, 1018, 1193; Peng Shuzhi
  seen as denying, 971, 1020; Soviet Union
  and, 953–6 959–60; Trotskyist reaction
  to victory of, 28–30, 132–3, 141, 847n, 949,

Chinese Revolution, Third (1949) (*cont.*)
968–9, 973; Trotsky's prognoses confirmed by, 830–1, 838, 843; Wang Fanxi on reasons for victory of, 29–30, 571–2, 575, 839, 967–82, 994, 997, 1001–24, 1192–3; Zheng Chaolin on reasons for victory of, 29n, 575, 1003–4. *See also* Chinese Civil War; People's Republic of China

Chinese Revolution character: as bourgeois-democratic, 130, 412, 424–5, 432, 828; CCP First Congress programme on, 668; Chen Duxiu on, 459–60, 666–7, 668, 715; Chinese Trotskyists' debates over, 482, 483–4, 488, 492, 665–6, 867–8; and democratic dictatorship of workers and peasants, 9, 336, 412, 613, 700, 794–5, 799; national revolution theory on, 597–9, 603; Peng Shuzhi on, 667–8, 1085–7; and revolutionary-democratic programme, 104, 351, 511–12, 569, 1014, 1015, 1022, 1128; Russian Revolution compared to, 284–5, 425–6, 597–8, 622, 937; and stages theory, 459, 796n, 814–15, 816; Stalin on, 858, 913; Trotsky on, 337–8, 453–7, 484, 488, 669, 803, 814–17, 828–30, 868, 876, 931–2; Wang Fanxi on, 668–9, 876; Zheng Chaolin on, 427–8, 464, 668–9, 1110

Chinese Trotskyism. *See* Left Opposition, Chinese (1928–31); Communist League of China (1931–41); Communist League of China—Struggle (Peng Shuzhi group, 1942–8); Communist League of China—Internationalist (Wang Fanxi/Zheng Chaolin group, 1942–9); Internationalist Workers' Party of China (1949–52); Revolutionary Communist Party of China (1948–)

Chinese Trotskyist membership: of Chinese Left Opposition groups, 8, 475n, 487, 491, 1097, 1098, 1099; of Communist League, 10, 66, 102, 112, 139–40, 576, 714–15, 872, 922, 1101; in Moscow, 349, 365, 393; of RCP and IWP, 12, 571, 846n, 1070

Chinese Trotskyist rehabilitation, 3, 155–6; calls for, 36–8, 45–6, 115–16, 563, 682, 683–4, 1113, 1130–1, 1181–2; of Chen Duxiu, 4, 35, 705–6, 1044, 1193

Chinese Trotskyists after 1949: arrests, 2, 13, 43, 113–14, 123, 143, 146, 149–51, 573–4, 847n, 1112, 1127, 1132–3, 1146, 1160, 1181; continued split of, 19–20, 1146; executions of, 574, 1128, 1161; Liu Renjing, 133–4, 485, 976; Lou Guohua, 19, 1176–7, 1197; Peng Shuzhi, 28, 112, 122, 132–3, 1183, 1189; political work by (1949–52), 123, 141, 146, 150, 573, 574, 1180–1; in prison, 13, 124–5, 1132–46, 1161; reaction to revolutionary victory by, 28–30, 132–3, 141, 847n, 949, 968–9, 973; release from prison of, 114–15, 124–5, 1061, 1067, 1113, 1117, 1127–31, 1145, 1146, 1181; situation today, 33, 847n; Wang Fanxi, 1, 2, 28, 113, 122, 132–3, 1191, 1192, 1193–4; Wang Guolong, 141, 146; Wang Mengzou, 550, 1146; Zhou Lüqiang, 123, 141, 146, 150

Chinese Trotskyists in Soviet Union: arrest and Siberian exile of, 343, 374, 382–3, 386, 632, 1069; clandestine work by, 340, 351–2, 631; executions of, 386, 1069; expulsion from party of, 70, 339, 632; growth of among Chinese students, 340–1, 342, 349, 351–2, 393; measures taken against, 352–3, 390–1, 632; membership of, 349, 365, 393; organisation of, 7–8, 341–2, 349, 365, 392–3, 631; and origins of Chinese Left Opposition, 468, 1068, 1094; participation in November 1927 demonstration, 375, 392, 630; return to China of, 358–9, 630, 631, 1068; Russian Opposition links to, 392; at Sun Yat-sen University, 7–8, 58–9, 119, 341, 375, 378, 391–2, 393, 468, 631, 1094

Chongqing, 98, 108, 121, 547, 578, 720, 729; Chen Duxiu living near, 581, 591; Guomindang government in, 720n, 741, 857, 860, 960; Trotskyists in, 567

Chow Tse-tsung, 1028

Clarté, 190, 208–9

colonial and semi-colonial countries, 880–1, 1022; Chen Duxiu on, 742, 751–2, 762–7; Trotsky on, 919, 931–2

Combat society. *See* Militant group

combined development, 592, 675

Comintern (Communist International), 72, 797, 928, 936–7, 1090; adventurist line on China by, 811–12, 893, 894–8, 1084; bureaucratic centrism of, 901–2, 910; and CCP's Guomindang entry, 3–4, 5, 207n, 231, 401, 405, 407, 780–1, 782, 783, 792, 821–2,

Comintern (Communist International) (*cont.*) 1185; Chen Duxiu and, 6–7, 211, 606–7, 610, 623–4, 628, 797, 1082, 1085; falsification of Marxism by, 943–4; Far Eastern Bureau of, 403, 596–7, 603, 653n; financing of CCP by, 49, 366; Guomindang as sympathising party of, 781, 796, 1091; Left Opposition formed within, 467; under Lenin and Trotsky, 208, 496–7; on national and colonial questions, 48, 779, 781, 820, 825, 1082; as source of CCP's opportunism, 43, 406–7, 408, 790, 938, 1091; Stalin-Trotsky debate on China in, 58, 129, 801–4; Stalinisation of, 494, 496, 820; statutes of, 312, 327; Twenty-One Conditions of, 67

Comintern congresses and plenums: Second Congress (1920), 5, 48, 779, 781, 820, 825; Fourth Congress (1922), 211, 317, 589, 1082; Fifth Congress (1924), 324, 368, 1085; Seventh ECCI Plenum (1926), 795–6, 822–3; Eighth ECCI Plenum (1927), 801–4, 893; Ninth ECCI Plenum (Feb. 1928), 329, 333, 336, 892, 895–6; Sixth Congress (July–Sept. 1928), 344–5, 347, 624, 811–12, 833, 901, 902; Tenth ECCI Plenum (1929), 361; Seventh Congress (1935), 510, 813

Communist League of China (1931–41): arrest of leadership of, 10–11, 90–3, 102, 132, 499, 645–50, 989, 1101; class composition of, 577; debate over Sino-Japanese War in, 553, 557–9, 568, 852–4, 870–5, 991, 992, 1111; factionalism in, 549–50, 551–3, 582; financial situation of, 514–15; founding and naming of, 576, 1101; in Fuzhou, 576, 582, 922; Glass financing of, 107, 514–15, 655, 1159, 1175; Glass report on, 576–82, 921–3; in Guangxi, 137, 508–9; Guomindang repression of, 577, 578, 856; in Hong Kong, 507–9, 576, 578, 714–15, 857, 922; influence of, 576–7; initial Central Committee of, 10, 87, 643, 1101; membership of, 10, 66, 102, 139–40, 576, 714–15, 872, 922, 1101; new members in, 582; November 1937 conference of, 851, 870; paralysis of after arrests, 851, 992; Peng Shuzhi report on, 851–63; Political Committee of, 872; political level of cadres in, 922; press organs of, 507, 511, 513, 516, 554, 579–80; printshop of, 507, 514, 579–80, 658; Provisional Central Committee of, 12, 507–8, 509, 534, 657n, 1174–5; publishing activities of, 515–16, 554–6, 579–1; reorganisation of leadership after arrests, 92, 652, 655; response to Lu Xun letter, 1038; second national conference of (1941), 559, 854, 985–6; in Shanghai, 507–8, 509, 549–50, 551–3, 576, 577, 578, 655, 714–15, 855, 922; split of 1942 in, 12, 18, 21, 557, 559, 568, 570, 669, 817, 851, 854–6, 869–71, 985–6, 993, 1111, 1180; and Stalinist threats, 577; Standing Committee of, 87, 476, 643, 645; in Wenzhou, 137, 138, 509–10, 859; work among industrial proletariat, 508. *See also* Unification Congress

Communist League of China—Internationalist (Wang Fanxi/Zheng Chaolin group, 1942–9), 559, 861–3, 878, 880–1, 1111; and Chinese Civil War, 568–9, 877; organisational work of, 570; programme of, 882–3; propaganda and publishing activities of, 561–2, 569, 570, 879; and Sino-Japanese War, 560–1, 861; struggle for legality by, 880; working-class orientation of, 561; youth group of, 570–1. *See also* Internationalist Workers' Party of China

Communist League of China — Struggle (Peng Shuzhi group, 1942–8), 561, 570, 571, 861, 874, 879; and anti-Kremlin demonstrations, 858, 861, 878; and Chinese Civil War, 859, 877–8, 879; and Guomindang repression, 856, 857–8, 879; propaganda and publishing activities of, 569–70, 859–60; work among proletariat by, 855, 856, 859. *See also* Revolutionary Communist Party of China

Communist Party of the Soviet Union (CPSU), 45, 368–9; anti-Trotsky campaign in, 321, 323, 604, 618, 783; banning of factions within, 559–60; Chinese Revolution as issue in, 68, 81, 129, 630; Chinese Trotskyist students and, 8, 312, 352–3, 1083; criticisms of Stalin by, 37, 43, 69, 683, 976, 1135; degeneration of, 497; expulsion of Oppositionists from, 340; under Lenin and Trotsky, 496–7; Purge Commission of, 374–6, 379, 381, 382, 383; Sixteenth

Communist Party of the Soviet Union (CPSU) (*cont.*)
  Congress of (1930), 837; Trotsky expulsion from, 58, 70, 389, 630; Twentieth Congress of (1956), 69, 976, 1135
Communist University of the Toilers of the East. *See* Sun Yat-sen University
Communist Youth League, 130, 240, 256, 317, 372, 603–4. *See also* Socialist Youth League
Communist Youth Party, 201, 202–4, 211–12, 1109, 1179; activities of, 202, 205–8; founding of, 195, 202; German branch of, 202, 300–1
Confucius and Confucianism, 164, 170, 209, 219, 566, 623, 710n; Chen Duxiu on, 176–7, 588, 592, 663–4, 745, 771; Marxism and, 209, 211, 214; Peng Shuzhi and, 77, 79, 306–7, 600; *Spring and Autumn Annals*, 178, 206, 313, 664n; Wang Fanxi and, 213, 214; Zheng Chaolin and, 176–7, 1179
Congress of the Toilers of the Far East (1922), 5–6, 303, 400, 1081–2
constituent assembly, 17, 511; Chen Duxiu on call for, 24, 409–10, 412–13, 675–6, 700, 715; Chinese terms for, 456–7n; debate in Trotskyist movement over, 349, 458, 482–3, 675–7, 868–9, 1019–20, 1157; Liu Renjing on call for, 11, 351, 480, 481, 483, 676, 868, 1019; Peng Shuzhi on call for, 11, 410, 458, 868, 1019–20; as Russian Revolution demand, 913–14; Stalinist attacks on demand for, 918; Trotsky on call for, 337–8, 349, 350–1, 456–7, 458, 675, 677, 813, 832, 913–14, 915, 988, 1013, 1019, 1020; Unification Congress call for, 493, 715n; Wang Fanxi/Zheng Chaolin on, 480–1, 869, 883, 1022, 1157
Creation Society, 217, 254, 1029; about, 435–6, 435n; CCP members in, 438, 442; Wang Fanxi and, 275, 287; Zheng Chaolin and, 435, 437–42
Cultural Revolution, 15n, 114, 135, 150, 655, 1160, 1171; Chen Duxiu denunciation during, 563n; Liu Renjing during, 133, 1071; Qu Qiubai affair during, 65–6; Wang Fanxi on, 847n, 848, 1116; Zheng Chaolin during, 1071, 1105, 1113, 1142–4

Dai Jitao, 283, 401, 402, 790, 1090; 'The Fundamentals of Sun Yat-senism', 789
Dai Qing, 1029n, 1031, 1193, 1196
Dalin, Sergei Alekseevich, 400, 821
Dan, Fyodor, 891, 910
Daoism, 177, 180
Daybreak (Poxiao), 554, 729–30, 737
defeatism: Chen Duxiu on, 721–2, 740–1; Lenin on, 28, 558, 720, 725, 729, 844, 873, 881, 1023; Peng Shuzhi on, 817, 853–4, 860–1, 874; Tang Baolin on, 1155–7; Trotsky on, 845, 872–3; Wang Fanxi on, 28, 861, 872, 873–4, 986, 994, 1023–4; Zheng Chaolin on, 28, 817, 852, 853–4, 861, 872, 873–4, 991, 992, 994, 1024
democracy, 1129; bourgeois and proletarian, 188, 591, 728, 733–7; Chen Duxiu on, 9–10, 16, 18, 23, 34–5, 516–17, 591, 699, 701, 702–3, 725–6, 728, 733–7, 739, 761, 774; and dictatorship of proletariat, 703; in revolutionary party, 17, 18, 21, 617, 699; and socialism, 9–10, 23, 33, 34–5; Trotsky on slogan of, 919
democratic centralism, 19–20, 560, 572, 986; Peng Shuzhi on, 20, 854, 863, 1102
democratic demands, 337, 457, 861–2, 1002, 1017–18, 1021; Trotsky on, 812–13, 815, 922, 988–9, 1013
democratic dictatorship of workers and peasants, 455, 484; Chen Duxiu on, 9, 412, 700; Chinese embodiments of, 613, 799; as Comintern formula, 336, 424, 907, 936–7; Lenin on, 424, 454–5, 935–6; Peng Shuzhi on, 794–5; Trotsky on, 337, 348, 816, 830, 907, 908
Deng Xiaoping, 50, 69, 91, 139, 848; rise to power of, 35, 1145; on Sino-Soviet dispute, 151; Zheng Chaolin and, 110, 111, 1067
Deng Yanda, 458, 675, 1034, 1201
Deng Zhongxia, 74, 78, 79, 130, 230, 233, 266n, 296, 595, 612; anti-Trotskyism in Moscow by, 384; and Guomindang, 232, 785; and Jiangsu Provincial Committee, 421, 610
Deutscher, Isaac, 1085; *Trotsky Trilogy*, 43, 143–4, 1051
Dewey, John, 216, 1046
Dewey Commission, 516, 682–3
dictatorship of the proletariat, 483–4, 492; Chen Duxiu on, 412, 483–4, 700, 702, 703, 734, 773–4; and democratic dictatorship, 9, 412; Lenin on, 454, 935–6; Third Chinese

dictatorship of the proletariat (*cont.*)
  Revolution establishment of, 816, 830–1;
  Trotsky on, as goal in China, 455–6; Wang
  Fanxi on, 1118–19; Zheng Chaolin on, 1110
Dimitrov, Georgi, 369, 373
Ding Ling (Jiang Bingzhi), 65, 436–7, 1030, 1034
Dong Biwu, 64, 372, 387, 688–9; biographical
  sketch, 688n, 1201; friendliness toward
  Trotskyists by, 546
Dong Yixiang, 99, 337, 384; biographical
  sketch, 1201; Moscow purge of, 375, 379,
  380, 382; as Moscow student, 334, 335, 372,
  380; Wang Ming framing of, 335, 380, 1201
Dongfang zazhi ('Oriental Magazine'), 1188
Dongli ('Motive Force'), 503, 629, 1047
Dongxiang ('Tendency'), 554, 580, 720, 1176
Douzheng. See *Struggle*
Du Weizhi (Tu Qingqi), 156, 502, 631; arrest
  and imprisonment of in 1952, 124, 134–5,
  1138; arrest of in 1932, 131–2, 652; becomes
  Trotskyist, 129, 131, 469; biographical
  sketch, 1201; expelled from CCP, 131; in final
  years, 126–8, 150; as student in Moscow,
  128; as translator, 124, 130, 132; Wu Jimin
  chapter on, 126–36
Dushu zazhi. See *Study*

eight-legged essays, 165, 167, 170, 178, 586, 721
Eighth Route Army, 433–4, 462, 539, 545, 972,
  1008; establishment of, 659, 686n, 972;
  Trotskyists shot in, 856. *See also* People's
  Liberation Army; Red Army, Chinese
Engels, Frederick, 663, 720, 725; Chinese
  publication of, 503, 580, 1046; writings:
  Dialectics of Nature, 132; *Socialism Utopian
  and Scientific*, 209
Esperanto, 314–15

factions, right of, 559–60
Fan Jinbiao, 59, 282–3, 479; biographical
  sketch, 1201–02; as Trotskyist in Moscow,
  332, 339, 341
Fang Zhimin: 'Beloved China!', 66
Far Eastern Bureau, of Comintern, 403, 596–7,
  603, 653n
fascism: Chen Duxiu on, 703, 719, 721–2, 723,
  724, 725–6, 728–9, 730, 736, 757; Trotsky
  on, 912–13

February Seventh Incident (1923), 229n, 230,
  231, 242, 784
Feigon, Lee, 16, 34, 697, 706, 1198
Feng Xuefeng, 62, 275, 1035n, 1202; as real
  author of Lu Xun letter, 44–5, 106–7, 1039,
  1041–3, 1044, 1178
Feng Yuxiang, 241, 268–9, 273, 276, 283, 405,
  539–40, 804
feudalism and feudal remnants, 69, 411–12,
  455, 665–6, 828, 1047
Finland, Soviet attack on, 730, 878, 883
First National Labour Congress (1922), 778
Four Books, 77, 160, 178, 710n
Fourth International: Belgian section of,
  926–7; Chinese Trotskyist links to, 27–8;
  General Council of, 925–7, 1175; Peng
  Shuzhi and, 112, 1189; on Sino-Japanese
  War, 845; Trotsky call for, 1007; Wang Fanxi
  on, 977; during World War II, 1175
France: Chinese workers in, 205; social
  situation in, 185, 190; work-study
  programme in, 174–5, 187, 188, 191–2,
  196–7, 205–6, 1179; Zheng Chaolin in,
  182–212
French Revolution, 322, 425–6, 930, 1103
Fu Lei, 1066, 1149
Fu Zhong, 50, 91
Fujian, 184, 813; Zheng Chaolin in, 443–5, 1108,
  1179–80
Fujian Incident (1933), 11–12, 25
Fuzhou, 650, 921; Trotskyists in, 576, 582, 922

Galen (Blücher), V. I., 84, 285–6, 683
'Gang of Four', 1067, 1129, 1145
Gao Feng, 240, 298, 302
Gao Shangde, 230, 236
Gao Suming, 120, 126–7
Gao Yuhan, 251, 543, 675–6; biographical
  sketch, 1202; on Chen Duxiu, 705, 1165–70;
  embrace of Trotskyism by, 62–3, 74
Gao Zili, 372, 387
Ge Chonge, 480, 485, 1202
Germany: Nazi, 732–3, 735, 736, 741, 747–8,
  817, 945, 1151–2; revolutionary prospects
  in, 732; revolutionary situation of 1923 in,
  320–1, 1150–1; solidarity with struggle in,
  360–4; Zheng Chaolin in, 299–301
Gide, André, 1046; *Retour de l'URSS*, 580, 1041,
  1065, 1180

Glass, Frank (Li Furen), 578, 884; biographical sketch, 1174, 1199, 1202; and Chen Duxiu, 656, 866; on Communist League of China, 576–82, 921–3; financing of Chinese Trotskyists by, 107, 514–15, 655, 1159, 1175; and Isaacs, 11, 395, 576, 655, 1174; as journalist in Shanghai, 655, 1174; letter to Trotsky, 920; and reorganisation of Trotskyists, 11, 12, 656, 657n; responsibilities in Chinese Trotskyist movement, 1174–5; on Sino-Japanese War, 558; Stalinist threats against, 577; Trotsky letter to, 865, 941–2; and Trotskyist printshop, 507, 580, 658; and Trotskyist unification, 576; visit to Trotsky by, 1175; Wang Fanxi on, 1158–9, 1173–6

Gu Shunzhang, 61, 250, 257, 260; biographical sketch, 1202; as traitor, 62, 63, 79, 89, 131, 132

Gu Yingfen, 49–50, 128

Guan Xiangying, 61, 344; biographical sketch, 1202; sympathy for Trotsky's views by, 347, 348, 624

Guangdong, 5, 174, 240–1, 417; mass movement in, 430, 433–4; Trotskyist guerrilla unit in, 27, 541, 550, 561, 579

Guangxi, 118, 651; Trotskyists in, 118, 119, 137, 508–9, 651

Guangzhou, 66, 81–2, 229, 280, 778, 791, 853, 1090; Peasant Training Institute in, 409, 429, 609; Shaji Incident in, 273, 789; Trotskyists in, 573, 856, 859, 922; Wang Fanxi in, 280–6; Zhongshan Gunboat Incident in, 45, 69, 80, 277, 664

Guangzhou–Hong Kong general strike (1925–6), 273, 280, 284, 789, 826

Guangzhou insurrection (1927), 341, 423–4, 443, 455, 590, 613; Peng Shuzhi on, 807–8; Stalin on, 832; Trotsky on, 894–5

guerrilla warfare: Chen Bilan on, 1016–17; Trotsky on, 990–1; Wang Fanxi on, 841, 1017–18. *See also* Chinese Civil War

Guide Weekly (*Xiangdao*), 233, 246, 255, 280, 316, 318, 417, 1112; Cai Hesen and, 227, 234, 241; as CCP organ, 218, 231; Chen Duxiu articles in, 234–5, 250, 691, 790, 1084; effort to revive, 267, 268; on labour movement, 244, 403; Peng Shuzhi articles in, 787, 793, 795, 1092; Qu Qiubai article in, 250, 784–5;

Zheng Chaolin and, 227, 234, 239, 250, 324, 609

Guo Moruo, 437, 438, 441, 1029

Guomindang: Borodin and, 48, 69, 81–2, 198n, 229, 401, 402–3, 785; and bourgeoisie, 246, 412; CCP alliance with, 218, 229, 404–5, 598, 1083–4; CCP flip-flops on, 512, 912–13; and Civil War, 557, 923, 952, 958–9; class struggle attacked by, 789; collapse of regime of, 511, 571–2, 955; Comintern Second Congress on, 821; as Comintern 'sympathising party', 781, 796, 1091; congresses of, 220, 785, 790; corruption and rottenness of, 571–2, 950–2; delegation to Moscow by, 318–20; factions within, 227, 232–3, 278, 280, 283; mentioned, 60, 400, 874, 877–8, 998–9; reorganisation of, 48, 82, 198, 229, 324, 401, 594–5, 785; repressive machinery of, 2, 517, 518–19, 522, 610, 659–60, 1187; and Second United Front, 3, 17, 29–30, 97, 433n, 511, 659, 704, 813–14, 834, 843–4, 851, 972; and Sino-Japanese War, 24, 61, 80, 286, 511, 557, 834, 914–15, 951, 998; Soviet aid to, 47–9, 81, 139, 229, 401, 594, 785–6; Stalin on, 4, 5, 405, 791, 799, 803–4, 806, 810, 814, 822, 886; and Three People's Principles, 48, 287–8, 528, 546n, 792, 1090; Trotsky on nature of, 4, 809, 815, 823, 913, 1084; US imperialism and, 571–2, 952, 955; and warlords, 174, 276. *See also* Chiang Kai-shek; Chinese Communist Party Guomindang entry

Guomindang entry by CCP, 785; CCP members' leadership responsibilities inside, 82, 229, 460, 594–5, 785, 790–1, 1085; Cai Hesen on, 227, 401, 786; Chen Duxiu initial opposition to, 3, 780–1, 790, 822, 823; Chen Duxiu later call for withdrawal, 81, 82, 401–2, 403, 405, 407, 459, 612, 664, 790, 792, 805, 824, 1090, 1091; Comintern directives on, 3–4, 5, 207n, 231, 401, 405, 407, 780–1, 782, 783, 792, 821–2, 1185; Mao Zedong on, 783–4; Peng Shuzhi on, 619, 780–6, 1084, 1088, 1185; restrictions imposed on CCP activities, 82, 402, 786, 1090; Sneevliet and, 5, 207n, 231, 401, 780, 782, 822; Stalin on, 781, 791; Sun Yat-sen on, 400, 401, 821; Third CCP Congress debate on, 231, 320, 782; Trotsky

INDEX   1245

Guomindang entry by CCP (*cont.*)
    on, 4, 81, 389, 446, 619, 777–8, 792, 809–10, 822, 824, 1088; Yin Kuan on, 207, 619
Guomindang 'left', 290–1; CCP and, 4–5, 290–1, 797–805, 880; and Guomindang 'right', 232–3, 280; internal contradictions within, 283; massacre of workers and peasants by, 5, 431, 822, 825, 893; Stalin's illusions in, 801–2, 1093; Trotsky on, 5, 805; Wang Jingwei as leader of, 4–5, 790, 798–9, 880, 1093

Han Jun, 517, 518, 534, 1202; Chen Duxiu and, 679, 711; and generational conflict, 551–3; Wang Fanxi on, 565–6
Han Qi, 200, 202–3, 205
Hangzhou, 257, 259, 260, 342, 653, 793; Wang Fanxi in, 215, 216, 218–21
Hankou, 4, 250, 265, 269, 578–9, 793
Hankou Government, 801–2, 803–4
He Jifeng, 538–41
He Jinliang (He Songlin), 236, 249, 258, 325, 326
He Long, 998, 1021; and Nanchang uprising, 806, 997; Southern Expedition of, 462, 831, 894
He Mengxiong, 465; biographical sketch, 1202; as conciliationist, 498, 499; opposition to Li Lisan by, 14, 131, 449–50, 616
He Shizhen, 232–3, 252
He Yingqin, 94, 650
He Zishen (He Zhiyu), 87, 138, 637, 732; arrest and imprisonment in 1931, 90, 92, 499, 647, 648–9; arrest and imprisonment in 1952, 123–4; biographical sketch, 1203; CCP responsibilities of, 445, 610; Chen Duxiu letter to, 743; and Chen Duxiu writings, 570, 591, 706; and Mao Zedong, 460, 461, 979; member of Internationalist Workers' Party leadership, 113, 122, 571; as Oppositionist within CCP, 6, 74, 445, 626; and Peng Shuzhi, 472, 602; and Proletarian group, 469–70, 473, 639, 644; release from prison of, 530, 660; and Unification Congress, 474–5, 476, 492, 640
He Zishu, 131, 364, 493
He Zizhen, 86, 387, 657, 658
Hirson, Baruch, 1199
History of the Russian Revolution (Trotsky), 535, 881; Chinese translation of, 112, 555–6, 569, 1111, 1180; Trotsky introduction to Chinese edition, 943–5
Hitler, Adolf, 732–3, 735, 736, 741, 747–8, 817, 945; Brüning comparison with, 721–2, 732; Trotsky on, 913
Hitler-Stalin pact, 517, 537, 681, 701, 703, 719n
Hong Kong, 228, 582; general strike in (1925–6), 250, 273, 280, 284, 789, 826; Trotskyists in, 8, 19, 28, 357, 486, 491, 507–9, 572, 576, 578, 630–1, 714–15, 856, 922, 1176–7, 1181, 1197; youth radicalisation in, 1116–17
Horse Day Incident (1927), 66, 460, 461
Hot Blood Daily (*Rexue ribao*), 248–9
Hu Feng (Zhang Guangren), 150; biographical sketch, 1203; and Lu Xun letter, 106–7, 1041–3, 1044, 1178; Trotskyist influence on, 1034–6; Wang Fanxi and, 275, 1034, 1192
Hu Qiuyuan, 744–5, 1033–4, 1203
Hu Shi (Hu Shih): at Beijing University, 273, 587; biographical sketch, 745n, 1203; break with Chen Duxiu and May Fourth Movement, 198n, 218, 589, 664; on Chen Duxiu, 697, 745, 1062, 1153; and Chen Duxiu writings, 591, 706–7; favours to Chen Duxiu by, 95, 97, 659; and Liang Qichao's 'Study Clique', 218, 219, 274; and Literary Reform Movement, 215, 769, 1028; writings: 'On the Literary Revolution', 1028; *Outline History of Chinese Philosophy*, 181–2, 209, 307
Hu Wenzhang (Hu Wenwei), 655, 656, 657
Hu Zongnan, 485, 650, 1203
Hua Lin, 267, 609, 654
Huang Gongdu, 118–19, 508
Huang Jiantong: arrest and imprisonment, 123–4, 134, 1137–38; biographical sketch, 1203; member of Internationalist Workers' Party leadership, 113, 122; Wu Jimin on, 108, 118–25, 123, 151, 156
Huang Jieran, 67, 68, 608n
Huang Ping, 236, 372
Huang Qisheng, 189, 205–6
Huang Wenrong, 256, 417, 452, 606; as Chen Duxiu secretary, 420, 611, 637
Huangpu (Whampoa) Military Academy, 50, 80, 252, 509; Chiang Kai-shek and, 229, 785, 789; establishment of, 229, 302n, 594, 785; selection process for, 256–7; Society

Huangpu (Whampoa) Military Academy (*cont.*)
for the Study of Sun Yat-senism at, 789;
Soviet financial support to, 49
Hubei Provincial Committee, 176, 418, 421, 610, 1109, 1179
Hubin bookshop and publishing company, 465, 469, 502, 625–6, 629
L'Humanité, 209, 211, 321, 324
Hunan, 801, 1078; Autumn Harvest uprisings in, 806–7; peasant movement in, 429–30, 793, 800, 826
Hundred Flowers campaign, 35, 981
Hungarian Revolution (1956), 976, 978, 981, 986
Huohua. See *Spark*
Huoxing ('Sparkle'), 508, 558

imperialism: future prospects of, 750–1; mass sentiment in China against, 512, 793, 834; nature of, 742, 763, 764; oppression of China by, 918; revolutionary struggle against, 286, 427, 429, 431–2, 897, 916–17; US, 557, 558, 858, 952, 955, 1011. See also Sino-Japanese War
International Left Opposition, 467, 903. *See also* Fourth International
International Lenin School (MLSh), 366–88; Chinese students at, 287, 371–5, 390; closing of, 386; curriculum at, 369–70; as elite Comintern school, 368–71; establishment of, 368; financing of, 368; instructors at, 370; rectors at, 368–9, 388; and Stalin purges, 374–87
International Proletarian Revolutionaries' Aid Organisation (MOPR), 367, 387
Internationalist (*Guoji zhuyizhe*), 12, 559, 561–2, 864, 879, 1111, 1138, 1180
Internationalist group. *See* Communist League of China – Internationalist (Wang Fanxi / Zheng Chaolin group
Internationalist Workers' Party of China (1949–52), 12, 846; decides to remain in China, 572–3; executive committee of, 113; founding congress of, 112–13, 122, 571, 572–3; membership of, 571, 846n, 1070; periodical readership and influence, 570; work in People's Republic by, 573; Zheng Chaolin and, 113, 122, 571, 1070, 1180–1
Isaacs, Harold R., 25n, 231, 507, 925; biographical sketch, 1203; and Glass, 11, 395, 576, 655, 1174; letter to Trotsky by, 920–1; Lu Xun friendship with, 1041; and Soong Qingling, 395; *The Tragedy of the Chinese Revolution*, 485, 578, 580, 657n, 928, 940; Trotsky discussion with, 1152–3

Japan: alliance with Germany, 817; begins Sino-Japanese War, 45, 96, 538, 659; and Chinese Revolution, 286, 916–17; Guomindang government concessions to, 61, 80, 286, 834, 951, 998; Manchuria invasion by, 510, 989, 998; Nanjing occupation by, 529–30, 532, 660; seizure of Shenyang by, 24, 61, 92, 652; Shanghai attacks and occupation by, 526–7, 556, 570, 652, 660, 788, 993, 998, 1188; and Soviet Union, 545, 557, 766, 853, 917–18; Trotskyists smeared as agents of, 16, 36, 43–5, 92, 99–100, 547–8, 577–8, 591, 678, 683, 716, 941, 1044, 1128, 1135, 1154; war aims of, 834, 939–40. *See also* Sino-Japanese War
Jiang Changshi: arrest of, 90, 647, 649; at Unification Congress, 86, 475, 492, 641
Jiang Guangchi, 242, 253, 436; return to China by, 308, 324; at Shanghai University, 232, 251; as student in Moscow, 310, 314, 318; and Sun Society, 438, 441; writings: *Des sans-culottes*, 602; *Young Wanderers*, 253–4
Jiang Zhendong, 112, 552, 651–2; biographical sketch, 1203; and Internationalist Workers' Party, 112, 122; release from prison (1979), 1127; at Unification Congress, 86, 475, 641; and workers' schools, 561
Jiangjin, 36, 100, 705, 706, 1165–6
Jiangsu Provincial Committee (CCP), 62, 438, 449, 465, 498, 627; Chen Duxiu-ites in, 6, 421, 610; resolution of, 448, 892–902; struggle with Central Committee by, 423, 616; Trotsky on, 448, 618–19
'Jiangsu-Zhejiang Provincial Association', 334–5, 339, 380–1, 382
Jiangxi, 226, 463n, 511, 794, 806, 813, 990
Jiefang ribao. See *Liberation Daily*
Jiujiang, 94, 131, 431–2, 793
Joffe, Adolf A.: suicide of, 84, 673–4; Sun Yat-sen joint manifesto with, 48, 781–2, 1083
Juewu ('Awakening'), 235, 315
Justice (*Gongli ribao*), 120, 248

Kamenev, Lev, 340, 356; in anti-Trotsky triumvirate, 321, 604, 618, 783; as Moscow Trial victim, 515; in United Opposition, 618
Kang Sheng, 65, 134–5; anti-Trotskyist campaign led by, 16n, 44, 45, 99, 547–8, 941, 1044, 1134, 1154; biographical sketch, 1204; at International Lenin School, 373; on uninterrupted revolution, 674–5
Kang Youwei, 167, 171, 176, 206, 663; biographical sketch, 586n, 1204; reform movement of, 586–7, 769, 1078
Katayama Sen, 323, 941, 1175, 1204
Kautsky, Karl, 399, 703, 744, 764n, 840, 1019, 1204; *The Class Struggle*, 585
Kerensky, Alexander, 872, 910, 1018
Khrushchev, Nikita, 1072; denunciation of Stalin by, 37, 69, 683; on Mao and Maoism, 113, 149, 151
Kirov, Sergei Mironovich, 396, 683, 1204
Kirsanova, Klavdia, 368, 370, 388
KUTV. *See* Sun Yat-sen University

labour movement, 430–1, 433; CCP work in, 229, 233, 242–4, 594–5, 778, 786–7; and February Seventh Incident, 229n, 230, 231, 242, 784; national congresses of, 247, 778, 787; Shanghai General Labour Union, 247–8, 249, 250, 260, 261, 262, 263, 788, 789; strikes by, 228, 233, 250, 273, 280, 284, 401, 428, 594–5, 778, 787, 788, 826, 920, 963–4. *See also* proletariat
Lai Yantang, 86, 475, 492, 643
land reform, 406, 932; CCP and, 958, 959, 964–5, 972, 990
Laozi, 156, 442; Zheng Chaolin and, 176, 180, 181, 1179
League of Left-Wing Writers, 62–3, 513, 1034, 1043n
Left Opposition (Soviet Union), 352, 604, 618; arrest and deportation of, 343, 344, 354; defeat of, 820; demonstration of 7 November 1927 by, 58, 118, 375, 392, 630; expulsion from CPSU of, 340; growing influence of, 353–4; Platform of, 332, 900; relations with Chinese students by, 363. *See also* United Opposition
Left Opposition, Chinese (1928–31), 451–77; division into four groups, 478–9, 481, 634, 1097–100; expulsion from CCP of, 9, 72,

339, 467–8, 626–9, 632, 1095–6; formal establishment of, 70, 71, 467; generational conflicts within, 551–3, 633, 1099; initial activities and organisation by, 356–8, 625–6, 628–9; literary and propaganda work by, 389, 499–503, 625; membership of, 8, 475n, 487, 491, 1097, 1098, 1099; motives for joining, 481–2; negotiations over unification of, 10, 86, 470–1, 473–4, 482, 484, 487–91, 634, 635, 639–40, 1100; origins of in Moscow, 468, 1068, 1094; programmatic documents of, 488, 628, 633, 1096, 1128, 1187; reasons for failure of, 14–15; Trotsky on need for unification of, 10, 85–6, 469, 482, 484, 489, 635, 1100–1; work within CCP by, 626, 1187. *See also* Militant group; October group; Our Word group; Proletarian group; Unification Congress
Lenin, V. I., 347, 467, 909, 1018; on British Labour Party, 972–3; on character of Russian Revolution, 454–5, 598–9, 670–4, 935; Chen Duxiu comparisons to, 697; Chen Duxiu on, 23, 416, 536, 591–2, 702, 728; on China, 47–8; death of, 322–3; defeatism during World War I by, 28, 558, 720, 725, 729, 844, 873, 881, 1023; and democratic centralism, 560; on democratic dictatorship formula, 424, 454–5, 935–6; on national and colonial questions, 5, 779, 781, 820, 825, 881, 1081; on Plekhanov, 564, 692–3; publication of works by, 503, 580; on revolutionary and nonrevolutionary situations, 456, 675; on revolutionary party, 416, 537, 840; on soviets, 810; and Trotsky, 53, 670–4, 935–6
— writings: April Theses, 936; 'Democracy and Narodnism in China', 47–8; *The Development of Capitalism in Russia*, 132; 'Fourth Anniversary of the October Revolution', 673; *Left-Wing Communism: An Infantile Disorder*, 316; 'Letters from Afar', 672; *The Military Programme of Proletarian Revolution*, 881; 'New Times and Old Mistakes in an Old Guise', 673; *State and Revolution*, 195; 'Theses on the National and Colonial Questions', 779, 781, 820, 825, 881; 'The Threatening Catastrophe and

Lenin, V. I. (*cont.*)
How to Fight It', 672–3; *Two Tactics of Social Democracy in the Democratic Revolution*, 671–2; *What Is to Be Done*, 840
Li Cailian, 25n, 481, 485; death of, 567, 1177; Wang Fanxi assessment of, 566–7
Li Chuli, 442, 466, 627; and Creation Society, 439–40, 441
Li Dazhao, 78, 79, 279, 324, 460, 589, 1204; arrest and execution of, 66, 287, 288–90, 1093; becomes Communist, 230, 500; and Chen Duxiu, 601; and founding of CCP, 218, 692; and Joffe, 48; leader of CCP Northern China committee, 278, 595; member of CCP Central Committee, 78, 238; member of Guomindang Central Committee, 785; and *New Youth*, 585, 587
Li Fuchun, 201, 449–50, 616
Li Furen. *See* Glass, Frank
Li Hanjun, 208, 231, 252; opposition to Guomindang entry by, 231, 320
Li Heling, 270, 271, 296, 320; Chen Lu assassination attempt by, 197–8, 299
Li Ji, 74, 442, 502, 1204; capitulation to Stalinists by, 133, 976; escapes arrest, 132, 652; as Shanghai University lecturer, 251, 252
Li Jishen, 66, 280, 302, 807, 808
Li Lisan (Li Longzhi), 78, 225–6, 264, 429, 605; becomes central CCP leader, 446, 448–9, 615, 1187; biographical sketch, 1204; and Chen Duxiu, 399, 421; in France, 192–3, 194, 195; at International Lenin School, 372; labour movement activity by, 233, 240, 242, 243, 248, 249–50, 251, 596, 616, 786–7; opposition within CCP to, 349, 448; ouster of, 61, 62, 444, 445, 495, 498; Stalin and, 130, 131; on Trotsky and Trotskyism, 415; ultraleft and adventurist line of, 14, 130–1, 494, 496, 498, 1013; work in Guomindang by, 785; and Zheng Chaolin, 615
Li Minzhi, 450, 616; and Creation Society, 438, 439, 441
Li Peize, 348, 372
Li Ping, 59, 1204
Li Qihan, 236, 786–7
Li Qiushi, 131, 326, 498, 499
Li Shizeng, 186, 187, 192, 303; anarchism of, 174, 699; Sino-French perspective of, 175, 182n, 190

Li Weihan, 204, 207, 240, 266n, 595; biographical sketch, 1204; at CCP Fourth Congress, 78, 236, 237–8; in France, 199, 200, 201, 205; at International Lenin School, 372; membership on CCP leadership bodies, 78, 238, 387, 418, 421, 609; opposition to Chen Duxiu by, 607; ouster from CCP leadership of, 61, 444, 445; polemic on Chinese Revolution's nature by, 424, 425, 613; and Socialist Youth League, 200, 201, 202; and Zheng Chaolin, 270, 443, 574, 1068, 1070
Li Weinong, 203, 240, 320; in France, 199, 200, 201, 207
Li Zhenying, 240, 266, 270, 329, 331, 443
Li Zhongsan, 532–3, 1205; and Unification Congress, 86, 474, 491–2
Li Zhongwu, 307, 309, 310, 318, 324
Li Zongren, 80, 118–19, 651
Lian Zhengxiang, 574, 1128, 1161
Liang Ganqiao, 1205; Chen Duxiu opinion of, 490; defection to Guomindang by, 87, 486, 490, 493, 650–1; as leader of Our Word group, 85, 474, 480, 486, 631; sent back from Moscow, 59, 70, 118; at Unification Congress, 86, 475, 476, 492, 641; in unification negotiations, 487, 488, 491, 635
Liang Qichao (Liang Rengong), 171, 209, 1168; biographical sketch, 1167n, 1205; and reform movement, 586, 663, 769; Study Clique of, 218, 219, 274
Liang Shuming: *Eastern and Western Culture and Philosophy*, 209
Liang Si, 1195, 1197, 1205
Liberation Daily (*Jiefang ribao*), 44, 1050–1, 1135, 1136
Liberation Weekly, 44, 97, 547–8
Lin Biao, 65, 387, 953; and events of 1971, 135, 1144
Lin Boqu, 64, 80, 98, 785; transmits Chen Duxiu proposals to Mao, 533, 687, 688
Lin Huanhua, 119, 507, 509, 571, 573, 1205
Lin Keyi, 316, 317–18, 324
Lin Yunan, 228, 498, 499
Lin Yunming: *Analysis of Ancient Literature*, 178
liquidationism, 338, 351, 545, 622, 812, 879
literature and art, 1027–47; CCP and, 35, 275, 436–7, 438, 442, 503, 513–14, 1027, 1029–30; Chen Duxiu and, 253–4, 1028; Lu Xun on,

literature and art (*cont.*)
1036; Mao Zedong on, 1030–1; proletarian, 254, 503, 513, 1027; Trotsky on, 1027; Trotskyist influence on, 1044–5; Wang Fanxi on, 499–503, 1027, 1045; Wang Shiwei on, 1055–7; Little Pan, 638, 660

Liu Bojian, 79, 196, 267, 299, 320, 617; as Chen Duxiu supporter within CCP, 445, 609, 615

Liu Bozhuang, 6, 212, 279, 449, 619; biographical sketch, 1205; as Peng Shuzhi supporter, 602, 640

Liu Jialiang, 534, 554, 872n; factional activity by, 549–50, 551–3, 655; Guomindang jailing of, 656; as leader of Revolutionary Communist Party, 19, 122; murder in Vietnam of, 2, 657, 1205; and Sino-Japanese War debate, 558, 872; on Third Chinese Revolution, 575, 975

Liu Jingzhen (Wu Jingru), 444, 450, 465, 466, 615, 1144; arrest and imprisonment of (1931), 90, 91, 499, 646, 648, 1171–2; arrest and imprisonment of (1952), 655, 1070–1, 1127, 1172; biographical sketch, 1171–3, 1205; during Cultural Revolution, 1171; death of, 1170, 1182; early Left Opposition work by, 74, 626, 1110; expulsion from CCP, 627; given Trotskyist documents, 619; Wang Fanxi obituary of, 1170–3; and Zheng Chaolin imprisonment, 654–5, 660, 662, 670, 1065–6, 1067, 1136, 1141, 1171; Zheng Chaolin marriage to, 1179

Liu Renjing, 110, 478, 502, 578, 646; after 1949, 133–4, 485, 976; allegations of capitulation against, 96, 581, 656, 657; arrest and imprisonment by Guomindang, 96, 509, 656; biographical sketch, 1206; at Comintern Fourth Congress, 1082; and constituent assembly slogan, 351, 480, 481, 483, 676, 868, 1019; criticisms of Chen Duxiu by, 11, 25, 452, 483, 920, 1152; and debate on Chinese Revolution character, 484, 488, 668–9, 735–6, 867; and dissemination of Trotskyism, 74–5, 468, 469, 620–1, 625, 632; drafts 'An Open Letter to All Comrades', 480; and Fourth International General Council, 925; memoirs and recollections by, 367; not elected to Trotskyist Central Committee, 87, 96, 493; and October group, 479, 481, 485, 633–4, 1098; on peasant war and economic upturn, 923; political weaknesses of, 485; and reorganisation of Communist League, 11–12, 25, 96, 655–7, 922; as student in Moscow, 372, 374, 377, 631; visit to Trotsky by, 9, 74–5, 358, 374, 464–5, 468, 631, 662–3, 1098; and Yun Daiying, 464–5, 631; and Zheng Chaolin, 465, 632

Liu Shaoqi, 65, 69, 327, 429, 543, 605; biographical sketch, 1206; dictatorship of proletariat announced in China, 816, 831; labour movement activity by, 240, 249, 596; Liu Renjing meeting with, 133; and Peng Shuzhi, 1081

Liu Yin: biographical sketch, 1206; defection to Guomindang by, 479, 493; as leader of Militant group, 469, 479, 481, 487, 633; in Moscow, 478–9; and Trotskyist work in CCP, 478, 631; in unification negotiations, 487, 635; and Yin Kuan, 635, 640

Lominadze, Vissarion, 608, 892; adventurist policy directed by, 498, 806, 807–8, 1094; and August 7 Emergency Conference, 265, 266; biographical sketch, 1206

Long March, 17, 64, 433, 511, 813, 990

Lou Guohua, 492, 534, 550, 559, 1193; arrest and imprisonment of, 90, 499, 647, 649, 1176; biographical sketch, 1176, 1206; on collapse of Stalinism, 46; and *Dongxiang*, 554, 1176; on Lu Xun, 1039, 1040–1, 1177–8; and Sino-Japanese War debate, 558; Wang Fanxi obituary of, 1176–8; work in Hong Kong after 1949, 19, 1176–7, 1197

Lou Shiyi, 62, 658, 1177, 1206; on Lu Xun, 1040–1; on Zheng Chaolin, 1063–6

Lu Dingyi, 240, 265, 604

Lu Xun: biographical sketch, 1206; and Chen Duxiu, 514, 1033; Chen Qichang letter to, 103–4; on Gide, 1041; and Isaacs, 1041; on literature of the masses, 1036; Lou Guohua on, 1039, 1040–1, 1177–8; on March Eighteenth Incident, 277; mentioned, 215, 274, 441, 587; and New Culture Movement, 1177–8; and Qu Qiubai, 64; on slandering of revolutionaries, 1039–40; Trotskyist influence on, 1032–4, 1035–6, 1044; Wang Shiwei on, 1056; Zheng Chaolin on, 438, 1044

— writings: 'How I Started Writing Novels', 1034; 'Mid Summer Jottings', 1040, 1043; *The True Story of Ah-Q*, 967n

Lu Xun 'letter to a Trotskyite', 507, 513–14, 1037–39; Feng Xuefeng authorship of, 44–5, 106–7, 1039, 1041–3, 1044, 1178; Hu Feng on story of, 106, 1041–3; text of, 104–5; use of after 1949, 1044

Lu Yucai, 1128, 1131

Lugouqiao Incident (1937), 45, 96, 538, 659

Luo Feng, 1030, 1034

Luo Han, 328, 342, 480, 533, 542–3; attempts to restore CCP-Chen Duxiu relations, 97, 98, 686–8, 710; biographical sketch, 1206; death of, 578; demand for rehabilitation of, 1131; in France, 192–3, 194; friendly relations with CCP by, 530, 531, 546; as October group member, 485; Stalinist slanders against, 547–8, 678, 683; and Unification Congress, 86, 87, 492, 493, 642, 643

Luo Jiao. *See* Luo Yinong

Luo Qiyuan, 419, 446, 637, 1206

Luo Shifan, 660, 662, 710; biographical sketch, 1207; with Chen Duxiu in prison, 95, 658, 727n; Chen Duxiu letter to, 709–12; Chen Duxiu view of, 679, 711; helps reorganise Central Executive, 92, 132; member of Proletarian group leadership, 469, 473, 629

Luo Yinong (Luo Jiao), 79, 83, 240, 306, 318, 421, 597; arrest and execution of, 66, 434, 610; at August 7 Emergency Conference, 266, 267; biographical sketch, 306; and CCP factional struggle, 269, 418–19, 599–601, 602; CCP leadership responsibilities of, 251, 257–8, 267, 418–19, 595, 599, 607, 608–9, 612; and Chen Duxiu-ites within CCP, 6, 404, 421, 609; and Chiang Kai-shek, 320; and Peng Shuzhi, 306–7, 421, 599–601, 602, 604; relations with Chen Duxiu, 611–12, 637; and Shanghai insurrection and massacre, 259, 264, 265, 797; as student in Moscow, 307, 310, 311, 313, 316; and Zheng Chaolin, 253, 258, 270, 614

Luo Zhanglong, 74, 78, 131, 230, 344, 605, 607; biographical sketch, 1207; as 'conciliationist' toward Chen Duxiu, 348–9, 463, 498, 1109–10; sympathy for Trotskyist views expressed by, 347, 348; and Zhang Guotao, 240, 596

Ma Renzhi, 91, 650; and Hubin Book Company, 465, 469, 625–6

Ma Yuansheng, 367; arrest and exile of, 375, 382–3; at International Lenin School, 374–5, 376–8, 379

Ma Yufu: biographical sketch, 91–2, 1207; as Chen Duxiu-ite, 6, 71, 74; expelled from CCP, 72, 627, 1096; given Trotskyist literature in Moscow, 452, 619; killing of, 92; member of Proletarian group leadership, 469, 473, 628; mentioned, 320, 464, 617, 618, 638; opposition to Li Lisan by, 449, 616; opposition to Trotskyist unification by, 473, 641; as traitor and informer, 91, 110, 148, 499, 644–5, 647, 648, 649, 650; Trotskyist work within CCP by, 466–7, 626; and Unification Congress, 474, 493; in unification negotiations, 470, 471, 472, 487, 488–9, 635, 639; and Zheng Chaolin, 452, 617

Malraux, André: *Les Conquérants*, 550, 580

Manchuria: Japanese occupation of, 510, 989, 998

Manuilsky, Dmitry, 386, 837–8

Mao Dun. *See* Shen Yanbing

Mao Hongjian, 119, 507, 509, 1207

Mao Zedong: accused of 'Trotskyism', 113, 149–50, 151; and 'anti-fascist' united front with Guomindang, 512, 858, 957, 1036; and Autumn Harvest uprisings, 807; and campaign against Trotskyism, 15–16, 1030, 1044; and Chen Duxiu, 97, 98, 461, 533, 563–4, 685, 710n; Chen Duxiu appreciation by, 16, 101, 585, 691–2; Chen Duxiu compared to, 700, 979; and Cultural Revolution, 65; death of, 1145; on Guomindang entry, 783–4; on literature and art, 1030–1; and Long March, 64; and Lu Xun letter, 105, 106, 1044; and Marxism, 1027–8, 1045, 1193; mentioned, 31, 61, 78, 79, 116, 225–6, 233, 266, 852, 981–2; on Moscow Trials, 15, 1032; on 'New Democracy', 875, 963; and Peasant Training Institute, 429, 460, 609; and Peng Shuzhi, 1191; policies after 1949 by, 30, 149, 831; on Qu Qiubai, 65; Rectification Campaign of, 64, 1030; on Red Army and armed struggle, 31, 32, 69,

INDEX   1251

Mao Zedong (cont.)
  155, 462, 806, 835, 836, 842, 951, 954, 1021;
  rejection of Stalin's directives by, 23, 30,
  544, 843–4, 980; during Second Chinese
  Revolution, 80, 605, 806; and Soviet
  denunciation of Stalin, 37, 69; Stalin suspicions about, 113, 149–50, 495, 979–80; and
  Stalinism, 37–8, 497, 978–9; on Stalin's
  mistakes, 69–70; takes over CCP leadership,
  388, 511, 543–4; on Trotskyist prisoners,
  114, 124, 133, 135; and Wang Ming, 30, 99,
  149–50, 497, 511, 543–4, 548–9, 979; on
  Wang Shiwei, 1032; work in Guomindang
  by, 82, 460, 785, 790, 1085; on Yin Kuan, 114
  — writings: 'Analysis of the Classes in
    Chinese Society', 599; 'On the People's
    Democratic Dictatorship', 564; 'Report
    on the Hunan Peasant Movement', 460,
    606; A Single Spark Can Start a Prairie
    Fire', 835; Talks on Art and Literature,
    1030; 'The Struggle in the Jinggang
    Mountains', 836, 1021n
Mao Zedong Selected Works, 599, 1144;
  annotation in, 3, 4, 155, 682, 1044, 1134–5;
  Zheng Chaolin reading in jail of, 1112–13,
  1140
Maoism, 30; as variant of Stalinism, 848,
  980–1; as variant of Trotskyism, 113,
  149–50, 151, 844
Marco Polo Bridge Incident (1937), 45, 538, 659
Maring. See Sneevliet, Henk
Marx, Karl, 1103; Chen Duxiu and, 206–7, 663;
  Chinese publication of, 503, 580, 1046;
  on Franco-Prussian War, 720, 725; writings:
  Communist Manifesto, 209, 585; *The
  Eighteenth Brumaire of Louis Bonaparte*,
  480
Marxism, 703, 934; and individual terror,
  299–300; Mao Zedong and, 1027–8, 1045,
  1193; Stalinist distortion of, 928, 943–4,
  1027–8; Trotskyist dissemination of, 1045,
  1193
Maslov, 328, 330–1
May Fourth Movement, 206, 211; about, 770n;
  Chen Duxiu and, 101, 589, 664, 677, 697,
  706, 772, 1087, 1165; impact of, 184, 186, 230,
  589, 706, 1183; May Thirtieth Movement as

outgrowth of, 499–500; Wang Fanxi and,
  213–15, 219, 1192; Zheng Chaolin and, 172–3,
  176, 181, 184, 186
May Thirtieth Movement: bourgeoisie and,
  246–7, 401; massacre leading to, 217,
  245–6, 788; Peng Shuzhi on, 788–90; as
  spark for Second Chinese Revolution, 217,
  426–7, 788–9; strike movement in, 247,
  249–50, 273n, 426–7, 788; Wang Fanxi
  and, 220, 273; Zheng Chaolin and, 244–6,
  248–9, 1109
Memoirs of a Chinese Revolutionary (Wang
  Fanxi), 34, 71, 73, 75–6, 107, 108, 118, 137;
  'Chen Duxiu, Chinese Trotskyists, and
  the War of Resistance', 532–56; 'Chinese
  Students in Moscow', 327–65; 'The
  Founding of *Struggle* and the Darkest
  Days of my Life', 507–31; 'From War to
  Revolution', 568–75; mentioned 'My
  First Contact with New Ideas', 213–29;
  'The Pacific War and a New Split in the
  Organisation', 557–67; postscript to,
  1116–17; prefaces to, 1118–19, 1120–3;
  publication of, 28, 1120, 1192, 1195;
  'Thinking in Solitude', 967–82; 'Two Years
  at University', 272–91; 'Unification of the
  Four Groups', 478–503; writing of, 113,
  1116, 1118
Mencius, 170, 213, 663, 1179
Meng Qingshu, 382, 391
Menshevism, 782, 783–4, 944–5, 974
Merezhkovsky, Dmitry: *Resurrection of the
  Gods*, 1065, 1113–14, 1182
Mif, Pavel, 1157; biographical sketch, 1207;
  CCP leadership role of, 61, 62, 344; Stalin's
  purge of, 84, 386, 1207; as Sun Yat-sen
  University rector, 7, 52, 58–9, 329–31,
  380, 385, 388, 1095; and Wang Ming, 330–1,
  384, 495
Militant (China). See *Zhandou*
Militant (US), 469, 633
Militant group, 75, 486, 634; delegates to
  Unification Congress from, 86, 475, 642;
  formation of, 469, 481, 633, 1099;
  membership of, 487, 491, 1099; and
  unification negotiations, 635. See also Left
  Opposition, Chinese

Miller, Joseph T., 22, 1075–102, 1198
Mingtian ('Tomorrow'), 469, 634
Montargis Middle School, 192, 194, 199
Moscow branch of CCP, 212, 312, 315, 319, 323–4, 327–9, 330, 595, 599, 1081
'Moscow group', 6, 21, 240, 596, 599, 600; split in, 602–7
Moscow Infantry Military School, 366, 375, 393
Moscow Trials, 548, 661; charges in, 515; 'confessions' given in, 522, 1154; Mao Zedong criticisms of, 15; rehabilitation of victims of, 682, 1113; Wang Shiwei condemnation of, 1031; work to expose truth of, 516, 682–3

Nanchang uprising (1927), 262, 1093; about, 806; Ye-He army and, 462, 806, 894, 997
Nanjing, 66, 167–71, 572, 652–3, 797, 859; Japanese occupation of, 529–30, 532, 660
Narodniks, 430, 454, 564, 907, 934
national assembly. *See* constituent assembly
national-democratic revolution, 405, 778, 1084; 'national revolution' theory on, 596–9, 603; Peng Shuzhi on, 597, 788; Second CCP Congress on, 778, 821; Trotsky on, 828, 829
national liberation: Bolsheviks and Comintern on, 919, 933–4, 1081–2; Chen Duxiu on, 591, 752–3, 762
nationalism, 760; Chinese, 198, 288, 512, 1077; Stalinism and, 980, 1128; Trotsky on, 919
Nationalist Party. *See* Guomindang
New Banner (*Xinqi*): as Internationalist group organ, 122, 569, 864, 879, 1111, 1138, 1180–1; Peng Shuzhi criticisms of, 861–2, 863; readership and influence of, 570
New Culture Movement, 663, 697, 1177. *See also* May Fourth Movement
New Fourth Army, 433–4, 442, 462, 545, 557. *See also* People's Liberation Army; Red Army, Chinese
New Thought Movement, 588
New Universe publishing company and bookshop, 357, 502, 630, 631
New Youth (*Xin qingnian*), 173, 190, 226, 319, 588; becomes CCP organ, 778; Chen Duxiu and, 208, 218, 324, 500, 585, 587, 691, 699, 1028; influence and impact of, 176, 177, 208, 280–1, 429, 589, 1078, 1108; Mao Zedong on, 101; Peng Shuzhi as editor of, 77, 235, 323–4, 599, 787, 1085; Trotsky speech printed in, 323; Zheng Chaolin work for, 234, 239
Nie Rongzhen, 61, 257, 264
Niel Sih. *See* Liu Renjing
Northern Expedition, 82, 280, 286, 403, 420, 604; CCP leadership discussion on, 82–3; Chen Duxiu on, 82–3, 459; Comintern support for, 402, 791, 792–3, 795–6; mass movement sparked by, 428–9, 430–1, 432–3; Peng Shuzhi on, 83, 1091; Zheng Chaolin on, 258, 259

October (*Shiyue*), 75, 468, 481, 485, 633, 1098
October group, 85, 468, 486, 634, 635; Chen Duxiu on, 468–9, 1098–9; delegates to Unification Congress from, 86, 475, 641–2; formation of, 75, 468–9, 480–1, 633, 1098; membership of, 485, 491, 1098. *See also* Left Opposition, Chinese
October Review (*Shiyue pinglun*), 1076, 1197
On the Question of the Chinese Revolution, 621, 625, 632
Oriental Book Company, 461, 502–3, 548, 554–5, 636; about, 515–16, 1046–7
The Original Way (*Yuan dao*), 177, 183
Ou Fang, 644, 1207; arrest and killing of, 486, 487; Communist League Central Committee member, 87, 643, 1101; expelled from CCP and sent back to China, 59, 70, 339, 480; member of Our Word group, 85, 474, 479, 486, 631; in unification negotiations, 487, 635; work among industrial proletariat by, 486, 508
Our Word (*Women de hua*), 8, 452, 676, 1097; establishment of, 70, 118, 357, 468, 630
Our Word group, 85, 468, 632–3, 634; delegates to Unification Congress from, 86, 475, 641–2; distrust of Chen Duxiu group by, 8–9, 73–4, 472, 478–9; formation of, 73, 135, 468, 481, 485, 630–1, 1097; internal disputes in, 474, 479; leadership of, 480, 485; membership of, 491, 1097; Peng Shuzhi opposition to, 9, 73–4, 76, 468, 1097; political activity of, 630–1; and

INDEX 1253

Our Word group (*cont.*)
  unification negotiations, 470, 474, 634–5, 639, 640–1. *See also* Left Opposition, Chinese
Ouyang Jixiu, 252, 438, 439, 441

Pablo, Michel, 29, 1189
Pan Hannian, 450, 659
Pan Jiachen, 269, 425
Pan Lanzhen, 73, 76, 92, 95
Pan Wenyu, 450, 465, 466, 468, 615, 1207
Pan Zinian, 659, 1064
Pantsov, Alexander V., 366–88, 389–96
peasant movement: Chen Duxiu on, 887–9; Comintern line on, 406, 897, 1091; in Hunan, 429–30, 793, 800, 826; during 1940s, 877, 957; Trotsky on, 836, 908, 913, 916
peasant war, 836–7, 923, 952–3; Trotsky on, 836, 838–9, 841–2, 887–9, 903–11, 912, 915, 1014–15. *See also* Chinese Civil War
peasantry: CCP and, 428, 833, 952–3, 965, 969–73, 997, 1005–6, 1008–09; Chen Duxiu view of, 31–2; and land question, 427–8, 916; in pre-revolutionary Russia, 430; Trotsky on, 906, 916, 932–3; Trotskyist view of, 31, 909
Peng Guiqiu, 90–1, 110, 502, 645
Peng Kang, 439, 441, 442–3, 657
Peng Pai, 13, 66, 271, 467–8, 1207; peasant movement led by, 430, 807
Peng Shuzhi: archives of, 1199; arrest and imprisonment of, 2, 11, 94, 530, 660, 989, 1101, 1187–8; and arrests of 1931, 91, 110, 132, 646, 650; assassination plots against, 2, 549; becomes Trotskyist, 73, 1083, 1095, 1187; in Beijing, 607, 610; bibliography of writings by, 1196; biographical sketch, 77, 112, 1076–80, 1183, 1207–08; Borodin meeting with, 402, 404, 791, 1090–1, 1185–6; and Cai Hesen, 78–9, 786, 1185; careerist claims about, 471, 600–1, 602, 641, 1089, 1102; at CCP Emergency Conference, 265; at CCP Fifth Congress, 798, 1093; at CCP Fourth Congress, 78, 236, 237, 1087–9, 1185; and CCP Northern Bureau, 84, 1093; and CCP Sixth Congress, 68, 435, 1095, 1186–7; and Chen Bilan, 73–4, 80, 87, 601; Chen Duxiu clung to by, 471–2, 600, 605, 638; Chen Duxiu criticised by, 11, 18, 448, 562–3, 703, 852; Chen Duxiu discussions with, 637, 638, 1079, 1185; Chen Duxiu on, 476, 644; Chen Duxiu relations with, 21, 472, 473, 536, 658, 709, 710, 711; Chen Duxiu supported by, 6, 77, 404, 421, 617; and Chen Qiaonian, 421, 471, 602, 604, 617; at Comintern gatherings, 1081, 1085; dislike of, 20–1, 421–2, 473, 602, 617, 651; in exile after 1949, 28, 112, 122, 132–3, 1183, 1189; expulsion from CCP of, 72, 465–6, 627, 1095–6, 1187; and Fourth International, 112, 1189; and guerrilla war, 27, 993; head of CCP Propaganda Department, 78, 256, 595, 600, 1087, 1089; as lecturer and professor, 145, 232, 251, 1083; living arrangements of, 225, 233, 644; and Luo Yinong, 306–7, 421, 599–601, 602, 604; made scapegoat for revolution's defeat, 83, 1186; and May Thirtieth Movement, 252–3, 788–90; member of CCP leadership committees, 78, 81, 228, 238, 239, 600, 601, 607, 786–7, 1087, 1089; member of Trotskyist leadership committees, 87, 92, 122, 476, 492–3, 534, 643, 652, 872n, 1101; mentioned, 121, 250, 442, 449, 502, 551, 679, 1154; and Moscow branch of CCP, 327, 599; as *New Youth* editor, 77, 235, 323–4, 599, 787, 1085; nicknamed 'Confucius', 77, 79, 306–7, 600; obituary of, 1182–91; and origins of Chinese Trotskyism, 71, 577, 621, 1094–6, 1099; and Our Word group, 9, 73–4, 76, 468, 1097; ousted from CCP leadership, 615, 1094; personal appearance of, 306; and Proletarian group, 469, 628, 1097; Qu Qiubai as opponent of, 235, 440, 471, 599, 606, 796n, 1093; receives Trotskyist documents, 9, 451, 619, 1095; and reorganisation of Trotskyist leadership, 92, 132, 642; return from Soviet Union, 324, 599, 1068; and Revolutionary Communist Party, 12, 122, 143, 1076, 1181; on revolutionary democratic dictatorship, 794–5; in Shanghai, 77, 225, 251, 550, 1091, 1183, 1185–6, 1188; signs 'Our Political Views', 74, 75, 1096; and split of 1942, 12, 122, 559–60; Stalinist slanders against, 547, 549, 578; at Sun Yat-sen University, 77, 306–7, 310, 311,

Peng Shuzhi (*cont.*)
313–14, 315, 317, 318, 319, 320, 321, 323–4, 1080–5, 1184–5; supports withdrawal from Guomindang, 82, 792, 1091; Trotskyist recruitment work by, 145, 626; and unification campaign, 10, 471, 472, 473, 476, 488, 489, 634, 635, 638, 639–40, 643–4, 1100; and Unification Congress, 86, 87, 474, 475n, 476, 492–3, 634, 635, 641, 642, 643–4; Wang Fanxi on, 19, 473, 488, 560, 867, 970, 971, 991, 1004–5, 1009–12, 1019, 1020; and Wang Guolong, 139, 140; won to communism, 240, 1184; Wu Jimin on, 77–84; in Wuhan, 606, 637, 638, 797; Xiang Jingyu affair with, 78, 79; Zheng Chaolin on, 20–1, 77, 79, 110, 262–3, 306–7, 471–3, 489, 601–2, 604, 617, 667–8, 788–90; and Zhou Enlai, 81, 791

— views: on CCP class character, 29, 840, 961–6, 970, 971, 1005–6, 1008–09; on Chen Duxiu embrace of Trotskyism, 621; on Chiang Kai-shek's counter-revolutionary plans, 793–5;on Chinese Revolution character, 458–9, 666; on constituent assembly demand, 11, 410, 458, 868, 1019–20; on course of Chinese Civil War, 572, 857–8, 860; on defeatism, 817, 853–4, 860–1, 874; on democratic centralism and party organisation, 18–19, 20, 21, 560, 854, 863, 1102; on Guomindang entry, 619, 780–6, 1084, 1088, 1185; on national revolution, 597, 599, 787, 1085–7, 1092; on Northern Expedition, 83, 1091; on permanent revolution, 667–8, 669, 674, 675, 796n, 867, 875, 949–50, 956; on policy in Second Chinese Revolution, 81, 82, 402, 789–90, 792–805, 806–8, 1085–94, 1185; on Qu Qiubai, 471, 602; on Sino-Japanese War, 28, 553, 558, 846, 870, 871–2, 874, 985, 991, 1016; on Soviet-Finnish war, 878, 883; on Third Chinese Revolution victory, 29, 575, 950–5, 995–6, 1003, 1004–5, 1009–12, 1018, 1193; on Trotsky's contributions, 808–18; on Wang Fanxi, 488, 817; on Zheng Chaolin, 1067;

— writings: 'After Reading Chiang Kai-shek's Speech of 21 February', 795; 'The Causes of the Victory of the Chinese Communist Party over Chiang Kai-shek', 949–60; 'The Closing of the Shanghai General Labour Union and the Present Responsibilities of the Workers', 789–90; 'Imperialism and the Boxer Movement', 77; introduction to *Leon Trotsky on China*, 777–818; 'Is Leninism Applicable to the National Peculiarities of China?', 796n, 1091–2; memoirs, 21–2, 1195–6; 'The Present Revolutionary Crisis of the Rightward Tendency', 793–5; 'Report to the International Secretariat of the Fourth International', 575; 'Return to the Road of Trotskyism', 986–7; 'Trotskyism in China', 851–63; 'Who Is the Leader of the National Revolution?', 77, 787, 1086

Peng Zexiang, 217, 307–8

People's Liberation Army, 541, 857–8, 953, 954, 1144; call for Guomindang overthrow by, 958–9; 'general offensive of', 951; Soviet aid to, 953–4, 999; victories by, 572, 975. *See also* Red Army, Chinese

People's Republic of China, 149, 154, 1160–1; anti-rightist campaign in, 150, 981–2; anticapitalist measures taken by, 30, 816; bureaucratic dictatorship in, 816–17, 1130; call for Trotskyists' rehabilitation in, 3, 36–8, 45–6, 115–16, 155–6, 563, 682, 683–4, 1113, 1130–1, 1181–2; Cultural Revolution in, 15n, 65–6, 114, 133, 135, 150, 563n, 655, 847n, 848, 1071, 1105, 1113, 1116, 1142–4, 1160, 1171; curbing of working class in, 963–4; democracy movement in, 1129, 1189–90; Deng Xiaoping reforms in, 1145; dictatorship of proletariat announced in, 816, 830–1; Hundred Flower campaign in, 35, 981; idealisation of capitalism in, 1129–30; imprisonment of Trotskyists in, 2, 13, 43, 113–14, 123, 124–5, 134, 143, 146, 149–51, 573–4, 655, 847n, 1070–1, 1112, 1127, 1132–3, 1137–38, 1139, 1146, 1181; land reform in, 964–5; release of Trotskyist prisoners in, 114–15, 124–5, 133, 134, 1066, 1067, 1117, 1127–31, 1145, 1181; and Soviet Union, 149, 151; Stalinist model in, 979–80; Trotskyist activity in, 150, 573, 1180–1; Trotskyist programme for, 817, 1128; and US

INDEX 1255

People's Republic of China (*cont.*)
  government, 149; workers' state
  established in, 816, 1009
permanent revolution, 123, 363, 453, 459, 618,
  619, 840; Chen Duxiu and, 667; as issue
  in 1942 split, 861, 875–6; Peng Shuzhi
  on, 667–8, 669, 674, 675, 796n, 867, 875,
  949–50, 956; Trotsky's theory of, 455–6,
  667, 669–75, 814, 815–17, 829–30, 876;
  Wang Fanxi on, 867–8, 1118–19, 1150–1
personality cult, 356, 362, 601, 980
petty bourgeoisie, 512, 739, 852; Trotsky on,
  826–8, 932. *See also* peasantry
Platform of the Opposition, 332, 900
Plekhanov, Georgi, 399, 665, 865; on
  bourgeois and socialist revolution in
  Russia, 934, 935, 936; Chen Duxiu as
  China's, 692, 697; Lenin recognition of,
  564, 692–3; translation into Chinese of,
  132, 324, 469, 555
popular front, 726, 938; CCP implementation
  of, 511, 512–13, 960; Stalinist policy around,
  510, 813, 944–5, 1151–2; Trotsky on policy
  of, 944–5
Poxiao. See *Daybreak*
Pravda, 323, 548, 837–8, 890, 917; Bukharin
  article on China in, 403, 792, 823; Chen
  Duxiu speech in, 885, 889; on Trotsky and
  Trotskyists, 340, 354–5
pre-revolutionary situations, 858, 860, 913, 1016
Preobrazhensky, Yevgeni A., 254n, 344, 815
printshops and printing presses, 268, 418, 507,
  569, 579–80, 655; internal struggles over,
  11–12, 25, 468–9, 507, 580, 656–7, 658
Proletarian (*Wuchanzhe*), 9, 470, 590, 668–9,
  1097; establishment of, 394, 628;
  publication and printing of, 75, 629
Proletarian group, 86, 474, 634; composition
  of, 486–7, 628, 1097–8; delegates to
  Unification Congress from, 86, 87, 475,
  641–2; formation of, 9, 469–70, 481, 1097–9;
  internal debates in, 472–4, 489, 641, 668–9;
  leadership of, 469, 628; membership
  of, 486–7, 491, 1098; periodical of, 503;
  political activity of, 629; and unification
  negotiations, 470, 634–5, 639, 641, 1100; Wu
  Jiyan group joins, 632–3; Zheng Chaolin
  and, 640–1. *See also* Left Opposition,
  Chinese

proletarian literature (proletkult), 254, 503,
  513, 1027
proletariat, 905–6, 913; CCP withdrawal from,
  921, 956, 962–3; in colonial and semi-
  colonial countries, 933, 956; conditions of,
  582; and May Thirtieth Movement, 247–8,
  249–50, 401; and Red Army, 839–40, 907;
  repression of after 1949, 963–4; role of in
  Chinese Revolution, 31, 228–9, 714, 715,
  738, 788–90, 793, 1084, 1086; strikes by, 23,
  228, 230, 231, 242–4, 250, 273, 280, 284, 286,
  401, 428, 595–6, 778, 784, 920, 963–4;
  subordination to bourgeoisie of, 907–8,
  937, 944; Trotskyist work within, 508, 561,
  629, 630–1, 838, 855, 856, 1070. *See also*
  labour movement
Pu Dezhi (Pu Qingquan, Xiliu), 87, 95, 631;
  arrest and imprisonment of, 90, 499, 647,
  649, 658, 727n; biographical information,
  537, 1208; on Chen Duxiu, 621, 639, 685;
  Chen Duxiu letters to, 719–22, 723–4,
  725–7, 731–7; Chen Duxiu relations with,
  538, 542, 658, 727n; and He Jifeng, 539, 540;
  release from prison of, 538, 652, 660;
  and reorganisation of Trotskyist leadership,
  92, 132; translation work by, 662; at
  Unification Congress, 86, 87, 492, 641–2,
  643; and unification negotiations, 10n, 635;
  Wang Fanxi and, 537–8
Pu Qingquan. *See* Pu Dezhi
publishing houses and outlets, 501–2; Hubin,
  465, 469, 502, 625–6, 629; New Life, 503;
  New Universe, 357, 502, 630, 631; Oriental
  Book Company, 461, 502–3, 515–16, 548,
  554–5, 636, 1046–7; Shenzhou Guoguang,
  502, 629; Sincere Press, 1177, 1197; Spring
  Swallow, 1176; Xiqi Library, 569; Zhouji
  hang, 1197

Qian Chuan, 123, 138; after 1949, 141, 146
Qian Huichu, 37, 145, 146
Qian Xuantong, 214, 587, 769
Qin Bangxian. *See* Bo Gu
Qin Zhigu, 189, 198, 202–3, 207
Qingnian ('Youth'), 587, 1169
Qiuzhen ('Seeking the Truth'), 122, 569, 851,
  1019, 1189
Qu Qiubai, 419, 444, 494, 596, 601, 605, 607;
  adventurist line of, 498, 590, 806, 1013; and

Qu Qiubai (*cont.*)
  Bao Pu, 315; and CCP 7 August Emergency Conference, 265, 266, 267, 1093, 1094; becomes central CCP leader, 267, 418, 419, 590, 608, 805, 1094; biographical sketch, 61, 226–7, 1208; and *Bolshevik*, 417–18, 423–4, 612, 615; and Cai Hesen, 422, 603; capture and execution of, 64, 94; at CCP Fourth Congress, 78, 236–7, 238, 1087–8; and Chen Duxiu, 68, 79, 399, 405, 420, 435, 604, 611–12, 637; and Comintern, 239, 422, 792; at Comintern Sixth Congress, 344, 345–6, 624; on Creation Society, 438; Cultural Revolution attacks on, 65–6; denunciation of Trotskyists by, 383–4, 1093; deposed as CCP leader, 61–2, 331, 494, 498; educational work by, 244, 256, 314, 1063; and Guangzhou insurrection, 807; *Guide Weekly* articles by, 250, 784–5; and Guomindang-CCP relations, 232, 405, 784–5; ill health of, 63–4; on Jiang Guangchi, 254; living arrangements of, 63, 225, 253, 268–9; and Lu Xun, 64; and Mao Zedong, 65, 461; during May Thirtieth events, 248, 249; and *New Youth*, 226–7, 235; and ouster of Chen Duxiu, 267, 606, 609, 805, 1109–10, 1186; Peng Shuzhi as opponent of, 235, 440, 471, 599, 606, 796n, 1093; Peng Shuzhi on, 471, 602; and Ren Bishi, 65, 604; on Second Chinese Revolution prospects, 404, 428; as Shanghai University professor, 226, 232, 233; and Soviet advisers, 227, 418, 498, 603; and soviets slogan, 350–1, 826; and Stalin, 130, 345, 346, 495; support for Northern Expedition by, 82, 604; Trotsky document read by, 345–6, 624; Wang Ming attacks on, 335, 346, 384, 494, 495, 496, 498; won to communism, 226; and Zheng Chaolin, 253, 268–9, 271, 614, 615, 1110; and Zhou Enlai, 61–2, 65–6
  — writings: *Introduction to Social Science*, 66; *On Luantan Opera and Other Things*, 66; *Against Peng Shuzhi-ism*, 83, 235, 599, 604, 606; 'Reform of the Guomindang and the National Revolutionary Movement', 784–5; *Some Controversial Questions in the Chinese Revolution*, 83; *Superfluous Words*, 64–6

Radek, Karl, 321, 1082; biographical sketch, 52, 1208; on Guomindang entry, 780–1; line on Chinese Revolution of, 55, 828, 890, 891; Moscow purge trial of, 1113; Sun Yat-sen University course taught by, 54, 120; as Sun Yat-sen University rector, 7, 52, 58, 369, 390–1, 630, 1094; in Trotskyist opposition, 321, 344, 815, 822, 890, 891
Raiskaia, Minna Yakovlevna, 370, 372–3, 384–5
Rechao ('Hot Tide'), 24
Rectification Campaign, 64, 1030
Red Army, Chinese, 131, 923, 953, 972; Chen Duxiu on, 25, 26n, 459–60, 463–4, 483; class composition of, 915–16; discussion on Trotskyist presence in, 987, 988, 989, 990, 1015; formation of, 32, 433–4, 460, 462–3, 806, 813; liquidation of, 814, 817, 834, 953, 990; Long March of, 17, 64, 511, 813, 990; and proletariat, 433–4, 907, 910–11, 921; reorganisation and name change of, 433n, 512, 659; Stalin and Manuilsky on, 837–8; system of ranks in, 1053–4; Trotsky on, 463, 838, 839, 905, 906–7, 908, 909, 910–29, 1014–15. *See also* People's Liberation Army
Red Flag (*Hongqi bao*), 466, 627, 674–5, 1144
Reform Movement of 1898, 769, 1078, 1168–9
Ren Bishi, 61, 78, 266n, 326, 602; and Chen Duxiu, 405, 435; as Communist Youth leader, 240, 307, 595, 603–4; and Qu Qiubai, 65, 604; as student in Moscow, 307, 310
Ren Xu, 421, 445, 602, 609, 615
Ren Zhuoxuan (Ye Qing), 100, 200, 201, 205
Ren Zuomin, 258n, 325, 595, 636–7, 1080; as CCP secretary, 234, 239
Republic Daily (*Minguo ribao*), 232, 235, 315
'Resolution on Certain Questions in the History of Our Party', 495–6
revolution: artists and, 1055–6; bourgeois and proletarian, 427; Chen Duxiu on, 738, 739; international character of, 623; nonschematic view of, 976, 1018–19; relationship of democratic and socialist, 867–8; stages theory of, 459, 796n, 814–15, 816; Trotsky on laws of, 930–1; war as mother of, 945. *See also* First Chinese Revolution; Second Chinese Revolution; Third Chinese Revolution; Chinese Revolution character

INDEX 1257

Revolutionary Communist Party of China (1948–), 575, 846, 851, 1076; establishment of, 12, 19, 112; founding congress of, 122, 571; leadership committee of, 122; leadership moved to Hong Kong, 572, 1181; membership of, 12, 571, 846n; political work of, 1189
'revolutionary victoryism', 28, 845, 1024, 1156
Rolland, Romain, 190, 207–8, 1043; *Jean Christophe*, 209
Rousseau, Jean-Jacques, 209, 588, 930
Roy, M. N., 406–7, 605n, 608, 804, 1208; at CCP Fifth Congress, 607, 798–9
Russell, Bertrand, 190, 216
Russian Communist Party. *See* Communist Party of the Soviet Union
Russian Revolution, 48; CCP as product of, 427, 812; Chen Duxiu and, 589, 751, 765; and Chinese Revolution, 284–5, 425–6, 597–8, 622, 937; and constituent assembly demand, 913–14; discussion over character of, 454–5, 456, 670–4, 934–5, 937–38; influence on China of, 500, 587; soviets in, 915; victory of, 1000, 1018–19

Scientific Research Institute of National and Colonial Issues (NIINKP), 366, 385, 387
Second All-China Labour Congress (1925), 247, 787
Second United Front, 23, 30, 433n, 511, 704, 834, 851; and abandonment of class struggle, 843–4, 972; formation of, 3, 97, 659, 813–14; as tactical manoeuvre, 29–30
sectarianism, 24–5, 512, 559, 852, 853, 861, 1152
Serge, Victor, 208; *From Lenin to Stalin*, 554, 580
Shachtman, Max, 29, 864, 875n, 1174
Shachtmanites, 854, 877–8, 883, 986
Shaji Incident (1925), 273, 789
Shandong, 173n, 240–1, 770n; Communist League of China in, 509–10, 856; Trotskyist guerrilla unit in, 27, 541, 561, 855–6, 1016, 1128
Shanghai: CCP in, 5, 83, 243, 250–1, 418, 419, 421, 503, 518, 549, 778; Guomindang in, 229, 232, 793, 1187; International Settlement and Concession in, 225, 245, 246, 507, 518, 547, 550, 553, 556, 920–1, 1188; Japanese attacks and occupation, 66, 526–7, 556, 570, 582, 652, 660, 993, 998, 1188; May Thirtieth movement in, 217, 220, 244–7, 249–50, 273, 401, 426–7, 788; Peng Shuzhi in, 77, 225, 251, 550, 1091, 1183, 1185–6, 1188; publishing in, 501, 553–4; strikes in, 428, 787, 788, 920; Trotskyists in (1930s), 8, 11, 24, 73, 139–40, 357, 486, 491, 507–8, 576, 577, 578, 640, 714–15, 855, 922; Trotskyists in (1940s), 145–6, 561, 570, 572; Trotskyists in (after 1949), 146, 573; upsurge of 1945–6 in, 957; Wang Fanxi in, 547, 550–2, 655; Zheng Chaolin in, 111–12, 115, 225–8, 250, 251, 252, 265, 326, 444, 645, 1066, 1070, 1073, 1109, 1111, 1113, 1182
Shanghai College, 278, 334, 335
Shanghai General Labour Union, 247–8, 249, 250, 260, 261, 262, 263, 788, 789
Shanghai insurrection (20–22 March 1927), 55, 129, 256–62, 796, 1092, 1186; Chiang Kai-shek massacre following, 4, 56, 66, 129, 262, 263–5, 289, 404, 428, 797–8, 1093; preparations for, 256–7, 793, 794; Zheng Chaolin on, 256–64
Shanghai's People's Political Consultative Conference, 115, 1066, 1073, 1113, 1182
Shanghai University, 226, 232, 233, 251–2, 645, 1109, 1179
Shao Lizi, 50, 232, 241, 796
She Liya, 298, 302, 316
Shen Bingquan, 652–3, 654, 1064, 1065
Shen Xuanlu, 78, 236, 318, 319, 320
Shen Yanbing (Mao Dun), 248, 253, 256, 447; biographical sketch, 1208; cultural views of, 435–7; and *Guide Weekly*, 268, 609; writings: *Disillusion, Wavering, Pursuance* trilogy of, 436; 'From Guling to Tokyo', 437; *Midnight*, 62; *One Day in China*, 658
Shen Zemin, 61, 129, 232, 242; and *Hot Blood Daily*, 248, 249; in Society for Literary Studies, 435–6; as student in Moscow, 59, 335
Shenbao, 65, 94, 190, 659, 712
Sheng Zhongliang (Sheng Yue): *Sun Yat-sen University in Moscow and the Chinese Revolution*, 54–7
Shenyang Incident (1931), 24, 61, 92, 652
Shenzhou Guoguang publishing house, 502, 629

Shi Cuntong, 79, 232–3, 251, 255n; anti-Confucian article by, 214; and Socialist Youth League, 201
Shi Fuliang, 100, 574, 1070
Shi Tang, 357, 487; arrest and murder of, 1207; expelled from CCP and deported to China, 70, 118; member of Our Word group, 85, 478, 486, 487, 631, 640–1; as Trotskyist in Guangxi, 118, 119, 137, 508–9, 651
Shi Zhe, 149, 150, 367
Shiyue. See October
Shiyue pinglun ('October Review'), 1076, 1197
Shumiatsky, Boris, 328, 329, 330–1
Si Chaosheng, 509, 1205; and Communist League leadership, 507, 655; in prison, 656, 657
Sincere Press publishing house, 1177, 1197
Sino-French Education Association, 182, 183, 192
Sino-Japanese War: causes of, 713–14; CCP line in, 23, 24–5, 528, 817; Chen Duxiu on, 24–5, 26, 96, 533, 535–7, 539–42, 553, 591, 661, 713–14, 717, 721, 741, 765–6, 865, 870, 991, 1192; Communist League debate over, 12, 25–6, 553, 568, 846, 880–1, 991; Guomindang regime and, 61, 80, 286, 557, 834, 914–15, 951, 998; Japanese aims in, 939–40; killing of Chinese Trotskyists during, 1128; outbreak of in 1937, 96, 526–7, 538, 659; Peng Shuzhi on, 28, 553, 558, 846, 870, 871–2, 874, 985, 991, 1016; popular movement around, 834; reaches Shanghai and Nanjing, 529–30, 556, 660; refugees caused by, 579; Soviet Union and, 557, 765–6; Trotsky on, 817–18, 834, 846, 872–3, 929, 990–1, 1155–6; Trotskyist cooperation with CCP sought during, 26, 92, 96, 533, 539–42, 1192; Trotskyist guerrillas during, 27, 541; US imperialism and, 557, 558; Wang Fanxi on, 28, 553, 557–9, 817, 845, 846, 870, 872, 873–4, 985, 986, 993, 994, 1016–17, 1023, 1156–7, 1192; Wuhan during, 533–4, 547, 853; Zheng Chaolin on, 28, 553, 817, 852, 870, 872, 873–4, 991, 992, 994, 1024, 1111, 1156, 1180. See also Second United Front
Sneevliet, Henk (Maring), 49, 84, 821, 1157; and CCP's Guomindang entry, 5, 207n, 231, 401, 780, 782, 822

Snow, Edgar, 563, 655, 1208; *Red Star Over China*, 585
Social-Revolutionary Party (Russia), 454–5, 910, 937–38, 961–2
socialism: backward nations and, 763–5; democracy and, 9–10, 23, 33, 34–5
'socialism in one country', 364, 433, 497, 681, 820, 1114–15, 1122
Socialist Workers Party (US), 854, 864, 878, 1175; on guerrilla warfare, 1017–18; split of 1940 in, 854, 869, 883, 986; Trotsky on, 942
Socialist Youth League, 218, 303–4, 312, 319, 320, 1079; becomes Communist Youth League, 240, 603; and CCP, 236, 304; founding of, 200–1, 589, 778. See also Communist Youth League
Society for Frugal Study by Means of Labour, 175n, 278–9
Society for the Study of Sun Yat-senism, 283, 789, 790
Song Fengchun, 479, 646, 652, 1155; arrest of, 90, 480, 499, 647, 658; expelled and deported back to China, 59, 479–80; member of Communist League leadership, 10, 87, 92, 132, 476, 492, 643; at Unification Congress, 86, 492, 641–2; in unification negotiations, 487, 635; and Wang Fanxi, 479–80, 481
Song Jingxiu, 486, 644, 651–2; at Unification Congress, 86, 474, 475, 492, 641, 643, 1101
Song Qingling (Soong Ching-ling), 25, 395, 806, 1041n, 1208
Sovereignty Protection Movement, 858, 861, 878
Soviet Union: aid to People's Liberation Army by, 953–4, 955, 999, 1011; bureaucracy of, 94–941; Chen Duxiu on, 516–17, 591–2, 681, 701, 704, 733–5, 759, 765–6, 767, 924; Chinese students in, 327–65; 366–88, and degenerated workers' state label, 681, 701, 704, 924, 978, 986; denunciation of Stalin's crimes by Khrushchev, 37, 43, 69, 683, 976, 1135; discussion over class character of, 516–17, 766, 924, 968, 986; foreign students studying in, 312, 366, 368; Guomindang regime relations with, 914–15, 917–18; and Japan, 545, 557, 766, 853, 917–18; Left Opposition in, 68, 118, 332, 340, 343, 344,

INDEX 1259

Soviet Union (*cont.*)
352, 353–4, 353–54, 363, 375, 392, 604, 618, 618, 630, 820, 900; material conditions in, 129, 311, 341, 364; Moscow Trials in, 15, 515, 516, 522, 548, 661, 682–3, 1031, 1113, 1154; November 7, 1927, demonstration in, 58, 118, 375, 392, 630; overseas Chinese living in, 325–6; and Sino-Japanese War, 557, 765–6; and Sino-Soviet dispute, 151; 'Sovereignty Protection Movement' on, 858, 861, 878; Stalin purges in, 374, 387, 497, 511; Stalin-Trotsky conflict in, 7–8, 58, 68, 81, 129, 332, 426, 630, 1083, 1186; Stalinist degeneration of, 231, 497, 728, 820; support to Guomindang by, 47–9, 81, 139, 198n, 229, 285, 401, 594, 781–2, 785–6; Trotskyist debate on defence of, 582, 882, 924; and victory of Third Chinese Revolution, 959–60; war with Finland, 730, 878, 883; and World War II, 730, 759, 767. *See also* Chinese Trotskyists in Soviet Union

soviets, 800; CCP and organisation of, 350, 779, 826; Chen Duxiu on slogan of, 412–13, 715, 726; Hailufeng movement for, 807; Stalinist attacks on call for, 801, 826; Trotsky on call for, 800, 802–3, 810–11, 815, 825–6, 832–3, 888–9, 915

Spark (*Huohua*), 773; Chen Duxiu articles in, 24, 701; as Communist League organ, 10, 90, 507, 516, 537, 579, 644, 645, 922; reply to Lu Xun letter in, 1038

stages theory, 459, 796n, 814–15, 816

Stalin, Josef I.: adventurist line on China of, 806, 811–12, 832, 997–8; and anti-Trotsky triumvirate, 321, 604, 618, 783; and assassination of Trotsky, 58; banning of factions by, 559–60; break with Bukharin by, 353, 356, 361, 368; and Chen Duxiu, 495, 590, 610; Chen Duxiu on, 23, 399–400, 591–2, 702, 734, 737, 924; on Chiang Kai-shek, 795–6, 813–14, 885; on Chinese bourgeoisie, 824–5, 827; and Chinese Communist dissidents, 389–90; on Chinese Red Army, 837, 838; on Chinese Revolution character and policy, 81, 332, 336, 337, 350–1, 416, 443, 801–2, 827, 828; and Comintern, 494, 497; deportation of Oppositionists by, 344, 354; falsification of history by, 370, 943–4; frame-up purges by, 683; on Guomindang, 4, 5, 405, 791, 799, 803–4, 806, 810, 814, 822, 886; Hitler pact with, 517, 537, 681, 701, 703, 719n; illusions in Guomindang Left, 801–2, 1093; at International Lenin School, 370; Khrushchev denunciation of, 37, 43, 69, 683, 976, 1135; and Li Lisan, 130, 131; and Mao Zedong, 23, 37–8, 113, 149–50, 495, 544, 979–80; personality cult of, 356, 362, 980; on Plekhanov, 693; popular front line of, 510, 944–5; pursues agreements with world bourgeoisie, 544–5; and Qu Qiubai, 130, 345, 346, 495; revolution by stages theory of, 796n, 814–15; 'socialism in one country' theory of, 364, 433, 681, 820, 1114; and Sun Yat-sen University, 49, 58, 59; on Third Period, 811; on Trotsky and Trotskyism, 13, 53, 99, 133, 155, 356, 395–6, 682, 1085; Wang Ming as favourite of, 495, 544; Zheng Chaolin view of in Moscow, 321, 323; Zhou Enlai and, 69, 130, 495
— writings: *Foundations of Leninism*, 1114; 'The October Revolution and the Tactics of the Russian Communists', 670; *Problems of Leninism*, 255, 670, 1113, 1140; 'Questions of the Chinese Revolution', 799

Stalin-Trotsky conflict: Chinese Revolution as issue in, 6, 58, 68, 81, 129, 332, 426, 630, 1186; Chinese students in Moscow and, 7–8, 340–1, 1083

Stalinism, 45, 732, 820; Chen Duxiu on nature of, 733–5; collapse of after 1989, 1120, 1122; Maoism and, 848, 980–1; Wang Fanxi on Stalinist parties, 973–5. *See also* Chinese Communist Party

Stalinist parties: anti-capitalist potential of, 974–6; CCP and, 955, 980–1; differentiation among, 978

state capitalism, 749, 971, 1003

strikes, 233, 401, 594–5, 778; Beijing railroad, 229n, 230, 231, 242, 784; CCP influence in, 242–4, 778; CCP repression of after 1949, 963–4; in Hong Kong, 228, 250, 273, 280, 284, 428, 826; in Shanghai, 428, 787, 788, 920

Struggle (*Douzheng*), 551, 557–8; circulation of, 579; as Communist League organ, 12, 507, 511, 513, 515, 559, 564, 657n, 855, 872, 1038; as Peng Shuzhi group journal, 561, 562, 879
Struggle Society. *See* Militant group
student movement, 217–21, 276, 578–9, 913, 916, 957, 998
Study (*Dushu zazhi*), 123, 141, 146, 503
Study Clique, 218, 274, 276, 285, 1167n
Su Zhaozheng, 130, 266n, 609n, 799, 805
Suhua bao ('Vernacular Magazine'), 587, 1028
Sun Chuanfang, 221, 636
Sun Ke, 82, 1154
Sun Liangsi. *See* Liang Si
Sun Maochi, 1165, 1166
Sun Society, 438, 441
Sun Xi, 709, 1208
Sun Yat-sen, 174, 209, 276, 281–2, 287–8; CCP and, 48, 218, 230, 938; on CCP entry into Guomindang, 400, 401, 821; Chen Duxiu collaboration with, 587; death of, 49, 241; and Guomindang formation, 229; Lenin on, 47; sends delegation to Soviet Union, 120, 318; Soviet advisers to, 785; on Soviet aid to Guomindang, 786; Soviet government joint declaration with, 48, 781–2, 1083; telegram on death of Lenin by, 323; testament of, 47; Three People's Principles of, 120–1, 254, 288, 420, 512; and Yuan Shikai, 201, 1169n
Sun Yat-sen University: anti-Trotskyist campaign at, 7, 52, 58–9, 329–31, 380–1, 382, 391; arrest of Trotskyist students at, 374, 393–4, 1069; Chinese student body at, 239, 303–6, 308–9, 310, 312–13, 329–30, 1079–81; Chinese students returning from, 324–6, 341, 380–1, 486, 595, 1068; composition of students at, 303–4, 334; curriculum at, 309; disbanding of, 59; division into two institutions, 385; entertainment at, 312; establishment of, 49, 303, 334, 390, 630; impact of Chinese Revolution at, 54–8, 129; living conditions and arrangements at, 51–2, 129, 310–11; mentioned, 91, 226, 448, 892; Mif as rector of, 7, 52, 58–9, 329–31, 380, 385, 388, 1095; military studies at, 328–9, 366; and Moscow branch of CCP, 312, 328–9, 595; name of, 309–10; Peng Shuzhi at, 306–7, 310, 311, 313–14, 315, 317, 318, 319, 320, 321, 323–4, 1079–80, 1083, 1184–5; Radek as rector of, 7, 52, 58, 369, 390–1, 630, 1094; selection of students for, 49–50, 128; Trotsky speech at, 53–4, 1084; Trotskyists in, 7–8, 58–9, 119, 341, 375, 378, 391–2, 393, 468, 631, 1094; Wang Fanxi and, 333, 335, 339; Wang Ming and, 7, 59, 120, 128, 129, 330–1, 334–5, 380–1, 382, 1095; wildcat demonstration by students at, 329; Wu Jimin on, 47–59; Zheng Chaolin at, 111, 313–14, 317, 1109, 1179; Zheng Chaolin on, 303–26

Tan Pingshan, 80, 380, 419, 607, 791; biographical sketch, 1209; and CCP Central Committee, 20, 78, 81, 238, 606; and Communist armed forces, 267, 419, 461, 608; Guomindang work by, 785; as scapegoat for revolution's defeat, 68, 70, 806, 1094; and Wuhan 'Left Guomindang' government, 605, 799, 805; Zhou Enlai on, 267
Tan Yankai, 49–50, 128, 404
Tang Baolin, 34–5, 1197, 1198; on Chen Duxiu's 'mistake', 1153; on defeatism and 'national betrayal', 1155–7; on imprisonment of Trotskyists, 1160–1; on National Assembly question, 1157; on permanent revolution, 1150–1; on Second Chinese Revolution, 1159–60; on Stalinist slander claims, 1153–5; on Trotskyists as 'slaves of a foreign master', 1157–9; and united front question, 1151–3; Wang Fanxi review of book by, 1149–61
Tang Shengzhi, 176, 405, 532, 801; CCP support for, 80, 460; massacre of Communists by, 318, 431
Tao Xisheng, 502, 503, 659, 1209
Third International. *See* Comintern
Third Party, 458, 508, 541–2, 992
Third-Period line, 494, 498, 811, 974
Three People's Principles, 48, 60, 120–1, 288, 420, 512, 614, 792, 1090
Today group, 307, 316, 317

INDEX

The Tragedy of the Chinese Revolution (Isaacs), 485, 578, 580, 657n, 928, 940; Trotsky introduction to, 928–40
Transitional Programme (Trotsky), 845, 853, 858, 880–2, 994; on China, 814, 990
Trotsky, Leon: assassination of, 58, 71, 839; biographical sketch, 52–3; on 'bloc of four classes', 4, 808–9, 815, 823; on Bolshevism's essence, 944; on CCP class nature, 833–4, 839–40, 961–2, 963, 970, 1006–7; on Chen Duxiu, 9, 85, 469, 478, 484, 489, 536, 633, 635, 662–5, 700, 865, 885–89, 925–7, 941–2, 1175; Chen Duxiu letters to, 96, 713–18; Chen Duxiu on, 70–1, 408, 411, 704, 728; Chiang Kai-shek on, 120; on Chinese Red Army, 463, 838–9, 842–3, 987–9; on Chinese Revolution character, 337–8, 453–7, 484, 488, 669, 814–17, 828–30, 868, 876, 931–2; on colonial bourgeoisie, 825, 1152–3; on constituent assembly slogan, 337–8, 349, 350–1, 456–7, 458, 675, 677, 813, 832, 913–14, 915, 988, 1013, 1019, 1020; on defeatism, 872–3; on defensive struggles and policy, 69, 338, 634, 812–13, 997–8; deported from Soviet Union, 354–5, 354, 356; expulsion from Soviet CP of, 58, 70, 389, 630; on feudal remnants, 69, 828; on guerrilla warfare, 987–9, 990–1; on Guomindang 'Left', 5, 805; on historical development, 210–11; influence on Chinese writers, 1032–6, 1044, 1153; on Jiangsu Provincial Committee resolution, 448, 618–19; on Lenin and Russian Revolution, 53, 670–4, 935–6; letter to Frank Glass, 865, 941–2; Liu Renjing visit to, 9, 74–5, 358, 374, 464–5, 468, 631, 662–3, 1098; on nature of Guomindang, 4, 809, 815, 823, 913, 1084; opposed Guomindang entry, 446, 619, 777–8, 809, 822, 1088; on peasant war, 836, 838–9, 841–3, 887–89, 903–11, 912, 915, 987–9, 1014–15; on peasantry, 836, 906, 908, 913, 916, 932–3; Peng Shuzhi on contributions of, 777, 808–18; permanent revolution theory of, 455–6, 667, 669–75, 814, 815–17, 829–30, 876, 1150–1; on progressive and reactionary wars, 844–5, 846–7; on proletarian literature, 1027; recognition of Chinese Revolution's defeat by, 17–18, 68–9, 618, 811–14, 831–3, 1013; on results of Unification Congress, 87–9; on role of petty bourgeoisie, 826–8; on Second United Front, 834–5; on Sino-Japanese War, 817–18, 834, 846, 872–3, 929, 990–1, 1155–6; Soviet rehabilitation of, 37; on Soviet Union, 522, 681, 733–4, 735, 1122; on soviets in China, 800, 802–3, 810–11, 815, 825, 832–3, 888–9, 915; speeches to Comintern, 58, 802–3, 1082; Stalinist slanders against, 15, 682–3, 917; at Sun Yat-sen University, 53–4, 323, 1084; support in Soviet Union for, 58–9, 322, 353–4, 356; supports withdrawal from Guomindang, 4, 81, 389, 778, 792, 809–10, 822, 824; on transitional demands, 812–13; on united front, 719n, 1150–3; urges unification of Chinese Trotskyists, 10, 85–6, 469, 482, 484, 489, 635, 1100–1; Wang Fanxi introduction to China writings of, 819–48; Zheng Chaolin summary of views by, 321, 453–7

— writings: 'A Strategy of Action and Not of Speculation', 912–19; 'Chen Duxiu and the General Council', 925–7; 'China and the Russian Revolution', 943–4; 'The Chinese Communist Party and the Guomindang', 809; 'The Chinese Question after the Sixth Congress', 68, 75, 349, 377, 458, 498, 620–1, 675, 832, 892, 988; 'The Chinese Revolution and the Theses of Comrade Stalin', 332; 'Class Relations in the Chinese Revolution', 824, 829–30; *A Criticism of the Draft Programme of the Communist International*, 337–8, 342, 345, 348, 377, 624, 876; *History of the Russian Revolution*, 112, 535, 555–6, 569, 881, 1111, 1180; 'I Stake My Life', 516, 564; introduction to *The Tragedy of the Chinese Revolution*, 928–40; 'Leon Sedov: Son, Friend Fighter', 142, 356; Letter to Chinese Left Opposition, 842–3; *Literature and Revolution*, 1027, 1032–3, 1035–6, 1044; *My Life*, 53, 503, 569; 'Nature of the Coming Chinese Revolution', 488; 'New Opportunities for the Chinese Revolution, New

Trotsky, Leon (*cont.*)
  Tasks and New Mistakes', 831; *1905*, 321; *From October to Brest-Litovsk*, 321; 'On the Eve of World War II', 555; 'Open Letter to the Workers of the USSR', 355; 'Peasant War in China and the Proletariat', 838–9, 903–11, 970, 1006; *The Permanent Revolution*, 569; 'The Political Situation in China and the Tasks of the Bolshevik-Leninist Opposition', 358, 620, 631, 632, 1101; *Problems of the Chinese Revolution*, 68, 75, 451, 559, 569, 845, 1176; 'A Remarkable Document on the Policy and the Régime of the Communist International', 892–900; 'Results and Prospects', 876; 'A Retreat in Full Disorder', 876; *The Revolution Betrayed*, 554, 662, 1180; 'The speech of Comrade Chen Duxiu on the Tasks of the Chinese Communist Party', 885–91; *The Stalin School of Falsification*, 580; 'Summary and Perspectives of the Chinese Revolution', 68, 75, 488, 620–1, 669; *Terrorism and Communism*, 517; 'To the Chinese Left Opposition', 1100–1; *Transitional Programme*, 814, 845, 853, 858, 880–2, 990, 994
Trotskyist guerrillas, 993; Chen Zhongxi, 550, 561; Cheong Li Ming, 856–7; Cheong Tzi Ching, 856; Li Su, 1128; in Shandong, 27, 541, 561, 855–6, 1016, 1128; Wang Changyao, 541, 561, 1128, 1209; Zhang Sanjie, 541, 561; in Zhongshan, 27, 541, 550, 561, 579
Tu Qingqi. *See* Du Weizhi
Tu Yangzhi, 467, 626

unification campaign: Chen Duxiu support for, 86, 470–1, 490, 573, 638–9; negotiations over, 10, 86, 470–1, 473–4, 482, 484, 487–91, 634, 635, 639–40, 1100; Peng Shuzhi and, 10, 471, 472, 473, 476, 489, 634, 635, 638, 639–40, 643–4, 1100; and political differences, 482–4; Wang Fanxi on, 478–503
Unification Congress (1931), 18, 66, 132, 492; Communist League of China name adopted by, 1101; delegates to, 86, 474, 475, 491, 492, 641–2; discussion and debate at, 87, 488, 492, 642–3; funding of, 474, 491–2; leadership bodies elected by, 10, 87, 475–6, 492–3, 643, 1101; messages to Trotsky from, 87–9, 493, 644; Peng Shuzhi and, 86, 87, 474, 475n, 476, 492–3, 634, 635, 641, 642, 643–4; political decisions taken by, 644, 715n; resolutions of, 475, 490–1, 1101; venue for, 474–5, 491–2; Wu Jimin on, 86–9; Zheng Chaolin on, 474–7, 641–4, 1110–11
united front, 719, 719n, 911, 1151–3
United Opposition (Soviet Union), 332, 453, 618, 630; *Platform* of, 332, 900; supports withdrawal from Guomindang, 4, 81, 822. *See also* Left Opposition (Soviet Union)
United States, 657, 747–8; and Chinese Revolution, 149; and Guomindang government, 557, 558, 858, 952, 955, 1011

'victoryism', 28, 845, 1024, 1156
Voitinsky, Grigori, 603, 608, 778, 821, 1157; and founding of Chinese Communist movement, 778, 1079; at Fourth CCP Congress, 236, 1087; Komsomol and, 604; and national revolution theory, 597, 603; opposition to Guomindang withdrawal by, 403, 1090; Peng Shuzhi and, 20, 597; and Sun Yat-sen University students, 1079, 1080

Wang Changyao, 541, 561, 1128, 1209
Wang Delin, 525, 1209
Wang Duqing, 502; biographical sketch, 1209; and Creation Society, 439, 440–2, 1029; and Trotskyists, 74, 554, 1029
Wang Fanxi: archives of, 1199; arrest and imprisonment of, 90, 92, 97–8, 499, 516, 518–29, 551, 646, 647, 649; becomes Trotskyist, 331–3, 338–9, 1192; in Beijing, 272–80, 286–91; biographical sketch, 113, 213, 214–15, 1191–4, 1209; in Britain, 1, 28, 1193–4; at business school, 215–17; CCP responsibilities of, 113, 277–9, 286–91, 631; Chen Bilan polemic with, 985–1000; Chen Duxiu appraisal by, 542, 562–4, 585–93, 697–8, 700, 773–4; Chen Duxiu letter to, 728–30; Chen Duxiu meetings with, 489–90, 515–16, 534–7, 538, 540; and Chen Qichang, 108, 490, 550, 551; and Confucianism, 213, 214; drafting of

Wang Fanxi (*cont.*)
  initial Trotskyist documents by, 480–1,
    488, 644; expulsion from CCP, 113, 479; in
    Guangzhou, 280–6; in Hangzhou, 215,
    216, 218–21; in Hong Kong, 2, 12n, 28, 113,
    507–9, 1116; and Hu Feng, 275, 1034, 1192;
    and Internationalist Workers' Party, 12n,
    112, 113, 122, 569; joins CCP, 113, 276, 1191;
    and Liu Renjing-Song Fengchun
    opposition, 479–80; in Macao, 2, 28, 113,
    122, 1191, 1192; on Mao Zedong, 700, 978–80;
    and May Fourth Movement, 213–15, 219,
    1192; and May Thirtieth Movement, 220,
    273; member of Communist League
    leadership, 10, 12, 87, 475, 476, 492, 493,
    643, 657n, 872n, 1101; mentioned, 5, 8, 36,
    138, 141, 577, 629, 1037n; in Moscow, 59,
    327–65, 1192; and October group, 468–9,
    481, 487, 633, 635, 1098–9; Peng Shuzhi on,
    488, 817; People's Republic publication
    of, 3; political education of, 220, 281; and
    Pu Dezhi, 537–8; release from prison, 530,
    532–3, 547; return from Soviet Union by,
    9, 365; sent abroad in 1949, 12n, 28, 122,
    132–3, 1191; in Shanghai, 547, 550–2, 655; as
    student activist, 217–21; suspicions toward
    Our Word group by, 73, 478, 479, 1098–9;
    translation work by, 342–3, 357, 502, 550,
    551, 555; and Unification Congress, 18, 86,
    484, 492, 641, 642, 644; 19; and unification
    negotiations (1930–1), 10n, 487, 491, 635,
    668–9, 1100; and unification negotiations
    (1978), and Wang Ming, 336, 359–61; and
    Wang Shiwei, 35, 275, 1031–2, 1034, 1192;
    Zheng Chaolin correspondence with, 1193;
    and Zhou Enlai, 113, 346, 490, 1192
  — views: on bureaucratic collectivism,
      971, 973, 978, 986, 1003, 1004; on CCP
      during Sino-Japanese War, 704, 1192; on
      CCP factional struggle, 493–9; on CCP
      nature, 29–30, 841, 969–73; on Chen
      Duxiu's last views, 23, 26, 517, 534–7,
      542, 723, 731–2, 737, 773–4; on
      constituent assembly, 480–1, 869, 883,
      1022, 1157; on Cultural Revolution,
      847n, 848, 1116; on Glass, 1158–9, 1173–6;
      on initial Trotskyist organisations,
      75–6, 481–7, 1099; on Liu Jialiang,
      549–50; on literature, 499–503, 1027,
      1045; on Liu Jingzhen, 1170–3; on Lou
      Guohua, 1176–8; on Lu Xun, 107, 1038,
      1041n; on Peng Shuzhi, 19, 473, 488, 560,
      867, 970, 971, 991, 1004–5, 1009–12, 1019,
      1020; on permanent revolution, 867–8,
      1118–19, 1150–1; on Sino-Japanese War,
      28, 553, 557–9, 817, 845, 846, 861, 870,
      872, 873–4, 985, 986, 993, 994, 1016–17,
      1023–4, 1156–7, 1192; and split of 1942,
      12, 21, 559–60; on Stalinist parties'
      anticapitalist potential, 974–6; on Tang
      Baolin book, 1149–61; on Third Chinese
      Revolution victory, 29, 571–2, 575,
      967–82, 994, 997, 1001–24, 1192–3; on
      Trotskyists as bystanders, 27, 32, 1016;
      on Zheng Chaolin, 1062, 1178–2
  — writings: 'An Open Letter to the CC of
      the CCP', 1003; 'Chen Duxiu, Founder
      of Chinese Communism', 585–93;
      'Guerrilla Warfare: The Lesson of
      China', 986–8; 'Leon Trotsky and
      Chinese Communism', 819–48; 'On the
      Causes of the CCP's Victory and the
      Failure of the Chinese Trotskyists in
      the Third Chinese Revolution', 1001–24;
      'Problems of Chinese Trotskyism',
      864–84; 'Some Ideological Questions
      Concerning the Chinese Revolution',
      1004, 1007–08; *The Soviet Union and
      Socialism*, 986; *Study of Mao Zedong
      Thought*, 1192. See also *Memoirs of a
      Chinese Revolutionary*
Wang Gui, 295, 300, 301, 302
Wang Guolong, 137, 138, 144, 148, 156;
  biographical sketch, 139–42, 1209;
  Guomindang imprisonment of, 140;
  imprisonments after 1949 of, 141, 146
Wang Hebo, 78, 83, 228, 324
Wang Huating. *See* Wang Shuben
Wang Jiaxiang, 61, 131; in Moscow, 59, 128, 129,
  335
Wang Jingwei, 182n; becomes open
  reactionary, 57, 405, 431, 804–5;
  biographical sketch, 1209; CCP
  illusions in, 290, 798–9, 880; Chen Duxiu
  meetings with, 83, 404, 606; as leader of
  Guomindang 'left', 4–5, 790, 798–9, 880,

Wang Jingwei (cont.)
  1093; Mao Zedong praised by, 460; massacre of workers and Communists by, 5, 431, 822, 825; during Shanghai insurrection, 262–3; Stalin urges support to, 4–5, 814, 1093; and Sun Yat-sen testament, 47; and Sun Yat-sen University, 49–50, 128; Trotsky warning on, 802
Wang Kequan, 466, 627, 1209
Wang Linghan, 298, 302
Wang Lixi, 120, 502
Wang Maoting, 445, 614
Wang Mengzou: after 1949, 550, 1146; biographical sketch, 515–16, 1209; and Chen Duxiu, 636, 637, 1169; and Oriental Book Company, 516, 1046–7
Wang Ming (Chen Shaoyu): anti-Trotskyist slander campaign by, 15–16, 43–4, 396, 543, 546, 548, 591, 918, 941, 1038, 1044, 1128, 1134, 1154; biographical sketch, 1210; 'Bolshevisation' under, 17, 495; and Chen Duxiu, 330; on 'conciliators', 349, 499; and Li Lisan, 131, 493–4; and Mao Zedong, 30, 99, 149–50, 497, 511, 543–4, 548–9, 979; mentioned, 14, 61, 62, 63, 916; and Mif, 330–1, 384, 495; motivations for anti-Trotskyism of, 99, 530–1; opposition to cooperation with Trotskyists, 98–9, 689; and Qu Qiubai, 335, 346, 384, 494, 495, 496, 498; retention of influence within CCP by, 544, 545–6n; on Second United Front, 843, 1036; 'shock troops' of, 352; as Stalin's favourite, 495, 544; and Sun Yat-sen University, 7, 59, 120, 128, 129, 330–1, 334–5, 380–1, 382, 1095; takes over CCP leadership, 61, 339, 494, 495–6, 497–8, 1027; and Wang Fanxi, 336, 359–61; and Xiang Zhongfa, 334, 381, 493, 494; and Zhou Enlai, 63, 344–5, 346–7, 494, 495
Wang Pingyi (Wang Boping): breaks with Trotskyism and joins Guomindang, 651; member of Militant group, 469, 633; and Trotskyist documents, 9, 452, 621, 625
Wang Ruofei, 79, 258, 296, 344, 434, 604; biographical sketch, 302, 348, 1210; at CCP Sixth Congress, 444, 445, 616; and Chen Duxiu, 68, 239, 423, 434–5, 610, 611, 612–13, 637, 687; as Chen Duxiu supporter, 6, 423, 445, 447, 448, 617, 1109; and Communist Youth movement, 200–1, 204; facilitates Liu Renjing visit to Trotsky, 74; in France, 192–3, 195, 199, 200–1, 205; and Huang Qisheng, 206; and Jiangsu Provincial Committee, 6, 421, 448, 610; on Peng Shuzhi, 421, 471, 602, 604, 617; personal appearance of, 297; as returning Moscow student, 387, 595, 1068; as student in Moscow, 302, 313, 316, 372, 375, 383; travels through Europe by, 297, 298, 300; Trotsky on article drafted by, 448, 618–19; Trotsky's view on China supported by, 347–8, 423, 445; won to communism, 195, 240; and Zheng Chaolin, 111, 242, 253, 422, 423, 614–15
Wang Shiwei: biographical sketch, 1210; and CCP membership, 1029, 1031; condemned by Yan'an Forum, 1048; criticism of Yan'an practices by, 1030, 1049–4; rehabilitation of, 1032, 1131; Stalinist killing of, 35, 567, 1032, 1128; as symbol of cultural freedom struggle, 35, 1029, 1030–1; trial of, 35, 1031–2; and Trotskyism, 1029, 1034, 1153; Wang Fanxi and, 35, 275, 1031–2, 1034, 1192; writings: 'Politicians, Artists', 1055–7; 'Wild Lily', 1032, 1048–4
Wang Shiyuan, 379, 380, 382
Wang Shouhua, 66, 78, 83
Wang Shuben (Wang Huating), 655; imprisonment and murder of, 567, 656, 658
Wang Songjiu, 561, 1210
Wang Songlu, 189–90, 191, 193, 196–7
Wang Wenyuan. *See* Wang Fanxi
Wang Xizhe, 33, 1193
Wang Yifei, 79, 251, 314; Military Committee work by, 257, 596; in Moscow, 307, 310
Wang Yuanfang, 461, 658, 1046, 1146
Wang Zekai, 203, 442, 465; CCP responsibilities of, 240, 326, 418, 429, 449, 595; and Chen Duxiu, 421, 446, 637; and Communist Youth Party, 202; early Left Opposition activities by, 626; expelled from CCP, 72, 465–6, 627, 1096; in France, 192, 199, 205; Peng Shuzhi supported by, 602, 617; punished as Chen Duxiu-ite, 445, 615; return to China by, 324, 326; as student in Moscow, 313, 320; won to Trotskyism, 9, 71, 451–2, 619

Wang Zhihuai, 652; arrest of, 90, 499, 647, 648; at Unification Congress, 86, 474, 475, 492, 641, 643; and Zheng Chaolin, 640, 644

War of Resistance. See Sino-Japanese War

warlordism, 48, 174, 221, 241, 256, 274, 286, 288, 425, 427, 780, 1086, 1167; decline of, 228, 229, 273, 290

Wenzhou, 137, 138; Trotskyists in, 137, 138, 143, 509–10, 859

Western Hills Conference faction, 278, 283

Women de hua. See *Our Word*

work-study programme (France), 174–5, 187, 188, 191–2, 196–7, 205–6, 1179; Communist Youth Party work among students in, 205–6

workers' state label, 681, 701, 704, 924, 978, 986

World War I, 1023; Chen Duxiu on outcome of, 750; China's participation in, 881; Lenin position on, 558, 720, 725, 729, 844, 873, 881, 1023

World War II: approach of, 510, 929; and arms production, 759–60; CCP stance toward, 853; Chen Duxiu support for Allies in, 723–4, 726, 728, 730, 732–3, 735–6, 738–9, 740–1, 754–5, 757–9, 761; and defeatism, 721–2, 873, 1023; Japan-German alliance during, 817; Japanese-American conflict in, 993; possible outcomes following, 732, 746–8; Soviet Union and, 730, 759, 767

Wu Jimin, 3, 11, 37; Chen Sihe preface to book by, 43–6; difficulty in publishing book by, 152–6; text by, 47–156

Wu Jingru. See Liu Jingzhen

Wu Jixian, 328, 502; and Trotskyist unification, 487, 488–9, 492

Wu Jiyan, 645; and 1931 arrests, 90, 132, 645–6; arrest in 1932 of, 652; biographical sketch, 1210; as leader of Proletarian group, 469, 629, 632–3, 638; as newspaper editor, 615, 629; as Trotskyist within CCP, 469, 621, 631; at Unification Congress, 644; in unification negotiations, 470, 471, 472, 635; on World War II, 732

Wu Peifu, 230n, 238, 241, 300, 753

Wu Xiuquan, 126–8

Wu Zhihui, 182n, 186, 290, 296, 303; and Guomindang, 263, 514; and work-study programme in France, 174, 175, 187, 188, 196–7, 206

Wuchanzhe. See *Proletarian*

Wuhan, 229n, 269–70, 290–1, 419, 532–3; CCP in, 5, 605–6, 778; Chen Duxiu in, 533, 606, 637–8; Guomindang 'left' government in, 376, 404–5, 539–40, 802, 805, 885, 886, 888, 890; and Northern Expedition, 83, 280, 430–1; Peng Shuzhi in, 606, 637, 638, 797; during Sino-Japanese War, 533–4, 547, 853, 1111; Wang Jingwei counter-revolutionary coup in, 57, 66, 831

Wulanfu (Yun Ze), 126–8, 129

Xi'an Incident (1936), 120, 350, 990

Xiandai pinglun ('Contemporary Review'), 274, 275

Xiang Delong. See Xiang Ying

Xiang Jingyu, 79, 194, 225, 233, 243; as Cai Hesen wife, 78, 192, 227, 253; CCP work by, 192, 234, 250; Guomindang murder of, 66; Peng Shuzhi affair with, 78, 79

Xiang Ying (Xiang Delong), 448; biographical sketch, 1210; and CCP Fourth Congress, 78, 238n; as 'conciliationist' toward Chen Duxiu, 463; labour movement activity by, 226, 233, 242, 596, 785, 786–7; opposition to Li Lisan by, 448–50, 616

Xiang Zhongfa, 61, 78, 266n, 329, 443, 445, 833; becomes traitor, 63; biographical sketch, 654, 1210; as CCP general secretary, 331, 335, 344, 444, 615; Chen Duxiu discussions with, 463, 666, 667n; lack of talent by, 495; and Sun Yat-sen University students, 329–30, 331; Wang Ming relations with, 334, 381, 493, 494

Xiangdao. See *Guide Weekly*

Xiao Changbin, 480, 1210

Xiao Jun, 1030, 1034

Xiao Ke, 33–4, 691–3, 705

Xiao Pusheng, 201, 202, 251

Xiao Zizhang, 204, 261, 300, 313, 324, 602, 604

Xie Danru, 62–3, 66, 495

Xie Depan (Xie Ligong), 90–1, 93, 94, 148, 646, 650, 654

Xiliu. See Pu Dezhi

Xin qingnian. See *New Youth*

Xinda chuban she, 1177, 1197

Xinhua ribao ('New China Daily'), 99–100, 548, 686, 720, 729; anti-Trotskyist slanders in, 543, 547, 678

Xinmiao ('New Sprouts'), 1132, 1197
Xinqi. See *New Banner*
Xiong Shihui, 302, 649
Xiong Weigeng, 201, 299
Xiong Xiong, 204, 295, 324; arrest and execution of, 302; in Berlin, 299, 301; in France, 189, 193; as student in Moscow, 302, 310, 312, 315–16, 319
Xiong Zhinan, 192–4
Xu Enzeng, 14–15, 95
Xu Kexiang, 66, 460, 800–1
Xu Maoyong, 513, 1039
Xu Teli, 64, 206
Xue Juezai, 417–18
Xue Shilun, 199, 200, 320, 324; as CCP secretary and treasurer, 234, 326, 595; recruitment of Zheng Chaolin by, 200
Xue Yue, 261, 811

Yan Changyi, 13, 253, 257, 467–8, 596
Yan Lingfeng, 90, 644, 645, 1047
Yan Zhong, 282–3, 332
Yan'an, 547–8, 813, 990; CCP abandonment of, 858, 958; CCP rule and conduct in, 1030, 1034, 1049–4; crackdown on writers in, 35, 1029–30, 1048
Yang Hucheng, 45, 491
Yang Xianjiang, 197, 253, 437, 465, 466, 627, 634
Yang Yin, 13, 66, 236, 238, 467–8
Yang Zhihua, 64, 239, 269, 271, 372
Yaroslavsky, Y. M., 329, 331, 355, 368
Ye-He army, 265, 417, 419, 462, 608
Ye Jianying, 1210; relationship with Trotskyists, 97–8, 530–1; relays Chen Duxiu proposals to Mao, 533, 686, 687, 688–9, 710n
Ye Qing. See Ren Zhuoxuan
Ye Ting, 348, 543; military forces of, 81, 791, 831, 998, 1021; and Nanchang uprising, 462, 806, 894, 997
Yin Kuan, 74, 112, 258, 447, 1063, 1096; arrest and imprisonment (1952), 114, 124, 134, 1136, 1137–8, 1139, 1141–2, 1160; arrests and imprisonments (by Guomindang), 132, 517, 651–2; becomes Trotskyist, 71, 73; biographical sketch, 114, 1211; CCP expulsion of, 1096; at CCP Fourth Congress, 78, 236; CCP responsibilities of, 251, 607, 610; and Chen Duxiu, 6, 463, 615, 620, 638, 711; and Communist Youth, 200, 201, 212; early Left Opposition work by, 625, 626; in France, 189–90, 191, 193, 199, 200, 201, 209; on Guomindang entry, 207, 619; and Liu Renjing, 11–12, 25, 468–9, 655–7; member of RCP political bureau, 122; on nature of Chinese Revolution, 464, 666, 667–8; and Peng Shuzhi, 112, 471–2, 487, 658; in Proletarian group, 468, 469, 473, 628; and reorganisation of Trotskyist leadership, 12, 92, 132, 655, 657; as returning Moscow student, 324, 1068; during Second Chinese Revolution, 264; and split of 1942, 570; as student in Moscow, 313, 320, 1179; Trotskyist documents brought to China by, 70, 451–2, 618, 621; and Unification Congress, 474, 476, 491; and unification negotiations, 487, 634–5, 639, 640; won to communism, 209, 240; and Zheng Chaolin, 253, 451, 618, 640
Young China, 185–6, 191
Young China Party, 285
Youth, 121, 204–5, 206
Youth and Women (Qingnian yu funü), 122, 569–70, 1189
Yu Dafu, 217, 435n
Yu Mutao, 90, 91, 645–6
Yu Qiaqing, 647, 1211
Yu Qiuyu, 151, 154
Yu Shiyi (Yu Shouyi), 1137–8, 1211
Yu Shuoyi: imprisonment of after 1952, 124, 134; as Internationalist Workers' Party leader, 122, 571, 572
Yu Xiusong, 128, 245, 327, 334, 384; biographical sketch, 1211; Moscow purge against (1927), 375–6, 380, 382; Stalinist frame-up and murder of (1937–38), 99, 1153, 1211
Yu Youren, 232, 251
Yuan Qingyun, 200, 228; about, 297–8, 302; and Communist Youth, 200, 211–12; European travels of, 295, 298, 299, 300; as student in Moscow, 309, 316, 323
Yuan Shikai, 201, 228, 457n, 587, 663n, 769n, 1169
Yuan Zizhen, 212, 320
Yun Daiying, 113, 232, 282, 1063; biographical sketch, 1211; Liu Renjing discussion with, 464–5, 631
Yusi ('Threads of Talk'), 274, 275, 417

INDEX

Zeng Meng: arrest in 1932 of, 138, 658; arrest in 1952 of, 139; biographical sketch, 137–9, 1211; dissemination of Trotskyist documents by, 137–8, 509
Zeng Qi, 185–6, 188, 191, 233
Zhandou ('Combat'), 75, 469, 633
Zhang Bojian, 203–4, 211, 227, 236, 244, 300; and CCP Propaganda Department, 233–4, 248; return to China by, 324, 595; and Socialist Youth League, 201–2; as student in Moscow, 313
Zhang Bojun, 508, 541–2
Zhang Bolin, 659, 1211
Zhang Chong, 65, 137–8, 139, 395
Zhang Dehan, 561, 1211
Zhang Deze, 561, 1211
Zhang Fakui, 806, 807, 808
Zhang Guangren. *See* Hu Feng
Zhang Guotao, 74, 79, 236, 253; arrest of, 231, 324; biographical sketch, 1212; on Chen Duxiu, 608n, 636, 689; as Chen Duxiu opponent, 20, 419, 421, 606; and Communist armed forces, 267, 419, 608; and General Labour Union faction, 596, 1109; as *Guide Weekly* editor, 268; on Guomindang entry, 231, 1090; on Hunan, 1078; labour movement activity by, 230, 238, 240, 249; and Mao Zedong, 388, 461; member of CCP leadership bodies, 78, 81, 230, 238, 601; member of Guomindang Central Committee, 785; memoirs by, 367, 608n; in Moscow (1928), 68, 344, 347, 444; Peng Shuzhi on, 471, 602; in Second Chinese Revolution, 14, 83, 604, 605, 791, 1090; as student in Moscow, 372, 375, 378–9, 383
Zhang Jingchen, 278, 291
Zhang Jiu, 86, 492, 1101
Zhang Sanjie, 541, 561
Zhang Shi, 631, 650
Zhang Shizhao, 289, 1212
Zhang Songnian, 190, 195, 203, 236; and Communist Youth Party, 204, 212, 235, 301; expulsion from CCP, 237, 305
Zhang Tailei, 79, 81, 225, 266n, 596, 605, 610, 791; at Fourth CCP Congress, 78, 236, 237–8; on Mao, 461; as secretary of Hubei Provincial Committee, 418, 419; work in Guomindang by, 232, 318, 319, 320; as Youth League leader, 240, 319, 320, 603–4
Zhang Te, 647, 651, 1155; biographical sketch, 1212; and Our Word group, 478, 479, 486, 631; went over to counter-revolution, 486, 508
Zhang Wentian (Luo Fu), 61, 65, 128; and Long March, 64; in Moscow, 59, 129, 335
Zhang Xiyuan, 50, 110
Zhang Xueliang, 45, 60, 813; kidnapping of Chiang Kai-shek by, 813–14, 834, 990
Zhang Yisen, 90, 450, 499, 618, 648, 1212
Zhang Zhidong, 754, 979
Zhang Ziping, 439, 440, 441
Zhang Zuolin, 55, 241n, 273n, 286, 289, 424, 1212
Zhao Ji, 90, 645; biographical sketch, 1212; Chen Duxiu letter to, 709–12; Chen Duxiu view of, 679, 711; and Militant group, 469, 479, 481, 487, 633; and reorganisation of Trotskyist leadership, 102; and Trotskyist work in CCP, 478, 631; at Unification Congress, 86, 491, 492, 644–5; and unification negotiations, 487, 635; and Wang Fanxi, 479; and Yin Kuan, 635, 640
Zhao Shiyan, 83, 211, 258, 326, 421, 1063; biographical sketch, 295; capture and murder of, 66, 302; CCP leadership responsibilities of, 251, 257, 595; and Communist Youth, 195, 200–1, 202, 204, 212, 324; European travels of, 295–6, 298, 300, 301; and Peng Shuzhi, 604; and Shanghai insurrection and massacre, 260, 264; as student in Moscow, 305, 309, 312, 313, 315–16, 323, 1179; won to Marxism and communism, 195, 240; and work-studies students in France, 192, 205; Zheng Chaolin and, 111, 253
Zhao Yangxing, 123, 141
Zhao Yuanren, 447, 1029, 1212
Zheng Boqi, 439, 441, 442
Zheng Chaolin: arrest and imprisonment (1952), 13, 114, 124, 1061, 1067, 1070, 1071, 1112–13, 1132–46, 1160, 1171, 1181; arrest and imprisonment (1931), 90–1, 92, 110, 111, 450, 451, 499, 646–59, 1064–6, 1069, 1110, 1111, 1179–80; becomes Trotskyist, 71, 73, 451–2, 613, 618–19, 1068, 1110, 1180;

Zheng Chaolin (*cont.*)
biographical sketch, 11, 111, 178, 1108, 1179, 1212; as *Bolshevik* editor, 111, 417–18, 615, 1109, 1110, 1179; and Cai Hesen, 244, 444–5; and Cai Zhende, 450, 452, 615, 617; call for rehabilitation of Trotskyists, 36, 46, 115–16, 1113, 1181–2; at CCP congresses and conferences, 110, 236, 265–9, 1087, 1088, 1089, 1109, 1179; and CCP Propaganda Department, 250, 326, 418, 444–5, 450, 595, 1109, 1179; Chen Duxiu contact with, 74–5, 612, 638, 660–2; Chen Duxiu on, 711, 730; as Chen Duxiu supporter, 6, 9, 21, 97, 181, 423, 466, 609, 1062, 1109–10; and Chen Qichang, 103, 108; Chinese scholars' interest in, 22, 34; and Communist Youth movement, 195, 200–8; and Confucianism, 176–7, 211; and Creation Society, 435, 437–42; during Cultural Revolution, 1071, 1105, 1113, 1140, 1142–4; and Deng Xiaoping, 110, 111, 1067; early Left Opposition work by, 626; expulsion from CCP, 466, 627, 1096; finances and livelihood, 139, 234, 625–6; in France, 111, 175–6, 182–212, 1067–8, 1108, 1179; in Fujian, 443–4; and *Guide Weekly*, 227, 234, 239, 250, 324, 609–10; and Guomindang, 207, 439; as head of Trotskyist propaganda work, 87, 476, 493, 643, 645, 1110, 1180; in Hubei, 607, 609, 1109, 1179; as Internationalist Workers' Party leader, 112, 113, 122, 569, 571, 572, 1111, 1180; joins CCP, 110, 315–16, 1179; knowledge of languages, 1067; and Laozi, 176, 180, 181, 1179; as lecturer at Shanghai University, 251, 252, 645; and Li Lisan, 615, 616; and Li Weihan, 270, 443, 574, 1068, 1070; as lifelong Trotskyist, 110, 1071–4 literary work by, 139, 1109, 1180–1; and Liu Renjing, 465, 632; living arrangements of, 225–6, 233, 253, 465, 615, 617, 632, 660; Lou Shiyi on, 1063–6; and Luo Yinong, 253, 258, 270, 614; and May Fourth Movement, 172–3, 176, 181, 184, 186; and May Thirtieth Movement, 244–6, 248–9, 1109, 1179; member of CCP leadership bodies, 250, 435, 577, 612, 1109; member of Communist League leadership, 10, 87, 476, 492, 643, 872n, 1101, 1110, 1180; in Moscow, 303–26, 1068–9, 1179; and *New Youth*, 234, 239, 324; nicknames and pseudonyms, 203, 314; Peng Shuzhi discussions with, 315, 668–9; Peng Shuzhi on, 667–8, 817, 852, 853–4, 881, 1067; personal appearance and qualities, 1061–2, 1063–4; poetry by, 1063, 1071, 1072–3, 1113, 1140–1; political work during 1949–52, 574, 1180–1; and Proletarian group, 640–1; prose style of, 1071; publication in People's Republic, 3, 594, 1106–7, 1113, 1182, 1195; and Qu Qiubai, 253, 268–9, 271, 614, 615, 1110; reading by, 179–81, 208–9; release from prison (1937), 111, 530, 660, 1070, 1111; release from prison (1979), 115, 1061, 1067, 1113, 1117, 1127–31, 1145, 1181; remains in China after 1949, 572–3, 1063, 1181; return from Soviet Union by, 324–6, 1068, 1109, 1179; as scholar and teacher, 111, 150, 562, 1063; in Shanghai, 111–12, 115, 225–8, 250, 251, 252, 265, 326, 444, 645, 1066, 1070, 1073, 1109, 1111, 1113, 1182; Shanghai's People's Political Consultative Conference member, 115, 1066, 1073, 1113, 1182; son's death, 1104; and split of 1942, 21, 122, 559, 669; translation work by, 111, 112, 254, 255, 465, 555, 625, 662, 1041, 1064, 1065, 1070, 1111, 1180, 1182; travels through Europe, 295–303; and Trotsky, 321, 323; Trotskyist documents introduced to, 618, 619; at Unification Congress, 86, 474, 475, 476, 492, 641, 1110, 1180; and unification negotiations, 10n, 86, 488; Wang Fanxi correspondence with, 1193; Wang Fanxi on, 1062, 1178–2; and Wang Ruofei, 111, 242, 253, 422, 423, 614–15; work in glass factory (1972–7), 115, 125, 1144–5; and work-study programme, 174–5, 191–2, 1179; Wu Jimin on, 110–17, 156; and Yin Kuan, 253, 451, 618, 640; and Zhou En Lai, 110, 111, 267, 1068; and Zhou Lüqiang, 147
— views: on character of Chinese Revolution, 424–6, 464, 668–9; on Chen Duxiu, 16, 68, 70, 594–684, 685–90, 703, 705; on colonial question, 881–2; on constituent assembly, 675–7, 869, 883; on Lu Xun letter, 438, 1044; on Peng Shuzhi, 20–1, 77, 79, 110, 262–3, 306–7, 471–3, 489, 601–2, 604, 617, 667–8, 788–90; on Second Chinese Revolution, 256–64,

Zheng Chaolin (*cont.*)
   417–50, 612–13, 1109; on Sino-Japanese war and defeatism, 28, 553, 817, 852, 853–4, 860, 870, 872, 873–4, 991, 992, 994, 1024, 1111, 1180; on socialism in one country, 1114–15; on state capitalism, 971, 1111, 1181; on Tang Baolin book, 1149–50; on Third Chinese Revolution victory, 29n, 575, 1003–4;
   — writings, 1111–12; *ABC of the Theory of Permanent Revolution*, 562, 569, 1070, 1111, 1180; 'A Brief Account of My Third Spell in Prison, 1132–46; 'Chen Duxiu and the Trotskyists', 594–684; *A Critical Biography of Chen Duxiu*, 562, 1070, 1180; *Dialogue Between Three Travellers*, 562, 1070, 1111, 1180; 'Memorial to Ding', 1072–3; 'On Cadreism', 1112, 1139–40, 1181; 'On State Capitalism', 1111; *The Permanent Revolution and the Chinese Revolution,* 881; 'Reading Mao Zedong's Selected Works in Prison', 1112–13, 1140; 'A Self-Description at the Age of Ninety', 1108–17; *On State Capitalism,* 971, 1181; *Surviving Poems by Yu Yin*, 1063, 1113, 1140–1
Zheng Chaolin's Memoirs, 1, 33; chapters from, 172–212, 225–71, 295–326, 451–77; honesty of, 1062; introduction to, 1061–74; postscript to 1987 edition, 1105–7; preface to, 1103–4; publication of, 594, 1061, 1106–7, 1113, 1182, 1195; writing of, 1061, 1105
Zheng Xuejia, 703, 744, 1033n, 1197–8
Zheng Yifan, 43, 155–6
Zhongguo qingnian. See *Chinese Youth*
Zhongshan, Guangdong, 491, 510; Trotskyist guerrilla unit in, 27, 541, 550, 561, 579
Zhongshan Gunboat Incident (1926), 45, 69, 80, 664; Lu Xun on, 277
Zhou Dawen, 372, 381, 384; Moscow purge of, 379, 380, 382
Zhou Enlai: biographical sketch, 1212; at CCP Fourth Congress, 78, 236; at CCP Sixth Congress, 61, 344–5; on Chen Duxiu, 267, 585, 692; Chen Duxiu discussions with, 463, 666, 667n; and Chen Duxiu relations, 68, 100, 101, 546, 660; and Chinese Trotskyists, 14, 71, 632; and Communist Youth movement, 200, 201, 204, 212, 1179; and Cultural Revolution, 65–6; death of, 1145; in Europe, 200, 201, 295, 299, 300–1, 327; heads CCP Military Commission, 83, 468, 618; heads CCP Organisational Department, 239, 468; at Huangpu Military Academy, 229; and Jiangsu Committee, 616; and Li Lisan Central Committee, 449; and Long March, 64; mentioned, 97, 203, 421, 438, 1136; and Nanchang uprising, 1093; and Peng Shuzhi, 81, 791; on policy in Second Chinese Revolution, 405, 791, 797; and Qu Qiubai, 61–2, 65–6; Second United Front arranged by, 528, 813–14, 990; and Shanghai insurrection and massacre, 260, 262–3, 264; and Stalin, 69, 130, 495; and Wang Fanxi, 113, 346, 490, 1192; and Wang Ming, 63, 344–5, 346–7, 494, 495; and Zeng Meng, 137, 139; and Zheng Chaolin, 110, 111, 267, 1068
Zhou Lüqiang, 149, 156; arrest and imprisonment of, 146–7, 150; becomes Trotskyist, 145, 148; biographical sketch, 144–7, 1213; Guomindang arrest of, 146; as last surviving Chinese Trotskyist, 36–7; Trotskyist work after 1949, 123, 141, 146, 150
Zhou Rensheng, 121, 138, 140–1, 150, 156; arrest and imprisonment of, 143–4; biographical sketch, 142–3, 148, 1213
Zhou Yueran, 233, 252
Zhou Zuoren, 214, 215, 587
Zhu Daijie, 374, 375, 379
Zhu De, 32, 69, 462, 806, 1145
Zhu Jintang, 78, 236
Zhu Xi, 170, 220
Zhuang Wengong (Han Baihua), 244, 251, 595; and Shanghai District Committee, 243–4, 250, 251
Zhuangzi, 176, 177, 180, 181, 1179
Zinoviev, Grigorii E., 692–3, 1082; in anti-Trotsky triumvirate, 604, 618, 783; capitulation to Stalin by, 340; Chinese students at speeches of, 79–80, 323, 370; on Guomindang entry, 81, 781, 822; as member of United Opposition, 4, 81, 332, 453, 618, 630, 822; as Moscow Trial victim, 515, 1031, 1154; on Peng Shuzhi, 77; *Theses on the Chinese Revolution*, 332
Zuo Quan, 50, 91, 99